COMPACT EDITION

Literature for Composition

Essays, Fiction, Poetry, and Drama

Edited by

Sylvan Barnet
Tufts University

William Burto
University of Lowell

William E. Cain
Wellesley College

Marcia Stubbs
Wellesley College

D0877608

Longman

New York   San Francisco   Boston
London   Toronto   Sydney   Tokyo   Singapore   Madrid
Mexico City   Munich   Paris   Cape Town   Hong Kong   Montreal

Vice President and Editor-in-Chief: Joseph Terry
Acquisitions Editor: Erika Berg
Development Manager: Janet Lanphier
Development Editor: Katharine Glynn
Senior Marketing Manager: Melanie Craig
Senior Supplements Editor: Donna Campion
Media Supplements Editor: Nancy Garcia
Production Manager: Donna DeBenedictis
Project Coordination, Text Design, and Electronic Page Makeup:
   The Clarinda Company
Cover Design Manager: John Callahan
Cover Designer: Mary McDonnell
Cover Image: Richard Diebenkorn, *Girl with Plant,* 1960, oil on canvas,
   80 × 69½ inches, acquired 1961, The Phillips Collection, Washington, D.C.
Photo Researcher: Photosearch, Inc.
Manufacturing Buyer: Roy Pickering
Printer and Binder: Quebecor World/Taunton
Cover Printer: The Lehigh Press, Inc.

For permission to use copyrighted material, grateful acknowledgment is made to the
copyright holders on pp. 776–780, which are hereby made part of this copyright
page.

Library of Congress Cataloging-in-Publication Data

Literature for composition : essays, fiction, poetry, and drama / edited by Sylvan Barnet
   ... [et al.].—Compact ed.
      p. cm.
   Includes index.
   ISBN 0-321-10780-2 (pbk.)
      1. College readers. 2. English language—Rhetoric—Problems, exercises, etc. 3.
   Criticism—Authorship—Problems, exercises, etc. 4. Academic writing—Problems,
   exercises, etc. I. Barnet, Sylvan.

   PE1417 .L633 2003
   808'.0427—dc21   2002040567

Please visit our website at http://www.ablongman.com/barnet

ISBN 0-321-09364-X (Complete Edition)
ISBN 0-321-10780-2 (Compact Edition)

1 2 3 4 5 6 7 8 9 10—WCT—05 04 03 02

Contents

PART I

Getting Started: From Response to Argument   1

CHAPTER 1   The Writer as Reader   3

CHAPTER 2   The Reader as Writer   12

C H A P T E R **3**   Reading Literature Closely: Explication   **37**

C H A P T E R **4**   Reading Literature Closely: Analysis   **61**

CHAPTER 5   Other Kinds of Writing about Literature   130

PART II

Up Close: Thinking Critically about Literary Works and Literary Forms

C H A P T E R 6   Critical Thinking: Asking Questions and Making Comparisons

C H A P T E R 7   Reading and Writing about Essays

CHAPTER **10** Reading and Writing about Drama **365**

CHAPTER **11**   Reading and Writing about Poetry   **625**

CHAPTER **12**   Thinking Critically about Poetry   686

PART III

*Standing Back: Arguing Interpretations and Evaluations,
and Understanding Critical Strategies*   697

CHAPTER **13**   Arguing an Interpretation   699

Contents by Genre

Poetry

Drama

List of Illustrations

Preface to Instructors

This book is based on the assumption that a relatively brief book *can* be designed for students taking a literature course that emphasizes composition. We believe that students who are developing their skills as writers should encounter first-rate writing—not simply competent prose but the powerful reports of experience that have been recorded by highly skilled writers of the past and present. We assume that you share our belief that the study of such writing offers pleasure and insight into life and that it also leads to increased skill in communicating.

If we were asked to give, very briefly, the key features of *Literature for Composition, Compact Edition,* here is what we would say:

KEY FEATURES

Comprehensive Instruction in Composition. Students are guided through the entire process of writing, beginning with getting ideas (for instance, by listing or by annotating a text), developing a thesis, and on through the final stages of documenting and editing.

Abundant Student Samples. More than a dozen sample student papers illustrate the writing process, and several student samples are accompanied by the preliminary journal entries and drafts that helped produce them.

Genre Anthology. After preliminary chapters on getting ideas and thinking critically, students encounter chapters devoted to essays, fiction, drama, and poetry. These chapters give students an introduction to the elements of each genre.

Four Case Studies. Case studies on Ralph Ellison, Flannery O'Connor, and Emily Dickinson give a variety of perspectives and opportunities for writing and research. The fourth case study, "Writing about Barbie and Gender," includes four short, lively essays that debate the issue of whether Barbie dolls send a harmful message about young women's appearance; two witty poems continue and expand the discussion, but using the techniques of literature rather than of argumentative prose. This case study offers good opportunities for both female and male students to examine and present arguments about gender, sexual identity, body shape and size, and cultural norms.

Helpful Material on Research Papers and the Internet. Because instructors are increasingly assigning research papers, this Compact Edition includes material on research papers on literature and provides up-to-date instruction on evaluating, using, and citing electronic sources.

Emphasis on Critical Thinking Connected to Reading and Writing. Critical thinking is at the heart of the first four chapters, and it is kept in view throughout the book, most visibly in the Topics for Critical Thinking and Writing that follow each literary selection and in two later chapters, "Arguing an Interpretation" and "Arguing an Evaluation."

Strategies for Writing Effective Arguments. *Literature for Composition, Compact Edition,* focuses on argument and evaluation, not only in the case studies but also in the Topics for Critical Thinking and Writing that follow almost all of the readings. We emphasize not only the importance of questioning your own assumptions—a key principle in critical thinking—but also the importance of setting forth thoughtful responses in the form of coherent, readable arguments.

Abundant Visual Material. The book is conspicuously rich in photographs and facsimiles of manuscripts. For example, we include photos of Buffalo Bill and a facsimile of a draft of E. E. Cummings's poem about Buffalo Bill (to our knowledge, never before published in a textbook).

ORGANIZATION

Literature for Composition, Compact Edition, offers comprehensive writing instruction along with a wonderful range of selections.

Part I, "Getting Started: From Response to Argument," consists of five chapters with 12 stories and 22 poems. The aim of all the chapters in Part I is to help students read and respond—in writing—to literature. The first two chapters discuss annotating, free writing, and listing; the third and fourth chapters discuss writing explications and analyses; and the fifth chapter discusses other kinds of writing, including parody, stories based on stories, and poems based on poems. These chapters include six examples of student writing, all of which are accompanied by the preliminary journal entries or drafts that helped produce them.

Part II, "Up Close: Thinking About Literary Works and Literary Forms," begins with a discussion of critical thinking (Chapter 6). This chapter invites students to analyze, especially by means of comparison, (1) a photograph of Buffalo Bill and Sitting Bull, (2) E. E. Cummings's poem "Buffalo Bill 's," and (3) the manuscript draft of the poem. The next nine chapters introduce the students to four genres: the essay (Chapter 7), fiction (Chapters 8 and 9), drama (Chapter 10), and poetry (Chapters 11 and 12). The chapter on the essay includes 5 essays. The two chapters on fiction present 11 stories, with case studies on Ralph Ellison's "Battle Royal" and Flannery O'Connor. The chapter on drama includes 7 plays, and the two chapters on poetry include 39 poems, with a case study on Emily Dickinson (the case study on Emily Dickinson also includes an essay by a student). Suggested topics for discussion and examples of student writing (annotations, journal entries, drafts, and final essays) help students think critically and develop arguments about the material. Part II, then, offers a compact but rich anthology of literature organized by genre, as well as abundant guidance in thinking and writing about literature.

Part III, "Standing Back: Arguing Interpretations and Evaluations, and Understanding Critical Strategies," consists of two chapters: "Arguing an Interpretation" (Chapter 13) and "Arguing an Evaluation" (Chapter 14). Our idea is this: If instructors begin the course by assigning some or all of the chapters in Parts I and II, by now the students have read enough literature to be in a good position to think further about the assumptions underlying the analytic interpretations and evaluations they are writing.

WHAT IS NEW IN *LITERATURE FOR COMPOSITION, COMPACT EDITION?*

Instructors familiar with earlier editions of the larger book will notice major new features in the Compact Edition, some of which we have already mentioned. Here, for the convenience of instructors who have used an earlier edition of the larger book, we will list the major changes:

Increased coverage of argument.   The emphasis on the connection between critical thinking—very largely a matter of arguing with yourself, i.e., questioning your assumptions and early responses—has been heightened and more evidently connected with issues of setting forth a thesis in an essay. Because instructors often assign students to explicate a passage and because students may think that an explication is merely a paraphrase, we have added a unit called "Explication as Argument."

New sample essays and checklists.   We have amplified the material on writing, partly by giving additional advice of our own, especially on evaluating evidence, developing a thesis, and explication as argument, but also by increasing the number of essays by students (usually prefaced with journal entries); the book includes more than a dozen sample essays. We have also increased to ten the number of checklists concerned with writing.

RESOURCES FOR STUDENTS AND INSTRUCTORS

Writing about Literature: Craft of Argument CD-ROM.   This highly interactive CD-ROM presents paintings, photographs, audio, and film accompanied by questions to spark student interest in the literary selections. ISBN 0-321-15446-0.

Instructor's Manual.   An instructor's manual with detailed comments and suggestions for teaching each selection is available. This important resource contains references to critical articles and books that we have found to be the most useful. ISBN 0-321-10776-4.

Literature for Composition Website.   The *Literature for Composition* Website can be found at <www.ablongman.com/barnet>. This site includes in-depth information about the text as well as helpful links to literature and research sites.

Coursecompass Generic Site, Longman English Resources for Introduction to Literature, Fiction, Creative Writing, and Drama Access Code Card, Second Edition.   This course provides a number of guides that will help students analyze literature, evaluate plays, critique and write about literature, and conduct research on-line. This course also includes a journal for writing about literature as well as a journal for creative writing. Instructors will find various additional resources, such as guides to teaching literature on-line and teaching multicultural literature. Available FREE when value-packed with *Literature for Composition, Compact Edition.* ISBN 0-321-14311-6; blackboard content ISBN 0-321-14313-2.

MLA Documentation Style: A Concise Guide for Students.   Replete with examples and clear explanations, this straightforward and accessible manual helps students understand and properly use the basic principles of MLA documentation. This brief guide includes information students need to properly cite works, avoid plagiarism, and format their papers. Available FREE when value-packed with *Literature for Composition, Compact Edition*. ISBN 0-321-10337-8.

Glossary of Literary and Critical Terms.   A quick, reliable, and portable resource, this easy-to-use glossary includes definitions, explanations, and examples for over 100 literary and critical terms which students commonly encounter in their readings or hear in their lectures and class discussions. Available FREE when value-packed with *Literature for Composition, Compact Edition*. ISBN 0-321-12691-2.

Literature Timeline.   This accessible and visually appealing timeline provides students with a chronological overview of major literary works. In addition, the timeline also lists the major sociocultural and political events that occurred contemporaneously with these major works of literature. Available FREE when value-packed with *Literature for Composition, Compact Edition*. ISBN 0-321-14315-9.

Responding to Literature: A Writer's Journal.   This free journal provides students with their own personal space for writing. Helpful writing prompts for responding to fiction, poetry, and drama are also included. Available FREE when value-packed with *Literature for Composition, Compact Edition*. ISBN 0-321-09542-1.

Evaluating a Performance.   Perfect for the student assigned to review a local production, this free supplement offers students a convenient place to record their evaluation. Useful tips and suggestions of things to consider when evaluating a production are included. Available FREE when value-packed with *Literature for Composition, Compact Edition*. ISBN 0-321-09541-3.

Analyzing Literature, Second Edition.   This brief supplement provides critical reading strategies, writing advice, and sample student papers to help students interpret and discuss literary works in a variety of genres. Suggestions for collaborative activities and on-line research on literary topics are also featured, as well as numerous exercises and writing assignments. Available FREE when value-packed with *Literature for Composition, Compact Edition*. ISBN 0-321-09338-0.

iSearch Guide for English.   A guide to on-line research. Featuring the Longman Internet Guide and access to the ContentSelect Research Database, each iSearch guide gives students and instructors instant access to thousands of academic journals and periodicals any time from any computer with an Internet connection. With helpful tips on the writing process, online research, and finding and citing valid sources, starting the research process has never been easier! Available FREE when value-packed with *Literature for Composition, Compact Edition*. ISBN 0-321-12411-1.

Merriam-Webster Collegiate Dictionary.   This hardcover comprehensive dictionary is available at a significant discount when packaged with any Longman text. ISBN 0-87779-709-9.

The English Pages Website *<http://www.ablongman.com/englishpages>*. This Website provides professors and students with resources for reading, writing, and research practice in four areas: composition, literature, technical writing, and basic skills. Features include simulated searches, first-person essays that show students how everyday men and women have applied what they have learned in composition to a wide variety of situations, and annotated links that provide the best information on a wide variety of writing issues and research topics.

Penguin Discount Novel Program. In cooperation with Penguin Putnam, Inc., one of our sibling companies, Longman is proud to offer a variety of Penguin paperbacks at a significant discount when packaged with any Longman title. Excellent additions to any literature course, Penguin titles give students the opportuniy to explore contemporary and classical fiction and drama. The available titles include works by authors as diverse as Toni Morrison, Julia Alvarez, Mary Shelley, and Shakespeare. To review the complete list of titles available, visit the Longman-Penguin-Putnam Website *<http://www.ablongman.com/ penguin>*.

The Longman Printed Test Bank for Literature. This printed test bank features various objective questions on major works of fiction, short fiction, poetry, and drama. A versatile and handy resource, this easy-to-use test bank can be used for all quizzing and testing needs. (Electronic version also available on CD.) Available FREE when value-packed with *Literature for Composition, Compact Edition.* ISBN 0-321-14312-4.

Teaching Literature On-Line, Second Edition. Concise and practical, *Teaching Literature On-Line* provides instructors with strategies and advice for incorporating elements of computer technology into the literature classroom. Available FREE when value-packed with *Literature for Composition, Compact Edition.* ISBN 0-321-10618-0.

Video Program. For qualified adopters, an impressive selection of videotapes is available to enrich students' experience of literature. Contact your sales representative.

Acknowledgments

For the compact edition, we want to thank the following reviewers: Jennifer Bruer, University of Florida; Sharon Buzzard, Quincy University; Bruce Danner, Xavier University of Louisiana; Phebe Davidson, University of South Carolina at Aiken; Jessica Beth Gordon, J. Sergeant Reynolds College; Ana B. Hernandez, Miami-Dade Community College at Wolfson; Alison Kuehner, Ohlone College; Robert Lynch, Longwood College; Maria Makowiecka, Bergen Community College; Phil Martin, Minneapolis Community and Technical College; Delma McLeod-Porter, McNeese State University; Linda McPherson, Indiana University of Pennsylvania; Jonathan Morrow, Mt. Hood Community College; Eric Otto, University of Florida; Janet Palmer, Caldwell Community College; Lois Sampson, Cowley College; Linda Scott, New Mexico Military Institute; Martha Ann Smith, Brookhaven College; Geri Strecker, Ball State University; David Sudol, Arizona State University; and Cary Wolfe, University of Albany, SUNY.

The following instructors offered invaluable advice: Jennifer Breuer, University of Florida; Phebe Davidson, University of South Carolina at Aiken; Robert Lynch, Longwood College; Steve Wozniak, Palomar College; and Cary Wolfe, State University of New York at Albany.

For many e-mails and conversations about the compact edition, and for help with its preparation, we are grateful to Erika Berg and Katharine Glynn at Longman. We wish also to thank Celeste Parker-Bates, who secured copyright permission for the texts, and Jennifer Sanfilippo, who secured permission for the images. Chris Thillen did an excellent job of copyediting the manuscript, and Richard Cairnes and Carol Singer did an equally good job with the proofreading. Gail Gavin at Clarinda Publication Services coordinated the efforts of publisher, authors, copyeditor, proofreader, and compositor; we owe her more than she can imagine. In short, we have been fortunate in our associates.

Bill Cain would like to thank his wife Barbara and his daughters Julia and Isabel for their love and support.

Sylvan Barnet
William Burto
William E. Cain
Marcia Stubbs

Letter to Students

We hope that you already enjoy reading literature and that *Literature for Composition, Compact Edition,* will help you enjoy it even more. But as you begin your course this semester with our book, we would like to say a little more to you about why we wrote it, how we believe it can help you, and in what ways we think it can deepen and enrich your pleasure in studying literature.

Throughout the process of writing and rewriting *Literature for Composition, Compact Edition,* we saw ourselves as teachers, bringing to you the kinds of suggestions and strategies that, over many years, have benefited the students we have taught.

As you can tell from a glance at the Contents, *Literature for Composition, Compact Edition,* includes a great deal of practical advice about reading and responding to literature and writing analytical papers, advice that comes directly from our experience not only as readers and writers but also as teachers. This experience derives from classrooms, from conferences with students, and from assignments we have given, read, responded to, and graded. We have learned from our experiences (we have revised this book five times, each time fairly extensively) and have done our best to give you the tools that will help you make yourself a more perceptive reader and a more careful, cogent writer.

Speaking of making and remaking, we are reminded of a short poem by William Butler Yeats, who was a persistent reviser of his work. (You can find three versions of his poem "Leda and the Swan" on pages 139–40.)

> The friends that have it I do wrong
> Whenever I remake a song,
> Should know what issue is at stake:
> It is myself that I remake.

Like Yeats, you will develop throughout your life: you will find you have new things to say, and you may even come to find that the tools you acquired in college—and that suited you for a while—are not fully adequate to the new self that you have become. We can't claim to equip you for the rest of your life—though some of these works of literature surely will remain in your mind for years—but we do claim that, with your instructor, we are helping you develop skills that are important for your mental progress. We have in mind skills useful not merely in the course in which you are now enrolled, or other literature courses, or even courses in the humanities in general that you may take. We go further. We think that these skills in reading and writing are important for your development as an educated adult. Becoming an alert reader and an effective writer should be among the central goals of your education, and they are goals that *Literature for Composition, Compact Edition,* is designed to help you reach.

The skills we stress in *Literature for Composition, Compact Edition,* will enable you to gain confidence as a reader of literary works so that you will increase your understanding of what literature offers. You need not enjoy all authors equally. You'll have your favorites—and also some authors whom you do not like much at all. There's nothing wrong with that; reading literature is very much a personal encounter. But, at the same time, the skills we highlight in *Literature for Composition, Compact Edition,* can help you know and explain why one author means much to you and another does not. In this respect, reading and studying literature is more than personal; as we share our responses and try to express them effectively in writing, the work that we perform becomes cooperative and communal, a type of cultural conversation among fellow students, teachers, and friends.

As you proceed through *Literature for Composition, Compact Edition,* and gain further experience as a reader and writer, you will start to see features of poems, stories, and plays that you had not noticed before, or that you had noticed but not really understood, or that you had understood but not, so to speak, fully experienced. You may even find yourself enjoying an author you thought you disliked and would never be able to understand. The study of literature calls for concentration, commitment, and discipline. It's work—sometimes hard, challenging work. But it is rewarding work, and we believe that it will lead you to find literature more engaging and more pleasurable.

We hope that *Literature for Composition, Compact Edition,* will have this effect for you. Feel free to contact us with your comments and suggestions. We are eager to know what in this book has served you well, and what we might do better. You can write to us in care of Literature Editor, Longman Publishers, 1185 Avenue of the Americas, New York, NY 10036.

Sylvan Barnet
William Burto
William E. Cain
Marcia Stubbs

PART I

Getting Started

From Response to Argument

1

The Writer as Reader

Interviewer: Did you know as a child you wanted to be a writer?
Toni Morrison: No. I wanted to be a reader.

READING AND RESPONDING

Learning to write is in large measure learning to read. The text you must read most carefully is the one you write, an essay you will ask someone else to read. It may start as a jotting in the margin of a book you are reading or as a brief note in a journal, and it will go through several drafts before it becomes an essay. To produce something that another person will find worth reading, you must read each draft with care, trying to imagine the effect your words are likely to have on your reader. In writing about literature, you will apply some of the same critical skills to your reading; that is, you will examine your responses to what you are reading and will try to account for them.

Let's begin by looking at a very short story by Kate Chopin (1851–1904). (The name is pronounced in the French way, something like "show pan.") Kate O'Flaherty, born into a prosperous family in St. Louis, in 1870 married Oscar Chopin, a French-Creole businessman from Louisiana. They lived in New Orleans, where they had six children. Oscar died of malaria in 1882, and in 1884 Kate returned to St. Louis, where, living with her mother and children, she began to write fiction.

KATE CHOPIN

Ripe Figs

Maman-Nainaine said that when the figs were ripe Babette might go to visit her cousins down on the Bayou-Lafourche where the sugar cane grows. Not that the ripening of figs had the least thing to do with it, but that is the way Maman-Nainaine was.

It seemed to Babette a very long time to wait; for the leaves upon the trees were tender yet, and the figs were like little hard, green marbles.

But warm rains came along and plenty of strong sunshine, and though Maman-Nainaine was as patient as the statue of la Madone, and Babette as restless as a humming-bird, the first thing they both knew it was hot summertime. Every day Babette danced out to where the fig-trees were in a long line against the fence. She walked slowly beneath them, carefully peering between the gnarled, spreading branches. But each time she came disconsolate away again. What she saw there finally was something that made her sing and dance the whole long day.

When Maman-Nainaine sat down in her stately way to breakfast, the following morning, her muslin cap standing like an aureole about her white, placid face, Babette approached. She bore a dainty porcelain platter, which she set down before her godmother. It contained a dozen purple figs, fringed around with their rich, green leaves.

"Ah," said Maman-Nainaine arching her eyebrows, "how early the figs have ripened this year!"

"Oh," said Babette. "I think they have ripened very late."

"Babette," continued Maman-Nainaine, as she peeled the very plumpest figs with her pointed silver fruit-knife, "you will carry my love to them all down on Bayou-Lafourche. And tell your Tante Frosine I shall look for her at Toussaint— when the chrysanthemums are in bloom."

[1893]

Reading as Re-creation

If we had been Chopin's contemporaries, we might have read this sketch in *Vogue* in 1893 or in an early collection of her works, *A Night in Acadie* (1897). But we are not Chopin's original readers, and, since we live more than a century later, we inevitably read "Ripe Figs" in a somewhat different way. And this gets us to an important truth about writing and reading. A writer writes, sets forth his or her meaning, and attempts to guide the reader's responses, as we all do when we write a letter home saying that we're thinking of dropping a course or asking for news or money. To this extent, the writer creates the written work and puts a meaning in it.

But the reader, whether reading that written work as a requirement or for recreation, *re-creates* it according to his or her experience and understanding. For instance, if the letter-writer's appeal for money is too indirect, the reader may miss it entirely or may sense it but feel that the need is not urgent. If, on the other hand, the appeal is direct or demanding, the reader may feel imposed upon, even assaulted. "Oh, but I didn't mean it that way," the writer later protests. Nevertheless, that's the way the reader took it. The letter is "out there," a physical reality standing between the writer and the reader, but its *meaning* is something the reader as well as the writer makes.

Since all readers bring themselves to a written work, they each bring something individual. Although many of Chopin's original readers knew that she wrote chiefly about the people of Louisiana, especially Creoles (descendants of the early French and Spanish settlers), Cajuns (descendants of the French whom the British had expelled from Canada in the eighteenth century), African Americans, and mulattoes, those readers must have varied in their attitudes about such people. And many of today's readers do *not* (before they read a work by Chopin) know anything about her subject. Some readers may know where Bayou-Lafourche is, and they may have notions about what it looks like, but most readers will not; indeed, many readers will not know that a bayou is a sluggish, marshy inlet or outlet of a river or lake. Moreover, even if a present-day reader in Chicago, Seattle, or Juneau knows what a bayou is, he or she may assume that "Ripe Figs" depicts a way of life still current, whereas a reader from Louisiana may see in the work a depiction of a lost way of life, a depiction of the good old days (or perhaps of the bad old days, depending on the reader's point of view). Much depends, we can say, on the reader's storehouse of experience.

To repeat: Reading is a *re*-creation; the author has tried to guide our responses, but inevitably our own experiences, as well as our ethnic background and education, contribute to our responses. You may find useful a distinction that E. D. Hirsch makes in *Validity in Interpretation* (1967). For Hirsch,

- the *meaning* in a text is the author's intended meaning;
- the *significance* is the particular relevance for each reader.

In this view, when you think about meaning you are thinking about what the author was trying to say and to do—for instance, to take an old theme and treat it in a new way. When you think about significance, you are thinking about what the work does for you—it enlarges your mind, deepens your understanding of love or grief, offends you by its depiction of women, or produces some other effect.

Making Reasonable Inferences

Does this mean, then, that there is no use talking (or writing) about literature, since all of us perceive it in our relatively private ways, rather like the seven blind men in the fable? One man, you will recall, touched the elephant's tail (or was it his trunk?) and said that the elephant is like a snake; another touched the elephant's side and said the elephant is like a wall; a third touched the elephant's leg and said the elephant is like a tree, and so on. This familiar story is usually told in order to illustrate human limitations, but notice, too, that each of the blind men *did* perceive an aspect of the elephant—an elephant is massive, like a wall or a tree, and an elephant is (in its way) remarkably supple, as you know if you have given peanuts to one.

As readers we can and should make an effort to understand what an author seems to be getting at. For instance, we should make an effort to understand unfamiliar words. Perhaps we shouldn't look up every word that we don't know, at least on the first reading, but if certain unfamiliar words are repeated and thus seem especially important, we will want to look them up. It happens that in "Ripe Figs" a French word appears: "*Tante* Frosine" means "*Aunt* Frosine." Fortunately, the meaning of the word is not crucial, and the context probably makes it clear that Frosine is an adult, which is all that we really need to know about her. But a reader who does not know that chrysanthemums bloom in late summer or early autumn will miss part of Chopin's meaning. The point is this: The writer is pitching, and she expects the reader to catch.

On the other hand, although writers tell us a good deal, they cannot tell us everything. We know that Maman-Nainaine is Babette's godmother, but we don't know exactly how old Maman-Nainaine and Babette are. Further, Chopin tells us nothing of Babette's parents. It *sounds* as though Babette and her godmother live alone, but readers' opinions may differ. One reader may argue that Babette's parents must be dead or ill, whereas another may say that the status of her parents is irrelevant and that what counts is that Babette is supervised by only one person, a mature woman. In short, a text includes **indeterminacies** (passages that careful readers agree are open to various interpretations) and **gaps** (things left unsaid in the story, such as why a godmother rather than a mother takes care of Babette).

As we work our way through a text, we keep reevaluating what we have read, pulling the details together to make sense of them, in a process called **consistency building**.

Whatever the gaps, careful readers are able to draw many reasonable inferences about Maman-Nainaine. What are some of these? We can list them:

> She is older than Babette.
> She has a "stately way," and she is "patient as the statue of la Madone."
> She has an odd way (is it exasperating, or engaging, or a little of each?) of connecting actions with the seasons.
> Given this last point, she seems to act slowly, to be very patient.
> She apparently is used to being obeyed.

You may at this point want to go back and reread "Ripe Figs," to see what else you can say about Maman-Nainaine.

And now what of Babette?

> She is young.
> She is active and impatient ("restless as a humming-bird").
> She is obedient.

And at this point, too, you may want to add to the list.

If you do add to the list, you might compare your additions with those of a classmate. The two of you may find that you disagree about what may reasonably be inferred from Chopin's words. Suppose, for instance, that your classmate said that although Babette is outwardly obedient, inwardly she probably hates Maman-Nainaine. Would you agree that this assertion is an acceptable inference? If you don't agree, how might you go about trying to convince your classmate that such a response is not justified? We are speaking here of an activity of mind called **critical thinking**, a topic discussed in the next chapter.

Reading with Pen in Hand

It's probably best to read a work of literature straight through, enjoying it and letting yourself be carried along to the end. But then, when you have an overall view, you'll want to read it again, noticing (for example) how certain innocent-seeming details given early in the work prove to be important later.

Perhaps the best way to read attentively is, after a first reading, to mark the text, underlining or highlighting passages that seem especially interesting, and to jot notes or queries in the margins. (*Caution:* Annotate and highlight, but don't get so carried away that you highlight whole pages.) Here is "Ripe Figs" once more, this time with the marks that a student added to it during and after a second reading.

KATE CHOPIN

Ripe Figs

Maman-Nainaine said that when the figs were ripe Babette might go to visit her cousins down on the Bayou-Lafourche where the sugar cane grows. Not that the ripening of figs had the least thing to do with it, but that is the way Maman-Nainaine was.

strange

?

It seemed to Babette a very long time to wait; for the leaves upon the trees were tender yet, and the figs were like little hard, green marbles.

But warm rains came along and plenty of strong sunshine, and though Maman-Nainaine was as patient as the statue of la Madone, and Babette as restless as a humming-bird, the first thing they both knew it was hot summertime. Every day Babette danced out to where the fig-trees were in a long line against the fence. She walked slowly beneath them, carefully peering between the gnarled, spreading branches. But each time she came disconsolate away again. What she saw there finally was something that made her sing and dance the whole long day.

contrast between M-N and B

When Maman-Nainaine sat down in her stately way to breakfast, the following morning, her muslin cap standing like an aureole about her white, placid face, Babette approached. She bore a dainty porcelain platter, which she set down before her godmother. It contained a dozen purple figs fringed around with their rich, green leaves.

Check ? this

another contrast

ceremonious

nice echo contrast like a song

"Ah," said Maman-Nainaine arching her eyebrows, "how early the figs have ripened this year!"

"Oh," said Babette. "I think they have ripened very late."

"Babette," continued Maman-Nainaine as she peeled the very plumpest figs with her pointed silver fruit-knife, "you will carry my love to them all down on Bayou-Lafourche. And tell your Tante Frosine I shall look for her at Toussaint—when the chrysanthemums are in bloom."

time passes fast for M-N slowly for B

is M-N herself like a plump fig?

B entrusted with a message of love

opens with figs; ends with chrys. (autumn)

fulfillment? Equivalent to figs ripening?

Recording Your First Responses

Another useful way of getting at the meaning of a work of literature is to jot down your initial responses to it, recording your impressions as they come to you in any order—almost as though you're talking to yourself. Since no one else is going to read your notes, you can be entirely free and at ease. You can write in sentences or not; it's up to you. You can jot down these responses either before or after you annotate the text. Some readers find that annotating the text helps to produce ideas for further jottings, but others prefer to jot down a few thoughts immediately after a first reading, and then, stimulated by these thoughts, they reread and annotate the text.

Write whatever comes into your mind, whatever the literary work triggers in your own imagination, whatever you think are the important ideas or values of your own experience.

Here is a student's first response to "Ripe Figs":

> This is a very short story. I didn't know stories were this short, but I
> like it because you can get it all quickly and it's no trouble to reread it
> carefully. The shortness, though, leaves a lot of gaps for the reader to fill
> in. So much is <u>not</u> said. Your imagination is put to work.
>
> But I can see Maman-N sitting at her table--pleasantly powerful--no
> one you would want to argue with. She's formal and distant--and definitely
> has quirks. She wants to postpone Babette's trip, but we don't know why.
> And you can sense B's frustration. But maybe she's <u>teaching</u> her that
> something really good is worth waiting for and that anticipation is as
> much fun as the trip. Maybe I can develop this idea.
>
> Another thing. I can tell they are not poor--from two things. The
> pointed silver fruit knife and the porcelain platter, and the fact that Maman
> sits down to breakfast in a "stately" way. They are the leisure class. But I
> don't know enough about life on the bayous to go into this. Their life is
> different from mine; no one I know has that kind of peaceful rural life.

Identifying Your Audience and Purpose

Now, suppose that you are beginning the process of writing about "Ripe Figs" for someone else, not for yourself. The first question to ask yourself is: "For whom am I writing?" That is, who is your *audience?* (Of course you probably are writing because an instructor has asked you to do so, but you must still imagine an audience. Your instructor may tell you, for instance, to write for your classmates, or to write for the readers of the college newspaper.)

- If you are writing for people who already are familiar with some of Chopin's work, you won't have to say much about the author, but
- if you are writing for an audience that perhaps has never heard of Chopin, you may want to include a brief biographical note of the sort we gave.
- If you are writing for an audience that, you have reason to believe, has read several works by Chopin, you may want to make some comparisons, explaining how "Ripe Figs" resembles or differs from Chopin's other work.

In a sense, the audience is your collaborator; it helps you to decide what you will say. You are also helped by your sense of *purpose.* If your aim is to introduce readers to Chopin, you will make certain points that reflect this purpose. If your aim is to tell people what you think "Ripe Figs" means to say about human relationships, or about time, you will say some different things. If your aim is to have a little fun and to entertain an audience that is already familiar with "Ripe Figs," you may decide to write a parody (a humorous imitation) of the story.

YOUR TURN: A WRITING ASSIGNMENT

Let's assume that you want to describe "Ripe Figs" to someone who has not read it. You will briefly summarize the action, such as it is, and will mention where it takes place; who the characters are, including what their relationship is; and what, if anything, happens to them. Beyond that, you'll try to explain as honestly as you can what makes "Ripe Figs" appealing or interesting—or trifling, or boring, or whatever. That is, you will *argue* a thesis, even though you almost surely will not say anything as formal as "In this essay I will argue that . . . " or "This essay will attempt to prove that . . ." Your essay nevertheless will essentially be an argument because (perhaps after a brief summary of the work) you will be pointing to the evidence that has caused you to respond as you did.

A Sample Essay by a Student: "Ripening"

Here is an essay that a student, Antonia Tenori, wrote for this assignment.

Images of Ripening in Kate Chopin's "Ripe Figs"

Very little happens in Kate Chopin's one-page story, "Ripe Figs." Maman-Nainaine tells her goddaughter Babette that she may "visit her cousins down on the Bayou-Lafourche" "when the figs were ripe"; the figs ripen, and Babette is given permission to go. So little happens in "Ripe Figs" that the story at first appears merely to be a character sketch that illustrates, through Babette and her godmother, the contrast between youth and age. But by means of the natural imagery of the tale, Chopin suggests more than this: She asks her readers to see the relationship of human time to nature's seasons, and she suggests that, try as we may to push the process of maturity, growth or "ripening" happens in its own time.

The story clearly contrasts the impatience of youth with the patience and dignity that come with age. Babette, whose name suggests she is still a "little baby," is "restless as a humming-bird." Each day when she eagerly goes to see if the figs have ripened, she doesn't simply walk but she dances. By contrast, Maman-Nainaine has a "stately way," she is "patient as the statue of la Madone," and there is an "aureole"--a radiance--"about her white, placid face." The brief dialog near the end of the story also emphasizes the difference between the two characters. When the figs finally ripen, Maman-Nainaine is surprised (she arches her eyebrows), and she exclaims, "how early the figs have ripened this year!" Babette replies, "I think they have ripened very late."

Chopin is not simply remarking here that time passes slowly for young people, and quickly for old people. She suggests that nature moves

at its own pace regardless of human wishes. Babette, young and "tender" as
the fig leaves, can't wait to "ripen." Her visit to Bayou-Lafourche is not a
mere pleasure trip, but represents her coming into her own season of
maturity. Babette's desire to rush this process is tempered by a condition
that her godmother sets: Babette must wait until the figs ripen, since
everything comes in its own season. Maman-Nainaine recognizes the
patterns of the natural world, the rhythms of life. By asking Babette to await
the ripening, the young girl is asked to pay attention to the patterns as well.

Chopin further suggests that if we pay attention and wait with
patience, the fruits of our own growth will be sweet, plump, and beautiful,
like the "dozen purple figs, fringed around with their rich, green leaves,"
that Babette finally offers her godmother. Chopin uses natural imagery
effectively, interweaving the young girl's growth with the rhythms of the
seasons. In this way, the reader is connected with both processes in an
intimate and inviting way.

The Argument Analyzed

- The title of the essay is informative; it clearly indicates the focus of the
  analysis. Notice, too, that it is much more interesting than "An Analysis of a
  Story" or "An Analysis of Kate Chopin's 'Ripe Figs'" or "'Ripe Figs': A Study"
  or "An Analysis of Imagery." In your own essays, construct titles that inform
  and interest.
- The first sentence names the author and title. Strictly speaking, this information is redundant, since it appears in the title, but it is customary to give
  the author's full name and the title of the work early in the essay, and it is
  essential to give such information if it is not in the title.
- The second sentence offers enough plot summary to enable the reader to
  follow the discussion. But notice that the essay as a whole is much more
  than a summary of the plot. Summary here is offered early, merely to
  make the analysis intelligible. Chiefly, the opening paragraph presents one
  view (the view that Antonia believes is inadequate); then, after a transitional "but," offers a second view and presents a thesis—the point that
  Antonia will argue. Perhaps the most common error students make in writing about literature is to confuse a summary of the plot with a thoughtful
  analysis of the work. A little plot-telling is acceptable, to remind your
  reader of what happens, but normally your essay will be devoted to setting
  forth a thesis about a work, and supporting the thesis with evidence. Your
  readers do not want to know what happens in the work; they want to

know what you make out of the work—how you interpret it, or why you like or dislike it.

- In the second paragraph, Antonia supports her thesis by providing brief quotations. These quotations are not padding; rather, they are evidence supporting her assertion that Chopin "contrasts the impatience of youth with the patience and dignity that come with age."
- In the third paragraph Antonia develops her thesis ("Chopin is not simply . . . She suggests . . .")
- The final paragraph begins with a helpful transition ("Chopin *further* suggests"), offers additional evidence, and ends with a new idea (about the reader's response to the story) that takes the discussion a step further. The essay avoids the deadliest kind of conclusion, a mere summary of the essay ("Thus we have seen," or some such words). Antonia's effective final sentence nicely draws the reader into the essay. (Effective final sentences are hard to write, but we give advice about them on page 85.)

Antonia Tenori wrote this paper for an assignment early in the semester, and it's worth noting that students were told to write "no more than a page." If

- the first question to ask is "To whom am I writing?"
- the second question to ask is, "What is the length of the assignment?"

The answer to this second question will provide two sorts of guidance: It will give you some sense of how much time you should devote to preparing the paper—obviously an instructor expects you to spend more time on a ten-page paper than on a one-page paper—and, second, it will give you a sense of how much detail you can include. For a short paper—say, 1–2 pages—you will need to make your main point with a special kind of directness; you will not have space for lots of details, just those that support the main point. This is what Antonia aims to achieve in her second and third paragraphs, where she highlights the term "ripens" and briefly, but effectively, develops its implications. For a longer paper, 3–5 pages, or one that is longer still, you can examine the characters, setting, and central themes in greater depth, and can focus on more details in the text to strengthen your analysis.

Other Possibilities for Writing

You might write a paper of a very different sort. Consider the following possibilities:

1. Write a sequel, moving from fall to spring.
2. Write a letter from Babette, at Bayou-Lafourche, to Maman-Nainaine.
3. Imagine that Babette is now an old woman, writing her memoirs. What does she say about Maman-Nainaine?
4. Write a narrative based on your own experience of learning a lesson in patience.

2

The Reader as Writer

*All there is to writing is having ideas. To learn
to write is to learn to have ideas.*

ROBERT FROST

DEVELOPING A THESIS, DRAFTING
AND WRITING AN ARGUMENT

Pre-writing: Getting Ideas

How do writers "learn to have ideas"? Among the methods are these: reading with
a pen or pencil in hand, so that (as we have already seen) you can annotate the
text; keeping a journal, in which you jot down reflections about your reading;
talking with others (including your instructor) about the reading. Let's take another look at the first of these, annotating.

Annotating a Text

In reading, if you own the book don't hesitate to mark it up, indicating (by highlighting or underlining or by making marginal notes) what puzzles you, what
pleases or interests you, and what displeases or bores you. Later you'll want to
think further about these responses, asking yourself, on rereading, if you still feel
that way, and if not, why not; but these first responses will get you started.

   Annotations of the sort given on page 7, which chiefly call attention to contrasts, indicate that the student is thinking about writing an analysis of the story.
That is, she is thinking of writing an essay in which she will examine the parts of
a literary work either in an effort to see how they relate to each other or in an effort to see how one part relates to the whole.

More about Getting Ideas:
A Second Story by Kate Chopin

Let's look at a story that is a little longer than "Ripe Figs," and then we'll discuss
how in addition to annotating you might get ideas for writing about it.

The Story of an Hour

Knowing that Mrs. Mallard was afflicted with a heart trouble, great care was taken
to break to her as gently as possible the news of her husband's death.

   It was her sister Josephine who told her, in broken sentences, veiled hints
that revealed in half concealing. Her husband's friend Richards was there, too,

near her. It was he who had been in the newspaper office when intelligence of the railroad disaster was received, with Brently Mallard's name leading the list of "killed." He had only taken the time to assure himself of its truth by a second telegram, and had hastened to forestall any less careful, less tender friend in bearing the sad message.

She did not hear the story as many women have heard the same, with a paralyzed inability to accept its significance. She wept at once, with sudden, wild abandonment, in her sister's arms. When the storm of grief had spent itself she went away to her room alone. She would have no one follow her.

There stood, facing the open window, a comfortable, roomy armchair. Into this she sank, pressed down by a physical exhaustion that haunted her body and seemed to reach into her soul.

5   She could see in the open square before her house the tops of trees that were all aquiver with the new spring life. The delicious breath of rain was in the air. In the street below a peddler was crying his wares. The notes of a distant song which some one was singing reached her faintly, and countless sparrows were twittering in the eaves.

There were patches of blue sky showing here and there through the clouds that had met and piled above the other in the west facing her window. She sat with her head thrown back upon the cushion of the chair quite motionless, except when a sob came up into her throat and shook her, as a child who has cried itself to sleep continues to sob in its dreams.

She was young, with a fair, calm face, whose lines bespoke repression and even a certain strength. But now there was a dull stare in her eyes, whose gaze was fixed away off yonder on one of those patches of blue sky. It was not a glance of reflection, but rather indicated a suspension of intelligent thought.

There was something coming to her and she was waiting for it, fearfully. What was it? She did not know; it was too subtle and elusive to name. But she felt it, creeping out of the sky, reaching toward her through the sounds, the scents, the color that filled the air.

Now her bosom rose and fell tumultuously. She was beginning to recognize this thing that was approaching to possess her, and she was striving to beat it back with her will—as powerless as her two white slender hands would have been.

10   When she abandoned herself a little whispered word escaped her slightly parted lips. She said it over and over under her breath: "Free, free, free!" The vacant stare and the look of terror that had followed it went from her eyes. They stayed keen and bright. Her pulses beat fast, and the coursing blood warmed and relaxed every inch of her body.

She did not stop to ask if it were not a monstrous joy that held her. A clear and exalted perception enabled her to dismiss the suggestion as trivial.

She knew that she would weep again when she saw the kind, tender hands folded in death; the face that had never looked save with love upon her, fixed and gray and dead. But she saw beyond that bitter moment a long procession of years to come that would belong to her absolutely. And she opened and spread her arms out to them in welcome.

There would be no one to live for her during those coming years; she would live for herself. There would be no powerful will bending her in that blind persistence with which men and women believe they have a right to impose a private will upon a fellow creature. A kind intention or a cruel intention made the act seem no less a crime as she looked upon it in that brief moment of illumination.

And yet she had loved him—sometimes. Often she had not. What did it matter! What could love, the unsolved mystery, count for in face of this possession of self-assertion which she suddenly recognized as the strongest impulse of her being.

15   "Free! Body and soul free!" she kept whispering.

Josephine was kneeling before the closed door with her lips to the keyhole, imploring for admission. "Louise, open the door! I beg; open the door—you will make yourself ill. What are you doing, Louise? For heaven's sake open the door."

"Go away. I am not making myself ill." No; she was drinking in a very elixir of life through that open window.

Her fancy was running riot along those days ahead of her. Spring days, and summer days, and all sorts of days that would be her own. She breathed a quick prayer that life might be long. It was only yesterday she had thought with a shudder that life might be long.

She arose at length and opened the door to her sister's importunities. There was a feverish triumph in her eyes, and she carried herself unwittingly like a goddess of Victory. She clasped her sister's waist, and together they descended the stairs. Richards stood waiting for them at the bottom.

20   Some one was opening the front door with a latchkey. It was Brently Mallard who entered, a little travel-stained, composedly carrying his gripsack and umbrella. He had been far from the scene of accident, and did not even know there had been one. He stood amazed at Josephine's piercing cry; at Richards' quick motion to screen him from the view of his wife.

But Richards was too late.

When the doctors came they said she had died of heart disease—of joy that kills.

[1894]

Brainstorming for Ideas for Writing

Unlike annotating, which consists of making brief notes and small marks on the printed page, "brainstorming"—the free jotting down of ideas—asks that you jot down whatever comes to mind, without inhibition. Don't worry about spelling, about writing complete sentences, or about unifying your thoughts; just let one thought lead to another. Later you can review your jottings, deleting some, connecting with arrows others that are related, expanding still others, but for now you want to get going, and so there is no reason to look back. Thus you might jot down something about the title:

> Title speaks of an hour, and story covers an hour, but maybe takes five minutes to read.

And then, perhaps prompted by "an hour," you might happen to add something to this effect:

> Doubt that a woman who got news of the death of her husband could move from grief to joy within an hour.

Your next jotting might have little or nothing to do with this issue; it might simply say

> Enjoyed "Hour" more than "Ripe Figs" partly because "Hour" is so shocking.

And then you might ask yourself

> By shocking, do I mean "improbable," or what? Come to think of it, maybe it's not so improbable. A lot depends on what the marriage was like.

Focused Free Writing

Focused, or directed, free writing is a method related to brainstorming that some writers use to uncover ideas they may want to write about. Concentrating on one issue—for instance, a question that strikes them as worth puzzling over (What kind of person is Mrs. Mallard?)—they write at length, nonstop, for perhaps five or ten minutes.

Writers who find free writing helpful put down everything they can think of that bears on the one issue or question they are examining. They do not stop at this stage to evaluate the results, and they do not worry about niceties of sentence structure or of spelling. They just pour out their ideas in a steady stream of writing, drawing on whatever associations come to mind. If they pause in their writing, it is only to refer to the text, to search for more detail—perhaps a quotation—that will help them answer their question.

After the free-writing session, these writers usually go back and reread what they have written, highlighting or underlining what seems to be of value. Of course they find much that is of little or no use, but they also usually find that some strong ideas have surfaced and have received some development. At this point the writers are often able to make a rough outline and then begin a draft.

Here is an example of one student's focused free writing:

> What do I know about Mrs. Mallard? Let me put everything down here I know about her or can figure out from what Kate Chopin tells me. When she finds herself alone after the death of her husband, she says, "Free. Body and soul free" and before that she said, "Free, free, free" Three times. So she has suddenly perceived that she has not been free; she has been under the influence of a "powerful will." In this case it has been her husband, but she says no one, man nor woman, should impose their will on anyone else. So it's not a feminist issue--it's a power issue. No one should push anyone else around is what I guess Chopin means, force someone to do what the other person wants. I used to have a friend that did that to me all the time; he had to run everything. They say that fathers--before the women's movement--used to run things, with the father in charge of all the decisions, so maybe this is an honest reaction to having been pushed around by a husband. I think Mrs. Mallard is a believable character, even if the plot is not all that believable--all those things happening in such quick succession.

Listing

In your preliminary thinking you may find it useful to make lists. In the previous chapter we saw that listing the traits of the two characters was helpful in thinking about Chopin's "Ripe Figs":

Maman-Nainaine
    older than Babette
    "stately way"

"patient as the statue of la Madone"
connects actions with seasons
expects to be obeyed
Babette
young
active and impatient
obedient

For "The Story of an Hour" you might list Mrs. Mallard's traits; or you might list the stages in her development. (Such a list is not the same as a summary of the plot. The list helps the writer to see the sequence of psychological changes.)

weeps (when she gets the news)
goes to room, alone
"pressed down by a physical exhaustion"
"dull stare"
"something coming to her"
strives to beat back "this thing"
"Free, free, free!" The "vacant stare went . . . from her eyes"
"A clear and exalted perception"
rejects Josephine
"she was drinking in a very elixir of life"
gets up, opens door, "a feverish triumph in her eyes"
sees B., and dies

Unlike brainstorming and annotating, which let you go in all directions, listing requires that you first make a decision about what you will be listing—traits of character, images, puns, or whatever. Once you make the decision, you can then construct the list, and with a list in front of you, you will probably see patterns that you were not fully conscious of earlier.

Asking Questions

If you feel stuck, ask yourself questions. (You'll recall that the assignment on "Ripe Figs" in effect asked the students to ask themselves questions about the work—for instance, questions about the relationship between the characters—and about their responses to it: "You'll try to explain as honestly as you can what makes 'Ripe Figs' appealing or interesting—or trifling, or boring."

If you are thinking about a work of fiction, ask yourself questions about the plot and the characters—are they believable, are they interesting, and what does it all add up to? What does the story mean to *you?* One student found it helpful to jot down the following questions:

Plot
   Ending false? Unconvincing? Or prepared for?
Character?
   Mrs. M. unfeeling? Immoral?
   Mrs. M. unbelievable character?
   What might her marriage have been like? Many gaps.
   (Can we tell what her husband was like?)
   "And yet she loved him--sometimes" Fickle? Realistic?
   What is "this thing that was approaching to possess her"?

    Symbolism
       Set on spring day = symbolic of new life?

You don't have to be as tidy as this student. You may begin by jotting down notes and queries about what you like or dislike and about what puzzles or amuses you. What follows are the jottings of another student, Janet Vong. They are, obviously, in no particular order—the student is "brainstorming," putting down whatever occurs to her—though it is equally obvious that one note sometimes led to the next:

> Title nothing special. What might be a better title?
> Could a woman who loved her husband be so heartless?
> Is she heartless? Did she love him?
> What are (were) Louise's feelings about her husband?
> Did she want too much? What did she want?
> Could this story happen today? Feminist interpretation?
> Sister (Josephine)--a busybody?
> Tricky ending--but maybe it could be true.
> "And yet she had loved him--sometimes. Often she had not."
>   Why does one love someone "sometimes"?
> Irony: plot has reversal. Are characters ironic too?

These jottings will help the reader-writer think about the story, find a special point of interest, and develop a thoughtful argument about it.

Keeping a Journal

A journal is not a diary, a record of what the writer did during the day ("today I read Chopin's 'Hour'"). Rather, a journal is a place to store some of the thoughts you may have inscribed on a scrap of paper or in the margin of the text, such as your initial response to the title of a work or to the ending. It is also a place to jot down further reflections, such as thoughts about what the work means to you, and what was said in the classroom about writing in general or specific works.

    You will get something out of your journal if you write an entry at least once a week, but you will get much more if you write entries after reading each assignment and after each class meeting. You may, for instance, want to reflect on why your opinion is so different from that of another student, or you may want to apply a concept such as *character* or *irony* or *plausibility* to a story that later you may write about in an essay. Comparisons are especially helpful: How does this work (or this character, or this rhyme scheme) differ from last week's reading?

    You might even make an entry in the form of a letter to the author or from one character to another. You might write a dialogue between characters in two works or between two authors, or you might record an experience of your own that is comparable to something in the work.

    A student who wrote about "The Story of an Hour" began with the following entry in his journal. In reading this entry, notice that one idea stimulates another. The student was, quite rightly, concerned with getting and exploring ideas, not with writing a unified paragraph.

> Apparently a "well-made" story, but seems clever rather than moving or real. Doesn't seem plausible. Mrs. M's change comes out of the blue--maybe some women might respond like this, but probably not most.

Does literature deal with unusual people, or with usual (typical?) people? Shouldn't it deal with typical? Maybe not. (Anyway, how can I know?) Is "typical" same as "plausible"? Come to think of it, prob. not.

Anyway, whether Mrs. M is typical or not, is her change plausible, believable? Think more about this.

Why did she change? Her husband dominated her life and controlled her actions; he did "impose a private will upon a fellow creature." She calls this a crime, even if well-intentioned. Is it a crime?

Arguing with Yourself: Critical Thinking

In our discussion of annotating, brainstorming, free writing, listing, asking questions, and keeping a journal, the emphasis has been on responding freely rather than in any highly systematic or disciplined way. Something strikes us (perhaps an idea, perhaps an uncertainty), and we jot it down. Even before we finish jotting it down we may go on to question it, but probably not; at this early stage it is enough to put onto paper some thoughts, rooted in our first responses, and to keep going.

The almost random play of mind that is evident in brainstorming and in the other activities already discussed is of course a kind of thinking, but the term **critical thinking** (which we addressed briefly in our first chapter) is reserved for something different. When we think critically, we skeptically scrutinize our own ideas—for example, by searching out our underlying assumptions, or by evaluating what we have quickly jotted down as evidence. We have already seen some examples of this sort of analysis of one's own thinking in the journal entries, where, for instance, a student wrote that literature should probably deal with "typical" people, then wondered if "typical" and "plausible" were the same, and then added "probably not."

Speaking broadly, critical thinking is rational, logical thinking. In thinking critically, writers

- scrutinize their assumptions;
- test the evidence they have collected, even to the extent of looking for counterevidence; and
- revise their thesis when necessary, in order to make the argument as complete and convincing as possible.

Let's start with assumptions. If I say that a story is weak because it is improbable, I ought to think about my assumption that improbability is a fault. I can begin by asking myself if all good stories—or all the stories that I value highly—are probable. I may recall that among my favorites is *Alice in Wonderland* (or *Gulliver's Travels* or *Animal Farm*)—so I probably have to withdraw my assumption that improbability in itself makes a story less than good. I may go on to refine the idea and decide that improbability is not a fault in satiric stories but is a fault in other kinds, but that is not the same as saying bluntly that improbability is a fault.

The second aspect of critical thinking that we have isolated—searching for counterevidence within the literary work—especially involves rereading the work to see if we have overlooked material or have taken a particular detail out of context. If, for instance, we say that in "The Story of an Hour" Josephine is a busybody, we should reexamine the work to make sure that she indeed is meddling needlessly and is not offering welcome or necessary assistance. Perhaps the original observation will stand up, but perhaps on rereading the story we may come to feel, as we examine each of Josephine's actions, that she cannot reasonably be characterized as a busybody.

Different readers may come to different conclusions; the important thing is that all readers should subject their initial responses to critical thinking, testing their responses against all of the evidence. Remember, your instructor probably expects you to hand in an essay that is essentially an **argument**, a paper that advances a thesis of your own, and therefore you will revise your drafts if you find counterevidence. The **thesis** (the point) might be that

- the story is improbable, or
- the story is typical of Chopin, or
- the story is anti-woman, or
- the story is a remarkable anticipation of contemporary feminist thinking.

Whatever your thesis, it should be able to withstand scrutiny. You may not convince every reader that you are unquestionably right, but you should make every reader feel that your argument is thoughtful. If you read your notes and then your drafts critically, you probably will write a paper that meets this standard.

One last point, or maybe it's two. Just as your first jottings probably won't be the products of critical thinking, your first reading of the literary work probably *won't* be a critical reading. It is entirely appropriate to begin by reading simply for enjoyment. After all, the reason we read literature (or listen to music, or go to an art museum, or watch dancers) is to derive pleasure. It happens, however, that in this course you are trying (among other things) to deepen your understanding of literature, so you are *studying* literature. On subsequent readings, therefore, you will read the work critically, carefully noting the writer's view of human nature and the writer's ways of achieving certain effects.

This business of critical thinking is important. We will discuss it yet again, in Chapters 6 and 13.

Arguing a Thesis

If you think critically about your early jottings and about the literary work itself, you probably will find that some of your jottings lead to dead ends, but some will lead to further ideas that hold up under scrutiny. What the **thesis** of the essay will be—the idea that will be asserted and *argued* (supported with evidence)—is still in doubt, but there is no doubt about one thing: A good essay will have a thesis, a point, an argument. You ought to be able to state your point in a **thesis sentence**.

Consider these candidates as possible thesis sentences:

  1. Mrs. Mallard dies soon after hearing that her husband has died.

True, but scarcely a point that can be argued or even developed. About the most the essayist can do with this sentence is amplify it by summarizing the plot of the story, a task not worth doing unless the plot is unusually obscure. An essay may include a sentence or two of summary to give readers their bearings, but a summary is not an essay.

  2. The story is a libel on women.

In contrast to the first statement, this one can be developed into an argument. Probably the writer will try to demonstrate that Mrs. Mallard's behavior is despicable. Whether this point can be convincingly argued is another matter; the thesis may be untenable, but it is a thesis. A second problem, however, is this: Even if the writer demonstrates that Mrs. Mallard's behavior is despicable, he or she will have to go on to demonstrate that the presentation of one despicable woman constitutes a libel on women in general. That's a pretty big order.

> **3. The story is clever but superficial because it is based on an unreal character.**

Here, too, is a thesis—a point of view that can be argued. Whether this thesis is true is another matter. The writer's job will be to support it by presenting evidence. Probably the writer will have no difficulty in finding evidence that the story is "clever"; the difficulty will be in establishing a case that the characterization of Mrs. Mallard is "unreal." The writer will have to set forth some ideas about what makes a character real and then will have to show that Mrs. Mallard is an unreal (unbelievable) figure.

> **4. The irony of the ending is believable partly because it is consistent with earlier ironies in the story.**

It happens that the student who wrote the essay printed on page 25 began by drafting an essay based on the third of these thesis topics, but as she worked on a draft she found that she couldn't support her assertion that the character was unconvincing. In fact, she came to believe that although Mrs. Mallard's joy was the reverse of what a reader might expect, several early reversals in the story helped to make Mrs. Mallard's shift from grief to joy acceptable.

DRAFTING YOUR ARGUMENT

After jotting down notes and then adding more notes stimulated by rereading and further thinking, you should be able to formulate a tentative thesis. At this point most writers find it useful to clear the air by glancing over their preliminary notes and by jotting down the thesis and a few especially promising notes—brief statements of what they think their key points may be. These notes may include some brief key quotations that the writer thinks will help to support the thesis.

Here are the selected notes (not the original brainstorming notes, but a later selection from them, with additions) and a draft (p. 21) that makes use of them.

> title? Ironies in an Hour (?) An Hour of Irony (?) Kate Chopin's
>   Irony (?)
> thesis: irony at end is prepared for by earlier ironies
> chief irony: Mrs. M. dies just as she is beginning to enjoy life
> smaller ironies: 1. "sad message" brings her joy
>   2. Richards is "too late" at end
>   3. Richards is too early at start

These notes are in effect a very brief **outline**. Some writers at this point like to develop a fuller outline, but most writers begin with only a brief outline, knowing that in the process of developing a draft from these few notes additional ideas will arise. For these writers, the time to jot down a detailed outline is *after* they have written a first or second draft. The outline of the written draft will, as we shall see, help them to make sure that their draft has an adequate organization, and that main points are developed.

A Sample Draft: "Ironies in an Hour"

Now for the student's draft—not the first version, but a revised draft with some of the irrelevancies of the first draft omitted and some evidence added.

The numbers in parentheses refer to the page numbers from which the quotations are drawn, though with so short a work as "The Story of an Hour," page references are hardly necessary. Check with your instructor to find out if you must always give citations. (Detailed information about how to document a paper is given on pp. 763–74.)

Ironies in an Hour

After we know how the story turns out, if we reread it we find irony at the very start, as is true of many other stories. Mrs. Mallard's friends assume, mistakenly, that Mrs. Mallard was deeply in love with her husband, Brently Mallard. They take great care to tell her gently of his death. The friends mean well, and in fact they do well. They bring her an hour of life, an hour of freedom. They think their news is sad. Mrs. Mallard at first expresses grief when she hears the news, but soon she finds joy in it. So Richards's "sad message" (13), though sad in Richards's eyes, is in fact a happy message.

Among the ironic details is the statement that when Mallard entered the house, Richards tried to conceal him from Mrs. Mallard, but "Richards was too late" (14). This is ironic because earlier Richards "hastened" (13) to bring his sad message; if he had at the start been "too late" (14), Brently Mallard would have arrived at home first, and Mrs. Mallard's life would not have ended an hour later but would simply have gone on as it had before. Yet another irony at the end of the story is the diagnosis of the doctors. The doctors say she died of "heart disease--of joy that kills" (14). In one sense the doctors are right: Mrs. Mallard has experienced a great joy. But of course the doctors totally misunderstand the joy that kills her.

The central irony resides not in the well-intentioned but ironic actions of Richards, or in the unconsciously ironic words of the doctors, but in her own life. In a way she has been dead. She "sometimes" (14) loved her husband, but in a way she has been dead. Now, his apparent death brings

her new life. This new life comes to her at the season of the year when "the

tops of trees . . . were all aquiver with the new spring life" (13). But,

ironically, her new life will last only an hour. She looks forward to "summer

days" (14) but she will not see even the end of this spring day. Her years of

marriage were ironic. They brought her a sort of living death instead of joy.

Her new life is ironic too. It grows out of her moment of grief for her

supposedly dead husband, and her vision of a new life is cut short.

[New page]

Work Cited

Chopin, Kate. "The Story of an Hour." <u>Literature for Composition, Compact</u>

<u>Edition</u>. Ed. Sylvan Barnet et al. New York: Longman, 2003, 12–14.

Revising an Argument

The draft, although thoughtful and clear, is not yet a finished essay. The student went on to improve it in many small but important ways.

First, the draft needs a good introductory paragraph, a paragraph that will let the **audience**—the readers—know where the writer will be taking them. (In Chapter 4 we discuss introductory paragraphs.) Doubtless you know from your own experience as a reader that readers can follow an argument more easily— and with more pleasure—if early in the discussion the writer alerts them to the gist of the argument. (The title, too, can strongly suggest the thesis.) Second, some of the paragraphs could be clearer.

In revising paragraphs—or, for that matter, in revising an entire draft—writers unify, organize, clarify, and polish.

1. **Unity** is achieved partly by eliminating irrelevancies. Notice that in the final version, printed on page 25 the writer has deleted "as is true of many other stories."
2. **Organization** is largely a matter of arranging material into a sequence that will assist the reader to grasp the point.
3. **Clarity** is achieved largely by providing concrete details and quotations— these provide evidence—to support generalizations and by providing helpful transitions ("for instance," "furthermore," "on the other hand," "however").
4. **Polish** is small-scale revision. For instance, the writer deletes unnecessary repetitions. In the second paragraph of the draft, the phrase "the doctors" appears four times, but it appears only three times in the final version of the paragraph. Similarly, in polishing, a writer combines choppy sentences into longer ones and breaks overly long sentences into shorter ones.

Later, after producing a draft that seems close to a finished essay, writers engage in yet another activity. They edit.

5. **Editing** includes checking the accuracy of quotations by comparing them with the original, checking a dictionary for the spelling of doubtful words, and checking a handbook for doubtful punctuation—for instance, whether a comma or a semicolon is needed in a particular sentence.

Outlining an Argument

Whether or not you draw up an outline as a preliminary guide to writing a draft, you will be able to improve your draft if you prepare an outline of what you have written. (If you write on a word processor it is probably especially important that you make an outline of your written draft. Writing on a word processor is—or seems—so easy, so effortless, that often we just tap away, filling screen after screen with loosely structured material.) For each paragraph in your draft, jot down the gist of the topic sentence or topic idea. Under each of these sentences, indented, jot down key words for the idea(s) developed in the paragraph. Thus, in an outline of the draft we have just looked at, for the first two paragraphs you might make these jottings:

> story ironic from start
> > friends think news is sad
> > Ms. M. finds joy
> some ironic details
> > Richards hastened, but "too late"
> > doctors right and also wrong

An outline of what you have written will help you to see if your draft is adequate in three important ways. The outline will show you:

1. the sequence of major topics
2. the degree of development of these topics
3. the argument, the thesis

By studying your outline you may see (for instance) that your first major point (probably after an introductory paragraph) would be more effective as your third point, and that your second point needs to be further developed.

An outline of this sort is essentially a brief version of your draft, perhaps even using some phrases from the draft. But consider making yet another sort of outline, an outline indicating not what each paragraph says but what each paragraph *does*. An attempt at such an outline of the three-paragraph draft of the essay on "The Story of an Hour" might look like something like this:

1. The action of the friends is ironic.
2. Gives some specific (minor) details about ironies.
3. Explains "central irony."

We ought to see a red flag here. The aim of this sort of outline is to indicate what each paragraph *does*, but the jotting for the first paragraph does not tell us what the paragraph does; rather, it more or less summarizes the content of the paragraph. Why? Because the paragraph doesn't *do* much of anything. It does not clearly introduce the thesis, or define a crucial term, or set the story in the context of Chopin's other work. An outline indicating the function of each paragraph will force you to see if your essay has an effective structure. We will see that the student later wrote a new opening paragraph for the essay on "The Story of an Hour."

Soliciting Peer Review

Your instructor may encourage (or even require) you to discuss your draft with another student or with a small group of students. That is, you may be asked to get a review from your peers. Such a procedure is helpful in several ways. First, it gives the writer a real audience, readers who can point to what pleases or puzzles them, who make suggestions, who may often disagree (with the writer or with each other), and who frequently, though not intentionally, *misread*. Though writers don't necessarily like everything they hear (they seldom hear "This is perfect. Don't change a word!"), reading and discussing their work with others almost always gives them a fresh perspective on their work, and a fresh perspective may stimulate thoughtful revision. (Having your intentions misread because your writing isn't clear enough can be particularly stimulating.)

The writer whose work is being reviewed is not the sole beneficiary. When students regularly serve as readers for each other, they become better readers of their own work and consequently better revisers. As we say in Chapter 1, learning to write is in large measure learning to read.

If peer review is a part of the writing process in your course, the instructor may distribute a sheet with some suggestions and questions. Here is an example of such a sheet.

QUESTIONS FOR PEER REVIEW   ENGLISH 125A
Read each draft once, quickly. Then read it again, with the following questions in mind.

1. What is the essay's topic? Is it one of the assigned topics, or a variation from it? Does the draft show promise of fulfilling the assignment?
2. Looking at the essay as a whole, what thesis (main idea) is stated or implied? If implied, state it in your own words.
3. Is the thesis plausible? How might the argument be strengthened?
4. Looking at each paragraph separately:
   a. What is the basic point? (If it isn't clear to you, ask for clarification.)
   b. How does the paragraph relate to the essay's main idea or to the previous paragraph?
   c. Should some paragraphs be deleted? Be divided into two or more paragraphs? Be combined? Be put elsewhere? (If you outline the essay by jotting down the gist of each paragraph, you will get help in answering these questions.)
   d. Is each sentence clearly related to the sentence that precedes and to the sentence that follows?
   e. Is each paragraph adequately developed?
   f. Are there sufficient details, perhaps brief, supporting quotations from the text?
5. What are the paper's chief strengths?
6. Make at least two specific suggestions that you think will assist the author to improve the paper.

Final Version of the Sample Essay: "Ironies of Life in Kate Chopin's 'The Story of an Hour'"

Here is the final version of the student's essay. The essay submitted to the instructor had been retyped; but here, so that you can easily see how the draft has been revised, we print the draft with the final changes written in by hand.

Ironies of Life in Kate Chopin's "The Story of an Hour"

~~Ironies in an Hour~~

Despite its title, Kate Chopin's "The Story of an Hour" ironically takes only a few minutes to read. In addition, the story turns out to have an ironic ending, but on rereading it one sees that the irony is not concentrated only in the outcome of the plot--Mrs. Mallard dies just when she is beginning to live--but is also present in many details.

After we know how the story turns out, if we reread it we find irony at the very start. ~~/as is true of many other stories.~~ Because Mrs. and her sister Mallard's friends assume, mistakenly, that ~~Mrs. Mallard~~ she was deeply in love with her husband, Brently Mallard./ They take great They care to tell her gently of his death. ~~The friends~~ mean well, and in ing joyous fact they do well./ ~~They~~ bring her an hour of life, an hour of but it is ironic that True, freedom/. They think their news is sad. Mrs. Mallard at first (unknown to her friends) expresses grief when she hears the news, but soon she finds joy in it. So Richards's "sad message" (12), though sad in Richards's eyes, is in fact a happy message.

small but significant near the end of the story Among the ironic details is the statement that when Mallard entered the house, Richards tried to conceal him from Mrs. almost at Mallard, but "Richards was too late" (13). This is ironic because the start of the story, in the second paragraph, ~~earlier~~ Richards "hastened" (12) to bring his sad message; if he had at the start been "too late" (13), Brently Mallard would have arrived at home first, and Mrs. Mallard's life would not have ended an hour later but would simply have gone on as it had before. Yet another irony at the end of the story is the diagnosis of the doctors. The doctors say she died of "heart disease--of joy that they for the last hour kills" (13). In one sense ~~the doctors~~ are right: Mrs. Mallard experienced a great joy. But of course the doctors totally misunderstand the joy that kills her. It is not joy at seeing her husband alive, but her realization that the great joy she experienced during the last hour is over.

All of these ironic details add richness to the story, but
∧ ~~T~~he central irony resides not in the well-intentioned but

ironic actions of Richards, or in the unconsciously ironic words of
                    Mrs. Mallard's
the doctors, but in ~~her~~ own life. ~~In a way she has been dead.~~ She

"sometimes" (13) loved her husband, but in a way she has been
a body subjected to her husband's will   Appropriately
dead~~,~~ Now, his apparent death brings her new life. ~~T~~his new
                                                        ∧
life comes to her at the season of the year when "the tops of

trees . . . were all aquiver with the new spring life" (13). But,
    She is "free, free, free"--but only until her husband walks through the
ironically, her new life will last only an hour. She looks   doorway.
                                                        ∧
forward to "summer days" (14) but she will not see even the
                        If
end of this spring day. ~~H~~er years of marriage were ironic~~.~~,
                        ∧
bringing
~~They brought~~ her a sort of living death instead of joy~~.~~, ~~H~~er
            not only because
new life is ironic too~~.~~, ~~I~~t grows out of her moment of grief for
                but also because her vision of "a long progression of years"
her supposedly dead husband, ~~and her vision of a new life~~ is
                            ∧
cut short~~.~~ within an hour on a spring day.

[New page]

Work Cited

Chopin, Kate. "The Story of an Hour." Literature for Composition, Compact

Edition. Ed. Sylvan Barnet et al. New York: Longman, 2003, 12–14.

A Brief Overview of the Final Version

Finally, as a quick review, let's look at several principles illustrated by this essay.

- The **title of the essay** is not merely the title of the work discussed; rather, it should give the reader a clue, a small idea of the essayist's topic. Because your title will create a crucial first impression, make sure that it is interesting.
- The **opening or introductory paragraph** does not begin by saying "In this story . . . " Rather, by naming the author and the title, it lets the reader know exactly what story is being discussed. It also develops the writer's thesis so readers know where they will be going.
- The **organization** is effective. The smaller ironies are discussed in the second and third paragraphs, the central (chief) irony in the last paragraph. That is, the essay does not dwindle or become anticlimactic; rather, it builds up from the least important to the most important point. Again, if you outline your draft you will see if it has an effective organization.
- Some **brief quotations** are used, both to provide evidence and to let the reader hear—even if only fleetingly—Kate Chopin's writing.

- The essay is chiefly devoted to **analysis** (how the parts relate to each other), not to summary (a brief restatement of the happenings). The writer, properly assuming that the reader has read the work, does not tell the plot in great detail. But, aware that the reader has not memorized the story, the writer gives helpful reminders.
- The **present tense** is used in narrating the action: "Mrs. Mallard dies"; "Mrs. Mallard's friends and relatives all assume."
- Although a **concluding paragraph** is often useful—if it does more than merely summarize what has already been clearly said—it is not essential in a short analysis. In this essay, the last sentence explains the chief irony and therefore makes an acceptable ending.
- Documentation is given according to the form set forth in Appendix B.
- There are no typographical errors. The author has proofread the paper carefully.

WRITING WITH A WORD PROCESSOR

In the preceding chapter we talked about "reading with pen in hand," and we really meant a pen—or a pencil—with which, in your early stage of interacting with the text, you will underline or circle or connect with arrows words and phrases. But when it comes to jotting down ideas, or sketching an outline, or drafting an essay, many students use a computer or a word processor. Further, you can receive valuable help from reference books and handbooks on style and usage, from computer programs (which check the spelling and grammar of documents), and from Internet resources. Users of this book, for example, can make good use of the many resources available at Longman's "English Pages" site: <http://longman.awl.com/englishpages/>. Here you will find a citation guide, advice on (and exercises for) developing your style, links to many additional sites and resources, and much more. Although no computer program or Internet site can write and revise a paper for you, it can help you to detect mistakes and weak spots in your work that you can then proceed to remedy.

✔ **CHECKLIST:** *Writing with a Word Processor*

Pre-writing

❏ Take notes. Try listing, then linking and clustering your ideas. Use an outline if you find it helpful.
❏ Check that your transcriptions are accurate if you quote.
❏ Keep your notes together in one file.
❏ Organize your sources in a bibliography.
❏ *Always back up your material.*
❏ Print out your notes.

Preparing a First Draft

❏ Use your notes—move them around in blocks. Expand on your ideas.
❏ Incorporate notes to yourself in your first draft.

❏ Read your draft on the screen to check for errors.
❏ Print out a copy of your first draft.

Working with Your Draft

❏ Revise your printed draft with pen or pencil. Incorporate these changes into your computer file.
❏ Read your corrected draft on the screen; then print out a fresh copy.
❏ Repeat these steps as many times as necessary.

Responding to Peer Review

❏ Give a copy to a peer for comments and suggestions.
❏ Respond appropriately to your reviewer, making changes in your computer file.
❏ Print out your revised version and reread it.

Preparing a Final Copy

❏ If there are only a few changes, make them on your printed copy. Otherwise, incorporate your changes in your computer file and print out your final copy.

YOUR TURN: TWO ADDITIONAL STORIES BY KATE CHOPIN

Désirée's Baby

As the day was pleasant, Madame Valmondé drove over to L'Abri to see Désirée and the baby.

It made her laugh to think of Désirée with a baby. Why, it seemed but yesterday that Désirée was little more than a baby herself; when Monsieur in riding through the gateway of Valmondé had found her lying asleep in the shadow of the big stone pillar.

The little one awoke in his arms and began to cry for "Dada." That was as much as she could do or say. Some people thought she might have strayed there of her own accord, for she was of the toddling age. The prevailing belief was that she had been purposely left by a party of Texans, whose canvas-covered wagon, late in the day, had crossed the ferry that Coton Maïs kept, just below the plantation. In time Madame Valmondé abandoned every speculation but the one that Désirée had been sent to her by a beneficent Providence to be the child of her affection, seeing that she was without child of the flesh. For the girl grew to be beautiful and gentle, affectionate and sincere—the idol of Valmondé.

It was no wonder, when she stood one day against the stone pillar in whose shadow she had lain asleep, eighteen years before, that Armand Aubigny riding by and seeing her there, had fallen in love with her. That was the way all the Aubignys fell in love, as if struck by a pistol shot. The wonder was that he had not loved her before; for he had known her since his father brought him home from Paris, a boy of eight, after his mother died there. The passion that awoke in him that day, when he saw her at the gate, swept along like an avalanche, or like a prairie fire, or like anything that drives headlong over all obstacles.

5   Monsieur Valmondé grew practical and wanted things well considered: that is, the girl's obscure origin. Armand looked into her eyes and did not care. He was reminded that she was nameless. What did it matter about a name when he could give her one of the oldest and proudest in Louisiana? He ordered the *corbeille*[1] from Paris, and contained himself with what patience he could until it arrived; then they were married.

Madame Valmondé had not seen Désirée and the baby for four weeks. When she reached L'Abri she shuddered at the first sight of it, as she always did. It was a sad looking place, which for many years had not known the gentle presence of a mistress, old Monsieur Aubigny having married and buried his wife in France, and she having loved her own land too well ever to leave it. The roof came down steep and black like a cowl, reaching out beyond the wide galleries that encircled the yellow stuccoed house. Big, solemn oaks grew close to it, and their thick-leaved, far-reaching branches shadowed it like a pall. Young Aubigny's rule was a strict one, too, and under it his negroes had forgotten how to be gay, as they had been during the old master's easy-going and indulgent lifetime.

The young mother was recovering slowly, and lay full length, in her soft white muslins and laces, upon a couch. The baby was beside her, upon her arm, where he had fallen asleep, at her breast. The yellow nurse woman sat beside a window fanning herself.

Madame Valmondé bent her portly figure over Désirée and kissed her, holding her an instant tenderly in her arms. Then she turned to the child.

"This is not the baby!" she exclaimed, in startled tones. French was the language spoken at Valmondé in those days.

10   "I knew you would be astonished," laughed Désirée, "at the way he has grown. The little *cochon de lait!*[2] Look at his legs, mamma, and his hands and fingernails,—real fingernails. Zandrine had to cut them this morning. Isn't it true, Zandrine?"

The woman bowed her turbaned head majestically, "Mais si,[3] Madame."

"And the way he cries," went on Désirée, "is deafening. Armand heard him the other day as far away as La Blanche's cabin."

Madame Valmondé had never removed her eyes from the child. She lifted it and walked with it over to the window that was lightest. She scanned the baby narrowly, then looked as searchingly at Zandrine, whose face was turned to gaze across the fields.

"Yes, the child has grown, has changed," said Madame Valmondé, slowly, as she replaced it beside its mother. "What does Armand say?"

15   Désirée's face became suffused with a glow that was happiness itself.

"Oh, Armand is the proudest father in the parish, I believe, chiefly because it is a boy, to bear his name; though he says not—that he would have loved a girl as well. But I know it isn't true. I know he says that to please me. And mamma," she added, drawing Madame Valmondé's head down to her, and speaking in a whisper, "he hasn't punished one of them—not one of them—since baby is born. Even Négrillon, who pretended to have burnt his leg that he might rest from work—he only laughed, and said Négrillon was a great scamp. Oh, mamma, I'm so happy; it frightens me."

---

[1]*corbeille* wedding gifts from the groom to the bride.   [2]*cochon de lait* suckling pig (French).
[3]*Mais si* certainly (French).

What Désirée said was true. Marriage, and later the birth of his son had softened Armand Aubigny's imperious and exacting nature greatly. This was what made the gentle Désirée so happy, for she loved him desperately. When he frowned she trembled, but loved him. When he smiled, she asked no greater blessing of God. But Armand's dark, handsome face had not often been disfigured by frowns since the day he fell in love with her.

When the baby was about three months old, Désirée awoke one day to the conviction that there was something in the air menacing her peace. It was at first too subtle to grasp. It had only been a disquieting suggestion; an air of mystery among the blacks; unexpected visits from far-off neighbors who could hardly account for their coming. Then a strange, an awful change in her husband's manner, which she dared not ask him to explain. When he spoke to her, it was with averted eyes, from which the old love-light seemed to have gone out. He absented himself from home; and when there, avoided her presence and that of her child, without excuse. And the very spirit of Satan seemed suddenly to take hold of him in his dealings with the slaves. Désirée was miserable enough to die.

She sat in her room, one hot afternoon, in her *peignoir*, listlessly drawing through her fingers the strands of her long, silky brown hair that hung about her shoulders. The baby, half naked, lay asleep upon her own great mahogany bed, that was like a sumptuous throne, with its satin-lined half-canopy. One of La Blanche's little quadroon boys—half naked too—stood fanning the child slowly with a fan of peacock feathers. Désirée's eyes had been fixed absently and sadly upon the baby, while she was striving to penetrate the threatening mist that she felt closing about her. She looked from her child to the boy who stood beside him, and back again; over and over. "Ah!" It was a cry that she could not help; which she was not conscious of having uttered. The blood turned like ice in her veins, and a clammy moisture gathered upon her face.

20   She tried to speak to the little quadroon boy; but no sound would come, at first. When he heard his name uttered, he looked up, and his mistress was pointing to the door. He laid aside the great, soft fan, and obediently stole away, over the polished floor, on his bare tiptoes.

She stayed motionless, with gaze riveted upon her child, and her face the picture of fright.

Presently her husband entered the room, and without noticing her, went to a table and began to search among some papers which covered it.

"Armand," she called to him, in a voice which must have stabbed him, if he was human. But he did not notice. "Armand," she said again. Then she rose and tottered towards him. "Armand," she panted once more, clutching his arm, "look at our child. What does it mean? tell me."

He coldly but gently loosened her fingers from about his arm and thrust the hand away from him. "Tell me what it means!" she cried despairingly.

25   "It means," he answered lightly, "that the child is not white; it means that you are not white."

A quick conception of all that this accusation meant for her nerved her with unwonted courage to deny it. "It is a lie; it is not true, I am white! Look at my hair, it is brown; and my eyes are gray, Armand, you know they are gray. And my skin is fair," seizing his wrist. "Look at my hand; whiter than yours, Armand," she laughed hysterically.

"As white as La Blanche's," he returned cruelly; and went away leaving her alone with their child.

When she could hold a pen in her hand, she sent a despairing letter to Madame Valmondé.

"My mother, they tell me I am not white. Armand has told me I am not white. For God's sake tell them it is not true. You must know it is not true. I shall die. I must die. I cannot be so unhappy, and live."

30   The answer that came was as brief:

"My own Désirée: Come home to Valmondé; back to your mother who loves you. Come with your child."

When the letter reached Désirée she went with it to her husband's study, and laid it open upon the desk before which he sat. She was like a stone image: silent, white, motionless after she placed it there.

In silence he ran his cold eyes over the written words. He said nothing. "Shall I go, Armand?" she asked in tones sharp with agonized suspense.

"Yes, go."

35   "Do you want me to go?"

"Yes, I want you to go."

He thought Almighty God had dealt cruelly and unjustly with him; and felt, somehow, that he was paying Him back in kind when he stabbed thus into his wife's soul. Moreover he no longer loved her, because of the unconscious injury she had brought upon his home and his name.

She turned away like one stunned by a blow, and walked slowly towards the door, hoping he would call her back.

"Good-by, Armand," she moaned.

40   He did not answer her. That was his last blow at fate.

Désirée went in search of her child. Zandrine was pacing the sombre gallery with it. She took the little one from the nurse's arms with no word of explanation, and descending the steps, walked away, under the live-oak branches.

It was an October afternoon; the sun was just sinking. Out in the still fields the negroes were picking cotton.

Désirée had not changed the thin white garment nor the slippers which she wore. Her hair was uncovered and the sun's rays brought a golden gleam from its brown meshes. She did not take the broad, beaten road which led to the far-off plantation of Valmondé. She walked across a deserted field, where the stubble bruised her tender feet, so delicately shod, and tore her thin gown to shreds.

She disappeared among the reeds and willows that grew thick along the banks of the deep, sluggish bayou; and she did not come back again.

45   Some weeks later there was a curious scene enacted at L'Abri. In the centre of the smoothly swept back yard was a great bonfire. Armand Aubigny sat in the wide hallway that commanded a view of the spectacle; and it was he who dealt out to a half dozen negroes the material which kept this fire ablaze.

A graceful cradle of willow, with all its dainty furbishings, was laid upon the pyre, which had already been fed with the richness of a priceless *layette*. Then there were silk gowns, and velvet and satin ones added to these; laces, too, and embroideries; bonnets and gloves; for the *corbeille* had been of rare quality.

The last thing to go was a tiny bundle of letters; innocent little scribblings that Désirée had sent to him during the days of their espousal. There was the remnant of one back in the drawer from which he took them. But it was not Désirée's; it was part of an old letter from his mother to his father. He read it. She was thanking God for the blessing of her husband's love:—

"But, above all," she wrote, "night and day, I thank the good God for having so arranged our lives that our dear Armand will never know that his mother, who adores him, belongs to the race that is cursed with the brand of slavery."

[1892]

Topics for Critical Thinking and Writing

1. Let's start with the ending. Readers find the ending powerful, but they differ in their interpretations of it. Do you think that when Armand reads the letter he learns something he had never suspected, or, instead, something that he had sensed about himself all along? Find evidence in the text to support your view.

2. Describe Désirée's feelings toward Armand. Do you agree with the student who told us, "She makes him into a god"?

3. Chopin writes economically: Each word counts, each phrase and sentence is significant. What is she revealing about Armand (and perhaps about the discovery he has made) when she writes, "And the very spirit of Satan seemed suddenly to take hold of him in his dealings with the slaves"?

4. Is this story primarily a character study, or is Chopin seeking to make larger points in it about race, slavery, and gender?

The Storm

I

The leaves were so still that even Bibi thought it was going to rain. Bobinôt, who was accustomed to converse on terms of perfect equality with his little son, called the child's attention to certain sombre clouds that were rolling with sinister intention from the west, accompanied by a sullen, threatening roar. They were at Friedheimer's store and decided to remain there till the storm had passed. They sat within the door on two empty kegs. Bibi was four years old and looked very wise.

"Mama'll be 'fraid, yes," he suggested with blinking eyes.

"She'll shut the house. Maybe she got Sylvie helpin' her this evenin'," Bobinôt responded reassuringly.

"No; she ent got Sylvie. Sylvie was helpin' her yistiday," piped Bibi.

5   Bobinôt arose and going across to the counter purchased a can of shrimps, of which Calixta was very fond. Then he returned to his perch on the keg and sat stolidly holding the can of shrimps while the storm burst. It shook the wooden store and seemed to be ripping great furrows in the distant field. Bibi laid his little hand on his father's knee and was not afraid.

II

Calixta, at home, felt no uneasiness for their safety. She sat at a side window sewing furiously on a sewing machine. She was greatly occupied and did not notice the approaching storm. But she felt very warm and often stopped to mop her face on which the perspiration gathered in beads. She unfastened her white sacque at the throat. It began to grow dark, and suddenly realizing the situation she got up hurriedly and went about closing windows and doors.

Out on the small front gallery[1] she had hung Bobinôt's Sunday clothes to air and she hastened out to gather them before the rain fell. As she stepped outside,

---

[1]**gallery** porch, or passageway along a wall, open to the air but protected by a roof supported by columns.

Alcée Laballière rode in at the gate. She had not seen him very often since her marriage, and never alone. She stood there with Bobinôt's coat in her hands, and the big rain drops began to fall. Alcée rode his horse under the shelter of a side projection where the chickens had huddled and there were plows and a harrow piled up in the corner.

"May I come and wait on your gallery till the storm is over, Calixta?" he asked.

"Come 'long in, M'sieur Alcée."

His voice and her own startled her as if from a trance, and she seized Bobinôt's vest. Alcée, mounting to the porch, grabbed the trousers and snatched Bibi's braided jacket that was about to be carried away by a sudden gust of wind. He expressed an intention to remain outside, but it was soon apparent that he might as well have been out in the open: the water beat in upon the boards in driving sheets, and he went inside, closing the door after him. It was even necessary to put something beneath the door to keep the water out.

"My! what a rain! It's good two years since it rain' like that," exclaimed Calixta as she rolled up a piece of bagging and Alcée helped her to thrust it beneath the crack.

She was a little fuller of figure than five years before when she married; but she had lost nothing of her vivacity. Her blue eyes still retained their melting quality; and her yellow hair, dishevelled by the wind and rain, kinked more stubbornly than ever about her ears and temples.

The rain beat upon the low, shingled roof with a force and clatter that threatened to break an entrance and deluge them there. They were in the dining room—the sitting room—the general utility room. Adjoining was her bed room, with Bibi's couch along side her own. The door stood open, and the room with its white, monumental bed, its closed shutters, looked dim and mysterious.

Alcée flung himself into a rocker and Calixta nervously began to gather up from the floor the lengths of a cotton sheet which she had been sewing.

"If this keeps up, *Dieu sait*[2] if the levees goin' to stan' it!" she exclaimed.

"What have you got to do with the levees?"

"I got enough to do! An' there's Bobinôt with Bibi out in that storm—if he only didn' left Friedheimer's!"

"Let us hope, Calixta, that Bobinôt's got sense enough to come in out of a cyclone."

She went and stood at the window with a greatly disturbed look on her face. She wiped the frame that was clouded with moisture. It was stiflingly hot. Alcée got up and joined her at the window, looking over her shoulder. The rain was coming down in sheets obscuring the view of far-off cabins and enveloping the distant wood in a gray mist. The playing of the lightning was incessant. A bolt struck a tall chinaberry tree at the edge of the field. It filled all visible space with a blinding glare and the crash seemed to invade the very boards they stood upon.

Calixta put her hands to her eyes, and with a cry, staggered backward. Alcée's arm encircled her, and for an instant he drew her close and spasmodically to him.

"Bonté!"[3] she cried, releasing herself from his encircling arm and retreating from the window, "the house'll go next! If I only knew w'ere Bibi was!" She would not compose herself; she would not be seated. Alcée clasped her shoulders and looked into her face. The contact of her warm, palpitating body when he had

---

[2]*Dieu sait* God only knows.   [3]*Bonté*! Heavens!

unthinkingly drawn her into his arms, had aroused all the old-time infatuation and desire for her flesh.

"Calixta," he said, "don't be frightened. Nothing can happen. The house is too low to be struck, with so many tall trees standing about. There! aren't you going to be quiet? say, aren't you?" He pushed her hair back from her face that was warm and steaming. Her lips were as red and moist as pomegranate seed. Her white neck and a glimpse of her full, firm bosom disturbed him powerfully. As she glanced up at him the fear in her liquid blue eyes had given place to a drowsy gleam that unconsciously betrayed a sensuous desire. He looked down into her eyes and there was nothing for him to do but to gather her lips in a kiss. It reminded him of Assumption.[4]

"Do you remember—in Assumption, Calixta?" he asked in a low voice broken by passion. Oh! she remembered; for in Assumption he had kissed her and kissed and kissed her; until his senses would well nigh fail, and to save her he would resort to a desperate flight. If she was not an immaculate dove in those days, she was still inviolate; a passionate creature whose very defenselessness had made her defense, against which his honor forbade him to prevail. Now—well, now— her lips seemed in a manner free to be tasted, as well as her round, white throat and her whiter breasts.

They did not heed the crashing torrents, and the roar of the elements made her laugh as she lay in his arms. She was a revelation in that dim, mysterious chamber; as white as the couch she lay upon. Her firm, elastic flesh that was knowing for the first time its birthright, was like a creamy lily that the sun invites to contribute its breath and perfume to the undying life of the world.

25   The generous abundance of her passion, without guile or trickery, was like a white flame which penetrated and found response in depths of his own sensuous nature that had never yet been reached.

When he touched her breasts they gave themselves up in quivering ecstasy, inviting his lips. Her mouth was a fountain of delight. And when he possessed her, they seemed to swoon together at the very borderland of life's mystery.

He stayed cushioned upon her, breathless, dazed, enervated, with his heart beating like a hammer upon her. With one hand she clasped his head, her lips lightly touching his forehead. The other hand stroked with a soothing rhythm his muscular shoulders.

The growl of the thunder was distant and passing away. The rain beat softly upon the shingles, inviting them to drowsiness and sleep. But they dared not yield.

The rain was over; and the sun was turning the glistening green world into a place of gems. Calixta, on the gallery, watched Alcée ride away. He turned and smiled at her with a beaming face; and she lifted her pretty chin in the air and laughed aloud.

III

30   Bobinôt and Bibi, trudging home, stopped without at the cistern to make themselves presentable.

"My! Bibi, w'at will yo' mama say! You ought to be ashame'. You oughtn' put on those good pants. Look at 'em! An' that mud on yo' collar! How you got that

---

[4]**Assumption** a parish (i.e., a county) in southeast Louisiana.

mud on yo' collar, Bibi? I never saw such a boy!" Bibi was the picture of pathetic resignation. Bobinôt was the embodiment of serious solicitude as he strove to remove from his own person and his son's the signs of their tramp over heavy roads and through wet fields. He scraped the mud off Bibi's bare legs and feet with a stick and carefully removed all traces from his heavy brogans. Then, prepared for the worst—the meeting with an over-scrupulous housewife, they entered cautiously at the back door.

Calixta was preparing supper. She had set the table and was dripping coffee at the hearth. She sprang up as they came in.

"Oh, Bobinôt! You back! My! but I was uneasy. W'ere you been during the rain? An' Bibi? he ain't wet? he ain't hurt?" She had clasped Bibi and was kissing him effusively. Bobinôt's explanations and apologies which he had been composing all along the way, died on his lips as Calixta felt him to see if he were dry, and seemed to express nothing but satisfaction at their safe return.

"I brought you some shrimps, Calixta," offered Bobinôt, hauling the can from his ample side pocket and laying it on the table.

35   "Shrimps! Oh, Bobinôt! you too good fo' anything!" and she gave him a smacking kiss on the cheek that resounded. "*J'vous reponds,*[5] we'll have a feas' to night! umph-umph!"

Bobinôt and Bibi began to relax and enjoy themselves, and when the three seated themselves at table they laughed much and so loud that anyone might have heard them as far away as Laballière's.

IV

Alcée Laballière wrote to his wife, Clarisse, that night. It was a loving letter, full of tender solicitude. He told her not to hurry back, but if she and the babies liked it at Biloxi, to stay a month longer. He was getting on nicely; and though he missed them, he was willing to bear the separation a while longer—realizing that their health and pleasure were the first things to be considered.

V

As for Clarisse, she was charmed upon receiving her husband's letter. She and the babies were doing well. The society was agreeable; many of her old friends and acquaintances were at the bay. And the first free breath since her marriage seemed to restore the pleasant liberty of her maiden days. Devoted as she was to her husband, their intimate conjugal life was something which she was more than willing to forego for a while.

So the storm passed and everyone was happy.

[1898]

[5]*J'vous reponds* Take my word; let me tell you.

Writing about "The Storm"

As we said earlier, what you write will depend partly on your audience and on your purpose, as well as on your responses (for instance, pleasure or irritation). Consider the *differences* among these assignments:

1. Assume that you are trying to describe "The Storm" to someone who has not read it. Briefly summarize the action, and then explain why you think "The Storm" is (or is not) worth reading.
2. Assume that your readers are familiar with "The Story of an Hour" and "The Storm." Compare the implied attitudes, as you see them, toward marriage.
3. Write an essay arguing that "The Storm" is (or is not) immoral, or (a different thing) amoral. (By the way, because one of her slightly earlier works, a short novel called *The Awakening*, was widely condemned as sordid, Chopin was unable to find a publisher for "The Storm.")
4. In Part IV we are told that Alcée wrote a letter to Clarisse. Write his letter (500 words). Or write Clarisse's response (500 words).
5. You are writing to a high school teacher, urging that one of the four stories by Chopin be taught in high school. Which one do you recommend, and why?
6. Do you think "The Storm" would make a good film? Why? (And while you are thinking about Chopin and film, think about what devices you might use to turn "Ripe Figs," "The Story of an Hour," or "Désirée's Baby" into an interesting film.)

A Note about Literary Evaluations

One other point—and it is a big one. Until a decade or two ago, Chopin was regarded as a minor writer who worked in a minor field. She was called a "local colorist," that is, a writer who emphasizes the unique speech, mannerisms, and ways of thinking of the charming and somewhat eccentric characters associated with a particular locale. Other late-nineteenth-century writers who are widely regarded as local colorists are Bret Harte (California), Sarah Orne Jewett and Mary E. Wilkins Freeman (New England), and Joel Chandler Harris (the old South). Because of the writer's alleged emphasis on the uniqueness and charm of a region, the reader's response is likely to be "How quaint" rather than "This is life as I feel it, or at least as I can imagine it."

Probably part of the reason for the relatively low value attributed to Chopin's work was that she was a woman, and it was widely believed that "serious and important literature" was (with a very few exceptions) written by men. In short, judgments, including literary evaluations, depend partly on cultural traditions.

A question: On the basis of the four stories by Chopin, do you think Chopin's interest went beyond presenting quaint folk for our entertainment? You might set forth your response in an essay of 500 words—after you have done some brainstorming, some thinking in a journal, and some drafting, revising, and editing.

3

Reading Literature Closely: Explication

WHAT IS LITERATURE?

Perhaps the first thing to say is that it is impossible to define *literature* in a way that will satisfy everyone. And perhaps the second thing to say is that in the last twenty years or so, some serious thinkers have argued that it is impossible to set off certain verbal works from all others, and on some basis or other to designate them as literature. For one thing, it is argued, a work is just marks on paper or sounds in the air. The audience (reader or listener) turns these marks or sounds into something with meaning, and different audiences will construct different meanings out of what they read or hear. There are *texts* (birthday cards, sermons, political speeches, magazines, novels that sell by the millions and novels that don't sell at all, poems, popular songs, editorials, and so forth), but there is nothing that should be given the special title of literature.

Although there is something to be said for the idea that *literature* is just an honorific word and not a body of work embodying eternal truths and eternal beauty, let's make the opposite assumption, at least for a start. Let's assume that certain verbal works are of a distinct sort—whether because the author shapes them, or because a reader perceives them a certain way—and that we can call these works literature. But what are these works like?

Literature and Form

We all know why we value a newspaper (for instance) or a textbook or an atlas, but why do we value a verbal work that doesn't give us the latest news or important information about business cycles or the names of the capitals of nations? About a thousand years ago a Japanese woman, Shikibu Murasaki, or Lady Murasaki (978?–1026), offered an answer in *The Tale of Genji*, a book often called the world's first novel. During a discussion about reading fiction, one of the characters gives an opinion as to why a writer tells a story:

> Again and again writers find something in their experience, or see something in the life around them, that seems so important they cannot bear to let it pass into oblivion. There must never come a time, the writer feels, when people do not know about this.

Literature is about human experiences, but the experiences embodied in literature are not simply the shapeless experiences—the chaotic passing scene—captured by a mindless, unselective video camera. Poets, dramatists, and storytellers find or impose a shape on scenes (for instance, the history of two lovers), giving readers things to value—written or spoken accounts that are memorable not only for their content but also for their *form*—the shape of the speeches, of the scenes, of the plots. (In a little while we will see that form and content are inseparable, but for the moment, for textbook purposes, we can talk about them separately.)

Because this discussion of literature is brief, we will illustrate the point by looking at one of the briefest literary forms, the proverb. Consider this statement:

A rolling stone gathers no moss.

Now let's compare it with a **paraphrase** (a restatement, a translation into other words):

If a stone is always moving around, vegetation won't have a chance to grow on it.

What makes the original version more powerful, more memorable? Surely much of the answer is that the original is more concrete and its form is more shapely. At the risk of being heavy-handed, we can analyze the shapeliness thus: *Stone* and *moss* (the two nouns in the sentence) each contain one syllable; *rolling* and *gathers* (the two words of motion) each contain two syllables, with the accent on the first syllable. Notice, too, the nice contrast between stone (hard) and moss (soft).

The reader probably *feels* this shapeliness unconsciously rather than perceives it consciously. That is, these connections become apparent when one starts to analyze, but the literary work can make its effect on a reader even before the reader analyzes. As T. S. Eliot said in his essay on Dante (1929), "Genuine poetry can communicate before it is understood." Indeed, our *first* reading of a work, when, so to speak, we are all eyes and ears (and the mind is highly receptive rather than sifting for evidence), is sometimes the most important reading. Experience proves that we can feel the effects of a work without yet understanding *how* the effects are achieved.

Probably most readers will agree that

- the words in the proverb are paired interestingly and meaningfully;
- the sentence is not simply some information but is also (to quote one of Robert Frost's definitions of literature) "a performance in words";
- what the sentence *is*, we might say, is no less significant than what the sentence *says*;
- the sentence as a whole forms a memorable picture, a small but complete world, hard and soft, inorganic and organic, inert and moving;
- the idea set forth is simple—partly because it is highly focused and therefore it leaves out a lot—but it is also complex;
- by virtue of the contrasts, and, again, even by the pairing of monosyllabic nouns and of disyllabic words of motion, it is unified into a pleasing whole.

For all of its specificity and its compactness—the proverb contains only six words—it expands our minds.

A Brief Exercise: Take a minute to think about some other proverb, for instance "Look before you leap," "Finders keepers," "Haste makes waste," or "Absence makes the heart grow fonder." Paraphrase it, and then ask yourself why the original is more interesting, more memorable, than your paraphrase.

Form and Meaning

Let's turn now to a work not much longer than a proverb—a very short poem by Robert Frost (1874–1963).

The Span of Life

The old dog barks backward without getting up.
I can remember when he was a pup.

Read the poem aloud once or twice, physically experiencing Frost's "performance in words." Notice that the first line is harder to say than the second line, which more or less rolls off the tongue. Why? Because in the first line we must pause between *old* and *dog*, between *backward* and *without*, and between *without* and *getting*—and in fact between *back* and *ward*. Further, when we read the poem aloud, or with the mind's ear, in the first line we hear four consecutive stresses in "old dog barks back," a noticeable contrast to the rather jingling "when he was a pup" in the second line. No two readers will read the lines in exactly the same way, but it is probably safe to say that most readers will agree that in the first line they may stress fairly heavily as many as eight syllables, whereas in the second line they may stress only three or four:

The óld dóg bárks báckward withoút gétting úp.
Í can remémber when hé was a púp.

And so we can say that the form (a relatively effortful, hard-to-speak line followed by a bouncy line) shapes and indeed is part of the content (a description of a dog that no longer has the energy or the strength to leap up, followed by a memory of the dog as a puppy).

Thinking further about Frost's poem, we notice something else about the form. The first line is about a dog, but the second line is about a dog *and* a human being ("*I* can remember"). The speaker must be getting on, too. And although nothing is said about the dog as a *symbol* of human life, surely the reader, prompted by the title of the poem, makes a connection between the life span of a dog and that of a human being. Part of what makes the poem effective is that this point is *not* stated explicitly, not belabored. Readers have the pleasure of making the connection for themselves—under Frost's careful guidance.

Everyone knows that puppies are frisky and that old dogs are not—though perhaps not until we encountered this poem did we think twice about the fact that "the old dog barks backward without getting up." Or let's put it this way:

- Many people may have noticed this behavior, but
- perhaps only Frost thought (to use Lady Murasaki's words), "There must never come a time . . . when people do not know about this." And,
- fortunately for all of us, Frost had the ability to put his perception into memorable words.

Part of what makes this performance in words especially memorable is, of course, the *relationship* between the two lines. Neither line in itself is anything very special, but because of the counterpoint the whole is more than the sum of the parts. Skill in handling language, obviously, is indispensable if the writer is to produce literature. A person may know a great deal about dogs and may be a great lover of dogs, but knowledge and love are not enough equipment to write even a two-line poem about a dog (or the span of life, or both). Poems, like other kinds of literature, are produced by people who know how to delight us with verbal performances.

The chief reason for opposing pornography is that it exerts a bad influence on those who consume it. If indeed books and pictures can exert a bad influence,

it seems reasonable to think that other books and pictures can exert a good influence. Fairness requires us to mention, however, that many thoughtful people disagree and argue that literature and art entertain us but do not really influence us
in any significant way. In trying to solve this debate, perhaps we can rely only on
our own experience.

We can easily see that Robert Frost's "The Span of Life" is a work of literature—a work that uses language in a special way—if we contrast it with another
short work in rhyme:

> Thirty days hath September,
> April, June, and November;
> All the rest have thirty-one
> Excepting February alone,
> Which has twenty-eight in fine,
> Till leap year gives it twenty-nine.

This information is important, but it is only information. The lines rhyme,
giving the work some form, but there is nothing very interesting about it. (This
is a matter of opinion; perhaps you will want to take issue.) It is true and therefore useful, but it is not of compelling interest, probably because it only *tells* us
facts rather than *shows* or *presents* human experience. We all remember the
lines, but they do not hold our interest. "Thirty days" offers neither the pleasure
of an insight nor the pleasure of an interesting tune. It has nothing of what the
poet Thomas Gray said characterizes literature: "Thoughts that breathe, and
words that burn."

READING IN SLOW MOTION

In this chapter, and in the next, we focus on the skills that careful study of literary
language requires. "Close reading" is perhaps the most familiar name for this technique of heightened responsiveness to the words on the page. But another, employed by the literary critics Reuben A. Brower and Richard Poirier, may be even
better. They refer to "reading in slow motion." Brower, for example, speaks of
"slowing down the process of reading to observe what is happening, in order to
attend very closely to the words, their uses, and their meanings." This sort of reading, he explains, involves looking and listening with special alertness, slowly,
without rushing or feeling impatient if a work puzzles us at first encounter.[1]

As Brower and Poirier point out, sometimes we are so intrigued or moved by
a writer's operations with words that we are led to "slow down" in our reading,
lingering over verbal details and vivid images—"a watersmooth-silver / stallion" in
Cummings's poem about Buffalo Bill (p. 155), or "Babette danced out to where
the fig-trees were," in Chopin's "Ripe Figs" (p. 3). Or else, we find that we want to
return to a poem, or to a key section of a story or scene in a play, to articulate—
"slow motion" style—why it has affected us as powerfully as it did.

"Close" or slow-motion reading can help you to understand and enjoy a work
that at first seems strange or obscure. When we examine a piece of literature with

---

[1] The quotation is taken from Brower's introduction to *In Defense of Reading: A Reader's
Approach to Literary Criticism*, ed. Reuben A. Brower and Richard Poirier (1962). See also
Brower, *The Fields of Light: An Experiment in Critical Reading* (1951); and Poirier, *Poetry and
Pragmatism* (1992).

care and intensity, we are not taking it apart in a destructive way but, instead, are seeking to satisfy our curiosity about how the writer organized it. And almost always, our increased *understanding* of the work results in increased *enjoyment*. Very few poems have been made worse by close reading, and many have been made better—made, that is, more accessible and interesting, deeper, and more rewarding.

This point becomes clearer when we recall what it's like to watch a scene from a movie in slow motion, or a TV replay in slow motion of a touchdown run in a football game. In slow-motion film we perceive details we might otherwise miss—the subtle changes in expression on an actress's face, for example, or the interplay of gestures among several performers at a climactic moment in the action. Similarly, seeing a touchdown multiple times in slow motion, and perhaps from a half-dozen camera angles, reveals to us how the play developed, who made the crucial blocks, where the defense failed. The touchdown was exciting when it took place; and it remains exciting—and frequently it becomes more so—when we slow it down in order to study and talk about it.

This chapter deals with explication, and the next with analysis. Both are based on the principle that responding well to literature means:

- acquiring the ability to read it closely;
- practicing this skill to become better and better at it;
- explaining and demonstrating in critical essays what we have learned.

But the two terms, while related to one another, differ in emphasis. An **explication** moves from beginning to end of an entire work (if it is fairly short) or of a section of a work; it is sustained, meticulous, thorough, systematic. An **analysis** builds upon the habits of attention that we have gained from explicating texts and passages of texts.

When we engage in analysis of literature, we are doing so as part of presenting an argument, a thesis, about a work. What is the central theme in this short story by Welty or that one by Updike? What is the most compelling insight into the nature of love that Rich offers in this or that group of poems about men and women? Does Hamlet delay—and if he does, why? To deal with questions like these, we have to read the text closely and study its language carefully, but we must be selective in the pieces of textual evidence that we offer. To be sure, we can explicate a single speech in Hamlet, or an exchange between characters. But it would be a daunting assignment in a short critical essay to explicate an entire scene, and impossible to explicate the entire play from start to finish.

Analysis goes hand in hand with the job of presenting and proving a thesis; it goes hand in hand with explication as well, taking that form of close reading, of reading in slow motion, as its foundation. But rather than say more about analysis here, let's turn to explication first and learn what we can discover about literature through it. As you'll see, one of the things we quickly realize is that close reading of literary works makes us not only better readers but also better writers attuned more sharply and sensitively to the organization of the language in our own prose.

EXPLICATION

A line-by-line or episode-by-episode commentary on what is going on in a text is an explication (literally, unfolding or spreading out). An explication does not deal with the writer's life and times, and it is not a paraphrase, a rewording—though it may include paraphrase. Rather, it is a commentary that reveals your sense of the meaning of the work and its structure. When we explicate a text, we ask questions about the meanings of words, the implications of metaphors and images, the speaker's tone of voice as we initially hear it and it develops and perhaps changes. How is this literary work put together? How did the writer organize it to prompt from me the response I had (and am having) to it? How does it begin, and what happens next, and next after that? And so on, through to the end.

It takes some skill to work your way along in an explication without saying, "In line one . . . In the second line . . . In the third line . . . " This sounds mechanical and formulaic. Make good use of transitional words and phrases, so that your commentary will feel to your reader more natural, with a better pace and rhythm. For example: "The speaker begins by suggesting . . . The poem then shifts in direction . . . In the next paragraph, however, the narrator implies . . . "

A Sample Explication

The following short poem is by Langston Hughes (1902–67), an African American writer. Hughes was born in Joplin, Missouri, lived part of his youth in Mexico, spent a year at Columbia University, served as a merchant seaman, and worked in a Paris nightclub, where he showed some of his poems to Alain Locke, an influential critic, educator, and strong advocate of African American literature. When he returned to the United States, Hughes went on to publish fiction, plays, essays, and biographies; he also founded theaters, gave public readings, and was, in short, an important force.

Harlem

What happens to a dream deferred?

    Does it dry up
    like a raisin in the sun?
    Or fester like a sore—   4
    And then run?
    Does it stink like rotten meat?
    Or crust and sugar over—
    like a syrupy sweet?   8

    Maybe it just sags
    like a heavy load.

    Or does it explode?

[1951]

Different readers will respond at least somewhat differently to any work. On the other hand, since writers want to communicate, they try to control their readers' responses, and they count on their readers to understand the denotations of words as they understand them. Thus, Hughes assumed that his readers knew that Harlem was the site of a large African American community in New York City. A reader who confuses the title of the poem with Haarlem in the Netherlands will wonder what this poem is saying about the tulip-growing center in northern Holland. Explication is based on the assumption that the poem contains a meaning and that by studying the work thoughtfully we can unfold the meaning or meanings.

Let's assume that the reader understands Hughes is talking about Harlem, New York, and that the "dream deferred" refers to the unfulfilled hopes of African Americans who live in a society dominated by whites. But Hughes does not say "hopes," he says "dream," and he does not say "unfulfilled," he says "deferred." You might ask yourself exactly what differences there are between these words. Next, after you have read the poem several times, you might think about which expression is better in the context, "unfulfilled hopes" or "dream deferred," and why.

Working Toward an Explication

In preparing to write an explication, first write on a computer, or type or hand-write, the complete text of the work that you will explicate—usually a poem but sometimes a short passage of prose. *Don't* photocopy it; the act of typing or writing it will help you to get into the piece, word by word, comma by comma. Type or write it *double-spaced*, so that you will have plenty of room for annotations as you study the piece. It's advisable to make a few photocopies (or to print a few copies, if you are using a word processor) before you start annotating, so that if one page gets too cluttered you can continue working on a clean copy. Or you may want to use one copy for a certain kind of annotations—let's say those concerning imagery—and other copies for other kinds of notes—let's say those concerning meter or wordplay. If you are writing on a word processor, you can highlight words, boldface them, put them in capitals (for instance, to indicate accented syllables), and so forth.

Let's turn to an explication of the poem, a detailed examination of the whole. Here are the preliminary jottings of a student, Bill Horner.

These annotations chiefly get at the structure of the poem, the relationship of the parts. Horner notices that the poem begins with a line set off by itself and ends with a line set off by itself, and he also notices that each of these lines is a question. Further, he indicates that each of these two lines is emphasized in other ways: The first begins farther to the left than any of the other lines—as though the other lines are subheadings or are in some way subordinate—and the last is italicized.

Some Journal Entries

Bill Horner later wrote entries in his journal:

Feb. 18. Since the title is "Harlem," it's obvious that the "dream" is by African American people. Also, obvious that Hughes thinks that if the "dream" doesn't become real there may be riots ("explode"). I like "raisin in the sun" (maybe because I like the play), and I like the business about "a syrupy sweet"--much more pleasant than the festering sore and the rotten meat. But if the dream becomes "sweet," what's wrong with that? Why should something "sweet" explode?

Feb. 21. Prof. McCabe said to think of structure or form of a poem as a sort of architecture, a building with a foundation, floors, etc., topped by a roof--but since we read a poem from top to bottom, it's like a building upside down. Title is foundation (even though it's at top); last line is roof, capping the whole. As you read, you add layers. Foundation of "Harlem" is a question (first line). Then, set back a bit from foundation, or built on it by white space, a tall room (7 lines high, with 4 questions); then, on top of this room, another room (lines, statement, not a question). Funny; I thought that in poems all stanzas are the same number of lines. Then--more white space, so another unit--the roof. Man, this roof is going to fall in-- "explodes." Not just the roof, maybe the whole house.

Feb. 21, p.m. I get it; one line at start, one line at end; both are questions, but the last sort of says (because it is in italics) that it is the most likely answer to the question of the first line. The last line is also a question, but it's still an answer. The big stanza (7 lines) has 4 questions: 2 lines, 2 lines, 1 line, 2 lines. Maybe the switch to 1 line is to give some variety, so as not to be dull? It's exactly in the middle of the poem. I get the progress from raisin in the sun (dried, but not so terrible), to festering sore and to stinking meat, but I still don't see what's so bad about "a syrupy sweet." Is Hughes saying that after things are very bad they will get better? But why, then, the explosion at the end?

Feb. 23. "Heavy load" and "sags" in next-to-last stanza seem to me to suggest slaves with bales of cotton, or maybe poor cotton pickers dragging big sacks of cotton. Or maybe people doing heavy labor in Harlem. Anyway, very tired. Different from running sore and stinking meat earlier; not disgusting, but pressing down, deadening. Maybe worse than a sore or rotten meat--a hard, hopeless life. And then the last line. Just one line, no fancy (and disgusting) simile. In fact, no simile at all. This is a metaphor, not a simile. Boom! Not just pressed down and tired, like maybe some racist whites think (hope?) blacks will be. Bang! Will there be survivors?

Drawing chiefly on these notes, Horner jotted down some key ideas to guide him through a draft of an analysis. (The organization of the draft posed no problem; the writer simply followed the organization of the poem.)

11 lines; short, but powerful; explosive
Question (first line)
answers (set off by space and also indented)
"raisin in the sun": shrinking
"sore" ⎫
"rotten meat" ⎬ *disgusting*
"syrupy sweet": relief from disgusting comparisons
final question (last line): explosion?
  explosive (powerful) because:
    short, condensed, packed
    in italics
    stands by self-like first line
    no fancy comparison; very direct

A Sample Essay by a Student (Final Version): "Langston Hughes's 'Harlem'"

Here is Bill Horner's final essay:

Langston Hughes's "Harlem"

"Harlem" is a poem that is only eleven lines long, but it is charged with power. It explodes. Hughes sets the stage, so to speak, by telling us in the title that he is talking about Harlem, and then he begins by asking, "What happens to a dream deferred?" The rest of the poem is set off by being indented, as though it is the answer to his question. This answer is in three parts (three stanzas, of different lengths).

In a way, it's wrong to speak of the answer, since the rest of the poem consists of questions, but I think Hughes means that each question (for instance, does a "deferred" hope "dry up / like a raisin in the sun?") really is an answer, something that really has happened and that will happen again. The first question, "Does it dry up / like a raisin in the sun?," is a famous line. To compare hope to a raisin dried in the sun is to suggest a terrible shrinking. The next two comparisons are to a "sore" and to "rotten meat." These comparisons are less clever, but they are very effective because they are disgusting. Then, maybe because of the disgusting comparisons, he gives a comparison that is not at all disgusting. In this comparison he says that maybe the "dream deferred" will "crust over-- / like a syrupy sweet."

The seven lines with four comparisons are followed by a stanza of two lines with just one comparison:

> Maybe it just sags
>
> like a heavy load.

So if we thought that this postponed dream might finally turn into something "sweet," we were kidding ourselves. Hughes comes down to earth, in a short stanza, with an image of a heavy load, which probably also calls to mind images of people bent under heavy loads, maybe of cotton, or maybe just any sort of heavy load carried by African Americans in Harlem and elsewhere.

The opening question ("What happens to a dream deferred?") was followed by four questions in seven lines, but now, with "Maybe it just sags / like a heavy load," we get a statement, as though the poet at last has found an answer. But at the end we get one more question, set off by itself and in italics: "Or does it explode?" This line itself is explosive for three reasons: It is short, it is italicized, and it is a stanza in itself. It's also interesting that this line, unlike the earlier lines, does not use a simile. It uses a metaphor. It's almost as though Hughes is saying, "O.K., we've had enough fancy ways of talking about this terrible situation; here it is, "boom."

Topics for Critical Thinking and Writing

1. The student's explication suggests that the comparison with "a syrupy sweet" deliberately misleads the reader into thinking the ending will be happy, and it thus serves to make the real ending even more powerful. In class another student suggested that Hughes may be referring to African Americans who play Uncle Tom, people who adopt a smiling manner in order to cope with an oppressive society. Which explanation do you prefer, and why? What do you think of combining the two?

Does some method or principle help us decide which interpretation is correct? Can we, in fact, talk about a "correct" interpretation, or only about a plausible or implausible interpretation and an interesting or uninteresting interpretation?

2. In *The Collected Poems of Langston Hughes* (1994), the editors title this poem "Harlem." But in the *Selected Poems of Langston Hughes* (1959), published when the poet was still alive, the poem is titled "Dream Deferred." Which title do you think is more effective? Do you interpret the poem differently depending on how it is titled? How might a reader—who knew nothing about Hughes—respond to the poem if he or she came upon it with the title "Dream Deferred"?

Note: Another explication (of W. B. Yeats's "The Balloon of the Mind") appears in Chapter 11.

Explication as Argument

We have said that an explication unfolds or opens up or interprets a work by calling attention to such things as the speaker's tone of voice and the implications in images. It might seem, then, to be an objective report, the sort of explanatory writing that is called expository rather than argumentative.

But in fact, because literature makes considerable use of connotations and symbolic meanings—"A rolling stone gathers no moss" is not essentially a statement about stones and moss but about something else—readers may differ in what they take the words to mean. The writer of an explication not only examines the meanings of specific words and images but also, having come to a conclusion about what the details add up to, argues an interpretation, supports a thesis.

What distinguishes argument from exposition is this: In argument, some statements are offered as *reasons* for others. Because writers of arguments assume that their readers may not at the outset share their views, in their writing they offer evidence to support their assertions.

If you reread Bill Horner's explication of "Harlem," you will notice, for instance, that in speaking of the line "Or does it explode?", Horner says, "This line is explosive for three reasons." He then specifies the three reasons. That is, he argues his case, presenting three pieces of supporting evidence: Hughes's line is short, it is italicized, and it is a stanza in itself.

True, much of Horner's explication does consist of expository writing, for instance when he says that the poem consists of "three parts (three stanzas, of different lengths)." There can be little disagreement between writer and reader here—although, come to think of it, a reader might respond, "No, the title is also part of the poem, so the poem consists of four parts." A reader who is looking for an argument—in the sense of a quarrel, not in the sense of a reasoned discussion—can find it with almost any piece of writing. But, again, our point is that because expository writing does not assume a difference of opinion, it chiefly sets forth information rather than seeks to make a case. Argumentative writing, on the other hand, assumes that it must set forth information in a way that persuades the reader of its truth, which means that it must give evidence.

Pure exposition—let's say, information about how to register for classes, or information about what is likely to be on the next examination—is not concerned with persuading readers to accept a thesis. But an explication, even though it might seem only to clarify the meanings of the words in a poem, essentially argues a thesis about the work as a whole. Notice Bill Horner's opening sentence:

> "Harlem" is a poem that is only eleven lines long, but it is charged
> with power.

What is Horner's thesis? Certainly not that the poem is "only eleven lines long"—a writer hardly needs to argue a reader into believing this assertion. Rather, Horner's thesis is that the poem "is charged with power." In the rest of the explication he offers evidence that supports this assertion. To persuade us, he points out that certain lines are indented, that certain figures of speech have certain implications, and that the last stanza is italicized and consists of only one line.

You may disagree: You may not think the poem "is charged with power," and you may think that Horner has misread certain lines. We have already mentioned, in our first "Topic for Critical Thinking and Writing," that when Horner offered this interpretation in class, another student saw a different meaning in "syrupy sweet" (line 8). But if you disagree, whether with the reading as a whole or with the interpretation of a single image, it's not enough to assert that you disagree. You will have to offer an argument, which is to say you will have to set forth reasons in your effort to persuade your readers.

Your goal, in an explication, is to present your insights about the details of the poem's language. But even more, you want these insights to add up to something as a whole. When related to one another, they should enable your reader to understand the poem, overall, more clearly, and to enjoy it more fully. Ask yourself, as you study the poem and develop your draft of the paper,

> **What is my thesis (my central point, my argument)?**

This question will help you to make your essay coherent and unified. It is a reminder that an explication is more than a set of observations about this and that detail. The best explications make use of the details to teach the reader something new about the poem as a whole.

✔ CHECKLIST: *Drafting an Explication*

Overall Considerations

❑ Does the poem imply a story of some sort, for instance the speaker's report of a love affair, or of a response to nature? If so, what is its beginning, middle, and end?

❑ If you detect a story in the speaker's mind, a change of mood—for instance a shift from bitterness that a love affair has ended to hope for its renewal—is this change communicated in part by the connotations of certain words? By syntax? By metrical shifts?

❑ Do the details all cohere into a meaningful whole? If so, your explication will largely be an argument on behalf of this thesis.

Detailed Considerations

❏ If the poem has a title other than the first line, what are the implications of the title?
❏ Are there clusters or patterns of imagery, for instance religious images, economic images, or images drawn from nature? If so, how do they contribute to the meaning of the poem?
❏ Is irony (understatement or overstatement) used? To what effect?
❏ How do the connotations of certain words (for instance, *dad* rather than *father*) help to establish the meaning?
❏ What are the implications of the syntax—for instance, of notably simple or notably complex sentences? What do such sentences tell us about the speaker?
❏ Do metrical variations occur, and if so, what is their significance?
❏ Do rhyming words have some meaningful connection, as in the clichés *moon* and *June, dove* and *love*?
❏ What are the implications of the poem's appearance on the page—for example, of an indented line, or of the stanzaic pattern? (For instance, if the poem consists of two stanzas of four lines each, does the second stanza offer a reversal of the first?)

WHY WRITE? PURPOSE AND AUDIENCE

In Chapter 1 we briefly talked about audience and purpose, but a few further words may be useful. People write explications (as well as other essays on literature) not only to communicate with others but also to clarify and to account for their responses to material that interests or excites or frustrates them. In putting words on paper you will have to take a second and a third look at what is in front of you and at what is within you. And so the process of writing is a way of learning. The last word is never said about complex thoughts and feelings, but when we write we hope to make at least a little progress in the difficult but rewarding job of talking about our responses. We learn, and then we hope to interest our reader because we are communicating our responses to material that for one reason or another is worth talking about.

When you write, you transform your responses into words that will let your reader share your perceptions, your enthusiasms, and even your doubts. This sharing is, in effect, teaching. Students often think that they are writing for the teacher, but this is a misconception. When you write, *you* are the teacher. An essay on literature is an attempt to help someone to see something as you see it.

If you are not writing for the teacher, for whom are you writing? For yourself, of course, but also for others. Occasionally, in an effort to help you develop an awareness that what you write depends partly on your audience, your instructor may specify an audience, suggesting that you write for high school students or for the readers of *The Atlantic* or *Ms.* But if an audience is not specified, write for your classmates.

> • If you keep your classmates in mind as your audience, you will *not* write, "William Shakespeare, England's most famous playwright," because such a remark seems to imply that your reader does not know Shakespeare's nationality or trade.

- On the other hand, you *will* write, "Sei Shōnagon, a lady of the court in medieval Japan," because you can reasonably assume that your classmates do not know who she is.

YOUR TURN: POEMS FOR EXPLICATION

The basic assignment is to explicate the poems, but your instructor may also ask you to respond to some or all of the questions that follow each poem.

WILLIAM SHAKESPEARE

William Shakespeare (1564–1616), born in Stratford-upon-Avon in England, is chiefly known as a dramatic poet, but he also wrote nondramatic poetry. In 1609 a volume of 154 of his sonnets was published, apparently without his permission. Probably he chose to keep his sonnets unpublished not because he thought that they were of little value but because it was more prestigious to be an amateur poet (unpublished) than a professional (published) poet. Although the sonnets were published in 1609, they were probably written in the mid-1590s, when there was a vogue for sonneteering. A contemporary writer in 1598 said that Shakespeare's "sugred Sonnets [circulate] among his private friends."

Sonnet 73

That time of year thou mayst in me behold
When yellow leaves, or none, or few, do hang
Upon those boughs which shake against the cold,
Bare ruined choirs° where late the sweet birds sang.   4
In me thou see'st the twilight of such day
As after sunset fadeth in the west,
Which by-and-by black night doth take away,
Death's second self that seals up all in rest,   8
In me thou see'st the glowing of such fire
That on the ashes of his youth doth lie,
As the deathbed whereon it must expire,
Consumed with that which it was nourished by.   12
    This thou perceiv'st, which makes thy love more strong,
    To love that well which thou must leave ere long.

4 choir the part of the church where services were sung.

Topics for Critical Thinking and Writing

1. In the first quatrain (the first four lines) to what "time of year" does Shakespeare compare himself? In the second quatrain (lines 5–8) to what does

he compare himself? In the third? If the sequence of the three quatrains were reversed, what would be gained or lost?

2. In line 8, what is "Death's second self"? What implications do you perceive in "seals up all in rest," as opposed, for instance, to "brings most welcome rest"?

3. In line 13, exactly what is "This"?

4. In line 14, suppose in place of "To love that well which thou must leave ere long," Shakespeare had written "To love me well whom thou must leave ere long." What if anything would have been gained or lost?

BEN JONSON

Ben Jonson (1572–1637), born in London, was Shakespeare's contemporary. Like Shakespeare, he wrote for the theater, and in fact Shakespeare acted in Jonson's first important play, Every Man in His Humor *(1598). But unlike Shakespeare, Jonson produced a fairly large body of nondramatic poetry.*

Jonson's son, born in 1596, died on his birthday in 1603. Like the father, the boy was named Benjamin, which in Hebrew means "son of the right hand," a phrase Jonson draws on in the first line of the poem.

On My First Son

Farewell, thou child of my right hand and joy;
    My sin was too much hope of thee, loved boy.
Seven years thou wert lent to me, and I thee pay,
    Exacted by thy fate, on the just day.
O, could I lose all father now! For why   5
    Will man lament the state he should envy?
To have so soon 'scaped world's and flesh's rage,
    And, if no other misery, yet age?
Rest in soft peace, and asked, say here doth lie
    Ben. Jonson, his best piece of poetry: 10
For whose sake, henceforth, all his vows be such,
    As what he loves may never like too much.

[1616]

Topics for Critical Thinking and Writing

1. In lines 6–9 Jonson sketches some of the pains of living, including the "misery" of old age. Why do we lament the loss of life, when we see the battering that most people ultimately undergo?

2. As a whole Jonson's language is plain and, it seems, eloquently straightforward. But his words and phrases in fact merit close study, and in certain cases may even be somewhat obscure, at least at first. What, for example, does Jonson mean by the word "just" in line 4? In line 5, what is the meaning of his cry, "O, could I lose all father now"? In line 10, how do you interpret Jonson's statement that his son is "his best piece of poetry"? And in the final line, what is the distinction he makes between "loves" and "like"?

3. Sentimentality, usually defined as excessive emotion, especially an excess of pity or sorrow, is often regarded as a defect in literature. No one is saying that a parent cannot be grief-stricken by the death of a child, but as readers, we can ask if the literary expression of the emotion is convincing, engaging, and moving. Would you call Jonson's poem sentimental, and if so, do you think the sentimentality is a fault?

WILLIAM BLAKE

William Blake (1757–1827) was born in London and at fourteen was apprenticed for seven years to an engraver. A Christian visionary poet, he made his living by giving drawing lessons and by illustrating books, including his own Songs of Innocence *(1789) and* Songs of Experience *(1794). These two books represent, he said, "two contrary states of the human soul." "London" comes from* Experience.) *In 1809 Blake exhibited his art, but the show was a failure. Not until he was in his sixties, when he stopped writing poetry, did he achieve any public recognition— and then it was as a painter.*

London

I wander through each chartered street,
Near where the chartered Thames does flow,
And mark in every face I meet
Marks of weakness, marks of woe.   4

In every cry of every man,
In every Infant's cry of fear,
In every voice, in every ban,
The mind-forged manacles I hear.   8

How the Chimney-sweeper's cry
Every black'ning Church appalls;
And the hapless Soldier's sigh
Runs in blood down Palace walls.   12

But most through midnight streets I hear
How the youthful Harlot's curse
Blasts the new-born Infant's tear,
And blights with plagues the Marriage hearse.   16

[1794]

Topics for Critical Thinking and Writing

1. What do you think Blake means by "mind-forged manacles" (line 8)? What might be some modern examples?
2. Paraphrase the second stanza.
3. Read the poem aloud, several times. How would you characterize the *tone*— sad, angry, or what? Of course the tone may vary from line to line, but what is the prevailing tone, if any?

4. An earlier version of the last stanza ran thus:

> But most the midnight harlot's curse
> From every dismal street I hear,
> Weaves around the marriage hearse
> And blasts the new-born infant's tear.

Compare the two versions closely. Then consider which you think is more effective, and explain why.

5. Write a poem or a paragraph setting forth your response to a city or town that you know well.

EMILY BRONTË

Emily Brontë (1818–48) spent most of her short life (she died of tuberculosis) in an English village on the Yorkshire moors. The sister of Charlotte Brontë (author of Jane Eyre) *and of Anne Brontë, Emily is best known for her novel* Wuthering Heights *(1847), but she was a considerable poet, and her first significant publication (1846) was in a volume of poems by the three sisters.*

Spellbound

The night is darkening round me,
The wild winds coldly blow;
But a tyrant spell has bound me
And I cannot, cannot go.   4

The giant trees are bending
Their bare boughs weighed with snow.
And the storm is fast descending,
And yet I cannot go.   8

Clouds beyond clouds above me,
Wastes beyond wastes below;
But nothing drear can move me;
I will not, cannot go.   12

[1837]

Topics for Critical Thinking and Writing

1. What exactly is a "spell," and what does it mean to be "spellbound"?
2. What difference, if any, would it make if the first line said "has darkened" instead of "is darkening"?
3. What difference would it make, if any, if lines 4 and 12 were switched?
4. What does "drear" (line 11) mean? Is this word too unusual? Should the poet have used a more familiar word?
5. Describe the speaker's state of mind. Have you ever experienced anything like this yourself? What was the situation and how did you move beyond it?

LI-YOUNG LEE

Li-Young Lee was born in 1957 in Jakarta, Indonesia, of Chinese parents. In 1964 his family brought him to the United States. He was educated at the University of Pittsburgh, the University of Arizona, and the State University of New York, Brockport. He now lives in Illinois, where he works as an artist.

I Ask My Mother to Sing

She begins, and my grandmother joins her.
Mother and daughter sing like young girls.
If my father were alive, he would play
his accordion and sway like a boat.   4

I've never been in Peking, or the Summer Palace,
nor stood on the great Stone Boat to watch
the rain begin on Kuen Ming Lake, the picnickers
running away in the grass.   8

But I love to hear it sung;
how the waterlilies fill with rain until
they overturn, spilling water into water,
then rock back, and fill with more.   12

Both women have begun to cry.
But neither stops her song.

[1986]

Topics for Critical Thinking and Writing

1. Why might the speaker ask the women to sing?
2. Why do the women cry? Why do they continue to sing?

E. E. CUMMINGS

Edwin Estlin Cummings (1894–1962), who used the pen name E. E. Cummings, grew up in Cambridge, Massachusetts, and was graduated from Harvard, where he became interested in modern literature and art, especially in the movements called Cubism and Futurism. His father, a conservative clergyman and a professor at Harvard, seems to have been baffled by the youth's interests, but Cummings's mother encouraged his artistic activities, including unconventional punctuation.

Politically liberal in his youth, Cummings became more conservative after a visit to Russia in 1931, but early and late his work emphasizes individuality and freedom of expression.

in Just-

in Just-
spring   when the world is mud-
luscious the little
lame balloonman

whistles   far   and wee   5

and eddieandbill come
running from marbles and
piracies and it's
spring

when the world is puddle-wonderful   10

the queer
old balloonman whistles
far   and   wee
and bettyandisbel come dancing

from hop-scotch and jump-rope and   15

it's
spring
and
        the
                goat-footed   20

balloonMan   whistles
far
and
wee

[1920]

Topics for Critical Thinking and Writing

1. Why "eddieandbill" and "bettyandisbel" rather than "eddie and bill" and "betty and isabel"? And why not "eddie and betty," and "bill and isabel"?
2. What are some effects that Cummings may be getting at by his unusual arrangement of words on the page? Compare, for instance, the physical appearance of "Whistles far and wee" in line 5 with the appearance of the same words in lines 12–13 and 21–24.
3. Because the balloonman is "lame" (line 4) or "goat-footed" (line 20), many readers find an allusion to the Greek god Pan, the goat-footed god of woods, fields, and flocks, and the inventor of a primitive wind instrument consisting of a series of reeds, "Pan's pipes." (If you are unfamiliar with Pan, consult an encyclopedia or a guide to mythology.) Do you agree that Cummings is alluding to Pan? If so, what is the point of the allusion?

Pieter Brueghel the Elder. *Landscape with the Fall of Icarus.* (Royal Museum of Fine Arts, Brussels, Belgium.)

W. H. AUDEN

Wystan Hugh Auden (1907–73) was born in York, England, and educated at Oxford. In the 1930s his left-wing poetry earned him wide acclaim as the leading poet of his generation. He went to Spain during the Spanish civil war, intending to serve as an ambulance driver for the Republicans in their struggle against fascism, but he was so distressed by the violence of the Republicans that he almost immediately returned to England. In 1939 he came to America, and in 1946 he became a citizen of the United States, though he spent his last years in England. Much of his poetry is characterized by a combination of colloquial diction and technical dexterity.

In the following poem, Auden offers a meditation triggered by a painting in the Museum of Fine Arts in Brussels. The painting, by Pieter Brueghel (c. 1525–69), is based on the legend of Icarus, told by the Roman poet Ovid (43 B.C.–A.D. 17) in his Metamorphoses. *The story goes thus: Daedalus, father of Icarus, was confined with his son on the island of Crete. To escape, Daedalus made wings for himself and Icarus by fastening feathers together with wax; but Icarus flew too near the sun, the wax melted, and Icarus fell into the sea. According to Ovid, the event—a boy falling through the sky—was witnessed with amazement by a plowman, a shepherd, and an angler. In the painting, however, these figures seem to pay no attention to Icarus, who is represented not falling through the sky but already in the water (in the lower right corner, near the ship), with only his lower legs still visible.*

Musée des Beaux Arts

About suffering they were never wrong,
The Old Masters: how well they understood
Its human position; how it takes place
While someone else is eating or opening a window or just walking dully along;
How, when the aged are reverently, passionately waiting   5
For the miraculous birth, there always must be
Children who did not specially want it to happen, skating
On a pond at the edge of the wood:
They never forgot
That even the dreadful martyrdom must run its course   10
Anyhow in a corner, some untidy spot
Where the dogs go on with their doggy life and the torturer's horse
Scratches its innocent behind on a tree.

In Brueghel's *Icarus,* for instance: how everything turns away
Quite leisurely from the disaster; the ploughman may   15
Have heard the splash, the forsaken cry,
But for him it was not an important failure; the sun shone
As it had to on the white legs disappearing into the green
Water; and the expensive delicate ship that must have seen
Something amazing, a boy falling out of the sky,   20
Had somewhere to get to and sailed calmly on.

[1938]

Topics for Critical Thinking and Writing

1. In your own words sum up what, according to the speaker (in lines 1–13), the Old Masters understood about human suffering. (The Old Masters were the great European painters who worked from about 1500 to about 1750.)
2. Suppose the first lines read:

   The Old Masters were never wrong about suffering.
   They understood its human position well.

   What (beside the particular rhymes) would change or be lost?
3. Reread the poem (preferably over the course of several days) a number of times, jotting down your chief responses after each reading. Then, in connection with a final reading, study your notes, and write an essay of 500 words setting forth the history of your final response to the poem. For example, you may want to report that certain difficulties soon were clarified and that your enjoyment increased. Or, conversely, you may want to report that the poem became less interesting (for reasons you will set forth) the more you studied it. Probably your history will be somewhat more complicated than these simple examples. Try to find a chief pattern in your experience, and shape it into a thesis.
4. Consider a picture, either in a local museum or reproduced in a book, and write a 500-word reflection on it. If the picture is not well known, include a reproduction (a postcard from the museum or a photocopy of a page of a book).

CLAUDE MCKAY

Born in Jamaica, Claude McKay (1890–1948) wrote his first poems there, in dialect that drew upon the island's folk culture. In 1912 he left Jamaica to pursue a literary career in the United States. McKay attended school and worked at a number of jobs in the 1910s, but above all he continued to write poems, which were well received. During the 1920s, he became part of the Harlem literary and cultural renaissance. A political radical, McKay also was active in left-wing groups and causes; in 1922–23, he traveled to the Soviet Union, where he lectured on politics and literature. McKay's books of poems include Songs of Jamaica *(1912) and* Harlem Shadows *(1922). His most notable novel is* Home to Harlem *(1928); it tells the story of an African American soldier who deserts from the army in France and then returns to the United States, and it was the first novel by an African American to become a best-seller. McKay's autobiography is* A Long Way from Home *(1937). "If We Must Die," printed here, is McKay's best-known poem. A response to a horrific outbreak of racial violence in the summer of 1919 in Chicago and other major cities, the poem was first published in July of that year in the radical journal* Liberator.

If We Must Die

If we must die, let it not be like hogs
Hunted and penned in an inglorious spot,
While round us bark the mad and hungry dogs,
Making their mock at our accursed lot.   4
If we must die, O let us nobly die,
So that our precious blood may not be shed
In vain: then even the monsters we defy
Shall be constrained to honor us though dead!   8
O kinsmen! we must meet the common foe!
Though far outnumbered let us show us brave,
And for their thousand blows deal one deathblow!
What though before us lies the open grave?   12
Like men we'll face the murderous, cowardly pack,
Pressed to the wall, dying, but fighting back!

[1919]

Topics for Critical Thinking and Writing

1. In line 9, the speaker refers to "the common foe." In what other ways in the poem is this "foe" characterized?
2. We know that "If We Must Die" is a poem about racial violence. How would you interpret the poem if you did not know this?
3. Some would argue that violence should never be the response to injustice, no matter how cruel the injustice might be. Do you believe this yourself? Or can you think of instances where violence might be justified?

ALFRED, LORD TENNYSON

Alfred, Lord Tennyson (1809–92), the son of an English clergyman, was born in Lincolnshire, where he began writing verse at age 5. Educated at Cambridge, he had to leave without a degree when his father died and Alfred had to accept responsibility for bringing up his brothers and sisters. In fact, the family had inherited ample funds, but for some years the money was tied up by litigation. Following Wordsworth's death in 1850, Tennyson was made poet laureate. With his government pension he moved with his family to the Isle of Wight, where he lived in comfort until his death.

The poem is relatively long, and your instructor will probably ask you to explicate only a few lines, for example lines 18–23 or perhaps the end, lines 56–70.

Ulysses*

It little profits that an idle king,
By this still hearth, among these barren crags,
Matched with an aged wife, I mete and dole
Unequal laws unto a savage race,
That hoard, and sleep, and feed, and know not me.   5
I cannot rest from travel; I will drink
Life to the lees. All times I have enjoyed
Greatly, have suffered greatly, both with those
That loved me, and alone; on shore, and when
Thro' scudding drifts the rainy Hyades   10
Vext the dim sea. I am become a name;
For always roaming with a hungry heart
Much have I seen and known,—cities of men
And manners, climates, councils, governments,
Myself not least, but honored of them all,—   15
And drunk delight of battle with my peers,
Far on the ringing plains of windy Troy.
I am a part of all that I have met
Yet all experience is an arch wherethro'
Gleams that untravelled world whose margin fades   20
For ever and for ever when I move.
How dull it is to pause, to make an end,
To rust unburnished, not to shine in use!
As tho' to breathe were life! Life piled on life
Were all too little, and of one to me   25
Little remains; but every hour is saved
From that eternal silence, something more,
A bringer of new things; and vile it were
For some three suns to store and hoard myself,
And this gray spirit yearning in desire   30
To follow knowledge like a sinking star
Beyond the utmost bound of human thought.

---

*Ulysses Odysseus, King of Ithaca, a leader of the Greeks in the Trojan War, famous for his ten years of journeying to remote places.

This is my son, mine own Telemachus,
To whom I leave the scepter and the isle,—
Well-loved of me, discerning to fulfill   35
This labor, by slow prudence to make mild
A rugged people, and thro' soft degrees
Subdue them to the useful and the good.
Most blameless is he, centered in the sphere
Of common duties, decent not to fail   40
In offices of tenderness, and pay
Meet adoration to my household gods,
When I am gone. He works his work, I mine.

    There lies the port; the vessel puffs her sail;
There gloom the dark, broad seas. My mariners,   45
Souls that have toiled, and wrought, and thought with me,—
That ever with a frolic welcome took
The thunder and the sunshine, and opposed
Free hearts, free foreheads,—you and I are old;
Old age hath yet his honor and his toil.   50
Death closes all; but something ere the end,
Some work of noble note, may yet be done,
Not unbecoming men that strove with Gods.
The lights begin to twinkle from the rocks;
The long day wanes; the slow moon climbs; the deep   55
Moans round with many voices. Come, my friends.
'Tis not too late to seek a newer world.
Push off, and sitting well in order smite
The sounding furrows; for my purpose holds
To sail beyond the sunset, and the baths   60
Of all the western stars, until I die.
It may be that the gulfs will wash us down;
It may be we shall touch the Happy Isles,
And see the great Achilles, whom we knew.
Tho' much is taken, much abides; and tho'   65
We are not now that strength which in old days
Moved earth and heaven, that which we are, we are.
One equal temper of heroic hearts,
Made weak by time and fate, but strong in will
To strive, to seek, to find, and not to yield.   70

[1833]

4

Reading Literature Closely: Analysis

ANALYSIS

Explication is a method used chiefly in the study of fairly short poems or brief extracts from essays, stories, novels, and plays. Of course, if a writer has world enough and time, he or she can set out to explicate all of *The Color Purple* or *Hamlet;* more likely, the writer will explicate only a paragraph or at most a page of the novel or a speech or two of the play. In writing about works longer than a page or two, a more common approach than explicating is **analyzing** (literally, separating into parts in order to better understand the whole). An analysis of, say, *The Color Purple* may consider the functions of the setting or the uses that certain minor characters serve; an analysis of *Hamlet* may consider the comic passages or the reasons for Hamlet's delay; an analysis of *Death of a Salesman* may consider the depiction of women or the causes of Willy Loman's failure.

Most of the writing that you will do in college—not only in your English courses but in courses in history, sociology, economics, fine arts, and philosophy—will be analytic. **Analysis** is a method we commonly use in thinking about complex matters and in attempting to account for our responses. Watching Steffi Graf play tennis, we may admire her serve, or her backhand, or the execution of several brilliant plays, and then think more generally about the concentration and flexibility that allow her to capitalize on her opponent's momentary weakness. And of course when we want to improve our own game, we try to analyze our performance. When writing is our game, we analyze our responses to a work, trying to name them and account for them. We analyze our notes, looking for ideas that connect, searching for significant patterns, and later we analyze our drafts, looking for strengths and weaknesses. Similarly, in peer review we analyze the draft of a fellow student, seeing how the parts (individual words, sentences, whole paragraphs, the tentative title, and so on) relate to one another and fit together as a whole.

To develop an analysis of a work, we tend, whether consciously or not, to formulate questions and then to answer them. We ask such questions as:

- What is the function of the setting in this story or play?
- Why has this character been introduced?
- What is the author trying to tell us?
- How exactly can I describe the tone?
- What is the difference in assumptions between this essay and that one?

This book contains an anthology of literary works for you to respond to and then write about, and after most of the works we pose some questions. We also pose general questions on essays, fiction, drama, and poetry. These questions may stimulate your thinking and thus help you write. Our concern as teachers of writing is not so much with the answers to these questions; we believe and we ask you to believe that there are in fact no "right answers," only more or less persuasive ones, to most questions about literature—as about life. Our aim is to help you to pose questions that will stimulate your thinking.

ANALYZING A STORY FROM THE HEBREW BIBLE: THE JUDGMENT OF SOLOMON

A brief analysis of a very short story about King Solomon, from the Hebrew Bible, may be useful here. Because the story is short, the analysis can consider all or almost all of the story's parts, and therefore the analysis can seem relatively complete. ("*Seem* relatively complete" because the analysis will in fact be far from complete, since the number of reasonable things that can be said about a work is almost as great as the number of readers. And a given reader might, at a later date, offer a different reading from what the reader offers today.)

The following story about King Solomon, customarily called the Judgment of Solomon, appears in the Hebrew Bible, in the latter part of the third chapter of the book called 1 Kings or First Kings, probably written in the mid-sixth century B.C. The translation is from the King James Version of the Bible (1611). Two expressions in the story need clarification: (1) The woman who "overlaid" her child in her sleep rolled over on the child and suffocated it; and (2) it is said of a woman that her "bowels yearned upon her son," that is, her heart longed for her son. (In Hebrew psychology, the bowels were thought to be the seat of emotion.)

The Judgment of Solomon

Then came there two women, that were harlots, unto the king, and stood before him. And the one woman said, "O my lord, I and this woman dwell in one house, and I was delivered of a child with her in the house. And it came to pass the third day after that I was delivered, that this woman was delivered also: and we were together; there was no stranger in the house, save we two in the house. And this woman's child died in the night; because she overlaid it. And she arose at midnight, and took my son from beside me, while thine handmaid slept, and laid it in her bosom, and laid her dead child in my bosom. And when I rose in the morning to give my child suck, behold, it was dead: but when I considered it in the morning, behold, it was not my son, which I did bear."

And the other woman said, "Nay; but the living is my son, and the dead is thy son." And this said, "No; but the dead is thy son, and the living is my son." Thus they spake before the king.

Then said the king, "The one saith, 'This is my son that liveth, and thy son is dead': and the other saith, 'Nay; but thy son is the dead, and my son is the living.'" And the king said, "Bring me a sword." And they brought a sword before the king. And the king said, "Divide the living child in two, and give half to the one, and half to the other."

Then spake the woman whose the living child was unto the king, for her bowels yearned upon her son, and she said, "O my lord, give her the living child, and in no wise slay it." But the other said, "Let it be neither mine nor thine, but divide it."

5   Then the king answered and said, "Give her the living child, and in no wise slay it: she is the mother thereof."

And all Israel heard of the judgment which the king had judged; and they feared the king, for they saw that the wisdom of God was in him to do judgment.

Analyzing the Story

Let's begin by analyzing the **form** or the shape of the story. One form or shape that we notice is this:

The story moves from a problem to a solution.

We can also say, still speaking of the overall form, that

the story moves from quarreling and talk of death to unity and talk of life.

In short, it has a happy ending, a form that (because it provides an optimistic view of life and also a sense of completeness) gives most people pleasure.

In thinking about a work of literature, it is always useful to take notice of the basic form of the whole, the overall structural pattern. Doubtless you are already familiar with many basic patterns, for example,

tragedy (joy yielding to sorrow) and
romantic comedy (angry conflict yielding to joyful union).

If you think even briefly about verbal works, you'll notice the structures or patterns that govern songs, episodes in soap operas, political speeches (beginning with the candidate's expression of pleasure at being in Duluth, and ending with "God bless you all"), detective stories, westerns, and so on. And just as viewers of a western film experience one western in the context of others, so readers experience one story in the context of similar stories, and one poem in the context of others.

Second, we can say that the Judgment of Solomon is a sort of detective story: There is a death, followed by a conflict in the testimony of the witnesses, and then a solution by a shrewd outsider. Consider Solomon's predicament. Ordinarily in literature characters are sharply defined and individualized, yet the essence of a detective story is that the culprit should *not* be easily recognized as wicked, and here nothing seems to distinguish the two petitioners. Solomon is confronted by "two women, that were harlots." Until late in the story—that is, up to the time Solomon suggests dividing the child—they are described only as "the one woman," "the other woman," "the one," "the other."

Does the story suffer from weak characterization? If we think analytically about this issue, we realize that the point surely is *not* to make each woman distinct. Rather, the point is (until late in the story) to make the women as alike as possible, so that we cannot tell which of the two is speaking the truth. Like Solomon, we have nothing to go on; neither witness is known to be more honest than the other, and there are no other witnesses to support or refute either woman.

Analysis is concerned with

- seeing the relationships between the parts of a work, but it is also concerned with
- taking notice of what is *not* in the work.

A witness would destroy the story, or turn it into an utterly different story. Another thing missing from this story is an explicit editorial comment or interpretation, except for the brief remark at the end that the people "feared the king." If we had read the story in the so-called Geneva Bible (1557–60), which is the translation of the Bible that Shakespeare was familiar with, we would have found a marginal comment: "Her motherly affection herein appeareth that she had rather endure the rigour of the lawe, than see her child cruelly slaine." Would you agree that it is better, at least in this story, for the reader to draw conclusions than for the storyteller explicitly to point them out?

Solomon wisely contrives a situation in which these two claimants, who seem so similar, will reveal their true natures: The mother will reveal her love, and the liar will reveal her hard heart. The early symmetry (the identity of the two women) pleases the reader, and so does the device by which we can at last distinguish between the two women.

But even near the end there is a further symmetry. To save the child's life, the true mother gives up her claim, crying out, "Give her the living child, and in no wise slay it." The author (or, rather, the translator who produced this part of the King James Version) takes these very words, with no change whatsoever, and puts them into Solomon's mouth as the king's final judgment. Solomon too says, "Give her the living child, and in no wise slay it," but now the sentence takes on a new meaning. In the first sentence, "her" refers to the liar (the true mother says to give the child to "her"); in Solomon's sentence, "her" refers to the true mother: "Give her the living child. . . ." Surely we take pleasure in the fact that the very words by which the mother renounces her child are the words that (1) reveal to Solomon the truth, and that (2) Solomon uses to restore the child to his mother.

This analysis has chiefly talked about the relations of parts, and especially it has tried to explain why the two women in this story are *not* distinct until Solomon finds a way to reveal their distinctive natures: If the story is to demonstrate Solomon's wisdom, the women must seem identical until Solomon can show that they differ. But the analysis could have gone into some other topic. Let's consider several possibilities.

A student might begin by asking this question: "Although it is important for the women to be highly similar, why are they harlots?" (It is too simple to say that the women in the story are harlots because the author is faithfully reporting a historical episode in Solomon's career. The story is widely recognized as a folktale, found also in other ancient cultures.) One possible reason for making the women harlots is that the story demands that there be no witnesses; by using harlots, the author disposed of husbands, parents, and siblings who might otherwise be expected to live with the women. A second possible reason is that the author wanted to show that Solomon's justice extended to all, not only to respectable folk. Third, perhaps the author wished to reject or to complicate the stereotype of the harlot as a thoroughly disreputable person. The author rejected or complicated the harlot by introducing another (and truer?) stereotype, the mother as motivated by overwhelming maternal love.

Other Possible Topics for Analysis

1. Another possible kind of analytic essay might go beyond the structure of the individual work, to the relation of the work to some larger whole. For instance, the writer might approach the Judgment of Solomon from the point of view of gender criticism: In this story, it might be argued, wisdom is an attribute only of a male; women are either deceitful or emotional. From this point the writer might set out to create a research essay on gender in a larger whole, certain books of the Hebrew Bible.

2. We might also analyze the story in the context of other examples of what scholars call Wisdom Literature (the Book of Proverbs, and Ecclesiastes, for instance). Notice that Solomon's judgment leads the people to *fear* him—because his wisdom is great, formidable, and God-inspired.

It happens that we do not know who wrote the Judgment of Solomon, but the authors of most later works of literature are known, and therefore some critics seek to analyze a given work within the context of the author's life. For some other critics, the larger context would be the reading process, which includes the psychology of the reader.

3. Still another analysis—again, remember that a work can be analyzed from many points of view—might examine two or more translations of the story. You do not need to know Hebrew in order to compare this early seventeenth-century translation with a twentieth-century version such as the New Jerusalem Bible or the Revised English Bible. You might argue that one version is, on literary grounds, more effective. Such an essay might include an attempt, by means of a comparison, to analyze the effect of the archaic language of the King James Version. Does the somewhat unfamiliar language turn a reader off, or does it add mystery or dignity or authority to the tale, valuable qualities perhaps not found in the modern version? (By the way, in the Revised English Bible, Solomon does *not* exactly repeat the mother's plea. The mother says, "Let her have the baby," and Solomon then says, "Give the living baby to the first woman." In the New Jerusalem Bible, after the mother says, "Let them give her the live child," Solomon says, "Give the live child to the first woman." If you prefer one version to the other two, why not try to analyze your preference?)

Finally, it should be mentioned that an analysis of the structure of a work, in which the relationships of the parts to the whole are considered, allows the work to be regarded as independent of the external world. If we insist, say, that literature should in all respects reflect life, and we want to analyze the work against reality as we see it, we may find ourselves severely judging the Judgment of Solomon. We might ask if it is likely that a great king would bother to hear the case of two prostitutes quarreling over a child, or if it is likely that the false claimant would really call for the killing of the child. Similarly, to take an absurd example, an analysis of this story in terms of its ability to evoke laughter would be laughable. The point: An analysis will be interesting and useful to a reader only insofar as the aim of the analysis seems reasonable.

ANALYZING A STORY FROM THE NEW TESTAMENT: THE PARABLE OF THE PRODIGAL SON

Let's now look at another brief story from the Bible, this one from the Gospel according to St. Luke, in the New Testament. Luke, the author of the third of the four Gospels, was a second-generation Christian. He probably was a Roman, though some early accounts refer to him as a Syrian; in any case, he wrote in

Greek, probably composing the Gospel about A.D. 80–85. In Chapter 15, verses 11–32, Luke reports a story that Jesus told. This story, which occurs only in Luke's Gospel, is of a type called a **parable**, an extremely brief narrative from which a moral may be drawn.

The Parable of the Prodigal Son

And he said, "A certain man had two sons: and the younger of them said to his father, 'Father, give me a portion of goods that falleth to me.' And he divided unto them his living. And not many days after, the younger son gathered all together, and took his journey into a far country, and there wasted his substance with riotous living.

"And when he had spent all, there arose a mighty famine in that land, and he began to be in want. And he went and joined himself to a citizen of that country, and he sent him into his fields to feed swine. And he would fain have filled his belly with the husks that the swine did eat: and no man gave unto him. And when he came to himself, he said, 'How many hired servants of my father's have bread enough and to spare, and I perish with hunger? I will arise and go to my father, and will say unto him, "Father, I have sinned against heaven, and before thee, and am no more worthy to be called thy son: make me as one of thy hired servants."'

"And he arose, and came to his father. But when he was yet a great way off, his father saw him, and had compassion, and ran, and fell on his neck, and kissed him. And the son said unto him, 'Father, I have sinned against heaven, and in thy sight, and am no more worthy to be called thy son.' But the father said to his servants, 'Bring forth the best robe, and put it on him, and put a ring on his hand, and shoes on his feet. And bring hither the fatted calf, and kill it, and let us eat, and be merry. For this my son was dead, and is alive again; he was lost, and is found.' And they began to be merry.

"Now his elder son was in the field, and as he came and drew nigh to the house, he heard music and dancing. And he called one of the servants, and asked what these things meant. And he said unto him 'Thy brother is come, and thy father hath killed the fatted calf, because he hath received him safe and sound.' And he was angry, and would not go in: therefore came his father out, and entreated him. And he answering said to his father 'Lo, these many years do I serve thee, neither transgressed I at any time thy commandment, and yet thou never gavest me a kid, that I might make merry with friends: but as soon as this thy son was come, which hath devoured thy living with harlots, thou hast killed for him the fatted calf.' And he said unto him, 'Son, thou art ever with me, and all that I have is thine. It was meet that we should make merry, and be glad: for this thy brother was dead, and is alive again: and was lost, and is found.'"

Topics for Critical Thinking and Writing

1. In talking about the Judgment of Solomon we commented on certain repetitions (e.g., *two* women) and contrasts (e.g., troubled beginning, happy ending), which help to give shape to the story. What parallels or contrasts (or

both) do you find in the parable of the prodigal son? What *function* does the older brother serve? If he were omitted, what if anything would be lost? (Characterize him, partly by comparing him with the younger brother and with the father.)

2. Is the father foolish and sentimental? Do you approve or disapprove of his behavior at the end? Why?

3. Jesus told the story, so it must have had a meaning consistent with his other teachings. Christians customarily interpret the story as meaning that God (like the father in the parable) rejoices in the return of a sinner. What meaning, if any, can it have for readers who are not Christians? Explain.

COMPARISON: AN ANALYTIC TOOL

Analysis frequently involves comparing. A moment ago we asked you to compare the older brother with the younger brother and the father in the parable of the prodigal son. When we compare, we examine things for their resemblances to and differences from other things. Strictly speaking, if you emphasize the differences rather than the similarities, you are contrasting rather than comparing, but we need not preserve this distinction: we can call both processes *comparing*.

Although your instructor may ask you to write a comparison of two works of literature, the *subject* of the essay is the works; comparison is simply an effective analytic technique to show some of the qualities in the works. You might compare Chopin's use of nature in "The Story of an Hour" (page 12) with the use of nature in another story, in order to reveal the subtle differences between the stories, but a comparison of works utterly unlike can hardly tell the reader or the writer anything.

Something should be said about organizing a comparison, say between the settings in two stories, between two characters in a novel (or even between a character at the end of a novel and the same character at the beginning), or between the symbolism of two poems. Probably, a student's first thought after making some jottings is to discuss one half of the comparison and then go on to the second half. Instructors and textbooks (though not this one) usually condemn such an organization, arguing that the essay breaks into two parts and that the second part involves a good deal of repetition of categories set up in the first part. Usually, they recommend that the students organize their thoughts differently, somewhat along these lines:

1. First similarity
   a. First work (or character, or characteristic)
   b. Second work
2. Second similarity
   a. First work
   b. Second work
3. First difference
   a. First work
   b. Second work
4. Second difference
   a. First work
   b. Second work

and so on, for as many additional differences as seem relevant. If you wish to compare *Huckleberry Finn* with *The Catcher in the Rye*, you might organize the material thus:

1. First similarity: the narrator and his quest
   a. Huck
   b. Holden
2. Second similarity: the corrupt world surrounding the narrator
   a. Society in *Huck*
   b. Society in *Catcher*
3. First difference: degree to which the narrator fulfills his quest and escapes from society
   a. Huck's plan to "light out" to the frontier
   b. Holden's breakdown

Another way of organizing a comparison and contrast:

1. First point: the narrator and his quest
   a. Similarities between Huck and Holden
   b. Differences between Huck and Holden
2. Second point: the corrupt world
   a. Similarities between the worlds in *Huck* and *Catcher*
   b. Differences between the worlds in *Huck* and *Catcher*
3. Third point: degree of success
   a. Similarities between Huck and Holden
   b. Differences between Huck and Holden

A comparison need not employ either of these structures. There is even the danger that an essay employing either of them may not come into focus until the essayist stands back from the seven-layer cake and announces in the concluding paragraph that the odd layers taste better. In your preparatory thinking, you may want to make comparisons in pairs:

- good-natured humor: the clown in *Othello*, the clownish grave-digger in *Hamlet*
- social satire: the clown in *Othello*, the grave-digger in *Hamlet*
- relevance to main theme: —
- length of role: —

But before writing the final version, you must come to some conclusions about what these add up to.

This final version should not duplicate the thought processes; rather, it should be organized so as to make the point—the thesis—clearly and effectively. After reflection, you may believe that

- although there are superficial similarities between the clown in *Othello* and the clownish grave-digger in *Hamlet*,
- there are essential differences.

In the finished essay, a writer will not wish to obscure the main point by jumping back and forth from play to play, working through a series of similarities and differences. It may be better to discuss the clown in *Othello* and then to point out that although the grave-digger in *Hamlet* resembles him in A, B, and C, the grave-digger also has other functions (D, E, and F) and is of greater consequence to *Hamlet* than the clown is to *Othello*. Some repetition in the second half of the essay ("The grave-digger's puns come even faster than the clown's . . . ") will bind the two halves into a meaningful whole, making clear the degree of similarity or difference. The point of the essay is not to list pairs of similarities or differences but to illuminate a work or works by making thoughtful comparisons.

Although in a long essay the writer cannot postpone until page 30 a discussion of the second half of the comparison, in an essay of fewer than ten pages nothing is wrong with setting forth one half of the comparison and then, in light of it, the second half. The essay will break into two unrelated parts if the second half makes no use of the first or if it fails to modify the first half, but not if the second half looks back to the first half and calls attention to differences that the new material reveals. Students ought to learn how to write an essay with interwoven comparisons, but they ought also to know that a comparison may be written in another, simpler and clearer way.

Finally, a reminder: **The purpose of a comparison is to call attention to the unique features of something by holding it up against something similar but significantly different**. You can compare Macbeth with Banquo (two men who hear a prophecy but who respond differently), or Macbeth with Lady Macbeth (a husband and wife, both eager to be monarchs but differing in their sense of the consequences), or Hamlet and Holden Caulfield (two people who see themselves as surrounded by a corrupt world), but you can hardly compare Holden with Macbeth or with Lady Macbeth—there simply aren't enough points of resemblance to make it worth your effort to call attention to subtle differences.

If the differences are great and apparent, a comparison is a waste of effort. ("Blueberries are different from elephants. Blueberries do not have trunks. And elephants do not grow on bushes.") Indeed, a comparison between essentially and evidently unlike things can only obscure, for by making the comparison the writer implies that significant similarities do exist, and readers can only wonder why they do not see them. The essays that do break into two halves are essays that make uninstructive comparisons: the first half tells the reader about five qualities in Alice Walker, the second half tells the reader about five different qualities in Toni Morrison.

A Sample Essay by a Student: "Two New Women"

A student in an introductory class was asked to compare any two of the three stories by Kate Chopin ("Ripe Figs," p. 3; "The Story of an Hour," p. 12; "The Storm," p. 32). She settled on "The Story of an Hour" and "The Storm." We print the final version of her essay, preceded by a page of notes (a synthesis of earlier notes) that she prepared shortly before she wrote her first draft.

> Resemblances or differences greater?
>
> Resemblances
> Theme: release from marital bonds; liberated women
> Setting: nature plays a role in both; springtime in "Hour," storm in
>   "Storm"
> Characterization: in both stories, no villains
>   forces of nature compel;
>   Clarisse presumably happier without husband
>   both seem to emphasize roles of women
>
> Differences
> Ending: "Hour" sad (LM unfulfilled); "Storm" happy; all characters
>   seem content

But endings different in that "Hour" ends suddenly, surprise; "Storm" not surprising at very end.

Overall view (theme?)

"Hour" very restricted view; only one person is of much interest (LM); Josephine interesting only in terms of LM (contrast).
In "Storm," Cal. and Alc. interesting; but also interesting are simple Bobinot and even the child, and also even Clarisse, who sort of has the last word

Possible titles

Two Women
New Women
Tragic Louise, Comic Calixta
Louise, Calixta, and Clarisse

Two New Women

It is not surprising that two stories by an author somewhat resemble each other. What is especially interesting about Kate Chopin's "The Story of an Hour" and "The Storm" is that although they both deal with women who achieve a sense of new life or growth outside of the bonds of marriage, the stories differ greatly in what we call tone. "The Story of an Hour" is bittersweet, or perhaps even bitter and tragic, whereas "The Storm" is romantic and in some ways comic.

The chief similarity is that Louise Mallard in "The Story of an Hour" and Calixta in "The Storm" both experience valuable, affirming, liberating sensations that a traditional moral view would condemn. Mrs. Mallard, after some moments of deep grief, feels a great sense of liberation when she learns of the death of her husband. She dies almost immediately after this experience, but even though she is never physically unfaithful to her husband, there is a sort of mental disloyalty, at least from a traditional point of view. Calixta's disloyalty is physical, not merely mental. Unlike Louise Mallard, Calixta does go to bed with a man who is not her husband. But Calixta, as we will see, is treated just about as sympathetically as is Mrs. Mallard.

Louise Mallard is sympathetic because she does grieve for her husband, and because Chopin suggests that Mallard's sense of freedom is natural, something associated with the spring, the "delicious breath of rain," and "the tops of trees that were all aquiver with the new spring life" (13). Furthermore, Chopin explicitly says that Mallard loved her husband. But Chopin also tells us that one aspect of the marriage was a "powerful will bending her" (13). For all of these reasons, then--Mrs. Mallard's genuine grief, the association of her new feeling with the power of nature, and the assertion that Mrs. Mallard loved her husband but was at least in some degree subject to his will--the reader sympathizes with Mrs. Mallard.

In her presentation of Calixta, too, Chopin takes care to make the unfaithful woman a sympathetic figure. As in "The Story of an Hour," nature plays a role. Here, instead of nature or the outside world being a parallel to the woman's emotions, nature in the form of a storm exerts pressure on the woman. We are told that "the water beat in upon the boards in driving sheets" (33), and a bolt of lightning causes Calixta to stagger backward, into Alcée's arms. These forces of outside nature are parallel to a force of nature within Calixta. Chopin tells us that during the sexual union Calixta's "firm, elastic flesh . . . was knowing for the first time its birthright" (34). And in one additional way, too, Chopin guards against the reader condemning Calixta. We learn, at the end of the story, that Alcée's wife, Clarisse, is quite pleased to be free from her husband for a while:

> And the first free breath since her marriage seemed to restore
> the pleasant liberty of her maiden days. Devoted as she was to
> her husband, their intimate conjugal life was something which
> she was more than willing to forego for a while. (35)

Since Clarisse is portrayed as somewhat pleased to be relieved of her husband for a while, we probably do not see Alcée as a villainous betrayer of his wife. The story seems to end pleasantly, like a comedy, with everybody happy.

In Louise Mallard and in Calixta we see two women who achieve new lives, although in the case of Louise Mallard the reader is surprised to learn in the last sentence that the achievement lasts only a few moments. By "new lives" I mean emancipation from their husbands, but what is especially interesting is that in both cases Chopin guides the reader to feel that although in fact both women behave in ways that would be strongly condemned by the codes of Chopin's day, and even by many people today, neither woman (as Chopin presents her) is blameworthy. Mrs. Mallard is presented almost as a tragic victim, and Calixta is presented almost as a figure in a very pleasant comedy.

[New page]

Work Cited

Barnet, Sylvan, et al., eds. <u>Literature for Composition, Compact Edition</u>.

New York: Longman, 2003.

Looking at the Essay

A few comments on this student's essay may be useful.

- The title announces the *topic*.
- The first paragraph announces the *thesis*, the point that will be argued.
- The second paragraph begins by getting directly to the point: "The chief similarity is . . . "
- The third paragraph clearly advances the argument by giving *evidence*, introduced by a word that implies reasoning, "because."
- The writer provides further evidence by using short relevant quotations from the story.
- The final paragraph summarizes but does not boringly repeat; i.e., it does not merely say "Thus we see, . . . " Rather, it presents the material freshly.

Topic for Critical Thinking and Writing

We like this essay, but perhaps you have a different view. In any case, what grade would you give this essay? Why? Be as specfic as possible in calling attention to what you see as its strengths and weaknesses.

✔ CHECKLIST: *Revising a Comparison*

❏ Does it makes sense to compare these things? (What question will the comparison help to answer? What do you hope your reader will learn?)
❏ Is the point of the comparison—the reason for making it—clear?
❏ Does the comparison cover all significant similarities and differences?
❏ Is the comparison readable; that is, is it clear and yet not tediously mechanical?
❏ Is the organization that is used—perhaps treating one text first and then the other, or perhaps shifting back and forth between texts—the best way to make this comparison?
❏ If the essay offers a value judgment, is the judgment fair? Does the essay offer enough evidence to bring a reader into at least partial agreement?

EVALUATION IN EXPLICATION AND ANALYSIS

When we evaluate, we say how good, how successful, how worthwhile, something is. If you reread the student's essay on "Harlem," you'll notice that he implies that the poem is worth reading. He doesn't say "In this excellent poem," but a reader of the essay probably comes away with the impression that the student thinks the poem is excellent. The writer might, of course, have included a more explicit evaluation, along these lines:

> In "Harlem," every word counts, and every word is effective. The image of the "heavy load" that "sags" is not as unusual as the image of the raisin in the sun, but it nevertheless is just right, adding a simple, powerful touch just before the explosive ending.

In any case, if an essay argues that the parts fit together effectively, it almost surely is implying a favorable evaluation. But only *"almost* surely." We might argue, for instance, that the parts fit, and so on, but that the work is immoral, or trivial, or unpleasant, or untrue to life. Even though it might be granted that the work is carefully constructed, the final evaluation of the work might be low. Evaluations are based on standards. If you offer an evaluation, make certain that your standards are clear to the reader.

Notice in the following three examples of evaluations of J. D. Salinger's *The Catcher in the Rye* that the writers let their readers know what their standards are. Each excerpt is from a review that was published when the book first appeared. In the first, Anne L. Goodman, writing in *The New Republic* (16 July 1951), began by praising Salinger's earlier short stories and then said of the novel:

> But the book as a whole is disappointing, and not merely because it is a reworking of a theme that one begins to suspect must obsess the author. Holden Caulfield, the main character who tells his own story, is an extraordinary portrait, but there is too much of him. He describes himself early on and, with the sureness of a wire recording, he remains strictly in character throughout.

Goodman then quotes a longish passage from *The Catcher*, and says,

> In the course of 277 pages the reader wearies of this kind of explicitness, repetition, and adolescence, exactly as one would weary of Holden himself.

Goodman lets us know that, in her opinion, (1) a book ought not simply to repeat a writer's earlier books, and that, again in her opinion, (2) it's not enough to give a highly realistic portrait of a character; if the character is not a sufficiently interesting person, in the long run the book will be dull.

Another reviewer, Virgilia Peterson, writing in the *New York Herald Tribune Book Review* (15 July 1951), found the book realistic in some ways, but unrealistic and therefore defective because its abundant profanity becomes unconvincing:

> There is probably not one phrase in the whole book that Holden Caulfield would not have used upon occasion, but when they are piled upon each other in cumulative monotony, the ear refuses to believe.

Ms. Peterson concluded her review, however, by confessing that she did not think she was in a position to evaluate a book about an adolescent, or at least *this* adolescent.

> . . . it would be interesting and highly enlightening to know what Holden Caulfield's contemporaries, male and female, think of him. Their opinion would constitute the real test of Mr. Salinger's validity. The question of authenticity is one to which no parent can really guess the reply.

Here again the standard is clear—authenticity—but the writer confesses that she isn't sure about authenticity in this matter, and she defers to her juniors. Peterson's review is a rare example of an analysis offered by a writer who confesses an inability to evaluate.

Finally, here is a brief extract from a more favorable review, written by Paul Engle and published in the *Chicago Sunday Tribune Magazine of Books* (15 July 1951):

> The book ends with Holden in a mental institution, for which the earlier events have hardly prepared the reader. But the story is an engaging and believable one for the most part, full of right observations and sharp insight, and a wonderful sort of grasp of how a boy can create his own world of fantasy and live form.

The first sentence implies that a good book prepares the reader for the end, and that in this respect *The Catcher* is deficient. The rest of the paragraph sets forth other standards that *The Catcher* meets (it is "engaging and believable," "full of right observations and sharp insight"), though one of the standards in Engle's last sentence ("live form") strikes us as obscure.

CHOOSING A TOPIC AND DEVELOPING A THESIS IN AN ANALYTIC PAPER

Because Hughes's "Harlem" is very short, the analysis may discuss the entire poem. But a short essay, or even a long one, can hardly discuss all aspects of a play or a novel or even of a long story. If you are writing about a long work, you'll have to single out an appropriate topic.

What is an appropriate topic? First, it must be a topic that you can work up some interest in or your writing will be mechanical and dull. (We say "work up some interest" because interest is commonly the result of some effort.) Second, an appropriate topic is compassable—that is, it is something you can cover with reasonable attention to detail in the few pages (and few days) you have to devote to it. If a work is fairly long, almost surely you will write an analysis of some part.

Unless you have an enormous amount of time for reflection and revision, you cannot write a meaningful essay of 500 words or even 1,000 words on "Shakespeare's *Hamlet*" or "The Fiction of Alice Walker." You cannot even write on "Character in *Hamlet*" or "Symbolism in Walker's *The Color Purple*." And probably you won't really want to write on such topics anyway. Probably *one* character or *one* symbol has caught your interest. Think of something in your annotations or "response" notes (described in Chapter 1) that has caught your attention. Trust your feelings; you are likely onto something interesting.

In Chapter 2 we talked about the value of asking yourself questions. To find an appropriate topic, ask yourself such questions as the following:

1. *What purpose does this serve?* For instance, why is this scene in the novel or play? Why is there a comic grave-digger in *Hamlet*? Why are these lines unrhymed? Why did the author call the work by this title?
2. *Why do I have this response?* Why do I feel that this work is more profound (or amusing, or puzzling) than that work? How did the author make this character funny or dignified or pathetic? How did the author communicate the idea that this character is a bore without boring me?

The first of these questions, "What purpose does this serve?" requires that you identify yourself with the author, wondering, for example, whether this opening scene is the best possible for this story. The second question, "Why do I have this response?" requires that you trust your feelings. If you are amused or puzzled or annoyed, assume that these responses are appropriate and follow them up, at least until a rereading of the work provides other responses. If you jot down notes reporting your responses and later think about them, you will probably find that you can select a topic.

A third valuable way to find a thesis is to test a published comment against your response to a particular work. Perhaps somewhere you have seen—for instance, in a textbook—a statement about the nature of fiction, poetry, or drama. Maybe you have heard that a tragic hero has a "flaw." Don't simply accept the remark. Test it against your reading of the work. And interpret the word *published* broadly. Students and instructors publish their opinions—offer them to a public— when they utter them in class. Think about something said in class; students who pay close attention to their peers learn a great deal.

Given an appropriate topic, you will find your essay easier to write and the finished version of it clearer and more persuasive if, at some point in your preparation, in note taking or in writing a first draft, you have converted your topic into a *thesis* (a proposition, a point, an argument) and constructed a *thesis statement* (a sentence stating your overall point).

Let's dwell a moment on the distinction between a topic and a thesis. It may be useful to think of it this way: A topic is a subject (for example, "The Role of Providence in *Hamlet*"); to arrive at a thesis, you have to make an arguable assertion (for example, "The role of Providence in *Hamlet* is not obvious, but it is crucial").

Of course some theses are more promising than others. Consider this thesis:

The role of Providence in <u>Hamlet</u> is interesting.

This sentence indeed asserts a thesis, but it is vague and provides little direction, little help in generating ideas and in shaping your essay. Let's try again. It's almost always necessary to try again and again, for the process of writing is in large part a process of trial and error, of generating better and better ideas by evaluating—selecting or rejecting—ideas and options.

The role of Providence is evident in the Ghost.

This is much better, and it could stimulate ideas for an interesting essay. Let's assume the writer rereads the play, looking for further evidence, and comes to believe that the Ghost is only one of several manifestations of Providence. The writer may stay with the Ghost or may (especially if the paper is long enough to allow for such a thesis to be developed) alter the thesis thus:

The role of Providence is not confined to the Ghost but is found also in the killing of Polonius, in the surprising appearance of the pirate ship, and in the presence of the poisoned chalice.

Strictly speaking, the thesis here is given in the first part of the sentence ("The role of Providence is not confined to the Ghost"); the rest of the sentence provides an indication of how the argument will be supported.

Every literary work suggests its own topics for analysis to an active reader, and all essayists must set forth their own theses, but if you begin by seeking to examine one of your responses, you will soon be able to stake out a topic and to formulate a thesis.

A suggestion: With two or three other students, formulate a thesis about Kate Chopin's "The Storm" (in Chapter 2). By practicing with a group you will develop a skill that you will use when you have to formulate a thesis on your own.

ANALYZING A STORY

If a story is short enough, you may be able to examine everything in it that you think is worth commenting on, but even if it is short you may nevertheless decide to focus on one element, such as the setting, or the construction of the plot, or the connection between two characters, or the degree of plausibility. Here is a story by James Thurber (1894–1961), the American humorist. It was first published in 1939.

JAMES THURBER
The Secret Life of Walter Mitty

"We're going through!" The Commander's voice was like thin ice breaking. He wore his full-dress uniform, with the heavily braided white cap pulled down rakishly over one cold gray eye. "We can't make it, sir. It's spoiling for a hurricane, if you ask me." "I'm not asking you, Lieutenant Berg," said the Commander. "Throw on the power lights! Rev her up to 8,500! We're going through!" The pounding of the cylinders increased: ta-pocketa-pocketa-pocketa-*pocketa-pocketa*.

The Commander stared at the ice forming on the pilot window. He walked over and twisted a row of complicated dials. "Switch on No. 8 auxiliary!" he shouted. "Switch on No. 8 auxiliary!" repeated Lieutenant Berg. "Full strength in No. 3 turret!" shouted the Commander. "Full strength in No. 3 turret!" The crew, bending to their various tasks in the huge, hurtling eight-engined Navy hydroplane, looked at each other and grinned. "The Old Man'll get us through," they said to one another. "The Old Man ain't afraid of Hell!" . . .

"Not so fast! You're driving too fast!" said Mrs. Mitty. "What are you driving so fast for?"

"Hmm?" said Walter Mitty. He looked at his wife, in the seat beside him, with shocked astonishment. She seemed grossly unfamiliar, like a strange woman who had yelled at him in a crowd. "You were up to fifty-five," she said. "You know I don't like to go more than forty. You were up to fifty-five." Walter Mitty drove on toward Waterbury in silence, the roaring of the SN202 through the worst storm in twenty years of Navy flying fading in the remote, intimate airways of his mind. "You're tensed up again," said Mrs. Mitty. "It's one of your days. I wish you'd let Dr. Renshaw look you over."

Walter Mitty stopped the car in front of the building where his wife went to have her hair done. "Remember to get those overshoes while I'm having my hair done," she said. "I don't need overshoes," said Mitty. She put her mirror back into her bag. "We've been all through that," she said, getting out of the car. "You're not a young man any longer." He raced the engine a little. "Why don't you wear your gloves? Have you lost your gloves?" Walter Mitty reached in a pocket and brought out the gloves. He put them on, but after she had turned and gone into the building and he had driven on to a red light, he took them off again. "Pick it up, brother!" snapped a cop as the light changed, and Mitty hastily pulled on his gloves and lurched ahead. He drove around the streets aimlessly for a time, and then he drove past the hospital on his way to the parking lot.

5   . . . "It's the millionaire banker, Wellington McMillan," said the pretty nurse. "Yes?" said Walter Mitty, removing his gloves slowly. "Who has the case?" "Dr. Renshaw and Dr. Benbow, but there are two specialists here, Dr. Remington from New York and Dr. Pritchard-Mitford from London. He flew over." A door opened down a long, cool corridor and Dr. Renshaw came out. He looked distraught and haggard. "Hello, Mitty," he said. "We're having the devil's own time with McMillan, the millionaire banker and close personal friend of Roosevelt. Obstreosis of the ductal tract. Tertiary. Wish you'd take a look at him." "Glad to," said Mitty.

In the operating room there were whispered introductions: "Dr. Remington, Dr. Mitty, Mr. Pritchard-Mitford, Dr. Mitty." "I've read your book on streptothricosis," said Pritchard-Mitford, shaking hands. "A brilliant performance, sir." "Thank you," said Walter Mitty. "Didn't know you were in the States, Mitty," grumbled Remington. "Coals to Newcastle, bringing Mitford and me up here for a tertiary." "You are very kind," said Mitty. A huge, complicated machine, connected to the operating table, with many tubes and wires, began at this moment to go pocketa-pocketa-pocketa. "The new anesthetizer is giving way!" shouted an interne. "There is no one in the East who knows how to fix it!" "Quiet, man!" said Mitty, in a low, cool voice. He sprang to the machine, which was now going pocketa-pocketa-queep-pocketa-queep. He began fingering delicately a row of glistening dials. "Give me a fountain pen!" he snapped. Someone handed him a fountain pen. He pulled a faulty piston out of the machine and inserted the pen in its place. "That will hold for ten minutes," he said. "Get on with the operation." A nurse hurried over and whispered to Renshaw, and Mitty saw the man turn pale. "Coreopsis has set in," said Renshaw nervously. "If you would take over, Mitty?" Mitty looked at him and at the craven figure of Benbow, who drank, and at the grave, uncertain faces of the two great specialists. "If you wish," he said. They slipped a white gown on him: he adjusted a mask and drew on thin gloves; nurses handed him shining . . .

"Back it up, Mac! Look out for that Buick!" Walter Mitty jammed on the brakes. "Wrong lane, Mac," said the parking-lot attendant, looking at Mitty closely. "Gee. Yeh," muttered Mitty. He began cautiously to back out of the lane marked "Exit Only." "Leave her sit there," said the attendant. "I'll put her away." Mitty got out of the car. "Hey, better leave the key." "Oh," said Mitty, handing the man the ignition key. The attendant vaulted into the car, backed it up with insolent skill, and put it where it belonged.

They're so damn cocky, thought Walter Mitty, walking along Main Street; they think they know everything. Once he had tried to take his chains off, outside New Milford, and he had got them wound around the axles. A man had had to come out in a wrecking car and unwind them, a young, grinning garageman. Since then Mrs. Mitty always made him drive to the garage to have the chains taken off. The next time, he thought, I'll wear my right arm in a sling; they won't grin at me then. I'll have my right arm in a sling and they'll see I couldn't possibly take the chains off myself. He kicked at the slush on the sidewalk. "Overshoes," he said to himself, and he began looking for a shoe store.

When he came out into the street again, with the overshoes in a box under his arm, Walter Mitty began to wonder what the other thing was his wife had told him to get. She had told him, twice, before they set out from their house for Waterbury. In a way he hated these weekly trips to town—he was always getting something wrong. Kleenex, he thought, Squibb's, razor blades? No. Toothpaste, toothbrush, bicarbonate, carborundum, initiative and referendum? He gave it up. But she would remember it. "Where's the what's-its-name?" she would ask. "Don't tell me you forgot the what's-its-name." A newsboy went by shouting something about the Waterbury trial.

10   . . . "Perhaps this will refresh your memory." The District Attorney suddenly thrust a heavy automatic at the quiet figure on the witness stand. "Have you ever seen this before?" Walter Mitty took the gun and examined it expertly. "This is my Webley-Vickers 50.80," he said calmly. An excited buzz ran around the courtroom. The Judge rapped for order. "You are a crack shot with any sort of firearms, I believe?" said the District Attorney, insinuatingly. "Objection!" shouted Mitty's attorney. "We have shown that the defendant could not have fired the shot. We have shown that he wore his right arm in a sling on the night of the fourteenth of July." Walter Mitty raised his hand briefly and the bickering attorneys were stilled. "With any known make of gun," he said evenly, "I could have killed Gregory Fitzhurst at three hundred feet *with my left hand*." Pandemonium broke loose in the courtroom. A woman's scream rose above the bedlam and suddenly a lovely, dark-haired girl was in Walter Mitty's arms. The District Attorney struck at her savagely. Without rising from his chair, Mitty let the man have it on the point of the chin. "You miserable cur!" . . .

"Puppy biscuit," said Walter Mitty. He stopped walking and the buildings of Waterbury rose up out of the misty courtroom and surrounded him again. A woman who was passing laughed. "He said 'Puppy biscuit,'" she said to her companion. "That man said 'Puppy biscuit' to himself." Walter Mitty hurried on. He went into an A. & P., not the first one he came to but a smaller one farther up the street. "I want some biscuit for small, young dogs," he said to the clerk. "Any special brand, sir?" The greatest pistol shot in the world thought a moment. "It says 'Puppies Bark for It' on the box," said Walter Mitty.

His wife would be through at the hairdresser's in fifteen minutes, Mitty saw in looking at his watch, unless they had trouble drying it; sometimes they had trouble drying it. She didn't like to get to the hotel first; she would want him to be there waiting for her as usual. He found a big leather chair in the lobby, facing a window, and he put the overshoes and the puppy biscuit on the floor beside it. He picked up an old copy of *Liberty* and sank down into the chair. "Can Germany Conquer the World through the Air?" Walter Mitty looked at the pictures of bombing planes and of ruined streets.

. . . "The cannonading has got the wind up in young Raleigh, sir," said the sergeant. Captain Mitty looked up at him through tousled hair. "Get him to bed," he said wearily. "With the others. I'll fly alone." "But you can't, sir," said the sergeant anxiously. "It takes two men to handle that bomber and the Archies are pounding hell out of the air. Von Richtman's circus is between here and Saulier." "Somebody's got to get that ammunition dump," said Mitty. "I'm going over. Spot of brandy?" He poured a drink for the sergeant and one for himself. War thundered and whined around the dugout and battered at the door. There was a rending of wood and splinters flew through the room. "A bit of a near thing," said Captain Mitty carelessly. "The box barrage is closing in," said the sergeant. "We only live once, Sergeant," said Mitty, with his faint, fleeting smile. "Or do we?" He poured another brandy and tossed it off. "I never see a man could hold his brandy like you, sir," said the sergeant. "Begging your pardon, sir." Captain Mitty stood up and strapped on his huge Webley-Vickers automatic. "It's forty kilometers through hell, sir," said the sergeant. Mitty finished one last brandy. "After all," he said softly, "what isn't?" The pounding of the cannon increased; there was the rat-tat-tatting of machine guns, and from somewhere came the menacing pocket-pocketa-pocketa of the new flame-throwers. Walter Mitty walked to the door of the dugout humming "Auprès de Ma Blonde." He turned and waved to the sergeant. "Cheerio!" he said. . . .

Something struck his shoulder. "I've been looking all over this hotel for you," said Mrs. Mitty. "Why do you have to hide in this old chair? How did you expect me to find you?" "Things close in," said Walter Mitty vaguely. "What?" Mrs. Mitty said. "Did you get the what's-its-name? The puppy biscuit? What's in that box?" "Overshoes," said Mitty. "Couldn't you have put them on in the store?" "I was thinking," said Walter Mitty. "Does it ever occur to you that I am sometimes thinking?" She looked at him. "I'm going to take your temperature when I get you home," she said.

15   They went out through the revolving doors that made a faintly derisive whistling sound when you pushed them. It was two blocks to the parking lot. At the drugstore on the corner she said, "Wait here for me. I forgot something. I won't be a minute." She was more than a minute. Walter Mitty lighted a cigarette. It began to rain, rain with sleet in it. He stood up against the wall of the drugstore, smoking. . . . He put his shoulders back and his heels together. "To hell with the handkerchief," said Walter Mitty scornfully. He took one last drag on his cigarette and snapped it away. Then, with that faint, fleeting smile playing about his lips, he faced the firing squad; erect and motionless, proud and disdainful, Walter Mitty the Undefeated, inscrutable to the last.

[1939]

Working Toward a Thesis: Journal Entries

Before reading the following entries about "The Secret Life of Walter Mitty," write some of your own. You may want to think about what (if anything) you found amusing in the story, or about whether the story is dated, or about some aspect of Mitty's character or of his wife's. But the choice is yours.

A student wrote the following entry in her journal after the story was discussed in class.

> March 21. Funny, I guess, especially the business about him as a doctor performing an operation. And that "pocketa-pocketa," but I don't think that it's as hysterical as everyone else seems to think it is. And how could anyone stand being married to a man like that? In fact, it's a good thing he has her to look after him. He ought to be locked up, driving into the "Exit Only" lane, talking to himself in the street, and having those crazy daydreams. No wonder the woman in the street laughs at him.

> March 24. He's certainly a case, and she's not nearly as bad as everyone was saying. So she tells him to put his overshoes on; well, he ought to put them on, since Thurber says there is slush in the street, and he's no kid anymore. About the worst I can say of her is that she seems a little unreasonable in always wanting him to wait for her, rather than sometimes the other way around, but probably she's really telling him not to wander off, because if he ever drifts away there'll be no finding him. The joke, I guess, is that he's supposed to have these daydreams because he's henpecked, and henpecked men are supposed to be funny. Would people find the story just as funny if she had the daydreams, and he bullied her?

Developing the Thesis: List Notes

In preparation for writing a draft, the student reread the story and jotted down some tentative notes based on her journal and on material that she had highlighted in the text. (At this point you may want to make your own list, based on your notes.)

> Mitty helpless: he _needs_ her
>   chains on tires
>   enters Exit Only
>   ~~Waterbury~~
>   cop tells him to get going
>   fantasies
> wife a nag?   causes his daydreams? Evidence?
>   makes him get to hotel first
>   overshoes
>   backseat driver?
> "Does it ever occur to you that I am sometimes thinking?" _Is_
> he thinking, or just having dreams?
> M. confuses Richthoven with someone called Richtman.
> Funny--or anti-woman? Would it be funny if he nagged her, and
> she had daydreams?

Next, the student wrote a draft; then she revised the draft and submitted the revision (printed here) to some classmates for peer review. (The number enclosed within parentheses cites the source of a quotation.) Before reading the student's draft, you may want to write a draft based on your own notes and lists.

Sample Draft by a Student: "Walter Mitty Is No Joke"

Walter Mitty Is No Joke

James Thurber's "The Secret Life of Walter Mitty" seems to be highly regarded as a comic story about a man who is so dominated by his wife that he has to escape through fantasies. In my high school course in English, everyone found Mitty's dreams and his wife's bullying funny, and everyone seems to find them funny in college, too. Everyone except me.

If we look closely at the story, we see that Mitty is a pitiful man who needs to be told what to do. The slightest glimpse of reality sets him off on a daydream, as when he passes a hospital and immediately begins to imagine that he is a famous surgeon, or when he hears a newsboy shouting a headline about a crime and he imagines himself in a courtroom. The point seems to be that his wife nags him, so he escapes into daydreams. But the fact is that she needs to keep after him, because he needs someone to tell him what to do. It depends on what one considers nagging. She tells him he is driving too fast, and (given the date of the story, 1939) he probably is, since he is going 55 on a slushy or snowy road. She tells him to wear overshoes, and he probably ought to, since the weather is bad. He resents all of these orders, but he clearly is incompetent, since he delays when the traffic light turns from red to green, and he enters an "Exit Only" lane in a parking lot. We are also told that he can't put chains on tires.

In fact, he can't do anything right. All he can do is daydream, and the dreams, though they are funny, are proof of his inability to live in the real world. When his wife asks him why he didn't put the overshoes on in the store, instead of carrying them in a box, he says, "Does it ever occur to you that I am sometimes thinking?" (79). But he <u>doesn't</u> "think," he just

daydreams. Furthermore, he can't even get things straight in his

daydreams, since he gets everything mixed up, confusing Richthoven with

Richtman, for example.

Is "The Secret Life of Walter Mitty" really a funny story about a man

who daydreams because he is henpecked? Probably it is supposed to be so,

but it's also a story about a man who is lucky to have a wife who can put up

with him and keep him from getting killed on the road or lost in town.

[New page]

Work Cited

Thurber, James. "The Secret Life of Walter Mitty." <u>Literature for</u>

<u>Composition, Compact Edition</u>. Ed. Sylvan Barnet et al. New York:

Longman, 2003, 76–79.

DEVELOPING AN ARGUMENT
Introductory Paragraphs

As the poet Byron said, at the beginning of a long part of a long poem, "Nothing so difficult as a beginning." Woody Allen thinks so, too. In an interview he said that the toughest part of writing is "to go from nothing to the first draft."

We can give two pieces of advice:

1. *The opening paragraph is unimportant.* It's great if you can write a paragraph that will engage your readers and let them know where the essay will be taking them, but if you can't come up with such a paragraph, just put down anything in order to prime the pump.
2. *The opening paragraph is extremely important.* It must engage your readers, and probably by means of a thesis sentence it should let the readers know where the essay will be taking them.

The contradiction is, however, only apparent, not real. The first point is relevant to the opening paragraph of a *draft*; the second point is relevant to the opening paragraph of the *final version*. Almost all writers—professionals as well as amateurs—find that the first paragraphs in their drafts are false starts. Don't worry too much about the opening paragraphs of your draft; you'll want to revise your opening later anyway. (Surprisingly often your first paragraph may simply be deleted; your second, you may find, is where your essay truly begins.)

When writing a first draft you merely need something—almost anything may do—to break the ice. But in your finished paper the opening cannot be mere throat-clearing. The opening should be interesting.

Among the commonest **uninteresting openings** are these:

1. A dictionary definition ("Webster says . . . ").
2. A restatement of your title. The title is (let's assume) "Romeo's Maturation," and the first sentence says, "This essay will study Romeo's maturation." True, there is an attempt at a thesis statement here, but no information beyond what has already been given in the title. There is no information about you, either, that is, no sense of your response to the topic, such as is present in, say, "*Romeo and Juliet* covers less than one week, but within this short period Romeo is impressively transformed from a somewhat comic infatuated boy to a thoughtful tragic hero."
3. A platitude, such as "Ever since the beginning of time men and women have fallen in love." Again, such a sentence may be fine if it helps you to start drafting, but because it sounds canned and because it is insufficiently interesting, it should not remain in your final version.

What is left? What *is* a good way for a final version to begin? Your introductory paragraph will be interesting if it gives information, and it will be pleasing if the information provides a focus—that is, if it goes beyond the title in letting the reader know exactly what your topic is and where you are headed.

Let's assume that you agree: An opening paragraph should be *interesting* and *focused*. Doubtless you will find your own ways of fulfilling these goals, but you might consider using one of the following time-tested methods.

1. *Establish a connection between life and literature.* We have already suggested that a platitude (for instance, "Ever since the beginning of time men and women have fallen in love") usually makes a poor beginning because it is dull, but you may find some other way of relating the work to daily experience. For instance:

   Doubtless the popularity of Romeo and Juliet (the play has been with us for more than four hundred years) is partly due to the fact that it deals with a universal experience. Still, no other play about love is so much a part of our culture that the mere mention of the names of the lovers immediately calls up an image. But when we say that So-and-so is "a regular Romeo," exactly what do we mean? And exactly what sort of lover is Romeo?

2. *Give an overview.* Here is an example:

   Langston Hughes's "Harlem" is about the destruction of the hopes of African Americans. More precisely, Hughes begins by asking "What happens to a dream deferred?" and then offers several possibilities, the last of which is that it may "explode."

3. *Include a quotation.* The previous example illustrates this approach, also. Here is another example:

> One line from Langston Hughes's poem "Harlem" has become
>
> famous, "A raisin in the sun," but its fame is, in a sense, accidental;
>
> Lorraine Hansberry happened to use it for the title of a play. Doubtless
>
> she used it because it is impressive, but in fact the entire poem is worthy
>
> of its most famous line.

4. *Use a definition.* We have already suggested that a definition such as "Webster says . . . " is boring and therefore unusable, but consider the following:

> When we say that a character is the hero of a story, we usually
>
> mean that he is the central figure, and we probably imply that he is
>
> manly. But in Kafka's "The Metamorphosis" the hero is most <u>unmanly</u>.

5. *Introduce a critical stance.* If your approach is feminist, or psychoanalytic, or Marxist, or whatever, you may want to say so at the start. Example:

> Feminists have called our attention to the unfunny sexism of
>
> mother-in-law jokes, comments about women hooking men into
>
> marriage, and so forth. We can now see that the stories of James
>
> Thurber, long thought to be wholesome fun, are unpleasantly sexist.

Caution: We are not saying that these are the only ways to begin, and we certainly are not suggesting that you pack all five into the opening paragraph. We are saying only that after you have done some brainstorming and written some drafts, you may want to think about using one of these methods for your opening paragraph.

An Exercise: Write (either by yourself or in collaboration with one or two other students) an opening paragraph for an essay on one of Kate Chopin's stories and another for an essay on Hughes's "Harlem." (To write a useful opening paragraph you will, of course, first have to settle on the essay's thesis.)

Middle Paragraphs

The middle, or body, of your essay will develop your thesis by offering supporting evidence. Ideas for the body should emerge from the sketchy outline that you made after you reviewed your brainstorming notes or journal.

1. *Be sure that each paragraph makes a specific point* and that the point is sufficiently developed with evidence (a brief quotation is often the best evidence).

2. *Be sure that each paragraph is coherent.* Read each sentence, starting with the second sentence, to see how it relates to the preceding sentence. Does it clarify, extend, reinforce, add an example? If you can't find the relationship, the sentence probably does not belong where it is. Rewrite it, move it, or strike it out.

3. *Be sure that the connections between paragraphs are clear.* Transitional words and phrases, such as "Furthermore," "On the other hand," and "In the next stanza," will often give readers all the help they need in seeing how your points are connected.

4. *Be sure that the paragraphs are in the best possible order.* A good way to test the organization is to jot down the topic sentence or topic idea of each paragraph, and then to see if your jottings are in a reasonable sequence.

Concluding Paragraphs

Concluding paragraphs, like opening paragraphs, are especially difficult, if only because they are so conspicuous. Readers often skim first paragraphs and last paragraphs to see if an essay is worth reading. With conclusions, as with openings, say something interesting. It is not interesting to say, "Thus we see that Mrs. Mitty . . . " (and here you go on to echo your title or your first sentence).

What to do? When you are revising a draft, you might keep in mind the following widely practiced principles. They are not inflexible rules, but they often work.

1. *Hint that the end is near.* Expressions such as "Finally," "One other point must be discussed," and "In short," alert the reader that the end is nigh and help to prevent the reader from feeling that the essay ends abruptly.

2. *Perhaps reassert the thesis, but put it in a slightly new light.* Not, "I have shown that Romeo and Hamlet are similar in some ways," but:

These similarities suggest that in some respects Romeo is an early study for Hamlet. Both are young men in love, both seek by the force of their passion to shape the world according to their own desires, and both die in the attempt. But compared with Hamlet, who at the end of the play understands everything that has happened, Romeo dies in happy ignorance; Romeo is spared the pain of knowing that his own actions will destroy Juliet, whereas Hamlet dies with the painful knowledge that his kingdom has been conquered by Norwegian invaders.

3. *Perhaps offer an evaluation.* You may find it appropriate to conclude your analysis with an evaluation, such as this:

Romeo is as convincing as he needs to be in a play about young lovers, but from first to last he is a relatively uncomplicated figure, the ardent lover. Hamlet is a lover, but he is also a good deal more, a figure whose complexity reveals a more sophisticated or a more mature author. Only five or six years separate <u>Romeo and Juliet</u> from <u>Hamlet</u>, but one feels that in those few years Shakespeare made a quantum leap in his grasp of human nature.

4. *Perhaps include a brief significant quotation from the work.* Example:

Romeo has won the hearts of audiences for almost four centuries, but, for all his charm, he is in the last analysis concerned only with fulfilling his own passion. Hamlet, on the other hand, at last fulfills not only his own wish but that of the Ghost, his father. "Remember me," the Ghost says, when he first appears to Hamlet and asks for revenge. Throughout the play Hamlet does remember the Ghost, and finally, at the cost of his own life, Hamlet succeeds in avenging his dead father.

Coherence in Paragraphs: Using Transitions

In addition to having a unified point and a reasonable organization, a good paragraph is **coherent;** that is, the connections between ideas in the paragraph are clear. Coherence can often be achieved by inserting the right transitional words or by taking care to repeat key words.

Richard Wagner, commenting on his work as a composer of operas, once said "The art of composition is the art of transition," for his art moved from note to note, measure to measure, scene to scene. **Transitions** establish connections between ideas; they alert readers to the way in which you are conducting your argument. Here are some of the most common transitional words and phrases.

1. **amplification or likeness:** similarly, likewise, and, also, again, second, third, in addition, furthermore, moreover, finally
2. **emphasis:** chiefly, equally, indeed, even more important
3. **contrast or concession:** but, on the contrary, on the other hand, by contrast, of course, however, still, doubtless, no doubt, nevertheless, granted that, conversely, although, admittedly
4. **example:** for example, for instance, as an example, specifically, consider as an illustration, that is, such as, like
5. **consequence or cause and effect:** thus, so, then, it follows, as a result, therefore, hence
6. **restatement:** in short, that is, in effect, in other words
7. **place:** in the foreground, further back, in the distance
8. **time:** afterward, next, then, as soon as, later, until, when, finally, last, at last
9. **conclusion:** finally, therefore, thus, to sum up

✔ CHECKLIST: *Revising Paragraphs*

❑ Does the paragraph *say* anything? Does it have substance?
❑ Does the paragraph have a topic sentence? If so, is it in the best place? If the paragraph doesn't have a topic sentence, might adding one improve the paragraph? Or does it have a clear topic idea?
❑ If the paragraph is an opening paragraph, is it interesting enough to attract and to hold a reader's attention? If it is a later paragraph, does it easily evolve out of the previous paragraph, and lead into the next paragraph?
❑ Does the paragraph contain some principle of development, for instance from general to particular?
❑ Does each sentence clearly follow from the preceding sentence? Have you provided transitional words or cues to guide your reader? Would it be useful to repeat certain key words, for clarity?
❑ What is the purpose of the paragraph? Do you want to summarize, or tell a story, or give an illustration, or concede a point, or what? Is your purpose clear to you, and does the paragraph fulfill your purpose?
❑ Is the closing paragraph effective, and not an unnecessary restatement of the obvious?

REVIEW: WRITING AN ANALYSIS

Each writing assignment will require its own kind of thinking, but here are a few principles that usually are relevant:

1. Assume that your reader has already read the work you are discussing but is not thoroughly familiar with it—and of course does not know what you think and how you feel about the work. Early in your essay name the author, the work, and your thesis.
2. Do not tell the plot (or, at most, summarize it very briefly); instead, tell your reader what the work is about (not what happens, but what the happenings add up to).
3. Whether you are writing about character or plot or meter or anything else, you will probably be telling your reader something about *how* the work works, that is, how it develops. The stages by which a work advances may sometimes be marked fairly clearly. For instance (to oversimplify), a poem of two stanzas may ask a question in the first and give an answer in the second, or it may express a hope in the first and reveal a doubt in the second. Novels, of course, are customarily divided into chapters, and even a short story may be printed with numbered parts. Virtually all works are built up out of parts, whether or not the parts are labeled.
4. In telling the reader how each part leads to the next, or how each part arises out of what has come before, you will probably be commenting on such things as (in a story) changes in a character's state of mind—marked perhaps by a change in the setting—or (in a poem) changes in the speaker's tone of voice—for instance from eager to resigned, or from cautious to enthusiastic. Probably you will in fact not only be describing the

development of character or of tone or of plot, but also (and more important) you will be advancing your own thesis.

A Note on Technical Terminology

Literature—like the law, medicine, the dance, and for that matter, cooking and
baseball—has given rise to technical terminology. A cookbook will tell you to
boil, or bake, or blend, and it will speak of a "slow" oven (300 degrees), a
"moderate" oven (350 degrees), or a "hot" oven (450 degrees). These are technical terms in the world of cookery. In watching a baseball game we find ourselves saying, "I think the hit-and-run is on," or "He'll probably bunt." We use
these terms because they convey a good deal in a few words; they are clear
and precise. Further, although we don't use them in order to impress our
hearer, in fact they do indicate that we have more than a superficial acquaintance with the game. That is, the better we know our subject, the more likely
we are to use the technical language of the subject. Why? *Because such language enables us to talk precisely and in considerable depth about the subject.*
Technical language, unlike jargon (pretentious diction that needlessly compli-
cates or obscures), is illuminating—provided that the reader is familiar with the
terms.

In writing about literature you will, for the most part, use the same language
that you use in your other courses, and you will not needlessly introduce the
technical vocabulary of literary study—but you *will* use this vocabulary when it
enables you to be clear, concise, and accurate.

A Lyric Poem and a Student's Essay

APHRA BEHN

*Aphra Behn (1640–89) is regarded as the first English woman to have made a liv-
ing by writing. Not much is known of her life, but she seems to have married a
London merchant of Dutch descent, and after his death to have served as a spy in
the Dutch Wars (1665–67). After her return to England she took up playwrighting,
and she gained fame with* The Rover *(1677). Behn also wrote novels, the most important of which is* Oroonoko, or The Royal Slave *(1688), which is among the first
works in English to express pity for enslaved Africans.*

Song: Love Armed

Love in fantastic triumph sate,
    Whilst bleeding hearts around him flowed,
For whom fresh pains he did create,
    And strange tyrannic power he showed:
From thy bright eyes he took his fire,   5
    Which round about in sport he hurled;
But 'twas from mine he took desire,
    Enough to undo the amorous world.
From me he took his sighs and tears:
    From thee, his pride and cruelty;   10

From me, his languishments and fears;
    And every killing dart from thee.
Thus thou and I the god have armed
    And set him up a deity;
But my poor heart alone is harmed,   15
    Whilst thine the victor is, and free.

[1676]

Topics for Critical Thinking and Writing

1. The speaker (a man, although the author is a woman) talks of the suffering he is undergoing. Can we nevertheless feel that he enjoys his plight? *Why*, by the way, do we often enjoy songs of unhappy love?
2. The woman ("thee") is said to exhibit "pride and cruelty" (line 10). Is the poem sexist? Is it therefore offensive?
3. Do you suppose that men can enjoy the poem more than women? Explain.

Journal Entries

The subject is Aphra Behn's "song." We begin with two entries in a journal, kept by a first-year student, Geoffrey Sullivan, and we follow these entries with Sullivan's completed essay.

October 10. The title "Love Armed" puzzled me at first; funny, I somehow was thinking of the expression "strong-armed" and at first I didn't understand that "Love" in this poem is a human--no, not a human, but the god Cupid, who has a human form--and that he is shown as armed, with darts and so forth.

October 13. This god of "Love" is Cupid, and so he is something like what is on a valentine card--Cupid with his bow and arrow. But valentine cards just show cute little Cupids, and in this poem Cupid is a real menace. He causes lots of pain ("bleeding hearts," "tears," "killing dart," etc.). So what is Aphra Behn telling us about the god of love, or love? That love hurts? And she is <u>singing</u> about it! But we <u>do</u> sing songs about how hard life is. But do we sing them when we are really hurting, or only when we are pretty well off and just thinking about being hurt?

When you love someone and they don't return your love, it hurts, but even when love isn't returned it still gives some intense pleasure. Strange, but I think true. I wouldn't say that love always has this two-sided nature, but I do see the idea that love <u>can</u> have two sides, pleasure and pain. And love takes two kinds of people, male and female. Well, for most people, anyway. Maybe there's also something to the idea that "opposites attract." Anyway, Aphra Behn seems to be talking about men vs. women, pain vs. pleasure, power vs. weakness, etc. Pairs, opposites. And in two stanzas (a pair of stanzas?).

A Sample Essay by a Student: "The Double Nature of Love"

The final essay makes use of some, but not of all, of the preliminary jottings, and it includes much that Sullivan did not think of until he reread his jottings, reread the poem, and began drafting the essay.

Geoffrey Sullivan

English 2G

15 October 2001

The Double Nature of Love

Aphra Behn's "Love Armed" is in two stanzas, and it is about two people, "me" and "thee," that is, you and I, the lover and the woman he loves. I think the speaker is a man, since according to the usual code men are supposed to be the active lovers and women are the (relatively) passive people who are loved. In this poem, the beloved--the woman, I think--has "bright eyes" (line 5) that provide the god of Love with fire, and she also provides the god with "pride and cruelty" (10). This of course is the way the man sees it if a woman doesn't respond to him; if she doesn't love him in return, she is (he thinks) arrogant and cruel. What does the man give to Love? He provides "desire" (7), "sighs and tears" (9), "languishments and fears" (11). None of this sounds very manly, but the joke is that the god of love--which means love--can turn a strong man into a crybaby when a woman does not respond to him.

Although both stanzas are clever descriptions of the god of love, the poem is not just a description. Of course there is not a plot in the way that a short story has a plot, but there is a sort of a switch at the end, giving the story something of a plot. The poem is, say, ninety percent expression of feeling and description of love, but during the course of expressing feelings and describing love something happens, so there is a tiny story. The first stanza sets the scene ("Love in fantastic triumph sate" [1]) and tells of some of the things that the speaker and the woman contributed to the god of Love. The woman's eyes provided Love with fire, and the man's feelings provided Love with "desire" (7). The second stanza goes on to mention other things that Love got from the speaker ("sighs and tears," etc. [9]), and other things that Love got from the beloved ("pride and cruelty," etc. [10]), and in line 13 the poet says, "Thus thou and I the god have armed," so the two humans share something. They have both given Love his weapons. But-- and this is the story I spoke of--the poem ends by emphasizing their difference: Only the man is "harmed," and the woman is the "victor" because her heart is not captured, as the man's heart is. In the battle that Love presides over, the woman is the winner; the man's heart has fallen for the woman, but, according to the last line, the woman's heart remains "free."

We have all seen the god of Love on valentine cards, a cute little Cupid armed with a bow and arrow. But despite the bow and arrow that the Valentine Day Cupid carries, I think that until I read Aphra Behn's "Love Armed" I had never really thought about Cupid as powerful and as capable of causing real pain. On valentine cards, he is just cute, but when I think about it, I realize the truth of Aphra Behn's concept of love. Love is (or can be) two-sided, whereas the valentine cards show only the sweet side.

I think it is interesting to notice that although the poem is about the destructive power of love, it is fun to read. I am not bothered by the fact that the lover is miserable. Why? I think I enjoy the poem, rather than am bothered by it, because he is enjoying his misery. After all, he is singing about it, sort of singing in the rain, telling anyone who will listen about how miserable he is, and he is having a very good time doing it.

[New page]

Work Cited

Behn, Aphra. "Love Armed." Literature for Composition, Compact Edition.

Ed. Sylvan Barnet et al. New York: Longman, 2003, 88–89.

Topics for Critical Thinking and Writing

1. What do you think of the title? Is it sufficiently interesting and focused?
2. What are the writer's chief points? Are they clear, and are they adequately developed?
3. Do you think the writer is too concerned with himself, and that he loses sight of the poem? Or do you find it interesting that he connects the poem with life?
4. Focus on the writer's use of quotations. Does he effectively introduce and examine quoted lines and phrases?
5. What grade would you give the essay? Why?

✔ CHECKLIST: *Editing a Draft*

- ❏ Is the title of my essay at least moderately informative and interesting?
- ❏ Do I identify the subject of my essay (author and title) early?
- ❏ What is my thesis? Do I state it soon enough (perhaps even in the title) and keep it in view?
- ❏ Is the organization reasonable? Does each point lead into the next without irrelevancies and without anticlimaxes?
- ❏ Is each paragraph unified by a topic sentence or a topic idea? Are there adequate transitions from one paragraph to the next?
- ❏ Are generalizations supported by appropriate concrete details, especially by brief quotations from the text?
- ❏ Is the opening paragraph interesting and, by its end, focused on the topic? Is the final paragraph conclusive without being repetitive?
- ❏ Is the tone appropriate? No sarcasm, no apologies, no condescension?
- ❏ If there is a summary, is it as brief as possible, given its purpose?
- ❏ Are the quotations adequately introduced, and are they accurate? Do they provide evidence and let the reader hear the author's voice, or do they merely add words to the essay?
- ❏ Is the present tense used to describe the author's work and the action of the work ("Shakespeare *shows*," "Hamlet *dies*")?
- ❏ Have I kept in mind the needs of my audience, for instance, by defining unfamiliar terms or by briefly summarizing works or opinions with which the reader may be unfamiliar?
- ❏ Is documentation provided where necessary?
- ❏ Are the spelling and punctuation correct? Are other mechanical matters (such as margins, spacing, and citations) in correct form? Have I proofread carefully?
- ❏ Is the paper properly identified—author's name, instructor's name, course number, and date?

YOUR TURN: SHORT STORIES AND POEMS FOR ANALYSIS

EDGAR ALLAN POE

Edgar Allan Poe (1809–49) was the son of traveling actors. His father abandoned the family almost immediately, and his mother died when he was two. The child was adopted—though never legally—by a prosperous merchant and his wife in Richmond. The tensions were great, aggravated by Poe's drinking and heavy gambling, and in 1827 Poe left Richmond for Boston. He wrote, served briefly in the army, attended West Point but left within a year, and became an editor for the remaining eighteen years of his life. It was during these years, too, that he wrote the poems, essays, and fiction—especially detective stories and horror stories—that have made him famous.

The Fall of the House of Usher

> *Son cœur est un luth suspendu;*
> *Sitôt qu'on le touche il résonne.*
> —*De Béranger*[1]

During the whole of a dull, dark, and soundless day in the autumn of the year, when the clouds hung oppressively low in the heavens, I had been passing alone, on horseback, through a singularly dreary tract of country, and at length found myself, as the shades of the evening drew on, within view of the melancholy House of Usher. I know not how it was—but, with the first glimpse of the building, a sense of insufferable gloom pervaded my spirit. I say insufferable; for the feeling was unrelieved by any of that half-pleasurable, because poetic, sentiment with which the mind usually receives even the sternest natural images of the desolate or terrible. I looked upon the scene before me—upon the mere house, and the simple landscape features of the domain—upon the bleak walls—upon the vacant eye-like windows—upon a few rank sedges—and upon a few white trunks of decayed trees—with an utter depression of soul which I can compare to no earthly sensation more properly than to the after-dream of the reveller upon opium—the bitter lapse into every-day life—the hideous dropping off of the veil. There was an iciness, a sinking, a sickening of the heart—an unredeemed dreariness of thought which no goading of the imagination could torture into aught of the sublime. What was it—I paused to think—what was it that so unnerved me in the contemplation of the House of Usher? It was a mystery all insoluble; nor could I grapple with the shadowy fancies that crowded upon me as I pondered. I was forced to fall back upon the unsatisfactory conclusion, that while, beyond doubt, there are combinations of very simple natural objects which have the power of thus affecting us, still the analysis of this power lies among considerations beyond our depth. It was possible, I reflected, that a mere different arrangement of the particulars of the scene, of the details of the picture, would be sufficient to modify, or perhaps to annihilate its capacity for sorrowful impression;

---

[1] From "Le Refus," by Pierre-Jean de Béranger. The lines may be translated thus: "His heart is a lute, tightly strung; / The instant one touches it, it resounds".

and, acting upon this idea, I reined my horse to the precipitous brink of a black and lurid tarn[2] that lay in unruffled lustre by the dwelling, and gazed down—but with a shudder even more thrilling than before—upon the remodelled and inverted images of the gray sedge, and the ghastly tree-stems, and the vacant and eye-like windows.

Nevertheless, in this mansion of gloom I now proposed to myself a sojourn of some weeks. Its proprietor, Roderick Usher, had been one of my boon companions in boyhood; but many years had elapsed since our last meeting. A letter, however, had lately reached me in a distant part of the country—a letter from him—which, in its wildly importunate nature, had admitted of no other than a personal reply. The MS. gave evidence of nervous agitation. The writer spoke of acute bodily illness—of a mental disorder which oppressed him—and of an earnest desire to see me, as his best and indeed his only personal friend, with a view of attempting, by the cheerfulness of my society, some alleviation of his malady. It was the manner in which all this, and much more, was said—it was the apparent *heart* that went with his request—which allowed me no room for hesitation; and I accordingly obeyed forthwith what I still considered a very singular summons.

Although, as boys, we had been even intimate associates, yet I really knew little of my friend. His reserve had been always excessive and habitual. I was aware, however, that his very ancient family had been noted, time out of mind, for a peculiar sensibility of temperament, displaying itself, through long ages, in many works of exalted art, and manifested, of late, in repeated deeds of munificent yet unobtrusive charity, as well as in a passionate devotion to the intricacies, perhaps even more than to the orthodox and easily recognizable beauties, of musical science. I had learned, too, the very remarkable fact, that the stem of the Usher race, all time-honored as it was, had put forth, at no period, any enduring branch; in other words, that the entire family lay in the direct line of descent, and had always, with very trifling and very temporary variation, so lain. It was this deficiency, I considered, while running over in thought the perfect keeping of the character of the premises with the accredited character of the people, and while speculating upon the possible influence which the one, in the long lapse of centuries, might have exercised upon the other—it was this deficiency, perhaps, of collateral issue, and the consequent undeviating transmission, from site to son, of the patrimony with the name, which had, at length, so identified the two as to merge the original title of the estate in the quaint and equivocal appellation of the "House of Usher"—an appellation which seemed to include, in the minds of the peasantry who used it, both the family and the family mansion.

I have said that the sole effect of my somewhat childish experiment—that of looking down within the tarn—had been to deepen the first singular impression. There can be no doubt that the consciousness of the rapid increase of my superstition—for why should I not so term it?—served mainly to accelerate the increase itself. Such, I have long known, is the paradoxical law of all sentiments having terror as a basis. And it might have been for this reason only, that, when I again uplifted my eyes to the house itself, from its image in the pool, there grew in my mind a strange fancy—a fancy so ridiculous, indeed, that I but mention it to show the vivid force of the sensations which oppressed me. I had so worked upon my imagination as really to believe that about the whole mansion and domain there

---

[2] **tarn** small mountain lake.

hung an atmosphere peculiar to themselves and their immediate vicinity—an atmosphere which had no affinity with the air of heaven, but which had reeked up from the decayed trees, and the gray wall, and the silent tarn—a pestilent and mystic vapor, dull, sluggish, faintly discernible, and leaden-hued.

5   Shaking off from my spirit what *must* have been a dream, I scanned more narrowly the real aspect of the building. Its principal features seemed to be that of an excessive antiquity. The discoloration of ages had been great. Minute fungi overspread the whole exterior, hanging in a fine tangled web-work from the eaves. Yet all this was apart from any extraordinary dilapidation. No portion of the masonry had fallen; and there appeared to be a wild inconsistency between its still perfect adaptation of parts, and the crumbling condition of the individual stones. In this there was much that reminded me of the specious totality of old wood-work which has rotted for long years in some neglected vault, with no disturbance from the breath of the external air. Beyond this indication of extensive decay, however, the fabric gave little token of instability. Perhaps the eye of a scrutinizing observer might have discovered a barely perceptible fissure, which, extending from the roof of the building in front, made its way down the wall in a zigzag direction, until it became lost in the sullen waters of the tarn.

Noticing these things, I rode over a short causeway to the house. A servant in waiting took my horse, and I entered the Gothic archway of the hall. A valet, of stealthy step, thence conducted me, in silence, through many dark and intricate passages in my progress to the *studio* of his master. Much that I encountered on the way contributed, I know not how, to heighten the vague sentiments of which I have already spoken. While the objects around me—while the carvings of the ceilings, the sombre tapestries of the walls, the ebon blackness of the floors, and the phantasmagoric armorial trophies which rattled as I strode, were but matters to which, or to such as which, I had been accustomed from my infancy—while I hesitated not to acknowledge how familiar was all this—I still wondered to find how unfamiliar were the fancies which ordinary images were stirring up. On one of the staircases, I met the physician of the family. His countenance, I thought, wore a mingled expression of low cunning and perplexity. He accosted me with trepidation and passed on. The valet now threw open a door and ushered me into the presence of his master.

The room in which I found myself was very large and lofty. The windows were long, narrow, and pointed, and at so vast a distance from the black oaken floor as to be altogether inaccessible from within. Feeble gleams of encrimsoned light made their way through the trellised panes, and served to render sufficiently distinct the more prominent objects around; the eye, however, struggled in vain to reach the remoter angles of the chamber, or the recesses of the vaulted and fretted ceiling. Dark draperies hung upon the walls. The general furniture was profuse, comfortless, antique, and tattered. Many books and musical instruments lay scattered about, but failed to give any vitality to the scene. I felt that I breathed an atmosphere of sorrow. An air of stern, deep, and irredeemable gloom hung over and pervaded all.

Upon my entrance, Usher arose from a sofa on which he had been lying at full length, and greeted me with a vivacious warmth which had much in it, I at first thought, of an overdone cordiality—of the constrained effort of the *ennuyé*[3] man of the world. A glance, however, at his countenance convinced me of his

---

[3] **ennuyé** bored.

perfect sincerity. We sat down; and for some moments, while he spoke not, I gazed upon him with a feeling half of pity, half of awe. Surely, man had never before so terribly altered, in so brief a period, as had Roderick Usher! It was with difficulty that I could bring myself to admit the identity of the wan being before me with the companion of my early boyhood. Yet the character of his face had been at all times remarkable. A cadaverousness of complexion; an eye large, liquid, and luminous beyond comparison; lips somewhat thin and very pallid but of a surpassingly beautiful curve; a nose of a delicate Hebrew model, but with a breadth of nostril unusual in similar formations; a finely moulded chin, speaking, in its want of prominence, of a want of moral energy; hair of a more than web-like softness and tenuity;—these features, with an inordinate expansion above the regions of the temple, made up altogether a countenance not easily to be forgotten. And now in the mere exaggeration of the prevailing character of these features, and of the expression they were wont to convey, lay so much of change that I doubted to whom I spoke, The now ghastly pallor of the skin, and the now miraculous lustre of the eye, above all things startled and even awed me. The silken hair, too, had been suffered to grow all unheeded, and as, in its wild gossamer texture, it floated rather than fell about the face, I could not, even with effort, connect its Arabesque[4] expression with any idea of simple humanity.

In the manner of my friend I was at once struck with an incoherence—an inconsistency; and I soon found this to arise from a series of feeble and futile struggles to overcome an habitual trepidancy—an excessive nervous agitation. For something of this nature I had indeed been prepared, no less by his letter, than by reminiscences of certain boyish traits, and by conclusions deduced from his peculiar physical confirmation and temperament. His action was alternately vivacious and sullen. His voice varied rapidly from a tremulous indecision (when the animal spirits seemed utterly in abeyance) to that species of energetic concision—that abrupt, weighty, unhurried, and hollow-sounding enunciation—that leaden, self-balanced, and perfectly modulated guttural utterance, which may be observed in the lost drunkard, or the irreclaimable eater of opium, during the periods of his most intense excitement.

10   It was thus that he spoke of the object of my visit, of his earnest desire to see me, and of the solace he expected me to afford him. He entered, at some length, into what he conceived to be the nature of his malady. It was, he said, a constitutional and a family evil, and one for which he despaired to find a remedy—a mere nervous affection, he immediately added, which would undoubtedly soon pass off. It displayed itself in a host of unnatural sensations. Some of these, as he detailed them, interested and bewildered me; although, perhaps, the terms and the general manner of their narration had their weight. He suffered much from a morbid acuteness of the senses; the most insipid food was alone endurable; he could wear only garments of certain texture; the odors of all flowers were oppressive; his eyes were tortured by even a faint light; and there were but peculiar sounds, and these from stringed instruments, which did not inspire him with horror.

To an anomalous species of terror I found him a bounden slave. "I shall perish," said he, "I *must* perish in this deplorable folly. Thus, thus, and not otherwise, I shall be lost. I dread the events of the future, not in themselves, but in their results. I shudder at the thought of any, even the most trivial, incident, which may

---

[4] **Arabesque** intricate.

operate upon this intolerable agitation of soul. I have, indeed, no abhorrence of danger, except in its absolute effect—in terror. In this unnerved, in this pitiable, condition I feel that the period will sooner or later arrive when I must abandon life and reason together, in some struggle with the grim phantasm, FEAR."

I learned, moreover, at intervals, and through broken and equivocal hints, another singular feature of his mental condition. He was enchained by certain superstitious impressions in regard to the dwelling which he tenanted, and whence, for many years, he had never ventured forth—in regard to an influence whose supposititious force was conveyed in terms too shadowy here to be re-stated—an influence which some peculiarities in the mere form and substance of his family mansion had, by dint of long sufferance, he said, obtained over his spirit—an effect which the *physique* of the gray walls and turrets, and of the dim tarn into which they all looked down, had, at length, brought about upon the *morale* of his existence.

He admitted, however, although with hesitation, that much of the peculiar gloom which thus afflicted him could be traced to a more natural and far more palpable origin—to the severe and long-continued illness—indeed to the evidently approaching dissolution—of a tenderly beloved sister, his sole companion for many long years, his last and only relative on earth. "Her decease," he said, with a bitterness which I can never forget, "would leave him (him, the hopeless and the frail) the last of the ancient race of the Ushers." While he spoke, the lady Madeline (for so was she called) passed through a remote portion of the apartment, and, without having noticed any presence, disappeared. I regarded her with an utter astonishment not unmingled with dread; and yet I found it impossible to account for such feelings. A sensation of stupor oppressed me as my eyes followed her retreating steps. When a door, at length, closed upon her, my glance sought instinctively and eagerly the countenance of the brother; but he had buried his face in his hands, and I could only perceive that a far more than ordinary wanness had overspread the emaciated fingers through which trickled many passionate tears.

The disease of the lady Madeline had long baffled the skill of her physicians. A settled apathy, a gradual wasting away of the person, and frequent although transient affections of a partially cataleptical character were the unusual diagnosis. Hitherto she had steadily borne up against the pressure of her malady, and had not betaken herself finally to bed; but on the closing in of the evening of my arrival at the house, she succumbed (as her brother told me at night with inexpressible agitation) to the prostrating power of the destroyer; and I learned that the glimpse I had obtained of her person would thus probably be the last I should obtain—that the lady, at least while living, would be seen by me no more.

15   For several days ensuing, her name was unmentioned by either Usher or myself; and during this period I was busied in earnest endeavors to alleviate the melancholy of my friend. We painted and read together, or I listened, as if in a dream, to the wild improvisations of his speaking guitar. And thus, as a closer and still closer intimacy admitted me more unreservedly into the recess of his spirit, the more bitterly did I perceive the futility of all attempt at cheering a mind from which darkness, as if an inherent positive quality, poured forth upon all objects of the moral and physical universe in one unceasing radiation of gloom.

I shall ever bear about me a memory of the many solemn hours I thus spent alone with the master of the House of Usher. Yet I should fail in any attempt to convey an idea of the exact character of the studies, or of the occupations, in which he involved me, or led me the way. An excited and highly distempered ideality threw a sulphureous luster over all. His long improvised dirges will ring forever in my ears. Among other things, I hold painfully in mind a certain singular perversion and amplification of the wild air of the last waltz of Von Weber. From the paintings over which his elaborate fancy brooded, and which grew, touch by touch, into vaguenesses at which I shuddered and more thrillingly, because I shuddered knowing not why—from these paintings (vivid as their images now are before me) I would in vain endeavor to educe more than a small portion which should lie within the compass of merely written words. By the utter simplicity, by the nakedness of his designs, he arrested and overawed attention. If ever mortal painted an idea, that mortal was Roderick Usher. For me at least, in the circumstances then surrounding me, there arose out of the pure abstractions which the hypochondriac contrived to throw upon his canvas, an intensity of intolerable awe, no shadow of which felt I ever yet in the contemplation of the certainly glowing yet too concrete reveries of Fuseli.

One of the phantasmagoric conceptions of my friend, partaking not so rigidly of the spirit of abstraction, may be shadowed forth, although feebly, in words. A small picture presented the interior of an immensely long and rectangular vault or tunnel, with low walls, smooth, white, and without interruption or device. Certain accessory points of the design served well to convey the idea that this excavation lay at an exceeding depth below the surface of the earth. No outlet was observed in any portion of its vast extent, and no torch or other artificial source of light was discernible; yet a flood of intense rays rolled throughout, and bathed the whole in a ghastly and inappropriate splendor.

I have just spoken of that morbid condition of the auditory nerve which rendered all music intolerable to the sufferer, with the exception of certain effects of stringed instruments. It was, perhaps, the narrow limits to which he thus confined himself upon the guitar which gave birth, in great measure, to the fantastic character of his performances. But the fervid *facility* of his *impromptus* could not be so accounted for. They must have been, and were, in the notes, as well as in the words of his wild fantasies (for he not unfrequently accompanied himself with rhymed verbal improvisations), the result of that intense mental collectedness and concentration to which I have previously alluded as observable only in particular moments of the highest artificial excitement. The words of one of these rhapsodies I have easily remembered. I was, perhaps, the more forcibly impressed with it as he gave it, because, in the under or mystic current of its meaning, I fancied that I perceived, and for the first time, a full consciousness on the part of Usher of the tottering of his lofty reason upon her throne. The verses, which were entitled "The Haunted Palace," ran very nearly, if not accurately, thus:—

I.

In the greenest of our valleys,
    By good angels tenanted,
Once a fair and stately palace—
    Radiant palace—reared its head.
In the monarch Thought's dominion—
    It stood there!
Never seraph spread a pinion
    Over fabric half so fair.

II.

Banners yellow, glorious, golden,
    On its roof did float and flow
(This—all this—was in the olden
    Time long ago);
And every gentle air that dallied,
    In that sweet day,
Along the ramparts plumed and pallid,
    A winged odor went away.

III.

Wanderers in that happy valley
 Through two luminous windows saw
Spirits moving musically
 To a lute's well-tunèd law;
Round about a throne, where sitting
 (Porphyrogene!)[5]
In state his glory well befitting,
 The ruler of the realm was seen.

IV.

And all with pearl and ruby glowing
 Was the fair palace door,
Through which came flowing,
 flowing, flowing
 And sparkling evermore,
A troop of Echoes whose sweet duty
 Was but to sing,
In voices of surpassing beauty,
 The wit and wisdom of their song.

V.

But evil things, in robes of sorrow,
 Assailed the monarch's high estate;
(Ah, let us mourn, for never morrow
 Shall dawn upon him, desolate!)
And, round about his home, the glory
 That blushed and bloomed
Is but a dim-remembered story
 Of the old time entombed.

VI.

And travellers now within that valley,
 Through the red-litten windows see
Vast forms that move fantastically
 To a discordant melody;
While, like a rapid ghastly river,
 Through the pale door;
A hideous throng rush out forever,
 And laugh—but smile no more.

 I well remember that suggestions arising from this ballad led us into a train of thought wherein there became manifest an opinion of Usher's which I mention not so much on account of its novelty (for other men have thought thus), as on account of the pertinacity with which he maintained it. This opinion, in its general form, was that of the sentience of all vegetable things. But, in his disordered fancy, the idea had assumed a more daring character, and trespassed, under certain conditions, upon the kingdom of inorganization. I lack words to express the full extent, or the earnest *abandon* of his persuasion. The belief, however, was connected (as I have previously hinted) with the gray stones of the home of his forefathers. The conditions of the sentence had been here, he imagined, fulfilled in the method of collocation of these stones—in the order of their arrangement, as well as in that of the many *fungi* which overspread them, and of the decayed trees which stood around—above all, in the long undisturbed endurance of this arrangement, and in its reduplication in the still waters of the tarn. Its evidence—the evidence of the sentience—was to be seen, he said (and I here started as he spoke), in the gradual yet certain condensation of an atmosphere of their own about the waters and their walls. The result was discoverable, he added, in that silent yet importunate and terrible influence which for centuries had moulded the destinies of his family, and which made *him* what I now saw him—what he was. Such opinions need no comment, and I will make none.

20 Our books—books which, for years, had formed no small portion of the mental existence of the invalid—were, as might be supposed, in strict keeping with this character of phantasm. We pored together over such works as the "Ververt et Chartreuse" of Gresset; the "Belphegor" of Machiavelli; the "Heaven and Hell" of Swedenborg; the "Subterranean Voyage of Nicholas Klimm" of Holberg; the "Chiromancy" of Robert Flud, of Jean D'Indaginé, and of Dela

---

[5] **Porphyrogene** born to the purple, i.e., royal.

"Now hear it?—yes, I hear it, and *have* heard it. Long—long—long—many minutes, many hours, many days, have I heard it—yet I dared not—oh, pity me, miserable wretch that I am!—I dared not—I *dared* not speak! *We have put her living in the tomb!* Said I not that my senses were acute? I *now* tell you that I heard her first feeble movements in the hollow coffin, I heard them—many, many days ago—yet I dared not—*I dared not speak!* And now—to-night—Ethelred—ha! ha!—the breaking of the hermit's door, and the death-cry of the dragon, and the clangor of the shield—say, rather, the rending of her coffin, and the grating of the iron hinges of her prison, and her struggles within the coppered archway of the vault! Oh! whither shall I fly? Will she not be here anon? Is she not hurrying to upbraid me for my haste? Have I not heard her footstep on the stair? Do I not distinguish that heavy and horrible beating of her heart? Madman!"—here he sprang furiously to his feet, and shrieked out his syllables, as if in the effort he were giving up his soul—"*Madman! I tell you that she now stands without the door!*"

40   As if in the superhuman energy of his utterance there had been found the potency of a spell, the huge antique panels to which the speaker pointed threw slowly back, upon the instant, their ponderous and ebony jaws. It was the work of the rushing gust—but then without those doors there *did* stand the lofty and enshrouded figure of the lady Madeline of Usher. There was blood upon her white robes, and the evidence of some bitter struggle upon every portion of her emaciated frame. For a moment she remained trembling and reeling to and fro upon the threshold—then, with a low moaning cry, fell heavily inward upon the person of her brother, and in her violent and now final death-agonies, bore him to the floor a corpse, and a victim to the terrors he had anticipated.

From that chamber, and from that mansion, I fled aghast. The storm was still abroad in all its wrath as I found myself crossing the old causeway. Suddenly there shot along the path a wild light, and I turned to see whence a gleam so unusual could have issued; for the vast house and its shadows were alone behind me. The radiance was that of the full, setting, and blood-red moon, which now shone vividly through that once barely discernible fissure, of which I have before spoken as extending from the roof of the building, in a zigzag direction, to the base. While I gazed, this fissure rapidly widened—there came a fierce breath of the whirlwind—the entire orb of the satellite burst at once upon my sight—my brain reeled as I saw the mighty walls rushing asunder—there was a long tumultuous shouting sound like the voice of a thousand waters—and the deep and dank tarn at my feet closed sullenly and silently over the fragments of the "*House of Usher.*"

[1839]

Topics for Critical Thinking and Writing

1. Is it reasonable to say that the decaying mansion is a metaphor for the mind of Roderick Usher? If so, what evidence supports this view?
2. What might have been Poe's reason(s) for introducing the romance of the knight and the dragon? In any case, what is the effect of this interpolated story?
3. There is very little drama, in the sense of scenes with dialogue. Rather, most of the story is devoted to the narrator's report of what happened. Why do you

suppose Poe chose this method? What is the effect of Poe's decision to let the narrator tell so much of the story in his own words?

4. Do you take the narrator to be a reliable narrator? Is it possible that he is insane? After all, can we believe (to take a single example) that Madeline broke open a coffin whose lid had been tightly screwed down, and pushed open a door of "massive iron"? Is the story, then, about a mad narrator?

VIRGINIA WOOLF

Virginia Woolf (1882–1941) is known chiefly as a novelist, but she was also the author of short stories and essays, and in recent years her distinguished work in these genres has been increasingly recognized.

Woolf was self-educated in the library of her father, Leslie Stephen, an important English scholar, literary critic, and biographer. (Four years before Virginia's birth Stephen had, as editor of the Cornhill Magazine, *published Henry James's* Daisy Miller.) *After Stephen's death she moved to Bloomsbury, an unfashionable part of London, where she was part of a brilliant circle of friends—the Bloomsbury group—that included Clive Bell and Roger Fry (art critics), J. M. Keynes (an economist), Lytton Strachey (a biographer), and E. M. Forster (novelist and essayist). In 1907 she married Leonard Woolf, with whom ten years later she established the Hogarth Press, which published some of the most interesting literature of the period, including her own novels. Her major novels are usually said to be* Mrs. Dalloway (1925), To the Lighthouse (1927), *and* The Waves (1931). *Woolf experienced several mental breakdowns, and in 1941, fearing yet another, she drowned herself.*

Some of her most interesting critical essays are reprinted in The Common Reader (1925) *and* The Second Common Reader (1932), *but additional invaluable comments can be found in the six volumes of her* Letters *and in the five volumes of her* Diary.

In her first novel, The Voyage Out (1915), *one of her characters probably voices Woolf's idea of what the writer of fiction should aim for:*

> *What I want to do in writing novels is very much what you want to do when you play the piano, I expect. We want to find out what's behind things, don't we?—Look at the lights down there scattered about anyhow. Things I feel come to me like lights. . . . I want to combine them. . . . Have you ever seen fireworks that make figures? . . . I want to make figures.*

A Haunted House

Whatever hour you woke there was a door shutting. From room to room they went, hand in hand, lifting here, opening there, making sure—a ghostly couple.

"Here we left it," she said. And he added, "Oh, but here too!" "It's upstairs," she murmured. "And in the garden," he whispered. "Quietly," they said, "or we shall wake them."

But it wasn't that you woke us. Oh, no. "They're looking for it; they're drawing the curtain," one might say, and so read on a page or two. "Now they've found it," one would be certain, stopping the pencil on the margin. And then, tired of reading, one might rise and see for oneself, the house all empty, the doors standing open, only the wood pigeons bubbling with content and the hum of the threshing machine sounding from the farm. "What did I come in here for? What did I want to find?" My hands are empty. "Perhaps it's upstairs then?" The apples were in the loft. And so down again, the garden still as ever, only the book had slipped into the grass.

But they had found it in the drawing-room. Not that one could ever see them. The window panes reflected apples, reflected roses; all the leaves were green in the glass. If they moved in the drawing-room, the apple only turned its yellow side. Yet, the moment after, if the door was opened, spread about the floor, hung upon the walls, pendant from the ceiling—what? My hands were empty. The shadow of a thrush crossed the carpet; from the deepest wells of silence the wood pigeon drew its bubble of sound. "Safe, safe, safe," the pulse of the house beat softly. "The treasure buried; the room . . . " the pulse stopped short. Oh, was that the buried treasure?

5   A moment later the light had faded. Out in the garden then? But the trees spun darkness for a wandering beam of sun. So fine, so rare, coolly sunk beneath the surface the beam I sought always burnt behind the glass. Death was the glass; death was between us; coming to the woman first, hundreds of years ago, leaving the house, sealing all the windows; the rooms were darkened. He left it, left her, went North, went East, saw the stars turned in the Southern sky; sought the house, found it dropped beneath the Downs. "Safe, safe, safe," the pulse of the house beat gladly. "The Treasure yours."

The wind roars up the avenue. Trees stoop and bend this way and that. Moonbeams splash and spill wildly in the rain. But the beam of the lamp falls straight from the window. The candle burns stiff and still. Wandering through the house, opening the windows, whispering not to wake us, the ghostly couple seek their joy.

"Here we slept," she says. And he adds, "Kisses without number." "Waking in the morning—" "Silver between the trees—" "Upstairs—" "In the garden—" "When summer came—" "In winter snowtime—" The doors go shutting far in the distance, gently knocking like the pulse of a heart.

Nearer they come; cease at the doorway. The wind falls, the rain slides silver down the glass. Our eyes darken; we hear no steps beside us; we see no lady spread her ghostly cloak. His hands shield the lantern. "Look," he breathes. "Sound asleep. Love upon their lips."

Stooping, holding their silver lamp above us, long they look and deeply. Long they pause. The wind drives straightly; the flame stoops slightly. Wild beams of moonlight cross both floor and wall, and, meeting, stain the faces bent; the faces pondering; the faces that search the sleepers and seek their hidden joy.

10   "Safe, safe, safe," the heart of the house beats proudly. "Long years—" he sighs. "Again you found me." "Here," she murmurs, "sleeping; in the garden reading; laughing, rolling apples in the loft. Here we left our treasure—" Stooping, their light lifts the lids upon my eyes. "Safe! safe! safe!" the pulse of the house beats wildly. Waking, I cry "Oh, is this *your* buried treasure? The light in the heart."

[1921]

Topics for Critical Thinking and Writing

1. In what ways does this brief story resemble a traditional ghost story? In what ways does it differ? Who are the characters in this story? What are they seeking? Do they find it? If so, where?

2. Who is the narrator? Does the narrator discover who the ghosts are? If not, does the narrator discover anything else?

GUY DE MAUPASSANT

Born and raised in Normandy, the French novelist and short-story writer Guy de Maupassant (1850–93) studied law in Paris, then served in the Franco-Prussian War. Afterwards he worked for a time as a clerk for the government until, with the support of the novelist Gustave Flaubert (a friend of Maupassant's mother) and later Emile Zola, he decided to pursue a career as a writer. Ironic and pointed, detached yet compassionate, Maupassant explores human folly and its both grim and comic consequences. His first great success came in April 1880, with the publication of the story "Boule de Suif" ("Ball of Fat"), about a prostitute traveling by coach, with a number of bourgeois companions, through Prussian-occupied France during wartime. Maupassant published six novels, including Bel-Ami *(1885) and* Pierre et Jean *(1888), and a number of collections of stories, before his untimely death from the effects of syphilis, a month short of his forty-third birthday. Like many of his stories, "The Necklace" uses realistic observation and keenly chosen detail to tell its story of a misunderstanding and the years of hard labor that follow from it.*

The Necklace

Translated by Marjorie Laurie

She was one of those pretty and charming girls who are sometimes, as if by a mistake of destiny, born in a family of clerks. She had no dowry, no expectations, no means of being known, understood, loved, wedded by any rich and distinguished man; and she let herself be married to a little clerk at the Ministry of Public Instruction.

She dressed plainly because she could not dress well, but she was as unhappy as though she had really fallen from her proper station, since with women there is neither caste nor rank: and beauty, grace and charm act instead of family and birth. Natural fineness, instinct for what is elegant, suppleness of wit, are the sole hierarchy, and make from women of the people the equals of the very greatest ladies.

She suffered ceaselessly, feeling herself born for all the delicacies and all the luxuries. She suffered from the poverty of her dwelling, from the wretched look of the walls, from the worn-out chairs, from the ugliness of the curtains. All those things, of which another woman of her rank would never even have been conscious, tortured her and made her angry. The sight of the little Breton peasant who did her humble housework aroused in her regrets which were despairing, and distracted dreams. She thought of the silent antechambers hung with Oriental tapestry, lit by tall bronze candelabra, and of the two great footmen in knee breeches who sleep in the big armchairs, made drowsy by the heavy warmth of the hot-air stove. She thought of the long *salons*[1] fitted up with ancient silk, of the delicate furniture carrying priceless curiosities, and of the coquettish perfumed boudoirs made for talks at five o'clock with intimate friends, with men famous and sought after, whom all women envy and whose attention they all desire.

---

[1] **salons** drawing-rooms.

When she sat down to dinner, before the round table covered with a table-cloth three days old, opposite her husband, who uncovered the soup tureen and declared with an enchanted air, "Ah, the good *pot-au-feu!*[2] I don't know anything better than that," she thought of dainty dinners, of shining silverware, of tapestry which peopled the walls with ancient personages and with strange birds flying in the midst of a fairy forest; and she thought of delicious dishes served on mar-velous plates, and of the whispered gallantries which you listen to with a sphinx-like smile, while you are eating the pink flesh of a trout or the wings of a quail.

5 She had no dresses, no jewels, nothing. And she loved nothing but that; she felt made for that. She would so have liked to please, to be envied, to be charm-ing, to be sought after.

She had a friend, a former schoolmate at the convent, who was rich, and whom she did not like to go and see any more, because she suffered so much when she came back.

But one evening, her husband returned home with a triumphant air, and holding a large envelope in his hand.

"There," said he. "Here is something for you."

She tore the paper sharply, and drew out a printed card which bore these words:

10 "The Minister of Public Instruction and Mme. Georges Ramponneau request the honor of M. and Mme. Loisel's company at the palace of the Ministry on Monday evening, January eighteenth."

Instead of being delighted, as her husband hoped, she threw the invitation on the table with disdain, murmuring:

"What do you want me to do with that?"

"But, my dear, I thought you would be glad. You never go out, and this is such a fine opportunity. I had awful trouble to get it. Everyone wants to go; it is very select, and they are not giving many invitations to clerks. The whole official world will be there."

She looked at him with an irritated glance, and said, impatiently:

15 "And what do you want me to put on my back?"

He had not thought of that; he stammered:

"Why, the dress you go to the theater in. It looks very well, to me."

He stopped, distracted, seeing his wife was crying. Two great tears de-scended slowly from the corners of her eyes toward the corners of her mouth. He stuttered:

"What's the matter? What's the matter?"

20 But, by violent effort, she had conquered her grief, and she replied, with a calm voice, while she wiped her wet cheeks:

"Nothing. Only I have no dress and therefore I can't go to this ball. Give your card to some colleague whose wife is better equipped than I."

He was in despair. He resumed:

"Come, let us see, Mathilde. How much would it cost, a suitable dress, which you could use on other occasions, something very simple?"

She reflected several seconds, making her calculations and wondering also what sum she could ask without drawing on herself an immediate refusal and a frightened exclamation from the economical clerk.

25 Finally, she replied, hesitatingly:

---

[2] **pot-au-feu** stew.

"I don't know exactly, but I think I could manage it with four hundred francs."

He had grown a little pale, because he was laying aside just that amount to buy a gun and treat himself to a little shooting next summer on the plain of Nanterre, with several friends who went to shoot larks down there, of a Sunday.

But he said:

"All right. I will give you four hundred francs. And try to have a pretty dress."

30   The day of the ball drew near, and Mme. Loisel seemed sad, uneasy, anxious. Her dress was ready, however. Her husband said to her one evening:

"What is the matter? Come, you've been so queer these last three days."

And she answered:

"It annoys me not to have a single jewel, not a single stone, nothing to put on. I shall look like distress. I should almost rather not go at all."

He resumed:

35   "You might wear natural flowers. It's very stylish at this time of the year. For ten francs you can get two or three magnificent roses."

She was not convinced.

"No; there's nothing more humiliating than to look poor among other women who are rich."

But her husband cried:

"How stupid you are! Go look up your friend Mme. Forestier, and ask her to lend you some jewels. You're quite thick enough with her to do that."

40   She uttered a cry of joy:

"It's true. I never thought of it."

The next day she went to her friend and told of her distress.

Mme. Forestier went to a wardrobe with a glass door, took out a large jewel-box, brought it back, opened it, and said to Mme. Loisel:

"Choose, my dear."

45   She saw first of all some bracelets, then a pearl necklace, then a Venetian cross, gold and precious stones of admirable workmanship. She tried on the ornaments before the glass, hesitated, could not make up her mind to part with them, to give them back. She kept asking:

"Haven't you any more?"

"Why, yes. Look. I don't know what you like."

All of a sudden she discovered, in a black satin box, a superb necklace of diamonds, and her heart began to beat with an immoderate desire. Her hands trembled as she took it. She fastened it around her throat, outside her high-necked dress, and remained lost in ecstasy at the sight of herself.

Then she asked, hesitating, filled with anguish:

50   "Can you lend me that, only that?"

"Why, yes, certainly."

She sprang upon the neck of her friend, kissed her passionately, then fled with her treasure.

The day of the ball arrived. Mme. Loisel made a great success. She was prettier than them all, elegant, gracious, smiling, and crazy with joy. All the men looked at her, asked her name, endeavored to be introduced. All the attachés of the Cabinet wanted to waltz with her. She was remarked by the minister himself.

She danced with intoxication, with passion, made drunk by pleasure, forgetting all, in the triumph of her beauty, in the glory of her success, in a sort of cloud of happiness composed of all this homage, of all this admiration, of all these awakened desires, and of that sense of complete victory which is so sweet to a woman's heart.

55   She went away about four o'clock in the morning. Her husband had been sleeping since midnight, in a little deserted anteroom, with three other gentlemen whose wives were having a very good time. He threw over her shoulders the wraps which he had brought, modest wraps of common life, whose poverty contrasted with the elegance of the ball dress. She felt this, and wanted to escape so as not to be remarked by the other women, who were enveloping themselves in costly furs.

Loisel held her back.

"Wait a bit. You will catch cold outside. I will go and call a cab."

But she did not listen to him, and rapidly descended the stairs. When they were in the street they did not find a carriage; and they began to look for one, shouting after the cabmen whom they saw passing by at a distance.

They went down toward the Seine, in despair, shivering with cold. At last they found on the quay one of those ancient noctambulant coupés which, exactly as if they were ashamed to show their misery during the day, are never seen round Paris until after nightfall.

60   It took them to their door in the Rue des Martyrs, and once more, sadly, they climbed up homeward. All was ended, for her. And as to him, he reflected that he must be at the Ministry at ten o'clock.

She removed the wraps which covered her shoulders, before the glass, so as once more to see herself in all her glory. But suddenly she uttered a cry. She no longer had the necklace around her neck!

Her husband, already half undressed, demanded:

"What is the matter with you?"

She turned madly toward him:

65   "I have—I have—I've lost Mme. Forestier's necklace."

He stood up, distracted.

"What!—how?—impossible!"

And they looked in the folds of her dress, in the folds of her cloak, in her pockets, everywhere. They did not find it.

He asked:

70   "You're sure you had it on when you left the ball?"

"Yes, I felt it in the vestibule of the palace."

"But if you had lost it in the street we should have heard it fall. It must be in the cab."

"Yes. Probably. Did you take his number?"

"No. And you, didn't you notice it?"

75   "No."

They looked, thunderstruck, at one another. At last Loisel put on his clothes.

"I shall go back on foot," said he, "over the whole route which we have taken to see if I can find it."

And he went out. She sat waiting on a chair in her ball dress, without strength to go to bed, overwhelmed, without fire, without a thought.

Her husband came back about seven o'clock. He had found nothing.

80   He went to Police Headquarters, to the newspaper offices, to offer a reward: he went to the cab companies—everywhere, in fact, whither he was urged by the least suspicion of hope.

She waited all day, in the same condition of mad fear before this terrible calamity.

Loisel returned at night with a hollow, pale face; he had discovered nothing.

"You must write to your friend," said he, "that you have broken the clasp of her necklace and that you are having it mended. That will give us time to turn round."

She wrote at his dictation.

85   At the end of a week they had lost all hope.

And Loisel, who had aged five years, declared:

"We must consider how to replace that ornament."

The next day they took the box which had contained it, and they went to the jeweler whose name was found within. He consulted his books.

"It was not I, madame, who sold that necklace; I must simply have furnished the case."

90   Then they went from jeweler to jeweler, searching for a necklace like the other, consulting their memories, sick both of them with chagrin and anguish.

They found, in a shop at the Palais Royal, a string of diamonds which seemed to them exactly like the one they looked for. It was worth forty thousand francs. They could have it for thirty-six.

So they begged the jeweler not to sell it for three days yet. And they made a bargain that he should buy it back for thirty-four thousand francs, in case they found the other one before the end of February.

Loisel possessed eighteen thousand francs which his father had left him. He would borrow the rest.

He did borrow, asking a thousand francs of one, five hundred of another, five louis here, three louis[3] there. He gave notes, took up ruinous obligations, dealt with usurers and all the race of lenders. He compromised all the rest of his life, risked his signature without even knowing if he could meet it; and, frightened by the pains yet to come, by the black misery which was about to fall upon him, by the prospect of all the physical privation and of all the moral tortures which he was to suffer, he went to get the new necklace, putting down upon the merchant's counter thirty-six thousand francs.

95   When Mme. Loisel took back the necklace, Mme. Forestier said to her, with a chilly manner:

"You should have returned it sooner; I might have needed it."

She did not open the case, as her friend had so much feared. If she had detected the substitution, what would she have thought, what would she have said? Would she not have taken Mme. Loisel for a thief?

Mme. Loisel now knew the horrible existence of the needy. She took her part, moreover, all of a sudden, with heroism. That dreadful debt must be paid. She would pay it. They dismissed their servant; they changed their lodgings; they rented a garret under the roof.

She came to know what heavy housework meant and the odious cares of the kitchen. She washed the dishes, using her rosy nails on the greasy pots and pans. She washed the dirty linen, the shirts, and the dishcloths, which she dried upon a line; she carried the slops down to the street every morning, and carried up the

---

[3] **louis** a gold coin worth 20 francs.

water, stopping for breath at every landing. And, dressed like a woman of the people, she went to the fruiterer, the grocer, the butcher, her basket on her arm, bargaining, insulted, defending her miserable money sou by sou.

100   Each month they had to meet some notes, renew others, obtain more time.

Her husband worked in the evening making a fair copy of some tradesman's accounts, and late at night he often copied manuscript for five sous a page.

And this life lasted for ten years.

At the end of ten years, they had paid everything, everything, with the rates of usury, and the accumulations of the compound interest.

Mme. Loisel looked old now. She had become the woman of impoverished households—strong and hard and rough. With frowsy hair, skirts askew, and red hands, she talked loud while washing the floor with great swishes of water. But sometimes, when her husband was at the office, she sat down near the window, and she thought of that gay evening of long ago, of the ball where she had been so beautiful and so fêted.

105   What would have happened if she had not lost that necklace? Who knows? Who knows? How life is strange and changeful! How little a thing is needed for us to be lost or to be saved!

But, one Sunday, having gone to take a walk in the Champs Elysées to refresh herself from the labor of the week, she suddenly perceived a woman who was leading a child. It was Mme. Forestier, still young, still beautiful, still charming.

Mme. Loisel felt moved. Was she going to speak to her? Yes, certainly. And now that she had paid, she was going to tell her all about it. Why not?

She went up.

"Good day, Jeanne."

110   The other, astonished to be familiarly addressed by this plain goodwife, did not recognize her at all, and stammered:

"But—madam!—I do not know—You must be mistaken."

"No. I am Mathilde Loisel."

Her friend uttered a cry.

"Oh, my poor Mathilde! How you are changed!"

115   "Yes, I have had days hard enough, since I have seen you, days wretched enough—and that because of you!"

"Of me! How so?"

"Do you remember that diamond necklace which you lent me to wear at the ministerial ball?"

"Yes. Well?"

"Well, I lost it."

120   "What do you mean? You brought it back."

"I brought you back another just like it. And for this we have been ten years paying. You can understand that it was not easy for us, us who had nothing. At last it is ended, and I am very glad."

Mme. Forestier had stopped.

"You say that you bought a necklace of diamonds to replace mine?"

"Yes. You never noticed it, then! They were very like."

125   And she smiled with a joy which was proud and naïve at once.

Mme. Forestier, strongly moved, took her two hands.

"Oh, my poor Mathilde! Why, my necklace was paste. It was worth at most five hundred francs!"

[1885]

Topics for Critical Thinking and Writing

1. What do we learn about Mme. Loisel from the first six paragraphs of the story? What is your response to the narrator's generalizations about women in paragraph 2?
2. Is Maupassant's point that Mme. Loisel is justly punished for her vanity and pride? What about her husband, and the impact of the apparent loss of the necklace on his life?
3. In paragraph 98, as Mme. Loisel decides she must pay the debt, Maupassant writes: "She took her part, moreover, all of a sudden, with heroism." Why the word "heroism"? Isn't this a strange way to characterize Mme. Loisel's behavior?
4. Maupassant, in a discussion of fiction, said that a serious writer's goal

   > is not to tell a story to entertain us, or to appeal to our feelings, but to make us to think, and to make us understand the hidden meaning of events. By dint of having observed and having meditated, the writer sees the world, facts, people, and things in a distinctive way, a way that is the result of all of his thoughtful observation. It is this personal view of the world that a writer strives to communicate to us. . . . To make the spectacle of life as moving to us as it has been to him, he must bring life before our eyes with scrupulous accuracy. He must construct his work with great skill—his art must seem artless—so that we cannot detect his contrivance or see his intentions.

   Among the big ideas in these few sentences are these: (a) The purpose of fiction is "to make us understand the hidden meaning of events"; (b) writers give us a "personal view"; (c) readers should be moved by the story but should not be aware that the artist has imposed a personal view on them. Do you agree with some or with all of these assertions? And do you think that "The Necklace" effectively illustrates Maupassant's points? What might be "the hidden meaning of events"? What would you guess is Maupassant's "personal view"? Would you agree that the story is so skillfully constructed that we are unaware of the author's methods and of his intentions?
5. Have you ever done something, tried to make up for it, and then discovered later that you had not done what you thought you did after all? How did this make you feel?

RAYMOND CARVER

Raymond Carver (1938–1988) was born in Clatskanie, a logging town in Oregon. In 1963 he graduated from Humboldt State College in northern California and then did further study at the University of Iowa.

His early years were not easy—he married while still in college, divorced a little later, and sometimes suffered from alcoholism. In his last years he found domestic happiness, but he died of cancer at the age of fifty.

As a young man he wrote poetry while working at odd jobs (janitor, delivery-man, etc.); later he turned to fiction, though he continued to write poetry. Most of his fiction is of a sort called "minimalist," narrating in a spare, understated style stories about bewildered and sometimes exhausted men and women.

We give two versions of a story: Carver published "Mine" in 1977 and then revised it, publishing the revised version in 1981, with the title "Popular Mechanics." In 1986 he reprinted the revised version but gave it a new title, "Little Things."

Mine	Little Things
During the day the sun had come out and the snow melted into dirty water. Streaks of water ran down from the little, shoulder-high window that faced the back yard. Cars slushed by on the street outside. It was getting dark, outside and inside.	Early that day the weather turned and the snow was melting into dirty water. Streaks of it ran down from the little shoulder-high window that faced the backyard. Cars slushed by on the street outside, where it was getting dark. But it was getting dark on the inside too.
He was in the bedroom pushing clothes into a suitcase when she came to the door.	He was in the bedroom pushing clothes into a suitcase when she came to the door.
I'm glad you're leaving. I'm glad you're leaving! she said. Do you hear?	I'm glad you're leaving! I'm glad you're leaving! she said. Do you hear?
He kept on putting his things into the suitcase and didn't look up.	He kept on putting his things into the suitcase.
5 Sonofabitch! I'm so glad you're leaving! She began to cry. You can't even look me in the face, can you? Then she noticed the baby's picture on the bed and picked it up.	5 Son a bitch! I'm so glad you're leaving! She began to cry. You can't even look me in the face, can you?
	Then she noticed the baby's picture on the bed and picked it up.
He looked at her and she wiped her eyes and stared at him before turning and going back to the living room.	He looked at her and she wiped her eyes and stared at him before turning and going back to the living room.
Bring that back.	Bring that back, he said.
Just get your things and get out, she said.	Just get your things and get out, she said.
He did not answer. He fastened the suitcase, put on his coat, and looked at the bedroom before turning off the light. Then he went out to the living room. She stood in the doorway of the little kitchen, holding the baby.	10 He did not answer. He fastened the suitcase, put on his coat, looked around the bedroom before turning off the light. Then he went out to the living room.
10 I want the baby, he said.	She stood in the doorway of the little kitchen, holding the baby.
Are you crazy?	I want the baby, he said.
No, but I want the baby. I'll get someone to come by for his things.	Are you crazy?
You can go to hell! You're not touching this baby.	No, but I want the baby. I'll get someone to come by for his things.
The baby had begun to cry and she uncovered the blanket from around its head.	15 You're not touching this baby, she said.

15   Oh, oh, she said, looking at the baby.

He moved towards her.

For God's sake! she said. She took a step back into the kitchen.

I want the baby.

Get out of here!

20   She turned and tried to hold the baby over in a corner behind the stove as he came up.

He reached across the stove and tightened his hands on the baby.

Let go of him, he said.

Get away, get away! she cried.

The baby was red-faced and screaming. In the scuffle they knocked down a little flower pot that hung behind the stove.

25   He crowded her into the wall then, trying to break her grip, holding onto the baby and pushing his weight against her arm.

Let go of him, he said.

Don't, she said, you're hurting him!

He didn't talk again. The kitchen window gave no light. In the near dark he worked on her fisted fingers with one hand and with the other hand he gripped the screaming baby up under an arm near the shoulder.

She felt her fingers being forced open and the baby going from her. No, she said, just as her hands came loose. She would have it, this baby whose chubby face gazed up at them from the picture on the table. She grabbed for the baby's other arm. She caught the baby around the wrist and leaned back.

30   He would not give. He felt the baby going out of his hands and he pulled back hard. He pulled back very hard.

In this manner they decided the issue.

[1977]

The baby had begun to cry and she uncovered the blanket from around his head.

Oh, oh, she said, looking at the baby.

He moved toward her.

For God's sake! she said. She took a step back into the kitchen.

20   I want the baby.

Get out of here!

She turned and tried to hold the baby over in a corner behind the stove.

But he came up. He reached across the stove and tightened his hands on the baby.

Let go of him, he said.

25   Get away, get away! she cried.

The baby was red-faced and screaming. In the scuffle they knocked down a flowerpot that hung behind the stove.

He crowded her into the wall then, trying to break her grip. He held on to the baby and pushed with all his weight.

Let go of him, he said.

Don't, she said. You're hurting the baby, she said.

I'm not hurting the baby, he said.

30   The kitchen window gave no light. In the near-dark he worked on her fisted fingers with one hand and with the other hand he gripped the screaming baby up under an arm near the shoulder.

She felt her fingers being forced open. She felt the baby going from her.

No! she screamed just as her hands came loose.

She would have it, this baby. She grabbed for the baby's other arm. She caught the baby around the wrist and leaned back.

35   But he would not let go. He felt the baby slipping out of his hands and he pulled back very hard.

In this manner, the issue was decided.

[1981]

Topics for Critical Thinking and Writing

1. Compare the opening paragraphs. Why do you think Carver made the changes that he made? Do you think the changes improve the story? Explain.
2. Which of the three titles—"Mine," "Popular Mechanics," and "Little Things"— do you think is the best title for this story? Why?

JOSÉ ARMAS

Born in 1944, José Armas has been a teacher (at the University of New Mexico and at the University of Albuquerque), publisher, critic, and community organizer. His interest in community affairs won him a fellowship, which in 1974–75 brought him into association with the Urban Planning Department at the Massachusetts Institute of Technology. In 1980 he was awarded a writing fellowship by the National Endowment for the Arts, and he now writes a column on Hispanic affairs for The Albuquerque Journal.

El Tonto del Barrio[1]

Romero Estrado was called "El Cotorro"[2] because he was always whistling and singing. He made nice music even though his songs were spontaneous compositions made up of words with sounds that he liked but which seldom made any sense. But that didn't seem to bother either Romero or anyone else in the Golden Heights Centro where he lived. Not even the kids made fun of him. It just was not permitted.

Romero had a ritual that he followed almost every day. After breakfast he would get his broom and go up and down the main street of the Golden Heights Centro whistling and singing and sweeping the sidewalks for all the businesses. He would sweep in front of the Tortillería America,[3] the XXX Liquor Store, the Tres Milpas[4] Bar run by Tino Gabaldon, Barelas' Barber Shop, the used furniture store owned by Goldstein, El Centro Market of the Avila family, the Model Cities Office, and Lourdes Printing Store. Then, in the afternoons, he would come back and sit in Barelas' Barber Shop and spend the day looking at magazines and watching and waving to the passing people as he sang and composed his songs without a care in the world.

When business was slow, Barelas would let him sit in the barber's chair. Romero loved it. It was a routine that Romero kept every day except Sundays and Mondays when Barelas' Barber Shop was closed. After a period of years, people in the barrio got used to seeing Romero do his little task of sweeping the sidewalks and sitting in Barelas' Barber Shop. If he didn't show up one day someone assumed the responsibility to go to his house to see if he was ill. People would

---

[1] **El Tonto del Barrio** the barrio dummy (in the United States, a barrio is a Spanish-speaking community) (all notes are by the editors).   [2] **El Cotorro** The Parrot.   [3] **Tortillería America** Tortilla Factory.   [4] **Tres Milpas** Three Cornfields.

stop to say hello to Romero on the street and although he never initiated a conversation while he was sober, he always smiled and responded cheerfully to everyone. People passing the barber shop in the afternoons made it a point to wave even though they couldn't see him; they knew he was in there and was expecting some salutation.

When he was feeling real good, Romero would sweep in front of the houses on both sides of the block also. He took his job seriously and took great care to sweep cleanly, between the cracks and even between the sides of buildings. The dirt and small scraps went into the gutter. The bottles and bigger pieces of litter were put carefully in cardboard boxes, ready for the garbage man.

5   If he did it the way he wanted, the work took him the whole morning. And always cheerful—always with some song.

Only once did someone call attention to his work. Frank Avila told him in jest that Romero had forgotten to pick up an empty bottle of wine from his door. Romero was so offended and made such a commotion that it got around very quickly that no one should criticize his work. There was, in fact, no reason to.

Although it had been long acknowledged that Romero was a little "touched," he fit very well into the community. He was a respected citizen.

He could be found at the Tres Milpas Bar drinking his occasional beer in the evenings. Romero had a rivalry going with the Ranchera songs on the jukebox. He would try to outsing the songs using the same melody but inserting his own selection of random words. Sometimes, like all people, he would "bust out" and get drunk.

One could always tell when Romero was getting drunk because he would begin telling everyone that he loved them.

10   "I looov youuu," he would sing to someone and offer to compose them a song.

"Ta bueno, Romero. Ta bueno, ya bete,"[5] they would tell him.

Sometimes when he got too drunk he would crap in his pants and then Tino would make him go home.

Romero received some money from Social Security but it wasn't much. None of the merchants gave him any credit because he would always forget to pay his bills. He didn't do it on purpose, he just forgot and spent his money on something else. So instead, the businessmen preferred to do little things for him occasionally. Barelas would trim his hair when things were slow. The Tortillería America would give him menudo[6] and fresh-made tortillas at noon when he was finished with his sweeping. El Centro Market would give him the overripe fruit and broken boxes of food that no one else would buy. Although it was unspoken and unwritten, there was an agreement that existed between Romero and the Golden Heights Centro. Romero kept the sidewalks clean and the barrio looked after him. It was a contract that worked well for a long time.

Then, when Seferino, Barelas' oldest son, graduated from high school he went to work in the barber shop for the summer. Seferino was a conscientious and sensitive young man and it wasn't long before he took notice of Romero and came to feel sorry for him.

15   One day when Romero was in the shop Seferino decided to act.

[5] **Ta bueno, ya bete** OK, now go away.   [6] **menudo** tripe soup.

"Mira, Romero. Yo te doy 50 centavos por cada día que me barres la ban-
queta. Fifty cents for every day you sweep the sidewalk for us. Qué te parece?"[7]

Romero thought about it carefully.

"Hecho! Done!" he exclaimed. He started for home right away to get his
broom.

"Why did you do that for, m'ijo?"[8] asked Barelas.

20   "It don't seem right, Dad. The man works and no one pays him for his work.
Everyone should get paid for what they do."

"He don't need no pay. Romero has everything he needs."

"It's not the same, Dad. How would you like to do what he does and be
treated the same way? It's degrading the way he has to go around getting scraps
and handouts."

"I'm not Romero. Besides you don't know about these things, m'ijo. Romero
would be unhappy if his schedule was upset. Right now everyone likes him and
takes care of him. He sweeps the sidewalks because he wants something to do,
not because he wants money."

"I'll pay him out of my money, don't worry about it then."

25   "The money is not the point. The point is that money will not help Romero.
Don't you understand that?"

"Look, Dad. Just put yourself in his place. Would you do it? Would you cut
hair for nothing?"

Barelas just knew his son was putting something over on him but he didn't
know how to answer. It seemed to make sense the way Seferino explained it. But
it still went against his "instinct." On the other hand, Seferino had gone and finished high school. He must know something. There were few kids who had finished high school in the barrio, and fewer who had gone to college. Barelas knew
them all. He noted (with some pride) that Seferino was going to be enrolled at
Harvard University this year. That must count for something, he thought. Barelas
himself had never gone to school. So maybe his son had something there. On the
other hand . . . it upset Barelas that he wasn't able to get Seferino to see the issue.
How can we be so far apart on something so simple, he thought. But he decided
not to say anything else about it.

Romero came back right away and swept the front of Barelas' shop again and
put what little dirt he found into the curb. He swept up the gutter, put the trash in
a shoe box and threw it in a garbage can.

Seferino watched with pride as Romero went about his job and when he was
finished he went outside and shook Romero's hand. Seferino told him he had
done a good job. Romero beamed.

30   Manolo was coming into the shop to get his hair cut as Seferino was giving
Romero his wages. He noticed Romero with his broom.

"What's going on?" he asked. Barelas shrugged his shoulders. "Qué tiene
Romero?[9] Is he sick or something?"

"No, he's not sick," explained Seferino, who had now come inside. He told
Manolo the story.

"We're going to make Romero a businessman," said Seferino. "Do you realize
how much money Romero would make if everyone paid him just fifty cents a day?
Like my dad says, 'Everyone should be able to keep his dignity, no matter how
poor.' And he does a job, you know."

---

[7] **Qué te parece?** How does that strike you?   [8] **m'ijo** (mi hijo), my son.   [9] **Qué tiene Romero?**
What's with Romero?

"Well, it makes sense," said Manolo.

35   "Hey, maybe I'll ask people to do that," said Seferino. "That way the poor old man could make a decent wage. Do you want to help, Manolo? You can go with me to ask people to pay him."

"Well," said Manolo as he glanced at Barelas, "I'm not too good at asking people for money."

This did not discourage Seferino. He went out and contacted all the businesses on his own, but no one else wanted to contribute. This didn't discourage Seferino either. He went on giving Romero fifty cents a day.

After a while, Seferino heard that Romero had asked for credit at the grocery store. "See, Dad. What did I tell you? Things are getting better for him already. He's becoming his own man. And look. It's only been a couple of weeks." Barelas did not reply.

But then the next week Romero did not show up to sweep any sidewalks. He was around but he didn't do any work for anybody the entire week. He walked around Golden Heights Centro in his best gray work pants and his slouch hat, looking important and making it a point to walk right past the barber shop every little while.

40   Of course, the people in the Golden Heights Centro noticed the change immediately, and since they saw Romero in the street, they knew he wasn't ill. But the change was clearly disturbing the community. They discussed him in the Tortillería America where people got together for coffee, and at the Tres Milpas Bar. Everywhere the topic of conversation was the great change that had come over Romero. Only Barelas did not talk about it.

The following week Romero came into the barber shop and asked to talk with Seferino in private. Barelas knew immediately something was wrong. Romero never initiated a conversation unless he was drunk.

They went into the back room where Barelas could not hear and then Romero informed Seferino, "I want a raise."

"What? What do you mean, a raise? You haven't been around for a week. You only worked a few weeks and now you want a raise?" Seferino was clearly angry but Romero was calm and insistent.

Romero correctly pointed out that he had been sweeping the sidewalks for a long time. Even before Seferino finished high school.

45   "I deserve a raise," he repeated after an eloquent presentation.

Seferino looked coldly at Romero. It was clearly a stand-off.

Then Seferino said, "Look, maybe we should forget the whole thing. I was just trying to help you out and look at what you do."

Romero held his ground. "I helped you out too. No one told me to do it and I did it anyway. I helped you many years."

"Well, let's forget about the whole thing then," said Seferino.

50   "I quit then," said Romero.

"Quit?" exclaimed Seferino as he laughed at Romero.

"Quit! I quit!" said Romero as he walked out the front of the shop past Barelas, who was cutting a customer's hair.

Seferino came out shaking his head and laughing.

"Can you imagine that old guy?"

55   Barelas did not seem too amused. He felt he could have predicted that something bad like this would happen.

Romero began sweeping the sidewalks again the next day with the exception that when he came to the barber shop he would go around it and continue sweeping the rest of the sidewalks. He did this for the rest of the week. And the following Tuesday he began sweeping the sidewalk all the way up to the shop and then pushing the trash to the sidewalk in front of the barber shop. Romero then stopped coming to the barber shop in the afternoon.

The barrio buzzed with fact and rumor about Romero. Tino commented that Romero was not singing anymore. Even if someone offered to buy him a beer he wouldn't sing. Frank Avila said the neighbors were complaining because he was leaving his TV on loud the whole day and night. He still greeted people but seldom smiled. He had run up a big bill at the liquor store and when the manager stopped his credit, he caught Romero stealing bottles of whiskey. He was also getting careless about his dress. He didn't shave and clean like he used to. Women complained that he walked around in soiled pants, that he smelled bad. Even one of the little kids complained that Romero had kicked his puppy, but that seemed hard to believe.

Barelas felt terrible. He felt responsible. But he couldn't convince Seferino that what he had done was wrong. Barelas himself stopped going to the Tres Milpas Bar after work to avoid hearing about Romero. Once he came across Romero on the street and Barelas said hello but with a sense of guilt. Romero responded, avoiding Barelas' eyes and moving past him awkwardly and quickly. Romero's behavior continued to get erratic and some people started talking about having Romero committed.

"You can't do that," said Barelas when he was presented with a petition.

60   "He's flipped," said Tino, who made up part of the delegation circulating the petition. "No one likes Romero more than I do, you know that Barelas."

"But he's really crazy," said Frank Avila.

"He was crazy before. No one noticed," pleaded Barelas.

"But it was a crazy we could depend on. Now he just wants to sit on the curb and pull up the women's skirts. It's terrible. The women are going crazy. He's also running into the street stopping the traffic. You see how he is. What choice do we have?"

"It's for his own good," put in one of the workers from the Model Cities Office. Barelas dismissed them as outsiders. Seferino was there and wanted to say something but a look from Barelas stopped him.

65   "We just can't do that," insisted Barelas. "Let's wait. Maybe he's just going through a cycle. Look. We've had a full moon recently, qué no?[10] That must be it. You know how the moon affects people in his condition."

"I don't know," said Tino. "What if he hurts. . . ."

"He's not going to hurt anyone," cut in Barelas.

"No, Barelas. I was going to say, what if he hurts himself. He has no one at home. I'd say, let him come home with me for a while but you know how stubborn he is. You can't even talk to him any more."

"He gives everyone the finger when they try to pull him out of the traffic," said Frank Avila. "The cops have missed him, but it won't be long before they see him doing some of his antics and arrest him. Then what? Then the poor guy is in real trouble."

70   "Well, look," said Barelas. "How many names you got on the list?"

Tino responded slowly, "Well, we sort of wanted you to start off the list."

"Let's wait a while longer," said Barelas. "I just know that Romero will come around. Let's wait just a while, okay?"

---

[10] **qué no?** right?

No one had the heart to fight the issue and so they postponed the petition.

There was no dramatic change in Romero even though the full moon had completed its cycle. Still, no one initiated the petition again and then in the middle of August Seferino left for Cambridge to look for housing and to register early for school. Suddenly everything began to change again. One day Romero began sweeping the entire sidewalk again. His spirits began to pick up and his strange antics began to disappear.

75   At the Tortillería America the original committee met for coffee and the talk turned to Romero.

"He's going to be all right now," said a jubilant Barelas. "I guarantee it."

"Well, don't hold your breath yet," said Tino. "The full moon is coming up again."

"Yeah," said Frank Avila dejectedly.

When the next full moon was in force the group was together again drinking coffee and Tino asked, "Well, how's Romero doing?"

80   Barelas smiled and said, "Well. Singing songs like crazy."

[1982]

Topics for Critical Thinking and Writing

1. What sort of man do you think Barelas is? In your response take account of the fact that the townspeople "sort of want" Barelas "to start off the list" of petitioners seeking to commit Romero.
2. The narrator, introducing the reader to Seferino, tells us that "Seferino was a conscientious and sensitive young man." Do you agree? Why, or why not?
3. What do you make of the last line of the story?
4. Do you think this story could take place in almost any community? If you did not grow up in a barrio, could it take place in your community?

LESLIE MARMON SILKO

Leslie Marmon Silko was born in 1948 in Albuquerque, New Mexico, and grew up on the Laguna Pueblo Reservation some fifty miles to the west. Of her family she says,

> *We are mixed blood—Laguna, Mexican, white. . . . All those languages, all those ways of living are combined, and we live somewhere on the fringes of all three. But I don't apologize for this any more—not to whites, not to full bloods—our origin is unlike any other. My poetry, my storytelling rise out of this source.*

After graduating from the University of New Mexico in 1969, Silko entered law school but soon left to become a writer. She taught for two years at Navajo Community College at Many Farms, Arizona, and then went to Alaska for two years where she studied Eskimo-Aleut culture and worked on a novel, Ceremony.

25   The priest turned away from Leon and looked out the window at the patio full of shadows and the dining-room windows of the nuns' cloister across the patio. The curtains were heavy, and the light from within faintly penetrated; it was impossible to see the nuns inside eating supper. "Why didn't you tell me he was dead? I could have brought the Last Rites anyway."

Leon smiled. "It wasn't necessary, Father."

The priest stared down at his scuffed brown loafers and the worn hem of his cassock. "For a Christian burial it was necessary."

His voice was distant, and Leon thought that his blue eyes looked tired.

"It's O.K., Father, we just want him to have plenty of water."

30   The priest sank down in the green chair and picked up a glossy missionary magazine. He turned the colored pages full of lepers and pagans without looking at them.

"You know I can't do that, Leon. There should have been the Last Rites and a funeral Mass at the very least."

Leon put on his green cap and pulled the flaps down over his ears. "It's getting late, Father. I've got to go."

When Leon opened the door Father Paul stood up and said, "Wait." He left the room and came back wearing a long brown overcoat. He followed Leon out the door and across the dim churchyard to the adobe steps in front of the church. They both stooped to fit through the low adobe entrance. And when they started down the hill to the graveyard only half of the sun was visible above the mesa.

The priest approached the grave slowly, wondering how they had managed to dig into the frozen ground, and then he remembered that this was New Mexico, and saw the pile of cold loose sand beside the hole. The people stood close to each other with little clouds of steam puffing from their faces. The priest looked at them and saw a pile of jackets, gloves, and scarves in the yellow, dry tumbleweeds that grew in the graveyard. He looked at the red blanket, not sure that Teofilo was so small, wondering if it wasn't some perverse Indian trick—something they did in March to ensure a good harvest—wondering if maybe old Teofilo was actually at sheep camp corraling the sheep for the night. But there he was, facing into a cold dry wind and squinting at the last sunlight, ready to bury a red wool blanket while the faces of the parishioners were in shadow with the last warmth of the sun on their backs.

35   His fingers were stiff, and it took them a long time to twist the lid off the holy water. Drops of water fell on the red blanket and soaked into dark icy spots. He sprinkled the grave and the water disappeared almost before it touched the dim, cold sand; it reminded him of something—he tried to remember what it was, because he thought if he could remember he might understand this. He sprinkled more water; he shook the container until it was empty, and the water fell through the light from sundown like August rain that fell while the sun was still shining, almost evaporating before it touched the wilted squash flowers.

The wind pulled at the priest's brown Franciscan robe and swirled away the corn meal and pollen that had been sprinkled on the blanket. They lowered the bundle into the ground, and they didn't bother to untie the stiff pieces of new rope that were tied around the ends of the blanket. The sun was gone, and over on the highway the eastbound lane was full of headlights. The priest walked away slowly. Leon watched him climb the hill, and when he had disappeared within the tall, thick walls, Leon turned to look up at the high blue mountains in the deep snow that reflected a faint red light from the west. He felt good because it was finished, and he was happy about the sprinkling of the holy water, now the old man could send them big thunderclouds for sure.

[1969]

Topics for Critical Thinking and Writing

1. How would you describe the response of Leon, Ken, Louise, and Teresa to Teofilo's death? To what degree does it resemble or differ from responses to death that you are familiar with?
2. How do the funeral rites resemble or differ from those of your community?
3. How well does Leon understand the priest? How well does the priest understand Leon?
4. At the end of the story we are told that Leon "felt good." Do you assume that the priest also felt good? Why, or why not?
5. From what point of view is the story told? Mark the passages where the narrator enters a character's mind, and then explain what, in your opinion, Silko gains (or loses) by doing so.

ELIZABETH BISHOP

Elizabeth Bishop (1911–79) was born in Worcester, Massachusetts. Because her father died when she was eight months old and her mother was confined to a sanitarium four years later, Bishop was raised by relatives in New England and Nova Scotia. After graduating from Vassar College in 1934, where she was co-editor of the student literary magazine, she lived (on a small private income) for a while in Key West, France, and Mexico, and then for much of her adult life in Brazil, before returning to the United States to teach at Harvard. Her financial independence enabled her to write without worrying about the sales of her books and without having to devote energy to distracting jobs.

Filling Station

Oh, but it is dirty!
—this little filling station,
oil-soaked, oil-permeated
to a disturbing, over-all
black translucency.   5
Be careful with that match!

Father wears a dirty,
oil-soaked monkey suit
that cuts him under the arms,
and several quick and saucy   10
and greasy sons assist him
(it's a family filling station),
all quite thoroughly dirty.

Do they live in the station?
It has a cement porch   15
behind the pumps, and on it
a set of crushed and grease-
impregnated wickerwork;
on the wicker sofa
a dirty dog, quite comfy.   20

Some comic books provide
the only note of color—
of certain color. They lie
upon a big dim doily
draping a taboret   25
(part of the set), beside
a big hirsute begonia.

Why the extraneous plant?
Why the taboret?
Why, oh why, the doily?   30
(Embroidered in daisy stitch
with marguerites, I think,
and heavy with gray crochet.)

Somebody embroidered the doily.
Somebody waters the plant,   35
or oils it, maybe. Somebody
arranges the rows of cans
so that they softly say:
ESSO°—so—so—so
to high-strung automobiles.   40
Somebody loves us all.

[1965]

39 **ESSO** a brand of gasoline, now Exxon (editors' note).

Topics for Critical Thinking and Writing

1. Taking into account only the first 14 lines, how would you characterize the speaker?
2. Robert Lowell, a poet and a friend of Elizabeth Bishop, said of her poems that they have "a tone of . . . grave tenderness and sorrowing amusement." Do you agree? If so, illustrate his comment by calling attention to specific passages in "Filling Station." If you disagree, how would you describe the tone?
3. In lines 21–30, what evidence suggests that the speaker feels that her taste is superior to the taste of the family? Does she change her mind by the end of the poem, or not?
4. "High-strung" in the last stanza *is* a rather odd way to characterize automobiles. What else strikes you as odd in the last stanza?

5. In two or three paragraphs, characterize a store, or stand, or territory that you
know. Focus on an aspect of it (as Bishop focuses on the dirt and oil) so that
readers can see what you find odd, or interesting, or striking about it.

The Fish

I caught a tremendous fish
and held him beside the boat
half out of water, with my hook
fast in a corner of his mouth.
He didn't fight.   5
He hadn't fought at all.
He hung a grunting weight,
battered and venerable
and homely. Here and there
his brown skin hung in strips   10
like ancient wall-paper,
and its pattern of darker brown
was like wall-paper:
shapes like full-blown roses
stained and lost through age.   15
He was speckled with barnacles,
fine rosettes of lime,
and infested
with tiny white sea-lice,
and underneath two or three   20
rags of green weed hung down.
While his gills were breathing in
the terrible oxygen
—the frightening gills,
fresh and crisp with blood,   25
that can cut so badly—
I thought of the coarse white flesh
packed in like feathers,
the big bones and the little bones,
the dramatic reds and blacks   30
of his shiny entrails,
and the pink swim-bladder
like a big peony.
I looked into his eyes
which were far larger than mine   35
but shallower, and yellowed,
the irises backed and packed
with tarnished tinfoil
seen through the lenses
of old scratched isinglass.   40
They shifted a little, but not
to return my stare.
—It was more like the tipping
of an object toward the light.

I admired his sullen face,   45
the mechanism of his jaw,
and then I saw
that from his lower lip
—if you could call it a lip—
grim, wet, and weapon-like,   50
hung five old pieces of fish-line,
or four and a wire leader
with the swivel still attached,
with all their five big hooks
grown firmly in his mouth.   55
A green line, frayed at the end
where he broke it, two heavier lines,
and a fine black thread
still crimped from the strain and snap
when it broke and he got away.   60
Like medals with their ribbons
frayed and wavering,
a five-haired beard of wisdom
trailing from his aching jaw.
I stared and stared   65
and victory filled up
the little rented boat,
from the pool of bilge
where oil had spread a rainbow
around the rusted engine   70
to the bailer rusted orange,
the sun-cracked thwarts,
the oarlocks on their strings,
the gunnels—until everything
was rainbow, rainbow, rainbow!   75
And I let the fish go.

[1946]

Topics for Critical Thinking and Writing

1. In line 9 Bishop calls the fish "homely" and in succeeding lines compares him to a series of stained, scratched, and tarnished domestic objects. When (in line 45) she reports that she "admired his sullen face," did that take you by surprise, or had she prepared you for her admiration? Explain.
2. In lines 66–67 we're told that "victory filled up / the little rented boat." Whose victory was it? Or do you think the lines are deliberately ambiguous?
3. Why does the speaker pause in her story to describe the condition of the rented boat? Is a comparison between the boat and the fish implied?
4. What causes the "rainbow" in line 69? How do you understand "everything / was rainbow, rainbow, rainbow!" in lines 74–75?
5. Why does the speaker let the fish go? Is this ending a surprise, or has it been prepared for? Explain.

One Art

The art of losing isn't hard to master;
so many things seem filled with the intent
to be lost that their loss is no disaster.   3

Lose something every day. Accept the fluster
of lost door keys, the hour badly spent.
The art of losing isn't hard to master.   6

Then practice losing farther, losing faster:
places, and names, and where it was you meant
to travel. None of these will bring disaster.   9

I lost my mother's watch. And look! my last, or
next-to-last, of three loved houses went.
The art of losing isn't hard to master.   12

I lost two cities, lovely ones. And, vaster,
some realms I owned, two rivers, a continent.
I miss them, but it wasn't a disaster.   15

—Even losing you (the joking voice, a gesture
I love) I shan't have lied. It's evident
the art of losing's not too hard to master
though it may look like (*Write* it!) like disaster.   19

[1976]

Topics for Critical Thinking and Writing

1. What was your response to the title when you first read it? Did your response change after you read the poem and studied it further?
2. "One Art" is a villanelle, a form consisting of an uneven number (usually five) of tercets (three-line units) that rhyme *aba* and a concluding quatrain that rhymes *abaa*. Is the form connected to the poem's theme? In what way?
3. Linger over line one: Why is "losing" an "art"? And why does Bishop echo the phrasing of the first line in lines later in the poem? Does the echo make the poem feel repetitive?
4. Follow Bishop's uses of the words "lose," "losing," and "loss" from one to the next. Do you find her reliance on these very closely related words to be important for the poem's meaning, or does it strike you as a lot or a little confusing? Can a poem be a lot or a little confusing and yet still be a good poem?
5. Can we tell what kind of loss Bishop is exploring? If we can, where does this kind of loss become clear?
6. Whom is Bishop addressing when she says (note the exclamation point) "*Write* it!"? Why is this command in the poem, and why is it in parentheses?
7. Has this poem helped you to understand a loss or losses that you have experienced yourself? Something, perhaps, that you did not understand before about what "losing" someone or something important means? Do you have an insight of your own into losing and loss that Bishop has not considered, at least not in this poem? Is this an insight that you would want to share with others—in a poem, for example—or keep to yourself?

5

Other Kinds of Writing about Literature

SUMMARY

The essay on "The Story of an Hour" in Chapter 2 does not include a *summary* because the writer knew that all of her readers were thoroughly familiar with Chopin's story. Sometimes, however, it is advisable to summarize the work you are writing about, thus reminding a reader who has not read the work recently, or even informing a reader who may never have read the work. A review of a new work of literature or of a new film, for instance, usually includes a summary, on the assumption that readers are unfamiliar with it.

A summary is a brief restatement or condensation of the plot. Consider this **summary** of Chopin's "The Story of an Hour."

> A newspaper office reports that Brently Mallard has been killed in a railroad accident. When the news is gently broken to Mrs. Mallard by her sister Josephine, Mrs. Mallard weeps wildly and then shuts herself up in her room, where she sinks into an armchair. Staring dully through the window, she sees the signs of spring, and then an unnameable sensation possesses her. She tries to reject it but finally abandons herself to it. Renewed, she exults in her freedom, in the thought that at last the days will be her own. She finally comes out of the room, embraces her sister, and descends the stairs. A moment later her husband--who in fact had not been in the accident--enters. Mrs. Mallard dies--of the joy that kills, according to the doctors' diagnosis.

Here are a few principles that govern summaries:

1. A summary is **much briefer than the original**. It is not a paraphrase—a word-by-word translation of someone's words into your own. A paraphrase is usually at least as long as the original, whereas a summary is rarely longer than one-fourth of the original and is usually much shorter. A novel may be summarized in a few paragraphs, or even in one paragraph.
2. A summary **usually achieves its brevity by omitting almost all of the concrete details of the original** and by omitting minor characters and episodes. Notice that the summary of "The Story of an Hour" omits the friend of the family, omits specifying the signs of spring, and omits the business of the sister imploring Mrs. Mallard to open the door.
3. A summary is **as accurate as possible**, given the limits of space. It has no value if it misrepresents the point of the original.
4. A summary is **normally written in the present tense**. Thus "A newspaper office reports . . . , Mrs. Mallard weeps. . . . "

5. If the summary is brief (say, fewer than 250 words), it **may be given as a single paragraph**. If you are summarizing a long work, you may feel that a longer summary is needed. In this case your reader will be grateful to you if you divide the summary into paragraphs. As you draft your summary, you may find **natural divisions**. For instance, the scene of the story may change midway, giving you the opportunity to use two paragraphs. Or you may want to summarize a five-act play in five paragraphs.

6. The writer of a summary **need not make the points in the same order as that of the original**. If the writer of an essay has delayed revealing the main point until the end of the essay, the summary may rearrange the order, stating the main point first. Occasionally, for instance, if the original author has presented an argument in a disorderly or confusing sequence, a summary is written to disengage the author's argument from its confusing structure.

7. Because a summary is openly based on someone else's views, it is usually **not necessary to use quotation marks** around key words or phrases from the original. Nor is it necessary to repeat "he says" or "she goes on to prove." From the opening sentence of a summary it should be clear that what follows is what the original author says.

Summaries have their place in essays, but remember that a summary is not an analysis; it is only a summary.

PARAPHRASE

What Paraphrase Is

A **paraphrase** is a restatement—a sort of translation in the same language—of material that may in its original form be somewhat obscure to a reader. A native speaker of English will not need a paraphrase of "Thirty days hath September," though a nonnative speaker might be puzzled by two things, the meaning of *hath* and the inverted word order. For such a reader, "September has thirty days" would be a helpful paraphrase.

Although a paraphrase seeks to make clear the gist of the original, if the original is even a little more complex than "Thirty days hath September" the paraphrase will—in the process of clarifying something—lose something, since the substitution of one word for another will change the meaning. For instance, "Shut up" and "Be quiet" do not say exactly the same thing; the former (in addition to asking for quiet) says that the speaker is rude, or perhaps it says that the speaker feels little respect for the auditor, but the paraphrase loses all of this.

The Value of Paraphrase

Still, a paraphrase can be a first step in helping a reader to understand a line that includes an obsolete word or phrase, or a word or phrase that is current only in one region. In a poem by Emily Dickinson (1830–86), the following line appears:

The sun engrossed the East. . . .

"Engrossed" here has (perhaps among other meanings) a special commercial meaning, "to acquire most or all of a commodity; to monopolize the market," so a paraphrase of the line might go thus:

> The sun took over all of the east.

(It's worth mentioning, parenthetically, that you should have at your elbow a good desk dictionary, such as *The American Heritage Dictionary of the English Language,* third edition. Writers—especially poets—expect you to pay close attention to every word. If a word puzzles you, look it up.)

Idioms, as well as words, may puzzle a reader. The Anglo-Irish poet William Butler Yeats (1865—1939) begins one poem with

> The friends that have it I do wrong. . . .

Because the idiom "to have it" (meaning "to believe that," "to think that") is unfamiliar to many American readers today, a discussion of the poem might include a paraphrase—a rewording, a translation into more familiar language, such as

> The friends who think that I am doing the wrong thing. . . .

Perhaps the rest of the poem is immediately clear, but in any case here is the entire poem, followed by a paraphrase:

> The friends that have it I do wrong
> When ever I remake a song,
> Should know what issue is at stake:
> It is myself that I remake.

Now for the paraphrase:

> The friends who think that I am doing the wrong thing when I revise one of my poems should be informed what the important issue is: I'm not just revising a poem—rather, I am revising myself (my thoughts, feelings).

Here, as with any paraphrase, the meaning is not translated exactly; there is some distortion. For instance, if "song" in the original is clarified by "poem" in the paraphrase, it is also altered; the paraphrase loses the sense of lyricism that is implicit in "song." Further, "Should know what issue is at stake" (in the original) is ambiguous. Does "should" mean "ought," as in "You should know better than to speak so rudely," or does it mean "deserve to be informed," as in "You ought to know that I am thinking about quitting"?

Granted that a paraphrase may miss a great deal, a paraphrase often helps you, or your reader, to understand at least the surface meaning, and the act of paraphrasing will usually help you to understand at least some of the implicit meaning. Furthermore, a paraphrase makes you see that the original writer's words (if the work is a good one) are exactly right, better than any words we might substitute. It becomes clear that the thing said in the original—not only the rough "idea" expressed but the precise tone with which it is expressed—is a sharply defined experience.

LITERARY RESPONSE

Anything that you write about a work of literature is a response, even if it seems to be as matter-of-fact as a summary. It's sometimes useful to compare your summary with that of a classmate. You may be surprised to find that the two summaries differ considerably—though when you think about it, it isn't really surprising. Two different people are saying what they think is the gist of the work, and their views are shaped, to some degree, by such things as their gender, their ethnicity, and their experience (including, of course, their *literary* experience).

But when we talk about writing a response, we usually mean something more avowedly personal, something like an entry in a journal, where the writer may set forth an emotional response, perhaps relating the work to one of his or her own experiences. (On journals, see pp. 17–18.)

Writing a Literary Response

You may want to rewrite a literary work, for instance by giving it a different ending or by writing an epilogue in which you show the characters 20 years later. (We have already talked about the possibility of writing a sequel to Chopin's "Ripe Figs," or writing a letter from Babette to Maman-Nainaine, or writing Babette's memoirs.) Or you might want to rewrite the work by presenting the characters from a different point of view. The student who in an essay on Thurber's "The Secret Life of Walter Mitty" argued that Mitty *needed* someone very much like Mrs. Mitty might well have rewritten Thurber's story along those lines. The fun for the reader would of course reside largely in hearing the story reinterpreted, in seeing the story turned inside out.

A Story by a Student: "The Ticket (A Different View of 'The Story of an Hour')"

Here is an example, written by Lola Lee Loveall for a course taught by Diana Muir at Solano Community College. Ms. Loveall's story is a response to Kate Chopin's "The Story of an Hour" (p. 12). Notice that Loveall's first sentence is close to her source—a good way to get started, but by no means the only way; notice, too, that elsewhere in her story she occasionally echoes Chopin—for instance, in the references to the treetops, the sparrows, and the latchkey. A reader enjoys detecting these echoes.

What is especially interesting, however, is that before she conceived her story Loveall presumably said to herself something like, "Well, Chopin's story is superb, but suppose we shift the focus a bit. Suppose we think about what it would be like, *from the husband's point of view*, to live with a woman who suffered from 'heart trouble,' a person whom one had to treat with 'great care'" (Chopin's words, in the first sentence of "The Story of an Hour"). "And what about Mrs. Mallard's sister, Josephine—so considerate of Mrs. Mallard? What, exactly, would *Mr.* Mallard think of her? Wouldn't he see her as a pain in the neck? And what might he be prompted to do? That is, how might this character in this situation respond?" And so Loveall's characters and her plot began to take shape. As part of the game, she committed herself to writing a plot that, in its broad outline, resembled Chopin's by being highly ironic. But read it yourself.

Lola Lee Loveall

English 6

The Ticket

(A Different View of "The Story of an Hour")

Knowing full well his wife was afflicted with heart trouble, Brently Mallard wondered how he was going to break the news about the jacket. As he strode along his boots broke through the shallow crust from the recent rain, and dust kicked up from the well-worn wagon road came up to flavor his breathing. At least, the gentle spring rain had settled the dusty powder even as it had sprinkled his stiffly starched shirt which was already dampened from the exertion of stamping along. The strenuous pace he set himself to cover the intervening miles home helped him regain his composure. Mr. Brently Mallard was always calm, cool, and confident.

However, he hadn't been this morning when he stepped aboard the train, took off his jacket and folded it neatly beside him, and settled in his seat on the westbound train. He had been wildly excited. Freedom was his. He was Free! He was off for California, devil take the consequences! He would be his old self again, let the chips fall where they may. And he would have been well on his way, too, if that accursed ticket agent hadn't come bawling out, "Mr. Mallard, you left your ticket on the counter!" just when Mallard himself had spied that nosy Jan Ardan bidding her sister goodbye several car lengths down the depot. How could he be so unfortunate as to run into them both twice this morning? Earlier, they had come into the bank just as the banker had extended the thick envelope.

"You understand, this is just an advance against the estate for a while?"

Only Mallard's persuasiveness could have extracted that amount from the cagey old moneybags. Mallard had carefully tucked it into his inside pocket.

This was the kind of spring day to fall in love--or lure an adventurer to the top of the next hill. Sparrows hovered about making happy sounds. Something about their movements reminded Mallard of his wife--quick, fluttering, then darting away.

He had loved her at first for her delicate ways. They had made a dashing pair--he so dark and worldly, she so fragile and fair--but her delicacy was a trap, for it disguised the heart trouble, bane of his life. Oh, he still took her a sip of brandy in bed in the morning as the doctor had suggested, although, of course, it wasn't his bed anymore. He had moved farther down the hall not long after her sister, Josephine, came to help, quick to come when Mrs. Mallard called, even in the middle of the night. After one such sudden appearance one night--"I thought I heard you call"-- he had given up even sharing the same bed with his wife, although there had been little real sharing there for some time.

"No children!" the doctor had cautioned.

Mallard concentrated harder on the problem of the missing jacket. What to say? She would notice. Maybe not right away, but she would be aware. Oh, he knew Louise's reaction. She would apparently take the news calmly, then make a sudden stab toward her side with her delicate hands, then straighten and walk away--but not before he observed. A new jacket would cost money. Discussing money made the little drama happen more often, so now Mr. Mallard handled all the financial affairs, protecting her the best he could. After all, it was her inheritance, and he took great care with it, but there were the added costs: doctors, Josephine living with them, the medications, even his wife's brandy. Why, he checked it daily to be sure it was the proper strength. Of course, a man had to have a few pleasures, even if the cards did seem to fall against him more often than not. He manfully kept trying.

Everyone has a limit, though, and Mr. Mallard had reached his several days ago when the doctor had cautioned him again.

"She may go on like she is for years, or she may just keel over any time. However, the chances are she will gradually go downhill and need continual care. It is impossible to tell."

Mallard could not face "gradually go downhill." His manhood revolted against it. He was young, full of life. Let Josephine carry the chamber pot! After Louise's demise (whenever that occurred!) the simple estate which she had inherited reverted to Josephine. Let her earn it. Also, good old friend Richards was always about with a suggestion here or a word of comfort there for Louise. They'd really not care too much if Mallard were a long time absent.

As he drew nearer his home, Mallard continued to try to calm his composure, which was difficult for he kept hearing the sound of the train wheels as it pulled away, jacket, envelope, and all, right before his panic-stricken eyes: CALIFORNIA; California; california; california.

DUTY! It was his duty not to excite Louise. As he thought of duty he unconsciously squared his drooping shoulders, and the image of Sir Galahad flitted across his mind.

The treetops were aglow in the strange afterlight of the storm. A shaft of sunlight shot through the leaves and fell upon his face. He had come home.

He opened the front door with the latchkey. Fortunately, it had been in his pants pocket.

Later, the doctors did not think Mr. Mallard's reaction unusual, even when a slight smile appeared on the bereaved husband's face. Grief causes strange reactions.

"He took it like a man," they said.

Only later, when the full significance of his loss reached him, did

he weep.

A Poem Based on a Poem

We begin with a poem by William Blake (1757–1827), an English Christian visionary poet.

The Tyger

Tyger! Tyger! burning bright
In the forests of the night,
What immortal hand or eye
Could frame thy fearful symmetry?   4

In what distant deeps or skies
Burnt the fire of thine eyes?
On what wings dare he aspire?
What the hand dare seize the fire?   8

And what shoulder, and what art,
Could twist the sinews of thy heart?
And, when thy heart began to beat,
What dread hand? and what dread feet?   12

What the hammer? what the chain?
In what furnace was thy brain?
What the anvil? What dread grasp
Dare its deadly terrors clasp?   16

When the stars threw down their spears,
And watered heaven with their tears,
Did he smile his work to see?
Did he who made the lamb make thee?   20

Tyger! Tyger! burning bright
In the forests of the night,
What immortal hand or eye,
Dare frame thy fearful symmetry?   24

[1794]

William Blake was the favorite poet of Allen Ginsberg (1926–97). Ginsberg, a New Yorker who established his fame in San Francisco, was noted for his declamatory poetry and his celebration of outsiders, especially protestors against the wars in Korea and Vietnam. He often chanted Blake's poems at his own poetry readings. In the following poem X. J. Kennedy pays homage to Ginsberg by adopting the form of one of Ginsberg's favorite poems. Kennedy alludes, in his poem, to Ginsberg's left-wing activities ("Taunter of the ultra right"), his view that his hearers should drop out of a corrupt and repressive society, his interest in Buddhist mantras (syllables laden with mystic power), his antiwar activity ("Mantra-minded flower child"), his homosexuality ("Queer," "Queen"), and his use of finger cymbals in some of his readings. *Om* (line 9) is a syllable that begins several mantras. Ginsberg often had his audience utter the sound.

X. J. KENNEDY

For Allen Ginsberg

Ginsberg, Ginsberg, burning bright,
Taunter of the ultra right,
What blink of the Buddha's eye
Chose the day for you to die?   4

Queer pied piper, howling wild,
Mantra-minded flower child,
Queen of Maytime, misrule's lord
Bawling, *Drop out! All aboard!*   8

Finger-cymbaled, chanting *Om*,
Foe of fascist, bane of bomb,
Proper poets' thorn-in-side,
Turner of a whole time's tide,   12

Who can fill your sloppy shoes?
What a catch for Death. We lose
Glee and sweetness, freaky light,
Ginsberg, Ginsberg, burning bright.   16

[1997]

REWRITING A POEM

WILLIAM BUTLER YEATS: "LEDA AND THE SWAN"

William Butler Yeats (1865–1939) was born in Dublin, Ireland. The early Yeats was much interested in highly lyrical, romantic poetry, often drawing on Irish mythology. The later poems, from about 1910 (and especially after Yeats met Ezra Pound in 1911), are usually more colloquial. Although these later poems often employ mythological references, too, one feels that the poems are more down-to-earth. Yeats was awarded the Nobel Prize in Literature in 1923.

According to Greek mythology, Zeus fell in love with Leda, disguised himself as a swan, and raped her. Among the offspring of this union were Helen and Clytemnestra. Paris abducted Helen, causing the Greeks to raze Troy; Clytemnestra, wife of Agamemnon, murdered her husband on his triumphant return to Greece. Yeats saw political significance in the myth of beauty and war engendered by a god, but, as he tells us, when he was composing "Leda and the Swan" the political significance evaporated:

> *After the individualistic, demagogic movements, founded by Hobbes and popularized by the Encyclopaedists and the French Revolution, we have a soil so exhausted that it cannot grow that crop again for centuries. Then I thought "Nothing is now possible but some movement, or birth from above, preceded by some violent annunciation." My fancy began to play with Leda and the Swan for metaphor, and I began this poem, but as I wrote, bird and lady took such possession of the scene that all politics went out of it.*

The first version, "Annunciation," is from a manuscript dated September 18, 1923; the second was printed in a magazine, June 1924; the third, first published in his Collected Poems *of 1933, is Yeats's final one. But this third version had been almost fully achieved by 1925; the 1933 version differs from the 1925 version only in two punctuation marks: The question marks at the ends of lines 6 and 8 in the latest version were, in 1925, respectively, a comma and a semicolon.*

Annunciation

Now can the swooping Godhead have his will
Yet hovers, though her helpless thighs are pressed
By the webbed toes; and that all powerful bill
Has suddenly bowed her face upon his breast,   4
How can those terrified vague fingers push
The feathered glory from her loosening thighs?
All the stretched body's laid on that white rush
And feels the strange heart beating where it lies   8
A shudder in the loins engenders there
The broken wall, the burning roof and tower
And Agamemnon dead . . .
                             Being so caught up   12
Did nothing pass before her in the air?
Did she put on his knowledge with his power
Before the indifferent beak could let her drop.   [1923]

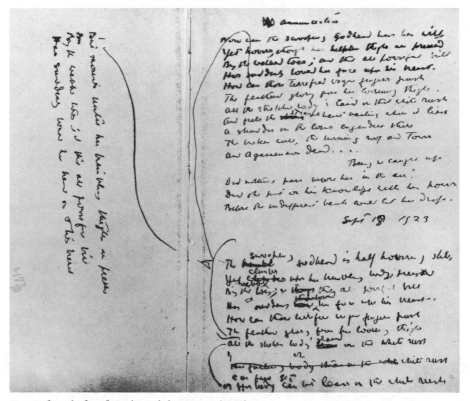

Yeats's first drafts of "Leda and the Swan" (1923).

Leda and the Swan

A rush, a sudden wheel, and hovering still
The bird descends, and her frail thighs are pressed
By the webbed toes, and that all-powerful bill
Has laid her helpless face upon his breast   4
How can those terrified vague fingers push
The feathered glory from her loosening thighs!
All the stretched body's laid on the white rush
And feels the strange heart beating where it lies;   8
A shudder in the loins engenders there
The broken wall, the burning roof and tower
And Agamemnon dead.
                   Being so caught up,   12
So mastered by the brute blood of the air,
Did she put on his knowledge with his power
Before the indifferent beak could let her drop?

                                                  [1924]

Leda and the Swan

A sudden blow: the great wings beating still
Above the staggering girl, her thighs caressed
By the dark webs, her nape caught in his bill,
He holds her helpless breast upon his breast.   4

How can those terrified vague fingers push
The feathered glory from her loosening thighs?
And how can body, laid in that white rush,
But feel the strange heart beating where it lies?   8

A shudder in the loins engenders there
The broken wall, the burning roof and tower
And Agamemnon dead.
                   Being so caught up,   12
So mastered by the brute blood of the air,
Did she put on his knowledge with his power
Before the indifferent beak could let her drop?

                                                  [1933]

MONA VAN DUYN

The first woman poet laureate of the United States (1992–93), Mona Van Duyn was born in Waterloo, Iowa, in 1921, and educated at the University of Northern Iowa and the University of Iowa. Her first books, Valentines to the Wide World *(1959) and* A Time of Bees *(1964), were praised for their "simple, human subjects" and adroit handling of traditional forms. In 1971, Van Duyn received the National Book Award for* To See, To Take *(1970), and she has since then published a number of other books, including* Letters from a Father, and Other Poems *(1982) and* Near Changes *(1990). Much of her work has been gathered in* If It Be Not I: Collected Poems 1959–1982 *(1993).*

The following poem, "Leda," was first published in To See, To Take. *This same book includes another, longer poem, titled "Leda Reconsidered." Both can be understood as poetic responses to Yeats's "Leda and the Swan."*

Leda

> *"Did she put on his knowledge with his power*
> *Before the indifferent beak could let her drop?"*

Not even for a moment. He knew, for one thing, what he was.
When he saw the swan in her eyes he could let her drop.
In the first look of love men find their great disguise,
and collecting these rare pictures of himself was his life.   4

Her body became the consequence of his juice,
while her mind closed on a bird and went to sleep.
Later, with the children in school, she opened her eyes
and saw her own openness, and felt relief.   8

In men's stories her life ended with his loss.
She stiffened under the storm of his wings to a glassy shape,
stricken and mysterious and immortal. But the fact is,
she was not, for such an ending, abstract enough.   12

She tried for a while to understand what it was
that had happened, and then decided to let it drop.
She married a smaller man with a beaky nose,
and melted away in the storm of everyday life.   16

[1971]

Topics for Critical Thinking and Writing

1. Van Duyn uses as an epigraph, in quotation marks and italicized, the last lines of Yeats's poem. How do you understand these lines? Why do you think that Van Duyn chose to use them as an epigraph, in quotation marks and italicized? What does her poem gain (or lose) from this epigraph?

2. In line 2 Van Duyn writes, "When he saw the swan in her eyes." Is Van Duyn talking about Zeus's reflection in Leda's eyes, or about something else? And in line 3 she writes of "the first look of love." Is she talking about Zeus's "look of love" or Leda's?

3. The poem begins with its focus, in stanza 1, on the swan; but then in stanza 2 the focus, the point of view, shifts to Leda. Do you find this to be awkward? Or does it strike you as effective—and if so, in what ways?

4. In the second stanza, line 7, we read of "the children in school." Who are Leda's children? What does it tell you about Leda to find that the children are "in school"?

5. Can you explain lines 5–6? And what does it mean to say, in lines 11–12, that Leda was not "abstract enough"?

6. Consider the phrases "to let it drop" and "with a beaky nose": What is the tone of each of these phrases, and of the final stanza as a whole?

7. Can Van Duyn's poem stand alone and be effective? Or do you think that it is truly meaningful only for a reader who knows Yeats's poem?

8. Yeats's "Leda and the Swan" is a sonnet. Try to describe the form of Van Duyn's poems. Where do you find rhymes, or off-rhymes (also called "half-rhymes" or "imperfect rhymes," such as "come" and "home," or "mirth" and "forth")?

9. Which poem, Yeats's or Van Duyn's, do you like better? Why is that?

PARODY

One special kind of response is the **parody**, a comic form that imitates the original in a humorous way. It is a caricature in words. A parody may imitate the style of the original—let's say, short, punchy sentences—but apply this style to a subject that the original author would not be concerned with. Thus, because Ernest Hemingway often wrote short, simple sentences about tough guys engaged in activities such as hunting, fishing, and boxing, parodists of Hemingway are likely to use the same style, but for their subject they may choose something like opening the mail or preparing a cup of tea.

We once heard on the radio a parody of an announcer doing a baseball game. It went something like this:

> Well, here's Bill Shakespeare now, approaching the desk. Like so many other writers, Bill likes to work at a desk. In fact, just about every writer we know writes at a desk, but every writer has a particular way of approaching the desk and sitting at it. Bill is sitting down now; now he's adjusting the chair, moving it forward a little. Oh, he's just pushed the chair back an inch or two. He likes his chair to be just right. Now he's picking up a pen. It's a gray quill. I think it's the pen he uses when he writes a tragedy, and he's due for a tragedy—of his last five plays, only one was a tragedy, and two were comedies and two were history plays. But you never can tell with Bill, or "The Bard" as his fans call him. Some people call him "The Swan of Avon," but I'm told that he really hates that. Well, he's at the desk, and, you know, in circumstances like these, he might even sneak in a sonnet or two. Oh, he's put down the gray quill, and now he's trying a white one. Oh boy, oh boy, he's written a *word. No,* he's going for *a whole sentence!*

Parodies are, in a way, critical, but they are usually affectionate too. In the best parodies the reader feels that the writer admires the author being parodied. The distinguished sociologist Daniel Bell wrote a deliberate parody of sociological writing. It begins thus:

The purpose of this scene is to present a taxonomic dichotomization which would allow for unilinear comparison. In this fashion we could hope to distinguish the relevant variables which determine the functional specificities of social movements.

The journalist H. L. Mencken (1880–1956), who had a love-hate relationship with what he called the Great American Booboisie, wrote a parody in which he set forth the Declaration of Independence as it might have been written (or spoken) by Joe Sixpack in the mid-twentieth century. Here the target is not the original document but the twentieth-century American. The original document, you will remember, begins in this way:

> When in the Course of human events, it becomes necessary for one people to dissolve the political bands which have connected them with another, and to assume among the powers of the earth, the separate and equal station to which the Laws of Nature and of Nature's God entitle them, a decent respect to the opinions of mankind requires that they should declare the causes which impel them to the separation.

Now for Mencken's version:

> When things get so balled up that the people of a country got to cut loose from some other country, and go it on their own hook, without asking no permission from nobody, excepting maybe God Almighty, then they ought to let everybody know why they done it, so that everybody can see they are not trying to put nothing over on nobody.

WILLIAM CARLOS WILLIAMS

William Carlos Williams (1883–1963) was the son of an English traveling salesman and a Basque-Jewish woman. The couple met in Puerto Rico and settled in Rutherford, New Jersey, where Williams was born. He spent his life there, practicing as a pediatrician and writing poems in the moments between seeing patients.

This Is Just to Say

I have eaten
the plums
that were in
the icebox   4

and which
you were probably
saving
for breakfast   8

Forgive me
they were delicious
so sweet
and so cold   12

[1934]

Here are three parodies of Williams's poem, written by our students. The first is by Edward Rothko, the second by Julia Alfaro, and the third by Holly Chung.

I let out
the air
that was stored
in the tires

and which
your car
so badly
needed

I'm sorry
I like them
flat

   *   *   *

In your e-mail you said
that during spring break
we should meet
on the beach at Daytona

and we would have
fun, but I misread it
and here I am in Dayton

and I can't
forgive myself

   *   . *   *

I always forget
to return
your phone calls

which you probably think
are so
important

Forgive me
but you are
such a pain
in the
neck

Topics for Critical Thinking and Writing

1. Do these poems sound like a poem by Williams? Why or why not? (We print another poem by Williams on page 681.)
2. Write your own parody of "This Is Just to Say," apologizing for some action (real or imagined). Follow Williams's basic pattern: In the first stanza, state what you supposedly have done, in the second state what the person to whom you are apologizing probably was planning, and in the third stanza ask for forgiveness.

REVIEWING A DRAMATIC PRODUCTION

A review also is a response, since it normally includes an evaluation of the work, but at least at first glance it may seem to be an analytic essay. We'll talk about a review of a production of a play, but you can easily adapt what we say to a review of a book.

A review requires analytic skill, but it is not identical with an analysis. First of all, a reviewer normally assumes that the reader is unfamiliar with the production being reviewed, and unfamiliar with the play if the play is not a classic. Thus, the first paragraph usually provides a helpful introduction, along these lines:

> Marsha Norman's recent play, '*night, Mother*, a tragedy with only two actors and one set, shows us a woman's preparation for suicide. Jesse has concluded that she no longer wishes to live, and so she tries to put her affairs into order, which chiefly means preparing her rather uncomprehending mother to get along without her.

Inevitably some retelling of the plot is necessary if the play is new, and a summary of a sentence or two is acceptable even for a familiar play, but the review will chiefly be concerned with

1. describing,
2. analyzing, and, especially,
3. evaluating.

By the way, don't confuse description with analysis. Description tells what something—for instance, the set or the costumes—looks like; analysis tells us how it works, what it adds up to, what it contributes to the total effect.) If the play is new, much of the evaluation may center on the play itself, but if the play is a classic, the evaluation probably will be devoted chiefly to the acting, the set, and the direction.

Other points:

1. **Save the playbill.** It will give you the names of the actors, and perhaps a brief biography of the author, a synopsis of the plot, and a photograph of the set, all of which may be helpful.
2. **Draft your review as soon as possible,** while the performance is still fresh in your mind. If you can't draft it immediately after seeing the play, at least jot down some notes about the setting and the staging, the acting, and the audience's responses.
3. If possible, **read the play**—ideally, before the performance and again after it.
4. **In your first draft, don't worry about limitations of space.** Write as long a review as you can, putting down everything that comes to mind. Later you can cut it to the required length, retaining only the chief points and the necessary supporting details. But in your first draft try to produce a fairly full record of the performance and your response to it, so that a day or two later, when you revise, you won't have to trust a fading memory for details.

A Sample Review by a Student: "An Effective *Macbeth*"

If you read reviews of plays in *Time, Newsweek,* or a newspaper, you will soon develop a sense of what reviews do. The following example, an undergraduate's

Concrete details to support evaluation

primitive, and somewhat sadistic world. The catwalk, though effectively used when Macbeth goes off to murder Duncan (whose room is presumably upstairs and offstage), is not much used in later scenes. For the most part it is an interesting piece of scenery but not otherwise helpful. For instance, there is no reason why the scene with Macduff's wife and children is staged on it. The costumes are not in any way Scottish—no plaids—but in several scenes the sound of a bagpipe is heard, adding another weird or primitive tone to the production.

Summary

This *Macbeth* appeals to the eye, the ear, and the mind. The director has given us a unified production that makes sense and that is faithful to the spirit of Shakespeare's play.

Work Cited

Documentation

Macbeth. By William Shakespeare. Dir. Mark Urice. With Stephen Beers, Tina Peters, and John Berens. University Theater, Medford, MA. 3 Mar. 1998.

The Review Reviewed

The marginal notes call attention to certain qualities in the review, but three additional points should be made:

1. The reviewer's feelings and evaluations are clearly expressed, not in such expressions as "furthermore I feel," and "it is also my opinion," but in such expressions as "a thoughtful and occasionally exciting production," "excellent," and "appeals to the eye, the ear, and the mind."
2. The evaluations are supported by details. For instance, the evaluation that the witches are effectively presented is supported by a brief description of their appearance.
3. The reviewer is courteous, even when (as in the discussion of the catwalk, in the next-to-last paragraph) she is talking about aspects of the production she doesn't care for.

PART II

Up Close

Thinking Critically about Literary Works and Literary Forms

almost surely set yourself thinking about how the parts relate to each other and to the whole, their context. Here are some typical questions:

- What expectations does the title arouse in a reader?
- Does the middle drag?
- Do certain characters or settings seem to be symbolic, suggesting more than themselves?
- Is the end satisfactory, and if so, why? Because it is surprising? Because, on the contrary, foreshadowing caused us to anticipate it, and it therefore fulfills our expectations?

When you ask yourself questions such as these, you will find that you are deepening your understanding of how a work (perhaps an essay, story, poem, or play in this book, perhaps an essay of your own) works. Because thinking about questions is an excellent way to deepen your understanding, we include questions along with most of the literature in this book. And we include numerous checklists—in effect, lists of questions for you to ask yourself when you are writing—in order to help you think about your own productions.

A process that in effect is synonymous with critical thinking is **analysis**; this word also comes from a Greek word, meaning *to separate into parts*. And because the point of analysis is to understand how things connect, how things work, and because the point of writing an analysis is to share your understanding with your readers, your essay normally will include a **synthesis**, "a putting together." It can almost be said that essays based on critical thinking will propose a **thesis**, and will support the thesis by giving **reasons**, that is, by giving evidence: "X is so, *because* . . . "

Writing of this sort, in which evidence is offered, commonly is the result of conscious reasoning, but it must be admitted that sometimes insights come unsought. Two examples are famous. Legend says that the Greek mathematician Archimedes (287–212 B.C.), asked by the ruler of Syracuse to determine if a gold crown really was pure gold or was alloyed with silver, was baffled. To relax, he visited a public bath, and idly observed the overflow of water. "*Eureka!*" ("I have found it"), he shouted, leaping out of the water and (in his excitement) running home naked. What he had found was not the cake of soap but the solution to the problem: Since gold is denser than silver, a given weight of gold represents a smaller volume than an equal weight of silver. A one-pound crown of gold will therefore displace less water than a one-pound crown that is made of gold alloyed with silver. (The crown in question *was* alloyed.) A second (and better documented) example is the discovery by the great German chemist F. A. Kekulé, who, dozing in front of the fireplace, developed the ring theory of the molecular structure of benzene. Kekulé dreamed of a snake biting its own tail, and according to his report, he "awoke as though from a flash of lightning," and spent the rest of the night in working out the consequences of the hypothesis.

Confronted with the difficult but exciting and rewarding job of writing a thoughtful paper, you cannot count on inspiration, no matter how many baths you take or how many fires you contemplate sleepily. You probably will find, like almost everyone else, that your best thoughts come to you when you start to put them into writing, whether with pencil and paper or with a keyboard and a computer. Although our chief concern in this book is with writing about literature, and in a moment we will look at a short poem, let's start indirectly by thinking analytically, thinking critically, about a picture. (Our method will be in accord with Polonius's advice in *Hamlet*, "By indirections find directions out.")

COMPARING AND CONTRASTING

This photograph of Sitting Bull and Buffalo Bill was taken by a Canadian photographer, William Notman. Buffalo Bill—William F. Cody—got his name from his activities as a supplier of buffalo meat for workers on the Kansas Pacific Railway, but his fame came chiefly from his exploits as an army scout and a fighter against the Sioux Indians, and later from Buffalo Bill's Wild West. Buffalo Bill's Wild West was a show (though he never used this word because he insisted that the exhibition recreated recent Western history) consisting of mock battles with Indians, an attack on a stage coach, and feats of horsemanship and sharpshooting. Sitting Bull, a Sioux chief, had defeated Custer at the Battle of Little Bighorn ten years before this picture was taken, but he had fled to Canada soon after the battle. In 1879 he was granted amnesty and returned to the United States, and in 1885 he appeared in Buffalo Bill's Wild West. The photograph, entitled *Foes in '76, Friends in '85*, was used to publicize the show.

In Chapter 4 we talked about writing a comparison (pages 67–69), but we now want to add a few things. The writer Howard Nemerov once said, "If you really want to see something, look at something else." He was talking about the

William Notman, *Foes in '76, Friends in '85*. The Sioux chief appeared for one season in William F. Cody's show, which was called *Buffalo Bill's Wild West*. Souvenir cards with this picture were sold. (Buffalo Bill Historical Center, Cody, WY)

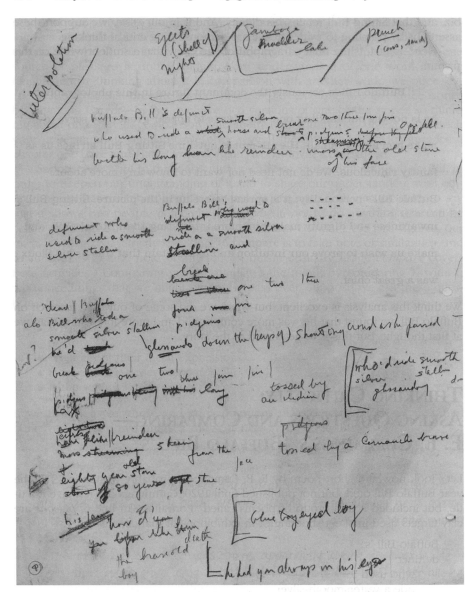

Manuscript of the draft of E. E. Cummings's poem (the final version is printed on page 155). (By permission of the Houghton Library, Harvard University. bMS Am 1823.7 [21], bMS Am 1823.7 [80].)

Ultimately you will want to ask your own questions about the poem and about your responses, but for a start you may find it useful to put down tentative answers to some or all of these questions:

1. What is the speaker's attitude toward Buffalo Bill? (How do you know? What *evidence* can you point to?)
2. In line 6, why do you suppose the poet ran the words together?
3. Why do you think Cummings spaced the poem as he does? One student suggested that the lines form an arrowhead pointing to the right. Do you

```
 1        buffalo Bill [is]'s defunct
 2                    smooth silver  break one two three four five  one fell.
 3        who used to ride a white,horse and shoot,pidgens before they fell.
 4                                    streaming from
 5                                       xx x
 6        with his long hair like reindeer moss,in the old stone
 7                                    of his face

 8                              Buffalo Bill's        - - - -
 9                                 who used to
10     defunct who          defunct  defunct      - - - -  -
11     used to ride a smooth    who
12     silver stallion      ride a a smooth silver  p - - - - -
13                          [horse] stallion and

14                              break
15                          break one
16     dead ‖Buffalo          two three  one  two  three
17            'd
18  alo Bill who rode a     four xxxx five
19     smooth silver stallion  pidgens
20     he'd break
21  how?            pidgens/    glissando down the (happy) shouting crowd as he passed
22     break break
23                   one    two
24                          three four  five  |               who'd ride smooth
25                                           |               silver ' stallion
26     pidgens pidgens being with his long      tossed by    glissandoing  do
27     ax                                    an indian
28     eighty-two
29     curls
30     hair like ‖ reindeer                    pidgens
31               streaming
32     moss streaming         from the         tossed by a Comanche brave
33                              face
34     x         old
35  xxx eighty year stone
36     stone xx 80 years xxx stone
37     his long
38          how d'you
39        you [like] you like [it] him    ┌ blue boy eye[o]d boy
40                        death           └─
41          the brave old
42          boy
43                              └ he had you always in his | ey[oo]e |
```

Modern transcription of the draft reproduced on the facing page. (By permission of the Houghton Library, Harvard University. bMS Am 1823.7 [21], bMS Am 1823.7 [80].)

find merit in this suggestion? If not, what better explanation(s) can you offer?

4. What do you make out of the address to "Mister Death"? Why "Mister Death" rather than "Mr. Death" or "Death"? If Mister Death could speak, what answer do you think he might give to the speaker's question?

5. What do you make of the use of "defunct" (as opposed to "dead") in line 2?

6. What do you make of "Jesus" in line 7? What is the effect of placing the word on a line by itself? Is Cummings being blasphemous? Is he inviting us

The Farewell Shot, 1910. A poster from
what was billed as a farewell performance.
(Buffalo Bill Historical Center, Cody, WY)

to compare Buffalo Bill with Jesus? Again, support your response with
evidence.

7. Compare the published poem with the manuscript draft. In the manuscript
(see page 156, and for a scholar's transcription of it, see page 157) you will
notice that Cummings wrote, near the start, "with his long hair like rein-
deer moss streaming from the old stone of his face." These words do not
appear in the final version. Do you think Cummings showed good judgment in deleting the line? Explain.

8. Some readers say that Cummings is satirizing Buffalo Bill, others that he is
satirizing death. Do you agree with either of these views? Why? (In a sentence or two define *satire*—feel free to consult a dictionary—and perhaps
give a clear example. By the way, it's possible to satirize the common human fear of death, but can death be satirized? How might that be done?
And what would be the point?)

You may want to discuss some or all of these questions, and others that you generate for yourself, with classmates and with your instructor. It will be interesting to
see whether at least some differences of opinion can be resolved by discussion,
by pointing to evidence.

Finally, after you have thought about the preceding questions, and any questions that you may initiate, consider these two opinions, from published discussions of the poem:

1. Buffalo Bill, in the poem, functions as a destroyer, an agent of death.

Buffalo Bill on a favorite horse, around 1910.
(Buffalo Bill Historical Center, Cody, WY)

2. The picture of Buffalo Bill on his "watersmooth-silver stallion," riding to the center of the tent to accept the adulation of the crowd before his demonstration of crack marksmanship is, I think, acidly ironic.

Do you agree with either, or with both? What evidence in the poem can you point to, in order to support or rebut these assertions?

Emily Dickinson: Three Versions of a Poem, and More

Here, for study and comparison, we present Emily Dickinson's "I felt a Funeral, in my Brain," in multiple versions: the poem as we know it today; the poem in manuscript; and the poem in its first published version. Then, two more poems, which are similar in phrasing to one another and show an affinity to "I felt a Funeral, in my Brain." Read each version carefully, asking questions about its style and structure and comparing it to the others. Look for details, and ask yourself why the detail—the use of a specific image, or a change in the organization of a line, for example—is significant.

This is the version of "I felt a Funeral, in my Brain" as we know it today. It is printed as #280 in *The Complete Poems of Emily Dickinson*, ed. Thomas H. Johnson (Boston: Little, Brown, and Company, 1957). This edition follows the text that Johnson presented in his three-volume scholarly edition, *The Poems of Emily*

Galway, Ireland, of Yeats's patron, Lady Gregory. (*Coole* is from an Irish word meaning "a niche" or "a retreat," hence its appropriateness for the name of a place of retirement or retreat.) Yeats was a frequent visitor there, beginning in 1897. Writing in 1916, in lines 7–8 he alludes to his first visit: "The nineteenth autumn has come upon me / Since I first made my count." At the time of this first visit, he was grieving because the woman he loved had rejected him. In a prose work he characterized his emotional state at the time of the first visit to Coole Park: "I was involved in a miserable love affair . . . My devotion might as well have been offered to an image in a milliner's window, or to a statue in a wax museum. . . ."

We follow Yeats's poem with an utterly unrelated work, Gwendolyn Brooks's "We Real Cool"—unrelated except for the accidental resemblance of "Coole" and "Cool." And we follow Brooks's poem with a witty piece by Andrew Hudgins, who brings the two preceding poems together by using Yeats's imagery and Brooks's lineation or versification. His work is a sort of parody of each author, but clearly—we think—he is motivated not by malice but by admiration and affection. And we end with an anonymous poem, set to music by Orlando Gibbons.

WILLIAM BUTLER YEATS

The Wild Swans at Coole

The trees are in their autumn beauty,
The woodland paths are dry,
Under the October twilight the water
Mirrors a still sky;
Upon the brimming water among the stones   5
Are nine-and-fifty swans.

The nineteenth autumn has come upon me
Since I first made my count;
I saw, before I had well finished,
All suddenly mount   10
And scatter wheeling in great broken rings
Upon their clamorous wings.

I have looked upon those brilliant creatures,
And now my heart is sore.
All's changed since I, hearing at twilight,   15
The first time on this shore,
The bell-beat of their wings above my head,
Trod with a lighter tread.

Unwearied still, lover by lover,
They paddle in the cold   20
Companionable streams or climb the air;
Their hearts have not grown old;
Passion or conquest, wander where they will,
Attend upon them still.

But now they drift on the still water,   25
Mysterious, beautiful;
Among what rushes will they build,
By what lake's edge or pool
Delight men's eyes when I awake some day
To find they have flown away?   30

[1916]

Topics for Critical Thinking and Writing

1. Do you find this a beautiful poem? Or would you be inclined to use a different term to characterize it? Is there a special element in this poem or in other poems you have read, or perhaps a special feeling that this poem or others give you, that leads you to say, "Now this is a beautiful poem"?

2. The key transition comes at line 15, in the exact middle: "All's changed since I. . . ." What is the scene that the speaker describes from lines 1–14? And what is the nature of the change that he describes in lines 15–30?

3. Yeats says in line 13 that the swans are "brilliant creatures." What does he mean by this phrase?

4. Can you explain the meaning of the question with which the speaker ends the poem? Do you think it is a good idea to end a poem with a question? What would be your argument in favor of such a choice? What would be your argument against it?

5. Have you ever had an experience similar to Yeats's—an experience, for example, of an eagle's flight, or of a group of horses in the wild, that has given you a feeling of connection? Or, maybe, a feeling of hope, or loss, or of something else that was powerful and profound? What was this experience? What was the response you had when it happened? Do you think about the experience differently now?

GWENDOLYN BROOKS

Gwendolyn Brooks (1917–2000) was born in Topeka, Kansas, but was raised on Chicago's South Side, where she spent most of her life. In 1950, when she won the Pulitzer Prize for Poetry, she became the first African American writer to win a Pulitzer Prize.

We Real Cool

The Pool Players.
Seven at the Golden Shovel.

We real cool. We
Left school. We

Lurk late. We
Strike straight. We   4

Sing sin. We
Thin gin. We

Jazz June. We
Die soon.   8

                                                                        [1960]

Topics for Critical Thinking and Writing

1. What does it mean for the pool players to say that they are "cool," and not just "cool," but "real cool"?
2. Why does Brooks give seven speakers? Why not simply one, as in "I real cool" and so on? Would that have been more focused and thus more effective?
3. The stanzas could have been written:

   We real cool.
   We left school.

   We lurk late.
   We strike straight.

   And so on. What does Brooks gain by organizing the lines as she does?
4. Brooks presents the poem in a first-person plural voice, "we." If someone claimed that Brooks would have made the poem more objective, and hence better, if she had presented it in third-personal plural, "they," what would be your argument in response?
5. One commentary we consulted says that this poem describes "pool-playing gang members at a bar called The Golden Shovel on the South Side of Chicago." Does this specific information add to or detract from your experience of the poem?

ANDREW HUDGINS

Andrew Hudgins was born in Killeen, Texas in 1951, and educated at Huntingdon College, the University of Alabama, and the University of Iowa. The author of a book of essays and of five volumes of poems, Hudgins has received numerous awards. He teaches at the University of Cincinnati.

The Wild Swans Skip School

We beat wings. We
fly rings. We

scorn Yeats. We
have mates. We   4

won't stay. We
fly 'way.

                                                                        [2001]

Topics for Critical Thinking and Writing

1. In what way is Hudgins responding to Yeats? In what way is he responding to Brooks? Why do you think he would want to do something like this?
2. Does this poem make you laugh, or at least smile? Does it seem silly to you?
3. Is there anything serious about this poem, or is it a comic poem and no more than that?
4. If you were unfamiliar with the poems by Yeats and Brooks, what would your response be to Hudgins's poem?
5. Imagine that someone says to you, "This poem isn't any good: it's too short and too simple." What kind of argument could you present to convince this person that this is in fact a good poem?
6. Now imagine that someone says to you, "This poem is short and simple and I find it delightful." What kind of argument could you present that takes a more skeptical point of view?

ANONYMOUS

The ancient Greeks thought that the swan was silent throughout its life until the moment just before death, when it sang melodiously, hence the term "swan song" to denote a person's last action or last words. The following poem was first published in Orlando Gibbons's First Set of Madrigals and Motets *(1612).*

Cantus I (soprano I) vocal part from Orlando Gibbons's five-voice setting of 1612.

The Silver Swan

The silver swan, who living had no note,
When death approached, unlocked her silent throat;
Leaning her breast against the reedy shore,
Thus sung her first and last, and sung no more:
"Farewell, all joys; Oh death, come close mine eyes;   5
More geese than swans now live, more fools than wise."

[1612]

Topics for Critical Thinking and Writing

1. It is untrue that swans are silent until just before their death, at which point
   they sing. In fact, it is doubly untrue: (a) when angry, swans make hissing
   sounds, and (b) no kind of swan utters anything that can reasonably be called
   a song (though the whistling swan does a bit more than hiss). But does the
   truth or falsehood of the legend have any relevance to the value of the poem?
2. Suppose the final two lines were:

   Farewell all joys; Oh death, come close mine eyes;
   I leave the water now, for heavenly skies.

   Or:

   Farewell all joys; Oh death, come close mine eyes;
   A swan sings only once before it dies.

   Which version do you prefer? Why?

7

Reading and Writing about Essays

The word *essay* entered the English language in 1597, when Francis Bacon called a small book of ten short prose pieces *Essays*. Bacon borrowed the word from Michel de Montaigne, a French writer who in 1580 had published some short prose pieces under the title *Essais*—that is, "testings," or "attempts," from the French verb *essayer*, "to try." Montaigne's title indicated that his graceful and personal jottings—the fruit of pleasant study and meditation—were not fully thought-out treatises but rather sketches that could be amplified and amended.

If you keep a journal, you are working in Montaigne's tradition. You jot down your tentative thoughts, perhaps your responses to a work of literature, partly to find out what you think and how you feel. Montaigne said, in the preface to his book, "I am myself the subject of my book," and in all probability you are the real subject of your journal. Your entries—your responses to other writers and your reflections on those responses—require you to examine yourself.

TYPES OF ESSAYS

If you have already taken a course in composition (or even if you haven't), you are probably familiar with the chief kinds of essays. Essays are usually classified—roughly, of course—along the following lines: meditation (or speculation or reflection), argument (or persuasion), exposition (or information), narration, and description.

Of these, the **meditative** (or **speculative** or **reflective**) **essay** is the closest to Montaigne. In a meditative essay, the writer seems chiefly concerned with exploring an idea or a feeling. The organization usually seems casual, not a careful and evident structure but a free flow of thought—what the Japanese (who wrote with brush and ink) called "following the brush." The essayist is thinking, but he or she is not especially concerned with arguing a case, or even with being logical. We think along with the essayist, chiefly because we find the writer's tentative thoughts engaging. Of course the writer may in the long run be pressing a point, advancing an argument, but the emphasis is on the free play of mind, not on an orderly and logical analysis.

In the **argumentative** (or **persuasive**) **essay**, the organization probably is apparent, and it is reasonable: For instance, the essay may announce a problem, define some terms, present and refute solutions that the writer considers to be inadequate, and then, by way of a knockdown ending, offer what the writer considers to be the correct solution.

The **expository essay**, in which the writer is chiefly concerned with giving information (for instance on how to annotate a text, or how to read a poem, or

169

how to use a word processor), ordinarily has an equally clear organization. A clear organization is necessary in such an essay because the reader is reading not in order to come into contact with an interesting mind that may keep doubling back on its thinking (as in a meditative essay), and not in order to come to a decision about some controversial issue (as in an argumentative essay), but in order to gain information.

Narrative and **descriptive essays** usually really are largely meditative essays. For instance, a narrative essay may recount some happening—often a bit of autobiography—partly to allow the writer and the reader to meditate on it. Similarly, a description, let's say of a spider spinning a web or of children playing in the street, usually turns out to be offered not so much as information—it thus is unlike the account of how to annotate a text—but rather as something for the writer and reader to enjoy in itself, and perhaps to think further about.

Of course most essays are not pure specimens. For instance, an informative essay, let's say on how to use a word processing program on a computer, may begin with a paragraph that seeks to persuade you to use this particular software. Or it might begin with a very brief narrative, an anecdote of a student who switched from program X to program Y, again in order to persuade the reader to use this software (Y, of course). Similarly, an argument—and probably most of the essays that you write in English courses will be arguments advancing a thesis concerning the meaning or structure of a literary work—may include some exposition, for instance a very brief summary to remind the reader of the gist of the work you will be arguing about.

THE ESSAYIST'S PERSONA

Many of the essays that give readers the most pleasure are, like entries in a journal, chiefly reflective. An essay of this kind sets forth the writer's attitudes or states of mind, and the reader's interest in the essay is almost entirely in the way the writer sees things. It's not so much *what* the writers see and say as *how* they say what they see. Even in essays that are narrative—that is, in essays that recount events, such as a bit of biography—our interest is more in the essayists' *responses* to the events than in the events themselves. When we read an essay, we almost say, "So that's how it feels to be you," and "Tell me more about the way you see things." The bit of history is less important than the memorable presence of the writer.

Voice

When you read an essay in this chapter or in a later chapter, try to imagine the kind of person who wrote it, the kind of person who seems to be speaking it. Then slowly reread the essay, noticing *how* the writer conveyed this personality or persona or "voice" (even while he or she was writing about a topic "out there"). The writer's persona may be revealed by common or uncommon words, for example, by short or long sentences, by literal or figurative language, or by familiar or erudite examples.

Let's take a simple, familiar example of words that establish a persona. Lincoln begins the Gettysburg Address with "Four score and seven years ago . . ." He might have said "Eighty-seven years ago"—but the language would have lacked the biblical echo, and the persona would thus have been that of an ordinary person rather than that of a man who has about him something of the tone of an Old Testament prophet. This religious tone of "four score and seven years" is entirely fitting, since

- President Lincoln was speaking at the dedication of a cemetery for "these hallowed dead" and
- he was urging the members of his audience to give all of their energies to ensure that the dead men had not died in vain.

By such devices as the choice of words, the length of sentences, and the sorts of evidence offered, an author sounds to the reader solemn or agitated or witty or genial or severe. If you are familiar with Martin Luther King's "I Have a Dream," you may recall that he begins the piece (originally it was a speech, delivered at the Lincoln Memorial on the one-hundredth anniversary of Lincoln's Emancipation Proclamation) with these words: "Five score years ago. . . ." King is deliberately echoing Lincoln's words, partly in tribute to Lincoln, but also to help establish himself as the spiritual descendant of Lincoln and, further back, of the founders of the Judeo-Christian tradition.

Tone

Only by reading closely can we hear in the mind's ear the writer's tone—friendly, or bitter, or indignant, or ironic (characterized by wry understatement or over-statement). Perhaps you have heard the line from Owen Wister's novel *The Virginian*: "When you call me that, smile!" Words spoken with a smile mean something different from the same words forced through clenched teeth. But while speakers can communicate—or, we might say, can guide the responses of their audience—by body language and by gestures, by facial expressions and by changes in tone of voice, writers have only words in ink on paper. As a writer, you are learning control of tone as you learn to take pains in your choice of words, in the way you arrange sentences, and even in the punctuation marks you may find yourself changing in your final draft. These skills will pay off doubly if you apply them to your reading, by putting yourself in the place of the writer whose work you are reading. As a reader, you must make some effort to "hear" the writer's tone as part of the meaning the words communicate. Skimming is not adequate to that task. Thinking carefully about the works in this book means, first of all, reading them carefully, listening for the sound of the speaking voice, so that you can respond to the persona—the personality or character the author presents in the essay.

Consider the following paragraph from the middle of "Black Men and Public Space," a short essay by Brent Staples. Staples is talking about growing up in a tough neighborhood. Of course the paragraph is only a small example; the tone depends, finally, on the entire essay, which we will print in a moment.

> As a boy, I saw countless tough guys locked away; I have since buried several, too. They were babies, really—a teenage cousin, a brother of twenty-two, a childhood friend in his mid-twenties—all gone down in episodes of bravado played out in the streets. I came to doubt the virtues of intimidation early on. I chose, perhaps unconsciously, to remain a shadow—timid, but a survivor.

Judging only from these few lines, what sense of Staples do we get? Perhaps you will agree that we can probably say something along these lines:

- He is relatively quiet and gentle. We sense this not simply because he tells us that he was "timid" but because (at least in this passage) he does not raise his voice either in a denunciation of white society for creating a system that produces black violence or in a denunciation of those blacks of his youth who engaged in violence.
- He is perceptive; he sees that the "tough guys," despite the fact that some were in their twenties, were babies; their bravado was infantile and destructive.
- He speaks with authority; he is giving a firsthand report.
- He doesn't claim to be especially shrewd; he modestly says that he may have "unconsciously" adopted the behavior that enabled him to survive.
- In saying that he is a "survivor" he displays a bit of wry humor. The usual image of a survivor is a guy in a Banana Republic outfit, gripping a knife, someone who survived a dog-eat-dog world by being tougher than the others. But Staples almost comically says he is a "survivor" who is "timid."

If your responses to the paragraph are somewhat different, jot them down and in a few sentences try to explain them.

Pre-writing: Identifying the Topic and Thesis

Although we have emphasized the importance of the essayist's personality, essayists also make a point. They have a thesis or argument, and an argument implies taking a specific viewpoint toward a topic. In reading an essay, then, try to identify the topic. The topic of "Do-It-Yourself Brain Surgery" can't really be brain surgery; it must be do-it-yourself books, and the attitude probably will be amused contempt for such books. Even an essay that is largely narrative, like Brent Staples's, recounting a personal experience or a bit of history, probably will include an attitude toward the event that is being narrated. It is that attitude—the interpretation of the event rather than the event itself—that may be the real topic of the essay.

It's time to look at Staples's essay. (Following the essay you will find a student's outline of it and another student's version of its thesis.)

Brent Staples

Brent Staples, born in 1951, received a bachelor's degree from Widener University in Chester, Pennsylvania, and a Ph.D. from the University of Chicago. After working as a journalist in Chicago, he joined The New York Times *in 1985, and he is now on the newspaper's editorial board, where he writes on politics and culture. His essay was first published in* Ms. *magazine in 1986 and reprinted in a slightly revised form—the form we give here—in* Harper's *in 1987.*

Black Men and Public Space

My first victim was a woman—white, well dressed, probably in her late twenties. I came upon her late one evening on a deserted street in Hyde Park, a relatively affluent neighborhood in an otherwise mean, impoverished section of Chicago.

As I swung onto the avenue behind her, there seemed to be a discreet, unin-flammatory distance between us. Not so. She cast back a worried glance. To her, the youngish black man—a broad six feet two inches with a beard and billowing hair, both hands shoved into the pockets of a bulky military jacket—seemed menacingly close. After a few more quick glimpses, she picked up her pace and was soon running in earnest. Within seconds, she disappeared into a cross street.

That was more than a decade ago. I was twenty-two years old, a graduate student newly arrived at the University of Chicago. It was in the echo of that terri-fied woman's footfalls that I first began to know the unwieldy inheritance I'd come into—the ability to alter public space in ugly ways. It was clear that she thought herself the quarry of a mugger, a rapist, or worse. Suffering a bout of in-somnia, however, I was stalking sleep, not defenseless wayfarers. As a softy who is scarcely able to take a knife to a raw chicken—let alone hold one to a person's throat—I was surprised, embarrassed, and dismayed all at once. Her flight made me feel like an accomplice in tyranny. It also made it clear that I was indistin-guishable from the muggers who occasionally seeped into the area from the sur-rounding ghetto. That first encounter, and those that followed, signified that a vast, unnerving gulf lay between nighttime pedestrians—particularly women—and me. And I soon gathered that being perceived as dangerous is a hazard in itself. I only needed to turn a corner into a dicey situation, or crowd some frightened, armed person in a foyer somewhere, or make an errant move after being pulled over by a policeman. Where fear and weapons meet—and they often do in urban America—there is always the possibility of death.

In that first year, my first away from my hometown, I was to become thor-oughly familiar with the language of fear. At dark, shadowy intersections, I could cross in front of a car stopped at a traffic light and elicit the *thunk*, thunk, thunk, thunk of the driver—black, white, male, or female—hammering down the door locks. On less traveled streets after dark, I grew accustomed to but never comfort-able with people crossing to the other side of the street rather than pass me. Then there were the standard unpleasantries with policemen, doormen, bouncers, cab-drivers, and others whose business it is to screen out troublesome individuals *before* there is any nastiness.

I moved to New York nearly two years ago and I have remained an avid night walker. In central Manhattan, the near-constant crowd cover minimizes tense one-on-one street encounters. Elsewhere—in SoHo, for example, where sidewalks are narrow and tightly spaced buildings shut out the sky—things can get very taut indeed.

5   After dark, on the warrenlike streets of Brooklyn where I live, I often see women who fear the worst from me. They seem to have set their faces on neutral, and with their purse straps strung across their chests bandolier-style, they forge ahead as though bracing themselves against being tackled. I understand, of course, that the danger they perceive is not a hallucination. Women are particu-larly vulnerable to street violence, and young black males are drastically overrep-resented among the perpetrators of that violence. Yet these truths are no solace against the kind of alienation that comes of being ever the suspect, a fearsome en-tity with whom pedestrians avoid making eye contact.

It is not altogether clear to me how I reached the ripe old age of twenty-two without being conscious of the lethality nighttime pedestrians attributed to me. Perhaps it was because in Chester, Pennsylvania, the small, angry industrial town where I came of age in the 1960s, I was scarcely noticeable against a backdrop of gang warfare, street knifings, and murders. I grew up one of the good boys, had perhaps a half-dozen fistfights. In retrospect, my shyness of combat has clear sources.

As a boy, I saw countless tough guys locked away; I have since buried several, too. They were babies, really—a teenage cousin, a brother of twenty-two, a childhood friend in his mid-twenties—all gone down in episodes of bravado played out in the streets. I came to doubt the virtues of intimidation early on. I chose, perhaps unconsciously, to remain a shadow—timid, but a survivor.

The fearsomeness mistakenly attributed to me in public places often has a perilous flavor. The most frightening of these confusions occurred in the late 1970s and early 1980s, when I worked as a journalist in Chicago. One day, rushing into the office of a magazine I was writing for with a deadline story in hand, I was mistaken for a burglar. The office manager called security and, with an ad hoc posse, pursued me through the labyrinthine halls, nearly to my editor's door. I had no way of proving who I was. I could only move briskly toward the company of someone who knew me.

Another time I was on assignment for a local paper and killing time before an interview. I entered a jewelry store on the city's affluent Near North Side. The proprietor excused herself and returned with an enormous red Doberman pinscher straining at the end of a leash. She stood, the dog extended toward me, silent to my questions, her eyes bulging nearly out of her head. I took a cursory look around, nodded, and bade her good night.

10   Relatively speaking, however, I never fared as badly as another black male journalist. He went to nearby Waukegan, Illinois, a couple of summers ago to work on a story about a murderer who was born there. Mistaking the reporter for the killer, police officers hauled him from his car at gunpoint and but for his press credentials would probably have tried to book him. Such episodes are not uncommon. Black men trade tales like this all the time.

Over the years, I learned to smother the rage I felt at so often being taken for a criminal. Not to do so would surely have led to madness. I now take precautions to make myself less threatening. I move about with care, particularly late in the evening. I give a wide berth to nervous people on subway platforms during the wee hours, particularly when I have exchanged business clothes for jeans. If I happen to be entering a building behind some people who appear skittish, I may walk by, letting them clear the lobby before I return, so as not to seem to be following them. I have been calm and extremely congenial on those rare occasions when I've been pulled over by the police.

And on late-evening constitutionals I employ what has proved to be an excellent tension-reducing measure: I whistle melodies from Beethoven and Vivaldi and the more popular classical composers. Even steely New Yorkers hunching toward nighttime destinations seem to relax, and occasionally they even join in the tune. Virtually everybody seems to sense that a mugger wouldn't be warbling bright, sunny selections from Vivaldi's *Four Seasons*. It is my equivalent of the cowbell that hikers wear when they know they are in bear country.

[1986]

SUMMARIZING

Summary should be clearly distinguished from analysis. The word *summary* is related to *sum*, the total something adds up to. (We say "adds *up* to" because the Greeks and Romans counted upward and wrote the total at the top.)

A summary is a condensation or abridgement; it briefly gives the reader the gist of a longer work. It boils down the longer work, resembling the longer work as a bouillon cube resembles a bowl of soup. A summary of Staples's "Black Men and Public Space" will reduce the essay, perhaps to a paragraph or two or even to a sentence. It will not call attention to Staples's various strategies, and it will not evaluate his views or his skill as a writer; it will merely present the gist of what he says.

Summary and Analysis

If, then, you are asked to write an analysis of something you have read, you should not hand in a summary. On the other hand, a very brief summary may appropriately appear within an analytic essay. Usually, in fact, the reader needs some information, and the writer of the essay will briefly summarize this information. For example, a student who wrote about Staples's essay is *summarizing* when she writes

> Staples says that he is aware that his presence frightens many whites, especially women.

She is summarizing because she is reporting, without personal comment, what Staples said.

On the other hand, she is *analyzing* when she writes

> By saying at the outset, "My first victim was a woman--white, well dressed, probably in her late twenties," Staples immediately catches the reader's attention and sets up expectations that will be undermined in the next paragraph.

In this sentence the writer is not reporting *what* Staples said but is explaining *how* he achieved an effect.

In Chapter 5 we discussed a few principles that govern summaries (see the list on pp. 130–31). Here is a summary of our comments on "summary":

> A summary is a condensation or abridgment. Its chief characteristics are that (1) it is rarely more than one-fourth as long as the original; (2) its brevity is usually achieved by leaving out most of the concrete details of the original; (3) it is accurate; (4) it may rearrange the organization of the original, especially if a rearrangement will make things clearer; (5) it normally is in the present tense; and (6) quoted words need not be enclosed in quotation marks.

Preparing a Summary

If you are summarizing an essay, you may find that the essay includes its own summary, perhaps at the start or more likely near the end. If it does, you're in luck.

If it doesn't, we suggest that on rereading you jot down, after reading each paragraph, a sentence summarizing the gist of the paragraph. (A very long or poorly unified paragraph may require two sentences, but make every effort to boil the paragraph down to a dozen or so words.) Of course if a paragraph consists merely of a transitional sentence or two ("We will now turn to another example") you will lump it with the next paragraph. Similarly, if for some reason you encounter a series of very short paragraphs—for instance, three examples, each briefly stated, and all illustrating the same point—you probably will find that you can cover them with a single sentence. But if a paragraph runs to half a page or more of print, it's probably worth its own sentence of summary. In fact, your author may summarize the paragraph in the paragraph's opening sentence or in its final sentence.

Here is a student's paragraph-by-paragraph summary of Staples's "Black Men and Public Space." The numbers refer to Staples's paragraphs.

1. "First victim" was a white woman in Chicago, who hurried away.
2. Age 22, he realized--to his surprise and embarrassment--that he (a "youngish black man") could be perceived by strangers as a mugger. And, since his presence created fear, he was in a dangerous situation.
3,4,5. At intersections he heard drivers of cars lock their doors, and elsewhere he sensed hostility of bouncers and others. In NY, lots of tension on narrow sidewalks. Women are esp. afraid of him; he knows why, but that's "no solace."
6. He's not sure why it took him 22 years to see that others fear him, but prob. because in his hometown of Chester, Pa., there was lots of adolescent violence, though he stayed clear of it.
7. As a boy, he saw young toughs killed, and he kept clear, "timid, but a survivor."
8,9,10. Though he is gentle, he looks fearsome. Once, working as a journalist, he was mistaken for a burglar. Another time, in a jewelry store, the clerk brought out a guard dog. Another black journalist was covering a crime, but the police thought the journalist was the killer. Many blacks have had such experiences.
11. He has learned to smother his rage--and he keeps away from nervous people.
12. Walking late at night, he whistles familiar classical music, trying to reassure others that he is not a mugger.

When you have written your sentence summarizing the last paragraph, you may have done enough if the summary was intended simply for your own private use, for example, to help you review material for an examination. But if you are going to use it as the basis of a summary within an essay you are writing, you probably won't want to include a summary longer than three or four sentences, so your job will be to reduce and combine the sentences you have jotted down. Indeed, you may even want to reduce the summary to a single sentence.

A Suggested Exercise: Assuming that you find the sentences summarizing "Black Men and Public Space" acceptable, reduce them to a summary no longer than four readable sentences. Then compare your version with the versions of two other students and, working as a group, produce a summary.

Stating the Thesis of an Essay

Summarizing each stage of the essay forces a reader to be attentive and can assist the reader to formulate a **thesis sentence**, a sentence that (in the reader's opinion) sets forth the writer's central point. If an essay is essentially an argument—for example, a defense of (or an argument against) capital punishment—it will probably include one or more sentences that directly assert the thesis. "Black Men and Public Space," chiefly a narrative essay, is much less evidently an argument, but it does have a point, and some of its sentences come pretty close to summarizing the point. Here are three of those sentences:

> And I soon gathered that being perceived as dangerous is a hazard in itself. (2)
>
> The fearsomeness mistakenly attributed to me in public places often has a perilous flavor. (8)
>
> I now take precautions to make myself less threatening. (11)

We asked our students to formulate their own thesis sentence for Staples's essay. One student came up with the following sentence after first drafting a couple of tentative versions and then rereading the essay in order to modify them:

> In "Black Men and Public Space" Staples recognizes that because many whites fear a young black man and therefore may do violence to him, he may do well to try to cool the situation by making himself unthreatening.

Notice, again, that a thesis sentence states the *point* of the work. Don't confuse a thesis sentence with a summary of a narrative, such as "Staples at the age of twenty-two came to realize that his presence was threatening to whites, and he has since taken measures to make himself less threatening." This sentence, though true, doesn't clearly get at the point of the essay, the generalization that can be drawn from Staples's example.

Look again at the student's formulation of a thesis sentence (*not* the narrative summary sentence that we have just given). If you don't think that it fairly represents Staples's point, you may (if you are writing an essay about Staples's essay) want to come up with a sentence that seems more precise to you. Whether you use the sentence we have quoted or a sentence that you formulate for yourself, you can in any case of course disagree very strongly with what you take to be Staples's point. Your version of Staples's thesis should accurately reflect your understanding of Staples's point, but you need not agree with the point. You may think, for instance, that Staples is hypersensitive or (to mention only one other possibility) that he is playing the Uncle Tom.

A thesis sentence, then, whether the words are your own or the author's, is a very brief summary of the argument (not of the narrative) of the work. If you are writing an essay about an essay, you'll probably want to offer a sentence that reminds your reader of the point of the work you are discussing or gives the reader the gist of an unfamiliar work:

> Black males, however harmless, are in a perilous situation because whites, especially white women, perceive them as threatening.

Or:

> In "Black Men and Public Space" Brent Staples recognizes that because many whites fear young black men and may therefore do violence to them, black men may do well to try to cool the situation by making themselves nonthreatening.

Drafting a Summary

Sometimes, however, a fuller statement may be useful. For instance, if you are writing about a complex essay that makes six points, you may help your reader if you briefly restate all six. The length of your summary will depend on your purpose and the needs of your audience.

The following principles may help you to write your summary:

1. First, after having written sentences that summarize each paragraph or group of paragraphs, formulate the essay's thesis sentence. Formulating the sentence in writing will help you to stay with what you take to be the writer's main point.
2. Next, write a first draft by turning your summaries of the paragraphs into fewer and better sentences. For example, the student who wrote the paragraph-by-paragraph summary (page 176) of Staples's essay turned her first five sentences (on Staples's first paragraphs) into this:

> Staples's "first victim" was a white woman in Chicago. When she hurried away from him, he realized--to his surprise and embarrassment--that because he was large and black and young he seemed to her to be a mugger. And since his presence created fear, he was in a dangerous situation. Other experiences, such as hearing drivers lock their cars when they were waiting at an intersection, have made him aware of the hostility of others. Women are especially afraid of him, and although he knows why, this knowledge is "no solace."

The student turned the remaining sentences of the outline into the following summary:

> Oddly, it took him twenty-two years to see that others fear him. Perhaps it took this long because he grew up in a violent neighborhood, though he kept clear, "timid, but a survivor." Because he is black and large, whites regard him as fearsome and treat him accordingly (once a clerk in a jewelry store brought out a guard dog), but other blacks have been treated worse. He has learned to smother his rage, and in order to cool things he tries to reassure nervous people by keeping away from them and (when he is walking late at night) by whistling classical music.

3. Write a lead-in sentence, probably incorporating the gist of the thesis sentence. Here is an example:

> Brent Staples, in "Black Men and Public Space," tells how his awareness that many white people regarded him as dangerous caused him to realize that he was in danger. His implicitly recommended

solution is to try to cool the anxiety by adopting nonthreatening behavior.

After writing a lead-in, revise the draft of your summary, eliminating needless repetition, providing transitions, and adding whatever you think may be needed to clarify the work for someone who is unfamiliar with it. You may rearrange the points if you think the rearrangement will clarify matters.

4. Edit your draft for errors in grammar, punctuation, and spelling. Read it aloud to test it once more for readability. Sometimes only by reading aloud do writers detect needless repetition or confusing phrases.

Some Writing Assignments

1. In a paragraph or two, set forth what you take to be Staples's *purpose*. Do you think he was writing chiefly to clarify some ideas for himself—for instance, to explore how he came to discover the "alienation that comes of being ever the suspect"? Or writing to assist blacks? Or to assist whites? Or what? (You may of course conclude that none of these suggestions, or all, are relevant.)

2. If you think the essay is effective, in a paragraph or two addressed to your classmates try to account for its effectiveness. Do certain examples strike you as particularly forceful? If so, why? Do certain sentences seem especially memorable? Again, why? For example, if the opening and concluding paragraphs strike you as effective, explain why. On the other hand, if you are unimpressed by part or all of the essay, explain why.

3. The success of a narrative as a piece of writing often depends on the reader's willingness to identify with the narrator. From an examination of "Black Men and Public Space," what explanations can you give for your willingness (or unwillingness) to identify yourself with Staples? (Probably you will want to say something about his persona as you sense it from the essay.) In the course of a 500-word essay explaining your position, very briefly summarize Staples's essay and state his thesis.

4. Have *you* ever unintentionally altered public space? For instance, you might recall an experience in which, as a child, your mere presence caused adults to alter their behavior—for instance, to stop quarreling.

   After a session of brainstorming, in which you produce some possible topics, you'll want to try to settle on one. After you have chosen a topic and produced a first draft, if you are not satisfied with your first paragraph—for instance, if you feel that it is not likely to get and hold the reader's attention—you may want to imitate the strategy that Staples adopted for his first paragraph.

5. If you have ever been in the position of one of Staples's "victims," that is, if you have ever shown fear or suspicion of someone who, it turned out, meant you no harm (or if you can imagine being in that position), write an essay from the "victim's" point of view. Explain what happened, what you did and thought. Did you think at the time about the feelings of the person you avoided or fled from? Has reading Staples's essay prompted further reflections on your experience? (Suggested length: 750 words.)

✎ CHECKLIST: *Getting Ideas for Writing about Essays*

Persona and Tone

❑ What sort of *persona* does the writer create?

❑ How does the writer create this persona? (For example, does the writer use colloquial language or formal language or technical language? Short sentences or long ones? Personal anecdotes? Quotations from authorities?)

❑ What is the *tone* of the essay? Is it, for example, solemn, or playful? Is the tone consistent? If not, how do the shifts affect your understanding of the writer's point or your identification of the writer's persona? Who is the *audience?*

Kind of Essay

❑ What kind of essay is it? Is it chiefly a presentation of facts (for example, an exposition, a report, a history)? Or is it chiefly an argument? Or a meditation? (Probably the essay draws on several kinds of writing, but which kind is it primarily? How are the other kinds related to the main kind?) What is the overall *purpose* of the essay?

❑ What does it seem to add up to? If the essay is chiefly meditative or speculative, how much emphasis is placed on the persona? That is, if the essay is a sort of thinking-out-loud, is your interest chiefly in the announced or ostensible topic, or in the writer's mood and personality? If the essay is chiefly a presentation of facts, does it also have a larger implication? For instance, if it narrates a happening (history), does the reader draw an inference—find a meaning—in the happening? If the essay is chiefly an argument, what is the thesis? How is the thesis supported? (Is it supported, for example, by induction, deduction, analogy, or emotional appeal?) Do you accept the assumptions (explicit and implicit)?

Structure

❑ Is the title appropriate? Propose a better title, if possible.

❑ Did the opening paragraph interest you? Why, or why not? Did the essay continue more or less as expected, or did it turn out to be rather different from what you anticipated?

❑ Prepare an outline of the essay. What effect does the writer seem to be aiming at by using this structure?

Value

❑ What is especially good (or bad) about the essay? Is it logically persuasive? Or entertaining? Or does it introduce an engaging persona? Or (if it is a narrative) does it tell a story effectively, using (where appropriate) description, dialogue, and commentary, and somehow make you feel that this story is worth reporting?

❑ Does the writer seem to hold values that you share? Or cannot share? Explain.

❑ Do you think that most readers will share your response, or do you think that for some reason—for example, your age, or your cultural background—your responses are unusual? Explain.

YOUR TURN: ESSAYS FOR ANALYSIS

GEORGE ORWELL

"George Orwell" was the pen name adopted in 1933 by Eric Blair (1903–50). Orwell was born in India, where his father was serving as a civil servant. The boy was brought up in England and educated at Eton, an exclusive school; but instead of going to a university, he joined the Imperial Indian Police and served for five years in Burma (now Myanmar, but a province of British India from 1886 until 1948). Disenchanted with imperialism, he resigned his post and went to Paris, where he hoped to earn a living as a writer but was forced to support himself with menial jobs. He then returned to England, tramped around, and in 1933 wrote his first book, Down and Out in Paris and London, *using for the first time the pseudonym that he was to use for all of his future writings. Three novels followed, including* Burmese Days *(1934). In 1936 the Spanish civil war broke out, and Orwell joined the Republican (anti-Franco) side as a common soldier, but his book on the experience,* Homage to Catalonia *(1938) did not at all please the Communists. Other books include* Animal Farm *(1945), a fable clearly critical of Stalinism but also implying that any form of government can easily become tyrannical; and* 1984 *(1949), a vision of a totalitarian England. Orwell's last book was* 1984; *he died of tuberculosis in 1950.*

We print an essay based on his days in Burma, but written after he could no longer stomach his duties as a police officer there.

A Hanging

It was in Burma, a sodden morning of the rains. A sickly light, like yellow tinfoil, was slanting over the high walls into the jail yard. We were waiting outside the condemned cells, a row of sheds fronted with double bars, like small animal cages. Each cell measured about ten feet by ten and was quite bare within except for a plank bed and a pot for drinking water. In some of them brown silent men were squatting at the inner bars, with their blankets draped round them. These were the condemned men, due to be hanged within the next week or two.

One prisoner had been brought out of his cell. He was a Hindu, a puny wisp of a man, with a shaven head and vague liquid eyes. He had a thick, sprouting moustache, absurdly too big for his body, rather like the moustache of a comic man on the films. Six tall Indian warders were guarding him and getting him ready for the gallows. Two of them stood by with rifles and fixed bayonets, while the others handcuffed him, passed a chain through his handcuffs and fixed it to their belts, and lashed his arms tight to his sides. They crowded very close about him, with their hands always on him in a careful, caressing grip, as though all the while feeling him to make sure he was there. It was like men handling a fish which is still alive and may jump back into the water. But he stood quite unresisting, yielding his arms limply to the ropes, as though he hardly noticed what was happening.

Eight o'clock struck and a bugle call, desolately thin in the wet air, floated from the distant barracks. The superintendent of the jail, who was standing apart from the rest of us, moodily prodding the gravel with his stick, raised his head at the sound. He was an army doctor, with a gray toothbrush moustache and a gruff voice. "For God's sake hurry up, Francis," he said irritably. "The man ought to have been dead by this time. Aren't you ready yet?"

Francis, the head jailer, a fat Dravidian in a white drill suit and gold spectacles, waved his black hand. "Yes sir, yes sir," he bubbled. "All iss satisfactorily prepared. The hangman iss waiting. We shall proceed."

5   "Well, quick march,[1] then. The prisoners can't get their breakfast till this job's over."

We set out for the gallows. Two warders marched on either side of the prisoner, with their rifles at the slope; two others marched close against him, gripping him by arm and shoulder, as though at once pushing and supporting him. The rest of us, magistrates and the like, followed behind. Suddenly, when we had gone ten yards, the procession stopped short without any order or warning. A dreadful thing had happened—a dog, come goodness knows whence, had appeared in the yard. It came bounding among us with a loud volley of barks, and leapt round us wagging its whole body, wild with glee at finding so many human beings together. It was a large woolly dog, half Airedale, half pariah. For a moment it pranced round us, and then, before anyone could stop it, it had made a dash for the prisoner and, jumping up, tried to lick his face. Everyone stood aghast, too taken aback even to grab at the dog.

"Who let that bloody brute in here?" said the superintendent angrily. "Catch it, someone!"

A warder, detached from the escort, charged clumsily after the dog, but it danced and gamboled just out of his reach, taking everything as part of the game. A young Eurasian jailer picked up a handful of gravel and tried to stone the dog away, but it dodged the stones and came after us again. Its yaps echoed from the jail walls. The prisoner, in the grasp of the two warders, looked on incuriously, as though this was another formality of the hanging. It was several minutes before someone managed to catch the dog. Then we put my handkerchief through its collar and moved off once more, with the dog still straining and whimpering.

It was about forty yards to the gallows. I watched the bare brown back of the prisoner marching in front of me. He walked clumsily with his bound arms, but quite steadily, with that bobbing gait of the Indian who never straightens his knees. At each step his muscles slid neatly into place, the lock of hair on his scalp danced up and down, his feet printed themselves on the wet gravel. And once, in spite of the men who gripped him by each shoulder, he stepped slightly aside to avoid a puddle on the path.

10   It is curious, but till that moment I had never realized what it means to destroy a healthy, conscious man. When I saw the prisoner step aside to avoid the puddle I saw the mystery, the unspeakable wrongness, of cutting a life short when it is in full tide. This man was not dying, he was alive just as we are alive. All the organs of his body were working—bowels digesting food, skin renewing itself, nails growing, tissues forming—all toiling away in solemn foolery. His nails would still be growing when he stood on the drop, when he was falling through the air with a tenth of a second to live. His eyes saw the yellow gravel and the gray walls, and his brain still remembered, foresaw, reasoned—reasoned even about puddles. He and we were a party of men walking together, seeing, hearing, feeling, understanding the same world; and in two minutes, with a sudden snap, one of us would be gone—one mind less, one world less.

The gallows stood in a small yard, separate from the main grounds of the prison, and overgrown with tall prickly weeds. It was a brick erection like three sides of a shed, with planking on top, and above that two beams and a crossbar with the rope dangling. The hangman, a gray-haired convict in the white uniform of the prison, was waiting beside his machine. He greeted us with a servile crouch

---

[1]**quick march** a marching pace of 120 steps per minute.

as we entered. At a word from Francis the two warders, gripping the prisoner more closely than ever, half led half pushed him to the gallows and helped him clumsily up the ladder. Then the hangman climbed up and fixed the rope round the prisoner's neck.

We stood waiting, five yards away. The warders had formed in a rough circle round the gallows. And then, when the noose was fixed, the prisoner began crying out to his god. It was a high, reiterated cry of "Ram! Ram! Ram! Ram!" not urgent and fearful like a prayer or cry for help, but steady, rhythmical, almost like the tolling of a bell. The dog answered the sound with a whine. The hangman, still standing on the gallows, produced a small cotton bag like a flour bag and drew it down over the prisoner's face. But the sound, muffled by the cloth, still persisted, over and over again: "Ram! Ram! Ram! Ram! Ram!"

The hangman climbed down and stood ready, holding the lever. Minutes seemed to pass. The steady, muffled crying from the prisoner went on and on, "Ram! Ram! Ram!" never faltering for an instant. The superintendent, his head on his chest, was slowly poking the ground with his stick; perhaps he was counting the cries, allowing the prisoner a fixed number—fifty, perhaps, or a hundred. Everyone had changed color. The Indians had gone gray like bad coffee, and one or two of the bayonets were wavering. We looked at the lashed, hooded man on the drop, and listened to his cries—each cry another second of life; the same thought was in all our minds: oh, kill him quickly, get it over, stop that abominable noise!

Suddenly the superintendent made up his mind. Throwing up his head he made a swift motion with his stick. "Chalo!"[2] he shouted almost fiercely.

15　　There was a clanking noise, and then dead silence. The prisoner had vanished, and the rope was twisting on itself. I let go of the dog, and it galloped immediately to the back of the gallows; but when it got there it stopped short, barked, and then retreated into a corner of the yard, where it stood among the weeds, looking timorously out at us. We went round the gallows to inspect the prisoner's body. He was dangling with his toes pointed straight downward, very slowly revolving, as dead as a stone.

The superintendent reached out with his stick and poked the bare brown body; it oscillated slightly. "*He's* all right," said the superintendent. He backed out from under the gallows, and blew out a deep breath. The moody look had gone out of his face quite suddenly. He glanced at his wrist watch. "Eight minutes past eight. Well, that's all for this morning, thank God."

The warders unfixed bayonets and marched away. The dog, sobered and conscious of having misbehaved itself, slipped after them. We walked out of the gallows yard, past the condemned cells with their waiting prisoners, into the big central yard of the prison. The convicts, under the command of warders armed with lathis,[3] were already receiving their breakfast. They squatted in long rows, each man holding a tin pannikin, while two warders with buckets marched round ladling out rice; it seemed quite a homely, jolly scene, after the hanging. An enormous relief had come upon us now that the job was done. One felt an impluse to sing, to break into a run, to snigger. All at once everyone began chattering gaily.

The Eurasian boy walking beside me nodded toward the way we had come, with a knowing smile: "Do you know, sir, our friend [he meant the dead man] when he heard his appeal had been dismissed, he pissed on the floor of his cell. From fright. Kindly take one of my cigarettes, sir. Do you not admire my new silver case, sir? From the boxwalah, two rupees eight annas. Classy European style."

---

[2]**Chalo!** Proceed!　[3]**lathis** bamboo canes fitted with iron, used as weapons.

Several people laughed—at what, nobody seemed certain.

20   Francis was walking by the superintendent, talking garrulously: "Well, sir, all hass passed off with the utmost satisfactoriness. It was all finished—flick! like that. It iss not always so—oah, no! I have known cases where the doctor wass obliged to go beneath the gallows and pull the prissoner's legs to ensure decease. Most disagreeable!"

"Wriggling about, eh? That's bad," said the superintendent.

"Ach, sir, it iss worse when they become refractory! One man, I recall, clung to the bars of hiss cage when we went to take him out. You will scarcely credit, sir, that it took six warders to dislodge him, three pulling at each leg. We reasoned with him. 'My dear fellow,' we said, 'think of all the pain and trouble you are causing to us!' But no, he would not listen! Ach, he wass very troublesome!"

I found that I was laughing quite loudly. Everyone was laughing. Even the superintendent grinned in a tolerant way. "You'd better all come out and have a drink," he said quite genially. "I've got a bottle of whisky in the car. We could do with it."

We went through the big double gates of the prison into the road. "Pulling at his legs!" exclaimed a Burmese magistrate suddenly, and burst into a loud chuckling. We all began laughing again. At that moment Francis' anecdote seemed extraordinarily funny. We all had a drink together, native and European alike, quite amicably. The dead man was a hundred yards away.

[1931]

Topics for Critical Thinking and Writing

1. The narrative of the hanging is pretty straightforward: The title tells us what we are in for, the first paragraph speaks of "condemned men," and the second paragraph introduces the "one prisoner" who soon will be hanged, and indeed he is soon hanged. But this narrative, brief though it is, is delayed by the intrusion of the dog (paragraphs 6–8), and again slightly delayed by the prisoner's "prayer or cry for help" (12–14). Would anything be gained or lost if Orwell had omitted these delays?

2. The narrative could end with paragraph 15 (when the prisoner is hanged) or paragraph 16 (when the superintendent confirms the death). But Orwell continues the essay, telling us (17) that "an enormous relief had come upon us now that the job was done," and he then continues for seven more paragraphs. Should he have ended after the sixteenth paragraph? Or after the seventeenth? Why?

3. What do you make of the detail in paragraph 9, when Orwell tells us that the condemned man "stepped aside to avoid a puddle" on the path to the gallows?

4. Consider the final two sentences: "We all had a drink together, native and European alike, quite amicably. The dead man was a hundred yards away." Orwell might have written, "We all had a drink together, native and European alike, quite amicably, although the dead man was only a hundred yards away." Or he could have written, "Although the dead man was only a hundred yards away, we all had a drink together, quite amicably, native and European alike." Of these three versions, which is the most effective? Why?

LOUIS OWENS

Louis Owens, born in 1948, describes himself as "a mixed-blood American of Choctaw, Cherokee, and Irish-American heritage." He is a professor of English at the University of New Mexico, where he specializes in Native American writing, but before he became a teacher and a writer he worked as a fire fighter and wilderness ranger.

Owens's essay should be read in the context of the Wilderness Act of 1964, which defines a wilderness thus: "A wilderness, in contrast with those areas where man and his own works dominate the landscape, is hereby recognized as an area where the earth itself and its community of life are untrammeled by man, where man himself is a visitor who does not remain."

The American Indian Wilderness

In the center of the Glacier Peak Wilderness in northern Washington, a magnificent, fully glaciated white volcano rises over a stunningly beautiful region of the North Cascades. On maps, the mountain is called Glacier Peak. To the Salishan people who have always lived in this part of the Cascades, however, the mountain is *Dakobed*, or the Great Mother, the place of emergence. For more than eighty years, a small, three-sided log shelter stood in a place called White Pass just below one shoulder of the great mountain, tucked securely into a meadow between thick stands of mountain hemlock and alpine fir.

In the early fall of seventy-six, while working as a seasonal ranger for the U.S. Forest Service, I drew the task of burning the White Pass shelter. After all those years, the shelter roof had collapsed like a broken bird wing under the weight of winter snow, and the time was right for fire and replanting. It was part of a Forest Service plan to remove all human-made objects from wilderness areas, a plan of which I heartily approved. So I backpacked eleven miles to the pass and set up camp, and for five days, while a bitter early storm sent snow driving horizontally out of the north, I dismantled the shelter and burned the old logs, piling and burning and piling and burning until nothing remained. The antique, hand-forged spikes that had held the shelter together I put into gunny sacks and cached to be packed out later by mule. I spaded up the earth beaten hard for nearly a century by boot and hoof, and transplanted plugs of vegetation from hidden spots on the nearby ridge.

At the end of those five days, not a trace of the shelter remained, and I felt good, very smug in fact, about returning the White Pass meadow to its "original" state. As I packed up my camp, the snowstorm had subsided to a few flurries and a chill that felt bone-deep with the promise of winter. My season was almost over, and as I started the steep hike down to the trailhead my mind was on the winter I was going to spend in sunny Arizona.

A half-mile from the pass I saw the two old women. At first they were dark, hunched forms far down on the last long switchback up the snowy ridge. But as we drew closer to one another, I began to feel a growing amazement that, by the time we were face-to-face, had become awe. Almost swallowed up in their baggy wool pants, heavy sweaters and parkas, silver braids hanging below thick wool caps, they seemed ancient, each weighted with at least seventy years as well as a small backpack. They paused every few steps to lean on their staffs and look out over the North Fork drainage below, a deep, heavily forested river valley that rose on the far side to the glaciers and sawtoothed black granite of the Monte Cristo Range. And they smiled hugely upon seeing me, clearly surprised and delighted to find another person in the mountains at such a time.

5   We stood and chatted for a moment, and as I did with all backpackers, I reluctantly asked them where they were going. The snow quickened a little, obscuring the view, as they told me that they were going to White Pass.

"Our father built a little house up here," one of them said, "when he worked for the Forest Service like you. Way back before we was born, before this century."

"We been coming up here each year since we was little," the other added. "Except last year when Sarah was not well enough."

"A long time ago, this was all our land," the one called Sarah said. "All Indi'n land everywhere you can see. Our people had houses up in the mountains, for gathering berries every year."

As they took turns speaking, the smiles never leaving their faces, I wanted to excuse myself, to edge around these elders and flee to the trailhead and my car, drive back to the district station and keep going south. I wanted to say, "I'm Indian too. Choctaw from Mississippi; Cherokee from Oklahoma"—as if mixed blood could pardon me for what I had done. Instead, I said, "The shelter is gone." Cravenly I added, "It was crushed by snow, so I was sent up to burn it. It's gone now."

10   I expected outrage, anger, sadness, but instead the sisters continued to smile at me, their smiles changing only slightly. They had a plastic tarp and would stay dry, they said, because a person always had to be prepared in the mountains. They would put up their tarp inside the hemlock grove above the meadow, and the scaly hemlock branches would turn back the snow. They forgave me without saying it—my ignorance and my part in the long pattern of loss which they knew so well.

Hiking out those eleven miles, as the snow of the high country became a drumming rain in the forests below, I had long hours to ponder my encounter with the sisters. Gradually, almost painfully, I began to understand that what I called "wilderness" was an absurdity, nothing more than a figment of the European imagination. Before the European invasion, there was no wilderness in North America; there was only the fertile continent where people lived in a hard-learned balance with the natural world. In embracing a philosophy that saw the White Pass shelter—and all traces of humanity—as a shameful stain upon the "pure" wilderness, I had succumbed to a five-hundred-year-old pattern of deadly thinking that separates us from the natural world. This is not to say that what we call wilderness today does not need careful safeguarding. I believe that White Pass really is better off now that the shelter doesn't serve as a magnet to backpackers and horsepackers who compact the soil, disturb and kill the wildlife, cut down centuries-old trees for firewood, and leave their litter strewn about. And I believe the man who built the shelter would agree. But despite this unfortunate reality, the global environmental crisis that sends species into extinction daily and threatens to destroy all life surely has its roots in the Western pattern of thought that sees humanity and "wilderness" as mutually exclusive.

In old-growth forests in the North Cascades, deep inside the official Wilderness Area, I have come upon faint traces of log shelters built by Suiattle and

Upper Skagit people for berry harvesting a century or more ago—just as the sisters said. Those human-made structures were as natural a part of the Cascade ecosystem as the burrows of marmots in the steep scree slopes. Our Native ancestors all over this continent lived within a complex web of relations with the natural world, and in doing so they assumed a responsibility for their world that contemporary Americans cannot even imagine. Unless Americans, and all human beings, can learn to imagine themselves as intimately and inextricably related to every aspect of the world they inhabit, with the extraordinary responsibilities such relationship entails—unless they can learn what the indigenous peoples of the Americas knew and often still know—the earth simply will not survive. A few square miles of something called wilderness will become the sign of failure everywhere.

[1994]

Topics for Critical Thinking and Writing

1. The Forest Service commissioned Owens to "dismantle" the shelter and then to burn the logs. Does it make sense to use human beings to create a "natural" space? Explain.
2. Suppose someone said to you that human beings are a part of nature, and that their creations—let's say the three-sided shelter at White Pass—are just as "natural" as a bird's nest. What response might you make?
3. In his second paragraph Owen tells us that the Forest Service had a plan "to remove all human-made objects from wilderness areas." What can be said in behalf of such a plan? What can be said against it? By the way, given the realities of life today, can we reasonably say that parts of the country can be unshaped by human activity? If, for instance, we restore wolves to a certain area that they have long been absent from, is this area of nature really natural?
4. In his final paragraph Owens says that unless people come to understand that they are "inextricably related to every aspect of the world, . . . a few square miles of something called wilderness will become the sign of failure everywhere." What does he mean?

MAY SARTON

May Sarton (1912–95), born in Belgium, was brought to the United States in 1916 and in 1924 she became a citizen. A teacher of writing and a distinguished writer herself, she received numerous awards for her fiction, poetry, and essays.

The Rewards of Living a Solitary Life

The other day an acquaintance of mine, a gregarious and charming man, told me he had found himself unexpectedly alone in New York for an hour or two between appointments. He went to the Whitney and spent the "empty" time looking at things in solitary bliss. For him it proved to be a shock nearly as great as falling in love to discover that he could enjoy himself so much alone.

What had he been afraid of, I asked myself? That, suddenly alone, he would discover that he bored himself, or that there was, quite simply, no self there to meet? But having taken the plunge, he is now on the brink of adventure; he is about to be launched into his own inner space, space as immense, unexplored, and sometimes frightening as outer space to the astronaut. His every perception will come to him with a new freshness and, for a time, seem startlingly original. For anyone who can see things for himself with a naked eye becomes, for a moment or two, something of a genius. With another human being present vision becomes double vision, inevitably. We are busy wondering, what does my companion see or think of this, and what do I think of it? The original impact gets lost, or diffused.

"Music I heard with you was more than music."[1] Exactly. And therefore music *itself* can only be heard alone. Solitude is the salt of personhood. It brings out the authentic flavor of every experience.

"Alone one is never lonely: the spirit adventures, walking/In a quiet garden, in a cool house, abiding single there."

5   Loneliness is most acutely felt with other people, for with others, even with a lover sometimes, we suffer from our differences of taste, temperament, mood. Human intercourse often demands that we soften the edge of perception, or withdraw at the very instant of personal truth for fear of hurting, or of being inappropriately present, which is to say naked, in a social situation. Alone we can afford to be wholly whatever we are, and to feel whatever we feel absolutely. That is a great luxury!

For me the most interesting thing about a solitary life, and mine has been that for the last twenty years, is that it becomes increasingly rewarding. When I can wake up and watch the sun rise over the ocean, as I do most days, and know that I have an entire day ahead, uninterrupted in which to write a few pages, take a walk with my dog, lie down in the afternoon for a long think (why does one think better in a horizontal position?), read and listen to music, I am flooded with happiness.

I am lonely only when I am overtired, when I have worked too long without a break, when for the time being I feel empty and need filling up. And I am lonely sometimes when I come back home after a lecture trip, when I have seen a lot of people and talked a lot, and am full to the brim with experience that needs to be sorted out.

Then for a little while the house feels huge and empty, and I wonder where my self is hiding. It has to be recaptured slowly by watering the plants, perhaps, and looking again at each one as though it were a person, by feeding the two cats, by cooking a meal.

It takes a while, as I watch the surf blowing up in fountains at the end of the field, but the moment comes when the world falls away, and the self emerges again from the deep unconscious, bringing back all I have recently experienced to be explored and slowly understood, when I can converse again with my hidden powers, and so grow, and so be renewed, till death do us part.

[1974]

------

[1] **"Music . . . music"** A line from Conrad Aiken's *Bread and Music* (1914).

Topics for Critical Thinking and Writing

1. The essay opens with an anecdote about an acquaintance of the author's. Why are we told at the outset that he is "a gregarious and charming man"?
2. In paragraph 2 Sarton compares inner space with outer space. And in paragraph 3 she writes, "Solitude is the salt of personhood." How do you interpret these metaphors? How do they enrich her main point, that solitude is rewarding?
3. What does Sarton mean when in her first paragraph she says, "Anyone who can see things for himself with a naked eye becomes, for a moment or two, something of a genius"? Does your own experience confirm her comment? Explain.
4. What phrase in the last paragraph connects the ending with the first paragraph?
5. Drawing on Sarton's essay, in a paragraph explain the distinction between being "alone" and being "lonely."
6. In an essay of about 500 words, explain the difference between loving and being in love.

JOHN UPDIKE

John Updike (b. 1932) grew up in Shillington, Pennsylvania, where his father was a teacher and his mother was a writer. After receiving a bachelor of arts degree from Harvard, he studied drawing at Oxford for a year, but an offer from The New Yorker *magazine brought him back to the United States. He at first served as a reporter for the magazine, but soon began contributing poetry, essays, and fiction. Today he is one of America's most prolific and well-known writers.*

The following essay on the destruction of the World Trade Center (September 11, 2001), was published in The New Yorker *about a week after the attack.*

Talk of the Town: September 11, 2001

Suddenly summoned to witness something great and horrendous, we keep fighting not to reduce it to our own smallness. From the viewpoint of a tenth-floor apartment in Brooklyn Heights, where I happened to be visiting some kin, the destruction of the World Trade Center twin towers had the false intimacy of television, on a day of perfect reception. A four-year-old girl and her babysitter called from the library, and pointed out through the window the smoking top of the north tower, not a mile away. It seemed, at that first glance, more curious than horrendous: smoke speckled with bits of paper curled into the cloudless sky, and strange inky rivulets ran down the giant structure's vertically corrugated surface. The W.T.C. had formed a pale background to our Brooklyn view of lower Manhattan, not beloved, like the stony, spired midtown thirties skyscrapers it had displaced as the city's tallest, but, with its pre-postmodern combination of unignorable immensity and architectural reticence, in some lights beautiful. As we watched the second tower burst into ballooning flame (an intervening building had hidden the approach of the second airplane), there persisted the notion that, as on television, this was not quite real; it could be fixed; the technocracy

2. How would you characterize the style of this essay? In your view, does Updike describe the actual event, or, instead, his own experience of the event? Is it possible to make a distinction between the two—a description of an event, on the one hand, and the description of one's personal experience of it, on the other?

3. Does Updike make a specific point in this piece of writing, or does he have some other intention in mind?

4. This essay was written and published very soon after the events of September 11, 2001. What is its impact when you read it today? How do you imagine that its first readers responded to it?

5. If you were the editor of *The New Yorker* magazine and this essay were submitted to you a few days after September 11 would you accept it for publication or not? What kind of letter would you write to the author, accepting or rejecting his essay, and/or asking for revisions?

8

Reading and Writing about Fiction

STORIES TRUE AND FALSE

The word *story* comes from *history*; the stories that historians, biographers, and journalists narrate are supposed to be true accounts of what happened. The stories of novelists and short-story writers, however, are admittedly untrue; they are "fiction," things made up, imagined, manufactured. As readers, we come to a supposedly true story with expectations different from those we bring to fiction.

Consider the difference between reading a narrative in a newspaper and one in a book of short stories. If, while reading a newspaper, we come across a story of, say, a subway accident, we assume that the account is true, and we read it for the information about a relatively unusual event. Anyone hurt? What sort of people? In our neighborhood? Whose fault? When we read a book of fiction, however, we do not expect to encounter literal truths; we read novels and short stories not for facts but for pleasure and for some insight or for a sense of what an aspect of life means to the writer. Consider the following short story by Grace Paley.

GRACE PALEY

Born in New York City, Grace Paley attended Hunter College and New York University but left without a degree. (She now is an affiliate faculty member at Sarah Lawrence College.) While raising two children she wrote poetry and then, in the 1950s, turned to writing fiction.

Paley's chief subject is the life of little people struggling in the Big City. Of life she has said, "How daily life is lived is a mystery to me. You write about what's mysterious to you. What is it like? Why do people do this?" Of the short story she has said, "It can be just telling a little tale, or writing a complicated philosophical story. It can be a song, almost."

Samuel

Some boys are very tough. They're afraid of nothing. They are the ones who climb a wall and take a bow at the top. Not only are they brave on the roof, but they make a lot of noise in the darkest part of the cellar where even the super hates to go. They also jiggle and hop on the platform between the locked doors of the subway cars.

Four boys are jiggling on the swaying platform. Their names are Alfred, Calvin, Samuel, and Tom. The men and the women in the cars on either side watch them. They don't like them to jiggle or jump but don't want to interfere. Of course some of the men in the cars were once brave boys like these. One of them had ridden the tail of a speeding truck from New York to Rockaway Beach without getting off, without his sore fingers losing hold. Nothing happened to him then or later. He had made a compact with other boys who preferred to watch: Starting at Eighth Avenue and Fifteenth Street, he would get to some specified place, maybe Twenty-third and the river, by hopping the tops of the moving trucks. This was hard to do when one truck turned a corner in the wrong direction and the nearest truck was a couple of feet too high. He made three or four starts before succeeding. He had gotten his idea from a film at school called *The Romance of Logging*. He had finished high school, married a good friend, was in a responsible job and going to night school.

These two men and others looked at the four boys jumping and jiggling on the platform and thought, It must be fun to ride that way, especially now the weather is nice and we're out of the tunnel and way high over the Bronx. Then they thought, These kids do seem to be acting sort of stupid. They *are* little. Then they thought of some of the brave things they had done when they were boys and jiggling didn't seem so risky.

The ladies in the car became very angry when they looked at the four boys. Most of them brought their brows together and hoped the boys could see their extreme disapproval. One of the ladies wanted to get up and say, Be careful you dumb kids, get off that platform or I'll call a cop. But three of the boys were Negroes and the fourth was something else she couldn't tell for sure. She was afraid they'd be fresh and laugh at her and embarrass her. She wasn't afraid they'd hit her, but she was afraid of embarrassment. Another lady thought, Their mothers never know where they are. It wasn't true in this particular case. Their mothers all knew that they had gone to see the missile exhibit on Fourteenth Street.

5   Out on the platform, whenever the train accelerated, the boys would raise their hands and point them up to the sky to act like rockets going off, then they rat-tat-tatted the shatterproof glass pane like machine guns, although no machine guns had been exhibited.

For some reason known only to the motorman, the train began a sudden slowdown. The lady who was afraid of embarrassment saw the boys jerk forward and backward and grab the swinging guard chains. She had her own boy at home. She stood up with determination and went to the door. She slid it open and said, "You boys will be hurt. You'll be killed. I'm going to call the conductor if you don't just go into the next car and sit down and be quiet."

Two of the boys said, "Yes'm," and acted as though they were about to go. Two of them blinked their eyes a couple of times and pressed their lips together. The train resumed its speed. The door slid shut, parting the lady and the boys. She leaned against the side door because she had to get off at the next stop.

The boys opened their eyes wide at each other and laughed. The lady blushed. The boys looked at her and laughed harder. They began to pound each other's back. Samuel laughed the hardest and pounded Alfred's back until Alfred coughed and the tears came. Alfred held tight to the chain hook. Samuel pounded him even harder when he saw the tears. He said, "Why you bawling? You a baby, huh?" and laughed. One of the men whose boyhood had been more watchful than brave became angry. He stood up straight and looked at the boys for a couple of seconds. Then he walked in a citizenly way to the end of the car, where he pulled the emergency cord. Almost at once, with a terrible hiss, the pressure of air abandoned the brakes and the wheels were caught and held.

People standing in the most secure places fell forward, then backward. Samuel had let go of his hold on the chain so he could pound Tom as well as Alfred. All the passengers in the cars whipped back and forth, but he pitched only forward and fell head first to be crushed and killed between the cars.

10 The train had stopped hard, halfway into the station, and the conductor called at once for the trainmen who knew about this kind of death and how to take the body from the wheels and brakes. There was silence except for passengers from other cars who asked, What happened! What happened! The ladies waited around wondering if he might be an only child. The men recalled other afternoons with very bad endings. The little boys stayed close to each other, leaning and touching shoulders and arms and legs.

When the policeman knocked at the door and told her about it, Samuel's mother began to scream. She screamed all day and moaned all night, though the doctors tried to quiet her with pills.

Oh, oh, she hopelessly cried. She did not know how she could ever find another boy like that one. However, she was a young woman and she became pregnant. Then for a few months she was hopeful. The child born to her was a boy. They brought him to be seen and nursed. She smiled. But immediately she saw that this baby wasn't Samuel. She and her husband together have had other children, but never again will a boy exactly like Samuel be known.

[1968]

Topics for Critical Thinking and Writing

1. Paley wrote the story, but an unspecified person *tells* it. Describe the voice of this narrator in the first paragraph. Is the voice neutral and objective, or do you hear some sort of attitude, a point of view? If you do hear an attitude, what words or phrases in the story indicate it?

2. What do you know about the setting—the locale—of "Samuel"? What can you infer about the neighborhood?

3. In the fourth paragraph we are told that "three of the boys were Negroes and the fourth was something else." Is race important in this story? Is Samuel "Negro" or "something else"? Does it matter?

4. Exactly *why* did a man walk "in a citizenly way to the end of the car, where he pulled the emergency cord"? Do you think the author blames him? What evidence can you offer to support your view? Do *you* blame him? Or do you blame the boys? Or anyone? Explain.

5. The story is called "Samuel," and it is, surely, about him. But what happens after Samuel dies? (You might want to list the events.) What else is the story about? (You might want to comment on why you believe the items in your list are important.)

6. Can you generalize about what the men think of the jigglers and about what the women think? Is Paley saying something about the sexes? About the attitudes of onlookers in a big city?

ELEMENTS OF FICTION

You might think about the ways in which "Samuel" differs from a newspaper story of an accident in a subway. (You might even want to write a newspaper version of the happening.) In some ways, of course, Paley's story faintly resembles an account that might appear in a newspaper. Journalists are taught to give information about

- who,
- what,
- when,
- where, and
- why,

and Paley does provide this material. Thus, the *characters* (Samuel and others) are the journalist's Who; the *plot* (the boys were jiggling on the platform, and when a man pulled the emergency cord one of them was killed) is the What; the *setting* (the subway, presumably in modern times) is the When and the Where; the *motivation* (the irritation of the man who pulls the emergency cord) is the Why.

To write about fiction you would think about these elements of fiction, asking yourself questions about each, both separately and how they work together. Much of the rest of this chapter will be devoted to examining such words as *character* and *plot*, but before you read those pages notice the questions we've posed about "Samuel" and try responding to them. Your responses will teach you a good deal about what fiction is, and some of the ways in which it works.

Plot and Character

In some stories, such as adventure stories, the emphasis is on physical action—wanderings and strange encounters. In Paley's "Samuel," however, although there is a violent death in the subway, the emphasis is less on an unusual happening than on other things: for instance, the contrast between some of the adults, the contrast between uptight adults and energetic children, and the impact of the death on Samuel's mother.

The novelist E. M. Forster, in a short critical study entitled *Aspects of the Novel* (1927), introduced a distinction between **flat characters** and **round characters**. A *flat character* is relatively simple and usually has only one trait: loving wife (or jealous wife), tyrannical husband (or meek husband), braggart, pedant, hypocrite, or whatever. Thus, in "Samuel" we are told about a man "whose boyhood had been more watchful than brave." This man walks "in a citizenly way" to the end of the subway car, where he pulls the emergency cord. He is, so to speak, the conventional solid citizen. He is flat, or uncomplicated, but that is probably part of what the author is getting at. A *round character*, on the other hand, embodies several or even many traits that cohere to form a complex personality. Of course in a story as short as "Samuel" we can hardly expect to find fully rounded characters, but we can say that, at least by comparison with the "citizenly" man, the man who had once been a wild kid, had gone to night school, and now holds a "responsible job" is relatively round. Paley's story asserts rather than shows the development of the character, but much fiction does show such a development. Whereas a flat character is usually *static* (at the end of the story the character is pretty much what he or she was at the start), a round character is likely to be *dynamic*, changing considerably as the story progresses.

A frequent assignment in writing courses is to set forth a character sketch, describing some person in the story or novel. In preparing such a sketch, take these points into consideration:

- what the character says (but consider that what he or she says need not be taken at face value; the character may be hypocritical, or self-deceived, or biased—you will have to detect this from the context),
- what the character does,
- what other characters say about the character, and
- what others *do*. (A character who serves as a contrast to another character is called a *foil*.)

A character sketch can be complex and demanding, but usually you will want to do more than write a character sketch. You will probably discuss the character's function, or trace the development of his or her personality, or contrast the character with another. (One of the most difficult topics, the narrator's personality, is discussed later in this chapter under the heading "Narrative Point of View.") In writing on one of these topics you will probably still want to keep in mind the four suggestions for getting at a character, but you will also want to go further, relating your findings to additional matters that we discuss later.

Most discussions of fiction are concerned with happenings and with *why* they happen. Why does Samuel die? Because (to put it too simply) his youthful high spirits clash with the values of a "citizenly" adult. Paley never explicitly says anything like this, but a reader of the story tries to make sense out of the details, filling in the gaps.

Things happen, in most good fiction, at least partly because the people have certain personalities or character traits (moral, intellectual, and emotional qualities) and, given their natures, because they respond plausibly to other personalities. What their names are and what they look like may help you to understand them, but probably the best guide to characters is what they do and what they say. As we get to know more about their drives and goals—and especially about the choices they make—we enjoy seeing the writer complete the portraits, finally presenting us with a coherent and credible picture of people in action. In this view, plot and character are inseparable. Plot is not simply a series of happenings, but happenings that come out of character, that reveal character, and that influence character. Henry James puts it thus: "What is character but the determination of incident? What is incident but the illustration of character?" James goes on: "It is an incident for a woman to stand up with her hand resting on a table and look out at you in a certain way."

Foreshadowing

Although some stories depend heavily on a plot with a surprise ending, other stories prepare the reader for the outcome, at least to some degree. The **foreshadowing** that would eliminate surprise, or greatly reduce it, and thus destroy a story that has nothing else to offer, is a powerful tool in the hands of a writer of serious fiction. In "Samuel," the reader perhaps senses even in the first paragraph that these "tough" boys who "jiggle and hop on the platform" may be vulnerable, may come to an unfortunate end. When a woman says, "You'll be killed," the reader doesn't yet know if she is right, but a seed has been planted.

figs had the least thing to do with it, but that is the way Maman-Nainaine was." The narrator sees nothing special—merely Maman-Nainaine's eccentricity—in the connection between the ripening of the figs and Babette's visit to her cousins. Readers, however, may see more than the narrator sees or says. They may see in Babette a young girl maturing; they may see in Maman-Nainaine an older woman who, almost collaborating with nature, helps Babette to mature.

And here, of course, as we talk about symbolism we are getting into the theme of the story. An apparently inconsequential and even puzzling action, such as is set forth in "Ripe Figs," may cast a long shadow. As Robert Frost once said,

> There is no story written that has any value at all, however straightforward it looks and free from doubleness, double entendre, that you'd value at all if it didn't have intimations of something more than itself.

The stranger, the more mysterious the story, the more likely we are to suspect some sort of significance, but even realistic stories such as Chopin's "The Storm" and "The Story of an Hour" may be rich in suggestions. This is not to say, however, that the suggestions (rather than the details of the surface) are what count. A reader does not discard the richly detailed, highly specific narrative (Mrs. Mallard learned that her husband was dead and reacted in such-and-such a way) in favor of some supposedly universal message or theme that it implies. We do not throw away the specific narrative—the memorable characters or the interesting things that happen in the story—and move on to some "higher truth." Robert Frost went on to say, "The anecdote, the parable, the surface meaning has got to be good and got to be sufficient in itself."

Narrative Point of View

An author must choose a **point of view** (or sometimes, several points of view) from which he or she will narrate the story. The choice will contribute to the total effect of the story.

Narrative points of view can be divided into two sorts: **participant** (or **first-person**) and **nonparticipant** (or **third-person**). That is, the narrator may or may not be a character who participates in the story. Each of these two divisions can be subdivided:

    I. Participant (first-person narrative)
        A. Narrator as a major character
        B. Narrator as a minor character
   II. Nonparticipant (third-person narrative)
        A. Omniscient
        B. Selective omniscient
        C. Objective

PARTICIPANT POINTS OF VIEW   Toni Bambara's "The Lesson" (p. 276) begins thus:

> Back in the days when everyone was old and stupid or young and foolish and me and Sugar were the only ones just right, this lady moved on our block with nappy hair and proper speech and no makeup.

In this story, the narrator is a major character. Bambara is the author, but the narrator—the person who tells us the story—is a young girl who speaks of "me and Sugar," and the story is chiefly about the narrator. We can say, then, that Bambara uses a first-person (or participant) point of view. She has invented a young girl who tells us about the impact a woman in the neighborhood had on her: "[Sugar] can run if she want to and even run faster. But ain't nobody gonna beat me at nuthin." The narrator is a major character. She, and not Bambara, tells the story.

But sometimes a first-person narrator tells a story that focuses on someone other than the narrator; he or she is a minor character, a peripheral witness, for example, to a story about Sally Jones, and we get the story of Sally filtered through, say, the eyes of her friend or brother or cat.

Whether a major or a minor character, a first-person narrator is a particular character, seeing things in a particular way. The reader should not assume that the speaker is necessarily a reliable source. Some, in fact, are notably **unreliable narrators**, for instance young children, mentally impaired adults, and psychopaths. A story told by an unreliable narrator, let's say by a man consumed with vengeful thoughts, depends largely on the reader's perception of the gap between what the narrator says and what the facts presumably are.

NONPARTICIPANT POINTS OF VIEW   In a nonparticipant (third-person) point of view, the teller of the tale does not introduce himself or herself as a character. If the point of view is **omniscient**, the narrator relates what he or she wants to relate about the thoughts as well as the deeds of all the characters. The omniscient teller can enter the mind of any character; the first-person narrator can only say, "I was angry" or "Jack seemed angry," but the omniscient teller can say, "Jack was inwardly angry but gave no sign; Jill continued chatting, but she sensed his anger." Thus, in Paley's "Samuel," the narrator tells us that Samuel's mother was "hopeful," but when the new baby was born "immediately she saw that this baby wasn't Samuel."

Furthermore, a distinction can be made between **neutral omniscience** (the narrator recounts deeds and thoughts but does not judge) and **editorial omniscience** (the narrator not only recounts but also judges). An editorially omniscient narrator knows what goes on in the minds of all the characters and might comment approvingly or disapprovingly: "He closed the book, having finished the story, but, poor fellow, he had missed the meaning."

Because a short story can scarcely hope to develop a picture of several minds effectively, authors may prefer to limit their omniscience to the minds of a few of their characters, or even to that of only one of the characters; that is, they may use **selective omniscience** as the point of view. Selective omniscience provides a focus, especially if it is limited to a single character. When thus limited, the author sees one character from both outside and inside, but sees the other characters only from the outside and from the impact they have on the mind of this selected receptor. When selective omniscience attempts to record mental activity ranging from consciousness to the unconscious, from clear perceptions to confused longings, it is sometimes labeled the **stream-of-consciousness** point of view.

Finally, sometimes a third-person narrator does not enter even a single mind but records only what crosses an apparently dispassionate eye and ear. Such a point of view is **objective** (sometimes called the **camera** or **fly-on-the-wall** point of view). The absence of editorializing and of dissection of the mind often produces the effect of a play; we see and hear the characters in action. Much of Chekhov's

"Misery" (p. 222) is objective, consisting of bits of dialogue that make the story look like a play:

> "My head aches," says one of the tall ones. "At the Dukmasovs' yesterday Vaska and I drank four bottles of brandy between us."
>
> "I can't make out why you talk such stuff," says the other tall one angrily. "You lie like a brute."
>
> "Strike me dead, it's the truth! . . . "
>
> "It's about as true as that a louse coughs."

Style and Point of View

Obviously a story told by a first-person narrator will have a distinctive style—let's say the voice of an adolescent boy, or an elderly widow, or a madman. The voice of a third-person narrator—especially the voice of a supposedly objective narrator—will be much less distinctive, but if, especially on rereading, you listen carefully, you will probably hear a distinctive tone. (Look, for instance, at the first paragraph of Grace Paley's "Samuel.") Put it this way: Even a supposedly objective point of view is not purely objective, since it represents the writer's choice of a style, a way of reporting material with an apparently dispassionate voice.

After reading a story, you may want to think at least briefly about what the story might be like if told from a different point of view. You may find it instructive, for instance, to rewrite "Samuel" from the "citizenly" man's point of view, or "Ripe Figs" from Babette's.

Theme

First, we can distinguish between story (or plot) and theme in fiction. *Story* is concerned with "How does it turn out? What happens?" But **theme** is concerned with "What is it about? What does it add up to? What motif holds the happenings together? What does it make of life, and, perhaps, what wisdom does it offer?" In a good work of fiction, the details add up, or, to use Flannery O'Connor's words, they are "controlled by some overall purpose." In F. Scott Fitzgerald's *The Great Gatsby*, for example, there are many references to popular music, especially to jazz. These references contribute to our sense of the reality of Fitzgerald's depiction of America in the 1920s, but they do more: They help to comment on the shallowness of the white middle-class characters, and they sometimes (very gently) remind us of an alternative culture. A reader might study Fitzgerald's references to music with an eye toward getting a deeper understanding of what the novel is about.

Suppose we think for a moment about the theme of Paley's "Samuel." Do we sense an "overall purpose" that holds the story together? Different readers inevitably will come up with different readings, that is, with different views of what the story is about. Here is one student's version:

Whites cannot understand the feelings of blacks.

This statement gets at an important element in the story—the conflict between the sober-minded adults and the jiggling boys—but it apparently assumes that all of the adults are white, an inference that cannot be supported by pointing to evidence in the story. Further, we cannot be certain that Samuel is black. And, finally, even if Samuel and his mother are black, surely white readers *do understand his youthful enthusiasm and his mother's inconsolable grief.*

Here is a second statement:

One should not interfere with the actions of others.

Does the story really offer such specific advice? This version of the theme seems to us to reduce the story to a too-simple code of action, a heartless rule of behavior, a rule that seems at odds with the writer's awareness of the mother's enduring grief.

A third version:

Middle-class adults, acting from what seem to them to be the best of motives, may cause irreparable harm and grief.

This last statement seems to us to be one that can be fully supported by checking it against the story, but other equally valid statements can probably be made. How would you put it?

ERNEST HEMINGWAY

Ernest Hemingway (1899–1961) was born in Oak Park, Illinois. After graduating from high school in 1917 he worked on the Kansas City Star, *but left to serve as a volunteer ambulance driver in Italy, where he was wounded in action. He returned home, married, and then served as European correspondent for the* Toronto Star, *but he soon gave up journalism for fiction. In 1922 he settled in Paris, where he moved in a circle of American expatriates that included Ezra Pound, Gertrude Stein, and F. Scott Fitzgerald. It was in Paris that he wrote stories and novels about what Gertrude Stein called a "lost generation" of rootless Americans in Europe. (For Hemingway's reminiscences of the Paris years, see his posthumously published* A Moveable Feast.) *He served as a journalist during the Spanish civil war and during the Second World War, but he was also something of a private soldier.*

After the Second World War his reputation sank, though he was still active as a writer (for instance, he wrote The Old Man and the Sea *in 1952). In 1954 Hemingway was awarded the Nobel Prize in Literature, but in 1961, depressed by a sense of failing power, he took his own life.*

Cat in the Rain

There were only two Americans stopping at the hotel. They did not know any of the people they passed on the stairs on their way to and from their room. Their room was on the second floor facing the sea. It also faced the public garden and the war monument. There were big palms and green benches in the public garden. In the good weather there was always an artist with his easel. Artists liked the way the palms grew and the bright colors of the hotels facing the gardens and the sea. Italians came from a long way off to look up at the war monument. It was made of bronze and glistened in the rain. It was raining. The rain dripped from the palm trees. Water stood in pools on the gravel paths. The sea broke in a long line in the rain and slipped back down the beach to come up and break again in a long line in the rain. The motor cars were gone from the square by the war monument. Across the square in the doorway of the café a waiter stood looking out at the empty square.

The American wife stood at the window looking out. Outside right under their window a cat was crouched under one of the dripping green tables. The cat was trying to make herself so compact that she would not be dripped on.

"I'm going down and get that kitty," the American wife said.

"I'll do it," her husband offered from the bed.

5   "No, I'll get it. The poor kitty is out trying to keep dry under a table."

The husband went on reading, lying propped up with the two pillows at the foot of the bed.

"Don't get wet," he said.

The wife went downstairs and the hotel owner stood up and bowed to her as she passed the office. His desk was at the far end of the office. He was an old man and very tall.

"Il piove,"[1] the wife said. She liked the hotel-keeper.

10   "Si, si, Signora, brutto tempo. It is very bad weather."

He stood behind his desk in the far end of the dim room. The wife liked him. She liked the deadly serious way he received any complaints. She liked his dignity. She liked the way he wanted to serve her. She liked the way he felt about being a hotel-keeper. She liked his old, heavy face and big hands.

Liking him she opened the door and looked out. It was raining harder. A man in a rubber cape was crossing the empty square to the café. The cat would be around to the right. Perhaps she could go along under the eaves. As she stood in the doorway an umbrella opened behind her. It was the maid who looked after their room.

"You must not get wet," she smiled, speaking Italian. Of course, the hotel-keeper had sent her.

With the maid holding the umbrella over her, she walked along the gravel path until she was under their window. The table was there, washed bright green in the rain, but the cat was gone. She was suddenly disappointed. The maid looked up at her.

15   "Ha perduto qualque cosa, Signora?"[2]

"There was a cat," said the American girl.

"A cat?"

"Si, il gatto."

"A cat?" the maid laughed. "A cat in the rain?"

20   "Yes," she said, "under the table." Then. "Oh. I wanted it so much. I wanted a kitty."

When she talked English the maid's face tightened.

"Come, Signora," she said. "We must get back inside. You will be wet."

"I suppose so," said the American girl.

They went back along the gravel path and passed in the door. The maid stayed outside to close the umbrella. As the American girl passed the office, the padrone bowed from his desk. Something felt very small and tight inside the girl. The padrone made her feel very small and at the same time really important. She had a momentary feeling of being of supreme importance. She went on up the stairs. She opened the door of the room. George was on the bed, reading.

25   "Did you get the cat?" he asked, putting the book down.

"It was gone."

---

[1]**Il piove** It's raining (Italian).   [2]**Ha . . . Signora** Have you lost something, Madam?

"Wonder where it went to," he said, resting his eyes from reading.

She sat down on the bed.

"I wanted it so much," she said. "I don't know why I wanted it so much. I wanted that poor kitty. It isn't any fun to be a poor kitty out in the rain."

30 George was reading again.

She went over and sat in front of the mirror of the dressing table looking at herself with the hand glass. She studied her profile, first one side and then the other. Then she studied the back of her head and her neck.

"Don't you think it would be a good idea if I let my hair grow out?" she asked, looking at her profile again.

George looked up and saw the back of her neck, clipped close like a boy's.

"I like it the way it is."

35 "I get so tired of it," she said. "I get so tired of looking like a boy."

George shifted his position in the bed. He hadn't looked away from her since she started to speak.

"You look pretty darn nice," he said.

She laid the mirror down on the dresser and went over to the window and looked out. It was getting dark.

"I want to pull my hair back tight and smooth and make a big knot at the back that I can feel," she said. "I want to have a kitty to sit on my lap and purr when I stroke her."

40 "Yeah?" George said from the bed.

"And I want to eat at a table with my own silver and I want candles. And I want it to be spring and I want to brush my hair out in front of a mirror and I want a kitty and I want some new clothes."

"Oh, shut up and get something to read," George said. He was reading again.

His wife was looking out of the window. It was quite dark now and still raining in the palm trees.

"Anyway, I want a cat," she said, "I want a cat. I want a cat now. If I can't have long hair or any fun, I can have a cat."

45 George was not listening. He was reading his book. His wife looked out of the window where the light had come on in the square.

Someone knocked at the door.

"Avanti,"[3] George said. He looked up from his book.

In the doorway stood the maid. She held a big tortoise-shell cat pressed tight against her and swung down against her body.

"Excuse me," she said, "the padrone asked me to bring this for the Signora."

[1925]

[3]**Avanti** Come in.

A Student's Notes and Journal Entries on "Cat in the Rain"

When you read a story—or, perhaps more accurately, when you reread a story before discussing it or writing about it—you'll find it helpful to jot an occasional note (for instance, a brief response or a question) in the margins and to underline or highlight passages that strike you as especially interesting. Here is part of the story, with the annotations of a student, Bill Yanagi.

Is he making a joke? Or maybe he just isn't even thinking about what he is saying?——

The cat was trying to make herself so compact that she would not be dripped on.

"I'm going down and get that kitty," the American wife said.

"I'll do it," her husband offered from the bed.

He doesn't make a move

"No, I'll get it. The poor kitty is out trying to keep dry under a table."

The husband went on reading, lying propped up with the two pillows at the foot of the bed.

"Don't get wet," he said.

still doesn't move

The wife went downstairs and the hotel owner stood up and bowed to her as she passed the office. His desk was at the far end of the office. He was an old man and very tall.

contrast with the husband

"Il piove," the wife said. She liked the hotel-keeper.

"Si, si, Signora, brutto tempo. It is very bad weather."

He stood behind his desk in the far end of the dim room. The wife liked him. She liked the deadly serious way he received any complaints. She liked his dignity. She liked the way he wanted to serve her. She liked the way he felt about being a hotel-keeper. She liked his old, heavy face and big hands.

She respects him and she is pleased by the attention he shows

Liking him she opened the door and looked out. It was raining harder. A man in a rubber cape was crossing the empty square to the café. The cat would be around to the right.

to emphasize the bad weather??

Asking Questions about a Story

Everything in a story presumably is important, but having read the story once, probably something has especially interested (or puzzled) you, such as the relationship between two people, or the way the end of the story is connected to the beginning. On rereading, then, pen in hand, you'll find yourself noticing things that you missed or didn't find especially significant on your first reading. Now that you know the end of the story, you will read the beginning in a different way.

And of course if your instructor asks you to think about certain questions, you'll keep these in mind while you reread, and you will find ideas coming to you. In "Cat in the Rain," suppose you are asked (or you ask yourself) if the story might just as well be about a dog in the rain. Would anything be lost?

Here are a few questions that you can ask of almost any story. (Later in this chapter, on pages 211–13, we give a fuller list.) After scanning the questions, you will want to reread the story, pen in hand, and then jot down your responses on a sheet of paper. As you write, doubtless you will go back and reread the story or at least parts of it.

1. *What happens?* In two or three sentences—say 25–50 words—summarize what happens in the story.
2. *What sorts of people are the chief characters?* In "Cat in the Rain" the chief characters are George, George's wife, and the innkeeper (the padrone). Jot

down the traits that each seems to possess, and next to each trait briefly
give some supporting evidence.

3. *What especially pleased or displeased you in the story?* Devote at least a
   sentence or two to the end of the story. Do you find the end satisfying?
   Why or why not?

4. *Have you any thoughts about the title?* If so, what are they? If the story did
   not have a title, what would you call it?

After you have made your own jottings, compare them with these responses
by a student. No two readers will respond in exactly the same way, but all readers
can examine their responses and try to account for them, at least in part. If your
responses are substantially different, how do you account for the differences?

1. A summary. A young wife, stopping with her husband at an Italian
   hotel, from her room sees a cat in the rain. She goes to get it, but it is
   gone, and so she returns empty-handed. A moment later the maid
   knocks at the door, holding a tortoise-shell cat.

2. The characters: The woman.
   kind-hearted (pities cat in rain)
   appreciates innkeeper's courtesy ("liked the way he wanted to serve her")
       and admires him ("She liked his dignity")
   unhappy (wants a cat, wants to change her hair, wants to eat at a table
       with her own silver)
   The husband, George.
   not willing to put himself out (says he'll go to garden to get cat but
       doesn't move)
   doesn't seem very interested in wife (hardly talks to her--he's reading;
       tells her to "shut up")
   but he does say he finds her attractive ("You look pretty darn nice")
   The innkeeper.
   serious, dignified ("She liked the deadly serious way he received any
       complaints. She liked his dignity")
   courteous, helpful (sends maid with umbrella; at end sends maid
       with cat)

3. Dislikes and likes. "Dislikes" is too strong, but I was disappointed that
   more didn't happen at the end. What is the husband's reaction to the cat?
   Or his final reaction to his wife? I mean, what did he think about his
   wife when the maid brings the cat? And, for that matter, what is the
   wife's reaction? Is she satisfied? Or does she realize that the cat can't
   really make her happy? Now for the likes. (1) I guess I did like the way
   it turned out; it's sort of a happy ending, I think, since she wants the cat
   and gets it. (2) I also especially like the innkeeper. Maybe I like him
   partly because the wife likes him, and if she likes him he must be nice.
   And he is nice--very helpful. And I also like the way Hemingway shows
   the husband. I don't mean that I like the man himself, but I like the way
   Hemingway shows he is such a bastard--not getting off the bed to get the
   cat, telling his wife to shut up and read.
       Another thing about him is that the one time he says something
   nice about her, it's about her hair, and she isn't keen on the way her hair
   is. She says it makes her look "like a boy," and she is "tired" of looking
   like a boy. There's something wrong with this marriage. George hardly

pays attention to his wife, but he wants her to look like a boy. Maybe the idea is that this macho guy wants to keep her looking like an inferior (immature) version of himself. Anyway, he certainly doesn't seem interested in letting her fulfill herself as a woman.

I think my feelings add up to this: I like the way Hemingway shows us the relation between the husband and wife (even though the relation is pretty bad), and I like the innkeeper. Even if the relation with the couple ends unhappily, the story has a sort of happy ending, so far as it goes, since the innkeeper does what he can to please his guest: he sends the maid, with the cat. There's really nothing more that he can do.

More about the ending. The more I think about it, the more I feel that the ending is as happy as it can be. George is awful. When his wife says "I want a cat and I want a cat now," Hemingway tells us "George was not listening." And then, a moment later, almost like a good fairy the maid appears and grants the wife's wish.

4. The title. I don't suppose that I would have called it "Cat in the Rain," but I don't know what I would have called it. Maybe "An American Couple in Italy." Or maybe "The Innkeeper." I really do think that the innkeeper is very important, even though he only has a few lines. He's very impressive--not only to the girl, but to me (and maybe to all readers), since at the end of the story we see how careful the innkeeper is.

But the more I think about Hemingway's title, the more I think that maybe it also refers to the girl. Like the "poor kitty" in the rain, the wife is in a pretty bad situation. "It isn't any fun to be a poor kitty out in the rain." Of course the woman is indoors, but her husband generates lots of unpleasant weather. She may as well be out in the rain. She says "I want to have a kitty to sit on my lap and purr when I stroke her." This shows that she wants to be affectionate and that she also wants to have someone respond to her affection. She is like a cat in the rain.

The responses of this student probably include statements that you want to take issue with. Or perhaps you feel that the student did not even mention some things that you think are important. You may want to jot down some notes and raise some questions in class.

A Sample Essay by a Student: "Hemingway's American Wife"

The responses that we have quoted were written by Bill Yanagi, who later wrote an essay developing one of them. Here is the essay.

Bill Yanagi

English 10B

20 October 2002

Hemingway's American Wife

My title alludes not to any of the four women to whom Hemingway was married, but to "the American wife" who is twice called by this term in his short story, "Cat in the Rain." We first meet her in the first sentence of the story ("There were only two Americans stopping at the hotel"), and the next time she is mentioned (apart from a reference to the wife and her husband as "they") it is as "the American wife," at the beginning of the second paragraph of the story. The term is used again at the end of the third paragraph.

She is, then, at least in the early part of this story, just an American or an American wife--someone identified only by her nationality and her marital status, but not at all by her personality, her individuality, her inner self. She first becomes something of an individual when she separates herself from her husband by leaving the hotel room and going to look for a cat that she has seen in the garden, in the rain. This act of separation, however, has not the slightest effect on her husband, who "went on reading" (204).

When she returns, without the cat, he puts down his book and speaks to her, but it is obvious that he has no interest in her, beyond as a physical object ("You look pretty darn nice"). This comment is produced when she says she is thinking of letting her hair grow out, because she is "so tired of looking like a boy" (205). Why, a reader wonders, does her husband, who has paid almost no attention to her up to now, assure her that she looks "pretty darn nice"? I think it is reasonable to conclude that he wants her to look like someone who is not truly a woman, in particular someone who is immature. That she does not feel she has much identity is evident when she continues to talk about letting her hair grow, and she says "I want to pull my hair back tight and smooth and make a big knot at the back that I can feel" (205). Long hair is, or at least was, the traditional sign of a woman; she wants long hair, and at the same time she wants to keep it under her control by tying it in a "big knot," a knot that she can feel, a knot whose presence reminds her, because she can feel it, of her feminine nature.

She goes on to say that she story does two things at once: It pro-
                                    e of life, and it also illuminates some
mirror." That is, she wants to see we feel is part of the essence of human
                                    but for the moment accept it. Do you
husband apparently--so far as we either or both of these specifications?

recognizes it or her. Perhaps her c

way of saying that she wants to ex

simply a neglected woman who is ——————————————————————

Hemingway tells us, however, that *for Writing about Fiction*

garden she could not find it, a sig stimulate ideas about stories. Not every
                                    ry; but if after reading a story and think-
man. At the end of the story the m these questions, you will probably find
                                    k further about the story—in short, that
cannot just be handed a new natur

find it herself, and in herself, so I t 's best to do your thinking with a pen or
                                    iestions seem to you to be especially rel-
wife" still nothing more than an A out, jot down—freely, without worrying
                                    iterrupting your writing only to glance
[New page]   to check the evidence.

                          Wc

Literature for Composition, Compa rs, or does it depend on chance or coin-
                                    you as irrelevant that later you perceived
    York: Longman, 2003.   strike you as irrelevant?
                                    or does foreshadowing? If surprise is very
A few comments and questions may cond time with any interest? If so, what

• Do you find the essay interesting? ? Conflicts of one character against an-
• Do you find the essay well writter ting, or against society? Conflicts within a
• Do you find the essay convincing
  it, or do you think its argument i hronological order? If so, were you puz-
  Rain," taking note of passages that he arrangement of episodes seem effec-
  gument, or that seem to challenge ations repeated? If so, what do you make
• We often say that a good critical e
  with a fresh point of view. Our re
  Does this essay change your readir

                                    interest? Why?
                                    erve? Do you find some who by their simi-
                    Topics fo   e each other or help to define the major
                                    iaracter defined—by his or her words, ac-
                                    ns), dress, setting, narrative point of view?
1. One student argued that the cat rep n the same, or in a similar, situation?
   have. Do you think there is something ter? By explicit authorial (editorial) com-
   refute it?   r hand, by revelation through dialogue?

❑ If you do believe that the story has symbolic elements, do you think they are adequately integrated within the story, or do they strike you as being too obviously stuck in?

Style

❑ How has the point of view shaped or determined the style?
❑ How would you characterize the style? Simple? Understated? Figurative? Or what, and why?
❑ Do you think that the style is consistent? If it isn't—for instance, if there are shifts from simple sentences to highly complex ones—what do you make of the shifts?

Theme

❑ Is the title informative? What does it mean or suggest? Did the meaning seem to change after you read the story? Does the title help you to formulate a theme? If you had written the story, what title would you use?
❑ Do certain passages—dialogue or description—seem to you to point especially toward the theme? Do you find certain repetitions of words or pairs of incidents highly suggestive and helpful in directing your thoughts toward stating a theme? Flannery O'Connor, in *Mystery and Manners*, says, "In good fiction, certain of the details will tend to accumulate meaning from the action of the story itself, and when that happens, they become symbolic in the way they work." Does this story work that way?
❑ Is the meaning of the story embodied in the whole story, or does it seem stuck in, for example in certain passages of editorializing?
❑ Suppose someone asked you to state the point—the theme—of the story. Could you? And if you could, would you say that the theme of a particular story reinforces values you hold, or does it to some degree challenge them? Or is the concept of a theme irrelevant to this story?

Your Turn: Short Stories for Analysis

Nathaniel Hawthorne

Nathaniel Hawthorne (1804–64) was born in Salem, Massachusetts, the son of a sea captain. Two of his ancestors were judges; one had persecuted Quakers, and another had served at the Salem witch trials. After graduating from Bowdoin College in Maine, Hawthorne went back to Salem in order to write in relative seclusion. In 1835 he published "Young Goodman Brown."

From 1839 to 1841 Hawthorne worked in the Boston Customs House and then spent a few months as a member of a communal society, Brook Farm. In 1842 he married. From 1846 to 1849 he was a surveyor at the Salem Customs House; from 1849 to 1850 he wrote The Scarlet Letter, *the book that made him famous. From*

Indian priests, or powwows, who had often scared their native forest with more hideous incantations than any known to English witchcraft.

"But where is Faith?" thought Goodman Brown; and, as hope came into his heart, he trembled.

Another verse of the hymn arose, a slow and mournful strain, such as the pious love, but joined to words which expressed all that our nature can conceive of sin, and darkly hinted at far more. Unfathomable to mere mortals is the lore of fiends. Verse after verse was sung; and still the chorus of the desert swelled between like the deepest tone of a mighty organ; and with the final peal of that dreadful anthem there came a sound, as if the roaring wind, the rushing streams, the howling beasts, and every other voice of the unconcerted wilderness were mingling and according with the voice of guilty man in homage to the prince of all. The four blazing pines threw up a loftier flame, and obscurely discovered shapes and visages of horror on the smoke wreaths above the impious assembly. At the same moment the fire on the rock shot redly forth and formed a glowing arch above its base, where now appeared a figure. With reverence be it spoken, the figure bore no slight similitude, both in garb and manner, to some grave divine of the New England churches.

"Bring forth the converts!" cried a voice that echoed through the field and rolled into the forest.

60   At the word, Goodman Brown stepped forth from the shadow of the trees and approached the congregation, with whom he felt a loathful brotherhood by the sympathy of all that was wicked in his heart. He could have well-nigh sworn that the shape of his own dead father beckoned him to advance, looking downward from a smoke wreath, while a woman, with dim features of despair, threw out her hand to warn him back. Was it his mother? But he had no power to retreat one step, nor to resist, even in thought, when the minister and good old Deacon Gookin seized his arms and led him to the blazing rock. Thither came also the slender form of a veiled female, led between Goody Cloyse, that pious teacher of the catechism, and Martha Carrier, who had received the devil's promise to be queen of hell. A rampant hag was she. And there stood the proselytes beneath the canopy of fire.

"Welcome, my children," said the dark figure, "to the communion of your race. Ye have found thus young your nature and your destiny. My children, look behind you!"

They turned; and flashing forth, as it were, in a sheet of flame, the fiend worshippers were seen; the smile of welcome gleamed darkly on every visage.

"There," resumed the sable form, "are all whom ye have reverenced from youth. Ye deemed them holier than yourselves, and shrank from your own sin, contrasting it with their lives of righteousness and prayerful aspirations heavenward. Yet here are they all in my worshipping assembly. This night it shall be granted you to know their secret deeds: how hoary-bearded elders of the church have whispered wanton words to the young maids of their households; how many a woman, eager for widows' weeds, has given her husband a drink at bedtime and let him sleep his last sleep in her bosom; how beardless youths have made haste to inherit their fathers' wealth; and how fair damsels—blush not, sweet ones—have dug little graves in the garden, and bidden me, the sole guest, to an infant's funeral. By the sympathy of your human hearts for sin ye shall scent out all the places—whether in church, bedchamber, street, field, or forest—where crime has been committed, and shall exult to behold the whole earth one stain of guilt, one mighty blood spot. Far more than this. It shall be yours to penetrate, in every bosom, the deep mystery of sin, the fountain of all wicked arts, and which inexhaustibly supplies more evil impulses than human power—than my power at its utmost—can make manifest in deeds. And now, my children, look upon each other."

They did so; and, by the blaze of the hell-kindled torches, the wretched man beheld his Faith, and the wife her husband, trembling before that unhallowed altar.

65 "Lo, there ye stand, my children," said the figure, in a deep and solemn tone, almost sad with its despairing awfulness, as if his once angelic nature could yet mourn for our miserable race. "Depending upon one another's hearts, ye had still hoped that virtue were not all a dream. Now are ye undeceived. Evil is the nature of mankind. Evil must be your only happiness. Welcome again, my children, to the communion of your race."

"Welcome," repeated the fiend worshippers, in one cry of despair and triumph.

And there they stood, the only pair, as it seemed, who were yet hesitating on the verge of wickedness in this dark world. A basin was hollowed, naturally, in the rock. Did it contain water, reddened by the lurid light? or was it blood? or, perchance, a liquid flame? Herein did the shape of evil dip his hand and prepare to lay the mark of baptism upon their foreheads, that they might be partakers of the mystery of sin, more conscious of the secret guilt of others, both in deed and thought, than they could now be of their own. The husband cast one look at his pale wife, and Faith at him. What polluted wretches would the next glance show them to each other, shuddering alike at what they disclosed and what they saw!

"Faith! Faith!" cried the husband, "look up to heaven, and resist the wicked one."

Whether Faith obeyed he knew not. Hardly had he spoken when he found himself amid calm night and solitude, listening to a roar of the wind which died heavily away through the forest. He staggered against the rock, and felt it chill and damp; while a hanging twig, that had been all on fire, besprinkled his cheek with the coldest dew.

70 The next morning young Goodman Brown came slowly into the street of Salem village, staring around him like a bewildered man. The good old minister was taking a walk along the graveyard to get an appetite for breakfast and meditate his sermon, and bestowed a blessing, as he passed, on Goodman Brown. He shrank from the venerable saint as if to avoid an anathema. Old Deacon Gookin was at domestic worship, and the holy words of his prayer were heard through the open window. "What God doth the wizard pray to?" quoth Goodman Brown. Goody Cloyse, that excellent old Christian, stood in the early sunshine at her own lattice, catechizing a little girl who had brought her a pint of morning's milk. Goodman Brown snatched away the child as from the grasp of the fiend himself. Turning the corner by the meeting-house, he spied the head of Faith, with the pink ribbons, gazing anxiously forth, and bursting into such joy at sight of him that she skipped along the street and almost kissed her husband before the whole village. But Goodman Brown looked sternly and sadly into her face, and passed on without a greeting.

Had Goodman Brown fallen asleep in the forest and only dreamed a wild dream of a witch-meeting?

Be it so if you will; but alas! it was a dream of evil omen for young Goodman Brown. A stern, a sad, a darkly meditative, a distrustful, if not a desperate man did he become from the night of that fearful dream. On the Sabbath day, when the

"Cabby, to the Police Bridge!" the hunchback cries in a cracked voice. "The three of us, . . . twenty kopecks!"

Iona tugs at the reins and clicks to his horse. Twenty kopecks is not a fair price, but he has no thoughts for that. Whether it is a rouble or whether it is five kopecks does not matter to him now so long as he has a fare. . . . The three young men, shoving each other and using bad language, go up to the sledge, and all three try to sit down at once. The question remains to be settled: Which are to sit down and which one is to stand? After a long altercation, ill-temper, and abuse, they come to the conclusion that the hunchback must stand because he is the shortest.

"Well, drive on," says the hunchback in his cracked voice, settling himself and breathing down Iona's neck. "Cut along! What a cap you've got, my friend! You wouldn't find a worse one in all Petersburg. . . ."

"He-he! . . . he-he! . . . " laughs Iona. "It's nothing to boast of!"

25   "Well, then, nothing to boast of, drive on! Are you going to drive like this all the way? Eh? Shall I give you one in the neck?"

"My head aches," says one of the tall ones. "At the Dukmasovs' yesterday Vaska and I drank four bottles of brandy between us."

"I can't make out why you talk such stuff," says the other tall one angrily. "You lie like a brute."

"Strike me dead, it's the truth! . . . "

"It's about as true as that a louse coughs."

30   "He-he!" grins Iona. "Me-er-ry gentlemen!"

"Tfoo! the devil take you!" cries the hunchback indignantly. "Will you get on, you old plague, or won't you? Is that the way to drive? Give her one with the whip. Hang it all, give it her well."

Iona feels behind his back the jolting person and quivering voice of the hunchback. He hears abuse addressed to him, he sees people, and the feeling of loneliness begins little by little to be less heavy on his heart. The hunchback swears at him, till he chokes over some elaborately whimsical string of epithets and is overpowered by his cough. His tall companions begin talking of a certain Nadyezhda Petrovna. Iona looks round at them. Waiting till there is a brief pause, he looks round once more and says:

"This week . . . er . . . my . . . er . . . son died!"

"We shall all die, . . . " says the hunchback with a sigh, wiping his lips after coughing. "Come, drive on! drive on! My friends, I simply cannot stand crawling like this! When will he get us there?"

35   "Well, you give him a little encouragement . . . one in the neck!"

"Do you hear, you old plague? I'll make you smart. If one stands on ceremony with fellows like you one may as well walk. Do you hear, you old dragon? Or don't you care a hang what we say?"

And Iona hears rather than feels a slap on the back of his neck.

"He-he! . . . " he laughs. "Merry gentlemen . . . God give you health!"

"Cabman, are you married?" asks one of the tall ones.

40   "I? He-he! Me-er-ry gentlemen. The only wife for me now is the damp earth. . . . He-ho-ho! . . . The grave that is! . . . Here my son's dead and I am alive. . . . It's a strange thing, death has come in at the wrong door. . . . Instead of coming for me it went for my son. . . ."

And Iona turns round to tell them how his son died, but at that point the hunchback gives a faint sigh and announces that, thank God! they have arrived at last. After taking his twenty kopecks, Iona gazes for a long while after the revelers, who disappear into a dark entry. Again he is alone and again there is silence for him. . . . The misery which has been for a brief space eased comes back again and tears his heart more cruelly than ever. With a look of anxiety and suffering Iona's eyes stray restlessly among the crowds moving to and fro on both sides of the street: can he not find among those thousands someone who will listen to him? But the crowds flit by heedless of him and his misery. . . . His misery is immense, beyond all bounds. If Iona's heart were to burst and his misery to flow out, it would flood the whole world, it seems, but yet it is not seen. It has found a hiding-place in such an insignificant shell that one would not have found it with a candle by daylight. . . .

Iona sees a house-porter with a parcel and makes up his mind to address him.

"What time will it be, friend?" he asks.

"Going on for ten. . . . Why have you stopped here? Drive on!"

45   Iona drives a few paces away, bends himself double, and gives himself up to his misery. He feels it is no good to appeal to people. But before five minutes have passed he draws himself up, shakes his head as though he feels a sharp pain, and tugs at the reins. . . . He can bear it no longer.

"Back to the yard!" he thinks. "To the yard!"

And his little mare, as though she knew his thoughts, falls to trotting. An hour and a half later Iona is sitting by a big dirty stove. On the stove, on the floor, and on the benches are people snoring. The air is full of smells and stuffiness. Iona looks at the sleeping figures, scratches himself, and regrets that he has come home so early. . . .

"I have not earned enough to pay for the oats, even," he thinks. "That's why I am so miserable. A man who knows how to do his work, . . . who has had enough to eat, and whose horse has had enough to eat, is always at ease. . . ."

In one of the corners a young cabman gets up, clears his throat sleepily, and makes for the waterbucket.

50   "Want a drink?" Iona asks him.

"Seems so."

"May it do you good. . . . But my son is dead, mate. . . . Do you hear? This week in the hospital. . . . It's queer business. . . ."

Iona looks to see the effect produced by his words, but he sees nothing. The young man has covered his head over and is already asleep. The old man sighs and scratches himself. . . . Just as the young man had been thirsty for water, he thirsts for speech. His son will soon have been dead a week, and he has not really talked to anybody yet. . . . He wants to talk of it properly, with deliberation. . . . He wants to tell how his son was taken ill, how he suffered, what he said before he died, how he died. . . . He wants to describe the funeral, and how he went to the hospital to get his son's clothes. He still has his daughter Anisya in the country. . . . And he wants to talk about her too. . . . Yes, he has plenty to talk about now. His listener ought to sigh and exclaim and lament. . . . It would be even better to talk to women. Though they are silly creatures, they blubber at the first word.

"Let's go out and have a look at the mare," Iona thinks. "There is always time for sleep. . . . You'll have sleep enough, no fear. . . ."

55   He puts on his coat and goes into the stables where his mare is standing. He thinks about oats, about hay, about the weather. . . . He cannot think about his son when he is alone. . . . To talk about him with someone is possible, but to think of him and picture him is insufferable anguish. . . .

"Are you munching?" Iona asks his mare, seeing her shining eyes. "There, munch away, munch away. . . . Since we have not earned enough for oats, we will eat hay. . . . Yes, . . . I have grown too old to drive. . . . My son ought to be driving, not I. . . . He was a real coachman. . . . He ought to have lived. . . ."

Iona is silent for a while, and then he goes on:

"That's how it is, old girl. . . . Kuzma Ionitch is gone. . . . He said goodby to me. . . . He went and died for no reason. . . . Now, suppose you had a little colt, and you were mother to that little colt. . . . And all at once that same little colt went and died. . . . You'd be sorry, wouldn't you? . . ."

The little mare munches, listens, and breathes on her master's hands. Iona is carried away and tells her all about it.

[1886]

Topics for Critical Thinking and Writing

1. What do you admire or not admire about Chekhov's story? Why?
2. Try to examine in detail your response to the ending. Do you think the ending is, in a way, a happy ending? Would you prefer a different ending? For instance, should the story end when the young cabman falls asleep? Or when Iona sets out for the stable? Or can you imagine a better ending? If so, what?

JAMES JOYCE

James Joyce (1882–1941) was born into a middle-class family in Dublin, Ireland. His father drank, became increasingly irresponsible and unemployable, and the family sank in the social order. Still, Joyce received a strong classical education at excellent Jesuit schools and at University College, Dublin, where he studied modern languages. In 1902, at the age of twenty, he left Ireland so that he might spend the rest of his life writing about life in Ireland. ("The shortest way to Tara," he said, "is via Holyhead," i.e., the shortest way to the heart of Ireland is to take ship away.) In Trieste, Zurich, and Paris he supported his family in a variety of ways, sometimes teaching English in a Berlitz language school. His fifteen stories, collected under the title of Dubliners, *were written between 1904 and 1907, but he could not get them published until 1914. Next came a highly autobiographical novel,* A Portrait of the Artist as a Young Man *(1916). Ulysses (1922), a large novel covering eighteen hours in Dublin, was for some years banned by the United States Post Office, though few if any readers today find it offensive. Joyce spent most of the rest of his life working on* Finnegans Wake *(1939).*

Nine years before he succeeded in getting Dubliners *published, Joyce described the manuscript in these terms:*

> My intention was to write a chapter of the moral history of my country and I chose Dublin for the scene because that city seemed to me the centre of paralysis. . . . I have written it for the most part in a style of scrupulous meanness and with the conviction that he is a very bold man who dares to alter in the presentment, still more to deform, whatever he has seen and heard.

Araby

North Richmond Street, being blind,[1] was a quiet street except at the hour when the Christian Brothers' School set the boys free. An uninhabited house of two stories stood at the blind end, detached from its neighbors in a square ground. The other houses of the street, conscious of decent lives within them, gazed at one another with brown imperturbable faces.

The former tenant of our house, a priest, had died in the back drawing-room. Air, musty from having long been enclosed, hung in all the rooms, and the waste room behind the kitchen was littered with old useless papers. Among these I found a few papercovered books, the pages of which were curled and damp: *The Abbot,* by Walter Scott, *The Devout Communicant* and *The Memoirs of Vidocq.*[2] I liked the last best because its leaves were yellow. The wild garden behind the house contained a central apple-tree and a few straggling bushes under one of which I found the late tenant's rusty bicycle-pump. He had been a very charitable priest; in his will he had left all his money to institutions and the furniture of his house to his sister.

When the short days of winter came dusk fell before we had well eaten our dinners. When we met in the street the houses had grown sombre. The space of sky above us was the colour of everchanging violet and towards it the lamps of the street lifted their feeble lanterns. The cold air stung us and we played till our bodies glowed. Our shouts echoed in the silent street. The career of our play brought us through the dark muddy lanes behind the houses where we ran the gauntlet of the rough tribes from the cottages, to the back doors of the dark dripping gardens where odours arose from the ashpits, to the dark odorous stables where a coachman smoothed and combed the horse or shook music from the buckled harness. When we returned to the street light from the kitchen windows had filled the areas. If my uncle was seen turning the corner we hid in the shadow until we had seen him safely housed. Or if Mangan's sister came out on the doorstep to call her brother in to his tea we watched her from our shadow peer up and down the street. We waited to see whether she would remain or go in and, if she remained, we left our shadow and walked up to Mangan's steps resignedly. She was waiting for us, her figure defined by the light from the half-opened door. Her brother always teased her before he obeyed and I stood by the railings looking at her. Her dress swung as she moved her body and the soft rope of her hair tossed from side to side.

Every morning I lay on the floor in the front parlour watching her door. The blind was pulled down to within an inch of the sash so that I could not be seen. When she came out on the doorstep my heart leaped. I ran to the hall, seized my books and followed her. I kept her brown figure always in my eye and, when we came near the point at which our ways diverged, I quickened my pace and passed her. This happened morning after morning. I had never spoken to her, except for a few casual words, and yet her name was like a summons to all my foolish blood.

5   Her image accompanied me even in places the most hostile to romance. On Saturday evenings when my aunt went marketing I had to go to carry some of the parcels. We walked through the flaring streets, jostled by drunken men and bar-

---

[1]**blind** a dead-end street. (All notes are by the editors.)   [2]***The Abbot*** one of Scott's popular historical romances; ***The Devout Communicant*** a Catholic religious manual; ***The Memoirs of Vidocq*** the memoirs of the chief of the French detective force.

gaining women, amid the curses of labourers, the shrill litanies of shop-boys who stood on guard by the barrels of pigs' cheeks, the nasal chanting of street-singers, who sang a *come-all-you* about O'Donovan Rossa,[3] or a ballad about the troubles in our native land. These noises converged in a single sensation of life for me: I imagined that I bore my chalice safely through a throng of foes. Her name sprang to my lips at moments in strange prayers and praises which I myself did not understand. My eyes were often full of tears (I could not tell why) and at times a flood from my heart seemed to pour itself out into my bosom. I thought little of the future. I did not know whether I would ever speak to her or not or, if I spoke to her, how I could tell her of my confused adoration. But my body was like a harp and her words and gestures were like fingers running upon the wires.

One evening I went into the back drawing-room in which the priest had died. It was a dark rainy evening and there was no sound in the house. Through one of the broken panes I heard the rain impinge upon the earth, the fine incessant needles of water playing in the sodden beds. Some distant lamp or lighted window gleamed below me. I was thankful that I could see so little. All my senses seemed to desire to veil themselves and, feeling that I was about to slip from them, I pressed the palms of my hands together until they trembled, murmuring: *O love! O love!* many times.

At last she spoke to me. When she addressed the first words to me I was so confused that I did not know what to answer. She asked me was I going to Araby. I forget whether I answered yes or no. It would be a splendid bazaar, she said; she would love to go.

—And why can't you? I asked.

10   While she spoke she turned a silver bracelet round and round her wrist. She could not go, she said, because there would be a retreat that week in her convent. Her brother and two other boys were fighting for their caps and I was alone at the railings. She held one of the spikes, bowing her head towards me. The light from the lamp opposite our door caught the white curve of her neck, lit up her hair that rested there and, falling, lit up the hand upon the railing. It fell over one side of her dress and caught the white border of a petticoat, just visible as she stood at ease.

—It's well for you, she said.

—If I go, I said, I will bring you something.

What innumerable follies laid waste my waking and sleeping thoughts after that evening! I wished to annihilate the tedious intervening days. I chafed against the work of school. At night in my bedroom and by day in the classroom her image came between me and the page I strove to read. The syllables of the word *Araby* were called to me through the silence in which my soul luxuriated and cast an Eastern enchantment over me. I asked for leave to go to the bazaar on Saturday night. My aunt was surprised and hoped it was not some Freemason[4] affair. I answered few questions in class, I watched my master's face pass from amiability to sternness; he hoped I was not beginning to idle. I could not call my wandering thoughts together. I had hardly any patience with the serious work of life which, now that it stood between me and my desire, seemed to me child's play, ugly monotonous child's play.

---

[3]**O'Donovan Rossa** Jeremiah O'Donovan (1831–1915), a popular Irish leader who was jailed by the British for advocating violent rebellion; *come-all-you* a topical song that began "Come all you gallant Irishmen." [4]**Freemason** Irish Catholics viewed the Masons as their Protestant enemies.

On Saturday morning I reminded my uncle that I wished to go to the bazaar in the evening. He was fussing at the hallstand, looking for the hat-brush, and answered me curtly:

15 —Yes, boy, I know.

As he was in the hall I could not go into the front parlour and lie at the window. I left the house in bad humour and walked slowly towards the school. The air was pitilessly raw and already my heart misgave me.

When I came home to dinner my uncle had not yet been home. Still it was early. I sat staring at the clock for some time and, when its ticking began to irritate me, I left the room. I mounted the staircase and gained the upper part of the house. The high cold empty gloomy rooms liberated me and I went from room to room singing. From the front window I saw my companions playing below in the street. Their cries reached me weakened and indistinct and, leaning my forehead against the cool glass, I looked over at the dark house where she lived. I may have stood there for an hour, seeing nothing but the brown-clad figure cast by my imagination, touched discreetly by the lamplight at the curved neck, at the hand upon the railings and at the border below the dress.

When I came downstairs again I found Mrs Mercer sitting at the fire. She was an old garrulous woman, a pawnbroker's widow, who collected used stamps for some pious purpose. I had to endure the gossip of the tea-table. The meal was prolonged beyond an hour and still my uncle did not come. Mrs Mercer stood up to go: she was sorry she couldn't wait any longer, but it was after eight o'clock and she did not like to be out late, as the night air was bad for her. When she had gone I began to walk up and down the room, clenching my fists. My aunt said:

—I'm afraid you may put off your bazaar for this night of Our Lord.

20 At nine o'clock I heard my uncle's latchkey in the halldoor. I heard him talking to himself and heard the hallstand rocking when it had received the weight of his overcoat. I could interpret these signs. When he was midway through his dinner I asked him to give me the money to go to the bazaar. He had forgotten.

—The people are in bed and after their first sleep now, he said.

I did not smile. My aunt said to him energetically:

—Can't you give him the money and let him go? You've kept him late enough as it is.

My uncle said he was very sorry he had forgotten. He said he believed in the old saying: *All work and no play makes Jack a dull boy*. He asked me where I was going and, when I had told him a second time he asked me did I know *The Arab's Farewell to His Steed*.[5] When I left the kitchen he was about to recite the opening lines of the piece to my aunt.

25 I held a florin tightly in my hand as I strode down Buckingham Street towards the station. The sight of the streets thronged with buyers and glaring with gas recalled to me the purpose of my journey. I took my seat in a third-class carriage of a deserted train. After an intolerable delay the train moved out of the station slowly. It crept onward among ruinous houses and over the twinkling river. At Westland Row Station a crowd of people pressed to the carriage doors; but the porters moved them back, saying that it was a special train for the bazaar. I remained alone in the bare carriage. In a few minutes the train drew up beside an improvised wooden platform. I passed out on to the road and saw by the lighted

[5]*The Arab's Farewell to His Steed* "The Arab to His Favorite Steed" was a popular sentimental poem by Caroline Norton (1808–77).

dial of a clock that it was ten minutes to ten. In front of me was a large building which displayed the magical name.

I could not find any sixpenny entrance and, fearing that the bazaar would be closed, I passed in quickly through a turnstile, handing a shilling to a weary-looking man. I found myself in a big hall girdled at half its height by a gallery. Nearly all the stalls were closed and the greater part of the hall was in darkness. I recognised a silence like that which pervades a church after a service. I walked into the center of the bazaar timidly. A few people were gathered about the stalls which were still open. Before a curtain, over which the words *Café Chantant* were written in coloured lamps, two men were counting money on a salver. I listened to the fall of the coins.

Remembering with difficulty why I had come I went over to one of the stalls and examined porcelain vases and flowered tea-sets. At the door of the stall a young lady was talking and laughing with two young gentlemen. I remarked their English accents and listened vaguely to their conversation.

—O, I never said such a thing!

—O, but you did!

30   —O, but I didn't!

—Didn't she say that?

—Yes! I heard her.

—O, there's a . . . fib!

Observing me the young lady came over and asked me did I wish to buy anything. The tone of her voice was not encouraging; she seemed to have spoken to me out of a sense of duty. I looked humbly at the great jars that stood like eastern guards at either side of the dark entrance to the stall and murmured:

35   —No, thank you.

The young lady changed the position of one of the vases and went back to the two young men. They began to talk of the same subject. Once or twice the young lady glanced at me over her shoulder.

I lingered before her stall, though I knew my stay was useless, to make my interest in her wares seem the more real. Then I turned away slowly and walked down the middle of the bazaar. I allowed the two pennies to fall against the sixpence in my pocket. I heard a voice call from one end of the gallery that the light was out. The upper part of the hall was now completely dark.

Gazing up into the darkness I saw myself as a creature driven and derided by vanity; and my eyes burned with anguish and anger.

[1905]

Topics for Critical Thinking and Writing

1. Joyce wrote a novel called *A Portrait of the Artist as a Young Man*. Write an essay of about 500 words on "Araby" as a portrait of the artist as a boy.

2. In an essay of about 500 words, consider the role of images of darkness and blindness and what they reveal to us about "Araby" as a story of the fall from innocence into painful awareness.

3. How old, approximately, is the narrator of "Araby" at the time of the experience he describes? How old is he at the time he tells his story? On what evidence do you base your estimates?

4. The boy, apparently an only child, lives with an uncle and aunt, rather than with parents. Why do you suppose Joyce put him in this family setting rather than some other?

5. The story is rich in images of religion. This in itself is not surprising, for the story is set in Roman Catholic Ireland, but the religious images are not simply references to religious persons or objects. In an essay of 500 to 750 words, discuss how these images reveal the narrator's state of mind.

CHARLOTTE PERKINS GILMAN

Charlotte Perkins Gilman (1860–1935), née Charlotte Perkins, was born in Hartford, Connecticut. Her father deserted the family soon after Charlotte's birth; she was brought up by her mother, who found it difficult to make ends meet. For a while Charlotte worked as an artist and teacher of art, and in 1884, when she was twenty-four, she married an artist. In 1885 she had a daughter, but soon after the birth of the girl Charlotte had a nervous breakdown. At her husband's urging she spent a month in the sanitarium of Dr. S. Weir Mitchell, a physician who specialized in treating women with nervous disorders. (Mitchell is specifically named in "The Yellow Wallpaper.") Because the treatment—isolation and total rest—nearly drove her to insanity, she fled Mitchell and her husband. In California she began a career as a lecturer and writer on feminist topics. (She also supported herself by teaching school and by keeping a boarding-house.) Among her books are Women and Economics *(1899) and* The Man-Made World *(1911), which have been revived by the feminist movement. In 1900 she married a cousin, George Gilman. From all available evidence, the marriage was successful. Certainly it did not restrict her activities as a feminist. In 1935, suffering from inoperable cancer, she took her own life.*

"The Yellow Wallpaper," written in 1892—that is, written after she had been treated by S. Weir Mitchell for her nervous breakdown—was at first interpreted either as a ghost story or as a Poe-like study of insanity. Only in recent years has it been seen as a feminist story. (One might ask oneself if these interpretations are mutually exclusive.)

The Yellow Wallpaper

It is very seldom that mere ordinary people like John and myself secure ancestral halls for the summer.

A colonial mansion, a hereditary estate. I would say a haunted house, and reach the height of romantic felicity—but that would be asking too much of fate!

Still I will proudly declare that there is something queer about it.

Else, why should it be let so cheaply? And why have stood so long untenanted?

5   John laughs at me, of course, but one expects that in marriage.

John is practical in the extreme. He has no patience with faith, an intense horror of superstition, and he scoffs openly at any talk of things not to be felt and seen and put down in figures.

John is a physician, and *perhaps*—(I would not say it to a living soul, of course, but this is dead paper and a great relief to my mind)—*perhaps* that is one reason I do not get well faster.

You see he does not believe I am sick!

And what can one do?

10   If a physician of high standing, and one's own husband, assures friends and relatives that there is really nothing the matter with one but temporary nervous depression—a slight hysterical tendency—what is one to do?

My brother is also a physician, and also of high standing, and he says the same thing.

So I take phosphates or phosphites—whichever it is, and tonics, and journeys, and air, and exercise, and am absolutely forbidden to "work" until I am well again.

Personally, I disagree with their ideas.

Personally, I believe that congenial work, with excitement and change, would do me good.

15   But what is one to do?

I did write for a while in spite of them: but it *does* exhaust me a good deal—having to be so sly about it, or else meet with heavy opposition.

I sometimes fancy that in my condition if I had less opposition and more society and stimulus—but John says the very worst thing I can do is to think about my condition, and I confess it always makes me feel bad.

So I will let it alone and talk about the house.

The most beautiful place! It is quite alone, standing well back from the road, quite three miles from the village. It makes me think of English places that you read about, for there are hedges and walls and gates that lock, and lots of separate little houses for the gardeners and people.

20   There is a *delicious* garden! I never saw such a garden—large and shady, full of box-bordered paths, and lined with long grapecovered arbors with seats under them.

There were greenhouses, too, but they are all broken now. There was some legal trouble. I believe, something about the heirs and coheirs: anyhow, the place has been empty for years.

That spoils my ghostliness. I am afraid, but I don't care—there is something strange about the house—I can feel it.

I even said so to John one moonlight evening, but he said what I felt was a *draught,* and shut the window.

I get unreasonably angry with John sometimes. I'm sure I never used to be so sensitive. I think it is due to this nervous condition.

25   But John says if I feel so, I shall neglect proper self-control: so I take pains to control myself—before him, at least, and that makes me very tired.

I don't like our room a bit. I wanted one downstairs that opened on the piazza and had roses all over the window, and such pretty old-fashioned chintz hangings! but John would not hear of it.

He said there was only one window and not room for two beds, and no near room for him if he took another.

He is very careful and loving, and hardly lets me stir without special direction.

I have a schedule prescription for each hour in the day: he takes all care from me, and so I feel basely ungrateful not to value it more.

30   He said we came here solely on my account, that I was to have perfect rest and all the air I could get. "Your exercise depends on your strength, my dear," said he, "and your food somewhat on your appetite; but air you can absorb all the time." So we took the nursery at the top of the house.

It is a big, airy room, the whole floor nearly, with windows that look all ways, and air and sunshine galore. It was nursery first and then playroom and gymnasium, I should judge; for the windows are barred for little children, and there are rings and things in the walls.

The paint and paper look as if a boys' school had used it. It is stripped off—the paper—in great patches all around the head of my bed, about as far as I can reach, and in a great place on the other side of the room low down. I never saw a worse paper in my life.

One of those sprawling flamboyant patterns committing every artistic sin.

It is dull enough to confuse the eye in following, pronounced enough to constantly irritate and provoke study, and when you follow the lame uncertain curves for a little distance they suddenly commit suicide—plunge off at outrageous angles, destroy themselves in unheard of contradictions.

35   The color is repellent, almost revolting: a smouldering unclean yellow, strangely faded by the slow-turning sunlight.

It is a dull yet lurid orange in some places, a sickly sulphur tint in others.

No wonder the children hated it! I should hate it myself if I had to live in this room long.

There comes John, and I must put this away,—he hates to have me write a word.

We have been here two weeks, and I haven't felt like writing before, since that first day.

40   I am sitting by the window now, up in this atrocious nursery, and there is nothing to hinder my writing as much as I please, save lack of strength.

John is away all day, and even some nights when his cases are serious.

I am glad my case is not serious!

But these nervous troubles are dreadfully depressing.

John does not know how much I really suffer. He knows there is no *reason* to suffer, and that satisfies him.

45   Of course it is only nervousness. It does weigh on me so not to do my duty in any way!

I meant to be such a help to John, such a real rest and comfort, and here I am a comparative burden already!

Nobody would believe what an effort it is to do what little I am able,—to dress and entertain, and order things.

It is fortunate Mary is so good with the baby. Such a dear baby!

And yet I *cannot* be with him, it makes me so nervous.

50   I suppose John never was nervous in his life. He laughs at me so about this wallpaper!

At first he meant to repaper the room, but afterwards he said that I was letting it get the better of me, and that nothing was worse for a nervous patient than to give way to such fancies.

He said that after the wallpaper was changed it would be the heavy bed-stead, and then the barred windows, and then that gate at the head of the stairs, and so on.

"You know the place is doing you good," he said, "and really, dear, I don't care to renovate the house just for a three months' rental."

"Then do let us go downstairs," I said, "there are such pretty rooms there."

55   Then he took me in his arms and called me a blessed little goose, and said he would go down to the cellar, if I wished, and have it whitewashed into the bargain.

But he is right enough about the beds and windows and things.

It is an airy and comfortable room as any one need wish, and, of course, I would not be so silly as to make him uncomfortable just for a whim.

I'm really getting quite fond of the big room, all but that horrid paper.

Out of one window I can see the garden, those mysterious deep-shaded arbors, the riotous old-fashioned flowers, and bushes and gnarly trees.

60   Out of another I get a lovely view of the bay and a little private wharf belonging to the estate. There is a beautiful shaded lane that runs down there from the house. I always fancy I see people walking in these numerous paths and arbors, but John has cautioned me not to give way to fancy in the least. He says that with my imaginative power and habit of story-making, a nervous weakness like mine is sure to lead to all manner of excited fancies, and that I ought to use my will and good sense to check the tendency. So I try.

I think sometimes that if I were only well enough to write a little it would relieve the press of ideas and rest me.

But I find I get pretty tired when I try.

It is so discouraging not to have any advice and companionship about my work. When I get really well, John says we will ask Cousin Henry and Julia down for a long visit; but he says he would as soon put fireworks in my pillow-case as to let me have those stimulating people about now.

I wish I could get well faster.

65   But I must not think about that. This paper looks to me as if it *knew* what a vicious influence it had!

There is a recurrent spot where the pattern lolls like a broken neck and two bulbous eyes stare at you upside down.

I get positively angry with the impertinence of it and the everlastingness. Up and down and sideways they crawl, and those absurd, unblinking eyes are everywhere. There is one place where two breadths didn't match, and the eyes go all up and down the line, one a little higher than the other.

I never saw so much expression in an inanimate thing before, and we all know how much expression they have! I used to lie awake as a child and get more entertainment and terror out of blank walls and plain furniture than most children could find in a toystore.

I remember what a kindly wink the knobs of our big, old bureau used to have, and there was one chair that always seemed like a strong friend.

70   I used to feel that if any of the other things looked too fierce I could always hop into that chair and be safe.

The furniture in this room is no worse than inharmonious, however, for we had to bring it all from downstairs. I suppose when this was used as a playroom they had to take the nursery things out, and no wonder! I never saw such ravages as the children have made here.

The wallpaper, as I said before, is torn off in spots, and it sticketh closer than a brother—they must have had perseverance as well as hatred.

Then the floor is scratched and gouged and splintered, the plaster itself is dug out here and there, and this great heavy bed which is all we found in the room, looks as if it had been through the wars.

But I don't mind it a bit—only the paper.

75   There comes John's sister. Such a dear girl as she is, and so careful of me! I must not let her find me writing.

She is a perfect and enthusiastic housekeeper, and hopes for no better profession. I verily believe she thinks it is the writing which made me sick!

But I can write when she is out, and see her a long way off from these windows.

There is one that commands the road, a lovely shaded winding road, and one that just looks off over the country. A lovely country, too, full of great elms and velvet meadows.

This wallpaper has a kind of sub-pattern in a different shade, a particularly irritating one, for you can only see it in certain lights, and not clearly then.

80 But in the places where it isn't faded and where the sun is just so—I can see a strange, provoking, formless sort of figure, that seems to skulk about behind that silly and conspicuous front design.

There's sister on the stairs!

Well, the Fourth of July is over! The people are all gone and I am tired out. John thought it might do me good to see a little company, so we just had mother and Nellie and the children down for a week.

Of course I didn't do a thing. Jennie sees to everything now. But it tired me all the same.

John says if I don't pick up faster he shall send me to Weir Mitchell in the fall.

85 But I don't want to go there at all. I had a friend who was in his hands once, and she says he is just like John and my brother, only more so!

Besides, it is such an undertaking to go so far.

I don't feel as if it was worth while to turn my hand over for anything, and I'm getting dreadfully fretful and querulous.

I cry at nothing, and cry most of the time.

Of course I don't when John is here, or anybody else, but when I am alone.

90 And I am alone a good deal just now. John is kept in town very often by serious cases, and Jennie is good and lets me alone when I want her to.

So I walk a little in the garden or down that lovely lane, sit on the porch under the roses, and lie down up here a good deal.

I'm getting really fond of the room in spite of the wallpaper. Perhaps *because* of the wallpaper.

It dwells in my mind so!

I lie here on this great immovable bed—it is nailed down, I believe—and follow that pattern about by the hour. It is as good as gymnastics, I assure you. I start, we'll say, at the bottom, down in the corner over there where it has not been touched, and I determine for the thousandth time that I *will* follow that pointless pattern to some sort of a conclusion.

95 I know a little of the principle of design, and I know this thing was not arranged on any laws of radiation, or alternation, or repetition, or symmetry, or anything else that I ever heard of.

It is repeated, of course, by the breadths, but not otherwise.

Looked at in one way each breadth stands alone, the bloated curves and flourishes—a kind of "debased Romanesque" with *delirium tremens*—go waddling up and down in isolated columns of fatuity.

But, on the other hand, they connect diagonally, and the sprawling outlines run off in great slanting waves of optic horror, like a lot of wallowing seaweeds in full chase.

The whole thing goes horizontally, too, at least it seems so, and I exhaust myself in trying to distinguish the order of its going in that direction.

100 They have used a horizontal breadth for a frieze, and that adds wonderfully to the confusion.

There is one end of the room where it is almost intact, and there, when the crosslights fade and the low sun shines directly upon it, I can almost fancy radiation after all,—the interminable grotesques seem to form around a common center and rush off in headlong plunges of equal distraction.

It makes me tired to follow it. I will take a nap I guess.

I don't know why I should write this.

I don't want to.

105   I don't feel able.

And I know John would think it absurd. But I *must* say what I feel and think in some way—it is such a relief.

But the effort is getting to be greater than the relief!

Half the time now I am awfully lazy, and lie down ever so much.

John says I mustn't lose my strength, and has me take cod liver oil and lots of tonics and things, to say nothing of ale and wine and rare meat.

110   Dear John! He loves me very dearly, and hates to have me sick. I tried to have a real earnest reasonable talk with him the other day, and tell him how I wish he would let me go and make a visit to Cousin Henry and Julia.

But he said I wasn't able to go, nor able to stand it after I got there: and I did not make out a very good case for myself, for I was crying before I had finished.

It is getting to be a great effort for me to think straight. Just this nervous weakness I suppose.

And dear John gathered me up in his arms, and just carried me upstairs and laid me on the bed, and sat by me and read to me till it tired my head.

He said I was his darling and his comfort and all he had, and that I must take care of myself for his sake, and keep well.

115   He says no one but myself can help me out of it, that I must use my will and self-control and not let any silly fancies run away with me.

There's one comfort, the baby is well and happy, and does not have to occupy this nursery with the horrid wallpaper.

If we had not used it, that blessed child would have! What a fortunate escape! Why, I wouldn't have a child of mine, an impressionable little thing, live in such a room for worlds.

I never thought of it before, but it is lucky that John kept me here after all. I can stand it so much easier than a baby, you see.

Of course I never mention it to them any more—I am too wise,—but I keep watch of it all the same.

120   There are things in that paper that nobody knows but me, or ever will.

Behind that outside pattern the dim shapes get clearer every day.

It is always the same shape, only very numerous.

And it is like a woman stooping down and creeping about behind that pattern. I don't like it a bit. I wonder—I begin to think—I wish John would take me away from here!

It is so hard to talk with John about my case, because he is so wise, and because he loves me so.

125   But I tried last night.

It was moonlight. The moon shines in all around just as the sun does.

I hate to see it sometimes, it creeps so slowly, and always comes in by one window or another.

John was asleep and I hated to waken him, so I kept still and watched the moonlight on that undulating wallpaper till I felt creepy.

The faint figure behind seemed to shake the pattern, just as if she wanted to get out.

130   I got up softly and went to feel and see if the paper *did* move, and when I came back John was awake.

"What is it, little girl?" he said. "Don't go walking about like that—you'll get cold."

I thought it was a good time to talk, so I told him that I really was not gaining here, and that I wished he would take me away.

"Why darling!" said he, "our lease will be up in three weeks, and I can't see how to leave before."

"The repairs are not done at home, and I cannot possibly leave town just now. Of course if you were in any danger, I could and would, but you really are better, dear, whether you can see it or not. I am a doctor, dear, and I know. You are gaining flesh and color, your appetite is better, I feel really much easier about you."

135   "I don't weigh a bit more," said I, "nor as much: and my appetite may be better in the evening when you are here, but it is worse in the morning when you are away!"

"Bless her little heart!" said he with a big hug, "she shall be as sick as she pleases! But now let's improve the shining hours by going to sleep, and talk about it in the morning!"

"And you won't go away?" I asked gloomily.

"Why, how can I, dear? It is only three weeks more and then we will take a nice little trip of a few days while Jennie is getting the house ready. Really dear you are better!"

"Better in body perhaps—" I began, and stopped short, for he sat up straight and looked at me with such a stern, reproachful look that I could not say another word.

140   "My darling," said he, "I beg of you, for my sake and for our child's sake, as well as for your own, that you will never for one instant let that idea enter your mind! There is nothing so dangerous, so fascinating, to a temperament like yours. It is a false and foolish fancy. Can you not trust me as a physician when I tell you so?"

So of course I said no more on that score, and we went to sleep before long. He thought I was asleep first, but I wasn't and lay there for hours trying to decide whether that front pattern and the back pattern really did move together or separately.

On a pattern like this, by daylight, there is a lack of sequence, a defiance of law, that is a constant irritant to a normal mind.

The color is hideous enough, and unreliable enough, and infuriating enough, but the pattern is torturing.

You think you have mastered it, but just as you get well underway in following, it turns a back-somersault and there you are. It slaps you in the face, knocks you down, and tramples upon you. It is like a bad dream.

145   The outside pattern is a florid arabesque, reminding one of a fungus. If you can imagine a toadstool in joints, an interminable string of toadstools, budding and sprouting in endless convolutions—why, that is something like it.

That is, sometimes!

There is one marked peculiarity about this paper, a thing nobody seems to notice but myself, and that is that it changes as the light changes.

When the sun shoots in through the east window—I always watch for that first long, straight ray—it changes so quickly that I never can quite believe it.

That is why I watch it always.

150   By moonlight—the moon shines in all night when there is a moon—I wouldn't know it was the same paper.

At night in any kind of light, in twilight, candle light, lamplight, and worst of all by moonlight, it becomes bars! The outside pattern I mean, and the woman behind it is as plain as can be.

I didn't realize for a long time what the thing was that showed behind, that dim sub-pattern, but now I am quite sure it is a woman.

By daylight she is subdued, quiet. I fancy it is the pattern that keeps her so still. It is so puzzling. It keeps me quiet by the hour.

I lie down ever so much now. John says it is good for me, and to sleep all I can.

155   Indeed he started the habit by making me lie down for an hour after each meal.

It is a very bad habit I am convinced, for you see I don't sleep.

And that cultivates deceit, for I don't tell them I'm awake—O no!

The fact is I am getting a little afraid of John.

He seems very queer sometimes, and even Jennie has an inexplicable look.

160   It strikes me occasionally, just as a scientific hypothesis—that perhaps it is the paper!

I have watched John when he did not know I was looking, and come into the room suddenly on the most innocent excuses, and I've caught him several times *looking at the paper!* And Jennie too. I caught Jennie with her hand on it once.

She didn't know I was in the room, and when I asked her in a quiet, a very quiet voice, with the most restrained manner possible, what she was doing with the paper—she turned around as if she had been caught stealing, and looked quite angry—asked me why I should frighten her so!

Then she said that the paper stained everything it touched, that she had found yellow smooches on all my clothes and John's, and she wished we would be more careful!

Did not that sound innocent? But I know she was studying that pattern, and I am determined that nobody shall find it out but myself!

165   Life is very much more exciting now than it used to be. You see I have something more to expect, to look forward to, to watch. I really do eat better, and am more quiet than I was.

John is so pleased to see me improve! He laughed a little the other day, and said I seemed to be flourishing in spite of my wallpaper.

I turned it off with a laugh. I had no intention of telling him it was *because* of the wallpaper—he would make fun of me. He might even want to take me away.

I don't want to leave now until I have found it out. There is a week more, and I think that will be enough.

I'm feeling ever so much better! I don't sleep much at night, for it is so interesting to watch developments, but I sleep a good deal in the daytime.

170   In the daytime it is tiresome and perplexing.

There are always new shoots on the fungus, and new shades of yellow all over it. I cannot keep count of them, though I have tried conscientiously.

It is the strangest yellow, that wallpaper! It makes me think of all the yellow things I ever saw—not beautiful ones like buttercups, but old foul, bad yellow things.

But there is something else about that paper—the smell! I noticed it the moment we came into the room, but with so much air and sun it was not bad. Now we have had a week of fog and rain, and whether the windows are open or not, the smell is here.

It creeps all over the house.

175   I find it hovering in the dining-room, skulking in the parlor, hiding in the hall, lying in wait for me on the stairs.

It gets into my hair.

Even when I go to ride, if I turn my head suddenly and surprise it—there is that smell!

Such a peculiar odor, too! I have spent hours in trying to analyze it, to find what it smelled like.

It is not bad—at first, and very gentle, but quite the subtlest, most enduring odor I ever met.

180   In this damp weather it is awful, I wake up in the night and find it hanging over me.

It used to disturb me at first. I thought seriously of burning the house—to reach the smell.

But now I am used to it. The only thing I can think of that it is like is the *color* of the paper! A yellow smell.

There is a very funny mark on this wall, low down, near the mopboard. A streak that runs round the room. It goes behind every piece of furniture, except the bed, a long, straight, even *smooch,* as if it had been rubbed over and over.

I wonder how it was done and who did it, and what they did it for. Round and round and round—round and round and round—it makes me dizzy!

185   I really have discovered something at last.

Through watching so much at night, when it changes so, I have finally found out.

The front pattern *does* move—and no wonder! The woman behind shakes it!

Sometimes I think there are a great many women behind, and sometimes only one, and she crawls around fast, and her crawling shakes it all over.

Then in the very bright spots she keeps still, and in the very shady spots she just takes hold of the bars and shakes them hard.

190   And she is all the time trying to climb through. But nobody could climb through that pattern—it strangles so: I think that is why it has so many heads.

They get through, and then the pattern strangles them off and turns them upside down, and makes their eyes white!

If those heads were covered or taken off it would not be half so bad.

I think that woman gets out in the daytime!

And I'll tell you why—privately—I've seen her!

195   I can see her out of every one of my windows!

It is the same woman, I know, for she is always creeping, and most women do not creep by daylight.

I see her on that long road under the trees, creeping along, and when a carriage comes she hides under the blackberry vines.

I don't blame her a bit. It must be very humiliating to be caught creeping by daylight!

I always lock the door when I creep by daylight. I can't do it at night, for I know John would suspect something at once.

200   And John is so queer now, that I don't want to irritate him. I wish he would take another room! Besides, I don't want anybody to get that woman out at night but myself.

I often wonder if I could see her out of all the windows at once.

But, turn as fast as I can, I can only see out of one at one time. And though I always see her, she *may* be able to creep faster than I can turn!

I have watched her sometimes away off in the open country, creeping as fast as a cloud shadow in a high wind.

If only that top pattern could be gotten off from the under one! I mean to try it, little by little.

205   I have found out another funny thing, but I shan't tell at this time! It does not do to trust people too much.

There are only two more days to get this paper off, and I believe John is beginning to notice. I don't like the look in his eyes.

And I heard him ask Jennie a lot of professional questions about me. She had a very good report to give.

She said I slept a good deal in the daytime.

John knows I don't sleep very well at night, for all I'm so quiet!

210   He asked me all sorts of questions, too, and pretended to be very loving and kind.

As if I couldn't see through him!

Still, I don't wonder he acts so, sleeping under this paper for three months.

It only interests me, but I feel sure John and Jennie are secretly affected by it.

Hurrah! This is the last day, but it is enough. John is to stay in town over night, and won't be out until this evening.

215   Jennie wanted to sleep with me—the sly thing! But I told her I should undoubtedly rest better for a night all alone.

That was clever, for really I wasn't alone a bit! As soon as it was moonlight and that poor thing began to crawl and shake the pattern, I got up and ran to help her.

I pulled and she shook, I shook and she pulled, and before morning we had peeled off yards of that paper.

A strip about as high as my head and half round the room. And then when the sun came and that awful pattern began to laugh at me, I declared I would finish it to-day!

We go away to-morrow, and they are moving all the furniture down again to leave things as they were before.

220   Jennie looked at the wall in amazement, but I told her merrily that I did it out of pure spite at the vicious thing.

She laughed and said she wouldn't mind doing it herself, but I must not get tired.

How she betrayed herself that time!

But I am here, and no person touches this paper but me—not *alive!*

She tried to get me out of the room—it was too patent! But I said it was so quiet and empty and clean now that I believed I would lie down again and sleep all I could; and not to wake me even for dinner—I would call when I woke.

225   So now she is gone, and the servants are gone, and the things are gone, and there is nothing left but that great bedstead nailed down, with the canvas mattress we found on it.

We shall sleep downstairs to-night, and take the boat home to-morrow.

I quite enjoy the room, now it is bare again.

How those children did tear about here!

This bedstead is fairly gnawed!

230   But I must get to work.

I have locked the door and thrown the key down into the front path.

I don't want to go out, and I don't want to have anybody come in, till John comes.

I want to astonish him.

I've got a rope up here that even Jennie did not find. If that woman does get out, and tries to get away, I can tie her!

235   But I forgot I could not reach far without anything to stand on! This bed will *not* move!

I tried to lift and push it until I was lame, and then I got so angry I bit off a little piece at one corner—but it hurt my teeth.

Then I peeled off all the paper I could reach standing on the floor. It sticks horribly and the pattern just enjoys it! All those strangled heads and bulbous eyes and waddling fungus growths just shriek with derision!

I am getting angry enough to do something desperate. To jump out of the window would be admirable exercise, but the bars are too strong even to try.

Besides I wouldn't do it. Of course not, I know well enough that a step like that is improper and might be misconstrued.

240   I don't like to *look* out of the windows even—there are so many of those creeping women, and they creep so fast.

I wonder if they all come out of that wallpaper as I did?

But I am securely fastened now by my well-hidden rope—you don't get *me* out in the road there!

I suppose I shall have to get back behind the pattern when it comes night, and that is hard!

It is so pleasant to be out in this great room and creep around as I please!

245   I don't want to go outside. I won't, even if Jennie asks me to.

For outside you have to creep on the ground, and everything is green instead of yellow.

But here I can creep smoothly on the floor, and my shoulder just fits in that long smooch around the wall, so I cannot lose my way.

Why there's John at the door!

It is no use, young man, you can't open it!

250   How he does call and pound!

Now he's crying for an axe.

It would be a shame to break down that beautiful door!

"John dear!" said I in the gentlest voice, "the key is down by the front steps, under a plantain leaf!"

That silenced him for a few moments.

255   Then he said—very quietly indeed, "Open the door, my darling!"

"I can't," said I. "The key is down by the front door under a plantain leaf!"

And then I said it again, several times, very gently and slowly, and said it so often that he had to go and see, and he got it of course, and came in. He stopped short by the door.

"What is the matter?" he cried. "For God's sake, what are you doing!"

I kept on creeping just the same, but I looked at him over my shoulder.

260   "I've got out at last," said I, "in spite of you and Jane. And I've pulled off most of the paper, so you can't put me back!"

Now why should that man have fainted? But he did, and right across my path by the wall, so that I had to creep over him every time!

[1892]

Topics for Critical Thinking and Writing

1. Is the narrator insane at the start of the story, or does she become insane at some point during the narrative? Or can't we be sure? Support your view with evidence from the story.

2. How reliable do you think the narrator's characterization of her husband is? Support your answer with reasons.

3. The narrator says that she cannot get better because her husband is a physician. What do you take this to mean? Do you think the story is about a husband who deliberately drives his wife insane?

LANGSTON HUGHES

Langston Hughes (1902–67), an African American writer, was born in Joplin, Missouri. He lived part of his youth in Mexico, spent a year at Columbia University, served as a merchant seaman, and worked in a Paris nightclub. After returning to the United States, he showed some of his poems to Dr. Alain Locke, a strong advocate of African American literature. Encouraged by Locke, Hughes continued to write, publishing fiction, plays, essays, and biographies; he also founded theaters, gave public readings, and was, in short, a highly visible presence.

One Friday Morning

The thrilling news did not come directly to Nancy Lee, but it came in little indirections that finally added themselves up to one tremendous fact: she had won the prize! But being a calm and quiet young lady, she did not say anything, although the whole high school buzzed with rumors, guesses, reportedly authentic announcements on the part of students who had no right to be making announcements at all—since no student really knew yet who had won this year's art scholarship.

But Nancy Lee's drawing was so good, her lines so sure, her colors so bright and harmonious, that certainly no other student in the senior art class at George Washington High was thought to have very much of a chance. Yet you never could tell. Last year nobody had expected Joe Williams to win the Artist Club scholarship with that funny modernistic water color he had done of the high-level bridge. In fact, it was hard to make out there was a bridge until you had looked at the picture a long time. Still, Joe Williams got the prize, was feted by the community's leading painters, club women, and society folks at a big banquet at the Park-Rose Hotel, and was now an award student at the Art School—the city's only art school.

Nancy Lee Johnson was a colored girl, a few years out of the South. But seldom did her high-school classmates think of her as colored. She was smart, pretty, and brown, and fitted in well with the life of the school. She stood high in scholarship, played a swell game of basketball, had taken part in the senior musical in a soft, velvety voice, and had never seemed to intrude or stand out, except in pleasant ways, so it was seldom even mentioned—her color.

Nancy Lee sometimes forgot she was colored herself. She liked her classmates and her school. Particularly she liked her art teacher, Miss Dietrich, the tall red-haired woman who taught her law and order in doing things; and the beauty of working step by step until a job is done; a picture finished; a design created; or a block print carved out of nothing but an idea and a smooth square of linoleum, inked, proofs made, and finally put down on paper—clean, sharp, beautiful, individual, unlike any other in the world, thus making the paper have a meaning nobody else could give it except Nancy Lee. That was the wonderful thing about true creation. You made something nobody else on earth could make—but you.

5   Miss Dietrich was the kind of teacher who brought out the best in her students—but their own best, not anybody else's copied best. For anybody else's
best, great though it might be, even Michelangelo's, wasn't enough to please Miss
Dietrich, dealing with the creative impulses of young men and women living in an
American city in the Middle West, and being American.

Nancy Lee was proud of being American, a Negro American with blood out
of Africa a long time ago, too many generations back to count. But her parents
had taught her the beauties of Africa, its strength, its song, its mighty rivers, its
early smelting of iron, its building of the pyramids, and its ancient and important
civilizations. And Miss Dietrich had discovered for her the sharp and humorous
lines of African sculpture, Benin, Congo, Makonde. Nancy Lee's father was a mail
carrier, her mother a social worker in a city settlement house. Both parents had
been to Negro colleges in the South. And her mother had gotten a further degree
in social work from a Northern university. Her parents were, like most Americans,
simple, ordinary people who had worked hard and steadily for their education.
Now they were trying to make it easier for Nancy Lee to achieve learning than it
had been for them. They would be very happy when they heard of the award to
their daughter—yet Nancy did not tell them. To surprise them would be better.
Besides, there had been a promise.

Casually, one day, Miss Dietrich asked Nancy Lee what color frame she
thought would be best on her picture. That had been the first inkling.

"Blue," Nancy Lee said. Although the picture had been entered in the Artist
Club contest a month ago, Nancy Lee did not hesitate in her choice of a color for
the possible frame, since she could still see her picture clearly in her mind's eye—
for that picture waiting for the blue frame had come out of her soul, her own life,
and had bloomed into miraculous being with Miss Dietrich's help. It was, she
knew, the best water color she had painted in her four years as a high-school art
student, and she was glad she had made something Miss Dietrich liked well
enough to permit her to enter in the contest before she graduated.

It was not a modernistic picture in the sense that you had to look at it a long
time to understand what it meant. It was just a simple scene in the city park on a
spring day, with the trees still leaflessly lacy against the sky, the new grass fresh
and green, a flag on a tall pole in the center, children playing, and an old Negro
woman sitting on a bench with her head turned. A lot for one picture, to be sure,
but it was not there in heavy and final detail like a calendar. Its charm was that
everything was light and airy, happy like spring, with a lot of blue sky; paper-
white clouds, and air showing through. You could tell that the old Negro woman
was looking at the flag, and that the flag was proud in the spring breeze, and that
the breeze helped to make the children's dresses billow as they played.

10   Miss Dietrich had taught Nancy Lee how to paint spring, people, and a breeze
on what was only a plain white piece of paper from the supply closet. But Miss
Dietrich had not said make it like any other spring-people-breeze ever seen before. She let it remain Nancy Lee's own. That is how the old Negro woman happened to be there looking at the flag—for in her mind the flag, the spring, and the
woman formed a kind of triangle holding a dream Nancy Lee wanted to express.
White stars on a blue field, spring, children, ever-growing life, and an old woman.
Would the judges at the Artist Club like it?

One wet, rainy April afternoon Miss O'Shay, the girls' vice-principal, sent for
Nancy Lee to stop by her office as school closed. Pupils without umbrellas or rain-
coats were clustered in doorways, hoping to make it home between showers.
Outside the skies were gray. Nancy Lee's thoughts were suddenly gray, too.

She did not think she had done anything wrong, yet that tight little knot came in her throat just the same as she approached Miss O'Shay's door. Perhaps she had banged her locker too often and too hard. Perhaps the note in French she had written to Sallie halfway across the study hall just for fun had never gotten to Sallie but into Miss O'Shay's hands instead. Or maybe she was failing in some subject and wouldn't be allowed to graduate. Chemistry! A pang went through the pit of her stomach.

She knocked on Miss O'Shay's door. That familiarly solid and competent voice said, "Come in."

Miss O'Shay had a way of making you feel welcome, even if you came to be expelled.

15   "Sit down, Nancy Lee Johnson," said Miss O'Shay. "I have something to tell you." Nancy Lee sat down. "But I must ask you to promise not to tell anyone yet."

"I won't, Miss O'Shay," Nancy Lee said, wondering what on earth the principal had to say to her.

"You are about to graduate," Miss O'Shay said. "And we shall miss you. You have been an excellent student, Nancy, and you will not be without honors on the senior list, as I am sure you know."

At that point there was a light knock on the door. Miss O'Shay called out, "Come in," and Miss Dietrich entered. "May I be a part of this, too?" she asked, tall and smiling.

"Of course," Miss O'Shay said. "I was just telling Nancy Lee what we thought of her. But I hadn't gotten around to giving her the news. Perhaps, Miss Dietrich, you'd like to tell her yourself."

20   Miss Dietrich was always direct. "Nancy Lee," she said, "your picture has won the Artist Club scholarship."

The slender brown girl's eyes widened, her heart jumped, then her throat tightened again. She tried to smile, but instead tears came to her eyes.

"Dear Nancy Lee," Miss O'Shay said, "we are so happy for you." The elderly white woman took her hand and shook it warmly while Miss Dietrich beamed with pride.

Nancy Lee must have danced all the way home. She never remembered quite how she got there through the rain. She hoped she had been dignified. But certainly she hadn't stopped to tell anybody her secret on the way. Raindrops, smiles, and tears mingled on her brown cheeks. She hoped her mother hadn't yet gotten home and that the house was empty. She wanted to have time to calm down and look natural before she had to see anyone. She didn't want to be bursting with excitement—having a secret to contain.

Miss O'Shay's calling her to the office had been in the nature of a preparation and a warning. The kind, elderly vice-principal said she did not believe in catching young ladies unawares, even with honors, so she wished her to know about the coming award. In making acceptance speeches she wanted her to be calm, prepared, not nervous, overcome, and frightened. So Nancy Lee was asked to think what she would say when the scholarship was conferred upon her a few days hence, both at the Friday morning high-school assembly hour, when the announcement would be made, and at the evening banquet of the Artist Club. Nancy Lee promised the vice-principal to think calmly about what she would say.

25   Miss Dietrich had then asked for some facts about her parents, her background, and her life, since such material would probably be desired for the papers. Nancy Lee had told her how, six years before, they had come up from the Deep South, her father having been successful in achieving a transfer from the

one post office to another, a thing he had long sought in order to give Nancy Lee a chance to go to school in the North. Now they lived in a modest Negro neighborhood, went to see the best plays when they came to town, and had been saving to send Nancy Lee to art school, in case she were permitted to enter. But the scholarship would help a great deal, for they were not rich people.

"Now Mother can have a new coat next winter," Nancy Lee thought, "because my tuition will all be covered for the first year. And once in art school, there are other scholarships I can win."

Dreams began to dance through her head, plans and ambitions, beauties she would create for herself, her parents, and the Negro people—for Nancy Lee possessed a deep and reverent race pride. She could see the old woman in her picture (really her grandmother in the South) lifting her head to the bright stars on the flag in the distance. A Negro in America! Often hurt, discriminated against, sometimes lynched—but always there were the stars on the blue body of the flag. Was there any other flag in the world that had so many stars? Nancy Lee thought deeply, but she could remember none in all the encyclopedias or geographies she had ever looked into.

"Hitch your wagon to a star," Nancy Lee thought, dancing home in the rain. "Who were our flag-makers?"

Friday morning came, the morning when the world would know—her high-school world, the newspaper world, her mother and dad. Dad could not be there at the assembly to hear the announcement, nor see her prize picture displayed on the stage, nor to listen to Nancy Lee's little speech of acceptance, but Mother would be able to come, although Mother was much puzzled as to why Nancy Lee was so insistent she be at school on that particular Friday morning.

30   When something is happening, something new and fine, something that will change your very life, it is hard to go to sleep at night for thinking about it, and hard to keep your heart from pounding, or a strange little knot of joy from gathering in your throat. Nancy Lee had taken her bath, brushed her hair until it glowed, and had gone to bed thinking about the next day, the big day, when before three thousand students, she would be the one student honored, her painting the one painting to be acclaimed as the best of the year from all the art classes of the city. Her short speech of gratitude was ready. She went over it in her mind, not word for word (because she didn't want it to sound as if she had learned it by heart), but she let the thoughts flow simply and sincerely through her consciousness many times.

When the president of the Artist Club presented her with the medal and scroll of the scholarship award, she would say:

"Judges and members of the Artist Club. I want to thank you for this award that means so much to me personally and through me to my people, the colored people of this city, who, sometimes, are discouraged and bewildered, thinking that color and poverty are against them. I accept this award with gratitude and pride, not for myself alone, but for my race that believes in American opportunity and American fairness—and the bright stars in our flag. I thank Miss Dietrich and the teachers who made it possible for me to have the knowledge and training that lie behind this honor you have conferred upon my painting. When I came here from the South a few years ago, I was not sure how you would receive me. You received me well. You have given me a chance and helped me along the road I wanted to follow. I suppose the judges know that every week here at assembly the students of this school pledge allegiance to the flag. I shall try to be worthy of that pledge, and of the help and friendship and understanding of my fellow citizens of whatever race or creed, and of our American dream of 'Liberty and justice for all'!"

That would be her response before the students in the morning. How proud and happy the Negro pupils would be, perhaps almost as proud as they were of the one colored star on the football team. Her mother would probably cry with happiness. Thus Nancy Lee went to sleep dreaming of a wonderful tomorrow.

The bright sunlight of an April morning woke her. There was breakfast with her parents—their half-amused and puzzled faces across the table, wondering what could be this secret that made her eyes so bright. The swift walk to school; the clock in the tower almost nine; hundreds of pupils streaming into the long, rambling old building that was the city's largest high school; the sudden quiet of the homeroom after the bell rang; then the teacher opening her record book to call the roll. But just before she began, she looked across the room until her eyes located Nancy Lee.

35   "Nancy," she said, "Miss O'Shay would like to see you in her office, please."

Nancy Lee rose and went out while the names were being called and the word *present* added its period to each name. Perhaps, Nancy Lee thought, the reporters from the papers had already come. Maybe they wanted to take her picture before assembly, which wasn't until ten o'clock. (Last year they had had the photograph of the winner of the award in the morning papers as soon as the announcement had been made.)

Nancy Lee knocked at Miss O'Shay's door.

"Come in."

The vice-principal stood at her desk. There was no one else in the room. It was very quiet.

40   "Sit down, Nancy Lee," she said. Miss O'Shay did not smile. There was a long pause. The seconds went by slowly. "I do not know how to tell you what I have to say," the elderly woman began, her eyes on the papers on her desk. "I am indignant and ashamed for myself and for this city." Then she lifted her eyes and looked at Nancy Lee in the neat blue dress, sitting there before her. "You are not to receive the scholarship this morning."

Outside in the hall the electric bells announcing the first period rang, loud and interminably long. Miss O'Shay remained silent. To the brown girl there in the chair, the room grew suddenly smaller, smaller, smaller, and there was no air. She could not speak.

Miss O'Shay said, "When the committee learned that you were colored, they changed their plans."

Still Nancy Lee said nothing, for there was no air to give breath to her lungs.

"Here is the letter from the committee, Nancy Lee." Miss O'Shay picked it up and read the final paragraph to her.

45   "'It seems to us wiser to arbitrarily rotate the award among the various high schools of the city from now on. And especially in this case since the student chosen happens to be colored, a circumstance which unfortunately, had we known, might have prevented this embarrassment. But there have never been any Negro students in the local art school, and the presence of one there might create difficulties for all concerned. We have high regard for the quality of Nancy Lee Johnson's talent, but we do not feel it would be fair to honor it with the Artist Club award.'" Miss O'Shay paused. She put the letter down.

"Nancy Lee, I am very sorry to have to give you this message."

"But my speech," Nancy Lee said, "was about. . . ." The words stuck in her throat. ". . . about America. . . ."

Miss O'Shay had risen; she turned her back and stood looking out the window at the spring tulips in the school yard.

"I thought, since the award would be made at assembly right after our oath of allegiance," the words tumbled almost hysterically from Nancy Lee's throat now, "I would put part of the flag salute in my speech. You know, Miss O'Shay, that part about 'liberty and justice for all.'"

50   "I know," said Miss O'Shay, slowly facing the room again. "But America is only what we who believe in it make it. I am Irish. You may not know, Nancy Lee, but years ago we were called the dirty Irish, and mobs rioted against us in the big cities, and we were invited to go back where we came from. But we didn't go. And we didn't give up, because we believed in the American dream, and in our power to make that dream come true. Difficulties, yes. Mountains to climb, yes. Discouragements to face, yes. Democracy to make, yes. That is it, Nancy Lee! We still have in this world of ours democracy to *make*. You and I, Nancy Lee. But the premise and the base are here, the lines of the Declaration of Independence and the words of Lincoln are here, and the stars in our flag. Those who deny you this scholarship do not know the meaning of those stars, but it's up to us to make them know. As a teacher in the public schools of this city, I myself will go before the school board and ask them to remove from our system the offer of any prizes or awards denied to any student because of race or color."

Suddenly Miss O'Shay stopped speaking. Her clear, clear blue eyes looked into those of the girl before her. The woman's eyes were full of strength and courage. "Lift up your head, Nancy Lee, and smile at me."

Miss O'Shay stood against the open window with the green lawn and the tulips beyond, the sunlight tangled in her gray hair, her voice an electric flow of strength to the hurt spirit of Nancy Lee. The Abolitionists who believed in freedom when there was slavery must have been like that. The first white teachers who went into the Deep South to teach the freed slaves must have been like that. All those who stand against ignorance, narrowness, hate, and mud on stars must be like that.

Nancy Lee lifted her head and smiled. The bell for assembly rang. She went through the long hall filled with students, toward the auditorium.

"There will be other awards," Nancy Lee thought. "There're schools in other cities. This won't keep me down. But when I'm a woman, I'll fight to see that these things don't happen to other girls as this has happened to me. And men and women like Miss O'Shay will help me."

55   She took her seat among the seniors. The doors of the auditorium closed. As the principal came onto the platform, the students rose and turned their eyes to the flag on the stage.

One hand went to the heart, the other outstretched toward the flag. Three thousand voices spoke. Among them was the voice of a dark girl whose cheeks were suddenly wet with tears, ". . . one nation indivisible, with liberty and justice for all."

"That is the land we must make," she thought.

[1941]

Topics for Critical Thinking and Writing

1. The third paragraph begins: "Nancy Lee Johnson was a colored girl. . . ." How would your response to the opening of the story change if this paragraph were placed at the very beginning?

2. Nancy Lee takes pride in her identity as both a "Negro" and an "American." How does she define and understand each of these terms? Does she perceive them to be at all at odds with one another? Is she admirable in her convictions, or is she simply naive?

3. This is a story about racism, but it is also a study (and an affirmation) of American ideals and principles. What is your response to Miss O'Shay's inspiring words to Nancy Lee at the end of the story? What is Nancy Lee's response to them, and your response to her? Does Hughes succeed in making us believe in, and accept, Nancy Lee's feelings at the conclusion?

WILLIAM FAULKNER

William Faulkner (1897–1962) was brought up in Oxford, Mississippi. His great-grandfather had been a Civil War hero, and his father was treasurer of the University of Mississippi in Oxford; the family was no longer rich, but it was still respected. In 1918 he enrolled in the Royal Canadian Air Force, though he never saw overseas service. After the war he returned to Mississippi and went to the university for two years. He then moved to New Orleans, where he became friendly with Sherwood Anderson, who was already an established writer. In New Orleans Faulkner worked for the Times-Picayune; *still later, even after he had established himself as a major novelist with* The Sound and the Fury *(1929), he had to do some work in Hollywood in order to make ends meet. In 1950 he was awarded the Nobel Prize in Literature.*

Almost all of Faulkner's writing is concerned with the people of Yoknapatawpha, an imaginary county in Mississippi. "I discovered," he said, "that my own little postage stamp of native soil was worth writing about and that I would never live long enough to exhaust it." Though he lived for brief periods in Canada, New Orleans, New York, Hollywood, and Virginia (where he died), he spent most of his life in his native Mississippi.

A Rose for Emily

I

When Miss Emily Grierson died, our whole town went to her funeral: the men through a sort of respectful affection for a fallen monument, the women mostly out of curiosity to see the inside of her house, which no one save an old manservant—a combined gardener and cook—had seen in at least ten years.

It was a big, squarish frame house that had once been white, decorated with cupolas and spires and scrolled balconies in the heavily lightsome style of the seventies, set on what had once been our most select street. But garages and cotton gins had encroached and obliterated even the august names of that neighborhood; only Miss Emily's house was left, lifting its stubborn and coquettish decay above the cotton wagons and the gasoline pumps—an eyesore among eyesores. And now Miss Emily had gone to join the representatives of those august names where they lay in the cedar-bemused cemetery among the ranked and anonymous graves of Union and Confederate soldiers who fell at the battle of Jefferson.

Alive, Miss Emily had been a tradition, a duty, and a care; a sort of hereditary obligation upon the town, dating from that day in 1894 when Colonel Sartoris, the mayor—he who fathered the edict that no Negro woman should appear on the streets without an apron—remitted her taxes, the dispensation dating from the death of her father on into perpetuity. Not that Miss Emily would have accepted charity. Colonel Sartoris invented an involved tale to the effect that Miss Emily's father had loaned money to the town, which the town, as a matter of business, preferred this way of repaying. Only a man of Colonel Sartoris' generation and thought could have invented it, and only a woman could have believed it.

When the next generation, with its more modern ideas, became mayors and aldermen, this arrangement created some little dissatisfaction. On the first of the year they mailed her a tax notice. February came, and there was no reply. They wrote her a formal letter, asking her to call at the sheriff's office at her convenience. A week later the mayor wrote her himself, offering to call or to send his car for her, and received in reply a note on paper of an archaic shape, in a thin, flowing calligraphy in faded ink, to the effect that she no longer went out at all. The tax notice was also enclosed, without comment.

5   They called a special meeting of the Board of Aldermen. A deputation waited upon her, knocked at the door through which no visitor had passed since she ceased giving china-painting lessons eight or ten years earlier. They were admitted by the old Negro into a dim hall from which a staircase mounted into still more shadow. It smelled of dust and disuse—a close, dank smell. The Negro led them into the parlor. It was furnished in heavy, leather-covered furniture. When the Negro opened the blinds of one window they could see that the leather was cracked; and when they sat down, a faint dust rose sluggishly about their thighs, spinning with slow motes in the single sunray. On a tarnished gilt easel before the fireplace stood a crayon portrait of Miss Emily's father.

They rose when she entered—a small, fat woman in black, with a thin gold chain descending to her waist and vanishing into her belt, leaning on an ebony cane with a tarnished gold head. Her skeleton was small and spare; perhaps that was why what would have been merely plumpness in another was obesity in her. She looked bloated, like a body long submerged in motionless water, and of that pallid hue. Her eyes, lost in the fatty ridges of her face, looked like two small pieces of coal pressed into a lump of dough as they moved from one face to another while the visitors stated their errand.

She did not ask them to sit. She just stood in the door and listened quietly until the spokesman came to a stumbling halt. Then they could hear the invisible watch ticking at the end of the gold chain.

Her voice was dry and cold. "I have no taxes in Jefferson. Colonel Sartoris explained it to me. Perhaps one of you can gain access to the city records and satisfy yourselves."

"But we have. We are the city authorities, Miss Emily. Didn't you get a notice from the sheriff, signed by him?"

10   "I received a paper, yes," Miss Emily said. "Perhaps he considers himself the sheriff. . . . I have no taxes in Jefferson."

"But there is nothing on the books to show that, you see. We must go by the—"

"See Colonel Sartoris. I have no taxes in Jefferson."

"But, Miss Emily—"

"See Colonel Sartoris." (Colonel Sartoris had been dead almost ten years.) "I have no taxes in Jefferson. Tobe!" The Negro appeared. "Show these gentlemen out."

II

15   So she vanquished them, horse and foot, just as she had vanquished their fathers thirty years before about the smell. That was two years after her father's death and a short time after her sweetheart—the one we believed would marry her—had deserted her. After her father's death she went out very little; after her sweetheart went away, people hardly saw her at all. A few of the ladies had the temerity to call, but were not received, and the only sign of life about the place was the Negro man—a young man then—going in and out with a market basket.

"Just as if a man—any man—could keep a kitchen properly," the ladies said; so they were not surprised when the smell developed. It was another link between the gross, teeming world and the high and mighty Griersons.

A neighbor, a woman, complained to the mayor, Judge Stevens, eighty years old.

"But what will you have me do about it, madam?" he said.

"Why, send her word to stop it," the woman said. "Isn't there a law?"

20   "I'm sure that won't be necessary," Judge Stevens said. "It's probably just a snake or a rat that nigger of hers killed in the yard. I'll speak to him about it."

The next day he received two more complaints, one from a man who came in diffident deprecation. "We really must do something about it, Judge. I'd be the last one in the world to bother Miss Emily, but we've got to do something." That night the Board of Aldermen met—three graybeards and one younger man, a member of the rising generation.

"It's simple enough," he said. "Send her word to have her place cleaned up. Give her a certain time to do it in, and if she don't . . . "

"Dammit, sir," Judge Stevens said, "will you accuse a lady to her face of smelling bad?"

So the next night, after midnight, four men crossed Miss Emily's lawn and slunk about the house like burglars, sniffing along the base of the brickwork and at the cellar openings while one of them performed a regular sowing motion with his hand out of a sack slung from his shoulder. They broke open the cellar door and sprinkled lime there, and in all the out-buildings. As they recrossed the lawn, a window that had been dark was lighted and Miss Emily sat in it, the light behind her, and her upright torso motionless as that of an idol. They crept quietly across the lawn and into the shadow of the locusts that lined the street. After a week or two the smell went away.

25   That was when people had begun to feel really sorry for her. People in our town remembering how old lady Wyatt, her great-aunt, had gone completely crazy at last, believed that the Griersons held themselves a little too high for what they really were. None of the young men were quite good enough for Miss Emily and such. We had long thought of them as a tableau; Miss Emily a slender figure in white in the background, her father a spraddled silhouette in the foreground, his back to her and clutching a horsewhip, the two of them framed by the back-flung front door. So when she got to be thirty and was still single, we were not pleased exactly, but vindicated; even with insanity in the family she wouldn't have turned down all of her chances if they had really materialized.

When her father died, it got about that the house was all that was left to her; and in a way, people were glad. At last they could pity Miss Emily. Being left alone, and a pauper, she had become humanized. Now she too would know the old thrill and the old despair of a penny more or less.

The day after his death all the ladies prepared to call at the house and offer condolence and aid, as is our custom. Miss Emily met them at the door, dressed as usual and with no trace of grief on her face. She told them that her father was not dead. She did that for three days, with the ministers calling on her, and the doctors, trying to persuade her to let them dispose of the body. Just as they were about to resort to law and force, she broke down, and they buried her father quickly.

We did not say she was crazy then. We believed she had to do that. We remembered all the young men her father had driven away, and we knew that with nothing left, she would have to cling to that which had robbed her, as people will.

III

She was sick for a long time. When we saw her again, her hair was cut short, making her look like a girl, with a vague resemblance to those angels in colored church windows—sort of tragic and serene.

30   The town had just let the contracts for paving the sidewalks, and in the summer after her father's death they began to work. The construction company came with niggers and mules and machinery, and a foreman named Homer Barron, a Yankee—a big, dark, ready man, with a big voice and eyes lighter than his face. The little boys would follow in groups to hear him cuss the niggers, and the niggers singing in time to the rise and fall of picks. Pretty soon he knew everybody in town. Whenever you heard a lot of laughing anywhere about the square, Homer Barron would be in the center of the group. Presently we began to see him and Miss Emily on Sunday afternoons driving in the yellow-wheeled buggy and the matched team of bays from the livery stable.

At first we were glad that Miss Emily would have an interest, because the ladies all said, "Of course a Grierson would not think seriously of a Northerner, a day laborer." But there were still others, older people, who said that even grief could not cause a real lady to forget *noblesse oblige*—without calling it *noblesse oblige*. They just said, "Poor Emily. Her kinsfolk should come to her." She had some kin in Alabama; but years ago her father had fallen out with them over the estate of old lady Wyatt, the crazy woman, and there was no communication between the two families. They had not even been represented at the funeral.

And as soon as the old people said, "Poor Emily," the whispering began. "Do you suppose it's really so?" they said to one another. "Of course it is. . . ." This behind their hands; rustling of craned silk and satin behind jalousies closed upon the sun of Sunday afternoon as the thin, swift clop-clop-clop of the matched team passed: "Poor Emily."

She carried her head high enough—even when we believed that she was fallen. It was as if she demanded more than ever the recognition of her dignity as the last Grierson; as if it had wanted that touch of earthiness to reaffirm her imperviousness. Like when she bought the rat poison, the arsenic. That was over a year after they had begun to say "Poor Emily," and while the two female cousins were visiting her.

"I want some poison," she said to the druggist. She was over thirty then, still a slight woman, though thinner than usual, with cold, haughty black eyes in a face the flesh of which was strained across the temples and about the eyesockets as you imagine a lighthouse-keeper's face ought to look. "I want some poison," she said.

35   "Yes, Miss Emily. What kind? For rats and such? I'd recom—"

"I want the best you have. I don't care what kind."

The druggist named several. "They'll kill anything up to an elephant. But what you want is—"

"Arsenic," Miss Emily said. "Is that a good one?"

"Is . . . arsenic? Yes ma'am. But what you want—"

40   "I want arsenic."

The druggist looked down at her. She looked back at him, erect, her face like a strained flag. "Why, of course," the druggist said. "If that's what you want. But the law requires you to tell what you are going to use it for."

Miss Emily just stared at him, her head tilted back in order to look him eye for eye, until he looked away and went and got the arsenic and wrapped it up. The Negro delivery boy brought her the package; the druggist didn't come back. When she opened the package at home there was written on the box, under the skull and bones: "For rats."

IV

So the next day we all said, "She will kill herself"; and we said it would be the best thing. When she had first begun to be seen with Homer Barron, we had said, "She will marry him." Then we said, "She will persuade him yet," because Homer himself had remarked—he liked men, and it was known that he drank with the younger men in the Elks' Club—that he was not a marrying man. Later we said, "Poor Emily," behind the jalousies as they passed on Sunday afternoon in the glittering buggy, Miss Emily with her head high and Homer Barron with his hat cocked and a cigar in his teeth, reins and whip in a yellow glove.

Then some of the ladies began to say that it was a disgrace to the town and a bad example to the young people. The men did not want to interfere, but at last the ladies forced the Baptist minister—Miss Emily's people were Episcopal—to call upon her. He would never divulge what happened during that interview, but he refused to go back again. The next Sunday they again drove about the streets, and the following day the minister's wife wrote to Miss Emily's relations in Alabama.

45   So she had blood-kin under her roof again and we sat back to watch developments. At first nothing happened. Then we were sure that they were to be married. We learned that Miss Emily had been to the jeweler's and ordered a man's toilet set in silver, with the letters H.B. on each piece. Two days later we learned that she had bought a complete outfit of men's clothing, including a nightshirt, and we said, "They are married." We were really glad. We were glad because the two female cousins were even more Grierson than Miss Emily had ever been.

So we were surprised when Homer Barron—the streets had been finished some time since—was gone. We were a little disappointed that there was not a public blowing-off but we believed that he had gone on to prepare for Miss Emily's coming, or to give a chance to get rid of the cousins. (By that time it was a cabal, and we were all Miss Emily's allies to help circumvent the cousins.) Sure enough, after another week they departed. And, as we had expected all along, within three days Homer Barron was back in town. A neighbor saw the Negro man admit him at the kitchen door at dusk one evening.

And that was the last we saw of Homer Barron. And of Miss Emily for some time. The Negro man went in and out with the market basket, but the front door remained closed. Now and then we would see her at a window for a moment, as the men did that night when they sprinkled the lime, but for almost six months she did not appear on the streets. Then we knew that this was to be expected too; as if that quality of her father which had thwarted her woman's life so many times had been too virulent and too furious to die.

When we next saw Miss Emily, she had grown fat and her hair was turning gray. During the next few years it grew grayer and grayer until it attained an even pepper-and-salt iron-gray, when it ceased turning. Up to the day of her death at seventy-four it was still that vigorous iron-gray, like the hair of an active man.

From that time on her front door remained closed, save for a period of six or seven years, when she was about forty, during which she gave lessons in china-painting. She fitted up a studio in one of the downstairs rooms, where the daughters and granddaughters of Colonel Sartoris' contemporaries were sent to her with the same regularity and in the same spirit that they were sent on Sundays with a twenty-five cent piece for the collection plate. Meanwhile her taxes had been remitted.

50   Then the newer generation became the backbone and the spirit of the town, and the painting pupils grew up and fell away and did not send their children to her with boxes of color and tedious brushes and pictures cut from the ladies' magazines. The front door closed upon the last one and remained closed for good. When the town got free postal delivery Miss Emily alone refused to let them fasten the metal numbers above her door and attach a mailbox to it. She would not listen to them.

Daily, monthly, yearly we watched the Negro grow grayer and more stooped, going in and out with the market basket. Each December we sent her a tax notice, which would be returned by the post office a week later, un-claimed. Now and then we could see her in one of the downstairs windows—she had evidently shut up the top floor of the house—like the carven torso of an idol in a niche, looking or not looking at us, we could never tell which. Thus she passed from generation to generation—dear, inescapable, impervious, tranquil, and perverse.

And so she died. Fell ill in the house filled with dust and shadows, with only a doddering Negro man to wait on her. We did not even know she was sick; we had long since given up trying to get any information from the Negro. He talked to no one, probably not even to her, for his voice had grown harsh and rusty, as if from disuse.

She died in one of the downstairs rooms, in a heavy walnut bed with a curtain, her gray head propped on a pillow yellow and moldy with age and lack of sunlight.

V

The Negro met the first of the ladies at the front door and let them in, with their hushed, sibilant voices and their quick, curious glances, and then he disappeared. He walked right through the house and out the back and was not seen again.

55   The two female cousins came at once. They held the funeral on the second day, with the town coming to look at Miss Emily beneath a mass of bought flowers, with the crayon face of her father musing profoundly above the bier and the ladies sibilant and macabre; and the very old men—some in their brushed

dust and shadows, with only a doddering negro man to wait on
her. We did not even know she was sick; we had long since given up
trying to get any information from the negro. He talked to no
one, probably not even to her, for his voice had grown ~~harsh~~
harsh and ~~so~~ rusty, as though with disuse; the sparse words
which he did speak sounded as though he had learned them that
morning by rote---just enough of them to carry him through
the day.

     She died in one of the downstairs rooms, in a heavy
walnut bed with a curtain, her gray head propped on a pillow
yellow and moldy with age and lack of sunlight, her voice
cold and strong to the last.

     "But not till I'm gone," she said. "Dont you let a
soul in until I'm gone, do you hear?" Standing beside the bed,
his head in the dim light nimbused by a faint halo of napped,
perfectly white hair, the negro made a brief gesture with his
hand. Miss Emily lay with her eyes open, gazing into the opposite shadows of the room. Upon the coverlet her hands lay on
her breast, gnarled, blue with age, motionless. "Hah," she said.
"Then they can. Let 'em go up there and see what's in that
room. ~~And you let them just~~ Fools. And Let
'em. ~~And you let them~~ Satisfy their minds that
I am crazy. Do you think I am?" The negro made no reply, no
movement. He stood above the bed, ~~stooped, hunched like an~~
~~ape~~ motionless, musing: a secret and unfathomable soul behind
the death-mask of an ape and haloed like an angel. "Let 'em
go up there and open that door. And you wont be the last one,

                           13.

The printed version of Faulkner's "A Rose for Emily" omitted several passages of dialogue (shown here in pages 13 to 15 of the typed manuscript) between Miss Emily and her long-time manservant.

either. Will you?"

        "I wont have to," the negro said. "I know what's in
that room. I dont have to see."

        "Hah," Miss Emily said. "You do, do you. How long have
you known?" Again he made that brief sign with his hand. Miss
Emily had not turned her head. She stared into the shadows where
the high ceiling was lost. "You should be glad. Now you can go
to Chicago, like you've been talking about for thirty years. And
with what you'll get for the house and furniture.... Colonel Sartoris has the will. He'll see they dont rob you."

        "I dont want any house," the negro said.

        "You cant help yourself. It's signed and sealed thirty-
five years ago. Wasn't that our agreement when I found I couldn't
pay you any wages? that you were to have everything that was left
if you outlived me, and I was to bury you Ɱ₥₥ in a coffin with
your name on a gold plate if I outlived you?" He said nothing.
"Wasn't it?" Miss Emily said.

        "I was young then. Wanted to be rich. But now I dont
want any house."

        "Not when you have wanted to go to Chicago for thirty
years?" Their breathing was alike: each that harsh, rasping
breath of the old, the short inhalations that do not reach the
bottom of the lungs: tireless, precarious, on the verge of cessation for all time, as if anything might suffice: a word, a
look. "What are you going to do, then?"

        "Going to the poorhouse."

        "The poorhouse? When I'm trying to fix you so you'll

have neither to worry nor lift your hand as long as you live?

"I dont want nothing," the negro said. "I'm going t.
the poorhouse. I already told them."

"Well," Miss Emily said. She had not moved her head,
not moved at all. "Do you mind telling me why you want to go
to the poorhouse?"

Again he mused. The room was still save for their brea
ing: it was as though they had both quitted all living and all
dying; all the travail of mortality and of breath. "So I can
set on that hill in the sun all day and watch them trains pass.
See them at night too, with the engine puffing and lights in
all the windows.

"Oh," Miss Emily said. Motionless, her knotted hands
lying on the yellowed coverlet beneath her chin and her chin
resting upon her breast, she appeared to muse intently, as
though she were listening to dissolution setting up within her.
"Hah," she said.

Then she died, and the negro met the first of the ladies at the front door and let them in, with their hushed sibilant voices and their quick curious glances, and he went on
to the back and disappeared. He walked right through the house
and out the back and was not seen again.

The two female cousins came at once. They held the
funeral on the second day, with the town coming to look at
Miss Emily beneath a mass of bought flowers, with the crayon
face of her father musing profoundly above the bier and the la-

15.

grin cemented into what had once been a pillow by a substance like
hardened sealing-wax. One side of the covers was flung back, as
though he were preparing to rise; we lifted the covers completely
away, liberating still another sluggish cloud of infinitesimal
dust, invisible and tainted. The body had apparently once lain
in the attitude of an embrace, but now the long sleep that outlasts love, that conquers even the grimace of love, had cuckolded
him: what was left of him lay beneath what was left of the
nightshirt, become inextricable with the bed in which he lay,
and upon him and upon the pillow beside him lay that even coating of the patient and biding dust. /¶/ Then we noticed that in
the second pillow was the indentation of a head; one of us
lifted something from it, and leaning forward, that faint and
invisible dust lean and acrid in the nostrils, we saw a long
strand of iron-gray hair.

The final paragraph of the typed manuscript was reworded and made into two paragraphs
in the published version.

Confederate uniforms—on the porch and the lawn, talking of Miss Emily as if she had been a contemporary of theirs, believing that they had danced with her and courted her perhaps, confusing time with its mathematical progression, as the old do, to whom all the past is not a diminishing road, but, instead, a huge meadow which no winter ever quite touches, divided from them now by the narrow bottleneck of the most recent decade of years.

Already we knew that there was one room in that region above stairs which no one had seen in forty years, and which would have to be forced. They waited until Miss Emily was decently in the ground before they opened it.

The violence of breaking down the door seemed to fill this room with pervading dust. A thin, acrid pall as of the tomb seemed to lie everywhere upon this room decked and furnished as for a bridal: upon the valance curtains of faded rose color, upon the rose-shaded lights, upon the dressing table, upon the delicate array of crystal and the man's toilet things backed with tarnished silver, silver so tarnished that the monogram was obscured. Among them lay a collar and tie, as if they had just been removed, which, lifted, left upon the surface a pale crescent in the dust. Upon a chair hung the suit, carefully folded; beneath it the two mute shoes and the discarded socks.

The man himself lay in the bed.

For a long while we just stood there, looking down at the profound and fleshless grin. The body had apparently once lain in the attitude of an embrace, but now the long sleep that outlasts love, that conquers even the grimace of love, had cuckolded him. What was left of him, rotted beneath what was left of the nightshirt, had become inextricable from the bed in which he lay; and upon him and upon the pillow beside him lay that even coating of the patient and biding dust.

60   Then we noticed that in the second pillow was the indentation of a head. One of us lifted something from it, and leaning forward, that faint and invisible dust dry and acrid in the nostrils, we saw a long strand of iron-gray hair.

[1930]

Topics for Critical Thinking and Writing

1. Why does the narrator begin with what is almost the end of the story—the death of Miss Emily—rather than save this information for later? What devices does Faulkner use to hold the reader's interest throughout?
2. In a paragraph, offer a conjecture about Miss Emily's attitudes toward Homer Barron after he was last seen alive.
3. In a paragraph or two, characterize Miss Emily, calling attention not only to her eccentricities or even craziness, but also to what you conjecture to be her moral values.
4. In paragraph 44 we are told that the Baptist minister "would never divulge what happened" during the interview with Miss Emily. Why do you suppose Faulkner does not narrate or describe the interview? Let's assume that in his first draft of the story he *did* give a paragraph of narration or a short dramatic scene. Write such an episode.

5. Suppose that Homer Barron's remains had been discovered before Miss Emily died, and that she was arrested and charged with murder. You are the prosecutor and you are running for a statewide political office. In 500 words, set forth your argument that—despite the fact that she is a public monument—she should be convicted. Or: You are the defense attorney, also running for office. In 500 words, set forth your defense.
6. Assume that Miss Emily kept a journal—perhaps even from her days as a young girl. Write some entries for the journal, giving her thoughts about some of the episodes reported in Faulkner's story.

EUDORA WELTY

Eudora Welty (1909–2001) was born in Jackson, Mississippi. Although she earned a bachelor's degree at the University of Wisconsin, and she spent a year studying advertising in New York City at the Columbia University Graduate School of Business, she lived almost all of her life in Jackson.

In the preface to her Collected Stories *she says:*

I have been told, both in approval and in accusation, that I seem to love all my characters. What I do in writing of any character is to try to enter into the mind, heart and skin of a human being who is not myself. Whether this happens to be a man or a woman, old or young, with skin black or white, the primary challenge lies in making the jump itself. It is the act of a writer's imagination that I set most high.

In addition to writing stories and novels, Welty wrote a book about fiction, The Eye of the Story *(1977), and a memoir,* One Writer's Beginnings *(1984).*

A Worn Path

It was December—a bright frozen day in the early morning. Far out in the country there was an old Negro woman with her head tied in a red rag, coming along a path through the pinewoods. Her name was Phoenix Jackson. She was very old and small and she walked slowly in the dark pine shadows, moving a little from side to side in her steps, with the balanced heaviness and lightness of a pendulum in a grandfather clock. She carried a thin, small cane made from an umbrella, and with this she kept tapping the frozen earth in front of her. This made a grave and persistent noise in the still air, that seemed meditative like the chirping of a solitary little bird.

She wore a dark striped dress reaching down to her shoe tops, and an equally long apron of bleached sugar sacks, with a full pocket: all neat and tidy, but every time she took a step she might have fallen over her shoelaces, which dragged from her unlaced shoes. She looked straight ahead. Her eyes were blue with age. Her skin had a pattern all its own of numberless branching wrinkles and as though a whole little tree stood in the middle of her forehead, but a golden color ran underneath, and the two knobs of her cheeks were illuminated by a yellow burning under the dark. Under the red rag her hair came down on her neck in the frailest of ringlets, still black, and with an odor like copper.

Now and then there was a quivering in the thicket. Old Phoenix said, "Out of my way, all you foxes, owls, beetles, jack rabbits, coons, and wild animals! . . . Keep out from under these feet, little bob-whites. . . . Keep the big wild hogs out of my path. Don't let none of those come running my direction. I got a long way." Under her small black-freckled hand her cane, limber as a buggy whip, would switch at the brush as if to rouse up any hiding things.

On she went. The woods were deep and still. The sun made the pine needles almost too bright to look at, up where the wind rocked. The cones dropped as light as feathers. Down in the hollow was the mourning dove—it was not too late for him.

5   The path ran up a hill. "Seem like there is chains about my feet, time I get this far," she said, in the voice of argument old people keep to use with themselves. "Something always take a hold of me on this hill—pleads I should stay."

After she got to the top she turned and gave a full, severe look behind her where she had come. "Up through pines," she said at length. "Now down through oaks."

Her eyes opened their widest, and she started down gently. But before she got to the bottom of the hill a bush caught her dress.

Her fingers were busy and intent, but her skirts were full and long, so that before she could pull them free in one place they were caught in another. It was not possible to allow the dress to tear. "I in the thorny bush," she said. "Thorns, you doing your appointed work. Never want to let folks pass—no sir. Old eyes thought you was a pretty little *green* bush."

Finally, trembling all over, she stood free, and after a moment dared to stoop for her cane.

10   "Sun so high!" she cried, leaning back and looking, while the thick tears went over her eyes. "The time getting all gone here."

At the foot of this hill was a place where a log was laid across the creek.

"Now comes the trial," said Phoenix.

Putting her right foot out, she mounted the log and shut her eyes. Lifting her skirt, levelling her cane fiercely before her, like a festival figure in some parade, she began to march across. Then she opened her eyes and she was safe on the other side.

"I wasn't as old as I thought," she said.

15   But she sat down to rest. She spread her skirts on the bank around her and folded her hands over her knees. Up above her was a tree in a pearly cloud of mistletoe. She did not dare to close her eyes, and when a little boy brought her a little plate with a slice of marble-cake on it she spoke to him. "That would be acceptable," she said. But when she went to take it there was just her own hand in the air.

So she left that tree, and had to go through a barbed-wire fence. There she had to creep and crawl, spreading her knees and stretching her fingers like a baby trying to climb the steps. But she talked loudly to herself: she could not let her dress be torn now, so late in the day, and she could not pay for having her arm or leg sawed off if she got caught fast where she was.

At last she was safe through the fence and risen up out in the clearing. Big dead trees, like black men with one arm, were standing in the purple stalks of the withered cotton field. There sat a buzzard.

"Who you watching?"

In the furrow she made her way along.

20   "Glad this not the season for bulls," she said, looking sideways, "and the good Lord made his snakes to curl up and sleep in the winter. A pleasure I don't see no two-headed snake coming around that tree, where it come once. It took a while to get by him, back in the summer."

She passed through the old cotton and went into a field of dead corn. It whispered and shook and was taller than her head. "Through the maze now," she said, for there was no path.

Then there was something tall, black, and skinny there, moving before her.

At first she took it for a man. It could have been a man dancing in the field. But she stood still and listened, and it did not make a sound. It was as silent as a ghost.

"Ghost," she said sharply, "who be you the ghost of? For I have heard of nary death close by."

25   But there was no answer—only the ragged dancing in the wind.

She shut her eyes, reached out her hand, and touched a sleeve. She found a coat and inside that an emptiness, cold as ice.

"You scarecrow," she said. Her face lighted. "I ought to be shut up for good," she said with laughter. "My senses is gone, I too old. I the oldest people I ever know. Dance, old scarecrow," she said, "while I dancing with you."

She kicked her foot over the furrow, and with mouth drawn down, shook her head once or twice in a little strutting way. Some husks blew down and whirled in streamers about her skirts.

Then she went on, parting her way from side to side with the cane, through the whispering field. At last she came to the end, to a wagon track where the silver grass blew between the red ruts. The quail were walking around like pullets, seeming all dainty and unseen.

30   "Walk pretty," she said. "This the easy place. This the easy going."

She followed the track, swaying through the quiet bare fields, through the little strings of trees silver in their dead leaves, past cabins silver from weather, with the doors and windows boarded shut, all like old women under a spell sitting there. "I walking in their sleep," she said, nodding her head vigorously.

In a ravine she went where a spring was silently flowing through a hollow log. Old Phoenix bent and drank. "Sweet-gum makes the water sweet," she said, and drank more. "Nobody know who made this well, for it was here when I was born."

The track crossed a swampy part where the moss hung as white as lace from every limb. "Sleep on, alligators, and blow your bubbles." Then the track went into the road.

Deep, deep the road went down between the high green-colored banks. Overhead the live-oaks met, and it was as dark as a cave.

35   A black dog with a lolling tongue came up out of the weeds by the ditch. She was meditating, and not ready, and when he came at her she only hit him a little with her cane. Over she went in the ditch, like a little puff of milk-weed.

Down there, her senses drifted away. A dream visited her, and she reached her hand up, but nothing reached down and gave her a pull. So she lay there and presently went to talking. "Old woman," she said to herself, "that black dog come up out of the weeds to stall you off, and now there he sitting on his fine tail, smiling at you."

A white man finally came [phoenix. She inclined her head in]
his dog on a chain. [s, but she could hear the gun] [on't you hear]
[came for the]

"Well, Granny!" he laughed

"Lying on my back like a [oak trees to the road like cur-] [rect and mo-]
said, reaching up her hand. [lled the river, and she saw a]

40   He lifted her up, gave he[rs of little black children whirled] [se said. "Tell]
broken, Granny?" [ls were ringing. She walked on.]

"No sir, them old dead we[re were red and green electric] [n across her]
had got her breath. "I thank yo[u turned on in the daytime. Old]

"Where do you live, Granny[distrusted her eyesight and de-] [forgot why I]
each other.

"Away back yonder, sir, be[people were passing by. A lady]

"On your way home?" [red-, green-, and silver-wrapped]

45   "No, sir, I going to town." [es in hot summer, and Phoenix] [giveness for] [o old at the]

"Why, that's too far! That's a [ducation. It]
something for my trouble." He [he held up her foot.] [forgot it in]
down a little closed claw. It was
terly to show it was dead. "Now[r out in the country, but wouldn'] [re voice to] [a little list.]

"I bound to go to town, mist[

He gave another laugh, fill[me put her packages down on the] [the same.]
people! Wouldn't miss going to t[es tightly.]

But something held Old Ph[Thank you, missy. I doesn't min[d] [swallow.]
into a fierce and different radiati[s out on the street."] [bund, and]
eyes a flashing nickel fall out of [ent into the big building and int[o]

50   "How old are you, Granny?"[round and around until her fee] [I have it,"]

"There is no telling, mister," s

Then she gave a little cry an[led up on the wall the documen] [aiting by]
here, dog! Look! Look at that d[framed in the gold frame, whic[h] [fer and it]
scared of nobody. He a big black[d.] [He wear]

"Watch me get rid of that cur,[and ceremonial stiffness over he] [ird. I re-]

Phoenix heard the dogs fight[[nduring]
sticks. She even heard a gunsho[nt who sat at the desk before he]
time, further and further forward[There was sweat on her face, th] [bottle of]
she were doing this in her sleep
The yellow palm of her hand ca[What's your name? We must hav[e] [it into]
slid down and along the ground [before? What seems to be the trou[]
care they would have in lifting an
straightened up, she stood erect,[e as if a fly were bothering her.] [a few]
bird flew by. Her lips moved. "[
stealing."

55   The man came back, and his [oid. "She doesn't come for herself—]
off that time," he said, and then h[s just as regular as clockwork. Sh] [el and]
Phoenix. [he bent down. "Well, Aunt Phoeni[x] [. She]

She stood straight and faced hi[you standing after your long trip]

"Doesn't the gun scare you?" h[e]

"No, sir, I seen plenty go off [the chair.] [y my]
done," she said, holding utterly still. [o be-]

He smiled, and shouldered the [iting,]
hundred years old, and scared of
money with me. But you take my [ght ahead, her face very solemn an] [ut of]
pen to you."

[941]

Topics for Critical Thinking and Writing

1. If you do not know the legend of the phoenix, look it up in a dictionary or, better, in an encyclopedia. Then carefully reread the story, to learn whether the story in any way connects with the legend.
2. What do you think of the hunter?
3. What would be lost if the episode (with all of its dialogue) of Phoenix falling into the ditch and being helped out of it by the hunter were omitted?
4. Is Christmas a particularly appropriate time in which to set the story? Why or why not?
5. What do you make of the title?

JOHN UPDIKE

John Updike (b. 1932) grew up in Shillington, Pennsylvania, where his father was a teacher and his mother was a writer. After receiving a B.A. degree from Harvard he studied drawing at Oxford for a year, but an offer from The New Yorker *magazine brought him back to the United States. He at first served as a reporter for the magazine, but soon began contributing poetry, essays, and fiction. Today he is one of America's most prolific and well-known writers.*

A & P

In walks these three girls in nothing but bathing suits. I'm in the third checkout slot, with my back to the door, so I don't see them until they're over by the bread. The one that caught my eye first was the one in the plaid green two-piece. She was a chunky kid, with a good tan and a sweet broad soft-looking can with those two crescents of white just under it, where the sun never seems to hit, at the top of the backs of her legs. I stood there with my hand on a box of HiHo crackers trying to remember if I rang it up or not. I ring it up again and the customer starts giving me hell. She's one of these cash-register-watchers, a witch about fifty with rouge on her cheekbones and no eyebrows, and I know it made her day to trip me up. She'd been watching cash registers for fifty years and probably never seen a mistake before.

By the time I got her feathers smoothed and her goodies into a bag—she gives me a little snort in passing, if she'd been born at the right time they would have burned her over in Salem—by the time I get her on her way the girls had circled around the bread and were coming back, without a pushcart, back my way along the counters, in the aisle between the checkouts and the Special bins. They didn't even have shoes on. There was this chunky one, with the two-piece—it was bright green and the seams on the bra were still sharp and her belly was still pretty pale so I guessed she just got it (the suit)—there was this one, with one of those chubby berry-faces, the lips all bunched together under her nose, this one, and a tall one, with black hair that hadn't quite frizzed right, and one of these sunburns right across under the eyes, and a chin that was too long—you know, the kind of girl other girls think is very "striking" and "attractive" but never quite makes it, as they very well know, which is why they like her so much—and then the third one, that wasn't quite so tall. She was the queen. She kind of led them, the other two peeking around and making their shoulders round. She didn't look color of water with olives and sprigs of mint in them. When my parents have somebody over they get lemonade and if it's a real racy affair Schlitz in tall glasses with "They'll Do It Every Time" cartoons stencilled on.

15   "That's all right," Lengel said. "But this isn't the beach." His repeating this struck me as funny, as if it had just occurred to him, and he had been thinking all these years the A & P was a great big dune and he was the head lifeguard. He didn't like my smiling—as I say he doesn't miss much—but he concentrates on giving the girls that sad Sunday-school-superintendent stare.

Queenie's blush was no sunburn now, and the plump one in plaid, that I liked better from the back—a really sweet can—pipes up, "We weren't doing any shopping. We just came in for the one thing."

"That makes no difference," Lengel tells her, and I could see from the way his eyes went that he hadn't noticed she was wearing a two-piece before. "We want you decently dressed when you come in here."

"We *are* decent," Queenie says suddenly, her lower lip pushing, getting sore now that she remembers her place, a place from which the crowd that runs the A & P must look pretty crummy. Fancy Herring Snacks flashed in her very blue eyes.

"Girls, I don't want to argue with you. After this come in here with your shoulders covered. It's our policy." He turns his back. That's policy for you. Policy is what the kingpins want. What the others want is juvenile delinquency.

20   All this while, the customers had been showing up with their carts but, you know, sheep, seeing a scene, they had all bunched up on Stokesie, who shook open a paper bag as gently as peeling a peach, not wanting to miss a word. I could feel in the silence everybody getting nervous, most of all Lengel, who asks me, "Sammy, have you rung up this purchase?"

I thought and said "No" but it wasn't about that I was thinking. I go through the punches, 4, 9, GROC, TOT—it's more complicated than you think and after you do it often enough, it begins to make a little song, that you hear words to, in my case "Hello (*bing*) there, you (*gung*) hap-py *peepul* (*splat*)!"—the *splat* being the drawer flying out. I uncrease the bill, tenderly as you may imagine, it just having come from between the two smoothest scoops of vanilla I had ever known were there, and pass a half and a penny into her narrow pink palm and nestle the herrings in a bag and twist its neck and hand it over, all the time thinking.

The girls, and who'd blame them, are in a hurry to get out, so I say "I quit" to Lengel quick enough for them to hear, hoping they'll stop and watch me, their un-suspected hero. They keep right on going, into the electric eye; the door flies open and they flicker across the lot to their car, Queenie and Plaid and Big Tall Goony-Goony (not that as raw material she was so bad), leaving me with Lengel and a kink in his eyebrow.

"Did you say something, Sammy?"

"I said I quit."

25   "I thought you did."

"You didn't have to embarrass them."

"It was they who were embarrassing us."

I started to say something that came out "Fiddle-de-doo." It's a saying of my grandmother's, and I know she would have been pleased.

"I don't think you know what you're saying," Lengel said.

30   "I know you don't," I said. "But I do." I pull the bow at the back of my apron and start shrugging it off my shoulders. A couple customers that had been heading for my slot begin to knock against each other, like scared pigs in a chute.

Lengel sighs and begins to look very patient and old and gray. He's been a friend of my parents for years. "Sammy, you don't want to do this to your Mom and Dad," he tells me. It's true, I don't. But it seems to me that once you begin a gesture it's fatal not to go through with it. I fold the apron, "Sammy" stitched in red on the pocket, and put it on the counter, and drop the bow tie on top of it. The bow tie is theirs, if you've ever wondered. "You'll feel this for the rest of your life," Lengel says, and I know that's true, too, but remembering how he made that pretty girl blush makes me so scrunchy inside I punch the No Sale tab and the machine whirs "pee-pul" and the drawer splats out. One advantage to this scene taking place in summer, I can follow this up with a clean exit, there's no fumbling around getting your coat and galoshes, I just saunter into the electric eye in my white shirt that my mother ironed the night before, and the door heaves itself open, and outside the sunshine is skating round on the asphalt.

I look around for my girls, but they're gone, of course. There wasn't anybody but some young married screaming with her children about some candy they didn't get by the door of a powder-blue Falcon station wagon. Looking back in the big windows, over the bags of peat moss and aluminum lawn furniture stacked on the pavement, I could see Lengel in my place in the slot, checking the sheep through. His face was dark gray and his back stiff, as if he'd just had an injection of iron, and my stomach kind of fell as I felt how hard the world was going to be to me hereafter.

[1962]

Topics for Critical Thinking and Writing

1. In what sort of community is this A & P located? To what extent does this community resemble yours?
2. Do you think Sammy is a male chauvinist pig? Why, or why not? And if you think he is, do you find the story offensive? Again, why or why not?
3. In the last line of the story Sammy says, "I felt how hard the world was going to be to me hereafter." Do you think the world is going to be hard to Sammy? Why, or why not? And if it is hard to him, is this because of a virtue or a weakness in Sammy?
4. Some of the young narrator's comments about women are sexist. The story was first published in 1962, when such remarks could usually be made with impunity. Do you think the story could be written and published today? Why, or why not? Do you think the narrator's kind of thinking still exists?
5. Write Lengel's version of the story (500–1000 words) as he might narrate it to his wife during dinner. Or write the story from Queenie's point of view.
6. In speaking of contemporary fiction, Updike said:

   I want stories to startle and engage me within the first few sentences, and in their middle to widen or deepen or sharpen my knowledge of human activity, and to end by giving me a sensation of completed statement.

   Let's assume that you share Updike's view of what a story should do. To what extent do you think "A & P" fulfills these demands? (You may want to put your response in the form of a letter to Updike.)

GLORIA NAYLOR

Gloria Naylor (b. 1950), a native of New York City, holds a bachelor's degree from Brooklyn College and a master's degree in Afro-American Studies from Yale University. "The Two" comes from The Women of Brewster Place *(1982), a book that won the American Book Award for First Fiction. Naylor has subsequently published two novels and* Centennial *(1986), a work of nonfiction.*

The Two

At first they seemed like such nice girls. No one could remember exactly when they had moved into Brewster. It was earlier in the year before Ben[1] was killed—of course, it had to be before Ben's death. But no one remembered if it was in the winter or spring of that year that the two had come. People often came and went on Brewster Place like a restless night's dream, moving in and out in the dark to avoid eviction notices or neighborhood bulletins about the dilapidated condition of their furnishings. So it wasn't until the two were clocked leaving in the mornings and returning in the evenings at regular intervals that it was quietly absorbed that they now claimed Brewster as home. And Brewster waited, cautiously prepared to claim them, because you never knew about young women, and obviously single at that. But when no wild music or drunken friends careened out of the corner building on weekends, and especially, when no slightly eager husbands were encouraged to linger around that first-floor apartment and run errands for them, a suspended sigh of relief floated around the two when they dumped their garbage, did their shopping, and headed for the morning bus.

The women of Brewster had readily accepted the lighter, skinny one. There wasn't much threat in her timid mincing walk and the slightly protruding teeth she seemed so eager to show everyone in her bell-like good mornings and evenings. Breaths were held a little longer in the direction of the short dark one—too pretty, and too much behind. And she insisted on wearing those thin Qiana dresses that the summer breeze molded against the maddening rhythm of the twenty pounds of rounded flesh that she swung steadily down the street. Through slitted eyes, the women watched their men watching her pass, knowing the bastards were praying for a wind. But since she seemed oblivious to whether these supplications went answered, their sighs settled around her shoulders too. Nice girls.

And so no one even cared to remember exactly when they had moved into Brewster Place, until the rumor started. It had first spread through the block like a sour odor that's only faintly perceptible and easily ignored until it starts growing in strength from the dozen mouths it had been lying in, among clammy gums and scum-coated teeth. And then it was everywhere—lining the mouths and whitening the lips of everyone as they wrinkled up their noses at its pervading smell, unable to pinpoint the source or time of its initial arrival. Sophie could—she had been there.

It wasn't that the rumor had actually begun with Sophie. A rumor needs no true parent. It only needs a willing carrier, and it found one in Sophie. She had been there—on one of those August evenings when the sun's absence is a mock-

---

[1]**Ben** the custodian of Brewster Place

ery because the heat leaves the air so heavy it presses the naked skin down on your body, to the point that a sheet becomes unbearable and sleep impossible. So most of Brewster was outside that night when the two had come in together, probably from one of those air-conditioned movies downtown, and had greeted the ones who were loitering around their building. And they had started up the steps when the skinny one tripped over a child's ball and the darker one had grabbed her by the arm and around the waist to break her fall. "Careful, don't wanna lose you now." And the two of them had laughed into each other's eyes and went into the building.

5   The smell had begun there. It outlined the image of the stumbling woman and the one who had broken her fall. Sophie and a few other women sniffed at the spot and then, perplexed, silently looked at each other. Where had they seen that before? They had often laughed and touched each other—held each other in joy or its dark twin—but where had they seen *that* before? It came to them as the scent drifted down the steps and entered their nostrils on the way to their inner mouths. They had seen that—done that—with their men. That shared moment of invisible communion reserved for two and hidden from the rest of the world behind laughter or tears or a touch. In the days before babies, miscarriages, and other broken dreams, after stolen caresses in barn stalls and cotton houses, after intimate walks from church and secret kisses with boys who were now long forgotten or permanently fixed in their lives—that was where. They could almost feel the odor moving about in their mouths, and they slowly knitted themselves together and let it out into the air like a yellow mist that began to cling to the bricks on Brewster.

So it got around that the two in 312 were *that* way. And they had seemed like such nice girls. Their regular exits and entrances to the block were viewed with a jaundiced eye. The quiet that rested around their door on the weekends hinted of all sorts of secret rituals, and their friendly indifference to the men on the street was an insult to the women as a brazen flaunting of unnatural ways.

Since Sophie's apartment windows faced theirs from across the air shaft, she became the official watchman for the block, and her opinions were deferred to whenever the two came up in conversation. Sophie took her position seriously and was constantly alert for any telltale signs that might creep out around their drawn shades, across from which she kept a religious vigil. An entire week of drawn shades was evidence enough to send her flying around with reports that as soon as it got dark they pulled their shades down and put on the lights. Heads nodded in knowing unison—a definite sign. If doubt was voiced with a "But I pull my shades down at night too," a whispered "Yeah, but you're not *that* way" was argument enough to win them over.

Sophie watched the lighter one dumping their garbage, and she went outside and opened the lid. Her eyes darted over the crushed tin cans, vegetable peelings, and empty chocolate chip cookie boxes. What do they do with all them chocolate chip cookies? It was surely a sign, but it would take some time to figure that one out. She saw Ben go into their apartment, and she waited and blocked his path as he came out, carrying his toolbox.

"What ya see?" She grabbed his arm and whispered wetly in his face.

10   Ben stared at her squinted eyes and drooping lips and shook his head slowly. "Uh, uh, uh, it was terrible."

"Yeah?" She moved in a little closer.

"Worst busted faucet I seen in my whole life." He shook her hand off his arm and left her standing in the middle of the block.

"You old sop bucket," she muttered, as she went back up on her stoop. A broken faucet, huh? Why did they need to use so much water?

Sophie had plenty to report that day. Ben had said it was terrible in there. No, she didn't know exactly what he had seen, but you can imagine—and they did. Confronted with the difference that had been thrust into their predictable world, they reached into their imaginations and, using an ancient pattern, weaved themselves a reason for its existence. Out of necessity they stitched all of their secret fears and lingering childhood nightmares into this existence, because even though it was deceptive enough to try and look as they looked, talk as they talked, and do as they did, it had to have some hidden stain to invalidate it—it was impossible for them both to be right. So they leaned back, supported by the sheer weight of their numbers and comforted by the woven barrier that kept them protected from the yellow mist that enshrouded the two as they came and went on Brewster Place.

15   Lorraine was the first to notice the change in the people on Brewster Place. She was a shy but naturally friendly woman who got up early, and had read the morning paper and done fifty sit-ups before it was time to leave for work. She came out of her apartment eager to start her day by greeting any of her neighbors who were outside. But she noticed that some of the people who had spoken to her before made a point of having something else to do with their eyes when she passed, although she could almost feel them staring at her back as she moved on. The ones who still spoke only did so after an uncomfortable pause, in which they seemed to be peering through her before they begrudged her a good morning or evening. She wondered if it was all in her mind and she thought about mentioning it to Theresa, but she didn't want to be accused of being too sensitive again. And how would Tee even notice anything like that anyway? She had a lousy attitude and hardly ever spoke to people. She stayed in that bed until the last moment and rushed out of the house fogged-up and grumpy, and she was used to being stared at—by men at least—because of her body.

Lorraine thought about these things as she came up the block from work, carrying a large paper bag. The group of women on her stoop parted silently and let her pass.

"Good evening," she said, as she climbed the steps.

Sophie was standing on the top step and tried to peek into the bag. "You been shopping, huh? What ya buy?" It was almost an accusation.

"Groceries." Lorraine shielded the top of the bag from view and squeezed past her with a confused frown. She saw Sophie throw a knowing glance to the others at the bottom of the stoop. What was wrong with this old woman? Was she crazy or something?

20   Lorraine went into her apartment. Theresa was sitting by the window, reading a copy of *Mademoiselle*. She glanced up from her magazine. "Did you get my chocolate chip cookies?"

"Why good evening to you, too, Tee. And how was my day? Just wonderful." She sat the bag down on the couch. "The little Baxter boy brought in a puppy for show-and-tell, and the damn thing pissed all over the floor and then proceeded to chew the heel off my shoe, but, yes, I managed to hobble to the store and bring you your chocolate chip cookies."

Oh, Jesus, Theresa thought, she's got a bug up her ass tonight.

"Well, you should speak to Mrs. Baxter. She ought to train her kid better than that." She didn't wait for Lorraine to stop laughing before she tried to stretch her good mood. "Here, I'll put those things away. Want me to make dinner so you can rest? I only worked half a day, and the most tragic thing that went down was a broken fingernail and that got caught in my typewriter."

Lorraine followed Theresa into the kitchen. "No, I'm not really tired, and fair's fair, you cooked last night. I didn't mean to tick off like that; it's just that . . . well, Tee, have you noticed that people aren't as nice as they used to be?"

Theresa stiffened. Oh, God, here she goes again. "What people, Lorraine? Nice in what way?"

"Well, the people in this building and on the street. No one hardly speaks anymore. I mean, I'll come in and say good evening—and just silence. It wasn't like that when we first moved in. I don't know, it just makes you wonder; that's all. What are they thinking?"

"I personally don't give a shit what they're thinking. And their good evenings don't put any bread on my table."

"Yeah, but you didn't see the way that woman looked at me out there. They must feel something or know something. They probably—"

"They, they, they!" Theresa exploded. "You know, I'm not starting up with this again, Lorraine. Who in the hell are they? And where in the hell are we? Living in some dump of a building in this God-forsaken part of town around a bunch of ignorant niggers with the cotton still under their fingernails because of you and your theys. They knew something in Linden Hills, so I gave up an apartment for you that I'd been in for the last four years. And then they knew in Park Heights, and you made me so miserable there we had to leave. Now these mysterious theys are on Brewster Place. Well, look out that window, kid. There's a big wall down that block, and this is the end of the line for me. I'm not moving anymore, so if that's what you're working yourself up to—save it!"

When Theresa became angry she was like a lump of smoldering coal, and her fierce bursts of temper always unsettled Lorraine.

"You see, that's why I didn't want to mention it." Lorraine began to pull at her fingers nervously. "You're always flying up and jumping to conclusions—no one said anything about moving. And I didn't know your life has been so miserable since you met me. I'm sorry about that," she finished tearfully.

Theresa looked at Lorraine, standing in the kitchen door like a wilted leaf, and she wanted to throw something at her. Why didn't she ever fight back? The very softness that had first attracted her to Lorraine was now a frequent cause for irritation. Smoked honey. That's what Lorraine had reminded her of, sitting in her office clutching that application. Dry autumn days in Georgia woods, thick bloated smoke under a beehive, and the first glimpse of amber honey just faintly darkened about the edges by the burning twigs. She had flowed just that heavily into Theresa's mind and had stuck there with a persistent sweetness.

But Theresa hadn't known then that this softness filled Lorraine up to the very middle and that she would bend at the slightest pressure, would be constantly seeking to surround herself with the comfort of everyone's goodwill, and would shrivel up at the least touch of disapproval. It was becoming a drain to be continually called upon for this nurturing and support that she just didn't understand. She had supplied it at first out of love for Lorraine, hoping that she would harden eventually, even as honey does when exposed to the cold. Theresa was growing tired of being clung to—of being the one who was leaned on. She didn't want a child—she wanted someone who could stand toe to toe with her and be willing to slug it out at times. If they practiced that way with each other, then they could turn back to back and beat the hell out of the world for trying to invade their territory. But she had found no such sparring partner in Lorraine, and the strain of fighting alone was beginning to show on her.

"Well, if it was that miserable, I would have been gone a long time ago," she said, watching her words refresh Lorraine like a gentle shower.

35   "I guess you think I'm some sort of a sick paranoid, but I can't afford to have people calling my job or writing letters to my principal. You know I've already lost a position like that in Detroit. And teaching is my whole life, Tee."

"I know," she sighed, not really knowing at all. There was no danger of that ever happening on Brewster Place. Lorraine taught too far from this neighborhood for anyone here to recognize her in that school. No, it wasn't her job she feared losing this time, but their approval. She wanted to stand out there and chat and trade makeup secrets and cake recipes. She wanted to be secretary of their block association and be asked to mind their kids while they ran to the store. And none of that was going to happen if they couldn't even bring themselves to accept her good evenings.

Theresa silently finished unpacking the groceries. "Why did you buy cottage cheese? Who eats that stuff?"

"Well, I thought we should go on a diet."

"If *we* go on a diet, then you'll disappear. You've got nothing to lose but your hair."

40   "Oh, I don't know. I thought that we might want to try and reduce our hips or something." Lorraine shrugged playfully.

"No, thank you. We are very happy with our hips the way they are," Theresa said, as she shoved the cottage cheese to the back of the refrigerator. "And even when I lose weight, it never comes off there. My chest and arms just get smaller, and I start looking like a bottle of salad dressing."

The two women laughed, and Theresa sat down to watch Lorraine fix dinner. "You know, this behind has always been my downfall. When I was coming up in Georgia with my grandmother, the boys used to promise me penny candy if I would let them pat my behind. And I used to love those jawbreakers—you know, the kind that lasted all day and kept changing colors in your mouth. So I was glad to oblige them, because in one afternoon I could collect a whole week's worth of jawbreakers."

"Really. That's funny to you? Having some boy feeling all over you."

Theresa sucked her teeth. "We were only kids, Lorraine. You know, you remind me of my grandmother. That was one straight-laced old lady. She had a fit when my brother told her what I was doing. She called me into the smokehouse and told me in this real scary whisper that I could get pregnant from letting little boys pat my butt and that I'd end up like my cousin Willa. But Willa and I had been thick as fleas, and she had already given me a step-by-step summary of how she'd gotten into her predicament. But I sneaked around to her house that night just to double-check her story, since that old lady had seemed so earnest. 'Willa, are you sure?' I whispered through her bedroom window. 'I'm tellin' ya, Tee,' she said. 'Just keep both feet on the ground and you home free.' Much later I learned that advice wasn't too biologically sound, but it worked in Georgia because those country boys didn't have much imagination."

45   Theresa's laughter bounced off of Lorraine's silent, rigid back and died in her throat. She angrily tore open a pack of the chocolate chip cookies.

"Yeah," she said, staring at Lorraine's back and biting down hard into the cookie, "it wasn't until I came up north to college that I found out there's a whole lot of things that a dude with a little imagination can do to you even with both feet on the ground. You see, Willa forgot to tell me not to bend over or squat or—"

"Must you!" Lorraine turned around from the stove with her teeth clenched tightly together.

"Must I what, Lorraine? Must I talk about things that are as much a part of life as eating or breathing or growing old? Why are you always so uptight about sex or men?"

"I'm not uptight about anything. I just think its disgusting when you go on and on about—"

50   "There's nothing disgusting about it, Lorraine. You've never been with a man, but I've been with quite a few—some better than others. There were a couple who I still hope to this day will die a slow, painful death, but then there were some who were good to me—in and out of bed."

"If they were so great, then why are you with me?" Lorraine's lips were trembling.

"Because—" Theresa looked steadily into her eyes and then down at the cookie she was twirling on the table. "Because," she continued slowly, "you can take a chocolate chip cookie and put holes in it and attach it to your ears and call it an earring, or hang it around your neck on a silver chain and pretend it's a necklace—but it's still a cookie. See—you can toss it in the air and call it a Frisbee or even a flying saucer, if the mood hits you, and it's still just a cookie. Send it spinning on a table—like this—until it's a wonderful blur of amber and brown light that you can imagine to be a topaz or rusted gold or old crystal, but the law of gravity has got to come into play, sometime, and it's got to come to rest—sometime. Then all the spinning and pretending and hoopla is over with. And you know what you got?"

"A chocolate chip cookie," Lorraine said.

"Uh-huh." Theresa put the cookie in her mouth and winked. "A lesbian." She got up from the table. "Call me when dinner's ready. I'm going back to read." She stopped at the kitchen door. "Now, why are you putting gravy on that chicken, Lorraine? You know it's fattening."

[1982]

Topics for Critical Thinking and Writing

1. The first sentence says, "At first they seemed like such nice girls." What do we know about the person who says it? What does it tell us (and imply) about the "nice girls"?
2. What is Sophie's role in the story?
3. In the second part of the story, who is the narrator? Does she or he know Theresa's thoughts, or Lorraine's, or both?
4. How does the story end? What do you think will happen between Lorraine and Theresa?
5. Try writing a page or less that is the *end* of a story about two people (men, women, children—but *people*) whose relationship is going to end soon, or is going to survive, because of, or despite, its difficulties.

TONI CADE BAMBARA

Toni Cade Bambara (1939–95), an African American writer, was born in New York City and grew up in black districts of the city. After studying at the University of Florence in Italy and at City College in New York, where she received a master's degree, she worked for awhile as a case investigator for the New York State Welfare Department. Later she directed a recreation program for hospital patients. After her literary reputation became established, she spent most of her time writing, though she also served as writer in residence at Spelman College in Atlanta.

The Lesson

Back in the days when everyone was old and stupid or young and foolish and me and Sugar were the only ones just right, this lady moved on our block with nappy hair and proper speech and no makeup. And quite naturally we laughed at her, laughed the way we did at the junk man who went about his business like he was some big-time president and his sorry-ass horse his secretary. And we kinda hated her too, hated the way we did the winos who cluttered up our parks and pissed on our handball walls and stank up our hallways and stairs so you couldn't halfway play hide-and-seek without a goddamn gas mask. Miss Moore was her name. The only woman on the block with no first name. And she was black as hell, cept for her feet, which were fish-white and spooky. And she was always planning these boring-ass things for us to do, us being my cousin, mostly, who lived on the block cause we all moved North the same time and to the same apartment then spread out gradual to breathe. And our parents would yank our heads into some kinda shape and crisp up our clothes so we'd be presentable for travel with Miss Moore, who always looked like she was going to church, though she never did. Which is just one of the things the grownups talked about when they talked behind her back like a dog. But when she came calling with some sachet she'd sewed up or some gingerbread she'd made or some book, why then they'd all be too embarrassed to turn her down and we'd get handed over all spruced up. She'd been to college and said it was only right that she should take responsibility for the young ones' education, and she not even related by marriage or blood. So they'd go for it. Specially Aunt Gretchen. She was the main gofer in the family. You got some ole dumb shit foolishness you want somebody to go for, you send for Aunt Gretchen. She been screwed into the go-along for so long, it's a blood-deep natural thing with her. Which is how she got saddled with me and Sugar and Junior in the first place while our mothers were in a la-de-da apartment up the block having a good ole time.

So this one day Miss Moore rounds us all up at the mailbox and it's puredee hot and she's knockin herself out about arithmetic. And school suppose to let up in summer I heard, but she don't never let up. And the starch in my pinafore scratching the shit outta me and I'm really hating this nappy-head bitch and her goddamn college degree. I'd much rather go to the pool or to the show where it's cool. So me and Sugar leaning on the mailbox being surly, which is a Miss Moore word. And Flyboy checking out what everybody brought for lunch. And Fat Butt already wasting his peanut-butter-and-jelly sandwich like the pig he is. And Junebug punchin on Q.T.'s arm for potato chips. And Rosie Giraffe shifting from one hip to the other waiting for somebody to step on her foot or ask her if she from Georgia so she can kick ass, preferably Mercedes'. And Miss Moore asking us do we know what money is, like we a bunch of retards. I mean real money, she say, like it's only poker chips or monopoly papers we lay on the grocer. So right away I'm tired of this and say so. And would much rather snatch Sugar and go to the Sunset and terrorize the West Indian kids and take their hair ribbons and their money too. And Miss Moore files that remark away for next week's lesson on brotherhood, I can tell. And finally I say we oughta get to the subway cause it's cooler and besides we might meet some cute boys. Sugar done swiped her mama's lipstick, so we ready.

So we heading down the street and she's boring us silly about what things cost and what our parents make and how much goes for rent and how money ain't divided up right in this country. And then she gets to the part about we all poor and live in the slums, which I don't feature. And I'm ready to speak on that, but she steps out in the street and hails two cabs just like that. Then she hustles half the crew in with her and hands me a five-dollar bill and tells me to calculate 10 percent tip for the driver. And we're off. Me and Sugar and Junebug and Flyboy hangin out the window and hollering to everybody, putting lipstick on each other cause Flyboy a faggot anyway, and making farts with our sweaty armpits. But I'm mostly trying to figure how to spend this money. But they all fascinated with the meter ticking and Junebug starts laying bets to how much it'll read when Flyboy can't hold his breath no more. Then Sugar lays bets as to how much it'll be when we get there. So I'm stuck. Don't nobody want to go for my plan, which is to jump out at the next light and run off to the first bar-b-que we can find. Then the driver tells us to get the hell out cause we there already. And the meter reads eighty-five cents. And I'm stalling to figure out the tip and Sugar say give him a dime. And I decide he don't need it as bad as I do, so later for him. But then he tries to take off with Junebug foot still in the door so we talk about his mama something fero-cious. Then we check out that we on Fifth Avenue and everybody dressed up in stockings. One lady in a fur coat, hot as it is. White folks crazy.

"This is the place," Miss Moore say, presenting it to us in the voice she uses at the museum. "Let's look in the windows before we go in."

5   "Can we steal?" Sugar asks very serious like she's getting the ground rules squared away before she plays. "I beg your pardon," say Miss Moore, and we fall out. So she leads us around the windows of the toy store and me and Sugar screamin, "This is mine, that's mine, I gotta have that, that was made for me, I was born for that," till Big Butt drowns us out.

"Hey, I'm goin to buy that there."

"That there? You don't even know what it is, stupid."

"I do so," he say punchin on Rosie Giraffe. "It's a microscope."

"Whatcha gonna do with a microscope, fool?"

10   "Look at things."

"Like what, Ronald?" ask Miss Moore. And Big Butt ain't got the first notion. So here go Miss Moore gabbing about the thousands of bacteria in a drop of wa-ter and the somethinorother in a speck of blood and the million and one living things in the air around us is invisible to the naked eye. And what she say that for? Junebug go to town on that "naked" and we rolling. Then Miss Moore ask what it cost. So we all jam into the window smudgin it up and the price tag say $300. So then she ask how long'd take for Big Butt and Junebug to save up their al-lowances. "Too long," I say. "Yeh," adds Sugar, "outgrown it by that time." And Miss Moore say no, you never outgrow learning instruments. "Why, even medical students and interns and," blah, blah, blah. And we ready to choke Big Butt for bringing it up in the first damn place.

"This here costs four hundred eighty dollars," say Rosie Giraffe. So we pile up all over her to see what she pointin out. My eyes tell me it's a chunk of glass cracked with something heavy, and different-color inks dripped into the splits, then the whole thing put into a oven or something. But for $480 it don't make sense.

"That's a paperweight made of semi-precious stones fused together under tremendous pressure," she explains slowly, and her hands doing the mining and all the factory work.

"So what's a paperweight?" asks Rosie Giraffe.

15   "To weigh paper with, dumbbell," say Flyboy, the wise man from the East.

"Not exactly," say Miss Moore, which is what she say when you warm or way off too. "It's to weigh paper down so it won't scatter and make your desk untidy." So right away me and Sugar curtsy to each other and then to Mercedes who is more the tidy type.

"We don't keep paper on top of the desk in my class," say Junebug, figuring Miss Moore crazy or lyin one.

"At home, then," she say. "Don't you have a calendar and a pencil case and a blotter and a letter-opener on your desk at home where you do your homework?" And she know damn well what our homes look like cause she nosys around in them every chance she gets.

"I don't even have a desk," say Junebug. "Do we?"

20   "No. And I don't get no homework neither," says Big Butt.

"And I don't even have a home," say Flyboy like he do at school to keep the white folks off his back and sorry for him. Send this poor kid to camp posters, is his specialty.

"I do," says Mercedes. "I have a box of stationery on my desk and a picture of my cat. My godmother bought the stationery and the desk. There's a big rose on each sheet and the envelopes smell like roses."

"Who wants to know about your smelly-ass stationery," say Rosie Giraffe fore I can get my two cents in.

"It's important to have a work area all your own so that . . ."

25   "Will you look at this sailboat, please," say Flyboy, cuttin her off and pointin to the thing like it was his. So once again we tumble all over each other to gaze at this magnificent thing in the toy store which is just big enough to maybe sail two kittens across the pond if you strap them to the posts tight. We all start reciting the price tag like we in assembly. "Handcrafted sailboat of fiberglass at one thousand one hundred ninety-five dollars."

"Unbelievable," I hear myself say and am really stunned. I read it again for myself just in case the group recitation put me in a trance. Same thing. For some reason this pisses me off. We look at Miss Moore and she lookin at us, waiting for I dunno what.

"Who'd pay all that when you can buy a sailboat set for a quarter at Pop's, a tube of glue for a dime, and a ball of string for eight cents? It must have a motor and a whole lot else besides," I say. "My sailboat cost me about fifty cents."

"But will it take water?" say Mercedes with her smart ass.

"Took mine to Alley Pond Park once," say Flyboy. "String broke. Lost it. Pity."

30   "Sailed mine in Central Park and it keeled over and sank. Had to ask my father for another dollar."

"And you got the strap," laugh Big Butt. "The jerk didn't even have a string on it. My old man wailed on his behind."

Little Q.T. was staring hard at the sailboat and you could see he wanted it bad. But he too little and somebody'd just take it from him. So what the hell. "This boat for kids, Miss Moore?"

"Parents silly to buy something like that just to get all broke up," say Rosie Giraffe.

"That much money it should last forever," I figure.

35   "My father'd buy it for me if I wanted it."

"Your father, my ass," say Rosie Giraffe getting a chance to finally push Mercedes.

"Must be rich people shop here," say Q.T.

"You are a very bright boy," say Flyboy. "What was your first clue?" And he rap him on the head with the back of his knuckles, since Q.T. the only one he could get away with. Though Q.T. liable to come up behind you years later and get his licks in when you half expect it.

"What I want to know is," I says to Miss Moore though I never talk to her, I wouldn't give the bitch that satisfaction, "is how much a real boat costs? I figure a thousand'd get you a yacht any day."

40   "Why don't you check that out," she says, "and report back to the group?" Which really pains my ass. If you gonna mess up a perfectly good swim day least you could do is have some answers. "Let's go in," she say like she got something up her sleeve. Only she don't lead the way. So me and Sugar turn the corner to where the entrance is, but when we get there I kinda hang back. Not that I'm scared, what's there to be afraid of, just a toy store. But I feel funny, shame. But what I got to be shamed about? Got as much right to go in as anybody. But somehow I can't seem to get hold of the door, so I step away for Sugar to lead. But she hangs back too. And I look at her and she looks at me and this is ridiculous. I mean, damn, I have never ever been shy about doing nothing or going nowhere. But then Mercedes steps up and then Rosie Giraffe and Big Butt crowd in behind and shove, and next thing we all stuffed into the doorway with only Mercedes squeezing past us, smoothing out her jumper and walking right down the aisle. Then the rest of us tumble in like a glued-together jigsaw done all wrong. And people lookin at us. And it's like the time me and Sugar crashed into the Catholic church on a dare. But once we got in there and everything so hushed and holy and the candles and the bowin and the handkerchiefs on all the drooping heads, I just couldn't go through with the plan. Which was for me to run up to the altar and do a tap dance while Sugar played the nose flute and messed around in the holy water. And Sugar kept givin me the elbow. Then later teased me so bad I tied her up in the shower and turned it on and locked her in. And she'd be there till this day if Aunt Gretchen hadn't finally figured I was lyin about the boarder takin a shower.

Same thing in the store. We all walkin on tiptoe and hardly touchin the games and puzzles and things. And I watched Miss Moore who is steady watchin us like she waitin for a sign. Like Mama Drewery watches the sky and sniffs the air and takes note of just how much slant is in the bird formation. Then me and Sugar bump smack into each other, so busy gazing at the toys, 'specially the sailboat. But we don't laugh and go into our fat-lady bumpstomach routine. We just stare at that price tag. Then Sugar run a finger over the whole boat. And I'm jealous and want to hit her. Maybe not her, but I sure want to punch somebody in the mouth.

"Whatcha bring us here for, Miss Moore?"

"You sound angry, Sylvia. Are you mad about something?" Givin me one of them grins like she tellin a grown-up joke that never turns out to be funny. And she's lookin very closely at me like maybe she plannin to do my portrait from memory. I'm mad, but I won't give her that satisfaction. So I slouch around the store bein very bored and say, "Let's go."

Me and Sugar at the back of the train watchin the tracks whizzin by large then small then gettin gobbled up in the dark. I'm thinkin about this tricky toy I saw in the store. A clown that somersaults on a bar then does chin-ups just cause you yank lightly at his leg. Cost $35. I could see me askin my mother for a $35 birthday clown. "You wanna who that costs what?" she'd say, cocking her head to the side to get a better view of the hole in my head. Thirty-five dollars could buy new bunk beds for Junior and Gretchen's boy. Thirty-five dollars and the whole household could go visit Granddaddy Nelson in the country. Thirty-five dollars would pay for the rent and the piano bill too. Who are these people that spend that much for performing clowns and $1000 for toy sailboats? What kinda work they do and how they live and how come we ain't in on it? Where we are is who we are, Miss Moore always pointin out. But it don't necessarily have to be that way, she always adds then waits for somebody to say that poor people have to wake up and demand their share of the pie and don't none of us know what kind of pie she talkin about in the first damn place. But she ain't so smart cause I still got her four dollars from the taxi and she sure ain't gettin it. Messin up my day with this shit. Sugar nudges me in my pocket and winks.

45   Miss Moore lines us up in front of the mailbox where we started from, seem like years ago, and I got a headache for thinkin so hard. And we lean all over each other so we can hold up under the draggy-ass lecture she always finishes us off with at the end before we thank her for borin us to tears. But she just looks at us like she readin tea leaves. Finally she say, "Well, what do you think of F. A. O. Schwarz?"

Rosie Giraffe mumbles, "White folks crazy."

"I'd like to go there again when I get my birthday money," says Mercedes, and we shove her out the pack so she has to lean on the mailbox by herself.

"I'd like a shower. Tiring day," say Flyboy.

Then Sugar surprises me by sayin, "You know, Miss Moore, I don't think all of us here put together eat in a year what that sailboat costs." And Miss Moore lights up like somebody goosed her. "And?" she say, urging Sugar on. Only I'm standin on her foot so she don't continue.

50   "Imagine for a minute what kind of society it is in which some people can spend on a toy what it would cost to feed a family of six or seven. What do you think?"

"I think," say Sugar pushing me off her feet like she never done before, cause I whip her ass in a minute, "that this is not much of a democracy if you ask me. Equal chance to pursue happiness means an equal crack at the dough, don't it?" Miss Moore is besides herself and I am disgusted with Sugar's treachery. So I stand on her foot one more time to see if she'll shove me. She shuts up, and Miss Moore looks at me, sorrowfully I'm thinkin. And somethin weird is goin on, I can feel it in my chest.

"Anybody else learn anything today?" lookin dead at me. I walk away and Sugar has to run to catch up and don't even seem to notice when I shrug her arm off my shoulder.

"Well, we got four dollars anyway," she says.

"Uh hunh."

55   "We could go to Hascombs and get half a chocolate layer and then go to the Sunset and still have plenty money for potato chips and ice cream sodas."

"Uh hunh."

"Race you to Hascombs," she say.

We start down the block and she gets ahead which is O.K. by me cause I'm going to the West End and then over to the Drive to think this day through. She can run if she want to and even run faster. But ain't nobody gonna beat me at nuthin.

[1972]

Topics for Critical Thinking and Writing

1. What is the point of Miss Moore's lesson? Why does Sylvia resist it?
2. Describe the relationship between Sugar and Sylvia. What is Sugar's function in the story?
3. What does the last line of the story suggest?
4. In a paragraph or two, characterize the narrator. Do not summarize the story—assume that your reader is familiar with it—but support your characterization by some references to episodes in the story and perhaps by a few brief quotations.

ALICE ELLIOTT DARK

Alice Elliott Dark received a B.A. in Oriental studies from the University of Pennsylvania, and an M.F.A. in creative writing from Antioch University. She has published a book of stories, Naked to the Waist *(1991), and she teaches at The Writer's Voice, in New York City.*

In the Gloaming

Her son wanted to talk again, suddenly. During the days, he still brooded, scowling at the swimming pool from the vantage point of his wheelchair, where he sat covered with blankets despite the summer heat. In the evenings, though, Laird became more like his old self—his *old* old self, really. He became sweeter, the way he'd been as a child, before he began to cloak himself with layers of irony and clever remarks. He spoke with an openness that astonished her. No one she knew talked that way—no man, at least. After he was asleep, Janet would run through the conversations in her mind, and realize what it was she wished she had said. She knew she was generally considered sincere, but that had more to do with her being a good listener than with how she expressed herself. She found it hard work to keep up with him, but it was the work she had pined for all her life.

A month earlier, after a particularly long and grueling visit with a friend who'd come up on the train from New York, Laird had declared a new policy: no visitors, no telephone calls. She didn't blame him. People who hadn't seen him for a while were often shocked to tears by his appearance, and, rather than having them cheer him up, he felt obliged to comfort them. She'd overheard bits of some of those conversations. The final one was no worse than the others, but he was fed up. He had said more than once that he wasn't cut out to be the brave one, the one who would inspire everybody to walk away from a visit with him feeling uplifted, shaking their heads in wonder. He had liked being the most handsome and missed it very much: he was not a good victim. When he had had enough he went into a self-imposed retreat, complete with a wall of silence and other ascetic practices that kept him busy for several weeks.

Then he softened. Not only did he want to talk again; he wanted to talk to *her*.

It began the night they ate outside on the terrace for the first time all summer. Afterward, Martin—Laird's father—got up to make a telephone call, but Janet stayed in her wicker chair, resting before clearing the table. It was one of those moments when she felt nostalgic for cigarettes. On nights like this, when the air was completely still, she used to blow her famous smoke rings for the children, dutifully obeying their commands to blow one through another or three in a row, or to make big, ropy circles that expanded as they floated up to the heavens. She did exactly what they wanted, for as long as they wanted, sometimes going through a quarter of a pack before they allowed her to stop. Incredibly, neither Anne nor Laird became smokers. Just the opposite; they nagged at her to quit, and were pleased when she finally did. She wished they had been just a little bit sorry; it was a part of their childhood coming to an end, after all.

5   Out of habit, she took note of the first lightning bug, the first star. The lawn darkened, and the flowers that had sulked in the heat all day suddenly released their perfumes. She laid her head back on the rim of the chair and closed her eyes. Soon she was following Laird's breathing, and found herself picking up the vital rhythms, breathing along. It was so peaceful, being near him like this. How many mothers spend so much time with their thirty-three-year-old sons? she thought. She had as much of him now as she had had when he was an infant; more, in a way, because she had the memory of the intervening years as well, to round out her thoughts about him. When they sat quietly together she felt as close to him as she ever had. It was still him in there, inside the failing shell. *She still enjoyed him.*

"The gloaming," he said, suddenly.

She nodded dreamily, automatically, then sat up. She turned to him. "What?" Although she had heard.

"I remember when I was little you took me over to the picture window and told me that in Scotland this time of day was called the 'gloaming.'"

Her skin tingled. She cleared her throat, quietly, taking care not to make too much of an event of his talking again. "You thought I said 'gloomy.'"

10   He gave a smile, then looked at her searchingly. "I always thought it hurt you somehow that the day was over, but you said it was a beautiful time because for a few moments the purple light made the whole world look like the Scottish Highlands on a summer night."

"Yes. As if all the earth were covered with heather."

"I'm sorry I never saw Scotland," he said.

"You're a Scottish lad nonetheless," she said. "At least on my side." She remembered offering to take him to Scotland once, but Laird hadn't been interested. By then, he was in college and already sure of his own destinations, which had diverged so thoroughly from hers. "I'm amazed you remember that conversation. You couldn't have been more than seven."

"I've been remembering a lot lately."

15   "Have you?"

"Mostly about when I was very small. I suppose it comes from having you take care of me again. Sometimes, when I wake up and see your face, I feel I can remember you looking in on me when I was in my crib. I remember your dresses."

"Oh, no!" She laughed lightly.

"You always had the loveliest expressions," he said.

She was astonished, caught off guard. Then, she had a memory, too—of her leaning over Laird's crib and suddenly having a picture of looking up at her own mother. "I know what you mean," she said.

20   "You do, don't you?"

He looked at her in a close, intimate way that made her self-conscious. She caught herself swinging her leg nervously, like a pendulum, and stopped.

"Mom," he said. "There are still a few things I need to do. I have to write a will, for one thing."

Her heart went flat. In his presence she had always maintained that he would get well. She wasn't sure she could discuss the other possibility.

"Thank you," he said.

25   "For what?"

"For not saying that there's plenty of time for that, or some similar sentiment."

"The only reason I didn't say it was to avoid the cliché, not because I don't believe it."

"You believe there is plenty of time?"

She hesitated; he noticed, and leaned forward slightly. "I believe there is time," she said.

30   "Even if I were healthy, it would be a good idea."

"I suppose."

"I don't want to leave it until it's too late. You wouldn't want me to suddenly leave everything to the nurses, would you?"

She laughed, pleased to hear him joking again. "All right, all right, I'll call the lawyer."

"That would be great." There was a pause. "Is this still your favorite time of day, Mom?"

35   "Yes, I suppose it is," she said, "although I don't think in terms of favorites anymore."

"Never mind favorites, then. What else do you like?"

"What do you mean?" she asked.

"I mean exactly that."

"I don't know. I care about all the ordinary things. You know what I like."

40   "Name one thing."

"I feel silly."

"Please?"

"All right. I like my patch of lilies of the valley under the trees over there. Now can we change the subject?"

"Name one more thing."

45   "Why?"

"I want to get to know you."

"Oh, Laird, there's nothing to know."

"I don't believe that for a minute."

"But it's true. I'm average. The only extraordinary thing about me is my children."

50   "All right," he said. "Then let's talk about how you feel about me."

"Do you flirt with your nurses like this when I'm not around?"

"I don't dare. They've got me where they want me." He looked at her. "You're changing the subject."

She smoothed her skirt. "I know how you feel about church, but if you need to talk I'm sure the minister would be glad to come over. Or if you would rather have a doctor . . . "

He laughed.

55   "What?"

"That you still call psychiatrists 'doctors.'"

She shrugged.

"I don't need a professional, Ma." He laced his hands and pulled at them as he struggled for words.

"What can I do?" she asked.

60   He met her gaze. "You're where I come from. I need to know about you."

That night she lay awake, trying to think of how she could help, of what, aside from her time, she had to offer. She couldn't imagine.

She was anxious the next day when he was sullen again, but the next night, and on each succeeding night, the dusk worked its spell. She set dinner on the table outside, and afterward, when Martin had vanished into the maw of his study, she and Laird began to speak. The air around them seemed to crackle with the energy they were creating in their effort to know and be known. Were other people so close, she wondered. She never had been, not to anybody. Certainly she and Martin had never really connected, not soul to soul, and with her friends, no matter how loyal and reliable, she always had a sense of what she could do that would alienate them. Of course, her friends had the option of cutting her off, and Martin could always ask for a divorce, whereas Laird was a captive audience. Parents and children were all captive audiences to each other; in view of this, it was amazing how little comprehension there was of one another's stories. Everyone stopped paying attention so early on, thinking they had figured it all out. She recognized that she was as guilty of this as anyone. She was still surprised whenever she went over to her daughter's house and saw how neat she was; in her mind, Anne was still a sloppy teenager who threw sweaters into the corner of her closet and candy wrappers under her bed. It still surprised her that Laird wasn't interested in girls. He had been, hadn't he? She remembered lying awake listening for him to come home, hoping that he was smart enough to apply what he knew about the facts of life, to take precautions.

Now she had the chance to let go of these old notions. It wasn't that she liked everything about Laird—there was much that remained foreign to her—but she wanted to know about all of it. As she came to her senses every morning in the moment or two after she awoke, she found herself aching with love and gratitude, as if he were a small, perfect creature again and she could look forward to a day of watching him grow. Quickly, she became greedy for their evenings. She replaced her half-facetious, half-hopeful reading of the horoscope in the daily newspaper with a new habit of tracking the time the sun would set, and drew satisfaction from seeing it come earlier as the summer waned; it meant she didn't have to wait as long. She took to sleeping late, shortening the day even more. It was ridiculous, she knew. She was behaving like a girl with a crush, behaving absurdly. It was a feeling she had thought she'd never have again, and now here it was. She immersed herself in it, living her life for the twilight moment when his eyes would begin to glow, the signal that he was stirring into consciousness. Then her real day would begin.

"Dad ran off quickly," he said one night. She had been wondering when he would mention it.

65   "He had a phone call to make," she said automatically.

Laird looked directly into her eyes, his expression one of gentle reproach. He was letting her know he had caught her in the central lie of her life, which was that she understood Martin's obsession with his work. She averted her gaze. The truth was that she had never understood. Why couldn't he sit with her for half an hour after dinner, or, if not with her, why not with his dying son?

She turned sharply to look at Laird. The word "dying" had sounded so loudly in her mind that she wondered if she had spoken it, but he showed no reaction. She wished she hadn't even thought it. She tried to stick to good thoughts in his presence. When she couldn't, and he had a bad night afterward, she blamed herself, as her efficient memory dredged up all the books and magazine articles she had read emphasizing the effect of psychological factors on the course of the disease. She didn't entirely believe it, but she felt compelled to give the benefit of the doubt to every theory that might help. It couldn't do any harm to think positively. And if it gave him a few more months . . . .

"I don't think Dad can stand to be around me."

"That's not true." It was true.

70   "Poor Dad. He's always been a hypochondriac—we have that in common. He must hate this."

"He just wants you to get well."

"If that's what he wants, I'm afraid I'm going to disappoint him again. At least this will be the last time I let him down."

He said this merrily, with the old, familiar light darting from his eyes. She allowed herself to be amused. He had always been fond of teasing, and held no subject sacred. As the de facto authority figure in the house—Martin hadn't been home enough to be the real disciplinarian—she had often been forced to reprimand Laird, but, in truth, she shared his sense of humor. She responded to it now by leaning over to cuff him on the arm. It was an automatic response, prompted by a burst of high spirits that took no notice of the circumstances. It was a mistake. Even through the thickness of his terrycloth robe, her knuckles knocked on bone. There was nothing left of him.

"It's his loss," she said, the shock of Laird's thinness making her serious again. It was the furthest she would go in criticizing Martin. She had always felt it her duty to maintain a benign image of him for the children. He had become a character of her invention, with a whole range of postulated emotions whereby he missed them when he was away on a business trip and thought of them every few minutes when he had to work late. Some years earlier, when she was secretly seeing a doctor—a psychiatrist—she had finally admitted to herself that Martin was never going to be the lover she had dreamed of. He was an ambitious, competitive, self-absorbed man who probably should never have got married. It was such a relief to be able to face it that she wanted to share the news with her children, only to discover that they were dependent on the myth. They could hate his work, but they could not bring themselves to believe he had any choice in the matter. She had dropped the subject.

75   "Thank you, Ma. It's his loss in your case, too."

A throbbing began behind her eyes, angering her. The last thing she wanted to do was cry. There would be plenty of time for that. "It's not all his fault," she

charm her: watercolors of her favorite vistas (unrecognizable without the cap-
tions), bouquets of violets self-consciously flung into her lap, chores performed
without prompting. He had always gone too far, then backtracked to regain even
footing. She had always allowed herself to be wooed.

She suddenly she realized: Laird had been the love of her life.

One night it rained hard. Janet decided to serve the meal in the kitchen, since
Martin was out. They ate in silence; she was freed from the compulsion to keep
up the steady stream of chatter that she used to affect when Laird hadn't talked at
all; now she knew she could save her words for afterward. He ate nothing but
comfort foods lately: mashed potatoes, vanilla ice cream, rice pudding. The days
of his strict macrobiotic regime, and all the cooking classes she had taken in order
to help him along with it, were past. His body was essentially a thing of the past,
too; when he ate, he was feeding what was left of his mind. He seemed to want
to recapture the cosseted feeling he'd had when he'd been sick as a child and she
would serve him flat ginger ale, and toast soaked in cream, and play endless card
games with him, using his blanket-covered legs as a table. In those days, too,
there'd been a general sense of giving way to illness: then, he let himself go completely because he knew he would soon be better and active and have a million
things expected of him again. Now he let himself go because he had fought long
enough.

Finally, he pushed his bowl toward the middle of the table, signaling that he
was finished. (His table manners had gone to pieces. Who cared?) She felt a light,
jittery excitement, the same jazzy feeling she got when she was in a plane that was
picking up speed on the runway. She arranged her fork and knife on the rim of
her plate and pulled her chair in closer. "I had an odd dream last night," she said.

His eyes remained dull.

130   She waited uncertainly, thinking that perhaps she had started to talk too
soon. "Would you like something else to eat?"

He shook his head. There was no will in his expression: his refusal was
purely physical, a gesture coming from the satiation in his stomach. An animal
walking away from its bowl, she thought.

To pass the time, she carried the dishes to the sink, gave them a good hot
rinse, and put them in the dishwasher. She carried the ice cream to the counter,
pulled a spoon from the drawer and scraped off a mouthful of the thick, creamy
residue that stuck to the inside of the lid. She ate it without thinking, so the sudden sweetness caught her by surprise. All the while she kept track of Laird, but
every time she thought she noticed signs of his readiness to talk and hurried back
to the table, she found his face still blank.

She went to the window. The lawn had become a floodplain and was filled
with broad pools; the branches of the evergreens sagged, and the sky was the
same uniform grayish yellow it had been since morning. She saw him focus his
gaze on the line where the treetops touched the heavens, and she understood.
There was no lovely interlude on this rainy night, no heathered dusk. The gray
landscape had taken the light out of him.

"I'm sorry," she said aloud, as if it were her fault.

135   He gave a tiny, helpless shrug.

She hovered for a few moments, hoping, but his face was slack, and she gave
up. She felt utterly forsaken, too disappointed and agitated to sit with him and
watch the rain. "It's all right," she said. "It's a good night to watch television."

She wheeled him to the den and left him with Maggie, then did not know
what to do with herself. She had no contingency plan for this time. It was usually

the one period of the day when she did not need the anesthesia of tennis games, bridge lessons, volunteer work, errands. She had not considered the present possibility. For some time, she hadn't given any thought to what Martin would call "the big picture." Her conversations with Laird had lulled her into inventing a parallel big picture of her own. She realized that a part of her had worked out a whole scenario: the summer evenings would blend into fall; then, gradually, the winter would arrive, heralding chats by the fire, Laird resting his feet on the pigskin ottoman in the den while she dutifully knitted her yearly Christmas sweaters for Anne's children.

She had allowed herself to imagine a future. That had been her mistake. This silent, endless evening was her punishment, a reminder of how things really were.

She did not know where to go in her own house, and ended up wandering through the rooms, propelled by a vague, hunted feeling. Several times, she turned around, expecting someone to be there, but, of course, no one ever was. She was quite alone. Eventually, she realized that she was imagining a person in order to give material properties to the source of her wounds. She was inventing a villain. There should be a villain, shouldn't there? There should be an enemy, a devil, an evil force that could be driven out. Her imagination had provided it with aspects of a corporeal presence so she could pretend, for a moment, that there was a real enemy hovering around her, someone she could have the police come and take away. But the enemy was part of Laird, and neither he nor she nor any of the doctors or experts or ministers could separate the two.

140   She went upstairs and took a shower. She barely paid attention to her own body anymore, and only noticed abstractly that the water was too hot, her skin turning pink. Afterward, she sat on the chaise longue in her bedroom and tried to read. She heard something; she leaned forward and cocked her head toward the sound. Was that Laird's voice? Suddenly she believed that he had begun to talk after all—she believed he was talking to Maggie. She dressed and went downstairs. He was alone in the den, alone with the television. He didn't hear or see her. She watched him take a drink from a cup, his hand shaking badly. It was a plastic cup with a straw poking through the lid, the kind used by small children while they are learning to drink. It was supposed to prevent accidents, but it couldn't stop his hands from trembling. He managed to spill the juice anyway.

Laird had always coveted the decadent pile of cashmere lap blankets she had collected over the years in the duty-free shops of the various British airports. Now he wore one around his shoulders, one over his knees. She remembered similar balmy nights when he would arrive home from soccer practice after dark, a towel slung around his neck.

"I suppose it has to be in the church," he said.

"I think it should," she said, "but it's up to you."

"I guess it's not the most timely moment to make a statement about my personal disbeliefs. But I'd like you to keep it from being too lugubrious. No lilies, for instance."

145   "God forbid."

"And have some decent music."

"Such as?"

"I had an idea, but now I can't remember."

He pressed his hands to his eyes. His fingers were so transparent that they looked as if he were holding them over a flashlight.

150   "Please buy a smashing dress, something mournful yet elegant."

"All right."

"And don't wait until the last minute."
She didn't reply.

Janet gave up on the idea of a rapprochement between Martin and Laird; she felt freer when she stopped hoping for it. Martin rarely came home for dinner anymore. Perhaps he was having an affair? It was a thought she'd never allowed herself to have before, but it didn't threaten her now. Good for him, she even decided, in her strongest, most magnanimous moments. Good for him if he's actually feeling bad and trying to do something to make himself feel better.

155   Anne was brave and chipper during her visits, yet when she walked back out to her car, she would wrap her arms around her ribs and shudder. "I don't know how you do it, Mom. Are you really all right?" she always asked, with genuine concern.

"Anne's become such a hopeless matron," Laird always said, with fond exasperation, when he and his mother were alone again later. Once, Janet began to tease him for finally coming to friendly terms with his sister, but she cut it short when she saw that he was blinking furiously.

They were exactly the children she had hoped to have: a companionable girl, a mischievous boy. It gave her great pleasure to see them together. She did not try to listen to their conversations but watched from a distance, usually from the kitchen as she prepared them a snack reminiscent of their childhood, like watermelon boats or lemonade. Then she would walk Anne to the car, their similar good shoes clacking across the gravel. They hugged, pressing each other's arms, and their brief embraces buoyed them up—forbearance and grace passing back and forth between them like a piece of shared clothing, designated for use by whoever needed it most. It was the kind of parting toward which she had aimed her whole life, a graceful, secure parting at the close of a peaceful afternoon. After Anne left, Janet always had a tranquil moment or two as she walked back to the house through the humid September air. Everything was so still. Occasionally there were the hums and clicks of a lawnmower or the shrieks of a band of children heading home from school. There were the insects and the birds. It was a straightforward, simple life she had chosen. She had tried never to ask for too much, and to be of use. Simplicity had been her hedge against bad luck. It had worked for so long. For a brief moment, as she stepped lightly up the single slate stair and through the door, her legs still harboring all their former vitality, she could pretend her luck was still holding.

Then she would glance out the window and there would be the heart-catching sight of Laird, who would never again drop by for a casual visit. Her chest would ache and flutter, a cave full of bats.

Perhaps she had asked for too much, after all.

160   "What did you want to be when you grew up?" Laird asked.
"I was expected to be a wife and mother. I accepted that. I wasn't a rebel."
"There must have been something else."
"No," she said. "Oh, I guess I had all the usual fantasies of the day, of being the next Amelia Earhart or Margaret Mead, but that was all they were—fantasies. I wasn't even close to being brave enough. Can you imagine me flying across the ocean on my own?" She laughed and looked over for his laughter, but he had fallen asleep.

A friend of Laird's had somehow got the mistaken information that Laird had died, so she and Martin received a condolence letter. There was a story about a time a few years back when the friend was with Laird on a bus in New York. They had been sitting behind two older women, waitresses who began to discuss their income taxes, trying to decide how much of their tip income to declare to sound realistic so they wouldn't attract an audit. Each woman offered up bits of folk wisdom on the subject, describing in detail her particular situation. During a lull in the conversation, Laird stood up.

165   "Excuse me, I couldn't help overhearing," he said, leaning over them. "May I have your names and addresses, please? I work for the IRS."

The entire bus fell silent as everyone watched to see what would happen next. Laird took a small notebook and pen from the inside pocket of his jacket. He faced his captive audience. "I'm part of a new IRS outreach program," he told the group. "For the next ten minutes I'll be taking confessions. Does anyone have anything he or she wants to tell me?"

Smiles. Soon the whole bus was talking, comparing notes—when they'd first realized he was kidding, and how scared they had been before they caught on. It was difficult to believe these were the same New Yorkers who were supposed to be so gruff and isolated.

"Laird was the most vital, funniest person I ever met," his friend wrote.

Now, in his wheelchair, he faced off against slow-moving flies, waving them away.

170   "The gloaming," Laird said.

Janet looked up from her knitting, startled. It was midafternoon, and the living room was filled with bright October sun. "Soon," she said.

He furrowed his brow. A little flash of confusion passed through his eyes, and she realized that for him it was already dark.

He tried to straighten his shawl, his hands shaking. She jumped up to help; then, when he pointed to the fireplace, she quickly laid the logs as she wondered what was wrong. Was he dehydrated? She thought she recalled that a dimming of vision was a sign of dehydration. She tried to remember what else she had read or heard, but even as she grasped for information, facts, her instincts kept interrupting with a deeper, more dreadful thought that vibrated through her, rattling her and making her gasp as she often did when remembering her mistakes, things she wished she hadn't said or done, wished she had the chance to do over. She knew what was wrong, and yet she kept turning away from the truth, her mind spinning in every other possible direction as she worked on the fire, only vaguely noticing how wildly she made the sparks fly as she pumped the old bellows.

Her work was mechanical—she had made hundreds of fires—and soon there was nothing left to do. She put the screen up and pushed him close, then leaned over to pull his flannel pajamas down to meet his socks, protecting his bare shins. The sun streamed in around him, making him appear trapped between bars of light. She resumed her knitting, with mechanical hands.

175   "The gloaming," he said again. It did sound somewhat like "gloomy," because his speech was slurred.

"When all the world is purple," she said, hearing herself sound falsely bright. She wasn't sure whether he wanted her to talk. It was some time since he had talked—not long, really, in other people's lives, perhaps two weeks—but she had gone on with their conversations, gradually expanding into the silence until she was telling him stories and he was listening. Sometimes, when his eyes closed, she trailed off and began to drift. There would be a pause that she didn't always realize she was making, but if it went on too long he would call out "Mom?" with an edge of panic in his voice, as if he were waking from a nightmare. Then she would resume, trying to create a seamless bridge between what she had been thinking and where she had left off.

"It was really your grandfather who gave me my love for the gloaming," she said. "Do you remember him talking about it?" She looked up politely, expectantly, as if Laird might offer her a conversational reply. He seemed to like hearing the sound of her voice, so she went on, her needles clicking. Afterward, she could never remember for sure at what point she had stopped talking and had floated off into a jumble of her own thoughts, afraid to move, afraid to look up, afraid to know at which exact moment she became alone. All she knew was that at a certain point the fire was in danger of dying out entirely, and when she got up to stir the embers she glanced at him in spite of herself and saw that his fingers were making knitting motions over his chest, the way people did as they were dying. She knew that if she went to get the nurse, Laird would be gone by the time she returned, so she went and stood behind him, leaning over to press her face against his, sliding her hands down his busy arms, helping him along with his fretful stitches until he finished this last piece of work.

Later, after the most pressing calls had been made and Laird's body had been taken away, Janet went up to his old room and lay down on one of the twin beds. She had changed the room into a guest room when he went off to college, replacing his things with guest room decor, thoughtful touches such as luggage racks at the foot of each bed, a writing desk stocked with paper and pens, heavy wooden hangers and shoe trees. She made an effort to remember the room as it had been when he was a little boy: she had chosen a train motif, then had to redecorate when Laird decided trains were silly. He had wanted it to look like a jungle, so she had hired an art student to paint a jungle mural on the walls. When he decided *that* was silly, he hadn't bothered her to do anything about it, but had simply marked time until he could move on.

Anne came over, offered to stay, but was relieved to be sent home to her children.

180   Presently, Martin came in. Janet was watching the trees turn to mere silhouettes against the darkening sky, fighting the urge to pick up a true-crime book, a debased urge. He lay down on the other bed.

"I'm sorry," he said.

"It's so wrong," she said angrily. She hadn't felt angry until that moment; she had saved it up for him. "A child shouldn't die before his parents. A young man shouldn't spend his early thirties wasting away talking to his mother. He should be out in the world. He shouldn't be thinking about me, or what I care about, or my opinions. He shouldn't have had to return my love to me—it was his to squander. Now I have it all back and I don't know what I'm supposed to do with it," she said.

She could hear Martin weeping in the darkness. He sobbed, and her anger veered away.

They were quiet for some time.

185   "Is there going to be a funeral?" Martin asked finally.

"Yes. We should start making the arrangements."

"I suppose he told you what he wanted."

"In general. He couldn't decide about the music."

She heard Martin roll onto his side, so that he was facing her across the narrow chasm between the beds. He was still in his office clothes. "I remember being very moved by the bagpipes at your father's funeral."

190   It was an awkward offering, to be sure, awkward and late, and seemed to come from someone on the periphery of her life who knew her only slightly. It didn't matter; it was perfectly right. Her heart rushed toward it.

"I think Laird would have liked that idea very much," she said.

It was the last moment of the gloaming, the last moment of the day her son died. In a breath, it would be night; the moon hovered behind the trees, already rising to claim the sky, and she told herself she might as well get on with it. She sat up and was running her toes across the bare floor, searching for her shoes, when Martin spoke again, in a tone she used to hear on those long-ago nights when he rarely got home until after the children were in bed and he relied on her to fill him in on what they'd done that day. It was the same curious, shy, deferential tone that had always made her feel as though all the frustrations and boredom and mistakes and rushes of feeling in her days as a mother did indeed add up to something of importance, and she decided that the next round of telephone calls could wait while she answered the question he asked her: "Please tell me—what else did my boy like?"

[1993]

Topics for Critical Thinking and Writing

1. Good writers give careful attention to their choice of titles. Describe your response to the title of this story when you first encountered it. And then describe your response to the title after you had read the story and taken note of how the phrase "in the gloaming" is used.
2. Janet feels a special connection to her son. What is the nature of this connection, and how is their relationship different from that between Janet and Martin, and Martin and Laird?
3. How much does Dark tell us about Laird's illness and how he acquired it? Should she have given us more information and background than she does? Explain why you think she chose not to.
4. Why does Dark conclude with a scene between Janet and Martin? Is this ending an effective one, or would a different ending—perhaps one that focuses on the final moments between Janet and Laird—have been more effective?

KATHERINE MIN

Katherine Min has published stories in several magazines notable for their excellent fiction, including Tri-Quarterly *and* Ploughshares. *She has received grants from the National Endowment for the Arts and from the New Hampshire State Arts Council, and she has twice been a fellow at the MacDowell Colony.*

Courting a Monk

When I first saw my husband he was sitting cross-legged under a tree on the quad, his hair as short as peach fuzz, large blue eyes staring upward, the smile on his face so wide and undirected as to seem moronic. I went flying by him every minute or two, guarding man-to-man, or chasing down a pass, and out of the corner of my eye I would see him watching and smiling. What I noticed about him most was his tremendous capacity for stillness. His hands were like still-life objects resting on his knees; his posture was impeccable. He looked so rooted there, like some cheerful, exotic mushroom, that I began to feel awkward in my exertion. Sweat funneled into the valley of my back, cooling and sticking when I stopped, hands on knees, to regain my breath. I tried to stop my gape-mouthed panting, refashioned my pony-tail, and wiped my hands on the soft front of my sweatpants.

He was still there two plays later when my team was down by one. Sully stole a pass and flipped to Graham. Graham threw me a long bomb that sailed wide and I leapt for it, sailing with the Frisbee for a moment in a parallel line—floating, flying, reaching—before coming down whap! against the ground. I groaned. I'd taken a tree root in the solar plexus. The wind was knocked out of me. I lay there, the taste of dry leaves in my mouth.

"Sorry, Gina. Lousy pass," Graham said, coming over. "You O.K.?"

"Fine," I gasped, fingering my ribs. "Just let me sit out for a while."

5   I sat down in the leaves, breathing carefully as I watched them play. The day was growing dark and the Frisbee was hard to see. Everyone was tired and played in a sloppy rhythm of errant throws and dropped passes.

Beside me on the grass crept the guy from under the tree. I had forgotten about him. He crouched shyly next to me, leaves cracking under his feet, and, when I looked up, he whispered, "You were magnificent," and walked away smiling.

I spotted him the next day in the vegetarian dining hall. I was passing through with my plate of veal cordon bleu when I saw him sitting by himself next to the window. He took a pair of wooden chopsticks out of the breast pocket of his shirt and poked halfheartedly at his tofu and wilted mung beans. I sat down across from him and demanded his life story.

It turned out he wanted to be a monk. Not the Chaucerian kind, bald-pated and stout, with a hooded robe, ribald humor and penchant for wine. Something even more baffling—a Buddhist. He had just returned from a semester in Nepal, studying in a monastery in the Himalayas. His hair was coming back in soft spikes across his head and he had a watchful manner—not cautious but receptive, waiting.

He was from King of Prussia, off the Philadelphia Main Line, and this made me mistrust the depth of his beliefs. I have discovered that a fascination for the East is often a prelude to a pass, a romantic overture set in motion by an "I think Oriental girls are so beautiful," and a vise-like grip on the upper thigh. But Micah was different. He understood I was not impressed by his belief, and he did not aim to impress.

10   "My father was raised Buddhist," I told him. "But he's a scientist now."

"Oh," said Micah. "So, he's not spiritual."

"Spirit's insubstantial," I said. "He doesn't hold with intangibility."

"Well, you can't hold atoms in your hand," Micah pointed out.

"Ah," I said, smiling, "but you can count them."

* * *

15   I told Micah my father was a man of science, and this was true. He was a man, also, of silence. Unlike Micah, whose reticence seemed calming, so undisturbed, like a pool of light on still water, my father's silence was like the lid on a pot, sealing off some steaming, inner pressure.

Words were not my father's medium. "Language," my father liked to say, "is an imprecise instrument." (For though he said little, when he hit upon a phrase he liked, he said it many times.) He was fond of Greek letters and numerals set together in intricate equations, symbolizing a certain physical law or experimental hypothesis. He filled yellow legal pads in a strong vertical hand, writing these beauties down in black, indelible felt-tip pen. I think it was a source of tremendous irritation to him that he could not communicate with other people in so ordered a fashion, that he could not simply draw an equals sign after something he'd said, have them solve for x or y.

That my father's English was not fluent was only part of it. He was not a garrulous man, even in Korean, among visiting relatives, or alone with my mother. And with me, his only child—who could speak neither of his preferred languages, Korean or science—my father had conspicuously little to say. "Pick up this mess," he would tell me, returning from work in the evening. "Homework finished?" he would inquire, raising an eyebrow over his rice bowl as I excused myself to go watch television.

He limited himself to the imperative mood, the realm of injunction and command; the kinds of statement that required no answer, that left no opening for discussion or rejoinder. These communications were my father's verbal equivalent to his neat numerical equations. They were hermetically sealed.

When I went away to college, my father's parting words constituted one of the longest speeches I'd heard him make. Surrounded by station wagons packed with suitcases, crates of books and study lamps, amid the excited chattering and calling out of students, among the adults with their nervous parental surveillance of the scene, my father leaned awkwardly forward with his hands in his pockets, looking at me intently. He said, "Study hard. Go to bed early. Do not goof off. And do not let the American boys take advantages."

20   This was the same campus my father had set foot on twenty years before, when he was a young veteran of the Korean War, with fifty dollars in his pocket and about that many words of English. Stories of his college years constituted family legend and, growing up, I had heard them so often they were as vivid and dream-like as my own memories. My father in the dorm bathroom over Christmas, vainly trying to hard-boil an egg in a sock by running it under hot water; his triumph in the physics lab where his ability with the new language did not impede him, and where his maturity and keen scientific mind garnered him highest marks and the top physics prize in his senior year—these were events I felt I'd witnessed, like some obscure, envious ghost.

In the shadow of my father's achievements then, on the same campus where he had first bowed his head to a microscope, lost in a chalk-dust mathematical dream, I pursued words. English words. I committed myself to expertise. I studied Shakespeare and Eliot, Hardy and Conrad, Joyce and Lawrence and Hemingway and Fitzgerald. It was important to get it right, every word, every nuance, to fill in my father's immigrant silences, the gaps he had left for me.

Other gaps he'd left. Staying up late and studying little, I did things my father would have been too shocked to merely disapprove. As for American boys, I heeded my father's advice and did not let them take advantage. Instead I took advantage of them, of their proximity, their good looks, and the amiable way they would fall into bed with you if you gave them the slightest encouragement. I liked the way they moved in proud possession of their bodies, the rough feel of their unshaven cheeks, their shoulders and smooth, hairless chests, the curve of their backs like burnished wood. I liked the way I could look up at them, or down, feeling their shuddering climax like a distant earthquake; I could make it happen, moving in undulant circles from above or below, watching them, holding them, making them happy. I collected boys like baubles, like objects not particularly val- ued, which you stash away in the back of some drawer. It was the pleasant inter- changeability of their bodies I liked. They were all white boys.

Micah refused to have sex with me. It became a matter of intellectual dis- agreement with us. "Sex saps the will," he said.

"Not necessarily," I argued. "Just reroutes it."

25   "There are higher forms of union," he said.

"Not with your clothes off," I replied.

"Gina," he said, looking at me with kindness, a concern that made me flush with anger. "What need do you have that sex must fill?"

"Fuck you, Micah," I said. "Be a monk, not a psychologist."

He laughed. His laughter was always a surprise to me, like a small distur- bance to the universe. I wanted to seduce him, this was true. I considered Micah the only real challenge among an easy field. But more than seduction, I wanted to rattle him, to get under that sense of peace, that inward contentment. No one my age, I reasoned, had the right to such self-possession.

30   We went for walks in the bird sanctuary, rustling along the paths slowly dis- cussing Emily Dickinson or maple syrup-making, but always I brought the subject around.

"What a waste of life," I said once. "Such indulgence. All that monkly devo- tion and quest for inner peace. Big deal. It's selfish. Not only is it selfish, it's a cop-out. An escape from this world and its messes."

Micah listened, a narrow smile on his lips, shaking his head regretfully. "You're so wonderfully passionate, Gina, so alive and in the world. I can't make you see. Maybe it is a cop-out as you say, but Buddhism makes no distinction be- tween the world outside or the world within the monastery. And historically, monks have been in the middle of political protest and persecution. Look at Tibet."

"I was thinking about, ahem, something more basic," I said.

Micah laughed. "Of course," he said. "You don't seem to understand, Gina, Buddhism is all about the renunciation of desire."

35   I sniffed. "What's wrong with desire? Without desire, you might as well not be alive."

The truth was that I was fascinated by this idea, the renunciation of desire. My life was fueled by longing, by vast and clamorous desires; a striving toward things I did not have and, perhaps, had no hope of having. I could vaguely imag- ine an end, some point past desiring, of satiety, but I could not fathom the laying down of desire, walking away in full appetite.

"The desire to renounce desire," I said now, "is still desire, isn't it?"

Micah sunk his hands into his pockets and smiled. "It's not," he said, walking ahead of me. "It's a conscious choice."

We came to a pond, sun-dappled in a clearing, bordered by white birch and maples with the bright leaves of mid-autumn. A fluttering of leaves blew from the trees, landing on the water as gently as if they'd been placed. The color of the pond was a deep canvas green; glints of light snapped like sparks above the surface. There was the lyric coo of a mourning dove, the chitter-chitter of late- second insects. Micah's capacity for appreciation was vast. Whether this had anything to do with Buddhism, I didn't know, but watching him stand on the edge of the pond, his head thrown back, his eyes eagerly taking in the light, I felt his peace and also his sense of wonder. He stood motionless for a long time.

40 I pulled at ferns, weaved their narrow leaves in irregular samplers, braided tendrils together, while Micah sat on a large rock and, taking his chopsticks from his breast pocket, began to tap them lightly against one another in a solemn rhythm.

"Every morning in the monastery," he said, "we woke to the prayer drum. Four o'clock and the sky would be dark and you'd hear the hollow wooden sound—plock, plock, plock—summoning you to meditation." He smiled dreamily. The chopsticks made a somewhat less effectual sound, a sort of ta ta ta. I imagined sunrise across a Himalayan valley—the wisps of pink-tinged cloud on a cold spring morning, the austerity of a monk's chamber.

Micah had his eyes closed, face to the sun. He continued to tap the chopsticks together slowly. He looked singular and new, sitting on that rock, like an advance scout for some new tribe, with his crest of hair and calm, and the attentiveness of his body to his surroundings.

I think it was then I fell in love with him, or, it was in that moment that my longing for him became so great that it was no longer a matter of simple gratification. I needed his response. I understood what desire was then, the disturbance of a perfect moment in anticipation of another.

"Wake-up call," I said. I peeled off my turtleneck and sweater in one clever motion and tossed them at Micah's feet. Micah opened his eyes. I pulled my pants off and my underwear and stood naked. "Plock, plock, who's there?"

45 Micah did not turn away. He looked at me, his chopsticks poised in the air. He raised one toward me and held it, as though he were an artist with a paintbrush raised for a proportion, or a conductor ready to lead an orchestra. He held the chopstick suspended in the space between us, and it was as though I couldn't move for as long as he held it. His eyes were fathomless blue. My nipples constricted with the cold. Around us leaves fell in shimmering lights to the water, making a soft rustling sound like the rub of stiff fabric. He brought his hand down and I was released. I turned and leapt into the water.

A few nights later I bought a bottle of cheap wine and goaded Micah into drinking it with me. We started out on the steps of the library after it had closed for the night, taking sloppy swigs from a brown paper bag. The lights of the Holyoke range blinked in the distance, across the velvet black of the freshman quad. From there we wandered the campus, sprawling on the tennis courts, bracing a stiff wind from the terrace of the science center, sedately rolling down Memorial Hill like a pair of tumbleweeds.

"J'a know what a koan is?" he asked me, when we were perched at the top of the bleachers behind home plate. We unsteadily contemplated the steep drop off the back side.

"You mean like ice cream?" I said.

"No, a ko-an. In Buddhism."

50 "Nope."

"It's a question that has no answer, sort of like a riddle. You know, like 'What is the sound of one hand clapping?' Or 'What was your face before you were born?'"

"'What was my face before I was born?' That makes no sense."

"Exactly. You're supposed to contemplate the koan until you achieve a greater awareness."

"Of what?"

55 "Of life, of meaning."

"Oh, O.K.," I said, "I've got it." I was facing backwards, the bag with the bottle in both my hands. "How 'bout, 'What's the sound of one cheek farting?'"

He laughed for a long time, then retched off the side of the bleachers. I got him home and put him to bed; his forehead was feverish, his eyes glassy with sickness.

"Sorry," I said. "I'm a bad influence." I kissed him. His lips were hot and slack.

"Don't mind," he murmured, half-asleep.

60 The next night we slept in the same bed together for the first time. He kept his underwear on and his hands pressed firmly to his sides, like Gandhi among his young virgins. I was determined to make it difficult for him. I kept brushing my naked body against him, draping a leg across his waist, stroking his narrow chest with my fingertips. He wiggled and pushed away, feigning sleep. When I woke in the morning, he was gone and the *Ode to Joy* was blasting from my stereo.

Graham said he missed me. We'd slept together a few times before I met Micah, enjoying the warm, healthful feeling we got from running or playing Ultimate, taking a quick sauna and falling into bed. He was good-looking, dark and broad, with sinewy arms and a tight chest. He made love to a woman like he was lifting Nautilus, all grim purpose and timing. It was hard to believe that had ever been appealing. I told him I was seeing someone else.

"Not the guy with the crew cut?" he said. "The one who looks like a baby seal?"

I shrugged.

Graham looked at me skeptically "He doesn't seem like your type," he said.

65 "No," I agreed. "But at least he's not yours."

Meanwhile I stepped up my attack. I asked endless questions about Buddhist teaching. Micah talked about *dukkha*[1]; the four noble truths; the five aggregates of attachment; the noble eightfold path to enlightenment. I listened dutifully, willing to acknowledge that it all sounded nice, that the goal of perfect awareness and peace seemed worth attaining. While he talked, I stretched my feet out until my toes touched his thigh; I slid my hand along his back; or leaned way over so he could see down my loose, barely-buttoned blouse.

"Too bad you aren't Tantric," I said. I'd been doing research.

Micah scoffed. "Hollywood Buddhism," he said. "Heavy breathing and theatrics."

"They believe in physical desire," I said. "They have sex."

70 "Buddha believes in physical desire," Micah said. "It's impermanent, that's all. Something to get beyond."

"To get beyond it," I said petulantly, "you have to do it."

Micah signed. "Gina," he said, "you are beautiful, but I can't. There are a lot of guys who will."

"A lot of them do."

He smiled a bit sadly. "Well, then . . . "

75 I leaned down to undo his shoelaces. I tied them together in double knots. "But I want you," I said.

---

[1]**dukkha** a Pali word meaning "suffering," particularly the suffering that is caused by desire.

My parents lived thirty miles from campus and my mother frequently asked me to come home for dinner. I went only once that year, and that was with Micah. My parents were not the kind of people who enjoyed the company of strangers. They were insular people who did not like to socialize much or go out—or anyway, my father was that way, and my mother accommodated herself to his preferences.

My mother had set the table in the dining room with blue linen. There were crystal wine glasses and silver utensils in floral patterns. She had made some dry baked chicken with overcooked peas and carrots—the meal she reserved for when Americans came to dinner. When it came to Korean cooking, my mother was a master. She made fabulous marinated short ribs and sautéed transparent bean noodles with vegetables and beef, pork dumplings and batter-fried shrimp, and cucumber and turnip kimchis[2] which she made herself and fermented in brown earthenware jars. But American cuisine eluded her; it bored her. I think she thought it was meant to be tasteless.

"Just make Korean," I had urged her on the phone. "He'll like that."

My mother was skeptical. "Too spicy," she said. "I know what Americans like."

80   "Not the chicken dish," I pleaded. "He's a vegetarian."

"We'll see," said my mother, conceding nothing.

Micah stared down at his plate. My mother smiled serenely. Micah nodded. He ate a forkful of vegetables, took a bite of bread. His Adam's apple seemed to be doing a lot of work. My father, too, was busy chewing, his Adam's apple moving up and down his throat like the ratchets of a tire jack. No one had said a thing since my father had uncorked the Chardonnay and read to us the description from his well-creased paperback edition of *The New York Times Guide to Wine*.

The sound of silverware scraping on ceramic plates seemed amplified. I was aware of my own prolonged chewing. My father cleared his throat. My mother looked at him expectantly. He coughed.

"Micah studied Buddhism in Nepal," I offered into the silence.

85   "Oh!" my mother exclaimed. She giggled.

My father kept eating. He swallowed exaggeratedly and looked up. "That so?" he said, sounding almost interested.

Micah nodded. "I was only there four months," he said. "Gina tells me you were brought up Buddhist."

My father grunted. "Well, of course," he said. "In Korea in those days, our families were all Buddhist. I do not consider myself a Buddhist now."

Micah and I exchanged a look.

90   "It's become quite fashionable, I understand," my father went on. "With you American college kids. Buddhism has become fad."

I saw Micah wince.

"I think it is wonderful, Hi Joon," my mother interceded, "for Americans to learn about Asian religion and philosophy. I was a philosophy major in college, Micah. I studied Whitehead,[3] American pragmatism."

My father leaned back in his chair and watched, frowning, while my mother and Micah talked. It was like he was trying to analyze Micah, not as a psychiatrist

---

[2]**kimchis** pickles.   [3]**Whitehead** Alfred North Whitehead (1861–1947), British mathematician and philosopher.

"O.K., this is going to stop," I said. I felt myself trembling. I pushed Micah back on the bed. I was furious. He had ruined it for me, the lightness, the skimming quality of my life. It had seemed easy, with the boys, the glib words and feelings, the simple heat and surface pleasures. It was like the sensation of flying, leaping for the Frisbee and sailing through the air. For a moment you lose a feeling for gravity, for the consciousness of your own skin or species. For a moment you are free.

I started to dance, fast, swinging and swaying in front of the bed. I closed my eyes and twirled wildly, bouncing off the walls like a pinball, stumbling on my own stockings. I danced so hard the stereo skipped, Jagger forced to stutter in throaty monosyllables, gulping repetitions. I whirled and circled, threw my head from side to side until I could feel the baffled blood, brought my hair up off my neck and held it with both hands.

Micah watched me dance. His body made an inverted-S upon my bed, his head propped by the pillar of his own arm. The expression on his face was the same as he'd had talking with my father, that look of deference, of fawn-eyed yielding. But I could see there was something hidden.

140   With white-knuckled fingers, I undid the buttons of my sweater and ripped my shirt lifting it off my head. I danced out of my skirt and underthings, kicking them into the corner, danced until the song was over, until I was soaked with sweat and burning—and then I jumped him.

It was like the taste of food after a day's starvation—unexpectedly strong and substantial. Micah responded to my fury, met it with his own mysterious passion; it was like a brawl, a fight, with something at stake that neither of us wanted to lose. Afterward we sat up in bed and listened to *Ode to Joy* while Micah, who had a surplus supply of chopsticks lying around the room, did his Leonard Bernstein impersonation. Later, we went out for a late-night snack to All-Star Dairy and Micah admitted to me that he was in love.

* * *

My father refused to attend the wedding. He liked Micah, but he did not want me to marry a Caucasian. It became a joke I would tell people. Korean custom, I said, to give the bride away four months before the ceremony.

Micah became a high-school biology teacher. I am an associate dean of students at the local college. We have two children. When Micah tells the story of our courtship, he tells it with great self-deprecation and humor. He makes it sound as though he were crazy to ever consider becoming a monk. "Think of it," he tells our kids. "Your dad."

Lately I've taken to reading books about Buddhism. Siddhartha Gotama was thirty-five years old when he sat under the Bodhi-tree on the bank of the river Neranjara and gained Enlightenment. Sometimes, when I see my husband looking at me across the breakfast table, or walking toward me from the other side of the room, I catch a look of distress on his face, a blinking confusion, as though he cannot remember who I am. I have happened on him a few times, on a Sunday when he has disappeared from the house, sitting on a bench with the newspaper in his lap staring across the town common, so immersed in his thoughts that he is not roused by my calling of his name.

145   I remember the first time I saw him, the tremendous stillness he carried, the contentment in his face. I remember how he looked on the rocks by that pond, like a pioneer in a new land, and I wonder if he regrets, as I do, the loss of his implausible faith. Does he miss the sound of the prayer drum, the call to an inner

life without the configuration of desire? I think of my father, running a sock under heated water thousands of miles from home, as yet unaware of the daughter he will raise with the same hopeful, determined, and ultimately futile, effort. I remember the way I used to play around with koans, and I wonder, "What is the sound of a life not lived?"

[1996]

Topics for Critical Thinking and Writing

1. Halfway through the story, in paragraph 43, the narrator says, "I think it was then I fell in love with him. . . ." Why does she fall in love with Micah at this moment? And how does she describe the feeling of love?
2. When we return to the beginning of the story—first, the Frisbee game, and, second, the scene at the dining hall—what signs do we see of the kind of relationship that will develop between the narrator and Micah? What do we learn about each of these persons and about what might draw them to one another?
3. What is your response to the narrator's father? Why do you think that Min chose to make him a scientist? Is our response to the father meant to be critical? Highly critical? Or, a lot or a little sympathetic?
4. Do you agree with Min's decision to include the brief scene with the narrator's former boyfriend, Graham, paragraphs 61–65? Is this scene important for the meaning of the story as a whole, or would you recommend that it be omitted?
5. Describe what happens during the love-making scene, beginning with paragraph 135. What is the narrator trying to do through her dance, and why? What leads Micah at last to respond to her?
6. Do sexual scenes in literature make you uncomfortable? Is there a right and a wrong way, in your view, to present such scenes?

9

Thinking and Writing Critically about Short Stories: Two Case Studies

Case Study: Writing about Ralph Ellison's "Battle Royal"

In this case study, we give a short story by the African American novelist and critic Ralph Ellison, "Battle Royal," first published in 1947 and later included as Chapter One in the novel *Invisible Man* (1952). We also give the following related material:

1. An influential, and controversial, speech delivered in 1895 by the African American educator Booker T. Washington (1856–1915), founder in 1881 and first president of Tuskegee Normal and Industrial Institute. The speech was reprinted in Washington's book, *Up from Slavery* (1901), which was among the most widely read books of the period.
2. Excerpts from *The Souls of Black Folk* (1903), by the African American historian, cultural critic, and man of letters W. E. B. Du Bois (1868–1963), which includes his critique of Washington's policies.
3. A photograph of the statue of Booker T. Washington at Tuskegee, to which Ellison's narrator refers.
4. A commentary on segregration in the South, from *An American Dilemma* (1944), a landmark study of race relations in the United States, written by the Swedish economist and sociologist Gunnar Myrdal (1898–1987).
5. An explanation by Ellison, from an interview published in 1955, of his use of folk material and myth in his fiction.
6. Ellison's reflections (1964) on his youth in Oklahoma and educational experiences at Tuskegee, where he was enrolled as a student in the 1930s.

RALPH ELLISON

Ralph Ellison (1914–94) was born in Oklahoma City. His father died when Ellison was three, and his mother supported herself and her child by working as a domestic. A trumpeter since boyhood, after graduating from high school Ellison went to study music at Tuskegee Institute, a black college in Alabama founded by Booker T. Washington. In 1936 he dropped out of Tuskegee and went to Harlem to study music composition and the visual arts; there he met Langston Hughes and Richard Wright, who encouraged him to turn to fiction. Ellison published stories and essays, and in 1942 became the managing editor of Negro Quarterly. *During the*

Second World War he served in the Merchant Marine. After the war he returned to writing and later taught in universities.

    "Battle Royal" was first published in 1947 and slightly revised (a transitional paragraph was added at the end of the story) for the opening chapter of Ellison's novel, Invisible Man *(1952), a book cited by Book-Week as "the most significant work of fiction written by an American" in the years between 1945 and 1965. In addition to publishing stories and one novel, Ellison published critical essays, which are brought together in* The Collected Essays of Ralph Ellison *(1995).*

Battle Royal

It goes a long way back, some twenty years. All my life I had been looking for something, and everywhere I turned someone tried to tell me what it was. I accepted their answers too, though they were often in contradiction and even self-contradictory. I was naïve. I was looking for myself and asking everyone except myself questions which I, and only I, could answer. It took me a long time and much painful boomeranging of my expectations to achieve a realization everyone else appears to have been born with: That I am nobody but myself. But first I had to discover that I am an invisible man!

    And yet I am no freak of nature, nor of history. I was in the cards, other things having been equal (or unequal) eighty-five years ago. I am not ashamed of my grandparents for having been slaves. I am only ashamed of myself for having at one time been ashamed. About eighty-five years ago they were told that they were free, united with others of our country in everything pertaining to the common good, and, in everything social, separate like the fingers of the hand. And they believed it. They exulted in it. They stayed in their place, worked hard, and brought up my father to do the same. But my grandfather is the one. He was an odd old guy, my grandfather, and I am told I take after him. It was he who caused the trouble. On his deathbed he called my father to him and said, "Son, after I'm gone I want you to keep up the good fight. I never told you, but our life is a war and I have been a traitor all my born days, a spy in the enemy's country ever since I give up my gun back in the Reconstruction. Live with your head in the lion's mouth. I want you to overcome 'em with yeses, undermine 'em with grins, agree 'em to death and destruction, let 'em swoller you till they vomit or bust wide open." They thought the old man had gone out of his mind. He had been the meekest of men. The younger children were rushed from the room, the shades drawn and the flame of the lamp turned so low that it sputtered on the wick like the old man's breathing. "Learn it to the younguns," he whispered fiercely; then he died.

    But my folks were more alarmed over his last words than over his dying. It was as though he had not died at all, his words caused so much anxiety. I was warned emphatically to forget what he had said and, indeed, this is the first time it has been mentioned outside the family circle. It has a tremendous effect upon me, however. I could never be sure of what he meant. Grandfather had been a quiet old man who never made any trouble, yet on his deathbed he had called himself a traitor and a spy, and he had spoken of his meekness as a dangerous activity. It became a constant puzzle which lay unanswered in the back of my mind. And whenever things went well for me I remembered my grandfather and felt guilty and uncomfortable. It was as though I was carrying out his advice in spite of myself. And to make it worse, everyone loved me for it. I was praised by the most lily-white men of the town. I was considered an example of desirable conduct—

Gordon Parks, *Ralph Ellison*.
Parks, an African American photographer with an international
reputation, has published many
books of photographs, including
Camera Portraits, where this picture appears.

just as my grandfather had been. And what puzzled me was that the old man had
defined it as *treachery*. When I was praised for my conduct I felt a guilt that in
some way I was doing something that was really against the wishes of the white
folks, that if they had understood they would have desired me to act just the opposite, that I should have been sulky and mean, and that that really would have
been what they wanted, even though they were fooled and thought they wanted
me to act as I did. It made me afraid that some day they would look upon me as
a traitor and I would be lost. Still I was more afraid to act any other way because
they didn't like that at all. The old man's words were like a curse. On my graduation day I delivered an oration in which I showed that humility was the secret, indeed, the very essence of progress. (Not that I believed this—how could I, remembering my grandfather?—I only believed that it worked.) It was a great
success. Everyone praised me and I was invited to give the speech at a gathering
of the town's leading white citizens. It was a triumph for our whole community.

It was in the main ballroom of the leading hotel. When I got there I discovered that it was on the occasion of a smoker, and I was told that since I was to be
there anyway I might as well take part in the battle royal to be fought by some of
my schoolmates as part of the entertainment. The battle royal came first.

5   All of the town's big shots were there in their tuxedoes, wolfing down the
buffet foods, drinking beer and whiskey and smoking black cigars. It was a large
room with a high ceiling. Chairs were arranged in neat rows around three sides of
a portable boxing ring. The fourth side was clear, revealing a gleaming space of
polished floor. I had some misgivings over the battle royal, by the way. Not from
a distaste for fighting, but because I didn't care too much for the other fellows

who were to take part. They were tough guys who seemed to have no grandfather's curse worrying their minds. No one could mistake their toughness. And besides, I suspected that fighting a battle royal might detract from the dignity of my speech. In those pre-invisible days I visualized myself as a potential Booker T. Washington. But the other fellows didn't care too much for me either, and there were nine of them. I felt superior to them in my way, and I didn't like the manner in which we were all crowded together into the servants' elevator. Nor did they like my being there. In fact, as the warmly lighted floors flashed past the elevator we had words over the fact that I, by taking part in the fight, had knocked one of their friends out of a night's work.

We were led out of the elevator through a rococo hall into an anteroom and told to get into our fighting togs. Each of us was issued a pair of boxing gloves and ushered out into the big mirrored hall, which we entered looking cautiously about us and whispering, lest we might accidentally be heard above the noise of the room. It was foggy with cigar smoke. And already the whiskey was taking effect. I was shocked to see some of the most important men of the town quite tipsy. They were all there—bankers, lawyers, judges, doctors, fire chiefs, teachers, merchants. Even one of the more fashionable pastors. Something we could not see was going on up front. A clarinet was vibrating sensuously and the men were standing up and moving eagerly forward. We were a small tight group, clustered together, our bare upper bodies touching and shining with anticipatory sweat; while up front the big shots were becoming increasingly excited over something we still could not see. Suddenly I heard the school superintendent, who had told me to come, yell. "Bring up the shines, gentlemen! Bring up the little shines!"

We were rushed up to the front of the ballroom, where it smelled even more strongly of tobacco and whiskey. Then we were pushed into place. I almost wet my pants. A sea of faces, some hostile, some amused, ringed around us, and in the center, facing us, stood a magnificent blonde—stark naked. There was dead silence. I felt a blast of cold air chill me. I tried to back away, but they were behind me and around me. Some of the boys stood with lowered heads, trembling. I felt a wave of irrational guilt and fear. My teeth chattered, my skin turned to goose flesh, my knees knocked. Yet I was strongly attracted and looked in spite of myself. Had the price of looking been blindness, I would have looked. The hair was yellow like that of a circus kewpie doll, the face heavily powdered and rouged, as though to form an abstract mask, the eyes hollow and smeared a cool blue, the color of a baboon's butt. I felt a desire to spit upon her as my eyes brushed slowly over her body. Her breasts were firm and round as the domes of East Indian temples, and I stood so close as to see the fine skin texture and beads of pearly perspiration glistening like dew around the pink and erected buds of her nipples. I wanted at one and the same time to run from the room, to sink through the floor, or go to her and cover her from my eyes and the eyes of the others with my body; to feel the soft thighs, to caress her and destroy her, to love her and murder her, to hide from her, and yet to stroke where below the small American flag tattooed upon her belly her thighs formed a capital V. I had a notion that of all in the room she saw only me with her impersonal eyes.

And then she began to dance, a slow sensuous movement; the smoke of a hundred cigars clinging to her like the thinnest of veils. She seemed like a fair bird-girl girdled in veils calling to me from the angry surface of some gray and threatening sea. I was transported. Then I became aware of the clarinet playing and the big shots yelling at us. Some threatened us if we looked and others if we did not. On my right I saw one boy faint. And now a man grabbed a silver pitcher from a table and stepped close as he dashed ice water upon him and stood him up and forced two of us to support him as his head hung and moans issued from his thick bluish lips. Another boy began to plead to go home. He was the largest of the group, wearing dark red fighting trunks much too small to conceal the erection which projected from him as though in answer to the insinuating low-registered moans of the clarinet. He tried to hide himself with his boxing gloves.

And all the while the blonde continued dancing, smiling faintly at the big shots who watched her with fascination, and faintly smiling at our fear. I noticed a certain merchant who followed her hungrily, his lips loose and drooling. He was a large man who wore diamond studs in a shirtfront which swelled with the ample paunch underneath, and each time the blonde swayed her undulating hips he ran his hand through the thin hair of his bald head and, with his arms upheld, his posture clumsy like that of an intoxicated panda, wound his belly in a slow and obscene grind. This creature was completely hypnotized. The music had quickened. As the dancer flung herself about with a detached expression on her face, the men began reaching out to touch her. I could see their beefy fingers sink into her soft flesh. Some of the others tried to stop them and she began to move around the floor in graceful circles, as they gave chase, slipping and sliding over the polished floor. It was mad. Chairs went crashing, drinks were spilt, as they ran laughing and howling after her. They caught her just as she reached a door, raised her from the floor, and tossed her as college boys are tossed at a hazing, and above her red, fixed-smiling lips I saw the terror and disgust in her eyes, almost like my own terror and that which I saw in some of the other boys. As I watched, they tossed her twice and her soft breasts seemed to flatten against the air and her legs flung wildly as she spun. Some of the more sober ones helped her to escape. And I started off the floor, heading for the anteroom with the rest of the boys.

10   Some were still crying and in hysteria. But as we tried to leave we were stopped and ordered to get into the ring. There was nothing to do but what we were told. All ten of us climbed under the ropes and allowed ourselves to be blindfolded with broad bands of white cloth. One of the men seemed to feel a bit sympathetic and tried to cheer us up as we stood with our backs against the ropes. Some of us tried to grin. "See that boy over there?" one of the men said. "I want you to run across at the bell and give it to him right in the belly. If you don't get him, I'm going to get you. I don't like his looks." Each of us was told the same. The blindfolds were put on. Yet even then I had been going over my speech. In my mind each word was as bright as flame. I felt the cloth pressed into place, and frowned so that it would be loosened when I relaxed.

But now I felt a sudden fit of blind terror. I was unused to darkness. It was as though I had suddenly found myself in a dark room filled with poisonous cotton-mouths. I could hear the bleary voices yelling insistently for the battle royal to begin.

"Get going in there!"

"Let me at that big nigger!"

I strained to pick up the school superintendent's voice, as though to squeeze some security out of that slightly more familiar sound.

15   "Let me at those black sonsabitches!" someone yelled.

"No, Jackson, no!" another voice yelled. "Here, somebody, help me hold Jack."

"I want to get at that ginger-colored nigger. Tear him limb from limb," the first voice yelled.

I stood against the ropes trembling. For in those days I was what they called ginger-colored, and he sounded as though he might crunch me between his teeth like a crisp ginger cookie.

Quite a struggle was going on. Chairs were being kicked about and I could hear voices grunting as with a terrific effort. I wanted to see, to see more desperately than ever before. But the blindfold was as tight as a thick skin-puckering scab and when I raised my gloved hands to push the layers of white aside a voice yelled, "Oh, no you don't, black bastard! Leave that alone!"

20   "Ring the bell before Jackson kills him a coon!" someone boomed in the sudden silence. And I heard the bell clang and the sound of the feet scuffling forward.

A glove smacked against my head. I pivoted, striking out stiffly as someone went past, and felt the jar ripple along the length of my arm to my shoulder. Then it seemed as though all nine of the boys had turned upon me at once. Blows pounded me from all sides while I struck out as best I could. So many blows landed upon me that I wondered if I were not the only blindfolded fighter in the ring, or if the man called Jackson hadn't succeeded in getting me after all.

Blindfolded, I could no longer control my motions. I had no dignity. I stumbled about like a baby or a drunken man. The smoke had become thicker and with each new blow it seemed to sear and further restrict my lungs. My saliva became like hot bitter glue. A glove connected with my head, filling my mouth with warm blood. It was everywhere. I could not tell if the moisture I felt upon my body was sweat or blood. A blow landed hard against the nape of my neck. I felt myself going over, my head hitting the floor. Streaks of blue light filled the black world behind the blindfold. I lay prone, pretending that I was knocked out, but felt myself seized by hands and yanked to my feet. "Get going, black boy! Mix it up!" My arms were like lead, my head smarting from blows. I managed to feel my way to the ropes and held on, trying to catch my breath. A glove landed in my mid-section and I went over again, feeling as though the smoke had become a knife jabbed into my guts. Pushed this way and that by the legs milling around me, I finally pulled erect and discovered that I could see the black, sweat-washed forms weaving in the smoky-blue atmosphere like drunken dancers weaving to the rapid drum-like thuds of blows.

Everyone fought hysterically. It was complete anarchy. Everybody fought everybody else. No group fought together for long. Two, three, four, fought one, then turned to fight each other, were themselves attacked. Blows landed below the belt and in the kidney, with the gloves open as well as closed, and with my eye partly opened now there was not so much terror. I moved carefully, avoiding blows, although not too many to attract attention, fighting from group to group. The boys groped about like blind, cautious crabs crouching to protect their mid-sections, their heads pulled in short against their shoulders, their arms stretched nervously before them, with their fists testing the smoke-filled air like the knobbed feelers of hypersensitive snails. In one corner I glimpsed a boy violently punching the air and heard him scream in pain as he smashed his hand against a ring post. For a second I saw him bent over holding his hand, then going down as a blow caught his unprotected head. I played one group against the other, slipping and throwing a punch then stepping out of range while pushing the others into the melee to take the blows blindly aimed at me. The smoke was agonizing and there were no rounds, no bells at three minute intervals to relieve our exhaustion. The room spun round me, a swirl of lights, smoke, sweating bodies surrounded by tense white faces. I bled from both nose and mouth, the blood spattering upon my chest.

The men kept yelling, "Slug him, black boy! Knock his guts out!"

25   "Uppercut him! Kill him! Kill that big boy!"

Taking a fake fall, I saw a boy going down heavily beside me as though we were felled by a single blow, saw a sneaker-clad foot shoot into his groin as the two who had knocked him down stumbled upon him. I rolled out of range, feeling a twinge of nausea.

The harder we fought the more threatening the men became. And yet, I had begun to worry about my speech again. How would it go? Would they recognize my ability? What would they give me?

I was fighting automatically and suddenly I noticed that one after another of the boys was leaving the ring. I was surprised, filled with panic, as though I had been left alone with an unknown danger. Then I understood. The boys had arranged it among themselves. It was the custom for the two men left in the ring to slug it out for the winner's prize. I discovered this too late. When the bell sounded two men in tuxedoes leaped into the ring and removed the blindfold. I found myself facing Tatlock, the biggest of the gang. I felt sick at my stomach. Hardly had the bell stopped ringing in my ears than it clanged again and I saw him moving swiftly toward me. Thinking of nothing else to do I hit him smash on the nose. He kept coming, bringing the rank sharp violence of stale sweat. His face was a black blank of a face, only his eyes alive—with hate of me and aglow with a feverish terror from what had happened to us all. I became anxious. I wanted to deliver my speech and he came at me as though he meant to beat it out of me. I smashed him again and again, taking his blows as they came. Then on a sudden impulse I struck him lightly as we clinched, I whispered, "Fake like I knocked you out, you can have the prize."

"I'll break your behind," he whispered hoarsely.

30   "For *them?*"

"For *me*, sonofabitch!"

They were yelling for us to break it up and Tatlock spun me half around with a blow, and as a joggled camera sweeps in a reeling scene, I saw the howling red faces crouching tense beneath the cloud of blue-gray smoke. For a moment the world wavered, unraveled, flowed, then my head cleared and Tatlock bounced before me. That fluttering shadow before my eyes was his jabbing left hand. Then falling forward, my head against his damp shoulder, I whispered,

"I'll make it five dollars more."

"Go to hell!"

35   But his muscles relaxed a trifle beneath my pressure and I breathed, "Seven!"

"Give it to your ma," he said, ripping me beneath the heart.

And while I still held him I butted him and moved away. I felt myself bombarded with punches. I fought back with hopeless desperation. I wanted to deliver my speech more than anything else in the world, because I felt that only these men could judge truly my ability, and now this stupid clown was ruining my chances. I began fighting carefully now, moving in to punch him and out again with my greater speed. A lucky blow to his chin and I had him going too—until I heard a loud voice yell, "I got my money on the big boy."

Hearing this, I almost dropped my guard. I was confused: Should I try to win against the voice out there? Would not this go against my speech, and was not this a moment for humility, for nonresistance? A blow to my head as I danced about sent my right eye popping like a jack-in-the-box and settled my dilemma. The room went red as I fell. It was a dream fall, my body languid and fastidious as to where to land, until the floor became impatient and smashed up to meet me. A moment later I came to. An hypnotic voice said FIVE emphatically. And I lay there, hazily watching a dark red spot of my own blood shaping itself into a butterfly, glistening and soaking into the soiled gray world of the canvas.

When the voice drawled TEN I was lifted up and dragged to a chair. I sat dazed. My eye pained and swelled with each throb of my pounding heart and I wondered if now I would be allowed to speak. I was wringing wet, my mouth still bleeding. We were grouped along the wall now. The other boys ignored me as they congratulated Tatlock and speculated as to how much they would be paid. One boy whimpered over his smashed hand. Looking up front, I saw attendants in white jackets rolling the portable ring away and placing a small square rug in the vacant space surrounded by chairs. Perhaps, I thought, I will stand on the rug to deliver my speech.

40   Then the M.C. called to us, "Come on up here boys and get your money."

We ran forward to where the men laughed and talked in their chairs, waiting. Everyone seemed friendly now.

"There it is on the rug," the man said. I saw the rug covered with coins of all dimensions and a few crumpled bills. But what excited me, scattered here and there, were the gold pieces.

"Boys, it's all yours," the man said. "You get all you grab."

"That's right, Sambo," a blond man said, winking at me confidentially.

45   I trembled with excitement, forgetting my pain. I would get the gold and the bills, I thought. I would use both hands. I would throw my body against the boys nearest me to block them from the gold.

"Get down around the rug now," the man commanded, "and don't anyone touch it until I give the signal."

"This ought to be good," I heard.

As told, we got around the square rug on our knees. Slowly the man raised his freckled hand as we followed it upward with our eyes.

I heard, "These niggers look like they're about to pray!"

50   Then, "Ready," the man said. "Go!"

I lunged for a yellow coin lying on the blue design of the carpet, touching it and sending a surprised shriek to join those rising around me. I tried frantically to remove my hand but could not let go. A hot, violent force tore through my body, shaking me like a wet rat. The rug was electrified. The hair bristled up on my head as I shook myself free. My muscles jumped, my nerves jangled, writhed. But I saw that this was not stopping the other boys. Laughing in fear and embarrassment, some were holding back and scooping up the coins knocked off by the painful contortions of the others. The men roared above us as we struggled.

"Pick it up, goddamnit, pick it up!" someone called like a bass-voiced parrot. "Go on, get it!"

I crawled rapidly around the floor, picking up the coins, trying to avoid the coppers and to get greenbacks and the gold. Ignoring the shock by laughing, as I brushed the coins off quickly, I discovered that I could contain the electricity—a contradiction, but it works. Then the men began to push us onto the rug. Laughing embarrassedly, we struggled out of their hands and kept after the coins. We were all wet and slippery and hard to hold. Suddenly I saw a boy lifted into the air, glistening with sweat like a circus seal, and dropped, his wet back landing flush upon the charged rug, heard him yell and saw him literally dance upon his back, his elbows beating a frenzied tattoo upon the floor, his muscles twitching like the flesh of a horse stung by many flies. When he finally rolled off, his face was gray and no one stopped him when he ran from the floor amid booming laughter.

"Get the money," the M.C. called. "That's good hard American cash!"

55   And we snatched and grabbed, snatched and grabbed. I was careful not to come too close to the rug now, and when I felt the hot whiskey breath descend upon me like a cloud of foul air I reached out and grabbed the leg of a chair. It was occupied and I held on desperately.

"Leggo, nigger! Leggo!"

The huge face wavered down to mine as he tried to push me free. But my body was slippery and he was too drunk. It was Mr. Colcord, who owned a chain of movie houses and "entertainment palaces." Each time he grabbed me I slipped out of his hands. It became a real struggle. I feared the rug more than I did the drunk, so I held on, surprising myself for a moment by trying to topple *him* upon the rug. It was such an enormous idea that I found myself actually carrying it out. I tried not to be obvious, yet when I grabbed his leg, trying to tumble him out of the chair, he raised up roaring with laughter, and, looking at me with soberness dead in the eye, kicked me viciously in the chest. The chair leg flew out of my hand. I felt myself going and rolled. It was as though I had rolled through a bed of hot coals. It seemed a whole century would pass before I would roll free, a century in which I was seared through the deepest levels of my body to the fearful breath within me and the breath seared and heated to the point of explosion. It'll all be over in a flash, I thought as I rolled clear. It'll all be over in a flash.

But not yet, the men on the other side were waiting, red faces swollen as though from apoplexy as they bent forward in their chairs. Seeing their fingers coming toward me I rolled away as a fumbled football rolls off the receiver's fingertips, back into the coals. That time I luckily sent the rug sliding out of place and heard the coins ringing against the floor and the boys scuffling to pick them up and the M.C. calling, "All right, boys, that's all. Go get dressed and get your money."

I was limp as a dish rag. My back felt as though it had been beaten with wires.

60   When we had dressed the M.C. came in and gave us each five dollars, except Tatlock, who got ten for being the last in the ring. Then he told us to leave. I was not to get a chance to deliver my speech, I thought. I was going out into the dim alley in despair when I was stopped and told to go back. I returned to the ballroom, where the men were pushing back their chairs and gathering in groups to talk.

The M.C. knocked on a table for quiet. "Gentlemen," he said, "we almost forgot an important part of the program. A most serious part, gentlemen. This boy was brought here to deliver a speech which he made at his graduation yesterday. . . ."

"Bravo!"

"I'm told that he is the smartest boy we've got out there in Greenwood. I'm told that he knows more big words than a pocket-sized dictionary."

Much applause and laughter.

65   "So now, gentlemen, I want you to give him your attention."

There was still laughter as I faced them, my mouth dry, my eye throbbing. I began slowly, but evidently my throat was tense, because they began shouting, "Louder! Louder!"

"We of the younger generation extol the wisdom of that great leader and educator," I shouted, "who first spoke these flaming words of wisdom: 'A ship lost at sea for many days suddenly sighted a friendly vessel. From the mast of the unfortunate vessel was seen a signal: "Water, water; we die of thirst!" The answer from the friendly vessel came back: "Cast down your bucket where you are." The captain of the distressed vessel, at last heeding the injunction, cast down his bucket, and it came up full of fresh sparkling water from the mouth of the Amazon River.' And like him I say, and in his words. 'To those of my race who depend upon bettering their condition in a foreign land, or who underestimate the importance of cultivating friendly relations with the Southern white man, who is his next-door neighbor. I would say: "Cast down your bucket where you are"—cast it down in making friends in every manly way of the people of all races by whom we are surrounded. . . .'"

I spoke automatically and with such fervor that I did not realize that the men were still talking and laughing until my dry mouth, filling up with blood from the cut, almost strangled me. I coughed, wanting to stop and go to one of the tall brass, sand-filled spittoons to relieve myself, but a few of the men, especially the superintendent, were listening and I was afraid. So I gulped it down, blood, saliva and all, and continued. (What powers of endurance I had during those days! What enthusiasm! What a belief in the rightness of things!) I spoke even louder in spite of the pain. But still they talked and still they laughed, as though deaf with cotton in dirty ears. So I spoke with greater emotional emphasis. I closed my ears and swallowed blood until I was nauseated. The speech seemed a hundred times as long as before, but I could not leave out a single word. All had to be said, each memorized nuance considered, rendered. Nor was that all. Whenever I uttered a word of three or more syllables a group of voices would yell for me to repeat it. I used the phrase "social responsibility" and they yelled:

"What's the word you say, boy?"

70   "Social responsibility," I said.

"What?"

"Social . . ."

"Louder."

". . . responsibility."

75   "More!"

"Respon—"

"Repeat!"

"—sibility."

The room filled with the uproar of laughter until, no doubt, distracted by having to gulp down my blood, I made a mistake and yelled a phrase I had often seen denounced in newspaper editorials, heard debated in private.

80   "Social . . ."

"What?" they yelled.

". . . equality—"

The laughter hung smokelike in the sudden stillness. I opened my eyes, puzzled. Sounds of displeasure filled the room. The M.C. rushed forward. They shouted hostile phrases at me. But I did not understand.

A small dry mustached man in the front row blared out, "Say that slowly, son!"

85   "What sir?"

"What you just said!"

"Social responsibility, sir," I said.

"You weren't being smart, were you, boy?" he said, not unkindly.

"No, sir!"

90   "You sure that about 'equality' was a mistake?"

"Oh, yes, sir," I said. "I was swallowing blood."

"Well, you had better speak more slowly so we can understand. We mean to do right by you, but you've got to know your place at all times. All right, now, go on with your speech."

I was afraid. I wanted to leave but I wanted also to speak and I was afraid they'd snatch me down.

"Thank you, sir," I said, beginning where I had left off, and having them ignore me as before.

95   Yet when I finished there was a thunderous applause. I was surprised to see the superintendent come forth with a package wrapped in white tissue paper, and gesturing for quiet, address the men.

"Gentlemen, you see that I did not overpraise this boy. He makes a good speech and some day he'll lead his people in the proper paths. And I don't have to tell you that that is important in these days and times. This is a good, smart boy, and so to encourage him in the right direction, in the name of the Board of Education I wish to present him a prize in the form of this . . . "

He paused, removing the tissue paper and revealing a gleaming calfskin brief case.

". . . in the form of this first-class article from Shad Whitmore's shop."

"Boy," he said, addressing me, "take this prize and keep it well. Consider it a badge of office. Prize it. Keep developing as you are and some day it will be filled with important papers that will help shape the destiny of your people."

100   I was so moved that I could hardly express my thanks. A rope of bloody saliva forming a shape like an undiscovered continent drooled upon the leather and I wiped it quickly away. I felt an importance that I had never dreamed.

"Open it and see what's inside," I was told.

My fingers a-tremble, I complied, smelling the fresh leather and finding an official-looking document inside. It was a scholarship to the state college for Negroes. My eyes filled with tears and I ran awkwardly off the floor.

I was overjoyed; I did not even mind when I discovered that the gold pieces I had scrambled for were brass pocket tokens advertising a certain make of automobile.

When I reached home everyone was excited. Next day the neighbors came to congratulate me. I even felt safe from grandfather, whose deathbed curse usually spoiled my triumphs. I stood beneath his photograph with my brief case in hand and smiled triumphantly into his stolid black peasant's face. It was a face that fascinated me. The eyes seemed to follow everywhere I went.

105   That night I dreamed I was at a circus with him and that he refused to laugh at the clowns no matter what they did. Then later he told me to open my brief case and read what was inside and I did, finding an official envelope stamped with the state seal; and inside the envelope I found another and another, endlessly, and I thought I would fall of weariness. "Them's years," he said. "Now open that one." And I did and in it I found an engraved document containing a short message in letters of gold. "Read it," my grandfather said. "Out loud."

"To Whom It May Concern," I intoned, "Keep This Nigger-Boy Running."

I awoke with the old man's laughter ringing in my ears.

(It was a dream I was to remember and dream again for many years after. But at the time I had no insight into its meaning. First I had to attend college.)

[1947]

Topics for Critical Thinking and Writing

1. Now that you have read the entire story, the opening paragraph may be clearer than it was when you first read it. What does the narrator mean when he declares at the end of this paragraph, "I am an invisible man?" Explain how the events described in the story taught him this painful truth.

2. The narrator says of his grandfather's dying speech, "I could never be sure of what he meant." What do you think the grandfather meant by calling himself a traitor and a spy in the enemy's territory?

3. What is the significance of the scene involving the naked blonde woman? How is this scene related to the narrator's discovery that he is invisible?

4. This story is a powerful, indeed shocking study of racism, but in essays and interviews Ellison often noted that he intended his stories and his novel *Invisible Man* to illuminate "universal truths" about human experience as well. In your view, does "Battle Royal" achieve this goal? What insights does it offer about the nature of self-knowledge and human identity?

Booker T. Washington
Atlanta Exposition Address

Mr. President and Gentlemen of the Board of Directors and Citizens:

One-third of the population of the South is of the Negro race. No enterprise seeking the material, civil, or moral welfare of this section can disregard this element of our population and reach the highest success. I but convey to you, Mr. President and Directors, the sentiment of the masses of my race when I say that in no way have the value and manhood of the American Negro been more fittingly and generously recognized than by the managers of this magnificent Exposition at every stage of its progress. It is a recognition that will do more to cement the friendship of the two races than any occurrence since the dawn of our freedom.

Not only this, but the opportunity here afforded will awaken among us a new era of industrial progress. Ignorant and inexperienced, it is not strange that in the first years of our new life we began at the top instead of at the bottom; that a seat in Congress or the state legislature was more sought than real estate or industrial skill; that the political convention or stump speaking had more attractions than starting a dairy farm or truck garden.

A ship lost at sea for many days suddenly sighted a friendly vessel. From the mast of the unfortunate vessel was seen a signal, "Water, water; we die of thirst!" The answer from the friendly vessel at once came back, "Cast down your bucket where you are." A second time the signal, "Water, water; send us water!" ran up from the distressed vessel, and was answered, "Cast down your bucket where you are." And a third and fourth signal for water was answered, "Cast down your bucket where you are." The captain of the distressed vessel, at last heeding the injunction, cast down his bucket, and it came up full of fresh, sparkling water from the mouth of the Amazon River. To those of my race who depend on bettering their condition in a foreign land or who underestimate the importance of cultivating friendly relations with the Southern white man, who is their next-door neighbour, I would say: "Cast down your bucket where you are"—cast it down in making friends in every manly way of the people of all races by whom we are surrounded.

Cast it down in agriculture, mechanics, in commerce, in domestic service, and in the professions. And in this connection it is well to bear in mind that whatever other sins the South may be called to bear, when it comes to business, pure and simple, it is in the South that the Negro is given a man's chance in the commercial world, and in nothing is this Exposition more eloquent than in emphasizing this chance. Our greatest danger is that in the great leap from slavery to freedom we may overlook the fact that the masses of us are to live by the productions of our hands, and fail to keep in mind that we shall prosper in proportion as we learn to dignify and glorify common labour and put brains and skill into the common occupations of life; shall prosper in proportion as we learn to draw the line between the superficial and the substantial, the ornamental gewgaws of life and the useful. No race can prosper till it learns that there is as much dignity in tilling a field as in writing a poem. It is at the bottom of life we must begin, and not at the top. Nor should we permit our grievances to overshadow our opportunities.

5   To those of the white race who look to the incoming of those of foreign birth and strange tongue and habits for the prosperity of the South, were I permitted I would repeat what I say to my own race, "Cast down your bucket where you are." Cast it down among the eight millions of Negroes whose habits you know, whose fidelity and love you have tested in days when to have proved treacherous meant the ruin of your firesides. Cast down your bucket among these people who have, without strikes and labour wars, tilled your fields, cleared your forests, builded your railroads and cities, and brought forth treasures from the bowels of the earth, and helped make possible this magnificent representation of the progress of the South. Casting down your bucket among my people, helping and encouraging them as you are doing on these grounds, and to education of head, hand, and heart, you will find that they will buy your surplus land, make blossom the waste places in your fields, and run your factories. While doing this, you can be sure in the future, as in the past, that you and your families will be surrounded by the most patient, faithful, law-abiding, and unresentful people that the world has seen. As we have proved our loyalty to you in the past, in nursing your children, watching by the sick-bed of your mothers and fathers, and often following them with tear-dimmed eyes to their graves, so in the future, in our humble way, we shall stand by you with a devotion that no foreigner can approach, ready to lay down our lives, if need be, in defence of yours, interlacing our industrial, commercial, civil, and religious life with yours in a way that shall make the interests of both races one. In all things that are purely social we can be as separate as the fingers, yet one as the hand in all things essential to mutual progress.

There is no defence or security for any of us except in the highest intelligence and development of all. If anywhere there are efforts tending to curtail the fullest growth of the Negro, let these efforts be turned into stimulating, encouraging, and making him the most useful and intelligent citizen. Effort or means so invested will pay a thousand per cent interest. These efforts will be twice blessed—"blessing him that gives and him that takes."

There is no escape through law of man or God from the inevitable:—

The laws of changeless justice bind
    Oppressor with oppressed;
And close as sin and suffering joined
    We march to fate abreast.

Nearly sixteen millions of hands will aid you in pulling the load upward, or they will pull against you the load downward. We shall constitute one-third and more of the ignorance and crime of the South, or one-third its intelligence and progress; we shall contribute one-third to the business and industrial prosperity of the South, or we shall prove a veritable body of death, stagnating, depressing, retarding every effort to advance the body politic.

Gentlemen of the Exposition, as we present to you our humble effort at an exhibition of our progress, you must not expect overmuch. Starting thirty years ago with ownership here and there in a few quilts and pumpkins and chickens (gathered from miscellaneous sources), remember the path that has led from these to the inventions and production of agricultural implements, buggies, steam-engines, newspapers, books, statuary, carving, paintings, the management of drug-stores and banks, has not been trodden without contact with thorns and thistles. While we take pride in what we exhibit as a result of our independent efforts, we do not for a moment forget that our part in this exhibition would fall far short of your expectations but for the constant help that has come to our educational life, not only from the Southern states, but especially from Northern philanthropists, who have made their gifts a constant stream of blessing and encouragement.

10   The wisest among my race understand that the agitation of questions of social equality is the extremest folly, and that progress in the enjoyment of all the privileges that will come to us must be the result of severe and constant struggle rather than of artificial forcing. No race that has anything to contribute to the markets of the world is long in any degree ostracized. It is important and right that all privileges of the law be ours, but it is vastly more important that we be prepared for the exercises of these privileges. The opportunity to earn a dollar in a factory just now is worth infinitely more than the opportunity to spend a dollar in an opera-house.

Charles Keck, *The Booker T. Washington Memorial* (1922). The statue shows Washington pulling away the veil of ignorance and revealing to the crouching black man the book of knowledge of life and the implements of industry that will enable African Americans to prosper. On the sides of the pedestal are Washington's words, "We shall prosper in proportion as we learn to dignify and glorify labor and put brains and skill into the common occupations of life." (Courtesy of Tuskegee University. Photograph by Eric J. Sundquist.)

In conclusion, may I repeat that nothing in thirty years has given us more hope and encouragement, and drawn us so near to you of the white race, as this opportunity offered by the Exposition; and here bending, as it were, over the altar that represents the results of the struggles of your race and mine, both starting practically empty-handed three decades ago, I pledge that in your effort to work out the great and intricate problem which God has laid at the doors of the South, you shall have at all times the patient, sympathetic help of my race; only let this be constantly in mind, that, while from representations in these buildings of the product of field, of forest, of mine, of factory, letters, and art, much good will come, yet far above and beyond material benefits will be that higher good, that, let us pray God, will come, in a blotting out of sectional differences and racial animosities and suspicions, in a determination to administer absolute justice, in a willing obedience among all classes to the mandates of law. This, this, coupled with our material prosperity, will bring into our beloved South a new heaven and a new earth.

[1895]

W. E. B. Du Bois
Of Our Spiritual Strivings

Between me and the other world there is ever an unasked question: unasked by some through feelings of delicacy; by others through the difficulty of rightly framing it. All, nevertheless, flutter round it. They approach me in a half-hesitant sort of way, eye me curiously or compassionately, and then, instead of saying directly, How does it feel to be a problem? they say, I know an excellent colored man in my town; or, I fought at Mechanicsville; or, Do not these Southern outrages make your blood boil? At these I smile, or am interested, or reduce the boiling to a simmer, as the occasion may require. To the real question, How does it feel to be a problem? I answer seldom a word.

And yet, being a problem is a strange experience,—peculiar even for one who has never been anything else, save perhaps in babyhood and in Europe. It is in the early days of rollicking boyhood that the revelation first bursts upon one, all in a day, as it were. I remember well when the shadow swept across me. I was a little thing, away up in the hills of New England, where the dark Housatonic winds between Hoosac and Taghkanic to the sea. In a wee wooden schoolhouse, something put it into the boys' and girls' heads to buy gorgeous visiting-cards—ten cents a package—and exchange. The exchange was merry, till one girl, a tall newcomer, refused my card,—refused it peremptorily, with a glance. Then it dawned upon me with a certain suddenness that I was different from the others; or like, mayhap, in heart and life and longing, but shut out from their world by a vast veil. I had thereafter no desire to tear down that veil, to creep through; I held all beyond it in common contempt, and lived above it in a region of blue sky and great wandering shadows. That sky was bluest when I could beat my mates at examination-time, or beat them at a foot-race, or even beat their stringy heads. Alas, with the years all this fine contempt began to fade; for the worlds I longed for, and all their dazzling opportunities, were theirs, not mine. But they should not keep these prizes, I said; some, all, I would wrest from them. Just how I would do it I could never decide: by reading law, by healing the sick, by telling the wonderful tales that swam in my head,—some way. With other black boys the strife was not so fiercely sunny: their youth shrunk into tasteless sycophancy, or into silent hatred of the pale world about them and mocking distrust of everything white; or wasted itself in a bitter cry, Why did God make me an outcast and a stranger in mine own house? The shades of the prison-house closed round about us all: walls strait and stubborn to the whitest, but relentlessly narrow, tall, and unscalable to sons of night who must plod darkly on in resignation, or beat unavailing palms against the stone, or steadily, half hopelessly, watch the streak of blue above.

After the Egyptian and Indian, the Greek and Roman, the Teuton and Mongolian, the Negro is a sort of seventh son, born with a veil, and gifted with second-sight in this American world,—a world which yields him no true self-consciousness, but only lets him see himself through the revelation of the other world. It is a peculiar sensation, this double-consciousness, this sense of always looking at one's self through the eyes of others, of measuring one's soul by the tape of a world that looks on in amused contempt and pity. One ever feels his two-ness,—an American, a Negro; two souls, two thoughts, two unreconciled strivings; two warring ideals in one dark body, whose dogged strength alone keeps it from being torn asunder.

The history of the American Negro is the history of this strife—this longing to attain self-conscious manhood, to merge his double self into a better and truer self. In this merging he wishes neither of the older selves to be lost. He would not Africanize America, for America has too much to teach the world and Africa. He would not bleach his Negro soul in a flood of white Americanism, for he knows that Negro blood has a message for the world. He simply wishes to make it possible for a man to be both a Negro and an American, without being cursed and spit upon by his fellows, without having the doors of Opportunity closed roughly in his face.

[1903]

W. E. B. Du Bois
Of Mr. Booker T. Washington and Others

Mr. Washington represents in Negro thought the old attitude of adjustment and submission; but adjustment at such a peculiar time as to make his programme unique. This is an age of unusual economic development, and Mr. Washington's programme naturally takes an economic cast, becoming a gospel of Work and Money to such an extent as apparently almost completely to overshadow the higher aims of life. Moreover, this is an age when the more advanced races are coming in closer contact with the less developed races, and the race-feeling is therefore intensified; and Mr. Washington's programme practically accepts the alleged inferiority of the Negro races. Again, in our own land, the reaction from the sentiment of war time has given impetus to race-prejudice against Negroes, and Mr. Washington withdraws many of the high demands of Negroes as men and American citizens. In other periods of intensified prejudice all the Negro's tendency to self-assertion has been called forth; at this period a policy of submission is advocated. In the history of nearly all other races and peoples the doctrine preached at such crises has been that manly self-respect is worth more than lands and houses, and that a people who voluntarily surrender such respect, or cease striving for it, are not worth civilizing.

In answer to this, it has been claimed that the Negro can survive only through submission. Mr. Washington distinctly asks that black people give up, at least for the present, three things,—

First, political power,
Second, insistence on civil rights,
Third, higher education of Negro youth,—

and concentrate all their energies on industrial education, the accumulation of wealth, and the conciliation of the South. This policy has been courageously and insistently advocated for over fifteen years, and has been triumphant for perhaps ten years. As a result of this tender of the palm-branch, what has been the return? In these years there have occurred:

1. The disfranchisement of the Negro.
2. The legal creation of a distinct status of civil inferiority for the Negro.
3. The steady withdrawal of aid from institutions for the higher training of the Negro.

These movements are not, to be sure, direct results of Mr. Washington's teachings; but his propaganda has, without a shadow of doubt, helped their speedier accomplishment. The question then comes: Is it possible, and probable, that nine millions of men can make effective progress in economic lines if they are deprived of political rights, made a servile caste, and allowed only the most meagre chance for developing their exceptional men? If history and reason give any distinct answer to these questions, it is an emphatic *No*. And Mr. Washington thus faces the triple paradox of his career:

10
1. He is striving nobly to make Negro artisans business men and property-owners; but it is utterly impossible, under modern competitive methods, for workingmen and property-owners to defend their rights and exist without the right of suffrage.
2. He insists on thrift and self-respect, but at the same time counsels a silent submission to civic inferiority such as is bound to sap the manhood of any race in the long run.
3. He advocates common-school and industrial training, and depreciates institutions of higher learning; but neither the Negro common-schools, nor Tuskegee itself, could remain open a day were it not for teachers trained in Negro colleges, or trained by their graduates.

This triple paradox in Mr. Washington's position is the object of criticism by two classes of colored Americans. One class is spiritually descended from Toussaint the Savior, through Gabriel, Vesey, and Turner, and they represent the attitude of revolt and revenge; they hate the white South blindly and distrust the white race generally, and so far as they agree on definite action, think that the Negro's only hope lies in emigration beyond the borders of the United States. And yet, by the irony of fate, nothing has more effectually made this programme seem hopeless than the recent course of the United States toward weaker and darker peoples in the West Indies, Hawaii, and the Philippines,—for where in the world may we go and be safe from lying and brute force?

The other class of Negroes who cannot agree with Mr. Washington has hitherto said little aloud. They deprecate the sight of scattered counsels, of internal disagreement; and especially they dislike making their just criticism of a useful and earnest man an excuse for a general discharge of venom from small-minded opponents. Nevertheless, the questions involved are so fundamental and serious that it is difficult to see how men like the Grimkes, Kelly Miller, J. W. E. Bowen, and other representatives of this group, can much longer be silent. Such men feel in conscience bound to ask of this nation three things:

15   **1.** The right to vote.
      2. Civic equality.
      3. The education of youth according to ability.

They acknowledge Mr. Washington's invaluable service in counselling patience and courtesy in such demands; they do not ask that ignorant black men vote when ignorant whites are debarred, or that any reasonable restrictions in the suffrage should not be applied; they know that the low social level of the mass of the race is responsible for much discrimination against it, but they also know, and the nation knows, that relentless color-prejudice is more often a cause than a result of the Negro's degradation; they seek the abatement of this relic of barbarism, and not its systematic encouragement and pampering by all agencies of social power from the Associated Press to the Church of Christ. They advocate, with Mr. Washington, a broad system of Negro common schools supplemented by thorough industrial training; but they are surprised that a man of Mr. Washington's insight cannot see that no such educational system ever has rested or can rest on any other basis than that of the well-equipped college and university, and they insist that there is a demand for a few such institutions throughout the South to train the best of the Negro youth as teachers, professional men, and leaders.

This group of men honor Mr. Washington for his attitude of conciliation toward the white South; they accept the "Atlanta Compromise" in its broadest interpretation; they recognize, with him, many signs of promise, many men of high purpose and fair judgment, in this section; they know that no easy task has been laid upon a region already tottering under heavy burdens. But, nevertheless, they insist that the way to truth and right lies in straightforward honesty, not in indiscriminate flattery; in praising those of the South who do well and criticising uncompromisingly those who do ill; in taking advantage of the opportunities at hand and urging their fellows to do the same, but at the same time in remembering that only a firm adherence to their higher ideals and aspirations will ever keep those ideals within the realm of possibility. They do not expect that the free right to vote, to enjoy civic rights, and to be educated, will come in a moment; they do not expect to see the bias and prejudices of years disappear at the blast of a trumpet; but they are absolutely certain that the way for a people to gain their reasonable rights is not by voluntarily throwing them away and insisting that they do not want them; that the way for a people to gain respect is not by continually belittling and ridiculing themselves; that, on the contrary, Negroes must insist continually, in season and out of season, that voting is necessary to modern manhood, that color discrimination is barbarism, and that black boys need education as well as white boys.

In failing thus to state plainly and unequivocally the legitimate demands of their people, even at the cost of opposing an honored leader, the thinking classes of American Negroes would shirk a heavy responsibility,—a responsibility to themselves, a responsibility to the struggling masses, a responsibility to the darker races of men whose future depends so largely on this American experiment, but especially a responsibility to this nation,—this common Fatherland. It is wrong to encourage a man or a people in evil-doing; it is wrong to aid and abet a national crime simply because it is unpopular not to do so. The growing spirit of kindliness and reconciliation between the North and South after the frightful differences of a generation ago ought to be a source of deep congratulation to all, and especially to those whose mistreatment caused the war; but if that reconciliation is to be marked by the industrial slavery and civic death of those same black men, with permanent legislation into a position of inferiority, then those black men, if they are really men, are called upon by every consideration of patriotism and loyalty to oppose such a course by all civilized methods, even though such opposition involves disagreement with Mr. Booker T. Washington. We have no right to sit silently by while the inevitable seeds are sown for a harvest of disaster to our children, black and white.

[1903]

GUNNAR MYRDAL
*On Social Equality**

I have heard few comments made so frequently and with so much emphasis and so many illustrations as the one that "Negroes are happiest among themselves" and that "Negroes really don't want white company but prefer to be among their own race." Even sociologists, educators, and interracial experts have informed me that, when the two groups keep apart, the wish for separation is as pronounced among Negroes as among whites. In the South, many liberals are eager to stress this assertion as part of the justification for their unwillingness to give up the Southern doctrine that the Negroes must not be allowed to aspire to "social equality." Southern conservatives will usually give a somewhat different twist to the argument and actually insist that Negroes are perfectly satisfied with their social status in the South. But the conservatives are more likely to contradict themselves bluntly in the next sentence by asserting that in the back of the Negro's mind there is a keen desire to be "like white people" and to "marry white girls."

For the moment, we shall leave it an open question whether the whites understand the Negroes correctly on this point. We shall start from the evident fact that—quite independent of whether or not, to what extent, and how the Negroes have accommodated themselves—*social segregation and discrimination is a system of deprivations forced upon the Negro group by the white group.* This is equally true in the North and in the South, though in this respect, as in all others, there is more segregation and discrimination in the South, and thus the phenomenon is easier to observe.

That segregation and discrimination are forced upon the Negroes by the whites becomes apparent in the *one-sidedness* of their application. Negroes are ordinarily never admitted to white churches in the South, but if a strange white man enters a Negro church the visit is received as a great honor. The guest will be ushered to a front seat or to the platform. The service will often be interrupted, an announcement will be made that there is a "white friend" present, and he will be asked to address the Negro audience, which will loudly testify its high appreciation. Likewise, a white stranger will be received with utmost respect and cordiality in any Negro school, and everything will be done to satisfy his every wish, whereas a Negro under similar circumstances would be pushed off the grounds of a white school. Whenever I have entered a Negro theater in the South, the girl in

* Editors' title.

the ticket office has regularly turned a bewildered face and told me that "it is a colored movie." But she has apparently done this because she thought I was making a mistake and wanted to spare me embarrassment. When I answered that I did not care, the ticket office girls usually sold the ticket and received my visit as a courtesy. I have never been refused service in a Negro restaurant in the South.

When the white conductor in a train has told me occasionally that I was in the wrong car, the underlying assumption has also been the same, that the separation was made in order to save white people from having to tolerate Negro company. Contrary to the laws—which are all written on the fiction of equality—he has, with a shrug of his shoulders, always left me where I was after I told him I had gone there purposely to have a look at the Negroes. A Negro who would disclose a similar desire to observe whites would, of course, be dealt with in quite another way. In the streetcars and buses the separation seems to be enforced fairly well in both directions. When, however, the conductor tells me, a white man, that I have taken the wrong seat, it is done in a spirit of respect and in order to help me preserve my caste status. The assumption is that I have made a mistake with no intention of overstepping the rules. In the case of a Negro the assumption is usually the contrary, that he is trying to intrude. In public buildings or private establishments of the South, I have never encountered any objection to my entering the spaces set aside for the Negroes, nor to my riding in the elevator set apart for Negroes if, for any reason, the white car was not there or was filled.

5   The rules are understood to be for the protection of whites and directed against Negroes. This applies also to social rituals and etiquette. The white man may waive most of the customs, as long as he does not demonstrate such a friendliness that he becomes known as a "nigger lover"; the reaction then comes, however, from the white society. He can recognize the Negro on the street and stop for a chat, or he can ignore him. He can offer his hand to shake, or he can keep it back. Negroes often complain about the uncertainty they experience because of the fact that the initiative in defining the personal situation always belongs to the white man. It is the white man who chooses between the alternatives as to the character of the contact to be established. The Negro, who often does not know how the white man has chosen, receives surprises in one direction or the other, which constantly push him off his balance.

. . .

In his first encounter with the American Negro problem, perhaps nothing perplexes the outside observer more than the popular term and the popular theory of "no social equality." He will be made to feel from the start that it has concrete implications and a central importance for the Negro problem in America. But, nevertheless, the term is kept vague and elusive, and the theory loose and ambiguous. One moment it will be stretched to cover and justify every form of social segregation and discrimination, and, in addition, all the inequalities in justice, politics and breadwinning. The next moment it will be narrowed to express only the denial of close personal intimacies and intermarriage. The very lack of precision allows the notion of "no social equality" to rationalize the rather illogical and wavering system of color caste in America.

The kernel of the popular theory of "no social equality" will, when pursued, be presented as a firm determination on the part of the whites to block amalgamation and preserve "the purity of the white race." The white man identifies himself with "the white race" and feels that he has a stake in resisting the dissipation of its racial identity. Important in this identification is the notion of "the absolute and unchangeable superiority of the white race." From this racial dogma will often be drawn the *direct* inference that the white man shall dominate in all spheres. But when the logic of this inference is inquired about, the inference will be made *indirect* and will be made to lead over to the danger of amalgamation, or, as it is popularly expressed, "intermarriage."

It is further found that the ban on intermarriage is focused on white women. For them it covers both formal marriage and illicit intercourse. In regard to white men it is taken more or less for granted that they would not stoop to marry Negro women, and that illicit intercourse does not fall under the same intense taboo. Their offspring, under the popular doctrine that maternity is more certain than paternity, become Negroes anyway, and the white race easily avoids pollution with Negro blood. To prevent "intermarriage" in this specific sense of sex relations between white women and Negro men, it is not enough to apply legal and social sanctions against . . . it—so the popular theory runs. In using the danger of intermarriage as a defense for the whole caste system, it is assumed both that Negro men have a strong desire for "intermarriage," and that white women would be open to proposals from Negro men, *if* they are not guarded from even meeting them on an equal plane. The latter assumption, of course, is never openly expressed, but is logically implicit in the popular theory. The conclusion follows that the whole system of segregation and discrimination is justified. Every single measure is defended as necessary to block "social equality" which in its turn is held necessary to prevent "intermarriage."

The basic role of the fear of amalgamation in white attitudes to the race problem is indicated by the popular magical concept of "blood." Educated white Southerners, who know everything about modern genetic and biological research, confess readily that they actually feel an irrational or "instinctive" repugnance in thinking of "intermarriage." These measures of segregation and discrimination are often of the type found in the true taboos and in the notion "not to be touched" of primitive religion. The specific taboos are characterized, further, by a different degree of excitement which attends their violation and a different degree of punishment to the violator: the closer the act to sexual association, the more furious is the public reaction. Sexual association itself is punished by death and is accompanied by tremendous public excitement; the other social relations meet decreasing degrees of public fury. Sex becomes in this popular theory the principle around which the whole structure of segregation of the Negroes—down to disfranchisement and denial of equal opportunities on the labor market—is organized. The reasoning is this: "For, say what we will, may not all the equalities be ultimately based on potential social equality, and that in turn on intermarriage? Here we reach the real *crux* of the question." In cruder language, but with the same logic, the Southern man on the street responds to any plea for social equality: "Would you like to have your daughter marry a Negro?"

10   This theory of color caste centering around the aversion to amalgamation determines, as we have just observed, the white man's rather definite rank order of the various measures of segregation and discrimination against Negroes. The relative significance attached to each of those measures is dependent upon their degree of expediency or necessity—in the view of white people—as means of upholding the ban on "intermarriage." In this rank order, (1) the ban on intermarriage and other sex relations involving white women and colored men takes precedence before everything else. It is the end for which the other restrictions are arranged as means. Thereafter follow: (2) all sorts of taboos and etiquettes in personal contacts; (3) segregation in schools and churches; (4) segregation in hotels, restaurants, and theaters, and other public places where people

meet socially; (5) segregation in public conveyances; (6) discrimination in public services; and, finally, inequality in (7) politics, (8) justice and (9) breadwinning and relief.

The degree of liberalism on racial matters in the white South can be designated mainly by the point on this rank order where a man stops because he believes further segregation and discrimination are not necessary to prevent "intermarriage." We have seen that white liberals in the South of the present day, as a matter of principle, rather unanimously stand up against inequality in breadwinning, relief, justice and politics. These fields of discrimination form the chief battleground and considerable changes in them are, as we have seen, on the way. When we ascend to the higher ranks which concern social relations in the narrow sense, we find the Southern liberals less prepared to split off from the majority opinion of the region. Hardly anybody in the South is prepared to go the whole way and argue that even the ban on intermarriage should be lifted. Practically all agree, not only upon the high desirability of preventing "intermarriage," but also that a certain amount of separation between the two groups is expedient and necessary to prevent it. Even the one who has his philosophical doubts on the point must, if he is reasonable, abstain from ever voicing them. The social pressure is so strong that it would be foolish not to conform. Conformity is a political necessity for having any hope of influence; it is, in addition, a personal necessity for not meeting social ostracism.

. . .

The fixation on the purity of white womanhood, and also part of the intensity of emotion surrounding the whole sphere of segregation and discrimination, are to be understood as the backwashes of the sore conscience on the part of white men for their own or their compeers' relations with, or desires for, Negro women. These psychological effects are greatly magnified because of the puritan *milieu* of America and especially of the South. The upper class men in a less puritanical people could probably have indulged in sex relations with, and sexual day-dreams of, lower caste women in a more matter-of-course way and without generating so much pathos about white womanhood. The Negro people have to carry the burden not only of the white men's sins but also of their virtues. The virtues of the honest, democratic, puritan white Americans in the South are great, and the burden upon the Negroes becomes ponderous.

Our practical conclusion is that it would have cleansing effects on race relations in America, and particularly in the South, to have an open and sober discussion in rational terms of this ever present popular theory of "intermarriage" and "social equality," giving matters their factual ground, true proportions and logical relations. Because it is, to a great extent, an opportunistic rationalization, and because it refers directly and indirectly to the most touchy spots in American life and American morals, tremendous inhibitions have been built up against a detached and critical discussion of this theory. But such inhibitions are gradually overcome when, in the course of secularized education, people become rational about their life problems. It must never be forgotten that in our increasingly intellectualized civilization even the plain citizen feels an urge for truth and objectivity, and that this rationalistic urge is increasingly competing with the opportunistic demands for rationalization and escape.

There are reasons to believe that a slow but steady cleansing of the American mind is proceeding as the cultural level is raised. The basic racial inferiority doctrine is being undermined by research and education. For a white man to have illicit relations with Negro women is increasingly meeting disapproval. Negroes themselves are more and more frowning upon such relations. This all must tend to dampen the emotional fires around "social equality." Sex and race fears are, however, even today the main defense for segregation and, in fact, for the whole caste order. The question shot at the interviewer touching any point of this order is still: "Would you like to have your daughter (sister) marry a Negro?"

[1944]

RALPH ELLISON
*On Negro Folklore**

INTERVIEWERS: How representative of the American nation would you say Negro folklore is?

ELLISON: The history of the American Negro is a most intimate part of American history. Through the very process of slavery came the building of the United States. Negro folklore, evolving within a larger culture which regarded it as inferior, was an especially courageous expression. It announced the Negro's willingness to trust his own experience, his own sensibilities as to the definition of reality, rather than allow his masters to define these crucial matters for him. His experience is that of America and the West, and is as rich a body of experience as one would find anywhere. We can view it narrowly as something exotic, folksy or "low-down," or we may identify ourselves with it and recognize it as an important segment of the larger American experience—not lying at the bottom of it, but intertwined, diffused in its very texture. I can't take this lightly or be impressed by those who cannot see its importance; it is important to *me*. One ironic witness to the beauty and the universality of this art is the fact that the descendants of the very men who enslaved us can now sing the spirituals and find in the singing an exaltation of their own humanity. Just take a look at some of the slave songs, blues, folk ballads; their possibilities for the writer are infinitely suggestive. Some of them have named human situations so well that a whole corps of writers could not exhaust their universality. For instance, here's an old slave verse:

> Ole Aunt Dinah, she's just like me
> She work so hard she want to be free
> But old Aunt Dinah's gittin' kinda ole
> She's afraid to go to Canada on account of the cold.
>
> Ole Uncle Jack, now he's a mighty "good nigger,"
> You tell him that you want to be free for a fac'
> Next thing you know they done stripped the skin off your back.
>
> Now old Uncle Ned, he want to be free
> He found his way north by the moss on the tree
> He cross that river floating in a tub
> The patateroller† give him a mighty close rub.

* Editors' title.   † Patroller.

It's crude, but in it you have three universal attitudes toward the problem of freedom. You can refine it and sketch in the psychological subtleties and historical and philosophical allusions, action and what not, but I don't think its basic definition can be exhausted. Perhaps some genius could do as much with it as Mann has done with the Joseph story.

INTERVIEWERS: Can you give us an example of the use of folklore in your own novel?

5   ELLISON: Well, there are certain themes, symbols and images which are based on folk material. For example, there is the old saying amongst Negroes: If you're black, stay back; if you're brown, stick around; if you're white, you're right. And there is the joke Negroes tell on themselves about their being so black they can't be seen in the dark. In my book this sort of thing was merged with the meanings which blackness and light have long had in Western mythology: evil and goodness, ignorance and knowledge, and so on. In my novel the narrator's development is one through blackness to light; that is, from ignorance to enlightenment: invisibility to visibility. He leaves the South and goes North; this, as you will notice in reading Negro folktales, is always the road to freedom, the movement upward. You have the same thing again when he leaves his underground cave for the open.

It took me a long time to learn how to adapt such examples of myth into my work—also ritual. The use of ritual is equally a vital part of the creative process. I learned a few things from Eliot, Joyce and Hemingway, but not how to adapt them. When I started writing, I knew that in both *The Waste Land* and *Ulysses* ancient myth and ritual were used to give form and significance to the material, but it took me a few years to realize that the myths and rites which we find functioning in our everyday lives could be used in the same way. In my first attempt at a novel—which I was unable to complete—I began by trying to manipulate the simple structural unities of *beginning, middle* and *end*, but when I attempted to deal with the psychological strata—the images, symbols and emotional configurations—of the experience at hand, I discovered that the unities were simply cool points of stability on which one could suspend the narrative line, but beneath the surface of apparently rational human relationships there seethed a chaos before which I was helpless. People rationalize what they shun or are incapable of dealing with; these superstitions and their rationalizations become ritual as they govern behavior. The rituals become social forms, and it is one of the functions of the artist to recognize them and raise them to the level of art.

I don't know whether I'm getting this over or not. Let's put it this way: take the "Battle Royal" passage in my novel, where the boys are blindfolded and forced to fight each other for the amusement of the white observers. This is a vital part of behavior pattern in the South, which both Negroes and whites thoughtlessly accept. It is a ritual in preservation of caste lines, a keeping of taboo to appease the gods and ward off bad luck. It is also the initiation ritual to which all greenhorns are subjected. This passage which states what Negroes will see I did not have to invent; the patterns were already there in society, so that all I had to do was present them in a broader context of meaning. In any society there are many rituals of situation which, for the most part, go unquestioned. They can be simple or elaborate, but they are the connective tissue between the work of art and the audience.

INTERVIEWERS: Do you think a reader unacquainted with this folklore can properly understand your work?

ELLISON: Yes, I think so. It's like jazz; there's no inherent problem which prohibits understanding but the assumptions brought to it. We don't all dig Shakespeare uniformly, or even Little Red Riding Hood. The understanding of art depends finally upon one's willingness to extend one's humanity and one's knowledge of human life. I noticed, incidentally, that the Germans, having no special caste assumptions concerning American Negroes, dealt with my work simply as a novel. I think the Americans will come to view it that way in twenty years—if it's around that long.

[1955]

RALPH ELLISON
*Life in Oklahoma City**

. . .

In the loosely structured community of that time, knowledge, news of other ways of living, ancient wisdom, the latest literary fads, hate literature—for years I kept a card warning Negroes away from the polls, which had been dropped by the thousands from a plane which circled over the Negro community—information of all kinds found its level, catch-as-catch-can, in the minds of those who were receptive to it. Not that there was no conscious structuring—I read my first Shaw and Maupassant, my first Harvard Classics in the home of a friend whose parents were products of that stream of New England education which had been brought to Negroes by the young and enthusiastic white teachers who staffed the schools set up for the freedmen after the Civil War. These parents were both teachers, and there were others like them in our town.

But the places where a rich oral literature was truly functional were the churches, the schoolyards, the barbershops, the cotton-picking camps—places where folklore and gossip thrived. The drug store where I worked was such a place, where on days of bad weather the older men would sit with their pipes and tell tall tales, hunting yarns and homely versions of the classics. It was here that I heard stories of searching for buried treasure and of headless horsemen, which I was told were my own father's versions told long before. There were even recitals of popular verse, "The Shooting of Dan McGrew," and, along with these, stories of Jesse James, of Negro outlaws and black United States marshals, of slaves who became the chiefs of Indian tribes, and of the exploits of Negro cowboys. There was both truth and fantasy in this, intermingled in the mysterious fashion of literature.

In their formative period, writers absorb into their consciousness much that has no special value until much later, and often much which is of no special value even then, perhaps, beyond the fact that it throbs with affect and mystery and in it "time and pain and royalty in the blood" are suspended in imagery. So, long before I thought of writing, I was claimed by weather, by speech rhythms, by Negro voices and their different idioms, by husky male voices and by the high shrill singing voices of certain Negro women, by music, by tight spaces and by wide spaces in which the eyes could wander, by death, by newly born babies, by manners of various kinds, company manners and street manners, the manners of white society and those of our own high society, and by interracial manners, by street fights, circuses and minstrel shows, by vaudeville and moving pictures, by

* Editors' title.

prize fights and foot races, baseball games and football matches. By spring floods and blizzards, catalpa worms and jack rabbits, honeysuckle and snapdragons (which smelled like old cigar butts), by sunflowers and hollyhocks, raw sugar cane and baked yams, pigs' feet, chili and blue haw ice cream. By parades, public dances and jam sessions, Easter sunrise ceremonies and large funerals. By contests between fire-and-brimstone preachers and by presiding elders who got "laughing-happy" when moved by the spirit of God.

I was impressed by expert players of the "dozens" and certain notorious bootleggers of corn whiskey. By jazz musicians and fortunetellers and by men who did anything well, by strange sicknesses and by interesting brick or razor scars, by expert cursing vocabularies as well as by exalted praying and terrifying shouting, and by transcendent playing or singing of the blues. I was fascinated by old ladies, those who had seen slavery and those who were defiant of white folk and black alike, by the enticing walks of prostitutes and by the limping walks affected by Negro hustlers, especially those who wore Stetson hats, expensive shoes with well-starched overalls, usually with a diamond stickpin (when not in hock) in their tireless collars as their gambling uniforms.

5   And there were the blind men who preached on corners, and the blind men who sang the blues to the accompaniment of washboard and guitar, and the white junkmen who sang mountain music and the famous hucksters of fruit and vegetables.

And there was the Indian-Negro confusion. There were Negroes who were part Indian and who lived on reservations, and Indians who had children who lived in towns as Negroes, and Negroes who were Indians and traveled back and forth between the groups with no trouble. And Indians who were as wild as wild Negroes, and others who were as solid and as steady as bankers. There were the teachers, too: inspiring teachers and villainous teachers who chased after the girl students, and certain female teachers who one wished would chase after young male students. And a handsome old principal of military bearing who had been blemished by his classmates at West Point when they discovered on the eve of graduation that he was a Negro. There were certain Jews, Mexicans, Chinese cooks, a German orchestra conductor and an English grocer who owned a Franklin touring car. And certain Negro mechanics—"Cadillac Slim," "Sticks" Walker, Buddy Bunn and Oscar Pitman—who had so assimilated the automobile that they seemed to be behind a steering wheel even as they walked the streets or danced with girls. And there were the whites who despised us and the others who shared our hardships and our joys.

There is much more, but this is sufficient to indicate some of what was present even in a segregated community to form the background of my work and my sense of life.

And now comes the next step. I went to Tuskegee to study music, hoping to become a composer of symphonies, and there, during my second year, I read *The Waste Land* and that, although I was then unaware of it, was the real transition to writing.

Mrs. L. C. McFarland had taught us much of Negro history in grade school, and from her I'd learned of the New Negro Movement of the twenties, of Langston Hughes, Countee Cullen, Claude McKay, James Weldon Johnson and the others. They had inspired pride and had given me a closer identification with poetry (by now, oddly enough, I seldom thought of my hidden name), but with music so much on my mind it never occurred to me to try to imitate them. Still, I read their work and was excited by the glamour of the Harlem which emerged from their poems, and it was good to know that there were Negro writers. Then came *The Waste Land*.

10   I was much more under the spell of literature than I realized at the time. *Wuthering Heights* had caused me an agony of unexpressible emotion, and the same was true of *Jude the Obscure*, but *The Waste Land* seized my mind. I was intrigued by its power to move me while eluding my understanding. Somehow its rhythms were often closer to those of jazz than were those of the Negro poets, and even though I could not understand then, its range of allusion was as mixed and as varied as that of Louis Armstrong. Yet there were its discontinuities, its changes of pace and its hidden system of organization which escaped me.

There was nothing to do but look up the references in the footnotes to the poem, and thus began my conscious education in literature. For this, the library at Tuskegee was quite adequate and I used it. Soon I was reading a whole range of subjects drawn upon by the poet, and this led, in turn, to criticism and to Pound, Ford Madox Ford, Sherwood Anderson, Gertrude Stein, Hemingway and Fitzgerald and "round about 'til I was come" back to Melville and Twain—the writers who are taught and doubtless overtaught today. Perhaps it was my good luck that they were not taught at Tuskegee; I wouldn't know. But at the time I was playing, having an intellectually interesting good time.

Having given so much attention to the techniques of music, the process of learning something of the craft and intention of modern poetry and fiction seemed quite familiar. Besides, it was absolutely painless because it involved no deadlines or credits. Even then, however, a process which I described earlier had begun to operate. The more I learned of literature in this conscious way, the more the details of my background became transformed. I heard undertones in remembered conversations which had escaped me before, local customs took on a more universal meaning, values which I hadn't understood were revealed, some of the people whom I had known were diminished, while others were elevated in stature. More important, I began to see my own possibilities with more objective and in some ways more hopeful eyes.

The summer of 1936 I went to New York seeking work, which I did not find, and remained there, but the personal transformation continued. Reading had become a conscious process of growth and discovery, a method of reordering the world. And that world had widened considerably.

At Tuskegee I had handled manuscripts which Prokofiev had given to Hazel Harrison, a Negro concert pianist who taught there and who had known him in Europe, and through Miss Harrison I had become aware of Prokofiev's symphonies. I had also become aware of the radical movement in politics and art, and in New York had begun reading the work of André Malraux, not only the fiction but chapters published from his *Psychology of Art*. And in my search for an expression of modern sensibility in the works of Negro writers I discovered Richard Wright. Shortly thereafter I was to meet Wright, and it was at his suggestion that I wrote both my first book review and my first short story.

15   These were fateful suggestions. For although I had tried my hand at poetry while at Tuskegee, it hadn't occurred to me that I might write fiction, but once he suggested it, it seemed the most natural thing to try. Fortunately for me, Wright, then on the verge of his first success, was eager to talk with a beginner, and I was able to save valuable time in searching out those works in which writing was discussed as a craft. He guided me to Henry James's prefaces, to Conrad, to Joseph

Warren Beach and to the letters of Dostoevsky. There were other advisers and other books involved, of course, but what is important here is that I was consciously concerned with the art of fiction, and that almost from the beginning I was grappling quite consciously with the art through which I wished to realize myself. But this was not done in isolation; the Spanish Civil War was now in progress and the Depression was still on. The world was being shaken up, and through one of those odd instances which occur to young provincials in New York, I was to hear Malraux make an appeal for the Spanish Loyalists at the same party where I first heard the folk singer Leadbelly perform. Wright and I were there seeking money for the magazine which he had come to New York to edit.

Art and politics: a great French novelist and a Negro folk singer, a young writer who was soon to publish *Uncle Tom's Children*, and I who had barely begun to study his craft. It is such accidents, such fortuitous meetings, which count for so much in our lives. I had never dreamed that I would be in the presence of Malraux, of whose work I became aware on my second day in Harlem when Langston Hughes suggested that I read *Man's Fate* and *Days of Wrath* before returning them to a friend of his. And it is this fortuitous circumstance which led to my selecting Malraux as a literary "ancestor," whom, unlike a relative, the artist is permitted to choose. There was in progress at the time all the agitation over the Scottsboro boys and the Herndon Case, and I was aware of both. I had to be; I myself had been taken off a freight train at Decatur, Alabama, only three years before while on my way to Tuskegee. But while I joined in the agitation for their release, my main energies went into learning to write.

I began to publish enough, and not too slowly, to justify my hopes for success, and as I continued, I made a most perplexing discovery—namely, that for all his conscious concern with technique, a writer did not so much create the novel as he was created *by* the novel. That is, one did not make an arbitrary gesture when one sought to write. And when I say that the novelist is created by the novel, I mean to remind you that fictional techniques are not a mere set of objective tools, but something much more intimate: a way of feeling, of seeing and of expressing one's sense of life. And the process of *acquiring* technique is a process of modifying one's responses, of learning to see and feel, to hear and observe, to evoke and evaluate the images of memory and of summoning up and directing the imagination, of learning to conceive of human values in the ways which have been established by the great writers who have developed and extended the art. And perhaps the writer's greatest freedom, as artist, lies precisely in his possession of technique, for it is through technique that he comes to possess and express the meaning of his life.

[1964]

Case Study: Writing about Flannery O'Connor

In this case study we give two short stories and several comments of O'Connor's on literature:

1. "A Good Man Is Hard to Find"
2. "Revelation"
3. Passages from five essays about fiction and a letter on "A Good Man Is Hard to Find"

We also include a page from the manuscript of "A Good Man Is Hard to Find," showing O'Connor's revisions.

Flannery O'Connor (1925–64)—her first name was Mary but she did not use it—was born in Savannah, Georgia, but spent most of her life in Milledgeville, Georgia, where her family moved when she was 12. She was educated in parochial schools and at the local college and then went to the School for Writers at the University of Iowa, where she earned an M.F.A. in 1946. For a few months she lived at a writers' colony in Saratoga Springs, New York, and then for a few weeks she lived in New York City, but most of her life was spent back in Milledgeville, where she tended her peacocks and wrote stories, novels, essays (posthumously published as Mystery and Manners *[1970]), and letters (posthumously published under the title* The Habit of Being *[1979]).*

In 1951, when she was 25, Flannery O'Connor discovered that she was a victim of lupus erythematosus, an incurable autoimmune disease that had crippled and then killed her father ten years before. She died at the age of 39. O'Connor faced her illness with stoic courage, Christian fortitude—and tough humor. Here is a glimpse, from one of her letters, of how she dealt with those who pitied her:

> *An old lady got on the elevator behind me and as soon as I turned around she fixed me with a moist gleaming eye and said in a loud voice, "Bless you, darling!" I felt exactly like the Misfit [in "A Good Man Is Hard to Find"] and I gave her a weakly lethal look, whereupon greatly encouraged she grabbed my arm and whispered (very loud) in my ear, "Remember what they said to John at the gate, darling!" It was not my floor but I got off and I suppose the old lady was astounded at how quick I could get away on crutches. I have a one-legged friend and I asked her what they said to John at the gate. She said she reckoned they said, "The lame shall enter first." This may be because the lame will be able to knock everybody else aside with their crutches.*

A devout Catholic, O'Connor forthrightly summarized the relation between her belief and her writing:

> *I see from the standpoint of Christian orthodoxy. This means that for me the meaning of life is centered in our Redemption by Christ and what I see in the world I see in its relation to that.*

A Good Man Is Hard to Find

The grandmother didn't want to go to Florida. She wanted to visit some of her connections in east Tennessee and she was seizing every chance to change Bailey's mind. Bailey was the son she lived with, her only boy. He was sitting on the edge of his chair at the table, bent over the orange sports section of the *Journal.* "Now look here, Bailey," she said, "see here, read this," and she stood with one hand on her thin hip and the other rattling the newspaper at his bald head. "Here this fellow that calls himself The Misfit is aloose from the Federal Pen and headed toward Florida and you read here what it says he did to these people. Just you read it. I wouldn't take my children in any direction with a criminal like that aloose in it. I couldn't answer to my conscience if I did."

Bailey didn't look up from his reading so she wheeled around then and faced the children's mother, a young woman in slacks, whose face was as broad and innocent as a cabbage and was tied around with a green headkerchief that had two points on the top like rabbit's ears. She was sitting on the sofa, feeding the baby his apricots out of a jar. "The children have been to Florida before," the old lady said. "You all ought to take them somewhere else for a change so they would see different parts of the world and be broad. They never have been to east Tennessee."

The children's mother didn't seem to hear her, but the eight-year-old boy, John Wesley, a stocky child with glasses, said. "If you don't want to go to Florida, why dontcha stay at home?" He and the little girl, June Star, were reading the funny papers on the floor.

"She wouldn't stay at home to be queen for a day," June Star said without raising her yellow head.

5   "Yes, and what would you do if this fellow, The Misfit, caught you?" the grandmother said.

"I'd smack his face," John Wesley said.

"She wouldn't stay at home for a million bucks," June Star said. "Afraid she'd miss something. She has to go everywhere we go."

"All right, Miss," the grandmother said. "Just remember that the next time you want me to curl your hair."

June Star said her hair was naturally curly.

10   The next morning the grandmother was the first one in the car, ready to go. She had her big black valise that looked like the head of a hippopotamus in one corner, and underneath it she was hiding a basket with Pitty Sing, the cat, in it. She didn't intend for the cat to be left alone in the house for three days because he would miss her too much and she was afraid he might brush against one of the gas burners and accidentally asphyxiate himself. Her son, Bailey, didn't like to arrive at a motel with a cat.

She sat in the middle of the back seat with John Wesley and June Star on either side of her. Bailey and the children's mother and the baby sat in front and they left Atlanta at eight forty-five with the mileage on the car at 55890. The grandmother wrote this down because she thought it would be interesting to say how many miles they had been when they got back. It took them twenty minutes to reach the outskirts of the city.

The old lady settled herself comfortably, removing her white cotton gloves and putting them up with her purse on the shelf in front of the back window. The children's mother still had on slacks and still had her head tied up in a green kerchief, but the grandmother had on a navy blue straw sailor hat with a bunch of white violets on the brim and a navy blue dress with a small white dot in the print. Her collars and cuffs were white organdy trimmed with lace and at her neckline she had pinned a purple spray of cloth violets containing a sachet. In case of an accident, anyone seeing her dead on the highway would know at once that she was a lady.

She said she thought it was going to be a good day for driving, neither too hot nor too cold, and she cautioned Bailey that the speed limit was fifty-five miles an hour and that the patrolmen hid themselves behind bill-boards and small clumps of trees and sped out after you before you had a chance to slow down. She pointed out interesting details of the scenery: Stone Mountain; the blue granite that in some places came up to both sides of the highway; the brilliant red clay banks slightly streaked with purple; and the various crops that made rows of

2.

the grandmother

~~Of course she~~ was the first one ready to load up the next morning at six
o'clock. She had Baby Brother's bucking bronco ~~that and~~ ~~xxxxxxxxx~~ what she
called her "~~xxxxx~~" and Pitty Sing, the cat, ~~xxxxxx~~ *put the* packed in the car before
Boatwrite had a chance to ~~gxtxxxxthingxxxxxx~~ ~~xxxx~~ ~~xxxxxxxxxxxxxxxxxx~~ with the
rest of the luggage out of the hall. They got off at seven-thirty, Boatwrite
and ~~Emy~~ the children's mother in the front and Granny, John Wesley, Baby Brother,
Little Sister Mayy Ann, Pitty Sing, and the bucking bronco in the back.

"Why the hell did you bring that goddam rocking horse?" Boatwrite asked
because as soon as ~~the car began to move,~~ *they were out of the city on the smooth highway* Baby Brother began to squall to get
on the bucking bronco. "He can't get on that thing in this car and that's final,"
his father who was a stern man said.

"Can we open the lunch now?" Little Sister ~~xxxxxxx~~ asked. "It'll shut
Baby Brother up. Mamma, can we open up the lunch?"

"No," their grandmother said. *It's only eight-thirty*

Their mother was ~~xxxx~~ reading SCREEN MOTHERS AND THEIR CHILDREN. "Yeah,
sure," she said without looking up. She was all dressed up today. She had on
a purple silk dress and a hat and ~~xxxxxxxx~~ a choker of pink beads and a new
her new pocket book, and high heel pumps.

"Let's go through Georgia quick so we won't have to look at it much," John
Wesley said. "~~xxxxxxxxxxxxxxxxx~~"

"You should see Tennessee," his grandmother said. "Now there is a *beautiful* state."

"Like hell," John Wesley said. "That's just a hillbilly dumping ground."

"Hah," his mother said, and nudged Boatwrite. "Didjer hear that?" *She was*
from Tennessee They ate their lunch and got along fine ~~after that~~ for a while until Pitty
Sing who had been asleep jumped into the front of the car and caused Boatwrite
to swerve to the right into a ditch. Pitty Sing was a large grey-striped cat
with a yellow hind leg and a ~~x~~ ~~long~~ soiled white face. Granny thought that she
was the only person in the world that he really loved but he had never ~~really~~ *he thought was*
looked ~~xxxxxxxxxxxxxxx~~ ~~xxx~~ farther *up* than her middle and he didn't even
like other cats. He jumped snarling into ~~the front seat and Boatwrite's~~ shoulders

Typescript page from "A Good Man Is Hard to Find" with O'Connor's handwritten
changes.

green lace-work on the ground. The trees were full of silver-white sunlight and
the meanest of them sparkled. The children were reading comic magazines and
their mother had gone back to sleep.

"Let's go through Georgia fast so we won't have to look at it much," John
Wesley said.

15   "If I were a little boy," said the grandmother, "I wouldn't talk about my native
state that way. Tennessee has the mountains and Georgia has the hills."

"Tennessee is just a hillbilly dumping ground," John Wesley said, "and Georgia is a lousy state too."

"You said it," June Star said.

"In my time," said the grandmother, folding her thin veined fingers, "children were more respectful of their native states and their parents and everything else. People did right then. Oh look at the cute little pickaninny!" she said and pointed to a Negro child standing in the door of a shack. "Wouldn't that make a picture, now?" she asked and they all turned and looked at the little Negro out of the back window. He waved.

"He didn't have any britches on," June Star said.

20   "He probably didn't have any," the grandmother explained. "Little niggers in the country don't have things like we do. If I could paint, I'd paint that picture," she said.

The children exchanged comic books.

The grandmother offered to hold the baby and the children's mother passed him over the front seat to her. She set him on her knee and bounced him and told him about the things they were passing. She rolled her eyes and screwed up her mouth and stuck her leathery thin face into his smooth bland one. Occasionally he gave her a faraway smile. They passed a large cotton field with five or six graves fenced in the middle of it, like a small island. "Look at the graveyard!" the grandmother said, pointing it out. "That was the old family burying ground. That belonged to the plantation."

"Where's the plantation?" John Wesley asked.

"Gone With the Wind," said the grandmother. "Ha. Ha."

25   When the children finished all the comic books they had brought, they opened the lunch and ate it. The grandmother ate a peanut butter sandwich and an olive and would not let the children throw the box and the paper napkins out the window. When there was nothing else to do they played a game by choosing a cloud and making the other two guess what shape it suggested. John Wesley took one the shape of a cow and June Star guessed a cow and John Wesley said, no, an automobile, and June Star said he didn't play fair, and they began to slap each other over the grandmother.

The grandmother said she would tell them a story if they would keep quiet. When she told a story, she rolled her eyes and waved her head and was very dramatic. She said once when she was a maiden lady she had been courted by a Mr. Edgar Atkins Teagarden from Jasper, Georgia. She said he was a very good-looking man and a gentleman and that he brought her a watermelon every Saturday afternoon with his initials cut in it, E.A.T. Well, one Saturday, she said, Mr. Teagarden brought the watermelon and there was nobody at home and he left it on the front porch and returned in his buggy to Jasper, but she never got the watermelon, she said, because a nigger boy ate it when he saw the initials, E.A.T.! This story tickled John Wesley's funny bone and he giggled and giggled but June Star didn't think it was any good. She said she wouldn't marry a man that just brought her a watermelon on Saturday. The grandmother said she would have done well to marry Mr. Teagarden because he was a gentleman and had bought Coca-Cola stock when it first came out and that he had died only a few years ago, a very wealthy man.

They stopped at The Tower for barbecued sandwiches. The Tower was a part-stucco and part-wood filling station and dance hall set in a clearing outside of Timothy. A fat man named Red Sammy Butts ran it and there were signs stuck here and there on the building and for miles up and down the highway saying,

TRY RED SAMMY'S FAMOUS BARBECUE. NONE LIKE FAMOUS RED SAMMY'S! RED SAM! THE FAT BOY
WITH THE HAPPY LAUGH. A VETERAN! RED SAMMY'S YOUR MAN!

Red Sammy was lying on the bare ground outside The Tower with his head
under a truck while a gray monkey about a foot high, chained to a small chinaberry tree, chattered nearby. The monkey sprang back into the tree and got on
the highest limb as soon as he saw the children jump out of the car and run toward him.

Inside, The Tower was a long dark room with a counter at one end and tables at the other and dancing space in the middle. They all sat down at a
broad table next to the nickelodeon and Red Sam's wife, a tall burnt-brown
woman with hair and eyes lighter than her skin, came and took their order.
The children's mother put a dime in the machine and played "The Tennessee
Waltz," and the grandmother said that tune always made her want to dance.
She asked Bailey if he would like to dance but he only glared at her. He didn't
have a naturally sunny disposition like she did and trips made him nervous.
The grandmother's brown eyes were very bright. She swayed her head from
side to side and pretended she was dancing in her chair. June Star said play
something she could tap to so the children's mother put in another dime and
played a fast number and June Star stepped out onto the dance floor and did
her tap routine.

30   "Ain't she cute?" Red Sam's wife said, leaning over the counter. "Would you
like to come be my little girl?"

"No, I certainly wouldn't," June Star said. "I wouldn't live in a broken-down
place like this for a million bucks!" and she ran back to the table.

"Ain't she cute?" the woman repeated, stretching her mouth politely.

"Aren't you ashamed?" hissed the grandmother.

Red Sam came in and told his wife to quit lounging on the counter and hurry
with these people's order. His khaki trousers reached just to his hip bones and his
stomach hung over them like a sack of meal swaying under his shirt. He came
over and sat down at a table nearby and let out a combination sigh and yodel.
"You can't win," he said. "You can't win," and he wiped his sweating red face off
with a gray handkerchief. "These days you don't know who to trust," he said.
"Ain't that the truth?"

35   "People are certainly not nice like they used to be," said the grandmother.

"Two fellers come in here last week," Red Sammy said, "driving a Chrysler. It
was an old beat-up car but it was a good one and these boys looked all right to
me. Said they worked at the mill and you know I let them fellers charge the gas
they bought? Now why did I do that?"

"Because you're a good man!" the grandmother said at once.

"Yes'm, I suppose so," Red Sam said as if he were struck with this answer.

His wife brought the orders, carrying the five plates all at once without a tray,
two in each hand and one balanced on her arm. "It isn't a soul in this green world
of God's that you can trust," she said. "And I don't count nobody out of that, not
nobody," she repeated, looking at Red Sammy.

40   "Did you read about that criminal, The Misfit, that's escaped?" asked the
grandmother.

"I wouldn't be a bit surprised if he didn't attack this place right here," said the
woman. "If he hears about it being here, I wouldn't be none surprised to see him.
If he hears it's two cent in the cash register, I wouldn't be a tall surprised if he . . . "

"That'll do," Red Sam said. "Go bring these people their Co'Colas," and the
woman went off to get the rest of the order.

"A good man is hard to find," Red Sammy said. "Everything is getting terrible. I remember the day you could go off and leave your screen door unlatched. Not no more."

He and the grandmother discussed better times. The old lady said that in her opinion Europe was entirely to blame for the way things were now. She said the way Europe acted you would think we were made of money and Red Sam said it was no use talking about it, she was exactly right. The children ran outside into the white sunlight and looked at the monkey in the lacy chinaberry tree. He was busy catching fleas on himself and biting each one carefully between his teeth as if it were a delicacy.

45   They drove off again into the hot afternoon. The grandmother took cat naps and woke up every five minutes with her own snoring. Outside of Toombsboro she woke up and recalled an old plantation that she had visited in this neighborhood once when she was a young lady. She said the house had six white columns across the front and that there was an avenue of oaks leading up to it and two little wooden trellis arbors on either side in front where you sat down with your suitor after a stroll in the garden. She recalled exactly which road to turn off to get to it. She knew that Bailey would not be willing to lose any time looking at an old house, but the more she talked about it, the more she wanted to see it once again and find out if the little twin arbors were still standing. "There was a secret panel in this house," she said craftily, not telling the truth but wishing that she were, "and the story went that all the family silver was hidden in it when Sherman came through but it was never found . . . "

"Hey!" John Wesley said. "Let's go see it! We'll find it! We'll poke all the woodwork and find it! Who lives there? Where do you turn off at? Hey, Pop, can't we turn off there?"

"We never have seen a house with a secret panel!" June Star shrieked. "Let's go to the house with the secret panel! Hey, Pop, can't we go see the house with the secret panel!"

"It's not far from here, I know," the grandmother said. "It wouldn't take over twenty minutes."

Bailey was looking straight ahead. His jaw was as rigid as a horseshoe. "No," he said.

50   The children began to yell and scream that they wanted to see the house with the secret panel. John Wesley kicked the back of the front seat and June Star hung over her mother's shoulder and whined desperately into her ear that they never had any fun even on their vacation, that they could never do what THEY wanted to do. The baby began to scream and John Wesley kicked the back of the seat so hard that his father could feel the blows in his kidney.

"All right!" he shouted and drew the car to a stop at the side of the road. "Will you all shut up? Will you all just shut up for one second? If you don't shut up, we won't go anywhere."

"It would be very educational for them," the grandmother murmured.

"All right," Bailey said, "but get this. This is the only time we're going to stop for anything like this. This is the one and only time."

"The dirt road that you have to turn down is about a mile back," the grandmother directed. "I marked it when we passed."

55   "A dirt road," Bailey groaned.

After they had turned around and were headed toward the dirt road, the grandmother recalled other points about the house, the beautiful glass over the front doorway and the candle lamp in the hall. John Wesley said that the secret panel was probably in the fireplace.

"You can't go inside this house," Bailey said. "You don't know who lives there."

"While you all talk to the people in front, I'll run around behind and get in a window," John Wesley suggested.

"We'll all stay in the car," his mother said.

60　　They turned onto the dirt road and the car raced roughly along in a swirl of pink dust. The grandmother recalled the times when there were no paved roads and thirty miles was a day's journey. The dirt road was hilly and there were sudden washes in it and sharp curves on dangerous embankments. All at once they would be on a hill, looking down over the blue tops of trees for miles around, then the next minute, they would be in a red depression with the dust-coated trees looking down on them.

"This place had better turn up in a minute," Bailey said, "or I'm going to turn around."

The road looked as if no one had traveled on it in months.

"It's not much farther," the grandmother said and just as she said it, a horrible thought came to her. The thought was so embarrassing that she turned red in the face and her eyes dilated and her feet jumped up, upsetting her valise in the corner. The instant the valise moved, the newspaper top she had over the basket under it rose with a snarl and Pitty Sing, the cat, sprang onto Bailey's shoulder.

The children were thrown to the floor and their mother, clutching the baby, was thrown out the door onto the ground; the old lady was thrown into the front seat. The car turned over once and landed right-side-up in a gulch on the side of the road. Bailey remained in the driver's seat with the cat—gray-striped with a broad white face and an orange nose—clinging to his neck like a caterpillar.

65　　As soon as the children saw they could move their arms and legs, they scrambled out of the car, shouting, "We've had an ACCIDENT!" The grandmother was curled up under the dashboard, hoping she was injured so that Bailey's wrath would not come down on her all at once. The horrible thought she had had before the accident was that the house she had remembered so vividly was not in Georgia but in Tennessee.

Bailey removed the cat from his neck with both hands and flung it out the window against the side of a pine tree. Then he got out of the car and started looking for the children's mother. She was sitting against the side of the red gutted ditch, holding the screaming baby, but she only had a cut down her face and a broken shoulder. "We've had an ACCIDENT!" the children screamed in a frenzy of delight.

"But nobody's killed," June Star said with disappointment as the grandmother limped out of the car, her hat still pinned to her head but the broken front brim standing up at a jaunty angle and the violet spray hanging off the side. They all sat down in the ditch, except the children, to recover from the shock. They were all shaking.

"Maybe a car will come along," said the children's mother hoarsely.

"I believe I have injured an organ," said the grandmother, pressing her side, but no one answered her. Bailey's teeth were clattering. He had on a yellow sport shirt with bright blue parrots designed in it and his face was as yellow as the shirt. The grandmother decided that she would not mention that the house was in Tennessee.

70   The road was about ten feet above and they could see only the tops of the trees on the other side of it. Behind the ditch they were sitting in there were more woods, tall and dark and deep. In a few minutes they saw a car some distance away on top of a hill, coming slowly as if the occupants were watching them. The grandmother stood up and waved both arms dramatically to attract their attention. The car continued to come on slowly, disappeared around a bend and appeared again, moving even slower on top of the hill they had gone over. It was a big black battered hearselike automobile. There were three men in it.

It came to a stop just over them and for some minutes, the driver looked down with a steady expressionless gaze to where they were sitting, and didn't speak. Then he turned his head and muttered something to the other two and they got out. One was a fat boy in black trousers and a red sweat shirt with a silver stallion embossed on the front of it. He moved around on the right side of them and stood staring, his mouth partly open in a kind of loose grin. The other had on khaki pants and a blue striped coat and a gray hat pulled down very low, hiding most of his face. He came around slowly on the left side. Neither spoke.

The driver got out of the car and stood by the side of it, looking down at them. He was an older man than the other two. His hair was just beginning to gray and he wore silver-rimmed spectacles that gave him a scholarly look. He had a long creased face and didn't have on any shirt or undershirt. He had on blue jeans that were too tight for him and was holding a black hat and a gun. The two boys also had guns.

"We've had an ACCIDENT!" the children screamed.

The grandmother had the peculiar feeling that the bespectacled man was someone she knew. His face was as familiar to her as if she had known him all her life but she could not recall who he was. He moved away from the car and began to come down the embankment, placing his feet carefully so that he wouldn't slip. He had on tan and white shoes and no socks, and his ankles were red and thin. "Good afternoon," he said. "I see you all had you a little spill."

75   "We turned over twice!" said the grandmother.

"Oncet," he corrected. "We seen it happen. Try their car and see will it run, Hiram," he said quietly to the boy with the gray hat.

"What you got that gun for?" John Wesley asked. "Whatcha gonna do with that gun?"

"Lady," the man said to the children's mother, "would you mind calling them children to sit down by you? Children make me nervous. I want all you to sit down right together there where you're at."

"What are you telling us what to do for?" June Star asked.

80   Behind them the line of woods gaped like a dark open mouth. "Come here," said their mother.

"Look here now," Bailey began suddenly, "we're in a predicament! We're in . . . "

The grandmother shrieked. She scrambled to her feet and stood staring. "You're The Misfit!" she said. "I recognized you at once!"

"Yes'm," the man said, smiling slightly as if he were pleased in spite of himself to be known, "but it would have been better for all of you, lady, if you hadn't of reckernized me."

Bailey turned his head sharply and said something to his mother that shocked even the children. The old lady began to cry and The Misfit reddened.

85   "Lady," he said, "don't you get upset. Sometimes a man says things he don't mean. I don't reckon he meant to talk to you thataway."

"You wouldn't shoot a lady, would you?" the grandmother said and removed a clean handkerchief from her cuff and began to slap at her eyes with it.

The Misfit pointed the toe of his shoe into the ground and made a little hole and then covered it up again. "I would hate to have to," he said.

"Listen," the grandmother almost screamed, "I know you're a good man. You don't look a bit like you have common blood. I know you must come from nice people!"

"Yes ma'm," he said, "finest people in the world." When he smiled he showed a row of strong white teeth. "God never made a finer woman than my mother and my daddy's heart was pure gold," he said. The boy with the red sweat shirt had come around behind them and was standing with his gun at his hip. The Misfit squatted down on the ground. "Watch them children, Bobby Lee," he said. "You know they make me nervous." He looked at the six of them huddled together in front of him and he seemed to be embarrassed as if he couldn't think of anything to say. "Ain't a cloud in the sky," he remarked, looking up at it. "Don't see no sun but don't see no cloud neither."

90   "Yes, it's a beautiful day," said the grandmother. "Listen," she said, "you shouldn't call yourself The Misfit because I know you're a good man at heart. I can just look at you and tell."

"Hush!" Bailey yelled, "Hush! Everybody shut up and let me handle this!" He was squatting in the position of a runner about to sprint forward but he didn't move.

"I pre-chate that, lady," The Misfit said and drew a little circle in the ground with the butt of his gun.

"It'll take a half a hour to fix this here car," Hiram called, looking over the raised hood of it.

"Well, first you and Bobby Lee get him and that little boy to step over yonder with you," The Misfit said, pointing to Bailey and John Wesley. "The boys want to ask you something," he said to Bailey. "Would you mind stepping back in them woods there with them?"

95   "Listen," Bailey began, "we're in a terrible predicament! Nobody realizes what this is," and his voice cracked. His eyes were as blue and intense as the parrots in his shirt and he remained perfectly still.

The grandmother reached up to adjust her hat brim as if she were going to the woods with him but it came off in her hand. She stood staring at it and after a second she let it fall on the ground. Hiram pulled Bailey up by the arm as if he were assisting an old man. John Wesley caught hold of his father's hand and Bobby Lee followed. They went off toward the woods and just as they reached the dark edge, Bailey turned and supporting himself against a gray naked pine trunk, he shouted, "I'll be back in a minute, Mamma, wait on me!"

"Come back this instant!" his mother shrilled but they all disappeared into the woods.

"Bailey Boy!" the grandmother called in a tragic voice but she found she was looking at The Misfit squatting on the ground in front of her. "I just know you're a good man," she said desperately. "You're not a bit common!"

"Nome, I ain't a good man," The Misfit said after a second as if he had considered her statement carefully, "but I ain't the worst in the world neither. My daddy said I was a different breed of dog from my brothers and sisters. 'You know,' Daddy said, 'It's some that can live their whole life without asking about it and it's others has to know why it is, and this boy is one of the latters. He's going to be into everything!'" He put on his black hat and looked up suddenly and then away

But we'll all blank along
To-geth-er,
And all along the blank
We'll hep each other out
Smile-ling in any kind of
Weath-ther!

Mrs. Turpin didn't catch every word but she caught enough to agree with the spirit of the song and it turned her thoughts sober. To help anybody out that needed it was her philosophy of life. She never spared herself when she found somebody in need, whether they were white or black, trash or decent. And of all she had to be thankful for, she was most thankful that this was so. If Jesus had said, "You can be high society and have all the money you want and be thin and svelte-like, but you can't be a good woman with it," she would have had to say, "Well don't make me that then. Make me a good woman and it don't matter what else, how fat or how ugly or how poor!" Her heart rose. He had not made her a nigger or white-trash or ugly! He had made her herself and given her a little of everything. Jesus, thank you! she said. Thank you thank you thank you! Whenever she counted her blessings she felt as buoyant as if she weighed one hundred and twenty-five pounds instead of one hundred and eighty.

75   "What's wrong with your little boy?" the pleasant lady asked the white-trashy woman.

"He has a ulcer," the woman said proudly. "He ain't give me a minute's peace since he was born. Him and her are just alike," she said, nodding at the old woman, who was running her leathery fingers through the child's pale hair. "Look like I can't get nothing down them two but Co'Cola and candy."

That's all you try to get down em, Mrs. Turpin said to herself. Too lazy to light the fire. There was nothing you could tell her about people like them that she didn't know already. And it was not just that they didn't have anything. Because if you gave them everything, in two weeks it would all be broken or filthy or they would have chopped it up for lightwood. She knew all this from her own experience. Help them you must, but help them you couldn't.

All at once the ugly girl turned her lips inside out again. Her eyes were fixed like two drills on Mrs. Turpin. This time there was no mistaking that there was something urgent behind them.

Girl, Mrs. Turpin exclaimed silently, I haven't done a thing to you! The girl might be confusing her with somebody else. There was no need to sit by and let herself be intimidated. "You must be in college," she said boldly, looking directly at the girl. "I see you reading a book there."

80   The girl continued to stare and pointedly did not answer.

Her mother blushed at this rudeness. "The lady asked you a question, Mary Grace," she said under her breath.

"I have ears," Mary Grace said.

The poor mother blushed again. "Mary Grace goes to Wellesley College," she explained. She twisted one of the buttons on her dress. "In Massachusetts," she added with a grimace. "And in the summer she just keeps right on studying. Just reads all the time, a real book worm. She's done real well at Wellesley; she's taking English and Math and History and Psychology and Social Studies," she rattled on, "and I think it's too much. I think she ought to get out and have fun."

The girl looked as if she would like to hurl them all through the plate glass window.

85   "Way up north," Mrs. Turpin murmured and thought, well, it hasn't done much for her manners.

"I'd almost rather to have him sick," the white-trash woman said, wrenching the attention back to herself. "He's so mean when he ain't. Look like some children just take natural to meanness. It's some gets bad when they get sick but he was the opposite. Took sick and turned good. He don't give me no trouble now. It's me waitin to see the doctor," she said.

If I was going to send anybody back to Africa, Mrs. Turpin thought, it would be your kind, woman. "Yes, indeed," she said aloud, but looking up at the ceiling, "it's a heap of things worse than a nigger." And dirtier than a hog, she added to herself.

"I think people with bad dispositions are more to be pitied than anyone on earth," the pleasant lady said in a voice that was decidedly thin.

"I thank the Lord he has blessed me with a good one," Mrs. Turpin said. "The day has never dawned that I couldn't find something to laugh at."

90   "Not since she married me anyways," Claud said with a comical straight face.

Everybody laughed except the girl and the white-trash.

Mrs. Turpin's stomach shook. "He's such a caution," she said, "that I can't help but laugh at him."

The girl made a loud ugly noise through her teeth.

Her mother's mouth grew thin and tight. "I think the worst thing in the world," she said, "is an ungrateful person. To have everything and not appreciate it. I know a girl," she said, "who has parents who would give her anything, a little brother who loves her dearly, who is getting a good education, who wears the best clothes, but who can never say a kind word to anyone, who never smiles, who just criticizes and complains all day long."

95   "Is she too old to paddle?" Claud asked.

The girl's face was almost purple.

"Yes," the lady said. "I'm afraid there's nothing to do but leave her to her folly. Some day she'll wake up and it'll be too late."

"It never hurt anyone to smile," Mrs. Turpin said. "It just makes you feel better all over."

"Of course," the lady said sadly, "but there are just some people you can't tell anything to. They can't take criticism."

100   "If it's one thing I am," Mrs. Turpin said with feeling, "it's grateful. When I think who all I could have been besides myself and what all I got, a little of everything, and a good disposition besides, I just feel like shouting, 'Thank you, Jesus, for making everything the way it is!' It could have been different!" For one thing, somebody else could have got Claud. At the thought of this, she was flooded with gratitude and a terrible pang of joy ran through her. "Oh thank you, Jesus, Jesus, thank you!" she cried aloud.

The book struck her directly over her left eye. It struck almost at the same instant that she realized the girl was about to hurl it. Before she could utter a sound, the raw face came crashing across the table toward her, howling. The girl's fingers sank like clamps into the soft flesh of her neck. She heard the mother cry out and Claud shout, "Whoa!" There was an instant when she was certain that she was about to be in an earthquake.

All at once her vision narrowed and she saw everything as if it were happening in a small room far away, or as if she were looking at it through the wrong end of a telescope. Claud's face crumpled and fell out of sight. The nurse ran in, then out, then in again. Then the gangling figure of the doctor rushed out of the inner door. Magazines flew this way and that as the table turned over. The girl fell with a thud and Mrs. Turpin's vision suddenly reversed itself and she saw everything large instead of small. The eyes of the white-trashy woman were staring hugely at the floor. There the girl, held down on one side by the nurse and on the other by her mother, was wrenching and turning in their grasp. The doctor was kneeling astride her, trying to hold her arm down. He managed after a second to sink a long needle into it.

Mrs. Turpin felt entirely hollow except for her heart which swung from side to side as if it were agitated in a great empty drum of flesh.

"Somebody that's not busy call for the ambulance," the doctor said in the offhand voice young doctors adopt for terrible occasions.

105   Mrs. Turpin could not have moved a finger. The old man who had been sitting next to her skipped nimbly into the office and made the call, for the secretary still seemed to be gone.

"Claud!" Mrs. Turpin called.

He was not in his chair. She knew she must jump up and find him but she felt like someone trying to catch a train in a dream, when everything moves in slow motion and the faster you try to run the slower you go.

"Here I am," a suffocated voice, very unlike Claud's, said.

He was doubled up in the corner on the floor, pale as paper, holding his leg. She wanted to get up and go to him but she could not move. Instead, her gaze was drawn slowly downward to the churning face on the floor, which she could see over the doctor's shoulder.

110   The girl's eyes stopped rolling and focused on her. They seemed a much lighter blue than before, as if a door that had been tightly closed behind them was now open to admit light and air.

Mrs. Turpin's head cleared and her power of motion returned. She leaned forward until she was looking directly into the fierce brilliant eyes. There was no doubt in her mind that the girl did know her, knew her in some intense and personal way, beyond time and place and condition. "What you got to say to me?" she asked hoarsely and held her breath, waiting, as for a revelation.

The girl raised her head. Her gaze locked with Mrs. Turpin's. "Go back to hell where you came from, you old wart hog," she whispered. Her voice was low but clear. Her eyes burned for a moment as if she saw with pleasure that her message had struck its target.

Mrs. Turpin sank back in her chair.

After a moment the girl's eyes closed and she turned her head wearily to the side.

115   The doctor rose and handed the nurse the empty syringe. He leaned over and put both hands for a moment on the mother's shoulders, which were shaking. She was sitting on the floor, her lips pressed together, holding Mary Grace's hand in her lap. The girl's fingers were gripped like a baby's around her thumb. "Go on to the hospital," he said. "I'll call and make the arrangements."

"Now let's see that neck," he said in a jovial voice to Mrs. Turpin. He began to inspect her neck with his first two fingers. Two little moonshaped lines like pink fish bones were indented over her windpipe. There was the beginning of an angry red swelling above her eye. His fingers passed over this also.

"Lea' me be," she said thickly and shook him off. "See about Claud. She kicked him."

"I'll see about him in a minute," he said and felt her pulse. He was a thin gray-haired man, given to pleasantries. "Go home and have yourself a vacation the rest of the day," he said and patted her on the shoulder.

Quit your pattin me, Mrs. Turpin growled to herself.

120   "And put an ice pack over that eye," he said. Then he went and squatted down beside Claud and looked at his leg. After a moment he pulled him up and Claud limped after him into the office.

Until the ambulance came, the only sounds in the room were the tremulous moans of the girl's mother, who continued to sit on the floor. The white-trash woman did not take her eyes off the girl. Mrs. Turpin looked straight ahead at nothing. Presently the ambulance drew up, a long dark shadow, behind the curtain. The attendants came in and set the stretcher down beside the girl and lifted her expertly onto it and carried her out. The nurse helped the mother gather up her things. The shadow of the ambulance moved silently away and the nurse came back in the office.

"That ther girl is going to be a lunatic, ain't she?" the white-trash woman asked the nurse, but the nurse kept on to the back and never answered her.

"Yes, she's going to be a lunatic," the white-trash woman said to the rest of them.

"Po' critter," the old woman murmured. The child's face was still in her lap. His eyes looked idly out over her knees. He had not moved during the disturbance except to draw one leg up under him.

125   "I thank Gawd," the white-trash woman said fervently, "I ain't a lunatic."

Claud came limping out and the Turpins went home.

As their pick-up truck turned into their own dirt road and made the crest of the hill, Mrs. Turpin gripped the window ledge and looked out suspiciously. The land sloped gracefully down through a field dotted with lavender weeds and at the start of the rise their small yellow frame house, with its little flower beds spread out around it like a fancy apron, sat primly in its accustomed place between two giant hickory trees. She would not have been startled to see a burnt wound between two blackened chimneys.

Neither of them felt like eating so they put on their house clothes and lowered the shade in the bedroom and lay down, Claud with his leg on a pillow and herself with a damp washcloth over her eye. The instant she was flat on her back, the image of a razor-backed hog with warts on its face and horns coming out behind its ears snorted into her head. She moaned, a low quiet moan.

"I am not," she said tearfully, "a wart hog. From hell." But the denial had no force. The girl's eyes and her words, even the tone of her voice, low but clear, directed only to her, brooked no repudiation. She had been singled out for the message, though there was trash in the room to whom it might justly have been applied. The full force of this fact struck her only now. There was a woman there who was neglecting her own child but she had been overlooked. The message had been given to Ruby Turpin, a respectable, hard-working, church-going woman. The tears dried. Her eyes began to burn instead with wrath.

130   She rose on her elbow and the washcloth fell into her hand. Claud was lying on his back, snoring. She wanted to tell him what the girl had said. At the same time she did not wish to put the image of herself as a wart hog from hell into his mind.

"Hey, Claud," she muttered and pushed his shoulder.

Claud opened one pale baby blue eye.

She looked into it warily. He did not think about anything. He just went his way.

"Wha, whasit?" he said and closed the eye again.

135   "Nothing," she said. "Does your leg pain you?"

"Hurts like hell," Claud said.

"It'll quit terreckly," she said and lay back down. In a moment Claud was snoring again. For the rest of the afternoon they lay there. Claud slept. She scowled at the ceiling. Occasionally she raised her fist and made a small stabbing motion over her chest as if she was defending her innocence to invisible guests who were like the comforters of Job, reasonable-seeming but wrong.

About five-thirty Claud stirred. "Got to go after those niggers," he sighed, not moving.

She was looking straight up as if there were unintelligible handwriting on the ceiling. The protuberance over her eye had turned a greenish-blue. "Listen here," she said.

140   "What"?

"Kiss me."

Claud leaned over and kissed her loudly on the mouth. He pinched her side and their hands interlocked. Her expression of ferocious concentration did not change. Claud got up, groaning and growling, and limped off. She continued to study the ceiling.

She did not get up until she heard the pick-up truck coming back with the Negroes. Then she rose and thrust her feet in her brown oxfords, which she did not bother to lace, and stumped out onto the back porch and got her red plastic bucket. She emptied a tray of ice cubes into it and filled it half full of water and went out into the back yard. Every afternoon after Claud brought the hands in, one of the boys helped him put out hay and the rest waited in the back of the truck until he was ready to take them home. The truck was parked in the shade under one one of the hickory trees.

"Hi yawl this evening?" Mrs. Turpin asked grimly, appearing with the bucket and the dipper. There were three women and a boy in the truck.

145   "Us doin nicely," the oldest woman said. "Hi you doin?" and her gaze stuck immediately on the dark lump on Mrs. Turpin's forehead. "You done fell down, ain't you?" she asked in a solicitous voice. The old woman was dark and almost toothless. She had on an old felt hat of Claud's set back on her head. The other two women were younger and lighter and they both had new bright green sun hats. One of them had hers on her head; the other had taken hers off and the boy was grinning beneath it.

Mrs. Turpin set the bucket down on the floor of the truck. "Yawl hep your-selves," she said. She looked around to make sure Claud had gone. "No. I didn't fall down," she said, folding her arms. "It was something worse than that."

"Ain't nothing bad happen to you!" the old woman said. She said it as if they all knew Mrs. Turpin was protected in some special way by Divine Providence. "You just had you a little fall."

"We were in town at the doctor's office for where the cow kicked Mr. Turpin," Mrs. Turpin said in a flat tone that indicated they could leave off their foolishness. "And there was this girl there. A big fat girl with her face all broke out. I could look at that girl and tell she was peculiar but I couldn't tell how. And me and her mama were just talking and going along and all of a sudden WHAM! She throws this big book she was reading at me and . . . "

"Naw!" the old woman cried out.

150   "And then she jumps over the table and commences to choke me."

"Naw!" they all exclaimed, "naw!"

"Hi come she do that?" the old woman asked. "What ail her?"

Mrs. Turpin only glared in front of her.

"Somethin ail her," the old woman said.

155   "They carried her off in an ambulance," Mrs. Turpin continued, "but before she went she was rolling on the floor and they were trying to hold her down to

give her a shot and she said something to me." She paused. "You know what she said to me?"

"What she say?" they asked.

"She said," Mrs. Turpin began, and stopped, her face very dark and heavy. The sun was getting whiter and whiter, blanching the sky overhead so that the leaves of the hickory tree were black in the face of it. She could not bring forth the words. "Something real ugly," she muttered.

"She sho shouldn't said nothin ugly to you," the old woman said. "You so sweet. You the sweetest lady I know."

"She pretty too," the one with the hat on said.

160   "And stout," the other one said. "I never knowed no sweeter white lady."

"That's the truth befo' Jesus," the old woman said. "Amen! You des as sweet and pretty as you can be.

Mrs. Turpin knew just exactly how much Negro flattery was worth and it added to her rage. "She said," she began again and finished this time with a fierce rush of breath, "that I was an old wart hog from hell."

There was an astounded silence.

"Where she at?" the youngest woman cried in a piercing voice.

165   "Lemme see her. I'll kill her!"

"I'll kill her with you!" the other one cried.

"She b'long in the sylum," the old woman said emphatically. "You the sweetest white lady I know."

"She pretty too," the other two said. "Stout as she can be and sweet. Jesus satisfied with her!"

"Deed he is," the old woman declared.

170   Idiots! Mrs. Turpin growled to herself. You could never say anything intelligent to a nigger. You could talk at them but not with them. "Yawl ain't drunk your water," she said shortly. "Leave the bucket in the truck when you're finished with it. I got more to do than just stand around and pass the time of day," and she moved off and into the house.

She stood for a moment in the middle of the kitchen. The dark protuberance over her eye looked like a miniature tornado cloud which might any moment sweep across the horizon of her brow. Her lower lip protruded dangerously. She squared her massive shoulders. Then she marched into the front of the house and out the side door and started down the road to the pig parlor. She had the look of a woman going single-handed, weaponless, into battle.

The sun was a deep yellow now like a harvest moon and was riding westward very fast over the far tree line as if it meant to reach the hogs before she did. The road was rutted and she kicked several good-sized stones out of her path as she strode along. The pig parlor was on a little knoll at the end of a lane that ran off from the side of the barn. It was a square of concrete as large as a small room, with a board fence about four feet high around it. The concrete floor sloped slightly so that the hog wash could drain off into a trench where it was carried to the field for fertilizer. Claud was standing on the outside, on the edge of the concrete, hanging onto the top board, hosing down the floor inside. The hose was connected to the faucet of a water trough nearby.

Mrs. Turpin climbed up beside him and glowered down at the hogs inside. There were seven long-snouted bristly shoats in it—tan with liver-colored spots— and an old sow a few weeks off from farrowing. She was lying on her side grunting. The shoats were running about shaking themselves like idiot children, their little slit pig eyes searching the floor for anything left. She had read that pigs were the most intelligent animal. She doubted it. They were supposed to be smarter than dogs. There had even been a pig astronaut. He had performed his assignment perfectly but died of a heart attack afterwards because they left him in his electric suit, sitting upright throughout his examination when naturally a hog should be on all fours.

A-gruntin and a-rootin and a-groanin.

175   "Gimme that hose," she said, yanking it away from Claud. "Go on and carry them niggers home and then get off that leg."

"You look like you might have swallowed a mad dog," Claud observed, but he got down and limped off. He paid no attention to her humors.

Until he was out of earshot, Mrs. Turpin stood on the side of the pen, holding the hose and pointing the stream of water at the hind quarter of any shoat that looked as if it might try to lie down. When he had had time to get over the hill, she turned her head slightly and her wrathful eyes scanned the path. He was nowhere in sight. She turned back again and seemed to gather herself up. Her shoulders rose and she drew in her breath.

"What do you send me a message like that for?" she said in a low fierce voice, barely above a whisper but with the force of a shout in its concentrated fury. "How am I a hog and me both? How am I saved and from hell too?" Her free fist was knotted and with the other she gripped the hose, blindly pointing the stream of water in and out of the eye of the old sow whose outraged squeal she did not hear.

The pig parlor commanded a view of the back pasture where their twenty beef cows were gathered around the hay-bales Claud and the boy had put out. The freshly cut pasture sloped down to the highway. Across it was their cotton field and beyond that a dark green dusty wood which they owned as well. The sun was behind the wood, very red, looking over the paling of trees like a farmer inspecting his own hogs.

180   "Why me?" she rumbled. "It's no trash around here, black or white, that I haven't given to. And break my back to the bone every day working. And do for the church."

She appeared to be the right size woman to command the arena before her. "How am I a hog?" she demanded. "Exactly how am I like them?" and she jabbed the stream of water at the shoats. "There was plenty of trash there. It didn't have to be me."

"If you like trash better, go get yourself some trash then," she railed. "You could have made me trash. Or a nigger. If trash is what you wanted why didn't you make me trash?" She shook her fist with the hose in it and a watery snake appeared momentarily in the air. "I could quit working and take it easy and be filthy," she growled. "Lounge about the sidewalks all day drinking root beer. Dip snuff and spit in every puddle and have it all over my face. I could be nasty."

"Or you could have made me a nigger. It's too late for me to be a nigger," she said with deep sarcasm, "but I could act like one. Lay down in the middle of the road and stop traffic. Roll on the ground."

In the deepening light everything was taking on a mysterious hue. The pasture was growing a peculiar glassy green and the streak of highway had turned lavender. She braced herself for a final assault and this time her voice rolled out over the pasture. "Go on," she yelled, "call me a hog! Call me a hog again. From hell. Call me a wart hog from hell. Put that bottom rail on top. There'll still be a top and bottom!"

185   A garbled echo returned to her.

A final surge of fury shook her and she roared, "Who do you think you are?"

The color of everything, field and crimson sky, burned for a moment with a transparent intensity. The question carried over the pasture and across the highway and the cotton field and returned to her clearly like an answer from beyond the wood.

She opened her mouth but no sound came out of it.

A tiny truck, Claud's, appeared on the highway, heading rapidly out of sight. Its gears scraped thinly. It looked like a child's toy. At any moment a bigger truck might smash into it and scatter Claud's and the niggers' brains all over the road.

190   Mrs. Turpin stood there, her gaze fixed on the highway, all her muscles rigid, until in five or six minutes the truck reappeared, returning. She waited until it had had time to turn into their own road. Then like a monumental statue coming to life, she bent her head slowly and gazed, as if through the very heart of the mystery, down into the pig parlor at the hogs. They had settled all in one corner around the old sow who was grunting softly. A red glow suffused them. They appeared to pant with a secret life.

Until the sun slipped finally behind the tree line, Mrs. Turpin remained there with her gaze bent to them as if she were absorbing some abysmal life-giving knowledge. At last she lifted her head. There was only a purple streak in the sky, cutting through a field of crimson and leading, like an extension of the highway, into the descending dusk. She raised her hands from the side of the pen in a gesture hieratic and profound. A visionary light settled in her eyes. She saw the streak as a vast swinging bridge extending upward from the earth through a field of living fire. Upon it a vast horde of souls were rumbling toward heaven. There were whole companies of white-trash, clean for the first time in their lives, and bands of black niggers in white robes, and battalions of freaks and lunatics shouting and clapping and leaping like frogs. And bringing up the end of the procession was a tribe of people whom she recognized at once as those who, like herself and Claud, had always had a little of everything and the God-given wit to use it right. She leaned forward to observe them closer. They were marching behind the others with great dignity, accountable as they had always been for good order and common sense and respectable behavior. They alone were on key. Yet she could see by their shocked and altered faces that even their virtues were being burned away. She lowered her hands and gripped the rail of the hog pen, her eyes small but fixed unblinkingly on what lay ahead. In a moment the vision faded but she remained where she was, immobile.

At length she got down and turned off the faucet and made her slow way on the darkening path to the house. In the woods around her the invisible cricket choruses had struck up, but what she heard were the voices of the souls climbing upward into the starry field and shouting hallelujah.

[1964]

REMARKS FROM ESSAYS AND LETTERS
From "The Fiction Writer and His Country"

In the greatest fiction, the writer's moral sense coincides with his dramatic sense, and I see no way for it to do this unless his moral judgment is part of the very act of seeing, and he is free to use it. I have heard it said that belief in Christian dogma is a hindrance to the writer, but I myself have found nothing further from the truth. Actually, it frees the storyteller to observe. It is not a set of rules which fixes what he sees in the world. It affects his writing primarily by guaranteeing his respect for mystery. . . .

When I look at stories I have written I find that they are, for the most part, about people who are poor, who are afflicted in both mind and body, who have little—or at best a distorted—sense of spiritual purpose, and whose actions do not apparently give the reader a great assurance of the joy of life.

Yet how is this? For I am no disbeliever in spiritual purpose and no vague believer. I see from the standpoint of Christian orthodoxy. This means that for me the meaning of life is centered in our Redemption by Christ and what I see in the world I see in its relation to that. . . .

The novelist with Christian concerns will find in modern life distortions which are repugnant to him, and his problem will be to make these appear as distortions to an audience which is used to seeing them as natural; and he may well be forced to take ever more violent means to get his vision across to this hostile audience. When you can assume that your audience holds the same beliefs you do, you can relax a little and use more normal means of talking to it; when you have to assume that it does not, then you have to make your vision apparent by shock—to the hard of hearing you shout, and for the almost-blind you draw large and startling figures.

From "Some Aspects of the Grotesque in Southern Fiction"

If the writer believes that our life is and will remain essentially mysterious, if he looks upon us as beings existing in a created order to whose laws we freely respond, then what he sees on the surface will be of interest to him only as he can go through it into an experience of mystery itself. His kind of fiction will always be pushing its own limits outward toward the limits of mystery, because for this kind of writer, the meaning of a story does not begin except at a depth where adequate motivation and adequate psychology and the various determinations have been exhausted. Such a writer will be interested in what we don't understand rather than in what we do. He will be interested in possibility rather than in probability. He will be interested in characters who are forced out to meet evil and grace and who act on a trust beyond themselves—whether they know very clearly what it is they act upon or not. To the modern mind, this kind of character, and his creator, are typical Don Quixotes, tilting at what is not there.

From "The Nature and Aim of Fiction"

The novel works by a slower accumulation of detail than the short story does. The short story requires more drastic procedures than the novel because more has to be accomplished in less space. The details have to carry more immediate weight. In good fiction, certain of the details will tend to accumulate meaning from the story itself, and when this happens, they become symbolic in their action.

Now the word *symbol* scares a good many people off, just as the word *art* does. They seem to feel that a symbol is some mysterious thing put in arbitrarily by the writer to frighten the common reader—sort of a literary Masonic grip that is only for the initiated. They seem to think that it is a way of saying something that you aren't actually saying, and so if they can be got to read a reputedly symbolic work at all, they approach it as if it were a problem in algebra. Find *x*. And when they do find or think they find this abstraction, *x*, then they go off with an elaborate sense of satisfaction and the notion that they have "understood" the story. Many students confuse the *process* of understanding a thing with understanding it.

I think that for the fiction writer himself, symbols are something he uses simply as a matter of course. You might say that these are details that, while having their essential place in the literal level of the story, operate in depth as well as on the surface, increasing the story in every direction. . . .

People have a habit of saying, "What is the theme of your story?" and they expect you to give them a statement: "The theme of my story is the economic pressure of the machine on the middle class"—or some such absurdity. And when they've got a statement like that, they go off happy and feel it is no longer necessary to read the story.

Some people have the notion that you read the story and then climb out of it into the meaning, but for the fiction writer himself the whole story is the meaning, because it is an experience, not an abstraction.

From "Writing Short Stories"

Being short does not mean being slight. A short story should be long in depth and should give us an experience of meaning. . . .

Meaning is what keeps the short story from being short. I prefer to talk about the meaning in a story rather than the theme of a story. People talk about the theme of a story as if the theme were like the string that a sack of chicken feed is tied with. They think that if you can pick out the theme, the way you pick the right thread in the chicken-feed sack, you can rip the story open and feed the chickens. But this is not the way meaning works in fiction.

When you can state the theme of a story, when you can separate it from the story itself, then you can be sure the story is not a very good one. The meaning of a story has to be embodied in it, has to be made concrete in it. A story is a way to say something that can't be said any other way, and it takes every word in the story to say what the meaning is. You tell a story because a statement would be inadequate. When anybody asks what a story is about, the only proper thing is to tell him to read the story. The meaning of fiction is not abstract meaning but experienced meaning, and the purpose of making statements about the meaning of a story is only to help you to experience that meaning more fully.

On Interpreting "A Good Man Is Hard to Find"

A professor of English had sent Flannery the following letter: "I am writing as spokesman for three members of our department and some ninety university students in three classes who for a week now have been discussing your story 'A Good Man Is Hard to Find.' We have debated at length several possible interpretations, none of which fully satisfies us. In general we believe that the appearance of the Misfit is not 'real' in the same sense that the incidents of the first half of the story are real. Bailey, we believe, imagines the appearance of the Misfit, whose activities have been called to his attention on the night before the trip and again during the stopover at the roadside restaurant. Bailey, we further believe, identifies himself with the Misfit and so plays two roles in the imaginary last half of the story. But we cannot, after great effort, determine the point at which reality fades into illusion or reverie. Does the accident literally occur, or is it a part of Bailey's dream? Please believe me when I say we are not seeking an easy way out of our difficulty. We admire your story and have examined it with great care, but we are convinced that we are missing something important which you intended for us to grasp. We will all be very grateful if you comment on the interpretation which I have outlined above and if you will give us further comments about your intention in writing 'A Good Man Is Hard to Find.'"

She replied:

To a Professor of English

28 March 61

The interpretation of your ninety students and three teachers is fantastic and about as far from my intentions as it could get to be. If it were a legitimate interpretation, the story would be little more than a trick and its interest would be simply for abnormal psychology. I am not interested in abnormal psychology.

There is a change of tension from the first part of the story to the second where the Misfit enters, but this is no lessening of reality. This story is, of course, not meant to be realistic in the sense that it portrays the everyday doings of people in Georgia. It is stylized and its conventions are comic even though its meaning is serious.

Bailey's only importance is as the Grandmother's boy and the driver of the car. It is the Grandmother who first recognizes the Misfit and who is most concerned with him throughout. The story is a duel of sorts between the Grandmother and her superficial beliefs and the Misfit's more profoundly felt involvement with Christ's action which set the world off balance for him.

The meaning of a story should go on expanding for the reader the more he thinks about it, but meaning cannot be captured in an interpretation. If teachers are in the habit of approaching a story as if it were a research problem for which any answer is believable so long as it is not obvious, then I think students will never learn to enjoy fiction. Too much interpretation is certainly worse than too little and where feeling for a story is absent, theory will not supply it.

My tone is not meant to be obnoxious. I am in a state of shock.

"A Reasonable Use of the Unreasonable"

Last fall I received a letter from a student who said she would be "graciously appreciative" if I would tell her "just what enlightenment" I expected her to get from each of my stories. I suspect she had a paper to write. I wrote her back to forget about the enlightenment and just try to enjoy them. I knew that was the most unsatisfactory answer I could have given because, of course, she didn't want to enjoy them, she just wanted to figure them out.

In most English classes the short story has become a kind of literary specimen to be dissected. Every time a story of mine appears in a Freshman anthology, I have a vision of it, with its little organs laid open, like a frog in a bottle.

I realize that a certain amount of this what-is-the-significance has to go on, but I think something has gone wrong in the process when, for so many students, the story becomes simply a problem to be solved, something which you evaporate to get Instant Enlightenment.

A story really isn't any good unless it successfully resists paraphrase, unless it hangs on and expands in the mind. Properly, you analyze to enjoy, but it's equally true that to analyze with any discrimination, you have to have enjoyed already, and I think that the best reason to hear a story read is that it should stimulate that primary enjoyment.

I don't have any pretensions to being an Aeschylus or Sophocles and providing you in this story with a cathartic experience out of your mythic background, though this story I'm going to read certainly calls up a good deal of the South's mythic background, and it should elicit from you a degree of pity and terror, even though its way of being serious is a comic one. I do think, though, that like the Greeks you should know what is going to happen in this story so that any element of suspense in it will be transferred from its surface to its interior.

I would be most happy if you have already read it, happier still if you knew it well, but since experience has taught me to keep my expectations along these lines modest, I'll tell you that this is the story of a family of six which, on its way driving to Florida, gets wiped out by an escaped convict who calls himself the Misfit. The family is made up of the Grandmother and her son, Bailey, and his children, John Wesley and June Star and the baby, and there is also the cat and the children's mother. The cat is named Pitty Sing, and the Grandmother is taking him with them, hidden in a basket.

Now I think it behooves me to try to establish with you the basis on which reason operates in this story. Much of my fiction takes its character from a reasonable use of the unreasonable, though the reasonableness of my use of it may not always be apparent. The assumptions that underlie this use of it, however, are those of the central Christian mysteries. These are assumptions to which a large part of the modern audience takes exception. About this I can only say that there are perhaps other ways than my own in which this story could be read, but none other by which it could have been written. Belief, in my own case anyway, is the engine that makes perception operate.

The heroine of this story, the Grandmother, is in the most significant position life offers the Christian. She is facing death. And to all appearances she, like the rest of us, is not too well prepared for it. She would like to see the event postponed. Indefinitely.

I've talked to a number of teachers who use this story in class and who tell their students that the Grandmother is evil, that in fact, she's a witch, even down to the cat. One of these teachers told me that his students, and particularly his Southern students, resisted this interpretation with a certain bemused vigor, and he didn't understand why. I had to tell him that they resisted it because they all had grandmothers or great-aunts just like her at home, and they knew, from personal experience, that the old lady lacked comprehension, but that she had a good heart. The Southerner is usually tolerant of those weaknesses that proceed from innocence, and he knows that a taste for self-preservation can be readily combined with the missionary spirit.

This same teacher was telling his students that morally the Misfit was several cuts above the Grandmother. He had a really sentimental attachment to the Misfit. But then a prophet gone wrong is almost always more interesting than your grandmother, and you have to let people take their pleasures where they find them.

It is true that the old lady is a hypocritical old soul; her wits are no match for the Misfit's, nor is her capacity for grace equal to his; yet I think the unprejudiced reader will feel that the Grandmother has a special kind of triumph in this story which instinctively we do not allow to someone altogether bad.

I often ask myself what makes a story work, and what makes it hold up as a story, and I have decided that it is probably some action, some gesture of a character that is unlike any other in the story, one which indicates where the real heart of the story lies. This would have to be an action or a gesture which was both totally right and totally unexpected; it would have to be one that was both in character and beyond character; it would have to suggest both the world and eternity. The action or gesture I'm talking about would have to be on the anagogical level, that is, the level which has to do with the Divine life and our participation in it. It would be a gesture that transcended any neat allegory that might have been intended or any pat moral categories a reader could make. It would be a gesture which somehow made contact with mystery.

There is a point in this story where such a gesture occurs. The Grandmother is at last alone, facing the Misfit. Her head clears for an instant and she realizes, even in her limited way, that she is responsible for the man before her and joined to him by ties of kinship which have their roots deep in the mystery she has been merely prattling about so far. And at this point, she does the right thing, she makes the right gesture.

I find that students are often puzzled by what she says and does here, but I think myself that if I took out this gesture and what she says with it, I would have no story. What was left would not be worth your attention. Our age not only does not have a very sharp eye for the almost imperceptible intrusions of grace, it no longer has much feeling for the nature of the violences which precede and follow them. The devil's greatest wile, Baudelaire has said, is to convince us that he does not exist.

I suppose the reasons for the use of so much violence in modern fiction will differ with each writer who uses it, but in my own stories I have found that violence is strangely capable of returning my characters to reality and preparing them to accept their moment of grace. Their heads are so hard that almost nothing else will do the work. This idea, that reality is something to which we must be returned at considerable cost, is one which is seldom understood by the casual reader, but it is one which is implicit in the Christian view of the world.

I don't want to equate the Misfit with the devil. I prefer to think that, however unlikely this may seem, the old lady's gesture, like the mustard-seed, will grow to be a great crow-filled tree in the Misfit's heart, and will be enough of a pain to him there to turn him into the prophet he was meant to become. But that's another story.

This story has been called grotesque, but I prefer to call it literal. A good story is literal in the same sense that a child's drawing is literal. When a child draws, he doesn't intend to distort but to set down exactly what he sees, and as his gaze is direct, he sees the lines that create motion. Now the lines of motion that interest the writer are usually invisible. They are lines of spiritual motion. And in this story you should be on the lookout for such things as the action of grace in the Grandmother's soul, and not for the dead bodies.

We hear many complaints about the prevalence of violence in modern fiction, and it is always assumed that this violence is a bad thing and meant to be an end in itself. With the serious writer, violence is never an end in itself. It is the extreme situation that best reveals what we are essentially, and I believe these are times when writers are more interested in what we are essentially than in the tenor of our daily lives. Violence is a force which can be used for good or evil, and among other things taken by it is the kingdom of heaven. But regardless of what can be taken by it, the man in the violent situation reveals those qualities least dispensable in his personality, those qualities which are all he will have to take into eternity with him; and since the characters in this story are all on the verge of eternity, it is appropriate to think of what they take with them. In any case, I hope that if you consider these points in connection with the story, you will come to see it as something more than an account of a family murdered on the way to Florida.

[1957]

10

Reading and Writing
about Drama

TYPES OF PLAYS

Most of the world's great plays written before the twentieth century may be regarded as one of two kinds: **tragedy** or **comedy**. Roughly speaking, tragedy dramatizes the conflict between the vitality of the individual life and the laws or limits of life. The tragic hero reaches a height, going beyond the experience of others but at the cost of his or her life. Comedy, on the other hand, dramatizes the vitality of the laws of social life. In comedy, the good life is seen to reside in the shedding of an individualism that isolates, in favor of a union with a genial and enlightened society. These points must be amplified a bit before we go on to the further point that, of course, any important play does much more than can be put into such crude formulas.

Tragedy

Tragic heroes usually go beyond the standards to which reasonable people adhere; they do some fearful deed which ultimately destroys them. This deed is often said to be an act of **hubris**, a Greek word meaning something like "overweening pride." It may involve, for instance, violating a taboo, such as that against taking life. But if the hubristic act ultimately destroys the man or woman who performs it, it also shows that person (paradoxically) to be in some way more fully a living being—a person who has experienced life more fully, whether by heroic action or by capacity for enduring suffering—than the other characters in the play. (If the tragic hero does not die, he or she is usually left in some deathlike state, as is the blind Oedipus in *Oedipus Rex*.) In tragedy we see humanity pushed to an extreme; the hero enters a world unknown to most and reveals magnificence. After the hero's departure from the stage, we are left in a world of littler people.

What has just been said may (or may not) be true of most tragedies, but it certainly is not true of all. If you are writing about a tragedy, you might consider whether the points just made are illustrated in your play. Is the hero guilty of hubris? Does the hero seem a greater person than the others in the play? An essay examining such questions probably requires not only a character sketch but also some comparison with other characters.

Tragedy commonly involves **irony** of two sorts: unconsciously ironic deeds and unconsciously ironic speeches. **Ironic deeds** have some consequence more or less the reverse of what the doer intends. Macbeth thinks that by killing Duncan he will gain happiness, but he finds that his deed brings him sleepless nights. Brutus thinks that by killing Caesar he will bring liberty to Rome, but he brings tyranny. In an **unconsciously ironic speech**, the words mean one thing to the speaker but something more significant to the audience, as when King Duncan, baffled by Cawdor's treason, says:

> There's no art
> To find the mind's construction in the face:
> He was a gentleman on whom I built
> An absolute trust.

At this moment Macbeth, whom we have already heard meditating the murder of Duncan, enters. Duncan's words are true, but he does not apply them to Macbeth, as the audience does. A few moments later Duncan praises Macbeth as "a peerless kinsman." Soon Macbeth will indeed become peerless, when he kills Duncan and ascends to the throne.[1] Sophocles' use of ironic deeds and speeches is so pervasive, especially in *Oedipus Rex,* that **Sophoclean irony** has become a critical term.

When the deed backfires or has a reverse effect, such as Macbeth's effort to gain happiness has, we have what Aristotle (the first—and still the greatest—drama critic) called a **peripeteia**, or a **reversal**. A character who comes to perceive what has happened (Macbeth's "I have lived long enough: my way of life / Is fall'n into the sere, the yellow leaf") experiences (in Aristotle's language) an **anagnorisis**, or **recognition**. Strictly speaking, for Aristotle the recognition was a matter of literal identification—for example, the recognition that Oedipus was the son of a man he killed. In *Macbeth,* the recognition in this sense is that Macduff, "from his mother's womb / Untimely ripped," is the man who fits the prophecy that Macbeth can be conquered only by someone not "of woman born."

In his analysis of drama, Aristotle says that the tragic hero comes to grief through his **hamartia**, a term sometimes translated as **tragic flaw** but perhaps better translated as **tragic error**, since *flaw* implies a moral fault. Thus it is a great error for Hamlet not to inspect the foils at the start of the deadly fencing match with Laertes; had he done so, he would have seen that one of the foils was blunt and one pointed. If we hold to the translation *flaw,* we begin to hunt for a fault in the tragic hero's character; and we say, for instance, that Hamlet is gullible, or some such thing. In doing this, we may diminish or even overlook the hero's grandeur.

Comedy

Although in tragedy the hero usually seems to embody certain values that are superior to those of the surrounding society, in comedy the fullest life is seen to reside *within* enlightened social norms: At the beginning of a comedy we find banished dukes, unhappy lovers, crabby parents, jealous husbands, and harsh laws; but at the end we usually have a unified and genial society, often symbolized by a marriage feast to which everyone, or almost everyone, is invited. Early in *A Midsummer Night's Dream,* for instance, we meet quarreling young lovers and a father who demands that his daughter either marry a man she does not love or enter a convent. Such is the Athenian law. At the end of the play the lovers are properly matched, to everyone's satisfaction.

---

[1]**Dramatic irony** (ironic deeds, or happenings, and unconsciously ironic speeches) must be distinguished from **verbal irony**, which is produced when the speaker is *conscious* that his words mean something different from what they say. In *Macbeth* Lennox says, "The gracious Duncan / Was pitied of Macbeth. Marry, he was dead! / And the right valiant Banquo walked too late./ . . . / Men must not walk too late." He *says* nothing about Macbeth having killed Duncan and Banquo, but he *means* that Macbeth has killed them.

Speaking broadly, most comedies fall into one of two classes: **satiric comedy** or **romantic comedy**. In satiric comedy, the emphasis is on the obstructionists—the irate fathers, hardheaded businessmen, and other members of the establishment who at the beginning of the play seem to hold all the cards, preventing joy from reigning. They are held up to ridicule because they are repressive monomaniacs enslaved to themselves, acting mechanistically (always irate, always hardheaded) instead of responding genially to the ups and downs of life. The outwitting of these obstructionists, usually by the younger generation, often provides the resolution of the plot. Ben Jonson, Molière, and George Bernard Shaw are in this tradition; their comedy, according to an ancient Roman formula, "chastens morals with ridicule"—that is, it reforms folly or vice by laughing at it. On the other hand, in romantic comedy (think of Shakespeare's *A Midsummer Night's Dream, As You Like It,* and *Twelfth Night*) the emphasis is on a pair or pairs of delightful people who engage our sympathies as they run their obstacle race to the altar. There are obstructionists here too, but the emphasis is on festivity.

In writing about comedy you may, of course, be concerned with the function of one scene or character. But whatever your topic, you may find it helpful to begin by trying to decide whether the play is primarily romantic or primarily satiric (or something else). One way of getting at this is to ask yourself to what degree you sympathize with the characters. Do you laugh *with* them, sympathetically, or on the other hand do you laugh *at* them, regarding them as at least somewhat contemptible?

ELEMENTS OF DRAMA

Theme

If we have read or seen a drama thoughtfully, we ought to be able to formulate its **theme**, its underlying idea—and perhaps we can even go so far as to say its moral attitudes, its view of life, its wisdom. Some critics, it is true, have argued that the concept of theme is meaningless. They hold that *Macbeth,* for example, gives us only an extremely detailed history of one imaginary man. In this view, *Macbeth* says nothing to you or me; it only says what happened to some imaginary man. Even *Julius Caesar* says nothing about the historical Julius Caesar or about the nature of Roman politics. Here we can agree; no one would offer Shakespeare's play as evidence of what the historical Caesar said or did. But surely the view that the concept of theme is meaningless, and that a work tells us only about imaginary creatures, is a desperate one. We *can* say that we see in *Julius Caesar* the fall of power, or (if we are thinking of Brutus) the vulnerability of idealism, or some such thing.

To the reply that these are mere truisms, we can counter: Yes, but the truisms are presented in such a way that they take on life and become a part of us rather than remain things of which we say, "I've heard it said, and I guess it's so." The play offers instruction, in a pleasant and persuasive way. And surely we are in no danger of equating the play with the theme that we sense underlies it. We recognize that the play presents the theme with such detail that our statement is only a wedge to help us enter into the play, so we can appreciate it more fully.

Some critics (influenced by Aristotle's statement that a drama is an imitation of an action) use **action** in a sense equivalent to theme. In this sense, the action is the underlying happening—the inner happening—for example, "the enlightenment of a character," or "the coming of unhappiness to a character," or "the finding of the self by self-surrender." It might be said that the theme of *Macbeth,* for example, is embodied in some words that Macbeth himself utters: "Blood will have blood." Of course this is not to say that these words and no other words embody the theme or the action; it is only to say that these words seem to the writer (and, if the essay is effective, to the reader) to bring us close to the center of the play.

Plot

Plot is variously defined, sometimes as equivalent to *story* (in this sense a synopsis of *Julius Caesar* has the same plot as *Julius Caesar*), but more often, and more usefully, as the dramatist's particular *arrangement of the story.* Thus, because Shakespeare's *Julius Caesar* begins with a scene dramatizing an encounter between plebeians and tribunes, its plot is different from that of a play on Julius Caesar in which such a scene (not necessary to the story) is omitted.

Handbooks on drama often suggest that a plot (arrangement of happenings) should have a **rising action**, a **climax**, and a **falling action**. This sort of plot can be diagramed as a pyramid: The tension rises through complications or **crises** to a climax, at which point the climax is the apex, and the tension allegedly slackens as we witness the **dénouement** (literally, *unknotting*). Shakespeare sometimes used a pyramidal structure, placing his climax neatly in the middle of what seems to us to be the third of five acts. In *Hamlet,* the protagonist proves to his own satisfaction Claudius's guilt in 3.2, with the play within the play; but almost immediately he begins to worsen his position, by failing to kill Claudius when he is an easy target (3.3) and by contaminating himself with the murder of Polonius (3.4). In *Romeo and Juliet,* the first half shows Romeo winning Juliet; but when in 3.1 he kills her cousin Tybalt, Romeo sets in motion the second half of the play, the losing of Juliet and of his own life.

Of course, no law demands such a structure, and a hunt for the pyramid usually causes the hunter to overlook all the crises but the middle one. William Butler Yeats once suggestively diagramed a good plot not as a pyramid but as a line moving diagonally upward, punctuated by several crises. Perhaps it is sufficient to say that a good plot has its moments of tension, but the location of these will vary with the play. They are the product of **conflict**, but it should be noted that not all conflict produces tension; there is conflict but little tension in a ball game when the home team is ahead 10–0 and the visiting pitcher comes to bat in the ninth inning with two out and none on base.

Regardless of how a plot is diagramed, the **exposition** is that part that tells the audience what it has to know about the past, the **antecedent action**. Two gossiping servants who tell each other that after a year away in Paris the young master is coming home tomorrow with a new wife are giving the audience the exposition. But the exposition may also extend far into the play, being given in small, explosive revelations.

Exposition has been discussed as though it consists simply of informing the audience about events, but exposition can do much more. It can give us an understanding of the characters who themselves are talking about other characters, it can evoke a mood, and it can generate tension. When we summarize the opening act, and treat it as "mere exposition," we are probably losing what is dramatic in it.

In fact, exposition usually includes **foreshadowing**. Details given in the exposition, which we may at first take as mere background, often turn out to be highly relevant to later developments. For instance, in the very short first scene of *Macbeth* the witches introduce the name of Macbeth, but in such words as "Fair is foul" and "when the battle's lost and won" they also give glimpses of what will happen: Macbeth will become foul, and though he will seem to win (he becomes king) he will lose the most important battle. Similarly, during the exposition in the second scene we learn that Macbeth has loyally defeated Cawdor, who betrayed King Duncan, and Macbeth has been given Cawdor's title. Later we will find that, like Cawdor, Macbeth betrays Duncan. That is, in giving us the background about Cawdor, the exposition is also telling us (though we don't know it, when we first see or read the play) something about what will happen to Macbeth.

In writing about an aspect of plot, you may want to consider one of the following topics:

- Is the plot improbable? If so, is the play therefore weak?
- Does a scene that might at first glance seem unimportant or even irrelevant serve an important function?
- If certain actions that could be shown onstage take place offstage, is there a reason? In *Macbeth,* for instance, why do you suppose the murder of Duncan takes place offstage, whereas Banquo and Macduff's family are murdered onstage? Why, then, might Shakespeare have preferred not to show us the murder of Duncan? What has he gained? (A good way to approach this sort of question is to think of what your own reaction would be if the action were shown on the stage.)
- If there are several conflicts—for example, between pairs of lovers or between parents and their children and also between the parents themselves—how are these conflicts related? Are they parallel? Or contrasting?
- Does the arrangement of scenes have a structure? For instance, do the scenes depict a rise and then a fall?
- Does the plot seem satisfactorily concluded? Are there loose threads? If so, is the apparent lack of a complete resolution a weakness in the play? Or does it serve a function?

Gestures

The language of a play, broadly conceived, includes the **gestures** that the characters make and the settings in which they make them. As Ezra Pound says, "The medium of drama is not words, but persons moving about on a stage using words." Because plays are meant to be seen, make every effort to visualize the action when you read a play. Ibsen is getting at something important when he tells us in a stage direction that Nora "walks cautiously over to the door to the study and listens." Her silent actions tell us as much about her as many of her speeches do.

Gesture can be interpreted even more broadly: The mere fact that a character enters, leaves, or does not enter may be highly significant. John Russell Brown comments on the actions and the absence of certain words that in *Hamlet* convey the growing separation between King Claudius and his wife, Gertrude:

> Their first appearance together with a public celebration of marriage is a large and simple visual effect, and Gertrude's close concern for her son suggests a simple, and perhaps unremarkable modification. . . . But Claudius enters without Gertrude for his "Prayer Scene" (3.2) and, for the first time, Gertrude enters without him for the Closet Scene (3.4) and is left alone, again for the first time, when Polonius hides behind the arras. Thereafter earlier accord is revalued by an increasing separation, often poignantly silent and unexpected.

When Claudius calls Gertrude to leave with him after Hamlet has dragged off Polonius' body, she makes no reply; twice more he urges her and she is still silent. But he does not remonstrate or question; rather he speaks of his own immediate concerns and, far from supporting her with assurances, becomes more aware of his own fears:

> O, come away!
> My soul is full of discord and dismay. (4.1.44–45)

Emotion has been so heightened that it is remarkable that they leave together without further words. The audience has been aware of a new distance between Gertrude and Claudius, of her immobility and silence, and of his self-concern, haste, and insistence.[2]

Setting

Drama of the nineteenth and early twentieth centuries (for example, the plays of Henrik Ibsen, Anton Chekhov, and George Bernard Shaw) is often thought to be "realistic," but even a realistic playwright or stage designer selects from among many available materials. A **realistic setting** (indication of the **locale**), then, can say a great deal, and can even serve as a symbol. Over and over again in Ibsen we find the realistic setting of a nineteenth-century drawing room, with its heavy draperies and its bulky furniture, helping to convey his vision of a bourgeois world that oppresses the individual who struggles to affirm other values.

Twentieth-century dramatists are often explicit about the symbolic qualities of the setting. Here is an example from Eugene O'Neill's *Desire Under the Elms;* only a part of the initial stage direction is given:

> The house is in good condition but in need of paint. Its walls are a sickly grayish, the green of the shutters faded. Two enormous elms are on each side of the house. They bend their trailing branches down over the roof. They appear to protect and at the same time subdue. There is a sinister maternity in their aspect, a crushing, jealous absorption.... They are like exhausted women resting their sagging breasts and hands and hair on its roof.

Not surprisingly, the action in the play includes deeds of "sinister maternity" (a mother kills her infant) and "jealous absorption."

In *The Glass Menagerie* Tennessee Williams tells us that

> the apartment faces an alley and is entered by a fire-escape, a structure whose name is a touch of accidental poetic truth, for all of these huge buildings are always burning with the slow and implacable fires of human desperation.

Characterization and Motivation

Characterization, or personality, is defined, as in fiction (see pp. 196–97), by what the characters do (a stage direction tells us that "Nora dances more and more wildly"), by what they say (she asks her husband to play the piano), by what others say about them, and by the setting in which they move. The characters are

---

[2]*Shakespeare's Plays in Performance* (New York: St. Martin's, 1967), p. 139.

also defined in part by other characters whom they in some degree resemble or from whom they in some degree differ. Hamlet, Laertes, and Fortinbras have each lost their fathers, but Hamlet spares the praying King Claudius, whereas Laertes, seeking vengeance on Hamlet for murdering Laertes's father, says he would cut Hamlet's throat in church; Hamlet meditates about the nature of action, but Fortinbras leads the Norwegians in a military campaign and ultimately acquires Denmark.

Other plays, of course, also provide examples of such **foils**, or characters who set one another off. Macbeth and Banquo both hear prophecies, but they act and react differently; Brutus is one kind of assassin, Cassius another, and Casca still another. Any analysis of a character, then, will probably have to take into account, in some degree, the other characters who help to show what he or she is, and who thus help to set forth his or her **motivation** (grounds for action, inner drives, goals).

ORGANIZING AN ANALYSIS OF A CHARACTER

As you read and reread, you'll annotate the text and will jot down (in whatever order they come to you) your thoughts about the character you are studying. Reading, with a view toward writing, you'll want to

1. jot down traits as they come to mind ("kind," "forgetful," "enthusiastic");
2. look back at the text, searching for supporting evidence (characteristic actions, brief supporting quotations); and of course you will also look for counterevidence so that you may modify your earlier impressions.

Brainstorming leads to an evaluation of your ideas and to a shaping of them. Evaluating and shaping lead to a tentative outline, and a tentative outline leads to the search for supporting evidence—the material that will constitute the body of your essay.

When you set out to write a first draft, review your annotations and notes and see if you can summarize your view of the character in one or two sentences:

X is . . . ,

or

Although X is . . . , she is also. . . .

That is, try to formulate a thesis sentence or a thesis paragraph, a proposition that you will go on to support.

You want to let your reader know early, probably in your first sentence—and almost certainly by the end of your first paragraph—which character you are writing about and what your overall thesis is.

First Draft

Here is the first draft of an **opening paragraph** that identifies the character and sets forth a thesis:

Romeo is a very interesting character, I think. In the beginning of the

play Romeo is very adolescent. Romeo is smitten with puppy love for a woman named Rosaline. He desires to show all of his friends that he knows

how a lover is supposed to act. When he sees Juliet he experiences true love.

From the point when he sees Juliet he experiences true love, and from this

point he steadily matures in <u>Romeo and Juliet.</u> He moves from a self-

centered man to a man who lives not for himself but only for Juliet.

Revised Draft

Later the student edited the draft. We reprint the original, with the additional editing in handwriting:

Romeo ~~is a very interesting character, I think. In the beginning~~
      begins as an
~~of the play Romeo is very~~ adolescent. ~~Romeo is~~ smitten with puppy
                              and a desire
love for ~~a woman named Rosaline.~~ ~~He desires~~ to show all of his friends
                                                              however,
that he knows how a lover is supposed to act. When he sees Juliet, he
          and,   *this*
experiences true love. ~~From the~~ point ~~when he sees Juliet he~~

~~experiences true love, and from this point~~ he steadily matures, in
          moving   *adolescent*
~~Romeo and Juliet.~~ ~~He moves~~ from a self-centered man to a man who

lives ~~not for himself but~~ only for Juliet.

Here is a revised version of another effective opening paragraph, effective
partly because it identifies the character and offers a thesis:

In the last speech of <u>Macbeth,</u> Malcolm characterizes Lady Macbeth as

"fiend-like," and indeed she invokes evil spirits and prompts her husband to

commit murder. But despite her bold pose, her role in the murder, and her

belief that she will be untroubled by guilt, she has a conscience that

torments her and that finally drives her to suicide. She is not a mere

heartless villain; she is a human being who is less strong—and more

moral—than she thinks she is.

Notice that

- the paragraph quotes a word ("fiend-like") from the text. It happens that
  the writer goes on to argue that this word is *not* a totally accurate description, but the quotation nevertheless helps to bring the reader into close
  contact with the subject of the essay.

- in writing about literature we do not ordinarily introduce the thesis formally. We do not, that is, say "In this paper it is my intention to prove that . . . " Such a sentence may be perfectly appropriate in a paper in political science, but in a paper on literature it sounds too stiff.

The body of your essay will be devoted, of course, to supporting your thesis. If you have asserted that although Lady Macbeth is cruel and domineering she nevertheless is endowed with a conscience, you will go on in your essay to support those assertions with references to passages that demonstrate them. This does *not* mean that you tell the plot of the whole work; an essay on a character is by no means the same as a summary of the plot. But since you must support your generalizations, you will have to make brief references to specific episodes that reveal her personality, and almost surely you will quote an occasional word or passage.

There are many possible **ways to organize** an essay on a character. Much will depend, of course, on your purpose and thesis. For instance,

- you may want to show how the character develops—gains knowledge, or matures, or disintegrates. Or, again,
- you may want to show what the character contributes to the story or play as a whole. Or, to give yet another example,
- you may want to show that the character is unbelievable.

Still, although no single organization is always right, two methods are common and effective. One is to let the organization of your essay follow closely the sequence of the literary work; that is, you might devote a paragraph to Lady Macbeth as we perceive her in the first act, and then in subsequent paragraphs go on to show that her character is later seen to be more complex than it at first appears. Such an essay may trace your changing responses. This does not mean that you need to write five paragraphs, one on her character in each of the five acts. But it does mean that you might begin with Lady Macbeth as you perceive her in, say, the first act, and then go on to the additional revelations of the rest of the play.

A second effective way of organizing an essay on a character is to set forth, early in the essay, the character's chief traits—let's say the chief strengths and two or three weaknesses—and then go on to study each trait you have listed. Here the organization would (to maintain the reader's interest) probably begin with the most obvious points and then move on to the less obvious, subtler points. The body of your essay, in any case, is devoted to offering evidence that supports your generalizations about the character.

What about a **concluding paragraph**? The concluding paragraph ought *not* to begin with the obviousness of "Thus we see," or "In conclusion," or "I recommend this play because . . . " In fact, after you have given what you consider a sound sketch of the character, it may be appropriate simply to quit. Especially if your essay has moved from the obvious traits to the more subtle and more important traits, and if your essay is fairly short (say, fewer than 500 words), a reader may not need a conclusion. Further, there probably is no reason to blunt what you have just said by adding an unnecessary and merely repetitive summary. But if you do feel that a conclusion is necessary, you may find it effective to write a summary of the character, somewhat as you did in your opening. For the conclusion, relate the character's character to the entire drama—that is, try to give the reader a sense of the role that the character plays.

✔ **C H E C K L I S T :** *Getting Ideas for Writing about Drama*

The following questions may help you to formulate ideas for an essay on a play.

Plot and Conflict

❑ Does the exposition introduce elements that will be ironically fulfilled? During the exposition do you perceive things differently from the way the characters perceive them?

❑ Are certain happenings or situations recurrent? If so, what significance do you attach to them?

❑ If there is more than one plot, do the plots seem to you to be related? Is one plot clearly the main plot and another plot a sort of subplot, a minor variation on the theme?

❑ Do any scenes strike you as irrelevant?

❑ Are certain scenes so strongly foreshadowed that you anticipated them? If so, did the happenings in these scenes merely fulfill your expectations, or did they also surprise you?

❑ What kinds of conflict are there? One character against another, one group against another, one part of a personality against another part in the same person?

❑ How is the conflict resolved? By an unambiguous triumph of one side or by a triumph that is also in some degree a loss for the triumphant side? Do you find the resolution satisfying, or unsettling, or what? Why?

Character

❑ A dramatic character is not likely to be thoroughly realistic, a copy of someone we might know. Still, we can ask if the character is consistent and coherent. We can also ask if the character is complex or is, on the other hand, a rather simple representative of some human type.

❑ How is the character defined? Consider what the character says and does and what others say about him or her and do to him or her. Also consider other characters who more or less resemble the character in question, because the similarities—and the differences—may be significant.

❑ How trustworthy are the characters when they characterize themselves? When they characterize others?

❑ Do characters change as the play goes on, or do we simply know them better at the end?

❑ What do you make of the minor characters? Are they merely necessary to the plot, or are they foils to other characters? Or do they serve some other functions?

❑ If a character is tragic, does the tragedy seem to you to proceed from a moral flaw, from an intellectual error, from the malice of others, from sheer chance, or from some combination of these?

❑ What are the character's goals? To what degree do you sympathize with them? If a character is comic, do you laugh *with* or *at* the character?

❑ Do you think the characters are adequately motivated?

❑ Is a given character so meditative that you feel he or she is engaged less in a dialogue with others than in a dialogue with the self? If so, do you feel that this character is in large degree a spokesperson for the author, commenting not only on the world of the play but also on the outside world?

Nonverbal Language

❑ If the playwright does not provide full stage directions, try to imagine for at least one scene what gestures and tones might accompany each speech. (The first scene is usually a good one to try your hand at.)

❑ What do you make of the setting? Does it help to reveal character? Do changes of scene strike you as symbolic? If so, symbolic of what?

THINKING ABOUT A FILMED VERSION OF A PLAY

If you have ever seen the filmed version of a novel that you have read, you know that because the camera is essentially visual rather than verbal, there are significant differences. The camera itself is a sort of narrator, commenting on the action, for instance by slow motion or by out-of-focus shots. And you have probably noticed that most filmed versions of plays use a musical background that in effect comments on the action. Except in the rare cases where a theatrical production has been filmed from, so to speak, the viewpoint of a spectator in the front row, center—no closeups, no long shots—the experience of watching a film is very different from the experience of watching a live production.

In preparing to write about a filmed version of a play, consider the following points:

• What has been added to the film? What has been omitted? Why?

• In the case of a film, has the film medium been used to advantage—for example, in focusing attention through close-ups or reaction shots (shots showing not the speaker but a person reacting to the speaker)?

• Do certain plays seem to be especially suited—maybe *only* suited—to the stage? Would they not work effectively as films? Is the reverse true—that is, are some plays best presented and best understood when they are done as films?

• Critics have sometimes said about this or that play that it cannot really be staged successfully or presented well on film—that the best way to appreciate and understand it is as something to be *read*, like a poem or novel. Are there plays you have studied for which this observation appears to be true? Which features of the work—its characters, settings, dialogue, central themes—might make it difficult to transfer the play from the page to the movie screen or the stage?

• Imagine that you are directing a film version. What important decisions would you have to make about character, setting, and pacing of the action? Would you be inclined to omit certain scenes? Would you, alternatively, add new scenes that are not in the work itself? What kinds of advice would you give to the performers about their roles?

✔ CHECKLIST: *Writing about a Filmed Play*

Preliminaries

❑ Is the title of the film the same as the title of the play? If not, what is implied?

Dramatic Adaptations

❑ Does the film closely follow its original and neglect the potentialities of the camera? Or does it so revel in cinematic devices that it distorts the original?
❑ Does the film do violence to the theme of the original? Is the film better than its source? Are the additions or omissions due to the medium or to a crude or faulty interpretation of the original?

Plot and Character

❑ Can film deal as effectively with inner action—mental processes—as with external, physical action? In a given film, how is the inner action conveyed? Olivier used voice-over for parts of Hamlet's soliloquies—that is, we hear Hamlet's voice but his lips do not move.
❑ Are shots and sequences adequately developed, or do they seem jerky? (A shot may be jerky by being extremely brief or at an odd angle; a sequence may be jerky by using discontinuous images or fast cuts. Sometimes, of course, jerkiness may be desirable.) If such cinematic techniques as wipes, dissolves, and slow motion are used, are they meaningful and effective?
❑ Are the characters believable?
❑ Are the actors appropriately cast?

Sound Track

❑ Does the sound track offer more than realistic dialogue? Is the music appropriate and functional? (Music may, among other things, imitate natural sounds, give a sense of locale or of ethnic group, suggest states of mind, provide ironic commentary, or—by repeated melodies—help establish connections.) Are volume, tempo, and pitch—whether of music or of such sounds as the wind blowing or cars moving—used to stimulate emotions?

YOUR TURN: PLAYS FOR ANALYSIS

A Note on Greek Tragedy

Little or nothing is known for certain about the origin of Greek tragedy. The most common hypothesis holds that it developed from improvised speeches during choral dances honoring Dionysus, a Greek nature god associated with spring, fertility, and wine. Thespis (who perhaps never existed) is said to have introduced an actor into these choral performances in the sixth century B.C. Aeschylus (525–456 B.C.), Greece's first great writer of tragedies, added the second actor, and Sophocles (496?–406 B.C.) added the third actor and fixed the size of the chorus at fifteen. (Because the chorus leader often functioned as an additional actor, and because the actors sometimes doubled in their parts, a Greek tragedy could have more characters than might at first be thought.)

All of the extant great Greek tragedy is of the fifth century B.C. It was performed at religious festivals in the winter and early spring, in large outdoor amphitheaters built on hillsides. Some of these theaters were enormous; the one at Epidaurus held about fifteen thousand people. The audience sat in tiers, looking down on the *orchestra* (a dancing place), with the acting area behind it and the *skene* (the scene building) yet farther back. The scene building served as dressing room, background (suggesting a palace or temple), and place for occasional entrances and exits. Furthermore, this building helped to provide good acoustics, for speech travels well if there is a solid barrier behind the speaker and a hard, smooth surface in front of him, and if the audience sits in tiers. The wall of the scene building provided the barrier; the orchestra provided the surface in front of the actors; and the seats on the hillside fulfilled the third requirement. Moreover, the acoustics were somewhat improved by slightly elevating the actors above the orchestra, but it is not known exactly when this platform was first constructed in front of the scene building.

A tragedy commonly begins with a *prologos* (prologue), during which the exposition is given. Next comes the *párodos,* the chorus's ode of entrance, sung while the chorus marches into the theater, through the side aisles, and onto the orchestra. The *epeisodion* (episode) is the ensuing scene; it is followed by a *stasimon* (choral song, ode). Usually there are four or five *epeisodia,* alternating with *stasima.* Each of these choral odes has a *strophe* (lines presumably sung while the chorus dances in one direction) and an *antistrophe* (lines presumably

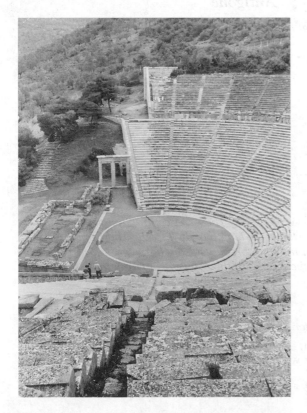

Greek theater at Epidaurus.
(Frederick Ayers/Photo
Researchers)

sung while the chorus retraces its steps). Sometimes a third part, an *epode,* concludes an ode. (In addition to odes that are *stasima,* there can be odes within
episodes; the fourth episode of *Antigonê* (here called Scene IV) contains an ode
complete with *epode.*) After the last part of the last ode comes the *exodos,* the epilogue or final scene.

The actors (all male) wore masks, and they seem to have chanted much of
the play. Perhaps the total result of combining speech with music and dancing
was a sort of music-drama roughly akin to opera with some spoken dialogue, like
Mozart's *Magic Flute.*

Thinking Critically about a Tragedy: Sophocles's *Antigonê*

SOPHOCLES

*One of the three great writers of tragedies in ancient Greece, Sophocles (496?–406
B.C.) was born in Colonus, near Athens, into a well-to-do family. Well educated, he
first won public acclaim as a tragic poet at the age of 27, in 468 B.C., when he defeated Aeschylus in a competition for writing a tragic play. He is said to have written some 120 plays, but only 7 tragedies are extant; among them are* Oedipus Rex,
Antigonê, *and* Oedipus at Colonus. *He died, much honored, in his ninetieth year,
in Athens, where he had lived his entire life.*

Antigonê

*An English Version by Dudley Fitts and Robert Fitzgerald**

LIST OF CHARACTERS

ANTIGONÊ
ISMENÊ
EURYDICÊ
CREON
HAIMON
TEIRESIAS
A SENTRY
A MESSENGER
CHORUS

SCENE: *Before the palace of* CREON, *king of Thebes. A central double door, and
two lateral doors. A platform extends the length of the façade, and from this
platform three steps lead down into the "orchestra," or chorus-ground.*
Time: *Dawn of the day after the repulse of the Argive army from the assault on
Thebes.*

Prologue

ANTIGONÊ *and* ISMENÊ *enter from the central door of the palace.*

ANTIGONÊ.   Ismenê, dear sister,
         You would think that we had already suffered enough

---

* Explanatory notes are indicated by a degree symbol (°) in the text and are keyed to the text by
line number.

Jane Lapotaire in *Antigonê*. National Theater, London, 1984. (Donald Cooper/Photo stage)

        For the curse on Oedipus.°
        I cannot imagine any grief
        That you and I have not gone through. And now—   5
        Have they told you of the new decree of our King Creon?
ISMENÊ. I have heard nothing: I know
        That two sisters lost two brothers, a double death
        In a single hour; and I know that the Argive army
        Fled in the night; but beyond this, nothing.   10
ANTIGONÊ.   I thought so. And this is why I wanted you
        To come out here with me. There is something we must do.
ISMENÊ. Why do you speak so strangely?
ANTIGONÊ.   Listen, Ismenê:
        Creon buried our brother Eteoclês   15
        With military honors, gave him a soldier's funeral,
        And it was right that he should; but Polyneicês,
        Who fought as bravely and died as miserably,—
        They say that Creon has sworn
        No one shall bury him, no one mourn for him,   20
        But his body must lie in the fields, a sweet treasure
        For carrion birds to find as they search for food.
        That is what they say, and our good Creon is coming here

3 Oedipus, once King of Thebes, was the father of Antigonê and Ismenê, and of their brothers Polyneicês and Eteoclês. Oedipus unwittingly killed his father, Laïos, and married his own mother, Iocastê. When he learned what he had done, he blinded himself and left Thebes. Eteoclês and Polyneicês quarreled; Polyneicês was driven out but returned to assault Thebes. In the battle each brother killed the other; Creon became king and ordered that Polyneicês be left to rot unburied on the battlefield as a traitor.

          To announce it publicly; and the penalty—
          Stoning to death in the public square!
                             There it is,   25
          And now you can prove what you are:
          A true sister, or a traitor to your family.

ISMENÊ.   Antigonê, you are mad! What could I possibly do?

ANTIGONÊ.   You must decide whether you will help me or not.

ISMENÊ.   I do not understand you. Help you in what?   30

ANTIGONÊ.   Ismenê. I am going to bury him. Will you come?

ISMENÊ.   Bury him! You have just said the new law forbids it.

ANTIGONÊ.   He is my brother. And he is your brother, too.

ISMENÊ.   But think of the danger! Think what Creon will do!

ANTIGONÊ.   Creon is not strong enough to stand in my way.   35

ISMENÊ.   Ah sister!
          Oedipus died, everyone hating him
          For what his own search brought to light, his eyes
          Ripped out by his own hand; and Iocastê died,
          His mother and wife at once: she twisted the cords   40
          That strangled her life; and our two brothers died,
          Each killed by the other's sword. And we are left:
          But oh, Antigonê,
          Think how much more terrible than these
          Our own death would be if we should go against Creon   45
          And do what he has forbidden! We are only women,
          We cannot fight with men, Antigonê!
          The law is strong, we must give in to the law
          In this thing, and in worse. I beg the Dead
          To forgive me, but I am helpless: I must yield   50
          To those in authority. And I think it is dangerous business
          To be always meddling.

ANTIGONÊ.   If that is what you think,
          I should not want you, even if you asked to come.
          You have made your choice, you can be what you want to be.
          But I will bury him; and if I must die,   55
          I say that this crime is holy: I shall lie down
          With him in death, and I shall be as dear
          To him as he to me.
                   It is the dead,
          Not the living, who make the longest demands:
          We die for ever. . . .
                    You may do as you like.   60
          Since apparently the laws of the gods mean nothing to you.

ISMENÊ.   They mean a great deal to me; but I have no strength
          To break laws that were made for the public good.

ANTIGONÊ.   That must be your excuse, I suppose. But as for me,
          I will bury the brother I love.

ISMENÊ.   Antigonê,   65
          I am so afraid for you!

ANTIGONÊ.   You need not be:
          You have yourself to consider, after all.

ISMENÊ.   But no one must hear of this, you must tell no one!
          I will keep it a secret, I promise!

ANTIGONÊ.   O tell it! Tell everyone!
  Think how they'll hate you when it all comes out   70
  If they learn that you knew about it all the time!
ISMENÊ. So fiery! You should be cold with fear.
ANTIGONÊ. Perhaps. But I am doing only what I must.
ISMENÊ. But can you do it? I say that you cannot.
ANTIGONÊ. Very well: when my strength gives out,
  I shall do no more.   75
ISMENÊ. Impossible things should not be tried at all.
ANTIGONÊ. Go away, Ismenê:
  I shall be hating you soon, and the dead will too,
  For your words are hateful. Leave me my foolish plan:
  I am not afraid of the danger; if it means death,   80
  It will not be the worst of deaths—death without honor.
ISMENÊ. Go then, if you feel that you must.
  You are unwise,
  But a loyal friend indeed to those who love you.

     Exit into the palace. ANTIGONÊ *goes off, left. Enter the* CHORUS.

      Párodos

CHORUS. Now the long blade of the sun, lying   *Strophe 1*
  Level east to west, touches with glory
  Thebes of the Seven Gates. Open, unlidded
  Eye of golden day! O marching light
  Across the eddy and rush of Dircê's stream,°   5
  Striking the white shields of the enemy
  Thrown headlong backward from the blaze of morning!
CHORAGOS.° Polyneicês their commander
  Roused them with windy phrases,
  He the wild eagle screaming   10
  Insults above our land,
  His wings their shields of snow,
  His crest their marshalled helms.
CHORUS. Against our seven gates in a yawning ring   *Antistrophe 1*
  The famished spears came onward in the night: 15
  But before his jaws were sated with our blood,
  Or pinefire took the garland of our towers,
  He was thrown back; and as he turned, great Thebes—
  No tender victim for his noisy power—
  Rose like a dragon behind him, shouting war.   20
CHORAGOS. For God hates utterly
  The bray of bragging tongues;
  And when he beheld their smiling,
  Their swagger of golden helms,
  The frown of his thunder blasted   25
  Their first man from our walls.
CHORUS. We heard his shout of triumph high in the air   *Strophe 2*
  Turn to a scream; far out in a flaming arc
  He fell with his windy torch, and the earth struck him.

Párodos 5 **Dircê's stream** a stream west of Thebes. **8 Choragos** leader of the Chorus.

And others storming in fury no less than his   30
Found shock of death in the dusty joy of battle.
CHORAGOS.   Seven captains at seven gates
Yielded their clanging arms to the god
That bends the battle-line and breaks it.
These two only, brothers in blood,   35
Face to face in matchless rage.
Mirroring each the other's death,
Clashed in long combat.
CHORUS.   But now in the beautiful morning of victory   *Antistrophe 2*
Let Thebes of the many chariots sing for joy!   40
With hearts for dancing we'll take leave of war:
Our temples shall be sweet with hymns of praise,
And the long nights shall echo with our chorus.

Scene I

CHORAGOS.   But now at last our new King is coming:
Creon of Thebes, Menoikeus' son.
In this auspicious dawn of his reign
What are the new complexities
That shifting Fate has woven for him?   5
What is his counsel? Why has he summoned
The old men to hear him?

Enter CREON *from the palace, center. He addresses the* CHORUS *from the top step.*

CREON.   Gentlemen: I have the honor to inform you that our Ship of State, which
recent storms have threatened to destroy, has come safely to harbor at last,
guided by the merciful wisdom of Heaven. I have summoned you here this   10
morning because I know that I can depend upon you: your devotion to King
Laïos was absolute; you never hesitated in your duty to our late ruler
Oedipus; and when Oedipus died, your loyalty was transferred to his children. Unfortunately, as you know, his two sons, the princes Eteoclês and
Polyneicês, have killed each other in battle; and I, as the next in blood, have   15
succeeded to the full power of the throne.
      I am aware, of course, that no Ruler can expect complete loyalty from his
subjects until he has been tested in office. Nevertheless, I say to you at the very
outset that I have nothing but contempt for the kind of Governor who is afraid,
for whatever reason, to follow the course that he knows is best for the State;   20
and as for the man who sets private friendship above the public welfare,—I
have no use for him, either. I call God to witness that if I saw my country
headed for ruin, I should not be afraid to speak out plainly; and I need hardly
remind you that I would never have any dealings with an enemy of the people.
No one values friendship more highly than I: but we must remember that   25
friends made at the risk of wrecking our Ship are not real friends at all.
      These are my principles, at any rate, and that is why I have made the fol-
lowing decision concerning the sons of Oedipus: Eteoclês, who died as a
man should die, fighting for his country, is to be buried with full military honors, with all the ceremony that is usual when the greatest heroes die; but his   30
brother Polyneicês, who broke his exile to come back with fire and sword
against his native city and the shrines of his fathers' gods, whose one idea
was to spill the blood of his blood and sell his own people into slavery—
Polyneicês, I say, is to have no burial: no man is to touch him or say the least

prayer for him; he shall lie on the plain, unburied; and the birds and the scav-   35
enging dogs can do with him whatever they like.

    This is my command, and you can see the wisdom behind it. As long as I
am King, no traitor is going to be honored with the loyal man. But whoever
shows by word and deed that he is on the side of the State—he shall have my
respect while he is living and my reverence when he is dead.   40

CHORAGOS.   If that is your will, Creon son of Menoikeus,
    You have the right to enforce it: we are yours.

CREON.   That is my will. Take care that you do your part.

CHORAGOS.   We are old men: let the younger ones carry it out.

CREON.   I do not mean that: the sentries have been appointed.   45

CHORAGOS.   Then what is it that you would have us do?

CREON.   You will give no support to whoever breaks this law.

CHORAGOS.   Only a crazy man is in love with death!

CREON.   And death it is; yet money talks, and the wisest
    Have sometimes been known to count a few coins too many.   50

    Enter SENTRY *from left.*

SENTRY.   I'll not say that I'm out of breath from running, King, because every time
I stopped to think about what I have to tell you, I felt like going back. And all
the time a voice kept saying, "You fool, don't you know you're walking
straight into trouble?"; and then another voice: "Yes, but if you let somebody
else get the news to Creon first, it will be even worse than that for you!" But   55
good sense won out, at least I hope it was good sense, and here I am with a
story that makes no sense at all; but I'll tell it anyhow, because, as they say,
what's going to happen's going to happen and—

CREON.   Come to the point. What have you to say?

SENTRY.   I did not do it. I did not see who did it. You must not punish me for what   60
    someone else has done.

CREON.   A comprehensive defense! More effective, perhaps, if I knew its purpose.
    Come: what is it?

SENTRY.   A dreadful thing . . . I don't know how to put it—

CREON.   Out with it!

SENTRY.   Well, then;   65
    The dead man—
           Polyneicês—

    Pause. The SENTRY *is overcome, fumbles for words.* CREON *waits impassively.*

                out there—
                     someone,—
    New dust on the slimy flesh!

    Pause. No sign from CREON.

    Someone has given it burial that way, and
    Gone. . . .

    Long pause. CREON *finally speaks with deadly control.*

CREON.   And the man who dared do this?

SENTRY.   I swear I   70
    Do not know! You must believe me!
                    Listen:
    The ground was dry, not a sign of digging, no,
    Not a wheeltrack in the dust, no trace of anyone.
    It was when they relieved us this morning: and one of them,

The corporal, pointed to it.
There it was,   75
The strangest—
Look:
The body, just mounded over with light dust: you see?
Not buried really, but as if they'd covered it
Just enough for the ghost's peace. And no sign
Of dogs or any wild animal that had been there.   80

And then what a scene there was! Every man of us
Accusing the other: we all proved the other man did it,
We all had proof that we could not have done it.
We were ready to take hot iron in our hands,
Walk through fire, swear by all the gods,   85
It was not I!
I do not know who it was, but it was not I!

CREON's *rage has been mounting steadily, but the* SENTRY *is too intent upon*
his story to notice it.

And then, when this came to nothing, someone said
A thing that silenced us and made us stare
Down at the ground: you had to be told the news,   90
And one of us had to do it! We threw the dice,
And the bad luck fell to me. So here I am,
No happier to be here than you are to have me:
Nobody likes the man who brings bad news.
CHORAGOS.   I have been wondering, King: can it be that the gods have done this?   95
CREON [*furiously*].   Stop!
Must you doddering wrecks
Go out of your heads entirely? "The gods"!
Intolerable!
The gods favor this corpse? Why? How had he served them?   100
Tried to loot their temples, burn their images,
Yes, and the whole State, and its laws with it!
Is it your senile opinion that the gods love to honor bad men?
A pious thought!—
No, from the very beginning
There have been those who have whispered together,   105
Stiff-necked anarchists, putting their heads together,
Scheming against me in alleys. These are the men,
And they have bribed my own guard to do this thing.
[*Sententiously.*] Money!
There's nothing in the world so demoralizing as money.   110
Down go your cities,
Homes gone, men gone, honest hearts corrupted.
Crookedness of all kinds, and all for money!
[*To* SENTRY.]   But you—!
I swear by God and by the throne of God,
The man who has done this thing shall pay for it!   115
Find that man, bring him here to me, or your death
Will be the least of your problems: I'll string you up

Alive, and there will be certain ways to make you
Discover your employer before you die;
And the process may teach you a lesson you seem to have missed: 120
The dearest profit is sometimes all too dear:
That depends on the source. Do you understand me?
A fortune won is often misfortune.

SENTRY.   King, may I speak?
CREON.   Your very voice distresses me.
SENTRY.   Are you sure that it is my voice, and not your conscience?   125
CREON.   By God, he wants to analyze me now!
SENTRY.   It is not what I say, but what has been done, that hurts you.
CREON.   You talk too much.
SENTRY.   Maybe; but I've done nothing.
CREON.   Sold your soul for some silver: that's all you've done.
SENTRY.   How dreadful it is when the right judge judges wrong!   130
CREON.   Your figures of speech
May entertain you now; but unless you bring me the man,
You will get little profit from them in the end.

                                                  Exit CREON *into the palace.*

SENTRY.   "Bring me the man"—!
I'd like nothing better than bringing him the man!   135
But bring him or not, you have seen the last of me here.
At any rate, I am safe!

                                                        [*Exit* SENTRY.]

Ode I

CHORUS.   Numberless are the world's wonders, but not   *Strophe 1*
More wonderful than man; the stormgray sea
Yields to his prows, the huge crests bear him high;
Earth, holy and inexhaustible, is graven
With shining furrows where his plows have gone   5
Year after year, the timeless labor of stallions.

The lightboned birds and beasts that cling to cover,   *Antistrophe 1*
The lithe fish lighting their reaches of dim water,
All are taken, tamed in the net of his mind;
The lion on the hill, the wild horse windy-maned,   10
Resign to him; and his blunt yoke has broken
The sultry shoulders of the mountain bull.

Words also, and thought as rapid as air,   *Strophe 2*
He fashions to his good use; statecraft is his,
And his the skill that deflects the arrows of snow,   15
The spears of winter rain: from every wind
He has made himself secure—from all but one:
In the late wind of death he cannot stand.

O clear intelligence, force beyond all measure!   *Antistrophe 2*
O fate of man, working both good and evil!   20
When the laws are kept, how proudly his city stands!
When the laws are broken, what of his city then?

> Never may the anarchic man find rest at my hearth,
> Never be it said that my thoughts are his thoughts.

Scene II

Reenter SENTRY *leading* ANTIGONÊ.

CHORAGOS.   What does this mean? Surely this captive woman
       Is the Princess, Antigonê. Why should she be taken?
SENTRY.   Here is the one who did it! We caught her
       In the very act of burying him.—Where is Creon?
CHORAGOS.   Just coming from the house.

Enter CREON, *center.*

CREON.   What has happened?   5
       Why have you come back so soon?
SENTRY [*expansively*].   O King,
       A man should never be too sure of anything:
       I would have sworn
       That you'd not see me here again: your anger
       Frightened me so, and the things you threatened me with;   10
       But how could I tell then
       That I'd be able to solve the case so soon?
       No dice-throwing this time: I was only too glad to come!
       Here is this woman. She is the guilty one:
       We found her trying to bury him.   15
       Take her, then; question her; judge her as you will.
       I am through with the whole thing now, and glad of it.
CREON.   But this is Antigonê! Why have you brought her here?
SENTRY.   She was burying him, I tell you!
CREON [*severely*].   Is this the truth?
SENTRY.   I saw her with my own eyes. Can I say more?   20
CREON.   The details: come, tell me quickly!
SENTRY.   It was like this:
       After those terrible threats of yours, King,
       We went back and brushed the dust away from the body.
       The flesh was soft by now, and stinking,
       So we sat on a hill to windward and kept guard.   25
       No napping this time! We kept each other awake.
       But nothing happened until the white round sun
       Whirled in the center of the round sky over us:
       Then, suddenly,
       A storm of dust roared up from the earth, and the sky   30
       Went out, the plain vanished with all its trees
       In the stinging dark. We closed our eyes and endured it.
       The whirlwind lasted a long time, but it passed;
       And then we looked, and there was Antigonê!
       I have seen   35
       A mother bird come back to a stripped nest, heard
       Her crying bitterly a broken note or two
       For the young ones stolen. Just so, when this girl
       Found the bare corpse, and all her love's work wasted,
       She wept, and cried on heaven to damn the hands   40
       That had done this thing.

And then she brought more dust
And sprinkled wine three times for her brother's ghost.

We ran and took her at once. She was not afraid,
Not even when we charged her with what she had done.
She denied nothing.
                      And this was a comfort to me,   45
And some uneasiness: for it is a good thing
To escape from death, but it is no great pleasure
To bring death to a friend.
                      Yet I always say
There is nothing so comfortable as your own safe skin!
CREON [*slowly, dangerously*].   And you, Antigonê,   50
      You with your head hanging,—do you confess this thing?
ANTIGONÊ.   I do. I deny nothing.
CREON [*to* SENTRY].   You may go.   [*Exit* SENTRY.]
      [*To* ANTIGONÊ.] Tell me, tell me briefly:
      Had you heard my proclamation touching this matter?
ANTIGONÊ.   It was public. Could I help hearing it?   55
CREON.   And yet you dared defy the law.
ANTIGONÊ.   I dared.
      It was not God's proclamation. That final Justice
      That rules the world below makes no such laws.

      Your edict, King, was strong.
      But all your strength is weakness itself against   60
      The immortal unrecorded laws of God.
      They are not merely now: they were, and shall be,
      Operative for ever, beyond man utterly.
      I knew I must die, even without your decree:
      I am only mortal. And if I must die   65
      Now, before it is my time to die,
      Surely this is no hardship: can anyone
      Living, as I live, with evil all about me,
      Think Death less than a friend? This death of mine
      Is of no importance; but if I had left my brother   70
      Lying in death unburied, I should have suffered.
      Now I do not.
                      You smile at me. Ah Creon,
      Think me a fool, if you like; but it may well be
      That a fool convicts me of folly.
CHORAGOS.   Like father, like daughter: both headstrong, deaf to reason!   75
      She has never learned to yield.
CREON.   She has much to learn.
      The inflexible heart breaks first, the toughest iron
      Cracks first, and the wildest horses bend their necks
      At the pull of the smallest curb.
                              Pride? In a slave?
      This girl is guilty of a double insolence,   80
      Breaking the given laws and boasting of it.
      Who is the man here,
      She or I, if this crime goes unpunished?

Sister's child, or more than sister's child,
Or closer yet in blood—she and her sister   85
Win bitter death for this!
[*To* SERVANTS.]   Go, some of you,
Arrest Ismenê. I accuse her equally.
Bring her: you will find her sniffling in the house there.

Her mind's a traitor: crimes kept in the dark
Cry for light, and the guardian brain shudders;   90
But how much worse than this
Is brazen boasting of barefaced anarchy!
ANTIGONÊ.   Creon, what more do you want than my death?
CREON.   Nothing.
That gives me everything.
ANTIGONÊ.   Then I beg you: kill me.
This talking is a great weariness: your words   95
Are distasteful to me, and I am sure that mine
Seem so to you. And yet they should not seem so:
I should have praise and honor for what I have done.
All these men here would praise me
Were their lips not frozen shut with fear of you.   100
[*Bitterly.*] Ah the good fortune of kings,
Licensed to say and do whatever they please!
CREON.   You are alone here in that opinion.
ANTIGONÊ.   No, they are with me. But they keep their tongues in leash.
CREON.   Maybe. But you are guilty, and they are not.   105
ANTIGONÊ.   There is no guilt in reverence for the dead.
CREON.   But Eteoclês—was he not your brother too?
ANTIGONÊ.   My brother too.
CREON.   And you insult his memory?
ANTIGONÊ [*softly*].   The dead man would not say that I insult it.
CREON.   He would: for you honor a traitor as much as him.   110
ANTIGONÊ.   His own brother, traitor or not, and equal in blood.
CREON.   He made war on his country. Eteoclês defended it.
ANTIGONÊ.   Nevertheless, there are honors due all the dead.
CREON.   But not the same for the wicked as for the just.
ANTIGONÊ.   Ah Creon, Creon,   115
Which of us can say what the gods hold wicked?
CREON.   An enemy is an enemy, even dead.
ANTIGONÊ.   It is my nature to join in love, not hate.
CREON [*finally losing patience*].   Go join them then; if you must have your love,
Find it in hell!   120
CHORAGOS.   But see, Ismenê comes:

Enter ISMENÊ, *guarded.*

Those tears are sisterly, the cloud
That shadows her eyes rains down gentle sorrow.
CREON.   You too, Ismenê,
Snake in my ordered house, sucking my blood   125
Stealthily—and all the time I never knew
That these two sisters were aiming at my throne!
                                    Ismenê,

Do you confess your share in this crime, or deny it?
Answer me.

ISMENÊ.   Yes, if she will let me say so. I am guilty.   130

ANTIGONÊ [*coldly*].   No, Ismenê. You have no right to say so.
You would not help me, and I will not have you help me.

ISMENÊ.   But now I know what you meant: and I am here
To join you, to take my share of punishment.

ANTIGONÊ.   The dead man and the gods who rule the dead   135
Know whose act this was. Words are not friends.

ISMENÊ.   Do you refuse me, Antigonê? I want to die with you:
I too have a duty that I must discharge to the dead.

ANTIGONÊ.   You shall not lessen my death by sharing it.

ISMENÊ.   What do I care for life when you are dead?   140

ANTIGONÊ.   Ask Creon. You're always hanging on his opinions.

ISMENÊ.   You are laughing at me. Why, Antigonê?

ANTIGONÊ.   It's a joyless laughter, Ismenê.

ISMENÊ.   But can I do nothing?

ANTIGONÊ.   Yes. Save yourself. I shall not envy you.
There are those who will praise you; I shall have honor, too.   145

ISMENÊ.   But we are equally guilty!

ANTIGONÊ.   No more, Ismenê.
You are alive, but I belong to Death.

CREON [*to the* CHORUS].   Gentlemen, I beg you to observe these girls:
One has just now lost her mind; the other,
It seems, has never had a mind at all.   150

ISMENÊ.   Grief teaches the steadiest minds to waver, King.

CREON.   Yours certainly did, when you assumed guilt with the guilty!

ISMENÊ.   But how could I go on living without her?

CREON.   You are.
She is already dead.

ISMENÊ.   But your own son's bride!

CREON.   There are places enough for him to push his plow.   155
I want no wicked women for my sons!

ISMENÊ.   O dearest Haimon, how your father wrongs you!

CREON.   I've had enough of your childish talk of marriage!

CHORAGOS.   Do you really intend to steal this girl from your son?

CREON.   No; Death will do that for me.

CHORAGOS.   Then she must die?   160

CREON [*ironically*].   You dazzle me.
                                        —But enough of this talk!

[*To* GUARDS.] You, there, take them away and guard them well:
For they are but women, and even brave men run
When they see Death coming.   *Exeunt* ISMENÊ, ANTIGONÊ, *and* GUARDS.

Ode II

CHORUS.   Fortunate is the man who has never tasted   *Strophe 1*
God's vengeance!
Where once the anger of heaven has struck, that house is shaken
For ever: damnation rises behind each child
Like a wave cresting out of the black northeast,

When the long darkness under sea roars up   5
And bursts drumming death upon the windwhipped sand.

I have seen this gathering sorrow from time long past   *Antistrophe 1*
Loom upon Oedipus' children: generation from generation
Takes the compulsive rage of the enemy god.
So lately this last flower of Oedipus' line   10
Drank the sunlight! but now a passionate word
And a handful of dust have closed up all its beauty.

What mortal arrogance   *Strophe 2*
Transcends the wrath of Zeus?
Sleep cannot lull him nor the effortless long months   15
Of the timeless gods: but he is young for ever,
And his house is the shining day of high Olympos.
All that is and shall be,
And all the past, is his.
No pride on earth is free of the curse of heaven.   20

The straying dreams of men   *Antistrophe 2*
May bring them ghosts of joy:
But as they drowse, the waking embers burn them;
Or they walk with fixed eyes, as blind men walk.
But the ancient wisdom speaks for our own time: 25

Fate works most for woe
With Folly's fairest show.

Man's little pleasure is the spring of sorrow.

Scene III

CHORAGOS.   But here is Haimon, King, the last of all your sons.
            Is it grief for Antigonê that brings him here,
            And bitterness at being robbed of his bride?

       Enter HAIMON.

CREON.   We shall soon see, and no need of diviners.
                                        —Son,
         You have heard my final judgment on that girl: 5
         Have you come here hating me, or have you come
         With deference and with love, whatever I do?
HAIMON.   I am your son, father. You are my guide.
          You make things clear for me, and I obey you.
          No marriage means more to me than your continuing wisdom.   10
CREON.   Good. That is the way to behave: subordinate
         Everything else, my son, to your father's will.
         This is what a man prays for, that he may get
         Sons attentive and dutiful in his house,
         Each one hating his father's enemies,   15
         Honoring his father's friends. But if his sons
         Fail him, if they turn out unprofitably,
         What has he fathered but trouble for himself
         And amusement for the malicious?
                                    So you are right

Not to lose your head over this woman.   20
Your pleasure with her would soon grow cold, Haimon,
And then you'd have a hellcat in bed and elsewhere.
Let her find her husband in Hell!
Of all the people in this city, only she
Has had contempt for my law and broken it.   25

Do you want me to show myself weak before the people?
Or to break my sworn word? No, and I will not.
The woman dies.
I suppose she'll plead "family ties." Well, let her.
If I permit my own family to rebel,   30
How shall I earn the world's obedience?
Show me the man who keeps his house in hand,
He's fit for public authority.
                         I'll have no dealings
With lawbreakers, critics of the government:
Whoever is chosen to govern should be obeyed—   35
Must be obeyed, in all things, great and small,
Just and unjust! O Haimon,
The man who knows how to obey, and that man only,
Knows how to give commands when the time comes.
You can depend on him, no matter how fast   40
The spears come: he's a good soldier, he'll stick it out.

Anarchy, anarchy! Show me a greater evil!
This is why cities tumble and the great houses rain down,
This is what scatters armies!
No, no: good lives are made so by discipline.   45
We keep the laws then, and the lawmakers,
And no woman shall seduce us. If we must lose,
    Let's lose to a man, at least! Is a woman stronger than we?
CHORAGOS.   Unless time has rusted my wits,
    What you say, King, is said with point and dignity.   50
HAIMON [*boyishly earnest*].   Father:
    Reason is God's crowning gift to man, and you are right
To warn me against losing mine. I cannot say—
I hope that I shall never want to say!—that you
Have reasoned badly. Yet there are other men   55
Who can reason, too; and their opinions might be helpful.
You are not in a position to know everything
That people say or do, or what they feel:
Your temper terrifies—everyone
Will tell you only what you like to hear.   60
But I, at any rate, can listen; and I have heard them
Muttering and whispering in the dark about this girl.
They say no woman has ever, so unreasonably,
Died so shameful a death for a generous act:
"She covered her brother's body. Is this indecent?   65
She kept him from dogs and vultures. Is this a crime?
Death?—She should have all the honor that we can give her!"

This is the way they talk out there in the city.

You must believe me:
Nothing is closer to me than your happiness.
What could be closer? Must not any son   70
Value his father's fortune as his father does his?
I beg you, do not be unchangeable:
Do not believe that you alone can be right.
The man who thinks that,
The man who maintains that only he has the power   75
To reason correctly, the gift to speak, the soul—
A man like that, when you know him, turns out empty.

It is not reason never to yield to reason!
In flood time you can see how some trees bend,   80
And because they bend, even their twigs are safe,
While stubborn trees are torn up, roots and all.
And the same thing happens in sailing:
Make your sheet fast, never slacken,—and over you go,
Head over heels and under: and there's your voyage.   85
Forget you are angry! Let yourself be moved!
I know I am young; but please let me say this:
The ideal condition
Would be, I admit, that men should be right by instinct;
But since we are all too likely to go astray,   90
The reasonable thing is to learn from those who can teach.
CHORAGOS.   You will do well to listen to him, King,
            If what he says is sensible. And you, Haimon,
            Must listen to your father.—Both speak well.
CREON.   You consider it right for a man of my years and experience   95
            To go to school to a boy?
HAIMON.   It is not right
            If I am wrong. But if I am young, and right,
            What does my age matter?
CREON.   You think it right to stand up for an anarchist?
HAIMON.   Not at all. I pay no respect to criminals.   100
CREON.   Then she is not a criminal?
HAIMON.   The City would deny it, to a man.
CREON.   And the City proposes to teach me how to rule?
HAIMON.   Ah. Who is it that's talking like a boy now?
CREON.   My voice is the one voice giving orders in this City!   105
HAIMON.   It is no City if it takes orders from one voice.
CREON.   The State is the King!
HAIMON.   Yes, if the State is a desert.
      Pause.

CREON.   This boy, it seems, has sold out to a woman.
HAIMON.   If you are a woman: my concern is only for you.
CREON.   So? Your "concern"! In a public brawl with your father!   110
HAIMON.   How about you, in a public brawl with justice?
CREON.   With justice, when all that I do is within my rights?
HAIMON.   You have no right to trample on God's right.
CREON [*completely out of control*].   Fool, adolescent fool! Taken in by a woman!

HAIMON.   You'll never see me taken in by anything vile.   115
CREON.   Every word you say is for her!
HAIMON [*quietly, darkly*].   And for you.
    And for me. And for the gods under the earth.
CREON.   You'll never marry her while she lives.
HAIMON.   Then she must die.—But her death will cause another.
CREON.   Another?   120
    Have you lost your senses? Is this an open threat?
HAIMON.   There is no threat in speaking to emptiness.
CREON.   I swear you'll regret this superior tone of yours!
    You are the empty one!
HAIMON.   If you were not my father,
    I'd say you were perverse.   125
CREON.   You girlstruck fool, don't play at words with me!
HAIMON.   I am sorry. You prefer silence.
CREON.   Now, by God—
    I swear, by all the gods in heaven above us,
    You'll watch it, I swear you shall!
    [*To the* SERVANTS.] Bring her out!
    Bring the woman out! Let her die before his eyes!   130
    Here, this instant, with her bridegroom beside her!
HAIMON.   Not here, no; she will not die here, King.
    And you will never see my face again.
    Go on raving as long as you've a friend to endure you.   *Exit* HAIMON.

CHORAGOS.   Gone, gone.   135
    Creon, a young man in a rage is dangerous!
CREON.   Let him do, or dream to do, more than a man can.
    He shall not save these girls from death.
CHORAGOS.   These girls?
    You have sentenced them both?
CREON.   No, you are right.
    I will not kill the one whose hands are clean.   140
CHORAGOS.   But Antigonê?
CREON. [*somberly*].   I will carry her far away
    Out there in the wilderness, and lock her
    Living in a vault of stone. She shall have food,
    As the custom is, to absolve the State of her death.
    And there let her pray to the gods of hell: 145
    They are her only gods:
    Perhaps they will show her an escape from death,
    Or she may learn,
            though late,
    That piety shown the dead is piety in vain.   [*Exit* CREON.]

Ode III

CHORUS.   Love, unconquerable   *Strophe*
    Waster of rich men, keeper
    Of warm lights and all-night vigil
    In the soft face of a girl:
    Sea-wanderer, forest-visitor!   5
    Even the pure Immortals cannot escape you,

And the mortal man, in his one day's dusk,
Trembles before your glory.

Surely you swerve upon ruin   *Antistrophe*
The just man's consenting heart,
As here you have made bright anger   10
Strike between father and son—
And none has conquered by Love!
A girl's glance working the will of heaven:
Pleasure to her alone who mocks us,
Merciless Aphroditê.°   15

Scene IV

CHORAGOS [*as* ANTIGONÊ *enters guarded*].   But I can no longer stand in awe of this,
     Nor, seeing what I see, keep back my tears.
     Here is Antigonê, passing to that chamber
     Where all find sleep at last.
ANTIGONÊ.   Look upon me, friends, and pity me   *Strophe 1*   5
     Turning back at the night's edge to say
     Good-by to the sun that shines for me no longer;
     Now sleepy Death
     Summons me down to Acheron,° that cold shore:
     There is no bridesong there, nor any music.   10
CHORUS.   Yet not unpraised, not without a kind of honor,
     You walk at last into the underworld;
     Untouched by sickness, broken by no sword.
     What woman has ever found your way to death?
ANTIGONÊ.   How often I have heard the story of Niobê,°   *Antistrophe 1*   15
     Tantalos' wretched daughter, how the stone
     Clung fast about her, ivy-close: and they say
     The rain falls endlessly
     And sifting soft snow; her tears are never done.
     I feel the loneliness of her death in mine.   20
CHORUS.   But she was born of heaven, and you
     Are woman, woman-born. If her death is yours,
     A mortal woman's, is this not for you
     Glory in our world and in the world beyond?
ANTIGONÊ.   You laugh at me. Ah, friends, friends   *Strophe 2*   25
     Can you not wait until I am dead? O Thebes,
     O men many-charioted, in love with Fortune,
     Dear springs of Dircê, sacred Theban grove,
     Be witnesses for me, denied all pity,
     Unjustly judged! and think a word of love   30
     For her whose path turns
     Under dark earth, where there are no more tears.
CHORUS.   You have passed beyond human daring and come at last

Ode III 16 Aphroditê goddess of love.   **9 Acheron** a river of the underworld, which was ruled
by Hades.   **15 Niobê** Niobê boasted of her numerous children, provoking Leto, the mother of
Apollo, to destroy them. Niobê wept profusely, and finally was turned to stone on Mount
Sipylus, whose streams are her tears.

Into a place of stone where Justice sits.
I cannot tell   35
What shape of your father's guilt appears in this.

ANTIGONÊ.   You have touched it at last: *Antistrophe 2*
That bridal bed
Unspeakable, horror of son and mother mingling:
Their crime, infection of all our family!
O Oedipus, father and brother!   40
Your marriage strikes from the grave to murder mine.
I have been a stranger here in my own land:
All my life
The blasphemy of my birth has followed me.

CHORUS.   Reverence is a virtue, but strength   45
Lives in established law: that must prevail.
You have made your choice,
Your death is the doing of your conscious hand.

ANTIGONÊ.   Then let me go, since all your words are bitter,   *Epode*
And the very light of the sun is cold to me.   50
Lead me to my vigil, where I must have
Neither love nor lamentation; no song, but silence.

    CREON *interrupts impatiently.*

CREON.   If dirges and planned lamentations could put off death,
Men would be singing for ever.
[*To the* SERVANTS.]   Take her, go!
You know your orders: take her to the vault   55
And leave her alone there. And if she lives or dies,
That's her affair, not ours: our hands are clean.

ANTIGONÊ.   O tomb, vaulted bride-bed in eternal rock,
Soon I shall be with my own again
Where Persephonê° welcomes the thin ghosts underground: 60
And I shall see my father again, and you, mother,
And dearest Polyneicês—
                dearest indeed
To me, since it was my hand
That washed him clean and poured the ritual wine:
And my reward is death before my time!   65
And yet, as men's hearts know, I have done no wrong,
I have not sinned before God. Or if I have,
I shall know the truth in death. But if the guilt
Lies upon Creon who judged me, then, I pray,
May his punishment equal my own.

CHORAGOS.   O passionate heart,   70
Unyielding, tormented still by the same winds!

CREON.   Her guards shall have good cause to regret their delaying.

ANTIGONÊ.   Ah! That voice is like the voice of death!

CREON.   I can give you no reason to think you are mistaken.

ANTIGONÊ.   Thebes, and you my fathers' gods,   75
And rulers of Thebes, you see me now, the last

60 Persephonê queen of the underworld.

Unhappy daughter of a line of kings,
Your kings, led away to death. You will remember
What things I suffer, and at what men's hands,
Because I would not transgress the laws of heaven.   80
[*To the* GUARDS, *simply.*] Come: let us wait no longer.

> [*Exit* ANTIGONÊ, *left, guarded.*]

Ode IV

CHORUS.   All Danaê's° beauty was locked away   *Strophe 1*
In a brazen cell where the sunlight could not come:
A small room, still as any grave, enclosed her.
Yet she was a princess too,
And Zeus in a rain of gold poured love upon her.   5
O child, child,
No power in wealth or war
Or tough sea-blackened ships
Can prevail against untiring Destiny!

And Dryas' son° also, that furious king,   *Antistrophe 1*
Bore the god's prisoning anger for his pride: 10
Sealed up by Dionysos in deaf stone,
His madness died among echoes.
So at the last he learned what dreadful power
His tongue had mocked:
For he had profaned the revels,   15
And fired the wrath of the nine
Implacable Sisters° that love the sound of the flute.

And old men tell a half-remembered tale   *Strophe 2*
Of horror where a dark ledge splits the sea
And a double surf beats on the gray shores: 20
How a king's new woman,° sick
With hatred for the queen he had imprisoned,
Ripped out his two sons' eyes with her bloody hands
While grinning Arês° watched the shuttle plunge
Four times: four blind wounds crying for revenge,   25

Crying, tears and blood mingled.—Piteously born,   *Antistrophe 2*
Those sons whose mother was of heavenly birth!
Her father was the god of the North Wind
And she was cradled by gales,
She raced with young colts on the glittering hills
And walked untrammeled in the open light: 30
But in her marriage deathless Fate found means
To build a tomb like yours for all her joy.

1 Danaê A princess shut into a tower by her father because of a prophecy that the king would be killed by his grandson. Zeus nevertheless entered Danaê's chamber in the form of a shower of gold and impregnated her. She gave birth to Perseus, who accidentally killed the king with a discus.   **10 Dryas' son** Lycurgus, King of Thrace.   **18 Sisters** the Muses.   **22 king's new woman** Eidothea, second wife of King Phineus, blinded her stepsons. Their mother, Cleopatra, had been imprisoned in a cave. Phineus was the son of a king, and Cleopatra, his first wife, was the daughter of Boreas, the North Wind, but this illustrious ancestry could not protect his sons from violence and darkness.   **25 Arês** god of war.

Scene V

Enter blind TEIRESIAS, *led by a boy. The opening speeches of* TEIRESIAS *should be in singsong contrast to the realistic lines of* CREON.

TEIRESIAS.   This is the way the blind man comes, Princes, Princes,
    Lock-step, two heads lit by the eyes of one.
CREON.   What new thing have you to tell us, old Teiresias?
TEIRESIAS.   I have much to tell you: listen to the prophet, Creon.
CREON.   I am not aware that I have ever failed to listen.   5
TEIRESIAS.   Then you have done wisely, King, and ruled well.
CREON.   I admit my debt to you. But what have you to say?
TEIRESIAS.   This, Creon: you stand once more on the edge of fate.
CREON.   What do you mean? Your words are a kind of dread.
TEIRESIAS.   Listen, Creon: 10
    I was sitting in my chair of augury, at the place
    Where the birds gather about me. They were all a-chatter,
    As is their habit, when suddenly I heard
    A strange note in their jangling, a scream, a
    Whirring fury; I knew that they were fighting,   15
    Tearing each other, dying
    In a whirlwind of wings clashing. And I was afraid.
    I began the rites of burnt-offering at the altar,
    But Hephaistos° failed me: instead of bright flame,
    There was only the sputtering slime of the fat thigh-flesh   20
    Melting: the entrails dissolved in gray smoke,
    The bare bone burst from the welter. And no blaze!

    This was a sign from heaven. My boy described it,
    Seeing for me as I see for others.

    I tell you, Creon, you yourself have brought   25
    This new calamity upon us. Our hearths and altars
    Are stained with the corruption of dogs and carrion birds
    That glut themselves on the corpse of Oedipus' son.
    The gods are deaf when we pray to them, their fire
    Recoils from our offering, their birds of omen   30
    Have no cry of comfort, for they are gorged
    With the thick blood of the dead.
                 O my son,
    These are no trifles! Think: all men make mistakes,
    But a good man yields when he knows his course is wrong,
    And repairs the evil. The only crime is pride.   35

    Give in to the dead man, then: do not fight with a corpse—
    What glory is it to kill a man who is dead?
    Think, I beg you:
    It is for your own good that I speak as I do.
    You should be able to yield for your own good.   40
CREON.   It seems that prophets have made me their especial province.
    All my life long

---

19 Hephaistos god of fire.

I have been a kind of butt for the dull arrows
Of doddering fortune-tellers!
                            No, Teiresias:
If your birds—if the great eagles of God himself   45
Should carry him stinking bit by bit to heaven,
I would not yield. I am not afraid of pollution:
No man can defile the gods.
                            Do what you will,
Go into business, make money, speculate
In India gold or that synthetic gold from Sardis,   50
Get rich otherwise than by my consent to bury him.
Teiresias, it is a sorry thing when a wise man
Sells his wisdom, lets out his words for hire!

TEIRESIAS.   Ah Creon! Is there no man left in the world—
CREON.   To do what?—Come, let's have the aphorism!   55
TEIRESIAS.   No man who knows that wisdom outweighs any wealth?
CREON.   As surely as bribes are baser than any baseness.
TEIRESIAS.   You are sick, Creon! You are deathly sick!
CREON.   As you say: it is not my place to challenge a prophet.
TEIRESIAS.   Yet you have said my prophecy is for sale.   60
CREON.   The generation of prophets has always loved gold.
TEIRESIAS.   The generation of kings has always loved brass.
CREON.   You forget yourself! You are speaking to your King.
TEIRESIAS.   I know it. You are a king because of me.
CREON.   You have a certain skill; but you have sold out.   65
TEIRESIAS.   King, you will drive me to words that—
CREON.   Say them, say them!
Only remember: I will not pay you for them.
TEIRESIAS.   No, you will find them too costly.
CREON.   No doubt. Speak:
Whatever you say, you will not change my will.
TEIRESIAS.   Then take this, and take it to heart!   70
The time is not far off when you shall pay back
Corpse for corpse, flesh of your own flesh.
You have thrust the child of this world into living night,
You have kept from the gods below the child that is theirs:
The one in a grave before her death, the other,   75
Dead, denied the grave. This is your crime:
And the Furies and the dark gods of Hell
Are swift with terrible punishment for you.

Do you want to buy me now, Creon?

                            Not many days,
And your house will be full of men and women weeping,   80
And curses will be hurled at you from far
Cities grieving for sons unburied, left to rot
Before the walls of Thebes.

These are my arrows, Creon: they are all for you.
[*To* BOY.] But come, child: lead me home.   85
Let him waste his fine anger upon younger men.

Maybe he will learn at last
To control a wiser tongue in a better head.   [*Exit* TEIRESIAS.]
CHORAGOS.   The old man has gone, King, but his words
Remain to plague us. I am old, too,   90
But I cannot remember that he was ever false.
CREON.   That is true. . . . It troubles me.
Oh it is hard to give in! but it is worse
To risk everything for stubborn pride.
CHORAGOS.   Creon: take my advice.
CREON.   What shall I do?   95
CHORAGOS.   Go quickly: free Antigonê from her vault
And build a tomb for the body of Polyneicês.
CREON.   You would have me do this!
CHORAGOS.   Creon, yes!
And it must be done at once: God moves
Swiftly to cancel the folly of stubborn men.   100
CREON.   It is hard to deny the heart! But I
Will do it: I will not fight with destiny.
CHORAGOS.   You must go yourself, you cannot leave it to others.
CREON.   I will go.
            —Bring axes, servants:
Come with me to the tomb. I buried her, I   105
Will set her free.
                  Oh quickly!
My mind misgives—
The laws of the gods are mighty, and a man must serve them
To the last day of his life!   [*Exit* CREON.]

Paean°

CHORAGOS.   God of many names   *Strophe 1*
CHORUS.   O Iacchos
                              son
of Kadmeian Sémelê
                  O born of the Thunder!
Guardian of the West
                  Regent
of Eleusis' plain
                  O Prince of Maenad Thebes
and the Dragon Field by rippling Ismenós:°   5
CHORAGOS.   God of many names   *Antistrophe 1*
CHORUS.   the flame of torches
flares on our hills
                  the nymphs of Iacchos
dance at the spring of Castalia:°

Paean a hymn (here dedicated to Iacchos, also called Dionysos. His father was Zeus, his mother
was Sémelê, daughter of Kadmos. Iacchos's worshipers were the Maenads, whose cry was
"*Evohé evohé*")   **5 Ismenós** a river east of Thebes (from a dragon's teeth, sown near the river,
there sprang men who became the ancestors of the Theban nobility).   **8 Castalia** a spring on
Mount Parnassos.

from the vine-close mountain
                                come ah come in ivy:
  Evohé evohé! sings through the streets of Thebes   10
CHORAGOS. God of many names   *Strophe 2*
CHORUS.   Iacchos of Thebes
 heavenly Child
    of Sémelê bride of the Thunderer!
 The shadow of plague is upon us:
         come
with clement feet
    oh come from Parnassos
 down the long slopes
     across the lamenting water   15
CHORAGOS. Iô Fire! Chorister of the throbbing stars!   *Antistrophe 2*
 O purest among the voices of the night!
 Thou son of God, blaze for us!
CHORUS. Come with choric rapture of circling Maenads
 Who cry *Iô Iacche!*
      God of many names!   20

       Exodos

 Enter MESSENGER *from left.*

MESSENGER. Men of the line of Kadmos,° you who live
 Near Amphion's citadel,°
         I cannot say
 Of any condition of human life "This is fixed,
 This is clearly good, or bad." Fate raises up,
 And Fate casts down the happy and unhappy alike: 5
 No man can foretell his Fate.
      Take the case of Creon:
 Creon was happy once, as I count happiness:
 Victorious in battle, sole governor of the land,
 Fortunate father of children nobly born.
 And now it has all gone from him! Who can say   10
 That a man is still alive when his life's joy fails?
 He is a walking dead man. Grant him rich,
 Let him live like a king in his great house:
 If his pleasure is gone, I would not give
 So much as the shadow of smoke for all he owns.   15
CHORAGOS. Your words hint at sorrow: what is your news for us?
MESSENGER. They are dead. The living are guilty of their death.
CHORAGOS. Who is guilty? Who is dead? Speak!
MESSENGER.   Haimon.
 Haimon is dead; and the hand that killed him
 Is his own hand.
CHORAGOS. His father's? or his own?   20

---

1 Kadmos, who sowed the dragon's teeth, was founder of Thebes. **2 Amphion's citadel**
Amphion played so sweetly on his lyre that he charmed stones to form a wall around Thebes.

MESSENGER.   His own, driven mad by the murder his father had done.
CHORAGOS.   Teiresias, Teiresias, how clearly you saw it all!
MESSENGER.   This is my news: you must draw what conclusions you can from it.
CHORAGOS.   But look: Eurydicê, our Queen:
                Has she overheard us?   25

Enter EURYDICÊ *from the palace, center.*

EURYDICE.   I have heard something, friends:
    As I was unlocking the gate of Pallas'° shrine,
    For I needed her help today, I heard a voice
    Telling of some new sorrow. And I fainted
    There at the temple with all my maidens about me.   30
    But speak again: whatever it is, I can bear it:
    Grief and I are no strangers.
MESSENGER.   Dearest Lady,
    I will tell you plainly all that I have seen.
    I shall not try to comfort you: what is the use,
    Since comfort could lie only in what is not true?   35
    The truth is always best.
                   I went with Creon
    To the outer plain where Polyneicês was lying,
    No friend to pity him, his body shredded by dogs.
    We made our prayers in the place to Hecatê
    And Pluto,° that they would be merciful. And we bathed   40
    The corpse with holy water, and we brought
    Fresh-broken branches to burn what was left of it,
    And upon the urn we heaped up a towering barrow
    Of the earth of his own land.
                  When we were done, we ran
    To the vault where Antigonê lay on her couch of stone.   45
    One of the servants had gone ahead,
    And while he was yet far off he heard a voice
    Grieving within the chamber, and he came back
    And told Creon. And as the King went closer,
    The air was full of wailing, the words lost,   50
    And he begged us to make all haste. "Am I a prophet?"
    He said, weeping, "And must I walk this road,
    The saddest of all that I have gone before?
    My son's voice calls me on. Oh quickly, quickly!
    Look through the crevice there, and tell me   55
    If it is Haimon, or some deception of the gods!"
    We obeyed; and in the cavern's farthest corner
    We saw her lying:
    She had made a noose of her fine linen veil
    And hanged herself. Haimon lay beside her,   60
    His arms about her waist, lamenting her,
    His love lost under ground, crying out
    That his father had stolen her away from him.

27 **Pallas** Pallas Athene, goddess of wisdom.   40 **Hecatê / And Pluto** Hecatê and Pluto (also known as Hades) were deities of the underworld.

When Creon saw him the tears rushed to his eyes
And he called to him: "What have you done, child?
Speak to me.   65
What are you thinking that makes your eyes so strange?
O my son, my son, I come to you on my knees!"
But Haimon spat in his face. He said not a word,
Staring—
        And suddenly drew his sword
And lunged. Creon shrank back, the blade missed; and the boy,   70
Desperate against himself, drove it half its length
Into his own side, and fell. And as he died
He gathered Antigonê close in his arms again,
Choking, his blood bright red on her white cheek.
And now he lies dead with the dead, and she is his   75
At last, his bride in the house of the dead.

                    Exit EURYDICÊ *into the palace.*

CHORAGOS.   She has left us without a word. What can this mean?
MESSENGER.   It troubles me, too; yet she knows what is best,
    Her grief is too great for public lamentation,
    And doubtless she has gone to her chamber to weep   80
    For her dead son, leading her maidens in his dirge.

    Pause.

CHORAGOS.   It may be so: but I fear this deep silence.
MESSENGER.   I will see what she is doing. I will go in.

                  Exit MESSENGER *into the palace.*

    Enter CREON *with attendants, bearing* HAIMON*'s body.*

CHORAGOS.   But here is the king himself: on look at him,
    Bearing his own damnation in his arms.   85
CREON.   Nothing you say can touch me any more.
    My own blind heart has brought me
    From darkness to final darkness. Here you see
    The father murdering, the murdered son—
    And all my civic wisdom!   90

    Haimon my son, so young, so young to die,
    I was the fool, not you; and you died for me.
CHORAGOS.   That is the truth; but you were late in learning it.
CREON.   This truth is hard to bear. Surely a god
    Has crushed me beneath the hugest weight of heaven,   95
    And driven me headlong a barbaric way
    To trample out the thing I held most dear.

    The pains that men will take to come to pain!

    Enter MESSENGER *from the palace.*

MESSENGER.   The burden you carry in your hands is heavy,
    But it is not all: you will find more in your house.   100
CREON.   What burden worse than this shall I find there?
MESSENGER.   The Queen is dead.
CREON.   O port of death, deaf world,
    Is there no pity for me? And you, Angel of evil,
    I was dead, and your words are death again.   105

Is it true, boy? Can it be true?
Is my wife dead? Has death bred death?
MESSENGER.   You can see for yourself.

The doors are opened and the body of EURYDICÊ *is disclosed within.*

CREON.   Oh pity!
All true, all true, and more than I can bear!   110
O my wife, my son!
MESSENGER.   She stood before the altar, and her heart
Welcomed the knife her own hand guided,
And a great cry burst from her lips for Megareus° dead,
And for Haimon dead, her sons; and her last breath   115
Was a curse for their father, the murderer of her sons.
And she fell, and the dark flowed in through her closing eyes.
CREON.   O God, I am sick with fear.
Are there no swords here? Has no one a blow for me?
MESSENGER.   Her curse is upon you for the deaths of both.   120
CREON.   It is right that it should be. I alone am guilty.
I know it, and I say it. Lead me in,
Quickly, friends.
I have neither life nor substance. Lead me in.
CHORAGOS.   You are right, if there can be right in so much wrong.   125
The briefest way is best in a world of sorrow.
CREON.   Let it come,
Let death come quickly, and be kind to me.
I would not ever see the sun again.
CHORAGOS.   All that will come when it will; but we, meanwhile,   130
Have much to do. Leave the future to itself.
CREON.   All my heart was in that prayer!
CHORAGOS.   Then do not pray any more: the sky is deaf.
CREON.   Lead me away. I have been rash and foolish.
I have killed my son and my wife.   135
I look for comfort; my comfort lies here dead.
Whatever my hands have touched has come to nothing.
Fate has brought all my pride to a thought of dust.

As CREON *is being led into the house, the* CHORAGOS *advances and speaks
directly to the audience.*

CHORAGOS.   There is no happiness where there is no wisdom;
No wisdom but in submission to the gods.   140
Big words are always punished,
And proud men in old age learn to be wise.

[c. 441 B.C.]

---

114 Megareus Megareus, brother of Haimon, had died in the assault on Thebes.

Topics for Critical Thinking and Writing

1. Would you use masks for some (or all) of the characters? If so, would they be
   masks that fully cover the face, Greek style, or some sort of half-masks? (A full
   mask enlarges the face, and conceivably the mouthpiece can amplify the voice,

404   *Chapter 10   Reading and Writing about Drama*

but only an exceptionally large theater might require such help. Perhaps half-masks are enough if the aim is chiefly to distance the actors from the audience and from daily reality, and to force the actors to develop resources other than facial gestures. One director, arguing in favor of half-masks, has said that an actor who wears even a half-mask learns to act not with his eyes but with his neck.)

2. How would you costume the players? Would you dress them as the Greeks might have? Why? One argument sometimes used by those who hold the modern productions of Greek drama should use classical costumes is that Greek drama *ought* to be remote and ritualistic. Evaluate this view. What sort of modern dress might be effective?

3. If you were directing a college production of *Antigonê*, how large a chorus would you use? (Sophocles is said to have used a chorus of 15.) Would you have the chorus recite (or chant) the odes in unison, or would you assign lines to single speakers?

4. Although Sophocles called his play *Antigonê*, many critics say that Creon is the real tragic hero, pointing out that Antigonê is absent from the last third of the play. Evaluate this view.

5. In some Greek tragedies, fate plays a great role in bringing about the downfall of the tragic hero. Though there are references to the curse on the House of Oedipus in *Antigonê*, do we feel that Antigonê goes to her death as a result of the workings of fate? Do we feel that fate is responsible for Creon's fall? Are both Antigonê and Creon the creators of their own tragedy?

6. Are the words *hamartia* (page 366) and *hubris* (page 365) relevant to Antigonê? To Creon?

7. Why does Creon, contrary to the Chorus's advice, bury the body of Polyneices before he releases Antigonê? Does his action show a zeal for piety as short-sighted as his earlier zeal for law? Is his action plausible, in view of the facts that Teiresias has dwelt on the wrong done to Polyneices and that Antigonê has ritual food to sustain her? Or are we not to worry about Creon's motive?

8. A *foil* is a character who, by contrast, sets off or helps define another character. To what extent is Ismenê a foil to Antigonê? Is she entirely without courage?

9. What function does Eurydicê serve? How deeply do we feel about her fate?

WILLIAM SHAKESPEARE

William Shakespeare (1564–1616) was born in Stratford, England, of middle-class parents. Nothing of interest is known about his early years, but by 1590 he was acting and writing plays in London. By the end of the following decade he had worked in all three Elizabethan dramatic genres—tragedy, comedy, and history. Romeo and Juliet, *for example, was written about 1595, the year of* Richard II. Hamlet *was probably written in 1600–01. Among the plays that followed were* Othello *(1603–04),* King Lear *(1605–06),* Macbeth *(1605–06), and several "romances"—plays that have happy endings but that seem more meditative and closer to tragedy than such comedies as* A Midsummer Night's Dream, As You Like It, *and* Twelfth Night.

Left, Johannes de Witt, a Continental visitor to London, made a drawing of the Swan Theater in about the year 1596. The original drawing is lost; this is Arend van Buchel's copy of it. (Copyright the British Museum.) *Right,* C. Walter Hodges's drawing (1965) of an Elizabethan playhouse. (Courtesy C. Walter Hodges)

A NOTE ON THE ELIZABETHAN THEATER

Shakespeare's theater was wooden, round or polygonal (the Chorus in *Henry V* calls it a "wooden O"). About eight hundred spectators could stand in the yard in front of—and perhaps along the two sides of—the stage that jutted from the rear wall, and another fifteen hundred or so spectators could sit in the three roofed galleries that ringed the stage.

That portion of the galleries that was above the rear of the stage was sometimes used by actors. For instance, in *The Tempest,* 3.3, a stage direction following line 17 mentions "Prospero on the top, invisible," that is, he is imagined to be invisible to the characters in the play.

Entry to the stage was normally gained by doors at the rear, but apparently on rare occasions use was made of a curtained alcove—or perhaps a booth—between the doors, which allowed characters to be "discovered" (revealed) as in the modern proscenium theater, which normally employs a curtain. Such "discovery" scenes are rare.

Although the theater as a whole was unroofed, the stage was protected by a roof, supported by two pillars. These could serve (by an act of imagination) as trees behind which actors might pretend to conceal themselves.

A performance was probably uninterrupted by intermissions or by long pauses for the changing of scenery; a group of characters leaves the stage, another enters, and if the locale has changed the new characters somehow tell us. (Modern editors customarily add indications of locales to help a reader, but it should be remembered that the action on the Elizabethan stage was continuous.)

A NOTE ON *HAMLET* ON THE STAGE

We know that *Hamlet* was popular during Shakespeare's lifetime, but the earliest illustration (1709) showing a scene from the play was engraved more than a century after the play was written, so we know little about what *Hamlet* looked like on Shakespeare's stage. Still, we do have at least some idea. We know, for instance, that at least in the first scene Hamlet wore black (he speaks of his "inky cloak"), and we know that when the Ghost first appears it is dressed in "the very armor he had on / When he the ambitious Norway combated" (1.1.64–65). We know, too, that when the Ghost appears later, in the Queen's chamber (3.4), he does not wear armor, a sign that his mood is different.

We also have a few tantalizing glimpses of Elizabethan acting. Thus, in the dumb show (pantomime) preceding "The Murder of Gonzago" that the touring players in 3.2 produce for the court, we get this stage direction: "Enter a King and a Queen very lovingly: the Queen embracing him and he her." A little later, when the Queen in this dumb show finds that the King has been poisoned, she "makes passionate action," but then, when the poisoner woos her, "she seems harsh a while but in the end accepts love."

We know something, too, of the sound effects. Possibly the play begins with the bell tolling twelve (in 1.1 Bernardo says, "'Tis now struck twelve"), and certainly in the first scene we hear the crowing of a cock, which causes the Ghost to depart. Later we hear the sound of drums, trumpets, and cannon when Claudius drinks toasts, and the play ends with the sound of cannon, when Fortinbras orders the soldiers to pay tribute to the dead Hamlet.

What about costumes? In their own day, Elizabethan plays were staged chiefly in contemporary dress—doublet (close-fitting jacket) and hose (tights) for the men, gowns of various sorts for the women (whose roles were played by boy actors)—though for classical plays such as *Julius Caesar* some attempt was made in the direction of ancient costume, at least for the major characters. The seventeenth and eighteenth centuries, too, staged the plays in the costume of the day, which of course was not Elizabethan. But in much of the nineteenth century, and in the first third of the twentieth, a strong sense that the plays were "Elizabethan" caused producers to use Elizabethan costumes, although these costumes—contemporary when the plays were first performed—now had become historical costume, marking the plays as of an age remote from our own. In 1925 Barry Jackson staged a modern-dress production in London, in an effort to emphasize the play's contemporary relevance. Today, productions tend to be in modern dress in the sense that they avoid Elizabethan costume. Usually, in an effort to add some color to the stage as well as some (but not a great) sense of remoteness, they use costumes of the nineteenth century, which allow for splendid gowns and for military uniforms with sashes.

The Tragedy of Hamlet, Prince of Denmark

DRAMATIS PERSONAE

GHOST *of Hamlet, the former King of Denmark*
CLAUDIUS, *King of Denmark, the former King's brother*
GERTRUDE, *Queen of Denmark, widow of the former King and now wife of Claudius*
HAMLET, *Prince of Denmark, son of the late King and of Gertrude*
POLONIUS, *councillor to the King*
LAERTES, *his son*
OPHELIA, *his daughter*
REYNALDO, *his servant*

HORATIO, *Hamlet's friend and fellow student*

VOLTIMAND,
CORNELIUS,
ROSENCRANTZ,
GUILDENSTERN, } *members of the Danish court*
OSRIC,
A GENTLEMAN,
A LORD,

BERNARDO,
FRANCISCO, } *officers and soldiers on watch*
MARCELLUS,

FORTINBRAS, *Prince of Norway*
CAPTAIN *in his army*
Three or Four PLAYERS, *taking the roles of* PROLOGUE, PLAYER KING, PLAYER QUEEN, and LUCIANUS
Two MESSENGERS
FIRST SAILOR
Two CLOWNS, *a gravedigger and his companion*
PRIEST
FIRST AMBASSADOR from England

Lords, Soldiers, Attendants, Guards, other Players, Followers of Laertes, other Sailors, another Ambassador or Ambassadors from England

SCENE: *Denmark*

1.1   *Enter* BERNARDO *and* FRANCISCO, *two sentinels* [*meeting*].

BERNARDO.   Who's there?
FRANCISCO.   Nay, answer me.° Stand and unfold yourself.°
BERNARDO.   Long live the King!
FRANCISCO.   Bernardo?
BERNARDO.   He.
FRANCISCO.   You come most carefully upon your hour.
BERNARDO.   'Tis now struck twelve. Get thee to bed, Francisco.   5
FRANCISCO.   For this relief much thanks. 'Tis bitter cold,
            And I am sick at heart.
BERNARDO.   Have you had quiet guard?
FRANCISCO.   Not a mouse stirring.
BERNARDO.   Well, good night.   10
            If you do meet Horatio and Marcellus,
            The rivals° of my watch, bid them make haste.

            Enter HORATIO *and* MARCELLUS.

FRANCISCO.   I think I hear them.—Stand, ho! Who is there?
HORATIO.   Friends to this ground.°
MARCELLUS.   And liegemen to the Dane.°   15
FRANCISCO.   Give° you good night.
MARCELLUS.   O, farewell, honest soldier. Who hath relieved you?
FRANCISCO.   Bernardo hath my place. Give you good night.   *Exit* FRANCISCO.
MARCELLUS.   Holla! Bernardo!
BERNARDO.   Say, what, is Horatio there?   20
HORATIO.   A piece of him.
BERNARDO.   Welcome, Horatio. Welcome, good Marcellus.
HORATIO.   What, has this thing appeared again tonight?
BERNARDO.   I have seen nothing.
MARCELLUS.   Horatio says 'tis but our fantasy,°   25
            And will not let belief take hold of him
            Touching this dreaded sight twice seen of us.
            Therefore I have entreated him along°
            With us to watch° the minutes of this night,
            That if again this apparition come   30
            He may approve° our eyes and speak to it.
HORATIO.   Tush, tush, 'twill not appear.
BERNARDO.   Sit down awhile,
            And let us once again assail your ears,
            That are so fortified against our story,
            What° we have two nights seen.   35

1.1 Location: Elsinore castle. A guard platform.   **2 me** (Francisco emphasizes that *he* is the
sentry currently on watch.);   **unfold yourself** reveal your identity.   **14 rivals** partners.
16 ground ground, land.   **17 liegemen to the Dane** men sworn to serve the Danish king.
18 Give i.e., may God give.   **27 fantasy** imagination.   **30 along** to come along.
31 watch keep watch during.   **33 approve** corroborate.   **37 What** with what.

HORATIO.   Well, sit we down,
　　And let us hear Bernardo speak of this.
BERNARDO.   Last night of all,°
　　When yond same star that's westward from the pole°   40
　　Had made his° course t' illume° that part of heaven
　　Where now it burns, Marcellus and myself,
　　The bell then beating one—

　　　　Enter GHOST.

MARCELLUS.   Peace, break thee off! Look where it comes again!
BERNARDO.   In the same figure like the King that's dead.   45
MARCELLUS.   Thou art a scholar.° Speak to it, Horatio.
BERNARDO.   Looks 'a° not like the King? Mark it, Horatio.
HORATIO.   Most like. It harrows me with fear and wonder.
BERNARDO.   It would be spoke to.°
MARCELLUS.   Speak to it, Horatio.
HORATIO.   What art thou that usurp'st° this time of night,   50
　　Together with that fair and warlike form
　　In which the majesty of buried Denmark°
　　Did sometime° march? By heaven, I charge thee, speak!
MARCELLUS.   It is offended.
BERNARDO.   See, it stalks away.
HORATIO.   Stay! Speak, speak! I charge thee, speak!   *Exit* GHOST.   55
MARCELLUS.   'Tis gone and will not answer.
BERNARDO.   How now, Horatio? You tremble and look pale.
　　Is not this something more than fantasy?
　　What think you on 't?°
HORATIO.   Before my God, I might not this believe   60
　　Without the sensible° and true avouch°
　　Of mine own eyes.
MARCELLUS.   Is it not like the King?
HORATIO.   As thou art to thyself.
　　Such was the very armor he had on
　　When he the ambitious Norway° combated.   65
　　So frowned he once when, in an angry parle,°
　　He smote the sledded° Polacks° on the ice.
　　'Tis strange.
MARCELLUS.   Thus twice before, and jump° at this dead hour,
　　With martial stalk° hath he gone by our watch.   70
HORATIO.   In what particular thought to work° I know not,
　　But in the gross and scope° of mine opinion
　　This bodes some strange eruption to our state.

39 Last . . . all i.e., this *very* last night (emphatic).   **40 pole** Pole Star, North Star.   **41 his** its;
illume illuminate.   **46 scholar** one learned enough to know how to question a ghost properly.
47 'a he.   **49 It . . . to** (It was commonly believed that a ghost could not speak until spoken
to.)   **50 usurp'st** wrongfully takes over.   **52 buried Denmark** the buried King of Denmark.
53 sometime formerly.   **59 on 't** of it.   **61 sensible** confirmed by the sense;   **avouch** warrant
evidence.   **65 Norway** King of Norway.   **66 parle** parley.   **67 sledded** traveling on sleds;
Polacks Poles.   **69 jump** exactly.   **70 stalk** stride.   **71 to work** i.e., to collect my thoughts and
try to understand this.   **72 gross and scope** general drift.

MARCELLUS.   Good now,° sit down, and tell me, he that knows,
          Why this same strict and most observant watch   75
          So nightly toils° the subject° of the land,
          And why such daily cast° of brazen cannon
          And foreign mart° for implements of war,
          Why such impress° of shipwrights, whose sore task
          Does not divide the Sunday from the week.   80
          What might be toward,° that this sweaty haste
          Doth make the night joint-laborer with the day?
          Who is 't that can inform me?
HORATIO.   That can I;
          At least, the whisper goes so. Our last king,
          Whose image even but now appeared to us,   85
          Was, as you know, by Fortinbras of Norway,
          Thereto pricked on° by a most emulate° pride,°
          Dared to the combat; in which our valiant Hamlet—
          For so this side of our known world° esteemed him—
          Did slay this Fortinbras; who by a sealed° compact   90
          Well ratified by law and heraldry
          Did forfeit, with his life, all those his lands
          Which he stood seized° of, to the conqueror;
          Against the° which a moiety competent°
          Was gagèd° by our king, which had returned°   95
          To the inheritance° of Fortinbras
          Had he been vanquisher, as, by the same cov'nant°
          And carriage of the article designed,°
          His fell to Hamlet. Now, sir, young Fortinbras,
          Of unimprovèd mettle° hot and full,   100
          Hath in the skirts° of Norway here and there
          Sharked up° a list° of lawless resolutes°
          For food and diet° to some enterprise
          That hath a stomach° in 't, which is no other—
          As it doth well appear unto our state—   105
          But to recover of us, by strong hand
          And terms compulsatory, those foresaid lands
          So by his father lost. And this, I take it,
          Is the main motive of our preparations,

74 Good now (An expression denoting entreaty or expostulation.)   **76 toils** causes to toil;
subject subjects.   **77 cast** casting.   **78 mart** buying and selling.   **79 impress** impressment,
conscription.   **81 toward** in preparation.   **87 pricked on** incited;   **emulate** emulous, ambitious;
Thereto . . . pride (Refers to old Fortinbras, not the Danish King.)   **89 this . . . world** i.e., all
Europe, the Western world.   **90 sealed** certified, confirmed.   **93 seized** possessed.   **94 Against
the** in return for;   **moiety competent** corresponding portion.   **95 gagèd** engaged, pledged;   **had
returned** would have passed.   **96 inheritance** possession.   **97 cov'nant** i.e., the *sealed compact*
on line 90.   **98 carriage . . . designed** carrying out of the article or clause drawn up to cover the
point.   **100 unimprovèd mettle** untried, undisciplined spirits.   **101 skirts** outlying regions,
outskirts.   **102 Sharked up** gathered up, as a shark takes fish;   **list** i.e., troop;
resolutes desperadoes.   **103 For food and diet** i.e., they are to serve as *food,* or "means," *to
some enterprises;* also they serve in return for the rations they get.   **104 stomach** (1) a spirit of
daring (2) an appetite that is fed by the *lawless resolutes.*

The source of this our watch, and the chief head°   110
Of this posthaste and rummage° in the land.
BERNARDO.   I think it be no other but e'en so.
Well may it sort° that this portentous figure
Comes armèd through our watch so like the King
That was and is the question° of these wars.   115
HORATIO.   A mote° it is to trouble the mind's eye.
In the most high and palmy° state of Rome,
A little ere the mightiest Julius fell,
The graves stood tenantless, and the sheeted° dead
Did squeak and gibber in the Roman streets;   120
As° stars with trains° of fire and dews of blood,
Disasters° in the sun; and the moist star°
Upon whose influence Neptune's° empire stands°
Was sick almost to doomsday° with eclipse.
And even the like precurse° of feared events,   125
As harbingers° preceding still° the fates
And prologue to the omen° coming on,
Have heaven and earth together demonstrated
Unto our climatures° and countrymen.

Enter GHOST.

But soft,° behold! Lo, where it comes again!   130
I'll cross° it, though it blast° me. [*It spreads his° arms.*]
    Stay, *illusion!*
If thou hast any sound or use of voice,
Speak to me!
If there be any good thing to be done
That may to thee do ease and grace to me,   135
Speak to me!
If thou art privy to° thy country's fate,
Which, happily,° foreknowing may avoid,
O, speak!
Or if thou hast uphoarded in thy life   140
Extorted treasure in the womb of earth,
For which, they say, you spirits oft walk in death,
Speak of it! [*The cock crows.*] Stay and speak!—Stop it, Marcellus.
MARCELLUS.   Shall I strike at it with my partisan?°
HORATIO.   Do, if it will not stand.   [*They strike at it.*]   145
BERNARDO.   'Tis here!
HORATIO.   'Tis here!   [*Exit* GHOST.]

---

110 head source.   **111 rummage** bustle, commotion.   **113 sort** suit.   **115 question** focus of
contention.   **116 mote** speck of dust.   **117 palmy** flourishing.   **119 sheeted** shrouded.
121 As (This abrupt transition suggests that matter is possibly omitted between lines 120 and
121.);   **trains** trails.   **122 Disasters** unfavorable signs or aspects;   **moist star** i.e., moon,
governing tides.   **123 Neptune** god of the sea;   **stands** depends.   **124 sick . . . doomsday** (See
Matthew 24:29 and Revelation 6:12.)   **125 precurse** heralding, foreshadowing.
126 harbingers forerunners;   **still** continually.   **127 omen** calamitous event.
129 climatures regions.   **130 soft** i.e., enough, break off.   **131 cross** stand in its path,
confront;   **blast** wither, strike with a curse;   **s.d. his** its.   **137 privy to** in on the secret of.
138 happily haply, perchance.   **144 partisan** long-handled spear.

MARCELLUS.   'Tis gone.
   We do it wrong, being so majestical,
   To offer it the show of violence,
   For it is as the air invulnerable,   150
   And our vain blows malicious mockery.
BERNARDO.   It was about to speak when the cock crew.
HORATIO.   And then it started like a guilty thing
   Upon a fearful summons. I have heard
   The cock, that is the trumpet° to the morn,   155
   Doth with his lofty and shrill-sounding throat
   Awake the god of day, and at his warning,
   Whether in sea or fire, in earth or air,
   Th' extravagant and erring° spirit hies°
   To his confine; and of the truth herein   160
   This present object made probation.°
MARCELLUS.   It faded on the crowing of the cock.
   Some say that ever 'gainst° that season comes
   Wherein our Savior's birth is celebrated,
   This bird of dawning singeth all night long,   165
   And then, they say, no spirit dare stir abroad;
   The nights are wholesome, then no planets strike,°
   No fairy takes,° nor witch hath power to charm,
   So hallowed and so gracious° is that time.
HORATIO.   So have I heard and do in part believe it.   170
   But, look, the morn in russet mantle clad
   Walks o'er the dew of yon high eastward hill.
   Break we our watch up, and by my advice
   Let us impart what we have seen tonight
   Unto young Hamlet; for upon my life,   175
   This spirit, dumb to us, will speak to him.
   Do you consent we shall acquaint him with it,
   As needful in our loves, fitting our duty?
MARCELLUS.   Let's do 't, I pray, and I this morning know
   Where we shall find him most conveniently.   *Exeunt.* 180

  1.2 *Flourish. Enter* CLAUDIUS, *King of Denmark,* GERTRUDE *the*
   Queen, [the] *Council, as°* POLONIUS *and his son* LAERTES, HAMLET,
    cum aliis° [*including* VOLTIMAND *and* CORNELIUS].

KING.   Though yet of Hamlet our° dear brother's death
   The memory be green, and that it us befitted
   To bear our hearts in grief and our whole kingdom
   To be contracted in one brow of woe,
   Yet so far hath discretion fought with nature
   That we with wisest sorrow think on him   5

156 trumpet trumpeter.   **160 extravagant and erring** wandering beyond bounds. (The words
have similar meaning.);   **hies** hastens.   **162 probation** proof.   **164 'gainst** just before.
168 strike destroy by evil influence.   **169 takes** bewitches.   **170 gracious** full of grace.
1.2. Location: The castle.   **s.d. as** i.e., such as, including;   **cum aliis** with others.   **1 our** my.
(The royal "we"; also in the following lines.)

Together with remembrance of ourselves.
Therefore our sometime° sister, now our queen,
Th' imperial jointress° to this warlike state,
Have we, as 'twere with a defeated joy—   10
With an auspicious and a dropping eye,°
With mirth in funeral and with dirge in marriage,
In equal scale weighing delight and dole°—
Taken to wife: Nor have we herein barred
Your better wisdoms, which have freely gone   15
With this affair along. For all, our thanks.
Now follows that you know° young Fortinbras,
Holding a weak supposal° of our worth,
Or thinking by our late dear brother's death
Our state to be disjoint and out of frame,   20
Co-leaguèd with° this dream of his advantage,°
He hath not failed to pester us with message
Importing° the surrender of those lands
Lost by his father, with all bonds° of law,
To our most valiant brother. So much for him.   25
Now for ourself and for this time of meeting.
Thus much the business is: we have here writ
To Norway, uncle of young Fortinbras—
Who, impotent° and bed-rid, scarcely hears
Of this his nephew's purpose—to suppress   30
His° further gait° herein, in that the levies,
The lists, and full proportions are all made
Out of his subject;° and we here dispatch
You, good Cornelius, and you, Voltimand,
For bearers of this greeting to old Norway,   35
Giving to you no further personal power
To business with the King more than the scope
Of these dilated° articles allow.   [*He gives a paper.*]
Farewell, and let your haste commend your duty.°
CORNELIUS, VOLTIMAND.   In that, and all things, will we show our duty.   40
KING.   We doubt it nothing.° Heartily farewell.

                     [*Exeunt* VOLTIMAND *and* CORNELIUS.]

And now, Laertes, what's the news with you?
You told us of some suit; what is 't, Laertes?
You cannot speak of reason to the Dane°
And lose your voice.° What wouldst thou beg, Laertes,   45
That shall not be my offer, not thy asking?

---

8 **sometime** former.   9 **jointress** woman possessing property with her husband.   11 **With . . .
eye** with one eye smiling and the other weeping.   13 **dole** grief.   17 **that you know** what you
know already, that; or, that you be informed as follows.   18 **weak supposal** low estimate.
21 **Co-leaguèd with** joined to, allied with; **dream . . . advantage** illusory hope of having the
advantage. (His only ally is this hope.)   23 **Importing** pertaining to.   24 **bonds** contracts.
29 **impotent** helpless.   31 **His** i.e., Fortinbras'; **gait** proceeding.   31–33 **in that . . .
subject** since the levying of troops and supplies is drawn entirely from the King of Norway's
own subjects.   38 **dilated** set out at length.   39 **let . . . duty** let your swift obeying of orders,
rather than mere words, express your dutifulness.   41 **nothing** not at all.   44 **the Dane** the
Danish king.   45 **lose your voice** waste your speech.

The head is not more native° to the heart,
The hand more instrumental° to the mouth,
Than is the throne of Denmark to thy father.
What wouldst thou have, Laertes?

LAERTES.   My dread lord,
Your leave and favor° to return to France,   50
From whence though willingly I came to Denmark
To show my duty in your coronation,
Yet now I must confess, that duty done,
My thoughts and wishes bend again toward France
And bow them to your gracious leave and pardon.°   55

KING.   Have you your father's leave? What says Polonius?

POLONIUS.   H'ath,° my lord, wrung from me my slow leave
By laborsome petition, and at last
Upon his will I sealed° my hard° consent.
I do beseech you, give him leave to go.   60

KING.   Take thy fair hour,° Laertes. Time be thine,
And thy best graces spend it at thy will!°
But now, my cousin° Hamlet, and my son—

HAMLET.   A little more than kin, and less than kind.°

KING.   How is it that the clouds still hang on you?   65

HAMLET.   Not so, my lord. I am too much in the sun.°

QUEEN.   Good Hamlet, cast thy nighted color° off,
And let thine eye look like a friend on Denmark.°
Do not forever with thy vailèd lids°
Seek for thy noble father in the dust.   70
Thou know'st 'tis common,° all that lives must die,
Passing through nature to eternity.

HAMLET.   Ay, madam, it is common.

QUEEN.   If it be,
Why seems it so particular° with thee?

HAMLET.   Seems, madam? Nay, it is. I know not "seems."   75
'Tis not alone my inky cloak, good Mother,
Nor customary° suits of solemn black,
Nor windy suspiration° of forced breath,

---

47 native closely connected, related.   **48 instrumental** serviceable.   **51 leave and favor** kind permission.   **56 bow . . . pardon** entreatingly make a deep bow, asking your permission to depart.   **58 H'ath** he has.   **60 sealed** (As if sealing a legal document.);   **hard** reluctant.
62 Take thy fair hour enjoy your time of youth.   **63 And . . . will** and may your finest qualities guide the way you choose to spend your time.   **64 cousin** any kin not of the immediate family.
65 A little . . . kind i.e., closer than an ordinary nephew (since I am stepson), and yet more separated in natural feeling (with pun on *kind* meaning "affectionate" and "natural," "lawful." This line is often read as an aside, but it need not be. The King chooses perhaps not to respond to Hamlet's cryptic and bitter remark.)   **67 the sun** i.e., the sunshine of the King's royal favor (with pun on *son*).   **68 nighted color** (1) mourning garments of black (2) dark melancholy.
69 Denmark the King of Denmark.   **70 vailèd lids** lowered eyes.   **72 common** of universal occurrence. (But Hamlet plays on the sense of "vulgar" in line 74.)   **75 particular** personal.
78 customary (1) socially conventional (2) habitual with me.   **79 suspiration** sighing.

No, nor the fruitful° river in the eye,   80
Nor the dejected havior° of the visage,
Together with all forms, moods,° shapes of grief,
That can denote me truly. These indeed seem,
For they are actions that a man might play.
But I have that within which passes show;   85
These but the trappings and the suits of woe.

KING. 'Tis sweet and commendable in your nature, Hamlet,
To give these mourning duties to your father.
But you must know your father lost a father,
That father lost, lost his, and the survivor bound   90
In filial obligation for some term
To do obsequious° sorrow. But to persever°
In obstinate condolement° is a course
Of impious stubbornness. 'Tis unmanly grief.
It shows a will most incorrect to heaven,   95
A heart unfortified,° a mind impatient,
An understanding simple° and unschooled.
For what we know must be and is as common
As any the most vulgar thing to sense,°
Why should we in our peevish opposition   100
Take it to heart? Fie, 'tis a fault to heaven,
A fault against the dead, a fault to nature,
To reason most absurd, whose common theme
Is death of fathers, and who still° hath cried,
From the first corpse° till he that died today,   105
"This must be so." We pray you, throw to earth
This unprevailing° woe and think of us
As of a father; for let the world take note,
You are the most immediate° to our throne,
And with no less nobility of love   110
Than that which dearest father bears his son
Do I impart toward° you. For° your intent
In going back to school° in Wittenberg,°
It is most retrograde° to our desire,
And we beseech you bend you° to remain   115
Here in the cheer and comfort of our eye,
Our chiefest courtier, cousin, and our son.

QUEEN. Let not thy mother lose her prayers, Hamlet.
I pray thee, stay with us, go not to Wittenberg.

---

80 fruitful abundant.   **81 havior** expression.   **82 moods** outward expression of feeling.
92 obsequious suited to obsequies or funerals;   **persever** persevere.
93 condolement sorrowing.   **96 unfortified** i.e., against adversity.   **97 simple** ignorant.   **99 As
. . . sense** as the most ordinary experience.   **104 still** always.   **105 the first corpse** (Abel's.)
107 unprevailing unavailing, useless.   **109 most immediate** next in succession.   **112 impart
toward** i.e., bestow my affection on;   **For** as for.   **113 to school** i.e., to your studies;
Wittenberg famous German university founded in 1502.   **114 retrograde** contrary.   **115 bend
you** incline yourself.

HAMLET.   I shall in all my best° obey you, madam.   120
KING.   Why, 'tis a loving and a fair reply.
      Be as ourself in Denmark. Madam, come.
      This gentle and unforced accord of Hamlet
      Sits smiling to° my heart, in grace° whereof
      No jocund° health that Denmark drinks today   125
      But the great cannon to the clouds shall tell,
      And the King's rouse° the heaven shall bruit again,°
      Respeaking earthly thunder.° Come away.

                          Flourish. Exeunt all but HAMLET.

HAMLET.   O, that this too too sullied° flesh would melt,
      Thaw, and resolve itself into a dew!   130
      Or that the Everlasting had not fixed
      His canon° 'gainst self-slaughter! O God, God,
      How weary, stale, flat, and unprofitable
      Seem to me all the uses° of this world!
      Fie on 't, ah fie! 'Tis an unweeded garden   135
      That grows to seed. Things rank and gross in nature
      Possess it merely.° That it should come to this!
      But two months dead—nay, not so much, not two.
      So excellent a king, that was to° this
      Hyperion° to a satyr,° so loving to my mother   140
      That he might not beteem° the winds of heaven
      Visit her face too roughly. Heaven and earth,
      Must I remember? Why, she would hang on him
      As if increase of appetite had grown
      By what it fed on, and yet within a month—   145
      Let me not think on 't; frailty, thy name is woman!—
      A little month, or ere° those shoes were old
      With which she followed my poor father's body,
      Like Niobe;° all tears, why she, even she—
      O God, a beast, that wants discourse of reason,°   150
      Would have mourned longer—married with my uncle,
      My father's brother, but no more like my father
      Than I to Hercules. Within a month,
      Ere yet the salt of most unrighteous tears
      Had left the flushing in her gallèd° eyes,   155
      She married. O, most wicked speed, to post°

120 in all my best to the best of my ability.   **124 to** i.e., at;   **grace** thanksgiving.
125 jocund merry.   **127 rouse** drinking of a draft of liquor;   **bruit again** loudly echo.
128 thunder i.e., of trumpet and kettledrum, sounded when the King drinks; see 1.4.8–12.
129 sullied defiled. (The early quartos read *sallied;* the Folio, *solid.*)   **132 canon** law.   **134 all
the uses** the whole routine.   **137 merely** completely.   **139 to** in comparison to.
140 Hyperion Titan sun-god, father of Helios;   **satyr** a lecherous creature of classical
mythology, half-human but with a goat's legs, tail, ears, and horns.   **141 beteem** allow.   **147 or
ere** even before.   **149 Niobe** Tantalus' daughter, Queen of Thebes, who boasted that she had
more sons and daughters than Leto; for this, Apollo and Artemis, children of Leto, slew her
fourteen children. She was turned by Zeus into a stone that continually dropped tears.
150 wants . . . reason lacks the faculty of reason.   **155 gallèd** irritated, inflamed.
156 post hasten.

With such dexterity to incestuous° sheets!
It is not, nor it cannot come to good.
But break, my heart, for I must hold my tongue.

Enter HORATIO, MARCELLUS *and* BERNARDO.

HORATIO.   Hail to your lordship!
HAMLET.   I am glad to see you well.   160
        Horatio!—or I do forget myself.
HORATIO.   The same, my lord, and your poor servant ever.
HAMLET.   Sir, my good friend; I'll change that name° with you.
        And what make you from° Wittenberg, Horatio?
        Marcellus.   165
MARCELLUS.   My good lord.
HAMLET.   I am very glad to see you. [*To* BERNARDO.] Good even, sir.—
        But what in faith make you from Wittenberg?
HORATIO.   A truant disposition, good my lord.
HAMLET.   I would not hear your enemy say so,   170
        Nor shall you do my ear that violence
        To make it truster of your own report
        Against yourself. I know you are no truant.
        But what is your affair in Elsinore?
        We'll teach you to drink deep ere you depart.   175
HORATIO.   My lord, I came to see your father's funeral.
HAMLET.   I prithee, do not mock me, fellow student;
        I think it was to see my mother's wedding.
HORATIO.   Indeed, my lord, it followed hard° upon.
HAMLET.   Thrift, thrift, Horatio! The funeral baked meats°   180
        Did coldly° furnish forth the marriage tables.
        Would I had met my dearest° foe in heaven
        Or ever° I had seen that day, Horatio!
        My father!—Methinks I see my father.
HORATIO.   Where, my lord?
HAMLET.   In my mind's eye, Horatio.   185
HORATIO.   I saw him once. 'A° was a goodly king.
HAMLET.   'A was a man. Take him for all in all,
        I shall not look upon his like again.
HORATIO.   My lord, I think I saw him yesternight.
HAMLET.   Saw? Who?   190
HORATIO.   My lord, the King your father.
HAMLET.   The King my father?
HORATIO.   Season your admiration° for a while
        With an attent° ear till I may deliver,
        Upon the witness of these gentlemen,   195
        This marvel to you.
HAMLET.   For God's love, let me hear!

157 incestuous (In Shakespeare's day, the marriage of a man like Claudius to his deceased brother's wife was considered incestuous.)   **163 change that name** i.e., give and receive reciprocally the name of "friend" (rather than talk of "servant").   **164 make you from** are you doing away from.   **179 hard** close.   **180 baked meats** meat pies.   **181 coldly** i.e., as cold leftovers.   **182 dearest** closest (and therefore deadliest).   **183 Or ever** before.   **186 'A** he. **193 Season your admiration** restrain your astonishment.   **194 attent** attentive.

HORATIO.   Two nights together had these gentlemen,
Marcellus and Bernardo, on their watch,
In the dead waste° and middle of the night,
Been thus encountered. A figure like your father,   200
Armèd at point° exactly, cap-à-pie,°
Appears before them, and with solemn march
Goes slow and stately by them. Thrice he walked
By their oppressed and fear-surprisèd eyes
Within his truncheon's° length, whilst they, distilled°   205
Almost to jelly with the act° of fear,
Stand dumb and speak not to him. This to me
In dreadful° secrecy impart they did,
And I with them the third night kept the watch,
Where, as they had delivered, both in time,   210
Form of the thing, each word made true and good,
The apparition comes. I knew your father;
These hands are not more like.

HAMLET.   But where was this?

MARCELLUS.   My lord, upon the platform where we watch.

HAMLET.   Did you not speak to it?

HORATIO.   My lord, I did,   215
But answer made it none. Yet once methought
It lifted up its head and did address
Itself to motion, like as it would speak;°
But even then° the morning cock crew loud,
And at the sound it shrunk in haste away   220
And vanished from our sight.

HAMLET.   'Tis very strange.

HORATIO.   As I do live, my honored lord, 'tis true,
And we did think it writ down in our duty
To let you know of it.

HAMLET.   Indeed, indeed, sirs. But this troubles me.   225
Hold you the watch tonight?

ALL.   We do, my lord.

HAMLET.   Armed, say you?

ALL.   Armed, my lord.

HAMLET.   From top to toe?

ALL.   My lord, from head to foot.   230

HAMLET.   Then saw you not his face?

HORATIO.   O, yes, my lord, he wore his beaver° up.

HAMLET.   What° looked he, frowningly?

HORATIO.   A countenance more in sorrow than in anger.

HAMLET.   Pale or red?   235

HORATIO.   Nay, very pale.

HAMLET.   And fixed his eyes upon you?

---

199 dead waste desolate stillness.   **201 at point** correctly in every detail;   **cap-à-pie** from head
to foot.   **205 truncheon** officer's staff;   **distilled** dissolved.   **206 act** action, operation.
208 dreadful full of dread.   **217–218 did . . . speak** began to move as though it were about to
speak.   **219 even then** at that very instant.   **232 beaver** visor on the helmet.   **233 What** how.

HORATIO.   Most constantly.

HAMLET.   I would I had been there.

HORATIO.   It would have much amazed you.   240

HAMLET.   Very like, very like. Stayed it long?

HORATIO.   While one with moderate haste might tell° a hundred.

MARCELLUS, BERNARDO.   Longer, longer.

HORATIO.   Not when I saw 't.

HAMLET.   His beard was grizzled°—no?   245

HORATIO.   It was, as I have seen it in his life,
      A sable silvered.°

HAMLET.   I will watch tonight.
      Perchance 'twill walk again.

HORATIO.   I warrant° it will.

HAMLET.   If it assume my noble father's person,
      I'll speak to it though hell itself should gape   250
      And bid me hold my peace. I pray you all,
      If you have hitherto concealed this sight,
      Let it be tenable° in your silence still,
      And whatsoever else shall hap tonight,
      Give it an understanding but no tongue.   255
      I will requite your loves. So, fare you well.
      Upon the platform twixt eleven and twelve
      I'll visit you.

ALL.   Our duty to your honor.

HAMLET.   Your loves, as mine to you. Farewell.   *Exeunt [all but* HAMLET].
      My father's spirit in arms! All is not well.   260
      I doubt° some foul play. Would the night were come!
      Till then sit still, my soul. Foul deeds will rise,
      Though all the earth o'erwhelm them, to men's eyes.   *Exit.*

            1.3 *Enter* LAERTES *and* OPHELIA, *his sister.*

LAERTES.   My necessaries are embarked. Farewell.
      And, sister, as the winds give benefit
      And convoy is assistant,° do not sleep
      But let me hear from you.

OPHELIA.   Do you doubt that?

LAERTES.   For Hamlet, and the trifling of his favor,   5
      Hold it a fashion and a toy in blood,°
      A violet in the youth of primy° nature,
      Forward,° not permanent, sweet, not lasting,
      The perfume and suppliance° of a minute—
      No more.

OPHELIA.   No more but so?

LAERTES.   Think it no more.   10

---

242 tell count.   **245 grizzled** gray.   **247 sable silvered** black mixed with white.
248 warrant assure you.   **253 tenable** held.   **261 doubt** suspect.   **1.3. Location: Polonius'
chambers.**   **3 convoy is assistant** means of conveyance are available.   **6 toy in blood** passing
amorous fancy.   **7 primy** in its prime, springtime.   **8 Forward** precocious.
9 suppliance supply, filler.

For nature crescent° does not grow alone
In thews° and bulk, but as this temple° waxes
The inward service of the mind and soul
Grows wide withal.° Perhaps he loves you now,
And now no soil° nor cautel° doth besmirch   15
The virtue of his will,° but you must fear,
His greatness weighed,° his will is not his own.
For he himself is subject to his birth.
He may not, as unvalued persons do,
Carve° for himself, for on his choice depends   20
The safety and health of this whole state,
And therefore must his choice be circumscribed
Unto the voice and yielding° of that body
Whereof he is the head. Then if he says he loves you,
It fits your wisdom so far to believe it   25
As he in his particular act and place°
May give his saying deed, which is no further
Than the main voice° of Denmark goes withal.°
Then weigh what loss your honor may sustain
If with too credent° ear you list° his songs,   30
Or lose your heart, or your chaste treasure open
To his unmastered importunity.
Fear it, Ophelia, fear it, my dear sister,
And keep you in the rear of your affection,°
Out of the shot and danger of desire.   35
The chariest° maid is prodigal enough
If she unmask her beauty° to the moon.°
Virtue itself scapes not calumnious strokes.
The canker galls° the infants of the spring
Too oft before their buttons° be disclosed,°   40
And in the morn and liquid dew° of youth
Contagious blastments° are most imminent.
Be wary then; best safety lies in fear.
Youth to itself rebels,° though none else near.

OPHELIA.   I shall the effect of this good lesson keep   45
As watchman to my heart. But, good my brother,
Do not, as some ungracious° pastors do,
Show me the steep and thorny way to heaven,
Whiles like a puffed° and reckless libertine

---

11 crescent growing, waxing.   **12 thews** bodily strength;   **temple** i.e., body.   **14 Grows wide
withal** grows along with it.   **15 soil** blemish;   **cautel** deceit.   **16 will** desire.   **17 His greatness
weighed** if you take into account his high position.   **20 Carve** i.e., choose.   **23 voice and
yielding** assent, approval.   **26 in . . . place** in his particular restricted circumstances.   **28 main
voice** general assent;   **withal** along with.   **30 credent** credulous;   **list** listen to.   **34 keep . . .
affection** don't advance as far as your affection might lead you (A military metaphor.)
36 chariest most scrupulously modest.   **37 If she unmask her beauty** if she does no more than
show her beauty;   **moon** (Symbol of chastity.)   **39 canker galls** canker-worm destroys.
40 buttons buds;   **disclosed** opened.   **41 liquid dew** i.e., time when dew is fresh and bright.
42 blastments blights.   **44 Youth . . . rebels** youth is inherently rebellious.
47 ungracious ungodly.   **49 puffed** bloated, or swollen with pride.

Himself the primrose path of dalliance treads,
And recks° not his own rede.°

Enter POLONIUS.

LAERTES.   O, fear me not.°
I stay too long. But here my father comes.
A double° blessing is a double grace;
Occasion smiles upon a second leave.°

POLONIUS.   Yet here, Laertes? Aboard, aboard, for shame!   55
The wind sits in the shoulder of your sail,
And you are stayed for. There—my blessing with thee!
And these few precepts in thy memory
Look° thou character.° Give thy thoughts no tongue,
Nor any unproportioned° thought his° act.   60
Be thou familiar,° but by no means vulgar.°
Those friends thou hast, and their adoption tried,°
Grapple them unto thy soul with hoops of steel,
But do not dull thy palm° with entertainment
Of each new-hatched, unfledged courage.° Beware   65
Of entrance to a quarrel, but being in,
Bear 't that° th' opposèd may beware of thee.
Give every man thy ear, but few thy voice;
Take each man's censure,° but reserve thy judgment.
Costly thy habit° as thy purse can buy,   70
But not expressed in fancy;° rich, not gaudy,
For the apparel oft proclaims the man,
And they in France of the best rank and station
Are of a most select and generous chief in that.°
Neither a borrower nor a lender be,   75
For loan oft loses both itself and friend,
And borrowing dulleth edge of husbandry.°
This above all: to thine own self be true,
And it must follow, as the night the day,
Thou canst not then be false to any man.   80
Farewell. My blessing season° this in thee!

LAERTES.   Most humbly do I take my leave, my lord.

POLONIUS.   The time invests° you. Go, your servants tend.°

LAERTES.   Farewell, Ophelia, and remember well
What I have said to you.   85

---

51 recks heeds;   **rede** counsel;   **fear me not** don't worry on my account.   **53 double** (Laertes has already bid his father good-bye.)   **54 Occasion . . . leave** happy is the circumstance that provides a second leave-taking. (The goddess Occasion, or Opportunity, smiles.)   **59 Look** be sure that;   **character** inscribe.   **60 unproportioned** badly calculated, intemperate;   **his** its.
61 familiar sociable;   **vulgar** common.   **62 and their adoption tried** and also their suitability for adoption as friends having been tested.   **64 dull thy palm** i.e., shake hands so often as to make the gesture meaningless.   **65 courage** young man of spirit.   **67 Bear 't that** manage it so that.
69 censure opinion, judgment.   **70 habit** clothing.   **71 fancy** excessive ornament, decadent fashion.   **74 Are . . . that** are of a most refined and well-bred preeminence in choosing what to wear.   **77 husbandry** thrift.   **81 season** mature.   **83 invests** besieges, presses upon;   **tend** attend, wait.

OPHELIA.   'Tis in my memory locked,
            And you yourself shall keep the key of it.
LAERTES.   Farewell.   *Exit* LAERTES.
POLONIUS.   What is 't, Ophelia, he hath said to you?
OPHELIA.   So please you, something touching the Lord Hamlet.   90
POLONIUS.   Marry,° well bethought.
            'Tis told me he hath very oft of late
            Given private time to you, and you yourself
            Have of your audience been most free and bounteous.
            If it be so—as so 'tis put on° me,   95
            And that in way of caution—I must tell you
            You do not understand yourself so clearly
            As it behooves° my daughter and your honor.
            What is between you? Give me up the truth.
OPHELIA.   He hath, my lord, of late made many tenders°   100
            Of his affection to me.
POLONIUS.   Affection? Pooh! You speak like a green girl,
            Unsifted° in such perilous circumstance.
            Do you believe his tenders, as you call them?
OPHELIA.   I do not know, my lord, what I should think.   105
POLONIUS.   Marry, I will teach you. Think yourself a baby
            That you have ta'en these tenders for true pay
            Which are not sterling.° Tender° yourself more dearly,
            Or—not to crack the wind° of the poor phrase,
            Running it thus—you'll tender me a fool.°   110
OPHELIA.   My lord, he hath importuned me with love
            In honorable fashion.
POLONIUS.   Ay, fashion° you may call it. Go to,° go to.
OPHELIA.   And hath given countenance° to his speech, my lord,
            With almost all the holy vows of heaven.   115
POLONIUS.   Ay, springes° to catch woodcocks.° I do know,
            When the blood burns, how prodigal° the soul
            Lends the tongue vows. These blazes, daughter,
            Giving more light than heat, extinct in both
            Even in their promise as it° is a-making,   120
            You must not take for fire. From this time
            Be something° scanter of your maiden presence.
            Set your entreatments° at a higher rate
            Than a command to parle.° For Lord Hamlet,

---

91 Marry i.e., by the Virgin Mary. (A mild oath.)   **95 put on** impressed on, told to.
98 behooves befits.   **100 tenders** offers.   **103 Unsifted** i.e., untried.   **108 sterling** legal
currency;   **Tender** hold, look after, offer.   **109 crack the wind** i.e., run it until it is broken-
winded.   **110 tender me a fool** (1) show yourself to me as a fool (2) show me up as a fool (3)
present me with a grandchild. (*Fool* was a term of endearment for a child.)   **113 fashion** mere
form, pretense;   **Go to** (An expression of impatience.)   **114 countenance** credit, confirmation.
116 springes snares;   **woodcocks** birds easily caught; here used to connote gullibility.
117 prodigal prodigally.   **120 it** i.e., the promise.   **122 something** somewhat.
123 entreatments negotiations for surrender. (A military term.)   **124 parle** discuss terms with
the enemy. (Polonius urges his daughter, in the metaphor of military language, not to meet with
Hamlet and consider giving in to him merely because he requests an interview.)

Believe so much in him° that he is young,
And with a larger tether may he walk
Than may be given you. In few,° Ophelia,
Do not believe his vows, for they are brokers,°
Not of that dye° which their investments° show,
But mere implorators° of unholy suits,   130
Breathing° like sanctified and pious bawds,
The better to beguile. This is for all:°
I would not, in plain terms, from this time forth
Have you so slander° any moment° leisure
As to give words or talk with the Lord Hamlet.   135
Look to 't, I charge you. Come your ways.°

OPHELIA.   I shall obey, my lord.   *Exeunt.*

1.4   *Enter* HAMLET, HORATIO, *and* MARCELLUS.

HAMLET.   The air bites shrewdly,° it is very cold.
HORATIO.   It is a nipping and an eager° air.
HAMLET.   What hour now?
HORATIO.   I think it lacks of° twelve.
MARCELLUS.   No, it is struck.
HORATIO.   Indeed? I heard it not.
It then draws near the season°   5
Wherein the spirit held his wont° to walk.
            A flourish of trumpets, and two pieces° go off [within].
What does this mean, my lord?
HAMLET.   The King doth wake° tonight and takes his rouse,°
Keeps wassail,° and the swaggering upspring° reels,°
And as he drains his drafts of Rhenish° down,   10
The kettledrum and trumpet thus bray out
The triumph of his pledge.°
HORATIO.   It is a custom?
HAMLET.   Ay, marry, is't,
But to my mind, though I am native here
And to the manner° born, it is a custom   15
More honored in the breach than the observance.°
This heavy-headed revel east and west°
Makes us traduced and taxed of° other nations.
They clepe° us drunkards, and with swinish phrase°

---

125 so . . . him this much concerning him.   **127 In few** briefly.   **128 brokers** go-betweens,
procurers.   **129 dye** color or sort;   **investments** clothes. (The vows are not what they seem.)
130 mere implorators out-and-out solicitors.   **131 Breathing** speaking.   **132 for all** once for
all, in sum.   **134 slander** abuse, misuse;   **moment** moment's.   **136 Come your ways** come
along.   **1.4. Location: The guard platform.**   **1 shrewdly** keenly, sharply.   **2 eager** biting.
3 lacks of is just short of.   **5 season** time.   **6 held his wont** was accustomed;   **s.d. pieces** i.e., of
ordnance, cannon.   **8 wake** stay awake and hold revel;   **takes his rouse** carouses.
9 wassail carousal;   **upspring** wild German dance;   **reels** dances.   **10 Rhenish** Rhine wine.
12 The triumph . . . pledge i.e., his feat in draining the wine in a single draft.
15 manner custom (of drinking).   **16 More . . . observance** better neglected than followed.
17 east and west i.e., everywhere.   **18 taxed of** censured by.   **19 clepe** call;   **with swinish
phrase** i.e., by calling us swine.

Soil our addition;° and indeed it takes   20
From our achievements, though performed at height,°
The pith and marrow of our attribute.°
So, oft it chances in particular men,
That for° some vicious mole of nature° in them,
As in their birth—wherein they are not guilty,   25
Since nature cannot choose his° origin—
By their o'ergrowth of some complexion,°
Oft breaking down the pales° and forts of reason,
Or by some habit that too much o'erleavens°
The form of plausive° manners, that these men,   30
Carrying, I say, the stamp of one defect,
Being nature's livery° or fortune's star,°
His virtues else,° be they as pure as grace,
As infinite as man may undergo,°
Shall in the general censure° take corruption   35
From that particular fault. The dram of evil
Doth all the noble substance often dout
To his own scandal.°

    Enter GHOST.

HORATIO.   Look, my lord, it comes!
HAMLET.   Angels and ministers of grace° defend us!
Be thou° a spirit of health° or goblin damned,   40
Bring° with thee airs from heaven or blasts from hell,
Be thy intents° wicked or charitable,
Thou com'st in such a questionable° shape
That I will speak to thee. I'll call thee Hamlet,
King, father, royal Dane. O, answer me!   45
Let me not burst in ignorance, but tell
Why thy canonized° bones, hearsèd° in death,
Have burst their cerements;° why the sepulcher
Wherein we saw thee quietly inurned°
Hath oped his ponderous and marble jaws   50
To cast thee up again. What may this mean,
That thou, dead corpse, again in complete steel,°

---

20 addition reputation.   **21 at height** outstandingly.   **22 The pith . . . attribute** the essence of
the reputation that others attribute to us.   **24 for** on account of;   **mole of nature** natural
blemish in one's constitution.   **26 his** its.   **27 their o'ergrowth . . . complexion** the excessive
growth in individuals of some natural trait.   **28 pales** palings, fences (as of a fortification).
29 o'erleavens induces a change throughout (as yeast works in dough).   **30 plausive** pleasing.
32 nature's livery sign of one's servitude to nature;   **fortune's star** the destiny that chance
brings.   **33 His virtues else** i.e., the other qualities of *these men* (line 30).   **34 may undergo** can
sustain.   **35 general censure** general opinion that people have of him.   **36–38 The dram . . .
scandal** i.e., the small drop of evil blots out or works against the noble substance of the whole
and brings it into disrepute. To *dout* is to blot out. (A famous crux.)   **39 ministers of
grace** messengers of God.   **40 Be thou** whether you are;   **spirit of health** good angel.
41 Bring whether you bring.   **42 Be thy intents** whether your intentions are.
43 questionable inviting question.   **47 canonized** buried according to the canons of the church;
hearsèd coffined.   **48 cerements** grave clothes.   **49 inurned** entombed.   **52 complete steel** full
armor.

Revisits thus the glimpses of the moon,°
Making night hideous, and we fools of nature°
So horridly to shake our disposition°   55
With thoughts beyond the reaches of our souls?
Say, why is this? Wherefore? What should we do?

[*The* GHOST] *beckons* [HAMLET].

HORATIO.   It beckons you to go away with it,
    As if it some impartment° did desire
    To you alone.
MARCELLUS.   Look with what courteous action   60
    It wafts you to a more removèd ground.
    But do not go with it.
HORATIO.   No, by no means.
HAMLET.   It will not speak. Then I will follow it.
HORATIO.   Do not, my lord!
HAMLET.   Why, what should be the fear?
    I do not set my life at a pin's fee,°   65
    And for my soul, what can it do to that,
    Being a thing immortal as itself?
    It waves me forth again. I'll follow it.
HORATIO.   What if it tempt you toward the flood,° my lord,
    Or to the dreadful summit of the cliff   70
    That beetles o'er° his° base into the sea,
    And there assume some other horrible form
    Which might deprive your sovereignty of reason°
    And draw you into madness? Think of it.
    The very place puts toys of desperation,°   75
    Without more motive, into every brain
    That looks so many fathoms to the sea
    And hears it roar beneath.
HAMLET.   It wafts me still.—Go on, I'll follow thee.
MARCELLUS.   You shall not go, my lord.   [*They try to stop him.*]
HAMLET.   Hold off your hands!   80
HORATIO.   Be ruled. You shall not go.
HAMLET.   My fate cries out,°
    And makes each petty° artery° in this body
    As hardy as the Nemean lion's° nerve.°
    Still am I called. Unhand me, gentlemen.
    By heaven, I'll make a ghost of him that lets° me!   85
    I say, away!—Go on, I'll follow thee.   *Exeunt* GHOST *and* HAMLET.
HORATIO.   He waxes desperate with imagination.
MARCELLUS.   Let's follow. 'Tis not fit thus to obey him.

---

53 glimpses of the moon pale and uncertain moonlight.   **54 fools of nature** mere men, limited
to natural knowledge and subject to nature.   **55 So . . . disposition** to distress our mental
composure so violently.   **59 impartment** communication.   **65 fee** value.   **69 flood** sea.
71 beetles o'er overhangs threateningly (like bushy eyebrows);   **his** its.   **73 deprive . . .
reason** take away the rule of reason over your mind.   **75 toys of desperation** fancies of
desperate acts, i.e., suicide.   **81 My fate cries out** my destiny summons me.   **82 petty** weak;
artery (through which the vital spirits were thought to have been conveyed).   **83 Nemean
lion** one of the monsters slain by Hercules in his twelve labors;   **nerve** sinew.   **85 lets** hinders.

HORATIO.   Have after.° To what issue° will this come?
MARCELLUS.   Something is rotten in the state of Denmark.
HORATIO.   Heaven will direct it.°   90
MARCELLUS.   Nay, let's follow him.   *Exeunt.*

1.5   *Enter* GHOST *and* HAMLET.

HAMLET.   Whither wilt thou lead me? Speak. I'll go no further.
GHOST.   Mark me.
HAMLET.   I will.
GHOST.   My hour is almost come,
            When I to sulfurous and tormenting flames
            Must render up myself.
HAMLET.   Alas, poor ghost!
GHOST.   Pity me not, but lend thy serious hearing
            To what I shall unfold.   5
HAMLET.   Speak. I am bound° to hear.
GHOST.   So art thou to revenge, when thou shalt hear.
HAMLET.   What?
GHOST.   I am thy father's spirit,
            Doomed for a certain term to walk the night,   10
            And for the day confined to fast° in fires,
            Till the foul crimes° done in my days of nature°
            Are burnt and purged away. But that° I am forbid
            To tell the secrets of my prison house,
            I could a tale unfold whose lightest word   15
            Would harrow up° thy soul, freeze thy young blood,
            Make thy two eyes like stars start from their spheres,°
            Thy knotted and combinèd locks° to part,
            And each particular hair to stand on end
            Like quills upon the fretful porcupine.   20
            But this eternal blazon° must not be
            To ears of flesh and blood. List, list, O, list!
            If thou didst ever thy dear father love—
HAMLET.   O God!
GHOST.   Revenge his foul and most unnatural murder.   25
HAMLET.   Murder?
GHOST.   Murder most foul, as in the best° it is,
            But this most foul, strange, and unnatural.
HAMLET.   Haste me to know't, that I, with wings as swift
            As meditation or the thoughts of love,   30
            May sweep to my revenge.

---

89 Have after let's go after him;   **issue** outcome.   **91 it** i.e., the outcome.   **1.5. Location: The battlements of the castle.**   **7 bound** (1) ready (2) obligated by duty and fate. (The Ghost, in line 8, answers in the second sense.)   **12 fast** do penance by fasting.   **13 crimes** sins;   **of nature** as a mortal.   **14 But that** were it not that.   **17 harrow up** lacerate, tear.   **18 spheres** i.e., eye-sockets, here compared to the orbits or transparent revolving spheres in which, according to Ptolemaic astronomy, the heavenly bodies were fixed.   **19 knotted . . . locks** hair neatly arranged and confined.   **22 eternal blazon** revelation of the secrets of eternity.   **28 in the best** even at best.

GHOST.   I find thee apt;
And duller shouldst thou be° than the fat° weed
That roots itself in ease on Lethe° wharf,
Wouldst thou not stir in this. Now, Hamlet, hear.   35
'Tis given out that, sleeping in my orchard,°
A serpent stung me. So the whole ear of Denmark
Is by a forgèd process° of my death
Rankly abused.° But know, thou noble youth,
The serpent that did sting thy father's life   40
Now wears his crown.

HAMLET.   O, my prophetic soul! My uncle!

GHOST.   Ay, that incestuous, that adulterate° beast,
With witchcraft of his wit, with traitorous gifts°—
O wicked wit and gifts, that have the power   45
So to seduce!—won to his shameful lust
The will of my most seeming-virtuous queen.
O Hamlet, what a falling off was there!
From me, whose love was of that dignity
That it went hand in hand even with the vow°   50
I made to her in marriage, and to decline
Upon a wretch whose natural gifts were poor
To° those of mine!
But virtue, as it° never will be moved,
Though lewdness court it in a shape of heaven,°   55
So lust, though to a radiant angel linked,
Will sate itself in a celestial bed°
And prey on garbage.
But soft, methinks I scent the morning air.
Brief let me be. Sleeping within my orchard,   60
My custom always of the afternoon,
Upon my secure° hour thy uncle stole,
With juice of cursèd hebona° in a vial,
And in the porches of my ears° did pour
The leprous distillment,° whose effect   65
Holds such an enmity with blood of man
That swift as quicksilver it courses through
The natural gates and alleys of the body,
And with a sudden vigor it doth posset°
And curd, like eager° droppings into milk,   70
The thin and wholesome blood. So did it mine,

---

33 shouldst thou be you would have to be;   **fat** torpid, lethargic.   **34⁸ Lethe** the river of
forgetfulness in Hades.   **36 orchard** garden.   **38 forgèd process** falsified account.
39 abused deceived.   **43 adulterate** adulterous.   **44 gifts** (1) talents (2) presents.   **50 even
with the vow** with the very vow.   **53 To** compared to.   **54 virtue, as it** as virtue.   **55 shape of
heaven** heavenly form.   **57 sate . . . bed** cease to find sexual pleasure in a virtuously lawful
marriage.   **62 secure** confident, unsuspicious.   **63 hebona** a poison. (The word seems to be a
form of *ebony,* though it is thought perhaps to be related to *benbane,* a poison, or to *ebenus,*
"yew.")   **64 porches of my ears** ears as a porch or entrance of the body.   **65 leprous
distillment** distillation causing leprosylike disfigurement.   **69 posset** coagulate, curdle.
70 eager sour, acid.

And a most instant tetter° barked° about,
Most lazar-like,° with vile and loathsome crust,
All my smooth body.
Thus was I, sleeping, by a brother's hand   75
Of life, of crown, of queen at once dispatched,°
Cut off even in the blossoms of my sin,
Unhouseled,° disappointed,° unaneled,°
No reckoning° made, but sent to my account
With all my imperfections on my head.   80
O, horrible! O, horrible, most horrible!
If thou hast nature° in thee, bear it not.
Let not the royal bed of Denmark be
A couch for luxury° and damnèd incest.
But, howsoever thou pursues this act,   85
Taint not thy mind nor let thy soul contrive
Against thy mother aught. Leave her to heaven
And to those thorns that in her bosom lodge,
To prick and sting her. Fare thee well at once.
The glowworm shows the matin° to be near,   90
And 'gins to pale his° uneffectual fire.
Adieu, adieu, adieu! Remember me.   [*Exit.*]
HAMLET.   O all you host of heaven! O earth! What else?
And shall I couple° hell? O, fie! Hold,° hold, my heart,
And you, my sinews, grow not instant° old,   95
But bear me stiffly up. Remember thee?
Ay, thou poor ghost, whiles memory holds a seat
In this distracted globe.° Remember thee?
Yea, from the table° of my memory
I'll wipe away all trivial fond° records,   100
All saws° of books, all forms,° all pressures° past
That youth and observation copied there,
And thy commandment all alone shall live
Within the book and volume of my brain,
Unmixed with baser matter. Yes, by heaven!   105
O most pernicious woman!
O villain, villain, smiling, damnèd villain!
My tables°—meet it is° I set it down
That one may smile, and smile, and be a villain.
At least I am sure it may be so in Denmark.   [*Writing.*]   110
So uncle, there you are.° Now to my word:
It is "Adieu, adieu! Remember me."
I have sworn 't.

72 **tetter** eruption of scabs;   **barked** recovered with a rough covering, like bark on a tree.
73 **lazar-like** leperlike.   76 **dispatched** suddenly deprived.   78 **Unhouseled** without having
received the Sacrament;   **disappointed** unready (spiritually) for the last journey;
unaneled without having received extreme unction.   79 **reckoning** settling of accounts.
82 **nature** i.e., the promptings of a son.   84 **luxury** lechery.   90 **matin** morning.   91 **his** its.
94 **couple** add;   **Hold** hold together.   95 **instant** instantly.   98 **globe** (1) head (2) world.
99 **table** tablet, slate.   100 **fond** foolish.   101 **saws** wise sayings;   **forms** shapes or images
copied onto the slate; general ideas;   **pressures** impressions stamped.   108 **tables** writing
tablets;   **meet it is** it is fitting.   111 **there you are** i.e., there, I've written that down against you.

Enter HORATIO *and* MARCELLUS.

HORATIO.   My lord, my lord!

MARCELLUS.   Lord Hamlet!   115

HORATIO.   Heavens secure him!°

HAMLET.   So be it.

MARCELLUS.   Hilo, ho, ho, my lord!

HAMLET.   Hillo, ho, ho, boy! Come, bird, come.°

MARCELLUS.   How is 't, my noble lord?   120

HORATIO.   What news, my lord?

HAMLET.   O, wonderful!

HORATIO.   Good my lord, tell it.

HAMLET.   No, you will reveal it.

HORATIO.   Not I, my lord, by heaven.   125

MARCELLUS.   Nor I, my lord.

HAMLET.   How say you, then, would heart of man once° think it?
    But you'll be secret?

HORATIO, MARCELLUS.   Ay, by heaven, my lord.

HAMLET.   There's never a villain dwelling in all Denmark
    But he's an arrant° knave.   130

HORATIO.   There needs no ghost, my lord, come from the grave
    To tell us this.

HAMLET.   Why, right, you are in the right.
    And so, without more circumstance° at all,
    I hold it fit that we shake hands and part,
    You as your business and desire shall point you—   135
    For every man hath business and desire,
    Such as it is—and for my own poor part,
    Look you, I'll go pray.

HORATIO.   These are but wild and whirling words, my lord.

HAMLET.   I am sorry they offend you, heartily;   140
    Yes, faith, heartily.

HORATIO.   There's no offense, my lord.

HAMLET.   Yes, by Saint Patrick,° but there is, Horatio,
    And much offense° too. Touching this vision here,
    It is an honest ghost,° that let me tell you.
    For your desire to know what is between us,   145
    O'ermaster 't as you may. And now, good friends,
    As you are friends, scholars, and soldiers,
    Give me one poor request.

HORATIO.   What is 't, my lord? We will.

HAMLET.   Never make known what you have seen tonight.   150

HORATIO, MARCELLUS.   My lord, we will not.

HAMLET.   Nay, but swear 't.

---

116 secure him keep him safe.   **119 Hillo . . . come** (A falconer's call to a hawk in air. Hamlet mocks the halloing as though it were a part of hawking.)   **127 once** ever.
130 arrant thoroughgoing.   **133 circumstance** ceremony, elaboration.   **142 Saint Patrick** (The keeper of Purgatory and patron saint of all blunders and confusion.)   **143 offense** (Hamlet deliberately changes Horatio's "no offense against all decency.")   **144 an honest ghost** i.e., a real ghost and not an evil spirit.

HORATIO.   In faith, my lord, not I.°
MARCELLUS.   Nor I, my lord, in faith.
HAMLET.   Upon my sword.°   [*He holds out his sword.*]   155
MARCELLUS.   We have sworn, my lord, already.°
HAMLET.   Indeed, upon my sword, indeed.
GHOST [*cries under the stage*].   Swear.
HAMLET.   Ha, ha, boy, sayst thou so? Art thou there, truepenny?°
    Come on, you hear this fellow in the cellarage.   160
    Consent to swear.
HORATIO.   Propose the oath, my lord.
HAMLET.   Never to speak of this that you have seen,
    Swear by my sword.
GHOST [*beneath*].   Swear.   [*They swear.*°]
HAMLET.   *Hic et ubique?*° Then we'll shift our ground.   165
                                 [*He moves to another spot.*]
    Come hither, gentlemen,
    And lay your hands again upon my sword.
    Swear by my sword
    Never to speak of this that you have heard.
GHOST [*beneath*].   Swear by his sword.   [*They swear.*]   170
HAMLET.   Well said, old mole. Canst work i' th' earth so fast?
    A worthy pioneer!°—Once more removed, good friends.
                                 [*He moves again.*]
HORATIO.   O day and night, but this is wondrous strange!
HAMLET.   And therefore as a stranger° give it welcome.
    There are more things in heaven and earth, Horatio,   175
    Than are dreamt of in your philosophy.°
    But come;
    Here, as before, never, so help you mercy,°
    How strange or odd soe'er I bear myself—
    As I perchance hereafter shall think meet   180
    To put an antic° disposition on—
    That you, at such times seeing me, never shall,
    With arms encumbered° thus, or this headshake,
    Or by pronouncing of some doubtful phrase
    As "Well, we know," or "We could, an if° we would,"   185
    Or "If we list° to speak," or "There be, an if they might,"°
    Or such ambiguous giving out,° to note°

---

153 In faith . . . I i.e., I swear not to tell what I have seen. (Horatio is not refusing to swear.)
155 sword i.e., the hilt in the form of a cross.   **156 We . . . already** i.e., we swore in *faith*.
159 truepenny honest old fellow.   **164 s.d. They swear** (Seemingly they swear here, and at
lines 170 and 190, as they lay their hands on Hamlet's sword. Triple oaths would have particular
force; these three oaths deal with what they have seen, what they have heard, and what they
promise about Hamlet's *antic disposition*.)   **165 Hic et ubique** here and everywhere (Latin).
172 pioneer foot soldier assigned to dig tunnels and excavations.   **174 as a stranger** i.e.,
needing your hospitality.   **176 your philosophy** this subject called "natural philosophy" or
"science" that people talk about.   **178 so help you mercy** as you hope for God's mercy when
you are judged.   **181 antic** fantastic.   **1831 encumbered** folded.   **185 an if** if.
186 list wished;   **There . . . might** i.e., there are people here (we, in fact) who could tell news if
we were at liberty to do so.   **187 giving out** intimation;   **note** draw attention to the fact.

That you know aught° of me—this do swear,
So grace and mercy at your most need help you.
GHOST [*beneath*].   Swear.   [*They swear.*]   190
HAMLET.   Rest, rest, perturbèd spirit! So, gentlemen,
With all my love I do commend me to you;°
And what so poor a man as Hamlet is
May do t' express his love and friending° to you,
God willing, shall not lack.° Let us go in together,   195
And still° your fingers on your lips, I pray.
The time° is out of joint. O cursèd spite°
That ever I was born to set it right!   [*They wait for him to leave first.*]
Nay, come, let's go together.°   *Exeunt.*

2.1   *Enter old* POLONIUS *with his man* [REYNALDO].

POLONIUS.   Give him this money and these notes, Reynaldo.
                                    [*He gives money and papers.*]
REYNALDO.   I will, my lord.
POLONIUS.   You shall do marvelous° wisely, good Reynaldo,
Before you visit him, to make inquire°
Of his behavior.
REYNALDO.   My lord, I did intend it.   5
POLONIUS.   Marry, well said, very well said. Look you, sir,
Inquire me first what Danskers° are in Paris,
And how, and who, what means,° and where they keep,°
What company, at what expense; and finding
By this encompassment° and drift° of question   10
That they do know my son, come you more nearer
Than your particular demands will touch it.°
Take you,° as 'twere, some distant knowledge of him,
As thus, "I know his father and his friends,
And in part him." Do you mark this, Reynaldo?   15
REYNALDO.   Ay, very well, my lord.
POLONIUS.   "And in part him, but," you may say, "not well.
But if 't be he I mean, he's very wild,
Addicted so and so," and there put on° him
What forgeries° you please—marry, none so rank°   20
As may dishonor him, take heed of that,
But, sir, such wanton,° wild, and usual slips
As are companions noted and most known
To youth and liberty.

---

188 aught i.e., something secret.   **192 do . . . you** entrust myself to you.
194 friending friendliness.   **195 lack** be lacking.   **196 still** always.   **197 The time** the state of
affairs;   **spite** i.e., the spite of Fortune.   **199 let's go together** (Probably they wait for him to
leave first, but he refuses this ceremoniousness.)   **2.1 Location: Polonius' chambers.**
3 marvelous marvelously.   **4 inquire** inquiry.   **7 Danskers** Danes.   **8 what means** what wealth
(they have);   **keep** dwell.   **10 encompassment** roundabout talking;   **drift** gradual approach or
course.   **11–12 come . . . it** you will find out more this way than by asking pointed questions
(*particular demands*).   **13 Take you** assume, pretend.   **19 put on** impute to.
20 forgeries invented tales;   **rank** gross.   **22 wanton** sportive, unrestrained.

REYNALDO.   As gaming, my lord.   25
POLONIUS.   Ay, or drinking, fencing, swearing,
     Quarreling, drabbing°—you may go so far.
REYNALDO.   My lord, that would dishonor him.
POLONIUS.   Faith, no, as you may season° it in the charge.
     You must not put another scandal on him   30
     That he is open to incontinency;°
     That's not my meaning. But breathe his faults so quaintly°
     That they may seem the taints of liberty,°
     The flash and outbreak of a fiery mind,
     A savageness in unreclaimèd blood,   35
     Of general assault.°
REYNALDO.   But, my good lord—
POLONIUS.   Wherefore should you do this?
REYNALDO.   Ay, my lord, I would know that.
POLONIUS.   Marry, sir, here's my drift,   40
     And I believe it is a fetch of warrant.°
     You laying these slight sullies on my son,
     As 'twere a thing a little soiled wi' the working,°
     Mark you,
     Your party in converse,° him you would sound,°   45
     Having ever° seen in the prenominate crimes°
     The youth you breathe° of guilty, be assured
     He closes with you in this consequence:°
     "Good sir," or so, or "friend," or "gentleman,"
     According to the phrase or the addition°   50
     Of man and country.
REYNALDO.   Very good, my lord.
POLONIUS.   And then, sir, does 'a this—'a does—what was I about to say? By the
     Mass, I was about to say something. Where did I leave?
REYNALDO.   At "closes in the consequence."
POLONIUS.   At "closes in the consequence," ay, marry.   55
     He closes thus: "I know the gentleman,
     I saw him yesterday," or "th' other day,"
     Or then, or then, with such or such, "and as you say,
     There was 'a gaming," "there o'ertook in 's rouse,"°
     "There falling out° at tennis," or perchance   60
     "I saw him enter such a house of sale,"
     Videlicet° a brothel, or so forth. See you now,
     Your bait of falsehood takes this carp° of truth;
     And thus do we of wisdom and of reach,°

---

27 drabbing whoring.   **29 season** temper, soften.   **31 incontinency** habitual sexual excess.
32 quaintly artfully, subtly.   **33 taints of liberty** faults resulting from free living.   **35–36 A
savageness . . . assault** a wildness in untamed youth that assails all indiscriminately.   **41 fetch of
warrant** legitimate trick.   **43 soiled wi' the working** soiled by handling while it is being made,
i.e., by involvement in the ways of the world.   **45 converse** conversation;   **sound** i.e., sound
out.   **46 Having ever** if he has ever;   **prenominate crimes** before-mentioned offenses.
47 breathe speak.   **48 closes . . . consequence** takes you into his confidence in some fashion, as
follows.   **50 addition** title.   **59 o'ertook in 's rouse** overcome by drink.   **60 falling
out** quarreling.   **62 Videlicet** namely.   **63 carp** a fish.   **64 reach** capacity, ability.

With windlasses° and with assays of bias,°   65
By indirections find directions° out.
So by my former lecture and advice
Shall you my son. You have° me, have you not?
REYNALDO.   My lord, I have.
POLONIUS.   God b'wi'° ye; fare ye well.
REYNALDO.   Good my lord.   70
POLONIUS.   Observe his inclination in yourself.°
REYNALDO.   I shall, my lord.
POLONIUS.   And let him ply his music.
REYNALDO.   Well, my lord.
POLONIUS.   Farewell.   *Exit* REYNALDO.

   Enter OPHELIA.

                    How now, Ophelia, what's the matter?   75
OPHELIA.   O my lord, my lord, I have been so affrighted!
POLONIUS.   With what, i' the name of God?
OPHELIA.   My lord, as I was sewing in my closet,°
Lord Hamlet, with his doublet° all unbraced,°
No hat upon his head, his stockings fouled,   80
Ungartered, and down-gyvèd° to his ankle,
Pale as his shirt, his knees knocking each other,
And with a look so piteous in purport°
As if he had been loosèd out of hell
To speak of horrors—he comes before me.   85
POLONIUS.   Mad for thy love?
OPHELIA.   My lord, I do not know,
But truly I do fear it.
POLONIUS.   What said he?
OPHELIA.   He took me by the wrist and held me hard.
Then goes he to the length of all his arm,
And, with his other hand thus o'er his brow   90
He falls to such perusal of my face
As° 'a would draw it. Long stayed he so.
At last, a little shaking of mine arm
And thrice his head thus waving up and down,
He raised a sigh so piteous and profound   95
As it did seem to shatter all his bulk°
And end his being. That done, he lets me go,
And with his head over his shoulder turned
He seemed to find his way without his eyes,
For out o' doors he went without their helps,   100
And to the last bended their light on me.

65 **windlasses** i.e., circuitous paths. (Literally, circuits made to head off the game in hunting); **assays of bias** attempts through indirection (like the curving path of the bowling ball, which is biased or weighted to one side). 66 **directions** i.e., the way things really are.
68 **have** understand. 69 **b' wi'** be with. 71 **in yourself** in your own person (as well as by asking questions). 78 **closet** private chamber. 79 **doublet** close-fitting jacket; **unbraced** unfastened. 81 **down-gyvèd** fallen to the ankles (like gyves or fetters). 83 **in purport** in what it expressed. 92 **As** as if (also in line 97). 96 **bulk** body.

POLONIUS.   Come, go with me. I will go seek the King.
　　　　This is the very ecstasy° of love,
　　　　Whose violent property° fordoes° itself
　　　　And leads the will to desperate undertakings　　　　　　　　105
　　　　As oft as any passion under heaven
　　　　That does afflict our natures. I am sorry.
　　　　What, have you given him any hard words of late?
OPHELIA.   No, my good lord, but as you did command
　　　　I did repel his letters and denied　　　　　　　　　　　　110
　　　　His access to me.
POLONIUS.　　　　　　　　That hath made him mad.
　　　　I am sorry that with better heed and judgment
　　　　I had not quoted° him. I feared he did but trifle
　　　　And meant to wrack° thee. But beshrew my jealousy!°
　　　　By heaven, it is as proper to our age°　　　　　　　　　　115
　　　　To cast beyond° ourselves in our opinions
　　　　As it is common for the younger sort
　　　　To lack discretion. Come, go we to the King.
　　　　This must be known,° which, being kept close,° might move
　　　　More grief to hide than hate to utter love.°　　　　　　　120
　　　　Come.　　　　　　　　　　　　　　　　　　　*Exeunt.*

　　　　　　2.2　*Flourish. Enter* KING *and* QUEEN, ROSENCRANTZ, *and*
　　　　　　　　　　　GUILDENSTERN [*with others*].

KING.   Welcome, dear Rosencrantz and Guildenstern.
　　　　Moreover that° we much did long to see you,
　　　　The need we have to use you did provoke
　　　　Our hasty sending. Something have you heard
　　　　Of Hamlet's transformation—so call it,　　　　　　　　　5
　　　　Sith nor° th' exterior nor the inward man
　　　　Resembles that° it was. What it should be,
　　　　More than his father's death, that thus hath put him
　　　　So much from th' understanding of himself,
　　　　I cannot dream of. I entreat you both　　　　　　　　　10
　　　　That, being of so young days° brought up with him,
　　　　And sith so neighbored to° his youth and havior,°
　　　　That you vouchsafe your rest° here in our court
　　　　Some little time, so by your companies
　　　　To draw him on to pleasures, and to gather　　　　　　　15

---

103 ecstasy madness.　**104 property** nature;　**fordoes** destroys.　**113 quoted** observed.
114 wrack ruin, seduce;　**beshrew my jealousy** a plague upon my suspicious nature.
115 proper . . . age characteristic of us (old) men.　**116 cast beyond** overshoot, miscalculate. (A
metaphor from hunting.)　**119 known** made known (to the King);　**close** secret.
119–120 might . . . love i.e., might cause more grief (because of what Hamlet might do) by
hiding the knowledge of Hamlet's strange behavior toward Ophelia than unpleasantness by
telling it.　**2.2. Location: The castle.**　**2 Moreover that** besides the fact that.　**6 Sith nor** since
neither.　**7 that** what.　**11 of . . . days** from such early youth.　**12 And sith so neighbored
to** and since you are (or, and since that time you are) intimately acquainted with;
havior demeanor.　**13 vouchsafe your rest** please to stay.

So much as from occasion° you may glean,
Whether aught to us unknown afflicts him thus
That, opened,° lies within our remedy.

QUEEN.   Good gentlemen, he hath much talked of you,
And sure I am two men there is not living   20
To whom he more adheres. If it will please you
To show us so much gentry° and good will
As to expend your time with us awhile
For the supply and profit of our hope,°
Your visitation shall receive such thanks   25
As fits a king's remembrance.°

ROSENCRANTZ.   Both Your Majesties
Might, by the sovereign power you have of° us,
Put your dread° pleasures more into command
Than to entreaty.

GUILDENSTERN.   But we both obey,
And here give up ourselves in the full bent°   30
To lay our service freely at your feet,
To be commanded.

KING.   Thanks, Rosencrantz and gentle Guildenstern.

QUEEN.   Thanks, Guildenstern and gentle Rosencrantz.
And I beseech you instantly to visit   35
My too much changèd son. Go, some of you,
And bring these gentlemen where Hamlet is.

GUILDENSTERN.   Heavens make our presence and our practices°
Pleasant and helpful to him!

QUEEN.   Ay, amen!

        Exeunt ROSENCRANTZ *and* GUILDENSTERN [*with some attendants*].

   Enter Polonius.

POLONIUS.   Th' ambassadors from Norway, my good lord,   40
Are joyfully returned.

KING.   Thou still° hast been the father of good news.

POLONIUS.   Have I, my lord? I assure my good liege
I hold° my duty, as° I hold my soul,
Both to my God and to my gracious king;   45
And I do think, or else this brain of mine
Hunts not the trail of policy° so sure
As it hath used to do, that I have found
The very cause of Hamlet's lunacy.

KING.   O, speak of that! That do I long to hear.   50

POLONIUS.   Give first admittance to th' ambassadors.
My news shall be the fruit° to that great feast.

KING.   Thyself do grace° to them and bring them in.   [*Exit* POLONIUS.]

---

16 occasion opportunity.   **18 opened** being revealed.   **22 gentry** courtesy.   **24 supply** . . .
hope aid and furtherance of what we hope for.   **26 As fits** . . . **remembrance** as would be a
fitting gift of a king who rewards true service.   **27 of** over.   **28 dread** inspiring awe.   **30 in** . . .
bent to the utmost degree of our capacity. (An archery metaphor.)   **38 practices** doings.
42 still always.   **44 hold** maintain; **as** firmly as.   **47 policy** sagacity.   **52 fruit** dessert.
53 grace honor (punning on *grace* said before a *feast,* line 52.)

He tells me, my dear Gertrude, he hath found
The head and source of all your son's distemper.   55
QUEEN.   I doubt° it is no other but the main,°
His father's death and our o'erhasty marriage.

Enter Ambassadors VOLTIMAND *and* CORNELIUS, *with* POLONIUS.

KING.   Well, we shall sift him.°—Welcome, my good friends!
Say, Voltimand, what from our brother° Norway?
VOLTIMAND.   Most fair return of greetings and desires.°   60
Upon our first,° he sent out to suppress
His nephew's levies, which to him appeared
To be a preparation 'gainst the Polack,
But, better looked into, he truly found
It was against Your Highness. Whereat grieved   65
That so his sickness, age, and impotence°
Was falsely borne in hand,° sends out arrests°
On Fortinbras, which he, in brief, obeys,
Receives rebuke from Norway, and in fine°
Makes vow before his uncle never more   70
To give th' assay° of arms against Your Majesty.
Whereon old Norway, overcome with joy,
Gives him three thousand crowns in annual fee
And his commission to employ those soldiers,
So levied as before, against the Polack,   75
With an entreaty, herein further shown,   [*giving a paper*]
That it might please you to give quiet pass
Through your dominions for this enterprise
On such regards of safety and allowance°
As therein are set down.
KING.   It likes° us well,   80
And at our more considered° time we'll read,
Answer, and think upon this business.
Meantime we thank you for your well-took labor.
Go to your rest; at night we'll feast together.
Most welcome home!   *Exeunt Ambassadors.*
POLONIUS.   This business is well ended.   85
My liege, and madam, to expostulate°
What majesty should be, what duty is,
Why day is day, night night, and time is time,
Were nothing but to waste night, day, and time.
Therefore, since brevity is the soul of wit,°   90
And tediousness the limbs and outward flourishes,
I will be brief. Your noble son is mad.

---

56 doubt fear, suspect;   **main** chief point, principal concern.   **58 sift him** question Polonius
closely.   **59 brother** fellow king.   **60 desires** good wishes.   **61 Upon our first** at our first
words on the business.   **66 impotence** helplessness.   **67 borne in hand** deluded, taken
advantage of;   **arrests** orders to desist.   **69 in fine** in conclusion.   **71 give th' assay** make trial
of strength, challenge.   **78 On . . . allowance** i.e., with such considerations for the safety of
Denmark and permission for Fortinbras.   **80 likes** pleases.   **81 considered** suitable for
deliberation.   **86 expostulate** expound, inquire into.   **90 wit** sense or judgment.

Mad call I it, for, to define true madness,
What is't but to be nothing else but mad?
But let that go.
QUEEN.   More matter, with less art.   95
POLONIUS.   Madam, I swear I use no art at all.
That he's mad, 'tis true; 'tis true 'tis pity.
And pity 'tis 'tis true—a foolish figure,°
But farewell it, for I will use no art.
Mad let us grant him, then, and now remains   100
That we find out the cause of this effect,
Or rather say, the cause of this defect,
For this effect defective comes by cause.°
Thus it remains, and the remainder thus.
Perpend.°   105
I have a daughter—have while she is mine—
Who, in her duty and obedience, mark,
Hath given me this. Now gather and surmise.°
[*He reads the letter.*] "To the celestial and my soul's idol, the most beauti-
fied Ophelia"—   110
That's an ill phrase, a vile phrase; "beautified" is a vile phrase. But you
shall hear. Thus: [*He reads.*]
"In her excellent white bosom,° these,° etc."
QUEEN.   Came this from Hamlet to her?
POLONIUS.   Good madam, stay° awhile, I will be faithful.°   [*He reads.*]   115

    "Doubt thou the stars are fire,
        Doubt that the sun doth move,
    Doubt° truth to be a liar,
        But never doubt I love.

O dear Ophelia, I am ill at these numbers.° I have not art to reckon° my   120
groans. But that I love thee best, O most best, believe it. Adieu.
        Thine evermore, most dear lady, whilst this machine° is to him,
                                                                    Hamlet."

This in obedience hath my daughter shown me,
And, more above,° hath his solicitings,   125
As they fell out° by° time, by means, and place,
All given to mine ear.°
KING.   But how hath she
Received his love?
POLONIUS.   What do you think of me?
KING.   As of a man faithful and honorable.
POLONIUS.   I would fain° prove so. But what might you think,   130

---

98 figure figure of speech.   **103 For ... cause** i.e., for this defective behavior, his madness, has
a cause.   **105 Perpend** consider.   **108 gather and surmise** draw your own conclusions.
113 In ... bosom (The letter is poetically addressed to her heart.);   **these** i.e., the letter.
115 stay wait;   **faithful** i.e., in reading the letter accurately.   **118 Doubt** suspect.   **120 ill ...**
numbers unskilled at writing verses.   **121 reckon** (1) count (2) number metrically, scan.
122 machine i.e., body.   **125 more above** moreover.   **126 fell out** occurred;   **by** according to.
127 given ... ear i.e., told me about.   **130 fain** gladly.

When I had seen this hot love on the wing—
As I perceived it, I must tell you that,
Before my daughter told me—what might you,
Or my dear Majesty your queen here, think,
If I had played the desk or table book,°   135
Or given my heart a winking,° mute and dumb,
Or looked upon this love with idle sight?°
What might you think? No, I went round° to work,
And my young mistress thus I did bespeak:°
"Lord Hamlet is a prince out of thy star;°   140
This must not be." And then I prescripts° gave her,
That she should lock herself from his resort,°
Admit no messengers, receive no tokens.
Which done, she took the fruits of my advice;
And he, repellèd—a short tale to make—   145
Fell into a sadness, then into a fast,
Thence to a watch,° thence into a weakness,
Thence to a lightness,° and by this declension°
Into the madness wherein now he raves,
And all we° mourn for.
KING [*to the* QUEEN].   Do you think 'tis this?   150
QUEEN.   It may be, very like.
POLONIUS.   Hath there been such a time—I would fain know that—
         That I have positively said "'Tis so,"
         When it proved otherwise?
KING.   Not that I know.
POLONIUS.   Take this from this,° if this be otherwise.   155
         If circumstances lead me, I will find
         Where truth is hid, though it were hid indeed
         Within the center.°
KING.   How may we try° it further?
POLONIUS.   You know sometimes he walks four hours together
         Here in the lobby.
QUEEN.   So he does indeed.   160
POLONIUS.   At such a time I'll loose° my daughter to him.
         Be you and I behind an arras° then.
         Mark the encounter. If he love her not
         And be not from his reason fall'n thereon,°

135 played . . . table book i.e., remained shut up, concealing the information.   136 given . . .
winking closed the eyes of my heart to this.   137 with idle sight complacently or
incomprehendingly.   138 round roundly, plainly.   139 bespeak address.   140 out of thy
star above your sphere, position.   141 prescripts orders.   142 his resort his visits.
147 watch state of sleeplessness.   148 lightness lightheadedness; declension decline,
deterioration (with a pun on the grammatical sense).   150 all we all of us, or, into everything
that we.   155 Take this from this (The actor probably gestures, indicating that he means his
head from his shoulders, or his staff of office or chain from his hands or neck, or something
similar.)   158 center middle point of the earth (which is also the center of the Ptolemaic
universe); try test, judge.   161 loose (As one might release an animal that is being mated.)
162 arras hanging, tapestry.   164 thereon on that account.

Let me be no assistant for a state,   165
     But keep a farm and carters.°
KING.   We will try it.

   Enter HAMLET [*reading on a book*].

QUEEN.   But look where sadly° the poor wretch comes reading.
POLONIUS.   Away, I do beseech you both, away.
     I'll board° him presently.° O, give me leave.°
                              Exeunt KING *and* QUEEN [*with attendants*].
     How does my good Lord Hamlet?   170
HAMLET.   Well, God-a-mercy.°
POLONIUS.   Do you know me, my lord?
HAMLET.   Excellent well. You are a fishmonger.°
POLONIUS.   Not I, my lord.
HAMLET.   Then I would you were so honest a man.   175
POLONIUS.   Honest, my lord?
HAMLET.   Ay, sir. To be honest, as this world goes, is to be one man picked out of
     ten thousand.
POLONIUS.   That's very true, my lord.
HAMLET.   For if the sun breed maggots in a dead dog, being a good kissing car-   180
     rion°—Have you a daughter?
POLONIUS.   I have, my lord.
HAMLET.   Let her not walk i' the sun.° Conception° is a blessing, but as your
     daughter may conceive, friend, look to 't.
POLONIUS [*aside*].   How say you by that? Still harping on my daughter. Yet he   185
     knew me not at first; 'a° said I was a fishmonger. 'A is far gone. And truly
     in my youth I suffered much extremity for love, very near this. I'll speak
     to him again.—What do you read, my lord?
HAMLET.   Words, words, words.
POLONIUS.   What is the matter,° my lord?   190
HAMLET.   Between who?
POLONIUS.   I mean, the matter that you read, my lord.
HAMLET.   Slanders, sir; for the satirical rogue says here that old men have gray
     beards, that their faces are wrinkled, their eyes purging° thick amber° and
     plum-tree gum, and that they have a plentiful lack of wit,° together with   195
     most weak hams. All which, sir, though I most powerfully and potently
     believe, yet I hold it not honesty° to have it thus set down, for yourself,
     sir, shall grow old° as I am, if like a crab you could go backward.
POLONIUS [*aside*].   Though this be madness, yet there is method in 't.—Will you
     walk out of the air,° my lord?   200

---

166 carters wagon drivers.   **167 sadly** seriously.   **169 board** accost;   **presently** at once;   **give
me leave** i.e., excuse me, leave me alone. (Said to those he hurries offstage, including the King
and Queen.)   **171 God-a-mercy** God have mercy, i.e., thank you.   **173 fishmonger** fish
merchant.   **180–181 a good kissing carrion** i.e., a good piece of flesh for kissing, or for the sun
to kiss.   **183 i' the sun** in public (with additional implication of the sunshine of princely favors);
Conception (1) understanding (2) pregnancy.   **186 'a** he.   **190 matter** substance. (But Hamlet
plays on the sense of "basis for a dispute.")   **194 purging** discharging;   **amber** i.e., resin, like
the resinous *plum-tree gum.*   **195 wit** understanding.   **197 honesty** decency, decorum.
198 old as old.   **200 out of the air** (The open air was considered dangerous for sick people.)

HAMLET.   Into my grave.

POLONIUS.   Indeed, that's out of the air. [*Aside.*] How pregnant° sometimes his
replies are! A happiness° that often madness hits on, which reason and
sanity could not so prosperously° be delivered of. I will leave him and
suddenly° contrive the means of meeting between him and my daugh-   205
ter.—My honorable lord, I will most humbly take my leave of you.

HAMLET.   You cannot, sir, take from me anything that I will more willingly part
withal°—except my life, except my life, except my life.

      Enter GUILDENSTERN *and* ROSENCRANTZ.

POLONIUS.   Fare you well, my lord.

HAMLET.   These tedious old fools!°   210

POLONIUS.   You go to seek the Lord Hamlet. There he is.

ROSENCRANTZ [*to* POLONIUS].   God save you, sir!   [*Exit* POLONIUS.]

GUILDENSTERN.   My honored lord!

ROSENCRANTZ.   My most dear lord!

HAMLET.   My excellent good friends! How dost thou, Guildenstern? Ah,   215
Rosencrantz! Good lads, how do you both?

ROSENCRANTZ.   As the indifferent° children of the earth.

GUILDENSTERN.   Happy in that we are not overhappy.
On Fortune's cap we are not the very button.

HAMLET.   Nor the soles of her shoe?   220

ROSENCRANTZ.   Neither, my lord.

HAMLET.   Then you live about her waist, or in the middle of her favors?°

GUILDENSTERN.   Faith, her privates we.°

HAMLET.   In the secret parts of Fortune? O, most true, she is a strumpet.°
What news?   225

ROSENCRANTZ.   None, my lord, but the world's grown honest.

HAMLET.   Then is doomsday near. But your news is not true. Let me question more
in particular. What have you, my good friends, deserved at the hands of
Fortune that she sends you to prison hither?

GUILDENSTERN.   Prison, my lord?   230

HAMLET.   Denmark's a prison.

ROSENCRANTZ.   Then is the world one.

HAMLET.   A goodly one, in which there are many confines,° wards,° and dun-
geons, Denmark being one o' the worst.

ROSENCRANTZ.   We think not so, my lord.   235

HAMLET.   Why then 'tis none to you, for there is nothing either good or bad but
thinking makes it so. To me it is a prison.

ROSENCRANTZ.   Why then, your ambition makes it one. 'Tis too narrow for your mind.

HAMLET.   O God, I could be bounded in a nutshell and count myself a king of infinite space, were it not that I have bad dreams.   240

---

202 pregnant quick-witted, full of meaning.   **203 happiness** felicity of expression.
204 prosperously successfully.   **205 suddenly** immediately.   **208 withal** with.   **210 old
fools** i.e., old men like Polonius.   **217 indifferent** ordinary, at neither extreme of fortune or
misfortune.   **222 favors** i.e., sexual favors.   **223 her privates we** i.e., (1) we are sexually
intimate with Fortune, the fickle goddess who bestows her favors indiscriminately (2) we are her
private citizens.   **224 strumpet** prostitute. (A common epithet for indiscriminate Fortune; see
line 452.)   **233 confines** places of confinement;   **wards** cells.

GUILDENSTERN. Which dreams indeed are ambition, for the very substance of the ambitious° is merely the shadow of a dream.

HAMLET. A dream itself is but a shadow.

ROSENCRANTZ. Truly, and I hold ambition of so airy and light a quality that it is but a shadow's shadow. 245

HAMLET. Then are our beggars bodies,° and our monarchs and outstretched° heroes the beggars' shadows. Shall we to the court? For, by my fay,° I cannot reason.

ROSENCRANTZ, GUILDENSTERN. We'll wait upon° you.

HAMLET. No such matter. I will not sort° you with the rest of my servants, for, to 250 speak to you like an honest man, I am most dreadfully attended.° But, in the beaten way° of friendship, what make° you at Elsinore?

ROSENCRANTZ. To visit you, my lord, no other occasion.

HAMLET. Beggar that I am, I am even poor in thanks; but I thank you, and sure, dear friends, my thanks are too dear a halfpenny.° Were you not sent for? 255 Is it your own inclining? Is it a free° visitation? Come, come, deal justly with me. Come, come. Nay, speak.

GUILDENSTERN. What should we say, my lord?

HAMLET. Anything but to the purpose.° You were sent for, and there is a kind of confession in your looks which your modesties° have not craft enough to 260 color.° I know the good King and Queen have sent for you.

ROSENCRANTZ. To what end, my lord?

HAMLET. That you must teach me. But let me conjure° you, by the rights of our fellowship, by the consonancy of our youth,° by the obligation of our everpreserved love, and by what more dear a better° proposer could charge° 265 you withal, be even° and direct with me whether you were sent for or no.

ROSENCRANTZ [*aside to* GUILDENSTERN]. What say you?

HAMLET [*aside*]. Nay, then, I have an eye of° you.—If you love me, hold not off.°

GUILDENSTERN. My lord, we were sent for.

HAMLET. I will tell you why; so shall my anticipation prevent your discovery,° and 270 your secrecy to the King and Queen molt no feather,° I have of late—but wherefore I know not—lost all my mirth, for-gone all custom of exercises; and indeed it goes so heavily with my disposition that this goodly frame, the earth, seems to me a sterile promontory; this most excellent canopy, the air, look you, this brave° o'erhanging firmament, this majesti- 275 cal roof fretted° with golden fire, why, it appeareth nothing to me but a

---

241–242 the very . . . ambitious that seemingly very substantial thing that the ambitious pursue. **246 bodies** i.e., solid substances rather than shadows (since beggars are not ambitious). **outstretched** (1) far-reaching in their ambition (2) elongated as shadows. **247 fay** faith. **249 wait upon** accompany, attend. (But Hamlet uses the phrase in the sense of providing menial service.) **250 sort** class, categorize. **251 dreadfully attended** waited upon in slovenly fashion. **252 beaten way** familiar path, tried-and-true course; **make** do. **255 too dear a halfpenny** (1) too expensive at even a halfpenny, i.e., of little worth (2) too expensive *by* a halfpenny in return for worthless kindness. **256 free** voluntary. **259 Anything but to the purpose** anything except a straightforward answer. (Said ironically.) **260 modesties** sense of shame. **261 color** disguise. **263 conjure** adjure, entreat. **264 the consonancy of our youth** our closeness in our younger days. **265 better** more skillful; **charge** urge. **266 even** straight, honest. **268 of** on; **hold not off** don't hold back. **270 so . . . discovery** in that way my saying it first will spare you from revealing the truth. **271 molt no feather** i.e., not diminish in the least. **275 brave** splendid. **276 fretted** adorned (with fretwork, as in a vaulted ceiling).

foul and pestilent congregation° of vapors. What a piece of work° is a man! How noble in reason, how infinite in faculties, in form and moving how express° and admirable, in action how like an angel, in apprehension° how like a god! The beauty of the world, the paragon of animals! And yet, to me, what is this quintessence° of dust? Man delights not me— no, nor woman neither, though by your smiling you seem to say so.   280

ROSENCRANTZ. My lord, there was no such stuff in my thoughts.

HAMLET. Why did you laugh, then, when I said man delights not me?

ROSENCRANTZ. To think, my lord, if you delight not in man, what Lenten entertainment° the players shall receive from you. We coted° them on the way, and hither are they coming to offer you service.   285

HAMLET. He that plays the king shall be welcome; His Majesty shall have tribute° of° me. The adventurous knight shall use his foil and target,° the lover shall not sigh gratis,° the humorous man° shall end his part in peace,° the clown shall make those laugh whose lungs are tickle o' the sear,° and the lady shall say her mind freely, or the blank verse shall halt° for 't. What players are they?   290

ROSENCRANTZ. Even those you were wont to take such delight in, the tragedians° of the city.   295

HAMLET. How chances it they travel? Their residence,° both in reputation and profit, was better both ways.

ROSENCRANTZ. I think their inhibition° comes by the means of the late° innovation.°

HAMLET. Do they hold the same estimation they did when I was in the city? Are they so followed?   300

ROSENCRANTZ. No, indeed are they not.

HAMLET. How comes it? Do they grow rusty?

ROSENCRANTZ. Nay, their endeavor keeps° in the wonted° pace. But there is, sir, an aerie° of children, little eyases,° that cry out on the top of question° and are most tyrannically° clapped for 't. These are now the fashion, and so berattle° the common stages°—so they call them—that many wearing rapiers° are afraid of goose quills° and dare scarce come thither.   305

HAMLET. What, are they children? Who maintains 'em? How are they escoted?° Will they pursue the quality° no longer than they can sing?° Will they not

277 congregation mass; **piece of work** masterpiece. **279 express** well-framed, exact, expressive. **279–280 apprehension** power of comprehending. **281 quintessence** the fifth essence of ancient philosophy, beyond earth, water, air, and fire, supposed to be the substance of the heavenly bodies and to be latent in all things. **285–286 Lenten entertainment** meager reception (appropriate to Lent); **coted** overtook and passed by. **288 tribute** (1) applause (2) homage paid in money. **289 of** from; **foil and target** sword and shield. **290 gratis** for nothing; **humorous man** eccentric character, dominated by one trait or "humor"; **in peace** i.e., with full license. **291 tickle o' the sear** easy on the trigger, ready to laugh easily. (A *sear* is part of a gunlock.) **292 halt** limp. **294 tragedians** actors. **296 residence** remaining in their usual place, i.e., in the city. **298 inhibition** formal prohibition (from acting plays in the city); **late** recent; **innovation** i.e., the new fashion in satirical plays performed by boy actors in the "private" theaters; or possibly a political uprising; or the strict limitations set on theaters in London in 1600. **303 keeps** continues; **wonted** usual. **304 aerie** nest; **eyases** young hawks; **cry . . . question** speak shrilly, dominating the controversy (in decrying the public theaters). **305 tyrannically** outrageously. **306 berattle** berate, clamor against; **common stages** public theaters. **306–307 many wearing rapiers** i.e., many men of fashion, afraid to patronize the common players for fear of being satirized by the poets writing for the boy actors; **goose quills** i.e., pens of satirists. **308 escoted** maintained. **309 quality** (acting) profession; **no longer . . . sing** i.e., only until their voices change.

say afterwards, if they should grow themselves to common° players—as   310
it is most like,° if their means are no better°—their writers do them
wrong to make them exclaim against their own succession?°

ROSENCRANTZ.   Faith, there has been much to-do° on both sides, and the nation holds
it no sin to tar° them to controversy. There was for a while no money bid for
argument unless the poet and the player went to cuffs in the question.°   315

HAMLET.   Is 't possible?

GUILDENSTERN.   O, there has been much throwing about of brains.

HAMLET.   Do the boys carry it away?°

ROSENCRANTZ.   Ay, that they do, my lord—Hercules and his load° too.°

HAMLET.   It is not very strange; for my uncle is King of Denmark, and those that   320
would make mouths° at him while my father lived give twenty, forty,
fifty, a hundred ducats° apiece for his picture in little.° 'Sblood,° there is
something in this more than natural, if philosophy° could find it out.

A flourish [of trumpets within].

GUILDENSTERN.   There are the players.

HAMLET.   Gentlemen, you are welcome to Elsinore. Your hands, come then.   325
Th' appurtenance° of welcome is fashion and ceremony. Let me comply°
with you in this garb,° lest my extent° to the players, which, I tell you,
must show fairly outwards,° should more appear like entertainment° than
yours. You are welcome. But my uncle-father and aunt-mother are
deceived.   330

GUILDENSTERN.   In what, my dear lord?

HAMLET.   I am but mad north-north-west.° When the wind is southerly I know a
hawk from a handsaw.°

Enter POLONIUS.

POLONIUS.   Well be with you, gentlemen!

HAMLET.   Hark you, Guildenstern, and you too; at each ear a hearer. That great   335
baby you see there is not yet out of his swaddling clouts.°

ROSENCRANTZ.   Haply° he is the second time come to them, for they say an old
man is twice a child.

HAMLET.   I will prophesy he comes to tell me of the players. Mark it.—You say
right, sir, o' Monday morning, 'twas then indeed.   340

---

310 **common** regular, adult.   311 **like** likely;   **if . . . better** if they find no better way to support
themselves.   312 **succession** i.e., future careers.   313 **to-do** ado.   314 **tar** set on (as dogs).
314–315 **There . . . question** i.e., for a while, no money was offered by the acting companies to
playwrights for the plot to a play unless the satirical poets who wrote for the boys and the adult
actors came to blows in the play itself.   318 **carry it away** i.e., win the day.   319 **Hercules . . .
load** (Thought to be an allusion to the sign of the Globe Theatre, which was Hercules bearing
the world on his shoulders.)   302–319 **How . . . load too** (The passage, omitted from the early
quartos, alludes to the so-called War of the Theaters, 1599–1602, the rivalry between the
children's companies and the adult actors.)   321 **mouths** faces.   322 **ducats** gold coins;   **in
little** in miniature;   **'Sblood** by God's (Christ's) blood.   323 **philosophy** i.e., scientific inquiry.
326 **appurtenance** proper accompaniment;   **comply** observe the formalities of courtesy.
327 **garb** i.e., manner;   **my extent** that which I extend, i.e., my polite behavior.   328 **show
fairly outwards** show every evidence of cordiality;   **entertainment** a (warm) reception.
332 **north-north-west** just off true north, only partly.   333 **hawk, handsaw** i.e., two very
different things, though also perhaps meaning a mattock (or *back*) and carpenter's cutting tools,
respectively; also birds, with a play on *bernshaw*, or heron.   336 **swaddling clouts** cloths in
which to wrap a newborn baby.   337 **Haply** perhaps.

POLONIUS.   My lord, I have news to tell you.

HAMLET.   My lord, I have news to tell you. When Roscius° was an actor in Rome—

POLONIUS.   The actors are come hither, my lord.

HAMLET.   Buzz,° buzz!

POLONIUS.   Upon my honor—   345

HAMLET.   Then came each actor on his ass.

POLONIUS.   The best actors in the world, either for tragedy, comedy, history, pastoral, pastoral-comical, historical-pastoral, tragical-historical, tragical-
comical-historical-pastoral, scene individable,° or poem unlimited.°
Seneca° cannot be too heavy, nor Plautus° too light. For the law of writ   350
and the liberty,° these° are the only men.

HAMLET.   O Jephthah, judge of Israel,°
what a treasure hadst thou!

POLONIUS.   What a treasure had he, my lord?

HAMLET.   Why,   355
"One fair daughter, and no more,
The which he lovèd passing° well."

POLONIUS [*aside*].   Still on my daughter.

HAMLET.   Am I not i' the right, old Jephthah?

POLONIUS.   If you call me Jephthah, my lord, I have a daughter that I love passing   360
well.

HAMLET.   Nay, that follows not.

POLONIUS.   What follows then, my lord?

HAMLET.   Why,
"As by lot,° God wot,"°   365
and then, you know,
"It came to pass, as most like° it was"—
the first row° of the pious chanson° will show you more, for look where
my abridgement° comes.

Enter the PLAYERS.

You are welcome, masters; welcome, all. I am glad to see thee well.   370
Welcome, good friends. O, old friend! Why, thy face is valanced° since I
saw thee last. Com'st thou to beard° me in Denmark? What, my young
lady° and mistress! By 'r Lady,° your ladyship is nearer to heaven than
when I saw you last, by the altitude of a chopine.° Pray God your voice,
like a piece of uncurrent° gold, be not cracked within the ring.° Masters,   375

---

342 Roscius a famous Roman actor who died in 62 B.C.   **344 Buzz** (An interjection used to
denote stale news.)   **349 scene individable** a play observing the unity of place; or perhaps one
that is unclassifiable, or performed without intermission;   **poem unlimited** a play disregarding
the unities of time and place; one that is all-inclusive.   **350 Seneca** writer of Latin tragedies;
Plautus writer of Latin comedies.   **350–351 law . . . liberty** dramatic composition both
according to the rules and disregarding the rules;   **these** i.e., the actors.   **352 Jephthah . . .
Israel** (Jephthah had to sacrifice his daughter; see Judges 11. Hamlet goes on to quote from a
ballad on the theme.)   **357 passing** surpassingly.   **365 lot** chance;   **wot** knows.
367 like likely, probable.   **368 row** stanza;   **chanson** ballad, song.   **369 my abridgement**
something that cuts short my conversation; also, a diversion.   **371 valanced** fringed (with a
beard).   **372 beard** confront, challenge (with obvious pun).   **372–373 young lady** i.e., boy
playing women's parts;   **By 'r Lady** by Our Lady.   **374 chopine** thick-soled shoe of Italian
fashion.   **375 uncurrent** not passable as lawful coinage;   **cracked . . . ring** i.e., changed from
adolescent to male voice, no longer suitable for women's roles. (Coins featured rings enclosing
the sovereign's head; if the coin was cracked within this ring, it was unfit for currency.)

William Shakespeare   445

you are all welcome. We'll e'en to 't° like French falconers, fly at anything
we see. We'll have a speech straight.° Come, give us a taste of your
quality.° Come, a passionate speech.

FIRST PLAYER.   What speech, my good lord?

HAMLET.   I heard thee speak me a speech once, but it was never acted, or if it   380
was, not above once, for the play, I remember, pleased not the million;
'twas caviar to the general.° But it was—as I received it, and others,
whose judgments in such matters cried in the top of° mine—an excellent
play, well digested° in the scenes, set down with as much modesty° as
cunning.° I remember one said there were no sallets° in the lines to   385
make the matter savory, nor no matter in the phrase that might indict°
the author of affectation, but called it an honest method, as wholesome
as sweet, and by very much more handsome° than fine.° One speech in
't I chiefly loved: 'twas Aeneas' tale to Dido, and thereabout of it especially when he speaks of Priam's slaughter.° If it live in your memory, be-   390
gin at this line: let me see, let me see—

"The rugged Pyrrhus,° like th' Hyrcanian beast°"—

'Tis not so. It begins with Pyrrhus:

"The rugged° Pyrrhus, he whose sable° arms,
Black as his purpose, did the night resemble   395
When he lay couchèd° in the ominous horse,°
Hath now this dread and black complexion smeared
With heraldry more dismal.° Head to foot
Now is he total gules,° horridly tricked°
With blood of fathers, mothers, daughters, sons,   400
Baked and impasted° with the parching streets,°
That lend a tyrannous° and a damnèd light
To their lord's° murder. Roasted in wrath and fire,
And thus o'ersizèd° with coagulate gore,
With eyes like carbuncles,° the hellish Pyrrhus   405
Old grandsire Priam seeks."

So proceed you.

---

376 e'en to 't go at it.   **377 straight** at once.   **378 quality** professional skill.   **382 caviar to the
general** caviar to the multitude, i.e., a choice dish too elegant for coarse tastes.   **383 cried in the
top of** i.e., spoke with greater authority than.   **384 digested** arranged, ordered;
modesty moderation, restraint.   **385 cunning** skill;   **sallets** i.e., something savory, spicy
improprieties.   **386 indict** convict.   **388 handsome** well-proportioned;   **fine** elaborately
ornamented, showy.   **390 Priam's slaughter** the slaying of the ruler of Troy, when the Greeks
finally took the city.   **392 Pyrrhus** a Greek hero in the Trojan War, also known as
Neoptolemus, son of Achilles—another avenging son;   **Hyrcanian beast** i.e., tiger. (On the
death of Priam, see Virgil, *Aeneid,* 2.506 ff.; compare the whole speech with Marlowe's *Dido
Queen of Carthage,* 2.1.214. ff. On the *Hyrcanian* tiger, see *Aeneid,* 4.366–367. Hyrcania is on
the Caspian Sea.)   **394 rugged** shaggy, savage;   **sable** black (for reasons of camouflage during
the episode of the Trojan horse).   **396 couchèd** concealed;   **ominous horse** fateful Trojan
horse, by which the Greeks gained access to Troy.   **398 dismal** ill-omened.   **399 total
gules** entirely red. (A heraldic term);   **tricked** spotted and smeared. (Heraldic.)
401 impasted crusted, like a thick paste;   **with . . . streets** by the parching heat of the streets
(because of the fires everywhere).   **402 tyrannous** cruel.   **403 their lord's** i.e., Priam's.
404 o'ersizèd covered as with size or glue.   **405 carbuncles** large fiery-red precious stones
thought to emit their own light.

POLONIUS.   'Fore God, my lord, well spoken, with good accent and good discretion.
FIRST PLAYER.   "Anon he finds him

> Striking too short at Greeks. His antique° sword,   410
> Rebellious to his arm, lies where it falls,
> Repugnant° to command. Unequal matched,
> Pyrrhus at Priam drives, in rage strikes wide,
> But with the whiff and wind of his fell° sword
> Th' unnervèd° father falls. Then senseless Ilium,°   415
> Seeming to feel this blow, with flaming top
> Stoops to his° base, and with a hideous crash
> Takes prisoner Pyrrhus' ear. For, lo! His sword,
> Which was declining° on the milky° head
> Of reverend Priam, seemed i' th' air to stick.   420
> So as a painted° tyrant Pyrrhus stood,
> And, like a neutral to his will and matter,°
> Did nothing.
> But as we often see against° some storm
> A silence in the heavens, the rack° stand still,   425
> The bold winds speechless, and the orb° below
> As hush as death, anon the dreadful thunder
> Doth rend the region,° so, after Pyrrhus' pause,
> A rousèd vengeance sets him new a-work
> And never did the Cyclops'° hammers fall   430
> On Mars's armor forged for proof eterne°
> With less remorse° than Pyrrhus' bleeding sword
> Now falls on Priam.
> Out, out, thou strumpet Fortune! All you gods
> In general synod° take away her power!   435
> Break all the spokes and fellies° from her wheel,
> And bowl the round nave° down the hill of heaven°
> As low as to the fiends!"

POLONIUS.   This is too long.
HAMLET.   It shall to the barber's with your beard.—Prithee, say on. He's for a jig°   440
    or a tale of bawdry, or he sleeps. Say on; come to Hecuba.°
FIRST PLAYER.   "But who, ah woe! had° seen the moblèd° queen"—
HAMLET.   "The moblèd queen?"
POLONIUS.   That's good. "Moblèd queen" is good.
FIRST PLAYER.   "Run barefoot up and down, threat'ning the flames°   445

---

410 antique ancient, long-used.   **412 Repugnant** disobedient, resistant.   **414 fell** cruel.
415 unnervèd strengthless;   **senseless Ilium** inanimate citadel of Troy.   **417 his** its.
419 declining descending;   **milky** white-haired.   **421 painted** i.e., painted in a picture.
422 like . . . matter i.e., as though suspended between his intention and its fulfillment.
424 against just before.   **425 rack** mass of clouds.   **426 orb** globe, earth.   **428 region** sky.
430 Cyclops giant armor makers in the smithy of Vulcan.   **431 proof eterne** eternal resistance
to assault.   **432 remorse** pity.   **435 synod** assembly.   **436 fellies** pieces of wood forming the
rim of a wheel.   **437 nave** hub;   **hill of heaven** Mount Olympus.   **440 jig** comic song and
dance often given at the end of a play.   **441 Hecuba** wife of Priam.   **442 who . . . had** anyone
who had (also in line 469);   **moblèd** muffled.   **445 threat'ning the flames** i.e., weeping hard
enough to dampen the flames.

With bisson rheum,° a clout° upon that head
Where late° the diadem stood, and, for a robe,
About her lank and all o'erteemd° loins
A blanket, in the alarm of fear caught up—
Who this had seen, with tongue in venom steeped,   450
'Gainst Fortune's state° would treason have pronounced.°
But if the gods themselves did see her then
When she saw Pyrrhus make malicious sport
In mincing with his sword her husband's limbs,
The instant burst of clamor that she made,   455
Unless things mortal move them not at all,
Would have made milch° the burning eyes of heaven,°
And passion° in the gods."

POLONIUS.   Look whe'er° he has not turned his color and has tears in 's eyes.
Prithee, no more.   460

HAMLET.   'Tis well; I'll have thee speak out the rest of this soon.—Good my lord, will
you see the players well bestowed?° Do you hear, let them be well used,
for they are the abstract° and brief chronicles of the time. After your death
you were better have a bad epitaph than their ill report while you live.

POLONIUS.   My lord, I will use them according to their desert.   465

HAMLET.   God's bodikin,° man, much better. Use every man after his desert, and
who shall scape whipping? Use them after° your own honor and dignity.
The less they deserve, the more merit is in your bounty. Take them in.

POLONIUS.   Come, sirs.   [*Exit.*]

HAMLET.   Follow him, friends. We'll hear a play tomorrow. [*As they start to leave,*   470
HAMLET *detains the* FIRST PLAYER.] Dost thou hear me, old friend? Can you
play *The Murder of Gonzago?*

FIRST PLAYER.   Ay, my lord.

HAMLET.   We'll ha 't° tomorrow night. You could, for a need, study° a speech of
some dozen or sixteen lines which I would set down and insert in 't,   475
could you not?

FIRST PLAYER.   Ay, my lord.

HAMLET.   Very well. Follow that lord, and look you mock him not. [*Exeunt* PLAYERS.]
My good friends, I'll leave you till night. You are welcome to Elsinore.

ROSENCRANTZ.   Good my lord!   *Exeunt* [ROSENCRANTZ *and* GUILDENSTERN].   480

HAMLET.   Ay, so, goodbye to you.—Now I am alone.
O, what a rogue and peasant slave am I!
Is it not monstrous that this player here,
But° in a fiction, in a dream of passion,
Could force his soul so to his own conceit°   485
That from her working° all his visage wanned,°

446 **bisson rheum** blinding tears;   **clout** cloth.   447 **late** lately.   448 **all o'erteemèd** utterly
worn out with bearing children.   451 **state** rule, managing;   **pronounced** proclaimed.
457 **milch** milky, moist with tears;   **burning eyes of heaven** i.e., heavenly bodies.
458 **passion** overpowering emotion.   459 **whe'er** whether.   462 **bestowed** lodged.
463 **abstract** summary account.   466 **God's bodikin** by God's (Christ's) little body, *bodykin.*
(Not to be confused with *bodkin,* "dagger.")   467 **after** according to.   474 **ha 't** have it;
study memorize.   484 **But** merely.   485 **force . . . conceit** bring his innermost being so entirely
into accord with his conception (of the role).   486 **from her working** as a result of, or in
response to, his soul's activity;   **wanned** grew pale.

Tears in his eyes, distraction in his aspect,°
A broken voice, and his whole function suiting
With forms to his conceit?° And all for nothing!
For Hecuba!   490
What's Hecuba to him, or he to Hecuba,
That he should weep for her? What would he do
Had he the motive and the cue for passion
That I have? He would drown the stage with tears
And cleave the general ear° with horrid° speech,   495
Make mad the guilty and appall° the free,°
Confound the ignorant,° and amaze° indeed
The very faculties of eyes and ears. Yet I,
A dull and muddy-mettled° rascal, peak°
Like John-a-dreams,° unpregnant of° my cause,   500
And can say nothing—no, not for a king
Upon whose property° and most dear life
A damned defeat° was made. Am I a coward?
Who calls me villain? Breaks my pate° across?
Plucks off my beard and blows it in my face?   505
Tweaks me by the nose? Gives me the lie i' the throat°
As deep as to the lungs? Who does me this?
Ha, 'swounds,° I should take it; for it cannot be
But I am pigeon-livered° and lack gall
To make oppression bitter,° or ere this   510
I should ha' fatted all the region kites°
With this slave's offal.° Bloody, bawdy villain!
Remorseless,° treacherous, lecherous, kindless° villain!
O, vengeance!
Why, what an ass am I! This is most brave,°   515
That I, the son of a dear father murdered,
Prompted to my revenge by heaven and hell,
Must like a whore unpack my heart with words
And fall a-cursing, like a very drab,°
A scullion!° Fie upon 't, foh! About,° my brains!   520
Hum, I have heard
That guilty creatures sitting at a play
Have by the very cunning° of the scene°

---

487 aspect look, glance.   **488–489 his whole . . . conceit** all his bodily powers responding with
actions to suit his thought.   **495 the general ear** everyone's ear;   **horrid** horrible.
496 appall (Literally, make pale.);   **free** innocent.   **497 Confound the ignorant,** i.e.,
dumbfound those who know nothing of the crime that has been committed;   **amaze** stun.
499 muddy-mettled dull-spirited;   **peak** mope, pine.   **500 John-a-dreams** a sleepy, dreaming
idler;   **unpregnant of** not quickened by.   **502 property** i.e., the crown; also character, quality.
503 damned defeat damnable act of destruction.   **504 pate** head.   **506 Gives . . . throat** calls
me an out-and-out liar.   **508 'swounds** by his (Christ's) wounds.   **509 pigeon-livered** (The
pigeon or dove was popularly supposed to be mild because it secreted no gall.)   **510 bitter** i.e.,
bitter to me.   **511 region kites** kites (birds of prey) of the air.   **512 offal** entrails.
513 Remorseless pitiless;   **kindless** unnatural.   **515 brave** fine, admirable. (Said ironically.)
519 drab whore.   **520 scullion** menial kitchen servant (apt to be foul-mouthed);   **About** about
it, to work.   **523 cunning** art, skill;   **scene** dramatic presentation.

Been struck so to the soul that presently°   525
They have proclaimed their malefactions;
For murder, though it have no tongue, will speak
With most miraculous organ. I'll have these players
Play something like the murder of my father
Before mine uncle. I'll observe his looks;
I'll tent° him to the quick.° If 'a do blench,°   530
I know my course. The spirit that I have seen
May be the devil, and the devil hath power
T' assume a pleasing shape; yea, and perhaps,
Out of my weakness and my melancholy,
As he is very potent with such spirits,°   535
Abuses° me to damn me. I'll have grounds
More relative° than this. The play's the thing
Wherein I'll catch the conscience of the King.   *Exit.*

3.1 *Enter* KING, QUEEN, POLONIUS, OPHELIA, ROSENCRANTZ, GUILDERNSTERN, *lords.*

KING. And can you by no drift of conference°
    Get from him why he puts on this confusion,
    Grating so harshly all his days of quiet
    With turbulent and dangerous lunacy?
ROSENCRANTZ. He does confess he feels himself distracted,   5
    But from what cause 'a will by no means speak.
GUILDENSTERN. Nor do we find him forward° to be sounded,°
    But with a crafty madness keeps aloof
    When we would bring him on to some confession
    Of his true state.
QUEEN.   Did he receive you well?   10
ROSENCRANTZ. Most like a gentleman.
GUILDENSTERN. But with much forcing of his disposition.°
ROSENCRANTZ. Niggard° of question,° but of our demands
    Most free in his reply.
QUEEN.   Did you assay° him
    To any pastime?   15
ROSENCRANTZ. Madam, it so fell out that certain players
    We o'erraught° on the way. Of these we told him,
    And there did seem in him a kind of joy
    To hear of it. They are here about the court,
    And, as I think, they have already order   20
    This night to play before him.
POLONIUS.   'Tis most true,
    And he beseeched me to entreat Your Majesties
    To hear and see the matter.
KING. With all my heart, and it doth much content me

524 **presently** at once. 530 **tent** probe; **the quick** the tender part of a wound, the core;
blench quail, flinch. 535 **spirits** humors (of melancholy). 536 **Abuses** deludes.
537 **relative** cogent, pertinent. **3.1. Location: The castle.** 1 **drift of conference** directing of
conversation. 7 **forward** willing; **sounded** questioned. 12 **dispositon** inclination.
13 **Niggard** stingy; **question** conversation. 14 **assay** try to win. 17 **o'erraught** overtook.

To hear him so inclined.   25
Good gentlemen, give him a further edge°
And drive his purpose into these delights.
ROSENCRANTZ.   We shall, my lord.   *Exeunt* ROSENCRANTZ *and* GUILDENSTERN.
KING.   Sweet Gertrude, leave us too
For we have closely° sent for Hamlet hither,
That he, as 'twere by accident, may here   30
Affront° Ophelia.
Her father and myself, lawful espials,°
Will so bestow ourselves that seeing, unseen,
We may of their encounter frankly judge,
And gather by him, as he is behaved,   35
If't be th' affliction of his love or no
That thus he suffers for.
QUEEN.   I shall obey you.
And for your part, Ophelia, I do wish
That your good beauties be the happy cause
Of Hamlet's wildness. So shall I hope your virtues   40
Will bring him to his wonted° way again,
To both your honors.
OPHELIA.   Madam, I wish it may.   [*Exit* QUEEN.]
POLONIUS.   Ophelia, walk you here.—Gracious,° so please you,
We will bestow° ourselves. [*To* OPHELIA.] Read on this book,
                                                  [*giving her a book*]
That show of such an exercise° may color°   45
Your loneliness.° We are oft to blame in this—
'Tis too much proved°—that with devotion's visage
And pious action we do sugar o'er
The devil himself.
KING [*aside*].   O 'tis too true!   50
How smart a lash that speech doth give my conscience!
The harlot's cheek, beautied with plastering art,
Is not more ugly to° the thing° that helps it
Than is my deed to my most painted word.
O heavy burden!   55
POLONIUS.   I hear him coming. Let's withdraw, my lord.
                                    [*The* KING *and* POLONIUS *withdraw.*°]

   Enter HAMLET. [OPHELIA *pretends to read a book.*]

HAMLET.   To be, or not to be, that is the question:
Whether 'tis nobler in the mind to suffer
The slings° and arrows of outrageous fortune,
Or to take arms against a sea of troubles   60

---

26 **edge** incitement.   29 **closely** privately.   31 **Affront** confront, meet.   32 **espials** spies.
41 **wonted** accustomed.   43 **Gracious** Your Grace (i.e., the King).   44 **bestow** conceal.
45 **exercise** religious exercise. (The book she reads is one of devotion.);   **color** give a plausible
appearance to.   46 **loneliness** being alone.   47 **too much proved** too often shown to be true,
too often practiced.   53 **to** compared to;   **the thing** i.e., the cosmetic.   56 **s.d. withdraw** (The
King and Polonius may retire behind an arras. The stage directions specify that they "enter"
again near the end of the scene.)   59 **slings** missiles.

And by opposing end them. To die, to sleep—
No more—and by a sleep to say we end
The heartache and the thousand natural shocks
That flesh is heir to. 'Tis a consummation
Devoutly to be wished. To die, to sleep;   65
To sleep, perchance to dream. Ay, there's the rub,°
For in that sleep of death what dreams may come,
When we have shuffled° off this mortal coil,°
Must give us pause. There's the respect°
That makes calamity of so long life.°   70
For who would bear the whips and scorns of time,
Th' oppressor's wrong, the proud man's contumely,°
The pangs of disprized° love, the law's delay,
The insolence of office,° and the spurns°
That patient merit of th' unworthy takes,°   75
When he himself might his quietus° make
With a bare bodkin?° Who would fardels° bear,
To grunt and sweat under a weary life,
But that the dread of something after death,
The undiscovered country from whose bourn°   80
No traveler returns, puzzles the will,
And makes us rather bear those ills we have
Than fly to others that we know not of?
Thus conscience does make cowards of us all;
And thus the native hue° of resolution   85
Is sicklied o'er with the pale cast° of thought,
And enterprises of great pitch° and moment°
With this regard° their currents° turn awry
And lose the name of action.—Soft you° now,
The fair Ophelia. Nymph, in thy orisons°   90
Be all my sins remembered.
OPHELIA.   Good my lord,
How does your honor for this many a day?
HAMLET.   I humbly thank you; well, well, well.
OPHELIA.   My lord, I have remembrances of yours,
That I have longèd long to redeliver.   95
I pray you, now receive them.   [*She offers tokens.*]
HAMLET.   No, not I, I never gave you aught.
OPHELIA.   My honored lord, you know right well you did,
And with them words of so sweet breath composed
As made the things more rich. Their perfume lost,   100

---

66 **rub** (Literally, an obstacle in the game of bowls.)   68 **shuffled** sloughed, cast;   **coil** turmoil.
69 **respect** consideration.   70 **of . . . life** so long-lived, something we willingly endure for so
long (also suggesting that long life is itself a calamity).   72 **contumely** insolent abuse.
73 **disprized** unvalued.   74 **office** officialdom;   **spurns** insults.   75 **of . . . takes** receives from
unworthy persons.   76 **quietus** acquitance; here, death.   77 **a bare bodkin** a mere dagger,
unsheathed;   **fardels** burdens.   80 **bourn** frontier, boundary.   85 **native hue** natural color,
complexion.   86 **cast** tinge, shade of color.   87 **pitch** height (as of a falcon's flight.);
moment importance.   88 **regard** respect, consideration;   **currents** courses.   89 **Soft you** i.e.,
wait a minute, gently.   90 **orisons** prayers.

Take these again, for to the noble mind
Rich gifts wax poor when givers prove unkind.
There, my lord.   *[She gives tokens.]*

HAMLET.   Ha, ha! Are you honest?°
OPHELIA.   My lord?   105
HAMLET.   Are you fair?°
OPHELIA.   What means your lordship?
HAMLET.   That if you be honest and fair, your honesty° should admit no discourse to° your beauty.
OPHELIA.   Could beauty, my lord, have better commerce° than with honesty?   110
HAMLET.   Ay, truly, for the power of beauty will sooner transform honesty from what it is to a bawd than the force of honesty can translate beauty into his° likeness. This was sometime° a paradox,° but now the time° gives it proof. I did love you once.
OPHELIA.   Indeed, my lord, you made me believe so.   115
HAMLET.   You should not have believed me, for virtue cannot so inoculate° our old stock but we shall relish of it.° I loved you not.
OPHELIA.   I was the more deceived.
HAMLET.   Get thee to a nunnery.° Why wouldst thou be a breeder of sinners? I am myself indifferent honest,° but yet I could accuse me of such things that it   120 were better my mother had not borne me: I am very proud, revengeful, ambitious, with more offenses at my beck° than I have thoughts to put them in, imagination to give them shape, or time to act them in. What should such fellows as I do crawling between earth and heaven? We are arrant knaves all; believe none of us. Go thy ways to a nunnery. Where's your father?   125
OPHELIA.   At home, my lord.
HAMLET.   Let the doors be shut upon him, that he may play the fool nowhere but in's own house. Farewell.
OPHELIA.   O, help him, you sweet heavens!
HAMLET.   If thou dost marry, I'll give thee this plague for thy dowry: be thou as   130 chaste as ice, as pure as snow, thou shalt not escape calumny. Get thee to a nunnery, farewell. Or, if thou wilt needs marry, marry a fool, for wise men know well enough what monsters° you° make of them. To a nunnery, go, and quickly too. Farewell.
OPHELIA.   Heavenly powers, restore him!   135
HAMLET.   I have heard of your paintings too, well enough. God hath given you one face, and you make yourselves another. You jig,° you amble,° and you lisp, you nickname God's creatures,° and make your wantonness your ignorance.° Go to, I'll no more on 't;° it hath made me mad. I say

104 honest (1) truthful (2) chaste.   **106 fair** (1) beautiful (2) just, honorable.   **108 your honesty** your chastity.   **108–109 discourse to** familiar dealings with.   **110 commerce** dealings, intercourse.   **113 his** its;   **sometime** formerly;   **a paradox** a view opposite to commonly held opinion;   **the time** the present age.   **116 inoculate** graft, be engrafted to.   **117 but . . . it** that we do not still have about us a taste of the old stock, i.e., retain our sinfulness.
119 nunnery convent (with possibly an awareness that the word was also used derisively to denote a brothel).   **120 indifferent honest** reasonably virtuous.   **122 beck** command.
133 monsters (An illusion to the horns of a cuckold.);   **you** i.e., you women.   **137 jig** dance;   **amble** move coyly.   **138 you nickname . . . creatures** i.e., you give trendy names to things in place of their God-given names.   **139 make . . . ignorance** i.e., excuse your affectation on the grounds of pretended ignorance;   **on 't** of it.

we will have no more marriage. Those that are married already—all but   140
one—shall live. The rest shall keep as they are. To a nunnery, go.

Exit.

OPHELIA.   O, what a noble mind is here o'erthrown!
  The courtier's, soldier's, scholar's, eye, tongue, sword,
  Th' expectancy° and rose° of the fair state,
  The glass of fashion and the mold of form,°   145
  Th' observed of all observers,° quite, quite down!
  And I, of ladies most deject and wretched,
  That sucked the honey of his music° vows,
  Now see that noble and most sovereign reason
  Like sweet bells jangled out of tune and harsh,   150
  That unmatched form and feature of blown° youth
  Blasted° with ecstasy.° O, woe is me,
  T' have seen what I have seen, see what I see!

  Enter KING *and* POLONIUS.

KING.   Love? His affections° do not that way tend;
  Nor what he spake, though it lacked form a little,   155
  Was not like madness. There's something in his soul
  O'er which his melancholy sits on brood,°
  And I do doubt° the hatch and the disclose°
  Will be some danger; which for to prevent,
  I have in quick determination   160
  Thus set it down:° he shall with speed to England
  For the demand of° our neglected tribute.
  Haply the seas and countries different
  With variable objects° shall expel
  This something-settled matter in his heart,°   165
  Whereon his brains still° beating puts him thus
  From fashion of himself.° What think you on 't?
POLONIUS.   It shall do well. But yet do I believe
  The origin and commencement of his grief
  Sprung from neglected love.—How now, Ophelia?   170
  You need not tell us what Lord Hamlet said;
  We heard it all.—My lord, do as you please,
  But, if you hold it fit, after the play
  Let his queen-mother° all alone entreat him
  To show his grief. Let her be round° with him;   175
  And I'll be placed, so please you, in the ear
  Of all their conference. If she find him not,°

144 expectancy hope;   **rose** ornament.   **145 The glass ... form** the mirror of true fashioning
and the pattern of courtly behavior.   **146 Th' observed ... observers** i.e., the center of attention
and honor in the court.   **148 music** musical, sweetly uttered.   **151 blown** blooming.
152 Blasted withered;   **ecstasy** madness.   **154 affections** emotions, feelings.   **157 sits on**
brood sits like a bird on a nest, about to *hatch* mischief (line 169).   **158 doubt** fear;
disclose disclosure, hatching.   **161 set it down** resolved.   **162 For ... of** to demand.
164 variable objects various sights and surroundings to divert him.   **165 This something ...**
heart the strange matter settled in his heart.   **166 still** continually.   **167 From ... himself** out
of his natural manner.   **174 queen-mother** queen and mother.   **175 round** blunt.   **177 find**
him not fails to discover what is troubling him.

> To England send him, or confine him where
> Your wisdom best shall think.

KING.   It shall be so.
> Madness in great ones must not unwatched go.   *Exeunt.*   180

3.2   *Enter* HAMLET *and three of the* PLAYERS.

HAMLET.   Speak the speech, I pray you, as I pronounced it to you, trippingly on
the tongue. But if you mouth it, as many of our players° do, I had as
lief° the town crier spoke my lines. Nor do not saw the air too much
with your hand, thus, but use all gently; for in the very torrent, tempest,
and, as I may say, whirlwind of your passion, you must acquire and   5
beget a temperance that may give it smoothness. O, it offends me to the
soul to hear a robustious° periwig-pated° fellow tear a passion to tatters,
to very rags, to split the ears of the groundlings,° who for the most part
are capable of° nothing but inexplicable dumb shows° and noise. I
would have such a fellow whipped for o'erdoing Termagant.° It out-   10
Herods Herod.° Pray you, avoid it.

FIRST PLAYER.   I warrant your honor.

HAMLET.   Be not too tame neither, but let your own discretion be your tutor. Suit
the action to the word, the word to the action, with this special observance, that you o'erstep not the modesty° of nature. For anything so o'er-   15
done is from° the purpose of playing, whose end, both at the first and
now, was and is to hold as 't were the mirror up to nature, to show virtue
her feature, scorn° her own image, and the very age and body of the
time° his° form and pressure.° Now this overdone or come tardy off,°
though it makes the unskillful° laugh, cannot but make the judicious   20
grieve, the censure of the which one° must in your allowance° o'erweigh
a whole theater of others. O, there be players that I have seen play, and
heard others praise, and that highly, not to speak it profanely,° that, neither having th' accent of Christians° nor the gait of Christian, pagan, nor
man,° have so strutted and bellowed that I have thought some of nature's   25
journeymen° had made men and not made them well, they imitated humanity so abominably.°

3.2. Location: The castle.   **2 our players** players nowadays.   **2–3 I had as lief** I would just as
soon.   **7 robustious** violent, boisterous;   **periwig-pated** wearing a wig.
8 groundlings spectators who paid least and stood in the yard of the theater.   **9 capable of** able
to understand;   **dumb shows** mimed performances, often used before Shakespeare's time to
precede a play or each act.   **10 Termagant** a supposed deity of the Mohammedans, not found
in any English medieval play but elsewhere portrayed as violent and blustering.
11 Herod Herod of Jewry. (A character in *The Slaughter of the Innocents* and other cycle plays.
The part was played with great noise and fury.)   **15 modesty** restraint, moderation.
16 from contrary to.   **18 scorn** i.e., something foolish and deserving of scorn.   **18–19 the very
. . . time** i.e., the present state of affairs;   **his** its;   **pressure** stamp, impressed character;   **come
tardy off** inadequately done.   **20 the unskillful** those lacking in judgment.   **21 the censure . . .
one** the judgment of even one of whom;   **your allowance** your scale of values.   **23 not . . .
profanely** (Hamlet anticipates his idea in lines 25–27 that some men were not made by God at
all.)   **24 Christians** i.e., ordinary decent folk.   **24–25 nor man** i.e., nor any human being at all.
26 journeymen laborers who are not yet masters in their trade.   **27 abominably** (Shakespeare's
usual spelling, *abhominably,* suggests a literal though etymologically incorrect meaning,
"removed from human nature.")

FIRST PLAYER.   I hope we have reformed that indifferently° with us, sir.

HAMLET.   O, reform it altogether. And let those that play your clowns speak no
more than is set down for them; for there be of them° that will them-   30
selves laugh, to set on some quantity of barren° spectators to laugh too,
though in the meantime some necessary question of the play be then to
be considered. That's villainous, and shows a most pitiful ambition in the
fool that uses it. Go make you ready.   [*Exeunt* PLAYERS.]

    Enter POLONIUS, GUILDENSTERN *and* ROSENCRANTZ.

    How now, my lord, will the King hear this piece of work?   35

POLONIUS.   And the Queen too, and that presently.°

HAMLET.   Bid the players make haste.   [*Exit* POLONIUS.]
    Will you two help to hasten them?

ROSENCRANTZ.   Ay, my lord.   *Exeunt they two.*

HAMLET.   What ho, Horatio!

    Enter HORATIO.

HORATIO.   Here, sweet lord, at your service.   40

HAMLET.   Horatio, thou art e'en as just a man
As e'er my conversation coped withal.°

HORATIO.   O, my dear lord—

HAMLET.   Nay, do not think I flatter,
For what advancement may I hope from thee
That no revenue hast but thy good spirits   45
To feed and clothe thee? Why should the poor be flattered?
No, let the candied° tongue lick absurd pomp,
And crook the pregnant° hinges of the knee
Where thrift° may follow fawning. Dost thou hear?
Since my dear soul was mistress of her choice   50
And could of men distinguish her election,°
Sh' hath sealed thee° for herself, for thou hast been
As one, in suffering all, that suffers nothing,
A man that Fortune's buffets and rewards
Hast ta'en with equal thanks; and blest are those   55
Whose blood° and judgment are so well commeddled°
That they are not a pipe for Fortune's finger
To sound what stop° she please. Give me that man
That is not passion's slave, and I will wear him
In my heart's core, ay, in my heart of heart,   60
As I do thee.—Something too much of this.—
There is a play tonight before the King.
One scene of it comes near the circumstance
Which I have told thee of my father's death.
I prithee, when thou seest that act afoot,   65

---

28 indifferently tolerably.   **30 of them** some among them.   **31 barren** i.e., of wit.
36 presently at once.   **42 my . . . withal** my dealings encountered.   **47 candied** sugared,
flattering.   **48 pregnant** compliant.   **49 thrift** profit.   **51 could . . . election** could make
distinguishing choices among persons.   **52 sealed thee** (Literally, as one would seal a legal
document to mark possession.)   **56 blood** passion;   **commeddled** commingled.   **58 stop** hole
in a wind instrument for controlling the sound.

Even with the very comment of thy soul°
Observe my uncle. If his occulted° guilt
Do not itself unkennel° in one speech,
It is a damnéd° ghost that we have seen,
And my imaginations are as foul   70
As Vulcan's stithy.° Give him heedful note,
For I mine eyes will rivet to his face,
And after we will both our judgments join
In censure of his seeming.°

HORATIO.   Well, my lord.
If 'a steal aught° the whilst this play is playing   75
And scape detecting, I will pay the theft.

[*Flourish.*] *Enter trumpets and kettledrums,* KING, QUEEN, POLONIUS, OPHELIA,
[ROSENCRANTZ, GUILDENSTERN, *and other lords, with guards carrying torches*].

HAMLET.   They are coming to the play. I must be idle.°
Get you a place.   [*The* KING, QUEEN, *and courtiers sit.*]

KING.   How fares our cousin° Hamlet?

HAMLET.   Excellent, i' faith, of the chameleon's dish:° I eat the air, promise-   80
crammed. You cannot feed capons° so.

KING.   I have nothing with° this answer, Hamlet. These words are not mine.°

HAMLET.   No, nor mine now.° [*To* POLONIUS.] My lord, you played once i' th' university, you say?

POLONIUS.   That did I, my lord, and was accounted a good actor.   85

HAMLET.   What did you enact?

POLONIUS.   I did enact Julius Caesar. I was killed i' the Capitol; Brutus killed me.

HAMLET.   It was a brute° part° of him to kill so capital a calf° there.—Be the players ready?

ROSENCRANTZ.   Ay, my lord. They stay upon° your patience.   90

QUEEN.   Come hither, my dear Hamlet, sit by me.

HAMLET.   No, good Mother, here's metal° more attractive.

POLONIUS [*to the* KING].   O, ho, do you mark that?

HAMLET.   Lady, shall I lie in your lap?   [*Lying down at* OPHELIA'*s feet.*]

OPHELIA.   No, my lord.   95

HAMLET.   I mean, my head upon your lap?

OPHELIA.   Ay, my lord.

---

66 very . . . soul your most penetrating observation and consideration.   **67 occulted** hidden.
68 unkennel (As one would say of a fox driven from its lair.)   **69 damnéd** in league with Satan.
71 stithy smithy, place of stiths (anvils).   **74 censure of his seeming** judgment of his appearance
or behavior.   **75 If 'a steal aught** if he gets away with anything.   **77 idle** (1) unoccupied (2)
mad.   **79 cousin** i.e., close relative.   **80 chameleon's dish** (Chameleons were supposed to feed
on air. Hamlet deliberately misinterprets the King's *fares* as "feeds." By his phrase *eat the air* he
also plays on the idea of feeding himself with the promise of succession, of being the *heir*.)
81 capons roosters castrated and *crammed* with feed to make them succulent.   **82 have . . .
with** make nothing of, or gain nothing from;   **are not mine** do not respond to what I asked.
83 nor mine now (Once spoken, words are proverbially no longer the speaker's own—and
hence should be uttered warily.)   **88 brute** (The Latin meaning of *brutus,* "stupid," was often
used punningly with the name Brutus.);   **part** (1)deed (2) role;   **calf** fool.   **90 stay
upon** await.   **92 metal** substance that is *attractive,* i.e., magnetic, but with suggestion also of
mettle, "disposition."

HAMLET.   Do you think I meant country matters?°
OPHELIA.   I think nothing, my lord.
HAMLET.   That's a fair thought to lie between maids' legs.   100
OPHELIA.   What is, my lord?
HAMLET.   Nothing.°
OPHELIA.   You are merry, my lord.
HAMLET.   Who, I?
OPHELIA.   Ay, my lord.   105
HAMLET.   O God, your only jig maker.° What should a man do but be merry? For
look you how cheerfully my mother looks, and my father died within 's°
two hours.
OPHELIA.   Nay, 'tis twice two months, my lord.
HAMLET.   So long? Nay then, let the devil wear black, for I'll have a suit of sables.°   110
O heavens! Die two months ago, and not forgotten yet? Then there's
hope a great man's memory may outlive his life half a year. But, by 'r
Lady, 'a must build churches, then, or else shall 'a suffer not thinking
on,° with the hobbyhorse, whose epitaph is
"For O, for O, the hobbyhorse is forgot."°   115

The trumpets sound. Dumb show follows.

*Enter a King and a Queen [very lovingly]; the Queen embracing him, and
he her. [She kneels, and makes show of protestation unto him.] He takes her up,
and declines his head upon her neck. He lies him down upon a bank of flowers.
She, seeing him asleep, leaves him. Anon comes in another man, takes off his
crown, kisses it, pours poison in the sleeper's ears, and leaves him. The Queen
returns, finds the King dead, makes passionate action. The Poisoner with some
three or four come in again, seem to condole with her. The dead body is carried
away. The Poisoner woos the Queen with gifts; she seems harsh awhile, but in the
end accepts love.*

[*Exeunt* PLAYERS.]

OPHELIA.   What means this, my lord?
HAMLET.   Marry, this' miching mallico;° it means mischief.
OPHELIA.   Belike° this show imports the argument° of the play.

Enter PROLOGUE.

HAMLET.   We shall know by this fellow. The players cannot keep counsel;° they'll
tell all.   120
OPHELIA.   Will 'a tell us what this show meant?

98 country matters sexual intercourse (making a bawdy pun on the first syllable of *country*).
102 Nothing the figure zero or naught, suggesting the female sexual anatomy. (*Thing* not
infrequently has a bawdy connotation of male or female anatomy, and the reference here could
be male.)   **106 only jig maker** very best composer of jigs, i.e., pointless merriment. (Hamlet
replies sardonically to Ophelia's observation that he is merry by saying, "If you're looking for
someone who is really merry, you've come to the right person.")   **107 within 's** within this (i.e.,
these).   **110 suit of sables** garments trimmed with the fur of the sable and hence suited for a
wealthy person, not a mourner (but with a pun on *sable*, "black," ironically suggesting mourning
once again).   **113–114 suffer . . . on** undergo oblivion.   **115 For . . . forgot** (Verse of a song
occurring also in *Love's Labor's Lost*, 3.1.27–28. The hobbyhorse was a character made up to
resemble a horse and rider, appearing in the morris dance and such May-game sports. This song
laments the disappearance of such customs under pressure from the Puritans.)   **117 this'
miching mallico** this is sneaking mischief.   **118 Belike** probably;   **argument** plot.
119 counsel secret.

HAMLET.   Ay, or any show that you will show him. Be not you° ashamed to show,
    he'll not shame to tell you what it means.

OPHELIA.   You are naught,° you are naught. I'll mark the play.

PROLOGUE.   For us, and for our tragedy,   125
    Here stooping° to your clemency,
    We beg your hearing patiently.   *[Exit.]*

HAMLET.   Is this a prologue, or the posy of a ring?°

OPHELIA.   'Tis brief, my lord.

HAMLET.   As woman's love.   130

> *Enter [two* PLAYERS *as] King and Queen.*

PLAYER KING.   Full thirty times hath Phoebus' cart° gone round
    Neptune's salt wash° and Tellus'° orbèd ground,
    And thirty dozen moons with borrowed° sheen
    About the world have times twelve thirties been,
    Since love our hearts and Hymen° did our hands   135
    Unite commutual° in most sacred bands.°

PLAYER QUEEN.   So many journeys may the sun and moon
    Make us again count o'er ere love be done!
    But, woe is me, you are so sick of late,
    So far from cheer and from your former state,   140
    That I distrust° you. Yet, though I distrust,
    Discomfort° you, my lord, it nothing° must.
    For women's fear and love hold quantity;°
    In neither aught, or in extremity.°
    Now, what my love is, proof° hath made you know,   145
    And as my love is sized,° my fear is so.
    Where love is great, the littlest doubts are fear;
    Where little fears grow great, great love grows there.

PLAYER KING.   Faith, I must leave thee, love, and shortly too;
    My operant powers° their functions leave to do.°   150
    And thou shalt live in this fair world behind,°
    Honored, beloved; and haply one as kind
    For husband shalt thou—

PLAYER QUEEN.   O, confound the rest!
    Such love must needs be treason in my breast.
    In second husband let me be accurst!   155
    None° wed the second but who° killed the first.

HAMLET.   Wormwood,° wormwood.

---

122 Be not you provided you are not.   **124 naught** indecent. (Ophelia is reacting to Hamlet's
pointed remarks about not being ashamed to show all.)   **126 stooping** bowing.   **128 posy . . .
ring** brief motto in verse inscribed in a ring.   **131 Phoebus' cart** the sun-god's chariot, making
its yearly cycle.   **132 salt wash** the sea;   **Tellus** goddess of the earth, of the *orbèd ground.*
133 borrowed i.e., reflected.   **135 Hymen** god of matrimony.   **136 commutual** mutually;
bands bonds.   **141 distrust** am anxious about.   **142 Discomfort** distress;   **nothing** not at all.
143 hold quantity keep proportion with one another.   **144 In . . . extremity** i.e., women fear
and love either too little or too much, but the two, fear and love, are equal in either case.
145 proof experience.   **146 sized** in size.   **150 operant powers** vital functions;   **leave to
do** cease to perform.   **151 behind** after I have gone.   **156 None** i.e., let no woman;   **but
who** except the one who.   **157 Wormwood** i.e., how bitter. (Literally, a bitter-tasting plant.)

PLAYER QUEEN.   The instances° that second marriage move°
      Are base respects of thrift,° but none of love.
      A second time I kill my husband dead   160
      When second husband kisses me in bed.
PLAYER KING.   I do believe you think what now you speak,
      But what we do determine oft we break.
      Purpose is but the slave to memory,°
      Of violent birth, but poor validity,°   165
      Which° now, like fruit unripe, sticks on the tree,
      But fall unshaken when they mellow be.
      Most necessary 'tis that we forget
      To pay ourselves what to ourselves is debt.°
      What to ourselves in passion we propose,   170
      The passion ending, doth the purpose lose.
      The violence of either grief or joy
      Their own enactures° with themselves destroy.
      Where joy most revels, grief doth most lament;
      Grief joys, joy grieves, on slender accident.°   175
      This world is not for aye,° nor 'tis not strange
      That even our loves should with our fortunes change;
      For 'tis a question left us yet to prove,
      Whether love lead fortune, or else fortune love.
      The great man down,° you mark his favorite flies;   180
      The poor advanced makes friends of enemies.°
      And hitherto° doth love on fortune tend;°
      For who not needs° shall never lack a friend,
      And who in want° a hollow friend doth try°
      Directly seasons him° his enemy.   185
      But, orderly to end where I begun,
      Our wills and fates do so contrary run°
      That our devices still° are overthrown;
      Our thoughts are ours, their ends° none of our own.
      So think thou wilt no second husband wed,   190
      But die thy thoughts when thy first lord is dead.
PLAYER QUEEN.   Nor° earth to me give food, nor heaven light,
      Sport and repose lock from me day and night,°
      To desperation turn my trust and hope,

---

158 instances motives;   **move** motivate.   **159 base . . . thrift** ignoble considerations of material prosperity.   **164 Purpose . . . memory** our good intentions are subject to forgetfulness.
165 validity strength, durability.   **166 Which** i.e., purpose.   **168–169 Most . . . debt** it's inevitable that in time we forget the obligations we have imposed on ourselves.
173 enactures fulfillments.   **174–175 Where . . . accident** the capacity for extreme joy and grief go together, and often one extreme is instantly changed into its opposite on the slightest provocation.   **176 aye** ever.   **180 down** fallen in fortune.   **181 The poor . . . enemies** when one of humble station is promoted, you see his enemies suddenly becoming his friends.
182 hitherto up to this point in the argument, or, to this extent;   **tend** attend.   **183 who not needs** he who is not in need (of wealth).   **184 who in want** he who, being in need;   **try** test (his generosity).   **185 seasons him** ripens him into.   **187 Our . . . run** what we want and what we get go so contrarily.   **188 devices still** intentions continually.   **189 ends** results.
192 Nor let neither.   **193 Sport . . . night** may day deny me its pastimes and night its repose.

An anchor's cheer° in prison be my scope!°   195
Each opposite that blanks° the face of joy
Meet what I would have well and it destroy!°
Both here and hence° pursue me lasting strife
If, once a widow, ever I be wife!

HAMLET.   If she should break it now!   200

PLAYER KING.   'Tis deeply sworn. Sweet, leave me here awhile;
My spirits° grow dull, and fain I would beguile
The tedious day with sleep.

PLAYER QUEEN.   Sleep rock thy brain,
And never come mischance between us twain!

[*He sleeps.*] *Exit* [PLAYER QUEEN].

HAMLET.   Madam, how like you this play?   205

QUEEN.   The lady doth protest too much,° methinks.

HAMLET.   O, but she'll keep her word.

KING.   Have you heard the argument?° Is there no offense in 't?

HAMLET.   No, no, they do but jest,° poison in jest. No offense° i' the world.

KING.   What do you call the play?   210

HAMLET.   *The Mousetrap.* Marry, how? Tropically.° This play is the image of a murder done in Vienna. Gonzago is the Duke's° name, his wife, Baptista.
You shall see anon. 'Tis a knavish piece of work, but what of that? Your
Majesty, and we that have free° souls, it touches us not. Let the galled
jade° wince, our withers° are unwrung.°   215

Enter LUCIANUS.

This is one Lucianus, nephew to the King.

OPHELIA.   You are as good as a chorus,° my lord.

HAMLET.   I could interpret° between you and your love, if I could see the puppets
dallying.°

OPHELIA.   You are keen,° my lord, you are keen.   220

HAMLET.   It would cost you a groaning to take off mine edge.

OPHELIA.   Still better, and worse.°

---

195 anchor's cheer anchorite's or hermit's fare;   **my scope** the extent of my happiness.
196 blanks causes to blanch or grow pale.   **196–197 Each . . . destroy** may every adverse thing
that causes the face of joy to turn pale meet and destroy everything that I desire to see prosper.
198 hence in the life hereafter.   **202 spirits** vital spirits.   **206 doth . . . much** makes too many
promises and protestations.   **208 argument** plot.   **209 jest** make believe.   **208–209 offense . . .
offense** cause for objection . . . actual injury, crime.   **211 Tropically** figuratively. (The First
Quarto reading, *trapically,* suggests a pun on *trap* in *Mousetrap.*)   **212 Duke's** i.e., King's (A
slip that may be due to Shakespeare's possible source, the alleged murder of the Duke of
Urbino by Luigi Gonzaga in 1538.)   **214 free** guiltless.   **214–215 galled jade** horse whose hide
is rubbed by saddle or harness.   **215 withers** the part between the horse's shoulder blades;
unwrung not rubbed sore.   **217 chorus** (In many Elizabethan plays, the forthcoming action was
explained by an actor known as the "chorus"; at a puppet show, the actor who spoke the
dialogue was known as an "interpreter," as indicated by the lines following.)   **218 interpret** (1)
ventriloquize the dialogue, as in a puppet show (2) act as pander.   **218–219 puppets
dallying** (With suggestion of sexual play, continued in *keen,* "sexually aroused," *groaning,*
"moaning in pregnancy," and *edge,* "sexual desire" or "impetuosity.")   **220 keen** sharp, bitter.
222 Still . . . worse more keen, always *bettering* what other people say with witty wordplay, but
at the same time more offensive.

HAMLET.   So° you mis-take° your husbands. Begin, murder; leave thy damnable
faces and begin. Come, the croaking raven doth bellow for revenge.

LUCIANUS.   Thoughts black, hands apt, drugs fit, and time agreeing,   225
Confederate season,° else° no creature seeing,°
Thou mixture rank, of midnight weeds collected,
With Hecate's ban° thrice blasted, thrice infected,
Thy natural magic and dire property°
On wholesome life usurp immediately.   230

[He pours the poison into the sleeper's ear.]

HAMLET.   'A poisons him i' the garden for his estate.° His° name's Gonzago. The
story is extant, and written in very choice Italian. You shall see anon how
the murderer gets the love of Gonzago's wife.

[CLAUDIUS *rises.*]

OPHELIA.   The King rises.
HAMLET.   What, frighted with false fire?°   235
QUEEN.   How fares my lord?
POLONIUS.   Give o'er the play.
KING.   Give me some light. Away!
POLONIUS.   Lights, lights, lights!

Exeunt all but HAMLET *and* HORATIO.

HAMLET.

"Why,° let the strucken deer go weep,   240
The hart ungallèd° play.
For some must watch,° while some must sleep;
Thus runs the world away."°

Would not this,° sir, and a forest of feathers°—if the rest of my fortunes
turn Turk with° me—with two Provincial roses° on my razed° shoes, get   245
me a fellowship in a cry° of players?°

HORATIO.   Half a share.
HAMLET.   A whole one, I.

"For thou dost know, O Damon° dear,
This realm dismantled° was   250

---

223 So even thus (in marriage);   **mis-take** take falseheartedly and cheat on. (The marriage vows
say "for better, for worse.")   **226 Confederate season** the time and occasion conspiring (to assist
the murderer);   **else** otherwise;   **seeing** seeing me.   **228 Hecate's ban** the curse of Hecate, the
goddess of witchcraft.   **229 dire property** baleful quality.   **231 estate** i.e., the kingship;
His i.e., the King's.   **235 false fire** the blank discharge of a gun loaded with powder but no
shot.   **240–243 Why . . . away** (Probably from an old ballad, with allusion to the popular belief
that a wounded deer retires to weep and die; compare with *As You Like It,* 2.1.33–66.)
241 ungallèd unafflicted.   **242 watch** remain awake.   **243 Thus . . . away** thus the world goes.
244 this i.e., the play;   **feathers** (Allusion to the plumes that Elizabethan actors were fond of
wearing.)   **245 turn Turk with** turn renegade against, go back on;   **Provincial roses** rosettes of
ribbon, named for roses grown in a part of France;   **razed** with ornamental slashing.
246 cry pack (of hounds);   **fellowship . . . players** partnership in a theatrical company.
249 Damon the friend of Pythias, as Horatio is friend of Hamlet; or, a traditional pastoral name.
250 dismantled stripped, divested.

Of Jove himself, and now reigns here
A very, very—pajock."°

HORATIO.   You might have rhymed.

HAMLET.   O good Horatio, I'll take the ghost's word for a thousand pound.
Didst perceive?   255

HORATIO.   Very well, my lord.

HAMLET.   Upon the talk of the poisoning?

HORATIO.   I did very well note him.

Enter ROSENCRANTZ *and* GUILDENSTERN.

HAMLET.   Aha! Come, some music! Come, the recorders.°

"For if the King like not the comedy,   260
Why then, belike, he likes it not, perdy."°

Come, some music.

GUILDENSTERN.   Good my lord, vouchsafe me a word with you.

HAMLET.   Sir, a whole history.

GUILDENSTERN.   The King, sir—   265

HAMLET.   Ay, sir, what of him?

GUILDENSTERN.   Is in his retirement° marvelous distempered.°

HAMLET.   With drink, sir?

GUILDENSTERN.   No, my lord, with choler.°

HAMLET.   Your wisdom should show itself more richer to signify this to the doctor,   270
for for me to put him to his purgation° would perhaps plunge him into
more choler.

GUILDENSTERN.   Good my lord, put your discourse into some frame° and start° not
so wildly from my affair.

HAMLET.   I am tame, sir. Pronounce.   275

GUILDENSTERN.   The Queen, your mother, in most great affliction of spirit, hath
sent me to you.

HAMLET.   You are welcome.

GUILDENSTERN.   Nay, good my lord, this courtesy is not of the right breed.° If it
shall please you to make me a wholesome answer, I will do your   280
mother's commandment; if not, your pardon° and my return shall be the
end of my business.

HAMLET.   Sir, I cannot.

ROSENCRANTZ.   What, my lord?

250–252 This realm . . . pajock i.e., Jove, representing divine authority and justice, has
abandoned this realm to its own devices, leaving in his stead only a peacock or vain pretender
to virtue (though the rhyme-word expected in place of *pajock* or "peacock" suggests that the
realm is now ruled over by an "ass").   **259 recorders** wind instruments of the flute kind.
261 perdy (A corruption of the French *par dieu,* "by God.")   **267 retirement** withdrawal to his
chambers;   **distempered** out of humor. (But Hamlet deliberately plays on the wider application
to any illness of mind or body, as in line 298, especially to drunkenness.)   **269 choler** anger.
(But Hamlet takes the word in its more basic humoral sense of "bilious disorder.")
271 purgation (Hamlet hints at something going beyond medical treatment to bloodletting and
the extraction of confession.)   **273 frame** order;   **start** shy or jump away (like a horse; the
opposite of *tame* in line 275).   **279 breed** (1) kind (2) breeding, manners.
281 pardon permission to depart.

HAMLET.   Make you a wholesome answer; my wit's diseased. But, sir, such answer   285
          as I can make, you shall command, or rather, as you say, my mother.
          Therefore no more, but to the matter. My mother, you say—

ROSENCRANTZ.   Then thus she says: your behavior hath struck her into amazement
          and admiration.°

HAMLET.   O wonderful son, that can so stonish a mother! But is there no sequel at   290
          the heels of this mother's admiration? Impart.

ROSENCRANTZ.   She desires to speak with you in her closet° ere you go to bed.

HAMLET.   We shall obey, were she ten times our mother. Have you any further
          trade with us?

ROSENCRANTZ.   My lord, you once did love me.   295

HAMLET.   And do still, by these pickers and stealers.°

ROSENCRANTZ.   Good my lord, what is your cause of distemper? You do surely bar
          the door upon your own liberty° if you deny° your griefs to your friend.

HAMLET.   Sir, I lack advancement.

ROSENCRANTZ.   How can that be, when you have the voice of the King himself for   300
          your succession in Denmark?

HAMLET.   Ay, sir, but "While the grass grows"°—the proverb is something° musty.

          Enter the PLAYERS° WITH RECORDERS.

          O, the recorders. Let me see one. [*He takes a recorder.*]
          To withdraw° with you: why do you go about to recover the wind° of
          me, as if you would drive me into a toil?°   305

GUILDENSTERN.   O, my lord, if my duty be too bold, my love is too unmannerly.°

HAMLET.   I do not well understand that.° Will you play upon this pipe?

GUILDENSTERN.   My lord, I cannot.

HAMLET.   I pray you.

GUILDENSTERN.   Believe me, I cannot.   310

HAMLET.   I do beseech you.

GUILDENSTERN.   I know no touch of it, my lord.

HAMLET.   It is as easy as lying. Govern these ventages° with your fingers and
          thumb, give it breath with your mouth, and it will discourse most elo-
          quent music. Look you, these are the stops.   315

GUILDENSTERN.   But these cannot I command to any utterance of harmony. I have
          not the skill.

HAMLET.   Why, look you now, how unworthy a thing you make of me! You would
          play upon me, you would seem to know my stops, you would pluck out
          the heart of my mystery, you would sound° me from my lowest note to   320
          the top of my compass,° and there is much music, excellent voice, in this
          little organ,° yet cannot you make it speak. 'Sblood, do you think I am

---

289 admiration bewilderment.   **292 closet** private chamber.   **296 pickers and stealers** i.e.,
hands. (So called from the catechism, "to keep my hands from picking and stealing.")
298 liberty i.e., being freed from *distemper,* line 297, but perhaps with a veiled threat as well;
deny refuse to share.   **302 While . . . grows** (The rest of the proverb is "the silly horse starves";
Hamlet may not live long enough to succeed to the kingdom.);   **something** somewhat;   **s.d.
Players** actors.   **304 withdraw** speak privately;   **recover the wind** get to the windward side
(thus driving the game into the *toil,* or "net").   **305 toil** snare.   **306 if . . . unmannerly** if I am
using an unmannerly boldness, it is my love that occasions it.   **307 I . . . that** i.e., I don't
understand how genuine love can be unmannerly.   **313 ventages** finger-holes or *stops* (line 319)
of the recorder.   **320 sound** (1) fathom (2) produce sound in.   **321 compass** range (of voice).
322 organ musical instrument.

easier to be played on than a pipe? Call me what instrument you will,
though you can fret° me, you cannot play upon me.

Enter POLONIUS.

God bless you, sir!   325
POLONIUS.   My lord, the Queen would speak with you, and presently.°
HAMLET.   Do you see yonder cloud that's almost in shape of a camel?
POLONIUS.   By the Mass and 'tis, like a camel indeed.
HAMLET.   Methinks it is like a weasel.
POLONIUS.   It is backed like a weasel.   330
HAMLET.   Or like a whale.
POLONIUS.   Very like a whale.
HAMLET.   Then I will come to my mother by and by.° [*Aside.*] They fool me° to the
top of my bent.°—I will come by and by.
POLONIUS.   I will say so.   [*Exit.*]   335
HAMLET.   "By and by" is easily said. Leave me, friends.

[*Exeunt all but* HAMLET.]

'Tis now the very witching time° of night,
When churchyards yawn and hell itself breathes out
Contagion to this world. Now could I drink hot blood
And do such bitter business as the day   340
Would quake to look on. Soft, now to my mother.
O heart, lose not thy nature!° Let not ever
The soul of Nero° enter this firm bosom.
Let me be cruel, not unnatural;
I will speak daggers to her, but use none.   345
My tongue and soul in this be hypocrites:
How in my words soever° she be shent,°
To give them seals° never my soul consent!   *Exit.*

3.3   *Enter* KING, ROSENCRANTZ, *and* GUILDENSTERN.

KING.   I like him° not, nor stands it safe with us
To let his madness range. Therefore prepare you.
I your commission will forthwith dispatch,°
And he to England shall along with you.
The terms of our estate° may not endure   5
Hazard so near 's as doth hourly grow
Out of his brows.°
GUILDENSTERN.   We will ourselves provide.
Most holy and religious fear° it is

---

324 fret irritate (with a quibble on *fret,* meaning the piece of wood, gut, or metal that regulates
the fingering on an instrument).   **326 presently** at once.   **333 by and by** quite soon.   **fool
me** trifle with me, humor my fooling.   **334 top of my bent** limit of my ability or endurance.
(Literally, the extent to which a bow may be bent.)   **337 witching time** time when spells are
cast and evil is abroad.   **342 nature** natural feeling.   **343 Nero** murderer of his mother,
Agrippina.   **347 How . . . soever** however much by my words;   **shent** rebuked.   **348 give
them seals** i.e., confirm them with deeds.   **3.3 Location: The castle.**   **1 him** i.e., his behavior.
3 dispatch prepare, cause to be drawn up.   **5 terms of our estate** circumstances of my royal
position.   **7 Out of his brows** i.e., from his brain, in the form of plots and threats.   **8 religious
fear** sacred concern.

To keep those many many bodies safe
That live and feed upon Your Majesty.   10
ROSENCRANTZ.   The single and peculiar° life is bound
With all the strength and armor of the mind
To keep itself from noyance,° but much more
That spirit upon whose weal depends and rests
The lives of many. The cess° of majesty   15
Dies not alone, but like a gulf° doth draw
What's near it with it; or it is a massy° wheel
Fixed on the summit of the highest mount,
To whose huge spokes ten thousand lesser things
Are mortised° and adjoined, which, when it falls,°   20
Each small annexment, petty consequence,°
Attends° the boisterous ruin. Never alone
Did the King sigh, but with a general groan.
KING.   Arm° you, I pray you, to this speedy voyage,
For we will fetters put about this fear,   25
Which now goes too free-footed.
ROSENCRANTZ.   We will haste us.

Exeunt gentlemen [ROSENCRANTZ *and* GUILDENSTERN].

Enter POLONIUS.

POLONIUS.   My lord, he's going to his mother's closet.
Behind the arras° I'll convey myself
To hear the process.° I'll warrant she'll tax him home,°
And, as you said—and wisely was it said—   30
'Tis meet° that some more audience than a mother,
Since nature makes them partial, should o'erhear
The speech, of vantage.° Fare you well, my liege.
I'll call upon you ere you go to bed
And tell you what I know.
KING.   Thanks, dear my lord.   *Exit* [POLONIUS].   35
O, my offense is rank! It smells to heaven.
It hath the primal eldest curse° upon't,
A brother's murder. Pray can I not,
Though inclination be as sharp as will;°
My stronger guilt defeats my strong intent,   40
And like a man to double business bound°
I stand in pause where I shall first begin,

---

11 **single and peculiar** individual and private.   13 **noyance** harm.   15 **cess** decease, cessation.
16 **gulf** whirlpool.   17 **massy** massive.   20 **mortised** fastened (as with a fitted joint);   **when it
falls** i.e., when it descends, like the wheel of Fortune, bringing a king down with it.   21 **Each
. . . consequence** i.e., every hanger-on and unimportant person or thing connected with the King.
22 **Attends** participates in.   24 **Arm** prepare.   28 **arras** screen of tapestry placed around the
walls of household apartments. (On the Elizabethan stage, the arras was presumably over a door
or discovery space in the tiring-house facade.)   29 **process** proceedings;   **tax him
home** reprove him severely.   31 **meet** fitting.   33 **of vantage** from an advantageous place, or, in
addition.   37 **the primal eldest curse** the curse of Cain, the first murderer; he killed his brother
Abel.   39 **Though . . . will** though my desire is as strong as my determination.   41 **bound**
(1) destined (2) obliged. (The King wants to repent and still enjoy what he has gained.)

And both neglect. What if this cursèd hand
Were thicker than itself with brother's blood,
Is there not rain enough in the sweet heavens   45
To wash it white as snow? Whereto serves mercy
But to confront the visage of offense?°
And what's in prayer but this twofold force,
To be forestallèd° ere we come to fall,
Or pardoned being down? Then I'll look up.   50
My fault is past. But O, what form of prayer
Can serve my turn? "Forgive me my foul murder"?
That cannot be, since I am still possessed
Of those effects for which I did the murder:
My crown, mine own ambition, and my Queen.   55
May one be pardoned and retain th' offense?°
In the corrupted currents° of this world
Offense's gilded hand° may shove by° justice,
And oft 'tis seen the wicked prize° itself
Buys out the law. But 'tis not so above.   60
There° is no shuffling,° there the action lies°
In his° true nature, and we ourselves compelled,
Even to the teeth and forehead° of our faults,
To give in° evidence. What then? What rests?°
Try what repentance can. What can it not?   65
Yet what can it, when one cannot repent?
O wretched state, O bosom black as death,
limèd° soul that, struggling to be free,
Art more engaged!° Help, angels! Make assay.°
Bow, stubborn knees, and heart with strings of steel,   70
Be soft as sinews of the newborn babe!
All may be well.   *[He kneels.]*

    Enter HAMLET.

HAMLET. Now might I do it pat,° now 'a is a-praying;
And now I'll do 't. *[He draws his sword.]* And so 'a goes to heaven,
And so am I revenged. That would be scanned:°   75
A villain kills my father, and for that,
I, his sole son, do this same villain send
To heaven.
Why, this is hire and salary, not revenge.
'A took my father grossly, full of bread,°   80

46–47 Whereto . . . offense what function does mercy serve other than to meet sin face to face?
49 forestallèd prevented (from sinning).   **56 th' offense** the thing for which one offended.
57 currents courses.   **58 gilded hand** hand offering gold as a bribe;   **shove by** thrust aside.
59 wicked prize prize won by wickendness.   **61 There** i.e., in heaven;   **shuffling** escape by
trickery;   **the action lies** the accusation is made manifest. (A legal metaphor.)   **62 his** its.
63 to the teeth and forehead face to face, concealing nothing.   **64 give in** provide;
rests remains.   **68 limèd** caught as with birdlime, a sticky substance used to ensnare birds.
69 engaged entangled;   **assay** trial. (Said to himself.)   **73 pat** opportunely.   **75 would be
scanned** needs to be looked into, or, would be interpreted as follows.   **80 grossly, full of
bread** i.e., enjoying his worldly pleasures rather than fasting. (See Ezekiel 16:49.)

With all his crimes broad blown,° as flush° as May;
And how his audit° stands who knows save° heaven?
But in our circumstance and course of thought°
'Tis heavy with him. And am I then revenged,
To take him in the purging of his soul   85
When he is fit and seasoned° for his passage?
No!
Up, sword, and know thou a more horrid hent.°

                                 [He puts up his sword.]

When he is drunk asleep, or in his rage,°
Or in th' incestuous pleasure of his bed,   90
At game,° a-swearing, or about some act
That has no relish° of salvation in 't—
Then trip him, that his heels may kick at heaven,
And that his soul may be as damned and black
As hell, whereto it goes. My mother stays.°   95
This physic° but prolongs thy sickly days.   *Exit.*

KING.   My words fly up, my thoughts remain below.
      Words without thoughts never to heaven go.   *Exit.*

          3.4 *Enter* [QUEEN] GERTRUDE *and* POLONIUS.

POLONIUS. 'A will come straight. Look you lay home° to him.
      Tell him his pranks have been too broad° to bear with,
      And that Your Grace hath screened and stood between
      Much heat° and him. I'll shroud° me even here.
      Pray you, be round° with him.   5
HAMLET [*within*]. Mother, Mother, Mother!
QUEEN. I'll warrant you, fear me not.
      Withdraw, I hear him coming.   [POLONIUS *hides behind the arras.*]

     Enter HAMLET.

HAMLET. Now, Mother, what's the matter?
QUEEN. Hamlet, thou hast thy father° much offended.   10
HAMLET. Mother, you have my father much offended.
QUEEN. Come, come, you answer with an idle° tongue.
HAMLET. Go, go, you question with a wicked tongue.
QUEEN. Why, how now, Hamlet?
HAMLET.   What's the matter now?

---

81 crimes broad blown sins in full bloom; **flush** vigorous. **82 audit** account; **save** except for.
83 in . . . thought as we see it from our mortal perspective. **86 seasoned** matured, readied.
88 know . . . hent await to be grasped by me on a more horrid occasion; **hent** act of seizing.
89 drunk . . . rage dead drunk, or in a fit of sexual passions. **91 game** gambling.
92 relish trace, savor. **95 stays** awaits (me). **96 physic** purging (by prayer), or, Hamlet's
postponement of the killing. **3.4 Location: The Queen's private chamber.** **1 lay home** thrust
to the heart, reprove him soundly. **2 broad** unrestrained. **4 Much heat** i.e., the King's anger;
shroud conceal. (With ironic fitness to Polonius' imminent death. The word is only in the First
Quarto: the Second Quarto and the Folio read "silence.") **5 round** blunt. **10 thy father** i.e.,
your stepfather, Claudius. **12 idle** foolish.

QUEEN.	Have you forgot me?°
HAMLET.	No, by the rood,° not so: 15
	You are the Queen your husband's brother's wife,
	And—would it were not so!—you are my mother.
QUEEN.	Nay, then, I'll set those to you that can speak.°
HAMLET.	Come, come, and sit you down; you shall not budge.
	You go not till I set you up a glass 20
	Where you may see the inmost part of you.
QUEEN.	What wilt thou do? Thou wilt not murder me?
	Help, ho!
POLONIUS [*behind the arras*].	What ho! Help!
HAMLET [*drawing*].	How now? A rat? Dead for a ducat,° dead! 25

[*He thrusts his rapier through the arras.*]

POLONIUS [*behind the arras*].	O, I am slain! [*He falls and dies.*]
QUEEN.	O me, what hast thou done?
HAMLET.	Nay, I know not. Is it the King?
QUEEN.	O, what a rash and bloody deed is this!
HAMLET.	A bloody deed—almost as bad, good Mother,
	As kill a King, and marry with his brother. 30
QUEEN.	As kill a King!
HAMLET.	Ay, lady, it was my word.

[*He parts the arras and discovers* POLONIUS.]

Thou wretched, rash, intruding fool, farewell!
I took thee for thy better. Take thy fortune.
Thou find'st to be too busy° is some danger.—
Leave wringing of your hands. Peace, sit you down,   35
And let me wring your heart, for so I shall,
If it be made of penetrable stuff,
If damnèd custom° have not brazed° it so
That it be proof° and bulwark against sense.°

QUEEN.	What have I done, that thou dar'st wag thy tongue
	In noise so rude against me? 40
HAMLET.	Such an act
	That blurs the grace and blush of modesty,
	Calls virtue hypocrite, takes off the rose
	From the fair forehead of an innocent love
	And sets a blister° there, makes marriage vows 45
	As false as dicers' oaths. O, such a deed
	As from the body of contraction° plucks
	The very soul, and sweet religion makes°
	A rhapsody° of words. Heaven's face does glow
	O'er this solidity and compound mass 50

15 forgot me i.e., forgotten that I am your mother; **rood** cross of Christ. **18 speak** i.e., to someone so rude. **25 Dead for a ducat** i.e., I bet a ducat he's dead; or, a ducat is his life's fee. **34 busy** nosey. **38 damnèd custom** habitual wickedness; **brazed** brazened, hardened. **39 proof** armor; **sense** feeling. **45 sets a blister** i.e., brands as a harlot. **47 contraction** the marriage contract. **48 sweet religion makes** i.e., makes marriage vows. **49 rhapsody** senseless string.

With tristful visage, as against the doom,
Is thought-sick at the act.°

QUEEN.   Ay me, what act,
That roars so loud and thunders in the index?°

HAMLET [*showing her two likenesses*].   Look here upon this picture, and on this,
The counterfeit presentment° of two brothers.   55
See what a grace was seated on this brow:
Hyperion's° curls, the front° of Jove himself,
An eye like Mars° to threaten and command,
A station° like the herald Mercury°
New-lighted° on a heaven-kissing hill—   60
A combination and a form indeed
Where every god did seem to set his seal°
To give the world assurance of a man.
This was your husband. Look you now what follows:
Here is your husband, like a mildewed ear,°   65
Blasting° his wholesome brother. Have you eyes?
Could you on this fair mountain leave° to feed
And batten° on this moor?° Ha, have you eyes?
You cannot call it love, for at your age
The heyday° in the blood° is tame, it's humble,   70
And waits upon the judgment, and what judgment
Would step from this to this? Sense,° sure, you have,
Else could you not have motion, but sure that sense
Is apoplexed,° for madness would not err,°
Nor sense to ecstasy was ne'er so thralled,   75
But° it reserved some quantity of choice
To serve in such a difference.° What devil was 't
That thus hath cozened° you at hoodman-blind?°
Eyes without feeling, feeling without sight,
Ears without hands or eyes, smelling sans° all   80
Or but a sickly part of one true sense
Could not so mope.° O shame, where is thy blush?
Rebellious hell,

49–52 Heaven's . . . act heaven's face blushes at this solid world compounded of the various elements, with sorrowful face as though the day of doom were near, and is sick with horror at the deed (i.e., Gertrude's marriage).   **54 index** table of contents, prelude or preface.
55 counterfeit presentment portrayed representation.   **57 Hyperion's** the sun god's;   **front** brow.
58 Mars god of war.   **59 station** manner of standing;   **Mercury** winged messenger of the gods.
60 New-lighted newly alighted.   **62 set his seal** i.e., affix his approval.   **65 ear** i.e., of grain.
66 Blasting blighting.   **67 leave** cease.   **68 batten** gorge;   **moor** barren or marshy ground (suggesting also "dark-skinned").   **70 heyday** state of excitement;   **blood** passion.
72 Sense perception through the five senses (the functions of the middle sensible soul).
74 apoplexed paralyzed (Hamlet goes on to explain that, without such a paralysis of will, mere madness would not so err, nor would the five senses so enthrall themselves to *ecstasy* or lunacy; even such deranged states of mind would be able to make the obvious choice between Hamlet Senior and Claudius.);   **err** so err.   **76 But** but that.   **77 To . . . difference** to help in making a choice between two such men.   **78 cozened** cheated;   **hoodman-blind** blindman's buff. (In this game, says Hamlet, the devil must have pushed Claudius toward Gertrude while she was blind-folded.)   **80 sans** without.   **82 mope** be dazed, act aimlessly.

        If thou canst mutine° in a matron's bones,
        To flaming youth let virtue be as wax   85
        And melt in her own fire.° Proclaim no shame
        When the compulsive ardor gives the charge,
        Since frost itself as actively doth burn,
        And reason panders will.°

QUEEN.   O Hamlet, speak no more!   90
        Thou turn'st mine eyes into my very soul,
        And there I see such black and grainèd° spots
        As will not leave their tinct.°

HAMLET.   Nay, but to live
        In the rank sweat of an enseamèd° bed,
        Stewed° in corruption, honeying and making love   95
        Over the nasty sty!

QUEEN.   O, speak to me no more!
        These words like daggers enter in my ears.
        No more, sweet Hamlet!

HAMLET.   A murderer and a villain,
        A slave that is not twentieth part the tithe°   100
        Of your precedent lord,° a vice° of kings,
        A cutpurse of the empire and the rule,
        That from a shelf the precious diadem stole
        And put it in his pocket!

QUEEN.   No more!   105

     Enter GHOST [*in his nightgown*].

HAMLET.   A king of shreds and patches°—
        Save me, and hover o'er me with your wings,
        You heavenly guards! What would your gracious figure?

QUEEN.   Alas, he's mad!

HAMLET.   Do you not come your tardy son to chide,   110
        That, lapsed° in time and passion, lets go by
        Th' important° acting of your dread command?
        O, say!

GHOST.   Do not forget. This visitation
        Is but to whet thy almost blunted purpose.   115
        But look, amazement° on thy mother sits.
        O, step between her and her fighting soul!
        Conceit° in weakest bodies strongest works.
        Speak to her, Hamlet.

---

84 mutine incite mutiny.   **85–86 be as wax . . . fire** melt like a candle or stick of sealing wax held over the candle flame.   **86–89 Proclaim . . . will** call it no shameful business when the compelling ardor of youth delivers the attack, i.e., commits lechery, since the *frost* of advanced age burns with as active a fire of lust and reason perverts itself by fomenting lust rather than restraining it.   **92 grainèd** dyed in grain, indelible.   **93 leave their tinct** surrender their color.   **94 enseamèd** saturated in the grease and filth of passionate lovemaking.   **95 Stewed** soaked, bathed (with a suggestion of "stew," brothel).   **100 tithe** tenth part.   **101 precedent lord** former husband;   **vice** buffoon. (A reference to the Vice of the morality plays.)   **106 shreds and patches** i.e., motley, the traditional costume of the clown or fool.   **111 lapsed** delaying.
112 important importunate, urgent.   **116 amazement** distraction.   **118 Conceit** imagination.

HAMLET.   How is it with you, lady?

QUEEN.   Alas, how is 't with you,   120
          That you do bend your eye on vacancy,
          And with th' incorporal° air do hold discourse?
          Forth at your eyes your spirits wildly peep,
          And, as the sleeping soldiers in th' alarm,°
          Your bedded° hair, like life in excrements,°   125
          Start up and stand on end. O gentle son,
          Upon the heat and flame of thy distemper°
          Sprinkle cool patience. Whereon do you look?

HAMLET.   On him, on him! Look you how pale he glares!
          His form and cause conjoined,° preaching to stones,   130
          Would make them capable.°—Do not look upon me,
          Lest with this piteous action you convert
          My stern effects.° Then what I have to do
          Will want true color—tears perchance for blood.°

QUEEN.   To whom do you speak this?   135

HAMLET.   Do you see nothing there?

QUEEN.   Nothing at all, yet all that is I see.

HAMLET.   Nor did you nothing hear?

QUEEN.   No, nothing but ourselves.

HAMLET.   Why, look you there, look how it steals away!   140
          My father, in his habit° as° he lived!
          Look where he goes even now out at the portal!   *Exit* GHOST.

QUEEN.   This is the very° coinage of your brain.
          This bodiless creation ecstasy
          Is very cunning in.°   145

HAMLET.   Ecstasy?
          My pulse as yours doth temperately keep time,
          And makes as healthful music. It is not madness
          That I have uttered. Bring me to the test,
          And I the matter will reword,° which madness   150
          Would gambol° from. Mother, for love of grace,
          Lay not that flattering unction° to your soul
          That not your trespass but my madness speaks.
          It will but skin° and film the ulcerous place,
          Whiles rank corruption, mining° all within,   155
          Infects unseen. Confess yourself to heaven,
          Repent what's past, avoid what is to come,

---

122 incorporal immaterial.   **124 as . . . alarm** like soldiers called out of sleep by an alarum.
125 bedded laid flat;   **like life in excrements** i.e., as though hair, an outgrowth of the body, had
a life of its own. (Hair was thought to be lifeless because it lacks sensation, and so its standing
on end would be unnatural and ominous.)   **127 distemper** disorder.   **130 His . . .
conjoined** his appearance joined to his cause for speaking.   **131 capable** receptive.
132–133 convert . . . effects divert me from my stern duty.   **134 want . . . blood** lack
plausibility so that (with a play on the normal sense of *color*) I shall shed colorless tears instead
of blood.   **141 habit** clothes;   **as** as when.   **143 very** mere.   **144–145 This . . . in** madness is
skillful in creating this kind of hallucination.   **150 reword** repeat word for word.
151 gambol skip away.   **152 unction** ointment.   **154 skin** grow a skin for.
155 mining working under the surface.

And do not spread the compost° on the weeds
To make them ranker. Forgive me this my virtue;°
For in the fatness° of these pursy° times   160
Virtue itself of vice must pardon beg,
Yea, curb° and woo for leave° to do him good.

QUEEN.   O Hamlet, thou hast cleft my heart in twain.
HAMLET.   O, throw away the worser part of it,
And live the purer with the other half.   165
Good night. But go not to my uncle's bed;
Assume a virtue, if you have it not.
That monster, custom, who all sense doth eat,°
Of habits devil,° is angel yet in this,
That to the use of actions fair and good   170
He likewise gives a frock or livery°
That aptly° is put on. Refrain tonight,
And that shall lend a kind of easiness
To the next abstinence; the next more easy;
For use° almost can change the stamp of nature,°   175
And either° . . . the devil, or throw him out
With wondrous potency. Once more, good night;
And when you are desirous to be blest,
I'll blessing beg of you.° For this same lord,   [*pointing to* POLONIUS.]
I do repent; but heaven hath pleased it so   180
To punish me with this, and this with me,
That I must be their scourge and minister.°
I will bestow° him, and will answer° well
The death I gave him. So, again, good night.
I must be cruel only to be kind.   185
This° bad begins, and worse remains behind.°
One word more, good lady.

QUEEN.   What shall I do?
HAMLET.   Not this by no means that I bid you do:
Let the bloat° King tempt you again to bed,
Pinch wanton° on your cheek, call you his mouse,   190
And let him, for a pair of reechy° kisses,
Or paddling° in your neck with his damned fingers,

---

158 compost manure.   **159 this my virtue** my virtuous talk in reproving you.
160 fatness grossness;   **pursy** flabby, out of shape.   **162 curb** bow, bend the knee;
leave permission.   **168 who . . . eat** which consumes all proper or natural feeling, all sensibility.
169 Of habits devil devil-like in prompting evil habits.   **171 livery** an outer appearance, a
customary garb (and hence a predisposition easily assumed in time of stress).
172 aptly readily.   **175 use** habit;   **the stamp of nature** our inborn traits.   **176 And either** (A
defective line, usually emended by inserting the word *master* after *either*, following the Fourth
Quarto and early editors.)   **178–179 when . . . you** i.e., when you are ready to be penitent and
seek God's blessing, I will ask your blessing as a dutiful son should.   **182 their scourge and
minister** i.e., agent of heavenly retribution. (By *scourge*, Hamlet also suggests that he himself will
eventually suffer punishment in the process of fulfilling heaven's will.)   **183 bestow** stow,
dispose of;   **answer** account or pay for.   **186 This** i.e., the killing of Polonius;   **behind** to
come.   **189 bloat** bloated.   **190 Pinch wanton** i.e., leave his love pinches on your cheeks,
branding you as wanton.   **191 reechy** dirty, filthy.   **192 paddling** fingering amorously.

Make you to ravel all this matter out°
That I essentially am not in madness,
But mad in craft.° 'Twere good° you let him know,   195
For who that's but a Queen, fair, sober, wise,
Would from a paddock,° from a bat, a gib,°
Such dear concernings° hide? Who would do so?
No, in despite of sense and secrecy,°
Unpeg the basket° on the house's top,   200
Let the birds fly, and like the famous ape,°
To try conclusions,° in the basket creep
And break your own neck down.°

QUEEN.   Be thou assured, if words be made of breath,
And breath of life, I have no life to breathe   205
What thou hast said to me.

HAMLET.   I must to England. You know that?

QUEEN.   Alack,
I had forgot. 'Tis so concluded on.

HAMLET.   There's letters sealed, and my two schoolfellows,
Whom I will trust as I will adders fanged,   210
They bear the mandate; they must sweep my way
And marshal me to knavery.° Let it work.°
For 'tis the sport to have the enginer°
Hoist with° his own petard,° and 't shall go hard
But I will° delve one yard below their mines°   215
And blow them at the moon. O, 'tis most sweet
When in one line° two crafts° directly meet.
This man shall set me packing.°
I'll lug the guts into the neighbor room.
Mother, good night indeed. This counselor   220
Is now most still, most secret, and most grave,
Who was in life a foolish prating knave.—
Come, sir, to draw toward an end° with you.—
Good night, Mother.

                         Exeunt [*separately,* HAMLET *dragging in* POLONIUS].

---

193 ravel . . . out unravel, disclose.   **195 in craft** by cunning;   **good** (Said sarcastically; also the following eight lines.)   **197 paddock** toad;   **gib** tomcat.   **198 dear concernings** important affairs.   **199 sense and secrecy** secrecy that common sense requires.   **200 Unpeg the basket** open the cage, i.e., let out the secret.   **201 famous ape** (In a story now lost.)   **202 try conclusions** test the outcome (in which the ape apparently enters a cage from which birds have been released and then tries to fly out of the cage as they have done, falling to its death).   **203 down** in the fall; utterly.   **211–212 sweep . . . knavery** sweep a path before me and conduct me to some *knavery* or treachery prepared for me;   **work** proceed.   **213 enginer** maker of military contrivances.   **214 Hoist with** blown up by;   **petard** an explosive used to blow in a door or make a breach.   **214–215 't shall . . . will** unless luck is against me, I will;   **mines** tunnels used in warfare to undermine the enemy's emplacements; Hamlet will countermine by going under their mines.   **217 in one line** i.e., mines and countermines on a collision course, or the countermines directly below the mines;   **crafts** acts of guile, plots.   **218 set me packing** set me to making schemes, and set me to lugging (him), and, also, send me off in a hurry.   **223 draw . . . end** finish up (with a pun on *draw*, "pull").

4.1   *Enter* KING *and* QUEEN,° *with* ROSENCRANTZ *and* GUILDENSTERN.

KING.   There's matter° in these sighs, these profound heaves.°
    You must translate; 'tis fit we understand them.
    Where is your son?
QUEEN.   Bestow this place on us a little while.

                      [*Exeunt* ROSENCRANTZ *and* GUILDENSTERN.]
    Ah, mine own lord, what have I seen tonight!   5
KING.   What, Gertrude? How does Hamlet?
QUEEN.   Mad as the sea and wind when both contend
    Which is the mightier. In his lawless fit,
    Behind the arras hearing something stir,
    Whips out his rapier, cries, "A rat, a rat!"   10
    And in this brainish apprehension° kills
    The unseen good old man.
KING.   O heavy° deed!
    It had been so with us,° had we been there.
    His liberty is full of threats to all—
    To you yourself, to us, to everyone.   15
    Alas, how shall this bloody deed be answered?°
    It will be laid to us, whose providence°
    Should have kept short,° restrained, and out of haunt°
    This mad young man. But so much was our love,
    We would not understand what was most fit,   20
    But, like the owner of a foul disease,
    To keep it from divulging,° let it feed
    Even on the pith of life. Where is he gone?
QUEEN.   To draw apart the body he hath killed,
    O'er whom his very madness, like some ore°   25
    Among a mineral° of metals base,
    Shows itself pure: 'a weeps for what is done.
KING.   O Gertrude, come away!
    The sun no sooner shall the mountains touch
    But we will ship him hence, and this vile deed   30
    We must with all our majesty and skill
    Both countenance° and excuse.—Ho, Guildenstern!

Enter ROSENCRANTZ *and* GUILDENSTERN.

    Friends both, go join you with some further aid.
    Hamlet in madness hath Polonius slain,
    And from his mother's closet hath he dragged him.   35

4.1 Location: The castle.   s.d. Enter . . . Queen (Some editors argue that Gertrude never exits
in 3.4 and that the scene is continuous here, as suggested in the Folio, but the Second Quarto
marks an entrance for her and at line 35 Claudius speaks of Gertrude's *closet* as though it were
elsewhere. A short time has elapsed, during which the King has become aware of her highly
wrought emotional state.)   **1 matter** significance;   **heaves** heavy sighs.   **11 brainish
apprehension** headstrong conception.   **12 heavy** grievous.   **13 us** i.e., me. (The royal "we";
also in line 15.)   **16 answered** explained.   **17 providence** foresight.   **18 short** i.e., on a short
tether;   **out of haunt** secluded.   **22 divulging** becoming evident.   **25 ore** vein of gold.
26 mineral mine.   **32 countenance** put the best face on.

Go seek him out, speak fair, and bring the body
Into the chapel. I pray you, haste in this.
                             [*Exeunt* ROSENCRANTZ *and* GUILDENSTERN.]
Come, Gertrude, we'll call up our wisest friends
And let them know both what we mean to do
And what's untimely done°.......   40
Whose whisper o'er the world's diameter,°
As level° as the cannon to his blank,°
Transports his poisoned shot, may miss our name
And hit the woundless° air. O, come away!
My soul is full of discord and dismay.   *Exeunt.*   45

4.2 *Enter* HAMLET.

HAMLET.   Safely stowed.
ROSENCRANTZ, GUILDENSTERN [*within*].   Hamlet! Lord Hamlet!
HAMLET.   But soft, what noise? Who calls on Hamlet? O, here they come.

  Enter ROSENCRANTZ *and* GUILDENSTERN.

ROSENCRANTZ.   What have you done, my lord, with the dead body?
HAMLET.   Compounded it with dust, whereto 'tis kin.   5
ROSENCRANTZ.   Tell us where 'tis, that we may take it thence
    And bear it to the chapel.
HAMLET.   Do not believe it.
ROSENCRANTZ.   Believe what?
HAMLET.   That I can keep your counsel and not mine own.° Besides, to be demanded   10
    of° a sponge, what replication° should be made by the son of a king?
ROSENCRANTZ.   Take you me for a sponge, my lord?
HAMLET.   Ay, sir, that soaks up the King's countenance,° his rewards, his authori-
    ties.° But such officers do the King best service in the end. He keeps
    them, like an ape, an apple, in the corner of his jaw, first mouthed to be   15
    last swallowed. When he needs what you have gleaned, it is but squeez-
    ing you, and, sponge, you shall be dry again.
ROSENCRANTZ.   I understand you not, my lord.
HAMLET.   I am glad of it. A knavish speech sleeps in° a foolish ear.
ROSENCRANTZ.   My lord, you must tell us where the body is and go with us to the   20
    King.
HAMLET.   The body is with the King, but the King is not with the body.°
    The King is a thing—

---

40 And . . . done (A defective line; conjectures as to the missing words include *So, haply, slander* [Capell and others]; *For, haply, slander* [Theobald and others]; and *So envious slander* [Jenkins].)   **41 diameter** extent from side to side.   **42 As level** with as direct aim;   **his blank** its target at point-blank range.   **44 woundless** invulnerable.   **4.2. Location: The castle.**
10 That . . . own i.e., that I can follow your advice (by telling where the body is) and still keep my own secret.   **10–11 demanded of** questioned by;   **replication** reply.
13 countenance favor.   **13–14 authorities** delegated power, influence.   **19 sleeps in** has no meaning to.   **22 The . . . body** (Perhaps alludes to the legal commonplace of "the king's two bodies," which drew a distinction between the sacred office of kingship and the particular mortal who possessed it at any given time. Hence, although Claudius' body is necessarily a part of him, true kingship is not contained in it. Similarly, Claudius will have Polonius' body when it is found, but there is no kingship in this business either.)

GUILDENSTERN.   A thing, my lord?

HAMLET.   Of nothing.° Bring me to him. Hide fox, and all after!°   25

                                                                    Exeunt [*running*].

4.3   *Enter* KING, *and two or three.*

KING.   I have sent to seek him, and to find the body.
            How dangerous is it that this man goes loose!
            Yet must not we put the strong law on him.
            He's loved of° the distracted° multitude,
            Who like not in their judgment, but their eyes,°   5
            And where 'tis so, th' offender's scourge° is weighed,°
            But never the offense. To bear all smooth and even,°
            This sudden sending him away must seem
            Deliberate pause.° Diseases desperate grown
            By desperate appliance° are relieved,   10
            Or not at all.

Enter ROSENCRANTZ, GUILDENSTERN, *and all the rest.*

                                    How now, what hath befall'n?

ROSENCRANTZ.   Where the dead body is bestowed, my lord,
            We cannot get from him.

KING.   But where is he?

ROSENCRANTZ.   Without, my lord; guarded, to know your pleasure.

KING.   Bring him before us.

ROSENCRANTZ.   Ho! Bring in the lord.   15

They enter [*with* HAMLET].

KING.   Now, Hamlet, where's Polonius?

HAMLET.   At supper.

KING.   At supper? Where?

HAMLET.   Not where he eats, but where 'a is eaten. A certain convocation of politic
            worms° are e'en° at him. Your worm° is your only emperor for diet.° We   20
            fat all creatures else to fat us, and we fat ourselves for maggots. Your fat
            king and your lean beggar is but variable service°—two dishes, but to
            one table. That's the end.

KING.   Alas, alas!

HAMLET.   A man may fish with the worm that hath eat° of a king, and eat of the   25
            fish that hath fed of that worm.

KING.   What dost thou mean by this?

---

25 Of nothing (1) of no account (2) lacking the essence of kingship, as in lines 24–25 and note;
Hide . . . after (An old signal cry in the game of hide-and-seek, suggesting that Hamlet now runs
away from them.)   **4.3 Location: The castle.   4 of** by;   **distracted** fickle, unstable.   **5 Who
. . . eyes** who choose not by judgment but by appearance.   **6 scourge** punishment. (Literally,
blow with a whip.);   **weighed** sympathetically considered.   **7 To . . . even** to manage the
business in an unprovocative way.   **9 Deliberate pause** carefully considered action.
10 appliance remedies.   **19–20 politic worms** crafty worms (suited to a master spy like
Polonius);   **e'en** even now;   **Your worm** your average worm. (Compare *your fat king and your
lean beggar* in lines 21–22.);   **diet** food, eating (with a punning reference to the Diet of Worms,
a famous *convocation* held in 1521).   **22 variable service** different courses of a single meal.
25 eat eaten. (Pronounced *et.*)

HAMLET.   Nothing but to show you how a king may go a progress° through the
          guts of a beggar.

KING.   Where is Polonius?   30

HAMLET.   In heaven. Send thither to see. If your messenger find him not there,
          seek him i' th' other place yourself. But if indeed you find him not
          within this month, you shall nose him as you go up the stairs into the
          lobby.

KING [*to some attendants*].   Go seek him there.   35

HAMLET.   'A will stay till you come.   [*Exeunt attendants.*]

KING.   Hamlet, this deed, for thine especial safety—
        Which we do tender,° as we dearly° grieve
        For that which thou hast done—must send thee hence
        With fiery quickness. Therefore prepare thyself.   40
        The bark° is ready, and the wind at help,
        Th' associates tend,° and everything is bent°
        For England.

HAMLET.   For England!

KING.   Ay, Hamlet.   45

HAMLET.   Good.

KING.   So is it, if thou knew'st our purposes.

HAMLET.   I see a cherub° that sees them. But come, for England!
          Farewell, dear mother.

KING.   Thy loving father, Hamlet.   50

HAMLET.   My mother. Father and mother is man and wife, man and wife is one
          flesh, and so, my mother. Come, for England!   *Exit.*

KING.   Follow him at foot;° tempt him with speed aboard.
        Delay it not. I'll have him hence tonight.
        Away! For everything is sealed and done   55
        That else leans on° th' affair. Pray you, make haste.
                                                       [*Exeunt all but the* KING.]
        And, England,° if my love thou hold'st at aught°—
        As my great power thereof may give thee sense,°
        Since yet thy cicatrice° looks raw and red
        After the Danish sword, and thy free awe°   60
        Pays homage to us—thou mayst not coldly set°
        Our sovereign process,° which imports at full,°
        By letters congruing° to that effect,
        The present° death of Hamlet. Do it, England,
        For like the hectic° in my blood he rages,   65
        And thou must cure me. Till I know 'tis done,
        Howe'er my haps,° my joys were ne'er begun.   *Exit.*

---

28 progress royal journey of state.   **38 tender** regard, hold dear;   **dearly** intensely.
41 bark sailing vessel.   **42 tend** wait;   **bent** in readiness.   **48 cherub** (Cherubim are angels of
knowledge. Hamlet hints that both he and heaven are onto Claudius' tricks.)   **53 at foot** close
behind, at heel.   **56 leans on** bears upon, is related to.   **57 England** i.e., King of England;   **at
aught** at any value.   **58 As . . . sense** for so my great power may give you a just appreciation of
the importance of valuing my love.   **59 cicatrice** scar.   **60 free awe** voluntary show of respect.
61 coldly set regard with indifference.   **62 process** command;   **imports at full** conveys specific
directions for.   **63 congruing** agreeing.   **64 present** immediate.   **65 hectic** persistent fever.
67 haps fortunes.

4.4   *Enter* FORTINBRAS *with his army over the stage.*

FORTINBRAS.   Go, Captain, from me greet the Danish king.
　　　　Tell him that by his license° Fortinbras
　　　　Craves the conveyance of° a promised march
　　　　Over his kingdom. You know the rendezvous.
　　　　If that His Majesty would aught with us,　　　　　　　　　　　5
　　　　We shall express our duty° in his eye;°
　　　　And let him know so.
CAPTAIN.   I will do 't, my lord.
FORTINBRAS.   Go softly° on.　　　　　　　　　　　 [*Exeunt all but the* CAPTAIN.]

　　　　Enter HAMLET, ROSENCRANTZ, [GUILDENSTERN,] *etc.*

HAMLET.   Good sir, whose powers° are these?　　　　　　　　　　10
CAPTAIN.   They are of Norway, sir.
HAMLET.   How purposed, sir, I pray you?
CAPTAIN.   Against some part of Poland.
HAMLET.   Who commands them, sir?
CAPTAIN.   The nephew to old Norway, Fortinbras.　　　　　　　　15
HAMLET.   Goes it against the main° of Poland, sir,
　　　　Or for some frontier?
CAPTAIN.   Truly to speak, and with no addition,°
　　　　We go to gain a little patch of ground
　　　　That hath in it no profit but the name.　　　　　　　　　　20
　　　　To pay° five ducats, five, I would not farm it;°
　　　　Nor will it yield to Norway or the Pole
　　　　A ranker° rate, should it be sold in fee.°
HAMLET.   Why, then the Polack never will defend it.
CAPTAIN.   Yes, it is already garrisoned.　　　　　　　　　　　　25
HAMLET.   Two thousand souls and twenty thousand ducats
　　　　Will not debate the question of this straw.°
　　　　This is th' impostume° of much wealth and peace,
　　　　That inward breaks, and shows no cause without
　　　　Why the man dies. I humbly thank you, sir.　　　　　　　　30
CAPTAIN.   God b' wi' you, sir.　　　　　　　　　　　　　 [*Exit.*]
ROSENCRANTZ.　　Will 't please you go, my lord?
HAMLET.   I'll be with you straight. Go a little before.

　　　　　　　　　　　　　　　　　 [*Exeunt all except* HAMLET.]

　　　　How all occasions do inform against° me
　　　　And spur my dull revenge! What is a man,　　　　　　　　35
　　　　If his chief good and market of° his time
　　　　Be but to sleep and feed? A beast, no more.
　　　　Sure he that made us with such large discourse,°
　　　　Looking before and after,° gave us not

4.4 **Location: The coast of Denmark.**   **2 license** permission.   **3 the conveyance of** escort
during.   **6 duty** respect; **eye** presence.   **9 softly** slowly, circumspectly.   **10 powers** forces.
16 main main part.   **18 addition** exaggeration.   **21 To pay** i.e., for a yearly rental of; **farm
it** take a lease on it.   **23 ranker** higher; **in fee** fee simple, outright.   **27 debate . . . straw** settle
this trifling matter.   **28 impostume** abscess.   **33 inform against** denounce, betray; take shape
against.   **35 market of** profit of, compensation for.   **37 discourse** power of reasoning.
38 Looking before and after able to review past events and anticipate the future.

That capability and godlike reason   40
To fust° in us unused. Now, whether it be
Bestial oblivion,° or some craven° scruple
Of thinking too precisely° on th' event°—
A thought which, quartered, hath but one part wisdom
And ever three parts coward—I do not know   45
Why yet I live to say "This thing's to do,"
Sith° I have cause, and will, and strength, and means
To do 't. Examples gross° as earth exhort me:
Witness this army of such mass and charge,°
Led by a delicate and tender° prince,   50
Whose spirit with divine ambition puffed
Makes mouths° at the invisible event,°
Exposing what is mortal and unsure
To all that fortune, death, and danger dare,°
Even for an eggshell. Rightly to be great   55
Is not to stir without great argument,
But greatly to find quarrel in a straw
When honor's at the stake.° How stand I, then,
That have a father killed, a mother stained,
Excitements of° my reason and my blood,   60
And let all sleep, while to my shame I see
The imminent death of twenty thousand men
That for a fantasy° and trick° of fame
Go to their graves like beds, fight for a plot°
Whereon the numbers cannot try the cause,°   65
Which is not tomb enough and continent°
To hide the slain? O, from this time forth
My thoughts be bloody or be nothing worth!   *Exit.*

    4.5 *Enter* HORATIO, [QUEEN] GERTRUDE, *and a* GENTLEMAN.

QUEEN.   I will not speak with her.
GENTLEMAN.   She is importunate,
    Indeed distract.° Her mood will needs be pitied.
QUEEN.   What would she have?
GENTLEMAN.   She speaks much of her father, says she hears
    There's tricks° i' the world, and hems,° and beats her heart,°   5
    Spurns enviously at straws,° speaks things in doubt°

---

41 fust grow moldy.   **42 oblivion** forgetfulness;   **craven** cowardly.   **43 precisely** scrupulously;
event outcome.   **47 Sith** since.   **48 gross** obvious.   **49 charge** expense.   **50 delicate and
tender** of fine and youthful qualities.   **52 Makes mouths** makes scornful faces;   **invisible event**
unforeseeable outcome.   **54 dare** could do (to him).   **55–58 Rightly . . . stake** true greatness
does not normally consist of rushing into action over some trivial provocation; however, when
one's honor is involved, even a trifling insult requires that one respond greatly (?);   **at the
stake** (A metaphor from gambling or bear-baiting.)   **60 Excitements of** promptings by.
63 fantasy fanciful caprice, illusion;   **trick** trifle, deceit.   **64 plot** plot of ground.   **65 Whereon
. . . cause** on which there is insufficient room for the soldiers needed to engage in a military
contest.   **66 continent** receptacle; container.   **4.5. Location: The castle.**   **2 distract** distracted.
5 tricks deceptions;   **hems** makes "hmm" sounds;   **heart** i.e., breast.   **6 Spurns . . . straws** kicks
spitefully, takes offense at trifles;   **in doubt** obscurely.

That carry but half sense. Her speech is nothing,
Yet the unshapèd use° of it doth move
The hearers to collection;° they yawn° at it,
And botch° the words up fit to their own thoughts,   10
Which,° as her winks and nods and gestures yield° them,
Indeed would make one think there might be thought,°
Though nothing sure, yet much unhappily.°

HORATIO.   'Twere good she were spoken with, for she may strew
Dangerous conjectures in ill-breeding° minds.   15

QUEEN.   Let her come in.   [*Exit* GENTLEMAN.]

[*Aside.*] To my sick soul, as sin's true nature is,
Each toy° seems prologue to some great amiss.°
So full of artless jealousy is guilt,
It spills itself in fearing to be spilt.°   20

Enter OPHELIA° [*distracted*].

OPHELIA.   Where is the beauteous majesty of Denmark?
QUEEN.   How now, Ophelia?
OPHELIA   [*she sings*].

"How should I your true love know
    From another one?   25
By his cockle hat° and staff,
    And his sandal shoon."°

QUEEN.   Alas, sweet lady, what imports this song?
OPHELIA.   Say you? Nay, pray you, mark.

"He is dead and gone, lady,   [*Song.*]   30
    He is dead and gone;
At his head a grass-green turf,
    At his heels a stone."

O, ho!

QUEEN.   Nay, but Ophelia—   35
OPHELIA.   Pray you, mark.   [*Sings.*]

"White his shroud as the mountain snow"—

Enter KING.

QUEEN.   Alas, look here, my lord.
OPHELIA.

"Larded° with sweet flowers;   [*Song.*]   40
Which bewept to the ground did not go
    With true-love showers."°

9 **unshapèd use** incoherent manner.   9 **collection** inference, a guess at some sort of meaning;
yawn gape, wonder; grasp. (The Folio reading, *aim,* is possible.)   10 **botch** patch.
11 **Which** which words;   **yield** deliver, represent.   12 **thought** intended.
13 **unhappily** unpleasantly near the truth, shrewdly.   15 **ill-breeding** prone to suspect the worst
and to make mischief.   18 **toy** trifle;   **amiss** calamity.   19–20 **So . . . split** guilt is so full of
suspicion that it unskilfully betrays itself in fearing betrayal.   **s.d. Enter Ophelia** (In the First
Quarto, Ophelia enters, "playing on a lute, and her hair down, singing.")   26 **cockle hat** hat
with cockle-shell stuck in it as a sign that the wearer had been a pilgrim to the shrine of Saint
James of Compostela in Spain.   27 **shoon** shoes.   40 **Larded** decorated.   42 **showers** i.e.,
tears.

KING.   How do you, pretty lady?

OPHELIA.   Well, God 'ild° you! They say the owl° was a baker's daughter.
Lord, we know what we are, but know not what we may be. God be at   45
your table!

KING.   Conceit° upon her father.

OPHELIA.   Pray let's have no words of this; but when they ask you what it means,
say you this:

> "Tomorrow is Saint Valentine's day,   [*Song.*]   50
>   All in the morning betime,°
> And I a maid at your window,
>   To be your Valentine.
> Then up he rose, and donned his clothes,
>   And dupped° the chamber door,   55
> Let in the maid, that out a maid
>   Never departed more."

KING.   Pretty Ophelia—

OPHELIA.   Indeed, la, without an oath, I'll make an end on 't: [*Sings.*]

> "By Gis° and by Saint Charity,   60
>   Alack, and fie for shame!
> Young men will do 't, if they come to 't;
>   By Cock,° they are to blame.
> Quoth she, 'Before you tumbled me,
>   You promised me to wed.'"   65

He answers:

> "'So would I ha' done, by yonder sun,
> An° thou hadst not come to my bed.'"

KING.   How long hath she been thus?

OPHELIA.   I hope all will be well. We must be patient, but I cannot choose but   70
weep to think they would lay him i' the cold ground. My brother shall
know of it. And so I thank you for your good counsel. Come, my
coach! Good night, ladies, good night, sweet ladies, good night, good
night.   [*Exit.*]

KING [*to* HORATIO].   Follow her close. Give her good watch, I pray you.   75

                          [*Exit* HORATIO.]

> O, this is the poison of deep grief; it springs
> All from her father's death—and now behold!
> O Gertrude, Gertrude,
> When sorrows come, they come not single spies,°
> But in battalions. First, her father slain;   80
> Next, your son gone, and he most violent author

---

44 God 'ild God yield or reward;   **owl** (Refers to a legend about a baker's daughter who was
turned into an owl for being ungenerous when Jesus begged a loaf of bread.)
47 Conceit brooding.   **51 betime** early.   **55 dupped** did up, opened.   **60 Gis** Jesus.
63 Cock (A perversion of "God" in oaths; here also with a quibble on the slang word for penis.)
68 An if.   **79 spies** scouts sent in advance of the main force.

Of his own just remove;° the people muddied,°
Thick and unwholesome in their thoughts and whispers
For good Polonius' death—and we have done but greenly,°
In hugger-mugger° to inter him; poor Ophelia   85
Divided from herself and her fair judgment,
Without the which we are pictures or mere beasts;
Last, and as much containing° as all these,
Her brother is in secret come from France,
Feeds on this wonder, keeps himself in clouds,°   90
And wants° not buzzers° to infect his ear
With pestilent speeches of his father's death,
Wherein necessity,° of matter beggared,°
Will nothing stick our person to arraign
In ear and ear.° O my dear Gertrude, this,   95
Like to a murdering piece,° in many places
Gives me superfluous death.°   *A noise within.*

QUEEN.   Alack, what noise is this?
KING.   Attend!°
Where is my Switzers?° Let them guard the door.   100

Enter a MESSENGER.

What is the matter?
MESSENGER.   Save yourself, my lord!
The ocean, overpeering of his list,°
Eats not the flats° with more impetuous° haste
Than young Laertes, in a riotous head,°
O'erbears your officers. The rabble call him lord,   105
And, as° the world were now but to begin,
Antiquity forgot, custom not known,
The ratifiers and props of every word,°
They cry, "Choose we! Laertes shall be king!"
Caps,° hands, and tongues applaud it to the clouds,   110
"Laertes shall be king, Laertes king!"
QUEEN.   How cheerfully on the false trail they cry!   *A noise within.*
O, this is counter,° you false Danish dogs!

Enter LAERTES *with others.*

82 remove removal;   muddied stirred up, confused.   84 greenly in an inexperienced way,
foolishly.   85 hugger-mugger secret haste.   88 as much containing as full of serious matter.
90 Feeds . . . clouds feeds his resentment or shocked grievance, holds himself inscrutable and
aloof amid all this rumor.   91 wants lacks;   buzzers gossipers, informers.   93 necessity i.e., the
need to invent some plausible explanation;   of matter beggared unprovided with facts.
94–95 Will . . . ear will not hesitate to accuse my (royal) person in everybody's ears.
96 murdering piece cannon loaded so as to scatter its shot.   97 Gives . . . death kills me over
and over.   99 Attend i.e., guard me.   100 Switzers Swiss guards, mercenaries.
102 overpeering of his list overflowing its shore, boundary.   103 flats i.e., flatlands near shore;
impetuous violent. (Perhaps also with the meaning of *impiteous* [*impitious,* Q2], "pitiless.")
104 head insurrection.   106 as as if.   108 The ratifiers . . . word i.e., *antiquity* (or tradition)
and *custom* ought to confirm (*ratify*) and underprop our every word or promise.
110 Caps (The caps are thrown in the air.)   113 counter (A hunting term, meaning to follow
the trail in a direction opposite to that which the game has taken.)

KING.   The doors are broke.

LAERTES.   Where is this King?—Sirs, stand you all without.   115

ALL.   No, let's come in.

LAERTES.   I pray you, give me leave.

ALL.   We will, we will.

LAERTES.   I thank you. Keep the door. [*Exeunt followers.*] O thou vile king,
    Give me my father!   120

QUEEN [*restraining him*].   Calmly, good Laertes.

LAERTES.   That drop of blood that's calm proclaims me bastard,
    Cries cuckold to my father, brands the harlot
    Even here, between° the chaste unsmirchèd brow
    Of my true mother.   125

KING.   What is the cause, Laertes,
    That thy rebellion looks so giantlike?
    Let him go, Gertrude. Do not fear our° person.
    There's such divinity doth hedge° a king
    That treason can but peep to what it would,°   130
    Acts little of his will.° Tell me, Laertes,
    Why thou art thus incensed. Let him go, Gertrude.
    Speak, man.

LAERTES.   Where is my father?

KING.   Dead.

QUEEN.   But not by him.

KING.   Let him demand his fill.   135

LAERTES.   How came he dead? I'll not be juggled with.°
    To hell, allegiance! Vows, to the blackest devil!
    Conscience and grace, to the profoundest pit!
    I dare damnation. To this point I stand,°
    That both the worlds I give to negligence,°   140
    Let come what comes, only I'll be revenged
    Most throughly° for my father.

KING.   Who shall stay you?

LAERTES.   My will, not all the world's.°
    And for° my means, I'll husband them so well   145
    They shall go far with little.

KING.   Good Laertes,
    If you desire to know the certainty
    Of your dear father, is 't writ in your revenge
    That, swoopstake,° you will draw both friend and foe,   150
    Winner and loser?

LAERTES.   None but his enemies.

KING.   Will you know them, then?

---

124 **between** in the middle of.   128 **fear our** fear for my.   129 **hedge** protect, as with a
surrounding barrier.   130 **can . . . would** can only peep furtively, as through a barrier, at what it
would intend.   131 **Acts . . . will** (but) performs little of what it intends.   136 **juggled
with** cheated, deceived.   139 **To . . . stand** I am resolved in this.   140 **both . . . negligence** i.e.
both this world and the next are of no consequence to me.   142 **throughly** thoroughly.
144 **My will . . . world's** I'll stop (*stay*) when my will is accomplished, not for anyone else's.
145 **for** as for.   150 **swoopstake** i.e., indiscriminately. (Literally, taking all stakes on the
gambling table at once. *Draw* is also a gambling term, meaning "taken from.")

LAERTES.   To his good friends thus wide I'll ope my arms,
And like the kind life-rendering pelican°   155
Repast° them with my blood.
KING.   Why, now you speak
Like a good child and a true gentleman.
That I am guiltless of your father's death,
And am most sensibly° in grief for it,   160
It shall as level° to your judgment 'pear
As day does to your eye.   *A noise within.*
LAERTES.   How now, what noise is that?

    Enter OPHELIA.

KING.   Let her come in.
LAERTES.   O heat, dry up my brains! Tears seven times salt
Burn out the sense and virtue° of mine eye!   165
By heaven, thy madness shall be paid with weight°
Till our scale turn the beam.° O rose of May!
Dear maid, kind sister, sweet Ophelia!
O heavens, is 't possible a young maid's wits
Should be as mortal as an old man's life?   170
Nature is fine in° love, and where 'tis fine
It sends some precious instance° of itself
After the thing it loves.°
OPHELIA.   [*Song.*]

    "They bore him barefaced on the bier,   175
      Hey non nonny, nonny, hey nonny,
    And in his grave rained many a tear—"

    Fare you well, my dove!
LAERTES.   Hadst thou thy wits and didst persuade° revenge,
It could not move thus.   180
OPHELIA.   You must sing "A-down a-down," and you "call him a-down-a."°
O, how the wheel° becomes it! It is the false steward° that stole his mas-
ter's daughter.
LAERTES.   This nothing's more than matter.°
OPHELIA.   There's rosemary,° that's for remembrance; pray you, love, remember.   185
And there is pansies;° that's for thoughts.
LAERTES.   A document° in madness, thoughts and remembrance fitted.

---

155 pelican (Refers to the belief that the female pelican fed its young with its own blood.)
156 Repast feed.   **160 sensibly** feelingly.   **161 level** plain.   **165 virtue** faculty, power.
166 paid with weight repaid, avenged equally or more.   **167 beam** crossbar of a balance.
171 fine in refined by.   **172 instance** token.   **173 After . . . loves** i.e., into the grave, along
with Polonius.   **179 persuade** argue cogently for.   **181 You . . . a-down-a** (Ophelia assigns the
singing of refrains, like her own "Hey non nonny," to others present.)   **182 wheel** spinning
wheel as accompaniment to the song, or refrain;   **false steward** (The story is unknown.)
184 This . . . matter this seeming nonsense is more eloquent than sane utterance.
185 rosemary (Used as a symbol of remembrance both at weddings and at funerals.)
186 pansies (Emblems of love and courtship; perhaps from French *pensées,* "thoughts.")
187 document instruction, lesson.

OPHELIA.   There's fennel° for you, and columbines.° There's rue° for you, and
here's some for me; we may call it herb of grace o' Sundays. You must
wear your rue with a difference.° There's a daisy.° I would give you   190
some violets,° but they withered all when my father died. They say 'a
made a good end—
[*Sings.*] "For bonny sweet Robin is all my joy."

LAERTES.   Thought° and affliction, passion,° hell itself,
She turns to favor° and to prettiness.   195

OPHELIA.   [*Song.*]

"And will 'a not come again?
And will 'a not come again?
    No, no, he is dead.
    Go to thy deathbed,   200
He never will come again.

"His beard was as white as snow,
All flaxen was his poll.°
    He is gone, he is gone,
    And we cast away moan.   205
God ha' mercy on his soul!"

And of all Christian souls, I pray God. God b' wi' you.
                                            [*Exit, followed by* GERTRUDE.]

LAERTES.   Do you see this, O God?

KING.   Laertes, I must commune with your grief,   210
Or you deny me right. Go but apart,
Make choice of whom° your wisest friends you will,
And they shall hear and judge twixt you and me.
If by direct or by collateral hand°
They find us touched,° we will our kingdom give,   215
Our crown, our life, and all that we call ours
To you in satisfaction; but if not,
Be you content to lend your patience to us,
And we shall jointly labor with your soul
To give it due content.

LAERTES.   Let this be so.   220
His means of death, his obscure funeral—
No trophy,° sword, nor hatchment° o'er his bones,
No noble rite, nor formal ostentation°—

188 **fennel** (Emblem of flattery.);   **columbines** (Emblems of unchastity or ingratitude.);
rue (Emblem of repentance—a signification that is evident in its popular name, *herb of grace.*)
190 **with a difference** (A device used in heraldry to distinguish one family from another on the
coat of arms, here suggesting that Ophelia and the others have different causes of sorrow and
repentance; perhaps with a play on *rue* in the sense of "ruth," "pity.");   **daisy** (Emblem of
dissembling, faithlessness.)   191 **violets** (Emblems of faithfulness.)   194 **Thought** melancholy;
passion suffering.   195 **favor** grace, beauty.   203 **poll** head.   212 **whom** whichever of.
214 **collateral hand** indirect agency.   215 **us touched** me implicated.   222 **trophy** memorial;
hatchment tablet displaying the armorial bearings of a deceased person.
223 **ostentation** ceremony.

Cry to be heard, as 'twere from heaven to earth,
That° I must call 't in question.°

KING.   So you shall,   225
And where th' offense is, let the great ax fall.
I pray you, go with me.   *Exeunt.*

4.6   *Enter* HORATIO *and others.*

HORATIO.   What are they that would speak with me?
GENTLEMAN.   Seafaring men, sir. They say they have letters for you.
HORATIO.   Let them come in.   [*Exit* GENTLEMAN.]
    I do not know from what part of the world
    I should be greeted, if not from Lord Hamlet.   5

Enter Sailors.

FIRST SAILOR.   God bless you, sir.
HORATIO.   Let him bless thee too.
FIRST SAILOR.   'A shall, sir, an 't° please him. There's a letter for you, sir—it came
    from th' ambassador° that was bound for England—if your name be
    Horatio, as I am let to know it is.   [*He gives a letter.*]   10
HORATIO [*reads*].   "Horatio, when thou shalt have overlooked° this, give these fel-
    lows some means° to the King; they have letters for him. Ere we were
    two days old at sea, a pirate of very warlike appointment° gave us chase.
    Finding ourselves too slow of sail, we put on a compelled valor, and in
    the grapple I boarded them. On the instant they got clear of our ship, so   15
    I alone became their prisoner. They have dealt with me like thieves of
    mercy,° but they knew what they did: I am to do a good turn for them.
    Let the King have the letters I have sent, and repair° thou to me with as
    much speed as thou wouldest fly death. I have words to speak in thine
    ear will make thee dumb, yet are they much too light for the bore° of the   20
    matter. These good fellows will bring thee where I am. Rosencrantz and
    Guildenstern hold their course for England. Of them I have much to tell
    thee. Farewell.
                    He that thou knowest thine, Hamlet."
    Come, I will give you way° for these your letters,   25
    And do 't the speedier that you may direct me
    To him from whom you brought them.   *Exeunt.*

4.7   *Enter* KING *and* LAERTES.

KING.   Now must your conscience my acquittance seal,°
    And you must put me in your heart for friend,
    Sith° you have heard, and with a knowing ear,
    That he which hath your noble father slain
    Pursued my life.

---

225 **That** so that;   **call 't in question** demand an explanation.   **4.6. Location: The castle.**
8 **an 't** if it.   9 **th' ambassador** (Evidently Hamlet. The sailor is being circumspect.)
11 **overlooked** looked over.   12 **means** means of access.   13 **appointment** equipage.
16–17 **thieves of mercy** merciful thieves.   18 **repair** come.   20 **bore** caliber, i.e., importance.
25 **way** means of access.   **4.7 Location: The castle.**   1 **my acquittance seal** confirm or
acknowledge my innocence.   3 **Sith** since.

LAERTES.   It well appears. But tell me   5
         Why you proceeded not against these feats°
         So crimeful and so capital° in nature,
         As by your safety, greatness, wisdom, all things else,
         You mainly° were stirred up.
KING.   O, for two special reasons,   10
         Which may to you perhaps seem much unsinewed,°
         But yet to me they're strong. The Queen his mother
         Lives almost by his looks, and for myself—
         My virtue or my plague, be it either which—
         She is so conjunctive° to my life and soul   15
         That, as the star moves not but in his° sphere,°
         I could not but by her. The other motive
         Why to a public count° I might not go
         Is the great love the general gender° bear him,
         Who, dipping all his faults in their affection,   20
         Work° like the spring° that turneth wood to stone,
         Convert his gyves° to graces, so that my arrows,
         Too slightly timbered° for so loud° a wind,
         Would have reverted° to my bow again
         But not where I had aimed them.   25
LAERTES.   And so have I a noble father lost,
         A sister driven into desperate terms,°
         Whose worth, if praises may go back° again,
         Stood challenger on mount° of all the age
         For her perfections. But my revenge will come.   30
KING.   Break not your sleeps for that. You must not think
         That we are made of stuff so flat and dull
         That we can let our beard be shook with danger
         And think it pastime. You shortly shall hear more.
         I loved your father, and we love ourself;   35
         And that, I hope, will teach you to imagine—

         Enter a MESSENGER *with letters.*

         How now? What news?
MESSENGER.   Letters, my lord, from Hamlet:
         This to Your Majesty, this to the Queen.   [*He gives letters.*]
KING.   From Hamlet? Who brought them?   40
MESSENGER.   Sailors, my lord, they say. I saw them not.
         They were given me by Claudio. He received them
         Of him that brought them.

---

6 feats acts.   **7 capital** punishable by death.   **9 mainly** greatly.   **11 unsinewed** weak.
15 conjunctive closely united. (An astronomical metaphor.)   **16 his** its;   **sphere** one of the
hollow spheres in which, according to Ptolematic astronomy, the planets were supposed to
move.   **18 count** account, reckoning, indictment.   **19 general gender** common people.
21 Work operate, act;   **spring** i.e., a spring with such a concentration of lime that it coats a
piece of wood with limestone, in effect gilding and petrifying it.   **22 gyves** fetters (which, gilded
by the people's praise, would look like badges of honor).   **23 slightly timbered** light;
loud (suggesting public outcry on Hamlet's behalf).   **24 reverted** returned.   **27 terms** state,
condition.   **28 go back** i.e., recall what she was.   **29 on mount** set up on high.

KING.   Laertes, you shall hear them.—
          Leave us.   [*Exit* MESSENGER.]   45
          [*He reads.*] "High and mighty, you shall know I am set naked° on your
          kingdom. Tomorrow shall I beg leave to see your kingly eyes, when I
          shall, first asking your pardon,° thereunto recount the occasion of my
          sudden and more strange return.   Hamlet."
          What should this mean? Are all the rest come back?   50
          Or is it some abuse,° and no such thing?°

LAERTES.   Know you the hand?

KING.   'Tis Hamlet's character.° "Naked!"
          And in a postscript here he says "alone."
          Can you devise° me?   55

LAERTES.   I am lost in it, my lord. But let him come.
          It warms the very sickness in my heart
          That I shall live and tell him to his teeth,
          "Thus didst thou."°

KING.   If it be so, Laertes—
          As how should it be so? How otherwise?°—   60
          Will you be ruled by me?

LAERTES.   .   Ay, my lord,
          So° you will not o'errule me to a peace.

KING.   To thine own peace. If he be now returned,
          As checking at° his voyage, and that° he means
          No more to undertake it, I will work him   65
          To an exploit, now ripe in my device,°
          Under the which he shall not choose but fall;
          And for his death no wind of blame shall breathe,
          But even his mother shall uncharge the practice°
          And call it accident.

LAERTES.   My lord, I will be ruled,   70
          The rather if you could devise it so
          That I might be the organ.°

KING.   It falls right.
          You have been talked of since your travel much,
          And that in Hamlet's hearing, for a quality   75
          Wherein they say you shine. Your sum of parts°
          Did not together pluck such envy from him
          As did that one, and that, in my regard,
          Of the unworthiest siege.°

LAERTES.   What part is that, my lord?   80

KING.   A very ribbon in the cap of youth,

46 naked destitute, unarmed, without following.   **48 pardon** permission.   **51 abuse** deceit;   **no
such thing** not what it appears.   **53 character** handwriting.   **55 devise** explain to.   **59 Thus
didst thou** i.e., here's for what you did to my father.   **60 As . . . otherwise** how can this
(Hamlet's return) be true? Yet how otherwise than true (since we have the evidence of his
letter)?   **62 So** provided that.   **64 checking at** i.e., turning aside from (like a falcon leaving the
quarry to fly at a chance bird);   **that** if.   **66 device** devising, invention.   **69 uncharge the
practice** acquit the stratagem of being a plot.   **72 organ** agent, instrument.   **76 Your . . .
parts** i.e., all your other virtues.   **79 unworthiest siege** least important rank.

Yet needful too, for youth no less becomes°
The light and careless livery that it wears
Than settled age his sables° and his weeds°
Importing health and graveness.° Two months since   85
Here was a gentleman of Normandy.
I have seen myself, and served against, the French,
And they can well° on horseback, but this gallant
Had witchcraft in 't; he grew unto his seat,
And to such wondrous doing brought his horse   90
As had he been incorpsed and demi-natured°
With the brave beast. So far he topped° my thought
That I in forgery° of shapes and tricks
Come short of what he did.

LAERTES.   A Norman was 't?

KING.   A Norman.   95

LAERTES.   Upon my life, Lamord.

KING.   The very same.

LAERTES.   I know him well. He is the brooch° indeed
And gem of all the nation.

KING.   He made confession° of you,   100
And gave you such a masterly report
For art and exercise in your defense,°
And for your rapier most especial,
That he cried out 'twould be a sight indeed
If one could match you. Th' escrimers° of their nation,   105
He swore, had neither motion, guard, nor eye
If you opposed them. Sir, this report of his
Did Hamlet so envenom with his envy
That he could nothing do but wish and beg
Your sudden° coming o'er, to play° with you.   110
Now, out of this—

LAERTES.   What out of this, my lord?

KING.   Laertes, was your father dear to you?
Or are you like the painting of a sorrow,
A face without a heart?

LAERTES.   Why ask you this?

KING.   Not that I think you did not love your father,   115
But that I know love is begun by time,°
And that I see, in passages of proof,°
Time qualifies° the spark and fire of it.
There lives within the very flame of love

---

82 no less becomes is no less suited by.   **84 his sables** its rich robes furred with sable;
weeds garments.   **85 Importing . . . graveness** signifying a concern for health and dignified
prosperity; also, giving an impression of comfortable prosperity.   **88 can well** are skilled.
91 As . . . demi-natured as if he had been of one body and nearly of one nature (like the
centaur).   **92 topped** surpassed.   **93 forgery** imagining.   **98 brooch** ornament.
100 confession testimonial, admission of superiority.   **102 For . . . defense** with respect to your
skill and practice with your weapon.   **105 escrimers** fencers.   **110 sudden** immediate;
play fence.   **116 begun by time** i.e., created by the right circumstance and hence subject to
change.   **117 passages of proof** actual instances that prove it.   **118 qualifies** weakens,
moderates.

A kind of wick or snuff° that will abate it,   120
And nothing is at a like goodness still,°
For goodness, growing to a pleurisy,°
Dies in his own too much.° That° we would do,
We should do when we would; for this "would" changes
And hath abatements° and delays as many   125
As there are tongues, are hands, are accidents,°
And then this "should" is like a spendthrift sigh,°
That hurts by easing.° But, to the quick o' th' ulcer:°
Hamlet comes back. What would you undertake
To show yourself in deed your father's son   130
More than in words?

LAERTES.   To cut his throat i' the church.

KING.   No place, indeed, should murder sanctuarize;°
Revenge should have no bounds. But good Laertes,
Will you do this,° keep close within your chamber.
Hamlet returned shall know you are come home.   135
We'll put on those shall° praise your excellence
And set a double varnish on the fame
The Frenchman gave you, bring you in fine° together,
And wager on your heads. He, being remiss,°
Most generous,° and free from all contriving,   140
Will not peruse the foils, so that with ease,
Or with a little shuffling, you may choose
A sword unbated,° and in a pass of practice°
Requite him for your father.

LAERTES.   I will do 't,
And for that purpose I'll anoint my sword.   145
I bought an unction° of a mountebank°
So mortal that, but dip a knife in it,
Where it draws blood no cataplasm° so rare,
Collected from all simples° that have virtue°
Under the moon,° can save the thing from death   150
That is but scratched withal. I'll touch my point
With this contagion, that if I gall° him slightly,
It may be death.

---

120 snuff the charred part of a candlewick.   **121 nothing . . . still** nothing remains at a constant level of perfection.   **122 pleurisy** excess, plethora. (Literally, a chest inflammation.)   **123 in . . . much** of its own excess;   **That** that which.   **125 abatements** diminutions.   **126 As . . . accidents** as there are tongues to dissuade, hands to prevent, and chance events to intervene.   **127 spendthrift sigh** (An allusion to the belief that sighs draw blood from the heart.)   **128 hurts by easing** i.e., costs the heart blood and wastes precious opportunity even while it affords emotional relief;   **quick o' th' ulcer** i.e., heart of the matter.   **132 sanctuarize** protect from punishment. (Alludes to the right of sanctuary with which certain religious places were invested.)   **134 Will you do this** if you wish to do this.   **136 put on those shall** arrange for some to.   **138 in fine** finally.   **139 remiss** negligently unsuspicious.   **140 generous** noble-minded.   **143 unbated** not blunted, having no button;   **pass of practice** treacherous thrust.   **146 unction** ointment;   **mountebank** quack doctor.   **148 cataplasm** plaster or poultice.   **149 simples** herbs;   **virtue** potency.   **150 Under the moon** i.e., anywhere (with reference perhaps to the belief that herbs gathered at night had a special power).   **152 gall** graze, wound.

KING.   Let's further think of this,
      Weigh what convenience both of time and means   155
      May fit us to our shape.° If this should fail,
      And that our drift look through our bad performance,°
      'Twere better not assayed. Therefore this project
      Should have a back or second, that might hold
      If this did blast in proof.° Soft, let me see.   160
      We'll make a solemn wager on your cunnings°—
      I ha 't!
      When in your motion you are hot and dry—
      As° make your bouts more violent to that end—
      And that he calls for drink, I'll have prepared him   165
      A chalice for the nonce,° whereon but sipping,
      If he by chance escape your venomed stuck,°
      Our purpose may hold there. [*A cry within.*] But stay, what noise?

    Enter QUEEN.

QUEEN.   One woe doth tread upon another's heel,
      So fast they follow. Your sister's drowned, Laertes.   170
LAERTES.   Drowned! O, where?
QUEEN.   There is a willow grows askant° the brook,
      That shows his hoar leaves° in the glassy stream;
      Therewith fantastic garlands did she make
      Of crowflowers, nettles, daisies, and long purples,°   175
      That liberal° shepherds give a grosser name,°
      But our cold° maids do dead men's fingers call them.
      There on the pendent° boughs her crownet° weeds
      Clamb'ring to hang, an envious sliver° broke,
      When down her weedy° trophies and herself   180
      Fell in the weeping brook. Her clothes spread wide,
      And mermaidlike awhile they bore her up,
      Which time she chanted snatches of old lauds,°
      As one incapable of° her own distress,
      Or like a creature native and endued°   185
      Unto that element. But long it could not be
      Till that her garments, heavy with their drink,
      Pulled the poor wretch from her melodious lay
      To muddy death.
LAERTES.   Alas, then she is drowned?
QUEEN.   Drowned, drowned.   190

---

156 shape part we propose to act.   **157 drift . . . performance** intention should be made visible by our bungling.   **160 blast in proof** burst in the test (like a cannon).   **161 cunnings** respective skills.   **164 As** i.e., and you should.   **166 nonce** occasion.   **167 stuck** thrust. (From *stoccado,* a fencing term.)   **172 askant** aslant.   **173 hoar leaves** white or gray undersides of the leaves. **175 long purples** early purple orchids.   **176 liberal** free-spoken;   **a grosser name** (The testicle-resembling tubers of the orchid, which also in some cases resemble *dead men's fingers,* have earned various slang names like "dogstones" and "cullions.")   **177 cold** chaste.
178 pendent over-hanging;   **crownet** made into a chaplet or coronet.   **179 envious sliver** malicious branch.   **180 weedy** i.e., of plants.   **183 lauds** hymns.   **184 incapable of** lacking capacity to apprehend.   **185 endued** adapted by nature.

LAERTES.   Too much of water hast thou, poor Ophelia,
And therefore I forbid my tears. But yet
It is our trick;° nature her custom holds,
Let shame say what it will. [*He weeps.*] When these are gone,
The woman will be out.° Adieu, my lord.   195
I have a speech of fire that fain would blaze,
But that this folly douts° it.   *Exit.*
KING.   Let's follow, Gertrude.
How much I had to do to calm his rage!
Now fear I this will give it start again;   200
Therefore let's follow.   *Exeunt.*

5.1   *Enter two* CLOWNS° [*with spades and mattocks*].

FIRST CLOWN.   Is she to be buried in Christian burial, when she willfully seeks her
own salvation?°
SECOND CLOWN.   I tell thee she is; therefore make her grave straight.° The
crowner° hath sat on her,° and finds it° Christian burial.
FIRST CLOWN.   How can that be, unless she drowned herself in her own defense?   5
SECOND CLOWN.   Why, 'tis found so.°
FIRST CLOWN.   It must be *se offendendo,*° it cannot be else. For here lies the point:
if I drown myself wittingly, it argues an act, and an act hath three
branches—it is to act, to do, and to perform. Argal,° she drowned herself
wittingly.   10
SECOND CLOWN.   Nay, but hear you, goodman° delver—
FIRST CLOWN.   Give me leave. Here lies the water; good. Here stands the man;
good. If the man go to this water and drown himself, it is, will he, nill he,°
he goes, mark you that. But if the water come to him and drown him, he
drowns not himself. Argal, he that is not guilty of his own death shortens   15
not his own life.
SECOND CLOWN.   But is this law?
FIRST CLOWN.   Ay, marry, is 't—crowner's quest° law.
SECOND CLOWN.   Will you ha' the truth on 't? If this had not been a gentlewoman,
she should have been buried out o' Christian burial.   20
FIRST CLOWN.   Why, there thou sayst.° And the more pity that great folk should have
countenance° in this world to drown or hang themselves, more than their
even-Christian.° Come, my spade. There is no ancient° gentlemen but gardeners, ditchers, and grave makers. They hold up° Adam's profession.

193 It is our trick i.e., weeping is our natural way (when sad).   **194–195 When . . . out** when
my tears are all shed, the woman in me will be expended, satisfied.   **197 douts** extinguishes.
(The Second Quarto reads "drowns.")   **5.1 Location: A churchyard.   s.d. Clowns** rustics.
2 salvation (A blunder for "damnation," or perhaps a suggestion that Ophelia was taking her
own shortcut to heaven.)   **3 straight** straightway, immediately. (But with a pun on *strait,*
"narrow.")   **4 crowner** coroner;   **sat on her** conducted an inquest on her case;   **finds it** gives
his official verdict that her means of death was consistent with.   **6 found so** determined so in
the coroner's verdict.   **7 se offendendo** (A comic mistake for *se defendendo,* a term used in
verdicts of justifiable homicide.)   **9 Argal** (Corruption of *ergo,* "therefore.")   **11 goodman** (An
honorific title often used with the name of a profession or craft.)   **13 will he, nill he** whether he
will or no, willy-nilly.   **18 quest** inquest.   **21 there thou sayst** i.e., that's right.
22 countenance privilege.   **23 even-Christian** fellow Christians;   **ancient** going back to ancient
times.   **24 hold up** maintain.

SECOND CLOWN.   Was he a gentleman?   25
FIRST CLOWN.   'A was the first that ever bore arms.°
SECOND CLOWN.   Why, he had none.
FIRST CLOWN.   What, art a heathen? How dost thou understand the Scripture? The
　　　Scripture says Adam digged. Could he dig without arms?° I'll put another
　　　question to thee. If thou answerest me not to the purpose, confess thy-   30
　　　self°—
SECOND CLOWN.   Go to.
FIRST CLOWN.   What is he that builds stronger than either the mason, the ship-
　　　wright, or the carpenter?
SECOND CLOWN.   The gallows maker, for that frame° outlives a thousand tenants.   35
FIRST CLOWN.   I like thy wit well, in good faith. The gallows does well.° But how
　　　does it well? It does well to those that do ill. Now thou dost ill to say the
　　　gallows is built stronger than the church. Argal, the gallows may do well
　　　to thee. To 't again, come.
SECOND CLOWN.   "Who builds stronger than a mason, a shipwright, or a carpenter?"   40
FIRST CLOWN.   Ay, tell me that, and unyoke.°
SECOND CLOWN.   Marry, now I can tell.
FIRST CLOWN.   To 't.
SECOND CLOWN.   Mass,° I cannot tell.

　　　Enter HAMLET *and* HORATIO ⌊*at a distance*⌋.

FIRST CLOWN.   Cudgel thy brains no more about it, for your dull ass will not mend   45
　　　his pace with beating; and when you are asked this question next, say "a
　　　grave maker." The houses he makes lasts till doomsday. Go get thee in
　　　and fetch me a stoup° of liquor.

　　　　　　　　　　　　　　　　　　[*Exit* SECOND CLOWN. FIRST CLOWN *digs.*]
　　　　　　　　　　　　　　　　　　　　　　　　　　　　　　　Song.

　　　"In youth, when I did love, did love,°
　　　　Methought it was very sweet,   50
　　　To contract—O—the time for—a—my behove,°
　　　　O, methought there—a—was nothing—a—meet."°

HAMLET.   Has this fellow no feeling of his business, 'a° sings in gravemaking?
HORATIO.   Custom hath made it in him a property of easiness.°
HAMLET.   'Tis e'en so. The hand of little employment hath the daintier sense.°   55
FIRST CLOWN.   *Song.*

　　　"But age with his stealing steps
　　　　Hath clawed me in his clutch,

26 bore arms (To be entitled to bear a coat of arms would make Adam a gentleman, but as one
who bore a spade, our common ancestor was an ordinary delver in the earth.)   **29 arms** i.e.,
the arms of the body.   **30–31 confess thyself** (The saying continues, "and be hanged.")
35 frame (1) gallows (2) structure.   **36 does well** (1) is an apt answer (2) does a good turn.
41 unyoke i.e., after this great effort, you may unharness the team of your wits.   **44 Mass** by
the Mass.   **48 stoup** two-quart measure.   **49 In . . . love** (This and the two following stanzas,
with nonsensical variations, are from a poem attributed to Lord Vaux and printed in *Tottel's
Miscellany*, 1557. The *O* and *a* [for "ah"] seemingly are the grunts of the digger.)   **51 To
contract . . . behove** i.e., to shorten the time for my own advantage. (Perhaps he means to
prolong it.)   **52 meet** suitable, i.e., more suitable.   **53 'a** that he.   **54 property of
easiness** something he can do easily and indifferently.   **55 daintier sense** more delicate sense of
feeling.

And hath shipped me into the land,°
As if I had never been such."   [*He throws up a skull.*]   60

HAMLET.   That skull had a tongue in it and could sing once. How the knave jowls°
it to the ground, as if 'twere Cain's jawbone, that did the first murder!
This might be the pate of a politician,° which this ass now o'erreaches,°
one that would circumvent God, might it not?

HORATIO.   It might, my lord.   65

HAMLET.   Or of a courtier, which could say, "Good morrow, sweet lord! How dost
thou, sweet lord?" This might be my Lord Such-a-one, that praised my
Lord Such-a-one's horse when 'a meant to beg it, might it not?

HORATIO.   Ay, my lord.

HAMLET.   Why, e'en so, and now my Lady Worm's, chapless,° and knocked about   70
the mazard° with a sexton's spade. Here's fine revolution,° an° we had
the trick to see° 't. Did these bones cost no more the breeding but to°
play at loggets° with them? Mine ache to think on 't.

FIRST CLOWN.   *Song.*

"A pickax and a spade, a spade,   75
    For and° a shrouding sheet;
O, a pit of clay for to be made
    For such a guest is meet."   [*He throws up another skull.*]

HAMLET.   There's another. Why may not that be the skull of a lawyer? Where be
his quiddities° now, his quillities,° his cases, his tenures,° and his tricks?   80
Why does he suffer this mad knave now to knock him about the sconce°
with a dirty shovel, and will not tell him of his action of battery?° Hum,
this fellow might be in 's time a great buyer of land, with his statutes, his
recognizances,° his fines, his double° vouchers,° his recoveries.° Is this
the fine of his fines and the recovery of his recoveries, to have his fine   85
pate full of fine dirt?° Will his vouchers vouch him no more of his pur-
chases, and double ones too, than the length and breadth of a pair of indentures?° The very conveyances° of his lands will scarcely lie in this
box,° and must th' inheritor° himself have no more, ha?

59 into the land i.e., toward my grave (?) (But note the lack of rhyme in *steps, land*.)
61 jowls dashes (with a pun on *jowl,* "jawbone"). **63 politician** schemer, plotter;
o'erreaches circumvents, gets the better of (with a quibble on the literal sense).
70 chapless having no lower jaw. **71 mazard** i.e., head (Literally, a drinking vessel.);
revolution turn of Fortune's wheel, change; **an** if. **72 trick to see** knack of seeing; **cost . . .
to** involve so little expense and care in upbringing that we may. **73 loggets** a game in which
pieces of hard wood shaped like Indian clubs or bowling pins are thrown to lie as near as
possible to a stake. **76 For and** and moreover. **80 quiddities** subtleties, quibbles. (From Latin
quid, "a thing."); **quillities** verbal niceties, subtle distinctions. (Variation of *quiddities.*);
tenures the holding of a piece of property or office, or the conditions or period of such holding.
81 sconce head. **82 action of battery** lawsuit about physical assault. **83–84 statutes,
recognizances** legal documents guaranteeing a debt by attaching land and property. **84 fines,
recoveries** ways of converting entailed estates into "fee simple" or freehold; **double** signed by
two signatories; **vouchers** guarantees of the legality of a title to real estate. **85–86 fine of his
fines . . . fine pate . . . fine dirt** end of his legal maneuvers . . . elegant head . . . minutely sifted
dirt. **87–88 pair of indentures** legal document drawn up in duplicate on a single sheet and
then cut apart on a zigzag line so that each pair was uniquely matched. (Hamlet may refer to
two rows of teeth or dentures.) **88 conveyances** deeds. **89 box** (1) deed box (2) coffin.
("Skull" has been suggested.); **inheritor** possessor, owner.

HORATIO.   Not a jot more, my lord.   90
HAMLET.   Is not parchment made of sheepskins?
HORATIO.   Ay, my lord, and of calves' skins too.
HAMLET.   They are sheep and calves which seek out assurance in that.° I will
    speak to this fellow.—Whose grave's this, sirrah?°
FIRST CLOWN.   Mine, sir.   [*Sings.*]   95

    "O, pit of clay for to be made
    For such a guest is meet."

HAMLET.   I think it be thine, indeed, for thou liest in 't.
FIRST CLOWN.   You lie out on 't, sir, and therefore 'tis not yours. For my part, I do
    not lie in 't, yet it is mine.   100
HAMLET.   Thou dost lie in 't, to be in 't and say it is thine. 'Tis for the dead, not for
    the quick;° therefore thou liest.
FIRST CLOWN.   'Tis a quick lie, sir; 'twill away again from me to you.
HAMLET.   What man dost thou dig it for?
FIRST CLOWN.   For no man, sir.   105
HAMLET.   What woman, then?
FIRST CLOWN.   For none, neither.
HAMLET.   Who is to be buried in 't?
FIRST CLOWN.   One that was a woman, sir, but, rest her soul, she's dead.
HAMLET.   How absolute° the knave is! We must speak by the card,° or equivoca-   110
    tion° will undo us. By the Lord, Horatio, this three years I have took°
    note of it: the age is grown so picked° that the toe of the peasant comes
    so near the heel of the courtier, he galls his kibe.°—How long hast thou
    been grave maker?
FIRST CLOWN.   Of all the days i' the year, I came to 't that day that our last king   115
    Hamlet overcame Fortinbras.
HAMLET.   How long is that since?
FIRST CLOWN.   Cannot you tell that? Every fool can tell that. It was that very day
    that young Hamlet was born—he that is mad and sent into England.
HAMLET.   Ay, marry, why was he sent into England?   120
FIRST CLOWN.   Why, because 'a was mad. 'A shall recover his wits there, or if 'a do
    not, 'tis no great matter there.
HAMLET.   Why?
FIRST CLOWN.   'Twill not be seen in him there. There the men are as mad as he.
HAMLET.   How came he mad?   125
FIRST CLOWN.   Very strangely, they say.
HAMLET.   How strangely?
FIRST CLOWN.   Faith, e'en with losing his wits.
HAMLET.   Upon what ground?°
FIRST CLOWN.   Why, here in Denmark. I have been sexton here, man and boy,   130
    thirty years.

---

93 assurance in that safety in legal parchments.   **94 sirrah** (A term of address to inferiors.)
102 quick living.   **110 absolute** strict, precise;   **by the card** i.e., with precision. (Literally, by
the mariner's compass-card, on which the points of the compass were marked.)
111–112 equivocation ambiguity in the use of terms.   **111 took** taken;   **picked** refined,
fastidious.   **113 galls his kibe** chafes the courtier's chilblain.   **129 ground** cause. (But, in the
next line, the gravedigger takes the word in the sense of "land," "country.")

HAMLET.   How long will a man lie i' th' earth ere he rot?

FIRST CLOWN.   Faith, if 'a be not rotten before 'a die—as we have many pocky°
corpses nowadays, that will scarce hold the laying in°—'a will last you°
some eight year or nine year. A tanner will last you nine year.   135

HAMLET.   Why he more than another?

FIRST CLOWN.   Why, sir, his hide is so tanned with his trade that 'a will keep out
water a great while, and your water is a sore° decayer of your whoreson°
dead body. [*He picks up a skull.*] Here's a skull now hath lien you° i' th'
earth three-and-twenty years.   140

HAMLET.   Whose was it?

FIRST CLOWN.   A whoreson mad fellow's it was. Whose do you think it was?

HAMLET.   Nay, I know not.

FIRST CLOWN.   A pestilence on him for a mad rogue! 'A poured a flagon of
Rhenish° on my head once. This same skull, sir, was, sir, Yorick's skull,   145
the King's jester.

HAMLET.   This?

FIRST CLOWN.   E'en that.

HAMLET.   Let me see. [*He takes the skull.*] Alas, poor Yorick! I knew him, Horatio, a
fellow of infinite jest, of most excellent fancy. He hath bore° me on his   150
back a thousand times, and now how abhorred in my imagination it is!
My gorge rises° at it. Here hung those lips that I have kissed I know not
how oft. Where be your gibes now? Your gambols, your songs, your
flashes of merriment that were wont° to set the table on a roar? Not one
now, to mock your own grinning?° Quite chopfallen?° Now get you to my   155
lady's chamber and tell her, let her paint an inch thick, to this favor° she
must come. Make her laugh at that. Prithee, Horatio, tell me one thing.

HORATIO.   What's that, my lord?

HAMLET.   Dost thou think Alexander looked o' this fashion i' th' earth?

HORATIO.   E'en so.   160

HAMLET.   And smelt so? Pah! [*He throws down the skull.*]

HORATIO.   E'en so, my lord.

HAMLET.   To what base uses we may return, Horatio! Why may not imagination
trace the noble dust of Alexander till 'a find it stopping a bunghole?°

HORATIO.   'Twere to consider too curiously° to consider so.   165

HAMLET.   No, faith, not a jot, but to follow him thither with modesty° enough, and
likelihood to lead it. As thus: Alexander died, Alexander was buried,
Alexander returneth to dust, the dust is earth, of earth we make loam,°
and why of that loam whereto he was converted might they not stop a
beer barrel?   170
Imperious° Caesar, dead and turned to clay,

---

133 pocky rotten, diseased. (Literally, with the pox, or syphilis.)   **134 hold the laying in** hold
together long enough to be interred;   **last you** last. (*You* is used colloquially here and in the
following lines.)   **138 sore** i.e., terrible, great;   **whoreson** i.e., vile, scurvy.   **139 lien you** lain.
(See the note at line 144.)   **145 Rhenish** Rhine wine.   **150 bore** borne.   **152 My gorge
rises** i.e., I feel nauseated.   **154 were wont** used.   **155 mock your own grinning** mock at the
way your skull seems to be grinning (just as you used to mock at yourself and those who
grinned at you);   **chopfallen** (1) lacking the lower jaw (2) dejected.   **156 favor** aspect,
appearance.   **164 bunghole** hole for filling or emptying a cask.   **165 curiously** minutely.
166 modesty plausible moderation.   **168 loam** mortar consisting chiefly of moistened clay and
straw.   **171 Imperious** imperial.

Might stop a hole to keep the wind away.
O, that that earth which kept the world in awe
Should patch a wall t' expel the winter's flaw!°

Enter KING, QUEEN, LAERTES, *and the corpse* [*of* OPHELIA, *in procession, with*
PRIEST, *lords, etc.*].

But soft,° but soft awhile! Here comes the King,   175
The Queen, the courtiers. Who is this they follow?
And with such maimèd° rites? This doth betoken
The corpse they follow did with desperate hand
Fordo° its own life. 'Twas of some estate.°
Couch we° awhile and mark.   180

[*He and* HORATIO *conceal themselves.* OPHELIA'*s body is taken to the grave.*]

LAERTES.   What ceremony else?
HAMLET [*to* HORATIO].   That is Laertes, a very noble youth. Mark.
LAERTES.   What ceremony else?
PRIEST.   Her obsequies have been as far enlarged
As we have warranty.° Her death was doubtful,   185
And but that great command o'ersways the order°
She should in ground unsanctified been lodged°
Till the last trumpet. For° charitable prayers,
Shards,° flints, and pebbles should be thrown on her.
Yet here she is allowed her virgin crants,°   190
Her maiden strewments,° and the bringing home
Of bell and burial.°
LAERTES.   Must there no more be done?
PRIEST.   No more be done.
We should profane the service of the dead   195
To sing a requiem and such rest° to her
As to peace-parted souls.°
LAERTES.   Lay her i' th' earth,
And from her fair and unpolluted flesh
May violets° spring! I tell thee, churlish priest,   200
A ministering angel shall my sister be
When thou liest howling.°
HAMLET [*to* HORATIO].   What, the fair Ophelia!
QUEEN [*scattering flowers*].   Sweets to the sweet! Farewell.
I hoped thou shouldst have been my Hamlet's wife.   205
I thought thy bride-bed to have decked, sweet maid,
And not t' have strewed thy grave.
LAERTES.   O, treble woe
Fall ten times treble on that cursèd head

174 **flaw** gust of wind.   175 **soft** i.e., wait, be careful.   177 **maimèd** mutilated, incomplete.
179 **Fordo** destroy;   **estate** rank.   180 **Couch we** let's hide, lie low.   185 **warranty** i.e.,
ecclesiastical authority.   186 **great . . . order** orders from on high overrule the prescribed
procedures.   187 **She should . . . lodged** she should have been buried in unsanctified ground.
188 **For** in place of.   189 **Shards** broken bits of pottery.   190 **crants** garlands betokening
maidenhood.   191 **strewments** flowers strewn on a coffin.   192 **bringing . . . burial** laying the
body to rest, to the sound of the bell.   196 **such rest** i.e., to pray for such rest.   197 **peace-
parted souls** those who have died at peace with God.   200 **violets** (See 4.5.191 and note.)
202 **howling** i.e., in hell.

Whose wicked deed thy most ingenious sense°
Deprived thee of! Hold off the earth awhile,   210
Till I have caught her once more in mine arms.

[*He leaps into the grave and embraces* OPHELIA.]

Now pile your dust upon the quick and dead,
Till of this flat a mountain you have made
T' o'ertop old Pelion or the skyish head
Of blue Olympus.°   215

HAMLET [*coming forward*].   What is he whose grief
Bears such an emphasis,° whose phrase of sorrow
Conjures the wandering stars° and makes them stand
Like wonder-wounded° hearers? This is I,
Hamlet the Dane.°   220

LAERTES [*grappling with him*°].   The devil take thy soul!

HAMLET.   Thou pray'st not well.
I prithee, take thy fingers from my throat,
For though I am not splenitive° and rash,
Yet have I in me something dangerous,   225
Which let thy wisdom fear. Hold off thy hand.

KING.   Pluck them asunder.

QUEEN.   Hamlet, Hamlet!

ALL.   Gentlemen!

HORATIO.   Good my lord, be quiet.   230

[HAMLET *and* LAERTES *are parted.*]

HAMLET.   Why, I will fight with him upon this theme
Until my eyelids will no longer wag.°

QUEEN.   O my son, what theme?

HAMLET.   I loved Ophelia. Forty thousand brothers
Could not with all their quantity of love   235
Make up my sum. What wilt thou do for her?

KING.   O, he is mad, Laertes.

QUEEN.   For love of God, forbear him.°

HAMLET.   'Swounds,° show me what thou'lt do.
Woo't° weep? Woo't fight? Woo't fast? Woo't tear thyself?   240
Woo't drink up° eisel?° Eat a crocodile?°
I'll do 't. Dost come here to whine?

---

209 ingenious sense a mind that is quick, alert, of fine qualities.   **214–215 Pelion,
Olympus** sacred mountains in the north of Thessaly; see also *Ossa,* below, at line 248.
217 emphasis i.e., rhetorical and florid emphasis. (*Phrase* has a similar rhetorical connotation.)
218 wandering stars planets.   **219 wonder-wounded** struck with amazement.   **220 the
Dane** (This title normally signifies the King; see 1.1.17 and note.)   **221 s.d. grappling with
him** (The testimony of the First Quarto that "*Hamlet leaps in after Laertes*" and the "Elegy on
Burbage" ("Oft have I seen him leap into the grave") seem to indicate one way in which this
fight was staged; however, the difficulty of fitting two contenders and Ophelia's body into a
confined space (probably the trapdoor) suggests to many editors the alternative, that Laertes
jumps out of the grave to attack Hamlet.)   **224 splenitive** quick-tempered.   **232 wag** move. (A
fluttering eyelid is a conventional sign that life has not yet gone.)   **238 forbear him** leave him
alone.   **239 'Swounds** by His (Christ's) wounds.   **240 Woo't** wilt thou.   **241 drink up** drink
deeply;   **eisel** vinegar;   **crocodile** (Crocodiles were tough and dangerous, and were supposed
to shed hypocritical tears.)

To outface me with leaping in her grave?
Be buried quick° with her, and so will I.
And if thou prate of mountains, let them throw   245
Millions of acres on us, till our ground,
Singeing his pate° against the burning zone,°
Make Ossa° like a wart! Nay, an° thou'lt mouth,°
I'll rant as well as thou.

QUEEN.   This is mere° madness,
And thus awhile the fit will work on him;   250
Anon, as patient as the female dove
When that her golden couplets° are disclosed,°
His silence will sit drooping.

HAMLET.   Hear you, sir,
What is the reason that you use me thus?
I loved you ever. But it is no matter.   255
Let Hercules himself do what he may,
The cat will mew, and dog will have his day.°   *Exit* HAMLET.

KING.   I pray thee, good Horatio, wait upon him.   [*Exit*] HORATIO.
[*To* LAERTES.] Strengthen your patience in° our last night's speech;
We'll put the matter to the present push.°—   260
Good Gertrude, set some watch over your son.—
This grave shall have a living° monument.
An hour of quiet° shortly shall we see;
Till then, in patience our proceeding be.   *Exeunt.*

5.2   *Enter* HAMLET *and* HORATIO.

HAMLET.   So much for this, sir; now shall you see the other.°
You do remember all the circumstance?

HORATIO.   Remember it, my lord!

HAMLET.   Sir, in my heart there was a kind of fighting
That would not let me sleep. Methought I lay   5
Worse than the mutines° in the bilboes.° Rashly,°
And praised be rashness for it—let us know°
Our indiscretion° sometimes serves us well
When our deep plots do pall,° and that should learn° us
There's a divinity that shapes our ends,   10

---

244 quick alive.   **247 his pate** its head, i.e., top;   **burning zone** zone in the celestial sphere
containing the sun's orbit, between the tropics of Cancer and Capricorn.   **248 Ossa** another
mountain in Thessaly. (In their war against the Olympian gods, the giants attempted to heap
Ossa on Pelion to scale Olympus.);   **an** if;   **mouth** i.e., rant.   **249 mere** utter.   **252 golden
couplets** two baby pigeons, covered with yellow down;   **disclosed** hatched.   **256–257 Let . . .
day** i.e., (1) even Hercules couldn't stop Laertes' theatrical rant (2) I, too, will have my turn; i.e.,
despite any blustering attempts at interference, every person will sooner or later do what he or
she must do.   **259 in** i.e., by recalling.   **260 present push** immediate test.   **262 living** lasting.
(For Laertes' private understanding, Claudius also hints that Hamlet's death will serve as such a
monument.)   **263 hour of quiet** time free of conflict.   **5.2. Location: The castle.   1 see the
other** hear the other news.   **6 mutines** mutineers;   **bilboes** shackles;   **Rashly** on impulse. (This
adverb goes with lines 12 ff.)   **7 know** acknowledge   **8 indiscretion** lack of foresight and
judgment (not an indiscreet act).   **9 pall** fail, falter, go stale;   **learn** teach.

Rough-hew° them how we will—

HORATIO.   That is most certain.

HAMLET.   Up from my cabin,
My sea-gown° scarfed° about me, in the dark
Groped I to find out them,° had my desire,
Fingered° their packet, and in fine° withdrew   15
To mine own room again, making so bold,
My fears forgetting manners, to unseal
Their grand commission; where I found, Horatio—
Ah, royal knavery!—an exact command,
Larded° with many several° sorts of reasons   20
Importing° Denmark's health and England's too,
With, ho! such bugs° and goblins in my life,°
That on the supervise,° no leisure bated,°
No, not to stay° the grinding of the ax,
My head should be struck off.

HORATIO.   Is't possible?   25

HAMLET [*giving a document*].
Here's the commission. Read it at more leisure.
But wilt thou hear now how I did proceed?

HORATIO.   I beseech you.

HAMLET.   Being thus benetted round with villainies—   30
Ere I could make a prologue to my brains,
They had begun the play°—I sat me down,
Devised a new commission, wrote it fair.°
I once did hold it, as our statists° do,
A baseness° to write fair, and labored much   35
How to forget that learning; but, sir, now
It did me yeoman's° service. Wilt thou know
Th' effect° of what I wrote?

HORATIO.   Ay, good my lord.

HAMLET.   An earnest conjuration° from the King,
As England was his faithful tributary,   40
As love between them like the palm° might flourish,
As peace should still° her wheaten garland° wear
And stand a comma° 'tween their amities,
And many suchlike "as"es° of great charge,°
That on the view and knowing of these contents,   45
Without debatement further more or less,
He should those bearers put to sudden death,

---

11 Rough-hew shape roughly.   **13 sea-gown** seaman's coat;   **scarfed** loosely wrapped.
14 them i.e., Rosencrantz and Guildenstern.   **15 Fingered** pilfered, pinched;   **in fine** finally, in
conclusion.   **20 Larded** garnished;   **several** different.   **21 Importing** relating to.
22 bugs bugbears, hobgoblins;   **in my life** i.e., to be feared if I were allowed to live.
23 supervise reading;   **leisure bated** delay allowed.   **24 stay** await.   **31–32 Ere . . . play** before
I could consciously turn my brain to the matter, it had started working on a plan.   **33 fair** in a
clear hand.   **34 statists** statesmen.   **35 baseness** i.e., lower-class trait.   **37 yeoman's** i.e.,
substantial, faithful, loyal.   **38 effect** purport.   **39 conjuration** entreaty.   **41 palm** (An image of
health; see Psalm 92:12.)   **42 still** always;   **wheaten garland** (Symbolic of fruitful agriculture, of
peace and plenty.)   **43 comma** (Indicating continuity, link.)   **44 "as"es** (1) the "whereases" of a
formal document (2) asses;   **charge** (1) import (2) burden (appropriate to asses).

Not shriving time° allowed.

HORATIO.   How was this sealed?

HAMLET.   Why, even in that was heaven ordinant.°
I had my father's signet° in my purse,   50
Which was the model° of that Danish seal;
Folded the writ° up in the form of th' other,
Subscribed° it, gave 't th' impression,° placed it safely,
The changeling° never known. Now, the next day
Was our sea fight, and what to this was sequent°   55
Thou knowest already.

HORATIO.   So Guildenstern and Rosencrantz go to 't.

HAMLET.   Why, man, they did make love to this employment.
They are not near my conscience. Their defeat°
Does by their own insinuation° grow.   60
'Tis dangerous when the baser° nature comes
Between the pass° and fell° incensèd points
Of mighty opposites.°

HORATIO.   Why, what a king is this!

HAMLET.   Does it not, think thee, stand me now upon°—
He that hath killed my king and whored my mother,   65
Popped in between th' election° and my hopes,
Thrown out his angle° for my proper° life,
And with such cozenage°—is 't not perfect conscience
To quit° him with this arm? And is 't not to be damned
To let this canker° of our nature come   70
In° further evil?

HORATIO.   It must be shortly known to him from England
What is the issue of the business there.

HAMLET.   It will be short. The interim is mine,
And a man's life's no more than to say "one."°   75
But I am very sorry, good Horatio,
That to Laertes I forgot myself,
For by the image of my cause I see
The portraiture of his. I'll court his favors.
But, sure, the bravery° of his grief did put me   80
Into a tow'ring passion.

HORATIO.   Peace, who comes here?

Enter a Courtier [OSRIC].

OSRIC.   Your lordship is right welcome back to Denmark.

---

48 shriving time time for confession and absolution.   **49 ordinant** directing.   **50 signet** small
seal.   **51 model** replica.   **52 writ** writing.   **53 Subscribed** signed (with forged signature);
impression i.e., with a wax seal.   **54 changeling** i.e., substituted letter. (Literally, a fairy child
substituted for a human one.)   **55 was sequent** followed.   **59 defeat** destruction.
60 insinuation intrusive intervention, sticking their noses in my business.   **61 baser** of lower
social station.   **62 pass** thrust;   **fell** fierce.   **63 opposites** antagonists.   **64 stand me now
upon** become incumbent on me now.   **66 election** (The Danish monarch was "elected" by a
small number of high-ranking electors.)   **67 angle** fishhook;   **proper** very.
68 cozenage trickery.   **69 quit** requite, pay back.   **70 canker** ulcer.   **70–71 come In** grow into.
75 a man's . . . "one" one's whole life occupies such a short time, only as long as it takes to
count to 1.   **80 bravery** bravado.

HAMLET.   I humbly thank you, sir. [*To* HORATIO.] Dost know this water fly?

HORATIO.   No, my good lord.

HAMLET.   Thy state is the more gracious, for 'tis a vice to know him. He hath   85
much land, and fertile. Let a beast be lord of beasts, and his crib° shall
stand at the King's mess.° 'Tis a chuff,° but, as I say, spacious in the possession of dirt.

OSRIC.   Sweet lord, if your lordship were at leisure, I should impart a thing to you
from His Majesty.   90

HAMLET.   I will receive it, sir, with all diligence of spirit.
Put your bonnet° to his° right use; 'tis for the head.

OSRIC.   I thank your lordship, it is very hot.

HAMLET.   No, believe me, 'tis very cold. The wind is northerly.

OSRIC.   It is indifferent° cold, my lord, indeed.   95

HAMLET.   But yet methinks it is very sultry and hot for my complexion.°

OSRIC.   Exceedingly, my lord. It is very sultry, as 'twere—I cannot tell how.
My lord, His Majesty bade me signify to you that 'a has laid a great wager
on your head. Sir, this is the matter—

HAMLET.   I beseech you, remember.   100

[HAMLET *moves him to put on his hat.*]

OSRIC.   Nay, good my lord; for my ease,° in good faith. Sir, here is newly
come to court Laertes—believe me, an absolute° gentleman, full of
most excellent differences,° of very soft society° and great showing.°
Indeed, to speak feelingly° of him, he is the card° or calendar° of
gentry,° for you shall find in him the continent of what part a gentle-   105
man would see.°

HAMLET.   Sir, his definement° suffers no perdition° in you,° though I know to divide him inventorially° would dozy° th' arithmetic of memory, and yet
but yaw° neither° in respect of° his quick sail. But, in the verity of extolment,° I take him to be a soul of great article,° and his infusion° of such   110
dearth and rareness° as, to make true diction° of him, his semblable° is
his mirror and who else would trace° him his umbrage,° nothing more.

OSRIC.   Your lordship speaks most infallibly of him.

---

86 crib manger.   **86–87 Let . . . mess** i.e., if a man, no matter how beastlike, is as rich in
livestock and possessions as Osric, he may eat at the King's table.   **87 chuff** boor, churl. (The
Second Quarto spelling, *chough,* is a variant spelling that also suggests the meaning here of
"chattering jackdaw.")   **92 bonnet** any kind of cap or hat;   **his** its.   **95 indifferent** somewhat.
96 complexion temperament.   **101 for my ease** (A conventional reply declining the invitation to
put his hat back on.)   **102 absolute** perfect.   **103 differences** special qualities;   **soft
society** agreeable manners;   **great showing** distinguished appearance.   **104 feelingly** with just
perception;   **card** chart, map;   **calendar** guide.   **105 gentry** good breeding.   **105–106 the
continent . . . see** one who contains in him all the qualities a gentleman would like to see. (A
continent is that which contains.)   **107 definement** definition (Hamlet proceeds to mock Osric
by throwing his lofty diction back at him);   **perdition** loss, diminution;   **you** your description.
107–108 divide him inventorially enumerate his graces;   **dozy** dizzy.   **109 yaw** swing
unsteadily off course. (Said of a ship.);   **neither** for all that;   **in respect of** in comparison with.
109–110 in . . . extolment in true praise (of him).   **110 of great article** one with many articles
in his inventory;   **infusion** essence, character infused into him by nature.   **111 dearth and
rareness** rarity;   **make true diction** speak truly;   **semblable** only true likeness.   **112 who . . .
trace** any other person who would wish to follow;   **umbrage** shadow.

HAMLET.   The concernancy,° sir? Why do we wrap the gentleman in our more
    rawer breath?°   115

OSRIC.   Sir?

HORATIO.   Is 't not possible to understand in another tongue?° You will do 't,° sir,
    really.

HAMLET.   What imports the nomination° of this gentleman?

OSRIC.   Of Laertes?   120

HORATIO [*to* HAMLET].   His purse is empty already; all 's golden words are spent.

HAMLET.   Of him, sir.

OSRIC.   I know you are not ignorant—

HAMLET.   I would you did, sir. Yet in faith if you did, it would not much approve°
    me. Well, sir?   125

OSRIC.   You are not ignorant of what excellence Laertes is—

HAMLET.   I dare not confess that, lest I should compare with him in excellence.
    But to know a man well were to know himself.°

OSRIC.   I mean, sir, for° his weapon; but in the imputation laid on him by them,°
    in his meed° he's unfellowed.°   130

HAMLET.   What's his weapon?

OSRIC.   Rapier and dagger.

HAMLET.   That's two of his weapons—but well.°

OSRIC.   The King, sir, hath wagered with him six Barbary horses, against the
    which he° has impawned,° as I take it, six French rapiers and poniards,°   135
    with their assigns,° as girdle, hangers,° and so.° Three of the carriages,°
    in faith, are very dear to fancy,° very responsive° to the hilts, most deli-
    cate° carriages, and of very liberal conceit.°

HAMLET.   What call you the carriages?

HORATIO [*to* HAMLET].   I knew you must be edified by the margent° ere you had   140
    done.

OSRIC.   The carriages, sir, are the hangers.

HAMLET.   The phrase would be more germane to the matter if we could carry a
    cannon by our sides; I would it might be hangers till then. But, on: six
    Barbary horses against six French swords, their assigns, and three liberal-   145
    conceited carriages; that's the French bet against the Danish. Why is this
    impawned, as you call it?

---

114 concernancy import, relevance.   **115 rawer breath** unrefined speech that can only come
short in praising him.   **118 to understand . . . tongue** i.e., for you, Osric, to understand when
someone else speaks your language. (Horatio twits Osric for not being able to understand the
kind of flowery speech he himself uses, when Hamlet speaks in such a vein. Alternatively, all
this could be said to Hamlet.);   **You will do 't** i.e., you can if you try, or, you may well have to
try (to speak plainly).   **119 nomination** naming.   **124 approve** commend.   **127–128 I dare
. . . himself** I dare not boast of knowing Laertes' excellence lest I seem to imply a comparable
excellence in myself. Certainly, to know another person well, one must know oneself.
129 for i.e., with;   **imputation . . . them** reputation given him by others.   **130 meed** merit;
unfellowed unmatched.   **133 but well** but never mind.   **135 he** i.e., Laertes;
impawned staked, wagered;   **poniards** daggers.   **136 assigns** appurtenances;   **hangers** straps
on the sword belt (*girdle*), from which the sword hung;   **and so** and so on;   **carriages** (An
affected way of saying *hangers;* literally, gun carriages.)   **137 dear to fancy** delightful to the
fancy;   **responsive** corresponding closely, matching or well adjusted.   **137–138 delicate** (i.e., in
workmanship);   **liberal conceit** elaborate design.   **140 margent** margin of a book, place for
explanatory notes.

OSRIC.   The King, sir, hath laid,° sir, that in a dozen passes° between yourself and
him, he shall not exceed you three hits. He hath laid on twelve for nine,
and it would come to immediate trial, if your lordship would vouchsafe   150
the answer.°

HAMLET.   How if I answer no?

OSRIC.   I mean, my lord, the opposition of your person in trial.

HAMLET.   Sir, I will walk here in the hall. If it please His Majesty, it is the breathing
time° of day with me. Let° the foils be brought, the gentleman willing,   155
and the King hold his purpose. I will win for him an I can; if not, I will
gain nothing but my shame and the odd hits.

OSRIC.   Shall I deliver you° so?

HAMLET.   To this effect, sir—after what flourish your nature will.

OSRIC.   I commend° my duty to your lordship.   160

HAMLET.   Yours, yours. [*Exit* OSRIC.] 'A does well to commend it himself; there are
no tongues else for 's turn.°

HORATIO.   This lapwing° runs away with the shell on his head.

HAMLET.   'A did comply with his dug° before 'a sucked it. Thus has he—and many
more of the same breed that I know the drossy° age dotes on—only got the   165
tune° of the time and, out of an habit of encounter,° a kind of yeasty° collection,° which carries them through and through the most fanned and win-
nowed opinions;° and do° but blow them to their trial, the bubbles are
out.°

Enter a LORD.

LORD.   My lord, His Majesty commended him to you by young Osric, who brings   170
back to him that you attend him in the hall. He sends to know if your
pleasure hold to play with Laertes, or that° you will take longer time.

HAMLET.   I am constant to my purposes; they follow the King's pleasure. If his fitness
speaks, mine is ready;° now or whensoever, provided I be so able as now.

LORD.   The King and Queen and all are coming down.   175

HAMLET.   In happy time.°

---

148 laid wagered;   **passes** bouts. (The odds of the betting are hard to explain. Possibly the King
bets that Hamlet will win at least five out of twelve, at which point Laertes raises the odds
against himself by betting he will win nine.)   **150–151 vouchsafe the answer** be so good as to
accept the challenge. (Hamlet deliberately takes the phrase in its literal sense of replying.)
154–155 breathing time exercise period;   **Let** i.e., if.   **158 deliver you** report what you say.
160 commend commit to your favor. (A conventional salutation, but Hamlet wryly uses a more
literal meaning, "recommend," "praise," in line 161.)   **162 for 's turn** for his purposes, i.e., to do
it for him.   **163 lapwing** (A proverbial type of youthful forwardness. Also, a bird that draws
intruders away from its nest and was thought to run about with its head in the shell when newly
hatched; a seeming reference to Osric's hat.)   **164 comply . . . dug** observe ceremonious
formality toward his nurse's or mother's teat.   **165 drossy** laden with scum and impurities,
frivolous.   **166 tune** temper, mood, manner of speech;   **an habit of encounter** a demeanor in
conversing (with courtiers of his own kind);   **yeasty** frothy.   **166–167 collection** i.e., of current
phrases.   **167–168 carries . . . opinions** sustains them right through the scrutiny of persons
whose opinions are select and refined. (Literally, like grain separated from its chaff. Osric is both
the chaff and the bubbly froth on the surface of the liquor that is soon blown away.)   **168 and
do** yet do.   **168–169 blow . . . out** test them by merely blowing on them, and their bubbles
burst.   **172 that** if.   **173–174 If . . . ready** if he declares his readiness, my convenience waits
on his.   **176 In happy time** (A phrase of courtesy indicating that the time is convenient.)

LORD.   The Queen desires you to use some gentle entertainment° to Laertes before you fall to play.

HAMLET.   She well instructs me.   [*Exit* LORD.]

HORATIO.   You will lose, my lord.   180

HAMLET.   I do not think so. Since he went into France, I have been in continual practice; I shall win at the odds. But thou wouldst not think how ill all's here about my heart; but it is no matter.

HORATIO.   Nay, good my lord—

HAMLET.   It is but foolery, but it is such a kind of gaingiving° as would perhaps   185
trouble a woman.

HORATIO.   If your mind dislike anything, obey it. I will forestall their repair° hither and say you are not fit.

HAMLET.   Not a whit, we defy augury. There is special providence in the fall of a sparrow. If it be now, 'tis not to come; if it be not to come, it will be   190
now; if it be not now, yet it will come. The readiness is all. Since no man of aught he leaves knows, what is 't to leave betimes? Let be.°

A table prepared. [*Enter*] *trumpets, drums, and officers with cushions;* KING,
QUEEN, [OSRIC,] *and all the state; foils, daggers,* [*and wine borne in;*] *and* LAERTES.

KING.   Come, Hamlet, come and take this hand from me.

[*The* KING *puts* LAERTES' *hand into* HAMLET'*s.*]

HAMLET [*to* LAERTES].   Give me your pardon, sir. I have done you wrong,
But pardon 't as you are a gentleman.   195
This presence° knows,
And you must needs have heard, how I am punished°
With a sore distraction. What I have done
That might your nature, honor, and exception°
Roughly awake, I here proclaim was madness.   200
Was 't Hamlet wronged Laertes? Never Hamlet.
If Hamlet from himself be ta'en away,
And when he's not himself does wrong Laertes,
Then Hamlet does it not, Hamlet denies it.
Who does it, then? His madness. If 't be so,   205
Hamlet is of the faction° that is wronged;
His madness is poor Hamlet's enemy.
Sir, in this audience
Let my disclaiming from a purposed evil
Free me so far in your most generous thoughts   210
That I have° shot my arrow o'er the house
And hurt my brother.

LAERTES.   I am satisfied in nature,°
Whose motive° in this case should stir me most
To my revenge. But in my terms of honor
I stand aloof, and will no reconcilement   215

---

177 entertainment greeting.   **185 gaingiving** misgiving.   **187 repair** coming.   **191–192 Since
. . . Let be** since no one has knowledge of what he is leaving behind, what does an early death
matter after all? Enough; don't struggle against it.   **196 presence** royal assembly.
197 punished afflicted.   **199 exception** disapproval.   **206 faction** party.   **211 That I have** as if
I had.   **212 in nature** i.e., as to my personal feelings.   **213 motive** prompting.

Till by some elder masters of known honor
I have a voice° and precedent of peace°
To keep my name ungored.° But till that time
I do receive your offered love like love,
And will not wrong it.

HAMLET.   I embrace it freely,   220
And will this brothers' wager frankly° play.—
Give us the foils. Come on.

LAERTES.   Come, one for me.

HAMLET.   I'll be your foil,° Laertes. In mine ignorance
Your skill shall, like a star i' the darkest night,
Stick fiery off° indeed.

LAERTES.   You mock me, sir.   225

HAMLET.   No, by this hand.

KING.   Give them the foils, young Osric. Cousin Hamlet,
You know the wager?

HAMLET.   Very well, my lord.
Your Grace has laid the odds o'° the weaker side.

KING.   I do not fear it; I have seen you both.   230
But since he is bettered,° we have therefore odds.

LAERTES.   This is too heavy. Let me see another.

                                    [*He exchanges his foil for another.*]

HAMLET.   This likes me° well. These foils have all a length?

                                    [*They prepare to play.*]

OSRIC.   Ay, my good lord.

KING.   Set me the stoups of wine upon that table.   235
If Hamlet give the first or second hit,
Or quit in answer of the third exchange,°
Let all the battlements their ordnance fire.
The King shall drink to Hamlet's better breath,°
And in the cup an union° shall he throw   240
Richer than that which four successive kings
In Denmark's crown have worn. Give me the cups,
And let the kettle° to the trumpet speak,
The trumpet to the cannoneer without,
The cannons to the heavens, the heaven to earth,   245
"Now the King drinks to Hamlet." Come, begin.   *Trumpets the while.*
And you, the judges, bear a wary eye.

HAMLET.   Come on, sir.

LAERTES.   Come, my lord.   [*They play.* HAMLET *scores a hit.*]

HAMLET.   One.   250

---

217 voice authoritative pronouncement;   **of peace** for reconciliation.   **218 name
ungored** reputation unwounded.   **221 frankly** without ill feeling or the burden of rancor.
223 foil thin metal background which sets a jewel off (with pun on the blunted rapier for
fencing).   **225 Stick fiery off** stand out brilliantly.   **229 laid the odds o'** bet on, backed.
231 is bettered has improved; is the odds-on favorite. (Laertes' handicap is the "three hits"
specified in line 149.)   **233 likes me** pleases me.   **237 Or . . . exchange** i.e., or requites Laertes
in the third bout for having won the first two.   **239 better breath** improved vigor.
240 union pearl. (So called, according to Pliny's *Natural History*, 9, because pearls are *unique*,
never identical.)   **243 kettle** kettledrum.

LAERTES.   No.

HAMLET.   Judgment.

OSRIC.   A hit, a very palpable hit.

                         Drum, trumpets, and shot. Flourish. A piece goes off.

LAERTES.   Well, again.

KING.   Stay, give me drink. Hamlet, this pearl is thine.

    [He drinks, and throws a pearl in HAMLET'*s cup.]*

    Here's to thy health. Give him the cup.   255

HAMLET.   I'll play this bout first. Set it by awhile.

    Come. *[They play.]* Another hit; what say you?

LAERTES.   A touch, a touch, I do confess 't.

KING.   Our son shall win.

QUEEN.   He's fat° and scant of breath.

    Here, Hamlet, take my napkin,° rub thy brows.   260

    The Queen carouses° to thy fortune, Hamlet.

HAMLET.   Good madam!

KING.   Gertrude, do not drink.

QUEEN.   I will, my lord, I pray you pardon me.   *[She drinks.]*

KING *[aside]*.   It is the poisoned cup. It is too late.   265

HAMLET.   I dare not drink yet, madam; by and by.

QUEEN.   Come, let me wipe thy face.

LAERTES *[to* KING*]*.   My lord, I'll hit him now.

KING.   I do not think 't.

LAERTES *[aside]*.   And yet it is almost against my conscience.   270

HAMLET.   Come, for the third, Laertes. You do but dally.

    I pray you, pass° with your best violence;

    I am afeard you make a wanton of me.°

LAERTES.   Say you so? Come on. *[They play.]*

OSRIC.   Nothing neither way.   275

LAERTES.   Have at you now!

    *[*LAERTES *wounds* HAMLET; *then, in scuffling, they change rapiers,° and* HAMLET

wounds LAERTES.*]*

KING.   Part them! They are incensed.

HAMLET.   Nay, come, again.   *[The* QUEEN *falls.]*

OSRIC.   Look to the Queen there, ho!

HORATIO.   They bleed on both sides. How is it, my lord?

OSRIC.   How is 't, Laertes?

LAERTES.   Why, as a woodcock° to mine own springe,° Osric;   280

    I am justly killed with mine own treachery.

HAMLET.   How does the Queen?

KING.   She swoons to see them bleed.

QUEEN.   No, no, the drink, the drink—O my dear Hamlet—

    The drink, the drink! I am poisoned.   *[She dies.]*

---

259 fat not physically fit, out of training.   **260 napkin** handkerchief.   **261 carouses** drinks a
toast.   **272 pass** thrust.   **273 make ... me** i.e., treat me like a spoiled child, trifle with me.
276 s.d. in scuffling, they change rapiers (This stage direction occurs in the Folio. According to a
widespread stage tradition, Hamlet receives a scratch, realizes that Laertes' sword is unbated,
and accordingly forces an exchange.)   **280 woodcock** a bird, a type of stupidity or as a decoy;
springe trap, snare.

HAMLET.   O villainy! Ho, let the door be locked!   285
    Treachery! Seek it out.   [LAERTES *falls. Exit* OSRIC.]
LAERTES.   It is here, Hamlet. Hamlet, thou art slain.
    No med'cine in the world can do thee good;
    In thee there is not half an hour's life.
    The treacherous instrument is in thy hand,   290
    Unbated° and envenomed. The foul practice°
    Hath turned itself on me. Lo, here I lie,
    Never to rise again. Thy mother's poisoned.
    I can no more. The King, the King's to blame.
HAMLET.   The point envenomed too? Then, venom, to thy work.   295

                                       [*He stabs the* KING.]

ALL.   Treason! Treason!
KING.   O, yet defend me, friends! I am but hurt.
HAMLET [*forcing the* KING *to drink.*]
    Here, thou incestuous, murderous, damnèd Dane,
    Drink off this potion. Is thy union° here?   300
    Follow my mother.   [*The* KING *dies.*]
LAERTES.   He is justly served.
    It is a poison tempered° by himself.
    Exchange forgiveness with me, noble Hamlet.
    Mine and my father's death come not upon thee,
    Nor thine on me!   [*He dies.*]   305
HAMLET.   Heaven make thee free of it! I follow thee.
    I am dead, Horatio. Wretched Queen, adieu!
    You that look pale and tremble at this chance,°
    That are but mutes° or audience to this act,
    Had I but time—as this fell° sergeant,° Death,   310
    Is strict° in his arrest°—O, I could tell you—
    But let it be. Horatio, I am dead;
    Thou livest. Report me and my cause aright
    To the unsatisfied.
HORATIO.   Never believe it.
    I am more an antique Roman° than a Dane.   315
    Here's yet some liquor left.

    [*He attempts to drink from the poisoned cup.* HAMLET *prevents him.*]

HAMLET.   As thou'rt a man,
    Give me the cup! Let go! By heaven, I'll ha 't.
    O God, Horatio, what a wounded name,
    Things standing thus unknown, shall I leave behind me!
    If thou didst ever hold me in thy heart,   320
    Absent thee from felicity awhile,
    And in this harsh world draw thy breath in pain

---

291 Unbated not blunted with a button;   practice plot.   300 union pearl. (See line 240; with
grim puns on the word's other meanings: marriage, shared death.)   302 tempered mixed.
308 chance mischance.   309 mutes silent observers. (Literally, actors with nonspeaking parts.)
310 fell cruel;   sergeant sheriff's officer.   311 strict (1) severely just (2) unavoidable;
arrest (1) taking into custody (2) stopping my speech.   315 Roman (Suicide was an honorable
choice for many Romans as an alternative to a dishonorable life.)

To tell my story.   *A march afar off* [*and a volley within*].
What warlike noise is this?

Enter OSRIC.

OSRIC.   Young Fortinbras, with conquest come from Poland,   325
To th' ambassadors of England gives
This warlike volley.

HAMLET.   O, I die, Horatio!
The potent poison quite o'ercrows° my spirit.
I cannot live to hear the news from England,
But I do prophesy th' election lights   330
On Fortinbras. He has my dying voice.°
So tell him, with th' occurents° more and less
Which have solicited°—the rest is silence.   [*He dies.*]

HORATIO.   Now cracks a noble heart. Good night, sweet prince,
And flights of angels sing thee to thy rest!   [*March within.*]   335
Why does the drum come hither?

Enter FORTINBRAS, *with the* [*English*] *Ambassadors* [*with drum, colors, and attendants*].

FORTINBRAS.   Where is this sight?

HORATIO.   What is it you would see?
If aught of woe or wonder, cease your search.

FORTINBRAS.   This quarry° cries on havoc.° O proud Death,
What feast° is toward° in thine eternal cell,   340
That thou so many princes at a shot
So bloodily hast struck?

FIRST AMBASSADOR.   The sight is dismal,
And our affairs from England come too late.
The ears are senseless that should give us hearing,
To tell him his commandment is fulfilled,   345
That Rosencrantz and Guildenstern are dead.
Where should we have our thanks?

HORATIO.   Not from his° mouth,
Had it th' ability of life to thank you.
He never gave commandment for their death.
But since, so jump° upon this bloody question,°   350
You from the Polack wars, and you from England,
And here arrived, give order that these bodies
High on a stage° be placèd to the view,
And let me speak to th' yet unknowing world
How these things came about. So shall you hear   355
Of carnal, bloody, and unnatural acts,
Of accidental judgments,° casual° slaughters,

---

328 o'ercrows triumphs over (like the winner in a cockfight).   **331 voice** vote.
332 occurrents events, incidents.   **333 solicited** moved, urged. (Hamlet doesn't finish saying what the events have prompted—presumably, his acts of vengeance, or his reporting of those events to Fortinbras.)   **339 quarry** heap of dead;   **cries on havoc** proclaims a general slaughter.
340 feast i.e., Death feasting on those who have fallen;   **toward** in preparation.   **347 his** i.e., Claudius'.   **350 jump** precisely, immediately;   **question** dispute, affair.   **353 stage** platform.
357 judgments retributions;   **casual** occurring by chance.

Of deaths put on° by cunning and forced cause,°
And, in this upshot, purposes mistook
Fall'n on th' inventors' heads. All this can I   360
Truly deliver.
FORTINBRAS.   Let us haste to hear it,
And call the noblest to the audience.
For me, with sorrow I embrace my fortune.
I have some rights of memory° in this kingdom,
Which now to claim my vantage° doth invite me.   365
HORATIO.   Of that I shall have also cause to speak,
And from his mouth whose voice will draw on more.°
But let this same be presently° performed,
Even while men's minds are wild, lest more mischance
On° plots and errors happen.
FORTINBRAS.   Let four captains   370
Bear Hamlet, like a soldier, to the stage,
For he was likely, had he been put on,°
To have proved most royal; and for his passage,°
The soldiers' music and the rite of war
Speak° loudly for him.   375
Take up the bodies. Such a sight as this
Becomes the field,° but here shows much amiss.
Go bid the soldiers shoot.
     Exeunt [marching, bearing off the dead bodies; a peal of ordnance is shot off].

358 put on instigated;   **forced cause** contrivance.   **364 of memory** traditional, remembered,
unforgotten.   **365 vantage** favorable opportunity.   **367 voice . . . more** vote will influence still
others.   **368 presently** immediately.   **370 On** on the basis of; on top of.   **372 put on** i.e.,
invested in royal office and so put to the test.   **373 passage** i.e., from life to death.
375 Speak let them speak.   **377 Becomes the field** suits the field of battle.

Topics for Critical Thinking and Writing

Act 1

1. The first scene (like many other scenes in this play) is full of expressions of uncertainty. What are some are these uncertainties? The Ghost first appears at
   1.1.43. Does his appearance surprise us, or have we been prepared for it? Or is
   there both preparation and surprise? Do the last four speeches of 1.1 help to
   introduce a note of hope? If so, how?
2. Does the King's opening speech in 1.2 reveal him to be an accomplished public speaker—or are lines 10–14 offensive? In his second speech (lines 41–49),
   what is the effect of naming Laertes four times? Claudius sometimes uses the
   royal pronouns ("we," "our"), sometimes the more intimate "I" and "my." Study
   his use of these in lines 1–4 and in 106–117. What do you think he is getting at?
3. Hamlet's first soliloquy (1.2.129–159) reveals that more than just his father's
   death distresses him. Be as specific as possible about the causes of Hamlet's
   anguish here. What traits does Hamlet reveal in his conversation with Horatio
   (1.2.160–258)?

4. What do you make of Polonius's advice to Laertes (1.3.55–81)? Is it sound? Sound advice, but here uttered by a fool? Ignoble advice? How would one follow the advice of line 78: "to thine own self be true"? In his words to Ophelia in 1.3.102–136, what does he reveal about himself?

5. Can 1.4.17–38 reasonably be taken as a speech on the "tragic flaw"? (On this idea, see page 366.) Or is the passage a much more limited discussion, a comment simply on Danish drinking habits?

6. Hamlet is convinced in 1.5.93–105 that the Ghost has told the truth, indeed, the only important truth. But do we detect in 105–112 a hint of a tone suggesting that Hamlet delights in hating villainy? If so, can it be said that later this delight grows, and that in some scenes (e.g., 3.3) we feel that Hamlet has almost become a diabolic revenger? Explain.

Act 2

1. Characterize Polonius on the basis of 2.1.1–75.

2. In light of what we have seen of Hamlet, is Ophelia's report of his strange behavior when he visits her understandable?

3. Why does 2.2.33–34 seem almost comic? How do these lines help us to form a view about Rosencrantz and Guildenstern?

4. Is "the hellish Pyrrhus" (2.2.405) Hamlet's version of Claudius? Or is he Hamlet, who soon will be responsible for the deaths of Polonius, Rosencrantz and Guildenstern, Claudius, Gertrude, Ophelia, and Laertes? Explain.

5. Is the speech that Hamlet and the First Player recite, with some interruptions (2.2.392–453), an absurdly bombastic speech? If so, why? To distinguish it from the poetry of the play itself? To characterize the bloody deeds that Hamlet cannot descend to?

6. In 2.2.482–520 Hamlet rebukes himself for not acting. Why has he not acted? Because he is a coward (line 503)? Because he has a conscience? Because no action can restore his father and his mother's purity? Because he doubts the Ghost? What reason(s) can you offer?

Act 3

1. What do you make out of Hamlet's assertion to Ophelia: "I loved you not" (3.1.117)? Of his characterization of himself as full of "offenses" (3.1.121–25)? Why is Hamlet so harsh to Ophelia?

2. In 3.3.36–72 Claudius's conscience afflicts him. But is he repentant? What makes you say so?

3. Is Hamlet other than abhorrent in 3.3.73–96? Do we want him to kill Claudius at this moment, when Claudius (presumably with his back to Hamlet) is praying? Why?

4. The Ghost speaks of Hamlet's "almost blunted purpose" (3.4.115). Is the accusation fair? Explain.

5. How would you characterize the Hamlet who speaks in 3.4.209–24?

Act 4

1. Is Gertrude protecting Hamlet when she says he is mad (4.1.7), or does she believe that he is mad? If she believes he is mad, does it follow that she no longer feels ashamed and guilty? Explain.

2. Why should Hamlet hide Polonius's body (in 4.2)? Is he feigning madness? Is he on the edge of madness? Explain.
3. How can we explain Hamlet's willingness to go to England (4.3.52)?
4. Judging from 4.5, what has driven Ophelia mad? Is Laertes heroic, or somewhat foolish? Consider also the way Claudius treats him in 4.7.

Act 5

1. Would anything be lost if the gravediggers in 5.1 were omitted?
2. To what extent do we judge Hamlet severely for sending Rosencrantz and Guildenstern to their deaths, as he reports in 5.2? On the whole, do we think of Hamlet as an intriguer? What other intrigues has he engendered? How successful were they?
3. Does 5.2.189–192 show a paralysis of the will, or a wise recognition that more is needed than mere human scheming? Explain.
4. Does 5.2.276 suggest that Laertes takes advantage of a momentary pause and unfairly stabs Hamlet? Is the exchange of weapons accidental, or does Hamlet (as in Olivier's film version), realizing that he has been betrayed, deliberately get possession of Laertes's deadly weapon?
5. Fortinbras is often cut from the play. How much is lost by the cut? Explain.
6. Fortinbras gives Hamlet a soldier's funeral. Is this ridiculous? Can it fairly be said that, in a sense, Hamlet has been at war? Explain.

General Questions

1. Hamlet in 5.2.10–11 speaks of a "divinity that shapes our ends." To what extent does "divinity" (or Fate or mysterious Chance) play a role in the happenings?
2. How do Laertes, Fortinbras, and Horatio help to define Hamlet for us?
3. T. S. Eliot says (in "Shakespeare and the Stoicism of Seneca") that Hamlet, having made a mess, "dies fairly well pleased with himself." Evaluate.

Henrik Ibsen

Henrik Ibsen (1828–1906) was born in Skien, Norway, of wealthy parents who soon after his birth lost their money. Ibsen worked as a pharmacist's apprentice, but at the age of 22 he had written his first play, a promising melodrama entitled Cataline. *He engaged in theater work first in Norway and then in Denmark and Germany. By 1865 his plays had won him a state pension that enabled him to settle in Rome. After writing romantic, historic, and poetic plays, he turned to realistic drama with* The League of Youth *(1869). Among the major realistic "problem plays" are* A Doll's House *(1879),* Ghosts *(1881), and* An Enemy of the People *(1882). In* The Wild Duck *(1884) he moved toward a more symbolic tragic comedy, and his last plays, written in the nineties, are highly symbolic.* Hedda Gabler *(1890) looks backward to the plays of the eighties rather than forward to the plays of the nineties.*

A Doll's House (Harvard Theatre Collection)

A Doll's House

Translated by James McFarlane

CHARACTERS

TORVALD HELMER, a lawyer
NORA, his wife
DR. RANK
MRS. KRISTINE LINDE
NILS KROGSTAD
ANNE MARIE, the nursemaid
HELENE, the maid
THE HELMERS' THREE CHILDREN
A PORTER

The action takes place in the Helmers' flat.

Act I

A pleasant room, tastefully but not expensively furnished. On the back wall, one door on the right leads to the entrance hall, a second door on the left leads to HELMER'S *study. Between these two doors, a piano. In the middle of the left wall, a door; and downstage from it, a window. Near the window a round table with armchairs and a small sofa. In the right wall, upstage, a door; and on the same wall downstage, a porcelain stove with a couple of armchairs and a rocking chair. Between the stove and the door a small table. Etchings on the walls. A whatnot with china and other small objets d'art; a small bookcase with books in handsome bindings. Carpet on the floor; a fire burns in the stove. A winter's day.*

The front door-bell rings in the hall; a moment later, there is the sound of the front door being opened. NORA *comes into the room, happily humming to herself. She is dressed in her outdoor things, and is carrying lots of parcels which she then puts down on the table, right. She leaves the door into the hall standing open; a* PORTER *can be seen outside holding a Christmas tree and a basket; he hands them to the* MAID *who has opened the door for them.*

NORA.   Hide the Christmas tree away carefully, Helene. The children mustn't see it till this evening when it's decorated. [*To the* PORTER, *taking out her purse.*] How much?

PORTER.   Fifty öre.

NORA.   There's a crown. Keep the change.

[*The* PORTER *thanks her and goes.* NORA *shuts the door. She continues to laugh quietly and happily to herself as she takes off her things. She takes a bag of macaroons out of her pocket and eats one or two; then she walks stealthily across and listens at her husband's door.*]

NORA.   Yes, he's in.

[*She begins humming again as she walks over to the table, right.*]

HELMER   [*in his study*].   Is that my little sky-lark chirruping out there?

NORA   [*busy opening some of the parcels*].   Yes, it is.

HELMER.   Is that my little squirrel frisking about?

NORA.   Yes!

HELMER.   When did my little squirrel get home?

NORA.   Just this minute. [*She stuffs the bag of macaroons in her pocket and wipes her mouth.*] Come on out, Torvald, and see what I've bought.

HELMER.   I don't want to be disturbed! [*A moment later, he opens the door and looks out, his pen in his hand.*] 'Bought', did you say? All that? Has my little spendthrift been out squandering money again?

NORA.   But, Torvald, surely this year we can spread ourselves just a little. This is the first Christmas we haven't had to go carefully.

HELMER.   Ah, but that doesn't mean we can afford to be extravagant, you know.

NORA.   Oh yes, Torvald, surely we can afford to be just a little bit extravagant now, can't we? Just a teeny-weeny bit. You are getting quite a good salary now, and you are going to earn lots and lots of money.

HELMER.   Yes, after the New Year. But it's going to be three whole months before the first pay cheque comes in.

NORA.   Pooh! We can always borrow in the meantime.

HELMER.   Nora! [*Crosses to her and takes her playfully by the ear.*] Here we go again, you and your frivolous ideas! Suppose I went and borrowed a thousand crowns today, and you went and spent it all over Christmas, then on New Year's Eve a slate fell and hit me on the head and there I was. . . .

NORA [*putting her hand over his mouth*].   Sh! Don't say such horrid things.

HELMER.   Yes, but supposing something like that did happen . . . what then?

NORA.   If anything as awful as that did happen, I wouldn't care if I owed anybody anything or not.

HELMER.   Yes, but what about the people I'd borrowed from?

NORA.   Them? Who cares about them! They are only strangers!

HELMER.   Nora, Nora! Just like a woman! Seriously though, Nora, you know what I think about these things. No debts! Never borrow! There's always something inhibited, something unpleasant, about a home built on credit and borrowed money. We two have managed to stick it out so far, and that's the way we'll go on for the little time that remains.

NORA [*walks over to the stove*].   Very well, just as you say, Torvald.

HELMER [*following her*].   There, there! My little singing bird mustn't go drooping her wings, eh? Has it got the sulks, that little squirrel of mine? [*Takes out his wallet.*] Nora, what do you think I've got here?

NORA [*quickly turning round*].   Money!

HELMER.   There! [*He hands her some notes.*] Good heavens, I know only too well how Christmas runs away with the housekeeping.

NORA [*counts*].   Ten, twenty, thirty, forty. Oh, thank you, thank you, Torvald! This will see me quite a long way.

HELMER.   Yes, it'll have to.

NORA.   Yes, yes, I'll see that it does. But come over here, I want to show you all the things I've bought. And so cheap! Look, some new clothes for Ivar . . . and a little sword. There's a horse and a trumpet for Bob. And a doll and a doll's cot for Emmy. They are not very grand but she'll have them all broken before long anyway. And I've got some dress material and some handkerchiefs for the maids. Though, really, dear old Anne Marie should have had something better.

HELMER.   And what's in this parcel here?

NORA [*shrieking*].   No, Torvald! You mustn't see that till tonight!

HELMER.   All right. But tell me now, what did my little spendthrift fancy for herself?

NORA.   For me? Puh, I don't really want anything.

HELMER.   Of course you do. Anything reasonable that you think you might like, just tell me.

NORA.   Well, I don't really know. As a matter of fact, though, Torvald . . .

HELMER.   Well?

NORA [*toying with his coat buttons, and without looking at him*].   If you did want to give me something, you could . . . you could always . . .

HELMER.   Well, well, out with it!

NORA [*quickly*].   You could always give me money, Torvald. Only what you think you could spare. And then I could buy myself something with it later on.

HELMER.   But Nora. . . .

NORA.   Oh, please, Torvald dear! Please! I beg you. Then I'd wrap the money up in some pretty gilt paper and hang it on the Christmas tree. Wouldn't that be fun?

HELMER.   What do we call my pretty little pet when it runs away with all the money?

NORA.   I know, I know, we call it a spendthrift. But please let's do what I said, Torvald. Then I'll have a bit of time to think about what I need most. Isn't that awfully sensible, now, eh?

HELMER [*smiling*].   Yes, it is indeed—that is, if only you really could hold on to the money I gave you, and really did buy something for yourself with it. But it just gets mixed up with the housekeeping and frittered away on all sorts of useless things, and then I have to dig into my pocket all over again.

NORA.   Oh but, Torvald. . . .

HELMER.   You can't deny it, Nora dear. [*Puts his arm round her waist.*] My pretty little pet is very sweet, but it runs away with an awful lot of money. It's incredible how expensive it is for a man to keep such a pet.

NORA.   For shame! How can you say such a thing? As a matter of fact I save everything I can.

HELMER [*laughs*].   Yes, you are right there. Everything you *can*. But you simply can't.

NORA [*hums and smiles quietly and happily*].   Ah, if you only knew how many expenses the likes of us sky-larks and squirrels have, Torvald!

HELMER.   What a funny little one you are! Just like your father. Always on the look-out for money, wherever you can lay your hands on it; but as soon as you've got it, it just seems to slip through your fingers. You never seem to know what you've done with it. Well, one must accept you as you are. It's in the blood. Oh yes, it is, Nora. That sort of thing is hereditary.

NORA.   Oh, I only wish I'd inherited a few more of Daddy's qualities.

HELMER.   And I wouldn't want my pretty little song-bird to be the least bit different from what she is now. But come to think of it, you look rather . . . rather . . . how shall I put it? . . . rather guilty today. . . .

NORA.   Do I?

HELMER.   Yes, you do indeed. Look me straight in the eye.

NORA [*looks at him*].   Well?

HELMER [*wagging his finger at her*].   My little sweet-tooth surely didn't forget herself in town today?

NORA.   No, whatever makes you think that?

HELMER.   She didn't just pop into the confectioner's for a moment?

NORA.   No, I assure you, Torvald . . . !

HELMER.   Didn't try sampling the preserves?

NORA.   No, really I didn't.

HELMER.   Didn't go nibbling a macaroon or two?

NORA.   No, Torvald, honestly, you must believe me . . . !

HELMER.   All right then! It's really just my little joke. . . .

NORA [*crosses to the table*].   I would never dream of doing anything you didn't want me to.

HELMER.   Of course not, I know that. And then you've given me your word. . . . [*Crosses to her.*] Well then, Nora dearest, you shall keep your little Christmas secrets. They'll all come out tonight, I dare say, when we light the tree.

NORA.   Did you remember to invite Dr. Rank?

HELMER.   No. But there's really no need. Of course he'll come and have dinner with us. Anyway, I can ask him when he looks in this morning. I've ordered some good wine. Nora, you can't imagine how I am looking forward to this evening.

NORA.   So am I. And won't the children enjoy it, Torvald!

HELMER.   Oh, what a glorious feeling it is, knowing you've got a nice, safe job, and a good fat income. Don't you agree? Isn't it wonderful, just thinking about it?

NORA.   Oh, it's marvellous!

HELMER.   Do you remember last Christmas? Three whole weeks beforehand you shut yourself up every evening till after midnight making flowers for the Christmas tree and all the other splendid things you wanted to surprise us with. Ugh, I never felt so bored in all my life.

NORA.   I wasn't the least bit bored.

HELMER [*smiling*].   But it turned out a bit of an anticlimax, Nora.

NORA.   Oh, you are not going to tease me about that again! How was I to know the cat would get in and pull everything to bits?

HELMER.   No, of course you weren't. Poor little Nora! All you wanted was for us to have a nice time—and it's the thought behind it that counts, after all. All the same, it's a good thing we've seen the back of those lean times.

NORA.   Yes, really it's marvellous.

HELMER.   Now there's no need for me to sit here all on my own, bored to tears. And you don't have to strain your dear little eyes, and work those dainty little fingers to the bone. . . .

NORA [*clapping her hands*].   No, Torvald, I don't, do I? Not any more. Oh, how marvellous it is to hear that! [*Takes his arm.*] Now I want to tell you how I've been thinking we might arrange things, Torvald. As soon as Christmas is over. . . . [*The door-bell rings in the hall.*] Oh, there's the bell. [*Tidies one or two things in the room.*] It's probably a visitor. What a nuisance!

HELMER.   Remember I'm not at home to callers.

MAID [*in the doorway*].   There's a lady to see you, ma'am.

NORA.   Show her in, please.

MAID [*to* HELMER].   And the doctor's just arrived, too, sir.

HELMER.   Did he go straight into my room?

MAID.   Yes, he did, sir.

[HELMER *goes into his study. The* MAID *shows in Mrs. Linde, who is in travelling clothes, and closes the door after her.*]

MRS. LINDE [*subdued and rather hesitantly*].   How do you do, Nora?

NORA [*uncertainly*].   How do you do?

MRS. LINDE.   I'm afraid you don't recognize me.

NORA.   No, I don't think I . . . And yet I seem to. . . . [*Bursts out suddenly.*] Why! Kristine! Is it really you?

MRS. LINDE.   Yes, it's me.

NORA.   Kristine! Fancy not recognizing you again! But how was I to, when . . . [*Gently.*] How you've changed, Kristine!

MRS. LINDE.   I dare say I have. In nine . . . ten years. . . .

NORA.   Is it so long since we last saw each other? Yes, it must be. Oh, believe me these last eight years have been such a happy time. And now you've come up to town, too? All that long journey in wintertime. That took courage.

MRS. LINDE.   I just arrived this morning on the steamer.

NORA.   To enjoy yourself over Christmas, of course. How lovely! Oh, we'll have such fun, you'll see. Do take off your things. You are not cold, are you? [*Helps her.*] There now! Now let's sit down here in comfort beside the stove. No, here, you take the armchair, I'll sit here on the rocking chair. [*Takes her hands.*] Ah, now you look a bit more like your old self again. It was just that when I first saw you. . . . But you are a little paler, Kristine . . . and perhaps even a bit thinner!

MRS. LINDE.   And much, much older, Nora.

NORA.   Yes, perhaps a little older . . . very, very little, not really very much. [*Stops suddenly and looks serious.*] Oh, what a thoughtless creature I am, sitting here chattering on like this! Dear, sweet Kristine, can you forgive me?

MRS. LINDE.   What do you mean, Nora?

NORA [*gently*].   Poor Kristine, of course you're a widow now.

MRS. LINDE.   Yes, my husband died three years ago.

NORA.   Oh, I remember now. I read about it in the papers. Oh, Kristine, believe me I often thought at the time of writing to you. But I kept putting it off, something always seemed to crop up.

MRS. LINDE.   My dear Nora, I understand so well.

NORA.   No, it wasn't very nice of me, Kristine. Oh, you poor thing, what you must have gone through. And didn't he leave you anything?

MRS. LINDE.   No.

NORA.   And no children?

MRS. LINDE.   No.

NORA.   Absolutely nothing?

MRS. LINDE.   Nothing at all . . . not even a broken heart to grieve over.

NORA [*looks at her incredulously*].   But, Kristine, is that possible?

MRS. LINDE [*smiles sadly and strokes* NORA's *hair*].   Oh, it sometimes happens, Nora.

NORA.   So utterly alone. How terribly sad that must be for you. I have three lovely children. You can't see them for the moment, because they're out with their nanny. But now you must tell me all about yourself. . . .

MRS. LINDE.   No, no, I want to hear about you.

NORA.   No, you start. I won't be selfish today. I must think only about your affairs today. But there's just one thing I really must tell you. Have you heard about the great stroke of luck we've had in the last few days?

MRS. LINDE.   No. What is it?

NORA.   What do you think? My husband has just been made Bank Manager!

MRS. LINDE.   Your husband? How splendid!

NORA.   Isn't it tremendous! It's not a very steady way of making a living, you know, being a lawyer, especially if he refuses to take on anything that's the least bit shady—which of course is what Torvald does, and I think he's quite right. You can imagine how pleased we are! He starts at the Bank straight after New Year, and he's getting a big salary and lots of commission. From now on we'll be able to live quite differently . . . we'll do just what we want. Oh, Kristine, I'm so happy and relieved. I must say it's lovely to have plenty of money and not have to worry. Isn't it?

MRS. LINDE.   Yes. It must be nice to have enough, at any rate.

NORA.   No, not just enough, but pots and pots of money.

MRS. LINDE [*smiles*].   Nora, Nora, haven't you learned any sense yet? At school you used to be an awful spendthrift.

NORA.   Yes, Torvald still says I am. [*Wags her finger.*] But little Nora isn't as stupid as everybody thinks. Oh, we haven't really been in a position where I could afford to spend a lot of money. We've both had to work.

MRS. LINDE.   You too?

NORA.   Yes, odd jobs—sewing, crochet-work, embroidery and things like that. [*Casually.*] And one or two other things, besides. I suppose you know that Torvald left the Ministry when we got married. There weren't any prospects of promotion in his department, and of course he needed to earn more money than he had before. But the first year he wore himself out completely. He had to take on all kinds of extra jobs, you know, and he found himself working all hours of the day and night. But he couldn't go on like that; and he became seriously ill. The doctors said it was essential for him to go South.

MRS. LINDE.   Yes, I believe you spent a whole year in Italy, didn't you?

NORA.   That's right. It wasn't easy to get away, I can tell you. It was just after I'd had Ivar. But of course we had to go. Oh, it was an absolutely marvellous trip. And it saved Torvald's life. But it cost an awful lot of money, Kristine.

MRS. LINDE.   That I can well imagine.

NORA.   Twelve hundred dollars. Four thousand eight hundred crowns. That's a lot of money, Kristine.

MRS. LINDE.   Yes, but in such circumstances, one is very lucky if one has it.

NORA.   Well, we got it from Daddy, you see.

MRS. LINDE.   Ah, that was it. It was just about then your father died, I believe, wasn't it?

NORA.   Yes, Kristine, just about then. And do you know, I couldn't even go and look after him. Here was I expecting Ivar any day. And I also had poor Torvald, gravely ill, on my hands. Dear, kind Daddy! I never saw him again, Kristine. Oh, that's the saddest thing that has happened to me in all my married life.

MRS. LINDE.   I know you were very fond of him. But after that you left for Italy?

NORA.   Yes, we had the money then, and the doctors said it was urgent. We left a month later.

MRS. LINDE.   And your husband came back completely cured?

NORA.   Fit as a fiddle!

MRS. LINDE.   But . . . what about the doctor?

NORA.   How do you mean?

MRS. LINDE.   I thought the maid said something about the gentleman who came at the same time as me being a doctor.

NORA.   Yes, that was Dr. Rank. But this isn't a professional visit. He's our best friend and he always looks in at least once a day. No, Torvald has never had a day's illness since. And the children are fit and healthy, and so am I. [*Jumps up and claps her hands.*] Oh God, oh God, isn't it marvellous to be alive, and to be happy, Kristine! . . . Oh, but I ought to be ashamed of myself . . . Here I go on talking about nothing but myself. [*She sits on a low stool near* MRS. LINDE *and lays her arms on her lap.*] Oh, please, you mustn't be angry with me! Tell me, is it really true that you didn't love your husband? What made you marry him, then?

MRS. LINDE.   My mother was still alive; she was bedridden and helpless. And then I had my two young brothers to look after as well. I didn't think I would be justified in refusing him.

NORA.   No, I dare say you are right. I suppose he was fairly wealthy then?

MRS. LINDE.   He was quite well off, I believe. But the business was shaky. When he died, it went all to pieces, and there just wasn't anything left.

NORA.   What then?

MRS. LINDE.   Well, I had to fend for myself, opening a little shop, running a little school, anything I could turn my hand to. These last three years have been one long relentless drudge. But now it's finished, Nora. My poor dear mother doesn't need me any more, she's passed away. Nor the boys either; they're at work now, they can look after themselves.

NORA.   What a relief you must find it. . . .

MRS. LINDE.   No, Nora! Just unutterably empty. Nobody to live for any more. [*Stands up restless.*] That's why I couldn't stand it any longer being cut off up there. Surely it must be a bit easier here to find something to occupy your mind. If only I could manage to find a steady job of some kind, in an office perhaps. . . .

NORA.   But, Kristine, that's terribly exhausting; and you look so worn out even before you start. The best thing for you would be a little holiday at some quiet little resort.

MRS. LINDE [*crosses to the window*].   I haven't any father I can fall back on for the money, Nora.

NORA [*rises*].   Oh, please, you mustn't be angry with me!

MRS. LINDE [*goes to her*].   My dear Nora, you mustn't be angry with me either. That's the worst thing about people in my position, they become so bitter. One has nobody to work for, yet one has to be on the look-out all the time.

Life has to go on, and one starts thinking only of oneself. Believe it or not,
when you told me the good news about your step up, I was pleased not so
much for your sake as for mine.

NORA.   How do you mean? Ah, I see. You think Torvald might be able to do
something for you.

MRS. LINDE.   Yes, that's exactly what I thought.

NORA.   And so he shall, Kristine. Just leave things to me. I'll bring it up so cleverly
. . . I'll think up something to put him in a good mood. Oh, I do so much
want to help you.

MRS. LINDE.   It is awfully kind of you, Nora, offering to do all this for me, particularly in your case, where you haven't known much trouble or hardship in
your own life.

NORA.   When I . . . ? I haven't known much . . . ?

MRS. LINDE [*smiling*].   Well, good heavens, a little bit of sewing to do and a few
things like that. What a child you are, Nora!

NORA [*tosses her head and walks across the room*].   I wouldn't be too sure of that,
if I were you.

MRS. LINDE.   Oh?

NORA.   You're just like the rest of them. You all think I'm useless when it comes to
anything really serious. . . .

MRS. LINDE.   Come, come. . . .

NORA.   You think I've never had anything much to contend with in this hard world.

MRS. LINDE.   Nora dear, you've only just been telling me all the things you've had
to put up with.

NORA.   Pooh! They were just trivialities! [*Softly.*] I haven't told you about the really
big thing.

MRS. LINDE.   What big thing? What do you mean?

NORA.   I know you rather tend to look down on me, Kristine. But you shouldn't, you
know. You are proud of having worked so hard and so long for your mother.

MRS. LINDE.   I'm sure I don't look down on anybody. But it's true what you say: I
am both proud and happy when I think of how I was able to make Mother's
life a little easier towards the end.

NORA.   And you are proud when you think of what you have done for your
brothers, too.

MRS. LINDE.   I think I have every right to be.

NORA.   I think so too. But now I'm going to tell you something, Kristine. I too
have something to be proud and happy about.

MRS. LINDE.   I don't doubt that. But what is it you mean?

NORA.   Not so loud. Imagine if Torvald were to hear! He must never on any account . . . nobody must know about it, Kristine, nobody but you.

MRS. LINDE.   But what is it?

NORA.   Come over here. [*She pulls her down on the sofa beside her.*] Yes, Kristine, I
too have something to be proud and happy about. I was the one who saved
Torvald's life.

MRS. LINDE.   Saved . . . ? How . . . ?

NORA.   I told you about our trip to Italy. Torvald would never have recovered but
for that. . . .

MRS. LINDE.   Well? Your father gave you what money was necessary. . . .

NORA [*smiles*].   That's what Torvald thinks, and everybody else. But . . .

MRS. LINDE.   But . . . ?

NORA.   Daddy never gave us a penny. I was the one who raised the money.

MRS. LINDE.   You? All that money?

NORA.   Twelve hundred dollars. Four thousand eight hundred crowns. What do you say to that!

MRS. LINDE.   But, Nora, how was it possible? Had you won a sweepstake or something?

NORA [*contemptuously*].   A sweepstake? Pooh! There would have been nothing to it then.

MRS. LINDE.   Where did you get it from, then?

NORA [*hums and smiles secretively*].   H'm, tra-la-la!

MRS. LINDE.   Because what you couldn't do was borrow it.

NORA.   Oh? Why not?

MRS. LINDE.   Well, a wife can't borrow without her husband's consent.

NORA [*tossing her head*].   Ah, but when it happens to be a wife with a bit of a sense for business . . . a wife who knows her way about things, then. . . .

MRS. LINDE.   But, Nora, I just don't understand. . . .

NORA.   You don't have to. I haven't said I did borrow the money. I might have got it some other way. [*Throws herself back on the sofa.*] I might even have got it from some admirer. Anyone as reasonably attractive as I am. . . .

MRS. LINDE.   Don't be so silly!

NORA.   Now you must be dying of curiosity, Kristine.

MRS. LINDE.   Listen to me now, Nora dear—you haven't done anything rash, have you?

NORA [*sitting up again*].   Is it rash to save your husband's life?

MRS. LINDE.   I think it was rash to do anything without telling him. . . .

NORA.   But the whole point was that he mustn't know anything. Good heavens, can't you see! He wasn't even supposed to know how desperately ill he was. It was me the doctors came and told his life was in danger, that the only way to save him was to go South for a while. Do you think I didn't try talking him into it first? I began dropping hints about how nice it would be if I could be taken on a little trip abroad, like other young wives. I wept, I pleaded. I told him he ought to show some consideration for my condition, and let me have a bit of my own way. And then I suggested he might take out a loan. But at that he nearly lost his temper, Kristine. He said I was being frivolous, that it was his duty as a husband not to give in to all these whims and fancies of mine—as I do believe he called them. All right, I thought, somehow you've got to be saved. And it was then I found a way. . . .

MRS. LINDE.   Did your husband never find out from your father that the money hadn't come from him?

NORA.   No, never. It was just about the time Daddy died. I'd intended letting him into the secret and asking him not to give me away. But when he was so ill . . . I'm sorry to say it never became necessary.

MRS. LINDE.   And you never confided in your husband?

NORA.   Good heavens, how could you ever imagine such a thing! When he's so strict about such matters! Besides, Torvald is a man with a good deal of pride—it would be terribly embarrassing and humiliating for him if he thought he owed anything to me. It would spoil everything between us; this happy home of ours would never be the same again.

MRS. LINDE.   Are you never going to tell him?

NORA [*reflectively, half-smiling*].   Oh yes, some day perhaps . . . in many years time, when I'm no longer as pretty as I am now. You mustn't laugh! What I mean of course is when Torvald isn't quite so much in love with me as he is

now, when he's lost interest in watching me dance, or get dressed up, or recite. Then it might be a good thing to have something in reserve. . . . [*Breaks
off.*] What nonsense! That day will never come. Well, what have you got to
say to my big secret, Kristine? Still think I'm not much good for anything? One
thing, though, it's meant a lot of worry for me, I can tell you. It hasn't always
been easy to meet my obligations when the time came. You know in business there is something called quarterly interest, and other things called instalments, and these are always terribly difficult things to cope with. So what
I've had to do is save a little here and there, you see, wherever I could. I
couldn't really save anything out of the housekeeping, because Torvald has
to live in decent style. I couldn't let the children go about badly dressed either—I felt any money I got for them had to go on them alone. Such sweet
little things!

MRS. LINDE.   Poor Nora! So it had to come out of your own allowance?

NORA.   Of course. After all, I was the one it concerned most. Whenever Torvald
gave me money for new clothes and such-like, I never spent more than half.
And always I bought the simplest and cheapest things. It's a blessing most
things look well on me, so Torvald never noticed anything. But sometimes I
did feel it was a bit hard, Kristine, because it is nice to be well dressed, isn't it?

MRS. LINDE.   Yes, I suppose it is.

NORA.   I have had some other sources of income, of course. Last winter I was
lucky enough to get quite a bit of copying to do. So I shut myself up every
night and sat and wrote through to the small hours of the morning. Oh, sometimes I was so tired, so tired. But it was tremendous fun all the same, sitting
there working and earning money like that. It was almost like being a man.

MRS. LINDE.   And how much have you been able to pay off like this?

NORA.   Well, I can't tell exactly. It's not easy to know where you are with transactions
of this kind, you understand. All I know is I've paid off just as much as I could
scrape together. Many's the time I was at my wit's end. [*Smiles.*] Then I used to sit
here and pretend that some rich old gentleman had fallen in love with me. . . .

MRS. LINDE.   What! What gentleman?

NORA.   Oh, rubbish! . . . and that now he had died, and when they opened his
will, there in big letters were the words: 'My entire fortune is to be paid over,
immediately and in cash, to charming Mrs. Nora Helmer.'

MRS. LINDE.   But my dear Nora—who is this man?

NORA.   Good heavens, don't you understand? There never was any old gentleman;
it was just something I used to sit here pretending, time and time again, when I
didn't know where to turn next for money. But it doesn't make very much difference; as far as I'm concerned, the old boy can do what he likes, I'm tired of
him; I can't be bothered any more with him or his will. Because now all my
worries are over. [*Jumping up.*] Oh God, what a glorious thought, Kristine! No
more worries! Just think of being without a care in the world . . . being able to
romp with the children, and making the house nice and attractive, and having
things just as Torvald likes to have them! And then spring will soon be here, and
blue skies. And maybe we can go away somewhere. I might even see something of the sea again. Oh yes! When you're happy, life is a wonderful thing!

[*The door-bell is heard in the hall.*]

MRS. LINDE [*gets up*].   There's the bell. Perhaps I'd better go.

NORA.   No, do stay, please. I don't suppose it's for me; it's probably somebody for
Torvald . . .

MAID   [*in the doorway*].   Excuse me, ma'am, but there's a gentleman here wants to see Mr. Helmer, and I didn't quite know . . . because the Doctor is in there. . . .

NORA.   Who is the gentleman?

KROGSTAD [*in the doorway*].   It's me, Mrs. Helmer.

[MRS. LINDE *starts, then turns away to the window.*]

NORA [*tense, takes a step towards him and speaks in a low voice*].   You? What is it? What do you want to talk to my husband about?

KROGSTAD.   Bank matters . . . in a manner of speaking. I work at the bank, and I hear your husband is to be the new manager. . . .

NORA.   So it's . . .

KROGSTAD.   Just routine business matters, Mrs. Helmer. Absolutely nothing else.

NORA.   Well then, please go into his study.

[*She nods impassively and shuts the hall door behind him; then she walks across and sees to the stove.*]

MRS. LINDE.   Nora . . . who was that man?

NORA.   His name is Krogstad.

MRS. LINDE.   So it really was him.

NORA.   Do you know the man?

MRS. LINDE.   I used to know him . . . a good many years ago. He was a solicitor's clerk in our district for a while.

NORA.   Yes, so he was.

MRS. LINDE.   How he's changed!

NORA.   His marriage wasn't a very happy one, I believe.

MRS. LINDE.   He's a widower now, isn't he?

NORA.   With a lot of children. There, it'll burn better now.

[*She closes the stove door and moves the rocking chair a little to one side.*]

MRS. LINDE.   He does a certain amount of business on the side, they say?

NORA.   Oh? Yes, it's always possible. I just don't know. . . . But let's not think about business . . . it's all so dull.

[DR. RANK *comes in from* HELMER's *study.*]

DR. RANK [*still in the doorway*].   No, no, Torvald, I won't intrude. I'll just look in on your wife for a moment. [*Shuts the door and notices* MRS. LINDE.] Oh, I beg your pardon. I'm afraid I'm intruding here as well.

NORA.   No, not at all! [*Introduces them.*] Dr. Rank . . . Mrs. Linde.

RANK.   Ah! A name I've often heard mentioned in this house. I believe I came past you on the stairs as I came in.

MRS. LINDE.   I have to take things slowly going upstairs. I find it rather a trial.

RANK.   Ah, some little disability somewhere, eh?

MRS. LINDE.   Just a bit run down, I think, actually.

RANK.   Is that all? Then I suppose you've come to town for a good rest—doing the rounds of the parties?

MRS. LINDE.   I have come to look for work.

RANK.   Is that supposed to be some kind of sovereign remedy for being run down?

MRS. LINDE.   One must live, Doctor.

RANK.   Yes, it's generally thought to be necessary.

NORA.   Come, come, Dr. Rank. You are quite as keen to live as anybody.

RANK.   Quite keen, yes. Miserable as I am, I'm quite ready to let things drag on as long as possible. All my patients are the same. Even those with a moral affliction are no different. As a matter of fact, there's a bad case of that kind in talking with Helmer at this very moment . . .

MRS. LINDE [*softly*].   Ah!

NORA.   Whom do you mean?

RANK.   A person called Krogstad—nobody you would know. He's rotten to the core. But even he began talking about having to *live*, as though it were something terribly important.

NORA.   Oh? And what did he want to talk to Torvald about?

RANK.   I honestly don't know. All I heard was something about the Bank.

NORA.   I didn't know that Krog . . . that this Mr. Krogstad had anything to do with the Bank.

RANK.   Oh yes, he's got some kind of job down there. [*To* MRS. LINDE.] I wonder if you've got people in your part of the country too who go rushing round sniffing out cases of moral corruption, and then installing the individuals concerned in nice, well-paid jobs where they can keep them under observation. Sound, decent people have to be content to stay out in the cold.

MRS. LINDE.   Yet surely it's the sick who most need to be brought in.

RANK [*shrugs his shoulders*].   Well, there we have it. It's that attitude that's turning society into a clinic.

[NORA, *lost in her own thoughts, breaks into smothered laughter and claps her hands.*]

RANK.   Why are you laughing at that? Do you know in fact what society is?

NORA.   What do I care about your silly old society? I was laughing about something quite different . . . something frightfully funny. Tell me, Dr. Rank, are all the people who work at the Bank dependent on Torvald now?

RANK.   Is that what you find so frightfully funny?

NORA [*smiles and hums*].   Never you mind! Never you mind! [*Walks about the room.*] Yes, it really is terribly amusing to think that we . . . that Torvald now has power over so many people. [*She takes the bag out of her pocket.*] Dr. Rank, what about a little macaroon?

RANK.   Look at this, eh? Macaroons. I thought they were forbidden here.

NORA.   Yes, but these are some Kristine gave me.

MRS. LINDE.   What? I . . .?

NORA.   Now, now, you needn't be alarmed. You weren't to know that Torvald had forbidden them. He's worried in case they ruin my teeth, you know. Still . . . what's it matter once in a while! Don't you think so, Dr. Rank? Here! [*She pops a macaroon into his mouth.*] And you too, Kristine. And I shall have one as well; just a little one . . . or two at the most. [*She walks about the room again.*] Really I am so happy. There's just one little thing I'd love to do now.

RANK.   What's that?

NORA.   Something I'd love to say in front of Torvald.

RANK.   Then why can't you?

NORA.   No, I daren't. It's not very nice.

MRS. LINDE.   Not very nice?

RANK.   Well, in that case it might not be wise. But to us, I don't see why. . . . What is this you would love to say in front of Helmer?

NORA.   I would simply love to say: 'Damn.'

RANK.   Are you mad!

MRS. LINDE.   Good gracious, Nora . . .!

RANK.   Say it! Here he is!

NORA [*hiding the bag of macaroons*].   Sh! Sh!

[HELMER *comes out of his room, his overcoat over his arm and his hat in his hand.*]

NORA [*going over to him*].   Well, Torvald dear, did you get rid of him?

HELMER.   Yes, he's just gone.

NORA.   Let me introduce you. This is Kristine, who has just arrived in town. . . .

HELMER.   Kristine . . . ? You must forgive me, but I don't think I know . . .

NORA.   Mrs. Linde, Torvald dear. Kristine Linde.

HELMER.   Ah, indeed. A school-friend of my wife's, presumably.

MRS. LINDE.   Yes, we were girls together.

NORA.   Fancy, Torvald, she's come all this long way just to have a word with you.

HELMER.   How is that?

MRS. LINDE.   Well, it wasn't really . . .

NORA.   The thing is, Kristine is terribly clever at office work, and she's frightfully keen on finding a job with some efficient man, so that she can learn even more. . . .

HELMER.   Very sensible, Mrs. Linde.

NORA.   And then when she heard you'd been made Bank Manager—there was a bit in the paper about it—she set off at once. Torvald please! You *will* try and do something for Kristine, won't you? For my sake?

HELMER.   Well, that's not altogether impossible. You are a widow, I presume?

MRS. LINDE.   Yes.

HELMER.   And you've had some experience in business?

MRS. LINDE.   A fair amount.

HELMER.   Well, it's quite probable I can find you a job, I think. . . .

NORA [*clapping her hands*].   There, you see!

HELMER.   You have come at a fortunate moment, Mrs. Linde. . . .

MRS. LINDE.   Oh, how can I ever thank you . . . ?

HELMER.   Not a bit. [*He puts on his overcoat.*] But for the present I must ask you to excuse me. . . .

RANK.   Wait. I'm coming with you.

[*He fetches his fur coat from the hall and warms it at the stove.*]

NORA.   Don't be long, Torvald dear.

HELMER.   Not more than an hour, that's all.

NORA.   Are you leaving too, Kristine?

MRS. LINDE [*putting on her things*].   Yes, I must go and see if I can't find my-self a room.

HELMER.   Perhaps we can all walk down the road together.

NORA [*helping her*].   What a nuisance we are so limited for space here. I'm afraid it just isn't possible. . . .

MRS. LINDE.   Oh, you mustn't dream of it! Goodbye, Nora dear, and thanks for everything.

NORA.   Goodbye for the present. But . . . you'll be coming back this evening, of course. And you too, Dr. Rank? What's that? If you are up to it? Of course you'll be up to it. Just wrap yourself up well.

[*They go out, talking, into the hall; children's voices can be heard on the stairs.*]

NORA.   Here they are! Here they are! [*She runs to the front door and opens it. Anne Marie, the* NURSEMAID, *enters with the children.*] Come in! Come in! [*She *bends down and kisses them.*] Ah! my sweet little darlings. . . . You see them, Kristine? Aren't they lovely!

RANK.   Don't stand here chattering in this draught!

HELMER.   Come along, Mrs. Linde. The place now becomes unbearable for anybody except mothers.

[DR. RANK, HELMER *and* MRS. LINDE *go down the stairs: the* NURSEMAID *comes into the room with the children, then* NORA, *shutting the door behind her.*]

NORA.   How fresh and bright you look! My, what red cheeks you've got! Like apples and roses. [*During the following, the children keep chattering away to her.*] Have you had a nice time? That's splendid. And you gave Emmy and Bob a ride on your sledge? Did you now! Both together! Fancy that! There's a clever boy, Ivar. Oh, let me take her a little while, Anne Marie. There's my sweet little baby-doll! [*She takes the youngest of the children from the* NURSE-MAID *and dances with her.*] All right, Mummy will dance with Bobby too. What? You've been throwing snowballs? Oh, I wish I'd been there. No, don't bother, Anne Marie, I'll help them off with their things. No, please, let me— I like doing it. You go on in, you look frozen. You'll find some hot coffee on the stove. [*The* NURSEMAID *goes into the room, left.* NORA *takes off the children's coats and hats and throws them down anywhere, while the children all talk at once.*] Really! A great big dog came running after you? But he didn't bite. No, the doggies wouldn't bite my pretty little dollies. You mustn't touch the parcels, Ivar! What are they? Wouldn't you like to know! No, no, that's nasty. Now? Shall we play something? What shall we play? Hide and seek? Yes, let's play hide and seek. Bob can hide first. Me first? All right, let me hide first.

[*She and the children play, laughing and shrieking, in this room and in the adjacent room on the right. Finally* NORA *hides under the table; the children come rushing in to look for her but cannot find her; they hear her stifled laughter, rush to the table, lift up the tablecloth and find her. Tremendous shouts of delight. She creeps out and pretends to frighten them. More shouts. Meanwhile there has been a knock at the front door, which nobody has heard. The door half opens, and* KROGSTAD *can be seen. He waits a little; the game continues.*]

KROGSTAD.   I beg your pardon, Mrs. Helmer. . . .

NORA [*turns with a stifled cry and half jumps up*].   Ah! What do you want?

KROGSTAD.   Excuse me. The front door was standing open. Somebody must have forgotten to shut it. . . .

NORA [*standing up*].   My husband isn't at home, Mr. Krogstad.

KROGSTAD.   I know.

NORA.   Well . . . what are you doing here?

KROGSTAD.   I want a word with you.

NORA.   With . . . ? [*Quietly, to the children.*] Go to Anne Marie. What? No, the strange man won't do anything to Mummy. When he's gone we'll have another game. [*She leads the children into the room, left, and shuts the door after them; tense and uneasy.*] You want to speak to me?

KROGSTAD.   Yes, I do.

NORA.   Today? But it isn't the first of the month yet. . . .

KROGSTAD.   No, it's Christmas Eve. It depends entirely on you what sort of Christmas you have.

NORA.   What do you want? Today I can't possibly . . .

KROGSTAD.   Let's not talk about that for the moment. It's something else. You've got a moment to spare?

NORA.   Yes, I suppose so, though . . .

KROGSTAD.   Good. I was sitting in Olsen's café, and I saw your husband go down the road . . .

NORA.   Did you?

KROGSTAD.   . . . with a lady.

NORA.   Well?

KROGSTAD.   May I be so bold as to ask whether that lady was a Mrs. Linde?

NORA.   Yes.

KROGSTAD.   Just arrived in town?

NORA.   Yes, today.

KROGSTAD.   And she's a good friend of yours?

NORA.   Yes, she is. But I can't see . . .

KROGSTAD.   I also knew her once.

NORA.   I know.

KROGSTAD.   Oh? So you know all about it. I thought as much. Well, I want to ask you straight: is Mrs. Linde getting a job in the Bank?

NORA.   How dare you cross-examine me like this, Mr. Krogstad? You, one of my husband's subordinates? But since you've asked me, I'll tell you. Yes, Mrs. Linde *has* got a job. And I'm the one who got it for her, Mr. Krogstad. Now you know.

KROGSTAD.   So my guess was right.

NORA [*walking up and down*].   Oh, I think I can say that some of us have a little influence now and again. Just because one happens to be a woman, that doesn't mean. . . . People in subordinate positions, ought to take care they don't offend anybody . . . who . . . hm . . .

KROGSTAD.   . . . has influence?

NORA.   Exactly.

KROGSTAD [*changing his tone*].   Mrs. Helmer, will you have the goodness to use your influence on my behalf?

NORA.   What? What do you mean?

KROGSTAD   Will you be so good as to see that I keep my modest little job at the Bank?

NORA.   What do you mean? Who wants to take it away from you?

KROGSTAD.   Oh, you needn't try and pretend to me you don't know. I can quite see that this friend of yours isn't particularly anxious to bump up against me. And I can also see now whom I can thank for being given the sack.

NORA.   But I assure you. . . .

KROGSTAD.   All right, all right. But to come to the point: there's still time. And I advise you to use your influence to stop it.

NORA.   But, Mr. Krogstad, I *have* no influence.

KROGSTAD.   Haven't you? I thought just now you said yourself . . .

NORA.   I didn't mean it that way, of course. Me? What makes you think I've got any influence of that kind over my husband?

KROGSTAD.   I know your husband from our student days. I don't suppose he is any more steadfast than other married men.

NORA.   You speak disrespectfully of my husband like that and I'll show you the door.

KROGSTAD.   So the lady's got courage.

NORA.   I'm not frightened of you any more. After New Year's I'll soon be finished with the whole business.

KROGSTAD [*controlling himself*].   Listen to me, Mrs. Helmer. If necessary I shall fight for my little job in the Bank as if I were fighting for my life.

NORA.   So it seems.

KROGSTAD.   It's not just for the money, that's the last thing I care about. There's something else . . . well, I might as well out with it. You see it's like this. You know as well as anybody that some years ago I got myself mixed up in a bit of trouble.

NORA.   I believe I've heard something of the sort.

KROGSTAD.   It never got as far as the courts; but immediately it was as if all paths were barred to me. So I started going in for the sort of business you know about. I had to do something, and I think I can say I haven't been one of the worst. But now I have to get out of it. My sons are growing up; for their sake I must try and win back what respectability I can. That job in the Bank was like the first step on the ladder for me. And now your husband wants to kick me off the ladder again, back into the mud.

NORA.   But in God's name, Mr. Krogstad, it's quite beyond my power to help you.

KROGSTAD.   That's because you haven't the will to help me. But I have ways of making you.

NORA.   You wouldn't go and tell my husband I owe you money?

KROGSTAD.   Suppose I did tell him?

NORA.   It would be a rotten shame. [*Half choking with tears.*] That secret is all my pride and joy—why should he have to hear about it in this nasty, horrid way . . . hear about it from *you*. You would make things horribly unpleasant for me. . . .

KROGSTAD.   Merely unpleasant?

NORA [*vehemently*].   Go on, do it then! It'll be all the worse for you. Because then my husband will see for himself what a bad man you are, and then you certainly won't be able to keep your job.

KROGSTAD.   I asked whether it was only a bit of domestic unpleasantness you were afraid of?

NORA.   If my husband gets to know about it, he'll pay off what's owing at once. And then we'd have nothing more to do with you.

KROGSTAD [*taking a pace towards her*].   Listen, Mrs. Helmer, either you haven't a very good memory, or else you don't understand much about business. I'd better make the position a little bit clearer for you.

NORA.   How do you mean?

KROGSTAD.   When your husband was ill, you came to me for the loan of twelve hundred dollars.

NORA.   I didn't know of anybody else.

KROGSTAD.   I promised to find you the money. . . .

NORA.   And you did find it.

KROGSTAD.   I promised to find you the money on certain conditions. At the time you were so concerned about your husband's illness, and so anxious to get the money for going away with, that I don't think you paid very much attention to all the incidentals. So there is perhaps some point in reminding you of them. Well, I promised to find you the money against an IOU which I drew up for you.

NORA.   Yes, and which I signed.

KROGSTAD.   Very good. But below that I added a few lines, by which your father was to stand security. This your father was to sign.

NORA.   Was to . . . ? He did sign it.

KROGSTAD.   I had left the date blank. The idea was that your father was to add the date himself when he signed it. Remember?

NORA.   Yes, I think. . . .

KROGSTAD.   I then gave you the IOU to post to your father. Wasn't that so?

NORA.   Yes.

KROGSTAD.   Which of course you did at once. Because only about five or six days later you brought it back to me with your father's signature. I then paid out the money.

NORA.   Well? Haven't I paid the instalments regularly?

KROGSTAD.   Yes, fairly. But . . . coming back to what we were talking about . . . that was a pretty bad period you were going through then, Mrs. Helmer.

NORA.   Yes, it was.

KROGSTAD.   Your father was seriously ill, I believe.

NORA.   He was very near the end.

KROGSTAD.   And died shortly afterwards?

NORA.   Yes.

KROGSTAD.   Tell me, Mrs. Helmer, do you happen to remember which day your father died? The exact date, I mean.

NORA.   Daddy died on 29 September.

KROGSTAD.   Quite correct. I made some inquiries. Which brings up a rather curious point [*takes out a paper*] which I simply cannot explain.

NORA.   Curious . . . ? I don't know . . .

KROGSTAD.   The curious thing is, Mrs. Helmer, that your father signed this document three days after his death.

NORA.   What? I don't understand. . . .

KROGSTAD.   Your father died on 29 September. But look here. Your father has dated his signature 2 October. Isn't that rather curious, Mrs. Helmer? [NORA *remains silent.*] It's also remarkable that the words '2 October' and the year are not in your father's handwriting, but in a handwriting I rather think I recognize. Well, perhaps that could be explained. Your father might have forgotten to date his signature, and then somebody else might have made a guess at the date later, before the fact of your father's death was known. There is nothing wrong in that. What really matters is the signature. And *that* is of course genuine, Mrs. Helmer? It really was your father who wrote his name here?

NORA   [*after a moment's silence, throws her head back and looks at him defiantly*]. No, it wasn't. It was me who signed father's name.

KROGSTAD.   Listen to me. I suppose you realize that that is a very dangerous confession?

NORA.   Why? You'll soon have all your money back.

KROGSTAD.   Let me ask you a question: why didn't you send that document to your father?

NORA.   It was impossible. Daddy was ill. If I'd asked him for his signature, I'd have to tell him what the money was for. Don't you see, when he was as ill as that I couldn't go and tell him that my husband's life was in danger. It was simply impossible.

KROGSTAD.   It would have been better for you if you had abandoned the whole trip.

NORA.   No, that was impossible. This was the thing that was to save my husband's life. I couldn't give it up.

KROGSTAD.   But did it never strike you that this was fraudulent . . . ?

NORA.   That wouldn't have meant anything to me. Why should I worry about you? I couldn't stand you, not when you insisted on going through with all those cold-blooded formalities, knowing all the time what a critical state my husband was in.

KROGSTAD.   Mrs. Helmer, it's quite clear you still haven't the faintest idea what it is you've committed. But let me tell you, my own offence was no more and no worse than that, and it ruined my entire reputation.

NORA.   You? Are you trying to tell me that you once risked everything to save your wife's life?

KROGSTAD.   The law takes no account of motives.

NORA.   Then they must be very bad laws.

KROGSTAD.   Bad or not, if I produce this document in court, you'll be condemned according to them.

NORA.   I don't believe it. Isn't a daughter entitled to try and save her father from worry and anxiety on his deathbed? Isn't a wife entitled to save her husband's life? I might not know very much about the law, but I feel sure of one thing: it must say somewhere that things like this are allowed. You mean to say you don't know that   you, when it's your job? You must be a rotten lawyer, Mr. Krogstad.

KROGSTAD.   That may be. But when it comes to business transactions—like the sort between us two—perhaps you'll admit I know something about *them?* Good. Now you must please yourself. But I tell you this: if I'm pitched out a second time, you are going to keep me company.

[*He bows and goes out through the hall.*]

NORA [*stands thoughtfully for a moment, then tosses her head*].   Rubbish! He's just trying to scare me. I'm not such a fool as all that. [*Begins gathering up the children's clothes; after a moment she stops.*] Yet . . . ? No, it's impossible! I did it for love, didn't I?

THE CHILDREN [*in the doorway, left*].   Mummy, the gentleman's just gone out of the gate.

NORA.   Yes, I know. But you mustn't say anything to anybody about that gentleman. You hear? Not even to Daddy!

THE CHILDREN.   All right, Mummy. Are you going to play again?

NORA.   No, not just now.

THE CHILDREN.   But Mummy, you promised!

NORA.   Yes, but I can't just now. Off you go now, I have a lot to do. Off you go, my darlings. [*She herds them carefully into the other room and shuts the door behind them. She sits down on the sofa, picks up her embroidery and works a few stitches, but soon stops.*] No! [*She flings her work down, stands up, goes to the hall door and calls out.*] Helene! Fetch the tree in for me, please. [*She walks across to the table, left, and opens the drawer; again pauses.*] No, really, it's quite impossible!

MAID [*with the Christmas tree*].   Where shall I put it, ma'am?

NORA.   On the floor there, in the middle.

MAID.   Anything else you want me to bring?

NORA.   No, thank you. I've got what I want.

[*The* MAID *has put the tree down and goes out.*]

NORA [*busy decorating the tree*].   Candles here . . . and flowers here—Revolting man! It's all nonsense! There's nothing to worry about. We'll have a lovely Christmas tree. And I'll do anything you want me to, Torvald; I'll sing for you, dance for you. . . .

[HELMER, *with a bundle of documents under his arm, comes in by the hall door.*]

NORA.   Ah, back again already?

HELMER.   Yes. Anybody been?

NORA.   Here? No.

HELMER.   That's funny. I just saw Krogstad leave the house.

NORA.   Oh? O yes, that's right. Krogstad was here a minute.

HELMER.   Nora, I can tell by your face he's been asking you to put a good word in for him.

NORA.   Yes.

HELMER.   And you were to pretend it was your own idea? You were to keep quiet about his having been here. He asked you to do that as well, didn't he?

NORA.   Yes, Torvald. But . . .

HELMER.   Nora, Nora, what possessed you to do a thing like that? Talking to a person like him, making him promises? And then on top of everything, to tell me a lie!

NORA.   A lie . . . ?

HELMER.   Didn't you say that nobody had been here? [*Wagging his finger at her.*] Never again must my little song-bird do a thing like that! Little song-birds must keep their pretty little beaks out of mischief; no chirruping out of tune! [*Puts his arm round her waist.*] Isn't that the way we want things to be? Yes, of course it is. [*Lets her go.*] So let's say no more about it. [*Sits down by the stove.*] Ah, nice and cosy here!

[*He glances through his papers.*]

NORA [*busy with the Christmas tree, after a short pause*].   Torvald!

HELMER.   Yes.

NORA.   I'm so looking forward to the fancy dress ball at the Stenborgs on Boxing Day.

HELMER.   And I'm terribly curious to see what sort of surprise you've got for me.

NORA.   Oh, it's too silly.

HELMER.   Oh?

NORA.   I just can't think of anything suitable. Everything seems so absurd, so pointless.

HELMER.   Has my little Nora come to *that* conclusion?

NORA [*behind his chair, her arms on the chairback*].   Are you very busy, Torvald?

HELMER.   Oh. . . .

NORA.   What are all those papers?

HELMER.   Bank matters.

NORA.   Already?

HELMER.   I have persuaded the retiring manager to give me authority to make any changes in organisation or personnel I think necessary. I have to work on it over the Christmas week. I want everything straight by the New Year.

NORA.   So that was why that poor Krogstad. . . .

HELMER.   Hm!

NORA [*still leaning against the back of the chair, running her fingers through his hair*].   If you hadn't been so busy, Torvald, I'd have asked you to do me an awfully big favour.

HELMER.   Let me hear it. What's it to be?

NORA.   Nobody's got such good taste as you. And the thing is I do so want to look my best at the fancy dress ball. Torvald, couldn't you give me some advice and tell me what you think I ought to go as, and how I should arrange my costume?

HELMER.   Aha! So my impulsive little woman is asking for somebody to come to her rescue, eh?

NORA.   Please, Torvald, I never get anywhere without your help.

HELMER.   Very well, I'll think about it. We'll find something.

NORA.   That's sweet of you. [*She goes across to the tree again; pause.*] How pretty
these red flowers look.—Tell me, was it really something terribly wrong this
man Krogstad did?

HELMER.   Forgery. Have you any idea what that means?

NORA.   Perhaps circumstances left him no choice?

HELMER.   Maybe. Or perhaps, like so many others, he just didn't think. I am not so
heartless that I would necessarily want to condemn a man for a single mistake like that.

NORA.   Oh no, Torvald, of course not!

HELMER.   Many a man might be able to redeem himself, if he honestly confessed
his guilt and took his punishment.

NORA.   Punishment?

HELMER.   But that wasn't the way Krogstad chose. He dodged what was due to
him by a cunning trick. And that's what has been the cause of his corruption.

NORA.   Do you think it would . . . ?

HELMER.   Just think how a man with a thing like that on his conscience will always
be having to lie and cheat and dissemble; he can never drop the mask, not
even with his own wife and children. And the children—*that's* the most terrible part of it, Nora.

NORA.   Why?

HELMER.   A fog of lies like that in a household, and it spreads disease and infection to every part of it. Every breath the children take in that kind of house is
reeking with evil germs.

NORA [*closer behind him*].   Are you sure of that?

HELMER.   My dear Nora, as a lawyer I know what I'm talking about. Practically all
juvenile delinquents come from homes where the mother is dishonest.

NORA.   Why mothers particularly?

HELMER.   It's generally traceable to the mothers, but of course fathers can have the
same influence. Every lawyer knows that only too well. And yet there's
Krogstad been poisoning his own children for years with lies and deceit. That's
the reason I call him morally depraved. [*Holds out his hands to her.*] That's why
my sweet little Nora must promise me not to try putting in any more good
words for him. Shake hands on it. Well? What's this? Give me your hand. There
now! That's settled. I assure you I would have found it impossible to work
with him. I quite literally feel physically sick in the presence of such people.

NORA [*draws her hand away and walks over to the other side of the Christmas tree*].
How hot it is in here! And I still have such a lot to do.

HELMER [*stands up and collects his papers together*].   Yes, I'd better think of getting
some of this read before dinner. I must also think about your costume. And I
might even be able to lay my hands on something to wrap in gold paper and
hang on the Christmas tree. [*He lays his hand on her head.*] My precious little
singing bird.

[*He goes into his study and shuts the door behind him.*]

NORA [*quietly, after a pause*].   Nonsense! It can't be. It's impossible. It *must* be impossible.

MAID [*in the doorway, left*].   The children keep asking so nicely if they can come
in and see Mummy.

NORA.   No, no, don't let them in! You stay with them, Anne Marie.

MAID.   Very well, ma'am.

[*She shuts the door.*]

NORA [*pale with terror*].   Corrupt my children . . . ! Poison my home? [*Short pause; she throws back her head.*] It's not true! It could never, never be true!

Act II

The same room. In the corner beside the piano stands the Christmas tree, stripped, bedraggled and with its candles burnt out. NORA's *outdoor things lie on the sofa.* NORA, *alone there, walks about restlessly; at last she stops by the sofa and picks up her coat.*

NORA [*putting her coat down again*].   Somebody's coming! [*Crosses to the door, listens.*] No, it's nobody. Nobody will come today, of course, Christmas Day— nor tomorrow, either. But perhaps. . . . [*She opens the door and looks out.*] No, nothing in the letter box; quite empty. [*Comes forward.*] Oh, nonsense! He didn't mean it seriously. Things like that *can't* happen. It's impossible. Why, I have three small children.

[*The* NURSEMAID *comes from the room, left, carrying a big cardboard box.*]

NURSEMAID.   I finally found it, the box with the fancy dress costumes.

NORA.   Thank you. Put it on the table, please.

NURSEMAID [*does this*].   But I'm afraid they are in an awful mess.

NORA.   Oh, if only I could rip them up into a thousand pieces!

NURSEMAID.   Good heavens, they can be mended all right, with a bit of patience.

NORA.   Yes, I'll go over and get Mrs. Linde to help me.

NURSEMAID.   Out again? In this terrible weather? You'll catch your death of cold, Ma'am.

NORA.   Oh, worse things might happen.—How are the children?

NURSEMAID.   Playing with their Christmas presents, poor little things, but . . .

NORA.   Do they keep asking for me?

NURSEMAID.   They are so used to being with their Mummy.

NORA.   Yes, Anne Marie, from now on I can't be with them as often as I was before.

NURSEMAID.   Ah well, children get used to anything in time.

NORA.   Do you think so? Do you think they would forget their Mummy if she went away for good?

NURSEMAID.   Good gracious—for good?

NORA.   Tell me, Anne Marie—I've often wondered—how on earth could you bear to hand your child over to strangers?

NURSEMAID.   Well, there was nothing else for it when I had to come and nurse my little Nora.

NORA.   Yes but . . . how could you *bring* yourself to do it?

NURSEMAID.   When I had the chance of such a good place? When a poor girl's been in trouble she must make the best of things. Because *he* didn't help, the rotter.

NORA.   But your daughter will have forgotten you.

NURSEMAID.   Oh no, she hasn't. She wrote to me when she got confirmed, and again when she got married.

NORA [*putting her arms round her neck*].   Dear old Anne Marie, you were a good mother to me when I was little.

NURSEMAID.   My poor little Nora never had any other mother but me.

NORA.   And if my little ones only had you, I know you would. . . . Oh, what am I talking about! [*She opens the box.*] Go in to them. I must . . . Tomorrow I'll let you see how pretty I am going to look.

NURSEMAID.   Ah, there'll be nobody at the ball as pretty as my Nora.

[*She goes into the room, left.*]

NORA [*begins unpacking the box, but soon throws it down*].   Oh, if only I dare go
out. If only I could be sure nobody would come. And that nothing would
happen in the meantime here at home. Rubbish—nobody's going to come. I
mustn't think about it. Brush this muff. Pretty gloves, pretty gloves! I'll put it
right out of my mind. One, two, three, four, five, six. . . . [*Screams.*] Ah, they
are coming. . . . [*She starts towards the door, but stops irresolute.* MRS. LINDE
comes from the hall, where she has taken off her things.] Oh, it's you, Kristine.
There's nobody else out there, is there? I'm so glad you've come.

MRS. LINDE.   I heard you'd been over looking for me.

NORA.   Yes, I was just passing. There's something you must help me with. Come
and sit beside me on the sofa here. You see, the Stenborgs are having a fancy
dress party upstairs tomorrow evening, and now Torvald wants me to go as a
Neapolitan fisher lass and dance the tarantella. I learned it in Capri, you know.

MRS. LINDE.   Well, well! So you are going to do a party piece?

NORA.   Torvald says I should. Look, here's the costume, Torvald had it made for
me down there. But it's got all torn and I simply don't know. . . .

MRS. LINDE.   We'll soon have that put right. It's only the trimming come away here
and there. Got a needle and thread? Ah, here's what we are after.

NORA.   It's awfully kind of you.

MRS. LINDE.   So you are going to be all dressed up tomorrow, Nora? Tell you
what—I'll pop over for a minute to see you in all your finery. But I'm quite
forgetting to thank you for the pleasant time we had last night.

NORA [*gets up and walks across the room*].   Somehow I didn't think yesterday was
as nice as things generally are.—You should have come to town a little earlier, Kristine.—Yes, Torvald certainly knows how to make things pleasant
about the place.

MRS. LINDE.   You too, I should say. You are not your father's daughter for nothing.
But tell me, is Dr. Rank always as depressed as he was last night?

NORA.   No, last night it was rather obvious. He's got something seriously wrong
with him, you know. Tuberculosis of the spine, poor fellow. His father was a
horrible man, who used to have mistresses and things like that. That's why
the son was always ailing, right from being a child.

MRS. LINDE [*lowering her sewing*].   But my dear Nora, how do you come to know
about things like that?

NORA [*walking about the room*].   Huh! When you've got three children, you get
these visits from . . . women who have had a certain amount of medical training. And you hear all sorts of things from them.

MRS. LINDE [*begins sewing again; short silence*].   Does Dr. Rank call in every day?

NORA.   Every single day. He was Torvald's best friend as a boy, and he's a good
friend of *mine*, too. Dr. Rank is almost like one of the family.

MRS. LINDE.   But tell me—is he really genuine? What I mean is: doesn't he sometimes rather turn on the charm?

NORA.   No, on the contrary. What makes you think that?

MRS. LINDE.   When you introduced me yesterday, he claimed he'd often heard my
name in this house. But afterwards I noticed your husband hadn't the faintest
idea who I was. Then how is it that Dr. Rank should. . . .

NORA.   Oh yes, it was quite right what he said, Kristine. You see Torvald is so terribly in love with me that he says he wants me all to himself. When we were
first married, it even used to make him sort of jealous if I only as much as mentioned any of my old friends from back home. So of course I stopped doing it.
But I often talk to Dr. Rank about such things. He likes hearing about them.

MRS. LINDE.   Listen, Nora! In lots of ways you are still a child. Now, I'm a good deal older than you, and a bit more experienced. I'll tell you something: I think you ought to give up all this business with Dr. Rank.

NORA.   Give up what business?

MRS. LINDE.   The whole thing, I should say. Weren't you saying yesterday something about a rich admirer who was to provide you with money. . . .

NORA.   One who's never existed, I regret to say. But what of it?

MRS. LINDE.   Has Dr. Rank money?

NORA.   Yes, he has.

MRS. LINDE.   And no dependents?

NORA.   No, nobody. But . . . ?

MRS. LINDE.   And he comes to the house every day?

NORA.   Yes, I told you.

MRS. LINDE.   But how can a man of his position want to pester you like this?

NORA.   I simply don't understand.

MRS. LINDE.   Don't pretend, Nora. Do you think I don't see now who you borrowed the twelve hundred from?

NORA.   Are you out of your mind? Do you really think that? A friend of ours who comes here every day? The whole situation would have been absolutely intolerable.

MRS. LINDE.   It *really* isn't him?

NORA.   No, I give you my word. It would never have occurred to me for one moment. . . . Anyway, he didn't have the money to lend then. He didn't inherit it till later.

MRS. LINDE.   Just as well for you, I'd say, my dear Nora.

NORA.   No, it would never have occurred to me to ask Dr. Rank. . . . All the same I'm pretty certain if I were to ask him . . .

MRS. LINDE.   But of course you won't.

NORA.   No, of course not. I can't ever imagine it being necessary. But I'm quite certain if ever I were to mention it to Dr. Rank. . . .

MRS. LINDE.   Behind your husband's back?

NORA.   I have to get myself out of that other business. That's also behind his back. I *must* get myself out of that.

MRS. LINDE.   Yes, that's what I said yesterday. But . . .

NORA [*walking up and down*].   A man's better at coping with these things than a woman. . . .

MRS. LINDE.   Your own husband, yes.

NORA.   Nonsense! [*Stops.*] When you've paid everything you owe, you do get your IOU back again, don't you?

MRS. LINDE.   Of course.

NORA.   And you can tear it up into a thousand pieces and burn it—the nasty, filthy thing!

MRS. LINDE [*looking fixedly at her, puts down her sewing and slowly rises*].   Nora, you are hiding something from me.

NORA.   Is it so obvious?

MRS. LINDE.   Something has happened to you since yesterday morning. Nora, what is it?

NORA [*going towards her*].   Kristine! [*Listens.*] Hush! There's Torvald back. Look, you go and sit in there beside the children for the time being. Torvald can't stand the sight of mending lying about. Get Anne Marie to help you.

MRS. LINDE [*gathering a lot of the things together*].   All right, but I'm not leaving until we have thrashed this thing out.

[*She goes into the room, left; at the same time* HELMER *comes in from the hall.*]

NORA [*goes to meet him*].   I've been longing for you to be back, Torvald, dear.

HELMER.   Was that the dressmaker . . . ?

NORA.   No, it was Kristine; she's helping me with my costume. I think it's going to
look very nice . . .

HELMER.   Wasn't that a good idea of mine, now?

NORA.   Wonderful! But wasn't it also nice of me to let you have your way?

HELMER [*taking her under the chin*].   Nice of you—because you let your husband
have his way? All right, you little rogue, I know you didn't mean it that way. But
I don't want to disturb you. You'll be wanting to try the costume on, I suppose.

NORA.   And I dare say you've got work to do?

HELMER.   Yes. [*Shows her a bundle of papers.*] Look at this. I've been down at the
Bank. . . .

[*He turns to go into his study.*]

NORA.   Torvald!

HELMER [*stopping*].   Yes.

NORA.   If a little squirrel were to ask ever so nicely . . . ?

HELMER.   Well?

NORA.   Would you do something for it?

HELMER.   Naturally I would first have to know what it is.

NORA.   Please, if only you would let it have its way, and do what it wants, it'd
scamper about and do all sorts of marvellous tricks.

HELMER.   What is it?

NORA.   And the pretty little sky-lark would sing all day long. . . .

HELMER.   Huh! It does that anyway.

NORA.   I'd pretend I was an elfin child and dance a moonlight dance for you,
Torvald.

HELMER.   Nora—I hope it's not that business you started on this morning?

NORA [*coming closer*].   Yes, it is, Torvald. I implore you!

HELMER.   You have the nerve to bring that up again?

NORA.   Yes, yes, you *must* listen to me. You must let Krogstad keep his job at the
Bank.

HELMER.   My dear Nora, I'm giving his job to Mrs. Linde.

NORA.   Yes, it's awfully sweet of you. But couldn't you get rid of somebody else
in the office instead of Krogstad?

HELMER.   This really is the most incredible obstinacy! Just because you go and make
some thoughtless promise to put in a good word for him, you expect me . . .

NORA.   It's not that, Torvald. It's for your own sake. That man writes in all the nas-
tiest papers, you told me that yourself. He can do you no end of harm. He
terrifies me to death. . . .

HELMER.   Aha, now I see. It's your memories of what happened before that are
frightening you.

NORA.   What do you mean?

HELMER.   It's your father you are thinking of.

NORA.   Yes . . . yes, that's right. You remember all the nasty insinuations those
wicked people put in the papers about Daddy? I honestly think they would
have had him dismissed if the Ministry hadn't sent you down to investigate,
and you hadn't been so kind and helpful.

HELMER.   My dear little Nora, there is a considerable difference between your father
and me. Your father's professional conduct was not entirely above suspicion.
Mine is. And I hope it's going to stay that way as long as I hold this position.

NORA.   But nobody knows what some of these evil people are capable of. Things
could be so nice and pleasant for us here, in the peace and quiet of our
home—you and me and the children, Torvald! That's why I implore you. . . .

HELMER.   The more you plead for him, the more impossible you make it for me to
keep him on. It's already known down at the Bank that I am going to give
Krogstad his notice. If it ever got around that the new manager had been
talked over by his wife. . . .

NORA.   What of it?

HELMER.   Oh, nothing! As long as the little woman gets her own stubborn way . . . !
Do you want me to make myself a laughing stock in the office? . . . Give people the idea that I am susceptible to any kind of outside pressure? You can
imagine how soon I'd feel the consequences of that! Anyway, there's one
other consideration that makes it impossible to have Krogstad in the Bank as
long as I am manager.

NORA.   What's that?

HELMER.   At a pinch I might have overlooked his past lapses. . . .

NORA.   Of course you could, Torvald!

HELMER.   And I'm told he's not bad at his job, either. But we knew each other
rather well when we were younger. It was one of those rather rash friend-
ships that prove embarrassing in later life. There's no reason why you
shouldn't know we were once on terms of some familiarity. And he, in his
tactless way, makes no attempt to hide the fact, particularly when other people are present. On the contrary, he thinks he has every right to treat me as
an equal, with his 'Torvald this' and 'Torvald that' every time he opens his
mouth. I find it extremely irritating, I can tell you. He would make my position at the Bank absolutely intolerable.

NORA.   Torvald, surely you aren't serious?

HELMER.   Oh? Why not?

NORA.   Well, it's all so petty.

HELMER.   What's that you say? Petty? Do you think I'm petty?

NORA.   No, not at all, Torvald dear! And that's why . . .

HELMER.   Doesn't make any difference! . . . You call my motives petty; so I must be
petty too. Petty! Indeed! Well, we'll put a stop to that, once and for all. [*He
opens the hall door and calls.*] Helene!

NORA.   What are you going to do?

HELMER [*searching among his papers*].   Settle things. [*The* MAID *comes in.*] See this
letter? I want you to take it down at once. Get hold of a messenger and get
him to deliver it. Quickly. The address is on the outside. There's the money.

MAID.   Very good, sir.

[*She goes with the letter.*]

HELMER [*putting his papers together*].   There now, my stubborn little miss.

NORA   [*breathless*].   Torvald . . . what was that letter?

HELMER.   Krogstad's notice.

NORA.   Get it back, Torvald! There's still time! Oh, Torvald, get it back! Please for
my sake, for your sake, for the sake of the children! Listen, Torvald, please!
You don't realize what it can do to us.

HELMER.   Too late.

NORA.   Yes, too late.

HELMER.   My dear Nora, I forgive you this anxiety of yours, although it is actually a bit of an insult. Oh, but it is, I tell you! It's hardly flattering to suppose that anything this miserable pen-pusher wrote could frighten *me!* But I forgive you all the same, because it is rather a sweet way of showing how much you love me. [*He takes her in his arms.*] This is how things must be, my own darling Nora. When it comes to the point, I've enough strength and enough courage, believe me, for whatever happens. You'll find I'm man enough to take everything on myself.

NORA [*terrified*].   What do you mean?

HELMER.   Everything, I said. . . .

NORA [*in command of herself*].   That is something you shall never, never do.

HELMER.   All right, then we'll share it, Nora—as man and wife. That's what we'll do. [*Caressing her.*] Does that make you happy now? There, there, don't look at me with those eyes, like a little frightened dove. The whole thing is sheer imagination.—Why don't you run through the tarantella and try out the tambourine? I'll go into my study and shut both the doors, then I won't hear anything. You can make all the noise you want. [*Turns in the doorway.*] And when Rank comes, tell him where he can find me.

[*He nods to her, goes with his papers into his room, and shuts the door behind him.*]

NORA [*wild-eyed with terror, stands as though transfixed*].   He's quite capable of doing it! He would do it! No matter what, he'd do it.—No, never in this world! Anything but that! Help? Some way out . . . ? [*The door-bell rings in the hall.*] Dr. Rank . . . ! Anything but that, *anything!* [*She brushes her hands over her face, pulls herself together and opens the door into the hall.* DR. RANK *is standing outside hanging up his fur coat. During what follows it begins to grow dark.*] Hello, Dr. Rank. I recognized your ring. Do you mind not going in to Torvald just yet, I think he's busy.

RANK.   And you?

[DR. RANK *comes into the room and she closes the door behind him.*]

NORA.   Oh, you know very well I've always got time for you.

RANK.   Thank you. A privilege I shall take advantage of as long as I am able.

NORA.   What do you mean—as long as you are able?

RANK.   Does that frighten you?

NORA.   Well, it's just that it sounds so strange. Is anything likely to happen?

RANK.   Only what I have long expected. But I didn't think it would come quite so soon.

NORA [*catching at his arm*].   What have you found out? Dr. Rank, you must tell me!

RANK.   I'm slowly sinking. There's nothing to be done about it.

NORA [*with a sigh of relief*].   Oh, it's *you* you're . . . ?

RANK.   Who else? No point in deceiving oneself. I am the most wretched of all my patients, Mrs. Helmer. These last few days I've made a careful analysis of my internal economy. Bankrupt! Within a month I shall probably be lying rotting up there in the churchyard.

NORA.   Come now, what a ghastly thing to say!

RANK.   The whole damned thing is ghastly. But the worst thing is all the ghastliness that has to be gone through first. I only have one more test to make; and when that's done I'll know pretty well when the final disintegration will start.

There's something I want to ask you. Helmer is a sensitive soul; he loathes anything that's ugly. I don't want him visiting me. . . .

NORA. But Dr. Rank. . . .

RANK. On no account must he. I won't have it. I'll lock the door on him.—As soon as I'm absolutely certain of the worst, I'll send you my visiting card with a black cross on it. You'll know then the final horrible disintegration has begun.

NORA. Really, you are being quite absurd today. And here was I hoping you would be in a thoroughly good mood.

RANK. With death staring me in the face? Why should I suffer for another man's sins? What justice is there in that? Somewhere, somehow, every single family must be suffering some such cruel retribution. . . .

NORA [*stopping up her ears*]. Rubbish! Do cheer up!

RANK. Yes, really the whole thing's nothing but a huge joke. My poor innocent spine must do penance for my father's gay subaltern life.

NORA [*by the table, left*]. Wasn't he rather partial to asparagus and *pâté de foie gras?*

RANK. Yes, he was. And truffles.

NORA. Truffles, yes. And oysters, too, I believe?

RANK. Yes, oysters, oysters, of course.

NORA. And all the port and champagne that goes with them. It does seem a pity all these delicious things should attack the spine.

RANK. Especially when they attack a poor spine that never had any fun out of them.

NORA. Yes, that is an awful pity.

RANK [*looks at her sharply*]. Hm. . . .

NORA [*after a pause*]. Why did you smile?

RANK. No, it was you who laughed.

NORA. No, it was you who smiled, Dr. Rank!

RANK [*getting up*]. You are a bigger rascal than I thought you were.

NORA. I feel full of mischief today.

RANK. So it seems.

NORA [*putting her hands on his shoulders*]. Dear, dear Dr. Rank, you mustn't go and die on Torvald and me.

RANK. You wouldn't miss me for long. When you are gone, you are soon forgotten.

NORA [*looking at him anxiously*]. Do you think so?

RANK. People make new contacts, then . . .

NORA. Who make new contacts?

RANK. Both you and Helmer will, when I'm gone. You yourself are already well on the way, it seems to me. What was this Mrs. Linde doing here last night?

NORA. Surely you aren't jealous of poor Kristine?

RANK. Yes, I am. She'll be my successor in this house. When I'm done for, I can see this woman. . . .

NORA. Hush! Don't talk so loud, she's in there.

RANK. Today as well? There you are, you see!

NORA. Just to do some sewing on my dress. Good Lord, how absurd you are! [*She sits down on the sofa.*] Now Dr. Rank, cheer up. You'll see tomorrow how nicely I can dance. And you can pretend I'm doing it just for you—and for Torvald as well, of course. [*She takes various things out of the box.*] Come here, Dr. Rank. I want to show you something.

RANK [*sits*]. What is it?

NORA. Look!

RANK. Silk stockings.

NORA.   Flesh-coloured! Aren't they lovely! Of course, it's dark here now, but to-morrow. . . . No, no, no, you can only look at the feet. Oh well, you might as well see a bit higher up, too.

RANK.   Hm. . . .

NORA.   Why are you looking so critical? Don't you think they'll fit?

RANK.   I couldn't possibly offer any informed opinion about that.

NORA [*looks at him for a moment*].   Shame on you. [*Hits him lightly across the ear with the stockings.*] Take that! [*Folds them up again.*]

RANK.   And what other delights am I to be allowed to see?

NORA.   Not another thing. You are too naughty. [*She hums a little and searches among her things.*]

RANK [*after a short pause*].   Sitting here so intimately like this with you, I can't imagine . . . I simply cannot conceive what would have become of me if I had never come to this house.

NORA [*smiles*].   Yes, I rather think you do enjoy coming here.

RANK [*in a low voice, looking fixedly ahead*].   And the thought of having to leave it all . . .

NORA.   Nonsense. You aren't leaving.

RANK [*in the same tone*].   . . . without being able to leave behind even the slightest token of gratitude, hardly a fleeting regret even . . . nothing but an empty place to be filled by the first person that comes along.

NORA.   Supposing I were to ask you to . . . ? No . . .

RANK.   What?

NORA.   . . . to show me the extent of your friendship . . .

RANK.   Yes?

NORA.   I mean . . . to do me a tremendous favour. . . .

RANK.   Would you really, for once, give me that pleasure?

NORA.   You have no idea what it is.

RANK.   All right, tell me.

NORA.   No, really I can't, Dr. Rank. It's altogether too much to ask . . . because I need your advice and help as well. . . .

RANK.   The more the better. I cannot imagine what you have in mind. But tell me anyway. You do trust me, don't you?

NORA.   Yes, I trust you more than anybody I know. You are my best and my most faithful friend. I know that. So I will tell you. Well then, Dr. Rank, there is something you must help me to prevent. You know how deeply, how passionately Torvald is in love with me. He would never hesitate for a moment to sacrifice his life for my sake.

RANK [*bending towards her*].   Nora . . . do you think he's the only one who . . . ?

NORA [*stiffening slightly*].   Who . . . ?

RANK.   Who wouldn't gladly give his life for your sake.

NORA [*sadly*].   Oh!

RANK.   I swore to myself you would know before I went. I'll never have a better opportunity. Well, Nora! Now you know. And now you know too that you can confide in me as in nobody else.

NORA [*rises and speaks evenly and calmly*].   Let me past.

RANK [*makes way for her, but remains seated*].   Nora. . . .

NORA [*in the hall doorway*].   Helene, bring the lamp in, please. [*Walks over to the stove.*] Oh, my dear Dr. Rank, that really was rather horrid of you.

RANK [*getting up*].   That I have loved you every bit as much as anybody? Is *that* horrid?

NORA.   No, but that you had to go and tell me. When it was all so unnecessary. . . .

RANK.   What do you mean? Did you know . . . ?

[*The* MAID *comes in with the lamp, puts it on the table, and goes out again.*]

RANK.   Nora . . . Mrs. Helmer . . . I'm asking you if you knew?

NORA.   How can I tell whether I did or didn't. I simply can't tell you. . . . Oh, how could you be so clumsy, Dr. Rank! When everything was so nice.

RANK.   Anyway, you know now that I'm at your service, body and soul. So you can speak out.

NORA [*looking at him*].   After this?

RANK.   I beg you to tell me what it is.

NORA.   I can tell you nothing now.

RANK.   You must. You can't torment me like this. Give me a chance—I'll do anything that's humanly possible.

NORA.   You can do nothing for me now. Actually, I don't really need any help. It's all just my imagination, really it is. Of course! [*She sits down in the rocking chair, looks at him and smiles.*] I must say, you are a nice one, Dr. Rank! Don't you feel ashamed of yourself, now the lamp's been brought in?

RANK.   No, not exactly. But perhaps I ought to go—for good?

NORA.   No, you mustn't do that. You must keep coming just as you've always done. You know very well Torvald would miss you terribly.

RANK.   And *you?*

NORA.   I always think it's tremendous fun having you.

RANK.   That's exactly what gave me wrong ideas. I just can't puzzle you out. I often used to feel you'd just as soon be with me as with Helmer.

NORA.   Well, you see, there are those people you love and those people you'd almost rather *be* with.

RANK.   Yes, there's something in that.

NORA.   When I was a girl at home, I loved Daddy best, of course. But I also thought it great fun if I could slip into the maids' room. For one thing they never preached at me. And they always talked about such exciting things.

RANK.   Aha! So it's their role I've taken over!

NORA [*jumps up and crosses to him*].   Oh, my dear, kind Dr. Rank, I didn't mean that at all. But you can see how it's a bit with Torvald as it was with Daddy. . . .

[*The* MAID *comes in from the hall.*]

MAID.   Please, ma'am . . . !

[*She whispers and hands her a card.*]

NORA [*glances at the card*].   Ah!

[*She puts it in her pocket.*]

RANK.   Anything wrong?

NORA.   No, no, not at all. It's just . . . it's my new costume. . . .

RANK.   How is that? There's your costume in there.

NORA.   That one, yes. But this is another one. I've ordered it. Torvald mustn't hear about it. . . .

RANK.   Ah, so that's the big secret, is it!

NORA.   Yes, that's right. Just go in and see him, will you? He's in the study. Keep him occupied for the time being. . . .

RANK.   Don't worry. He shan't escape me.

[*He goes into* HELMER's *study.*]

NORA [*to the* MAID].   Is he waiting in the kitchen?

MAID.   Yes, he came up the back stairs. . . .

NORA.   But didn't you tell him somebody was here?

MAID.   Yes, but it was no good.

NORA.   Won't he go?

MAID.   No, he won't till he's seen you.

NORA.   Let him in, then. But quietly. Helene, you mustn't tell anybody about this. It's a surprise for my husband.

MAID.   I understand, ma'am. . . .

[*She goes out.*]

NORA.   Here it comes! What I've been dreading! No, no, it can't happen, it can't happen.

[*She walks over and bolts* HELMER's *door. The* MAID *opens the hall door for* KROGSTAD *and shuts it again behind him. He is wearing a fur coat, over-shoes, and a fur cap.*]

NORA [*goes towards him*].   Keep your voice down, my husband is at home.

KROGSTAD.   What if he is?

NORA.   What do you want with me?

KROGSTAD.   To find out something.

NORA.   Hurry, then. What is it?

KROGSTAD.   You know I've been given notice.

NORA.   I couldn't prevent it, Mr. Krogstad, I did my utmost for you, but it was no use.

KROGSTAD.   Has your husband so little affection for you? He knows what I can do to you, yet he dares. . . .

NORA.   You don't imagine he knows about it!

KROGSTAD.   No, I didn't imagine he did. It didn't seem a bit like my good friend Torvald Helmer to show that much courage. . . .

NORA.   Mr. Krogstad, I must ask you to show some respect for my husband.

KROGSTAD.   Oh, sure! All due respect! But since you are so anxious to keep this business quiet, Mrs. Helmer, I take it you now have a rather clearer idea of just what it is you've done, than you had yesterday.

NORA.   Clearer than *you* could ever have given me.

KROGSTAD.   Yes, being as I am such a rotten lawyer. . . .

NORA.   What do you want with me?

KROGSTAD.   I just wanted to see how things stood, Mrs. Helmer. I've been thinking about you all day. Even a mere money-lender, a hack journalist, a—well, even somebody like me has a bit of what you might call feeling.

NORA.   Show it then. Think of my little children.

KROGSTAD.   Did you or your husband think of mine? But what does it matter now? There was just one thing I wanted to say: you needn't take this business too seriously. I shan't start any proceedings, for the present.

NORA.   Ah, I knew you wouldn't.

KROGSTAD.   The whole thing can be arranged quite amicably. Nobody need know. Just the three of us.

NORA.   My husband must never know.

KROGSTAD.   How can you prevent it? Can you pay off the balance?

NORA.   No, not immediately.

KROGSTAD.   Perhaps you've some way of getting hold of the money in the next few days.

NORA.   None I want to make use of.

KROGSTAD.   Well, it wouldn't have been very much help to you if you had. Even if you stood there with the cash in your hand and to spare, you still wouldn't get your IOU back from me now.

NORA.   What are you going to do with it?

KROGSTAD.   Just keep it—have it in my possession. Nobody who isn't implicated need know about it. So if you are thinking of trying any desperate remedies . . .

NORA.   Which I am. . . .

KROGSTAD.   . . . if you happen to be thinking of running away . . .

NORA.   Which I am!

KROGSTAD.   . . . or anything worse . . .

NORA.   How did you know?

KROGSTAD.   . . . forget it!

NORA.   How did you know I was thinking of *that?*

KROGSTAD.   Most of us think of *that,* to begin with. I did, too; but I didn't have the courage. . . .

NORA [*tonelessly*].   I haven't either.

KROGSTAD [*relieved*].   So you haven't the courage either, eh?

NORA   No, I haven't! I haven't!

KROGSTAD.   It would also be very stupid. There'd only be the first domestic storm to get over. . . . I've got a letter to your husband in my pocket here. . . .

NORA.   And it's all in there?

KROGSTAD.   In as tactful a way as possible.

NORA [*quickly*].   He must never read that letter. Tear it up. I'll find the money somehow.

KROGSTAD.   Excuse me, Mrs. Helmer, but I've just told you. . . .

NORA.   I'm not talking about the money I owe you. I want to know how much you are demanding from my husband, and I'll get the money.

KROGSTAD.   I want no money from your husband.

NORA.   What do you want?

KROGSTAD.   I'll tell you. I want to get on my feet again, Mrs. Helmer; I want to get to the top. And your husband is going to help me. For the last eighteen months I've gone straight; all that time it's been hard going; I was content to work my way up, step by step. Now I'm being kicked out, and I won't stand for being taken back again as an act of charity. I'm going to get to the top, I tell you. I'm going back into that Bank—with a better job. Your husband is going to create a new vacancy, just for me. . . .

NORA.   He'll never do that!

KROGSTAD.   He will do it. I know him. He'll do it without so much as a whimper. And once I'm in there with him, you'll see what's what. In less than a year I'll be his right-hand man. It'll be Nils Krogstad, not Torvald Helmer, who'll be running that Bank.

NORA.   You'll never live to see that day!

KROGSTAD.   You mean you . . . ?

NORA.   Now I have the courage.

KROGSTAD.   You can't frighten me! A precious pampered little thing like you. . . .

NORA.   I'll show you! I'll show you!

KROGSTAD.   Under the ice, maybe? Down in the cold, black water? Then being washed up in the spring, bloated, hairless, unrecognizable. . . .

NORA.   You can't frighten me.

KROGSTAD.   You can't frighten me, either. People don't do that sort of thing, Mrs. Helmer. There wouldn't be any point to it, anyway, I'd still have him right in my pocket.

NORA.   Afterwards? When I'm no longer . . .

KROGSTAD.   Aren't you forgetting that your reputation would then be entirely in my hands? [NORA *stands looking at him, speechless.*] Well, I've warned you. Don't do anything silly. When Helmer gets my letter, I expect to hear from him. And don't forget: it's him who is forcing me off the straight and narrow again, your own husband! That's something I'll never forgive him for. Goodbye, Mrs. Helmer.

[*He goes out through the hall.* NORA *crosses to the door, opens it slightly, and listens.*]

NORA.   He's going. He hasn't left the letter. No, no, that would be impossible! [*Opens the door further and further.*] What's he doing? He's stopped outside. He's not going down the stairs. Has he changed his mind? Is he . . . ? [*A letter falls into the letter-box. Then* KROGSTAD's *footsteps are heard receding as he walks downstairs.* NORA *gives a stifled cry, runs across the room to the sofa table; pause.*] In the letter-box! [*She creeps stealthily across to the hall door.*] There it is! Torvald, Torvald! It's hopeless now!

MRS. LINDE [*comes into the room, left, carrying the costume*].   There, I think that's everything. Shall we try it on?

NORA [*in a low, hoarse voice*].   Kristine, come here.

MRS. LINDE [*throws the dress down on the sofa*].   What's wrong with you? You look upset.

NORA.   Come here. Do you see that letter? *There,* look! Through the glass in the letter-box.

MRS. LINDE.   Yes, yes, I can see it.

NORA.   It's a letter from Krogstad.

MRS. LINDE.   Nora! It was Krogstad who lent you the money!

NORA.   Yes. And now Torvald will get to know everything.

MRS. LINDE.   Believe me, Nora, it's best for you both.

NORA.   But there's more to it than that. I forged a signature. . . .

MRS. LINDE.   Heavens above!

NORA.   Listen, I want to tell you something, Kristine, so you can be my witness.

MRS. LINDE.   What do you mean 'witness'? What do you want me to . . . ?

NORA.   If I should go mad . . . which might easily happen . . .

MRS. LINDE.   Nora!

NORA.   Or if anything happened to me . . . which meant I couldn't be here. . . .

MRS. LINDE.   Nora, Nora! Are you out of your mind?

NORA.   And if somebody else wanted to take it all upon himself, the whole blame, you understand. . . .

MRS. LINDE.   Yes, yes. But what makes you think . . . ?

NORA.   Then you must testify that it isn't true, Kristine. I'm not out of my mind; I'm quite sane now. And I tell you this: nobody else knew anything, I alone was responsible for the whole thing. Remember that!

MRS. LINDE.   I will. But I don't understand a word of it.

NORA.   Why should you? You see something miraculous is going to happen.

MRS. LINDE.   Something miraculous?

NORA.   Yes, a miracle. But something so terrible as well, Kristine—oh, it must *never* happen, not for anything.

MRS. LINDE.   I'm going straight over to talk to Krogstad.

NORA.   Don't go. He'll only do you harm.

MRS. LINDE.   There was a time when he would have done anything for me.

NORA.   Him!

MRS. LINDE.   Where does he live?

NORA.   How do I know . . . ? Wait a minute. [*She feels in her pocket.*] Here's his card. But the letter, the letter . . . !

HELMER [*from his study, knocking on the door*].   Nora!

NORA [*cries out in terror*].   What's that? What do you want?

HELMER.   Don't be frightened. We're not coming in. You've locked the door. Are you trying on?

NORA.   Yes, yes, I'm trying on. It looks so nice on me, Torvald.

MRS. LINDE [*who has read the card*].   He lives just round the corner.

NORA.   It's no use. It's hopeless. The letter is there in the box.

MRS. LINDE.   Your husband keeps the key?

NORA.   Always.

MRS. LINDE.   Krogstad must ask for his letter back unread, he must find some sort of excuse. . . .

NORA.   But this is just the time that Torvald generally . . .

MRS. LINDE.   Put him off! Go in and keep him busy. I'll be back as soon as I can.

[*She goes out hastily by the hall door.* NORA *walks over to* HELMER*'s door, opens it and peeps in.*]

NORA.   Torvald!

HELMER [*in the study*].   Well, can a man get into his own living-room again now? Come along, Rank, now we'll see . . . [*In the doorway.*] But what's this?

NORA.   What, Torvald dear?

HELMER.   Rank led me to expect some kind of marvellous transformation.

RANK [*in the doorway*].   That's what I thought too, but I must have been mistaken.

NORA.   I'm not showing myself off to anybody before tomorrow.

HELMER.   Nora dear, you look tired. You haven't been practising too hard?

NORA.   No, I haven't practised at all yet.

HELMER.   You'll have to, though.

NORA.   Yes, I certainly must, Torvald. But I just can't get anywhere without your help: I've completely forgotten it.

HELMER.   We'll soon polish it up.

NORA.   Yes, do help me, Torvald. Promise? I'm so nervous. All those people. . . . You must devote yourself exclusively to me this evening. Pens away! Forget all about the office! Promise me, Torvald dear!

HELMER.   I promise. This evening I am wholly and entirely at your service . . . helpless little thing that you are. Oh, but while I remember, I'll just look first . . .

[*He goes towards the hall door.*]

NORA.   What do you want out there?

HELMER.   Just want to see if there are any letters.

NORA.   No, don't, Torvald!

HELMER.   Why not?

NORA.   Torvald, *please!* There aren't any.

HELMER.   Just let me see.

[*He starts to go.* NORA, *at the piano, plays the opening bars of the tarantella.*]

HELMER [*at the door, stops*].   Aha!

NORA.   I shan't be able to dance tomorrow if I don't rehearse it with you.

HELMER [*walks to her*].   Are you really so nervous, Nora dear?

NORA.   Terribly nervous. Let me run through it now. There's still time before sup-per. Come and sit here and play for me, Torvald dear. Tell me what to do, keep me right—as you always do.

HELMER.   Certainly, with pleasure, if that's what you want.

[*He sits at the piano.* NORA *snatches the tambourine out of the box, and also a long gaily-coloured shawl which she drapes round herself, then with a bound she leaps forward.*]

NORA. [*shouts*].   Now play for me! Now I'll dance!

[HELMER *plays and* NORA *dances;* DR. RANK *stands at the piano behind* HELMER *and looks on.*]

HELMER [*playing*].   Not so fast! Not so fast!

NORA.   I can't help it.

HELMER.   Not so wild, Nora!

NORA.   This is how it has to be.

HELMER [*stops*].   No, no, that won't do at all.

NORA [*laughs and swings the tambourine*].   Didn't I tell you?

RANK.   Let me play for her.

HELMER [*gets up*].   Yes, do. Then I'll be better able to tell her what to do.

[RANK *sits down at the piano and plays.* NORA *dances more and more wildly.* HELMER *stands by the stove giving her repeated directions as she dances; she does not seem to hear them. Her hair comes undone and falls about her shoulders; she pays no attention and goes on dancing.* MRS. LINDE *enters.*]

MRS. LINDE [*standing as though spellbound in the doorway*].   Ah . . . !

NORA [*dancing*].   See what fun we are having, Kristine.

HELMER.   But my dear darling Nora, you are dancing as though your life de-pended on it.

NORA.   It does.

HELMER.   Stop, Rank! This is sheer madness. Stop, I say.

[RANK *stops playing and* NORA *comes to a sudden halt.*]

HELMER [*crosses to her*].   I would never have believed it. You have forgotten every-thing I ever taught you.

NORA [*throwing away the tambourine*].   There you are, you see.

HELMER.   Well, some more instruction is certainly needed there.

NORA.   Yes, you see how necessary it is. You must go on coaching me right up to the last minute. Promise me, Torvald?

HELMER.   You can rely on me.

NORA.   You mustn't think about anything else but me until after tomorrow . . . mustn't open any letters . . . mustn't touch the letter-box.

HELMER.   Ah, you are still frightened of what that man might . . .

NORA.   Yes, yes, I am.

HELMER.   I can see from your face there's already a letter there from him.

NORA.   I don't know. I think so. But you mustn't read anything like that now. We don't want anything horrid coming between us until all this is over.

RANK [*softly to* HELMER].   I shouldn't cross her.

HELMER [*puts his arm round her*].   The child must have her way. But tomorrow night, when your dance is done. . . .

NORA.   Then you are free.

MAID [*in the doorway, right*].   Dinner is served, madam.

NORA.   We'll have champagne, Helene.

MAID.   Very good, madam.

   [*She goes.*]

HELMER.   Aha! It's to be quite a banquet, eh?

NORA.   With champagne flowing until dawn. [*Shouts.*] And some macaroons, Helene . . . lots of them, for once in a while.

HELMER [*seizing her hands*].   Now, now, not so wild and excitable! Let me see you being my own little singing bird again.

NORA.   Oh yes, I will. And if you'll just go in . . . you, too, Dr. Rank. Kristine, you must help me to do my hair.

RANK [*softly, as they leave*].   There isn't anything . . . anything as it were, impending, is there?

HELMER.   No, not at all, my dear fellow. It's nothing but these childish fears I was telling you about.

   [*They go out to the right.*]

NORA.   Well?

MRS. LINDE.   He's left town.

NORA.   I saw it in your face.

MRS. LINDE.   He's coming back tomorrow evening. I left a note for him.

NORA.   You shouldn't have done that. You must let things take their course. Because really it's a case for rejoicing, waiting like this for the miracle.

MRS. LINDE.   What is it you are waiting for?

NORA.   Oh, you wouldn't understand. Go and join the other two. I'll be there in a minute.

   [MRS. LINDE *goes into the dining-room.* NORA *stands for a moment as though to collect herself, then looks at her watch.*]

NORA.   Five. Seven hours to midnight. Then twenty-four hours till the next midnight. Then the tarantella will be over. Twenty-four and seven? Thirty-one hours to live.

HELMER [*in the doorway, right*].   What's happened to our little sky-lark?

NORA [*running towards him with open arms*].   Here she is!

Act III

The same room. The round table has been moved to the centre of the room, and the chairs placed round it. A lamp is burning on the table. The door to the hall stands open. Dance music can be heard coming from the floor above. MRS. LINDE *is sitting by the table, idly turning over the pages of a book; she tries to read, but does not seem able to concentrate. Once or twice she listens, tensely, for a sound at the front door.*

MRS. LINDE [*looking at her watch*].   Still not here. There isn't much time left. I only hope he hasn't . . . [*She listens again.*] Ah, there he is. [*She goes out into the hall, and cautiously opens the front door. Soft footsteps can be heard on the stairs. She whispers.*] Come in. There's nobody here.

KROGSTAD [*in the doorway*].   I found a note from you at home. What does it all mean?

MRS. LINDE.   I *had* to talk to you.

KROGSTAD.   Oh? And did it have to be here, in this house?

MRS. LINDE.   It wasn't possible over at my place, it hasn't a separate entrance. Come in. We are quite alone. The maid's asleep and the Helmers are at a party upstairs.

KROGSTAD [*comes into the room*].   Well, well! So the Helmers are out dancing tonight! Really?

MRS. LINDE.   Yes, why not?

KROGSTAD.   Why not indeed!

MRS. LINDE.   Well then, Nils. Let's talk.

KROGSTAD.   Have we two anything more to talk about?

MRS. LINDE.   We have a great deal to talk about.

KROGSTAD.   I shouldn't have thought so.

MRS. LINDE.   That's because you never really understood me.

KROGSTAD.   What else was there to understand, apart from the old, old story? A heartless woman throws a man over the moment something more profitable offers itself.

MRS. LINDE.   Do you really think I'm so heartless? Do you think I found it easy to break it off?

KROGSTAD.   Didn't you?

MRS. LINDE.   You didn't really believe that?

KROGSTAD.   If that wasn't the case, why did you write to me as you did?

MRS. LINDE.   There was nothing else I could do. If I had to make the break, I felt in duty bound to destroy any feeling that you had for me.

KROGSTAD [*clenching his hands*].   So that's how it was. And all that . . . was for money!

MRS. LINDE.   You mustn't forget I had a helpless mother and two young brothers. We couldn't wait for you, Nils. At that time you hadn't much immediate prospect of anything.

KROGSTAD.   That may be. But you had no right to throw me over for somebody else.

MRS. LINDE.   Well, I don't know. Many's the time I've asked myself whether I was justified.

KROGSTAD [*more quietly*].   When I lost you, it was just as if the ground had slipped away from under my feet. Look at me now: a broken man clinging to the wreck of his life.

MRS. LINDE.   Help might be near.

KROGSTAD.   It was near. Then you came along and got in the way.

MRS. LINDE.   Quite without knowing, Nils. I only heard today it's you I'm supposed to be replacing at the Bank.

KROGSTAD.   If you say so, I believe you. But now you do know, aren't you going to withdraw?

MRS. LINDE.   No, that wouldn't benefit you in the slightest.

KROGSTAD.   Benefit, benefit . . . ! I would do it just the same.

MRS. LINDE.   I have learned to go carefully. Life and hard, bitter necessity have taught me that.

KROGSTAD.   And life has taught me not to believe in pretty speeches.

MRS. LINDE.   Then life has taught you a very sensible thing. But deeds are something you surely must believe in?

KROGSTAD.   How do you mean?

MRS. LINDE.   You said you were like a broken man clinging to the wreck of his life.

KROGSTAD.   And I said it with good reason.

MRS. LINDE.   And I am like a broken woman clinging to the wreck of her life. Nobody to care about, and nobody to care for.

KROGSTAD.   It was your own choice.

MRS. LINDE.   At the time there was no other choice.

KROGSTAD.   Well, what of it?

MRS. LINDE.   Nils, what about us two castaways joining forces?

KROGSTAD.   What's that you say?

MRS. LINDE.   Two of us on one wreck surely stand a better chance than each on his own.

KROGSTAD.   Kristine!

MRS. LINDE.   Why do you suppose I came to town?

KROGSTAD.   You mean, you thought of me?

MRS. LINDE.   Without work I couldn't live. All my life I have worked, for as long as I can remember; that has always been my one great joy. But now I'm completely alone in the world, and feeling horribly empty and forlorn. There's no pleasure in working only for yourself. Nils, give me somebody and something to work for.

KROGSTAD.   I don't believe all this. It's only a woman's hysteria, wanting to be all magnanimous and self-sacrificing.

MRS. LINDE.   Have you ever known me hysterical before?

KROGSTAD.   Would you really do this? Tell me—do you know all about my past?

MRS. LINDE.   Yes.

KROGSTAD.   And you know what people think about me?

MRS. LINDE.   Just now you hinted you thought you might have been a different person with me.

KROGSTAD.   I'm convinced I would.

MRS. LINDE.   Couldn't it still happen?

KROGSTAD.   Kristine! You know what you are saying, don't you? Yes, you do. I can see you do. Have you really the courage . . . ?

MRS. LINDE.   I need someone to mother, and your children need a mother. We two need each other. Nils, I have faith in what, deep down, you are. With you I can face anything.

KROGSTAD [*seizing her hands*].   Thank you, thank you, Kristine. And I'll soon have everybody looking up to me, or I'll know the reason why. Ah, but I was forgetting. . . .

MRS. LINDE.   Hush! The tarantella! You must go!

KROGSTAD.   Why? What is it?

MRS. LINDE.   You hear that dance upstairs? When it's finished they'll be coming.

KROGSTAD.   Yes, I'll go. It's too late to do anything. Of course, you know nothing about what steps I've taken against the Helmers.

MRS. LINDE.   Yes, Nils, I do know.

KROGSTAD.   Yet you still want to go on. . . .

MRS. LINDE.   I know how far a man like you can be driven by despair.

KROGSTAD.   Oh, if only I could undo what I've done!

MRS. LINDE.   You still can. Your letter is still there in the box.

KROGSTAD.   Are you sure?

MRS. LINDE.   Quite sure. But . . .

KROGSTAD [*regards her searchingly*].   Is that how things are? You want to save your friend at any price? Tell me straight. Is that it?

MRS. LINDE.   When you've sold yourself *once* for other people's sake, you don't do it again.

KROGSTAD.   I shall demand my letter back.

MRS. LINDE.   No, no.

KROGSTAD.   Of course I will, I'll wait here till Helmer comes. I'll tell him he has to give me my letter back . . . that it's only about my notice . . . that he mustn't read it. . . .

MRS. LINDE.   No, Nils, don't ask for it back.

KROGSTAD.   But wasn't that the very reason you got me here?

MRS. LINDE.   Yes, that was my first terrified reaction. But that was yesterday, and it's quite incredible the things I've witnessed in this house in the last twenty-four hours. Helmer must know everything. This unhappy secret must come out. Those two must have the whole thing out between them. All this secrecy and deception, it just can't go on.

KROGSTAD.   Well, if you want to risk it. . . . But one thing I can do, and I'll do it at once. . . .

MRS. LINDE [*listening*].   Hurry! Go, go! The dance has stopped. We aren't safe a moment longer.

KROGSTAD.   I'll wait for you downstairs.

MRS. LINDE.   Yes, do. You must see me home.

KROGSTAD.   I've never been so incredibly happy before.

[*He goes out by the front door. The door out into the hall remains standing open.*]

MRS. LINDE [*tidies the room a little and gets her hat and coat ready*].   How things change! How things change! Somebody to work for . . . to live for. A home to bring happiness into. Just let me get down to it. . . . I wish they'd come. . . . [*Listens.*] Ah, there they are. . . . Get my things.

[*She takes her coat and hat. The voices of* HELMER *and* NORA *are heard outside. A key is turned and* HELMER *pushes* NORA *almost forcibly into the hall. She is dressed in the Italian costume, with a big black shawl over it. He is in evening dress, and over it a black cloak, open.*]

NORA [*still in the doorway, reluctantly*].   No, no, not in here! I want to go back up again. I don't want to leave so early.

HELMER.   But my dearest Nora . . .

NORA.   Oh, please, Torvald, I beg you. . . . *Please,* just for another hour.

HELMER.   Not another minute, Nora my sweet. You remember what we agreed. There now, come along in. You'll catch cold standing there.

[*He leads her, in spite of her resistance, gently but firmly into the room.*]

MRS. LINDE.   Good evening.

NORA.   Kristine!

HELMER.   Why, Mrs. Linde. You here so late?

MRS. LINDE.   Yes. You must forgive me but I did so want to see Nora all dressed up.

NORA.   Have you been sitting here waiting for me?

MRS. LINDE.   Yes, I'm afraid I wasn't in time to catch you before you went upstairs. And I felt I couldn't leave again without seeing you.

HELMER [*removing Nora's shawl*].   Well take a good look at her. I think I can say she's worth looking at. Isn't she lovely, Mrs. Linde?

MRS. LINDE.   Yes, I must say. . . .

HELMER.   Isn't she quite extraordinarily lovely? That's what everybody at the party thought, too. But she's dreadfully stubborn . . . the sweet little thing! And what shall we do about that? Would you believe it, I nearly had to use force to get her away.

NORA. Oh Torvald, you'll be sorry you didn't let me stay, even for half an hour.

HELMER. You hear that, Mrs. Linde? She dances her tarantella, there's wild applause—which was well deserved, although the performance was perhaps rather realistic . . . I mean, rather more so than was strictly necessary from the artistic point of view. But anyway! The main thing is she was a success, a tremendous success. Was I supposed to let her stay after that? Spoil the effect? No thank you! I took my lovely little Capri girl—my capricious little Capri girl, I might say—by the arm, whisked her once round the room, a curtsey all round, and then—as they say in novels—the beautiful vision vanished. An exit should always be effective, Mrs. Linde. But I just can't get Nora to see that. Phew! It's warm in here. [*He throws his cloak over a chair and opens the door to his study.*] What? It's dark. Oh yes, of course. Excuse me. . . .

[*He goes in and lights a few candles.*]

NORA [*quickly, in a breathless whisper*]. Well?

MRS. LINDE [*softly*]. I've spoken to him.

NORA. And . . . ?

MRS. LINDE. Nora . . . you must tell your husband everything.

NORA [*tonelessly*]. I knew it.

MRS. LINDE. You've got nothing to fear from Krogstad. But you must speak.

NORA. I won't.

MRS. LINDE. Then the letter will.

NORA. Thank you, Kristine. Now I know what's to be done. Hush . . . !

HELMER [*comes in again*]: Well, Mrs. Linde, have you finished admiring her?

MRS. LINDE. Yes. And now I must say good night.

HELMER. Oh, already? Is this yours, this knitting?

MRS. LINDE [*takes it*]. Yes, thank you. I nearly forgot it.

HELMER. So you knit, eh?

MRS. LINDE. Yes.

HELMER. You should embroider instead, you know.

MRS. LINDE. Oh? Why?

HELMER. So much prettier. Watch! You hold the embroidery like this in the left hand, and then you take the needle in the right hand, like this, and you describe a long, graceful curve. Isn't that right?

MRS. LINDE. Yes, I suppose so. . . .

HELMER. Whereas knitting on the other hand just can't help being ugly. Look! Arms pressed into the sides, the knitting needles going up and down—there's something Chinese about it. . . . Ah, that was marvellous champagne they served tonight.

MRS. LINDE. Well, good night, Nora! And stop being so stubborn.

HELMER. Well said, Mrs. Linde!

MRS. LINDE. Good night, Mr. Helmer.

HELMER [*accompanying her to the door*]. Good night, good night! You'll get home all right, I hope? I'd be only too pleased to. . . . But you haven't far to walk. Good night, good night! [*She goes; he shuts the door behind her and comes in again.*] There we are, got rid of her at last. She's a frightful bore, that woman.

NORA. Aren't you very tired, Torvald?

HELMER. Not in the least.

NORA.   Not sleepy?

HELMER.   Not at all. On the contrary, I feel extremely lively. What about you? Yes, you look quite tired and sleepy.

NORA.   Yes, I'm very tired. I just want to fall straight off to sleep.

HELMER.   There you are, you see! Wasn't I right in thinking we shouldn't stay any longer?

NORA.   Oh, everything you do is right.

HELMER [*kissing her forehead*].   There's my little sky-lark talking common sense. Did you notice how gay Rank was this evening?

NORA.   Oh, was he? I didn't get a chance to talk to him.

HELMER.   I hardly did either. But it's a long time since I saw him in such a good mood. [*Looks at Nora for a moment or two, then comes nearer her.*] Ah, it's wonderful to be back in our own home again, and quite alone with you. How irresistibly lovely you are, Nora!

NORA.   Don't look at me like that, Torvald!

HELMER.   Can't I look at my most treasured possession? At all this loveliness that's mine and mine alone, completely and utterly mine.

NORA [*walks round to the other side of the table*].   You mustn't talk to me like that tonight.

HELMER [*following her*].   You still have the tarantella in your blood, I see. And that makes you even more desirable. Listen! The guests are beginning to leave now. [*Softly.*] Nora . . . soon the whole house will be silent.

NORA.   I should hope so.

HELMER.   Of course you do, don't you, Nora my darling? You know, whenever I'm out at a party with you . . . do you know why I never talk to you very much, why I always stand away from you and only steal a quick glance at you now and then . . . do you know why I do that? It's because I'm pretending we are secretly in love, secretly engaged and nobody suspects there is anything between us.

NORA.   Yes, yes. I know your thoughts are always with me, of course.

HELMER.   And when it's time to go, and I lay your shawl round those shapely, young shoulders, round the exquisite curve of your neck . . . I pretend that you are my young bride, that we are just leaving our wedding, that I am taking you to our new home for the first time . . . to be alone with you for the first time . . . quite alone with your young and trembling loveliness! All evening I've been longing for you, and nothing else. And as I watched you darting and swaying in the tarantella, my blood was on fire . . . I couldn't bear it any longer . . . and that's why I brought you down here with me so early. . . .

NORA.   Go away, Torvald! Please leave me alone. I won't have it.

HELMER.   What's this? It's just your little game isn't it, my little Nora. Won't! Won't! Am I not your husband. . . ?

[*There is a knock on the front door.*]

NORA [*startled*].   Listen . . . !

HELMER [*going towards the hall*].   Who's there?

RANK [*outside*].   It's me. Can I come in for a minute?

HELMER [*in a low voice, annoyed*].   Oh, what does he want now? [*Aloud.*] Wait a moment. [*He walks across and opens the door.*] How nice of you to look in on your way out.

RANK.   I fancied I heard your voice and I thought I would just look in. [*He takes a quick glance round.*] Ah yes, this dear, familiar old place! How cosy and comfortable you've got things here, you two.

HELMER.   You seemed to be having a pretty good time upstairs yourself.

RANK.   Capital! Why shouldn't I? Why not make the most of things in this world? At least as much as one can, and for as long as one can. The wine was excellent. . . .

HELMER.   Especially the champagne.

RANK.   You noticed that too, did you? It's incredible the amount I was able to put away.

NORA.   Torvald also drank a lot of champagne this evening.

RANK.   Oh?

NORA.   Yes, and that always makes him quite merry.

RANK.   Well, why shouldn't a man allow himself a jolly evening after a day well spent?

HELMER.   Well spent? I'm afraid I can't exactly claim that.

RANK [*clapping him on the shoulder*].   But I can, you see!

NORA.   Dr. Rank, am I right in thinking you carried out a certain laboratory test today?

RANK.   Exactly.

HELMER.   Look at our little Nora talking about laboratory tests!

NORA.   And may I congratulate you on the result?

RANK.   You may indeed.

NORA.   So it was good?

RANK.   The best possible, for both doctor and patient—certainty!

NORA [*quickly and searchingly*].   Certainty?

RANK.   Absolute certainty. So why shouldn't I allow myself a jolly evening after that?

NORA.   Quite right, Dr. Rank.

HELMER.   I quite agree. As long as you don't suffer for it in the morning.

RANK.   Well, you never get anything for nothing in this life.

NORA.   Dr. Rank . . . you are very fond of masquerades, aren't you?

RANK.   Yes, when there are plenty of amusing disguises. . . .

NORA.   Tell me, what shall we two go as next time?

HELMER.   There's frivolity for you . . . thinking about the next time already!

RANK.   We two? I'll tell you. You must go as Lady Luck. . . .

HELMER.   Yes, but how do you find a costume to suggest *that?*

RANK.   Your wife could simply go in her everyday clothes. . . .

HELMER.   That was nicely said. But don't you know what you would be?

RANK.   Yes, my dear friend, I know exactly what I shall be.

HELMER.   Well?

RANK.   At the next masquerade, I shall be invisible.

HELMER.   That's a funny idea!

RANK.   There's a big black cloak . . . haven't you heard of the cloak of invisibility? That comes right down over you, and then nobody can see you.

HELMER [*suppressing a smile*].   Of course, that's right.

RANK.   But I'm clean forgetting what I came for. Helmer, give me a cigar, one of the dark Havanas.

HELMER.   With the greatest of pleasure.

[*He offers his case.*]

RANK [*takes one and cuts the end off*].   Thanks.

NORA [*strikes a match*].   Let me give you a light.

RANK.   Thank you. [*She holds out the match and he lights his cigar.*] And now, goodbye!

HELMER.   Goodbye, goodbye, my dear fellow!

NORA.   Sleep well, Dr. Rank.

RANK.   Thank you for that wish.

NORA.   Wish me the same.

RANK.   You? All right, if you want me to. . . . Sleep well. And thanks for the light.

> [*He nods to them both, and goes.*]

HELMER [*subdued*].   He's had a lot to drink.

NORA [*absently*].   Very likely.

> [HELMER *takes a bunch of keys out of his pocket and goes out into the hall.*]

NORA.   Torvald . . . what do you want there?

HELMER.   I must empty the letter-box, it's quite full. There'll be no room for the papers in the morning. . . .

NORA.   Are you going to work tonight?

HELMER.   You know very well I'm not. Hello, what's this? Somebody's been at the lock.

NORA.   At the lock?

HELMER.   Yes, I'm sure of it. Why should that be? I'd hardly have thought the maids . . . ? Here's a broken hair-pin. Nora, it's one of yours. . . .

NORA [*quickly*].   It must have been the children. . . .

HELMER.   Then you'd better tell them not to. Ah . . . there . . . I've managed to get it open. [*He takes the things out and shouts into the kitchen.*] Helene! . . . Helene, put the light out in the hall. [*He comes into the room again with the letters in his hand and shuts the hall door.*] Look how it all mounts up. [*Runs through them.*] What's this?

NORA.   The letter! Oh no, Torvald, no!

HELMER.   Two visiting cards . . . from Dr. Rank.

NORA.   From Dr. Rank?

HELMER [*looking at them*].   Dr. Rank, Medical Practitioner. They were on top. He must have put them in as he left.

NORA.   Is there anything on them?

HELMER.   There's a black cross above his name. Look. What an uncanny idea. It's just as if he were announcing his own death.

NORA.   He is.

HELMER.   What? What do you know about it? Has he said anything to you?

NORA.   Yes. He said when these cards came, he would have taken his last leave of us. He was going to shut himself up and die.

HELMER.   Poor fellow! Of course I knew we couldn't keep him with us very long. But so soon. . . . And hiding himself away like a wounded animal.

NORA.   When it has to happen, it's best that it should happen without words. Don't you think so, Torvald?

HELMER [*walking up and down*].   He had grown so close to us. I don't think I can imagine him gone. His suffering and his loneliness seemed almost to provide a background of dark cloud to the sunshine of our lives. Well, perhaps it's all for the best. For him at any rate. [*Pauses.*] And maybe for us as well, Nora. Now there's just the two of us. [*Puts his arms round her.*] Oh, my darling wife, I can't hold you close enough. You know, Nora . . . many's the time I wish you were threatened by some terrible danger so I could risk everything, body and soul, for your sake.

NORA [*tears herself free and says firmly and decisively*].   Now you must read your letters, Torvald.

HELMER.   No, no, not tonight. I want to be with you, my darling wife.

NORA.   Knowing all the time your friend is dying . . . ?

HELMER.   You are right. It's been a shock to both of us. This ugly thing has come between us . . . thoughts of death and decay. We must try to free ourselves from it. Until then . . . we shall go our separate ways.

NORA [*her arms round his neck*].   Torvald . . . good night! Good night!

HELMER [*kisses her forehead*].   Goodnight, my little singing bird. Sleep well, Nora, I'll just read through my letters.

[*He takes the letters into his room and shuts the door behind him.*]

NORA [*gropes around her, wild-eyed, seizes* HELMER*'s cloak, wraps it round herself, and whispers quickly, hoarsely, spasmodically*].   Never see him again. Never, never, never. [*Throws her shawl over her head.*] And never see the children again either. Never, never. Oh, that black icy water. Oh, that bottomless . . . ! If only it were all over! He's got it now. Now he's reading it. Oh no, no! Not yet! Torvald, goodbye . . . and my children. . . .

[*She rushes out in the direction of the hall; at the same moment Helmer flings open his door and stands there with an open letter in his hand.*]

HELMER.   Nora!

NORA [*shrieks*].   Ah!

HELMER.   What is this? Do you know what is in this letter?

NORA.   Yes, I know. Let me go! Let me out!

HELMER [*holds her back*].   Where are you going?

NORA [*trying to tear herself free*].   You mustn't try to save me, Torvald!

HELMER [*reels back*].   True! Is it true what he writes? How dreadful! No, no, it can't possibly be true.

NORA.   It *is* true. I loved you more than anything else in the world.

HELMER.   Don't come to me with a lot of paltry excuses!

NORA [*taking a step towards him*].   Torvald . . . !

HELMER.   Miserable woman . . . what is this you have done?

NORA.   Let me go. I won't have you taking the blame for me. You mustn't take it on yourself.

HELMER.   Stop play-acting! [*Locks the front door.*] You are staying here to give an account of yourself. Do you understand what you have done? Answer me! Do you understand?

NORA [*looking fixedly at him, her face hardening*].   Yes, now I'm really beginning to understand.

HELMER [*walking up and down*].   Oh, what a terrible awakening this is. All these eight years . . . this woman who was my pride and joy . . . a hypocrite, a liar, worse than that, a criminal! Oh, how utterly squalid it all is! Ugh! Ugh! [*Nora remains silent and looks fixedly at him.*] I should have realized something like this would happen. I should have seen it coming. All your father's irresponsible ways. . . . Quiet! All your father's irresponsible ways are coming out in you. No religion, no morals, no sense of duty. . . . Oh, this is my punishment for turning a blind eye to him. It was for your sake I did it, and this is what I get for it.

NORA.   Yes, this.

HELMER.   Now you have ruined my entire happiness, jeopardized my whole future. It's terrible to think of. Here I am, at the mercy of a thoroughly unscrupulous person; he can do whatever he likes with me, demand anything he wants, order me about just as he chooses . . . and I daren't even whimper. I'm done for, a miserable failure, and it's all the fault of a feather-brained woman!

NORA.   When I've left this world behind, you will be free.

HELMER.   Oh, stop pretending! Your father was just the same, always ready with fine phrases. What good would it do me if you left this world behind, as you put it? Not the slightest bit of good. He can still let it all come out, if he likes; and if he does, people might even suspect me of being an accomplice in these criminal acts of yours. They might even think I was the one behind it all, that it was I who pushed you into it! And it's you I have to thank for this . . . and when I've taken such good care of you, all our married life. Now do you understand what you have done to me?

NORA [*coldly and calmly*].   Yes.

HELMER.   I just can't understand it, it's so incredible. But we must see about putting things right. Take that shawl off. Take it off, I tell you! I must see if I can't find some way or other of appeasing him. The thing must be hushed up at all costs. And as far as you and I are concerned, things must appear to go on exactly as before. But only in the eyes of the world, of course. In other words you'll go on living here; that's understood. But you will not be allowed to bring up the children, I can't trust you with them. . . . Oh, that I should have to say this to the woman I loved so dearly, the woman I still. . . . Well, that must be all over and done with. From now on, there can be no question of happiness. All we can do is save the bits and pieces from the wreck, preserve appearances. . . . [*The front door-bell rings.* HELMER *gives a start.*] What's that? So late? How terrible, supposing. . . . If he should . . . ? Hide, Nora! Say you are not well.

[NORA *stands motionless.* HELMER *walks across and opens the door into the hall.*]

MAID [*half dressed, in the hall*].   It's a note for Mrs. Helmer.

HELMER.   Give it to me. [*He snatches the note and shuts the door.*] Yes, it's from him. You can't have it. I want to read it myself.

NORA.   You read it then.

HELMER [*by the lamp*].   I hardly dare. Perhaps this is the end, for both of us. Well, I must know. [*He opens the note hurriedly, reads a few lines, looks at another enclosed sheet, and gives a cry of joy.*] Nora! [*Nora looks at him inquiringly.*] Nora! I must read it again. Yes, yes, it's true! I am saved! Nora, I am saved!

NORA.   And me?

HELMER.   You too, of course, we are both saved, you as well as me. Look, he's sent your IOU back. He sends his regrets and apologies for what he has done. . . . His luck has changed. . . . Oh, what does it matter what he says. We are saved, Nora! Nobody can do anything to you now. Oh, Nora, Nora . . . but let's get rid of this disgusting thing first. Let me see. . . . [*He glances at the IOU.*] No, I don't want to see it. I don't want it to be anything but a dream. [*He tears up the IOU and both letters, throws all the pieces into the stove and watches them burn.*] Well, that's the end of that. He said in his note you'd known since Christmas Eve. . . . You must have had three terrible days of it, Nora.

NORA.   These three days haven't been easy.

HELMER.   The agonies you must have gone through! When the only way out seemed to be. . . . No, let's forget the whole ghastly thing. We can rejoice and say: It's all over! It's all over! Listen to me, Nora! You don't seem to understand: it's all over! Why this grim look on your face? Oh, poor little Nora, of course I understand. You can't bring yourself to believe I've forgiven you. But I have, Nora, I swear it. I forgive you everything. I know you did what you did because you loved me.

NORA. That's true.

HELMER. You loved me as a wife should love her husband. It was simply that you didn't have the experience to judge what was the best way of going about things. But do you think I love you any the less for that; just because you don't know how to act on your own responsibility? No, no, you just lean on me, I shall give you all the advice and guidance you need. I wouldn't be a proper man if I didn't find a woman doubly attractive for being so obviously helpless. You mustn't dwell on the harsh things I said in that first moment of horror, when I thought everything was going to come crashing down about my ears. I have forgiven you, Nora, I swear it! I have forgiven you!

NORA. Thank you for your forgiveness.

  [*She goes out through the door, right.*]

HELMER. No, don't go! [*He looks through the doorway.*] What are you doing in the spare room?

NORA. Taking off this fancy dress.

HELMER [*standing at the open door*]. Yes, do. You try and get some rest, and set your mind at peace again, my frightened little song-bird. Have a good long sleep; you know you are safe and sound under my wing. [*Walks up and down near the door.*] What a nice, cosy little home we have here, Nora! Here you can find refuge. Here I shall hold you like a hunted dove I have rescued unscathed from the cruel talons of the hawk, and calm your poor beating heart. And that will come, gradually, Nora, believe me. Tomorrow you'll see everything quite differently. Soon everything will be just as it was before. You won't need me to keep on telling you I've forgiven you; you'll feel convinced of it in your own heart. You don't really imagine me ever thinking of turning you out, or even of reproaching you? Oh, a real man isn't made that way, you know, Nora. For a man, there's something indescribably moving and very satisfying in knowing that he has forgiven his wife—forgiven her, completely and genuinely, from the depths of his heart. It's as though it made her his property in a double sense: he has, as it were, given her a new life, and she becomes in a way both his wife and at the same time his child. That is how you will seem to me after today, helpless, perplexed little thing that you are. Don't you worry your pretty little head about anything, Nora. Just you be frank with me, and I'll take all the decisions for you. . . . What's this? Not in bed? You've changed your things?

NORA [*in her everyday dress*]. Yes, Torvald, I've changed.

HELMER. What for? It's late.

NORA. I shan't sleep tonight.

HELMER. But my dear Nora. . . .

NORA [*looks at her watch*]. It's not so terribly late. Sit down, Torvald. We two have a lot to talk about.

  [*She sits down at one side of the table.*]

HELMER. Nora, what is all this? Why so grim?

NORA. Sit down. It'll take some time. I have a lot to say to you.

HELMER [*sits down at the table opposite her*]. You frighten me, Nora. I don't understand you.

NORA. Exactly. You don't understand me. And I have never understood you, either—until tonight. No, don't interrupt. I just want you to listen to what I have to say. We are going to have things out, Torvald.

HELMER. What do you mean?

NORA.   Isn't there anything that strikes you about the way we two are sitting here?

HELMER.   What's that?

NORA.   We have now been married eight years. Hasn't it struck you this is the first time you and I, man and wife, have had a serious talk together?

HELMER.   Depends what you mean by 'serious.'

NORA.   Eight whole years—no, more, ever since we first knew each other—and never have we exchanged one serious word about serious things.

HELMER.   What did you want me to do? Get you involved in worries that you couldn't possibly help me to bear?

NORA.   I'm not talking about worries. I say we've never once sat down together and seriously tried to get to the bottom of anything.

HELMER.   But, my dear Nora, would that have been a thing for you?

NORA.   That's just it. You have never understood me ... I've been greatly wronged, Torvald. First by my father, and then by you.

HELMER.   What! Us two! The two people who loved you more than anybody?

NORA [*shakes her head*].   You two never loved me. You only thought how nice it was to be in love with me.

HELMER.   But, Nora, what's this you are saying?

NORA.   It's right, you know, Torvald. At home, Daddy used to tell me what he thought, then I thought the same. And if I thought differently, I kept quiet about it, because he wouldn't have liked it. He used to call me his baby doll, and he played with me as I used to play with my dolls. Then I came to live in your house. . . .

HELMER.   What way is that to talk about our marriage?

NORA [*imperturbably*].   What I mean is: I passed out of Daddy's hands into yours. You arranged everything to your tastes, and I acquired the same tastes. Or I pretended to ... I don't really know ... I think it was a bit of both, some-times one thing and sometimes the other. When I look back, it seems to me I have been living here like a beggar, from hand to mouth. I lived by doing tricks for you, Torvald. But that's the way you wanted it. You and Daddy did me a great wrong. It's your fault that I've never made anything of my life.

HELMER.   Nora, how unreasonable ... how ungrateful you are! Haven't you been happy here?

NORA.   No, never. I thought I was, but I wasn't really.

HELMER.   Not ... not happy!

NORA.   No, just gay. And you've always been so kind to me. But our house has never been anything but a play-room. I have been your doll wife, just as at home I was Daddy's doll child. And the children in turn have been my dolls. I thought it was fun when you came and played with me, just as they thought it was fun when I went and played with them. That's been our marriage, Torvald.

HELMER.   There is some truth in what you say, exaggerated and hysterical though it is. But from now on it will be different. Play-time is over; now comes the time for lessons.

NORA.   Whose lessons? Mine or the children's?

HELMER.   Both yours and the children's, my dear Nora.

NORA.   Ah, Torvald, you are not the man to teach me to be a good wife for you.

HELMER.   How can you say that?

NORA.   And what sort of qualifications have I to teach the children?

HELMER.   Nora!

NORA.   Didn't you say yourself, a minute or two ago, that you couldn't trust me with that job?

HELMER.   In the heat of the moment! You shouldn't pay any attention to that.

NORA.   On the contrary, you were quite right. I'm not up to it. There's another problem needs solving first. I must take steps to educate myself. You are not the man to help me there. That's something I must do on my own. That's why I'm leaving you.

HELMER [*jumps up*].   What did you say?

NORA.   If I'm ever to reach any understanding of myself and the things around me, I must learn to stand alone. That's why I can't stay here with you any longer.

HELMER.   Nora! Nora!

NORA.   I'm leaving here at once. I dare say Kristine will put me up for tonight. . . .

HELMER.   You are out of your mind! I won't let you! I forbid you!

NORA.   It's no use forbidding me anything now. I'm taking with me my own personal belongings. I don't want anything of yours, either now or later.

HELMER.   This is madness!

NORA.   Tomorrow I'm going home—to what used to be my home, I mean. It will be easier for me to find something to do there.

HELMER.   Oh, you blind, inexperienced . . .

NORA.   I must set about *getting* experience, Torvald.

HELMER.   And leave your home, your husband and your children? Don't you care what people will say?

NORA.   That's no concern of mine. All I know is that this is necessary for me.

HELMER.   This is outrageous! You are betraying your most sacred duty.

NORA.   And what do you consider to be my most sacred duty?

HELMER.   Does it take me to tell you that? Isn't it your duty to your husband and your children?

NORA.   I have another duty equally sacred.

HELMER.   You have not. What duty might *that* be?

NORA.   My duty to myself.

HELMER.   First and foremost, you are a wife and mother.

NORA.   That I don't believe any more. I believe that first and foremost I am an individual, just as much as you are—or at least I'm going to try to be. I know most people agree with you, Torvald, and that's also what it says in books. But I'm not content any more with what most people say, or with what it says in books. I have to think things out for myself, and get things clear.

HELMER.   Surely you are clear about your position in your own home? Haven't you an infallible guide in questions like these? Haven't you your religion?

NORA.   Oh, Torvald, I don't really know what religion is.

HELMER.   What do you say!

NORA.   All I know is what Pastor Hansen said when I was confirmed. He said religion was this, that and the other. When I'm away from all this and on my own, I'll go into that, too. I want to find out whether what Pastor Hansen told me was right—or at least whether it's right for *me*.

HELMER.   This is incredible talk from a young woman! But if religion cannot keep you on the right path, let me at least stir your conscience. I suppose you do have some moral sense? Or tell me—perhaps you don't?

NORA.   Well, Torvald, that's not easy to say. I simply don't know. I'm really very confused about such things. All I know is my ideas about such things are very different from yours. I've also learnt that the law is different from what I thought; but I simply can't get it into my head that that particular law is right. Apparently a woman has no right to spare her old father on his deathbed, or to save her husband's life, even. I just don't believe it.

HELMER.   You are talking like a child. You understand nothing about the society you live in.

NORA.   No, I don't. But I shall go into that too. I must try to discover who is right, society or me.

HELMER.   You are ill, Nora. You are delirious. I'm half inclined to think you are out of your mind.

NORA.   Never have I felt so calm and collected as I do tonight.

HELMER.   Calm and collected enough to leave your husband and children?

NORA.   Yes.

HELMER.   Then only one explanation is possible.

NORA.   And that is?

HELMER.   You don't love me any more.

NORA.   Exactly.

HELMER.   Nora! Can you say that?

NORA.   I'm desperately sorry, Torvald. Because you have always been so kind to me. But I can't help it. I don't love you any more.

HELMER [*struggling to keep his composure*].   Is that also a 'calm and collected' decision you've made?

NORA.   Yes, absolutely calm and collected. That's why I don't want to stay here.

HELMER.   And can you also account for how I forfeited your love?

NORA.   Yes, very easily. It was tonight, when the miracle didn't happen. It was then I realized you weren't the man I thought you were.

HELMER.   Explain yourself more clearly. I don't understand.

NORA.   For eight years I have been patiently waiting. Because, heavens, I knew miracles didn't happen every day. Then this devastating business started, and I became absolutely convinced the miracle *would* happen. All the time Krogstad's letter lay there, it never so much as crossed my mind that you would ever submit to that man's conditions. I was absolutely convinced you would say to him: Tell the whole wide world if you like. And when that was done . . .

HELMER.   Yes, then what? After I had exposed my own wife to dishonour and shame . . . !

NORA.   When that was done, I was absolutely convinced you would come forward and take everything on yourself, and say: I am the guilty one.

HELMER.   Nora!

NORA.   You mean I'd never let you make such a sacrifice for my sake? Of course not. But what would my story have counted for against yours?—That was the miracle I went in hope and dread of. It was to prevent it that I was ready to end my life.

HELMER.   I would gladly toil day and night for you, Nora, enduring all manner of sorrow and distress. But nobody sacrifices his *honour* for the one he loves.

NORA.   Hundreds and thousands of women have.

HELMER.   Oh, you think and talk like a stupid child.

NORA.   All right. But you neither think nor talk like the man I would want to share my life with. When you had got over your fright—and you weren't concerned about me but only about what might happen to you—and when all danger was past, you acted as though nothing had happened. I was your little sky-lark again, your little doll, exactly as before; except you would have to protect it twice as carefully as before, now that it had shown itself to be so weak and fragile. [*Rises.*] Torvald, that was the moment I realised that for eight years I'd been living with a stranger, and had borne him three children. . . . Oh, I can't bear to think about it! I could tear myself to shreds.

HELMER [*sadly*].   I see. I see. There is a tremendous gulf dividing us. But, Nora, is there no way we might bridge it?

NORA.   As I am now, I am no wife for you.

HELMER.   I still have it in me to change.

NORA.   Perhaps . . . if you have your doll taken away.

HELMER.   And be separated from you! No, no, Nora, the very thought of it is inconceivable.

NORA [*goes into the room, right*].   All the more reason why it must be done.

[*She comes back with her outdoor things and a small travelling bag which she puts on the chair beside the table.*]

HELMER.   Nora, Nora, not now! Wait till the morning.

NORA [*putting on her coat*].   I can't spend the night in a strange man's room.

HELMER.   Couldn't we go on living here like brother and sister . . . ?

NORA [*tying on her hat*].   You know very well that wouldn't last. [*She draws the shawl round her.*] Goodbye, Torvald. I don't want to see the children. I know they are in better hands than mine. As I am now, I can never be anything to them.

HELMER.   But some day, Nora, some day . . . ?

NORA.   How should I know? I've no idea what I might turn out to be.

HELMER.   But you are my wife, whatever you are.

NORA.   Listen, Torvald, from what I've heard, when a wife leaves her husband's house as I am doing now, he is absolved by law of all responsibility for her. I can at any rate free you from all responsibility. You must not feel in any way bound, any more than I shall. There must be full freedom on both sides. Look, here's your ring back. Give me mine.

HELMER.   That too?

NORA.   That too.

HELMER.   There it is.

NORA.   Well, that's the end of that. I'll put the keys down here. The maids know where everything is in the house—better than I do, in fact. Kristine will come in the morning after I've left to pack up the few things I brought with me from home. I want them sent on.

HELMER.   The end! Nora, will you never think of me?

NORA.   I dare say I'll often think about you and the children and this house.

HELMER.   May I write to you, Nora?

NORA.   No, never. I won't let you.

HELMER.   But surely I can send you . . .

NORA.   Nothing, nothing.

HELMER.   Can't I help you if ever you need it?

NORA.   I said 'no.' I don't accept things from strangers.

HELMER.   Nora, can I never be anything more to you than a stranger?

NORA [*takes her bag*].   Ah, Torvald, only by a miracle of miracles . . .

HELMER.   Name it, this miracle of miracles!

NORA.   Both you and I would have to change to the point where. . . . Oh, Torvald, I don't believe in miracles any more.

HELMER.   But I *will* believe. Name it! Change to the point where . . . ?

NORA.   Where we could make a real marriage of our lives together. Goodbye!

[*She goes out through the hall door.*]

HELMER   [*sinks down on a chair near the door, and covers his face with his hands*]. Nora! Nora! [*He rises and looks round.*] Empty! She's gone! [*With sudden hope.*] The miracle of miracles . . . ?

[*The heavy sound of a door being slammed is heard from below.*]

[1879]

Topics for Critical Thinking and Writing

1. Near the beginning of the play, how does Mrs. Linde's presence help to define Nora's character? How does Nora's response to Krogstad's entrance tell us something about Nora?
2. What does Dr. Rank contribute to the play? If he were eliminated, what would be lost?
3. Can it be argued that although at the end Nora goes out to achieve self-realization, her abandonment of her children—especially to Torvald's loathsome conventional morality—is a crime? (By the way, exactly why does Nora leave the children? She seems to imply, in some passages, that because she forged a signature she is unfit to bring them up. But do you agree with her?)
4. Michael Meyer, in his splendid biography *Henrik Ibsen,* says that the play is not so much about women's rights as about "the need of every individual to find out the kind of person he or she really is, and to strive to become that person." What evidence can you offer to support or refute this interpretation?
5. In *The Quintessence of Ibsenism* Bernard Shaw says that Ibsen, reacting against a common theatrical preference for strange situations,

> saw that . . . the more familiar the situation, the more interesting the play. Shakespear had put ourselves on the stage but not our situations. Our uncles seldom murder our fathers and . . . marry our mothers. . . . Ibsen . . . gives us not only ourselves, but ourselves in our own situations. The things that happen to his stage figures are things that happen to us. One consequence is that his plays are much more important to us than Shakespear's. Another is that they are capable both of hurting us cruelly and of filling us with excited hopes of escape from idealistic tyrannies, and with visions of intenser life in the future.

How much of this do you believe?

SUSAN GLASPELL

Susan Glaspell (1882–1948) was born in Davenport, Iowa, and educated at Drake University in Des Moines. In 1903 she married George Cram Cook and, with Cook and other writers, actors, and artists, in 1915 founded the Provincetown Players, a group that remained vital until 1929. Glaspell wrote Trifles *(1916) for the Provincetown Players, but she also wrote stories, novels, and a biography of her husband. In 1931 she won a Pulitzer Prize for* Alison's House, *a play about the family of a deceased poet who in some ways resembles Emily Dickinson.*

Trifles

SCENE: *The kitchen in the now abandoned farmhouse of* JOHN WRIGHT, *a gloomy kitchen, and left without having been put in order—unwashed pans under the sink, a loaf of bread outside the breadbox, a dish towel on the table—other signs of incompleted work. At the rear the outer door opens, and the* SHERIFF *comes in, followed by the* COUNTY ATTORNEY *and* HALE. *The* SHERIFF *and* HALE *are men in middle life, the* COUNTY ATTORNEY *is a young man; all are much bundled up and go at once to the stove. They are followed by the two women—the* SHERIFF'S WIFE *first; she is a slight wiry woman, a thin nervous face.* MRS. HALE *is larger and would ordinarily be called more comfortable looking, but she is disturbed now and looks fearfully about as she enters. The women have come in slowly and stand close together near the door.*

COUNTY ATTORNEY [*rubbing his hands*].   This feels good. Come up to the fire, ladies.

MRS. PETERS [*after taking a step forward*].   I'm not—cold.

SHERIFF [*unbuttoning his overcoat and stepping away from the stove as if to the beginning of official business*].   Now, Mr. Hale, before we move things about, you explain to Mr. Henderson just what you saw when you came here yesterday morning.

COUNTY ATTORNEY.   By the way, has anything been moved? Are things just as you left them yesterday?

SHERIFF [*looking about*].   It's just the same. When it dropped below zero last night, I thought I'd better send Frank out this morning to make a fire for us—no use getting pneumonia with a big case on; but I told him not to touch anything except the stove—and you know Frank.

COUNTY ATTORNEY.   Somebody should have been left here yesterday.

SHERIFF.   Oh—yesterday. When I had to send Frank to Morris Center for that man who went crazy—I want you to know I had my hands full yesterday. I knew

Photo of the original production (1916) of *Trifles*. (New York Public Library)

you could get back from Omaha by today, and as long as I went over everything here myself—

COUNTY ATTORNEY.   Well, Mr. Hale, tell just what happened when you came here
yesterday morning.

HALE.   Harry and I had started to town with a load of potatoes. We came along
the road from my place; and as I got here, I said, "I'm going to see if I can't
get John Wright to go in with me on a party telephone." I spoke to Wright
about it once before, and he put me off, saying folks talked too much anyway, and all he asked was peace and quiet—I guess you know about how
much he talked himself; but I thought maybe if I went to the house and
talked about it before his wife, though I said to Harry that I didn't know as
what his wife wanted made much difference to John—

COUNTY ATTORNEY.   Let's talk about that later, Mr. Hale. I do want to talk about
that, but tell now just what happened when you got to the house.

HALE.   I didn't hear or see anything; I knocked at the door, and still it was all
quiet inside. I knew they must be up, it was past eight o'clock. So I knocked
again, and I thought I heard somebody say, "Come in." I wasn't sure, I'm not
sure yet, but I opened the door—this door [*indicating the door by which the
two women are still standing*], and there in that rocker—[*pointing to it*] sat
Mrs. Wright. [*They all look at the rocker.*]

COUNTY ATTORNEY.   What—was she doing?

HALE.   She was rockin' back and forth. She had her apron in her hand and was
kind of—pleating it.

COUNTY ATTORNEY.   And how did she—look?

HALE.   Well, she looked queer.

COUNTY ATTORNEY.   How do you mean—queer?

HALE.   Well, as if she didn't know what she was going to do next. And kind of
done up.

COUNTY ATTORNEY.   How did she seem to feel about your coming?

HALE.   Why, I don't think she minded—one way or other. She didn't pay much attention. I said, "How do, Mrs. Wright, it's cold, ain't it?" And she said, "Is it?"—
and went on kind of pleating at her apron. Well, I was surprised; she didn't
ask me to come up to the stove, or to set down, but just sat there, not even
looking at me, so I said, "I want to see John." And then she—laughed. I guess
you would call it a laugh. I thought of Harry and the team outside, so I said a
little sharp: "Can't I see John?" "No," she says, kind o' dull like. "Ain't he
home?" says I. "Yes," says she, "he's home." "Then why can't I see him?" I
asked her, out of patience. "'Cause he's dead," says she. "*Dead?*" says I. She
just nodded her head, not getting a bit excited, but rockin' back and forth.
"Why—where is he?" says I, not knowing what to say. She just pointed upstairs—like that [*himself pointing to the room above*]. I got up, with the idea of
going up there. I walked from there to here—then I says, "Why, what did he
die of?" "He died of a rope around his neck," says she, and just went on
pleatin' at her apron. Well, I went out and called Harry. I thought I might—
need help. We went upstairs, and there he was lyin'—

COUNTY ATTORNEY.   I think I'd rather have you go into that upstairs, where you can
point it all out. Just go on now with the rest of the story.

HALE.   Well, my first thought was to get that rope off. I looked . . . [*Stops, his face
twitches.*] . . . but Harry, he went up to him, and he said, "No, he's dead all
right, and we'd better not touch anything." So we went back downstairs. She
was still sitting that same way. "Has anybody been notified?" I asked. "No,"

says she, unconcerned. "Who did this, Mrs. Wright?" said Harry. He said it businesslike—and she stopped pleatin' of her apron. "I don't know," she says. "You don't *know?*" says Harry. "No," says she. "Weren't you sleepin' in the bed with him?" says Harry. "Yes," says she, "but I was on the inside." "Somebody slipped a rope round his neck and strangled him, and you didn't wake up?" says Harry. "I didn't wake up," she said after him. We must 'a looked as if we didn't see how that could be, for after a minute she said, "I sleep sound." Harry was going to ask her more questions, but I said maybe we ought to let her tell her story first to the coroner, or the sheriff, so Harry went fast as he could to Rivers' place, where there's a telephone.

COUNTY ATTORNEY.   And what did Mrs. Wright do when she knew that you had gone for the coroner?

HALE.   She moved from that chair to this over here . . . [*Pointing to a small chair in the corner.*] . . . and just sat there with her hands held together and looking down. I got a feeling that I ought to make some conversation, so I said I had come in to see if John wanted to put in a telephone, and at that she started to laugh, and then she stopped and looked at me—scared. [*The* COUNTY ATTOR-NEY, *who has had his notebook out, makes a note.*] I dunno, maybe it wasn't scared. I wouldn't like to say it was. Soon Harry got back, and then Dr. Lloyd came, and you, Mr. Peters, and so I guess that's all I know that you don't.

COUNTY ATTORNEY [*looking around*].   I guess we'll go upstairs first—and then out to the barn and around there. [*To the* SHERIFF.] You're convinced that there was nothing important here—nothing that would point to any motive?

SHERIFF.   Nothing here but kitchen things. [*The* COUNTY ATTORNEY, *after again look-ing around the kitchen, opens the door of a cupboard closet. He gets up on a chair and looks on a shelf. Pulls his hand away, sticky.*]

COUNTY ATTORNEY.   Here's a nice mess. [*The women draw nearer.*]

MRS. PETERS [*to the other woman*].   Oh, her fruit; it did freeze. [*To the* LAWYER.] She worried about that when it turned so cold. She said the fire'd go out and her jars would break.

SHERIFF.   Well, can you beat the women! Held for murder and worryin' about her preserves.

COUNTY ATTORNEY.   I guess before we're through she may have something more serious than preserves to worry about.

HALE.   Well, women are used to worrying over trifles.

[*The two women move a little closer together.*]

COUNTY ATTORNEY [*with the gallantry of a young politician*].   And yet, for all their worries, what would we do without the ladies? [*The women do not unbend. He goes to the sink, takes a dipperful of water from the pail and, pouring it into a basin, washes his hands. Starts to wipe them on the roller towel, turns it for a cleaner place.*] Dirty towels! [*Kicks his foot against the pans under the sink.*] Not much of a housekeeper, would you say, ladies?

MRS. HALE [*stiffly*].   There's a great deal of work to be done on a farm.

COUNTY ATTORNEY.   To be sure. And yet . . . [*With a little bow to her.*] . . . I know there are some Dickson county farmhouses which do not have such roller towels. [*He gives it a pull to expose its full length again.*]

MRS. HALE.   Those towels get dirty awful quick. Men's hands aren't always as clean as they might be.

COUNTY ATTORNEY.   Ah, loyal to your sex, I see. But you and Mrs. Wright were neighbors. I suppose you were friends, too.

MRS. HALE [*shaking her head*]. I've not seen much of her of late years. I've not been in this house—it's more than a year.

COUNTY ATTORNEY.   And why was that? You didn't like her?

MRS. HALE.   I liked her all well enough. Farmers' wives have their hands full, Mr. Henderson. And then—

COUNTY ATTORNEY.   Yes—?

MRS. HALE [*looking about*].   It never seemed a very cheerful place.

COUNTY ATTORNEY.   No—it's not cheerful. I shouldn't say she had the homemaking instinct.

MRS. HALE.   Well, I don't know as Wright had, either.

COUNTY ATTORNEY.   You mean that they didn't get on very well?

MRS. HALE.   No, I don't mean anything. But I don't think a place'd be any cheerfuler for John Wright's being in it.

COUNTY ATTORNEY.   I'd like to talk more of that a little later. I want to get the lay of things upstairs now. [*He goes to the left, where three steps lead to a stair door.*]

SHERIFF.   I suppose anything Mrs. Peters does'll be all right. She was to take in some clothes for her, you know, and a few little things. We left in such a hurry yesterday.

COUNTY ATTORNEY.   Yes, but I would like to see what you take, Mrs. Peters, and keep an eye out for anything that might be of use to us.

MRS. PETERS.   Yes, Mr. Henderson.

[*The women listen to the men's steps on the stairs, then look about the kitchen.*]

MRS. HALE.   I'd hate to have men coming into my kitchen, snooping around and criticizing. [*She arranges the pans under sink which the* LAWYER *had shoved out of place.*]

MRS. PETERS.   Of course it's no more than their duty.

MRS. HALE.   Duty's all right, but I guess that deputy sheriff that came out to make the fire might have got a little of this on. [*Gives the roller towel a pull.*] Wish I'd thought of that sooner. Seems mean to talk about her for not having things slicked up when she had to come away in such a hurry.

MRS. PETERS [*who has gone to a small table in the left rear corner of the room, and lifted one end of a towel that covers a pan*].   She had bread set. [*Stands still.*]

MRS. HALE [*eyes fixed on a loaf of bread beside the breadbox, which is on a low shelf at the other side of the room. Moves slowly toward it*].   She was going to put this in there. [*Picks up loaf, then abruptly drops it. In a manner of returning to familiar things.*] It's a shame about her fruit. I wonder if it's all gone. [*Gets up on the chair and looks.*] I think there's some here that's all right, Mrs. Peters. Yes—here; [*Holding it toward the window.*] this is cherries, too. [*Looking again.*] I declare I believe that's the only one. [*Gets down, bottle in her hand. Goes to the sink and wipes it off on the outside.*] She'll feel awful bad after all her hard work in the hot weather. I remember the afternoon I put up my cherries last summer. [*She puts the bottle on the big kitchen table, center of the room, front table. With a sigh, is about to sit down in the rocking chair. Before she is seated realizes what chair it is; with a slow look at it, steps back. The chair, which she has touched, rocks back and forth.*]

MRS. PETERS.   Well, I must get those things from the front room closet. [*She goes to the door at the right, but after looking into the other room steps back.*] You coming with me, Mrs. Hale? You could help me carry them. [*They go into the other room; reappear,* MRS. PETERS *carrying a dress and skirt, Mrs. Hale following with a pair of shoes.*]

MRS. PETERS.   My, it's cold in there. [*She puts the cloth on the big table, and hurries to the stove.*]

MRS. HALE [*examining the skirt*].   Wright was close. I think maybe that's why she kept so much to herself. She didn't even belong to the Ladies' Aid. I suppose she felt she couldn't do her part, and then you don't enjoy things when you feel shabby. She used to wear pretty clothes and be lively, when she was Minnie Foster, one of the town girls singing in the choir. But that—oh, that was thirty years ago. This all you was to take in?

MRS. PETERS.   She said she wanted an apron. Funny thing to want, for there isn't much to get you dirty in jail, goodness knows. But I suppose just to make her feel more natural. She said they was in the top drawer in this cupboard. Yes, here. And then her little shawl that always hung behind the door. [*Opens stair door and looks.*] Yes, here it is. [*Quickly shuts door leading upstairs.*]

MRS. HALE [*abruptly moving toward her*].   Mrs. Peters?

MRS. PETERS.   Yes, Mrs. Hale?

MRS. HALE.   Do you think she did it?

MRS. PETERS [*in a frightened voice*].   Oh, I don't know.

MRS. HALE.   Well, I don't think she did. Asking for an apron and her little shawl. Worrying about her fruit.

MRS. PETERS [*starts to speak, glances up, where footsteps are heard in the room above. In a low voice*].   Mr. Peters says it looks bad for her. Mr. Henderson is awful sarcastic in speech, and he'll make fun of her sayin' she didn't wake up.

MRS. HALE.   Well, I guess John Wright didn't wake when they was slipping that rope under his neck.

MRS. PETERS.   No, it's strange. It must have been done awful crafty and still. They say it was such a—funny way to kill a man, rigging it all up like that.

MRS. HALE.   That's just what Mr. Hale said. There was a gun in the house. He says that's what he can't understand.

MRS. PETERS.   Mr. Henderson said coming out that what was needed for the case was a motive; something to show anger, or—sudden feeling.

MRS. HALE [*who is standing by the table*].   Well, I don't see any signs of anger around here. [*She puts her hand on the dish towel which lies on the table, stands looking down at the table, one half of which is clean, the other half messy.*] It's wiped here. [*Makes a move as if to finish work, then turns and looks at loaf of bread outside the breadbox. Drops towel. In that voice of coming back to familiar things.*] Wonder how they are finding things upstairs? I hope she had it a little more red-up there. You know, it seems kind of *sneaking*. Locking her up in town and then coming out here and trying to get her own house to turn against her!

MRS. PETERS.   But, Mrs. Hale, the law is the law.

MRS. HALE.   I s'pose 'tis. [*Unbuttoning her coat.*] Better loosen up your things, Mrs. Peters. You won't feel them when you go out.

[MRS. PETERS *takes off her fur tippet, goes to hang it on hook at the back of room, stands looking at the under part of the small corner table.*]

MRS. PETERS.   She was piecing a quilt. [*She brings the large sewing basket, and they look at the bright pieces.*]

MRS. HALE.   It's log cabin pattern. Pretty, isn't it? I wonder if she was goin' to quilt or just knot it?

[*Footsteps have been heard coming down the stairs. The* SHERIFF *enters, followed by* HALE *and the* COUNTY ATTORNEY.]

SHERIFF.   They wonder if she was going to quilt it or just knot it. [*The men laugh, the women look abashed.*]

COUNTY ATTORNEY [*rubbing his hands over the stove*].   Frank's fire didn't do much up there, did it? Well, let's go out to the barn and get that cleared up.

[*The men go outside.*]

MRS. HALE [*resentfully*].   I don't know as there's anything so strange, our takin' up our time with little things while we're waiting for them to get the evidence. [*She sits down at the big table, smoothing out a block with decision.*] I don't see as it's anything to laugh about.

MRS. PETERS [*apologetically*].   Of course they've got awful important things on their minds. [*Pulls up a chair and joins* MRS. HALE *at the table.*]

MRS. HALE [*examining another block*].   Mrs. Peters, look at this one. Here, this is the one she was working on, and look at the sewing! All the rest of it has been so nice and even. And look at this! It's all over the place! Why, it looks as if she didn't know what she was about! [*After she has said this, they look at each other, then started to glance back at the door. After an instant* MRS. HALE *has pulled at a knot and ripped the sewing.*]

MRS. PETERS.   Oh, what are you doing, Mrs. Hale?

MRS. HALE [*mildly*].   Just pulling out a stitch or two that's not sewed very good. [*Threading a needle.*] Bad sewing always made me fidgety.

MRS. PETERS [*nervously*].   I don't think we ought to touch things.

MRS. HALE.   I'll just finish up this end. [*Suddenly stopping and leaning forward.*] Mrs. Peters?

MRS. PETERS.   Yes, Mrs. Hale?

MRS. HALE.   What do you suppose she was so nervous about?

MRS. PETERS.   Oh—I don't know. I don't know as she was nervous. I sometimes sew awful queer when I'm just tired. [MRS. HALE *starts to say something, looks at* MRS. PETERS, *then goes on sewing.*] Well, I must get these things wrapped up. They may be through sooner than we think. [*Putting apron and other things together.*] I wonder where I can find a piece of paper, and string.

MRS. HALE.   In that cupboard, maybe.

MRS. PETERS [*looking in cupboard*].   Why, here's a birdcage. [*Holds it up.*] Did she have a bird, Mrs. Hale?

MRS. HALE.   Why, I don't know whether she did or not—I've not been here for so long. There was a man around last year selling canaries cheap, but I don't know as she took one; maybe she did. She used to sing real pretty herself.

MRS. PETERS [*glancing around*].   Seems funny to think of a bird here. But she must have had one, or why should she have a cage? I wonder what happened to it?

MRS. HALE.   I s'pose maybe the cat got it.

MRS. PETERS.   No, she didn't have a cat. She's got that feeling some people have about cats—being afraid of them. My cat got in her room, and she was real upset and asked me to take it out.

MRS. HALE.   My sister Bessie was like that. Queer, ain't it?

MRS. PETERS [*examining the cage*].   Why, look at this door. It's broke. One hinge is pulled apart.

MRS. HALE [*looking, too*].   Looks as if someone must have been rough with it.

MRS. PETERS.   Why, yes. [*She brings the cage forward and puts it on the table.*]

MRS. HALE.   I wish if they're going to find any evidence they'd be about it. I don't like this place.

MRS. PETERS.   But I'm awful glad you came with me, Mrs. Hale. It would be lonesome for me sitting here alone.

MRS. HALE. It would, wouldn't it? [*Dropping her sewing.*] But I tell you what I do wish, Mrs. Peters. I wish I had come over sometimes when *she* was here. I—[*Looking around the room.*]—wish I had.

MRS. PETERS. But of course you were awful busy, Mrs. Hale—your house and your children.

MRS. HALE. I could've come. I stayed away because it weren't cheerful—and that's why I ought to have come. I—I've never liked this place. Maybe because it's down in a hollow, and you don't see the road. I dunno what it is, but it's a lonesome place and always was. I wish I had come over to see Minnie Foster sometimes. I can see now—[*Shakes her head.*]

MRS. PETERS. Well, you mustn't reproach yourself, Mrs. Hale. Somehow we just don't see how it is with other folks until—something comes up.

MRS. HALE. Not having children makes less work—but it makes a quiet house, and Wright out to work all day, and no company when he did come in. Did you know John Wright, Mrs. Peters?

MRS. PETERS. Not to know him; I've seen him in town. They say he was a good man.

MRS. HALE. Yes—good; he didn't drink, and kept his word as well as most, I guess, and paid his debts. But he was a hard man, Mrs. Peters. Just to pass the time of day with him. [*Shivers.*] Like a raw wind that gets to the bone. [*Pauses, her eye falling on the cage.*] I should think she would 'a wanted a bird. But what do you suppose went with it?

MRS. PETERS. I don't know, unless it got sick and died. [*She reaches over and swings the broken door, swings it again; both women watch it.*]

MRS. HALE. You weren't raised round here, were you? [MRS. PETERS *shakes her head.*] You didn't know—her?

MRS. PETERS. Not till they brought her yesterday.

MRS. HALE. She—come to think of it, she was kind of like a bird herself—real sweet and pretty, but kind of timid and—fluttery. How—she—did—change. [*Silence; then as if struck by a happy thought and relieved to get back to every-day things.*] Tell you what, Mrs. Peters; why don't you take the quilt in with you? It might take up her mind.

MRS. PETERS. Why, I think that's a real nice idea, Mrs. Hale. There couldn't possibly be any objection to it, could there? Now, just what would I take? I wonder if her patches are in here—and her things. [*They look in the sewing basket.*]

MRS. HALE. Here's some red. I expect this has got sewing things in it [*Brings out a fancy box.*] What a pretty box. Looks like something somebody would give you. Maybe her scissors are in here. [*Opens box. Suddenly puts her hand to her nose.*] Why—[MRS. PETERS *bends nearer, then turns her face away.*] There's something wrapped up in this piece of silk.

MRS. PETERS. Why, this isn't her scissors.

MRS. HALE [*lifting the silk*]. Oh, Mrs. Peters—it's—[MRS. PETERS *bends closer.*]

MRS. PETERS. It's the bird.

MRS. HALE [*jumping up*]. But, Mrs. Peters—look at it. Its neck! Look at its neck! It's all—other side *to.*

MRS. PETERS. Somebody—wrung—its neck.

[*Their eyes meet. A look of growing comprehension of horror. Steps are heard outside.* MRS. HALE *slips box under quilt pieces, and sinks into her chair. Enter* SHERIFF *and* COUNTY ATTORNEY. MRS. PETERS *rises.*]

COUNTY ATTORNEY [*as one turning from serious things to little pleasantries*]. Well, ladies, have you decided whether she was going to quilt it or knot it?

MRS. PETERS.   We think she was going to—knot it.

COUNTY ATTORNEY.   Well, that's interesting, I'm sure. [*Seeing the birdcage.*] Has the bird flown?

MRS. HALE [*putting more quilt pieces over the box*].   We think the—cat got it.

COUNTY ATTORNEY [*preoccupied*].   Is there a cat?

[MRS. HALE *glances in a quick covert way at* MRS. PETERS.]

MRS. PETERS.   Well, not now. They're superstitious, you know. They leave.

COUNTY ATTORNEY [*to* SHERIFF, *continuing an interrupted conversation*].   No sign at all of anyone having come from the outside. Their own rope. Now let's go up again and go over it piece by piece. [*They start upstairs.*] It would have to have been someone who knew just the—[MRS. PETERS *sits down. The two women sit there not looking at one another, but as if peering into something and at the same time holding back. When they talk now, it is the manner of feeling their way over strange ground, as if afraid of what they are saying, but as if they cannot help saying it.*]

MRS. HALE.   She liked the bird. She was going to bury it in that pretty box.

MRS. PETERS [*in a whisper*].   When I was a girl—my kitten—there was a boy took a hatchet, and before my eyes—and before I could get there—[*Covers her face an instant.*] If they hadn't held me back, I would have—[*Catches herself, looks upstairs where steps are heard, falters weakly.*]—hurt him.

MRS. HALE [*with a slow look around her*].   I wonder how it would seem never to have had any children around. [*Pause.*] No, Wright wouldn't like the bird—a thing that sang. She used to sing. He killed that, too.

MRS. PETERS [*moving uneasily*].   We don't know who killed the bird.

MRS. HALE.   I knew John Wright.

MRS. PETERS.   It was an awful thing was done in this house that night, Mrs. Hale. Killing a man while he slept, slipping a rope around his neck that choked the life out of him.

MRS. HALE.   His neck. Choked the life out of him.

[*Her hand goes out and rests on the birdcage.*]

MRS. PETERS [*with a rising voice*].   We don't know who killed him. We don't *know*.

MRS. HALE [*her own feeling not interrupted*].   If there'd been years and years of nothing, then a bird to sing to you, it would be awful—still, after the bird was still.

MRS. PETERS [*something within her speaking*].   I know what stillness is. When we homesteaded in Dakota, and my first baby died—after he was two years old, and me with no other then—

MRS. HALE [*moving*].   How soon do you suppose they'll be through, looking for evidence?

MRS. PETERS.   I know what stillness is. [*Pulling herself back.*] The law has got to punish crime, Mrs. Hale.

MRS. HALE [*not as if answering that*].   I wish you'd seen Minnie Foster when she wore a white dress with blue ribbons and stood up there in the choir and sang. [*A look around the room.*] Oh, I *wish* I'd come over here once in a while! That was a crime! That was a crime! Who's going to punish that?

MRS. PETERS [*looking upstairs*].   We mustn't—take on.

MRS. HALE.   I might have known she needed help! I know how things can be—for women. I tell you, it's queer, Mrs. Peters. We live close together and we live far apart. We all go through the same things—it's all just a different kind of the same thing. [*Brushes her eyes, noticing the bottle of fruit, reaches out for it.*] If I was you, I wouldn't tell her her fruit was gone. Tell her it *ain't*. Tell her it's all right. Take this in to prove it to her. She—she may never know whether it was broke or not.

MRS. PETERS [*takes the bottle, looks about for something to wrap it in; takes petticoat from the clothes brought from the other room, very nervously begins winding this around the bottle. In a false voice*].   My, it's a good thing the men couldn't hear us. Wouldn't they just laugh! Getting all stirred up over a little thing like a—dead canary. As if that could have anything to do with—with—wouldn't they *laugh!*

[*The men are heard coming downstairs.*]

MRS. HALE [*under her breath*]   Maybe they would—maybe they wouldn't.

COUNTY ATTORNEY.   No, Peters, it's all perfectly clear except a reason for doing it. But you know juries when it comes to women. If there was some definite thing. Something to show—something to make a story about—a thing that would connect up with this strange way of doing it.

[*The women's eyes meet for an instant. Enter* HALE *from outer door.*]

HALE.   Well, I've got the team around. Pretty cold out there.

COUNTY ATTORNEY.   I'm going to stay here awhile by myself. [*To the* SHERIFF.] You can send Frank out for me, can't you? I want to go over everything. I'm not satisfied that we can't do better.

SHERIFF.   Do you want to see what Mrs. Peters is going to take in?

[*The* LAWYER *goes to the table, picks up the apron, laughs.*]

COUNTY ATTORNEY.   Oh I guess they're not very dangerous things the ladies have picked up. [*Moves a few things about, disturbing the quilt pieces which cover the box. Steps back.*] No, Mrs. Peters doesn't need supervising. For that matter, a sheriff's wife is married to the law. Ever think of it that way, Mrs. Peters?

MRS. PETERS.   Not—just that way.

SHERIFF [*chuckling*].   Married to the law. [*Moves toward the other room.*] I just want you to come in here a minute, George. We ought to take a look at these windows.

COUNTY ATTORNEY [*scoffingly*].   Oh, windows!

SHERIFF.   We'll be right out, Mr. Hale.

[HALE *goes outside. The* SHERIFF *follows the* COUNTY ATTORNEY *into the other room. Then* MRS. HALE *rises, hands tight together, looking intensely at* MRS. PETERS, *whose eyes take a slow turn, finally meeting,* MRS. HALE*'s. A moment* MRS. HALE *holds her, then her own eyes point the way to where the box is concealed. Suddenly* MRS. PETERS *throws back quilt pieces and tries to put the box in the bag she is wearing. It is too big. She opens box, starts to take the bird out, cannot touch it, goes to pieces, stands there helpless. Sound of a knob turning in the other room.* MRS. HALE *snatches the box and puts it in the pocket of her big coat. Enter* COUNTY ATTORNEY *and* SHERIFF.]

COUNTY ATTORNEY [*facetiously*].   Well, Henry, at least we found out that she was not going to quilt it. She was going to—what is it you call it, ladies?

MRS. HALE [*her hand against her pocket*].   We call it—knot it, Mr. Henderson.

CURTAIN

[1916]

Topics for Critical Thinking and Writing

1. Briefly describe the setting, indicating what it "says" and what atmosphere it evokes.

2. Even before the first word of dialogue is spoken, what do you think the play tells us (in the entrance of the characters) about the distinction between the men and the women?

3. How would you characterize Mr. Henderson, the county attorney?

4. In what way or ways are Mrs. Peters and Mrs. Hale different from each other?

5. Several times the men "laugh" or "chuckle." In their contexts, what do these expressions of amusement convey?

6. On page 571, "*the women's eyes meet for an instant.*" What do you think this bit of action "says"? What do you understand by the exchange of glances?

7. On page 570, when Mrs. Peters tells of the boy who killed her cat, she says, "If they hadn't held me back, I would have—(*Catches herself, looks upstairs where steps are heard, falters weakly.*)—hurt him." What do you think she was about to say before she faltered? Why do you suppose Glaspell included this speech about Mrs. Peters's girlhood?

8. On page 567, Mrs. Hale, looking at a quilt, wonders whether Mrs. Wright "was goin' to quilt it or just knot it." The men are amused by the women's concern with this topic, and the last line of the play returns to the issue. What do you make of this emphasis on the matter?

9. We never see Mrs. Wright on stage. Nevertheless, by the end of *Trifles* we know a great deal about her. In an essay of 500–750 words explain both what we know about her—physical characteristics, habits, interests, personality, life before her marriage and after—and *how* we know these things.

10. The title of the play is ironic—the "trifles" are important. What other ironies do you find in the play?

11. Do you think the play is immoral? Explain.

12. Assume that the canary has been found, thereby revealing a possible motive, and that Minnie Wright is indicted for murder. You are the defense attorney. In 500 words set forth your defense. (Take any position you wish. For instance, you may want to argue that she committed justifiable homicide or that—on the basis of her behavior as reported by Mr. Hale—she is innocent by reason of insanity.)

13. Assume that the canary had been found and Minnie Wright convicted. Compose the speech you think she might have delivered before the sentence was given.

TENNESSEE WILLIAMS

Tennessee Williams (1914–83) was born Thomas Lanier Williams in Columbus, Mississippi. During his childhood his family moved to St. Louis, where his father had accepted a job as manager of a shoe company. Williams has written that neither he nor his sister Rose could adjust to the change from the South to the Midwest, but the children had already been deeply troubled. Nevertheless, at the age of 16 he achieved some distinction as a writer when his prize-winning essay in a nationwide contest was published. After high school he attended the University of Missouri but flunked ROTC and was therefore withdrawn from school by his father. He worked in a shoe factory for a while, then attended Washington University, where he wrote several plays. He finally graduated from the University of Iowa with a major in playwrighting. After graduation he continued to write, supporting himself with odd jobs such as waiting on tables and running elevators. His first commercial success was The Glass Menagerie *(produced in Chicago in 1944, and in New York in 1945); among his other plays are* A Streetcar Named Desire *(1947),* Cat on a Hot Tin Roof *(1955), and* Suddenly Last Summer *(1958).*

The Glass Menagerie

> *nobody, not even the rain, has such small hands.*
> —*e. e. cummings*

LIST OF CHARACTERS

AMANDA WINGFIELD, the mother. A little woman of great but confused vitality clinging frantically to another time and place. Her characterization must be carefully created, not copied from type. She is not paranoiac, but her life is paranoia. There is much to admire in Amanda, and as much to love and pity as there is to laugh at. Certainly she has endurance and a kind of heroism, and though her foolishness makes her unwittingly cruel at times, there is tenderness in her slight person.

LAURA WINGFIELD, her daughter. Amanda, having failed to establish contact with reality, continues to live vitally in her illusions, but Laura's situation is even graver. A childhood illness has left her crippled, one leg slightly shorter than the other, and held in a brace. This defect need not be more than suggested on the stage. Stemming from this, Laura's separation increases till she is like a piece of her own glass collection, too exquisitely fragile to move from the shelf.

TOM WINGFIELD, her son. And the narrator of the play. A poet with a job in a warehouse. His nature is not remorseless, but to escape from a trap he has to act without pity.

JIM O'CONNOR, the gentleman caller. A nice, ordinary, young man.

SCENE. *An alley in St. Louis.*
PART I. *Preparation for a Gentleman Caller.*
PART II. *The Gentleman Calls.*
TIME. *Now and the Past.*

Scene I

The Wingfield apartment is in the rear of the building, one of those vast hive-like conglomerations of cellular living-units that flower as warty growths in overcrowded urban centers of lower middle-class population and are symptomatic of the impulse of this largest and fundamentally enslaved section of American society to avoid fluidity and differentiation and to exist and function as one interfused mass of automatism.

The apartment faces an alley and is entered by a fire-escape, a structure whose name is a touch of accidental poetic truth, for all of these huge buildings are always burning with the slow and implacable fires of human desperation. The fire-escape is included in the set—that is, the landing of it and steps descending from it.

The scene is memory and is therefore nonrealistic. Memory takes a lot of poetic license. It omits some details; others are exaggerated, according to the emotional value of the articles it touches, for memory is seated predominantly in the heart. The interior is therefore rather dim and poetic.

At the rise of the curtain, the audience is faced with the dark, grim rear wall of the Wingfield tenement. This building, which runs parallel to the footlights, is flanked on both sides by dark, narrow alleys which run into murky canyons of tangled clotheslines, garbage cans and the sinister latticework of neighboring fire-escapes. It is up and down these side alleys that exterior entrances and exits are made, during the play. At the end of TOM's *opening commentary, the dark tenement wall slowly reveals (by means of a transparency) the interior of the ground floor Wingfield apartment.*

Downstage is the living room, which also serves as a sleeping room for LAURA, *the sofa unfolding to make her bed. Upstage, center, and divided by a wide arch or second proscenium with transparent faded portieres (or second curtain), is the dining room. In an old-fashioned what-not in the living room are seen scores of transparent glass animals. A blown-up photograph of the father hangs on the wall of the living room, facing the audience, to the left of the archway. It is the face of a very handsome young man in a doughboy's First World War cap. He is gallantly smiling, ineluctably smiling, as if to say, "I will be smiling forever."*

The audience hears and sees the opening scene in the dining room through both the transparent fourth wall of the building and the transparent gauze portieres of the dining-room arch. It is during this revealing scene that the fourth wall slowly ascends, out of sight.

This transparent exterior wall is not brought down again until the very end of the play, during TOM's *final speech.*

The narrator is an undisguised convention of the play. He takes whatever license with dramatic convention as is convenient to his purposes.

TOM *enters dressed as a merchant sailor from alley, stage left, and strolls across the front of the stage to the fire-escape. There he stops and lights a cigarette. He addresses the audience.*

TOM.   Yes, I have tricks in my pocket, I have things up my sleeve. But I am the opposite of a stage magician. He gives you illusion that has the appearance of truth. I give you truth in the pleasant disguise of illusion. To begin with, I turn back time. I reverse it to that quaint period, the thirties, when the huge middle class of America was matriculating in a school for the blind. Their eyes had failed them, or they had failed their eyes, and so they were having their fingers pressed forcibly down on the fiery Braille alphabet of a dissolving economy. In Spain there was revolution. Here there was only shouting and confusion. In Spain there was Guernica. Here there were disturbances of labor, sometimes pretty violent, in otherwise peaceful cities such as Chicago, Cleveland, Saint Louis. . . . This is the social background of the play.

[*Music.*]

The play is memory. Being a memory play, it is dimly lighted, it is sentimental, it is not realistic. In memory everything seems to happen to music. That explains the fiddle in the wings. I am the narrator of the play, and also a character in it. The other characters are my mother, Amanda, my sister, Laura, and a gentleman caller who appears in the final scenes. He is the most realistic character in the play, being an emissary from a world of reality that we were somehow set apart from. But since I have a poet's weakness for symbols, I am using this character also as a symbol; he is the long delayed but always expected something that we live for. There is a fifth character in the play who doesn't appear except in this larger-than-life photograph over the mantel. This is our father who left us a long time ago. He was a telephone man who fell in love with long distances; he gave up his job with the telephone company and skipped the light fantastic out of town. . . . The last we heard of him was a picture post-card from Mazatlan, on the Pacific coast of Mexico, containing a message of two words—"Hello—Goodbye!" and no address. I think the rest of the play will explain itself. . . .

AMANDA's *voice becomes audible through the portieres.*
[*Legend on Screen: "Où Sont les Neiges?"*]
He divides the portieres and enters the upstage area.
AMANDA *and* LAURA *are seated at a drop-leaf table. Eating is indicated by gestures without food or utensils.* AMANDA *faces the audience.* TOM *and* LAURA *are seated in profile.*
The interior has lit up softly and through the scrim we see AMANDA *and* LAURA *seated at the table in the upstage area.*

AMANDA [*calling*].   Tom?
TOM.   Yes, Mother.
AMANDA.   We can't say grace until you come to the table!
TOM.   Coming, Mother. [*He bows slightly and withdraws reappearing a few moments later in his place at the table.*]
AMANDA [*to her son*].   Honey, don't *push* with your *fingers*. If you have to push with something, the thing to push with is a crust of bread. And chew—chew! Animals have sections in their stomachs which enable them to digest food without mastication, but human beings are supposed to chew their food before they swallow it down. Eat food leisurely, son, and really enjoy it. A well-cooked meal has lots of delicate flavors that have to be held in the mouth for appreciation. So chew your food and give your salivary glands a chance to function!

TOM *deliberately lays his imaginary fork down and pushes his chair back from the table.*

TOM.   I haven't enjoyed one bite of this dinner because of your constant directions on how to eat it. It's you that makes me rush through meals with your hawk-like attention to every bite I take. Sickening—spoils my appetite—all this discussion of animals' secretion—salivary glands—mastication!
AMANDA [*lightly*].   Temperament like a Metropolitan star! [*He rises and crosses downstage.*] You're not excused from the table.
TOM.   I am getting a cigarette.
AMANDA.   You smoke too much.

LAURA *rises*.

LAURA.   I'll bring in the blanc mange.

He remains standing with his cigarette by the portieres during the following.

AMANDA [*rising*].   No, sister, no, sister—you be the lady this time and I'll be the darky.

LAURA.   I'm already up.

AMANDA.   Resume your seat, little sister—I want you to stay fresh and pretty—for gentlemen callers!

LAURA.   I'm not expecting any gentlemen callers.

AMANDA [*crossing out to kitchenette. Airily*].   Sometimes they come when they are least expected! Why, I remember one Sunday afternoon in Blue Mountain— [*Enters kitchenette.*]

TOM.   I know what's coming!

LAURA.   Yes. But let her tell it.

TOM.   Again?

LAURA.   She loves to tell it.

AMANDA *returns with bowl of dessert*.

AMANDA.   One Sunday afternoon in Blue Mountain—your mother received— *seventeen!*—gentlemen callers! Why, sometimes there weren't chairs enough to accommodate them all. We had to send the nigger over to bring in folding chairs from the parish house.

TOM [*remaining at portieres*].   How did you entertain those gentlemen callers?

AMANDA.   I understood the art of conversation!

TOM.   I bet you could talk.

AMANDA.   Girls in those days *knew* how to talk, I can tell you.

TOM.   Yes?

[*Image:* AMANDA *as a Girl on a Porch Greeting Callers.*]

AMANDA.   They knew how to entertain their gentlemen callers. It wasn't enough for a girl to be possessed of a pretty face and a graceful figure—although I wasn't slighted in either respect. She also needed to have a nimble wit and a tongue to meet all occasions.

TOM.   What did you talk about?

AMANDA.   Things of importance going on in the world! Never anything coarse or common or vulgar. [*She addresses* TOM *as though he were seated in the vacant chair at the table though he remains by portieres. He plays this scene as though he held the book.*] My callers were gentlemen—all! Among my callers were some of the most prominent young planters of the Mississippi Delta— planters and sons of planters!

TOM *motions for music and a spot of light on* AMANDA.

Her eyes lift, her face glows, her voice becomes rich and elegiac. [*Screen Legend: "Où Sont les Neiges?"*]

There was young Champ Laughlin who later became vice-president of the Delta Planters Bank. Hadley Stevenson who was drowned in Moon Lake and left his widow one hundred and fifty thousand in Government bonds. There were the Cutrere brothers, Wesley and Bates. Bates was one of my bright particular beaux! He got in a quarrel with that wild Wainright boy. They shot it out on the floor of Moon Lake Casino. Bates was shot through the stomach. Died in the ambulance on his way to Memphis. His widow was also well-provided for, came into eight or ten thousand acres, that's all. She married him on the rebound—never loved her—carried my picture on him the night he died! And there was that boy that every girl in Delta had set her cap for! That beautiful, brilliant young Fitzhugh boy from Green County!

TOM.   What did he leave his widow?

AMANDA.   He never married! Gracious, you talk as though all of my old admirers had turned up their toes to the daisies!

TOM.   Isn't this the first you mentioned that still survives?

AMANDA.   That Fitzhugh boy went North and made a fortune—came to be known as the Wolf of Wall Street! He had the Midas touch, whatever he touched turned to gold! And I could have been Mrs. Duncan J. Fitzhugh, mind you! But—I picked your *father!*

LAURA [*rising*].   Mother, let me clear the table.

AMANDA.   No dear, you go in front and study your typewriter chart. Or practice your shorthand a little. Stay fresh and pretty!—It's almost time for our gentlemen callers to start arriving. [*She flounces girlishly toward the kitchenette.*] How many do you suppose we're going to entertain this afternoon?

TOM *throws down the paper and jumps up with a groan.*

LAURA [*alone in the dining room*].   I don't believe we're going to receive any, Mother.

AMANDA [*reappearing, airily*].   What? No one—not one? You must be joking! [LAURA *nervously echoes her laugh. She slips in a fugitive manner through the half-open portieres and draws them gently behind her. A shaft of very clear light is thrown on her face against the faded tapestry of the curtains.*] [*Music: "The Glass Menagerie" Under Faintly.*] [*Lightly.*] Not one gentleman caller? It can't be true! There must be a flood, there must have been a tornado!

LAURA.   It isn't a flood, it's not a tornado, Mother. I'm just not popular like you were in Blue Mountain. . . . [TOM *utters another groan.* LAURA *glances at him with a faint, apologetic smile. Her voice catching a little.*] Mother's afraid I'm going to be an old maid.

[*The Scene Dims Out with "Glass Menagerie" Music.*]

Scene II
"Laura, Haven't You Ever Liked Some Boy?"

On the dark stage the screen is lighted with the image of blue roses. Gradually LAURA's *figure becomes apparent and the screen goes out. The music subsides.*

LAURA *is seated in the delicate ivory chair at the small clawfoot table.*

She wears a dress of soft violet material for a kimono—her hair tied back from her forehead with a ribbon.

She is washing and polishing her collection of glass.

AMANDA *appears on the fire-escape steps. At the sound of her ascent,* LAURA *catches her breath, thrusts the bowl of ornaments away and seats herself stiffly before the diagram of the typewriter keyboard as though it held her spellbound. Something has happened to* AMANDA. *It is written in her face as she climbs to the landing: a look that is grim and hopeless and a little absurd.*

She has on one of those cheap or imitation velvety-looking cloth coats with imitation fur collar. Her hat is five or six years old, one of those dreadful cloche hats that were worn in the late twenties, and she is clasping an enormous black patent-leather pocketbook with nickel clasp and initials. This is her full-dress outfit, the one she usually wears to the D.A.R.

Before entering she looks through the door.

She purses her lips, opens her eyes wide, rolls them upward and shakes her head.

Then she slowly lets herself in the door. Seeing her mother's expression LAURA *touches her lips with a nervous gesture.*

LAURA.   Hello, Mother, I was—[*She makes a nervous gesture toward the chart on the wall.* AMANDA *leans against the shut door and stares at* LAURA *with a martyred look.*]

AMANDA.   Deception? Deception? [*She slowly removes her hat and gloves, continuing the swift suffering stare. She lets the hat and gloves fall on the floor—a bit of acting.*]

LAURA [*shakily*].   How was the D.A.R. meeting? [AMANDA *slowly opens her purse and removes a dainty white handkerchief which she shakes out delicately and delicately touches to her lips and nostrils.*] Didn't you go to the D.A.R. meeting, Mother?

AMANDA [*faintly, almost inaudibly*].   —No.—No. [*Then more forcibly.*] I did not have the strength—to go to the D.A.R. In fact, I did not have the courage! I wanted to find a hole in the ground and hide myself in it forever! [*She crosses slowly to the wall and removes the diagram of the typewriter keyboard. She holds it in front of her for a second, staring at it sweetly and sorrowfully—then bites her lips and tears it in two pieces.*]

LAURA [*faintly*].   Why did you do that, Mother? [AMANDA *repeats the same procedure with the chart of the Gregg Alphabet.*] Why are you—

AMANDA.   Why? Why? How old are you, Laura?

LAURA.   Mother, you know my age.

AMANDA.   I thought that you were an adult; it seems that I was mistaken. [*She crosses slowly to the sofa and sinks down and stares at* LAURA.]

LAURA.   Please don't stare at me, Mother.

AMANDA *closes her eyes and lowers her head. Count ten.*

AMANDA.   What are we going to do, what is going to become of us, what is the future?

Count ten.

LAURA.   Has something happened, Mother? [AMANDA *draws a long breath and takes out the handkerchief again. Dabbing process.*] Mother, has—something happened?

AMANDA.   I'll be all right in a minute. I'm just bewildered—[*count five*]—by life. . . .

LAURA.   Mother, I wish that you would tell me what's happened.

AMANDA.   As you know, I was supposed to be inducted into my office at the D.A.R. this afternoon. [*Image: A Swarm of Typewriters.*] But I stopped off at Rubicam's Business College to speak to your teachers about your having a cold and ask them what progress they thought you were making down there.

LAURA.   Oh. . . .

AMANDA.   I went to the typing instructor and introduced myself as your mother. She didn't know who you were. Wingfield, she said. We don't have any such student enrolled at the school! I assured her she did, that you had been going to classes since early in January. "I wonder," she said, "if you could be talking about that terribly shy little girl who dropped out of school after only a few days' attendance?" "No," I said, "Laura, my daughter, has been going to school every day for the past six weeks!" "Excuse me," she said. She took the attendance book out and there was your name, unmistakably printed, and all the dates you were absent until they decided that you had dropped out of school. I still said, "No, there must have been some mistake! There must have been some mix-up in the records!" And she said, "No—I remember her perfectly now. Her hand shook so that she couldn't hit the right keys! The first time we gave a speed-test, she broke down completely—was sick at the stomach and almost had to be carried into the wash-room! After that morning she never

showed up any more. We phoned the house but never got any answer"—
while I was working at Famous and Barr, I suppose, demonstrating those—
Oh! I felt so weak I could barely keep on my feet. I had to sit down while
they got me a glass of water! Fifty dollars' tuition, all of our plans—my hopes
and ambitions for you—just gone up the spout, just gone up the spout like
that. [LAURA *draws a long breath and gets awkwardly to her feet. She crosses to
the victrola and winds it up.*] What are you doing?

LAURA.   Oh! [*She releases the handle and returns to her seat.*]

AMANDA.   Laura, where have you been going when you've gone out pretending
that you were going to business college?

LAURA.   I've just been going out walking.

AMANDA.   That's not true.

LAURA.   It is. I just went walking.

AMANDA.   Walking? Walking? In winter? Deliberately courting pneumonia in that
light coat? Where did you walk to, Laura?

LAURA.   It was the lesser of two evils, Mother. [*Image: Winter Scene in Park.*] I
couldn't go back up. I—threw up—on the floor!

AMANDA.   From half past seven till after five every day you mean to tell me you
walked around in the park, because you wanted to make me think that you
were still going to Rubicam's Business College?

LAURA.   It wasn't as bad as it sounds. I went inside places to get warmed up.

AMANDA.   Inside where?

LAURA.   I went in the art museum and the bird-houses at the Zoo. I visited the
penguins every day! Sometimes I did without lunch and went to the movies.
Lately I've been spending most of my afternoons in the Jewel-box, that big
glass house where they raise the tropical flowers.

AMANDA.   You did all this to deceive me, just for the deception? [LAURA *looks
down.*] Why?

LAURA.   Mother, when you're disappointed, you get that awful suffering look on
your face, like the picture of Jesus' mother in the museum!

AMANDA.   Hush!

LAURA.   I couldn't face it.

> *Pause. A whisper of strings.*
> [*Legend: "The Crust of Humility."*]

AMANDA [*hopelessly fingering the huge pocketbook*].   So what are we going to do the
rest of our lives? Stay home and watch the parades go by? Amuse ourselves with
the glass menagerie, darling? Eternally play those worn-out phonograph
records your father left as a painful reminder of him? We won't have a business
career—we've given that up because it gave us nervous indigestion! [*Laughs
wearily.*] What is there left but dependency all our lives? I know so well what
becomes of unmarried women who aren't prepared to occupy a position. I've
seen such pitiful cases in the South—barely tolerated spinsters living upon the
grudging patronage of sister's husband or brother's wife!—stuck away in some
little mousetrap of a room—encouraged by one in-law to visit another—little
birdlike women without any nest—eating the crust of humility all their life! Is
that the future that we've mapped out for ourselves? I swear it's the only alternative I can think of! It isn't a very pleasant alternative, is it? Of course—some girls
do marry. [LAURA *twists her hands nervously.*] Haven't you ever liked some boy?

LAURA.   Yes. I liked one once. [*Rises.*] I came across his picture a while ago.

AMANDA [*with some interest*].   He gave you his picture?

LAURA.   No, it's in the year-book.

AMANDA [*disappointed*].   Oh—a high-school boy.

[*Screen Image:* JIM *as a High-School Hero Bearing a Silver Cup.*]

LAURA.   Yes. His name was Jim. [LAURA *lifts the heavy annual from the clawfoot table.*] Here he is in *The Pirates of Penzance.*

AMANDA [*absently*].   The what?

LAURA.   The operetta the senior class put on. He had a wonderful voice and we sat across the aisle from each other Mondays, Wednesdays and Fridays in the Aud. Here he is with the silver cup for debating! See his grin?

AMANDA [*absently*].   He must have had a jolly disposition.

LAURA.   He used to call me—Blue Roses.

[*Image: Blue Roses.*]

AMANDA.   Why did he call you such a name as that?

LAURA.   When I had that attack of pleurosis—he asked me what was the matter when I came back. I said pleurosis—he thought that I said Blue Roses! So that's what he always called me after that. Whenever he saw me, he'd holler, "Hello, Blue Roses!" I didn't care for the girl that he went out with. Emily Meisenbach. Emily was the best-dressed girl at Soldan. She never struck me, though, as being sincere. . . . It says in the Personal Section—they're engaged. That's—six years ago! They must be married by now.

AMANDA.   Girls that aren't cut out for business careers usually wind up married to some nice man. [*Gets up with a spark of revival.*] Sister, that's what you'll do!

LAURA *utters a startled, doubtful laugh. She reaches quickly for a piece of glass.*

LAURA.   But, Mother—

AMANDA.   Yes? [*Crossing to photograph.*]

LAURA [*in a tone of frightened apology*].   I'm—crippled!

[*Image: Screen.*]

AMANDA.   Nonsense! Laura, I've told you never, never to use that word. Why, you're not crippled, you just have a little defect—hardly noticeable, even! When people have some slight disadvantage like that, they cultivate other things to make up for it—develop charm—and vivacity—and—*charm!* That's all you have to do! [*She turns again to the photograph.*] One thing your father had *plenty of*—was *charm!*

TOM *motions to the fiddle in the wings.*
[*The Scene Fades out with Music.*]

Scene III

[*Legend on the Screen: "After the Fiasco— "*]
TOM *speaks from the fire-escape landing.*

TOM.   After the fiasco at Rubicam's Business College, the idea of getting a gentleman caller for Laura began to play a more important part in Mother's calculations. It became an obsession. Like some archetype of the universal unconscious, the image of the gentleman caller haunted our small apartment. . . . [*Image: Young Man at Door with Flowers.*] An evening at home rarely passed without some allusion to this image, this specter, this hope. . . . Even when he wasn't mentioned, his presence hung in Mother's preoccupied look and in my sister's frightened, apologetic manner—hung like a sentence passed upon the Wingfields! Mother was a woman of action as well as words. She began to take logical steps in the planned direction. Late that winter and in the early spring—realizing that extra money would be needed to properly feather the nest and plume the bird—she conducted a vigorous campaign on the telephone, roping in subscribers to one of those magazines for matrons called *The Home-maker's Companion,* the type of journal that features the serialized sublimations of ladies of letters who think in terms of delicate cuplike breasts, slim, tapering waists, rich, creamy thighs, eyes like wood-smoke in autumn, fingers that soothe and caress like strains of music, bodies as powerful as Etruscan sculpture.

[*Screen Image: Glamor Magazine Cover.*]

AMANDA *enters with phone on long extension cord. She is spotted in the dim* stage.

AMANDA.   Ida Scott? This is Amanda Wingfield! We *missed* you at the D.A.R. last Monday! I said to myself: She's probably suffering with that sinus condition! How is that sinus condition? Horrors! Heaven have mercy!—You're a Christian martyr, yes, that's what you are, a Christian martyr! Well, I just now happened to notice that your subscription to the *Companion*'s about to expire! Yes, it expires with the next issue, honey!—just when that wonderful new serial by Bessie Mae Hopper is getting off to such an exciting start. Oh, honey, it's something that you can't miss! You remember how *Gone With the Wind* took everybody by storm? You simply couldn't go out if you hadn't read it. All everybody *talked* was Scarlett O'Hara. Well, this is a book that critics already compare to *Gone With the Wind*. It's the *Gone With the Wind* of the post-World War generation—What?—Burning?—Oh, honey, don't let them burn, go take a look in the oven and I'll hold the wire! Heavens—I think she's hung up!

[*Dim Out.*]

[*Legend on Screen:* "*You Think I'm in Love with Continental Shoemakers?*"]

Before the stage is lighted, the violent voices of TOM *and* AMANDA *are heard. They are quarreling behind the portieres. In front of them stands* LAURA *with clenched hands and panicky expression.*

A clear pool of light on her figure throughout this scene.

TOM.   What in Christ's name am I—

AMANDA [*shrilly*].   Don't you use that—

TOM.   Supposed to do!

AMANDA.   Expression! Not in my—

TOM.   Ohhh!

AMANDA.   Presence! Have you gone out of your senses?

TOM.   I have, that's true, *driven* out!

AMANDA.   What is the matter with you, you—big—big—IDIOT!

TOM.   Look—I've got *no thing,* no single thing—

AMANDA.   Lower your voice!

TOM.   In my life here that I can call my OWN! Everything is—

AMANDA.   Stop that shouting!

TOM.   Yesterday you confiscated my books! You had the nerve to—

AMANDA.   I took that horrible novel back to the library—yes! That hideous book by that insane Mr. Lawrence. [TOM *laughs wildly.*] I cannot control the output of diseased minds or people who cater to them—[TOM *laughs still more wildly.*] BUT I WON'T ALLOW SUCH FILTH BROUGHT INTO MY HOUSE! No, no, no, no, no!

TOM.   House, house! Who pays rent on it, who makes a slave of himself to—

AMANDA [*fairly screeching*].   Don't you DARE to—

TOM.   No, no, *I* mustn't say things! *I've* got to just—

AMANDA.   Let me tell you—

TOM.   I don't want to hear any more! [*He tears the portieres open. The upstage area is lit with a turgid smoky red glow.*]

AMANDA*'s hair is in metal curlers and she wears a very old bathrobe, much too large for her slight figure, a relic of the faithless Mr. Wingfield.*

An upright typewriter and a wild disarray of manuscripts are on the dropleaf table. The quarrel was probably precipitated by AMANDA*'s interruption of his creative labor. A chair lying overthrown on the floor.*

Their gesticulating shadows are cast on the ceiling by the fiery glow.

AMANDA.   You *will* hear more, you—

TOM.   No, I won't hear more, I'm going out!

AMANDA.   You come right back in—

TOM.   Out, out, out! Because I'm—

AMANDA.   Come back here, Tom Wingfield! I'm not through talking to you!

TOM.   Oh, go—

LAURA [*desperately*].   Tom!

AMANDA.   You're going to listen, and no more insolence from you! I'm at the end of my patience! [*He comes back toward her.*]

TOM.   What do you think I'm at? Aren't I supposed to have any patience to reach the end of, Mother? I know, I know. It seems unimportant to you, what I'm *doing*—what I *want* to do—having a little *difference* between them! You don't think that—

AMANDA.   I think you've been doing things that you're ashamed of. That's why you act like this. I don't believe that you go every night to the movies. Nobody goes to the movies night after night. Nobody in their right minds goes to the movies as often as you pretend to. People don't go to the movies at nearly midnight, and movies don't let out at two A.M. Come in stumbling. Muttering to yourself like a maniac! You get three hours' sleep and then go to work. Oh, I can picture the way you're doing down there. Moping, doping, because you're in no condition.

TOM [*wildly*].   No, I'm in no condition!

AMANDA.   What right have you got to jeopardize your job? Jeopardize the security of us all? How do you think we'd manage if you were—

TOM.   Listen! You think I'm crazy *about* the *warehouse?* [*He bends fiercely toward her slight figure.*] You think I'm in love with the Continental Shoemakers? You think I want to spend fifty-five *years* down there in that—*celotex interior!* with—*fluorescent—tubes!* Look! I'd rather somebody picked up a crowbar and battered out my brains—than go back mornings! *I go!* Every time you come in yelling that God damn *"Rise and Shine!" "Rise and Shine!"* I say to myself *"How lucky dead people are!"* But I get up. I *go!* For sixty-five dollars a month I give up all that I dream of doing and being *ever!* And you say self—*self*'s all I ever think of. Why, listen, if self is what I thought of, Mother, I'd be where he is—GONE! [*Pointing to father's picture.*] As far as the system of transportation reaches! [*He starts past her. She grabs his arm.*] Don't grab at me, Mother!

AMANDA.   Where are you going?

TOM.   I'm going to the *movies!*

AMANDA.   I don't believe that lie!

TOM [*crouching toward her, overtowering her tiny figure. She backs away, gasping*].   I'm going to opium dens! Yes, opium dens, dens of vice and criminals' hang-outs, Mother. I've joined the Hogan gang, I'm a hired assassin, I carry a tommy-gun in a violin case! I run a string of cat-houses in the Valley! They call

me Killer, Killer Wingfield, I'm leading a double-life, a simple, honest warehouse worker by day, by night a dynamic *czar* of the *underworld, Mother.* I go
to gambling casinos, I spin away fortunes on the roulette table! I wear a patch
over one eye and a false mustache, sometimes I put on green whiskers. On
those occasions they call me—*El Diablo!* Oh, I could tell you things to make
you sleepless! My enemies plan to dynamite this place. They're going to blow
us all sky-high some night! I'll be glad, very happy, and so will you! You'll go
up, up on a broomstick, over Blue Mountain with seventeen gentlemen callers!
You ugly—babbling old—*witch....* [*He goes through a series of violent,
clumsy movements, seizing his overcoat, lunging to the door, pulling it fiercely
open. The women watch him, aghast. His arm catches in the sleeve of the coat
as he struggles to pull it on. For a moment he is pinioned by the bulky garment.
With an outraged groan he tears the coat off again, splitting the shoulders of it
and hurls it across the room. It strikes against the shelf of* LAURA's *glass collection, there is a tinkle of shattering glass.* LAURA *cries out as if wounded.*]

[*Music Legend: "The Glass Menagerie."*]

LAURA [*shrilly*].   My glass!—menagerie.... [*She covers her face and turns away.*]

But AMANDA *is still stunned and stupefied by the "ugly witch" so that she
barely notices this occurrence. Now she recovers her speech.*

AMANDA [*in an awful voice*].   I won't speak to you—until you apologize!

[*She crosses through portieres and draws them together behind her.* TOM *is
left with* LAURA. LAURA *clings weakly to the mantel with her face averted.* TOM *stares
at her stupidly for a moment. Then he crosses to shelf. Drops, awkwardly to his
knees to collect the fallen glass, glancing at* LAURA *as if he would speak but
couldn't.*)

"The Glass Menagerie" steals in as
[*The Scene Dims Out.*]

Scene IV

The interior is dark. Faint light in the alley.

*A deep-voiced bell in a church is tolling the hour of five as the scene
commences.*

TOM *appears at the top of the alley. After each solemn boom of the bell in the
tower, he shakes a little noise-maker or rattle as if to express the tiny spasm of man
in contrast to the sustained power and dignity of the Almighty. This and the
unsteadiness of his advance make it evident that he has been drinking.*

As he climbs the few steps to the fire-escape landing light steals up inside.
LAURA *appears in night-dress, observing* TOM's *empty bed in the front room.*

TOM *fishes in his pockets for the door-key, removing a motley assortment of
articles in the search, including a perfect shower of movie-ticket stubs and an
empty bottle. At last he finds the key, but just as he is about to insert it, it slips from
his fingers. He strikes a match and crouches below the door.*

TOM [*bitterly*].   One crack—and it falls through!

LAURA *opens the door.*

LAURA.   Tom! Tom, what are you doing?

TOM.   Looking for a door-key.

LAURA.   Where have you been all this time?

TOM.   I have been to the movies.

LAURA.   All this time at the movies?

TOM.   There was a very long program. There was a Garbo picture and a Mickey Mouse and a travelogue and a newsreel and a preview of coming attractions. And there was an organ solo and a collection for the milk-fund—simultaneously—which ended up in a terrible fight between a fat lady and an usher!

LAURA [*innocently*].   Did you have to stay through everything?

TOM.   Of course! And, oh, I forgot! There was a big stage show! The headliner on this stage show was Malvolio the Magician. He performed wonderful tricks, many of them, such as pouring water back and forth between pitchers. First it turned to wine and then it turned to beer and then it turned to whiskey. I know it was whiskey it finally turned into because he needed somebody to come up out of the audience to help him, and I came up—both shows! It was Kentucky Straight Bourbon. A very generous fellow, he gave souvenirs. [*He pulls from his back pocket a shimmering rainbow-colored scarf.*] He gave me this. This is his magic scarf. You can have it, Laura. You wave it over a canary cage and you get a bowl of gold-fish. You wave it over the gold-fish bowl and they fly away canaries. . . . But the wonderfullest trick of all was the coffin trick. We nailed him into a coffin and he got out of the coffin without removing one nail. [*He has come inside.*] There is a trick that would come in handy for me—get me out of this 2 by 4 situation! [*Flops onto bed and starts removing shoes.*]

LAURA.   Tom—Shhh!

TOM.   What you shushing me for?

LAURA.   You'll wake up Mother.

TOM.   Goody, goody! Pay 'er back for all those "Rise an' Shines." [*Lies down, groaning.*] You know it don't take much intelligence to get yourself into a nailed-up coffin, Laura. But who in hell ever got himself out of one without removing one nail?

As if in answer, the father's grinning photograph lights up.
[*Scene Dims Out*]
Immediately following: The church bell is heard striking six. At the sixth stroke the alarm clock goes off in AMANDA'*s room, and after a few moments we hear her calling: "Rise and Shine! Rise and Shine!* LAURA, *go tell your brother to rise and shine!"*

TOM.   [*sitting up slowly*]. I'll rise—but I won't shine.

The light increases.

AMANDA.   Laura, tell your brother his coffee is ready.

LAURA *slips into front room.*

LAURA.   Tom! it's nearly seven. Don't make Mother nervous. [*He stares at her stupidly. Beseechingly.*] Tom, speak to Mother this morning. Make up with her, apologize, speak to her!

TOM.   She won't to me. It's her that started not speaking.

LAURA.   If you just say you're sorry she'll start speaking.

TOM.   Her not speaking—is that such a tragedy?

LAURA.   Please—please!

AMANDA [*calling from kitchenette*].   Laura, are you going to do what I asked you to do, or do I have to get dressed and go out myself?

LAURA.   Going, going—soon as I get on my coat! [*She pulls on a shapeless felt hat with nervous, jerky movement, pleadingly glancing at* TOM. *Rushes awkwardly for coat. The coat is one of* AMANDA'*s, inaccurately made-over, the sleeves too short for* LAURA.] Butter and what else?

AMANDA [*entering upstage*].   Just butter. Tell them to charge it.

LAURA.   Mother, they make such faces when I do that.

AMANDA.   Sticks and stones may break my bones, but the expression on Mr. Garfinkel's face won't harm us! Tell your brother his coffee is getting cold.

LAURA [*at door*].   Do what I asked you, will you, will you, Tom?

> *He looks sullenly away.*

AMANDA.   Laura, go now or just don't go at all!

LAURA [*rushing out*].   Going—going! [*A second later she cries out.* TOM *springs up and crosses to the door.* AMANDA *rushes anxiously in.* TOM *opens the door.*]

TOM.   Laura?

LAURA.   I'm all right. I slipped, but I'm all right.

AMANDA [*peering anxiously after her*].   If anyone breaks a leg on those fire-escape steps, the landlord ought to be sued for every cent he possesses!

> [*She shuts door. Remembers she isn't speaking and returns to other room.*]
>
> As TOM *enters listlessly for his coffee, she turns her back to him and stands rigidly facing the window on the gloomy gray vault of the areaway. Its light on her face with its aged but childish features is cruelly sharp, satirical as a Daumier print.*
>
> [*Music Under: "Ave Maria."*]
>
> TOM *glances sheepishly but sullenly at her averted figure and slumps at the table. The coffee is scalding hot; he sips it and gasps and spits it back in the cup. At his gasp,* AMANDA *catches her breath and half turns. Then catches herself and turns back to window.*
>
> TOM *blows on his coffee, glancing sidewise at his mother. She clears her throat.* TOM *clears his. He starts to rise. Sinks back down again, scratches his head, clears his throat again.* AMANDA *coughs.* TOM *raises his cup in both hands to blow on it, his eyes staring over the rim of it at his mother for several moments. Then he slowly sets the cup down and awkwardly and hesitantly rises from the chair.*

TOM [*hoarsely*].   Mother. I—I apologize. Mother. [AMANDA *draws a quick, shuddering breath. Her face works grotesquely. She breaks into childlike tears.*] I'm sorry for what I said, for everything that I said, I didn't mean it.

AMANDA [*sobbingly*].   My devotion has made me a witch and so I make myself hateful to my children!

TOM.   No you *don't*.

AMANDA.   I worry so much, don't sleep, it makes me nervous!

TOM [*gently*].   I understand that.

AMANDA.   I've had to put up a solitary battle all these years. But you're my right-hand bower! Don't fall down, don't fail!

TOM [*gently*].   I try, Mother.

AMANDA [*with great enthusiasm*].   Try and you will SUCCEED! [*The notion makes her breathless.*] Why, you—you're just *full* of natural endowments! Both of my children—they're *unusual* children! Don't you think I know it? I'm so—*proud!* Happy and—feel I've—so much to be thankful for but—Promise me one thing, son!

TOM.   What, Mother?

AMANDA.   Promise, son, you'll—never be a drunkard!

TOM [*turns to her grinning*].   I will never be a drunkard, Mother.

AMANDA.   That's what frightened me so, that you'd be drinking! Eat a bowl of Purina!

TOM.   Just coffee, Mother.

AMANDA.   Shredded wheat biscuit?

TOM.   No. No, Mother, just coffee.

AMANDA.   You can't put in a day's work on an empty stomach. You've got ten minutes—don't gulp! Drinking too-hot liquids makes cancer of the stomach. . . . Put cream in.

TOM.   No, thank you.

AMANDA.   To cool it.

TOM.   No! No, thank you, I want it black.

AMANDA.   I know, but it's not good for you. We have to do all that we can to build ourselves up. In these trying times we live in, all that we have to cling to is— each other. . . . That's why it's so important to—Tom, I—I sent out your sister so I could discuss something with you. If you hadn't spoken I would have spoken to you. [*Sits down.*]

TOM [*gently*].   What is it, Mother, that you want to discuss?

AMANDA.   Laura!

> TOM *puts his cup down slowly.*
> [*Legend on Screen: "Laura."*]
> [*Music: "The Glass Menagerie."*]

TOM.   —Oh.—Laura . . .

AMANDA [*touching his sleeve*].   You know how Laura is. So quiet but—still water runs deep! She notices things and I think she—broods about them. [TOM *looks up.*] A few days ago I came in and she was crying.

TOM.   What about?

AMANDA.   You.

TOM.   Me?

AMANDA.   She has an idea that you're not happy here.

TOM.   What gave her that idea?

AMANDA.   What gives her any idea? However, you do act strangely. I—I'm not criticizing, understand *that!* I know your ambitions do not lie in the warehouse, that like everybody in the whole wide world—you've had to—make sacrifices, but—Tom—Tom—life's not easy, it calls for—Spartan endurance! There's so many things in my heart that I cannot describe to you! I've never told you but I—*loved* your father. . . .

TOM [*gently*].   I know that, Mother.

AMANDA.   And you—when I see you taking after his ways! Staying out late— and—well, you *had* been drinking the night you were in that—terrifying condition! Laura says that you hate the apartment and that you go out nights to get away from it! Is that true, Tom?

TOM.   No. You say there's so much in your heart that you can't describe to me. That's true of me, too. There's so much in my heart that I can't describe to *you!* So let's respect each other's—

AMANDA.   But, why—*why,* Tom—are you always so *restless?* Where do you go to, nights?

TOM.   I—go to the movies.

AMANDA.   Why do you go to the movies so much, Tom?

TOM.   I go to the movies because—I like adventure. Adventure is something I don't have much of at work, so I go to the movies.

AMANDA.   But, Tom, you go to the movies *entirely too much!*

TOM.   I like a lot of adventure.

> AMANDA *looks baffled, then hurt. As the familiar inquisition resumes he becomes hard and impatient again.* AMANDA *slips back into her querulous attitude toward him.*
> [*Image on Screen: Sailing Vessel with Jolly Roger.*]

AMANDA.   Most young men find adventure in their careers.

TOM.   Then most young men are not employed in a warehouse.

AMANDA.   The world is full of young men employed in warehouses and offices and factories.

TOM.   Do all of them find adventure in their careers?

AMANDA.   They do or they do without it! Not everybody has a craze for adventure.

TOM.   Man is by instinct a lover, a hunter, a fighter, and none of those instincts are given much play at the warehouse!

AMANDA.   Man is by instinct! Don't quote instinct to me! Instinct is something that people have got away from! It belongs to animals! Christian adults don't want it!

TOM.   What do Christian adults want, then, Mother?

AMANDA.   Superior things! Things of the mind and the spirit! Only animals have to satisfy instincts! Surely your aims are somewhat higher than theirs! Than monkeys—pigs—

TOM.   I reckon they're not.

AMANDA.   You're joking. However, that isn't what I wanted to discuss.

TOM [*rising*].   I haven't much time.

AMANDA [*pushing his shoulders*].   Sit down.

TOM.   You want me to punch in red at the warehouse, Mother?

AMANDA.   You have five minutes. I want to talk about Laura.

   [*Legend: "Plans and Provisions."*]

TOM.   All right! What about Laura?

AMANDA.   We have to be making plans and provisions for her. She's older than you, two years, and nothing has happened. She just drifts along doing nothing. It frightens me terribly how she just drifts along.

TOM.   I guess she's the type that people call home girls.

AMANDA.   There's no such type, and if there is, it's a pity! That is unless the home is hers, with a husband!

TOM.   What?

AMANDA.   Oh, I can see the handwriting on the wall as plain as I see the nose in the front of my face! It's terrifying! More and more you remind me of your father! He was out all hours without explanation—Then *left! Goodbye!* And me with the bag to hold. I saw that letter you got from the Merchant Marine. I know what you're dreaming of. I'm not standing here blindfolded. Very well, then. Then *do* it! But not till there's somebody to take your place.

TOM.   What do you mean?

AMANDA.   I mean that as soon as Laura has got somebody to take care of her, married, a home of her own, independent—why, then you'll be free to go wherever you please, on land, on sea, whichever way the wind blows! But until that time you've got to look out for your sister. I don't say me because I'm old and don't matter! I say for your sister because she's young and dependent. I put her in business college—a dismal failure! Frightened her so it made her sick to her stomach. I took her over to the Young People's League at the church. Another fiasco. She spoke to nobody, nobody spoke to her. Now all she does is fool with those pieces of glass and play those worn-out records. What kind of a life is that for a girl to lead!

TOM.   What can I do about it?

AMANDA.   Overcome selfishness! Self, self, self is all that you ever think of! [TOM *springs up and crosses to get his coat. It is ugly and bulky. He pulls on a cap with earmuffs.*] Where is your muffler? Put your wool muffler on! [*He snatches it angrily from the closet and tosses it around his neck and pulls both ends tight.*] Tom! I haven't said what I had in mind to ask you.

TOM.   I'm too late to—

AMANDA [*catching his arms—very importunately. Then shyly*].   Down at the warehouse, aren't there some—nice young men?

TOM.   No!

AMANDA.   There *must* be—*some*.

TOM.   Mother—

> *Gesture.*

AMANDA.   Find out one that's clean-living—doesn't drink and—ask him out for sister!

TOM.   What?

AMANDA.   For *sister!* To *meet!* Get *acquainted!*

TOM [*stamping to door*].   Oh, my go-osh!

AMANDA.   Will you? [*He opens door. Imploringly.*] Will you? [*He starts down.*] Will you? *Will* you dear?

TOM [*calling back*].   YES!

AMANDA *closes the door hesitantly and with a troubled but faintly hopeful expression.*

[*Screen Image: Glamor Magazine Cover.*]

Spot AMANDA *at phone.*

AMANDA.   Ella Cartwright? This is Amanda Wingfield! How are you honey? How is that kidney condition? [*Count five.*] *Horrors!* [*Count five.*] You're a Christian martyr, yes, honey, that's what you are, a Christian martyr! Well, I just happened to notice in my little red book that your subscription to the *Companion* has just run out! I knew that you wouldn't want to miss out on the wonderful serial starting in this new issue. It's by Bessie Mae Hopper, the first thing she's written since *Honeymoon for Three.* Wasn't that a strange and interesting story? Well, this one is even lovelier, I believe. It has a sophisticated society background. It's all about the horsey set on Long Island!

[*Fade Out.*]

Scene V

[*Legend on Screen: "Annunciation."*] *Fade with music.*

It is early dusk of a spring evening. Supper has just been finished at the Wingfield apartment. AMANDA *and* LAURA *in light colored dresses are removing dishes from the table, in the upstage area, which is shadowy, their movements formalized almost as a dance or ritual, their moving forms as pale and silent as moths.*

TOM, *in white shirt and trousers, rises from the table and crosses toward the fire-escape.*

AMANDA [*as he passes her*].   Son, will you do me a favor?

TOM.   What?

AMANDA.   Comb your hair! You look so pretty when your hair is combed! [TOM *slouches on sofa with evening paper. Enormous caption "Franco Triumphs."*] There is only one respect in which I would like you to emulate your father.

TOM.   What respect is that?

AMANDA.   The care he always took of his appearance. He never allowed himself to look untidy. [*He throws down the paper and crosses to fire-escape.*] Where are you going?

TOM.   I'm going out to smoke.

AMANDA.   You smoke too much. A pack a day at fifteen cents a pack. How much would that amount to in a month? Thirty times fifteen is how much, Tom? Figure it out and you will be astounded at what you could save. Enough to give you a night-school course in accounting at Washington U! Just think what a wonderful thing that would be for you, son!

   TOM *is unmoved by the thought.*

TOM.   I'd rather smoke. [*He steps out on landing, letting the screen door slam.*]

AMANDA [*sharply*].   I know! That's the tragedy of it. . . . [*Alone, she turns to look at her husband's picture.*]

   [*Dance Music: "All the World Is Waiting for the Sunrise!"*]

TOM [*to the audience*].   Across the alley from us was the Paradise Dance Hall. On evenings in spring the windows and doors were open and the music came outdoors. Sometimes the lights were turned out except for a large glass sphere that hung from the ceiling. It would turn slowly about and filter the dusk with delicate rainbow colors. Then the orchestra played a waltz or a tango, something that had a slow and sensuous rhythm. Couples would come outside, to the relative privacy of the alley. You could see them kissing behind ashpits and telephone poles. This was the compensation for lives that passed like mine, without any change or adventure. Adventure and change were imminent in this year. They were waiting around the corner for all these kids. Suspended in the mist over Berchtesgaden, caught in the folds of Chamberlain's umbrella—In Spain there was Guernica! But here there was only hot swing music and liquor, dance halls, bars, and movies, and sex that hung in the gloom like a chandelier and flooded the world with brief, deceptive rainbows. . . . All the world was waiting for bombardments!

   AMANDA *turns from the picture and comes outside.*

AMANDA [*sighing*].   A fire-escape landing's a poor excuse for a porch. [*She spreads a newspaper on a step and sits down, gracefully and demurely as if she were settling into a swing on a Mississippi veranda.*] What are you looking at?

TOM.   The moon.

AMANDA.   Is there a moon this evening?

TOM.   It's rising over Garfinkel's Delicatessen.

AMANDA.   So it is! A little silver slipper of a moon. Have you made a wish on it yet?

TOM.   Um-hum.

AMANDA.   What did you wish for?

TOM.   That's a secret.

AMANDA.   A secret, huh? Well, I won't tell mine either. I will be just as mysterious as you.

TOM.   I bet I can guess what yours is.

AMANDA.   Is my head so transparent?

TOM.   You're not a sphinx.

AMANDA.   No, I don't have secrets. I'll tell you what I wished for on the moon. Success and happiness for my precious children! I wish for that whenever there's a moon, and when there isn't a moon, I wish for it, too.

TOM.   I thought perhaps you wished for a gentleman caller.

AMANDA.   Why do you say that?

TOM.   Don't you remember asking me to fetch one?

AMANDA.   I remember suggesting that it would be nice for your sister if you brought some nice young man from the warehouse. I think I've made that suggestion more than once.

TOM.   Yes, you have made it repeatedly.

AMANDA.   Well?

TOM.   We are going to have one.

AMANDA.   *What?*

TOM.   A gentleman caller!

> [*The Annunciation Is Celebrated with Music.*]
> AMANDA *rises.*
> [*Image on Screen: Caller with Bouquet.*]

AMANDA.   You mean you have asked some nice young man to come over?

TOM.   Yep. I've asked him to dinner.

AMANDA.   You really did?

TOM.   I did!

AMANDA.   You did, and did he—*accept?*

TOM.   He did!

AMANDA.   Well, well—well, well! That's—lovely!

TOM.   I thought that you would be pleased.

AMANDA.   It's definite, then?

TOM.   Very definite.

AMANDA.   Soon?

TOM.   Very soon.

AMANDA.   For heaven's sake, stop putting on and tell me some things, will you?

TOM.   What things do you want me to tell you?

AMANDA.   Naturally I would like to know when he's *coming!*

TOM.   He's coming tomorrow.

AMANDA.   *Tomorrow?*

TOM.   Yep. Tomorrow.

AMANDA.   But, Tom!

TOM.   Yes, Mother?

AMANDA.   Tomorrow gives me no time!

TOM.   Time for what?

AMANDA.   Preparations! Why didn't you phone me at once, as soon as you asked him, the minute that he accepted? Then, don't you see, I could have been getting ready!

TOM.   You don't have to make any fuss.

AMANDA.   Oh, Tom, Tom, Tom, of course I have to make a fuss! I want things nice, not sloppy! Not thrown together. I'll certainly have to do some fast thinking, won't I?

TOM.   I don't see why you have to think at all.

AMANDA.   You just don't know. We can't have a gentleman caller in a pigsty! All my wedding silver has to be polished, the monogrammed table linen ought to be laundered! The windows have to be washed and fresh curtains put up. And how about clothes? We have to *wear* something, don't we?

TOM.   Mother, this boy is no one to make a fuss over!

AMANDA.   Do you realize he's the first young man we've introduced to your sister? It's terrible, dreadful, disgraceful that poor little sister has never received a single gentleman caller! Tom, come inside! [*She opens the screen door.*]

TOM.   What for?

AMANDA.   I want to ask you some things.

TOM.   If you're going to make such a fuss, I'll call it off, I'll tell him not to come.

AMANDA.   You certainly won't do anything of the kind. Nothing offends people worse than broken engagements. It simply means I'll have to work like a

Turk! We won't be brilliant, but we'll pass inspection. Come on inside. [TOM *follows, groaning.*] Sit down.

TOM. Any particular place you would like me to sit?

AMANDA. Thank heavens I've got that new sofa! I'm also making payments on a floor lamp I'll have sent out! And put the chintz covers on, they'll brighten things up! Of course I'd hoped to have these walls repapered. . . . What is the young man's name?

TOM. His name is O'Connor.

AMANDA. That, of course, means fish—tomorrow is Friday! I'll have that salmon loaf—with Durkee's dressing! What does he do? He works at the warehouse?

TOM. Of course! How else would I—

AMANDA. Tom, he—doesn't drink?

TOM. Why do you ask me that?

AMANDA. Your father *did!*

TOM. Don't get started on that!

AMANDA. He *does* drink, then?

TOM. Not that I know of!

AMANDA. Make sure, be certain! The last thing I want for my daughter's a boy who drinks!

TOM. Aren't you being a little premature? Mr. O'Connor has not yet appeared on the scene!

AMANDA. But will tomorrow. To meet your sister, and what do I know about his character? Nothing! Old maids are better off than wives of drunkards!

TOM. Oh, my God!

AMANDA. Be still!

TOM [*leaning forward to whisper*].   Lots of fellows meet girls whom they don't marry!

AMANDA. Oh, talk sensibly, Tom—and don't be sarcastic! [*She has gotten a hair-brush.*]

TOM. What are you doing?

AMANDA. I'm brushing that cow-lick down! What is this young man's position at the warehouse?

TOM [*submitting grimly to the brush and the interrogation*].   This young man's position is that of a shipping clerk, Mother.

AMANDA. Sounds to me like a fairly responsible job, the sort of a job *you* would be in if you just had more *get-up*. What is his salary? Have you got any idea?

TOM. I would judge it to be approximately eighty-five dollars a month.

AMANDA. Well—not princely, but—

TOM. Twenty more than I make.

AMANDA. Yes, how well I know! But for a family man, eighty-five dollars a month is not much more than you can just get by on. . . .

TOM. Yes, but Mr. O'Connor is not a family man.

AMANDA. He might be, mightn't he? Some time in the future?

TOM. I see. Plans and provisions.

AMANDA. You are the only man that I know of who ignores the fact that the future becomes the present, the present the past, and the past turns into everlasting regret if you don't plan for it!

TOM. I will think that over and see what I can make of it.

AMANDA. Don't be supercilious with your mother! Tell me some more about this—what do you call him?

TOM. James D. O'Connor. The D. is for Delaney.

AMANDA.   Irish on *both* sides! *Gracious!* And doesn't drink?

TOM.   Shall I call him up and ask him right this minute?

AMANDA.   The only way to find out about those things is to make discreet inquiries at the proper moment. When I was a girl in Blue Mountain and it was suspected that a young man drank, the girl whose attentions he had been receiving, if any girl *was,* would sometimes speak to the minister of his church, or rather her father would if her father was living, and sort of feel him out on the young man's character. That is the way such things are discreetly handled to keep a young woman from making a tragic mistake!

TOM.   Then how did you happen to make a tragic mistake?

AMANDA.   That innocent look of your father's had everyone fooled! He *smiled*— the world was *enchanted!* No girl can do worse than put herself at the mercy of a handsome appearance! I hope that Mr. O'Connor is not too good-looking.

TOM.   No, he's not too good-looking. He's covered with freckles and hasn't too much of a nose.

AMANDA.   He's not right-down homely, though?

TOM.   Not right-down homely. Just medium homely, I'd say.

AMANDA.   Character's what to look for in a man.

TOM.   That's what I've always said, Mother.

AMANDA.   You've never said anything of the kind and I suspect you would never give it a thought.

TOM.   Don't be suspicious of me.

AMANDA.   At least I hope he's the type that's up and coming.

TOM.   I think he really goes in for self-improvement.

AMANDA.   What reason have you to think so?

TOM.   He goes to night school.

AMANDA [*beaming*].   Splendid! What does he do, I mean study?

TOM.   Radio engineering and public speaking!

AMANDA.   Then he has visions of being advanced in the world! Any young man who studies public speaking is aiming to have an executive job some day! And radio engineering? A thing for the future! Both of these facts are very illuminating. Those are the sort of things that a mother should know concerning any young man who comes to call on her daughter. Seriously or—not.

TOM.   One little warning. He doesn't know about Laura. I didn't let on that we had dark ulterior motives. I just said, why don't you come have dinner with us? He said okay and that was the whole conversation.

AMANDA.   I bet it was! You're eloquent as an oyster. However, he'll know about Laura when he gets here. When he sees how lovely and sweet and pretty she is, he'll thank his lucky stars he was asked to dinner.

TOM.   Mother, you mustn't expect too much of Laura.

AMANDA.   What do you mean?

TOM.   Laura seems all those things to you and me because she's ours and we love her. We don't even notice she's crippled any more.

AMANDA.   Don't say crippled! You know that I never allow that word to be used!

TOM.   But face facts, Mother. She is and—that's not all—

AMANDA.   What do you mean "not all"?

TOM.   Laura is very different from other girls.

AMANDA.   I think the difference is all to her advantage.

TOM.   Not quite all—in the eyes of others—strangers—she's terribly shy and lives in a world of her own and those things make her seem a little peculiar to people outside the house.

AMANDA. Don't say peculiar.

TOM. Face the facts. She is.

[*The Dance-Hall Music Changes to a Tango that Has a Minor and Somewhat Ominous Tone.*]

AMANDA. In what way is she peculiar—may I ask?

TOM [*gently*]. She lives in a world of her own—a world of—little glass ornaments, Mother. . . . [*Gets up.* AMANDA *remains holding brush, looking at him, troubled.*] She plays old phonograph records and—that's about all—[*He glances at himself in the mirror and crosses to door.*]

AMANDA [*sharply*]. Where are you going?

TOM. I'm going to the movies. [*Out screen door.*]

AMANDA. Not to the movies, every night to the movies! [*Follows quickly to screen door.*] I don't believe you always go to the movies! [*He is gone.* AMANDA *looks worriedly after him for a moment. Then vitality and optimism return and she turns from the door. Crossing to portieres.*] Laura! Laura! [LAURA *answers from kitchenette.*]

LAURA. Yes, Mother.

AMANDA. Let those dishes go and come in front! [*Laura appears with dish towel. Gaily.*] Laura, come here and make a wish on the moon!

LAURA [*entering*]. Moon—moon?

AMANDA. A little silver slipper of a moon. Look over your left shoulder, Laura, and make a wish! [LAURA *looks faintly puzzled as if called out of sleep.* AMANDA *seizes her shoulders and turns her at angle by the door.*] Now! Now, darling, *wish!*

LAURA. What shall I wish for, Mother?

AMANDA. [*her voice trembling and her eyes suddenly filling with tears*]. Happiness! Good Fortune!

The violin rises and the stage dims out.

Scene VI

[*Image: High School Hero.*]

TOM. And so the following evening I brought Jim home to dinner. I had known Jim slightly in high school. In high school Jim was a hero. He had tremendous Irish good nature and vitality with the scrubbed and polished look of white chinaware. He seemed to move in a continual spotlight. He was a star in basketball, captain of the debating club, president of the senior class and the glee club and he sang the male lead in the annual light operas. He was always running or bounding, never just walking. He seemed always at the point of defeating the law of gravity. He was shooting with such velocity through his adolescence that you would logically expect him to arrive at nothing short of the White House by the time he was thirty. But Jim apparently ran into more interference after his graduation from Soldan. His speed had definitely slowed. Six years after he left high school he was holding a job that wasn't much better than mine.

[*Image: Clerk.*]

He was the only one at the warehouse with whom I was on friendly terms. I was valuable to him as someone who could remember his former glory, who had seen him win basketball games and the silver cup in debating. He knew of my secret practice of retiring to a cabinet of the washroom to work on poems when business was slack in the warehouse. He called me Shakespeare. And while the other boys in the warehouse regarded me with suspicious hostility, Jim took a humorous attitude toward me. Gradually his attitude affected the others, their hostility wore off and they also began to smile at me as people smile at an oddly fashioned dog who trots across their path at some distance.

I knew that Jim and Laura had known each other at Soldan, and I had heard Laura speak admiringly of his voice. I didn't know if Jim remembered her or not. In high school Laura had been as unobtrusive as Jim had been astonishing. If he did remember Laura, it was not as my sister, for when I asked him to dinner, he grinned and said, "You know, Shakespeare, I never thought of you as having folks!"

He was about to discover that I did. . . .

[*Light up Stage*]

[*Legend on Screen: "The Accent of a Coming Foot."*]

Friday evening. It is about five o'clock of a late spring evening which comes "scattering poems in the sky."

A delicate lemony light is in the Wingfield apartment.

AMANDA *has worked like a Turk in preparation for the gentleman caller. The results are astonishing. The new floor lamp with its rose-silk shade is in place, a colored paper lantern conceals the broken light fixture in the ceiling, new billowing white curtains are at the windows, chintz covers are on chairs and sofa, a pair of new sofa pillows make their initial appearance.*

Open boxes and tissue paper are scattered on the floor.

LAURA *stands in the middle with lifted arms while* AMANDA *crouches before her, adjusting the hem of the new dress, devout and ritualistic. The dress is colored and designed by memory. The arrangement of* LAURA*'s hair is changed; it is softer and more becoming. A fragile, unearthly prettiness has come out in* LAURA: *she is like a piece of translucent glass touched by light, given a momentary radiance, not actual, not lasting.*

AMANDA [*impatiently*].   Why are you trembling?

LAURA.   Mother, you've made me so nervous!

AMANDA.   How have I made you nervous?

LAURA.   By all this fuss! You make it seem so important!

AMANDA.   I don't understand you, Laura. You couldn't be satisfied with just sitting home, and yet whenever I try to arrange something for you, you seem to resist it. [*She gets up.*] Now take a look at yourself. No, wait! Wait just a moment—I have an idea!

LAURA.   What is it now?

AMANDA *produces two powder puffs which she wraps in handkerchiefs and stuffs in* LAURA*'s bosom.*

LAURA.   Mother, what are you doing?

AMANDA.   They call them "Gay Deceivers"!

LAURA.   I won't wear them!

AMANDA.   You will!

LAURA.   Why should I?

AMANDA.   Because, to be painfully honest, your chest is flat.

LAURA.   You make it seem like we were setting a trap.

AMANDA.   All pretty girls are a trap, a pretty trap, and men expect them to be. [*Legend: "A Pretty Trap."*] Now look at yourself, young lady. This is the prettiest you will ever be! I've got to fix myself now! You're going to be surprised by your mother's appearance! [*She crosses through portieres, humming gaily.*]

LAURA *moves slowly to the long mirror and stares solemnly at herself.*

A wind blows the white curtains inward in a slow, graceful motion and with a faint sorrowful sighing.

AMANDA [*off stage*].   It isn't dark enough yet. [*She turns slowly before the mirror with a troubled look.*]

[*Legend on Screen: "This Is My Sister: Celebrate Her with Strings!" Music.*]

AMANDA [*laughing, off*].   I'm going to show you something. I'm going to make a spectacular appearance!

LAURA.   What is it, Mother?

AMANDA.   Possess your soul in patience—you will see! Something I've resurrected from that old trunk! Styles haven't changed so terribly much after all. . . . [*She parts the portieres.*] Now just look at your mother! [*She wears a girlish frock of yellowed voile with a blue silk sash. She carries a bunch of jonquils—the legend of her youth is nearly revived. Feverishly.*] This is the dress in which I led the cotillion. Won the cakewalk twice at Sunset Hill, wore one spring to the Governor's ball in Jackson! See how I sashayed around the ballroom, Laura? [*She raises her skirt and does a mincing step around the room.*] I wore it on Sundays for my gentlemen callers! I had it on the day I met your father—I had malaria fever all that spring. The change of climate from East Tennessee to the Delta—weakened resistance—I had a little temperature all the time—not enough to be serious—just enough to make me restless and giddy! Invitations poured in—parties all over the Delta!—"Stay in bed," said Mother, "you have fever!"—but I just wouldn't.—I took quinine but kept on going, going!—Evenings, dances!—Afternoons, long, long rides! Picnics—lovely!—So lovely, that country in May.—All lacy with dogwood, literally flooded with jonquils!—That was the spring I had the craze for jonquils. Jonquils became an absolute obsession. Mother said, "Honey, there's no more room for jonquils." And still I kept bringing in more jonquils. Whenever, wherever I saw them, I'd say, "Stop! Stop! I see jonquils!" I made the young men help me gather the jonquils! It was a joke, Amanda and her jonquils! Finally there were no more vases to hold them, every available space was filled with jonquils. No vases to hold them? All right, I'll hold them myself! And then I—[*She stops in front of the picture.*] [*Music.*] met your father! Malaria fever and jonquils and then—this—boy. . . . [*She switches on the rose-colored lamp.*] I hope they get here before it starts to rain. [*She crosses upstage and places the jonquils in bowl on table.*] I gave your brother a little extra change so he and Mr. O'Connor could take the service car home.

LAURA [*with altered look*].   What did you say his name was?

AMANDA.   O'Connor.

LAURA.   What is his first name?

AMANDA.   I don't remember. Oh, yes, I do. It was—Jim!

LAURA *sways slightly and catches hold of a chair.*
[*Legend on Screen: "Not Jim!"*]

LAURA [*faintly*].   Not—Jim!

AMANDA.   Yes, that was it, it was Jim! I've never known a Jim that wasn't nice!

[*Music: Ominous.*]

LAURA.   Are you sure his name is Jim O'Connor?

AMANDA.   Yes. Why?

LAURA.   Is he the one that Tom used to know in high school?

AMANDA.   He didn't say so. I think he just got to know him at the warehouse.

LAURA.   There was a Jim O'Connor we both knew in high school—[*Then, with ef-fort.*] If that is the one that Tom is bringing to dinner—you'll have to excuse me, I won't come to the table.

AMANDA.   What sort of nonsense is this?

LAURA.   You asked me once if I'd ever liked a boy. Don't you remember I showed you this boy's picture?

AMANDA.   You mean the boy you showed me in the year-book?

LAURA.   Yes, that boy.

AMANDA.   Laura, Laura, were you in love with that boy?

LAURA.   I don't know, Mother. All I know is I couldn't sit at the table if it was him!

AMANDA.   It won't be him! It isn't the least bit likely. But whether it is or not, you will come to the table. You will not be excused.

LAURA.   I'll have to be, Mother.

AMANDA.   I don't intend to humor your silliness, Laura. I've had too much from you and your brother, both! So just sit down and compose yourself till they come. Tom has forgotten his key so you'll have to let them in, when they arrive.

LAURA [*panicky*].   Oh, Mother—*you* answer the door!

AMANDA   [*lightly*].   I'll be in the kitchen—busy!

LAURA.   Oh, Mother, please answer the door, don't make me do it!

AMANDA [*crossing into kitchenette*].   I've got to fix the dressing for the salmon. Fuss, fuss—silliness!—over a gentleman caller!

> *Door swings shut.* LAURA *is left alone.*
> [*Legend: "Terror!"*]
> *She utters a low moan and turns off the lamp—sits stiffly on the edge of the sofa, knotting her fingers together.*
> [*Legend on Screen: "The Opening of a Door!"*]
> TOM *and* JIM *appear on the fire-escape steps and climb to landing. Hearing their approach,* LAURA *rises with a panicky gesture. She retreats to the portieres.*
> *The doorbell.* LAURA *catches her breath and touches her throat. Low drums.*

AMANDA [*calling*].   Laura, sweetheart! The door!

> LAURA *stares at it without moving.*

JIM.   I think we just beat the rain.

TOM.   Uh-huh. [*He rings again, nervously.* JIM *whistles and fishes for a cigarette.*]

AMANDA [*very, very gaily*].   Laura, that is your brother and Mr. O'Connor! Will you let them in, darling?

> LAURA *crosses toward kitchenette door.*

LAURA [*breathlessly*].   Mother—you go to the door!

> AMANDA *steps out of kitchenette and stares furiously at* LAURA. *She points imperiously at the door.*

LAURA.   Please, please!

AMANDA [*in a fierce whisper*].   What is the matter with you, you silly thing?

LAURA [*desperately*].   Please, you answer it, *please!*

AMANDA.   I told you I wasn't going to humor you, Laura. Why have you chosen this moment to lose your mind?

LAURA.   Please, please, please, you go!

AMANDA.   You'll have to go to the door because I can't!

LAURA [*despairingly*].   I can't either!

AMANDA.   Why?

LAURA.   I'm *sick!*

AMANDA.   I'm sick, too—of your nonsense! Why can't you and your brother be normal people? Fantastic whims and behavior! [TOM *gives a long ring.*] Preposterous goings on! Can you give me one reason—[*Calls out lyrically.*] COMING! JUST ONE SECOND!—why should you be afraid to open a door? Now you answer it, Laura!

LAURA.   Oh, oh, oh . . . [*She returns through the portieres. Darts to the victrola and winds it frantically and turns it on.*]

AMANDA.   Laura Wingfield, you march right to that door!

LAURA.   Yes—yes, Mother!

   A faraway, scratchy rendition of "Dardanella" softens the air and gives her strength to move through it. She slips to the door and draws it cautiously open.
   TOM enters with caller, JIM O'CONNOR.

TOM.   Laura, this is Jim. Jim, this is my sister, Laura.

JIM [*stepping inside*].   I didn't know that Shakespeare had a sister!

LAURA [*retreating stiff and trembling from the door*].   How—how do you do?

JIM [*heartily extending his hand*].   Okay!

   LAURA *touches it hesitantly with hers.*

JIM.   Your hand's *cold,* Laura!

LAURA.   Yes, well—I've been playing the victrola. . . .

JIM.   Must have been playing classical music on it! You ought to play a little hot swing music to warm you up!

LAURA.   Excuse me—I haven't finished playing the victrola. . . .

   She turns awkwardly and hurries into the front room. She pauses a second by the victrola. Then catches her breath and darts through the portieres like a frightened deer.

JIM [*grinning*].   What was the matter?

TOM.   Oh—with Laura? Laura is—terribly shy.

JIM.   Shy, huh? It's unusual to meet a shy girl nowadays. I don't believe you ever mentioned you had a sister.

TOM.   Well, now you know. I have one. Here is the *Post Dispatch.* You want a piece of it?

JIM.   Uh-huh.

TOM.   What piece? The comics?

JIM.   Sports! [*Glances at it*]. Ole Dizzy Dean is on his bad behavior.

TOM [*disinterest*].   Yeah? [*Lights cigarette and crosses back to fire-escape door.*]

JIM.   Where are *you* going?

TOM.   I'm going out on the terrace.

JIM [*goes after him*].   You know, Shakespeare—I'm going to sell you a bill of goods!

TOM.   What goods?

JIM.   A course I'm taking.

TOM.   Huh?

JIM.   In public speaking! You and me, we're not the warehouse type.

TOM.   Thanks—that's good news. But what has public speaking got to do with it?

JIM.   It fits you for—executive positions!

TOM.   Awww.

JIM.   I tell you it's done a helluva lot for me.

   [*Image: Executive at Desk.*]

TOM.   In what respect?

JIM.   In every! Ask yourself what is the difference between you an' me and men in the office down front? Brains?—No!—Ability?—No! Then what? Just one little thing—

TOM.   What is that one little thing?

JIM.   Primarily it amounts to—social poise! Being able to square up to people and hold your own on any social level!

AMANDA [*off stage*].   Tom?

TOM.   Yes, Mother?

AMANDA.   Is that you and Mr. O'Connor?

TOM.   Yes, Mother.

AMANDA.   Well, you just make yourselves comfortable in there.

TOM.   Yes, Mother.

AMANDA.   Ask Mr. O'Connor if he would like to wash his hands.

JIM.   Aw—no—no—thank you—I took care of that at the warehouse. Tom—

TOM.   Yes?

JIM.   Mr. Mendoza was speaking to me about you.

TOM.   Favorably?

JIM.   What do you think?

TOM.   Well—

JIM.   You're going to be out of a job if you don't wake up.

TOM.   I am waking up—

JIM.   You show no signs.

TOM.   The signs are interior.

[*Image on Screen: The Sailing Vessel with Jolly Roger Again.*]

TOM.   I'm planning to change. [*He leans over the rail speaking with quiet exhilaration. The incandescent marquees and signs of the first-run movie houses light his face from across the alley. He looks like a voyager.*] I'm right at the point of committing myself to a future that doesn't include the warehouse and Mr. Mendoza or even a night-school course in public speaking.

JIM.   What are you gassing about?

TOM.   I'm tired of the movies.

JIM.   Movies!

TOM.   Yes, movies! Look at them—[*a wave toward the marvels of Grand Avenue.*] All of those glamorous people—having adventures—hogging it all, gobbling the whole thing up! You know what happens? People go to the *movies* instead of *moving!* Hollywood characters are supposed to have all the adventures for everybody in America, while everybody in America sits in a dark room and watches them have them! Yes, until there's a war. That's when adventure becomes available to the masses! *Everyone's* dish, not only Gable's! Then the people in the dark room come out of the dark room to have some adventures themselves—Goody, goody—It's our turn now, to go to the South Sea Island—to make a safari—to be exotic, far-off—But I'm not patient. I don't want to wait till then. I'm tired of the *movies* and I am *about* to *move!*

JIM [*incredulously*].   Move?

TOM.   Yes.

JIM.   When?

TOM.   Soon!

JIM.   Where? Where?

[*Theme three music seems to answer the question, while* TOM *thinks it over. He searches among his pockets.*]

TOM.   I'm starting to boil inside. I know I seem dreamy, but inside—well, I'm boiling! Whenever I pick up a shoe, I shudder a little thinking how short life is and what I am doing!—Whatever that means. I know it doesn't mean shoes—except as something to wear on a traveler's feet [*Finds paper.*] Look—

JIM.   What?

TOM.   I'm a member.

JIM [*reading*].   The Union of Merchant Seamen.

TOM.   I paid my dues this month, instead of the light bill.

JIM.   You will regret it when they turn the lights off.

TOM.   I won't be here.

JIM.   How about your mother?

TOM.   I'm like my father. The bastard son of a bastard! See how he grins? And he's been absent going on sixteen years!

JIM.   You're just talking, you drip. How does your mother feel about it?

TOM.   Shhh—Here comes Mother! Mother is not acquainted with my plans!

AMANDA [*enters portieres*].   Where are you all?

TOM.   On the terrace, Mother.

They start inside. She advances to them. TOM *is distinctly shocked at her appearance. Even* JIM *blinks a little. He is making his first contact with girlish Southern vivacity and in spite of the night-school course in public speaking is somewhat thrown off the beam by the unexpected outlay of social charm.*

Certain responses are attempted by JIM *but are swept aside by* AMANDA's *gay laughter and chatter.* TOM *is embarrassed but after the first shock* JIM *reacts very warmly. Grins and chuckles, is altogether won over.*

[Image: AMANDA *as a Girl.]*

AMANDA [*coyly smiling, shaking her girlish ringlets*].   Well, well, well, so this is Mr. O'Connor. Introductions entirely unnecessary. I've heard so much about you from my boy. I finally said to him, Tom—good gracious!—why don't you bring this paragon to supper? I'd like to meet this nice young man at the warehouse!—Instead of just hearing him sing your praises so much! I don't know why my son is so standoffish—that's not Southern behavior! Let's sit down and—I think we could stand a little more air in here! Tom, leave the door open. I felt a nice fresh breeze a moment ago. Where has it gone? Mmm, so warm already! And not quite summer, even. We're going to burn up when summer really gets started. However, we're having—we're having a very light supper. I think light things are better fo' this time of year. The same as light clothes are. Light clothes an' light food are what warm weather calls fo'. You know our blood gets so thick during th' winter—it takes a while fo' us to *adjust* ou'selves!—when the season changes. . . . It's come so quick this year, I wasn't prepared. All of a sudden—heavens! Already summer!—I ran to the trunk an' pulled out this light dress—Terribly old! Historical almost! But feels so good—so good an' co-ol, y'know. . . .

TOM.   Mother—

AMANDA.   Yes, honey?

TOM.   How about—supper?

AMANDA.   Honey, you go ask Sister if supper is ready! You know that Sister is in full charge of supper! Tell her you hungry boys are waiting for it. [*To* JIM.] Have you met Laura?

JIM.   She—

AMANDA.   Let you in? Oh, good, you've met already! It's rare for a girl as sweet an' pretty as Laura to be domestic! But Laura is, thank heavens, not only pretty but also very domestic. I'm not at all. I never was a bit. I never could make a thing but angel-food cake. Well, in the South we had so many servants. Gone, gone, gone. All vestiges of gracious living! Gone completely! I wasn't prepared for what the future brought me. All of my gentlemen callers were sons of planters and so of course I assumed that I would be married to one and raise my family on a large piece of land with plenty of servants. But man proposes—and woman accepts the proposal!—To vary that old, old saying a little bit—I married no planter! I married a man who worked for the telephone company!—that gallantly smiling gentleman over there! [*Points to the picture.*] A telephone man who—fell in love with long distance!—Now he travels and I don't even know where!—But what am I going on for about my—tribulations! Tell me yours—I hope you don't have any! Tom?

TOM [*returning*].   Yes, Mother?

AMANDA.   Is supper nearly ready?

TOM.   It looks to me like supper is on the table.

AMANDA.   Let me look—[*She rises prettily and looks through portieres.*] Oh, lovely—But where is Sister?

TOM.   Laura is not feeling well and she says that she thinks she'd better not come to the table.

AMANDA.   What?—Nonsense!—Laura? Oh, Laura!

LAURA [*off stage, faintly*].   Yes, Mother.

AMANDA.   You really must come to the table. We won't be seated until you come to the table! Come in, Mr. O'Connor. You sit over there and I'll—Laura? Laura Wingfield! You're keeping us waiting, honey! We can't say grace until you come to the table!

The back door is pushed weakly open and LAURA *comes in. She is obviously quite faint, her lips trembling, her eyes wide and staring. She moves unsteadily toward the table.*
    [*Legend: "Terror!"*]
    Outside a summer storm is coming abruptly. The white curtains billow inward at the windows and there is a sorrowful murmur and deep blue dusk.
    LAURA *suddenly stumbles—She catches a chair with a faint moan.*

TOM.   Laura!

AMANDA.   Laura! [*There is a clap of thunder.*] [*Legend: "Ah!"*] [*Despairingly.*] Why, Laura, you *are* sick, darling! Tom, help your sister into the living room, dear! Sit in the living room, Laura—rest on the sofa. Well! [*To the gentleman caller.*] Standing over the hot stove made her ill!—I told her that it was just too warm this evening, but—[TOM *comes back in.* LAURA *is on the sofa.*] Is Laura all right now?

TOM.   Yes.

AMANDA.   What is that? Rain? A nice cool rain has come up! [*She gives the gentleman caller a frightened look.*] I think we may—have grace—now . . . [TOM *looks at her stupidly.*] Tom, honey—you say grace!

TOM.   Oh . . . "For these and all thy mercies—" [*They bow their heads.* AMANDA *stealing a nervous glance at* JIM. *In the living room* LAURA, *stretched on the sofa, clenches her hand to her lips, to hold back a shuddering sob.*] God's Holy Name be praised—

    [*The Scene Dims Out.*]

Scene VII
A Souvenir

Half an hour later. Dinner is just being finished in the upstage area which is concealed by the drawn portieres.
    As the curtain rises LAURA *is still huddled upon the sofa, her feet drawn under her, her head resting on a pale blue pillow, her eyes wide and mysteriously*

watchful. The new floor lamp with its shade of rose-colored silk gives a soft, becoming light to her face, bringing out the fragile, unearthly prettiness which usually escapes attention. There is a steady murmur of rain, but it is slackening and stops soon after the scene begins; the air outside becomes pale and luminous as the moon breaks out.

    A moment after the curtain rises, the lights in both rooms flicker and go out.

JIM. Hey, there, Mr. Light Bulb!

    AMANDA *laughs nervously.*

    [*Legend: "Suspension of a Public Service."*]

AMANDA. Where was Moses when the lights went out? Ha-ha. Do you know the answer to that one, Mr. O'Connor?

JIM. No, ma'am, what's the answer?

AMANDA. In the dark! [JIM *laughs appreciatively.*] Everybody sit still. I'll light the candles. Isn't it lucky we have them on the table? Where's a match? Which of you gentlemen can provide a match?

JIM. Here.

AMANDA. Thank you, sir.

JIM. Not at all, Ma'am!

AMANDA. I guess the fuse has burnt out. Mr. O'Connor, can you tell a burnt-out fuse? I know I can't and Tom is a total loss when it comes to mechanics. [*Sound: Getting Up: Voices Recede a Little to Kitchenette.*] Oh, be careful you don't bump into something. We don't want our gentleman caller to break his neck. Now wouldn't that be a fine howdy-do?

JIM. Ha-ha! Where is the fuse-box?

AMANDA. Right here next to the stove. Can you see anything?

JIM. Just a minute.

AMANDA. Isn't electricity a mysterious thing? Wasn't it Benjamin Franklin who tied a key to a kite? We live in such a mysterious universe, don't we? Some people say that science clears up all the mysteries for us. In my opinion it only creates more! Have you found it yet?

JIM. No, Ma'am. All these fuses look okay to me.

AMANDA. Tom!

TOM. Yes, Mother?

AMANDA. That light bill I gave you several days ago. The one I told you we got the notices about?

TOM. Oh.—Yeah.

    [*Legend: "Ha!"*]

AMANDA. You didn't neglect to pay it by any chance?

TOM. Why, I—

AMANDA. Didn't! I might have known it!

JIM. Shakespeare probably wrote a poem on that light bill, Mrs. Wingfield.

AMANDA. I might have known better than to trust him with it! There's such a high price for negligence in this world!

JIM. Maybe the poem will win a ten-dollar prize.

AMANDA. We'll just have to spend the remainder of the evening in the nineteenth century, before Mr. Edison made the Mazda lamp!

JIM. Candlelight is my favorite kind of light.

AMANDA. That shows you're romantic! But that's no excuse for Tom. Well, we got through dinner. Very considerate of them to let us get through dinner before they plunged us into everlasting darkness, wasn't it, Mr. O'Connor?

JIM. Ha-ha!

AMANDA. Tom, as a penalty for your carelessness you can help me with the dishes.

JIM.   Let me give you a hand.

AMANDA.   Indeed you will not!

JIM.   I ought to be good for something.

AMANDA.   Good for something? [*Her tone is rhapsodic.*] *You?* Why, Mr. O'Connor, nobody, *nobody's* given me this much entertainment in years—as you have!

JIM.   Aw, now, Mrs. Wingfield!

AMANDA.   I'm not exaggerating, not one bit! But Sister is all by her lonesome. You go keep her company in the parlor! I'll give you this lovely old candelabrum that used to be on the altar at the Church of the Heavenly Rest. It was melted a little out of shape when the church burnt down. Lightning struck it one spring. Gypsy Jones was holding a revival at the time and he intimated that the church was destroyed because the Episcopalians gave card parties.

JIM.   Ha ha.

AMANDA.   And how about coaxing Sister to drink a little wine? I think it would be good for her! Can you carry both at once?

JIM.   Sure. I'm Superman!

AMANDA.   Now, Thomas, get into this apron!

The door of kitchenette swings closed on AMANDA'*s gay laughter; the flickering light approaches the portieres.*

LAURA *sits up nervously as he enters. Her speech at first is low and breathless from the almost intolerable strain of being alone with a stranger.*

[*Legend: "I Don't Suppose You Remember Me at All!"*]

In her first speeches in this scene, before JIM'*s warmth overcomes her paralyzing shyness,* LAURA'*s voice is thin and breathless as though she has run up a steep flight of stairs.*

JIM'*s attitude is gently humorous. In playing this scene it should be stressed that while the incident is apparently unimportant, it is to* LAURA *the climax of her secret life.*

JIM.   Hello, there, Laura.

LAURA [*faintly*].   Hello.   [*She clears her throat.*]

JIM.   How are you feeling now? Better?

LAURA.   Yes. Yes, thank you.

JIM.   This is for you. A little dandelion wine. [*He extends it toward her with extravagant gallantry.*]

LAURA.   Thank you.

JIM.   Drink it—but don't get drunk! [*He laughs heartily.* LAURA *takes the glass uncertainly; laughs shyly.*] Where shall I set the candles?

LAURA.   Oh—oh, anywhere . . .

JIM.   How about here on the floor? Any objections?

LAURA.   No.

JIM.   I'll spread a newspaper under to catch the drippings. I like to sit on the floor. Mind if I do?

LAURA.   Oh, no.

JIM.   Give me a pillow?

LAURA.   What?

JIM.   A pillow!

LAURA.   Oh . . . [*Hands him one quickly.*]

JIM.   How about you? Don't you like to sit on the floor?

LAURA.   Oh—yes.

JIM.   Why don't you, then?

LAURA.   I—will.

JIM.   Take a pillow! [LAURA *does. Sits on the other side of the candelabrum.* JIM *crosses his legs and smiles engagingly at her.*] I can't hardly see you sitting way over there.

LAURA.   I can—see you.

JIM.   I know, but that's not fair, I'm in the limelight. [LAURA *moves her pillow closer.*] Good! Now I can see you! Comfortable?

LAURA.   Yes.

JIM.   So am I. Comfortable as a cow. Will you have some gum?

LAURA.   No, thank you.

JIM.   I think that I will indulge, with your permission [*Musingly unwraps it and holds it up.*] Think of the fortune made by the guy that invented the first piece of chewing gum. Amazing, huh? The Wrigley Building is one of the sights of Chicago.—I saw it summer before last when I went up to the Century of Progress. Did you take in the Century of Progress?

LAURA.   No, I didn't.

JIM.   Well, it was quite a wonderful exposition. What impressed me most was the Hall of Science. Gives you an idea of what the future will be in America, even more wonderful than the present time is! [*Pause. Smiling at her.*] Your brother tells me you're shy. Is that right, Laura?

LAURA.   I—don't know.

JIM.   I judge you to be an old-fashioned type of girl. Well, I think that's a pretty good type to be. Hope you don't think I'm being too personal—do you?

LAURA [*hastily, out of embarrassment*].   I believe I *will* take a piece of gum, if you—don't mind. [*Clearing her throat.*] Mr. O'Connor, have you—kept up with your singing?

JIM.   Singing? Me?

LAURA.   Yes. I remember what a beautiful voice you had.

JIM.   When did you hear me sing?

[*Voice Offstage in the Pause*]
Voice [*offstage*].

> O blow, ye winds, heigh-ho.
> A-roving I will go!
> I'm off to my love
> With a boxing glove—
> Ten thousand miles away!

JIM.   You say you've heard me sing?

LAURA.   Oh, yes! Yes, very often . . . I—don't suppose you remember me—at all?

JIM [*smiling doubtfully*].   You know I have an idea I've seen you before. I had that idea soon as you opened the door. It seemed almost like I was about to re-member your name. But the name that I started to call you—wasn't a name! And so I stopped myself before I said it.

LAURA.   Wasn't it—Blue Roses?

JIM [*springs up, grinning*].   Blue Roses! My gosh, yes—Blue Roses! That's what I had on my tongue when you opened the door! Isn't it funny what tricks your memory plays? I didn't connect you with the high school somehow or other. But that's where it was; it was high school. I didn't even know you were Shakespeare's sister! Gosh, I'm sorry.

LAURA.   I didn't expect you to. You—barely knew me!

JIM.   But we did have a speaking acquaintance, huh?

LAURA.   Yes, we—spoke to each other.

JIM.   When did you recognize me?

LAURA.   Oh, right away!

JIM.   Soon as I came in the door?

LAURA.   When I heard your name I thought it was probably you. I knew that Tom used to know you a little in high school. So when you came in the door— Well, then I was—sure.

JIM.   Why didn't you *say* something, then?

LAURA [*breathlessly*].   I didn't know what to say, I was—too surprised!

JIM.   For goodness' sakes! You know, this sure is funny!

LAURA.   Yes! Yes, isn't it, though. . . .

JIM.   Didn't we have a class in something together?

LAURA.   Yes, we did.

JIM.   What class was that?

LAURA.   It was—singing—Chorus!

JIM.   Aw!

LAURA.   I sat across the aisle from you in the Aud.

JIM.   Aw.

LAURA.   Mondays, Wednesdays and Fridays.

JIM.   Now I remember—you always came in late.

LAURA.   Yes, it was so hard for me, getting upstairs. I had a brace on my leg—it clumped so loud!

JIM.   I never heard any clumping.

LAURA [*wincing at the recollection*].   To me it sounded like—thunder!

JIM.   Well, well, well. I never even noticed.

LAURA.   And everybody was seated before I came in. I had to walk in front of all those people. My seat was in the back row. I had to go clumping all the way up the aisle with everyone watching!

JIM.   You shouldn't have been self-conscious.

LAURA.   I know, but I was. It was always such a relief when the singing started.

JIM.   Aw, yes, I've placed you now! I used to call you Blue Roses. How was it that I got started calling you that?

LAURA.   I was out of school a little while with pleurosis. When I came back you asked me what was the matter. I said I had pleurosis—you thought I said Blue Roses. That's what you always called me after that!

JIM.   I hope you didn't mind.

LAURA.   Oh, no—I liked it. You see, I wasn't acquainted with many—people. . . .

JIM.   As I remember you sort of stuck by yourself.

LAURA.   I—I—never had much luck at—making friends.

JIM.   I don't see why you wouldn't.

LAURA.   Well, I—started out badly.

JIM.   You mean being—

LAURA.   Yes, it sort of—stood between me—

JIM.   You shouldn't have let it!

LAURA.   I know, but it did, and—

JIM.   You were shy with people!

LAURA.   I tried not to be but never could—

JIM.   Overcome it?

LAURA.   No, I—I never could!

JIM.   I guess being shy is something you have to work out of kind of gradually.

LAURA [*sorrowfully*].   Yes—I guess it—

JIM.   Takes time!

LAURA.   Yes—

JIM.   People are not so dreadful when you know them. That's what you have to remember! And everybody has problems, not just you, but practically everybody has got some problems. You think of yourself as having the only problems, as being the only one who is disappointed. But just look around you and you will see lots of people as disappointed as you are. For instance, I hoped when I was going to high school that I would be further along at this time, six years after, than I am now—You remember that wonderful write-up I had in *The Torch?*

LAURA.   Yes! [*She rises and crosses to table.*]

JIM.   It said I was bound to succeed in anything I went into! [LAURA *returns with the annual.*] Holy Jeez! *The Torch!* [*He accepts it reverently. They smile across it with mutual wonder.* LAURA *crouches beside him and they begin to turn through it.* LAURA*'s shyness is dissolving in his warmth.*]

LAURA.   Here you are in *Pirates of Penzance!*

JIM [*wistfully*].   I sang the baritone lead in that operetta.

LAURA [*rapidly*].   So—*beautifully!*

JIM [*protesting*].   Aw—

LAURA.   Yes, yes—beautifully—beautifully!

JIM.   You heard me?

LAURA.   All three times!

JIM.   No!

LAURA.   Yes!

JIM.   All three performances?

LAURA [*looking down*].   Yes.

JIM.   Why?

LAURA.   I—wanted to ask you to—autograph my program.

JIM.   Why didn't you ask me to?

LAURA.   You were always surrounded by your own friends so much that I never had a chance to.

JIM.   You should have just—

LAURA.   Well, I—thought you might think I was—

JIM.   Thought I might think you was—what?

LAURA.   Oh—

JIM [*with reflective relish*].   I was beleaguered by females in those days.

LAURA.   You were terribly popular!

JIM.   Yeah—

LAURA.   You had such a—friendly way—

JIM.   I was spoiled in high school.

LAURA.   Everybody—liked you!

JIM.   Including you?

LAURA.   I—yes, I—I did, too—[*She gently closes the book in her lap.*]

JIM.   Well, well, well!—Give me that program, Laura. [*She hands it to him. He signs it with a flourish.*] There you are—better late than never!

LAURA.   Oh, I—what a—surprise!

JIM.   My signature isn't worth very much right now. But some day—maybe—it will increase in value! Being disappointed is one thing and being discouraged is something else. I am disappointed but I'm not discouraged. I'm twenty-three years old. How old are you?

LAURA.   I'll be twenty-four in June.

JIM.   That's not old age!

LAURA.   No, but—

JIM.   You finished high school?

LAURA [*with difficulty*].   I didn't go back.

JIM.   You mean you dropped out?

LAURA.   I made bad grades in my final examinations. [*She rises and replaces the book and the program. Her voice strained.*] How is—Emily Meisenbach getting along?

JIM.   Oh, that kraut-head!

LAURA.   Why do you call her that?

JIM.   That's what she was.

LAURA.   You're not still—going with her?

JIM.   I never see her.

LAURA.   It said in the Personal Section that you were—engaged!

JIM.   I know, but I wasn't impressed by that—propaganda!

LAURA.   It wasn't—the truth?

JIM.   Only in Emily's optimistic opinion!

LAURA.   Oh—

> [*Legend: "What Have You Done since High School?"*]

> JIM *lights a cigarette and leans indolently back on his elbows smiling at*
LAURA *with a warmth and charm which light her inwardly with altar candles. She remains by the table and turns in her hands a piece of glass to cover her tumult.*

JIM [*after several reflective puffs on a cigarette*].   What have you done since high school? [*She seems not to hear him.*] Huh? [LAURA *looks up.*] I said what have you done since high school, Laura?

LAURA.   Nothing much.

JIM.   You must have been doing something these six long years.

LAURA.   Yes.

JIM.   Well, then, such as what?

LAURA.   I took a business course at business college—

JIM.   How did that work out?

LAURA.   Well, not very—well—I had to drop out, it gave me—indigestion—

> JIM *laughs gently.*

JIM.   What are you doing now?

LAURA.   I don't do anything—much. Oh, please don't think I sit around doing nothing! My glass collection takes up a good deal of my time. Glass is something you have to take good care of.

JIM.   What did you say—about glass?

LAURA.   Collection I said—I have one—[*She clears her throat and turns away again, acutely shy.*]

JIM [*abruptly*].   You know what I judge to be the trouble with you? Inferiority complex! Know what that is? That's what they call it when someone low-rates himself! I understand it because I had it, too. Although my case was not so aggravated as yours seems to be. I had it until I took up public speaking, developed my voice, and learned that I had an aptitude for science. Before that time I never thought of myself as being outstanding in any way whatsoever! Now I've never made a regular study of it, but I have a friend who says I can analyze people better than doctors that make a profession of it. I don't claim that to be necessarily true, but I can sure guess a person's psychology, Laura! [*Takes out his gum.*] Excuse me, Laura. I always take it out when the flavor is gone. I'll use this scrap of paper to wrap it in. I know how it is to get it stuck on a shoe. Yep—that's what I judge to be your principal trouble. A lack of confidence in yourself as a person. You don't have the proper amount of faith in yourself. I'm basing that fact on a number of your remarks and also on certain observations I've made. For instance that clumping you thought was so awful in high school. You say that you even dreaded to walk into class. You see what you did? You dropped out of school, you gave up an education because of a clump, which as far as I know was practically nonexistent! A little physical defect is what you have. Hardly noticeable even! Magnified thousands of times by imagination! You know what my strong advice to you is? Think of yourself as *superior* in some way!

LAURA.   In what way would I think?

JIM.   Why, man alive, Laura! Just look about you a little. What do you see? A world full of common people! All of 'em born and all of 'em going to die! Which of them has one-tenth of your good points! Or mine! Or anyone else's, as far as that goes—Gosh! Everybody excels in some one thing. Some in many! [*Unconsciously glances at himself in the mirror.*] All you've got to do is discover in *what!* Take me, for instance. [*He adjusts his tie at the mirror.*] My interest happens to be in electrodynamics. I'm taking a course in radio engineering at night school, Laura, on top of a fairly responsible job at the warehouse. I'm taking that course and studying public speaking.

LAURA.   Ohhhh

JIM.   Because I believe in the future of television! [*Turning back to her.*] I wish to be ready to go up right along with it. Therefore I'm planning to get in on the ground floor. In fact, I've already made the right connections and all that remains is for the industry itself to get under way! Full steam—[*His eyes are starry.*] *Knowledge*—Zzzzzp! *Money*—Zzzzzzp!—*Power!* That's the cycle democracy is built on! [*His attitude is convincingly dynamic.* LAURA *stares at him, even her shyness eclipsed in her absolute wonder. He suddenly grins.*] I guess you think I think a lot of myself!

LAURA.   No—o-o-o, I—

JIM.   Now how about you? Isn't there something you take more interest in than anything else?

LAURA.   Well, I do—as I said—have my—glass collection—

A peal of girlish laughter from the kitchen.

JIM.   I'm not right sure I know what you're talking about. What kind of glass is it?

LAURA.   Little articles of it, they're ornaments mostly! Most of them are little animals made out of glass, the tiniest little animals in the world. Mother calls them a glass menagerie! Here's an example of one, if you'd like to see it! This one is one of the oldest. It's nearly thirteen. [*He stretches out his hand.*] [*Music: "The Glass Menagerie."*] Oh, be careful—if you breathe, it breaks!

JIM.   I'd better not take it. I'm pretty clumsy with things.

LAURA.   Go on, I trust you with him! [*Places it in his palm.*] There now—you're holding him gently! Hold him over the light, he loves the light! You see how the light shines through him?

JIM.   It sure does shine!

LAURA.   I shouldn't be partial, but he is my favorite one.

JIM.   What kind of a thing is this one supposed to be?

LAURA.   Haven't you noticed the single horn on his forehead?

JIM.   A unicorn, huh?

LAURA.   Mmm-hmmm!

JIM.   Unicorns, aren't they extinct in the modern world?

LAURA.   I know!

JIM.   Poor little fellow, he must feel sort of lonesome.

LAURA [*smiling*].   Well, if he does he doesn't complain about it. He stays on a shelf with some horses that don't have horns and all of them seem to get along nicely together.

JIM.   How do you know?

LAURA [*lightly*].   I haven't heard any arguments among them!

JIM [*grinning*].   No arguments, huh? Well, that's a pretty good sign! Where shall I set him?

LAURA.   Put him on the table. They all like a change of scenery once in a while!

JIM [*stretching*].   Well, well, well, well—Look how big my shadow is when I stretch!

LAURA.   Oh, oh, yes—it stretches across the ceiling!

JIM [*crossing to door*].   I think it's stopped raining. [*Opens fire-escape door.*] Where does the music come from?

LAURA.   From the Paradise Dance Hall across the alley.

JIM.   How about cutting the rug a little, Miss Wingfield?

LAURA.   Oh, I—

JIM.   Or is your program filled up? Let me have a look at it. [*Grasps imaginary card.*] Why, every dance is taken! I'll just have to scratch some out. [*Waltz Music: "La Golondrina."*] Ahhh, a waltz! [*He executes some sweeping turns by himself then holds his arms toward* LAURA.]

LAURA [*breathlessly*].   I—can't dance!

JIM.   There you go, that inferiority stuff!

LAURA.   I've never danced in my life!

JIM.   Come on, try!

LAURA.   Oh, but I'd step on you!

JIM.   I'm not made out of glass.

LAURA.   How—how—how do we start?

JIM.   Just leave it to me. You hold your arms out a little.

LAURA.   Like this?

JIM.   A little bit higher. Right. Now don't tighten up, that's the main thing about it—relax.

LAURA [*laughing breathlessly*].   It's hard not to.

JIM.   Okay.

LAURA.   I'm afraid you can't budge me.

JIM.   What do you bet I can't? [*He swings her into motion.*]

LAURA.   Goodness, yes, you can!

JIM.   Let yourself go, now, Laura, just let yourself go.

LAURA.   I'm—

JIM.   Come on!

LAURA.   Trying!

JIM.   Not so stiff—Easy does it!

LAURA.   I know but I'm—

JIM.   Loosen th' backbone! There now, that's a lot better.

LAURA.   Am I?

JIM.   Lots, lots better! [*He moves her about the room in a clumsy waltz.*]

LAURA.   Oh, my!

JIM.   Ha-ha!

LAURA.   Goodness, yes you can!

JIM.   Ha-ha-ha! [*They suddenly bump into the table.* JIM *stops.*] What did we hit on?

LAURA. Table.

JIM. Did something fall off it? I think—

LAURA. Yes.

JIM. I hope that it wasn't the little glass horse with the horn!

LAURA. Yes.

JIM. Aw, aw, aw. Is it broken?

LAURA. Now it is just like all the other horses.

JIM. It's lost its—

LAURA. Horn! It doesn't matter. Maybe it's a blessing in disguise.

JIM. You'll never forgive me. I bet that that was your favorite piece of glass.

LAURA. I don't have favorites much. It's no tragedy, Freckles. Glass breaks so easily. No matter how careful you are. The traffic jars the shelves and things fall
off them.

JIM. Still I'm awfully sorry that I was the cause.

LAURA [*smiling*]. I'll just imagine he had an operation. The horn was removed to
make him feel less—freakish! [*They both laugh.*] Now he will feel more at
home with the other horses, the ones that don't have horns . . .

JIM. Ha-ha, that's very funny! [*Suddenly serious.*] I'm glad to see that you have a
sense of humor. You know—you're—well—very different! Surprisingly different from anyone else I know! [*His voice becomes soft and hesitant with a genuine feeling.*] Do you mind me telling you that? [LAURA *is abashed beyond
speech.*] You make me feel sort of—I don't know how to put it! I'm usually
pretty good at expressing things, but—This is something that I don't know
how to say! LAURA *touches her throat and clears it—turns the broken unicorn
in her hands.*] [*Even softer*] Has anyone ever told you that you were pretty?
[*Pause: Music.*] [LAURA *looks up slowly, with wonder, and shakes her head.*]
Well, you are! In a very different way from anyone else. And all the nicer because of the difference, too. [*His voice becomes low and husky.* LAURA *turns
away, nearly faint with the novelty of her emotions.*] I wish that you were my
sister. I'd teach you to have some confidence in yourself. The different people
are not like other people, but being different is nothing to be ashamed of.
Because other people are not such wonderful people. They're one hundred
times one thousand. You're one times one! They walk all over the earth. You
just stay here. They're common as—weeds, but—you—well, you're *Blue
Roses!*

[*Image on Screen: Blue Roses.*]
[*Music Changes.*]

LAURA. But blue is wrong for—roses . . .

JIM. It's right for you—You're—pretty!

LAURA. In what respect am I pretty?

JIM. In all respects—believe me! Your eyes—your hair—are pretty! Your hands
are pretty! [*He catches hold of her hand.*] You think I'm making this up because I'm invited to dinner and have to be nice. Oh, I could do that! I could
put on an act for you, Laura, and say lots of things without being very sincere. But this time I am. I'm talking to you sincerely. I happened to notice
you had this inferiority complex that keeps you from feeling comfortable with
people. Somebody needs to build your confidence up and make you proud
instead of shy and turning away and—blushing—Somebody ought to—ought
to—*kiss* you. Laura! [*His hand slips slowly up her arm to her shoulder.*] [*Music
Swells Tumultuously.*] [*He suddenly turns her about and kisses her on the lips.*

When be releases her LAURA *sinks on the sofa with a bright, dazed look.* JIM *backs away and fishes in his pocket for a cigarette.] [Legend on Screen: "Souvenir."]* Stumble-john! [*He lights the cigarette, avoiding her look. There is a peal of girlish laughter from* AMANDA *in the kitchen.* LAURA *slowly raises and opens her hand. It still contains the little broken glass animal. She looks at it with a tender, bewildered expression.]* Stumble-john! I shouldn't have done that—That was way off the beam. You don't smoke, do you? [*She looks up, smiling, not hearing the question. He sits beside her a little gingerly. She looks at him speechlessly—waiting. He coughs decorously and moves a little farther aside as he considers the situation and senses her feelings, dimly, with perturbation. Gently.]* Would you—care for a—mint? [*She doesn't seem to hear him but her look grows brighter even.]* Peppermint—Life Saver? My pocket's a regular drug store—wherever I go . . . [*He pops a mint in his mouth. Then gulps and decides to make a clean breast of it. He speaks slowly and gingerly.]* Laura, you know, if I had a sister like you, I'd do the same thing as Tom. I'd bring out fellows—introduce her to them. The right type of boys of a type to—appreciate her. Only—well—he made a mistake about me. Maybe I've got no call to be saying this. That may not have been the idea in having me over. But what if it was? There's nothing wrong about that. The only trouble is that in my case—I'm not in a situation to—do the right thing. I can't take down your number and say I'll phone. I can't call up next week and—ask for a date. I thought I had better explain the situation in case you misunderstood it and—hurt your feelings. . . . [*Pause. Slowly, very slowly,* LAURA*'s look changes, her eyes returning slowly from his to the ornament in her palm.*]

AMANDA *utters another gay laugh in the kitchen.*

LAURA [*faintly*].   You—won't—call again?

JIM.   No, Laura, I can't [*He rises from the sofa.*] As I was just explaining, I've—got strings on me, Laura, I've—been going steady! I go out all the time with a girl named Betty. She's a home-girl like you, and Catholic, and Irish, and in a great many ways we—get along fine. I met her last summer on a moonlight boat trip up the river to Alton, on the *Majestic.* Well—right away from the start it was—love! [*Legend: Love!*] [LAURA *sways slightly forward and grips the arm of the sofa. He fails to notice, now enrapt in his own comfortable being.*] Being in love has made a new man of me! [*Leaning stiffly forward, clutching the arm of the sofa,* LAURA *struggles visibly with her storm. But* JIM *is oblivious, she is a long way off.*] The power of love is really pretty tremendous! Love is something that—changes the whole world, Laura! [*The storm abates a little and* LAURA *leans back. He notices her again.*] It happened that Betty's aunt took sick, she got a wire and had to go to Centralia. So Tom—when he asked me to dinner—I naturally just accepted the invitation, not knowing that you—that he—that I—[*He stops awkwardly.*] Huh—I'm a stumble-john! [*He flops back on the sofa. The holy candles in the altar of* LAURA*'s face have been snuffed out! There is a look of almost infinite desolation.* JIM *glances at her uneasily.*] I wish that you would—say something. [*She bites her lip which was trembling and then bravely smiles. She opens her hand again on the broken glass ornament. Then she gently takes his hand and raises it level with her own. She carefully places the unicorn in the palm of his hand, then pushes his fingers closed upon it.*] What are you—doing that for? You want me to have him?—Laura? [*She nods.*] What for?

LAURA.   A—souvenir . . .

She rises unsteadily and crouches beside the victrola to wind it up.

[*Legend on Screen: "Things Have a Way of Turning Out So Badly."*]
[*Or Image: "Gentleman Caller Waving Good-Bye!—Gaily."*]

At this moment AMANDA *rushes brightly back in the front room. She bears a pitcher of fruit punch in an old-fashioned cut-glass pitcher and a plate of macaroons. The plate has a gold border and poppies painted on it.*

AMANDA.   Well, well, well! Isn't the air delightful after the shower? I've made you children a little liquid refreshment. [*Turns gaily to the gentleman caller.*] Jim, do you know that song about lemonade?

> "Lemonade, lemonade
> Made in the shade and stirred with a spade—
> Good enough for any old maid!"

JIM [*uneasily*].   Ha-ha! No—I never heard it.

AMANDA.   Why, Laura! You look so serious!

JIM.   We were having a serious conversation.

AMANDA.   Good! Now you're better acquainted!

JIM [*uncertainly*].   Ha-ha! Yes.

AMANDA.   You modern young people are much more serious-minded than my generation. I was so gay as a girl!

JIM.   You haven't changed, Mrs. Wingfield.

AMANDA.   Tonight I'm rejuvenated! The gaiety of the occasion, Mr. O'Connor! [*She tosses her head with a peal of laughter. Spills lemonade.*] Oooo! I'm baptizing myself!

JIM.   Here—let me—

AMANDA [*setting the pitcher down*].   There now. I discovered we had some maraschino cherries. I dumped them in, juice and all!

JIM.   You shouldn't have gone to that trouble, Mrs. Wingfield.

AMANDA.   Trouble, trouble? Why it was loads of fun! Didn't you hear me cutting up in the kitchen? I bet your ears were burning! I told Tom how outdone with him I was for keeping you to himself so long a time! He should have brought you over much, much sooner! Well, now that you've found your way, I want you to be a very frequent caller! Not just occasional but all the time. Oh, we're going to have a lot of gay times together! I see them coming! Mmm, just breathe that air! So fresh, and the moon's so pretty! I'll skip back out—I know where my place is when young folks are having a—serious conversation!

JIM.   Oh, don't go out, Mrs. Wingfield. The fact of the matter is I've got to be going.

AMANDA.   Going, now? You're joking! Why, it's only the shank of the evening, Mr. O'Connor!

JIM.   Well, you know how it is.

AMANDA.   You mean you're a young workingman and have to keep workingmen's hours. We'll let you off early tonight. But only on the condition that next time you stay later. What's the best night for you? Isn't Saturday night the best night for you workingmen?

JIM.   I have a couple of time-clocks to punch, Mrs. Wingfield. One at morning, another one at night!

AMANDA.   My, but you *are* ambitious! You work at night, too?

JIM.   No, Ma'am, not work but—Betty! [*He crosses deliberately to pick up his hat. The band at the Paradise Dance Hall goes into a tender waltz.*]

AMANDA.   Betty? Betty? Who's—Betty! [*There is an ominous cracking sound in the sky.*]

JIM.   Oh, just a girl. The girl I go steady with! [*He smiles charmingly. The sky falls.*]

[*Legend: "The Sky Falls."*]

AMANDA [*a long-drawn exhalation*].   Ohhh .... Is it a serious romance, Mr. O'Connor?

JIM.   We're going to be married the second Sunday in June.

AMANDA.   Ohhhh—how nice! Tom didn't mention that you were engaged to be married.

JIM.   The cat's not out of the bag at the warehouse yet. You know how they are. They call you Romeo and stuff like that. [*He stops at the oval mirror to put on his hat. He carefully shapes the brim and the crown to give a discreetly dashing effect.*] It's been a wonderful evening, Mrs. Wingfield. I guess this is what they mean by Southern hospitality.

AMANDA.   It really wasn't anything at all.

JIM.   I hope it don't seem like I'm rushing off. But I promised Betty I'd pick her up at the Wabash depot, an' by the time I get my jalopy down there her train'll be in. Some women are pretty upset if you keep 'em waiting.

AMANDA.   Yes, I know—The tyranny of women! [*Extends her hand.*] Good-bye, Mr. O'Connor. I wish you luck—and happiness—and success! All three of them, and so does Laura!—Don't you, Laura?

LAURA.   Yes!

JIM [*taking her hand*].   Goodbye, Laura. I'm certainly going to treasure that souvenir. And don't you forget the good advice I gave you. [*Raises his voice to a cheery shout.*] So long, Shakespeare! Thanks again, ladies—good night!

He grins and ducks jauntily out.
Still bravely grimacing, AMANDA *closes the door on the gentleman caller.*
Then she turns back to the room with a puzzled expression. She and LAURA *don't dare to face each other.* LAURA *crouches beside the victrola to wind it.*

AMANDA [*faintly*].   Things have a way of turning out so badly. I don't believe that I would play the victrola. Well, well—well—Our gentleman caller was engaged to be married! Tom!

TOM [*from back*].   Yes, Mother?

AMANDA.   Come in here a minute. I want to tell you something awfully funny.

TOM [*enters with macaroon and a glass of the lemonade*].   Has the gentleman caller gotten away already?

AMANDA.   The gentleman caller has made an early departure. What a wonderful joke you played on us!

TOM.   How do you mean?

AMANDA.   You didn't mention that he was engaged to be married.

TOM.   Jim? Engaged?

AMANDA.   That's what he just informed us.

TOM.   I'll be jiggered! I didn't know about that.

AMANDA.   That seems very peculiar.

TOM.   What's peculiar about it?

AMANDA.   Didn't you call him your best friend down at the warehouse?

TOM.   He is, but how did I know?

AMANDA.   It seems extremely peculiar that you wouldn't know your best friend was going to be married!

TOM.   The warehouse is where I work, not where I know things about people!

AMANDA.   You don't know things anywhere! You live in a dream; you manufacture
   illusions! [*He crosses to door.*] Where are you going?
TOM.   I'm going to the movies.
AMANDA.   That's right, now that you've had us make such fools of ourselves. The
   effort, the preparations, all the expense! The new floor lamp, the rug, the
   clothes for Laura! All for what? To entertain some other girl's fiancé! Go to the
   movies, go! Don't think about us, a mother deserted, an unmarried sister
   who's crippled and has no job! Don't let anything interfere with your selfish
   pleasure! Just go, go, go—to the movies!
TOM.   All right, I will! The more you shout about my selfishness to me the quicker
   I'll go, and I won't go to the movies!
AMANDA.   Go, then! Then go to the moon—you selfish dreamer!

   TOM *smashes his glass on the floor. He plunges out on the fire-escape,*
slamming the door. LAURA *screams—cut by door.*
   Dance-hall music up. TOM *goes to the rail and grips it desperately, lifting his*
face in the chill white moonlight penetrating the narrow abyss of the alley.
   [*Legend on Screen: "And So Good-Bye . . ."*]
   TOM*'s closing speech is timed with the interior pantomime. The interior scene*
is played as though viewed through sound-proof glass. AMANDA *appears to be*
making a comforting speech to LAURA *who is huddled upon the sofa. Now that we*
cannot hear the mother's speech, her silliness is gone and she has dignity and
tragic beauty. LAURA*'s dark hair hides her face until at the end of the speech she*
lifts it to smile at her mother. AMANDA*'s gestures are slow and graceful, almost*
dancelike, as she comforts the daughter. At the end of her speech she glances a
moment at the father's picture—then withdraws through the portieres. At close of
TOM*'s speech,* LAURA *blows out the candles, ending the play.*

TOM.   I didn't go to the moon, I went much further—for time is the longest distance
   between two places—Not long after that I was fired for writing a poem on the
   lid of a shoe-box. I left Saint Louis. I descended the steps of this fire-escape for
   a last time and followed, from then on, in my father's footsteps, attempting to
   find in motion what was lost in space—I traveled around a great deal. The
   cities swept about me like dead leaves, leaves that were brightly colored but
   torn away from the branches. I would have stopped, but I was pursued by
   something. It always came upon me unawares, taking me altogether by surprise. Perhaps it was a familiar bit of music. Perhaps it was only a piece of
   transparent glass—Perhaps I am walking along a street at night, in some
   strange city, before I have found companions. I pass the lighted window of a
   shop where perfume is sold. The window is filled with pieces of colored glass,
   tiny transparent bottles in delicate colors, like bits of a shattered rainbow. Then
   all at once my sister touches my shoulder. I turn around and look into her eyes
   . . . Oh, Laura, Laura, I tried to leave you behind me, but I am more faithful
   than I intended to be! I reach for a cigarette, I cross the street, I run into the
   movies or a bar, I buy a drink, I speak to the nearest stranger—anything that
   can blow your candles out! [LAURA *bends over the candles.*]—for nowadays the
   world is lit by lightning! Blow out your candles, Laura—and so good-bye . . .

   She blows the candles out.
   [*The Scene Dissolves.*]

                                                                    [1944]

Topics for Critical Thinking and Writing

1. When the play was produced in New York, the magic-lantern slides were omitted. Is the device an extraneous gimmick? Might it even interfere with the play, by oversimplifying and thus in a way belittling the actions?
2. What does the Victrola offer to Laura? Why is the typewriter a better symbol (for the purposes of the play) than, say, a piano? After all, Laura could have been taking piano lessons. Explain the symbolism of the unicorn, and the loss of its horn. What is Laura saying to Jim in the gesture of giving him the unicorn?
3. Laura escapes to her glass menagerie. To what do Amanda and Tom escape? How complete is Tom's escape at the end of the play?
4. What is meant at the end when Laura blows out the candles? Is she blowing out illusions? Or life? Or both?
5. Did Williams make a slip in having Amanda say Laura is "crippled" on page 613?
6. There is an implication that had Jim not been going steady he might have rescued Laura, but Jim also seems to represent (for example, in his lines about money and power) the corrupt outside world that no longer values humanity. Is this a slip on Williams's part, or is it an interesting complexity?
7. On page 613 Williams says, in a stage direction, "Now that we cannot hear the mother's speech, her silliness is gone and she has dignity and tragic beauty." Is Williams simply dragging in the word "tragic" because of its prestige, or is it legitimate? "Tragedy" is often distinguished from "pathos": In the tragic, the suffering is experienced by persons who act and are in some measure responsible for their suffering; in the pathetic, the suffering is experienced by the passive and the innocent. For example, in discussing Aeschylus's *The Suppliants* (in *Greek Tragedy*), H. D. F. Kitto says, "The Suppliants are not only pathetic, as the victims of outrage, but also tragic, as the victims of their own misconceptions." Given this distinction, to what extent are Amanda and Laura tragic? pathetic?

LUIS VALDEZ

Luis Valdez was born into a family of migrant farm workers in Delano, California, in 1940. After completing high school he entered San Jose State College on a scholarship. He wrote his first plays while still an undergraduate, and after receiving his degree (in English and drama) from San Jose in 1964 he joined the San Francisco Mime Troupe, a left-wing group that performed in parks and streets. Revolutionary in technique as well as in political content, the Mime Troupe rejected the traditional forms of drama and instead drew on the traditions of the circus and the carnival.

In 1965 Valdez returned to Delano, where Cesar Chavez had organized a strike of farm workers and a boycott against grape growers. It was here, under the wing of the United Farm Workers, that he established El Teatro Campesino (the Farm Workers' Theater), which at first specialized in doing short, improvised, satirical skits called actos. *When the* teatro *moved to Del Rey, California, it expanded its repertoire beyond farm issues, and it became part of a cultural center that gave workshops (in English and Spanish) in such subjects as history, drama, and politics.*

The actos, *performed by amateurs on college campuses and on flatbed trucks and at the edges of vineyards, were highly political. Making use of stereotypes (the boss, the scab), the* actos *sought not to present the individual thoughts of a gifted playwright but to present the social vision of ordinary people—the* pueblo—*though it was acknowledged that in an oppressive society the playwright might have to help guide the people to see their own best interests.*

Valdez moved from actos *to* mitos *(myths)—plays that drew on Aztec mythology, Mexican folklore, and Christianity—and then to* Zoot Suit, *a play that ran for many months in California and that became the first Mexican American play to be produced on Broadway. More recently he wrote and directed a hit movie,* La Bamba, *and in 1991 received an award from the AT&T Foundation for his musical,* Bandido, *presented by El Teatro Campesino.*

Los Vendidos was written in 1967, when Ronald Reagan was governor of California.*

Los Vendidos*

LIST OF CHARACTERS

HONEST SANCHO
SECRETARY
FARM WORKER
JOHNNY
REVOLUCIONARIO
MEXICAN-AMERICAN

SCENE: *Honest Sancho's Used Mexican Lot and Mexican Curio Shop. Three models are on display in Honest* SANCHO's *shop: to the right, there is a* REVOLUCIONARIO, *complete with sombrero, carrilleras,[1] and carabina 30-30. At center, on the floor, there is the* FARM WORKER *under a broad straw sombrero. At stage left is the* PACHUCO,[2] *filero[3] in hand.*

[*Honest* SANCHO *is moving among his models, dusting them off and preparing for another day of business.*]

SANCHO. Bueno, bueno, mis monos, vamos a ver a quien vendemos ahora, ¿no?[4]
  [*To audience.*] ¡Quihubo! I'm Honest Sancho and this is my shop. Antes fui contratista pero ahora logré tener mi negocito.[5] All I need now is a customer. [*A bell rings offstage.*] Ay, a customer!
SECRETARY. [*Entering*] Good morning, I'm Miss Jiménez from—
SANCHO. ¡Ah, una chicana! Welcome, welcome Señorita Jiménez.
SECRETARY. [*Anglo pronunciation*] JIM-enez.
SANCHO. ¿Qué?
SECRETARY. My name is Miss JIM-enez. Don't you speak English? What's wrong with you?
SANCHO. Oh, nothing, Señorita JIM-enez. I'm here to help you.
SECRETARY. That's better. As I was starting to say, I'm a secretary from Governor Reagan's office, and we're looking for a Mexican type for the administration.

* **Los Vendidos** the sellouts. [1]**carrilleras** cartridge belts. [2]**Pachuco** an urban tough guy. [3]**filero** blade. [4]**Bueno . . . no?** Well, well darlings, let's see who we can sell now, O.K.? [5]**Antes . . . negocito** I used to be a contractor, but now I've succeeded in having my little business.

SANCHO.   Well, you come to the right place, lady. This is Honest Sancho's Used
     Mexican lot, and we got all types here. Any particular type you want?

SECRETARY.   Yes, we were looking for somebody suave—

SANCHO.   Suave.

SECRETARY.   Debonair.

SANCHO.   De buen aire.

SECRETARY.   Dark.

SANCHO.   Prieto.

SECRETARY.   But of course not too dark.

SANCHO.   No muy prieto.

SECRETARY.   Perhaps, beige.

SANCHO.   Beige, just the tone. Así como cafecito con leche,[6] ¿no?

SECRETARY.   One more thing. He must be hard-working.

SANCHO.   That could only be one model. Step right over here to the center of the
     shop, lady. [*They cross to the* FARM WORKER.] This is our standard farm worker
     model. As you can see, in the words of our beloved Senator George Murphy,
     he is "built close to the ground." Also take special notice of his four-ply
     Goodyear huaraches, made from the rain tire. This wide-brimmed sombrero
     is an extra added feature—keeps off the sun, rain, and dust.

SECRETARY.   Yes, it does look durable.

SANCHO.   And our farm worker model is friendly. Muy amable.[7] Watch. [*Snaps his
     fingers.*]

FARM WORKER   [*Lifts up head*]. Buenos días, señorita. [*His head drops.*]

SECRETARY.   My, he's friendly.

SANCHO.   Didn't I tell you? Loves his patrones! But his most attractive feature is
     that he's hard working. Let me show you. [*Snaps fingers,* FARM WORKER *stands.*]

FARM WORKER.   ¡El jale![8] [*He begins to work.*]

SANCHO.   As you can see, he is cutting grapes.

SECRETARY.   Oh, I wouldn't know.

SANCHO.   He also picks cotton. [*Snap.* FARM WORKER *begins to pick cotton.*]

SECRETARY.   Versatile isn't he?

SANCHO.   He also picks melons. [*Snap.* FARM WORKER *picks melons.*] That's his slow
     speed for late in the season. Here's his fast speed. [*Snap.* FARM WORKER *picks
     faster.*]

SECRETARY.   ¡Chihuahua! . . . I mean, goodness, he sure is a hard worker.

SANCHO   [*Pulls the* FARM WORKER *to his feet*]. And that isn't the half of it. Do you see
     these little holes on his arms that appear to be pores? During those hot slug-
     gish days in the field, when the vines or the branches get so entangled, it's al-
     most impossible to move; these holes emit a certain grease that allow our
     model to slip and slide right through the crop with no trouble at all.

SECRETARY.   Wonderful. But is he economical?

SANCHO.   Economical? Señorita, you are looking at the Volkswagen of Mexicans.
     Pennies a day is all it takes. One plate of beans and tortillas will keep him go-
     ing all day. That, and chile. Plenty of chile. Chile jalapeños, chile verde, chile
     colorado. But, of course, if you do give him chile [*Snap.* FARM WORKER *turns
     left face. Snap.* FARM WORKER *bends over.*] then you have to change his oil filter
     once a week.

SECRETARY.   What about storage?

---

[6]**Así . . . leche** like coffee with milk.   [7]**Muy amable** very friendly.   [8]**El jale** the job.

SANCHO.   No problem. You know these new farm labor camps our Honorable Governor Reagan has built out by Parlier or Raisin City? They were designed with our model in mind. Five, six, seven, even ten in one of those shacks will give you no trouble at all. You can also put him in old barns, old cars, river banks. You can even leave him out in the field overnight with no worry!

SECRETARY.   Remarkable.

SANCHO.   And here's an added feature: Every year at the end of the season, this model goes back to Mexico and doesn't return, automatically, until next Spring.

SECRETARY.   How about that. But tell me: does he speak English?

SANCHO.   Another outstanding feature is that last year this model was programmed to go out on STRIKE! [*Snap.*]

FARM WORKER.   ¡HUELGA! ¡HUELGA! Hermanos, sálganse de esos files.[9] [*Snap. He stops.*]

SECRETARY.   No! Oh no, we can't strike in the State Capitol.

SANCHO.   Well, he also scabs. [*Snap.*]

FARM WORKER.   Me vendo barato, ¿y qué?[10] [*Snap.*]

SECRETARY.   That's much better, but you didn't answer my question. Does he speak English?

SANCHO.   Bueno . . . no, pero[11] he has other—

SECRETARY.   No.

SANCHO.   Other features.

SECRETARY.   NO! He just won't do!

SANCHO.   Okay, okay pues. We have other models.

SECRETARY.   I hope so. What we need is something a little more sophisticated.

SANCHO.   Sophisti—¿qué?

SECRETARY.   An urban model.

SANCHO.   Ah, from the city! Step right back. Over here in this corner of the shop is exactly what you're looking for. Introducing our new 1969 JOHNNY PACHUCO model! This is our fast-back model. Streamlined. Built for speed, low-riding, city life. Take a look at some of these features. Mag shoes, dual exhausts, green chartreuse paint-job, dark-tint windshield, a little poof on top. Let me just turn him on. [*Snap.* JOHNNY *walks to stage center with a pachuco bounce.*]

SECRETARY.   What was that?

SANCHO.   That, señorita, was the Chicano shuffle.

SECRETARY.   Okay, what does he do?

SANCHO.   Anything and everything necessary for city life. For instance, survival: He knife fights. [*Snap.* JOHNNY *pulls out switchblade and swings at* SECRETARY.]

   [SECRETARY *screams.*]

SANCHO.   He dances. [*Snap.*]

JOHNNY   [*Singing*]. "Angel Baby, my Angel Baby . . . " [*Snap.*]

SANCHO.   And here's a feature no city model can be without. He gets arrested, but not without resisting, of course. [*Snap.*]

JOHNNY.   ¡En la madre, la placa![12] I didn't do it! I didn't do it! [JOHNNY *turns and stands up against an imaginary wall, legs spread out, arms behind his back.*]

SECRETARY.   Oh no, we can't have arrests! We must maintain law and order.

---

[9]**¡Huelga . . . files** Strike! Strike! Brothers, leave those rows.   [10]**Me . . . qué?** I come cheap. So what?   [11]**Bueno . . . no, pero** Well, no, but.   [12]**¡En . . . la placa!** Wow, the cops!

SANCHO.   But he's bilingual!

SECRETARY.   Bilingual?

SANCHO.   Simón que yes.[13] He speaks English! Johnny, give us some English. [*Snap.*]

JOHNNY.   [*Comes downstage*]. Fuck-you!

SECRETARY   [*Gasps*]. Oh! I've never been so insulted in my whole life!

SANCHO.   Well, he learned it in your school.

SECRETARY.   I don't care where he learned it.

SANCHO.   But he's economical!

SECRETARY.   Economical?

SANCHO.   Nickels and dimes. You can keep Johnny running on hamburgers, Taco Bell tacos, Lucky Lager beer, Thunderbird wine, yesca—

SECRETARY.   Yesca?

SANCHO.   Mota.

SECRETARY.   Mota?

SANCHO.   Leños[14] . . . Marijuana. [*Snap;* JOHNNY *inhales on an imaginary joint.*]

SECRETARY.   That's against the law!

JOHNNY   [*Big smile, holding his breath*]. Yeah.

SANCHO.   He also sniffs glue. [*Snap.* JOHNNY *inhales glue, big smile.*]

JOHNNY.   That's too much man, ése.[15]

SECRETARY.   No, Mr. Sancho, I don't think this—

SANCHO.   Wait a minute, he has other qualities I know you'll love. For example, an inferiority complex. [*Snap.*]

JOHNNY.   [*To* SANCHO]. You think you're better than me, huh ése? [*Swings switchblade.*]

SANCHO.   He can also be beaten and he bruises, cut him and he bleeds; kick him and he—[*He beats, bruises and kicks* PACHUCO.] would you like to try it?

SECRETARY.   Oh, I couldn't.

SANCHO.   Be my guest. He's a great scapegoat.

SECRETARY.   No, really.

SANCHO.   Please.

SECRETARY.   Well, all right. Just once. [*She kicks* PACHUCO.] Oh, he's so soft.

SANCHO.   Wasn't that good? Try again.

SECRETARY   [*Kicks* PACHUCO]. Oh, he's so wonderful! [*She kicks him again.*]

SANCHO.   Okay, that's enough, lady. You ruin the merchandise. Yes, our Johnny Pachuco model can give you many hours of pleasure. Why, the L.A.P.D. just bought twenty of these to train their rookie cops on. And talk about maintenance. Señorita, you are looking at an entirely self-supporting machine. You're never going to find our Johnny Pachuco model on the relief rolls. No, sir, this model knows how to liberate.

SECRETARY.   Liberate?

SANCHO.   He steals. [*Snap.* JOHNNY *rushes the* SECRETARY *and steals her purse.*]

JOHNNY.   ¡Dame esa bolsa, vieja![16] [*He grabs the purse and runs. Snap by* SANCHO. *He stops.*]

[SECRETARY *runs after* JOHNNY *and grabs purse away from him, kicking him as she goes.*]

---

[13]**Simón que yes** Yea, sure.   [14]**Leños** joints (marijuana).   [15]**ése** fellow.   [16]**¡Dame . . . vieja!** Give me that bag, old lady!

SECRETARY.   No, no, no! We can't have any *more* thieves in the State Administration. Put him back.

SANCHO.   Okay, we still got other models. Come on, Johnny, we'll sell you to some old lady. [SANCHO *takes* JOHNNY *back to his place.*)

SECRETARY.   Mr. Sancho, I don't think you quite understand what we need. What we need is something that will attract the women voters. Something more traditional, more romantic.

SANCHO.   Ah, a lover. [*He smiles meaningfully.*] Step right over here, señorita. Introducing our standard Revolucionario and/or Early California Bandit type. As you can see he is well-built, sturdy, durable. This is the International Harvester of Mexicans.

SECRETARY.   What does he do?

SANCHO.   You name it, he does it. He rides horses, stays in the mountains, crosses deserts, plains, rivers, leads revolutions, follows revolutions, kills, can be killed, serves as a martyr, hero, movie star—did I say movie star? Did you ever see *Viva Zapata? Viva Villa? Villa Rides? Pancho Villa Returns? Pancho Villa Goes Back? Pancho Villa Meets Abbott and Costello*—

SECRETARY.   I've never seen any of those.

SANCHO.   Well, he was in all of them. Listen to this. [*Snap.*]

REVOLUCIONARIO   [*Scream*]. ¡VIVA VILLAAAAA!

SECRETARY.   That's awfully loud.

SANCHO.   He has a volume control. [*He adjusts volume. Snap.*]

REVOLUCIONARIO   [*Mousey voice*]. ¡Viva Villa!

SECRETARY.   That's better.

SANCHO.   And even if you didn't see him in the movies, perhaps you saw him on TV. He makes commercials. [*Snap.*]

REVOLUCIONARIO.   Is there a Frito Bandito in your house?

SECRETARY.   Oh yes, I've seen that one!

SANCHO.   Another feature about this one is that he is economical. He runs on raw horsemeat and tequila.

SECRETARY.   Isn't that rather savage?

SANCHO.   Al contrario,[17] it makes him a lover. [*Snap.*]

REVOLUCIONARIO   [*To* SECRETARY]. ¡Ay, mamasota, cochota, ven pa'ca![18] [*He grabs* SECRETARY *and folds her back—Latin-Lover style.*]

SANCHO   [*Snap.* REVOLUCIONARIO *goes back upright.*]. Now wasn't that nice?

SECRETARY.   Well, it was rather nice.

SANCHO.   And finally, there is one outstanding feature about this model I KNOW the ladies are going to love: He's a GENUINE antique! He was made in Mexico in 1910!

SECRETARY.   Made in Mexico?

SANCHO.   That's right. Once in Tijuana, twice in Guadalajara, three times in Cuernavaca.

SECRETARY.   Mr. Sancho, I thought he was an American product.

SANCHO.   No, but—

SECRETARY.   No, I'm sorry. We can't buy anything but American-made products. He just won't do.

SANCHO.   But he's an antique!

---

[17]**Al contrario** on the contrary.   [18]**¡Ay . . . pa'ca!** —, get over here!

SECRETARY.   I don't care. You still don't understand what we need. It's true we need Mexican models such as these, but it's more important that he be *American*.

SANCHO.   American?

SECRETARY.   That's right, and judging from what you've shown me, I don't think you have what we want. Well, my lunch hour's almost over: I better—

SANCHO.   Wait a minute! Mexican but American?

SECRETARY.   That's correct.

SANCHO.   Mexican but . . . [*A sudden flash.*] AMERICAN! Yeah, I think we've got exactly what you want. He just came in today! Give me a minute. [*He exits. Talks from backstage.*] Here he is in the shop. Let me just get some papers off. There. Introducing our new 1970 Mexican-American! Ta-ra-ra-ra-ra-ra-RA-RAAA!

[SANCHO *brings out the* MEXICAN-AMERICAN *model, a clean-shaven middle-class type in a business suit, with glasses.*]

SECRETARY   [*Impressed*]. Where have you been hiding this one?

SANCHO.   He just came in this morning. Ain't he a beauty? Feast your eyes on him! Sturdy US STEEL frame, streamlined, modern. As a matter of fact, he is built exactly like our Anglo models except that he comes in a variety of darker shades: naugahyde, leather, or leatherette.

SECRETARY.   Naugahyde.

SANCHO.   Well, we'll just write that down. Yes, señorita, this model represents the apex of American engineering! He is bilingual, college educated, ambitious! Say the word "acculturate" and he accelerates. He is intelligent, well-mannered, clean—did I say clean? [*Snap.* MEXICAN-AMERICAN *raises his arm.*] Smell.

SECRETARY   [*Smells*]. Old Sobaco, my favorite.

SANCHO   [*Snap.* MEXICAN-AMERICAN *turns toward* SANCHO]. Eric! [*To* SECRETARY.] We call him Eric García. [*To* ERIC.] I want you to meet Miss JIM-enez, Eric.

MEXICAN-AMERICAN.   Miss JIM-enez, I am delighted to make your acquaintance. [*He kisses her hand.*]

SECRETARY.   Oh, my, how charming!

SANCHO.   Did you feel the suction? He has seven especially engineered suction cups right behind his lips. He's a charmer all right!

SECRETARY.   How about boards? Does he function on boards?

SANCHO.   You name them, he is on them. Parole boards, draft boards, school boards, taco quality control boards, surf boards, two-by-fours.

SECRETARY.   Does he function in politics?

SANCHO.   Señorita, you are looking at a political MACHINE. Have you ever heard of the OEO, EOC, COD, WAR ON POVERTY? That's our model! Not only that, he makes political speeches.

SECRETARY.   May I hear one?

SANCHO.   With pleasure. [*Snap.*] Eric, give us a speech.

MEXICAN-AMERICAN.   Mr. Congressman, Mr. Chairman, members of the board, honored guests, ladies and gentlemen. [SANCHO *and* SECRETARY *applaud.*] Please, please. I come before you as a Mexican-American to tell you about the problems of the Mexican. The problems of the Mexican stem from one thing and one thing alone: He's stupid. He's uneducated. He needs to stay in school. He needs to be ambitious, forward-looking, harder-working. He needs to think American, American, American, AMERICAN, AMERICAN, AMERICAN. GOD BLESS AMERICA! GOD BLESS AMERICA! GOD BLESS AMERICA!! [*He goes out of control.*]

[SANCHO *snaps frantically and the* MEXICAN-AMERICAN *finally slumps forward, bending at the waist.*]

SECRETARY. Oh my, he's patriotic too!

SANCHO. Sí, señorita, he loves his country. Let me just make a little adjustment here. [*Stands* MEXICAN-AMERICAN *up.*]

SECRETARY. What about upkeep? Is he economical?

SANCHO. Well, no, I won't lie to you. The Mexican-American costs a little bit more, but you get what you pay for. He's worth every extra cent. You can keep him running on dry Martinis, Langendorf bread.

SECRETARY. Apple pie?

SANCHO. Only Mom's. Of course, he's also programmed to eat Mexican food on ceremonial functions, but I must warn you: an overdose of beans will plug up his exhaust.

SECRETARY. Fine! There's just one more question: HOW MUCH DO YOU WANT FOR HIM?

SANCHO. Well, I tell you what I'm gonna do. Today and today only, because you've been so sweet, I'm gonna let you steal this model from me! I'm gonna let you drive him off the lot for the simple price of—let's see taxes and license included—$15,000.

SECRETARY. Fifteen thousand DOLLARS? For a MEXICAN!

SANCHO. Mexican? What are you talking, lady? This is a Mexican-AMERICAN! We had to melt down two pachucos, a farm worker and three gabachos[19] to make this model! You want quality, but you gotta pay for it! This is no cheap run-about. He's got class!

SECRETARY. Okay, I'll take him.

SANCHO. You will?

SECRETARY. Here's your money.

SANCHO. You mind if I count it?

SECRETARY. Go right ahead.

SANCHO. Well, you'll get your pink slip in the mail. Oh, do you want me to wrap him up for you? We have a box in the back.

SECRETARY. No, thank you. The Governor is having a luncheon this afternoon, and we need a brown face in the crowd. How do I drive him?

SANCHO. Just snap your fingers. He'll do anything you want.

[SECRETARY *snaps.* MEXICAN-AMERICAN *steps forward.*]

MEXICAN-AMERICAN. RAZA QUERIDA, ¡VAMOS LEVANTANDO ARMAS PARA LIBER-ARNOS DE ESTOS DESGRACIADOS GABACHOS QUE NOS EXPLOTAN! VA-MOS.[20]

SECRETARY. What did he say?

SANCHO. Something about lifting arms, killing white people, etc.

SECRETARY. But he's not supposed to say that!

SANCHO. Look, lady, don't blame me for bugs from the factory. He's your Mexican-American; you bought him, now drive him off the lot!

SECRETARY. But he's broken!

SANCHO. Try snapping another finger.

[SECRETARY *snaps.* MEXICAN-AMERICAN *comes to life again.*]

---

[19]**gabachos** whites. [20]**Raza . . . Vamos** Beloved Raza [persons of Mexican descent], let's take up arms to liberate ourselves from those damned whites who exploit us. Let's get going.

MEXICAN-AMERICAN.   ¡ESTA GRAN HUMANIDAD HA DICHO BASTA! Y SE HA
   PUESTO EN MARCHA! ¡BASTA! ¡BASTA! ¡VIVA LA RAZA! ¡VIVA LA CAUSA!
   ¡VIVA LA HUELGA! ¡VIVAN LOS BROWN BERETS! ¡VIVAN LOS ESTUDI-
   ANTES!²¹ ¡CHICANO POWER!

[*The* MEXICAN-AMERICAN *turns toward the* SECRETARY, *who gasps and backs up.*
He keeps turning toward the PACHUCO, FARM WORKER, *and* REVOLUCIONARIO *snapping*
his fingers and turning each of them on, one by one.]

PACHUCO   [*Snap. To* SECRETARY]. I'm going to get you, baby! ¡Viva La Raza!
FARM WORKER   [*Snap. To* SECRETARY]. ¡Viva la huelga! ¡Viva la Huelga! ¡VIVA LA
   HUELGA!
REVOLUCIONARIO   [*Snap. To* SECRETARY]. ¡Viva la revolución! ¡VIVA LA REVOLUCIÓN!

[*The three models join together and advance toward the* SECRETARY *who*
backs up and runs out of the shop screaming. SANCHO *is at the other end of the*
shop holding his money in his hand. All freeze. After a few seconds of silence, the
PACHUCO *moves and stretches, shaking his arms and loosening up. The* FARM
WORKER *and* REVOLUCIONARIO *do the same.* SANCHO *stays where he is, frozen to his*
spot.]

JOHNNY.   Man, that was a long one, ése.²² [*Others agree with him.*]
FARM WORKER.   How did we do?
JOHNNY.   Perty good, look at all that lana,²³ man! [*He goes over to* SANCHO *and re-*
   moves the money from his hand. SANCHO *stays where he is.*]
REVOLUCIONARIO.   En la madre, look at all the money.
JOHNNY.   We keep this up, we're going to be rich.
FARM WORKER.   They think we're machines.
REVOLUCIONARIO.   Burros.
JOHNNY.   Puppets.
MEXICAN-AMERICAN.   The only thing I don't like is—how come I always got to play
   the godamn Mexican-American?
JOHNNY.   That's what you get for finishing high school.
FARM WORKER.   How about our wages, ése?
JOHNNY.   Here it comes right now. $3,000 for you, $3,000 for you, $3,000 for you,
   and $3,000 for me. The rest we put back into the business.
MEXICAN-AMERICAN.   Too much, man. Heh, where you vatos²⁴ going tonight?
FARM WORKER.   I'm going over to Concha's. There's a party.
JOHNNY.   Wait a minute, vatos. What about our salesman? I think he needs an oil job.
REVOLUCIONARIO.   Leave him to me.

[*The* PACHUCO, FARM WORKER, *and* MEXICAN-AMERICAN *exit, talking loudly about*
their plans for the night. The REVOLUCIONARIO *goes over to* SANCHO, *removes his*
derby hat and cigar, lifts him up and throws him over his shoulder. SANCHO *hangs*
loose, lifeless.]

REVOLUCIONARIO   [*To audience*]. He's the best model we got! ¡Ajua!²⁵

[*Exit.*]

THE END

[1967]

---

²¹**¡Esta . . . Estudiantes!** This great mass of humanity has said enough! And it has begun to
march. Enough! Enough! Long live La Raza! Long live the Cause! Long live the strike! Long live
the Brown Berets! Long live the students!   ²²**ése** man.   ²³**lana** money.   ²⁴**vatos** guys.
²⁵**¡Ajua!** Wow!

Topics for Critical Thinking and Writing

1. If you are an Anglo (shorthand for a Caucasian with traditional northern European values), do you find the play deeply offensive? Why, or why not? If you are a Mexican American, do you find the play entertaining—or do you find parts of it offensive? What might Anglos enjoy in the play, and what might Mexican Americans find offensive?

2. What stereotypes of Mexican Americans are presented here? At the end of the play, what image of the Mexican American is presented? How does it compare with the stereotypes?

3. If you are a member of some other minority group, in a few sentences indicate how *Los Vendidos* might be adapted into a play about that group.

4. Putting aside the politics of the play (and your own politics), what do you think are the strengths of *Los Vendidos?* What do you think are the weaknesses?

5. The play was written in 1967. Putting aside a few specific references, for instance to Governor Reagan, do you find it dated? If not, why not?

6. In 1971 when *Los Vendidos* was produced by El Teatro de la Esperanza, the group altered the ending by having the men decide to use the money to build a community center. Evaluate this ending.

7. When the play was videotaped by KNBC in Los Angeles for broadcast in 1973, Valdez changed the ending. In the revised version we discover that a scientist (played by Valdez) masterminds the operation, placing Mexican American models wherever there are persons of Mexican descent. These models soon will become Chicanos (as opposed to persons with Anglo values) and will aid rather than work against their fellows. Evaluate this ending.

8. In his short essay "The Actos," Valdez says, "Actos: Inspire the audience to social action. Illuminate specific points about social problems. Satirize the opposition. Show or hint at a solution. Express what people are feeling." How many of these do you think *Los Vendidos* docs?

9. Many people assume that politics gets in the way of serious art. That is, they assume that artists ought to be concerned with issues that transcend politics. Does this point make any sense to you? Why, or why not?

11

Reading and Writing about Poetry

ELEMENTS OF POETRY

The Speaker and the Poet

The **speaker**, or **voice**, or **mask**, or **persona** (Latin for *mask*) that speaks a poem is not usually identical with the poet who writes it. The author assumes a role, or counterfeits the speech of a person in a particular situation. The nineteenth-century English poet Robert Browning, for instance, in "My Last Duchess" invented a Renaissance Italian duke who, in his palace, talks about his first wife and his art collection with an emissary from a count who is negotiating to offer his daughter in marriage to the duke.

In reading a poem, then, the first and most important question to ask yourself is this: Who is speaking? If an audience and a setting are suggested, keep them in mind, too, although these are not always indicated in a poem. Consider, for example, the following poem.

EMILY DICKINSON (1830–1886)

I'm Nobody! Who are you?
Are you—Nobody—too?
Then there's a pair of us!
Don't tell! they'd banish us—you know!   4

How dreary—to be—Somebody!
How public—like a Frog—
To tell your name—the livelong June—
To an admiring Bog!   8

[1861?]

We can't quite say that the speaker is Emily Dickinson, though if we have read a fair number of her poems we can say that the voice in this poem is familiar, and perhaps here we *can* talk of Dickinson rather than of "the speaker of the poem," since this speaker (unlike Browning's Renaissance duke) clearly is not a figure utterly remote from the poet.

Let's consider the sort of person we hear in "I'm Nobody! Who are you?" (Read it aloud, to see if you agree with what we say. In fact, you should test each of our assertions by reading the poem aloud.)

- The voice in the first line is rather like that of a child playing a game with a friend.
- In the second and third lines the speaker sees the reader as a fellow spirit ("Are you—Nobody—too?") and invites the reader to join her ("Then there's a pair of us!"), to form a sort of conspiracy of silence against outsiders ("Don't tell!").

In "they'd banish us," however, we hear a word that a child would not be likely to use, and we probably feel that the speaker is a shy but (with the right companion) playful adult, who here is speaking to an intimate friend, the reader. By means of "banish," a word that brings to mind images of a king's court, the speaker almost comically inflates and thereby makes fun of the "they" who are opposed to "us."

In the second stanza, or we might better say in the space between the two stanzas, the speaker puts aside the childlike manner. In "How dreary," the first words of the second stanza, we hear a sophisticated voice, one might even say a world-weary voice or a voice perhaps with more than a touch of condescension. But since by now we are paired with the speaker in a conspiracy against outsiders, we enjoy the contrast that the speaker makes between the Nobodies and the Somebodies. Who are these Somebodies, these people who would imperiously "banish" the speaker and the friend? What are the Somebodies like?

How dreary—to be—Somebody!
How public—like a Frog—
To tell your name—the livelong June—
To an admiring Bog!

The last two lines do at least two things:

- They amusingly explain to the speaker's new friend (the reader) in what way a Somebody is public (it proclaims its presence all day), and
- they indicate the absurdity of the Somebody-Frog's behavior (the audience is "an admiring Bog").

By the end of the poem we are quite convinced that it is better to be a Nobody (like Dickinson and the reader?) than a Somebody (a loudmouth).

Dickinson did not always speak in this persona, however. In "Wild Nights," probably written in the same year as "I'm Nobody! Who are you?", Dickinson speaks as an impassioned lover, but we need not assume that the beloved is actually in the presence of the lover. In fact, since the second line says, "Were I with thee," the reader must assume that the person addressed is *not* present. The poem apparently represents a state of mind—a sort of talking to oneself—rather than an address to another person.

Wild Nights—Wild Nights,
Were I with Thee
Wild Nights should be
Our luxury   4

Futile—the Winds
To a Heart in port—
Done with the Compass—
Done with the Chart!   8

Rowing in Eden—
Ah, the Sea!
Might I but moor—Tonight—
In Thee.   12

[c. 1861]

Clearly the speaker is someone passionately in love. The following questions
invite you to look more closely at how the speaker of "Wild Nights" is characterized.

Topics for Critical Thinking and Writing

1. How does this poem communicate the speaker's state of mind? For example, in
   the first stanza (lines 1–4), what—beyond the meaning of the words—is communicated by the repetition of "Wild Nights"? In the last stanza (lines 9–12),
   what is the tone of "Ah, the Sea!"? ("Tone" means something like emotional
   coloring, as for instance a "businesslike tone," a "bitter tone," or an "eager
   tone.")
2. Paraphrase (that is, put into your own words) the second stanza. What does
   this stanza communicate about the speaker's love for the beloved? Compare
   your paraphrase and the original. What does the form of the original sentences
   (the *omission,* for instance, of the verbs of lines 5 and 6 and of the subject in
   lines 7 and 8) communicate?
3. Paraphrase the last stanza. How does "Ah, the Sea!" fit into your paraphrase? If
   you had trouble fitting it in, do you think the poem would be better off without it? If not, why not?

The voice speaking a poem may, of course, have the ring of the author's own
voice, and to make a distinction between speaker and author may at times seem
perverse. In fact, some poetry (especially contemporary American poetry) is
highly autobiographical. Still, even in autobiographical poems it may be convenient to distinguish between author and speaker. The speaker of a given poem is,
let's say, Sylvia Plath in her role as parent, or Sylvia Plath in her role as daughter,
not simply Sylvia Plath the poet.

The Language of Poetry: Diction and Tone

How is a voice or mask or persona created? From the whole of language, the author consciously or unconsciously selects certain words and grammatical constructions; this selection constitutes the persona's diction. It is, then, partly by the diction that we come to know the speaker of a poem. Just as in life there is a
difference between people who speak of a "belly button," a "navel," or an "umbilicus," so in poetry there is a difference between speakers who use one word
rather than another. Of course it is also possible that all three of these words are
part of a given speaker's vocabulary, and the speaker's choice among the three
would depend on the situation. That is, in addressing a child, the speaker would
probably use the word "belly button"; in addressing an adult other than a family
member or close friend, the speaker might be more likely to use "navel"; and if
the speaker is a physician addressing an audience of physicians, he or she might

be most likely to use "umbilicus." But this is only to say, again, that the dramatic situation in which you find yourself helps to define yourself, helps to establish the particular role that you are playing.

Of course some words are used in virtually all poems: *I, see, and,* and the like. Still, the grammatical constructions in which they appear may help to define the speaker. In Dickinson's "Wild Nights," for instance, expressions such as "Were I with Thee" and "Might I" indicate a speaker of an earlier century than ours, and probably an educated speaker.

Speakers have attitudes toward

- themselves,
- their subjects, and
- their audiences,

and, consciously or unconsciously, they choose their words, pitch, and modulation accordingly; all these add up to their tone. In written literature, tone must be detected without the aid of the ear, although it's a good idea to read poetry aloud, trying to find the appropriate tone of voice. That is, the reader must understand by the selection and sequence of words the way the words are meant to sound—playful, angry, confidential, or ironic, for example. The reader must catch what Frost calls "the speaking tone of voice somehow entangled in the words and fastened to the page for the ear of the imagination."

Writing about the Speaker

Robert Frost once said:

> Everything written is as good as it is dramatic. . . . [A poem is] heard as sung or spoken by a person in a scene—in a character, in a setting. By whom, where and when is the question. By the dreamer of a better world out in a storm in autumn; by a lover under a window at night.

Suppose, in reading a poem Frost published in 1916, we try to establish "by whom, where and when" it is spoken. We may not be able to answer all three questions in great detail, but let's see what the poem suggests. As you read it, you'll notice—alerted by the quotation marks—that there are *two* speakers; the poem is a tiny drama. Thus, the closing quotation marks at the end of line 9 signal to us that the first speech is finished.

ROBERT FROST (1874–1963)

The Telephone

"When I was just as far as I could walk
From here today
There was an hour
All still
When leaning with my head against a flower   5
I heard you talk.
Don't say I didn't, for I heard you say—
You spoke from that flower on the window sill—
Do you remember what it was you said?"

"First tell me what it was you thought you heard."   10
"Having found the flower and driven a bee away,
I leaned my head,
And holding by the stalk,
I listened and I thought I caught the word—
What was it? Did you call me by my name?   15
Or did you say—
Someone said 'Come'—I heard it as I bowed."

"I may have thought as much, but not aloud."

"Well, so I came."

                                                                  [1916]

Suppose we ask: Who are these two speakers? What is their relationship? What's going on between them? Where are they? We don't think that these questions can be answered with absolute certainty, but we do think some answers are more probable than others. For instance, line 8 ("You spoke from that flower on the window sill") tells us that the speakers are in a room, probably of a home— rather than, say, in a railroad station—but we can't say whether the home is a farmhouse, or a house in a village, town, or city, or an apartment.

Let's put the questions (even if they may turn out to be unanswerable) into a more specific form.

Topics for Critical Thinking and Writing

1. One speaker speaks lines 1–9, 11–17, and 19. The other speaks lines 10 and 18. Do you think you can tell the gender of each speaker? For sure, probably, or not at all? On what do you base your answer?
2. Try to visualize this miniature drama. In line 7 the first speaker says, "Don't say I didn't, . . . " What happens—what do you see in your mind's eye—after line 6 that causes the speaker to say this?
3. Why do you suppose the speaker of lines 10 and 18 says so little? How would you characterize the tone of these two lines? What sort of relationship do you think exists between the two speakers?
4. How would you characterize the tone of lines 11–17? Of the last line of the poem?

If you haven't jotted down your responses, we suggest that you do so before reading what follows.

Journal Entries

Given questions somewhat like the preceding ones, students were asked to try to identify the speakers by sex, to speculate on their relationship, and then to add whatever they wished to say. One student recorded the following thoughts:

> These two people care about each other--maybe husband and wife, or lovers--and a man is doing most of the talking, though I can't prove it. He has walked as far as possible--that is, as far as possible and still get back on

the same day--and he seemed to hear the other person call him. He claims that she spoke to him "from that flower on the window sill," and that's why I think the second person is a woman. She's at home, near the window. Somehow I even imagine she was at the window near the kitchen sink, maybe working while he was out on this long walk.

Then she speaks one line; she won't say if she did or didn't speak. She is very cautious, or suspicious: "First tell me what it was you thought you heard." Maybe she doesn't want to say something and then have her husband embarrass her by saying, "No, that's not what I thought." Or maybe she just doesn't feel like talking. Then he claims that he heard her speaking through a flower, as though the flower was a telephone, just as though it was hooked up to the flower on the window sill. But at first he won't say what he supposedly heard, or "thought" he heard. Instead, he says that maybe it was someone else: "Someone said 'Come'." Is he teasing her? Pretending that she may have a rival?

Then she speaks--again just one line, saying, "I may have thought as much, but not aloud." She won't admit that she did think this thought. And then the man says, "Well, so I came." Just like that; short and sweet. No more fancy talk about flowers as telephones. He somehow (through telepathy?) got the message, and so here he is. He seems like a sensitive guy, playful (the stuff about the flowers as telephones), but also he knows when to stop kidding around.

Another student also identified the couple as a man and woman and thought that this dialogue occurs after a quarrel:

As the poem goes on, we learn that the man wants to be with the woman, but it starts by telling us that he walked as far away from her as he could. He doesn't say why, but I think from the way the woman speaks later in the poem, they had a fight and he walked out. Then, when he stopped to rest, he thought he heard her voice. He really means that he was thinking of her and he was hoping she was thinking of him. So he returns, and he tells her he heard her calling him, but he pretends he heard her call him through a flower on their window sill. He can't admit that he was thinking about her. This seems very realistic to me; when someone feels a bit ashamed, it's sometimes hard to admit that you were wrong, and you want the other person to tell you that things are OK anyhow. And judging from line 7, when he says "Don't say I didn't," it seems that she is going to interrupt him by denying it. She is still angry, or maybe she doesn't want to make up too quickly. But he wants to pretend that she called him back. So when he says, "Do you remember what it was you said?" she won't admit that she was thinking of him, and she says, "First tell me what it was you thought you heard." She's testing him a little. So he goes on, with the business about flowers as telephones, and he says "someone" called him. He understands that she doesn't want to be pushed into forgiving him, so he backs off. Then she is willing to admit that she did think about him, but still she doesn't quite admit it. She is too proud to say openly that she wants him back but she does say, "I may have thought as much, . . . " And then, since they both have preserved their dignity, and also both have admitted that they care about the other, he can say, "Well, so I came."

Topics for Writing

1. In a paragraph or two or three, *evaluate* one of these two entries recorded by students. Do you think the comments are weak, plausible, or convincing, and *why* do you think so? Can you offer additional supporting evidence or, on the other hand, counterevidence? You may want to set forth your own scenario.

2. Two small questions: In a sentence or two, offer a suggestion as to why in line 11 Frost wrote, "and driven a bee away." After all, the bee plays no role in the poem. Second, in line 17 Frost has the speaker say, "I heard it as I bowed." Of course "bowed" rhymes with "aloud," but let's assume that the need for a rhyme did not dictate the choice of this word. Do you think "I heard it as I bowed" is better than, say, "I heard it as I waited," or "I heard it as I listened"? Why?

3. Write an essay of 500 words either about an uncanny experience of your own or about a quarrel or disagreement that was resolved in a way you had not expected.

Figurative Language

Robert Frost has said, "Poetry provides the one permissible way of saying one thing and meaning another." This, of course, is an exaggeration, but it shrewdly suggests the importance of figurative language—saying one thing in terms of something else. Words have their literal meanings, but they can also be used so that something other than the literal meaning is implied. "My love is a rose" is, literally, nonsense, for a person is not a five-petaled, many-stamened plant with a spiny stem. But the suggestions of *rose* (at least for Robert Burns, who compared his beloved to a rose in the line "My love is like a red, red rose"), include "delicate beauty," "soft," and "perfumed," and thus the word *rose* can be meaningfully applied—figuratively rather than literally—to "my love." The girl is fragrant; her skin is perhaps like a rose in texture and (in some measure) color; she will not keep her beauty long. The poet, that is, has communicated his perception very precisely.

People who write about poetry have found it convenient to name the various kinds of figurative language. Just as the student of geology employs such special terms as *kames* and *eskers*, the student of literature employs special terms to name things as accurately as possible. The following paragraphs discuss the most common terms.

In a **simile**, items from different classes are explicitly compared by a connective such as *like, as,* or *than,* or by a verb such as *appears* or *seems.* (If the objects compared are from the same class, for example, "Tokyo is like Los Angeles," no simile is present.)

Float like a butterfly, sting like a bee.

—Muhammad Ali

It is a beauteous evening, calm and free.
The holy time is quiet as a Nun,
Breathless with adoration.

—William Wordsworth

All of our thoughts will be fairer than doves.

—Elizabeth Bishop

Seems he a dove? His feathers are but borrowed.

—Shakespeare

A **metaphor** asserts the identity, without a connective such as *like* or a verb such as *appears,* of terms that are literally incompatible.

Umbrellas clothe the beach in every hue.

—Elizabeth Bishop

whirlwind fife-and-drum of the storm bends the salt
marsh grass

—Marianne Moore

Two common types of metaphor have Greek names. In **synecdoche** the whole is replaced by the part, or the part by the whole. For example, *bread* in "Give us this day our daily bread" replaces all sorts of food. In **metonymy** something is named that replaces something closely related to it. For example, James Shirley names certain objects, using them to replace social classes (royalty and the peasantry) to which they are related:

Scepter and crown must tumble down
And in the dust be equal made
With the poor crooked scythe and spade.

The attribution of human feelings or characteristics or abstractions to inanimate objects is called **personification**.

Memory,
that exquisite blunderer.

—Amy Clampitt

There's Wrath who has learnt every trick of guerilla warfare,
The shamming dead, the night-raid, the feinted retreat.

—W. H. Auden

Hope, thou bold taster of delight.

—Richard Crashaw

Crashaw's personification, "Hope, thou bold taster of delight," is also an example of the figure called **apostrophe**, an address to a person or thing not literally listening. Wordsworth begins a sonnet by apostrophizing Milton:

Milton, thou shouldst be living at this hour.

What conclusions can we draw about figurative language? First, figurative language, with its literally incompatible terms, forces the reader to attend to the **connotations** (suggestions, associations) rather than to the **denotations** (dictionary definitions) of one of the terms. Second, although figurative language is said to differ from ordinary speech, it is found in ordinary speech as well as in poetry and other literary forms. "It rained cats and dogs," "War is hell," "Don't be a pig," "Mr. Know-it-all," and other tired figures are part of our daily utterances. But through repeated use, these, and most of the figures we use, have lost whatever impact they once had and are only a shade removed from expressions which, though once figurative, have become literal: the *eye* of a needle, a *branch* office, the *face* of a clock. Third, good figurative language is usually concrete, condensed, and interesting.

We should mention, too, that figurative language is not limited to literary writers; it is used by scientists and social scientists—by almost everyone who is concerned with effective expression. Take, for instance, R. H. Tawney's *Religion and the Rise of Capitalism* (1926), a classic of economics. Among the titles of Tawney's chapters are "The Economic Revolution," "The Puritan Movement," and "The New Medicine for Poverty," all of which include metaphors. (To take only the last: Poverty is seen as a sick person or a disease.) Or take this sentence from Tawney (almost any sentence will serve equally well to reveal his bent for metaphor): "By the end of the sixteenth century the divorce between religious theory and economic realities had long been evident." Figures are not a fancy way of speaking. Quite the opposite: Writers use figures because they are forceful and exact. Literal language would not only be less interesting, it would also be less precise.

Imagery and Symbolism

When we read *rose* we may more or less call to mind a picture of a rose, or perhaps we are reminded of the odor or texture of a rose. Whatever in a poem appeals to any of our senses (including sensations of heat as well as of sight, smell, taste, touch, sound) is an image. In short, images are the sensory content of a work, whether literal or figurative. When a poet says "My rose" and is speaking about a rose, we have no figure of speech—though we still have an image. If, however, "My rose" is a shortened form of "My love is a rose," some would say that the poet is using a metaphor; but others would say that because the first term is omitted ("My love is"), the rose is a symbol. A poem about the transience of a rose might compel the reader to feel that the transience of female beauty is the larger theme even though it is never explicitly stated.

Some symbols are **conventional symbols**—people have agreed to accept them as standing for something other than their literal meanings: A poem about the cross would probably be about Christianity; similarly, the rose has long been a symbol for love. In Virginia Woolf's novel *Mrs. Dalloway,* the husband communicates his love by proffering this conventional symbol: "He was holding out flowers—roses, red and white roses. (But he could not bring himself to say he loved her; not in so many words.)" Objects that are not conventional symbols, however, may also give rise to rich, multiple, indefinable associations. The following poem uses the traditional symbol of the rose, but uses it in a nontraditional way.

WILLIAM BLAKE (1757–1827)

The Sick Rose

O rose, thou art sick!
The invisible worm
That flies in the night,
In the howling storm,

4

Has found out thy bed
Of crimson joy,
And his dark secret love

Does thy life destroy.   8

[1794]

A reader might perhaps argue that the worm is invisible (line 2) merely because it is hidden within the rose, but an "invisible worm / That flies in the night"
is more than a long, slender, soft-bodied, creeping animal; and a rose that has, or
is, a "bed / Of crimson joy" is more than a gardener's rose. Blake's worm and rose
suggest things beyond themselves—a stranger, more vibrant world than the world
we are usually aware of. They are, in short, symbolic, though readers will doubtless differ in their interpretations. Perhaps we find ourselves half thinking, for example, that the worm is male, the rose female, and that the poem is about the violation of virginity. Or that the poem is about the destruction of beauty: Woman's
beauty, rooted in joy, is destroyed by a power that feeds on her.

But these interpretations are not fully satisfying: The poem presents a worm
and a rose, and yet it is not merely about a worm and a rose. These objects res-
onate, stimulating our thoughts toward something else, but the something else is
elusive. This is not to say, however, that symbols mean whatever any reader says
they mean. A reader could scarcely support, we imagine, an interpretation arguing
that the poem is about the need to love all aspects of nature. All interpretations
are not equally valid; it's the writer's job to offer a reasonably persuasive interpretation.

A symbol, then, is an image so loaded with significance that it is not simply
literal, and it does not simply stand for something else; it is both itself *and* something else that it richly suggests, a kind of manifestation of something too complex
or too elusive to be otherwise revealed. Blake's poem is about a blighted rose and
at the same time about much more. In a symbol, as Thomas Carlyle wrote, "the
Infinite is made to blend with the Finite, to stand visible, and as it were, attainable
there."

Verbal Irony and Paradox

Among the most common devices in poems is **verbal irony**. The speaker's words
mean more or less the opposite of what they seem to say. Sometimes verbal irony
takes the form of **overstatement**, or **hyperbole**, as when Lady Macbeth says, while
sleepwalking, "All the perfumes of Arabia will not sweeten this little hand."
Sometimes it takes the form of **understatement**, as when Andrew Marvell's
speaker in "To His Coy Mistress" remarks with cautious wryness, "The grave's a
fine and private place, / But none, I think, do there embrace," or when Sylvia
Plath sees an intended suicide as "the big strip tease." Speaking broadly, intensely
emotional contemporary poems like those of Plath often use irony to undercut—
and thus make acceptable—the emotion presented.

Another common device in poems is **paradox**: the assertion of an apparent
contradiction, as in Marvell's "am'rous birds of prey" in "To His Coy Mistress."
Normally we think of amorous birds as gentle—doves, for example—and not as
birds of prey, such as hawks. Another example of an apparent contradiction: In
"Auld Lang Syne" there is the paradox that the remembrance of joy evokes a kind
of sadness.

Structure

The arrangement of the parts, the organization of the entire poem, is its **structure**. Sometimes the poem is divided into blocks of, say, four lines each, but even if the poem is printed as a solid block it probably has some principle of organization. It may move, for example, from sorrow in the first two lines to joy in the next two or from a question in the first three lines to an answer in the last line.

Consider this short poem by an English poet of the seventeenth century.

ROBERT HERRICK (1591–1674)

Upon Julia's Clothes

Whenas in silks my Julia goes,
Then, then (methinks) how sweetly flows
That liquefaction of her clothes.

Next, when I cast mine eyes, and see
That brave° vibration, each way free   5
O, how that glittering taketh me.

[1648]

5 **brave** splendid.

A Sample Essay by a Student: "Herrick's Julia, Julia's Herrick"

One student, Stan Wylie, began thinking about this poem by copying it, double-spaced, and by making the following notes on his copy:

Upon Julia's Clothes

cool tone?

Whenas in silks (my Julia) goes,

3 { Then, then (methinks) how sweetly flows

That liquefaction of her clothes.

"Then, then"—
more
excited?
Almost at
a loss
for words?

3 { Next, when I cast mine eyes, and see

That brave vibration, each way free,

O, how that glittering taketh me.

emotional?

free to do what?
free from what?

Stan got some further ideas by thinking about several of the questions that, in the checklist on pages 649–51, we suggest you ask yourself while rereading a poem. Among the questions are these:

- Does the poem proceed in a straightforward way, or at some point or points does the speaker reverse course, altering his or her tone or perception?
- What is the effect on you of the form?

With such questions in mind, Stan was stimulated to see if there is some sort of reversal or change in Herrick's poem, and if there is, how it is related to the structure. After rereading the poem several times, thinking about it in the light of these questions and perhaps others that came to mind, he produced the following notes:

Two stanzas, each of three lines, with the same structure
Basic structure of first stanza: When X (one line), then Y (two lines)
Basic structure of second stanza: Next (one line), then Z (two lines)

When he marked the text, after reading the poem a few times, Stan noticed that the last line—an exclamation of delight ("O, how that glittering taketh me")—is much more personal than the rest of the poem. A little further thought enabled him to refine this last perception:

Although the pattern of stanzas is repeated, the somewhat analytic, detached tone of the beginning ("Whenas," "Then," "Next") changes to an open, enthusiastic confession of delight in what the poet sees.

Further thinking led to this:

Although the title is "Upon Julia's Clothes," and the first five lines describe Julia's silken dress, the poem finally is not only about Julia's clothing but about the effect of Julia (moving in silk that liquefies or seems to become a liquid) on the poet.

This is a nice observation, but when Stan looked again at the poem the next day, and started to write about it, he found that he was able to refine his observation.

Even at the beginning, the speaker is not entirely detached, for he speaks of "my Julia."

In writing about Herrick's "Upon Julia's Clothes," Stan tells us, the thoughts did not come quickly or neatly. After two or three thoughts, he started to write. Only after drafting a paragraph, and rereading the poem, did he notice that the personal element appears not only in the last line ("taketh *me*") but even in the first line ("*my* Julia"). In short, for almost all of us, the only way to get to a good final essay is to read, to think, to jot down ideas, to write a draft, and to revise and revise again. Having gone through such processes, Stan came up with the following excellent essay.

By the way, Stan did not hit on the final version of his title ("Herrick's Julia, Julia's Herrick") until shortly before he typed his final version. His preliminary title was

Structure and Personality in
Herrick's "Upon Julia's Clothing"

That's a bit heavy-handed but at least it is focused, as opposed to such an uninformative title as "On a Poem." He soon revised his tentative title to

Julia, Julia's Clothing, and Julia's Poet

That's quite a good title: It is neat, and it is appropriate, since it moves (as the poem and the essay do) from Julia and her clothing to the poet. Of course it doesn't tell the reader exactly what the essay will be about, but it does stimulate the reader's interest. The essayist's final title, however, is even better:

Herrick's Julia, Julia's Herrick

Again, it is neat (the balanced structure, and structure is part of the student's topic), and it moves (as the poem itself moves) from Julia to the poet.

Herrick's Julia, Julia's Herrick

Robert Herrick's "Upon Julia's Clothes" begins as a description of Julia's clothing and ends as an expression of the poet's response not just to Julia's clothing but to Julia herself. Despite the apparently objective or detached tone of the first stanza and the first two lines of the second stanza, the poem finally conveys a strong sense of the speaker's excitement.

The first stanza seems to say, "Whenas" X (one line), "Then" Y (two lines). The second stanza repeats this basic structure of one line of assertion and two lines describing the consequence: "Next" (one line), "then" (two lines). But the logic or coolness of "Whenas," "Then," and "Next," and of such rather scientific language as "liquefaction" (a more technical-sounding word than "melting") and "vibration," is undercut by the breathlessness or excitement of "Then, then" (that is very different from a simple "Then"). It is also worth mentioning that although there is a personal rather than a fully detached note even in the first line, in "<u>my</u> Julia," this expression scarcely reveals much feeling. In fact, it reveals a touch of male chauvinism, a suggestion that the woman is a possession of the speaker's. Not until the last line does the speaker reveal that, far from Julia being his possession, he is possessed by Julia: "O, how that glittering taketh me." If he begins coolly, objectively, and somewhat complacently, and uses a structure that suggests a somewhat detached mind, in the exclamatory "O" he nevertheless at last confesses (to our delight) that he is enraptured by Julia.

The Analysis Analyzed

Other things, of course, might be said about this poem. For instance, the writer says nothing about the changes in the basic iambic meter and their contributions to the poem. We have in mind not so much the trochees (a trochee is a metrical foot with a stressed syllable followed by an unstressed one) at the beginning of some lines, which is a fairly routine variation, but the spondees (two consecutive stresses) in "Then, then" and "O, how" and the almost-spondees in "Next, when," "each way free," and "that glittering." Also of interest are the two run-on lines (line 2 runs into 3, and 4 runs into 5) introducing related expressions, "That lique-faction" and "that brave vibration."

He also doesn't comment on the *s* and *z* sounds (*Whenas, silk, goes, thinks, sweetly flows*), which presumably imitate the sound of a silk gown in motion, a sound that can be said to resemble the sound of liquid, hence *liquefaction*— though the dress in motion also visually resembles flowing liquid. But the present essay seems excellent to us, and the neglected topics—sound effects in the poem—might be material for another essay.

EDNA ST. VINCENT MILLAY

Edna St. Vincent Millay (1892–1950) was born in Rockland, Maine. Even as a child she wrote poetry, and by the time she graduated from Vassar College (1917) she had achieved some note as a poet. Millay settled for a while in Greenwich Village, a center of Bohemian activity in New York City, where she wrote, performed in plays, and engaged in feminist causes. In 1923, the year she married, she became the first woman to win the Pulitzer Prize for Poetry. Numerous other awards followed. Though she is best known as a lyric poet—especially as a writer of sonnets—she also wrote memorable political poetry and nature poetry as well as short stories, plays, and a libretto for an opera.

Love Is Not All: It Is Not Meat nor Drink

Love is not all: it is not meat nor drink
Nor slumber nor a roof against the rain;
Nor yet a floating spar to men that sink
And rise and sink and rise and sink again;   4
Love can not fill the thickened lung with breath,
Nor clean the blood, nor set the fractured bone;
Yet many a man is making friends with death
Even as I speak, for lack of love alone.   8

It well may be that in a difficult hour,
Pinned down by pain and moaning for release,
Or nagged by want past resolution's power,
I might be driven to sell your love for peace,   12
Or trade the memory of this night for food.
It well may be. I do not think I would.

[1931]

Topics for Critical Thinking and Writing

1. "Love Is Not All" is a sonnet. Using your own words, briefly summarize the ar-gument of the octet (the first 8 lines). Next, paraphrase the sestet, line by line.

On the whole, does the sestet repeat the idea of the octet, or does it add a new idea? Whom did you imagine to be speaking the octet? What does the sestet add to your knowledge of the speaker and the occasion? (And how did you paraphrase line 11?)

2. The first and last lines of the poem consist of words of one syllable, and both lines have a distinct pause in the middle. Do you imagine the lines to be spoken in the same tone of voice? If not, can you describe the difference and account for it?

3. Lines 7 and 8 appear to mean that the absence of love can be a cause of death. To what degree do you believe that to be true?

4. Would you call "Love Is Not All" a love poem? Why or why not? Describe the kind of person who might include the poem in a love letter or valentine, or who would be happy to receive it. (One of our friends recited it at her wedding. What do you think of that idea?)

CHRISTINA ROSSETTI (1830–1894)

In an Artist's Studio

One face looks out from all his canvases,
    One selfsame figure sits or walks or leans:
    We found her hidden just behind those screens,
That mirror gave back all her loveliness.   4
A queen in opal or in ruby dress,
    A nameless girl in freshest summer-greens
    A saint, an angel—every canvas means
The same one meaning, neither more nor less.   8
He feeds upon her face by day and night,
    And she with true kind eyes looks back on him,
Fair as the moon and joyful as the light:
    Not wan with waiting, not with sorrow dim;   12
Not as she is, but was when hope shone bright;
    Not as she is, but as she fills his dream.

                               [1856]

This poem is a sonnet. We discuss the form later, on page 649, but if you study the rhymes here you will notice that the first eight lines are united by rhymes, and the next six by different rhymes. A reader might, for a start at least, think about whether what is said has any relation to these units. The first eight lines are about the model, but are the next six equally about her or about someone else?

Topics for Critical Thinking

1. What do we know about the model in the first eight lines? What do we know about her in the last two lines?

2. How are the contrasts (between then and now, between model and painter) communicated by the repetition of "Not as she is," in lines 13 and 14?

EXPLICATION

As we said in Chapter 3, a line-by-line commentary on what is going on in a text is an explication (literally, unfolding, or spreading out). Although your explication will for the most part move steadily from the beginning to the end of the selection, try to avoid writing along these lines (or, we might say, along this one line): "In the first line. . . . In the second line. . . . In the third line. . . ." That is, don't hesitate to write such things as

> The poem begins. . . . In the next line. . . . The speaker immediately adds. . . .
> He then introduces. . . . The next stanza begins by complicating the tone. . . .

And of course you can discuss the second line before the first if that seems the best way of handling the passage.

An explication is not a paraphrase (a rewording, a sort of translation)—though it may include paraphrase if a passage in the original seems unclear, perhaps because of an unusual word or an unfamiliar expression. On the whole, however, an explication goes beyond paraphrase, seeking to make explicit what the reader perceives as implicit in the work. It is chiefly concerned with

- Connotations of words—for instance, "look" versus "behold"
- Implications of syntax—for instance, whether it is notably complex (thereby implying one sort of speaker) or notably simple (implying a very different sort of speaker)
- Implications of rhyme—for instance, the implied connection in meaning between "throne" and "alone"
- Patterns of imagery—for instance, commercial imagery in a love poem

As we said in Chapters 3 and 4, explication and analysis are not clearly distinct from each other; it is reasonable to think of explication as a kind of analysis operating on the level of verbal details.

An Example

Take this short poem (published in 1917) by the Irish poet William Butler Yeats. The "balloon" in the poem is a dirigible, a blimp.

WILLIAM BUTLER YEATS (1865–1939)

The Balloon of the Mind

Hands, do what you're bid:
Bring the balloon of the mind
That bellies and drags in the wind
Into its narrow shed.

[1917]

Annotations and Journal Entries

A student, Tina Washington, began thinking about the poem by copying it, double-spaced. Then she jotted down her first thoughts:

sounds abrupt

Hands, do what you're bid:

                                      --balloon imagined by the
                                      mind? Or a mind like a

Bring the balloon of the mind   *balloon?*

That bellies and drags in the wind   *no real rhymes?*

Into its narrow shed.   *line seems to drag--*
                                        it's so long!

Later she wrote some notes in a journal:

> I'm still puzzled about the meaning of the words "The balloon of the mind." Does "balloon of the mind" mean a balloon that belongs to the mind, sort of like "a disease of the heart"? If so, it means a balloon that the mind has, a balloon that the mind possesses, I guess by imagining it. Or does it mean that the mind is like a balloon, as when you say "he's a pig of a man," meaning he is like a pig, he is a pig? Can it mean both? What's a balloon that the mind imagines? Something like dreams of fame, wealth? Castles in Spain.
>
> Is Yeats saying that the "hands" have to work hard to make dreams a reality? Maybe. But maybe the idea really is that the mind is like a balloon-- hard to keep under control, floating around. Very hard to keep the mind on the job. If the mind is like a balloon, it's hard to get it into the hangar (shed).
>
> "Bellies." Is there such a verb? In this poem it seems to mean something like "puffs out" or "flops around in the wind." Just checked The American Heritage Dictionary, and it says "belly" can be a verb, "to swell out," "to bulge." Well, you learn something every day.

A later entry:

> OK; I think the poem is about a writer trying to keep his balloon-like mind from floating around, trying to keep the mind under control, trying to keep it working at the job of writing something, maybe writing something with the "clarity, unity, and coherence" I keep hearing about in this course.

A Sample Essay by a Student: Explication of W. B. Yeats's "The Balloon of the Mind"

Here is Tina Washington's final version of the explication:

> Yeats's "Balloon of the Mind" is about writing poetry, specifically about the difficulty of getting one's floating thoughts down in lines on the page. The first line, a short, stern, heavily stressed command to the speaker's hands, perhaps implies by its severe or impatient tone that these hands will be disobedient or inept or careless if not watched closely: the

poor bumbling body so often fails to achieve the goals of the mind. The bluntness of the command in the first line is emphasized by the fact that all the subsequent lines have more syllables. Furthermore, the first line is a grammatically complete sentence, whereas the thought of line 2 spills over into the next lines, implying the difficulty of fitting ideas into confining spaces, that is, of getting one's thoughts into order, especially into a coherent poem.

Lines 2 and 3 amplify the metaphor already stated in the title (the product of the mind is an airy but unwieldy balloon), and they also contain a second command, "Bring." Alliteration ties this command, "Bring," to the earlier "bid"; it also ties both of these verbs to their object, "balloon," and to the verb that most effectively describes the balloon, "bellies." In comparison with the abrupt first line of the poem, lines 2 and 3 themselves seem almost swollen, bellying and dragging, an effect aided by using adjacent unstressed syllables ("of the," "[bell]ies and," "in the") and by using an eye rhyme ("mind" and "wind") rather than an exact rhyme. And then comes the short last line: almost before we could expect it, the cumbersome balloon-- here, the idea that is to be packed into the stanza--is successfully lodged in its "narrow shed." Aside from the relatively colorless "into," the only words of more than one syllable in the poem are "balloon," "bellies," and "narrow," and all three emphasize the difficulty of the task. But after "narrow"--the word itself almost looks long and narrow, in this context like a hangar--we get the simplicity of the monosyllable "shed." The difficult job is done, the thought is safely packed away, the poem is completed--but again with an off-rhyme ("bid" and "shed"), for neatness can go only so far when hands and mind and a balloon are involved.

Note: The reader of an explication needs to see the text, and because the explicated text is usually short, it is advisable to quote it all. (Remember, your imagined audience probably consists of your classmates; even if they have already read the work you are explicating, they have not memorized it, and so you helpfully remind them of the work by quoting it.) You can quote the entire text at the outset, or you can quote the first unit (for example, a stanza), then explicate that unit, and then quote the next unit, and so on. And if the poem or passage of prose is longer than, say, six lines, it is advisable to number each line at the right for easy reference.

✔ CHECKLIST: *Explication*

On pages 48–49 we provided an Explication Checklist. We include it again here, for convenience.

Overall Considerations

❏ Does the poem imply a story of some sort, for instance the speaker's report of a love affair, or of a response to nature? If so, what is its beginning, middle, and end?
❏ If you detect a story in the speaker's mind, a change of mood—for instance, a shift from bitterness that a love affair has ended to hope for its renewal—is this change communicated in part by the connotations of certain words? By syntax? By metrical shifts?

Detailed Considerations

❏ If the poem has a title other than the first line, what are the implications of the title?
❏ Are there clusters or patterns of imagery, for instance religious images, economic images, or images drawn from nature? If so, how do they contribute to the meaning of the poem?
❏ Is irony (understatement or overstatement) used? To what effect?
❏ How do the connotations of certain words (for instance, "dad" rather than "father") help to establish the meaning?
❏ What are the implications of the syntax—for instance, of notably simple or notably complex sentences? What do such sentences tell us about the speaker?
❏ Do metrical variations occur, and if so, what is their significance?
❏ Do rhyming words have some meaningful connection, as in the clichés "moon" and "June," "dove" and "love"?
❏ What are the implications of the appearance of the poem on the page—for example, of an indented line, or of the stanzaic pattern? (For instance, if the poem consists of two stanzas of four lines each, does the second stanza offer a reversal of the first?)

RHYTHM AND VERSIFICATION: A GLOSSARY FOR REFERENCE

Rhythm (most simply, in English poetry, stresses at regular intervals) has a power of its own. A highly pronounced rhythm is common in such forms of poetry as charms, college yells, and lullabies; all of them are aimed at inducing a special effect magically. It is not surprising that *carmen,* the Latin word for poem or song, is also the Latin word for *charm* and the word from which our word *charm* is derived.

In much poetry, rhythm is only half heard, but its presence is suggested by the way poetry is printed. Prose (from Latin *prorsus,* "forward," "straight on") keeps running across the paper until the right-hand margin is reached; then, merely because the paper has given out, the writer or printer starts again at the left, with a small letter. But verse (Latin *versus,* "a turning") often ends well short of the right-hand margin. The next line begins at the left—usually with a capital—not because paper has run out but because the rhythmic pattern begins again. Lines of poetry are continually reminding us that they have a pattern.

Note that a mechanical, unvarying rhythm may be good to put the baby to sleep, but it can be deadly to readers who want to stay awake. Poets vary their rhythm according to their purposes; they ought not to be so regular that they are (in W. H. Auden's words) "accentual pests." In competent hands, rhythm contributes to meaning; it says something. Ezra Pound had a relevant comment: "Rhythm *must* have meaning. It can't be merely a careless dash off, with no grip and no real hold to the words and sense, a tumty tum tumty tum tum ta."

Consider this description of Hell from John Milton's *Paradise Lost* (stressed syllables are marked by ´, unstressed syllables by ˘:

Rócks, cáves, lákes, féns, bógs, déns, ănd shádes ŏf déath.

The normal line in *Paradise Lost* is written in iambic feet—alternate unstressed and stressed syllables—but in this line Milton immediately follows one heavy stress with another, helping to communicate the "meaning"—the oppressive monotony of Hell. As a second example, consider the function of the rhythm in two lines by Alexander Pope:

Whĕn Ájax strĭves sŏme róck's vást wéight tŏ thrów,
Thĕ líne tóo lábŏrs, ănd thĕ wórds móve slów.

The stressed syllables do not merely alternate with the unstressed ones; rather the great weight of the rock is suggested by three consecutive stressed words, "rock's vast weight," and the great effort involved in moving it is suggested by another three consecutive stresses, "line too labors," and by yet another three, "words move slow." Note also the abundant pauses within the lines. In the first line, for example, unless one's speech is slovenly, one must pause at least slightly after "Ajax," "strives," "rock's," "vast," "weight," and "throw." The grating sounds in "Ajax" and "rock's" do their work, too, and so do the explosive *t*'s.

When Pope wishes to suggest lightness, he reverses his procedure, and he groups *un*stressed syllables:

Not so, when swift Camilla scours the plain,
Fliĕs o'ĕr th' ŭnbénding córn, ănd skíms ălŏng thĕ máin.

This last line has twelve syllables and is thus longer than the line about Ajax, but the addition of *along* helps to communicate lightness and swiftness because in this line (it can be argued) neither syllable of *along* is strongly stressed. If *along* is omitted, the line still makes grammatical sense and becomes more "regular," but it also becomes less imitative of lightness.

The very regularity of a line may be meaningful too. Shakespeare begins a sonnet thus:

Whĕn Í dŏ cóunt thĕ clóck thăt télls thĕ tíme.

This line about a mechanism runs with appropriate regularity. (It is worth noting, too, that "count the clock" and "tells the time" emphasize the regularity by the repetition of sounds and syntax.) But notice what Shakespeare does in the middle of the next line:

> Aňd sée tȟe bráve dáy súnk ĭn hídeŏus níght.

The technical vocabulary of **prosody** (the study of the principles of verse structure, including meter, rhyme and other sound effects, and stanzaic patterns) is large. An understanding of these terms will not turn anyone into a poet, but it will enable you to write about some aspects of poetry more efficiently. The following are the chief terms of prosody.

Meter

Most poetry written in English has a pattern of stressed (accented) sounds. This pattern is the **meter** (from the Greek word for "measure"). Strictly speaking, we really should not talk of "unstressed" or "unaccented" syllables, since to utter a syllable—however lightly—is to give it some stress. It is really a matter of *relative* stress, but the fact is that "unstressed" or "unaccented" are parts of the established terminology of versification.

In a line of poetry, the **foot** is the basic unit of measurement. It is on rare occasions a single stressed syllable; but generally a foot consists of two or three syllables, one of which is stressed. The repetition of feet, then, produces a pattern of stresses throughout the poem.

Two cautions:

- A poem will seldom contain only one kind of foot throughout; significant variations usually occur, but one kind of foot is dominant.
- In reading a poem, one chiefly pays attention to the sense, not to presupposed metrical pattern. By paying attention to the sense, one often finds (reading aloud is a great help) that the stress falls on a word that according to the metrical pattern would be unstressed. Or a word that according to the pattern would be stressed may be seen to be unstressed. Furthermore, by reading for sense one finds that not all stresses are equally heavy; some are almost as light as unstressed syllables, and sometimes there is a **hovering stress**—that is, the stress is equally distributed over two adjacent syllables. To repeat: One reads for sense, allowing the syntax to help indicate the stresses.

METRICAL FEET The most common feet in English poetry are the six listed here. **Iamb** (adjective: **iambic**): one unstressed syllable followed by one stressed syllable. The iamb, said to be the most common pattern in English speech, is surely the most common in English poetry. The following example has four iambic feet:

> Mý héart ĭs líke ă sínging bírd.
>
> —Christina Rossetti

Trochee (trochaic): one stressed syllable followed by one unstressed.

> Wé wĕre véry tírĕd, wé wĕre véry mérřy
>
> —Edna St. Vincent Millay

Anapest (anapestic): two unstressed syllables followed by one stressed.

Thĕre ărĕ mánў whŏ sáy thăt ă dóg hăs h̆is dáy.

—Dylan Thomas

Dactyl (dactylic): one stressed syllable followed by two unstressed. This trisyllabic foot, like the anapest, is common in light verse or verse suggesting joy, but its use is not limited to such material, as Longfellow's *Evangeline* shows. Thomas Hood's sentimental "The Bridge of Sighs" begins

Táke hĕr ŭp ténderlў.

Spondee (spondaic): two stressed syllables; most often used as a substitute for an iamb or trochee.

Smárt lád, t̆o slip bĕtímĕs ăwáy.

—A. E. Housman

Pyrrhic: two unstressed syllables; it is often not considered a legitimate foot in English.

METRICAL LINES   A metrical line consists of one or more feet and is named for the number of feet in it. The following names are used:

monometer: one foot   **pentameter**: five feet
dimeter: two feet   **hexameter**: six feet
trimeter: three feet   **heptameter**: seven feet
tetrameter: four feet

A line is scanned for the kind and number of feet in it, and the **scansion** tells you if it is, say, anapestic trimeter (three anapests):

Ăs Ĭ cáme t̆o thĕ édge ŏf thĕ wóods.

—Robert Frost

Or, in another example, iambic pentameter:

Thĕ súmmĕr thúndĕr, lĭke ă wóodĕn bĕll

—Louise Bogan

A line ending with a stress has a **masculine ending**; a line ending with an extra unstressed syllable has a **feminine ending**. The **caesura** (usually indicated by the symbol / /) is a slight pause within the line. It need not be indicated by punctuation (notice the fourth and fifth lines in the following quotation), and it does not affect the metrical count:

Awake, my St. John! / / leave all meaner things
To low ambition, / / and the pride of kings.
Let us / / (since Life can little more supply
Than just to look about us / / and to die)
Expatiate free / / o'er all this scene of Man;
A mighty maze! / / but not without a plan;
A wild, / / where weeds and flowers promiscuous shoot;
Or garden, / / tempting with forbidden fruit.

—Alexander Pope

The varying position of the caesura helps to give Pope's lines an informality that plays against the formality of the pairs of rhyming lines.

An **end-stopped line** concludes with a distinct syntactical pause, but a **run-on line** has its sense carried over into the next line without syntactical pause. (The running-on of a line is called **enjambment**.) In the following passage, only the first is a run-on line:

> Yet if we look more closely we shall find
> Most have the seeds of judgment in their mind:
> Nature affords at least a glimmering light;
> The lines, though touched but faintly, are drawn right.
>
> —Alexander Pope

Meter produces **rhythm**, recurrences at equal intervals, but rhythm (from a Greek word meaning "flow") is usually applied to larger units than feet. Often it depends most obviously on pauses. Thus, a poem with run-on lines will have a different rhythm from a poem with end-stopped lines, even though both are in the same meter. And prose, though it is unmetrical, can have rhythm, too.

In addition to being affected by syntactical pause, rhythm is affected by pauses attributable to consonant clusters and to the length of words. Polysyllabic words establish a different rhythm from monosyllabic words, even in metrically identical lines. We can say, then, that rhythm is altered by shifts in meter, syntax, and the length and ease of pronunciation. But even with no such shift, even if a line is repeated verbatim, a reader may sense a change in rhythm. The rhythm of the final line of a poem, for example, may well differ from that of the line before, even though in all other respects the lines are identical, as in Frost's "Stopping by Woods on a Snowy Evening" (p. 704), which concludes by repeating "And miles to go before I sleep." The reader may simply sense that this final line ought to be spoken, say, more slowly and with more stress on "miles."

Patterns of Sound

Though rhythm is basic to poetry, **rhyme**—the repetition of identical or similar stressed sound or sounds—is not. Rhyme is, presumably, pleasant in itself; it suggests order; and it also may be related to meaning, for it brings two words sharply together, often implying a relationship, as in the now trite *dove* and *love*, or in the more imaginative *throne* and *alone*.

Perfect rhyme (or **exact rhyme**): Differing consonant sounds are followed by identical stressed vowel sounds, and the following sounds, if any, are identical (*foe— toe; meet—fleet; buffer—rougher*). Notice that perfect rhyme involves identity of sound, not of spelling. *Fix* and *sticks,* like *buffer* and *rougher,* are perfect rhymes.

Half-rhyme (or **off-rhyme**): Only the final consonant sounds of the words are identical; the stressed vowel sounds as well as the initial consonant sounds, if any, differ (*soul—oil; mirth—forth; trolley—bully*).

Eye rhyme: The sounds do not in fact rhyme, but the words look as though they would rhyme (*cough—bough*).

Masculine rhyme: The final syllables are stressed and, after their differing initial consonant sounds, are identical in sound (*stark—mark; support—retort*).

Feminine rhyme (or **double rhyme**): Stressed rhyming syllables are followed by identical unstressed syllables (*revival—arrival; flatter—batter*). **Triple rhyme** is a kind of feminine rhyme in which identical stressed vowel sounds are followed by two identical unstressed syllables (*machinery—scenery; tenderly—slenderly*).

End rhyme (or **terminal rhyme**): The rhyming words occur at the ends of the lines.

Internal rhyme: At least one of the rhyming words occurs within the line (Oscar Wilde's "Each narrow *cell* in which we *dwell*").

Alliteration: sometimes defined as the repetition of initial sounds ("*A*ll the *a*wful *a*uguries," or "*B*ring me my *b*ow of *b*urning gold"), and sometimes as the prominent repetition of a consonant ("*a*f*t*er li*f*e's *fit*ful *f*ever").

Assonance: the repetition, in words of proximity, of identical vowel sounds preceded and followed by differing consonant sounds. Whereas *tide* and *hide* are rhymes, *tide* and *mine* are assonantal.

Consonance: the repetition of identical consonant sounds and differing vowel sounds in words in proximity (*fail—feel; rough—roof; pitter—patter*). Sometimes consonance is more loosely defined merely as the repetition of a consonant (*fail—peel*).

Onomatopoeia: the use of words that imitate sounds, such as *hiss* and *buzz*. There is a mistaken tendency to see onomatopoeia everywhere—for example, in *thunder* and *horror*. Many words sometimes thought to be onomatopoeic are not clearly imitative of the thing they refer to; they merely contain some sounds that, when we know what the word means, seem to have some resemblance to the thing they denote. Tennyson's lines from "Come down, O maid" are usually cited as an example of onomatopoeia:

> The moan of doves in immemorial elms
> And murmuring of innumerable bees.

Stanzaic Patterns

Lines of poetry are commonly arranged in a rhythmical unit called a stanza (from an Italian word meaning "room" or "stopping-place"). Usually all the stanzas in a poem have the same rhyme pattern. A stanza is sometimes called a **verse**, though *verse* may also mean a single line of poetry. (In discussing stanzas, rhymes are indicated by identical letters. Thus, *abab* indicates that the first and third lines rhyme with each other, while the second and fourth lines are linked by a different rhyme. An unrhymed line is denoted by *x*.) Common stanzaic forms in English poetry are the following:

Couplet: a stanza of two lines, usually, but not necessarily, with end-rhymes. *Couplet* is also used for a pair of rhyming lines. The **octosyllabic couplet** is iambic or trochaic tetrameter:

> Had we but world enough, and time,
> This coyness, lady, were no crime.

> —Andrew Marvell

Heroic couplet: a rhyming couplet of iambic pentameter, often "closed," that is, containing a complete thought, with a fairly heavy pause at the end of the first line and a still heavier one at the end of the second. Commonly, there is a parallel or an *antithesis* (contrast) within a line or between the two lines. It is called heroic because in England, especially in the eighteenth century, it was much used for heroic (epic) poems.

> Some foreign writers, some our own despise;
> The ancients only, or the moderns, prize.

> —Alexander Pope

Triplet (or **tercet**): a three-line stanza, usually with one rhyme:

> Whenas in silks my Julia goes
> Then, then (methinks) how sweetly flows
> That liquefaction of her clothes.

—Robert Herrick

Quatrain: a four-line stanza, rhymed or unrhymed. The **heroic** (or **elegiac**) **quatrain** is iambic pentameter, rhyming *abab*. That is, the first and third lines rhyme (so they are designated *a*), and the second and fourth lines rhyme (so they are designated *b*).

Sonnet: a fourteen-line poem, predominantly in iambic pentameter. The rhyme is usually according to one of two schemes. The **Italian** (or **Petrarchan**[1] **sonnet** has two divisions: The first eight lines (rhyming *abba abba*) are the **octave**, and the last six (rhyming *cd cd cd*, or a variant) are the **sestet** (page 711). The second kind of sonnet, the **English** (or **Shakespearean**) **sonnet**, is usually arranged into three quatrains and a couplet, rhyming *abab cdcd efef gg*. (For an example see page 50.) In many sonnets there is a marked correspondence between the rhyme scheme and the development of the thought. Thus an Italian sonnet may state a generalization in the octave and a specific example in the sestet. Or an English sonnet may give three examples—one in each quatrain—and draw a conclusion in the couplet.

Blank Verse and Free Verse

A good deal of English poetry is unrhymed, much of it in **blank verse**, that is, un-rhymed iambic pentameter. Introduced into English poetry by Henry Howard, Earl of Surrey, in the middle of the sixteenth century, late in the century it became the standard medium (especially in the hands of Christopher Marlowe and Shakespeare) of English drama. In the seventeenth century, Milton used blank verse for *Paradise Lost,* and it has continued to be used in both dramatic and non-dramatic literature. For an example, see the first scene of *Hamlet* (p. 408), until the Ghost appears.

The second kind of unrhymed poetry fairly common in English, especially in the twentieth century, is **free verse** (or **vers libre**): rhythmical lines varying in length, adhering to no fixed metrical pattern and usually unrhymed. The pattern is often largely based on repetition and parallel grammatical structure. For an example, see T. S. Eliot's "The Love Song of J. Alfred Prufrock" (p. 715).

✔ **CHECKLIST:** *Getting Ideas for Writing about Poetry*

If you are going to write about a fairly short poem (say, under thirty lines), it's not a bad idea to copy out the poem, writing or typing it double-spaced. By writing it out you will be forced to notice details, down to the punctuation. After you have copied the poem, proofread it carefully against the original. Catching an error—even the addition or omission of a comma—may help you to notice a detail in the original

---

[1]So called after Francesco Petrarch (1304–74), the Italian poet who perfected and popularized the form.

that you might otherwise have overlooked. And of course, now that you have the poem with ample space between the lines, you have a worksheet with room for jottings.

A good essay is based on a genuine response to a poem; a response may be stimulated in part by first reading the poem aloud and then considering the following questions.

First Response

❏ What was your response to the poem on first reading? Did some parts especially please or displease you, or puzzle you? After some study—perhaps checking the meanings of some of the words in a dictionary and reading the poem several times—did you modify your initial response to the parts and to the whole?

Speaker and Tone

❏ Who is the speaker? (Consider age, sex, personality, frame of mind, and tone of voice.) Is the speaker defined fairly precisely (for instance, an older woman speaking to a child), or is the speaker simply a voice meditating? (Jot down your first impressions, then reread the poem and make further jottings, if necessary.)
❏ Do you think the speaker is fully aware of what he or she is saying, or does the speaker unconsciously reveal his or her personality and values? What is your attitude toward this speaker?
❏ Is the speaker narrating or reflecting on an earlier experience or attitude? If so, does he or she convey a sense of new awareness, such as of regret for innocence lost?

Audience

❏ To whom is the speaker speaking? What is the situation (including time and place)? (In some poems, a listener is strongly implied, but in others, especially those in which the speaker is meditating, there may be no audience other than the reader, who "overhears" the speaker.)

Structure and Form

❏ Does the poem proceed in a straightforward way, or at some point or points does the speaker reverse course, altering his or her tone or perception? If there is a shift, what do you make of it?
❏ Is the poem organized into sections? If so, what are these sections—stanzas, for instance—and how does each section (characterized, perhaps, by a certain tone of voice, or a group of rhymes) grow out of what precedes it?
❏ What is the effect on you of the form—say, quatrains (stanzas of four lines) or blank verse (unrhymed lines of ten syllables)? If the sense overflows the form, running without pause from (for example) one quatrain into the next, what effect is created?

Center of Interest and Theme

❏ What is the poem about? Is the interest chiefly in a distinctive character, or in meditation? That is, is the poem chiefly psychological or chiefly philosophical?
❏ Is the theme stated explicitly (directly) or implicitly? How might you state the theme in a sentence?

Diction

❏ Do certain words have rich and relevant associations that relate to other words and help to define the speaker or the theme or both?

❏ What is the role of figurative language, if any? Does it help to define the speaker or the theme?

❏ What do you think is to be taken figuratively or symbolically, and what literally?

Sound Effects

❏ What is the role of sound effects, including repetitions of sound (for instance, alliteration) and of entire words, and shifts in versification?

❏ If there are off-rhymes (for instance "dizzy" and "easy," or "home" and "come"), what effect do they have on you? Do they, for instance, add a note of tentativeness or uncertainty?

❏ If there are unexpected stresses or pauses, what do they communicate about the speaker's experience? How do they affect you?

YOUR TURN: POEMS ABOUT PEOPLE, PLACES, AND THINGS

People

ANDREW MARVELL

Born in 1621 near Hull in England, Marvell attended Trinity College, Cambridge, and graduated in 1638. During the Civil War he was tutor to the daughter of Sir Thomas Fairfax in Yorkshire at Nun Appleton House, where most of his best-known poems were written. In 1657 he was appointed assistant to John Milton, the Latin Secretary for the Commonwealth. After the Restoration of the monarchy in 1659 until his death, Marvell represented Hull as a member of Parliament. Most of his poems were not published until after his death in 1678.

To His Coy Mistress

Had we but world enough, and time.
This coyness, lady, were no crime.
We would sit down, and think which way
To walk, and pass our long love's day.
Thou by the Indian Ganges' side   5
Should'st rubies find: I by the tide
Of Humber° would complain.° I would
Love you ten years before the Flood,
And you should, if you please, refuse
Till the conversion of the Jews.   10
My vegetable° love should grow
Vaster than empires, and more slow.
An hundred years should go to praise
Thine eyes, and on thy forehead gaze:
Two hundred to adore each breast: 15
But thirty thousand to the rest.
An age at least to every part,
And the last age should show your heart.

---

7 Humber river in England;   **complain** write love poems.   **11 vegetable** slowly growing.

For, lady, you deserve this state,
Nor would I love at lower rate,   20
    But at my back I always hear
Time's winged chariot hurrying near;
And yonder all before us lie
Deserts of vast eternity.
Thy beauty shall no more be found,   25
Nor in thy marble vault shall sound
My echoing song; then worms shall try
That long preserved virginity,
And your quaint honor turn to dust,
And into ashes all my lust.   30
The grave's a fine and private place,
But none, I think, do there embrace.
        Now therefore, while the youthful hue
Sits on thy skin like morning dew,
And while thy willing soul transpires   35
At every pore with instant fires,
Now let us sport us while we may;
And now, like am'rous birds of prey,
Rather at once our time devour,
Than languish in his slow-chapt° power,   40
Let us roll all our strength, and all
Our sweetness, up into one ball;
And tear our pleasures with rough strife
Thorough° the iron gates of life.
Thus, though we cannot make our sun   45
Stand still, yet we will make him run.

                                                                    [1641]

40 **slow-chapt** slowly devouring.   44 **thorough** through.

Topics for Critical Thinking and Writing

1. What does "coy" mean in the title, and "coyness" in line 2?
2. Do you think that the speaker's claims in lines 1–20 are so inflated that we detect behind them a playfully ironic tone? Explain. Why does the speaker say in line 8 that he would love "ten years before the Flood," rather than merely "since the Flood"?
3. What do you make of lines 21–24? Why is time behind the speaker, and eternity in front of him? Is this "eternity" the same as the period discussed in lines 1–20? Discuss the change in the speaker's tone after line 20.

ROBERT BROWNING

Born in a suburb of London into a middle-class family, Browning (1812–89) was educated primarily at home, where he read widely. For a while he wrote for the stage, and in 1846 he married Elizabeth Barrett—herself a poet—and lived with her in Italy until her death in 1861. He then returned to England and settled in London with their son. Regarded as one of the most distinguished poets of the Victorian period, he is buried in Westminster Abbey.

My Last Duchess

Ferrara*

That's my last Duchess painted on the wall,
Looking as if she were alive. I call
That piece a wonder, now; Frà Pandolf's° hands
Worked busily a day, and there she stands.
Will't please you sit and look at her? I said   5
"Frà Pandolf" by design, for never read
Strangers like you that pictured countenance,
The depth and passion of its earnest glance,
But to myself they turned (since none puts by
The curtain I have drawn for you, but I)   10
And seemed as they would ask me, if they durst,
How such a glance came there; so, not the first
Are you to turn and ask thus. Sir, 'twas not
Her husband's presence only, called that spot
Of joy into the Duchess' cheek; perhaps   15
Frà Pandolf chanced to say "Her mantle laps
Over my lady's wrist too much," or, "Paint
Must never hope to reproduce the faint
Half-flush that dies along her throat." Such stuff
Was courtesy, she thought, and cause enough   20
For calling up that spot of joy. She had
A heart—how shall I say?—too soon made glad,
Too easily impressed; she liked whate'er
She looked on, and her looks went everywhere.
Sir, 'twas all one! My favor at her breast,   25
The dropping of the daylight in the west,
The bough of cherries some officious fool
Broke in the orchard for her, the white mule
She rode with round the terrace—all and each
Would draw from her alike the approving speech,   30
Or blush, at least. She thanked men—good! but thanked
Somehow—I know not how—as if she ranked
My gift of a nine-hundred-years-old name
With anybody's gift. Who'd stoop to blame
This sort of trifling? Even had you skill   35
In speech—(which I have not)—to make your will
Quite clear to such an one, and say, "Just this
Or that in you disgusts me; here you miss,

---

* **Ferrara** town in Italy.   **3 Frà Pandolf** a fictitious painter.

Or there exceed the mark"—and if she let
Herself be lessoned so, nor plainly set   40
Her wits to yours, forsooth, and made excuse,
—E'en then would be some stooping; and I choose
Never to stoop. Oh, Sir, she smiled, no doubt,
Whene'er I passed her; but who passed without
Much the same smile? This grew; I gave commands;   45
Then all smiles stopped together. There she stands
As if alive. Will't please you rise? We'll meet
The company below, then. I repeat,
The Count your master's known munificence
Is ample warrant that no just pretense   50
Of mine for dowry will be disallowed;
Though his fair daughter's self, as I avowed
At starting, is my object. Nay, we'll go
Together down, Sir. Notice Neptune, though,
Taming a sea-horse, thought a rarity,   55
Which Claus of Innsbruck° cast in bronze for me!

                                                                      [1842]

56 Claus of Innsbruck a fictitious sculptor.

Topics for Critical Thinking and Writing

1. Who is speaking to whom? On what occasion?
2. What words or lines especially convey the speaker's arrogance? What is our attitude toward the speaker? Loathing? Fascination? Respect? Explain.
3. The time and place are Renaissance Italy; how do they affect our attitude toward the duke? What would be the effect if the poem were set in the twentieth century?
4. Years after writing this poem, Browning explained that the duke's "commands" (line 45) were "that she should be put to death, or he might have had her shut up in a convent." Should the poem have been more explicit? Does Browning's later uncertainty indicate that the poem is badly thought out? Suppose we did not have Browning's comment on line 45; could the line then mean only that he commanded her to stop smiling and that she obeyed? Explain.
5. Elizabeth Barrett (not yet Mrs. Browning) wrote to Robert Browning that it was not "by the dramatic medium that poets teach most impressively. . . . It is too difficult for the common reader to analyze, and to discern between the vivid and the earnest." She went on, urging him to teach "in the directest and most impressive way, the mask thrown off." What teaching, if any, is in this poem? If there is any teaching here, would it be more impressive if Browning had not used the mask of a Renaissance duke? Explain.
6. You are the envoy, writing to the count, your master, a 500-word report of your interview with the duke. What do you write?
7. You are the envoy, writing to the count, advising—as diplomatically as possible—for or against this marriage. Notice that this exercise, unlike #6, which calls for a *report,* calls for an *argument.*

Edward S. Curtis. *The Vanishing Race,* c. 1904. (Platinum print. San Francisco Museum of Modern Art; extended loan of Van Deren Coke.)

ROBERT FROST

For a biographical note on Robert Frost (1875–1963), see pages 703–04.

The Vanishing Red

He is said to have been the last Red Man
In Acton.° And the Miller is said to have laughed—
If you like to call such a sound a laugh.
But he gave no one else a laugher's license.
For he turned suddenly grave as if to say,   5
'Whose business—if I take it on myself,
Whose business—but why talk round the barn?—
When it's just that I hold with getting a thing done with.'
You can't get back and see it as he saw it.
It's too long a story to go into now.   10
You'd have to have been there and lived it.
Then you wouldn't have looked on it as just a matter
Of who began it between the two races.

---

2 Acton a town in Massachusetts, not far from where Frost spent part of his childhood.

Some guttural exclamation of surprise
The Red Man gave in poking about the mill   15
Over the great big thumping shuffling mill-stone
Disgusted the Miller physically as coming
From one who had no right to be heard from.
'Come, John,' he said, 'you want to see the wheel pit?'°

He took him down below a cramping rafter,   20
And showed him, through a manhole in the floor,
The water in desperate straits like frantic fish,
Salmon and sturgeon, lashing with their tails.
Then he shut down the trap door with a ring in it

That jangled even above the general noise,   25
And came up stairs alone—and gave that laugh,
And said something to a man with a meal-sack
That the man with the meal-sack didn't catch—then.
Oh, yes, he showed John the wheel pit all right.

                                                                    [1916]

19 **wheel pit** the pit containing the wheel that, agitated by the water, drives the mill.

E. E. CUMMINGS

E. E. Cummings was the pen name of Edwin Estlin Cummings (1894–1962), who grew up in Cambridge, Massachusetts, and was graduated from Harvard, where he became interested in modern literature and art, especially in the movements called Cubism and Futurism. His father, a conservative clergyman and a professor at Harvard, seems to have been baffled by the youth's interests, but Cummings's mother encouraged his artistic activities, including his use of unconventional punctuation and capitalization.

Politically liberal in his youth, Cummings became more conservative after a visit to Russia in 1931, but early and late his work emphasizes individuality and freedom of expression.

anyone lived in a pretty how town

anyone lived in a pretty how town
(with up so floating many bells down)
spring summer autumn winter
he sang his didn't he danced his did.   4

Women and men (both little and small)
cared for anyone not at all
they sowed their isn't they reaped their same
sun moon stars rain   8

children guessed (but only a few
and down they forgot as up they grew
autumn winter spring summer)
that noone loved him more by more   12

when by now and tree by leaf
she laughed his joy she cried his grief
bird by snow and stir by still
anyone's any was all to her   16

someones married their everyones
laughed their cryings and did their dance
(sleep wake hope and then) they
said their nevers they slept their dream   20

stars rain sun moon
(and only the snow can begin to explain
how children are apt to forget to remember
with up so floating many bells down)   24

one day anyone died i guess
(and noone stopped to kiss his face)
busy folk buried them side by side
little by little and was by was   28

all by all and deep by deep
and more by more they dream their sleep
noone and anyone earth by april
wish by spirit and if by yes.   32

Women and men (both dong and ding)
summer autumn winter spring
reaped their sowing and went their came
sun moon stars rain   36

[1940]

Topics for Critical Thinking and Writing

1. Put into normal order (as far as possible) the words of the first two stanzas and then compare your version with Cummings's. What does Cummings gain—or lose?
2. Characterize the "anyone" who "sang his didn't" and "danced his did." In your opinion, how does he differ from the people who "sowed their isn't they reaped their same"?
3. Some readers interpret "anyone died" (line 25) to mean that the child matured and became as dead as the other adults. How might you support or refute this interpretation?

ROBERT HAYDEN

Robert Hayden (1913–80) was born in Detroit, Michigan. His parents divorced when he was a child, and he was brought up by a neighboring family, whose name he adopted. In 1942, at the age of 29, he graduated from Detroit City College (now Wayne State University); he received a master's degree from the University of Michigan. He taught at Fisk University from 1946 to 1969 and after that, for the remainder of his life, at the University of Michigan. In 1979 he was appointed Consultant in Poetry to the Library of Congress, the first African American to hold the post.

Those Winter Sundays

Sundays too my father got up early
and put his clothes on in the blueblack cold,
then with cracked hands that ached
from labor in the weekday weather made
banked fires blaze. No one ever thanked him.   5

I'd wake and hear the cold splintering, breaking.
When the rooms were warm, he'd call,
and slowly I would rise and dress,
fearing the chronic angers of that house.

Speaking indifferently to him,   10
who had driven out the cold
and polished my good shoes as well.
What did I know, what did I know
of love's austere and lonely offices?

[1962]

Topics for Critical Thinking and Writing

1. In line 1, what does the word "too" tell us about the father? What does it suggest about the speaker and the implied hearer of the poem?
2. How old do you believe the speaker was at the time he recalls in the second and third stanzas? What details suggest this age?
3. What is the meaning of "offices" in the last line? What does this word suggest that other words Hayden might have chosen do not?
4. What do you take to be the speaker's present attitude toward his father? What circumstances, do you imagine, prompted his memory of "Those Winter Sundays"?
5. In a page or two, try to get down the exact circumstances when you spoke "indifferently," or not at all, to someone who had deserved your gratitude.

MITSUYE YAMADA

Mitsuye Yamada, the daughter of Japanese immigrants to the United States, was born in Japan in 1923, during her mother's return visit to her native land. Yamada was raised in Seattle, but in 1942 she and her family were incarcerated and then relocated in a camp in Idaho, when Executive Order 9066 gave military authorities the right to remove any and all persons from "military areas." In 1954 she became an American citizen. Later, she became a member of the Asian American Studies Program at the University at California at Irvine. She is the author of poems and stories.

To the Lady

The one in San Francisco who asked:
Why did the Japanese Americans let
the government put them in
those camps without protest?

Come to think of it I   5
   should've run off to Canada
   should've hijacked a plane to Algeria
   should've pulled myself up from my
   bra straps
   and kicked'm in the groin   10
   should've bombed a bank
   should've tried self-immolation
   should've holed myself up in a
   woodframe house
   and let you watch me   15
   burn up on the six o'clock news
   should've run howling down the street
   naked and assaulted you at breakfast
   by AP wirephoto
   should've screamed bloody murder   20
   like Kitty Genovese°

Then
YOU would've
   come to my aid in shining armor
   laid yourself across the railroad track   25
   marched on Washington
   tatooed a Star of David on your arm
   written six million enraged
   letters to Congress

21 Kitty Genovese In 1964 Kitty Genovese of Kew Gardens, New York, was stabbed to death when she left her car and walked toward her home. Thirty-eight persons heard her screams, but no one came to her assistance.

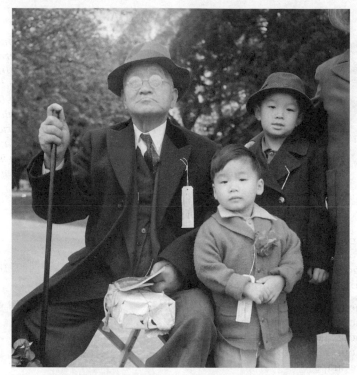

Dorothea Lange. "Grandfather and Grandchildren Awaiting Evacuation Bus." (War Relocation Authority/The National Archives)

But we didn't draw the line
anywhere
law and order Executive Order 9066°
social order moral order internal order

You let'm
I let'm   35
All are punished.

[1976]

32 **Executive Order 9066** an authorization, signed in 1941 by President Franklin D. Roosevelt, allowing military authorities to relocate Japanese and Japanese Americans who resided on the Pacific Coast of the United States.

Topics for Critical Thinking and Writing

1. Has the lady's question (lines 2–4) ever crossed your mind? If so, what answers did you think of?
2. What, in effect, is the speaker really saying in lines 5–21? And in lines 24–29?
3. Explain the last line.

SYLVIA PLATH

Sylvia Plath (1932–63) was born in Boston, the daughter of German immigrants. While still an undergraduate at Smith College, she published in Seventeen *and* Mademoiselle, *but her years at college, like her later years, were marked by manic-depressive periods. After graduating from college she went to England to study at Cambridge University, where she met the English poet Ted Hughes, whom she married in 1956. The marriage was unsuccessful, and they separated. One day she committed suicide by turning on the kitchen gas.*

Daddy

You do not do, you do not do
Any more, black shoe
In which I have lived like a foot
For thirty years, poor and white,
Barely daring to breathe or Achoo.   5

Daddy, I have had to kill you.
You died before I had time—
Marble-heavy, a bag full of God,
Ghastly statue with one gray toe
Big as a Frisco seal   10

And a head in the freakish Atlantic
Where it pours bean green over blue
In the waters off beautiful Nauset.
I used to pray to recover you.
Ach, du.°   15

In the German tongue, in the Polish town
Scraped flat by the roller
Of wars, wars, wars.
But the name of the town is common.
My Polack friend   20

Says there are a dozen or two.
So I never could tell where you
Put your foot, your root,
I never could talk to you.
The tongue stuck in my jaw.   25

It stuck in a barb wire snare.
Ich, ich, ich, ich,°
I could hardly speak.
I thought every German was you.
And the language obscene   30

15 Ach, du O, you (German).   **27 Ich, ich, ich, ich** I, I, I, I.

An engine, an engine
Chuffing me off like a Jew.
A Jew to Dachau, Auschwitz, Belsen.°
I began to talk like a Jew.
I think I may well be a Jew.   35

The snows of the Tyrol, the clear beer of Vienna
Are not very pure or true.
With my gypsy ancestress and my weird luck
And my Taroc pack and my Taroc pack
I may be a bit of a Jew.   40

I have always been scared of *you,*
With your Luftwaffe,° your gobbledygoo.
And your neat moustache
And your Aryan eye, bright blue,
Panzer-man,° panzer-man, O You—   45

Not God but a swastika
So black no sky could squeak through.
Every woman adores a Fascist,
The boot in the face, the brute
Brute heart of a brute like you.   50

You stand at the blackboard, daddy,
In the picture I have of you,
A cleft in your chin instead of your foot
But no less a devil for that, no not
Any less the black man who   55

Bit my pretty red heart in two.
I was ten when they buried you.
At twenty I tried to die
And get back, back, back to you.
I thought even the bones would do.   60

But they pulled me out of the sack,
And they stuck me together with glue,
And then I knew what to do.
I made a model of you,
A man in black with a Meinkampf° look   65

And a love of the rack and the screw.
And I said I do, I do.
So daddy, I'm finally through.
The black telephone's off at the root,
The voices just can't worm through.   70

33 **Dachau, Auschwitz, Belson** concentration camps.   42 **Luftwaffe** German air force.
45 **Panzer-man** member of a tank crew.   65 **Mein Kampf** *My Struggle* (title of Hitler's
autobiography).

If I've killed one man, I've killed two—
The vampire who said he was you
And drank my blood for a year,
Seven years, if you want to know.
Daddy, you can lie back now.   75

There's a stake in your fat black heart
And the villagers never liked you.
They are dancing and stamping on you.
They always *knew* it was you.
Daddy, daddy, you bastard, I'm through.   80

[1965]

Topics for Critical Thinking and Writing

1. Many readers find in this poem something that reminds them of nursery rhymes. If you are among these readers, specify the resemblance(s).
2. Some critics have called parts of the poem "surrealistic." Check a college dictionary, and then argue in a paragraph or two why the word is or is not appropriate.
3. Is this a poem whose experience a reader can share? Explain.

LOUISE ERDRICH

Louise Erdrich was born in Little Falls, Minnesota, in 1954 and raised in North Dakota; her father (born in Germany) and her mother (French Ojibwe) both worked for the Bureau of Indian Affairs. After graduating from Dartmouth College in 1976, she returned to North Dakota to teach in the Poetry in the Schools Program. In 1979 she received a master's degree in creative writing from Johns Hopkins University. She was married to late author and anthropologist Michael Dorris, a professor of Native American Studies at Dartmouth, and they successfully collaborated on multicultural literature. She now lives in Minneapolis, Minnesota, with her youngest three children. Although Erdrich is most widely known as a novelist, she has also won a reputation as a poet.

Indian Boarding School: The Runaways

Home's the place we head for in our sleep.
Boxcars stumbling north in dreams
don't wait for us. We catch them on the run.
The rails, old lacerations that we love,
shoot parallel across the face and break   5
just under Turtle Mountains.° Riding scars

---

6 Turtle Mountains mountains in North Dakota and Manitoba.

you can't get lost. Home is the place they cross.
The lame guard strikes a match and makes the dark

less tolerant. We watch through cracks in boards
as the land starts rolling, rolling till it hurts   10
to be here, cold in regulation clothes.
We know the sheriff's waiting at midrun
to take us back. His car is dumb and warm.
The highway doesn't rock, it only hums
like a wing of long insults. The worn-down welts   15
of ancient punishment lead back and forth.

All runaways wear dresses, long green ones,
the color you would think shame was. We scrub
the sidewalks down because it's shameful work.
Our brushes cut the stone in watered arcs   20
and in the soak frail outlines shiver clear
a moment, things us kids pressed on the dark
face before it hardened, pale, remembering
delicate old injuries, the spines of names and leaves.

[1984]

Topics for Critical Thinking and Writing

1. In line 4 the railroad tracks are called "old lacerations." What is the connection between the two?
2. What other imagery of injury do you find in the poem? In lines 20–24, what—literally—is "the dark / face" that "hardened, pale"?

HUDDIE LEDBETTER

Huddie Ledbetter (c. 1888–1949), better known as Leadbelly, was born on a plantation north of Shreveport, Louisiana, on the Louisiana-Texas line. By the age of 15 he was playing the accordion and the guitar at local dances; at 16 he was in Fannin Street, a red-light district where he heard jazz and blues. In 1908 he moved to Dallas, where he met Blind Lemon Jefferson, regarded as the greatest blues singer of the period, and the two performed together for several years.

In 1915 Ledbetter was convicted of assault and sent to a chain gang, but he escaped. In 1917 he was convicted of murder and imprisoned; but he was pardoned in 1925, after singing the governor a song that asked for the pardon. In 1930 he was again convicted of assault, and in 1934 he was again pardoned, this time routinely. After leaving prison he was employed by John A. Lomax, who had heard him sing in prison in 1933 and had recorded his songs for the Library of Congress. Lomax helped publicize Ledbetter in New York City, with radio shows, interviews, and bookings on college campuses. Ultimately Ledbetter made a series of recordings for Folkways. His greatest popularity in the late 1930s and '40s was with white socialist groups, though today his best-known songs, including "Irene" and "Midnight Special," are not overtly political.

The Titanic *sank on the night of April 14–15, 1912, after crashing into an iceberg in the North Atlantic. More than 1,500 lives were lost. In line 7 of his song Leadbelly refers to John Arthur Johnson (1878–1946), popularly called Jack Johnson, the first African American heavyweight boxing champion. It was widely though incorrectly believed that Johnson had sought passage on the* Titanic *but was rejected by Captain Edward John Smith, who allegedly (again, the story is untrue) said, "I ain't haulin' no coal." On the other hand, it is true that there were no persons of color on the ship.*

De Titanic

Captain Smith, when he got his load,
Might 'a' heard him holl'in', "All aboa'd!"
Cryin', "Fare thee, *Titanic,* fare thee well!"

Captain Smith, when he got his load,
Might 'a' heard him holl'in', "All aboa'd!"   5
Cryin', "Fare thee, *Titanic,* fare thee well!"

Jack Johnson wanted to get on boa'd;
Captain Smith hollered, "I ain' haulin' no coal."
Cryin', "Fare thee, *Titanic,* fare thee well!"

It was midnight on the sea,   10
Band playin', "Nearer My God to Thee."
Cryin', "Fare thee, *Titanic,* fare thee well!"

Titanic was sinking down,
Had them lifeboats aroun'.
Cryin', "Fare thee, *Titanic,* fare thee well!"   15

Had them lifeboats aroun',
Savin' the women, lettin' the men go down.
Cryin', "Fare thee, *Titanic,* fare thee well!"

When the women got out on the land,
Cryin', "Lawd, have mercy on my man."   20
Cryin', "Fare thee, *Titanic,* fare thee well!"

Jack Johnson heard the mighty shock,
Might 'a' seen the black rascal doin' th' Eagle Rock."°
Cryin', "Fare thee, *Titanic,* fare thee well!"

Black man oughta shout for joy,   25
Never lost a girl or either a boy.
Cryin', "Fare thee, *Titanic,* fare thee well!"

23 Eagle Rock a dance step.

Loud and swinging

♩ = 152–176, somewhat free

Cap - tain   Smith, when he got his load,   Might 'a'

heared him holl' - in', "All   a - bo - a'd."   Cry - in',

"Fare   thee,   *Ti - tan - ic,*   fare thee   well."

Cap - tain

Smith,   when he   got his load,   Might   'a'

heared him holl' - in', "All   a - bo - a'd."   Cry - in',

"Fare   thee,   *Ti - tan - ic,*   fare thee   well."

Topic for Critical Thinking and Writing

As we mentioned in our introduction to this song, there is no historical truth to the assertion that Jack Johnson was refused passage because of his color. On the other hand, there were no persons of color on the ship—every passenger and every member of the crew was white. Is it reasonable, then, to say that although in its reference to Johnson the song is wrong, in a way it is right?

ETHERIDGE KNIGHT

Etheridge Knight, born in Corinth, Mississippi, in 1931, dropped out of school in the eighth grade. He served in the U. S. Army from 1947 to 1951, but after his discharge became addicted to drugs and soon was involved in a life of crime. Arrested for robbery in 1960, Knight began to write poetry while in prison, encouraged by the African American poets Dudley Randall, Sonia Sanchez, and Gwendolyn Brooks. His first book, Poems from Prison, *was published in 1968 by Randall's Broadside Press. Knight was a leading figure in the Black Arts movement of the 1960s and 1970s, a form of radical cultural activity (related to the broader Black Power movement) that promoted "social engagement" as a crucial feature of literary practice. His* Belly Song and Other Poems *(1973) was one of the most influential books of the period for African American writers and critics. Knight died in 1985.*

The following poem was written a year after the assassination of the charismatic African American militant, writer, and orator Malcolm X (nicknamed "Red"). Born in Omaha, Nebraska, in 1925, Malcolm Little moved to Boston in the early 1940s, and there and in New York City, he was a drug dealer and a thief. He was arrested in 1946 for armed robbery and spent the next six years in prisons in Massachusetts. While still in prison, he became acquainted with the teachings of Elijah Muhammed, the leader of the Nation of Islam, and he embarked upon an intensive program of self-education, especially in history. Upon his release from

Malcolm X, June 29, 1963.

prison, Malcolm Little changed his name to Malcolm X, the "X" signifying the name, unknown to him, of his African ancestors who had been sold into slavery. He broke with Elijah Muhammed in 1963 and formed a rival organization, the Muslim Mosque, Inc. He then made a pilgrimage to Mecca, converted to orthodox Islam, and, while remaining a militant black nationalist, stated that he was no longer a racial separatist. In the Audubon Ballroom in Harlem, on February 21, 1965, Malcolm X was murdered by members of the Nation of Islam, though controversy still surrounds the conspiracy that led to his death. Malcolm X's writings and speeches are included in his Autobiography *(as told to Alex Haley, 1964) and* Malcolm X Speaks *(1965).*

For Malcolm, a Year After

Compose for Red a proper verse;
Adhere to foot and strict iamb;
Control the burst of angry words
Or they might boil and break the dam.
Or they might boil and overflow   5
And drench me, drown me, drive me mad.
So swear no oath, so shed no tear,
And sing no song blue Baptist sad.
Evoke no image, stir no flame,
And spin no yarn across the air.   10
Make empty anglo tea lace words—
Make them dead and white and dry bone bare.

Compose a verse for Malcolm man,
And make it rime and make it prim.
The verse will die—as all men do—   15
But not the memory of him!
Death might come singing sweet like C,
Or knocking like the old folk say,
The moon and stars may pass away,
But not the anger of that day.   20

[1966]

Topics for Critical Thinking and Writing

1. Knight's poem is both about Malcolm X and about the writing of a poem about him. Why might Knight have wanted to connect the subject of this poem to the act of writing the poem in the first place? Do you think that Knight should have presented a more straightforward tribute?
2. Explain the meaning of line 8. And of line 11. Which line is more effective? Are these lines more or less effective than other lines in the poem?
3. Are the first two lines of the second stanza puzzling? Why the word "prim"?
4. What is the relationship of the fourth line of the second stanza to the final line of the poem?

5. Do you think that Knight's poem remains powerful today? How does a poem keyed to a specific historical event or person retain its power decades after the event or after the person's death? Or is it the case, in your view, that the passing of time always diminishes the impact of a poem like this one?

RITA DOVE

Rita Dove was born in 1952 in Akron, Ohio. After graduating summa cum laude from Miami University (Ohio), she earned an M.F.A. at the Iowa Writers' Workshop. She has been awarded fellowships from the Guggenheim Foundation and the National Endowment for the Arts, and she now teaches at the University of Virginia. In 1993 she was appointed poet laureate for 1993–94. Dove is currently writing a book about the experiences of an African American volunteer regiment in France during World War I.

Daystar

She wanted a little room for thinking:
but she saw diapers steaming on the line,
a doll slumped behind the door.
So she lugged a chair behind the garage
to sit out the children's naps.   5

Sometimes there were things to watch—
the pinched armor of a vanished cricket,
a floating maple leaf. Other days
she stared until she was assured
when she closed her eyes   10
she'd see only her own vivid blood.

She had an hour, at best, before Liza appeared
pouting from the top of the stairs.
And just *what* was mother doing
out back with the field mice? Why,   15

building a palace. Later
that night when Thomas rolled over and
lurched into her, she would open her eyes
and think of the place that was hers
for an hour—where   20
she was nothing,
pure nothing, in the middle of the day.

[1986]

Topics for Critical Thinking and Writing

1. How would you characterize the woman who is the subject of the poem?
2. What do you make of the title?

Places

BASHO

If the name of any Japanese poet is known in the United States, it is probably Matsuo Basho (1644–94). He lived most of his life in Edo (now called Tokyo), but he enjoyed traveling on foot in Japan and writing about his experiences. His most famous work, The Narrow Road to the Deep North *(1694), is a poetic diary recording one of his extended journeys. (It is available in several English translations.)*

We give here, however, a short poem in the form known as **haiku**. *A haiku has 17 syllables, arranged in 3 lines of 5, 7, and 5 syllables. Japanese poetry is unrhymed, but English versions—which may or may not follow the Japanese syllabic pattern—sometimes rhyme the first and third lines, as in the following translation of one of Basho's haiku:*

> *On the withered bough*
> *A crow alone is perching;*
> *Autumn evening now.*

The American poet Richard Wright wrote a number of poems grouped under the title "Hokku" (a variant of haiku*), one of which goes thus:*

> *Keep straight down this block*
> *Then turn right where you will find*
> *A peach tree blooming.*

The subject matter of a haiku *can be high or low—the Milky Way or the screech of automobile brakes—but usually it is connected with the seasons, and it is described objectively and sharply. Here is Basho's most famous* haiku. *(The translation does not preserve the syllabic count of the original.)*

An Old Pond

> An old pond;
> A frog jumps in—
> The sound of the water.

Topic for Writing

Write at least one haiku. You need not use the 5-7-5 system if you don't want to; on the other hand, you may use rhyme if you wish. Some tips:

1. For a start, take some ordinary experience—tying your shoelaces, or seeing a cat at the foot of the stairs, or glancing out a window and seeing unexpected snowflakes, or hearing the alarm clock—and present it interestingly.
2. One way to make the experience interesting is to construct the poem in two parts—the first line balanced against the next two lines, or the first two lines balanced against the last line. If you construct a poem on this principle, the two sections should be related to each other, but they should also in some degree make a contrast with each other. Here is an example: "This handsome rooster / Struts before the clucking hens; / Inside, the pot is boiling." A second example, this one

offering a contrast between pleasant sociability (the first two lines) and loneliness: "'Look, O look, there go / Fireflies,' I would like to say— / But I am alone."

WILLIAM BUTLER YEATS

William Butler Yeats (1865–1939) was born in Dublin, Ireland. The early Yeats was much interested in highly lyrical, romantic poetry, often drawing on Irish mythology. The later poems, from about 1910 (and especially after Yeats met Ezra Pound in 1911), are often more colloquial. Although these later poems often employ mythological references too—"Leda and the Swan" on page 140 is an example—many believe that the poems are more down-to-earth. Yeats was awarded the Nobel Prize in Literature in 1923.

In the seventh century B.C. *the ancient Greeks founded the city of Byzantium in Thrace, where Istanbul, Turkey, now stands. (Constantine, the first Christian ruler of the Roman Empire, built a new city there in 330* A.D. *Named Constantinople, the city served as the capital of the Roman Empire until 1453, when the Turks captured it. In 1930 the name was officially changed to Istanbul.) The capital of the Roman Empire and the "holy city" of the Greek Orthodox Church, Byzantium had two golden ages. The first, in its early centuries, continued the traditions of the antique Greco-Roman world. The second, which is what Yeats had in mind, extended from the mid-ninth to the mid-thirteenth century and was a distinctive blend of classical, Christian, Slavic, and even Islamic culture. This period is noted for mysticism, for the preservation of ancient learning, and for exquisitely refined symbolic art. In short, Byzantium (as Yeats saw it) was wise and passionless. In* A Vision, *his prose treatment of his complex mystical system, Yeats says:*

> *I think that in early Byzantium, maybe never before or since in recorded history, religious, aesthetic and practical life were one, that architect and artificers—though not, it may be, poets, for language has been the instrument of controversy and must have grown abstract—spoke to the multitude and the few alike. The painter, the mosaic worker, the worker in gold and silver, the illuminator of sacred books, were almost impersonal, almost perhaps without the consciousness of individual design, absorbed in their subject matter and that the vision of the whole people. They could copy out of old Gospel books those pictures that seemed as sacred as the text, and yet weave all into a vast design, the work of many that seemed the work of one, that made building, picture, pattern, metal-work of rail and lamp, seem but a single image.*

Sailing to Byzantium

I

That is no country for old men. The young
In one another's arms, birds in the trees
—Those dying generations—at their song,
The salmon-falls, the mackerel-crowded seas,
Fish, flesh, or fowl, commend all summer long   5
Whatever is begotten, born, and dies.
Caught in that sensual music all neglect
Monuments of unaging intellect.

II

An aged man is but a paltry thing,
A tattered coat upon a stick, unless   10
Soul clap its hands and sing, and louder sing
For every tatter in its mortal dress.
Nor is there singing school but studying
Monuments of its own magnificence;
And therefore I have sailed the seas and come   15
To the holy city of Byzantium.

III

O sages standing in God's holy fire
As in the gold mosaic of a wall,
Come from the holy fire, perne° in a gyre,
And be the singing-masters of my soul.   20
Consume my heart away; sick with desire
And fastened to a dying animal
It knows not what it is; and gather me
Into the artifice of eternity.

IV

Once out of nature I shall never take   25
My bodily form from any natural thing,
But such a form as Grecian goldsmiths make
Of hammered gold and gold enameling
To keep a drowsy Emperor awake;
Or set upon a golden bough to sing   30
To lords and ladies of Byzantium
Of what is past, or passing, or to come.

[1926]

19 **perne** whirl down.

Topics for Critical Thinking and Writing

1. What is "that . . . country," mentioned in the first line?
2. By the end of the first stanza, the speaker seems to be dismissing the natural world. Do you agree that even in this stanza, however, he sounds attracted to it?
3. The poem is filled with oppositions, for instance "old men" versus "the young" (both in line 1), and "birds in the trees" (line 2) versus the mechanical bird in the final stanza. List as many opposites as you see in the poem, and then explain what Yeats is getting at.
4. The first stanza speaks of "monuments of unaging intellect." What might be some examples of these?
5. After reading and rereading this poem, do you think you will—even if only briefly—*act* differently, redirect any of your choices?

6. Have you ever visited any place—perhaps the place where you or your parents or grandparents were born, or perhaps a house of worship, or perhaps a college campus—that you have come to see symbolically, standing for a way of life or for some aspect of life? If so, describe the place and the significance that you give it.

JAMES WRIGHT

James Wright (1927–80) was born in Martins Ferry, Ohio, which provided him with the locale for many of his poems. He is often thought of as a poet of the Midwest, but (as in the example that we give) his poems move beyond the scenery. Wright was educated at Kenyon College in Ohio and at the University of Washington. He wrote several books of poetry and published many translations of European and Latin American poetry.

Lying in a Hammock at William Duffy's Farm in Pine Island, Minnesota

Over my head, I see the bronze butterfly,
Asleep on the black trunk,
Blowing like a leaf in green shadow.
Down the ravine behind the empty house,
The cowbells follow one another   5
Into the distances of the afternoon.
To my right,
In a field of sunlight between two pines,
The droppings of last year's horses
Blaze up into golden stones.   10
I lean back, as the evening darkens and comes on.
A chicken hawk floats over, looking for home.
I have wasted my life.

[1963]

Topics for Critical Thinking and Writing

1. How important is it that the poet is "lying in a hammock"? That he is at some place other than his own home?
2. Do you take the last line as a severe self-criticism, or as a joking remark, or as something in between, or what?
3. Imagine yourself lying in a hammock—perhaps you can recall an actual moment in a hammock—or lying in bed, your eye taking in the surroundings. Write a description ending with some sort of judgment or concluding comment, as Wright does. You may want to parody Wright's poem, but you need

not. (Keep in mind that the best parodies are written by people who regard the original with affection.)

YUSEF KOMUNYAKAA

Yusef Komunyakaa was born in 1947 in Bogalusa, Louisiana. After graduating from high school he entered the army and served in Vietnam, where he was awarded the Bronze Star. On his return to the United States he earned a bachelor's degree at the University of Colorado, and then earned an M.A. at Colorado State University and an M.F.A. in creative writing at the University of California, Irvine. The author of several books of poetry, he has been teaching at Indiana University in Bloomington since 1985. "Facing It" is the last poem in a book of poems about Vietnam, Dien Cai Dau *(1988). The title of the book is a slang word for crazy.*

Facing It

My black face fades,
hiding inside the black granite.
I said I wouldn't,
dammit: No tears.
I'm stone. I'm flesh.   5
My clouded reflection eyes me
like a bird of prey, the profile of night
slanted against morning. I turn
this way—the stone lets me go.
I turn that way—I'm inside   10
the Vietnam Veterans Memorial
again, depending on the light
to make a difference.
I go down the 58,022 names,
half-expecting to find   15
my own in letters like smoke.
I touch the name Andrew Johnson;
I see the booby trap's white flash.
Names shimmer on a woman's blouse
but when she walks away   20
the names stay on the wall.
Brushstrokes flash, a red bird's
wings cutting across my stare.
The sky. A plane in the sky.
A white vet's image floats   25
closer to me, then his pale eyes
look through mine. I'm a window.
He's lost his right arm
inside the stone. In the black mirror
a woman's trying to erase names: 30
No, she's brushing a boy's hair.

[1988]

Vietnam Veterans Memorial, Washington, D.C.

Topics for Critical Thinking and Writing

1. The poem's title is "Facing It." What is the speaker facing? How would you describe his attitude?
2. Three people, whose names we don't know, briefly appear on the wall. How might we describe their actions? Try to paraphrase: "I'm a window. / He's lost his right arm / inside the stone."
3. At the poem's end, has the speaker "faced it"? What is your evidence?
4. If you have seen the Vietnam Veterans Memorial, describe it and your reaction to it in a paragraph or two. If you haven't seen it, try to describe it from "Facing It" and any written or photographic accounts you have seen.

DEREK WALCOTT

Derek Walcott, born in 1930 on the Caribbean island of St. Lucia, was awarded the Nobel Prize for Literature in 1992. Although in the United States he is known chiefly as a poet, Walcott is also an important playwright and director of plays. Much of his work is concerned with his mixed heritage—a black writer from the Caribbean, whose language is English and who lives part of the year in Massachusetts, where he teaches in the Creative Writing Program at Boston University. Walcott's books include Collected Poems *(1986) and* Omeros *(1989), a Caribbean epic that echoes Homer's* Iliad *and* Odyssey *as it explores the Caribbean's past and present.*

A Far Cry from Africa

A wind is ruffling the tawny pelt
Of Africa. Kikuyu,° quick as flies,
Batten upon the bloodstreams of the veldt.°
Corpses are scattered through a paradise.
Only the worm, colonel of carrion, cries: 5
'Waste no compassion on these separate dead!'
Statistics justify and scholars seize
The salients of colonial policy.
What is that to the white child hacked in bed?
To savages, expendable as Jews?   10

Threshed out by beaters, the long rushes break
In a white dust of ibises whose cries
Have wheeled since civilization's dawn
From the parched river or beast-teeming plain.
The violence of beast on beast is read   15
As natural law, but upright man
Seeks his divinity by inflicting pain.
Delirious as these worried beasts, his wars
Dance to the tightened carcass of a drum,
While he calls courage still that native dread   20
Of the white peace contracted by the dead.

Again brutish necessity wipes its hands
Upon the napkins of a dirty cause, again
A waste of our compassion, as with Spain,°
The gorilla wrestles with the superman.   25

I who am poisoned with the blood of both,
Where shall I turn, divided to the vein?
I who have cursed
The drunken officer of British rule, how choose
Between this Africa and the English tongue I love?   30
Betray them both, or give back what they give?
How can I face such slaughter and be cool?
How can I turn from Africa and live?

[1962]

2 **Kikuyu** an African tribe that fought against British colonialists.   3 **veldt** grassland in southern Africa.   24 **Spain** a reference to the triumph of fascism in Spain after the civil war of 1936–39.

Topics for Critical Thinking and Writing

1. Now that you have read the poem, explain the meaning of the title.
2. Do you find the first stanza hard to understand? Why, or why not?
3. Focus on lines 15–17: What is Walcott saying here? Do you think that the poem might be even more effective if these lines were placed at the beginning? Or do they belong exactly where they are?

4. Imagine that Walcott sent this poem to you with a letter that asked for your response. In a letter ("Dear Mr. Walcott. . .) of one page in length, give your response to the poem.
5. What is the meaning of line 25?
6. Walcott uses the first-person "I" in the final stanza. How would you answer each of the questions he asks in it? Or do you think the point is that these questions cannot be answered?
7. What is your own experience of Africa? Have you lived or traveled there? Would you like to? Has Walcott given you a new perspective on Africa, its history and culture?

ANONYMOUS

Among the most memorable hymns produced in the United States are the spirituals, or Sorrow Songs, created by black slaves in the United States, chiefly in the first half of the nineteenth century. The origins of the spirituals are still a matter of some dispute, but most specialists agree that the songs represent a distinctive fusion of African rhythms with European hymns, and of course many of the texts derive ultimately from biblical sources. A chief theme is the desire for release, sometimes presented with imagery drawn from ancient Israel. Examples include references to crossing the River Jordan (a river that runs from north of the Sea of Galilee to the Dead Sea), the release of the Israelites from slavery in Egypt (Exodus), Jonah's release from the whale (Book of Jonah), Daniel's deliverance from the lions' den (Book of Daniel, chapter 6), and the deliverance of Shadrach, Meshach, and Abednego from a fiery funace (Book of Daniel, chapter 3).

The texts were collected and published especially in the 1860s, for instance in Slave Songs of the United States (1867). These books usually sought to reproduce the singers' pronunciation, and we have followed the early texts in the example that we give here, where we print "chillun" for "children."

Very slowly (with expression)

Deep————— riv - er, my home is ov - er

Jor- dan,————— Deep———— riv - er, Lord. I

want to cross o - ver in - to camp ground.

Deep River

Deep river, my home is over Jordan, Deep river,
Lord, I want to cross over into campground,
Lord, I want to cross over into campground,
Lord, I want to cross over into campground.

Oh, chillun, Oh, don't you want to go to that gospel feast,   5
That promised land, that land, where all is peace?
Walk into heaven, and take my seat,
And cast my crown at Jesus' feet,
Lord, I want to cross over into campground,
Lord, I want to cross over into campground,   10
Lord, I want to cross over into campground.

Deep river, my home is over Jordan, Deep river
Lord, I want to cross over into campground,
Lord, I want to cross over into campground,
Lord, I want to cross over into campground, Lord!   15

Topic for Critical Thinking and Writing

Can a reader who does not believe in an afterlife enjoy this song?

WALT WHITMAN

Walt Whitman (1819–92) was born in a farmhouse in rural Long Island, New York, but was brought up in Brooklyn, then an independent city in New York. He attended public school for a few years (1825–30), apprenticed as a printer in the 1830s, and then worked as a typesetter, journalist, and newspaper editor. In 1855 he published the first edition of a collection of his poems, Leaves of Grass, *a book that he revised and republished throughout the remainder of his life. During the Civil War, he served as a volunteer nurse for the Union army.*

In the third edition of Leaves of Grass *(1860) Whitman added two groups of poems, one called "Children of Adam" and the other (named for an aromatic grass that grows near ponds and swamps) called "Calamus." "Children of Adam" celebrates heterosexual relations, whereas "Calamus" celebrates what Whitman called "manly love." Although the "Calamus" poems seem clearly homosexual, perhaps the very fact that Whitman published them made them seem relatively innocent; in any case, those nineteenth-century critics who condemned Whitman for the sexuality of his writing concentrated on the poems in "Children of Adam."*

We give a poem from the "Calamus" section. It was originally published in the third edition of Leaves of Grass *(1860) and was revised into its final form in the 1867 edition, which is the version that we print. We also reprint the manuscript for the poem, showing it in its earliest version.*

II

I saw in Louisiana a
   live-oak growing,
All alone stood it, and the
   moss hung down from the
   branches,
Without any companion it grew
   there, glistening out with
   joyous leaves of dark green,
And its look, rude, unbending,
   lusty, made me think of
   myself;
But I wondered how it could
   utter joyous leaves, standing
   alone there without its friend
   its lover – For I knew I could
   not;
And I plucked a twig with
   a certain number of leaves
   upon it, and twined around
   it a little moss, and brought
   it away – And I have placed
   it in sight in my room,

2

Walt Whitman, "I Saw in Louisiana a Live-Oak Growing," manuscript of 1860. On the first
leaf, in line 3 Whitman deleted "with." On the second leaf, in the third line (line 8 of the
printed text) he added, with a caret, "lately." In the sixth line on this leaf he deleted, "I
write these pieces, and name them after it," replacing the deletion with "it makes me think

(continued)

It is not needed to remind me as of my friends, (for I believe lately I think of little else than of them,)
Yet it remains to me a curious token — it makes me think of manly love, ~~I wrote these pieces and name them after it~~ ;
For all that, and though the ~~tree~~ live oak glistens there in Louisiana, solitary in a wide flat space, uttering joyous leaves all its life, without a friend, a lover, near — I know very well I could not.

3

of manly love." In the next line he deleted "tree" and inserted "live oak." When he reprinted the poem in the 1867 version of *Leaves of Grass,* he made further changes, as you will see if you compare the printed text with this manuscript version. (Walt Whitman Collection, Clifton Waller Barrett Library, Manuscripts Division, University of Virginia Library.)

I Saw in Louisiana a Live-Oak Growing

I saw in Louisiana a live-oak growing,
All alone stood it and the moss hung down from the branches,
Without any companion it grew there uttering joyous leaves of dark green,
And its look, rude, unbending, lusty, made me think of myself,
But I wonder'd how it could utter joyous leaves standing alone there without
    its friend near, for I knew I could not,   5
And I broke off a twig with a certain number of leaves upon it, and twined
    around it a little moss,
And brought it away, and I have placed it in sight in my room,
It is not needed to remind me as of my own dear friends,
(For I believe lately I think of little else than of them,)
Yet it remains to me a curious token, it makes me think of manly love;   10
For all that, and though the live-oak glistens there in Louisiana solitary in a
    wide flat space,
Uttering joyous leaves all its life without a friend a lover near,
I know very well I could not.

[1867]

Topic for Critical Thinking and Writing

Compare the final version (1867) of the poem with the manuscript version of 1860. Which version do you prefer? Why?

Things

WILLIAM CARLOS WILLIAMS

William Carlos Williams (1883–1963) was the son of an English traveling sales-man and a Basque-Jewish woman. The couple met in Puerto Rico and settled in Rutherford, New Jersey, where Williams was born. He spent his life there, practic-ing as a pediatrician and writing poems in the moments between seeing patients who were visiting his office.

The Red Wheelbarrow

so much depends
upon

a red wheel
barrow   4

glazed with rain
water

beside the white
chickens.   8

[1923]

Topics for Critical Thinking and Writing

1. Suppose lines 3 and 4 were printed as one line, and lines 5 and 6 were printed as one line. What difference, if any, would it make?
2. What, if anything, depends on a wet wheelbarrow next to white chickens?

WALT WHITMAN

Walt Whitman (1819–92) was born on Long Island, the son of a farmer. The young Whitman taught school and worked as a carpenter, a printer, a newspaper editor, and, during the Civil War, as a volunteer nurse on the Union side. After the war he supported himself by doing secretarial jobs. In Whitman's own day his poetry was highly controversial because of its unusual form (formlessness, many people said) and (though not in the following poem) its abundant erotic implications.

A Noiseless Patient Spider

A noiseless patient spider,
I mark'd where on a little promontory it stood isolated,
Mark'd how to explore the vacant vast surrounding,
It launch'd forth filament, filament, filament, out of itself,
Ever unreeling them, ever tirelessly speeding them.   5

And you O my soul where you stand,
Surrounded, detached, in measureless oceans of space,
Ceaselessly musing, venturing, throwing, seeking the spheres to connect them,
Till the bridge you will need be form'd, till the ductile anchor hold,
Till the gossamer thread you fling catch somewhere, O my soul.   10

[1862–63]

Topics for Critical Thinking and Writing

1. How are the suggestions in "launch'd" (line 4) and "unreeling" (line 5) continued in the second stanza?
2. How are the varying lengths of lines 1, 4, and 8 relevant to their ideas?
3. The second stanza is not a complete sentence. Why? The poem is unrhymed. What effect does the near-rhyme (*hold—soul*) in the last two lines have on you?

MARY OLIVER

Mary Oliver, born in Cleveland in 1935, attended Ohio State University and Vassar College. She is the author of six books of poetry—American Primitive *received the Pulitzer Prize for Poetry in 1984, and* New and Selected Poems *received a National Book Award in 1992—and she has served as a visiting professor or a poet in residence at several colleges.*

Two of her prose comments may be of special interest. Of today's readers she has said, "The question asked today is: What does it mean? Nobody says, how does it feel?" And of her work she has said, "I am trying in my poems to vanish and have the reader be the experiencer. I do not want to be there. It is not even a walk we take together."

Hawk

This morning
  the hawk
    rose up
      out of the meadow's browse

and swung over the lake—   5
  it settled
    on the small black dome
      of a dead pine,

alert as an admiral,
  its profile   10
    distinguished with sideburns
      the color of smoke,

and I said: remember
  this is not something
    of the red fire, this is   15
      heaven's fistful

of death and destruction,
  and the hawk hooked
    one exquisite foot
      onto a last twig   20

to look deeper
  into the yellow reeds
    along the edges of the water
      and I said: remember

the tree, the cave,   25
  the white lily of resurrection,
    and that's when it simply lifted
      its golden feet and floated

into the wind, belly-first,
  and then it cruised along the lake—   30

all the time its eyes fastened
    harder than love on some

unimportant rustling in the
    yellow reeds—and then it
        seemed to crouch high in the air, and then it   35
        turned into a white blade, which fell.

[1992]

Topics for Critical Thinking and Writing

1. As an experiment, rewrite the first eight lines, dividing them into two prose sentences. What is the difference between the two sentences in this form and the two stanzas of verse that Oliver has composed? How do the "same" words affect us differently?

2. The poem seems serious, even solemn (for example, lines 15–16), yet in places it seems witty, perhaps even on the edge of being comic, in its details (for example, lines 9–10, line 19). Do you find the speaker's tone and choices of language to be complicated and coherent, or simply confusing?

3. What is the nature of the speaker's relationship to the hawk? Does it mean something special to her, or is she really just concerned with giving a precise, accurate description of it?

4. How do you interpret lines 25–26? Are these lines to be understood in a secular or Christian context, or both?

12

Thinking Critically about Poetry

Case Study: Writing about Emily Dickinson

In this case study we give the texts of eleven poems and an essay by a student, on Dickinson's religious poetry.

 Emily Dickinson (1830–86) was born into a proper New England family in Amherst, Massachusetts. Although she spent her seventeenth year a few miles away, at Mount Holyoke Seminary (now Mount Holyoke College), in the next twenty years she left Amherst only five or six times, and in her last twenty years she may never have left her house. Her brother was probably right when he said that having seen something of the rest of the world—she had visited Washington with her father, when he was a member of Congress—"she could not resist the feeling that it was painfully hollow. It was to her so thin and unsatisfying in the face of the Great Realities of Life." Dickinson lived with her parents (a somewhat reclusive mother and an austere, remote father) and a younger sister; a married brother lived in the house next door. She formed some passionate attachments, to women as well as men, but there is no evidence that they found physical expression.

By the age of twelve Dickinson was writing witty letters, but she apparently did not write more than an occasional poem before her late twenties. At her death— she died in the house where she was born—she left 1,775 poems, only seven of which had been published (anonymously) during her lifetime.

I heard a Fly buzz—when I died—

I heard a Fly buzz—when I died—
The Stillness in the Room
Was like the Stillness in the Air—
Between the Heaves of Storm—   4

The Eyes around—had wrung them dry—
And Breaths were gathering firm
For the last Onset—when the King
Be witnessed—in the Room—   8

I willed my Keepsakes—Signed away
What portion of me be
Assignable—and then it was
There interposed a Fly—   12

Manuscript of Emily Dickinson's "I heard a Fly buzz—when I died—"
(Reprinted by permission of the publishers and the Trustees of Amherst
College from *The Poems of Emily Dickinson,* Thomas H. Johnson, ed.
Cambridge, Mass.: The Belknap Press of Harvard University Press. Copyright ©
1951, 1955, 1979, 1983 by the President and Fellows of Harvard College.)

With Blue—uncertain stumbling Buzz—
Between the light—and me—
And then the Windows failed—and then
I could not see to see—   16

[c. 1862]

The Soul selects her own Society

The Soul selects her own Society—
Then—shuts the Door—
To her divine Majority—
Present no more—   4

Unmoved—she notes the Chariots—pausing—
At her low Gate—
Unmoved—an Emperor be kneeling
Upon her Mat—   8

I've known her—from an ample nation—
Choose One—
Then—close the Valves° of her attention—
Like Stone—   12

[1862]

11 **Valves** the two halves of a hinged door, such as is now found on old telephone booths. Possibly also an allusion to a bivalve, such as an oyster or a clam, having a shell consisting of two hinged parts.

These are the days when Birds come back

These are the days when Birds come back—
A very few—a Bird or two—
To take a backward look.

These are days when skies resume
The old—old sophistries° of June—   5
A blue and gold mistake.

O fraud that cannot cheat the Bee—
Almost thy plausibility
Induces my belief.

Till ranks of seeds their witness bear—   10
And softly thro' the altered air
Hurries a timid leaf.

Oh Sacrament of summer days,
Oh Last Communion in the Haze—
Permit a child to join.   15

Thy sacred emblems to partake—
Thy consecrated bread to take
And thine immortal wine!

[1859]

5 **sophistries** deceptively subtle arguments.

Papa above!

Papa above!
Regard a Mouse
O'erpowered by the Cat!
Reserve within thy kingdom
A "Mansion" for the Rat!   5

Snug in seraphic Cupboards
To nibble all the day,
While unsuspecting Cycles°
Wheel solemnly away!

[c. 1859]

8 **Cycles** long periods, eons.

There's a certain Slant of light

There's a certain Slant of light,
Winter Afternoons—
That oppresses, like the Heft°
Of Cathedral Tunes—   4

Heavenly Hurt, it gives us—
We can find no scar,
But internal difference,
Where the Meanings, are—   8

None may teach it—Any—
'Tis the Seal Despair—
An imperial affliction
Sent us of the Air—   12

When it comes, the Landscape listens—
Shadows—hold their breath—
When it goes, 'tis like the Distance
On the look of Death—   16

[c. 1861]

3 **Heft** weight.

This World is not Conclusion

This World is not Conclusion.
A Species stands beyond—
Invisible, as Music—
But positive, as Sound—
It beckons, and it baffles—   5
Philosophy—dont know—
And through a Riddle, at the last—

Sagacity, must go—
To guess it, puzzles scholars—
To gain it, Men have borne   10
Contempt of Generations
And Crucifixion, shown—
Faith slips—and laughs, and rallies—
Blushes, if any see—
Plucks at a twig of Evidence—   15
And asks a Vane, the way—
Much Gesture, from the Pulpit—
Strong Hallelujahs roll—
Narcotics cannot still the Tooth
That nibbles at the soul—   20

[c. 1862]

I got so I could hear his name—

I got so I could hear his name—
Without—Tremendous gain—
That Stop-sensation—on my Soul—
And Thunder—in the Room—   4

I got so I could walk across
That Angle in the floor,
Where he turned so, and I turned—how—
And all our Sinew tore—   8

I got so I could stir the Box—
In which his letters grew
Without that forcing, in my breath—
As Staples—driven through—   12

Could dimly recollect a Grace—
I think, they call it "God"—
Renowned to ease Extremity—
When Formula, had failed—   16

And shape my Hands—
Petition's way,
Tho' ignorant of a word
That Ordination°—utters—   20

My Business, with the Cloud,
If any Power behind it, be,
Not subject to Despair—

It care, in some remoter way,   24
For so minute affair
As Misery—
Itself, too great, for interrupting—more—

[1861]

20 Ordination the ministry.

Because I could not stop for Death

Because I could not stop for Death—
He kindly stopped for me—
The Carriage held but just Ourselves—
And Immortality.   4

We slowly drove—He knew no haste
And I had put away
My labor and my leisure too,
For His Civility—   8

We passed the School, where Children strove
At Recess—in the Ring—
We passed the Fields of Gazing Grain—
We passed the Setting Sun—   12

Or rather—He passed Us—
The Dews drew quivering and chill—
For only Gossamer, my Gown—
My Tippet°—only Tulle°—   16

We paused before a House that seemed
A Swelling of the Ground—
The Roof was scarcely visible—
The Cornice—in the Ground—   20

Since then—'tis Centuries—and yet
Feels shorter than the Day
I first surmised the Horses' Heads
Were toward Eternity—   24
                                                        [c. 1863]

16 Tippet shawl;   **Tulle** net of silk.

Those—dying, then

Those—dying, then
Knew where they went
They went to God's Right Hand—
The Hand is amputated now
And God cannot be found—   5

The abdication of Belief
Makes the Behavior small—
Better an ignis fatuus°
Than no illume at all—

                                                        [1882]

8 ignis fatuus a phosphorescent light that hovers over swampy ground, hence something deceptive.

Apparently with no surprise

Apparently with no surprise
To any happy Flower
The Frost beheads it at its play—
In accidental power—
The blonde Assassin passes on—   5
The Sun proceeds unmoved
To measure off another Day
For an Approving God.

[c. 1884]

Tell all the Truth but tell it slant

Tell all the Truth but tell it slant—
Success in Circuit lies
Too bright for our infirm Delight
The Truth's superb surprise   4

As Lightning to the Children eased
With explanation kind
The Truth must dazzle gradually
Or every man be blind—   8

[c. 1868]

A SAMPLE ESSAY BY A STUDENT: "RELIGION AND RELIGIOUS IMAGERY IN EMILY DICKINSON"

Peter Gottsegen

English 150G

April 12, 2001

Religion and Religious Imagery in Emily Dickinson

Emily Dickinson was not a preacher but a poet, so if we read her

poetry about God we should not be surprised if we do not find a simple,

consistent view, or even a clear development from one view--for instance,

belief--to another--for instance, loss of faith. Rather, judging from some

examples of her poetry, she explored various views, and we should not try

to convert this variety into unity.

We can begin by looking at extreme views, first two poems of faith, and then a poem of doubt. One of the poems of faith, "Papa above" (527), begins with a childlike or almost playful version of the Lord's Prayer. (In Matthew 6.9 Jesus begins a prayer by saying, "Our Father who art in heaven.") I think this poem says that God will see to it that even a mouse or rat will get into heaven, and will remain there for eternity. But Dickinson's God is not always concerned for all of the creatures of the world. In another poem that expresses belief in the existence of God, "Apparently with no surprise" (530), Dickinson describes the frost as beheading a flower--that is, beauty perishes--and she goes on to make the point that this occurs under the eyes of "an Approving God." Here she seems to be saying that evil takes place, and God approves of it. It is important to realize that in this poem Dickinson still says that God exists, even if he is indifferent to suffering.

In another poem, "Those--dying, then" (529), Dickinson expresses doubt that God exists. In olden days, she says, people mistakenly thought that God would protect them, but now, she says, "God cannot be found." She uses a particularly terrifying image to convey the loss of God. In the past, Dickinson says, the faithful went to "God's Right Hand," but, she goes on to say, "The Hand is amputated now. . . ." The faith in God that earlier people had was an illusion, but it was something, and it was "better" than the nothingness we now experience. This nothingness, or something not much more than nothingness, is the subject of "I heard a Fly buzz--when I died" (524–26). In this poem, the speaker expects "the King" (God) to appear to her as she dies, but all she sees is a fly, and then she hears its buzz. God ("the King") never appears.

Even these few poems show that Dickinson held a variety of views about God and religion, and it is difficult or perhaps impossible for us to say exactly what her religious beliefs were. But what is certain is that religious ideas were so important to her, so much a part of her mind, that even when she was not explicitly writing about the existence of a benevolent God or the absence of God, she used religious imagery--for instance, to describe impressive things in the natural world around her. In "These are the days when Birds come back" (526), she talks about what we call Indian summer, fall days that are like summer days. But the poem is filled with religious words: "belief," "Sacrament," "Communion," "consecrated bread," "immortal wine." The fifth stanza goes like this:

> Oh Sacrament of summer days,
>
> Oh Last Communion in the Haze--
>
> Permit a child to join.

I don't think Dickinson is really talking about traditional religion here. Instead, she is using religious imagery to talk about a particular precious moment in the seasons. As a second example of her use of religious imagery in a poem that is about nature and not about God, we might look at "There's a certain Slant of light" (527). In this poem she says that on "Wintry Afternoons" this particular light has "the Heft / Of Cathedral Tunes." That is, the wintry light has the solidity, the feel, the "heft" of religious music. When we see this light, Dickinson says, we are moved, in a way that we are moved by music in church. She is not saying anything here about whether God is benevolent or not, or whether he exists or not. Rather, she is drawing on experiences in church--probably experiences shared by many people even today--to help us to see nature more effectively.

Speaking as someone who was brought up with traditional religious beliefs but who does not go to church now, I can say that Dickinson effectively represents the ideas of a believer and also of a non-believer. But what I think is especially impressive is that she sees that someone who no longer is a believer can't help but still think in religious terms when he or she sees something exceptionally beautiful, for instance on a winter day "a certain Slant of light."

[New page]

Work Cited

Barnet, Sylvan, et al. <u>Literature for Composition, Compact Edition</u>. New

York: Longman, 2003.

Topics for Critical Thinking and Writing

1. In this essay Gottsegen comments on the following poems: "Papa above," "Apparently with no surprise," "Those—dying, then," "I heard a Fly buzz—when I died," "These are the days when Birds come back," and "There's a certain Slant of light." Read or reread each of these poems to see if you agree with Gottsegen's interpretations.
2. Are there other poems in the case study that you think Gottsegen could have used with better effect than some that he did use? Explain.
3. Reread the concluding paragraph. Do you think it is effective? Explain.

PART III

Standing Back

Arguing Interpretations and Evaluations, and Understanding Critical Strategies

13

Arguing an Interpretation

In Chapter 2 we discussed arguing with yourself as a way of developing ideas; in Chapter 3 we discussed arguing about meanings or interpretations; and in Chapter 7 we discussed supporting arguments with evidence. Nevertheless, we have more to say about writing an argument, and we will say some of it in this chapter and in the next two chapters where we will consider assumptions and evidence.

INTERPRETATION AND MEANING

We can define **interpretation** as

- a setting forth of the meaning, or, better,
- a setting forth of one or more of the meanings of a work of literature.

This question of *meaning* versus *meanings* deserves a brief explanation. Although some critics believe that a work of literature has a single meaning, the meaning it had for the author, most critics hold that a work has several meanings, for instance the meaning it had for the author, the meaning(s) it had for its first readers (or viewers, if the work is a drama), the meaning(s) it had for later readers, and the meaning(s) it has for us today. Take *Hamlet* (1600–01), for example. Perhaps this play about a man who has lost his father had a very special meaning for Shakespeare, who had recently lost his own father. Further, Shakespeare had earlier lost a son named Hamnet, a variant spelling of Hamlet. The play, then, may have had important psychological meanings for Shakespeare—but the audience could not have shared (or even known) these meanings.

What *did* the play mean to Shakespeare's audience? Perhaps the original audience of *Hamlet*—people living in a monarchy, presided over by Queen Elizabeth I—were especially concerned with the issue (specifically raised in *Hamlet*) of whether a monarch's subjects ever have the right to overthrow the monarch. But obviously for twenty-first-century Americans the interest in the play lies elsewhere, and the play must mean something else. If we are familiar with Freud, we may see in the play a young man who subconsciously lusts after his mother and seeks to kill his father (in the form of Claudius, Hamlet's uncle). Or we may see the play as largely about an alienated young man in a bourgeois society. Or—but the interpretations are countless.

Is the Author's Intention a Guide to Meaning?

Shouldn't we be concerned, you might ask, with the *intentions* of the author? The question is reasonable, but there are difficulties, as the members of the Supreme Court find when they try to base their decisions on the original intent of the writers of the Constitution. First, for older works we almost never know what the intention is. Authors did not leave comments about their intentions. We have *Hamlet,* but we do not have any statement of Shakespeare's intention concerning this or any other play. It might be argued that we can deduce Shakespeare's intention from the play itself, but to argue that we should study the play in the light of Shakespeare's intention, and that we can know his intention by studying the play, is to argue in a circle. We can say that Shakespeare must have intended to write a tragedy (if he intended to write a comedy he failed), but we can't go much further in talking about his intention.

Even if an author has gone on record expressing an intention, we may think twice before accepting the statement as decisive. The author may be speaking facetiously, deceptively, mistakenly, or (to be brief) unconvincingly. For instance, Thomas Mann said, probably sincerely and accurately, that he wrote one of his novels merely in order to entertain his family—but we may nevertheless take the book seriously and find it profound.

What Characterizes a Sound Interpretation?

Even the most vigorous advocates of the idea that meaning is indeterminate do not believe that all interpretations are equally significant. Rather, they believe that an interpretive essay is offered against a background of ideas, shared by essayist and reader, as to what constitutes a *persuasive argument.* Thus, an essay (even if it is characterized as "interpretive free play" or "creative engagement") will have to be

- coherent,
- plausible, and
- rhetorically effective.

The *presentation*—the rhetoric—as well as the interpretation is significant. This means (to repeat a point made in Chapter 2) that the essayist cannot merely set down random expressions of feeling or unsupported opinions. The essayist must, on the contrary, convincingly *argue* a thesis—must point to evidence so that the reader will not only know what the essayist believes but will also understand why he or she believes it.

There are lots of ways of making sense (and even more ways of making non-sense), but one important way of helping readers to see things from your point of view is to do your best to face all of the complexities of the work. Put it this way: Some interpretations strike a reader as better than others because they are *more inclusive,* that is, because they *account for more of the details of the work.* The less satisfactory interpretations leave a reader pointing to some aspects of the work—to some parts of the whole—and saying, "Yes, but your explanation doesn't take account of . . ." This does not mean, of course, that a reader must feel that a persuasive interpretation says the last word about the work. We always realize that the work—if we value it highly—is richer than the discussion; but, again, for us to value an interpretation we must find the interpretation plausible and inclusive.

Interpretation often depends not only on making connections among various elements of the work (for instance, among the characters in a story or among the images in a poem), and among the work and other works by the author, but also on making connections between the particular work and a **cultural context.** The cultural context usually includes other writers and specific works of literature, since a given literary work participates in a tradition. That is, if a work looks toward life, it also looks toward other works. A sonnet, for example, is about human experience, but it is also part of a tradition of sonnet writing. The more works of literature you are familiar with, the better equipped you are to interpret any particular work. Here is the way Robert Frost put it, in the preface to *Aforesaid:*

> A poem is best read in the light of all the other poems ever written. We read A the better to read B (we have to start somewhere; we may get very little out of A). We read B the better to read C, C the better to read D, D the better to go back and get something more out of A. Progress is not the aim, but circulation. The thing is to get among the poems where they hold each other apart in their places as the stars do.

An Example: Interpreting Pat Mora's "Immigrants"

Let's think about interpreting a short poem by a contemporary poet, Pat Mora.

Immigrants

wrap their babies in the American flag,
feed them mashed hot dogs and apple pie,
name them Bill and Daisy,
buy them blonde dolls that blink   5
blue eyes or a football and tiny cleats
before the baby can even walk,
speak to them in thick English,
    hallo, babee, hallo.
whisper in Spanish or Polish   10
when the babies sleep, whisper
in a dark parent bed, that dark
parent fear, "Will they like
our boy, our girl, our fine american
boy, our fine american girl?"   15

                         [1986]

Perhaps most readers will agree that the poem expresses or dramatizes a desire, attributed to "immigrants," that their child grow up in an Anglo mode. (Mora is not saying that *all* immigrants have this desire; she has simply invented one speaker who says such-and-such. Of course *we* may say that Mora says all immigrants have this desire, but that is our interpretation.) For this reason the parents call their children Bill and Daisy (rather than, say, José and Juanita) and give them blonde dolls and a football (rather than dark-haired dolls and a soccer ball). Up to this point, the parents seem a bit silly in their mimicking of Anglo ways. But the second part of the poem gives the reader a more interior view of the parents, brings out the fear and hope and worried concern that lies behind the behavior: Some unspecified "they" may not "like / our boy, our girl." Who are "they"? Most readers probably will agree that "they" refers to native-born citizens, especially the blond, blue-eyed "all-American" Anglo types that until recently constituted the establishment in the United States.

We can raise further questions about the interpretation of the poem.

- Exactly what does the poet mean when she says that immigrants "wrap their babies in the American flag"? Are we to take this literally?
- If not, how are we to take it?

- And why in the last two lines is the word "american" not capitalized? Is Mora imitating the non-native speaker's uncertain grasp of English punctuation? (But if so, why does Mora capitalize "American" in the first line and "Spanish" and "Polish" later in the poem?) Or is she perhaps implying some mild reservation about becoming 100 percent American, some suggestion that in changing from Spanish or Polish to "american" there is some sort of loss?

A reader might seek Mora out and ask her why she didn't capitalize "american" in the last line, but Mora might not be willing to answer, or she might not give a straight answer, or she might say that she doesn't really know why—it just seemed right when she wrote the poem. Most authors do in fact take this last approach. When they are working as writers, they work by a kind of instinct, a kind of feel for the material. Later they can look critically at their writing, but that's another sort of experience.

To return to our basic question: What characterizes a good interpretation? The short answer is, *Evidence,* and especially evidence that seems to cover all relevant issues. In an essay it is not enough merely to assert an interpretation. Your readers don't expect you to make an airtight case, but because you are trying to help readers to understand a work—to see a work the way you do—you are obliged to

- offer reasonable supporting evidence, and
- take account of what might be set forth as counterevidence to your thesis.

Of course your essay may originate in an intuition or an emotional response, a sense that the work is about such-and-such, but this intuition or emotion must then be examined, and it must stand a test of reasonableness. (It's usually a good idea to jot down in a journal your first responses to a work, and in later entries to reflect on them.) It is not enough in an essay merely to set forth your response. Your readers will expect you to *demonstrate* that the response is something that they can to a large degree share. They may not be convinced that the interpretation is right or true, but they must at least feel that the interpretation is plausible and in accord with the details of the work, rather than, say, highly eccentric and irreconcilable with some details.

This book includes ten case studies, some of which include essays by critics advancing interpretations. When you read these interpretations, think about *why* you find some interpretations more convincing than others.

THINKING CRITICALLY ABOUT RESPONSES TO LITERATURE

Usually you will begin with a strong *response* to your reading—interest, boredom, bafflement, annoyance, shock, pleasure, or whatever. Fine. Then, if you are going to think critically about the work, you will go on to *examine* your response in order to understand it, or to deepen it, or to change it.

How can you change a response? Critical thinking involves seeing an issue from all sides, to as great a degree as possible. As you know, in ordinary language *to criticize* usually means to find fault, but in literary studies the term does not have a negative connotation. Rather, it means "to examine carefully." (The word *criticism* comes from a Greek verb meaning "to distinguish," "to decide," "to judge.") Nevertheless, in one sense the term *critical thinking* does approach the usual meaning, since critical thinking requires you to take a skeptical view of your response. You will, so to speak, argue with yourself, seeing if your response can stand up to doubts.

Let's say that you have found a story implausible. Question yourself:

- Exactly what is implausible in it?
- Is implausibility always a fault?
- If so, exactly why?

Your answers may deepen your response. Usually, in fact, you will find supporting evidence for your response, but in your effort to distinguish and to decide and to judge, try also (if only as an exercise) to find **counterevidence.** See what can be said against your position. (The best lawyers, it is said, prepare two cases—their own, and the other side's.) As you consider the counterevidence you will sometimes find that it requires you to adjust your thesis. Fine. You may even find yourself developing an entirely different response. That's also fine, though of course the paper that you ultimately hand in should clearly argue a thesis.

Critical thinking, in short, means examining or exploring one's own responses, by questioning and testing them. Critical thinking is not so much a skill (though it does involve the ability to understand a text) as it is a *habit of mind,* or, rather, several habits, including

- Open-mindedness
- Intellectual curiosity
- Willingness to work

It may involve, for instance, willingness to discuss the issues with others and to do research, a topic that will be treated separately in Appendix B, on writing a research paper.

Two Interpretations by Students

Robert Frost, "Stopping by Woods on a Snowy Evening"

Read Frost's "Stopping by Woods on a Snowy Evening," and then read the first interpretation, written by a first-year student. This interpretation is followed by a discussion that is devoted chiefly to two questions:

- What is the essayist's thesis?
- Does the essayist offer convincing evidence to support the thesis?

A second essay by another first-year student, offering a different interpretation of the poem, provides further material for you to analyze critically.

ROBERT FROST

Robert Frost (1874–1963) was born in California. After his father's death in 1885 Frost's mother brought the family to New England, where she taught in high schools in Massachusetts and New Hampshire. Frost studied for part of one term at Dartmouth College in New Hampshire, then did odd jobs (including teaching), and from 1897 to 1899 was enrolled as a special student at Harvard. He then farmed in New Hampshire, published a few poems in local newspapers, left the farm and taught again, and in 1912 left for England, where he hoped to achieve more popular success as a writer. By 1915 he had won a

*considerable reputation, and he returned to the United States, settling on a farm in
New Hampshire and cultivating the image of the country-wise farmer-poet. In fact
he was well read in the classics, the Bible, and English and American literature.*

Stopping by Woods on a Snowy Evening

Whose woods these are I think I know.
His house is in the village though;
He will not see me stopping here
To watch his woods fill up with snow.   4

My little horse must think it queer
To stop without a farmhouse near
Between the woods and frozen lake
The darkest evening of the year.   8

He gives his harness bells a shake
To ask if there is some mistake.
The only other sound's the sweep
Of easy wind and downy flake.   12

The woods are lovely, dark and deep.
But I have promises to keep,
And miles to go before I sleep,
And miles to go before I sleep.   16

[1923]

Manuscript version of Frost's "Stopping by Woods on a Snowy Evening." The first part is lost. (Courtesy of the Jones Library, Inc., Amherst, Mass.)

Sample Essay by a Student:
"Stopping by Woods—and Going On"

Darrel MacDonald

Stopping by Woods--and Going On

Robert Frost's "Stopping by Woods on a Snowy Evening" is about what the title says it is. It is also about something more than the title says.

When I say it is about what the title says, I mean that the poem really does give us the thoughts of a person who pauses (that is, a person who is "stopping") by woods on a snowy evening. (This person probably is a man, since Robert Frost wrote the poem and nothing in the poem clearly indicates that the speaker is not a man. But, and this point will be important, the speaker perhaps feels that he is not a very masculine man. As we will see, the word "queer" appears in the poem, and, also, the speaker uses the word "lovely," which sounds more like the word a woman would use than a man.) In line 3 the speaker says he is "stopping here," and it is clear that "here" is by woods, since "woods" is mentioned not only in the title but also in the first line of the poem, and again in the second stanza, and still again in the last stanza. It is equally clear that, as the title says, there is snow, and that the time is evening. The speaker mentions "snow" and "downy flake," and he says this is "The darkest evening of the year."

But in what sense is the poem about <u>more</u> than the title? The title does not tell us anything about the man who is "stopping by woods," but the poem--the man's meditation--tells us a lot about him. In the first stanza he reveals that he is uneasy at the thought that the owner of the woods may see him stopping by the woods. Maybe he is uneasy because he is trespassing, but the poem does not actually say that he has illegally entered someone else's property. More likely, he feels uneasy, almost ashamed, of watching the "woods fill up with snow." That is, he would not want anyone to see that he actually is enjoying a beautiful aspect of nature and is not hurrying about whatever his real business is in thrifty Yankee style.

The second stanza gives more evidence that he feels guilty about enjoying beauty. He feels so guilty that he even thinks the horse thinks there is something odd about him. In fact, he says that the horse thinks he is "queer," which of course may just mean odd, but also (as is shown by The American Heritage Dictionary) it can mean "gay," "homosexual." A real man, he sort of suggests, wouldn't spend time looking at snow in the woods.

So far, then, the speaker in two ways has indicated that he feels insecure, though perhaps he does not realize that he has given himself away. First, he expresses uneasiness that someone might see him watching the woods fill up with snow. Second, he expresses uneasiness when he suggests that even the horse thinks he is strange, maybe even "queer" or unmanly, or at least unbusinesslike. And so in the last stanza, even though he finds the woods beautiful, he decides <u>not</u> to stop and to see the woods fill up with snow. And his description of the woods as "lovely"--a woman's word--sounds as though he may be something less than a he-man. He seems to feel ashamed of himself for enjoying the sight of the snowy woods and for seeing them as "lovely," and so he tells himself that he has spent enough time looking at the woods and that he must go on about his business. In fact, he tells himself <u>twice</u> that he has business to attend to. Why? Perhaps he is insisting too much. Just as we saw that he was excessively nervous in the first stanza, afraid that someone might see him trespassing and enjoying the beautiful spectacle, now at the end he is again afraid that someone might see him loitering, and so he very firmly, using repetition as a form of emphasis, tries to reassure himself that he is not too much attracted by beauty and is a man of business who keeps his promises.

Frost gives us, then, a man who indeed is seen "stopping by woods on

a snowy evening," but a man who, afraid of what society will think of him,

is also afraid to "stop" long enough to fully enjoy the sight that attracts

him, because he is driven by a sense that he may be seen to be trespassing

and also may be thought to be unmanly. So after only a brief stop in the

woods he forces himself to go on, a victim (though he probably doesn't

know it) of the work ethic and of an over-simple idea of manliness.

Let's examine this essay briefly.

The title is interesting. It gives the reader a good idea of which literary work will be discussed ("Stopping by Woods") *and* it arouses interest, in this case by a sort of wordplay ("Stopping . . . Going On"). A title of this sort is preferable to a title that merely announces the topic, such as "An Analysis of Frost's 'Stopping by Woods'" or "On a Poem by Robert Frost."

The opening paragraph helpfully names the exact topic (Robert Frost's poem) and arouses interest by asserting that the poem is about something more than its title. The writer's thesis presumably will be a fairly specific assertion concerning what else the poem is "about."

The body of the essay, beginning with the second paragraph, begins to develop the thesis. (The **thesis** perhaps can be summarized thus: "The speaker, insecure of his masculinity, feels ashamed that he responds with pleasure to the sight of the snowy woods.") The writer's evidence in the second paragraph is that the word "queer" (a word sometimes used of homosexuals) appears, and that the word "lovely" is "more like the word a woman would use than a man." Readers of MacDonald's essay may at this point be unconvinced by this evidence, but probably they suspend judgement. In any case, he has offered what he considers to be evidence in support of his thesis.

The next paragraph dwells on what is said to be the speaker's uneasiness, and the following paragraph returns to the word "queer," which, MacDonald correctly says, can mean "gay, homosexual." The question of course is whether *here*, in this poem, the word has this meaning. Do we agree with MacDonald's assertion, in the last sentence of this paragraph, that Frost is suggesting that "A real man . . . wouldn't spend time looking at snow in the woods"? Clearly this is the way MacDonald takes the poem—but is his response to these lines reasonable? After all, what Frost says is this: "My little horse must think it queer / To stop without a farmhouse near." Is it reasonable to see a reference to homosexuality (rather than merely to oddness) in *this* use of the word "queer"? Hasn't MacDonald offered a response that, so to speak, is private? It is *his* response—but are we likely to share it, to agree that we see it in Frost's poem?

The next paragraph, amplifying the point that the speaker is insecure, offers as evidence the argument that "lovely" is more often a woman's word than a man's. Probably most readers will agree on this point, though many or all might deny that only a gay man would use the word "lovely." And what do you think of MacDonald's assertions that the speaker of the poem "was excessively nervous in the first stanza" and is now "afraid that someone might see him loitering"? In your opinion, does the text lend much support to MacDonald's view?

The concluding paragraph effectively reasserts and clarifies MacDonald's thesis, saying that the speaker hesitates to stop and enjoy the woods because "he is driven by a sense that he may be seen to be trespassing and also may be thought to be unmanly."

The big questions, then, are these:

- Is the thesis *argued* rather than merely asserted, and
- Is it argued *convincingly?*

Or, to put it another way,

- Is the evidence adequate?

MacDonald certainly does argue (offer reasons) rather than merely assert, but does he offer enough evidence to make you think that his response is one that you can share? Has he helped you to enjoy the poem by seeing things that you may not have noticed—or has he said things that, however interesting, seem to you not to be in close contact with the poem as you see it?

Here is another interpretation of the same poem.

Sample Essay by a Student: "'Stopping by Woods on a Snowy Evening' as a Short Story"

Sara Fong

"Stopping by Woods on a Snowy Evening" as a Short Story

Robert Frost's "Stopping by Woods on a Snowy Evening" can be read as a poem about a man who pauses to observe the beauty of nature, and it can also be read as a poem about a man with a death wish, a man who seems to long to give himself up completely to nature and thus escape his responsibilities as a citizen. Much depends, apparently, on what a reader wants to emphasize. For instance, a reader can emphasize especially appealing lines about the beauty of nature: "The only other sound's the sweep / Of easy wind and downy flake," and "The woods are lovely, dark and deep." On the other hand, a reader can emphasize lines that show the speaker is fully aware of the responsibilities that most of us agree we have. For instance, at the very start of the poem he recognizes that the woods are not his but are owned by someone else, and at the end of the poem he recognizes that he has "promises to keep" and that before he sleeps (dies?) he must accomplish many things (go for "miles").

Does a reader have to choose between these two interpretations? I don't think so; to the contrary, I think it makes sense to read the poem as a kind of very short story, with a character whose developing thoughts make up a plot with four stages. In the first stage, the central figure is an ordinary person with rather ordinary thoughts. His very first thought is of the owner of the woods. He knows who the owner is, and since the owner lives in the village, the poet feels safe in trespassing, or at least in watching the woods "fill up with snow." Then, very subtly, the poet begins to tell us that although this seems to be an ordinary person thinking ordinary thoughts, he is a somewhat special person in a special situation. First of all, the horse thinks something is strange. He shakes his bells, wondering why the driver doesn't keep moving, as presumably ordinary drivers would. Second, we are told that this is "The darkest evening of the year." Frost could simply have said that the evening is dark, but he goes out of his way to make the evening a special evening.

We are now through with the first ten lines, and only six lines remain, yet in these six lines the story goes through two additional phases. The first three of these lines ("The only other sound's the sweep / Of easy wind and downy flake" and "The woods are lovely, dark and deep") are probably the most beautiful lines, in the sense that they are the ones that make us say, "I wish I were there," or "I'd love to experience this." We feel that the poet has moved from the ordinary thoughts of the first stanza, about such businesslike things as who owns the woods and where the owner's house is, to less materialistic thoughts, thoughts about the beauty of the nonhuman world of nature. And now, with the three final lines, we get the fourth stage of the story, the return to the ordinary world of people, the world of "promises." But this world that we get at the end is not exactly the same as the world we got at the beginning. The world at the beginning

of the poem is a world of property (who owns the woods, and where the
house is), but the world at the end of the poem is a world of unspecified and
rather mysterious responsibilities ("promises to keep," "miles to go before I
sleep"). It is almost as though the poet's experience of the beauty of nature--
a beauty that for a moment made him forget the world of property--has in
fact served to sharpen his sense that human beings have responsibilities.
He clearly sees that "The woods are lovely, dark and deep," and then he says
(I add the italics), "_But_ I have promises to keep." The "but" would be logical
if after saying that the woods are lovely, dark and deep, he had said
something like "But in the daylight they look different," or "But one can
freeze to death in them." The logic of what Frost says, however, is not at all
clear: "The woods are lovely, dark and deep, / But I have promises to keep."
What is the logical connection? We have to supply one, something like "but,
because we are human beings we have responsibilities; we can refresh
ourselves by perceiving the beauties of nature, and we can even for a
moment get so caught up that we seem to enter an enchanted forest ('the
woods are lovely, dark and deep'), but we cannot forget our responsibilities."

My point is not that Frost ends with an important moral, and it is
also not that we have to choose between saying it is a poem about nature or
a poem about a man with a death wish. Rather, my point is that the poem
takes us through several stages and that, although the poem begins and
ends with the speaker in the woods, the speaker has undergone mental
experiences--has, we might say, gone through a plot with a conflict (the
appeal of the snowy woods versus the call to return to the human world).
It's not a matter of good versus evil and of one side winning. Frost in no
way suggests that it is wrong to feel the beauty of nature--even to the
momentary exclusion of all other thoughts. But the poem is certainly not
simply a praise of the beauty of nature. Frost shows us, in this mini-story
or mini-drama, one character who sees the woods as property, then sees

them as a place of almost overwhelming beauty, and then (maybe refreshed

by this experience) rejoins the world of chores and responsibilities.

Topics for Critical Thinking and Writing

1. What is the thesis of the essay?
2. Does the essayist offer convincing evidence to support the thesis?
3. Do you consider the essay to be well written, poorly written, or something in between? On what evidence do you base your opinion?

YOUR TURN: POEMS FOR INTERPRETATION

JOHN MILTON

John Milton (1608–74) was born into a well-to-do family in London, where from childhood he was a student of languages, mastering at an early age Latin, Greek, Hebrew, and a number of modern languages. Instead of becoming a minister in the Anglican Church, he resolved to become a poet and spent five years at his family's country home, reading. His attacks against the monarchy secured him a position in Oliver Cromwell's Puritan government as Latin secretary for foreign affairs. He became totally blind, but he continued his work through secretaries, one of whom was Andrew Marvell, author of "To His Coy Mistress" (page 651). With the restoration of the monarchy in 1660, Milton was for a time confined but was later pardoned in the general amnesty. Until his death he continued to work on many subjects, including his greatest poem, the epic Paradise Lost.

When I Consider How My Light Is Spent

When I consider how my light is spent
 Ere half my days, in this dark world and wide,
 And that one talent which is death to hide°
Lodged with me useless,° though my soul more bent   4
To serve therewith my Maker, and present
 My true account, lest he returning chide;
 "Doth God exact day-labor, light denied?"
I fondly° ask; but Patience to prevent°   8
That murmur, soon replies, "God doth not need
 Either man's work or his own gifts; who best
 Bear his mild yoke, they serve him best. His state
Is kingly. Thousands at his bidding speed   12
 And post o'er land and ocean without rest:
 They also serve who only stand and wait."

[1655]

3 There is a pun in *talent,* relating Milton's literary talent to Christ's Parable of the Talents (Matthew 25.14 ff.), in which a servant is rebuked for not putting his talent (a unit of money) to use. **4 useless** a pun on *use,* i.e., usury, interest. **8 fondly** foolishly. **prevent** forestall.

Topics for Critical Thinking and Writing

1. This Petrarchan sonnet (see p. 649) is sometimes called "On His Blindness," though Milton never gave it a title. Do you think this title gets toward the heart of the poem? Explain. If you were to give it a title, what would the title be?
2. Read the parable in Matthew 25.14–30, and then consider how close the parable is to Milton's life as Milton describes it in this poem.

ROBERT FROST (1874–1963)
Mending Wall

Something there is that doesn't love a wall,
That sends the frozen-ground-swell under it,
And spills the upper boulders in the sun;
And makes gaps even two can pass abreast.
The work of hunters is another thing: 5
I have come after them and made repair
Where they have left not one stone on a stone,
But they would have the rabbit out of hiding,
To please the yelping dogs. The gaps I mean,
No one has seen them made or heard them made,   10
But at spring mending-time we find them there.
I let my neighbor know beyond the hill;
And on a day we meet to walk the line
And set the wall between us once again.
We keep the wall between us as we go.   15
To each the boulders that have fallen to each.
And some are loaves and some so nearly balls
We have to use a spell to make them balance:
"Stay where you are until our backs are turned!"
We wear our fingers rough with handling them.   20
Oh, just another kind of outdoor game,
One on a side. It comes to little more:
There where it is we do not need the wall:
He is all pine and I am apple orchard.
My apple trees will never get across   25
And eat the cones under his pines, I tell him.
He only says, "Good fences make good neighbors."
Spring is the mischief in me, and I wonder
If I could put a notion in his head:
"*Why* do they make good neighbors? Isn't it   30
Where there are cows? But here there are no cows.
Before I built a wall I'd ask to know
What I was walling in or walling out,
And to whom I was like to give offense.
Something there is that doesn't love a wall,   35
That wants it down." I could say "Elves" to him,
But it's not elves exactly, and I'd rather

He said it for himself. I see him there
Bringing a stone grasped firmly by the top
In each hand, like an old-stone savage armed.   40
He moves in darkness as it seems to me,
Not of woods only and the shade of trees.
He will not go behind his father's saying,
And he likes having thought of it so well
He says again, "Good fences make good neighbors."   45

[1914]

Topics for Critical Thinking and Writing

1. The poem includes a scene, or action, in which the speaker and a neighbor are engaged. Briefly summarize the scene. What indicates that the scene has been enacted before and will be again?
2. Compare and contrast the speaker and the neighbor.
3. Notice that the speaker, not the neighbor, initiates the business of repairing the wall (line 12). Why do you think he does this?
4. Both the speaker and the neighbor repeat themselves; they each make one point twice in identical language. What do they say? And why does Frost allow the neighbor to have the last word?
5. "Something there is that doesn't love a wall" adds up to "Something doesn't love a wall." Or does it? Within the context of the poem, what is the difference between the two statements?
6. Write an essay of 500 words, telling of an experience in which you came to conclude that "good fences make good neighbors." Or tell of an experience that led you to conclude that fences (they can be figurative fences, of course) are "like to give offense" (see lines 32–34).

WILLIAM WORDSWORTH

William Wordsworth (1770–1850) grew up in the Lake District in England. After graduating from Cambridge University in 1791, he spent a year in France, where he fell in love with a French girl and fathered her child. His enthusiasm for the French Revolution waned, and he returned alone to England, where he devoted his life to poetry. We print a poem, written in 1799, that is one of five poems customarily called "Lucy poems," even though this particular poem, unlike the other four, does not mention the woman's name. It is not known if the poems refer to a real person.

A Slumber Did My Spirit Seal

A slumber did my spirit seal;
    I had no human fears;
She seemed a thing that could not feel
    The touch of earthly years.   4

No motion has she now, no force;
    She neither hears nor sees;
Rolled round in earth's diurnal course,
    With rocks, and stones, and trees.   8

[1799]

Topics for Critical Thinking and Writing

Each of the following assertions represents a brief interpretation. Evaluate each, citing evidence to support or rebut it.

1. The first stanza expresses the speaker's comforting but naive view (his *spirit,* i.e., his intelligence, was in a *slumber*) that his beloved was exempt from the pressures of this world; the second stanza expresses his horrified realization that, now dead, she is mere inanimate matter mechanistically hurled into violent motion.
2. The poem, by a pantheist—someone who identifies the Deity with everything in the universe—is about the poet's realization that the woman he loved, who seemed to be apart from everything else, is now (through her death) assimilated into the grandeur of all that is on the Earth; her death is a return to the life of nature.
3. The poem is ambiguous—just as, say, the following sentence is ambiguous: "Martha's mother died when she was twenty." (Who was twenty, Martha or her mother?) There is no way to decide between the first and second views expressed.
4. The word *diurnal* ("daily") adds a solemnity that makes it impossible to see the poem as a statement about the brutality of Lucy's death. Further, *diurnal* contains the word *urn,* thereby affirming that the entire Earth is her funeral urn.
5. Even if the second view correctly summarizes Wordsworth's pantheism, *for today's readers* the poem is about the brute fact of death.
6. The language is ambiguous, so the only intelligent way to decide between conflicting interpretations is to choose the interpretation that best fits in with what we know about the author.
7. Here, as in most poetry by males, the female is allowed no significant identity. She is a "thing" (line 3), she is the object of the poet's love, she seems to be above nature (thus she is the traditional woman on a pedestal), she is a nature spirit, she is the poet's inspiration—she is lots of things, but she is not a person.

If none of the preceding statements seems to you to be just what you would say if you were asked to summarize your interpretation, set forth your own view, in 50–75 words, and then support it by pointing to details in the poem.

T. S. ELIOT

Thomas Stearns Eliot (1888–1965) was born into a New England family that had moved to St. Louis. He attended a preparatory school in Massachusetts, then graduated from Harvard and did further study in literature and philosophy in France, Germany, and England. In 1914 he began working for Lloyd's Bank in London, and three years later he published his first book of poems (it included "Prufrock"). In 1925 he joined a publishing firm, and in 1927 he became a British citizen and a member of the Church of England. Much of his later poetry, unlike "The Love Song of J. Alfred Prufrock," is highly religious. In 1948 Eliot received the Nobel Prize for Literature.

The Love Song of J. Alfred Prufrock

S'io credesse che mia risposta fosse
A persona che mai tornasse al mondo,
Questa fiamma staria senza piu scosse.
Ma perciocche giammai di questo fondo
Non torno vivo alcun. s'i' odo il vero,
*Senza tema d'infama ti rispondo.**

Let us go then, you and I,
When the evening is spread out against the sky
Like a patient etherized upon a table;
Let us go, through certain half-deserted streets,
The muttering retreats   5
Of restless nights in one-night cheap hotels
And sawdust restaurants with oyster-shells:
Streets that follow like a tedious argument
Of insidious intent
To lead you to an overwhelming question . . .   10
Oh, do not ask, "What is it?"
Let us go and make our visit.

In the room the women come and go
Talking of Michelangelo.

The yellow fog that rubs its back upon the window-panes,   15
The yellow smoke that rubs its muzzle on the window-panes
Licked its tongue into the corners of the evening,
Lingered upon the pools that stand in drains,
Let fall upon its back the soot that falls from chimneys,
Slipped by the terrace, made a sudden leap,   20
And seeing that it was a soft October night,
Curled once about the house, and fell asleep.

And indeed there will be time
For the yellow smoke that slides along the street,
Rubbing its back upon the window-panes;   25
There will be time, there will be time
To prepare a face to meet the faces that you meet;
There will be time to murder and create,
And time for all the works and days° of hands
That lift and drop a question on your plate;   30
Time for you and time for me,
And time yet for a hundred indecisions,
And for a hundred visions and revisions,
Before the taking of a toast and tea.

---

*In Dante's *Inferno* XXVII:61–66, a damned soul who had sought absolution before committing a crime addresses Dante, thinking that his words will never reach the Earth: "If I believed that my answer were to a person who could ever return to the world, this flame would no longer quiver. But because no one ever returned from this depth, if what I hear is true without fear of infamy, I answer you." **29 works and days** "Works and Days" is the title of a poem on farm life by Hesiod (eighth century B.C.).

In the room the women come and go   35
Talking of Michelangelo.

And indeed there will be time
To wonder, "Do I dare?" and, "Do I dare?"
Time to turn back and descend the stair,
With a bald spot in the middle of my hair—   40
[They will say: "How his hair is growing thin!"]
My morning coat, my collar mounting firmly to the chin,
My necktie rich and modest, but asserted by a simple pin—
[They will say: "But how his arms and legs are thin!"]
Do I dare   45
Disturb the universe?
In a minute there is time
For decisions and revisions which a minute will reverse.

For I have known them all already, known them all:—
Have known the evenings, mornings, afternoons,   50
I have measured out my life with coffee spoons;
I know the voices dying with a dying fall°
Beneath the music from a farther room.
    So how should I presume?

And I have known the eyes already, known them all—   55
The eyes that fix you in a formulated phrase,
And when I am formulated, sprawling on a pin,
When I am pinned and wriggling on the wall,
Then how should I begin
To spit out all the butt-ends of my days and ways?   60
    And how should I presume?

And I have known the arms already, known them all—
Arms that are braceleted and white and bare
[But in the lamplight, downed with light brown hair!]

Is it perfume from a dress   65
That makes me so digress?
Arms that lie along a table, or wrap about a shawl.
    And should I then presume?
    And how should I begin?

                              . . . .

Shall I say, I have gone at dusk through narrow streets   70
And watched the smoke that rises from the pipes
Of lonely men in shirt-sleeves, leaning out of windows? . . .

I should have been a pair of ragged claws
Scuttling across the floors of silent seas.

                              . . . .

And the afternoon, the evening, sleeps so peacefully!   75
Smoothed by long fingers,
Asleep . . . tired . . . or it malingers,

52 **dying fall** this line echoes Shakespeare's *Twelfth Night* 1.1.4.

Stretched on the floor, here beside you and me.
Should I, after tea and cakes and ices,
Have the strength to force the moment to its crisis?   80
But though I have wept and fasted, wept and prayed,
Though I have seen my head [grown slightly bald]
   brought in upon a platter,°
I am no prophet—and here's no great matter;
And I have seen the moment of my greatness flicker,
And I have seen the eternal Footman hold my coat, and snicker,   85
And in short, I was afraid.

And would it have been worth it, after all,
After the cups, the marmalade, the tea,
Among the porcelain, among some talk of you and me,
Would it have been worth while,   90
To have bitten off the matter with a smile,
To have squeezed the universe into a ball°
To roll it toward some overwhelming question,
To say: "I am Lazarus,° come from the dead,
Come back to tell you all, I shall tell you all"—   95
If one, settling a pillow by her head,
   Should say: "That is not what I meant at all.
   That is not it, at all."

And would it have been worth it, after all,
Would it have been worth while,   100
After the sunsets and the dooryards and the sprinkled streets.
After the novels, after the teacups, after the skirts that trail along the floor—
And this, and so much more?—
It is impossible to say just what I mean!
But as if a magic lantern threw the nerves in patterns on a screen: 105
Would it have been worth while
If one, settling a pillow or throwing off a shawl,
And turning toward the window, should say:
   "That is not it at all,
   That is not what I meant at all."   110

No! I am not Prince Hamlet, nor was meant to be;
Am an attendant lord, one that will do
To swell a progress, start a scene or two,
Advise the prince; no doubt, an easy tool,
Deferential, glad to be of use,   115
Politic, cautious, and meticulous;
Full of high sentence,° but a bit obtuse;°
At times, indeed, almost ridiculous—
Almost, at times, the Fool.

81–83 But . . . platter these lines allude to John the Baptist (see Matthew 14.1–11). **92 To have . . . ball** this line echoes lines 41–42 of Marvell's "To His Coy Mistress" (see p. 651). **94 Lazarus** see Luke 16 and John 11.   **117 full of high sentence** see Chaucer's description of the Clerk of Oxford in the *Canterbury Tales*.   **112–117 Am . . . obtuse** these lines allude to Polonius and perhaps other figures in *Hamlet*.

I grow old . . . I grow old . . .   120
I shall wear the bottoms of my trousers rolled.

Shall I part my hair behind? Do I dare to eat a peach?
I shall wear white flannel trousers, and walk upon the beach.
I have heard the mermaids singing, each to each.
I do not think that they will sing to me.   125

I have seen them riding seaward on the waves
Combing the white hair of the waves blown back
When the wind blows the water white and black.

We have lingered in the chambers of the sea
By sea-girls wreathed with seaweed red and brown   130
Till human voices wake us, and we drown.

[1910–11]

Topics for Critical Thinking and Writing

1. How does the speaker's name help to characterize him? What suggestions—of class, race, personality—do you find in it? Does the title of this poem strike you as ironic? If so, how or why?
2. What qualities of big-city life are suggested in the poem? How are these qualities linked to the speaker's mood? What other details of the setting—the weather, the time of day—express or reflect his mood? What images do you find especially striking?
3. The speaker's thoughts are represented in a stream-of-consciousness monologue, that is, in what appears to be an unedited flow of thought. Nevertheless, they reveal a story. What is the story?
4. In a paragraph, characterize Prufrock as he might be characterized by one of the women in the poem, and then, in a paragraph or two, offer your own characterization of him.
5. Consider the possibility that the "you" whom Prufrock is addressing is not a listener but is one aspect of Prufrock, and the "I" is another. Given this possibility, in a paragraph characterize the "you," and in another paragraph characterize the "I."
6. Prufrock has gone to a therapist, a psychiatrist, or a member of the clergy for help. Write a 500-word transcript of their session.

14

Arguing an Evaluation

CRITICISM AND EVALUATION

Although, as previously noted, in ordinary usage *criticism* implies finding fault, and therefore implies evaluation—"This story is weak"—in fact most literary criticism is *not* concerned with evaluation. Rather, it is chiefly concerned with *interpretation* (the setting forth of meaning) and with *analysis* (examination of relationships among the parts, or of causes and effects). For instance, an interpretation may argue that in *Death of a Salesman* Willy Loman is the victim of a cruel capitalistic economy, and an analysis may show how the symbolic setting of the play (a stage direction tells us that "towering, angular shapes" surround the salesman's house) contributes to the meaning. In our discussion of "What Is Literature?" we saw that an analysis of Robert Frost's "The Span of Life" (p. 39) called attention to the contrast between the meter of the first line (relatively uneven or irregular, with an exceptional number of heavy stresses) and the meter of the second (relatively even and jingling). The analysis also called attention to the contrast between the content of the first line (the old dog) and the second (the speaker's memory of a young dog):

> The old dog barks backward without getting up.
> I can remember when he was a pup.

In our discussion we did not worry about whether this poem deserves an A, B, or C, nor did we consider whether it was better or worse than some other poem by Frost, or by some other writer. And, to repeat, if you read books and journals devoted to literary study, you find chiefly discussions of meaning. For the most part, critics assume that the works they are writing about have value and are good enough to merit attention, so critics largely concern themselves with other matters.

Still, some critical writing is indeed concerned with evaluation—with saying that works are good or bad, dated or classic, major or minor. (The language need not be as explicit as these words are: Evaluation can also be conveyed through words like *moving, successful, effective, important,* or, on the other hand, *tedious, unsuccessful, weak,* and *trivial.*) In reviews of plays, books, musical and dance performances, and films, professional critics usually devote much of their space to evaluating the work or the performance, or both. The reviewer seeks, finally, to tell readers whether to buy a book or a ticket—or to save their money and their time.

In short, although in our independent reading we read what we like, and we need not argue that one work is better than another, the issue of evaluation is evident all around us.

ARE THERE CRITICAL STANDARDS?

One approach to evaluating a work of literature, or, indeed, to evaluating anything at all, is to rely on personal taste. This approach is evident in a statement such as "I don't know anything about modern art, but I know what I like." The idea is old, at least as old as the Roman saying *De gustibus non est disputandum* ("There is no disputing tastes").

If we say "This is a good work" or "This book is greater than that book," are we saying anything beyond "I like this" and "I like this better than that"? Are all expressions of evaluation really nothing more than expressions of taste? Most people believe that if there are such things as works of art, or works of literature, there must be standards by which they can be evaluated, just as most other things are evaluated by standards. The standards for evaluating a scissors, for instance, are perfectly clear: It ought to cut cleanly, it ought not to need frequent sharpening, and it ought to feel comfortable in the hand. We may also want it to look nice (perhaps to be painted—or on the contrary to reveal its stainless steel), and to be inexpensive, rustproof, and so on, but in any case we can easily state our standards. Similarly, there are agreed-upon standards for evaluating figure skating, gymnastics, fluency in language, and so on.

But what are the standards for evaluating literature? In earlier pages we have implied one standard: In a good work of literature, all of the parts contribute to the whole, making a unified work. Some people would add that mere unity is not enough; a work of high quality needs not only to be unified but also to be complex. The writer offers a "performance in words" (Frost's words, again), and when we read, we can see if the writer has successfully kept all of the Indian clubs in the air. If, for instance, the stated content of the poem is mournful, yet the meter jingles, we can probably say that the performance is unsuccessful; at least one of the juggler's Indian clubs is clattering on the floor.

Here are some of the standards commonly set forth:

- Personal taste
- Truth, realism
- Moral content
- Esthetic qualities, for instance unity

Let's look at some of these in detail.

Morality and Truth as Standards

"It is always a writer's duty to make the world better." Thus wrote Samuel Johnson, in 1765, in his "Preface to Shakespeare." In this view, **morality** plays a large role: A story that sympathetically treats lesbian or gay love is, from a traditional Judeo-Christian perspective, probably regarded as a bad story, or at least not as worthy as a story that celebrates heterosexual married love. On the other hand, a gay or lesbian critic, or anyone not committed to Judeo-Christian values, might regard the story highly because, in such a reader's view, it helps to educate readers and thereby does something "to make the world better."

But there are obvious problems. For one thing, a gay or lesbian story might strike even a reader with traditional values as a work that is effectively told, with believable and memorable characters, whereas a story of heterosexual married love might be unbelievable, awkwardly told, trite, sentimental. (More about sentimentality in a moment.) How much value should we give to the ostensible content of the story, the obvious moral or morality, and how much value should we give to the artistry exhibited in telling the story?

People differ greatly about moral (and religious) issues. Edward Fitzgerald's 1859 translation of *The Rubáiyát of Omar Khayyám* (a twelfth-century Persian poem) suggests that God doesn't exist, or—perhaps worse—if He does exist, He doesn't care about us. That God does not exist is a view held by many moral people; it is also a view opposed by many moral people. The issue then may become a matter of **truth**. Does the value of the poem depend on which view is right? In fact, does a reader have to subscribe to Fitzgerald's view to enjoy (and to evaluate highly) the following stanza from the poem, in which Fitzgerald suggests that the pleasures of this world are the only paradise that we can experience?

> A book of verses underneath the bough,
> A jug of wine, a loaf of bread—and thou
>   Beside me singing in the wilderness—
> Oh, wilderness were paradise enow!

Some critics can give high value to a literary work only if they share its beliefs, if they think that the work corresponds to reality. They measure the work against their vision of the truth.

Other readers can highly value a work of literature that expresses ideas they do not believe, arguing that literature does not require us to believe in its views. Rather, this theory claims, literature gives a reader a strong sense of *what it feels like* to hold certain views—even though the reader does not share those views. Take, for instance, a lyric poem in which Christina Rossetti (1830–94), a devout Anglican, expresses both spiritual numbness and spiritual hope. Here is one stanza from "A Better Resurrection":

> My life is like a broken bowl.
>   A broken bowl that cannot hold
> One drop of water for my soul
>   Or cordial in the searching cold:
> Cast in the fire the perished thing:
>   Melt and remould it, till it be
> A royal cup for Him, my King:
>   O Jesus, drink of me.

One need not be an Anglican suffering a crisis to find this poem of considerable interest. It offers insight into a state of mind, and the truth or falsity of religious belief is not at issue. Similarly, we can argue that although *The Divine Comedy* by Dante Alighieri (1265–1321) is deeply a Roman Catholic work, the non-Catholic reader can read it with interest and pleasure because of (for example) its rich portrayal of a wide range of characters, the most famous of whom perhaps are the pathetic lovers Paolo and Francesca. In Dante's view, they are eternally damned because they were unrepentant adulterers, but a reader need not share this belief.

Other Ways of Thinking about Truth and Realism

Other solutions to the problem of whether a reader must share a writer's beliefs have been offered. One extreme view says that beliefs are irrelevant, since literature has nothing to do with truth. In this view, a work of art does not correspond to anything "outside" itself, that is, to anything in the real world. If a work of art has any "truth," it is only in the sense of being internally consistent. Thus Shakespeare's *Macbeth,* like, say, "Rock-a-bye Baby," isn't making assertions about reality. *Macbeth* has nothing to do with the history of Scotland, just as (in this view) Shakespeare's *Julius Caesar* has nothing to do with the history of Rome, although Shakespeare borrowed some of his material from history books. These tragedies, like lullabies, are worlds in themselves—not to be judged against historical accounts of Scotland or Rome—and we are interested in the characters in the plays only as they exist *in the plays.* We may require, for instance, that the characters be consistent, believable, and engaging, but we cannot require that they correspond to historical figures. Literary works are neither true nor false; they are only (when successful) coherent and interesting. The poet William Butler Yeats (1865–1939) perhaps had in mind something along these lines when he said that you can refute a philosopher, but you cannot refute the song of sixpence. And indeed "Sing a song of sixpence, / Pocket full of rye" has endured for a couple of centuries, perhaps partly because it has nothing to do with truth or falsity; it has created its own engaging world.

And yet it's possible to object, offering a commonsense response: Surely when we see a play, or read an engaging work of literature, whether it is old or new, we feel that somehow the work says something about the life around us, the real world. True, some of what we read—let's say, detective fiction—is chiefly fanciful: We read it to test our wits, or to escape, or to kill time. But most literature seems to be connected to life. This commonsense view, that literature is related to life, has an ancient history, and in fact almost everyone in the Western world believed it from the time of the ancient Greeks until the nineteenth century. And of course many people—including authors and highly skilled readers—still believe it today.

Certainly a good deal of literature, most notably the realistic short story and the novel, is devoted to giving a detailed picture that at least *looks like* the real world. One reason we read the fiction of Kate Chopin is to find out what "the real world" of Creole New Orleans in the late nineteenth century was like—as seen through Chopin's eyes, of course. (You need not be a Marxist to believe, with Karl Marx, that you can learn more about industrial England from the novels of Dickens and Mrs. Gaskell than from economic treatises.) Writers of stories, novels, and plays are concerned to give plausible, indeed precise and insightful, images of the relationships between people. Writers of lyric poems presumably are specialists in presenting human feelings—the experience of love, for instance, or of the loss of faith. And presumably we are invited to compare the writer's created world to the world that we live in, perhaps to be reminded that our own lives can be richer than they are.

Even when a writer describes an earlier time, the implication is that the description is accurate, and especially that people *did* behave the way the writer says they did—and the way our own daily experience shows us that people do behave. Here is George Eliot at the beginning of her novel *Adam Bede* (1859):

> With a single drop of ink for a mirror, the Egyptian sorcerer undertook to reveal to any chance comer far-reaching visions of the past. This is what I undertake to do for you, reader. With this drop of ink at the end of my pen, I will show you the roomy workshop of Jonathan Burge, carpenter and builder in the village of Hayslope, as it appeared on the 18th of June, in the year of Our Lord, 1799.

Why do novelists like George Eliot give us detailed pictures, and cause us to become deeply involved in the lives of their characters? Another novelist, D. H. Lawrence, offers a relevant comment in the ninth chapter of *Lady Chatterley's Lover* (1928):

> It is the way our sympathy flows and recoils that really determines our lives. And here lies the vast importance of the novel, properly handled. It can inform and lead into new places the flow of our sympathetic consciousness, and it can lead our sympathy away in recoil from things gone dead. Therefore, the novel, properly handled, can reveal the most secret places of life.

In Lawrence's view, we can evaluate a novel in terms of its moral effect on the reader: The good novel, Lawrence claims, leads us into worlds—human relationships—that deserve our attention, and leads us away from "things gone dead," presumably relationships and values—whether political, moral, or religious—that no longer deserve to survive. To be blunt, Lawrence claims that good books improve us. His comment is similar to a more violent comment, quoted earlier, by Franz Kafka: "A book must be an ice-axe to break the frozen sea inside us."

Realism, of course, is not the writer's only tool. In *Gulliver's Travels* Swift gives us a world of Lilliputians, people about six inches tall. Is his book pure fancy, unrelated to life? Not at all. We perceive that the Lilliputians are (except for their size) pretty much like ourselves, and we realize that their tiny stature is an image of human pettiness, an *un*realistic device that helps us to see the real world more clearly.

The view that we have been talking about—that writers do connect us to the world—does not require realism, but it does assume that writers see, understand, and, through the medium of their writings, give us knowledge, deepen our understanding, and even perhaps improve our character. If, the argument goes, a work distorts reality—let's say because the author sees women superficially—the work is inferior. Some such assumption is found, for instance, in a comment by Elaine Savory Fido, who says that the work of Derek Walcott, a Caribbean poet and dramatist, is successful when Walcott deals with racism and with colonialism but is unsuccessful when he deals with women. "His treatment of women," Fido says in an essay in *Journal of Commonwealth Literature* (1986),

> is full of clichés, stereotypes and negativity. I shall seek to show how some of his worst writing is associated with these portraits of women, which sometimes lead him to the brink of losing verbal control, or give rise to a retreat into abstract, conventional terms which prevent any real treatment of the subject. (109)

We need not here be concerned with whether Fido's evaluations of Walcott's works about women and about colonialism are convincing: What concerns us is her assumption that works can be—should be—evaluated in terms of the keenness of the writer's perception of reality.

Although we *need* not be concerned with an evaluation, we may wish to be concerned with it—and if so, we will probably find, perhaps to our surprise, that in the very process of arguing our evaluation (perhaps only to ourselves) we are also interpreting and reinterpreting. That is, we find ourselves observing passages closely, from a new point of view, and we may therefore find ourselves seeing them differently, finding new meanings in them.

YOUR TURN: POEMS AND STORIES FOR EVALUATION

MATTHEW ARNOLD

Matthew Arnold (1822–88) was the son of a famous educator, Dr. Thomas Arnold, the headmaster of Rugby School. After graduating from Oxford, Matthew Arnold became an inspector of schools, a post he held until two years before his death. Besides writing poetry, Arnold wrote literary criticism and was appointed professor of poetry at Oxford from 1857 to 1867. He traveled widely on the Continent and lectured in the United States.

Dover Beach

The sea is calm to-night.
The tide is full, the moon lies fair
Upon the straits;—on the French coast the light
Gleams and is gone; the cliffs of England stand
Glimmering and vast, out in the tranquil bay.   5
Come to the window, sweet is the night-air!
Only, from the long line of spray
Where the sea meets the moon-blanch'd land,
Listen! you hear the grating roar
Of pebbles which the waves draw back, and fling,   10
At their return, up the high strand,
Begin, and cease, and then again begin,
With tremulous cadence slow, and bring
The eternal note of sadness in.

Sophocles long ago   15
Heard it on the Ægean, and it brought
Into his mind the turbid ebb and flow
Of human misery; we
Find also in the sound a thought,
Hearing it by this distant northern sea.   20

The Sea of Faith
Was once, too, at the full, and round earth's shore
Lay like the folds of a bright girdle furl'd.

But now I only hear
Its melancholy, long, withdrawing roar,   25
Retreating, to the breath
Of the night-wind, down the vast edges drear
And naked shingles° of the world.

Ah, love, let us be true
To one another! for the world, which seems   30
To lie before us like a land of dreams,
So various, so beautiful, so new,

28 shingles pebbled beaches.

Hath really neither joy, nor love, nor light,
Nor certitude, nor peace, nor help for pain;
And we are here as on a darkling plain   35
Swept with confused alarms of struggle and flight,
Where ignorant armies clash by night.

[c. 1851]

Topics for Critical Thinking and Writing

1. How would you characterize the speaker's tone of voice? Does the tone stay
   the same throughout?
2. What do we learn about the relationship between the speaker and the person
   whom he addresses? How is this relationship connected to the speaker's reflections on the general sorrow of life and the loss of faith?
3. What is your response to the simile that Arnold uses in line 23?
4. "Dover Beach" is included in many anthologies of literature and collections of
   verse. In your view, does this fact bear witness to the force of habit, or is
   there something about this poem that makes it especially important and memorable?

ANTHONY HECHT

*Anthony Hecht was born in New York City in 1923, and edu-
cated at Bard College and Columbia University. He has taught
at several institutions (since 1985 he has been at Georgetown
University), and he has served as poetry consultant to the Library of Congress.*

*Like "The Dover Bitch," which assumes a reader's familiar-
ity with Matthew Arnold's "Dover Beach," much of Hecht's work
glances at earlier literature.*

The Dover Bitch

A Criticism of Life
For Andrews Wanning

So there stood Matthew Arnold and this girl
With the cliffs of England crumbling away behind them,
And he said to her, "Try to be true to me,
And I'll do the same for you, for things are bad
All over, etc., etc."   5
Well now, I knew this girl. It's true she had read
Sophocles in a fairly good translation
And caught that bitter allusion to the sea.
But all the time he was talking she had in mind
The notion of what his whiskers would feel like   10
On the back of her neck. She told me later on
That after a while she got to looking out

At the lights across the channel, and really felt sad,
Thinking of all the wine and enormous beds
And blandishments in French and the perfumes.   15
And then she got really angry. To have been brought
All the way down from London, and then be addressed
As sort of a mournful cosmic last resort
Is really tough on a girl, and she was pretty.
Anyway, she watched him pace the room   20
And finger his watch-chain and seem to sweat a bit,
And then she said one or two unprintable things.
But you mustn't judge her by that. What I mean to say is,
She's really all right. I still see her once in a while
And she always treats me right.   25
We have a drink
And I give her a good time, and perhaps it's a year
Before I see her again, but there she is,
Running to fat, but dependable as they come,
And sometimes I bring her a bottle of *Nuit d'Amour.*   30

[1967]

Topics for Critical Thinking and Writing

1. Do you think that the first six lines of Hecht's poem are too chatty and informal? What might be the poet's purpose in writing in this style?
2. Line 8 seems somewhat puzzling. Is "that bitter allusion to the sea" the kind of phrase that the speaker of the first few lines would use? Take note as well of the word "blandishments" in line 15, and the phrase "mournful cosmic last resort," line 18. Are the tone and diction of these lines consistent with that of the rest of the poem?
3. What, finally, is the point of Hecht's poem? Is he simply making fun of the stuffy, solemn author of "Dover Beach," or, beyond that, does he seek to present and explore a point of view of his own—for example, on the nature of male/female relationships?
4. Does "The Dover Bitch," to be effective, require that we know "Dover Beach"? If you came across Hecht's poem by itself, and had never read Arnold's poem, what do you imagine your response to "The Dover Bitch" would be?

ROBERT FROST

Robert Frost (1874–1963) was born in California. After his father's death in 1885 Frost's mother brought the family to New England, where she taught in high schools in Massachusetts and New Hampshire. Frost studied for part of one term at Dartmouth College in New Hampshire, then did odd jobs (including teaching), and from 1897 to 1899 was enrolled as a special student at Harvard. He then farmed in New Hampshire, published a few poems in local newspapers, left the farm and taught again, and in 1912 left for England, where he hoped to achieve more popular success as a writer. By 1915 he had won a considerable reputation, and he returned to the United States, settling on a farm in New Hampshire and cultivating the image of the country-wise farmer-poet. In fact he was well read in the classics, the Bible, and English and American literature.

Design

I found a dimpled spider, fat and white,
On a white heal-all, holding up a moth
Like a white piece of rigid satin cloth—
Assorted characters of death and blight   4
Mixed ready to begin the morning right,
Like the ingredients of a witches' broth—
A snow-drop spider, a flower like a froth,
And dead wings carried like a paper kite.   8

What had that flower to do with being white,
The wayside blue and innocent heal-all?
What brought the kindred spider to that height,
Then steered the white moth thither in the night?   12
What but design of darkness to appall?—
If design govern in a thing so small.

[1936]

Topics for Critical Thinking and Writing

1. Do you find the spider, as described in line 1, cute or disgusting? Why?
2. What is the effect of "If" in the last line?
3. The word "design" can mean "pattern" (as in "a pretty design"), or it can mean "intention," especially an evil intention (as in "He had designs on her"). Does Frost use the word in one sense or in both? Explain.

IRA GERSHWIN

Ira (originally Israel) Gershwin (1896–1983) was born in the Lower East Side of New York City, of Russian-Jewish immigrant parents. He attended City College of New York for two years (1914–16), but dropped out so that he could concentrate on his work for musical comedies. A writer of lyrics, he collaborated with his younger brother George on some twenty Broadway musicals, as well as with others—notably Moss Hart, Kurt Weill, Jerome Kern, and Harold Arlen. In 1932 he and his collaborators (Morrie Ryskind and George S. Kaufman) received a Pulitzer Prize for the musical satire, Of Thee I Sing *(1931).*

Among his best-known songs (in addition to "The Man That Got Away") are "The Man I Love," "I Got Rhythm," "Embraceable You," and (from Porgy and Bess *[1935]) "Summertime," "I Got Plenty o' Nuttin'," and "It Ain't Necessarily So." "The Man That Got Away" (music by Harold Arlen) was written for Judy Garland, in* A Star Is Born *(1954).*

Judy Garland (1922–69) is best known for her roles in such film musicals as The Wizard of Oz *(1939),* Meet Me in St. Louis *(1944), and* Easter Parade *(1948). In* A Star Is Born, *the tragic story of an aging actor who helps a young, aspiring actress to fame, Garland excelled in both her musical and dramatic work.*

The Man That Got Away

The night is bitter,
The stars have lost their glitter,
The winds grow colder
And suddenly you're older—
And all because of the man that got away.   5

No more his eager call,
The writing's on the wall;
The dreams you've dreamed have all
    Gone astray.

The man that won you   10
Has run off and undone you.
That great beginning
Has seen the final inning.
Don't know what happened. It's all a crazy game.

No more that all-time thrill,   15
For you've been through the mill—
And never a new love will
    Be the same.

Good riddance, good bye!
    Ev'ry trick of his you're on to.   20
But, fools will be fools—
    And where's he gone to?

The road gets rougher,
It's lonelier and tougher.
With hope you burn up—   25
Tomorrow he may turn up.
There's just no let-up the live-long night and day.

Ever since this world began
    There is nothing sadder than
        A one man woman looking for   30
        The man that got away . . .
        The man that got away.

[1954]

Topics for Critical Thinking and Writing

1. Are these lyrics trash as poetry but great as lyrics for a song? Explain. While you are thinking about this issue, you may want to ponder some words by Edgar Allan Poe: "There are few cases in which mere popularity should be considered a proper test of merit; but the case of song-writing is, I think, one of the few."

2. Is the speaker making too much of a fuss? After all, it's only a man that she has lost.

3. Gershwin, in *Lyrics on Several Occasions* (1973), comments on the song. He mentions that some reviewers mistakenly called it "The Man Who Got Away," but, Gershwin says, this title is unacceptable because (1) it sounds like a whodunit title, and (2) it loses the echo of the fisherman's "You should have seen the one that got away." How valuable do you find these comments?

4. Gershwin also mentions that the word "man" in the title of a song usually limits it to female vocalists. Even if one makes some minimal switches (in "The Man I Love," changing to "the girl I love," and so forth) one is still left with something like "the girl I love; / And she'll be big and strong," which, Gershwin says, gives her "some undesirable attributes." But because Frank Sinatra wanted to do a recording of "The *Gal* That Got Away," Gershwin changed the ending thus:

Ever since this world began
There is nothing sadder than
A lost, lost loser looking for
The gal that got away.

What do you think of this revision? Try your hand at producing a better one.

FRANK O'HARA

Frank O'Hara (1926–1966), was born in Baltimore, and died in a tragic accident—he was run over by a beach vehicle—on Fire Island, New York. O'Hara was not only a prolific writer of verse but also an astute critic of sculpture and painting who worked as an assistant curator at the Museum of Modern Art, in New York, and as an editor of Art News. *O'Hara's first volume of poetry was* A City Winter, and Other Poems *(1952);* Collected Poems *was issued in 1971, but it was not complete. It has been supplemented by two additional volumes,* Early Poems *(1977) and* Poems Retrieved *(1977).*

Homosexuality

So we are taking off our masks, are we, and keeping
our mouths shut? as if we'd been pierced by a glance!

The song of an old cow is not more full of judgment
than the vapors which escape one's soul when one is sick;

so I pull the shadows around me like a puff   5
and crinkle my eyes as if at the most exquisite moment

of a very long opera, and then we are off!
without reproach and without hope that our delicate feet

will touch the earth again, let alone "very soon."
It is the law of my own voice I shall investigate.   10

I start like ice, my finger to my ear, my ear
to my heart, that proud cur at the garbage can

in the rain. It's wonderful to admire oneself
with complete candor, tallying up the merits of each

of the latrines. 14th Street is drunken and credulous,   15
53rd tries to tremble but is too at rest. The good

love a park and the inept a railway station,
and there are the divine ones who drag themselves up

and down the lengthening shadow of an Abyssinian head
in the dust, trailing their long elegant heels of hot air   20

crying to confuse the brave "It's a summer day,
and I want to be wanted more than anything else in the world."

[1971]

Topics for Critical Thinking and Writing

1. Describe your response to the word that O'Hara chooses for his title. In what
   ways does the poem define and explore the meanings of this word and our responses to it?
2. Characterize the point of view and tone of the speaker. Who is or are the "we"
   named in line 1?
3. In line 1 the speaker declares that "we are taking off our masks," but then immediately seems to confuse or contradict his point when he says "we" are
   "keeping / our mouths shut." Explain as clearly as you can what the speaker is
   suggesting in this first stanza.
4. Some of the language in this poem is ugly or unpleasant—for example, the
   "cur at the garbage can," "the latrines." What is the purpose of such language?
   What is its place in the structure of the poem as a whole?

AMBROSE BIERCE

*Ambrose Bierce (1842–1914?) was born in Horse Creek, Ohio, but his family soon
moved to Indiana, where at the age of nineteen he enlisted in the Union Army. In
the next four years he fought in several of the bloodiest battles of the Civil War, was
wounded twice, and rose to the rank of lieutenant. After the war he worked as a
journalist in San Francisco, in England, and again in San Francisco. In 1912 he
went to Mexico to cover the Mexican Revolution, but he disappeared there and it is
assumed that he died in 1914.*

*Bierce's literary reputation rests chiefly on one story, reprinted here, but he
wrote other stories of interest—some about the supernatural—as well as a witty,
cynical book called* The Devil's Dictionary. *Sample definition: "Marriage. The state
or condition of a community consisting of a master, a mistress, and two slaves,
making in all, two."*

The Orange and Alexandria Railroad Bridge. (Library of Congress)

"An Occurrence at Owl Creek Bridge" is set during the Civil War. The Civil War is widely regarded as the first modern total war, not so much because of new weapons (though breach-loading rifles were introduced) but because the railroad, the steamship, and the electric telegraph greatly expanded the battlefield. Because railroads allowed armies to depend for supplies on remote sources, Confederate forces would blow up bridges in order to impede Union advances. Similarly, when Sherman undertook his "march to the sea" through Georgia, he destroyed the railroads in order to stop the northward flow of supplies to Lee's army in Richmond. In the photograph above, a Union engineer inspects a repaired bridge that is guarded by Union soldiers. (In Bierce's story, notice in paragraph 10 the reference to Union forces "repairing the railroads. . . . They have reached the Owl Creek bridge, put it in order . . .")

An Occurrence at Owl Creek Bridge

1

A man stood upon a railroad bridge in northern Alabama, looking down into the swift water twenty feet below. The man's hands were behind his back, the wrists bound with a cord. A rope closely encircled his neck. It was attached to a stout cross-timber above his head and the slack fell to the level of his knees. Some loose boards laid upon the sleepers[1] supporting the metals of the railway supplied a footing for him and his executioners—two private soldiers of the Federal army, directed by a sergeant who in civil life may have been a deputy sheriff. At a short

---

[1]**sleepers** railroad crossties. (All notes to this story are the editors'.)

remove upon the same temporary platform was an officer in the uniform of his rank, armed. He was a captain. A sentinel at each end of the bridge stood with his rifle in the position known as "support," that is to say, vertical in front of the left shoulder, the hammer resting on the forearm thrown straight across the chest—a formal and unnatural position, enforcing an erect carriage of the body. It did not appear to be the duty of these two men to know what was occurring at the center of the bridge; they merely blockaded the two ends of the foot planking that traversed it.

Beyond one of the sentinels nobody was in sight; the railroad ran straight away into a forest for a hundred yards, then, curving, was lost to view. Doubtless there was an outpost farther along. The other bank of the stream was open ground—a gentle acclivity topped with a stockade of vertical tree trunks, loop-holed for rifles, with a single embrasure through which protruded the muzzle of a brass cannon commanding the bridge. Midway of the slope between bridge and fort were the spectators—a single company of infantry in line, at "parade rest," the butts of the rifles on the ground, the barrels inclining slightly backward against the right shoulder, the hands crossed upon the stock. A lieutenant stood at the right of the line, the point of his sword upon the ground, his left hand resting upon his right. Excepting the group of four at the center of the bridge, not a man moved. The company faced the bridge, staring stonily, motionless. The sentinels, facing the banks of the stream, might have been statues to adorn the bridge. The captain stood with folded arms, silent, observing the work of his subordinates, but making no sign. Death is a dignitary who when he comes announced is to be received with formal manifestations of respect, even by those most familiar with him. In the code of military etiquette silence and fixity are forms of deference.

The man who was engaged in being hanged was apparently about thirty-five years of age. He was a civilian, if one might judge from his habit, which was that of a planter. His features were good—a straight nose, firm mouth, broad forehead, from which his long, dark hair was combed straight back, falling behind his ears to the collar of his well-fitting frock-coat. He wore a mustache and pointed beard, but no whiskers; his eyes were large and dark gray, and had a kindly expression which one would hardly have expected in one whose neck was in the hemp. Evidently this was no vulgar assassin. The liberal military code makes provision for hanging many kinds of persons, and gentlemen are not excluded.

The preparations being complete, the two private soldiers stepped aside and each drew away the plank upon which he had been standing. The sergeant turned to the captain, saluted and placed himself immediately behind that officer, who in turn moved apart one pace. These movements left the condemned man and the sergeant standing on the two ends of the same plank, which spanned three of the crossties of the bridge. The end upon which the civilian stood almost, but not quite, reached a fourth. This plank had been held in place by the weight of the captain; it was now held by that of the sergeant. At a signal from the former the latter would step aside, the plank would tilt and the condemned man go down between two ties. The arrangement commended itself to his judgment as simple and effective. His face had not been covered nor his eyes bandaged. He looked a moment at his "unsteadfast footing," then let his gaze wander to the swirling water of the stream racing madly beneath his feet. A piece of dancing driftwood caught his attention and his eyes followed it down the current. How slowly it appeared to move! What a sluggish stream!

5   He closed his eyes in order to fix his last thoughts upon his wife and children. The water, touched to gold by the early sun, the brooding mists under the banks

at some distance down the stream, the fort, the soldiers, the piece of drift—all had distracted him. And now he became conscious of a new disturbance. Striking through the thought of his dear ones was a sound which he would neither ignore nor understand, a sharp, distinct, metallic percussion like the stroke of a black-smith's hammer upon the anvil; it had the same ringing quality. He wondered what it was, and whether immeasurably distant or near by—it seemed both. Its recurrence was regular, but as slow as the tolling of a death knell. He awaited each stroke with impatience and—he knew not why—apprehension. The intervals of silence grew progressively longer; the delays became maddening. With their greater infrequency the sounds increased in strength and sharpness. They hurt his ear like the thrust of a knife; he feared he would shriek. What he heard was the ticking of his watch.

He unclosed his eyes and saw again the water below him. "If I could free my hands," he thought, "I might throw off the noose and spring into the stream. By diving I could evade the bullets and, swimming vigorously, reach the bank, take to the woods and get away home. My home, thank God, is as yet outside their lines; my wife and little ones are still beyond the invader's farthest advance."

As these thoughts, which have here to be set down in words, were flashed into the doomed man's brain rather than evolved from it the captain nodded to the sergeant. The sergeant stepped aside.

2

Peyton Farquhar was a well-to-do planter, of an old and highly respected Alabama family. Being a slave owner and like other slave owners a politician he was naturally an original secessionist and ardently devoted to the Southern cause. Circumstances of an imperious nature, which it is unnecessary to relate here, had prevented him from taking service with the gallant army that had fought the disastrous campaigns ending with the fall of Corinth, and he chafed under the inglorious restraint, longing for the release of his energies, the larger life of the soldier, the opportunity for distinction. That opportunity, he felt, would come, as it comes to all in war time. Meanwhile he did what he could. No service was too humble for him to perform in aid of the South, no adventure too perilous for him to undertake if consistent with the character of a civilian who was at heart a soldier, and who in good faith and without too much qualification assented to at least a part of the frankly villainous dictum that all is fair in love and war.

One evening while Farquhar and his wife were sitting on a rustic bench near the entrance to his grounds, a gray-clad soldier rode up to the gate and asked for a drink of water. Mrs. Farquhar was only too happy to serve him with her own white hands. While she was fetching the water her husband approached the dusty horseman and inquired eagerly for news from the front.

10   "The Yanks are repairing the railroads," said the man, "and are getting ready for another advance. They have reached the Owl Creek bridge, put it in order and built a stockade on the north bank. The commandant has issued an order, which is posted everywhere, declaring that any civilian caught interfering with the railroad, its bridges, tunnels or trains will be summarily hanged. I saw the order."

"How far is it to the Owl Creek bridge?" Farquhar asked.

"About thirty miles."

"Is there no force on this side the creek?"

"Only a picket post half a mile out, on the railroad, and a single sentinel at this end of the bridge."

15   "Suppose a man—a civilian and student of hanging—should elude the picket post and perhaps get the better of the sentinel," said Farquhar, smiling, "what could he accomplish?"

The soldier reflected. "I was there a month ago," he replied. "I observed that the flood of last winter had lodged a great quantity of driftwood against the wooden pier at this end of the bridge. It is now dry and would burn like tow."

The lady had now brought the water, which the soldier drank. He thanked her ceremoniously, bowed to her husband and rode away. An hour later, after nightfall, he repassed the plantation, going northward in the direction from which he had come. He was a Federal scout.

3

As Peyton Farquhar fell straight downward through the bridge he lost consciousness and was as one already dead. From this state he was awakened—ages later, it seemed to him—by the pain of a sharp pressure upon his throat, followed by a sense of suffocation. Keen, poignant agonies seemed to shoot from his neck downward through every fiber of his body and limbs. These pains appeared to flash along well-defined lines of ramification and to beat with an inconceivably rapid periodicity. They seemed like streams of pulsating fire heating him to an intolerable temperature. As to his head, he was conscious of nothing but a feeling of fullness—of congestion. These sensations were unaccompanied by thought. The intellectual part of his nature was already effaced; he had power only to feel, and feeling was torment. He was conscious of motion. Encompassed in a luminous cloud, of which he was now merely the fiery heart, without material substance, he swung through unthinkable arcs of oscillation, like a vast pendulum. Then all at once, with terrible suddenness, the light about him shot upward with the noise of a loud plash; a frightful roaring was in his ears, and all was cold and dark. The power of thought was restored; he knew that the rope had broken and he had fallen into the stream. There was no additional strangulation; the noose about his neck was already suffocating him and kept the water from his lungs. To die of hanging at the bottom of a river!—the idea seemed to him ludicrous. He opened his eyes in the darkness and saw above him a gleam of light, but how distant, how inaccessible! He was still sinking, for the light became fainter and fainter until it was a mere glimmer. Then it began to grow and brighten, and he knew that he was rising toward the surface—knew it with reluctance, for he was now very comfortable. "To be hanged and drowned," he thought, "that is not so bad; but I do not wish to be shot. No; I will not be shot; that is not fair."

He was not conscious of an effort, but a sharp pain in his wrist apprised him that he was trying to free his hands. He gave the struggle his attention, as an idler might observe the feat of a juggler, without interest in the outcome. What splendid effort!—what magnificent, what superhuman strength! Ah, that was a fine endeavor! Bravo! The cord fell away; his arms parted and floated upward, the hands dimly seen on each side in the growing light. He watched them with new interest as first one and then the other pounced upon the noose at his neck. They tore it away and thrust it fiercely aside, its undulations resembling those of a water-snake. "Put it back, put it back!" He thought he shouted these words to his hands, for the undoing of the noose had been succeeded by the direst pang that he had yet experienced. His neck ached horribly; his brain was on fire; his heart, which had been fluttering faintly, gave a great leap, trying to force itself out at his mouth.

His whole body was racked and wrenched with an insupportable anguish! But his disobedient hands gave no heed to the command. They beat the water vigorously with quick, downward strokes, forcing him to the surface. He felt his head emerge; his eyes were blinded by the sunlight; his chest expanded convulsively, and with a supreme and crowning agony his lungs engulfed a great draught of air, which instantly he expelled in a shriek!

20 He was now in full possession of his physical senses. They were, indeed, preternaturally keen and alert. Something in the awful disturbance of his organic system had so exalted and refined them that they made record of things never before perceived. He felt the ripples upon his face and heard their separate sounds as they struck. He looked at the forest on the bank of the stream, saw the individual trees, the leaves and the veining of each leaf—saw the very insects upon them: the locusts, the brilliant-bodied flies, the gray spiders stretching their webs from twig to twig. He noted the prismatic colors in all the dewdrops upon a million blades of grass. The humming of the gnats that danced above the eddies of the stream, the beating of the dragon-flies' wings, the strokes of water-spiders' legs, like oars which had lifted their boat—all these made audible music. A fish slid along beneath his eyes and he heard the rush of its body parting the water.

He had come to the surface facing down the stream; in a moment the visible world seemed to wheel slowly round, himself the pivotal point, and he saw the bridge, the fort, the soldiers upon the bridge, the captain, the sergeant, the two privates, his executioners. They were in silhouette against the blue sky. They shouted and gesticulated, pointing at him. The captain had drawn his pistol, but did not fire; the others were unarmed. Their movements were grotesque and horrible, their forms gigantic.

Suddenly he heard a sharp report and something struck the water smartly within a few inches of his head, spattering his face with spray. He heard a second report, and saw one of the sentinels with his rifle at his shoulder, a light cloud of blue smoke rising from the muzzle. The man in the water saw the eye of the man on the bridge gazing into his own through the sights of the rifle. He observed that it was a gray eye and remembered having read that gray eyes were keenest, and that all famous marksmen had them. Nevertheless, this one had missed.

A counter-swirl had caught Farquhar and turned him half round; he was again looking into the forest on the bank opposite the fort. The sound of a clear, high voice in a monotonous singsong now rang out behind him and came across the water with a distinctness that pierced and subdued all other sounds, even the beating of the ripples in his ears. Although no soldier, he had frequented camps enough to know the dread significance of that deliberate, drawling, aspirated chant; the lieutenant on shore was taking a part in the morning's work. How coldly and pitilessly—with what an even, calm intonation, presaging, and enforcing tranquility in the men—with what accurately measured intervals fell those cruel words:

"Attention, company! . . . Shoulder arms! . . . Ready! . . . Aim! . . . Fire!"

25 Farquhar dived—dived as deeply as he could. The water roared in his ears like the voice of Niagara, yet he heard the dulled thunder of the volley and, rising again toward the surface, met shining bits of metal, singularly flattened, oscillating slowly downward. Some of them touched him on the face and hands, then fell away, continuing their descent. One lodged between his collar and neck; it was uncomfortably warm and he snatched it out.

As he rose to the surface, gasping for breath, he saw that he had been a long time under water; he was perceptibly farther down stream—nearer to safety. The soldiers had almost finished reloading; the metal ramrods flashed all at once in the sunshine as they were drawn from the barrels, turned in the air, and thrust into their sockets. The two sentinels fired again, independently and ineffectually.

The hunted man saw all this over his shoulder; he was now swimming vigorously with the current. His brain was as energetic as his arms and legs; he thought with the rapidity of lightning.

"The officer," he reasoned, "will not make that martinet's error a second time. It is as easy to dodge a volley as a single shot. He had probably already given the command to fire at will. God help me, I cannot dodge them all!"

An appalling plash within two yards of him was followed by a loud, rushing sound, *diminuendo,* which seemed to travel back through the air to the fort and died in an explosion which stirred the very river to its deeps! A rising sheet of water curved over him, fell down upon him, blinded him, strangled him! The cannon had taken a hand in the game. As he shook his head free from the commotion of the smitten water he heard the deflected shot humming through the air ahead, and in an instant it was cracking and smashing the branches in the forest beyond.

30   "They will not do that again," he thought; "the next time they will use a charge of grape.[2] I must keep my eye upon the gun; the smoke will apprise me—the report arrives too late; it lags behind the missile. That is a good gun."

Suddenly he felt himself whirled round and round—spinning like a top. The water, the banks, the forests, the now distant bridge, fort and men—all were commingled and blurred. Objects were represented by their colors only; circular horizontal streaks of color—that was all he saw. He had been caught in a vortex and was being whirled on with a velocity of advance and gyration that made him giddy and sick. In a few moments he was flung upon the gravel at the foot of the left bank of the stream—the southern bank—and behind a projecting point which concealed him from his enemies. The sudden arrest of his motion, the abrasion of one of his hands on the gravel, restored him, and he wept with delight. He dug his fingers into the sand, threw it over himself in handfuls and audibly blessed it. It looked like diamonds, rubies, emeralds; he could think of nothing beautiful which it did not resemble. The trees upon the bank were giant garden plants; he noted a definite order in their arrangement, inhaled the fragrance of their blooms. A strange, roseate light shone through the spaces among their trunks and the wind made in their branches the music of aeolian harps. He had no wish to perfect his escape—was content to remain in that enchanting spot until retaken.

A whiz and rattle of grapeshot among the branches high above his head roused him from his dream. The baffled cannoneer had fired him a random farewell. He sprang to his feet, rushed up the sloping bank, and plunged into the forest.

All that day he traveled, laying his course by the rounding sun. The forest seemed interminable; nowhere did he discover a break in it, not even a woodman's road. He had not known that he lived in so wild a region. There was something uncanny in the revelation.

By nightfall he was fatigued, footsore, famishing. The thought of his wife and children urged him on. At last he found a road which led him in what he knew to be the right direction. It was as wide and straight as a city street, yet it seemed untraveled. No fields bordered it, no dwelling anywhere. Not so much as the barking of a dog suggested human habitation. The black bodies of the trees formed a straight wall on both sides, terminating on the horizon in a point, like a diagram in

---

[2]**grape** grapeshot, a cluster of small iron balls fired from a cannon.

a lesson in perspective. Overhead, as he looked up through this rift in the wood, shone great golden stars looking unfamiliar and grouped in strange constellations. He was sure they were arranged in some order which had a secret and malign significance. The wood on either side was full of singular noises, among which—once, twice, and again—he distinctly heard whispers in an unknown tongue.

35   His neck was in pain and lifting his hand to it he found it horribly swollen. He knew that it had a circle of black where the rope had bruised it. His eyes felt congested; he could no longer close them. His tongue was swollen with thirst; he relieved its fever by thrusting it forward from between his teeth into the cold air. How softly the turf had carpeted the untraveled avenue—he could no longer feel the roadway beneath his feet!

Doubtless, despite his suffering, he had fallen asleep while walking, for now he sees another scene—perhaps he has merely recovered from a delirium. He stands at the gate of his own home. All is as he left it, and all bright and beautiful in the morning sunshine. He must have traveled the entire night. As he pushes open the gate and passes up the wide white walk, he sees a flutter of female garments; his wife, looking fresh and cool and sweet, steps down from the veranda to meet him. At the bottom of the steps she stands waiting, with a smile of ineffable joy, an attitude of matchless grace and dignity. Ah, how beautiful she is! He springs forward with extended arms. As he is about to clasp her he feels a stunning blow upon the back of the neck; a blinding white light blazes all about him with a sound like the shock of a cannon—then all is darkness and silence!

Peyton Farquhar was dead; his body, with a broken neck, swung gently from side to side beneath the timbers of the Owl Creek bridge.

[1890]

Topics for Critical Thinking and Writing

1. Is the story merely a clever trick, or is it a significant work of art, something with enduring power? You may find it useful to begin by thinking about a remark made by the poet and literary critic Samuel Taylor Coleridge, in which he asserts that *suspense* (or *expectation*) is superior to *surprise*. (In literature, suspense is usually achieved by foreshadowing—hints of what is to come.) Coleridge said that Shakespeare gives us not surprise but expectation, and then the satisfaction of perfect knowledge: "As the feeling with which we startle at a shooting star, compared with that of watching the sunrise at the pre-established moment, such and so low is surprise compared with expectation." Can you think of literary works (including films) that support or weaken his argument? Does Bierce's story support or weaken it?

2. Some readers of "An Occurrence at Owl Creek Bridge" have censured the story as sentimental, or as melodramatic, or as both. (You may want to check these terms in a good dictionary of literary terms, such as Meyer Abrams, *A Glossary of Literary Terms*, J. A. Cuddon, *A Dictionary of Literary Terms and Literary Theory*, C. Hugh Holman and William Harmon, *A Handbook to Literature*, or Ross Murfin and Supryia M. Ray, *The Bedford Glossary of Critical and Literary Terms*.) How much merit do you find in these accusations?

3. Presumably we can never know if in fact someone in the second before he or she dies can have a vision comparable to Farquhar's. Does our evaluation of Bierce's story depend on our view of whether it is psychologically sound?

Explain. (You may want to argue, for example, that the experience may indeed be possible—just as it is possible for long-lost twins to be reunited on their one-hundredth birthday and to die at the same moment—but it is so freakish that it cannot speak to us in the way we expect art to speak to us.)

KATHERINE MANSFIELD

Katherine Mansfield (1888–1923), née Kathleen Mansfield Beauchamp, was born in New Zealand. In 1902 she went to London for schooling; in 1906 she returned to New Zealand, but dissatisfied with its provincialism, in 1908 she returned to London to become a writer. After a disastrous marriage and a love affair, she went to Germany, where she wrote stories; in 1910 she returned to London, published a book of stories in 1911, and in 1912 met and began living with the writer John Middleton Murry. In 1918, after her first husband at last divorced her, she married Murry. She died of tuberculosis in 1923, a few months after her thirty-fourth birthday.

Mansfield published about seventy stories, and left some others unpublished. An early admirer of Chekhov, she read his works in German translations before they were translated into English.

Miss Brill

Although it was so brilliantly fine—the blue sky powdered with gold and great spots of light like white wine splashed over the Jardins Publiques[1]—Miss Brill was glad that she had decided on her fur. The air was motionless, but when you opened your mouth there was just a faint chill, like a chill from a glass of iced water before you sip, and now and again a leaf came drifting—from nowhere, from the sky. Miss Brill put up her hand and touched her fur. Dear little thing! It was nice to feel it again. She had taken it out of its box that afternoon, shaken out the moth-powder, given it a good brush, and rubbed the life back into the dim little eyes. "What has been happening to me?" said the sad little eyes. Oh, how sweet it was to see them snap at her again from the red eiderdown! . . . But the nose, which was of some black composition, wasn't at all firm. It must have had a knock, somehow. Never mind—a little dab of black sealing-wax when the time came—when it was absolutely necessary. . . . Little rogue! Yes, she really felt like that about it. Little rogue biting its tail just by her left ear. She could have taken it off and laid it on her lap and stroked it. She felt a tingling in her hands and arms, but that came from walking, she supposed. And when she breathed, something light and sad—no, not sad, exactly—something gentle seemed to move in her bosom.

There were a number of people out this afternoon, far more than last Sunday. And the band sounded louder and gayer. That was because the Season had begun. For although the band played all year round on Sundays, out of season it was never the same. It was like some one playing with only the family to listen; it didn't care how it played if there weren't any strangers present. Wasn't the conductor wearing a new coat, too? She was sure it was new. He scraped with his foot and flapped his arms like a rooster about to crow, and the bandsmen sitting in the green rotunda blew out their cheeks and glared at the music. Now there came a little "flutey" bit—very pretty!—a little chain of bright drops. She was sure it would be repeated. It was; she lifted her head and smiled.

[1]**Jardins Publiques** Public Gardens (French).

Only two people shared her "special" seat: a fine old man in a velvet coat, his hands clasped over a huge carved walking-stick, and a big old woman, sitting upright, with a roll of knitting on her embroidered apron. They did not speak. This was disappointing, for Miss Brill always looked forward to the conversation. She had become really quite expert, she thought, at listening as though she didn't listen, at sitting in other people's lives just for a minute while they talked round her.

She glanced, sideways, at the old couple. Perhaps they would go soon. Last Sunday, too, hadn't been as interesting as usual. An Englishman and his wife, he wearing a dreadful Panama hat and she button boots. And she'd gone on the whole time about how she ought to wear spectacles; she knew she needed them; but that it was no good getting any; they'd be sure to break and they'd never keep on. And he'd been so patient. He'd suggested everything—gold rims, the kind that curved round your ears, little pads inside the bridge. No, nothing would please her. "They'll always be sliding down my nose!" Miss Brill had wanted to shake her.

5   The old people sat on the bench, still as statues. Never mind, there was always the crowd to watch. To and fro, in front of the flower-beds and the band rotunda, the couples and groups paraded, stopped to talk, to greet, to buy a handful of flowers from the old beggar who had his tray fixed to the railings. Little children ran among them, swooping and laughing; little boys with big white silk bows under their chins, little girls, little French dolls, dressed up in velvet and lace. And sometimes a tiny staggerer came suddenly rocking into the open from under the trees, stopped, stared, as suddenly sat down "flop," until its small high-stepping mother, like a young hen, rushed scolding to its rescue. Other people sat on the benches and green chairs, but they were nearly always the same, Sunday after Sunday, and—Miss Brill had often noticed—there was something funny about nearly all of them. They were odd, silent, nearly all old, and from the way they stared they looked as though they'd just come from dark little rooms or even— even cupboards!

Behind the rotunda the slender trees with yellow leaves down drooping, and through them just a line of sea, and beyond the blue sky with gold-veined clouds.

Tum-tum-tum tiddle-um! tiddle-um! tum tiddley-um tum ta! blew the band.

Two young girls in red came by and two young soldiers in blue met them, and they laughed and paired and went off arm-in-arm. Two peasant women with funny straw hats passed, gravely, leading beautiful smoke-colored donkeys. A cold, pale nun hurried by. A beautiful woman came along and dropped her bunch of violets, and a little boy ran after to hand them to her, and she took them and threw them away as if they'd been poisoned. Dear me! Miss Brill didn't know whether to admire that or not! And now an ermine toque[2] and a gentleman in grey met just in front of her. He was tall, stiff, dignified, and she was wearing the ermine toque she'd bought when her hair was yellow. Now everything, her hair, her face, even her eyes, was the same color as the shabby ermine, and her hand, in its cleaned glove, lifted to dab her lips, was a tiny yellowish paw. Oh, she was so pleased to see him—delighted! She rather thought they were going to meet that afternoon. She described where she'd been—everywhere, here, there, along by the sea. The day was so charming—didn't he agree? And wouldn't he, perhaps? . . . But he shook his head, lighted a cigarette, slowly breathed a great deep puff into her face, and, even while she was still talking and laughing, flicked the match away and walked on. The ermine toque was alone; she smiled more brightly than

[2]**toque** a brimless, close-fitting woman's hat.

ever. But even the band seemed to know what she was feeling and played more softly, played tenderly, and the drum beat, "The Brute! The Brute!" over and over. What would she do? What was going to happen now? But as Miss Brill wondered, the ermine toque turned, raised her hand as though she'd seen some one else, much nicer, just over there, and pattered away. And the band changed again and played more quickly, more gaily than ever, and the old couple on Miss Brill's seat got up and marched away, and such a funny old man with long whiskers hobbled along in time to the music and was nearly knocked over by four girls walking abreast.

Oh, how fascinating it was! How she enjoyed it! How she loved sitting here, watching it all! It was like a play. It was exactly like a play. Who could believe the sky at the back wasn't painted? But it wasn't till a little brown dog trotted on solemn and then slowly trotted off, like a little "theatre" dog, a little dog that had been drugged, that Miss Brill discovered what it was that made it so exciting. They were all on the stage. They weren't only the audience, not only looking on; they were acting. Even she had a part and came every Sunday. No doubt somebody would have noticed if she hadn't been there; she was part of the performance after all. How strange she'd never thought of it like that before! And yet it explained why she made such a point of starting from home at just the same time each week—so as not to be late for the performance—and it also explained why she had quite a queer, shy feeling at telling her English pupils how she spent her Sunday afternoons. No wonder! Miss Brill nearly laughed out loud. She was on the stage. She thought of the old invalid gentleman to whom she read the newspaper four afternoons a week while he slept in the garden. She had got quite used to the frail head on the cotton pillow, the hollowed eyes, the open mouth and the high pinched nose. If he'd been dead she mightn't have noticed for weeks; she wouldn't have minded. But suddenly he knew he was having the paper read to him by an actress! "An actress!" The old head lifted; two points of light quivered in the old eyes. "An actress—are ye?" And Miss Brill smoothed the newspaper as though it were the manuscript of her part and said gently: "Yes, I have been an actress for a long time."

10   The band had been having a rest. Now they started again. And what they played was warm, sunny, yet there was just a faint chill—a something, what was it?—not sadness—no, not sadness—a something that made you want to sing. The tune lifted, lifted, the light shone; and it seemed to Miss Brill that in another moment all of them, all the whole company, would begin singing. The young ones, the laughing ones who were moving together, they would begin, and the men's voices, very resolute and brave, would join them. And then she too, she too, and the others on the benches—they would come in with a kind of accompaniment—something low, that scarcely rose or fell, something so beautiful—moving. . . . And Miss Brill's eyes filled with tears and she looked smiling at all the other members of the company. Yes, we understand, we understand, she thought—though what they understood she didn't know.

Just at that moment a boy and a girl came and sat down where the old couple had been. They were beautifully dressed; they were in love. The hero and heroine, of course, just arrived from his father's yacht. And still soundlessly singing, still with that trembling smile, Miss Brill prepared to listen.

"No, not now," said the girl. "Not here, I can't."

"But why? Because of that stupid old thing at the end there?" asked the boy. "Why does she come here at all—who wants her? Why doesn't she keep her silly old mug at home?"

"It's her fu-fur which is so funny," giggled the girl. "It's exactly like a fried whiting."[3]

15   "Ah, be off with you!" said the boy in an angry whisper. Then: "Tell me, my petite chère[4]—"

"No, not here," said the girl. "Not *yet*."

On her way home she usually bought a slice of honey-cake at the baker's. It was her Sunday treat. Sometimes there was an almond in her slice, sometimes not. It made a great difference. If there was an almond it was like carrying home a tiny present—a surprise—something that might very well not have been there. She hurried on the almond Sundays and struck the match for the kettle in quite a dashing way.

But today she passed the baker's by, climbed the stairs, went into the little dark room—her room like a cupboard—and sat down on the red eiderdown. She sat there for a long time. The box that the fur came out of was on the bed. She unclasped the necklet quickly; quickly, without looking, laid it inside. But when she put the lid on she thought she heard something crying.

[1920]

[3]**whiting** a kind of fish.   [4]*petite chère* darling.

Topics for Critical Thinking and Writing

1. Why do you think Mansfield did not give Miss Brill a first name?
2. What would be lost (or gained?) if the first paragraph were omitted?
3. Suppose someone said that the story is about a woman who is justly punished for her pride. What might be your response?

15

Case Study:
Writing about Barbie and Gender

Barbie is said to be the most popular toy ever made. Here is an abbreviated chronology, listing the chief events in her life.

1959   Barbie is introduced by Mattel. Historians say that she was a knock-off of a German doll that was designed for men, a sort of three-dimensional pinup, to be put on dashboards. Barbie's measurements, if she were a human, supposedly would be a most unrealistic 38-18-34.

1961   Ken is created; in due time he will be (among many other roles) an airline captain, a doctor, a soldier, a sailor, a cowboy, a college student, a lifeguard, and a rock star. Rather slender at first, he later became hunkier.

1965   Ken and Barbie get bendable legs.

1967   The revised Barbie gains eyelashes and a rotating waist ("Twist 'N Turn Barbie").

1970   Barbie swivels at the waist, wrists, knees, ankles; arms swing around (the advertisement says that Barbie is "As posable as you are").

"Barbie" is big business, and the buyers are not always the parents of little girls. This browser at a Barbie convention may well be looking to add a doll to his own collection.

Astronaut Barbie dolls at the Smithsonian's National Air and Space Museum. Left to right: from the 60s, the 80s, and the 90s. There were Barbie astronauts before the U.S. space program took the idea of women astronauts seriously.

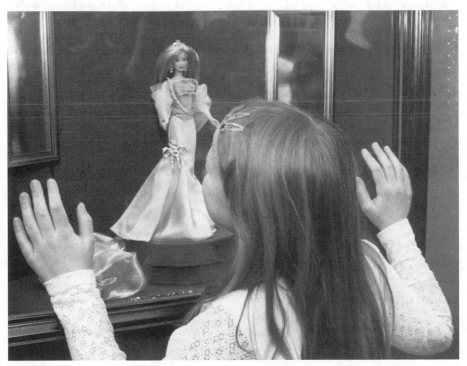

Stephanie Claire Oliver, age eight, and the owner of 62 Barbie dolls, looks at the world's most expensive Barbie doll. Valued at $80,000, this Barbie's gown is decorated with 160 diamonds.

1980   Black Barbie appears, along with several International Barbies (e.g., French, Spanish, Hawaiian).

1998   Barbie's bust is decreased, her waist is increased, and she can stand on her own two feet.

2000   "Barbie for President" is introduced, in three models: black, Hispanic, and white. The absence of an Asian American model is noticed, and some groups protest the absence.

Although we now have Doctor Barbie, Business-Woman Barbie, and so on, and we have Barbies of various colors, some people have protested that the essential message conveyed by the doll still is that successful women are blonde, pretty, slender, and big-busted. In this case study we offer essays and poems that take various points of view.

ANONYMOUS

The following editorial appeared in the San Francisco Chronicle *on November 19, 1997. The same issue of the newspaper included an article by Kevin Leary, which we reprint after the editorial.*

Beauty and the Barbie Doll

Ask most any grade-school girl to cite an example of glamour, and chances are good the name "Barbie" will figure in the response. Then take a look at the stacks of Barbies in any toy store, and you have an overpowering message about how society defines beauty—blonde hair and exaggeratedly large breasts, tiny waists and curved buttocks.

Oh, Mattel has made a few concessions since the days when success could only mean a date at the prom with the androgynous Ken. Today's Barbie also can be gainfully employed, such as the popular "Sea World" worker in a sleek black wetsuit. And then there's "Doctor Barbie," an African American with smock and stethoscope—and, of course, high heels and clingy mini-dress.

Barbie is hardly the only purveyor of an unsettling message about the importance of a certain "look," but she is a powerful one. The consequences of this tortured ideal of beauty are very real. They are apparent in the dieting school-age girls of average build who view themselves as woefully overweight. They are apparent in the number of women who assume the risk of breast implants, or other cosmetic surgery, to attain a beauty denied by nature.

Mattel has just announced that some of its 1999 Barbies will have more realistic proportions. The healthy change is just what Doctor Barbie would have ordered.

KEVIN LEARY

Kevin Leary writes editorials for the San Francisco Chronicle. *Here is his response to the preceding* Chronicle *editorial.*

Barbie Curtsies to Political Correctness

Chalk up a victory for political correctness in Toyland. Barbie Doll, the shapely, 11½-inch tall, plastic queen of the toy world, has become a victim of her own elaborate beauty and is about to be overhauled to look more like her critics.

Mattel Inc., the El Segundo–based toy company, has decided to downgrade the doll with a thicker waist, slimmer hips and a bust reduction.

It will give the doll a "more contemporary" and "natural" look, they say.

Why not give her a mustache, cellulite and varicose veins, too? And while they're at it, how about giving Skipper acne and Ken a beer gut and a receding hairline?

5 Have they gone mad at Mattel? They have marketed the most successful toy in the history of the world, a glamorous fantasy vehicle for little girls that has become an international icon. And they want to change it.

More than a billion Barbies have been sold since it was introduced in 1959. Placed head to toe that many dolls would circle the Earth more than seven times. Worldwide sales this year will be about $2 billion. One is sold every two seconds.

The average American girl, ages 3 to 11, owns 10 Barbies. Little girls—and many boys—appreciate Barbie the way she is, exquisitely slim, with long, well-formed legs, a tiny waist and extraordinary mamelonation for her size.

It didn't take long for salacious adults to calculate that if she were a life-size 5-foot-6, her measurements would be 38-19-34. That set off more feminist cawing about sexuality and impossible physical standards of beauty.

Shrieking Barbie-bashers—with a lot of time on their hands—insist the doll is a brainless clotheshorse and a symbol of materialism and sexist stereotyping. They blame Barbie for an epidemic of anorexia and low self-esteem among young girls.

10 That, of course, is thoroughgoing nonsense. Barbie dolls are toys. They are not meant to be role models or major influences in a kid's life.

But even as mere toys, the dolls have been models of women's liberation and success, as well as physical attractiveness. During her 38 years, Barbie has been a doctor, a nurse, a stewardess, a broadcaster, an Olympic gold medalist in several sports. She was an astronaut in 1965, nearly 20 years before Sally Ride.

She has broken barriers of race and disability. There are black Barbies, Latina Barbies, Asian Barbies and a Barbie in a wheelchair. All of them shapely.

The relentless criticism frequently focuses on the doll's physique. But anyone who has observed young girls playing with Barbies—including Skipper, Ken, Courtney, Tommy and the rest of the doll gang—knows that the dolls are not about sex and materialism.

They are simply attractive dolls with lots of clothes and accessories that encourage children to be anything or do anything they can imagine.

15 Barbie and her plastic companions provide the characters that children use to create a magical world of unlimited imagination where everyone is beautiful, rich and accomplished. It's a gilded world of pure fun—beach houses, fancy cars, boats, mobile homes, exciting jobs and a vast wardrobe. It's a world without the warped political correctness that is trying to take the fun out of childhood.

It's too bad that Mattel is bowing to decades of relentless silliness, but the company's marketeers are not stupid. Mattel will introduce 24 new Barbie models in January, and only one of them will bear the new dumpy look.

The others will retain the familiar tush conformation that has contributed to Barbie's huge popularity in 150 countries around the world. We'll see how the new, homelier model sells.

MEG WOLITZER

Meg Wolitzer, a resident of New York, is the author of short stories, novels, and essays. This essay originally appeared in a collection of essays edited by Yona Zeldis McDonough, Barbie Chronicles *(1999).*

Barbie as Boy Toy

My boys are playing with Barbie again. They have spent much of the day building a hideout, talking on the walkie-talkie headphones sent to them by their aunt, and watching Scooby-Doo cartoons on TV, and now it is nighttime and Barbie has been extracted from the toy chest and brought into the fray. It wouldn't have occurred to me to buy a Barbie doll for my sons, but through a series of events too boring to recount here, one happened to find its way into our home. I never thought the doll would be of more than a passing interest to my sons, since, throughout their lives, neither has ever showed the slightest interest in dolls. They have always, however, responded to all things vehicular; the soundtrack in our household is often a low-level *Vrrrrmmm . . .* as a car is pushed along the arm of a sofa. But the day Barbie arrived in the household, my sons quickly liberated her from her plastic box, and she has remained a surprisingly popular plaything ever since.

"Barbieeeeee!" screams Charlie, who's three, as he flings the doll across the living room toward his seven-year-old brother, Gabriel. Gabriel reaches out and neatly catches the doll in one hand. As I head across the living room, the doll whizzes back toward my younger son like a well-dressed missile. If I was the mother of girls, I might fear that the presence of a Barbie doll in their lives was sending them subliminal antifeminist messages about women. I would have to work hard to teach them that looks aren't everything, and try to get them to give the doll interests beyond dressing up in front of a vanity mirror in order to entice the male doll in her life.

My own mother worried about such matters back in the late sixties and early seventies, and when my sister and I requested a Barbie doll, the request was denied. My mother never came right out and said that she disapproved of Barbie on political grounds; actually, I don't think she'd ever really given it that much thought. But I feel that she had an innate sense of Barbie as being somehow illicit, an object that should be kept out of our home if at all possible. A compromise eventually was reached; my sister and I were never given an actual Barbie doll, but were instead given Barbie's younger sister, Skipper: a less-threatening, presexual version of Barbie. Whether my mother's precautions had any tangible effect can't be known, although I do remain a strong feminist with little interest in "accessories," and my sister is a lesbian.

But as far as my two boys go, I don't need to worry unduly about the political "message" aspect of Barbie, because, for the most part, neither of my sons dwells on her anatomy or wardrobe or vacuous, made-up face. (Although I have to say that just the other day, Charlie did peer under Barbie's blouse and, noticing her two nipple-free swells, commented admiringly, "She's got big muscles!") No, for them Barbie is merely another *thing* to be played with, manipulated, occasionally talked to, but mostly flung. Barbie is highly throwable, and highly catchable, too, what with that ample head of hair. I needn't worry that my boys are learning to be disrespectful of women through their behavior toward this doll. In truth, she has never actually been humanized by them.

5   I have a friend whose little boy was given a baby doll when he was eighteen months old. At first he ignored her, but finally, when he saw that her eyes opened and closed, he became interested. From then on, he would move the doll repeatedly up and down so he could see this mechanical phenomenon in action. When someone asked him what his doll's name was, he proudly said, "Eye."

Dolls as machines; dolls as projectiles. Why is it that most boys don't simply sit down and dress and feed and pamper and talk to dolls? Why is it that most boys don't even *like* dolls? Back in the 1970s, *Free to Be You and Me* was a popular TV special devoted to promoting nonsexist attitudes in children. One of the song-stories was about a little boy who, to his parents' chagrin, craves a doll. His mother and father buy him a baseball and bat to try and distract him, but these gifts don't do the trick. One day, his grandmother arrives bearing a coveted, verboten doll. While William's parents begin to freak out, his grandmother explains that a doll is a wonderful present for a boy because it will teach him how to be a loving father someday.

Before I had children of my own, this story used to move me; if I had a boy someday, I swore, I would definitely let him have a doll. I would be the kind of nonsexist parent who allowed my son to express himself freely. He could have a doll—oh, what the hell, he could have an entire, well-equipped Dream House! But I never imagined that I would one day have two boys who enjoyed dolls only insofar as they could serve as rough-and-tumble objects.

Which isn't to say that my sons aren't loving and tender; they certainly are. They are kind to other children, and surprisingly sensitive to people's feelings. But these qualities don't always overtly appear in the actual *ways* in which they play. I've watched a mother in my son's preschool sit discreetly to the side of the room and beam as her daughter took care of a "sick" doll. "Oh, poor thing, you're burning hot!" the girl said, and she stuck a pretend digital thermometer in the doll's ear and announced that her fever was quite high. Liquid Tylenol was dispensed, as were a series of kisses and hugs, and the doll was tucked into bed and sung an entire medley of lullabies. It was gratifying for that mother to see the way in which her daughter used that doll as a vessel for empathy, for burgeoning maternal feelings. The little girl had clearly been treated similarly, and the results of good mothering were evident.

But what about boys, my own and others? What can be said about who they are from the way in which they go *Vrmmmm, vrmmm,* or scrutinize the moving parts of a toy, or toss a Barbie doll around a room? The truth is that I beam, too, when I watch my sons deeply involved in their play. I see how free they are in the world, how comfortable they are taking an object and creating an entire imagined universe for it. And if Barbie's tiny rosebud mouth could ever speak, I'm certain she would say she has a lot more fun with Gabriel and Charlie than she ever did with Ken.

Yona Zeldis McDonough

Yona Zeldis McDonough is the author of Anne Frank, *a biography for children. The essay that we reprint originally appeared in* The New York Times Magazine, *on January 25, 1998, and later appeared in* The Barbie Chronicles.

Sex and the Single Doll

Now that my son is six and inextricably linked to the grade-school social circuit, he gets invited to birthday parties. Lots of them. Whenever I telephone to say he's coming, I always ask for hints on what might be a particularly coveted gift for the birthday child. And whenever that child is a girl, I secretly hope the answer will be the dirty little word I am longing to hear: *Barbie.*

No such luck. In the liberal Brooklyn neighborhood where we live, there is a definite bias against the poor doll, a veritable Barbie backlash. "My daughter loves her, but I can't stand her," laments one mother. "I won't let her in the house," asserts another. "Oh, please!" sniffs a third.

But I love Barbie. I loved her in 1963, when she made her entrance into my life. She was blond, with a Jackie Kennedy bouffant hairdo. Her thickly painted lids (carved out of plastic) and pouty, unsmiling mouth gave her a look both knowing and sullen. She belonged to a grown-up world of cocktail dresses, cigarette smoke, and perfume. I loved her in the years that followed, too, when she developed bendable joints; a twist-and-turn waist; long, silky ash-blond hair; and feathery, lifelike eyelashes. I never stopped loving her. I never will.

I've heard all the arguments against her: She's a bimbo and an airhead; she's an insatiable consumer—for tarty clothes, a dream house filled with garish pink furniture, a pink Barbie-mobile—who teaches little girls that there is nothing in life quite so exciting as shopping. Her body, with its buoyant breasts, wasplike waist, and endless legs defies all human proportion. But at six, I inchoately understood Barbie's appeal: pure sex. My other dolls were either babies or little girls, with flat chests and chubby legs. Even the other so-called fashion dolls—Tammy, in her aqua-and-white playsuit, and Tressy, with that useless hank of hair, couldn't compete. Barbie was clearly a woman doll, and a woman was what I longed to be.

5   When I was eight, and had just learned about menstruation, I fashioned a small sanitary napkin for her out of neatly folded tissues. Rubber bands held it in place. "Oh, look," said my bemused mother, "Barbie's got her little period. Now she can have a baby." I was disappointed, but my girlfriends all snickered in a much more satisfying way. You see, I wanted Barbie to be, well, dirty. We all did.

Our Barbies had sex, at least our childish version of it. They hugged and kissed the few available boy dolls we had—clean-cut and oh-so-square Ken, the more relaxed and sexy Allan. They also danced, pranced, and strutted, but mostly they stripped, showing off their amazing, no-way-in-the-world human bodies. An adult friend tells me how she used to put her Barbie's low-backed bathing suit on backwards so the doll's breasts were exposed. I liked dressing mine in her pink-and-white candy-striped baby-sitter's apron—and nothing else.

I've also heard that Barbie is a poor role model for little girls. Is there such widespread contempt for the intelligence of children that we really imagine they are stupid enough to be shaped by a doll? Girls learn how to be women from the women around them. Most often this means Mom. My own was a march-to-a-different-drummer bohemian in the early sixties. She eschewed the beauty parlor, cards, and mah-jongg that the other moms in the neighborhood favored. Instead, she wore her long, black hair loose, her earrings big and dangling, and her lipstick dark. She made me a Paris bistro birthday party, with candles stuck in old wine bottles, red-and-white-checked tablecloths for decorations; she read the poetry of T. S. Eliot to the assembled group of enchanted ten-year-olds. She was, in those years, an aspiring painter, and her work graced not only the walls of our apartment, but also the shower curtain, bathroom mirror, and a chest of drawers in my room. She—not an eleven-and-a-half-a-inch doll—was the most powerful female role model in my life. What she thought of Barbie I really don't know, but she had the good sense to back off and let me use the doll my own way.

Barbie has become more politically correct over the years. She no longer looks so vixenish, and has traded the sultry expression I remember for one that is more wholesome and less covert. She now exists in a variety of "serious" incarnations: teacher, Olympic athlete, dentist. And Mattel recently introduced the Really Rad Barbie, a doll whose breasts and hips are smaller and whose waist is thicker, thus reflecting a more real (as if children wanted their toys to be real) female body. None of this matters one iota. Girls will still know the reason they love her, a reason that has nothing to do with new professions or a subtly amended figure.

Fortunately, my Barbie love will no longer have to content itself with buying gifts for my son's friends and the daughters of my own. I have a daughter now, and although she is just two, she already has half a dozen Barbies.

They are, along with various articles of clothing, furniture, and other essential accouterments, packed away like so many sleeping princesses in translucent pink plastic boxes that line my basement shelves. But the magic for which they wait is no longer the prince's gentle kiss. Instead, it is the heart and mind of my little girl as she picks them up and begins to play. I can hardly wait.

MARGE PIERCY
Barbie Doll

This girlchild was born as usual
and presented dolls that did pee-pee
and miniature GE stoves and irons
and wee lipsticks the color of cherry candy.
Then in the magic of puberty, a classmate said: 5
You have a great big nose and fat legs.

She was healthy, tested intelligent,
possessed strong arms and back,
abundant sexual drive and manual dexterity.
She went to and fro apologizing.   10
Everyone saw a fat nose on thick legs.

She was advised to play coy,
exhorted to come on hearty,
exercise, diet, smile and wheedle.
Her good nature wore out   15
like a fan belt.
So she cut off her nose and her legs
and offered them up.

In the casket displayed on satin she lay
with the undertaker's cosmetics painted on,   20
a turned-up putty nose,
dressed in a pink and white nightie.
Doesn't she look pretty? everyone said.
Consummation at last.
To every woman a happy ending.   25

[1969]

DENISE DUHAMEL

Denise Duhamel was born in 1961 in Woonsocket, Rhode Island, and educated at Emerson College and Sarah Lawrence College. She has published several books of poems, and she has received a New York Foundation for the Arts Fellowship and the Poets and Writers' Exchange Award. Her most recent book is Queen for a Day: Selected and New Poems *(2001).*

In the following poem, Gautama (line 3) refers to Siddhartha Gautama, who became the Buddha ("The Enlightened"; "Gautama" is the family or clan name). He was born ca. 560 B.C. in what is now Nepal, near the Indian border, and he is thought to have died ca. 480 B.C. Although Gautama is the Buddha, or The Historical Buddha, anyone who achieves enlightenment can become a Buddha. Enlightenment begins with comprehending the Four Noble Truths: (1) Human life is characterized by suffering (physical and mental); (2) Suffering is caused by craving (desire, for instance lust, or even the desire for approval); (3) It is possible to end suffering; (4) The way to end suffering is to follow the Eightfold Path, which includes such things as "Right Speech" (e.g., avoid telling lies, avoid angry words) and "Right Action" (e.g., avoid killing any living creature, avoid drinking intoxicants). (Any book on Buddhism will explain the Eightfold Path in detail; or you can begin with an account in an encyclopedia and then, if you are taken with what you find, consult some of the references it cites.) The idea is to recognize that nothing has a fixed, independent nature, hence "all is emptiness" (line 3 of Duhamel's poem) and "There is no self" (line 4). (The Sanskrit word translated as "emptiness" is sunyata *or* shunyata, *pronounced "shoon-YA-ta"; the word translated as "no self" is* anatman, *pronounced "un-AT-mun.") If we understand that all is emptiness, that there is no enduring self, we can empty our transient selves of desire, of attachment to things—even of desire for or attachment to things we can consider noble, such as love of humanity, or of our parents or our country.*

Images of the Buddha vary—sometimes he is shown as an ascetic, the bones evident beneath the skin; sometimes he is fleshy; but the pot-bellied laughing or smiling figures (see lines 7–8 of Duhamel's poem) in shops that sell Asian knickknacks do not represent the Buddha. Rather, they are representations of a Chinese folk deity, Putai (Japanese: Hotei), widely regarded as a god of good luck, though indeed Putai came to be regarded as a Buddha-to-be.

Buddhist Barbie

In the 5th century B.C.
an Indian philosopher
Gautama teaches "All is emptiness"
and "There is no self."
In the 20th century A.D.
Barbie agrees, but wonders how a man
with such a belly could pose,
smiling, and without a shirt.

[1997]

Topics for Critical Thinking and Writing

1. What evidence can you offer to support or refute the idea that Barbie has had a bad effect on young women? Speaking more generally, do you think that toys help to shape behavior? Does anything in your own experience confirm or refute this view?

2. Do you think that little boys should be obliged to play with dolls and that little girls should be obliged to play with toy guns as a way of breaking down stereotypes about, and conventional views of, gender roles?

3. The essay by Leary is pretty much a reply to the anonymous editorial that precedes it. Write your own reply, either to the anonymous essay or to Leary's. Or write a dialogue setting forth what these two writers might say to each other after they had read the other's essay.
4. If you had boys who played with Barbie the way Wolitzer's boys do, what—if anything—might you say to them?
5. Evaluate the first two paragraphs of McDonough's essay as opening paragraphs. Did they hold your interest? Why or why not? Are they appropriate to the rest of the essay?
6. In an essay of 500–750 words, explain what Piercy is saying about women in general in "Barbie Doll." Does her view seem to you fair, slightly exaggerated, or greatly exaggerated?
7. Write a poem—or an essay of 50 words—about Ken, Barbie's companion doll. If you wish, closely imitate Marge Piercy's poem.
8. Write—in verse or prose—Guatama's response to Duhamel's "Buddhist Barbie."

Appendix A

Remarks about Manuscript Form

BASIC MANUSCRIPT FORM

Much of what follows is nothing more than common sense.

- Use good quality $8\frac{1}{2}'' \times 11''$ paper. Make a photocopy, or, if you have written on a word processor print out a second copy, in case the instructor's copy goes astray.
- If you write on a word processor, **double-space,** and print on one side of the page only; set the printer for professional or best quality. If you submit handwritten copy, use lined paper and write on one side of the page only in black or dark blue ink, on every other line.
- Use **one-inch margins** on all sides.
- Within the top margin, put your last name and then (after hitting the space bar twice) the **page number** (in arabic numerals), so that the number is flush with the right-hand margin.
- On the first page, below the top margin and flush with the left-hand margin, put your **full name,** your **instructor's name,** the **course number** (including the section), and the **date,** one item per line, double-spaced.
- **Center the title** of your essay. Remember that the title is important—it gives the readers their first glimpse of your essay. **Create your own title**—one that reflects your topic or thesis. For example, a paper on Charlotte Perkins Gilman's "The Yellow Wallpaper" should not be called "The Yellow Wallpaper" but might be called

Disguised Tyranny in Gilman's "The Yellow Wallpaper"

or

How to Drive a Woman Mad

These titles do at least a little in the way of rousing a reader's interest.
- **Capitalize the title thus:** Begin the first word of the title with a capital letter, and capitalize each subsequent word except articles (*a, an, the*), conjunctions (*and, but, if, when,* etc.), and prepositions (*in, on, with,* etc.):

A Word on Behalf of Love

Notice that you do *not* enclose your title within quotation marks, and you do *not* underline it—though if it includes the title of a poem or a story, *that* is enclosed within quotation marks, or if it includes the title of a novel or play, *that* is underlined (to indicate italics), thus:

Gilman's "The Yellow Wallpaper" and Medical Practice

and

Gender Stereotypes in <u>Hamlet</u>

- **After writing your title, double-space,** indent five spaces, and begin your first sentence.
- Unless your instructor tells you otherwise, **use a staple** to hold the pages together. (Do not use a stiff binder; it will only add to the bulk of the instructor's stack of papers.)
- Extensive revisions should have been made in your drafts, but minor **last-minute revisions** may be made—neatly—on the finished copy. Proofreading may catch some typographical errors, and you may notice some small weaknesses. You can make corrections using the following proofreader's symbols.

CORRECTIONS IN THE FINAL COPY

Changes in wording may be made by crossing through words and rewriting them:

The influence of Poe and Hawthorne ~~have~~ *has* greatly diminished.

Additions should be made above the line, with a caret below the line at the appropriate place:

The influence of Poe and Hawthorne has *greatly* diminished.

Transpositions of letters may be made thus:

The inᶠˡuence of Poe and Hawthorne has diminished.

Deletions are indicated by a horizontal line through the word or words to be deleted. Delete a single letter by drawing a vertical or diagonal line through it; then indicate whether the letters on either side are to be closed up by drawing a connecting arc:

The influence of Poe and Hawthorne has great̷ly diminished.

Separation of words accidentally run together is indicated by a vertical line, closure by a curved line connecting the letters to be closed up:

The influence/of Poe and Hawthorne has g‿reatly diminished.

Paragraphing may be indicated by the symbol ¶ before the word that is to begin the new paragraph:

The influence of Poe and Hawthorne has greatly diminished. ¶ The

influence of Borges has very largely replaced that of earlier writers of

fantasy.

QUOTATIONS AND QUOTATION MARKS

First, a word about the *point* of using quotations. Don't use quotations to pad the length of a paper. Rather, give quotations from the work you are discussing so that your readers will see the material being considered and (especially in a research paper) so that your readers will know what some of the chief interpretations are and what your responses to them are.

Note: The next few paragraphs do *not* discuss how to include citations of sources, a topic taken up in the next appendix under the heading "How to Document: Footnotes, Internal Parenthetical Citations, and a List of Works Cited."

The Golden Rule: If you quote, *comment on* the quotation. Let the reader know what you make of it and why you quote it.

Additional principles:

1. Identify the speaker or writer of the quotation so that the reader is not left with a sense of uncertainty. Usually, in accordance with the principle of letting readers know where they are going, this identification precedes the quoted material, but occasionally it may follow the quotation, especially if it will provide something of a pleasant surprise. For instance, in a discussion of Flannery O'Connor's stories, you might quote a disparaging comment on one of the stories and then reveal that O'Connor herself was the speaker.

2. If the quotation is part of your own sentence, **be sure to fit the quotation grammatically and logically into your sentence.**

> *Incorrect:* Holden Caulfield tells us very little about "what my lousy childhood was like."

> *Correct:* Holden Caulfield tells us very little about what his "lousy childhood was like."

3. Indicate any omissions or additions. The quotation must be exact. Any material that you add—even one or two words—must be enclosed within square brackets, thus:

> Hawthorne tells us that "owing doubtless to the depth of the gloom at that
>
> particular spot [in the forest], neither the travellers nor their steeds were
>
> visible."

If you wish to omit material from within a quotation, indicate the ellipsis by three spaced periods enclosed within a pair of square brackets. That is, at the point where you are omitting material, type a space, an opening square bracket, a period, a space, a period, a space, a third period, and a closing square bracket (no space between the last of these three periods and the closing bracket). If you are omitting material from the end of a sentence, type a space after the last word that you quote, then an opening square, a period, a space, a period, a space, a third period, the closing square bracket, and a period to indicate the end of the sentence. The following example is based on a quotation from the sentences immediately above this one:

> The instructions say, "If you [. . .] omit material from within a quotation,
>
> [you must] indicate the ellipsis [. . .]. If you are omitting material from the
>
> end of a sentence, type [. . .] then a period to indicate the end [. . .].

Notice that although material preceded "If you," periods are not needed to indicate the omission because "If you" began a sentence in the original. Customarily, initial and terminal omissions are indicated only when they are part of the sentence you are quoting. Even such omissions need not be indicated when the quoted material is obviously incomplete—when, for instance, it is a word or phrase.

4. Distinguish between short and long quotations, and treat each appropriately. **Short quotations** (usually defined as fewer than five lines of typed prose or three lines of poetry) are enclosed within quotation marks and run into the text (rather than being set off, without quotation marks), as in the following example:

> Hawthorne begins the story by telling us that "Young Goodman Brown came forth at sunset into the street at Salem village," thus at the outset connecting the village with daylight. A few paragraphs later, when Hawthorne tells us that the road Brown takes was "darkened by all of the gloomiest trees of the forest," he begins to associate the forest with darkness--and a very little later with evil.

If your short quotation is from a poem, be sure to follow the capitalization of the original, and use a slash mark (with a space before and after it) to indicate separate lines. Give the line numbers, if your source gives them, in parentheses, immediately after the closing quotation marks and before the closing punctuation, thus:

> In "Diving into the Wreck," Adrienne Rich's speaker says that she puts on "body-armor" (5). Obviously the journey is dangerous.

To set off a **long quotation** (more than four typed lines of prose or more than two lines of poetry), indent the entire quotation ten spaces from the left margin. Usually, a long quotation is introduced by a clause ending with a colon—for instance, "The following passage will make this point clear:" or "The closest we come to hearing an editorial voice is a long passage in the middle of the story:" or some such lead-in. After typing your lead-in, double-space, and then type the quotation, indented and double-spaced.

5. Commas and periods go inside the quotation marks.

> Chopin tells us in the first sentence that "Mrs. Mallard was afflicted with heart trouble," and in the last sentence the doctors say that Mrs. Mallard "died of heart disease."

Exception: If the quotation is immediately followed by material in parentheses or in square brackets, close the quotation, then give the parenthetic or bracketed material, and then—after closing the parenthesis or bracket—insert the comma or period.

Chopin tells us in the first sentence that "Mrs. Mallard was afflicted with

heart trouble" (12), and in the last sentence the doctors say that Mrs.

Mallard "died of heart disease" (14).

Semicolons, colons, and dashes go outside the closing quotation marks.

Question marks and exclamation points go inside if they are part of the quotation, outside if they are your own.

In the following passage from a student's essay, notice the difference in the position of the question marks. The first question mark is part of the quotation, so it is enclosed within the quotation marks. The second question mark, however, is the student's, so it comes after the closing quotation marks.

The older man says to Goodman Brown, "Sayest thou so?" Doesn't a reader

become uneasy when the man immediately adds, "We are but a little way in

the forest yet"?

Quotation Marks or Underlining?

Use quotation marks around titles of short stories and other short works—that is, titles of chapters in books, essays, and poems that might not be published by themselves. Underline (to indicate italics) titles of books, periodicals, collections of essays, plays, and long poems such as *The Rime of the Ancient Mariner.* Word processing software will let you use italic type (instead of underlining) if you wish.

A Note on the Possessive

It is awkward to use the possessive case for titles of literary works and secondary sources. Rather than "*The Great Gatsby*'s final chapter," write instead "the final chapter of *The Great Gatsby.*" Not "*The Oxford Companion to American Literature*'s entry on Emerson," but, instead, "the entry on Emerson in *The Oxford Companion to American Literature.*"

Appendix **B**

Writing a Research Paper

WHAT RESEARCH IS NOT, AND WHAT RESEARCH IS

Because a research paper requires its writer to collect and interpret evidence—usually including the opinions of earlier investigators—it is sometimes said that a research paper, unlike a critical essay, is not the expression of personal opinion. But such a view is unjust both to criticism and to research. A critical essay is not a mere expression of personal opinions; if it is any good, it offers evidence that supports the opinions and thus persuades the reader of their objective rightness. And a research paper is in the final analysis largely personal, because the author continuously uses his or her own judgment to evaluate the evidence, deciding what is relevant and convincing. A research paper is not the mere presentation of what a dozen scholars have already said about a topic; it is a thoughtful evaluation of the available evidence, and so it is, finally, an expression of what the author thinks the evidence adds up to.

PRIMARY AND SECONDARY MATERIALS

The materials of literary research can be conveniently divided into two sorts, primary and secondary. The *primary materials,* or sources, are the real subject of study; the *secondary materials* are critical and historical accounts already written about these primary materials. For example, Langston Hughes wrote poems, stories, plays, and essays. For a student of Hughes, these works are the primary materials. If you want to study his ways of representing African American speech, or his representations of whites, or his collaboration with Zora Neale Hurston, you will read the primary material—his own writings (and Hurston's, in the case of the collaborative work). But in an effort to reach a thoughtful understanding of some aspect of his work, you will also want to look at later biographical and critical studies of his works and perhaps also at scholarly writing on such topics as Black English. You may even find yourself looking at essays on Black English that do not specifically mention Hughes but that nevertheless may prove helpful.

Similarly, if you are writing about Charlotte Perkins Gilman (we include one of her stories), the primary material includes not only other stories but also her social and political writing. If you are writing about her views of medical treatment of women, you will want to look not only at the story we reprint ("The Yellow Wallpaper") but also at her autobiography. Further, you will also want to look at some secondary material, such as recent scholarly books and articles on medical treatment of women in the late nineteenth and early twentieth centuries.

Locating Materials: First Steps

The easiest way to locate articles and books on literature written in a modern language—that is, on a topic other than literature of the ancient world—is to consult the

> *MLA International Bibliography of Books and Articles in the Modern Languages and Literatures* (1922–),

which until 1969 was published as part of *PMLA* (*Publications of the Modern Language Association*) and since 1969 has been published separately. It is also available on CD-ROM through WilsonDisc, and in fact the disc is preferable since it is updated quarterly, whereas the print version is more than a year behind the times. Many college and university libraries also now offer the *MLA International Bibliography* as part of their package of online resources for research, and it is even more up-to-date.

   MLA International Bibliography lists scholarly studies—books as well as articles in academic journals—published in a given year. Because of the great number of items listed, the print version of the bibliography runs to more than one volume, but material on writing in English (including, for instance, South African authors who write in English) is in one volume. To see what has been published on Langston Hughes in a given year, then, in this volume you turn to the section on American literature (as opposed to British, Canadian, Irish, and so forth), and then to the subsection labeled 1900–99, to see if anything that sounds relevant is listed.

   Because your time is limited, you probably cannot read everything published on your topic. At least for the moment, therefore, you will use only the last five or ten years of this bibliography. Presumably, any important earlier material will have been incorporated into some of the recent studies listed. When you come to read these recent studies, if you find references to an article of, say, 1975 that sounds essential, of course you will read that article too.

   Although *MLA International Bibliography* includes works on American literature, if you are doing research on an aspect of American literature you may want to begin with

> *American Literary Scholarship* (1965–).

This annual publication is noted for its broad coverage of articles and books on major and minor American writers, and is especially valuable for its frank comments on the material that it lists.

   On some recent topics—for instance, the arguments for and against dropping *Huckleberry Finn* from high school curricula—there may be few or no books, and there may not even be material in the scholarly journals indexed in *MLA International Bibliography*. Popular magazines, however, such as *Atlantic, Ebony,* and *Newsweek*—unlisted in *MLA*—may include some useful material. These magazines, and about 200 others, are indexed in

> *Readers' Guide to Periodical Literature* (1900–).

If you want to write a research paper on the controversy over *Huckleberry Finn,* or on the popular reception given to Kenneth Branagh's films of Shakespeare's *Henry V, Much Ado about Nothing,* and *Hamlet,* you can locate material (for instance, reviews of Branagh's films) through *Readers' Guide*. For that matter, you can also locate reviews of older films, let's say Olivier's films of Shakespeare's plays, by consulting the volumes for the years in which the films were released.

On many campuses *Readers' Guide* has been supplanted by

InfoTrac (1985–)

on CD-ROM. The disc is preinstalled in a microcomputer that can be accessed from a computer terminal. This index to authors and subjects in popular and scholarly magazines and in newspapers provides access to several database indexes, including

- The *General Periodicals Index,* available in the Academic Library Edition (about 1,100 general and scholarly periodicals) and in the Public Library Edition (about 1,100 popular magazines)
- The *Academic Index* (400 general-interest publications, all of which are also available in the Academic Library Edition of the *General Periodicals Index*)
- The *Magazine Index Plus* (the four most recent years of the *New York Times,* the two most recent months of the *Wall Street Journal,* and 400 popular magazines, all of which are included in the Public Library Edition of the *General Periodicals Index*)
- The *National Newspaper Index* (the four most recent years of the *New York Times,* the *Christian Science Monitor,* the *Washington Post,* and the *Los Angeles Times*)

Once again, many college and university libraries are now making available online versions of these and similar resources for research. Some students (and faculty) prefer to use the books on the shelf, but the electronic editions have significant advantages. Often, it is easier to perform "searches" using them; and in many cases they are updated well before the next print editions are published.

Other Bibliographic Aids

There are hundreds of guides to publications and to reference works. *The Oxford Companion to African American Literature* (1997), edited by William L. Andrews, Frances Smith Foster, and Trudier Harris, provides detailed entries on authors, literary works, and many literary, historical, and cultural topics and terms, as well as suggestions for further reading. *Reader's Guide to Literature in English* (1996), edited by Mark Hawkins-Dady, is a massive work (nearly 1,000 pages) that gives thorough summaries of recent critical and scholarly writing on English and American authors.

How do you find such books? Two invaluable guides to reference works (that is, to bibliographies and to such helpful compilations as handbooks of mythology, place names, and critical terms) are

James L. Harner, *Literary Research Guide: A Guide to Reference Sources for the Study of Literatures in English and Related Topics,* 3rd ed. (1998)

and

Michael J. Marcuse, *A Reference Guide for English Studies* (1990).

And there are guides to these guides: reference librarians. If you don't know where to turn to find something, turn to the librarian.

TAKING NOTES

Let's assume now that you have checked some bibliographies and that you have a fair number of references you must read to have a substantial knowledge of the evidence and the common interpretations of the evidence. Most researchers find it convenient, when examining bibliographies and the library catalog, to write down each reference on a 3″ × 5″ index card—one title per card. On the card, put the author's full name (last name first), the exact title of the book or article, and the name of the journal (with dates and pages). Titles of books and periodicals (publications issued periodically—for example, monthly or four times a year) are underlined; titles of articles and of essays in books are enclosed in quotation marks. It's also a good idea to put the library catalog number on the card to save time if you need to get the item for a second look.

Next, start reading or scanning the materials whose titles you have collected. Some of these items will prove irrelevant or silly; others will prove valuable in themselves and also in the leads they give you to further references, which you should duly record on index cards. Notes—aside from these bibliographic notes—are best taken on larger index cards. The 3″ × 5″ cards are too small for summaries of useful materials; we use 4″ × 6″ cards, which allow you to record a moderate amount of information. Using these medium-sized cards rather than larger ones serves as a reminder that you need not take notes on everything. Be selective in taking notes.

Two Mechanical Aids: The Photocopier and the Word Processor

Use the **photocopier** to make copies of material from the library (including material that does not circulate) that you know you need, or that you might want to refer to later. But remember that sometimes it is even more efficient to

- read the material in the library,
- select carefully what pertains to the purpose of your research, and
- take your notes on it.

The **word processor** or **computer** is useful not only in the final stage, to produce a neat copy, but also in the early stages of research, when you are getting ideas and taking notes. With the help of the computer, you can brainstorm ideas, make connections, organize and reorganize material; develop (and change) outlines. This file can be a kind of creative "work space" for your research paper.

A Guide to Note-Taking

Some students use note cards—we have already mentioned that we use 4″ × 6″ cards—for taking notes during the process of research. Others write on separate sheets of a notebook, or on the sheets of a yellow legal pad. Still others take their notes using a computer or word processor, and then organize and rearrange this body of material by copying and pasting, moving the notes into a coherent order. (We advise you not to delete material that, when you reread your notes, strikes you as irrelevant. It *probably* is irrelevant; but on the other hand, it may turn out to be valuable after all. Just put unwanted material into a file called "rejects," or some such thing, until you have completed the paper.)

Whichever method you prefer, keep in mind the following:

- **For everything you consult or read in detail, always specify the source,** so that you know exactly from where you have taken a key point or a quotation.
- **Write summaries (abridgments), not paraphrases (restatements).**
- **Quote sparingly.** Remember that this is *your* paper—it will present your thesis, not the thesis and arguments and analyses of someone else. Quote directly only those passages that are particularly effective, or crucial, or memorable. In your finished paper these quotations will provide authority and emphasis.
- **Quote accurately.** After copying a quotation, check your note against the original, correct any misquotation, and then put a checkmark after your quotation to indicate that it is accurate. Verify the page number also, and then put a checkmark on your note after the page number. If a quotation runs from the bottom of, say, page 306 to the top of 307, on your note put a distinguishing mark (for instance two parallel vertical lines after the last word of the first page), so that if you later use only part of the quotation, you will know the page on which it appeared.

  Use ellipses (three spaced periods) to indicate the omission of any words within a sentence. If the omitted words are at the end of the quoted sentence, put a period where you end the sentence, and then add three spaced periods to indicate the omission:

  If the . . . words were at the end of the quoted sentence, put a period

  where you end. . . .

  Use square brackets to indicate your additions to the quotation. Here is an example:

  Here is an [uninteresting] example.

- **Never copy a passage by changing an occasional word,** under the impression that you are thereby putting it into your own words. Notes of this sort may find their way into your paper, your reader will sense a style other than yours, and suspicions of plagiarism may follow. (For a detailed discussion of plagiarism, see pages 763–64.)
- **Comment on your notes** as you do your work, and later as you reflect on what you have jotted down from the sources. Make a special mark—we

recommend using double parentheses ((. . .)) or a different-colored pen to write, for example, "Jones seriously misreads the passage," or "Smith makes a good point but fails to see its implications." As you work, consider it your obligation to *think* about the material, evaluating it and using it as a stimulus to further thought.

- **In the upper corner of each note card, write a brief key**—for example, "Swordplay in *Hamlet*"—so that later you can tell at a glance what is on the note.

DRAFTING THE PAPER

The difficult job of writing up your findings remains, but if you have taken good notes and have put useful headings on each note, you are well on your way.

- Read through the notes and sort them into packets of related material. Remove all notes that you now see are irrelevant to your paper. (Do not destroy them, however; you may want them later.) Go through the notes again and again, sorting and resorting, putting together what belongs together.
- Probably you will find that you have to do a little additional research—somehow you aren't quite clear about this or that—but after you have done this additional research, you should be able to arrange the packets into a reasonable and consistent sequence. You now have a kind of first draft, or at least a tentative organization for your paper.
- Beware of the compulsion to include every note in your essay; that is, beware of telling the reader, "A says . . . ; B says . . . ; C says . . . "
- You must have a point, a thesis. Make sure that you state it early, and that you keep it evident to your readers.
- Make sure that the organization is evident to the reader. When you were doing your research, and even perhaps when you were arranging your notes, you were not entirely sure where you where going; but by now, with your notes arranged into what seems to you to be the right sequence, you think you know what everything adds up to. Doubtless in the process of drafting you will make important changes in your focus, but do not abandon a draft until you think it not only says what you want to say, but says it in what seems to you to be a reasonable order. The final version of the paper should be a finished piece of work, without the inconsistencies, detours, and occasional dead ends of an early draft. Your readers should feel that they are moving toward a conclusion (by means of your thoughtful evaluation of the evidence) rather than merely reading an anthology of commentary on the topic. And so we should get some such structure as "There are three common views on. . . . The first two are represented by A and B; the third, and by far the most reasonable, is C's view that. . . . A argues . . . but. . . . The second view, B's, is based on . . . but. . . . Although the third view, C's, is not conclusive, still. . . . Moreover, C's point can be strengthened when we consider a piece of evidence that she does not make use of. . . ."
- Preface all or almost all quotations with a lead-in, such as "X concisely states the common view" or "Z, without offering any proof, asserts that . . . "

Let the reader know where you are going, or, to put it a little differently, let the reader know how the quotation fits into your argument.

Quotations and summaries, in short, are accompanied by judicious analyses of your own. By the end of the paper, your readers have not only read a neatly typed paper (see page 752) and gained an idea of what previous writers have said but also are persuaded that under your guidance they have seen the evidence, heard the arguments justly summarized, and reached a sound conclusion.

A bibliography or list of works consulted (see pages 769–74) is usually appended to a research paper so that readers may easily look further into the primary and secondary material if they wish; but if you have done your job well, readers will be content to leave the subject where you left it, grateful that you have set matters straight.

FOCUS ON PRIMARY SOURCES

Remember that your paper should highlight *primary* sources, the materials that are your real subject (as opposed to the secondary sources, the critical and historical discussion of these primary materials). It should be, above all, *your* paper, a paper in which you present a thesis that you have developed about the literary work or works that you have chosen to examine. By using secondary sources, you can enrich your analysis, as you place yourself in the midst of the scholarly community interested in this author or authors. But keep a judicious proportion between primary sources, which should receive the greater emphasis, and secondary sources, which should be used selectively.

To help you succeed in this balancing act, when you review your draft, mark with a red pen the quotations from and references to primary sources, and then with a blue pen do the same marking for secondary sources. If, when you scan the pages of your paper-in-progress, you see a lot more blue than red, you should change the emphasis, the proportion, to what it should be. Guard against the tendency to rely heavily on the secondary sources you have compiled. The point of view that really counts is your own.

DOCUMENTATION

What to Document: Avoiding Plagiarism

Honesty requires that you acknowledge your indebtedness for material, not only when you quote directly from a work but also when you appropriate an idea that is not common knowledge. Not to acknowledge such borrowing is plagiarism. If in doubt whether to give credit, give credit.

You ought, however, to develop a sense of what is considered **common knowledge.** Definitions in a dictionary can be considered common knowledge, so there is no need to say, "According to Webster, a novel is . . . " (This is weak in three ways: It's unnecessary, it's uninteresting, and it's unclear, since "Webster" appears in the titles of several dictionaries, some good and some bad.) Similarly, the date of first publication of *The Scarlet Letter* (1850) can be considered common knowledge. Few can give it when asked, but it can be found out from innumerable sources, and no one need get the credit for providing you with the date. The idea that Hamlet delays is also a matter of common knowledge. But if you are impressed by so-and-so's argument that Claudius has been much maligned, you should give credit to so-and-so.

Suppose that in the course of your research for a paper on Langston Hughes you happen to come across Arnold Rampersad's statement, in an essay in *Voices and Visions* (ed. Helen Vendler), that

> Books alone could not save Hughes from loneliness, let alone give him the strength to be a writer. At least one other factor was essential in priming him for creative obsession. In the place in his heart, or psychology, vacated by his parents entered the black masses. (355)

This is an interesting idea, and in the last sentence the shift from heart to psychology is perhaps especially interesting. You certainly *cannot* say—with the implication that the idea and the words are your own—something like

> Hughes let enter into his heart, or his psychology--a place vacated by his
>
> parents--the black masses.

The writer is simply lifting Rampersad's ideas and making only tiny changes in the wording. But even a larger change in the wording is unacceptable unless Rampersad is given credit. Here is a restatement that is an example of plagiarism even though the words differ from Rampersad's:

> Hughes took into himself ordinary black people, thus filling the gap
>
> created by his mother and father.

In this version, the writer presents Rampersad's idea as if it were the writer's own—and presents it less effectively than Rampersad.

What to do? Give Rampersad credit, perhaps along these lines:

> As Arnold Rampersad has said, "in the place in his heart, or his
>
> psychology" where his parents had once been, Hughes now substituted
>
> ordinary black people (355).

You can use another writer's ideas, and even some of the very words, but you must give credit, and you must use quotation marks when you quote.

You can

- Give credit and quote directly, or
- Give credit and summarize the writer's point, or
- Give credit and summarize the point but include—within quotation marks —some phrase you think is especially interesting

How to Document: Footnotes, Internal Parenthetical Citations, and a List of Works Cited (MLA Format)

Documentation tells your reader exactly what your sources are. Until fairly recently, the standard form was the footnote, which, for example, told the reader that the source of such and such a quotation was a book by so-and-so. But in 1984 the Modern Language Association, which had established the footnote form used in hundreds of journals, university presses, and classrooms, substituted a new form. It is this newer form—parenthetical citation *within* the text (rather than at the foot of the page or the end of the essay)—that we will discuss at length. Keep in mind, though, that footnotes still have their uses.

FOOTNOTES   If you are using only one source, your instructor may advise you to give the source in a footnote. (Check with your instructors to find out their preferred forms of documentation.)

Let's say that your only source is this textbook. Let's say, too, that all of your quotations will be from a single story—Kate Chopin's "The Story of an Hour"— printed in this book on pages 12–14. If you use a word processor, the software program can probably format the note for you. If, however, you are using a typewriter, type the digit 1 (elevated, and *without* a period after it) after your first reference to (or quotation from) the story, and then put a footnote at the bottom of the page, explaining where the story can be found. After your last line of text on the page, triple-space, indent five spaces from the left-hand margin, and type the arabic number 1, elevated. Do *not* put a period after it. Then type a statement (double-spaced) to the effect that all references are to this book.

Notice that although the footnote begins by being indented five spaces, if the note runs to more than one line the subsequent lines are given flush left.

[1]Chopin's story appears in Sylvan Barnet et al., eds. Literature for

Composition, Compact Edition. (New York: Longman, 2003), 12-14.

(If a book has more than three authors or editors, give the name of only the first author or editor, and follow it with a comma and *et al.,* the Latin abbreviation for "and others.")

Even if you are writing a comparison of, say, two stories in this book, you can use a note of this sort. It might run thus:

[1]All page references given parenthetically within the essay refer to

stories in Sylvan Barnet et al., eds. Literature for Composition, Compact

Edition. (New York: Longman, 2003).

If you use such a note, you do not need to use a footnote after each quotation that follows. You can give the citations right in the body of the paper, by putting the page references in parentheses after the quotations.

INTERNAL PARENTHETICAL CITATIONS   On page 755 we distinguish between embedded quotations (which are short, are run right into your own sentence, and are enclosed in quotation marks) and quotations that are set off on the page and are not enclosed in quotation marks (for example, three or more lines of poetry, five or more lines of typed prose).

For an embedded quotation, put the page reference in parentheses immediately after the closing quotation marks *without* any intervening punctuation. Then, after the parenthesis that follows the number, insert the necessary punctuation (for instance, a comma or a period):

> Brent Staples says that his "first victim was a woman" (172). Doubtless the
>
> reader thinks the victim was robbed or killed, but Staples has a surprise for
>
> the reader.

The period comes *after* the parenthetical citation. In the next example *no* punctuation comes after the first citation—because none is needed—and a comma comes *after* (not before or within) the second citation, because a comma is needed in the sentence:

> This is ironic because almost at the start of the story, in the second
>
> paragraph, Richards with the best of motives "hastened" (13) to bring his
>
> sad message; if he had at the start been "too late" (14), Mallard would have
>
> arrived at home first.

For a quotation that is not embedded within the text but is set off (by being indented ten spaces), put the parenthetical citation on the last line of the quotation, one space *after* the period that ends the quoted sentence.

Four additional points:

- The abbreviations *p., pg.,* and *pp.* are *not* used in citing pages.
- If a story is very short, perhaps running for only a page or two, your instructor may tell you there is no need to keep citing the page reference for each quotation. Simply mention in the footnote that the story appears on, say, pages 12–14.
- If you are referring to a poem, your instructor may tell you to use parenthetical citations of line numbers rather than of page numbers. But, again, your footnote will tell the reader that the poem can be found in this book, and on what page.
- If you are referring to a play with numbered lines, your instructor may prefer that in your parenthetical citations you give act, scene, and line, rather than page numbers. Use arabic (not roman) numerals, separating the act from the scene, and the scene from the line, by periods. Here, then, is how a reference to Act 3, Scene 2, line 118 would be given:

(3.2.118)

PARENTHETICAL CITATIONS AND LIST OF WORKS CITED   Footnotes have fallen into disfavor. Parenthetical citations are now usually clarified not by means of a footnote but by means of a list, headed "Works Cited," given at the end of the essay. In this list you give alphabetically (last name first) the authors and titles that you have quoted or referred to in the essay.

Briefly, the idea is that the reader of your paper encounters an author's name and a parenthetical citation of pages. By checking the author's name in Works

Cited, the reader can find the passage in the book. Suppose you are writing about Kate Chopin's "The Story of an Hour." Let's assume that you have already mentioned the author and the title of the story—that is, you have let the reader know the subject of the essay—and now you introduce a quotation from the story in a sentence such as this. (Notice the parenthetical citation of page numbers immediately after the quotation.)

> True, Mrs. Mallard at first expresses grief when she hears the news, but
>
> soon (unknown to her friends) she finds joy in it. So, Richards's "sad
>
> message" (13), though sad in Richards's eyes, is in fact a happy message.

Turning to Works Cited, the reader, knowing the quoted words are by Chopin, looks for Chopin and finds the following:

> Chopin, Kate. "The Story of an Hour." Literature for Composition, Compact
>
> Edition. Ed. Sylvan Barnet et al. New York: Longman, 2003.

Thus the essayist is informing the reader that the quoted words ("sad message") are to be found on page 13 of this anthology.

If you have not mentioned Chopin's name in some sort of lead-in, you will have to give her name within the parentheses so that the reader will know the author of the quoted words:

> What are we to make out of a story that ends by telling us that the leading
>
> character has died "of joy that kills" (Chopin 14)?

The closing quotation marks come immediately after the last word of the quotation; the citation and the final punctuation—in this case, the essayist's question mark—come *after* the closing quotation marks.

If you are comparing Chopin's story with Gilman's "The Yellow Wallpaper," in Works Cited you will give a similar entry for Gilman—her name, the title of the story, the book in which it is reprinted, and the page numbers that the story occupies.

If you are referring to several works reprinted within one volume, instead of listing each item fully, it is acceptable in Works Cited to list each item simply by giving the author's name, the title of the work, then a period, a space, and the name of the anthologist, followed by the page numbers that the selection spans. Thus a reference to Chopin's "The Story of an Hour" would be followed only by: Barnet 12–14. This form requires that the anthology itself be cited under the name of the first-listed editor, thus:

> Barnet, Sylvan, et al., eds. Literature for Composition, Compact Edition.
>
> New York: Longman, 2003.

If you are writing a research paper, you will use many sources. In the essay itself you will mention an author's name, quote or summarize from this author, and follow the quotation or summary with a parenthetical citation of the pages. In Works Cited you will give the full title, place of publication, and other bibliographic material.

Here are a few examples, all referring to an article by Joan Templeton, "The *Doll House* Backlash: Criticism, Feminism, and Ibsen." The article appeared in *PMLA* 104 (1989): 28–40, but this information is given only in Works Cited, not within the text of the student's essay.

If in the text of your essay you mention the author's name, the citation following a quotation (or a summary of a passage) is merely a page number in parentheses, followed by a period, thus:

> In 1989 Joan Templeton argued that many critics, unhappy with
>
> recognizing Ibsen as a feminist, sought "to render Nora inconsequential"
>
> (29).

Or:

> In 1989 Joan Templeton noted that many critics, unhappy with recognizing
>
> Ibsen as a feminist, have sought to make Nora trivial (29).

If you don't mention the name of the author in a lead-in, you will have to give the name within the parenthetical citation:

> Many critics, attempting to argue that Ibsen was not a feminist, have tried
>
> to make Nora trivial (Templeton 29).

Notice in all of these examples that the final period comes after the parenthetical citation. *Exception:* If the quotation is longer than four lines and is therefore set off by being indented ten spaces from the left margin, end the quotation with the appropriate punctuation (period, question mark, or exclamation mark), hit the space bar twice, and type (in parentheses) the page number. In this case, do not put a period after the citation.

Another point: If your list of Works Cited includes more than one work by an author, in your essay when you quote or refer to one or the other you'll have to identify *which* work you are drawing on. You can provide the title in a lead-in, thus:

> In "The Doll House Backlash: Criticism, Feminism, and Ibsen," Templeton
>
> says, "Nora's detractors have often been, from the first, her husband's
>
> defenders" (30).

Or you can provide the information in the parenthetic citation, giving a shortened version of the title. This usually consists of the first word, unless it is *A, An,* or *The,* in which case including the second word is usually enough. Certain titles may require still another word or two, as in this example:

> According to Templeton, "Nora's detractors have often been, from the first,
>
> her husband's defenders" ("Doll House Backlash" 30).

FORMS OF CITATION IN WORKS CITED   In looking over the following samples of entries in Works Cited, remember:

- The list of Works Cited appears at the end of the paper. It begins on a new page, and the page continues the numbering of the text.
- The list of Works Cited is arranged alphabetically by author (last name first).
- If a work is anonymous, list it under the first word of the title unless the first word is *A, An,* or *The,* in which case list it under the second word.
- If a work is by two authors, although the book is listed alphabetically under the first author's last name, the second author's name is given in the normal order, first name first.
- If you list two or more works by the same author, the author's name is not repeated but is represented by three hyphens followed by a period and a space.
- Each item begins flush left, but if an entry is longer than one line, subsequent lines in the entry are indented five spaces.

For details about almost every imaginable kind of citation, consult Joseph Gibaldi, *MLA Handbook for Writers of Research Papers,* 5th ed. (New York: Modern Language Association, 1999). We give here, however, information concerning the most common kinds of citations.

For citations of electronic sources, see page 775.

Here are samples of the kinds of citations you are most likely to include in your list of Works Cited.

A book by one author:

Douglas, Ann. The Feminization of American Culture. New York: Knopf,

1977.

Notice that the author's last name is given first, but otherwise the name is given as on the title page. Do not substitute initials for names written out on the title page, but you may shorten the publisher's name—for example, from Little, Brown and Company to Little.

Take the title from the title page, not from the cover or the spine, but disregard unusual typography—for instance, the use of only capital letters or the use of & for *and.* Underline the title and subtitle with one continuous underline, but do not underline the period. The place of publication is indicated by the name of the city. If the city is not well known or if several cities have the same name (for instance, Cambridge, Massachusetts, and Cambridge, England) the name of the state or country is added. If the title page lists several cities, give only the first.

A book by more than one author:

Gilbert, Sandra, and Susan Gubar. The Madwoman in the Attic: The Woman

Writer and the Nineteenth-Century Literary Imagination. New Haven:

Yale UP, 1979.

Notice that the book is listed under the last name of the first author (Gilbert) and that the second author's name is then given with first name (Susan) first. *If the book has more than three authors,* give the name of the first author only (last name first) and follow it with *et al.* (Latin for "and others").

A book in several volumes:

McQuade, Donald, et al., eds. The Harper American Literature. 2nd ed.

2 vols. New York: HarperCollins, 1994.

Pope, Alexander. The Correspondence of Alexander Pope. 5 vols. Ed. George

Sherburn. Oxford: Clarendon, 1955.

The total number of volumes is given after the title, regardless of the number that you have used.

If you have used more than one volume, within your essay you will parenthetically indicate a reference to, for instance, page 30 of volume 3 thus: (3: 30). If you have used only one volume of a multivolume work—let's say you used only volume 2 of McQuade's anthology—in your entry in Works Cited write, after the period following the date, Vol. 2. In your parenthetical citation within the essay you will therefore cite only the page reference (without the volume number), since the reader will (on consulting Works Cited) understand that in this example the reference is in volume 2.

If, instead of using the volumes as a whole, you used only an independent work within one volume—say, an essay in volume 2—in Works Cited omit the abbreviation *Vol.* Instead, give an arabic 2 (indicating volume 2) followed by a colon, a space, and the page numbers that encompass the selection you used:

McPherson, James Alan. "Why I Like Country Music." The Harper

American Literature. 2nd ed. 2 vols. New York: HarperCollins, 1994.

2: 2304-15.

Notice that this entry for McPherson specifies not only that the book consists of two volumes, but also that only one selection ("Why I Like Country Music," occupying pages 2304–15 in volume 2) was used. If you use this sort of citation in Works Cited, in the body of your essay a documentary reference to this work will be only to the page; the volume number will *not* be added.

A book with a separate title in a set of volumes:

Churchill, Winston. The Age of Revolution. Vol. 3 of A History of the

English-Speaking Peoples. New York: Dodd, 1957.

Jonson, Ben. The Complete Masques. Ed. Stephen Orgel. Vol. 4 of The Yale

Ben Jonson. New Haven: Yale UP, 1969.

A revised edition of a book:

Chaucer, Geoffrey. <u>The Riverside Chaucer</u>. Ed. Larry Benson. 3rd ed.

Boston: Houghton, 1987.

Ellmann, Richard. <u>James Joyce</u>. Rev. ed. New York: Oxford UP, 1982.

A reprint, such as a paperback version of an older hardcover book:

Rourke, Constance. <u>American Humor</u>. 1931. Garden City, New York:

Doubleday, 1953.

Notice that the entry cites the original date (1931) but indicates that the writer is using the Doubleday reprint of 1953.

An edited book other than an anthology:

Keats, John. <u>The Letters of John Keats</u>. Ed. Hyder Edward Rollins. 2 vols.

Cambridge, Mass.: Harvard UP, 1958.

An anthology: You can list an anthology either under the editor's name or under the title.

A work in a volume of works by one author:

Sontag, Susan. "The Aesthetics of Silence." In <u>Styles of Radical Will</u>. New

York: Farrar, 1969, 3-34.

This entry indicates that Sontag's essay, called "The Aesthetics of Silence," appears in a book of hers entitled *Styles of Radical Will*. Notice that the page numbers of the short work are cited (not page numbers that you may happen to refer to, but the page numbers of the entire piece).

A work in an anthology, that is, in a collection of works by several authors: Begin with the author and the title of the work you are citing, not with the name of the anthologist or the title of the anthology. The entry ends with the pages occupied by the selection you are citing:

Ng, Fae Myenne. "A Red Sweater." <u>Charlie Chan Is Dead: An Anthology of</u>

<u>Contemporary Asian American Fiction</u>. Ed. Jessica Hagedorn. New

York: Penguin, 1993. 358-68.

Normally, you will give the title of the work you are citing (probably an essay, short story, or poem) in quotation marks. If you are referring to a book-length work (for instance, a novel or a full-length play), underline it to indicate italics. If the work is translated, after the period that follows the title, write *Trans.* and give the name of the translator, followed by a period and the name of the anthology.

If the collection is a multivolume work and you are using only one volume, in Works Cited you will specify the volume, as in the example (p. 770) of McPherson's essay. Because the list of Works Cited specifies the volume, your parenthetical documentary reference within your essay will specify (as mentioned earlier) only the page numbers, not the volume. Thus, although McPherson's essay appears on pages 2304–15 in the second volume of a two-volume work, a parenthetical citation will refer only to the page numbers because the citation in Works Cited specifies the volume.

Remember that the pages specified in the entry in your list of Works Cited are to the *entire selection,* not simply to pages you may happen to refer to within your paper.

If you are referring to a *reprint of a scholarly article,* give details of the original publication, as in the following example:

> Mack, Maynard. "The World of Hamlet." Yale Review 41 (1952): 502-23. Rpt.
>
> in Hamlet. By William Shakespeare. Ed. Sylvan Barnet. New York:
>
> Penguin Putnam, 1998. 265-87.

Two or more works in an anthology: If you are referring to more than one work in an anthology in order to avoid repeating all the information about the anthology in each entry in Works Cited, under each author's name (in the appropriate alphabetical place) give the author and title of the work, then a period, a space, and the name of the anthologist, followed by the page numbers that the selection spans. Thus, a reference to Shakespeare's *Hamlet* would be followed only by

> Barnet 407-510

rather than by a full citation of Barnet's anthology. This form requires that the anthology itself also be listed, under Barnet.

Two or more works by the same author: Notice that the works are given in alphabetical order (*Fables* precedes *Fools*) and that the author's name is not repeated but is represented by three hyphens followed by a period and a space. If the author is the translator or editor of a volume, the three hyphens are followed not by a period but by a comma, then a space, then the appropriate abbreviation (*Trans.* or *Ed.*), then the title:

> Frye, Northrop. Fables of Identity: Studies in Poetic Mythology. New York:
>
> Harcourt, 1963.
>
> ---. Fools of Time: Studies in Shakespearean Tragedy. Toronto: U of Toronto
>
> P, 1967.

A translated book:

> Gogol, Nikolai. Dead Souls. Trans. Andrew McAndrew. New York: New
>
> American Library, 1961.

If you are discussing the translation itself, as opposed to the book, list the work under the translator's name. Then put a comma, a space, and "trans." After the period following "trans," skip a space, then give the title of the book, a period, a space, and then "By" and the author's name, first name first. Continue with information about the place of publication, publisher, and date, as in any entry for a book.

An introduction, foreword, or afterword, or other editorial apparatus:

> Fromm, Erich. Afterword. 1984. By George Orwell. New American Library,
>
> 1961.

Usually a book with an introduction or some such comparable material is listed under the name of the author of the book rather than the name of the author of the editorial material (see the citation to Pope on p. 770). But if you are referring to the editor's apparatus rather than to the work itself, use the form just given.

Words such as *preface, introduction, afterword,* and *conclusion* are capitalized in the entry but are neither enclosed within quotation marks nor underlined.

A book review: First, here is an example of a review that does not have a title.

> Vendler, Helen. Rev. of Essays on Style. Ed. Roger Fowler. Essays in
>
> Criticism 16 (1966): 457-63.

If the review has a title, give the title after the period following the reviewer's name, before "Rev." If the review is unsigned, list it under the first word of the title, or the second word if the first word is *A, An,* or *The.* If an unsigned review has no title, begin the entry with "Rev. of" and alphabetize it under the title of the work being reviewed.

An encyclopedia: The first example is for a signed article, the second for an unsigned article.

> Lang, Andrew. "Ballads." Encyclopaedia Britannica. 1910 ed.

> "Metaphor." The New Encyclopaedia Britannica: Micropaedia. 1974 ed.

An article in a scholarly journal: Some journals are paginated consecutively; that is, the pagination of the second issue picks up where the first issue left off. Other journals begin each issue with a new page 1. The forms of the citations in Works Cited differ slightly.

First, the citation of a *journal that uses continuous pagination:*

> Burbick, Joan. "Emily Dickinson and the Economics of Desire." American
>
> Literature 58 (1986): 361–78.

This article appeared in volume 58, which was published in 1986. (Notice that the volume number is followed by a space, then by the year in parentheses, and then by a colon, a space, and the page numbers of the entire article.) Although each volume consists of four issues, you do *not* specify the issue number when the journal is paginated continuously.

For a *journal that paginates each issue separately* (a quarterly journal will have four page 1's each year), give the issue number directly after the volume number and a period, with no spaces before or after the period:

> Spillers, Hortense J. "Martin Luther King and the Style of the Black
>
> Sermon." The Black Scholar 3.1 (1971): 14–27.

An article in a weekly, biweekly, or monthly publication:

> McCabe, Bernard. "Taking Dickens Seriously." Commonweal 14 May 1965:
>
> 24.

Notice that the volume number and the issue number are omitted for popular weeklies or monthlies such as *Time* and *Atlantic*.

An article in a newspaper: Because newspapers usually consist of several sections, a section number may precede the page number. The example indicates that an article begins on page 3 of section 2 and is continued on a later page:

> Wu, Jim. "Authors Praise New Forms." New York Times 8 Mar. 1996, sec. 2:
>
> 3+.

You may also have occasion to cite something other than a printed source, for instance, a lecture. Here are the forms for the chief nonprint sources.

An interview:

> Saretta, Howard. Personal interview. 3 Nov. 1998.

A lecture:

> Heaney, Seamus. Lecture. Tufts University. 15 Oct. 1998.

A television or radio program:

> 60 Minutes. CBS. 30 Jan. 1994.

A film or videotape:

> Modern Times. Dir. Charles Chaplin. United Artists, 1936.

A recording:

> Frost, Robert. "The Road Not Taken." Robert Frost Reads His Poetry.
>
> Caedmon, TC 1060, 1956.

A performance:

> The Cherry Orchard. By Anton Chekhov. Dir. Ron Daniels. American
>
> Repertory Theatre, Cambridge, Mass. 3 Feb. 1994.

Reminder: For the form of citations of electronic material, see page 775.

✔ **C H E C K L I S T :** *Researching a Literary-Historical Paper*

❑ Consult a range of reference books as you are getting launched on a literary-historical paper—it will take less time than you think, and it will be time invested wisely.

❑ Pay attention to *when* the books were published and how up-to-date they are in their suggestions for additional reading.

❑ Even as you acquire familiarity with the subject in general, take special note of where the historical record *makes connections* to the literature that you are studying. The real reward comes when you can perceive the relationship between history and the structure and themes of the literary works.

✔ **C H E C K L I S T :** *Evaluating Sources on the World Wide Web*

❑ *Focus* the topic of your research as precisely as you can before you embark on a WWW search. Lots of surfing and browsing can sometimes turn up good material, but using the WWW without a focus can prove distracting and unproductive. It takes you away from library research (where the results might be better) and from the actual planning and writing of the paper.

❑ Ask the following questions:
  ❑ Does this site or page look like it can help me in my assignment?
  ❑ Whose site or page is this?
  ❑ What is the intended audience?
  ❑ Can you determine the point of view? Are there signs of a specific slant or bias?
  ❑ What is detail, depth, and quality of the material presented?
  ❑ Is the site well constructed and well organized?
  ❑ Is the text well written?
  ❑ Can this WWW information be corroborated or supported by print sources?
  ❑ When was the site or page made available? Has it been recently revised or updated? *Reminder:* Your browser will enable you to get this information; if you are using Netscape 4.7, for example, go to View, and choose Page Info.
  ❑ Can the person or institution, company, or agency responsible for this site or page receive e-mail comments, questions, criticisms?

✔ **C H E C K L I S T :** *Citing Sources on the World Wide Web*

Provide the following information:

❑ Author
❑ Title
❑ Publication information
❑ Title of archive or database
❑ Date (if given) when the site was posted; sometimes termed the "revision" or "modification" date
❑ Name of institution or organization that supports or is associated with this site
❑ Date that you accessed this source
❑ URL

Literary Credits

Photo Credits

54: Photograph © Dorothy Alexander; 56: Royal Museum of Fine Arts, Brussels, Belgium; 113: Photograph © Jerry Bauer; 116: Photograph courtesy of Jose Armas; 121: Photograph © Nancy Crampton; 125: Photograph by Thomas Victor, Courtesy of Harriet Spurlin; 138: © Hulton-Duetsch Collection/CORBIS; 139: Manuscripts and Archives Division, New York Public Library, Astor, Lenox, and Tilden Foundations; 153: Buffalo Bill Historical Center, Cody, WY; P.69.2125; 156: Reprinted by permission of the Houghton Library, Harvard University. bMS Am 1823.7 (21); 157: Reprinted by permission of the Houghton Library, Harvard University. bMS Am 1823.7 (80); 158: Buffalo Bill Historical Center, Cody, WY; 1.69.137; 159: Buffalo Bill Historical Center, Cody, WY; P.69.862; 160–161: Reprinted by permission of the Houghton Library, Harvard University. (MS Am 11183.5 (53)). © The President and Fellows of Harvard College; 185: Jay Ann Cox; 190: Krista Niles/The New York Times; 191: © Reuters NewMedia Inc./CORBIS; 193: Hulton|Archive/Getty Images; 203: AP/Wide World Photos; 226: Hulton|Archive/Getty Images; 231: © Bettmann/CORBIS; 248: © B. Keating/Black Star/Stock Photo; 254–257: Faulkner Collection, University of Virginia Library; 259: AP/Wide World Photos; 270: AP/Wide World Photos; 276: Photograph by Annie Valva; 281: Photograph © Jerry Bauer; 307: Photograph © Gordon Parks; 318: Photograph by Eric J. Sundquist/Courtesy of Tuskegee University; 333: AP/Wide World Photos; 377: © Frederick Ayer/Photo Researchers; 379: © Donald Cooper/Photostage; 405, left: Reprinted by permission of the British Library, London; 405, right: Courtesy of C. Walter Hodges; 513: The Harvard Theater Collection, The Houghton Library; 562: AP/Wide World Photos; 563: Billy Rose Theatre Collection, The New York Public Library for the Performing Arts, Astor, Lenox and Tilden Foundations; 573: © Bettmann/CORBIS; 638: AP/Wide World Photos; 655: Christopher Cardozo Fine Art; 656: AP/Wide World Photos; 658: Scott, Foresman Library; 659: Courtesy Rutgers University Press; 660: National Archives; 661: © Bettmann/CORBIS; 663: Photograph © Nancy Crampton; 667: ©1963 Bob Adelman/Magnum Photos, Inc.; 673: AP/Wide World Photos; 675: AP/Wide World Photos; 679–680: Walt Whitman Collection, University of Virginia Library; 683: AP/Wide World Photos; 686: Amherst College Archives and Special Collections. Reprinted by permission of the Trustees of Amherst College; 687: Amherst College Archives and Special Collections. Reprinted by permission of the Trustees of Amherst College; 703: Hulton|Archive/Getty Images; 704: Reprinted by permission of the Jones Library, Inc., Amherst, MA; 714: Reprinted by permission of the Houghton Library, Harvard University, AC9.E1464.Zzx Box 2, env. 3a; 725: Photograph © Dorothy Alexander; 727: © Bettmann/CORBIS; 729: Hulton|Archive/Getty Images; 731: Library of Congress; 742: © Natasha Lane/Sipa Press; 743, top: AP/Wide World Photos; 743, bottom: AP/Wide World Photos.

Index of Authors, Titles, and First Lines of Poems

Index of Terms

2. It is sometimes said that a good short story does two things at once: It provides a believable picture of the surface of life, and it also illuminates some moral or psychological complexity that we feel is part of the essence of human life. This dual claim may not be true, but for the moment accept it. Do you think that Hemingway's story fulfills either or both of these specifications? Support your view.

✔ **CHECKLIST:** *Getting Ideas for Writing about Fiction*

Here are some questions that may help to stimulate ideas about stories. Not every question is, of course, relevant to every story; but if after reading a story and thinking about it, you then run your eye over these questions, you will probably find some questions that will help you to think further about the story—in short, that will help you to get ideas.

As we have said in earlier chapters, it's best to do your thinking with a pen or pencil in hand. If some of the following questions seem to you to be especially relevant to the story you will be writing about, jot down—freely, without worrying about spelling—your initial responses, interrupting your writing only to glance again at the story when you feel the need to check the evidence.

Plot

❑ Does the plot grow out of the characters, or does it depend on chance or coincidence? Did something at first strike you as irrelevant that later you perceived as relevant? Do some parts continue to strike you as irrelevant?
❑ Does surprise play an important role, or does foreshadowing? If surprise is very important, can the story be read a second time with any interest? If so, what gives it this further interest?
❑ What conflicts does the story include? Conflicts of one character against another? Of one character against the setting, or against society? Conflicts within a single character?
❑ Are certain episodes narrated out of chronological order? If so, were you puzzled? Annoyed? On reflection, does the arrangement of episodes seem effective? Why, or why not? Are certain situations repeated? If so, what do you make out of the repetitions?

Character

❑ Which character chiefly engages your interest? Why?
❑ What purposes do minor characters serve? Do you find some who by their similarities and differences help to define each other or help to define the major character? How else is a particular character defined—by his or her words, actions (including thoughts and emotions), dress, setting, narrative point of view? Do certain characters act differently in the same, or in a similar, situation?
❑ How does the author reveal character? By explicit authorial (editorial) comment, for instance, or, on the other hand, by revelation through dialogue?

Through depicted action? Through the actions of other characters? How are the author's methods especially suited to the whole of the story?

❑ Is the behavior plausible—that is, are the characters well motivated?

❑ If a character changes, why and how does he or she change? (You may want to jot down each event that influences a change.) Or did you change your attitude toward a character not because the character changes but because you came to know the character better?

❑ Are the characters round or flat? Are they complex, or, on the other hand, highly typical (for instance, one-dimensional representatives of a social class or age)? Are you chiefly interested in a character's psychology, or does the character strike you as standing for something, such as honesty or the arrogance of power?

❑ How has the author caused you to sympathize with certain characters? How does your response—your sympathy or lack of sympathy—contribute to your judgment of the conflict?

Point of View

❑ Who tells the story? How much does the narrator know? Does the narrator strike you as reliable? What effect is gained by using this narrator?

❑ How does the point of view help shape the theme? After all, the basic story of "Little Red Riding Hood"—what happens—remains unchanged whether told from the wolf's point of view or the girl's, but (to simplify grossly) if we hear the story from the wolf's point of view, we may feel that the story is about terrifying yet pathetic compulsive behavior; if from the girl's point of view, about terrified innocence.

❑ It is sometimes said that the best writers are subversive, forcing readers to see something they do not want to see—something that is true but that violates their comfortable conventional ideas. Does this story oppose comfortable conventional views?

❑ Does the narrator's language help you to construct a picture of the narrator's character, class, attitude, strengths, and limitations? (Jot down some evidence, such as colloquial or—on the other hand—formal expressions, ironic comments, figures of speech.) How far can you trust the narrator? Why?

Setting

❑ Do you have a strong sense of the time and place? Is the story very much about, say, New England Puritanism, or race relations in the South in the late nineteenth century, or midwestern urban versus small-town life? If time and place are important, how and at what points in the story has the author conveyed this sense? If you do not strongly feel the setting, do you think the author should have made it more evident?

❑ What is the relation of the setting to the plot and the characters? (For instance, do houses or rooms or their furnishings say something about their residents?) Would anything be lost if the descriptions of the setting were deleted from the story or the setting were changed?

Symbolism

❑ Do certain characters seem to you to stand for something in addition to themselves? Does the setting—whether a house, a farm, a landscape, a town, a period—have an extra dimension?